THE OXFORD HANDB

MODERN DIPLOMACY

At a time when diplomatic practices and the demands imposed on diplomats are changing quite radically, and many foreign ministries feel they are being left behind, there is a need to understand the various forces that are affecting the profession. Diplomacy remains a salient activity in today's world in which the basic authoritative actor is still the state. At the same time, in some respects the practice of diplomacy is undergoing significant, even radical, changes to the context, tools, actors and domain of the trade. These changes spring from the changing nature of the state, the changing nature of the world order, and the interplay between them. One way of describing this is to say that we are seeing increased interaction between two forms of diplomacy, 'club diplomacy' and 'network diplomacy'. The former is based on a small number of players, a highly hierarchical structure, based largely on written communication and on low transparency; the latter is based on a much larger number of players (particularly of civil society), a flatter structure, a more significant oral component, and greater transparency.

The Oxford Handbook of Modern Diplomacy is an authoritative reference tool for those studying and practicing modern diplomacy. It provides an up-to-date compendium of the latest developments in the field. Written by practitioners and scholars, the Handbook describes the elements of constancy and continuity and the changes that are affecting diplomacy. The Handbook goes further and gives insight to where the profession is headed in the future. Co-edited by three distinguished academics and former practitioners, the Handbook provides comprehensive analysis and description of the state of diplomacy in the 21st Century and is an essential resource for diplomats, practitioners and academics.

THE OXFORD HANDBOOK OF

MODERN DIPLOMACY

Edited by

ANDREW F. COOPER, JORGE HEINE,

and

RAMESH THAKUR

OXFORD
UNIVERSITY PRESS

OXFORD
UNIVERSITY PRESS

Great Clarendon Street, Oxford, OX2 6DP,
United Kingdom

Oxford University Press is a department of the University of Oxford.
It furthers the University's objective of excellence in research, scholarship,
and education by publishing worldwide. Oxford is a registered trade mark of
Oxford University Press in the UK and in certain other countries

Published in the United States of America by Oxford University Press
198 Madison Avenue, New York, NY 10016, United States of America

British Library Cataloguing in Publication Data
Data available

Library of Congress Cataloging in Publication Data
Data available

ISBN 978–0–19–958886–2 (Hbk.)
ISBN 978–0–19–874366–8 (Pbk.)

Contents

PART III MODES OF PRACTICE

PART IV TOOLS AND INSTRUMENTS

PART V ISSUE AREAS

PART VI CASE STUDIES

PREFACE

A central purpose of public policy think tanks is to bring under one roof people of shared interests, yet different backgrounds, to let creative sparks fly, new ideas germinate, and exciting projects emerge. In 2008 the three co-editors of this volume became closely connected as Distinguished Fellows at the Centre for International Governance Innovation (CIGI). We all shared a passion to understand better the changing nature of the international system in the new century, to grasp more precisely the role of intellectual endeavours in effecting these changes, and to craft more finely the tools needed to translate conceptual capacity into operational practice.

We hail from three different continents and have come to our current interest in the study of diplomacy via different routes. Cooper, by way of an extended trajectory in foreign policy research in many countries around the world, with a special focus on middle and small powers; Heine, as a political scientist and practitioner, with eight years as an ambassador accredited first to South Africa and then to India; Thakur, as an international relations scholar who served for nine years as the Senior Vice Rector, at the rank of UN Assistant Secretary General, at the United Nations University in Tokyo. We had all been associated, in one way or another, with CIGI from its inception: Cooper, as the founding associate director; Heine, as a founding member of the International Board of Governors; and Thakur, as an advisor and leading participant in many of CIGI's initial conferences and activities. In that capacity, we were to be witnesses to and part of an extraordinary process reflecting the power of ideas to change the way the world is run.

From day one, that is, from its establishment in 2001, CIGI's mandate was ambitious: to improve the multilateral governance of world affairs. In 2003, Paul Martin, shortly before becoming prime minister of Canada, gave this broad mandate a specific focus: he asked CIGI to put the proposal of a G20 at leaders' level—an L20, as the acronym at the time had it—on the table of the international marketplace of ideas. As Canada's minister of finance, Martin had played a leading role in establishing and then running the G20 at finance ministers' level. He was keen to take it one step further. Martin's view was that the world's global challenges needed urgent attention from a small and manageable group, a steering group rather than a central committee, at the highest possible level—that is, that of heads of state or government.

As Canada's minister of finance for much of the 1990s, Martin had seen first-hand the central challenge that the forces of globalization pose to governments all over the world. On the one hand, the ability of transnational firms to pack up and leave whenever taxation rates are deemed too high or regulations too tight triggers an unseemly race to the bottom in the matter of tax rates and business regulations. On the other hand, the inequality and growing disparity of incomes and wealth within and among nations, triggered by those very same forces, generates enormous popular pressures on governments to redress those inequalities, something for which governments are ill prepared as government revenue dwindles.

Lax business regulations, particularly in issues like finance, generate problems of their own, as the global financial crisis of 2008–2009 made only too apparent. Though there are no easy answers to these challenges, a grouping of the leaders of the world's key nations that meets regularly does at least get a chance to come up with them. Martin was also convinced that the G7/8, whatever its other virtues, was unable to cope with an environment in which emerging powers such as Brazil, China, and India were turning into the growth engines of the world economy, displacing the North Atlantic economies which had played that role for so long.

Over the next five years, CIGI promoted the idea of the G20 in a variety of fora, put together conferences and workshops, and published books, articles, policy briefs, and opinion pieces on the subject. It partnered with sister institutions in the United States and elsewhere in this endeavour and otherwise beat the drums about the advantages of such an enlarged, more representative group to take on global economic challenges. All three editors were closely involved in this project. Many others were sceptical, arguing that the United States would never acquiesce to be part of such an undertaking, one that would seemingly dilute its role as the world's only superpower and its largest economy. Others insisted that the George W. Bush administration, given its distrust of multilateral institutions, would be particularly opposed to such an initiative. Yet, perhaps to the surprise of many, it was President George W. Bush himself who called the first meeting of the G20 at leaders' level, to be held in Washington DC on 15 November 2008. A scarce seven years after its founding, CIGI's main public policy proposal on global governance, what has come to be known as 'the steering committee of the world economy', and something that *The Economist* has termed as the best thing to come out of the global financial crisis, had come into being. Since then, the G20, meeting once or twice a year, has become a regular part of the landscape of global international institutions. Many would say that it played a key role in stopping the world economy from falling off the cliff in the aftermath of what turned out to be the biggest recession since the Great Depression of the 1930s.

It was in the weeks after that very gratifying moment in November 2008 that the idea for this book developed. The three of us had worked together on a variety of different projects in the past, mostly on themes related to global governance, but also in the field of diplomatic studies. Heine was also fortunate in being able to watch first-hand, if as a ringside observer, the emergence of South Africa from the dark days of apartheid under the inspiring leadership of Nelson Mandela, and then the rise of India as a significant player in world affairs. Thakur was one of the international commissioners who formulated the responsibility to protect principle, which many observers have called one of the most significant normative advances since the Second World War. Cooper attended the first four G20 summits and wrote extensively about the shape-shifting of diplomatic processes. All three of us felt that the practice of the ancient craft of diplomacy was undergoing seismic changes, changes that were not reflected in the curricula of most diplomatic academies, let alone in the day-to-day management of many foreign ministries and diplomatic missions. The communications and IT revolutions have transformed a profession traditionally known for its glacial pace and long-form reporting. Nothing could be farther from the 21st-century world of 24-hour TV news channels, Twitter, and Facebook. The spread of instant global communications that these technologies has spurred have changed the pace and rhythm of diplomacy. They have also added new ways of doing things to the exercise of this 'labour in exile'. To chart these changing circumstances in a manner accessible to diplomats, policy-makers, students, and scholars of international relations is the purpose of this volume.

After discussing the project at some length among ourselves, we concluded that a brainstorming session in which we could lay it out and subject it to the critique and suggestions of our colleagues would be the best way to kick-start it. This session, sponsored by CIGI, took place at Woerner House, in Cambridge, Ontario, on 11 May 2009. The meeting brought together eighteen scholars and practitioners, mostly CIGI-affiliated, several of whom are contributors to this volume, who generously shared their insights on the changing nature of diplomacy and the key topics any such volume ought to address. Our thanks go to Alan Alexandroff, Manmohan Agarwal, Gregory Chin, Jennifer Clapp, John Curtis, John English, Louise Fréchette, Patricia Goff, Paul Heinbecker, Eric Helleiner, Bessma Momani, Daniel Schwanen, Mark Sedra, Andrew Thompson, and David Welch for participating in it. The help provided by Deanne Leifso and Joseph F. (Joe) Turcotte in coordinating that event and documenting the deliberations was also critical in allowing us to move forward with the project.

We then proceeded to assemble the necessary group of contributors to meet the ambitious goals of the project. We aimed for a global and eclectic mix of practitioners and scholars. We are fortunate to have had a positive response from such a broadly representative group of distinguished authors from all five continents. We were especially delighted that Prime Minister Paul Martin accepted our invitation to write a chapter on the G20, whose creation was one of the great diplomatic breakthroughs of our time.

Close to two years after our Woerner House retreat, from 14–16 March 2011, we had an authors' workshop in Ottawa, at the headquarters of the International Development Research Centre (IDRC). A little over half of the contributors to this volume presented first drafts of their chapters. Our thanks go to the IDRC team, especially to its president, David M. Malone, for his generous support for this project. Bruce Currie-Alder and Elizabeth Mohan and the rest of the IDRC team were instrumental in arranging the workshop and in making it a successful event. Wilfrid Laurier University, as the recipient of the IDRC grant, ensured its administration flowed smoothly.

Since the Ottawa workshop, we have also brought *The Oxford Handbook of Modern Diplomacy* project to the meetings of the American Political Science Association (APSA). The Annual Meetings in Seattle in 2011 provided us with a valuable platform to present earlier versions of our chapters. Andrew Cooper, David Forsythe, Patti Goff, Jorge Heine, and Carlos Portales participated in a panel on the changing nature of diplomacy in Seattle in September 2011. We thank Irene Wu of the Practising Politics Group of the APSA, as well as APSA's Foreign Policy Division, for their unwavering support for our panel proposal, that enabled these deliberations to take place.

As this preface shows, much time and many hands have gone into putting this book together. For much of the time, CIGI provided us with the infrastructure and human resource assistance needed to bring such an ambitious project to completion. Thanks to it, Joe Turcotte, now a PhD student in Communication and Culture at York University in Toronto, has been able to work on this project throughout and effectively coordinate it. Indeed, Joe's talents as an editor, honed in his time as a senior editor of *The Cord*, the student newspaper at Wilfrid Laurier University, have been instrumental in helping us bring this project to completion. The Balsillie School of International Affairs, whose new building was inaugurated in September 2011, and is now the home of half a dozen of the contributors, provided a stimulating environment in which to carry out our work, as did the University of Waterloo for Andrew Cooper, Wilfrid Laurier University for Jorge Heine, and the Australian National University for Ramesh Thakur from 2011 onwards.

Our final thanks go to Dominic Byatt from Oxford University Press, who so warmly and enthusiastically supported this project from the very beginning. He and his editorial team at OUP, in which Sarah Parker took the lead in managing this project, made our work especially rewarding.

Andrew F. Cooper and Jorge Heine, Waterloo, Ontario
Ramesh Thakur, Canberra, Australia
April 2012

FIGURES

TABLES

Boxes

ABBREVIATIONS

ABM	Anti-Ballistic Missile
ACP	*African, Caribbean, and Pacific Group of States*
AFTA	ASEAN Free Trade Area
ANC	African National Congress
AOSIS	Alliance of Small Island States
APEC	Asia-Pacific Economic Cooperation
APSA	American Political Science Association
ARF	ASEAN Regional Forum
AR4	Fourth Assessment Report (IPCC)
ASEAN	Association of Southeast Nations
ASEM	Asia–Europe Meeting
ASP	Assembly of States Parties (ICC)
ATTAC	Association for the Taxation of financial Transactions and Aid to Citizens
AU	African Union
BASIC	Brazil, South Africa, India, China
BATNA	Best Alternative to a Negotiated Agreement
BBC	British Broadcasting Corporation
BCBS	Basel Committee on Banking Supervision
BIAs	Bilateral Immunity Agreements
BIS	Bank for International Settlements
BITs	Bilateral Investment Treaties
BRIC	Brazil, Russia, India, China
BRICSAM	Brazil, Russia, India, China, South Africa, Mexico
BUSA	Business Unity South Africa
BWC	Biological and Toxin Weapons Convention
BWI	Bretton Woods Institutions
CAFTA	China–ASEAN Free Trade Area
CAS	Court of Arbitration for Sport
CBDR	common but differentiated responsibilities
CCWC	United Nations Convention on Certain Conventional Weapons
CD	Conference on Disarmament
CEO	Chief Executive Officer
CERF	Central Emergency Response Fund
CFA	Committee on Food Aid Policies (WFP)

CFAC	Conference of Central American Armed Forces
CFC	chlorofluorocarbon
CFS	Committee on World Food Security
CHOGM	Commonwealth Heads of Government Meeting
CIA	Central Intelligence Agency
CICC	Coalition for the International Criminal Court
CIDE	Mexican Centre for Economic Research and Development
CIGI	Centre for International Governance Innovation
CINDE	Costa Rican Investment Promotion Agency
CITES	Convention on International Trade in Endangered Species
CMC	Cluster Munitions Convention
CMI	Crisis Management Initiative
COMEXI	Mexican Council on Foreign Relations
COP	Conference of the Parties
COSATU	Congress of South African Trades Unions
CSIS	Center for Security and International Studies
CSO	civil society organization
CSR	corporate social responsibility
CSSD	Consultative Subcommittee on Surplus Disposal
CTBT	Comprehensive Nuclear Test Ban Treaty
DAC	Development Assistance Committee (OECD)
DDA	Doha Development Agenda
DFAIT	Department of Foreign Affairs and International Trade Canada
DPKO	United Nations Department of Peacekeeping Operations
DPRK	Democratic People's Republic of Korea
DRC	Democratic Republic of the Congo
DSM	Dispute Settlement Mechanism
EC	European Community
ECHR	European Court of Human Rights
ECOMOG	Economic Community of West African States Monitoring Group
ECOSOC	United Nations Economic and Social Council
ECOSOCC	Economic, Social, and Cultural Council (Africa)
ECOWAS	Economic Community of West African States
EDB	Economic Development Board (Singapore)
EEAS	European External Action Service
ENDA	Enda Tiers Monde
EU	European Union
ExComm	Executive Committee of the National Security Council (US)
FAC	Food Aid Convention
FAC	Food Assistance Convention
FANs	Friends of Anti-Dumping Negotiation

FAO	Food and Agriculture Organization
FCO	British Foreign and Commonwealth Office
FCTC	Framework Convention on Tobacco Control
FDI	foreign direct investment
FIDH	International Federation for Human Rights
FIFA	Fédération Internationale de Football Association
FIG	Fédération Internationale de Gymnastique
FMCT	Fissile Material Cut-off Treaty
FRBNY	Federal Reserve Bank of New York
FRIDE	Fundación para las Relaciones Internacionales y el Diálogo Exterior
FSB	Financial Stability Board
FSF	Financial Stability Forum
FTAA	Free Trade Area of the Americas
GAM	Free Aceh Movement
GATT	General Agreement on Tariffs and Trade
GCC	Gulf Cooperation Council
GDP	gross domestic product
GDR	German Democratic Republic
GEF	Global Environment Facility
GHG	greenhouse gas
GMO	genetically modified organism
GPA	Government Procurement Agreement
G6	Group of Six
G7	Group of Seven
G8	Group of Eight
G20	Group of Twenty
G77	Group of Seventy-Seven
GWOT	global war on terror
HLP	High-Level Panel on Threats, Challenges, and Change
HSBC	Hong Kong and Shanghai Banking Corporation
HSGIC	Heads of State and Government Implementation Committee
IAAF	International Amateur Athletics Federation/International Association of Athletics Federations
IAEA	International Atomic Energy Agency
IANSA	International Action Network on Small Arms
IBRD	International Bank of Reconstruction and Development
IBSA	India, Brazil, South Africa
ICBL	International Campaign to Ban Landmines
ICC	International Chamber of Commerce
ICC	International Criminal Court
ICISS	International Commission on Intervention and State Sovereignty

ICJ	International Court of Justice
ICNND	International Commission on Nuclear Non-proliferation and Disarmament
ICRC	International Committee of the Red Cross
ICSU	International Council of Scientific Unions
ICT	Information and Communications Technology
ICTR	International Criminal Tribunal for Rwanda
ICTSD	International Centre for Trade and Sustainable Development
ICTY	International Criminal Tribunal for the Former Yugoslavia
IDB	Inter-American Development Bank
IDF	Israeli Defence Forces
IDP	internally displaced person
IDRC	International Development Research Centre
IE	International Enterprise (Singapore)
IFAD	International Fund for Agricultural Development
IGC	International Grains Council
IGO	intergovernmental organization
IHL	international humanitarian law
IHR	International Health Regulations
IISS	International Institute for Strategic Studies (London)
ILC	International Law Commission
ILO	International Labour Organization
IMF	International Monetary Fund
IMFC	International Monetary Fund Conference
IMO	International Maritime Organization
INC	Intergovernmental Negotiating Committee
INF Treaty	Intermediate-Range Nuclear Forces Treaty
IOC	International Olympic Committee
IOM	Independent Oversight Mechanism
IO	international organization
IPCC	United Nations Intergovernmental Panel on Climate Change
IR	International Relations
IRC	International Rescue Committee
ISAF	International Security Assistance Force
ISI	Inter-Services Intelligence Directorate (Pakistan)
ISOs	International Sports Organizations
IT	information technology
ITA	Information Technology Agreement
ITTF	International Table Tennis Federation
ITU	International Telecommunications Union
IUCN	International Union for the Conservation of Nature
KFOR	Kosovo Force

KSA	Kingdom of Saudi Arabia
LDCs	least developed countries
LMG	like-minded group
LOCOG	London Organizing Committee for the Olympics Games
LTTE	Liberation Tigers of Tamil Eelam
MAI	Multilateral Investment Agreement
MAP	Mutual Assessment Process
MDB	multinational development banks
MDGs	Millennium Development Goals
MEAs	Multilateral Environment Agreements
Mercosur	Mercado Común del Sur
MFAs	Ministries of Foreign Affairs
MIFH	Multinational Interim Force for Haiti
MIGA	Multilateral Investment Guarantee Agency
MIKT	Mexico, Indonesia, South Korea, and Turkey
MINUSTAH	United Nations Mission for the Stabilization of Haiti
MNC	multinational corporation
MOP	Meeting of Parties
NAFTA	North America Free Trade Agreement
NAM	Non-Aligned Movement
NAMA	Non-Agricultural Market Access
NATO	North Atlantic Treaty Organization
NEDLAC	National Economic Development and Labour Council (South Africa)
NEPAD	New Partnership for Africa's Development
NGO	non-governmental organization
NNWS	non-nuclear-weapon state
NOCs	National Olympic Committees
NPT	Treaty on the Non-Proliferation of Nuclear Weapons
NPTREC	Non-Proliferation Treaty Review and Extension Conference (1995)
NPTREVCON	Non-Proliferation Treaty Review Conference
NRDC	Natural Resources Defence Council
NSG	Nuclear Suppliers Group
NTB	non-tariff barrier
NTI	Nuclear Threat Initiative
NWS	nuclear-weapon states
OAS	Organization of American States
OAU	Organization for African Unity
OCHA	United Nations Office for the Coordination of Humanitarian Affairs
OECD	Organisation for Economic Cooperation and Development

OEF	Operation Enduring Freedom
OHMD	The Oxford Handbook of Modern Diplomacy
OIC	Organization of the Islamic Conference
ONUCI	United Nations Operation in Côte d'Ivoire
OPCW	Organization for the Prohibition of Chemical Weapons
OPEC	Organization of Petroleum Exporting Countries
OSCE	Organization for Security and Cooperation in Europe
OTP	Office of the Prosecutor (ICC)
PD	public diplomacy
P5	Five Permanent Members of the United Nations Security Council
PKO	Peacekeeping Operation
PLO	Palestine Liberation Organization
PPP	public—private partnership
PR	public relations
PRC	people's republic of China
PrepCom	NPT Preparatory Committee Meeting
PSI	Proliferation Security initiative
PTBT	Partial Test Ban Treaty
QDDR	Quadrennial Diplomacy and Development Review
RAMs	Recently Acceded Members
RCG	Regional Consultative Groups
R&D	Research and Development
REDD+	Reducing Emissions from Deforestation and Degradation
RIM	Research in Motion
RS	Rome Statute of the International Criminal Court
RTA	Regional Trade Agreement
RTI	Radio Television Ivoirienne
R2P	Responsibility to Protect
SAARC	South Asian Association for Regional Cooperation
SADC	Southern African Development Community
SALW	Programme of Action on Small Arms and Light Weapons
SANROC	South African Non-Racial Olympic Committee
SDH	social determinants of health
SDRs	Special Drawing Rights
SICA	Central American Integration System
SIRG	Summit Implementation Review Group (Summit of the Americas)
SOM	Senior Officials Meeting
SRSG	Special Representative of the Secretary-General
SSBs	Standard Setting Bodies
SSOD I	First Special Session on Disarmament (1978)
START	Strategic Arms Reduction Treaty

SVCS	small and vulnerable coastal states
SVEs	small and vulnerable economies
SWAPO	Southwest African People's Organization
SWGCA	Special Working Group on the Crime of Aggression
TRIPS	Agreement on Trade-Related Aspects of Intellectual Property Rights
UCIL	Union Carbide India Ltd
UN	United Nations
UNAIDS	United Nations Joint Programme on HIV/AIDS
UNAMA	United Nations Assistance Mission in Afghanistan
UNASUR	South American Union of Nations
UNCCC	United Nations Convention on Climate Change
UNCHE	United Nations Conference on the Human Environment
UNCT	United Nations Country Team
UNCTAD	United Nations Conference on Trade and Development
UNDCP	United Nations Drug Control Programme
UNDP	United Nations Development Programme
UNEP	United Nations Environment Programme
UNESCO	United Nations Educational, Scientific, and Cultural Organization
UNFCCC	United Nations Framework Convention on Climate Change
UNFPA	United Nations Population Fund
UNGA	United Nations General Assembly
UNHCR	United Nations High Commissioner for Refugees
UNHRC	United Nations Human Rights Council
UNICEF	United Nations Children's Fund
UNIFIL	United Nations Interim Force in Lebanon
UNMOGIP	United Nations Military Observer Group in India and Pakistan
UNPKO	United Nations Peacekeeping Operation
UNPROFOR	United Nations Protection Force in Former Yugoslavia
UNSC	United Nations Security Council
UNTAET	United Nations Transitional Administration in East Timor
UNTAG	United Nations Transition Assistance Group
UNTSO	United Nations Truce Supervision Organization
URAA	Uruguay Round Agreement on Agriculture
US	United States
USD	United States dollars
USIA	United States Information Agency
USSR	Union of Soviet Socialist Republics
VANOC	The Vancouver Organizing Committee for the 2010 Olympic and Paralympic Winter Games

VCCR	Vienna Convention on Consular Relations
VCDR	Vienna Convention on Diplomatic Relations
VVAF	Vietnam Veterans of America Foundation
WADA	World Anti-Doping Agency
WFP	World Food Programme
WHO	World Health Organization
WIPO	World Intellectual Property Organization
WMD	weapons of mass destruction
WMO	World Meteorological Organization
WTO	World Trade Organization
WWF	World Wildlife Fund

About the Contributors

Pamela Aall is a senior vice president at the US Institute of Peace and provost of USIP's Academy for International Conflict Management and Peacebuilding.

Martti Ahtisaari was the 10th President of Finland (1994–2000). He received the Nobel Peace Prize in 2008.

Lloyd Axworthy is President and Vice-Chancellor of The University of Winnipeg. He served as Canada's Foreign Affairs Minister from 1996 to 2000.

Sir Nicholas Bayne is a Fellow at the International Trade Policy Unit of the London School of Economics and Political Science.

David Black is Director of the Centre for Foreign Policy Studies and Professor of Political Science and International Development Studies (IDS) at Dalhousie University.

Alicia Buenrostro is Consul General of Mexico in Hong Kong.

Simon Chesterman is Dean of the National University of Singapore Faculty of Law.

General Juan Emilio Cheyre (R) is the founding Director of the Centre of International Studies at the Catholic University of Chile. He served as Commander in Chief, Chilean Army, from 2002 to 2006.

Gregory Chin is an Associate Professor of Political Science at York University, and The China Research Chair at The Centre for International Governance Innovation.

Jennifer Clapp is Faculty of Environment chair in Global Environmental Governance in the Department of Environment and Resource Studies at the University of Waterloo and a Professor at the Balsillie School of International Affairs.

Daryl Copeland, a former Canadian diplomat, is an analyst specializing in diplomacy, international policy, global issues, and public management. He holds teaching appointments at Ottawa, Otago (New Zealand) and East Anglia (London Academy of Diplomacy) Universities, and is a Senior Fellow at the Canadian Defence and Foreign Affairs Institute.

Andrew F. Cooper is Professor at the Balsillie School of International Affairs and Department of Political Science at the University of Waterloo.

Chester A. Crocker is the James R. Schlesinger Professor of Strategic Studies at Georgetown University's Walsh School of Foreign Service. He served as the US Assistant Secretary of State for African Affairs from 1981 to 1989.

Jayantha Dhanapala is a former United Nations Under-Secretary-General for Disarmament Affairs and a former Ambassador of Sri Lanka to the United States and to the UN in Geneva.

Sanderijn Duquet is a Junior Member of the Leuven Centre for Global Governance Studies, KULeuven.

Jan Egeland is the Deputy Director of Human Rights Watch, Director of Human Rights Watch Europe, and former Director of the Norwegian Institute of International Affairs.

Lorraine Elliott is Professor, Department of International Relations, School of International, Political, and Strategic Studies at the Australian National University.

John English is Distinguished Senior Fellow at the Munk School of Global Affairs and Distinguished Visiting Professor at the Canadian Forces College.

Gareth Evans is Chancellor and Honorary Professonal Fellow of the Australian National University, President Emeritus of the International Crisis Group and a former Foreign Minister of Australia (1988–1996).

Tom Farer is University Professor at the University of Denver. He previously served as Dean of the University's Josef Korbel School of International Studies (1996–2010), President of the University of New Mexico (1985–1986), and President of the Inter-American Commission on Human Rights (1980–1982).

Richard Feinberg is professor of international political economy at the Graduate School of International Relations and Pacific Studies, University of California, San Diego. He served as President Bill Clinton's director for Latin American affairs in The White House.

David P. Fidler is James Louis Calamaras Professor of Law at the Maurer School of Law, Indiana University-Bloomington.

David P. Forsythe is University Professor and Charles J. Mach Distinguished Professor of Political Science, Emeritus, at the University of Nebraska-Lincoln.

Louise Fréchette is a Distinguished Fellow at The Centre for International Governance Innovation and former Deputy Secretary-General of the United Nations.

Patricia M. Goff is Associate Professor of Political Science at Wilfrid Laurier University.

Sir Jeremy Greenstock is Chairman of the UN Association in the UK and Chairman of the strategic advisory company Gatehouse Advisory Partners Ltd. He is a former United Kingdom Permanent Representative to the United Nations.

A.J.R. Groom is Emeritus Professor of International Relations at the University of Kent and Visiting Professor of Politics at Canterbury Christ Church University.

Fen Osler Hampson is Chancellor's Professor and Director of the Norman Patterson School of International Affairs and Professor of International Affairs at Carleton University.

Jorge Heine is Ambassador of Chile to the People's Republic of China. A Wilson Center Global Fellow, he is on leave from his position as Professor of Political Science, Balsillie School of International Affairs, Wilfrid Laurier University. He was previously Ambassador to India (2003–2007) and to South Africa (1994–1999).

Eric Helleiner is Faculty of Arts Chair in International Political Economy and Professor in the Department of Political Science and Balsillie School of International Affairs, University of Waterloo.

Kathryn Hochstetler is CIGI Chair of Governance in the Americas at the Balsillie School of International Affairs and Professor of Political Science at the University of Waterloo.

Kal Holsti is University Killam Professor Emeritus, and a Research Associate with the Centre for International Relations in the Liu Institute, the University of British Columbia.

Rebecca Johnson is Director of the Acronym Institute for Disarmament Diplomacy in London, Co-Chair of the International Campaign to Abolish Nuclear Weapons, and a Member of the International Panel on Fissile Materials.

Margaret P. Karns is Professor Emerita of Political Science at the University of Dayton. She was also the founding director of the University of Dayton's Center for International Programs.

Kishore Mahbubani is Dean and Professor in the Practice of Public Policy of the Lee Kuan Yew School of Public Policy at the National University of Singapore. He previously served twice as Singapore's Permanent Representative to the United Nations.

William Maley is Professor and Director of the Asia-Pacific College of Diplomacy at the Australian National University.

David M. Malone is President of Canada's International Development Research Centre (IDRC). He served previously as a Canadian Ambassador to the United Nations and as High Commissioner to India.

The Right Honourable Paul Martin was the 21st Prime Minister of Canada from 2003 to 2006 and the Minister of Finance from 1993 to 2002.

Jan Melissen is Director of Research at the Netherlands Institute of International Relations 'Clingendael', The Hague, and Professor of Diplomacy at the University of Antwerp.

Katrien Meuwissen is Junior Member of the Leuven Centre for Global Governance Studies, KULeuven.

Greg Mills is the Director of the Brenthurst Foundation in Johannesburg. He was the National Director of the South African Institute of International Affairs (SAIIA) from 1996 to 2004.

Karen A. Mingst is Lockwood Chair in the Patterson School of Diplomacy and International Commerce and Professor of Political Science at the University of Kentucky.

Amrita Narlikar is the Director of the Centre for Rising Powers, and Reader in International Political Economy at the Department of Politics and International Studies, University of Cambridge.

Joseph S. Nye Jr. is University Distinguished Service Professor at Harvard University and former Dean of the Kennedy School of Government. He served as US Assistant Secretary of Defense for International Security Affairs from 1994 to 1995.

Maaike Okano-Heijmans is a senior research fellow for diplomatic studies and Asia studies at the Netherlands Institute of International Relations 'Clingendael'.

Byron Peacock is a PhD student in the Department of Political Science, Dalhousie University.

Geoffrey Allen Pigman is a Research Associate and Visiting Fellow in the Department of Political Sciences, University of Pretoria, and a Research Associate at the Institute for Global Dialogue, Pretoria, South Africa.

Shawn Powers is an Assistant Professor at Georgia State University and an Associate Director at the Center on International Media Education.

Kristiina Rintakoski the Director for Advocacy at the Finnish Evangelical Lutheran Mission (FELM).

Andrés Rozental is the founding president of the Mexican Council on Foreign Relations. He served previously as Mexico's Deputy Minister of Foreign Affairs, and as ambassador to the United Nations in Geneva, the United Kingdom, and Sweden.

Benjamin N. Schiff is William G. and Jeanette Williams Smith Professor of Politics at Oberlin College.

Pierre Schori is President of the Olafe Palme Fund and Chair of the Board of International Alert. He was Sweden's Ambassador to the UN between 2000 and 2004, and served from 2005 until the beginning of 2007 as Special Representative of the UN Secretary-General and Head of Mission in Côte d'Ivoire.

Su Changhe is Professor at the Department of Diplomacy, School of International Relations and Public Affairs, Fudan University.

Ramesh Thakur is Professor of International Relations in the Asia-Pacific College of Diplomacy and Director of the Centre for Nuclear Non-proliferation and Disarmament (CNND), the Australian National University.

Diana Tussie heads the Department of International Relations at FLACSO/Argentina and is the founding director of the Latin American Trade Network (LATN).

Thomas G. Weiss is Director, Ralph Bunche Institute for International Studies and Presidential Professor at The Graduate Center, The City University of New York.

David A. Welch is Director of the Balsillie School of International Affairs, where he holds the CIGI Chair in Security. He is also Professor of Political Science at the University of Waterloo.

Stephen Woolcock is Programme Director for the Master's in International Political Economy at the London School of Economics and Political Science.

Jan Wouters is Professor of International Law and International Organizations, Jean Monnet Chair ad personam EU and Global Governance, and Director of the Leuven Centre for Global Governance Studies and the Institute for International Law at the University of Leuven, Belgium.

FOREWORD
Diplomacy: Old Trade, New Challenges

LOUISE FRÉCHETTE

I became a diplomat by accident. It all started with a small poster on a university billboard with the words 'interested in working abroad?' written in big bold letters. It informed me that the Foreign Service exam would be held in a few hours in a conference room nearby. I had nothing better to do that night so I went. In truth, I did not realize I was applying to join the diplomatic service of Canada until my first day on the job. I had never been inside an embassy and knew no one in the profession.

The Department of External Affairs of Canada, as it was then called, did not have a diplomatic academy and offered only minimal training to its new recruits. We were left to learn 'on-the-job' by observing our colleagues. I wish I had had a Handbook such as this one at my disposal to teach me the rudiments of my new profession.

An early 1970s Handbook of Diplomacy, which is when I joined the foreign ministry, would have been quite different from this one. Modern diplomacy takes place in a more complex environment than four decades ago. As this volume demonstrates, new players, new methods, new topics have entered the scene.[1] The distinction between domestic and international issues is increasingly blurred.

Yet contemporary diplomacy is built on ancient foundations and practices. Modern-day diplomats need to understand them as much as they need to be attuned to the more recent trends. One of the many merits of this *Handbook* is that it offers a comprehensive examination of the practice of diplomacy in all of its dimensions.

Of all the changes that have occurred in my time as a diplomat, none has had a more significant impact than the twin and linked phenomena of globalization and the communications revolution spurred by new information technologies.

Forty years ago, transmitting information was a slow process, especially if this information had to be encrypted. International telephone communications were costly and unreliable. In times of crisis, diplomats were often cut off from their headquarters and had to make judgement calls on the spot. In their letters of credentials ambassadors are still described as 'plenipotentiary' but nowadays they rarely if ever have the opportunity to use their 'full powers' to bind their government. Headquarters are often consulted up to the minute. As a result, the margin of initiative of envoys has shrunk considerably, at least when sensitive issues are concerned.

The communications revolution has also shortened the time available for making decisions. The advent of 24-hour news coverage and multiple information outlets forces governments to react to developments quickly or risk being portrayed as indecisive. The new media environment also creates expectations and standards of performance that are often set unreasonably high.[2] Anyone involved in the management of a humanitarian crisis knows how quickly the media will focus on deficiencies in the delivery of relief supplies, for instance.

Traditional diplomacy has often traded in secrecy and unacknowledged understandings. Many 'backroom negotiations' still take place but few of them remain secret for long.[3] The trend towards greater transparency is irreversible. Contemporary diplomats must pay as much attention to the public impact of their actions and recommendations as to their substantive merits.

Another major difference from my early days as a diplomat is the growing number of summit meetings and, more generally, the personal and ongoing involvement of leaders and ministers in the conduct of day-to-day diplomacy. This is of course not an entirely new phenomenon. There are many examples in history of kings and presidents coming together to make peace or divide the spoils of war. But they did so only in extraordinary circumstances. Now, political leaders meet on a regular basis. Most countries are members of many organizations that hold summits every few years, even, in some cases, on a yearly basis. At any opening session of the United Nations General Assembly, more than a third of the entire membership of 193 states will be represented at the head-of-state or head-of-government level. The Millennium Summit in 2000 was attended by no fewer than 150 leaders.[4]

These gatherings build enormous pressures on the leaders to deliver results. Too often, they yield minimal agreement wrapped up in grand-sounding declarations. Are these numerous summits worth all the efforts (and money) that go into them? Judging by their outcomes, it is not hard to conclude that the law of diminishing returns has set in. But let us remember these meetings bring other benefits to their participants. They are occasions to conduct a great deal of bilateral business in the course of a few days. Furthermore, leaders get to know one another personally and develop a measure of camaraderie, which may help to steer relations away from confrontation when a crisis occurs.

Summits have become magnets for civil society gatherings of, at times, gigantic proportions. The role of non-governmental organizations (NGOs) in international relations has grown exponentially over the last few decades. Easy communication and cheap travel have allowed NGOs to mobilize themselves across borders. Individual governments and international organizations have had to adjust and give them opportunities to be heard.

The United Nations (UN) has a long experience with NGOs. The UN Charter makes specific mention of them in article 71, which stipulates that the Economic and Social Council (ECOSOC) 'may make suitable arrangements for consultations with non-governmental organizations which are concerned with matters within its competence'. Such consultations have extended well beyond the ECOSOC to include practically every issue before the General Assembly.

In the last decade or so, the Security Council has adopted the practice of holding regular, informal consultations with NGOs. The latter have proved to be an invaluable source of information on the fate of civilian populations in conflict zones as well as being indispensable partners of the UN humanitarian agencies in the field.

Traditional NGOs now share the scene with many other interest groups including business associations, think tanks, labour groups, charitable foundations, religious leaders, scientists, artists, and many others. Parliamentarians have always played a role nationally in the formulation of foreign policy. Nowadays, they too seek to make their views heard internationally, through their various international associations.

In many countries, major foreign policy decisions are often preceded by extensive consultations. As Kathryn Hochstetler describes in Chapter 9 of this volume, modern diplomats may be called upon to meet with a vast array of civil society representatives and must be able to interact constructively with people who come to the issues at hand from widely varying perspectives. They will at times find themselves at the receiving end of sharp criticisms and vigorous pressure. Agreement will not come easily, if at all. NGOs are, almost by definition, single-issue driven. Diplomacy, on the other hand, usually requires reconciling different and often conflicting objectives.

In my experience, interaction with NGOs can be rewarding for both sides, even on the most controversial issues. Taking the time to explain one's position is never time wasted. For their part, most civil society representatives welcome encounters with diplomats, provided the latter are prepared to listen and engage in an honest conversation.

The last several decades have also seen a global reordering of foreign policy priorities. The risks of global war have receded and interstate conflicts are less frequent than in the past, while concerns for human rights and the protection of innocent civilians in internal conflicts have moved up the international agenda.

Since the end of the cold war, the international community has taken action to stop abuses in situations that would have been considered off-limits in earlier times. UN peacekeeping, which Pierre Schori discusses in detail in Chapter 43 of this volume, has evolved from the simple interposition of lightly-armed soldiers to the deployment of thousands of soldiers, police officers, and civilian staff mandated to maintain law and order, protect civilian populations, rebuild institutions, and help with the reconstruction of war-torn societies. Recent institutions like the International Criminal Courts[5] and norms like the 'responsibility to protect'[6] have embedded the new ethical trends in far-reaching governance tools.

Contemporary diplomatic agendas are also increasingly focused on issues that used to be within the purview of domestic policies but have now crossed over to the foreign policy realm because of significant cross-borders dimensions. Most prominent among them are numerous environmental questions such as climate change, water pollution, biodiversity, and desertification. Modern-day diplomats have to be fully conversant with questions, many of which are discussed in Part V of this *Handbook*, as diverse as infectious diseases, drugs smuggling and international crimes, food security, human trafficking, cyber-security, terrorism, weapons of mass destruction, and many, many others.

Diplomats used to form a separate 'brotherhood' within their national bureaucracy, exercising almost complete control over their country's foreign relations. With the growing globalization of issues that used to be confined to the domestic realm, experts from outside the foreign ministry have become much more active on the international scene. This poses many challenges to governments and their professional diplomats.

One such challenge is the risk of incoherence and ineffectiveness in a country's international projection, as each domestic department unwittingly ends up running its own foreign policy, suited to fit its own particular priorities and concerns. All governments are struggling to find effective ways of coordinating the bewildering array of international engagements. 'Joined-up government' and 'whole-of-government' are but a few examples of terms used to describe attempts to bring a little order in the international relations houses of nations big and small.

Diplomats are often best placed to note contradictions and discrepancies in the foreign activities of the various arms of their government. They have a natural coordination role to play, but that role can be played effectively only if all the stakeholders involved accept it. That, in turn, rests on the ability of diplomats and the foreign ministries to add genuine value to the treatment of issues 'owned' by specialized departments.

In an age of over-abundant information, easy travel, and instantaneous communications, some are tempted to conclude that the services of professional diplomats are no longer required. As former Canadian Prime Minister Pierre Trudeau is reported to have said several decades ago, 'Why pay good money to keep an army of diplomats abroad so they can report something I have already read in my morning newspaper?'.

Of course, diplomats do a lot more than just report on events in their country of accreditation and the smart ones have long since stopped trying to compete with the media in this regard. Their value added is the profound understanding of the outside world that they can bring to bear on the consideration of issues of interest to their country. Such understanding cannot be acquired simply by watching the news on television, by exchanging emails with distant partners, or by occasional visits to distant lands. This is the fruit of a life-long commitment to the field of international relations and a willingness to spend a good part of one's life away from home, steeped in the realities of foreign societies and cultures. Professional diplomats will never match the knowledge of technical experts and should not pretend that they do. But they are best placed to map out the strategy and identify the tactics to achieve national goals internationally.

Diplomacy is an art, not a science. Once one has mastered the history, studied the norms, understood the institutions, and figured out the players, there is one last, crucial lesson to learn. It has to do with the very human dimension of diplomacy.

Diplomacy is about persuasion, not coercion. It is about looking for and finding common ground, about forging agreement and achieving a balance of benefits that will allow each party to go home with at least some degree of satisfaction.

Trust is an essential element of successful diplomacy. The old joke that a diplomat is a person sent abroad to lie for his country could not be further from the reality. I was taught from the very beginning of my career that 'a good diplomat never lies'. She may not be able to share everything that she knows with her interlocutor but she realizes that she will lose all ability to build trust if she takes too many liberties with the truth.

Needless to say, a certain amount of discretion is essential. If every piece of information, every comment received in confidence is liable to find itself on the front page of a newspaper, the conduct of diplomacy will be severely undermined. Without assurances of confidentiality, it may be impossible to build the kind of personal rapport that is so often key to convincing rivals, competitors, or enemies to take that one final step to seal a deal, to lay down arms, to forge a new partnership. Total transparency in diplomacy is not a virtue, no more than it is in private life.

Diplomacy requires patience and an open mind. A diplomat who shows genuine interest in the history and culture of the country to which she is accredited, who refrains from passing peremptory judgements on the behaviour of its political leaders and the mores of its people, who listens more than she preaches will easily win the hearts and the confidence of her interlocutors.

Diplomacy remains, in many respects, an old-fashioned trade. Diplomats no longer have the monopoly of diplomatic transactions, if they ever did, but they continue to enjoy a special status in the countries and institutions where they serve. The rituals that surround the presentation of credentials are more than traditions. They serve as a reminder of the basic rules of civility, agreed to centuries ago, that underpin relations among states to this day. It is a great honour to be able to serve one's country as an ambassador. It is never without some emotion and a justified sense of pride that a new ambassador presents his or her credentials.

It is true that with globalization and interdependence everybody is forced to be a diplomat of sorts from time to time, but the intermediation of a cadre of professionals remains an essential tool for the conduct of any country's foreign relations. This *Handbook* will make the job of learning the tricks of this noble and ancient trade a little easier for the next generation of diplomats.

Louise Fréchette

Notes

1. For more, see Part I of this volume, where the co-editors chart the changing landscape of diplomacy in the 21st century.
2. Shawn M. Powers describes this changing media situation in Chapter 11, this volume.

3. A fact that Daryl Copeland addresses in Chapter 25, this volume, through his treatment of WikiLeaks.
4. For more on this, see Richard Feinberg's Chapter 16 on 'Summit Diplomacy' in this volume.
5. For more, see Benjamin Schiff's Chapter 41 in this volume.
6. Thomas G. Weiss explores this further in Chapter 42 of this volume.

INTRODUCTION:
THE CHALLENGES
OF 21ST-CENTURY
DIPLOMACY

ANDREW F. COOPER, JORGE HEINE,
AND RAMESH THAKUR

'Can it be that in wading through the plethora of business plans, capability reviews . . . and other excrescences of the management age, we have indeed forgotten what diplomacy is all about?'—Sir Ivor Roberts, the departing British ambassador to Italy.[1]

THE essence of diplomacy has never disappeared. Yet amid the complexities of the 21st century, the manner by which these core ingredients express themselves can be overshadowed by a myriad of contextual factors both structural and situational. The aim of *The Oxford Handbook of Modern Diplomacy* (OHMD) is to display the importance of diplomacy along with its attendant capacity—albeit with many constraints and frustrations—for adaptation. Modern diplomacy in terms of practice may have lost some of its image of exceptionalism, in the sense that it has to compete and interact with a much wider dynamic of agency, conduct itself in a more time-sensitive manner, and be applied with a greater technical orientation. Furthermore, to a far greater extent than in the past, diplomacy is wrapped up with domestic policy-making and political/societal demands about governance across an extended spectrum of issue areas. Such a template, if inculcating some considerable anxieties about the current and future performance of diplomacy, however, confirms both the salience of diplomacy in terms of the form, scope, and intensity of operational activity and the necessary focus of an extended and conceptually informed mode of analysis.

What underpins the OHMD is the ambitious and exciting scale of the project. Diplomacy today takes place among multiple sites of authority, power, and influence:

mainly states, but also including religious organizations, non-governmental organizations (NGOs), multinational corporations, and even individuals, whether they be celebrities, philanthropists, or terrorists. With over fifty contributions, the OHMD covers the repertoire of diplomacy in comprehensive fashion with respect to objectives, interfaces, norms, tools, sites, and impact. Richness of detail is meshed with a consistency of thematic approach: the interplay between what is termed the club and network models of diplomacy.

Before delving deeper into this core typology, nonetheless, there is a need to go back to some of the basic if textured questions about the nature and meaning of diplomacy, its emerging patterns of practice, and relevance for not only policy-makers but a wider cast of actors and set of social interaction.

Diplomacy at its essence is the conduct of relationships, using peaceful means, by and among international actors, at least one of whom is usually governmental.[2] The typical international actors are states and the bulk of diplomacy involves relations between states directly, or between states, international organizations, and other international actors.

There is, it must be acknowledged, some confusion between foreign policy and diplomacy. Books on the diplomacy and diplomatic history of many countries are often treatises on those countries' foreign policy and the history of their foreign relations. Policy is the provenance of governments. The civil service may shape and influence policy, but is not normally considered to be a policy-maker: that is the domain of the political heads of civil service departments, namely heads of government and cabinet ministers individually and the legislature and political executive collectively.

While the formulation and adoption of policy is the responsibility of leaders and ministers, its implementation or execution is the job description of public servants and, in the case of foreign policy, diplomats. Such delivery relies on a mix-and-match set of techniques and tools of persuasion-cum-negotiation and pressure-cum-coercion that draw on soft and hard power assets in various combinations. A nation's diplomat, required to function as his or her country's eyes, ears, and voice abroad, must be aware of national interests and values while being able to understand foreign politics and cultures. The skills required of professional diplomats include intelligence, tact, discretion, circumspection, patience, self-control, teamwork, adaptability, creative imagination, the ability to signal and communicate messages precisely to the target audience while being able to point to plausible alternative meanings to other audiences, and the intellectual facility and linguistic agility to present necessary compromises and accommodation resulting from intense bargaining as win-win outcomes. Matters of state call for delicacy as well as soundness of judgement and failures of either can lead to catastrophic consequences. The diplomat steps aside and the soldier takes over when the government concludes that the goals being pursued can best be achieved through the use of military force—or when the diplomat has bungled. While the threat of use of force, whether explicit or implicit, is still part of the diplomat's arsenal, the actual use of force is required because diplomacy has failed and must be substituted by other instruments of statecraft.

0.1 ANTECEDENTS

The word 'diplomacy' is of surprisingly recent vintage. The *Encyclopaedia Britannica*, defining it as 'the art of conducting the intercourse of nations with each other', noted that 'It is singular that a term of so much practical importance in politics and history should be so recent in its adoption that it is not to be found in Johnson's dictionary.'[3] The *Oxford English Dictionary* defines it as 'The management of international relations by negotiation; the method by which these relations are adjusted and managed by ambassadors and envoys.'[4] It is derived from a Greek word—a diploma—meaning an official document or state paper. Trained archivists who organized such documents were the first to be called diplomats or 'those who dealt with diplomas or archives'.[5] By the end of the 17th century, words like 'diplomaticus' and 'diplomatique' were applied more restrictively to treaties or state papers dealing with international relations; diplomats were officials dealing with such matters; 'diplomatic body'[6] referred collectively to ambassadors, envoys, and officials attached to foreign missions; and 'diplomatic service' denoted the part of the career public service from which were drawn the personnel working in the permanent missions in other countries.

The term ambassador, on the other hand, has been in common usage throughout recorded history. The *Oxford English Dictionary* provides three definitions:[7]

1. a. An official messenger sent...by or to a sovereign or public body; an envoy, commissioner, or representative. *esp* b. A minister of high rank sent by one sovereign or state on a mission to another.
2. A minister at a foreign court, of the highest rank, who there permanently represents his sovereign or country.
3. An appointed or official messenger generally.

The practice of sending official envoys to foreign political jurisdictions to represent a sovereign political entity is very ancient. Rulers in Greece, Persia, India, and China exchanged messages and gifts, negotiated treaties and alliances (often through marriage), signed peace agreements, and sometimes mediated disputes between neighbouring sovereigns. Thus diplomats and the profession of diplomacy existed well before the word was invented to refer to them collectively as a class. Some of the more famous ones from European history include Machiavelli (1469–1527), Cardinal Richelieu (1585–1642), Talleyrand (1754–1838), Metternich (1773–1859), and Bismarck (1815–1898). Sir Thomas Roe was the British 'lord ambassador' at the court of Mughal Emperor Jehangir (1615–1618). The office or institution of ambassador therefore has a long lineage. Many rituals, conventions, and etiquettes have accumulated over centuries to endow the office with distinction, mystique, and glamour.

According to *Satow's Diplomatic Practice*, the earliest known 'diplomatic document' is a copy of a letter from the Mesopotamian Kingdom of Ebla to that of Amazi (about 1000 km away) that was inscribed on a 2500 BC cuneiform tablet.[8] In the 4th–5th centuries BC, the Greek city-states exchanged duly accredited ambassadors who presented their case to rulers and citizens' assemblies and enjoyed a measure of immunity that went beyond the prevailing standards of local hospitality towards foreigners.[9] Being a good public speaker was a key requirement of ambassadors at the time, since they were expected to address the citizens of the city-state they were accredited to at the 'agora', or public square. Customs, ceremonies, and rules of procedure were established and institutionalized. The Greeks began the practice of selecting a local citizen in a foreign state as a resident consul who served the interests of a foreign state and yet was held in high esteem. The Greek city-states also struggled with the tension between efficient negotiation that rests on confidential discussions and the openness and transparency demanded by the citizens of a democracy or a republic. The first diplomatic conference as such was the celebrated Sparta Conference of 432 BC to debate whether or not to declare war on Athens. Thus the Greeks 'developed an elaborate apparatus of foreign relations together with a substantial body of diplomatic practice which ... endured for several centuries.'[10]

The Romans refined the role of emissaries to include trained observation and interpretation of conditions and opinions in the host country and negotiation in pursuit of the empire's interests. Important innovations included the extension of diplomatic immunity, and the practice of international arbitration through commissions. On the other side of the world, in India, the *Arthashastra*,[11] a treatise on statecraft, military strategy, and economic policy by Kautilya (ca. 350–283 BC, prime minister of India's first great emperor Chandragupta Maurya), classified diplomatic representatives into plenipotentiaries (fully empowered to represent the king), envoys with limited negotiating authority, and simple messengers. All were to be accorded special international protection. Kautilya also anticipated Machiavelli in the amoral and ruthless nature of his advice on statecraft to the prince.

The institution of residential diplomacy—'the most important innovation in diplomatic practice'[12]—has its origins in the second half of the 15th century among the Italian city-states. Envoys were soon stationed also in important capitals like Paris, Madrid, and Vienna to communicate messages and observe and interpret shifting moods and alliances and dynastic struggles for power in kingdoms most likely to intervene in the Italian Wars (1494–1559).[13] Many of the standard practices associated with modern diplomacy—the use of couriers and the use of secretaries—as well as elaborate written reports on developments in the host country were refined during this period.

The age of classical European diplomacy began with the Treaty of Westphalia (1648) which marks the transition from Christendom to the modern states system. In the Thirty Years' War (1618–1648), Cardinal Richelieu, by aligning France with the Protestants at the cost of the expansion of the Holy Roman Empire that would have weakened the French king, elevated state interests above the values of the religious community as the guiding principle of foreign policy. The seminal treatise on interstate relations was Emmerich de Vattel's *Law of Nations* (1758). The Congress of Vienna codified diplomacy as a characteristic institution of the new states system in 1815 and set out the international codes of conduct governing diplomatic discourse among sovereign states in the interests of the nation as a whole rather than of any given dynasty.

As indicated by the transformation of the European order after Westphalia, the content and practice of diplomacy is shaped by the changing nature of sovereign political actors. Following the Congress of Vienna, Europe enjoyed a hundred years free of major war under the Concert system. But its collapse under the weight of the First World War discredited the system of clandestine alliances and secret diplomacy. The age of democracy brought accompanying pressures for open and transparent diplomacy, negotiations, and treaties: 'open covenants openly arrived at', as US President Woodrow Wilson famously put it. Article 102 of the UN Charter requires member states to register all international agreements and deposit the texts with the Secretary-General. The end of the First World War also saw the first instance of summit diplomacy in the modern era: much of the Treaty of Versailles was negotiated between Wilson, Georges Clemenceau, and Lloyd George—just as many of the most important clauses of the UN Charter were negotiated between Franklin Roosevelt, Joseph Stalin, and Winston Churchill in summit meetings at Tehran and Yalta, and of Harry Truman, Stalin, and Churchill (followed by Clement Attlee) at Potsdam, during and after the Second World War.

The interwar period opened new channels and modes of diplomacy. New diplomatic procedures consolidated and initiated by the League included multilateral diplomacy, public debates, international parliamentary procedures, and collective decision-making. A parallel innovation was the tripartite representation of government, labour, and business in the International Labour Organization (ILO) where labour and management could vote independently of their governments. Many of the diplomatic practices and conventions have been codified in the 1946 Convention on the Privileges and Immunities of the United Nations (UN), the 1961 Vienna Convention on Diplomatic Relations, and the 1963 Vienna Convention on Consular Relations.

The amount of discretion and latitude permitted to ambassadors and envoys is partly a function of the prevailing technology of transportation and communications. In ancient times, when direct consultations and back-and-forth communications were not feasible, the monarch or republic was far more dependent on the ambassador's judgement and skills on the spot. Today all important matters are referred back to the ambassador's own capital. Advances in the ease and speed of travel have allowed leaders or their designates to engage in shuttle diplomacy—over and around embassy officials. At the same time, a systematic and persistent disregard of departmental analyses and advice increases the risks of costly mistakes.

Most importantly for present purposes, the world of international relations—the 'field' in which diplomats operate—has changed substantially since the First World War. The business of the world has changed almost beyond recognition over the last century. We operate today in a global environment that is vastly more challenging, complex, and demanding than the world of 1914. Just consider the vocabulary and metaphors of the new age: Srebrenica, Rwanda, DRC, Sierra Leone, Kosovo, East Timor, Darfur, Libya; child soldiers, ethnic cleansing, blood diamonds, 9/11, regime change, Islamophobia, HIV/AIDS, global warming, climate change; Microsoft, Google, iPod, Blackberry, Facebook, Twitter, YouTube, Flickr, WikiLeaks; metrosexual, heteropolitan, localitarian—the list is endless and endlessly changing.

In particular, as described in Figure 0.1, there has been a fivefold change in the world of diplomacy:

i. In the rapidly expanding *numbers and types of actors*, from governments to national private sector firms, multinational corporations (MNCs), non-governmental organizations (NGOs), and regional and intergovernmental organizations (IGOs).

ii. In the *domain and scope* of the subject matter or content, expanding rapidly to a very broad array of the different sectors of public policy and government activity that extend well beyond traditional 'high issue' foreign policy.

iii. In the *levels* at which diplomatic engagement and activity take place, from the local through the domestic-national to the bilateral, regional, and global, with globalization reducing the height of separation between the different layers.

iv. In the *apparatus and machinery* of foreign relations and diplomacy.

v. In the *modes, types, and techniques* of diplomacy.

We will shortly raise the question as to how much these changes can be encapsulated in the conceptual shift from 'club' to 'network' diplomacy. But first it is necessary to elaborate on the changes themselves.

0.1.1 Actors

The number of actors in world affairs has grown enormously, the types of actors have changed very substantially, the interactions between them have grown more dense, and the agenda of international public policy has been altered in line with the changing circumstances. Four decades ago Raymond Aron argued that 'the ambassador and the soldier *live* and *symbolize* international relations which, insofar as they are inter-state

Levels	Local, Domestic, National, Bilateral, Regional, Global
Scope	Broad array of public policy issues
Actors	Governments, Private Firms, MNCs, Civil Society Actors
Machinery	Ministry of Foreign Affairs, Ministry of International Trade, Department of Defence, Ministry of International Affairs
Modes	Summits, Shuttle, Track Two, Celebrity

FIGURE 0.1. Complexity management in network diplomacy

Adapted from: Jorge Heine, 'On the Manner of Practising the New Diplomacy', *CIGI Working Paper* No. 11 (Waterloo, Ontario: Centre for International Governance Innovation, October 2006), 15.

relations, concern diplomacy and war'.[14] Today, alongside the hordes of national diplomats and soldiers, the international lawyer, the multinational merchant, the cross-border financier, the World Bank and International Monetary Fund (IMF) technocrat, the UN peacekeeper, the World Health Organization (WHO) health official, the International Atomic Energy Agency (IAEA) inspector, 'Eurocrats' and officials of other regional organizations, and the humanitarian worker jostle for space on the increasingly congested stage of international diplomacy.

0.1.1.1 *States*

States are the basic and enduring entity in international relations and their number has grown manifold in the last hundred years, producing an exponential jump in the number of diplomatic interactions between them. One of the historic phenomena of the last century was the emergence of large swathes of humanity from colonial rule to independence. The first great wave of the retreat of European colonialism from Asia and Africa (1950s–1960s) and the South Pacific (1970s) was followed by the collapse of the large land-based Soviet empire and a fresh burst of newly independent countries in Eastern Europe and Central Asia (1990s). The number of independent state actors has quadrupled since 1945. And there is a great diversity among states, ranging from one superpower, two billion-strong, and nine nuclear-armed states to numerous mini-states, microstates, and failing states in a system of sovereign states that has famously been described as organized hypocrisy.[15]

There are several resulting diplomatic challenges. For most former colonies, from Africa and the South Pacific to Southeast and South Asia, the triple challenge of national integration, state-building, and economic development remains imperative. Several are struggling to avert state collapse and failure and the resulting humanitarian emergencies. This explains the importance of goals like the achievement of the Millennium Development Goals (MDGs), nation- and peace-building in places like Iraq, Afghanistan, and Haiti, and aid diplomacy, as major preoccupations of contemporary diplomacy. At the same time, former colonial powers and settler societies have to be sensitive to the foreign policy input of historical trauma, while former colonies must make an effort to escape the trap of viewing current events and motives from a historical prism. One of the clearest examples of the dual danger is in relation to providing international assistance to victims of atrocities inside sovereign borders.[16]

In addition to the number of state actors having grown, there is a military, financial, political, and moral rebalancing underway in the world's power structure. The end of the cold war terminated the US—Soviet great-power rivalry, brought victory for the liberal over a totalitarian ideology, and marked the triumph of the market over the command economy. The elimination of countervailing power to check the exercise of US power ushered in a quasi-imperial order that posed a major challenge for diplomacy: how to interact with a unipolar Washington that viewed itself as uniquely virtuous, resistant to 'Gulliverization',[17] and exempt from restrictions that applied to all others. A second and related challenge was how to interact with one another without always routing relations through Washington in a hub-and-spoke model.

While the four-trillion-dollar wars in Iraq and Afghanistan have contributed to the massive American debt load, outsourcing manufacturing to China and services to India has enfeebled US capacity to produce enough goods and services to pay its bills. The US economy, once the biggest, best balanced, and most productive and innovative, now seems saddled with debts, deficits, and distortions. If by the decade's end the US is still the world's biggest borrower, as Larry Summers mused,[18] will it still be the world's biggest power?

All actors engaged in the world of diplomacy have to adjust their goals and actions to the emerging reality of the power shift from the Atlantic to Asia and the Pacific. The future economic potential of Brazil, China, and India has already translated into present political clout, as witnessed acutely in areas such as multilateral trade negotiations and climate change. The demonstration of the limits to US and NATO power in Iraq and Afghanistan has left many less fearful of 'superior' Western power. Abusive practices in the 'war on terror' and the financial crisis have made them less respectful of Western values. Their own resilience in the financial emergency enhanced their self-confidence. Westerners have lost their once-dominant capacity to set standards and rules of behaviour for the whole world. Not just the process but the structures and rules of the game for conducting international negotiations must be reset. The minor adjustments in voting rights in the IMF and World Bank are harbingers of more significant changes that will be made in the foreseeable future.

As the various actors attempt to recalibrate foreign policy and diplomacy to realign them with the changing world order, some stress is inevitable. For example, as Japan readjusted to the changing equation between its traditional protector the US and its traditional rival China, it generated tension in relations with Washington and provoked a debate in Washington on whether to persuade Tokyo by the diplomacy of reassurance or coerce it by the diplomacy of pressure into honouring the previous government's commitments on the positioning and relocation of US troops and bases in Okinawa.[19]

Historically, a systemic rebalancing among major powers is rarely accomplished without a major war. In the contemporary, highly interdependent world, the costs of going to war would far exceed any potential gains. Indeed, the costs of delinking are so high as to suggest that the major powers must not just eschew armed conflict as the default mode of adjusting their relative status; on many global problems they must also deepen collaboration. That is, the realities of interdependence, globalization, and the technology of destructiveness mark a fundamental transformation in the diplomacy of major power relations, with flow-on implications for the diplomacy of all other actors in international society.

0.1.1.2 *International Organizations*

The role of contemporary governments in setting and implementing policy is increasingly constrained by multinational merchants, international financiers, global banks, regional, international, and supranational organizations, NGOs, and even sub-national public authorities like provincial and municipal governments in Canada, Germany, Spain, Brazil, and the US, to name just a few. There was a spurt in the number and types of international organizations in the 20th century. Their number climbed from 37 in

1909 and 123 in 1951 to about 7,000 in 2000; the number of NGOs increased from 176 to 48,000 in the corresponding period.[20] They have added greatly to the institutional complexity of international relations. Few issues today lie completely outside the purview of one international organization or another.

Napoleon Bonaparte imposed temporary order and unity on Europe through conquest. The other European powers set up an alternative Concert system in reaction and transformed the original impulse of a military alliance for the single purpose of defeating Napoleon into the longer-term political goal of preventing a similar domination of Europe by any one power in the future. The Concert of Europe was the most comprehensive attempt until then to construct new machinery for keeping the peace among and by the great powers. Although there was an ideological (anti-revolutionary) component to this process, the prime concern was the maintenance of order on a hierarchical basis.

The Hague Conferences of 1899 and 1907 signalled the broadening of international relations in participation and agenda. They pointed to an emergent extra-European international system. Emergent powers such as the US and Japan took their place on the world stage. Moreover, lesser powers would demand a say; and, with their emphasis upon mediation, conciliation, and enquiry, they demonstrated a rationalistic and legalistic approach to the problem of international disputes.

The two major international organizations of the 20th century were the League of Nations after the First and the United Nations after the Second World War. The League was built around Europe as the core of the international political system.[21] It accepted the sovereign state as the central unit of international affairs and great powers as the dominant participants. It did not challenge any of the fundamental principles of the traditional multistate system. The closeness with which the UN was modelled upon the League was testimony to the fact that while the League had failed, people still had faith in the *idea* of an umbrella international organization to oversee world peace and cooperation. While many of the UN Charter provisions were borrowed directly from the League Covenant, others represented substantial codifications of League procedures or logical developments of nascent League ideas.

International organizations are not merely sites of global governance but, in some limited yet important respects and the principal—agent problem notwithstanding, actors in their own right as well.[22] If the United Nations is an actor, who are the relevant policy-makers? Is 'international' policy made and implemented by international organizations or by national authorities meeting and interacting in international forums? To what extent has the policy paralysis over Darfur been the result of a policy gap on the part of the UN as opposed to weak political will among key member states? How well suited is the UN to determine the ends of policy, or to guide the processes by which it is made?[23] The one person with some claim to be the world's top diplomat is the UN Secretary-General who symbolizes as well as represents the organization and is expected to set the collective interest of the UN above the partisan interests of member states.[24]

International organizations have tempered the dictum handed down to posterity by Thucydides that 'the strong do what they can and the weak suffer what they must'.[25] UN multilateral diplomacy differs from traditional interstate diplomacy in some important respects.[26]

Guided by Charter principles, it offsets somewhat, albeit not totally, the unfavourable position of the weaker party. It aims to establish a just peace as well as a stable balance of power. And it takes into account the interests of member states as well as the disputants, thereby broadening the support base for any solutions reached. There will be occasions also when political leaders will welcome the UN's ability to provide a 'golden bridge' across which national governments can retire to safety, as well as a 'lightning rod' for deflecting and burying the more violent political reactions at home to international events.[27]

The UN system also includes very many agencies, funds, and programmes, some of which collectively and in the person of their chief executives are also influential international actors: the UN high commissioners for human rights and for refugees, the IAEA and the WHO and their directors-general, the UN Development Programme (UNDP) and its Administrator, the UN Children's Fund (UNICEF) and its chief, not to mention the World Bank and the IMF and their heads.

There has also been a spurt in the number of regional organizations (for example the African Union (AU), the Organization of American States (OAS), the Association of Southeast Nations (ASEAN), and the Asia-Pacific Economic Cooperation (APEC)), many with their own permanent secretariats and secretaries-general, as well as organizations serving historical links like the Commonwealth of Nations or a religious community like the Organization of the Islamic Conference (OIC). The European Union (EU) is unique as a supranational organization with its own president, foreign minister, foreign ministry, and overseas resident missions. In more recent times, the so-called new regionalism entails direct relations among regional organizations themselves, as for example in the summit meetings between ASEAN and the EU.[28] These too add to the institutional congestion and complexity of modern diplomacy.

0.1.1.3 *Civil Society*

'Civil society' refers to the social and political space where voluntary associations attempt to shape norms and policies for regulating public life in social, political, economic, and environmental dimensions.[29] Like national society, international society too is becoming more plural and diverse. There has been an exponential growth in the number of civil society actors and in the volume of transnational networks in which they are embedded.[30] They bridge the 'disconnect between the political geography of the state on the one side and the new geography of economic and social relations on the other'.[31] The expanding worldwide civil society networks embrace almost every level of organization, from the village community to global summits; and almost every sector of public life, from the provision of micro-credit and the delivery of paramedical assistance, to environmental and human rights norm promotion and activism.

Civil society actors can play one or more of the following roles: research; outreach education; advocacy and norm promotion; agenda-setting; lobbying governments and intergovernmental organizations to adopt and police laws, policies, and courses of action; implementing programmes and delivering services and humanitarian assistance; monitoring implementation of international commitments; and direct action. With respect to multilateralism, civil society actors have contributed in three ways: by advocating multilateral solutions to global problems, cultivating popular constituencies for multilateralism, and connecting local and national struggles to global norms and international institutions.[32]

Kofi Annan noted that NGOs are not merely 'disseminators of information or providers of services but also…shapers of policy, be it in peace and security matters, in development or in humanitarian affairs.'[33] More than 3,000 NGOs have been granted consultative status with the UN Economic and Social Council (ECOSOC). The agenda-setting capacity of NGOs—Amnesty International, Human Rights Watch, the International Committee of the Red Cross (ICRC),[34] Greenpeace, World Wildlife Fund (WWF), the International Union for the Conservation of Nature (IUCN)—is greater than that of many governments. The Cardoso Panel urged the UN to promote 'networked governance' by fostering greater interaction between governments and citizens.[35] It noted that many NGOs had become frustrated at being able to speak in the United Nations but not heard, with their participation producing little impact on outcomes.[36]

Nevertheless, NGOs face many challenges to their legitimacy as they are often seen as unelected, unaccountable, unrepresentative, self-serving, and irresponsible. Hugo Slim writes of 'voice accountability': the reliability and credibility of *what* they say (an empirical question: can you prove it?), and the *locus of their authority* for saying it (a political question: from where do you get your authority to speak?).[37] The engagement of governments and international organizations with unelected civil society actors can sometimes cut across and undermine the role of democratically elected representatives.[38] Recipient countries, for example Afghanistan, can resent the NGO community as competitors for siphoning off aid from governments.[39] 'For all the talk of coordination and accountability, the need to maintain market share continues to trump sound humanitarian practice—at least in crises like the [December 2004] tsunami, where the Western public and Western donor governments are attentive and engaged.'[40] Recognizing the validity of many of the complaints, civil society groups have begun to address the need for a system of self-regulation that rejects violence and lawlessness, and to broaden their membership to incorporate people from developing countries.

Civil society operating on the soft and well-lit side of the international street poses fewer and lesser problems than 'uncivil' society: non-state actors operating among the shadows on the rough and dark side of the international street who too have become increasingly globalized and interlinked in their operations, funnelling women and children, drugs, arms, hot money, and terrorists across state borders.[41]

The threefold challenge for diplomacy is how to counter uncivil society, give voice to civil society, but neither a vote nor a veto to them: for that would be an abdication of responsibility to govern on behalf of all citizens. NGOs usually focus on a single issue, while governments are multipurpose organizations. For some NGOs, one of their most important tasks is to hold the feet of governments to the fire of normative and legal commitments by monitoring their performance and scrutinizing their actions. Thus while in some cases they may be included in official delegations, acting as paradiplomats in harmony with governmental goals, in other cases they may have an adversarial relationship with their own government, for example with respect to reporting human rights violations to international agencies. In 2010, Greenpeace activists harassed Japanese whaling boats and thereby complicated official bilateral relations between Australia and Japan. Like Japan and Norway with whaling, Canada has been at the receiving end of protests by European NGO activists who object to seal hunting, and the Canadian government itself cannot but take into account NGO views in shaping its Myanmar policy. One of the best-known examples of the power of a domestic lobby over foreign policy is the role of Cuban-Americans in Florida in shaping US policy on Cuba. A more controversial example is the alleged power of the Israeli lobby in determining US policy on the Israel—Palestine conflict.[42] These established groups have been joined by the transnational activities of communities such as the Armenians and Sri Lankan Tamils.

0.1.1.4 *Multinational Corporations (MNCs)*

If some of the popular caricatures are to be believed, MNCs control and dominate world affairs. If anything, the opposite is true, that they are more severely disenfranchised in global decision-making bodies than NGOs and deserve a seat at the table and a voice in the room commensurate with their role and influence. Several multinational corporations employ agents to liaise and negotiate directly with foreign governments to obtain concessions, modify laws or taxes, permit repatriation of profits or duty-free entry of necessary parts and inputs, provide facilities or subsidies, relax labour and environmental standards and regulations, and so on. In 2009 the Australian-Chinese head of a major Australian firm was arrested by China and accused of industrial espionage and corruption, creating a diplomatic tiff between the two Asia-Pacific nations. The Global Compact was an effort led by Annan to instil civic virtue in the global marketplace by urging international business to adopt voluntary codes of conduct that incorporated human rights, environmental and labour standards into their operations.[43] Where MNCs (or more accurately, MNC executives) have been ascendant are in informal clubs and networks such as the Bilderberg group, the Trilateral Commission, the World Economic Forum (Davos), and the Clinton Global Initiative which merge the worlds of politics and business.

0.1.2 Issues

The issues and preoccupations of the new millennium present new and different types of challenges from those that faced the world in 1918 and again in 1945. With the new realities and challenges have come corresponding new expectations for action and new standards of conduct in national and international affairs.

Until the Second World War, war was an institution of the states system, with distinctive rules, etiquette, norms, and stable patterns of practices.[44] The number of armed conflicts rose steadily until the end of the cold war, peaked in the early 1990s, and has declined since then. The nature of armed conflict itself has changed, with most being internal struggles for power, dominance, and resources rather than militarized interstate confrontations.[45] Battle lines, if they exist at all, are fluid and shifting rather than territorially demarcated and static. The line between war as a political act and organized criminality has become increasingly blurred. Even most 'internal' conflicts have regional and transnational elements. Because they merge seamlessly with sectarian divides, contemporary conflicts are often rooted in, reproduce, and replicate past intergroup atrocities, thereby perpetuating hard-edged cleavages that are perceived as zero-sum games by all parties. Thus all sides are trapped in a never-ending cycle of suspicions, atrocities, and recriminations. The net result is that non-combatants are now on the frontline of modern battles. The need to help and protect civilians at risk of death and displacement caused by armed conflict is paramount. Diplomats will be judged on how well they discharge or dishonour their international responsibility to protect.

The multiplication of internal conflicts was accompanied by a worsening of the abuses of the human rights of millions of people. Conscious of the atrocities committed by the Nazis while the world looked silently away, the UN adopted the Universal Declaration of Human Rights in 1948. The two covenants in 1966 added force and specificity, affirming both civil-political and social-economic-cultural rights without privileging either set. The United Nations has also adopted scores of other legal instruments on human rights and in his major reform report in 2005 Annan elevated human rights alongside security and development as the three great normative mandates of the organization.[46] The parallel expansion of the reach and scope of international humanitarian law, and the rise of domestic, regional, international, and non-governmental institutions championing, monitoring, and enforcing human rights and international humanitarian law, has generated additional tasks and challenges for diplomacy.

The rise of environmental consciousness, the need to husband resources more frugally and nurture our fragile ecosystems more tenderly as our common legacy for future generations, was another great social movement of the last century that contributed greatly to the greening of the agenda of international affairs. The concept of 'sustainable development' was one of the major norm shifts, with the Bruntland Commission being the midwife.[47] How best to operationalize the concept in concrete policy and actual practice remains intensely contentious and thus a major diplomatic challenge.

Nothing illustrates this better than climate change. There is substantial agreement among scientists that the rate of climate change driven by human activity dwarfs the natural rates of change. The speed and amount of global warming will be determined by the increase in greenhouse gases and will in turn determine the rise in sea levels. But there is disagreement about the exact role and relative potency of different natural, cyclical, and human causes of global warming; about the costs, scale, timing, and distribution of the harmful consequences; about the urgency, costs, and benefits of the different mitigation and adaptation courses of action; and about the relative net costs and benefits of different courses of action for tackling different problems confronting human beings today. How much should rich and poor nations sacrifice their present and future lifestyles for the sake of the other? Or the present generation for the sake of future generations? Having entered the world of public health policy, how relevant is the precautionary principle to the world of international environmental diplomacy?

In 2007, the *foreign* ministers of seven countries—Norway, Brazil, France, Indonesia, Senegal, South Africa, and Thailand—issued the Oslo Ministerial Declaration calling for more attention to *health* as a foreign policy issue. They noted that 'Health is deeply interconnected with the environment, trade, economic growth, social development, national security, and human rights and dignity.' They linked health to human security: 'While national security focuses on the defence of the state from external attack, national health security relates to defence against internal and external public-health risks and threats', adding that 'These are risks and threats that by their very nature do not respect borders, as people, animals, and goods travel around the world faster than ever before.'[48] Among their concerns were a recognition that investment in health was fundamental to economic growth, development, and poverty eradication; imbalances in the global health workforce market (the persistent lack of skilled health workers and their uneven distribution within and among countries); and the protection of peoples' health in situations of crises. More frequent travel and contact among people from different countries and continents have been accompanied by the risk of major global pandemics like HIV/ AIDS, avian flu, SARS, and so on, creating pressures for governments to harmonize national and cross-border surveillance mechanisms and emergency responses. This also requires international data collection and standardization of measures.

Brink Lindsey described the 1990s as the age of abundance with rising incomes, growing capital markets, and accelerating flows of money and investment.[49] Untroubled by want and scarcity, Americans fought over values both domestically, leading to culture wars, and internationally, leading to expanding interest in human rights and the international protection agenda. By the end of the first decade of the 21st century, the age of scarcity seemed to have made a stunning comeback with alarmist scenarios of food, fuel, and water scarcity, fragile financial and banking systems and vulnerable ecosystems.

Financial crises of the 1990s in Asia, Latin America, and Russia and of 2008–2012 in the US and Europe showed how much, and how quickly, regional crises take on systemic character through rapid contagion. They also highlighted the unequal distribution of costs among the victims of financial crises. Hence the claim by Michel Camdessus, the former managing director of the IMF (1987–2000), that to the duty of domestic excellence and rectitude we must add the ethic of global responsibility in the management of national economies. He goes on to describe the widening inequality within and among nations as 'morally outrageous, economically wasteful, and socially explosive'.[50] A considerable portion of national and international diplomacy in 2007–2012 was devoted to grappling with the financial crisis.

The movement of people in large numbers, whether seeking fresh opportunities in new lands through migration or escaping cycles of violence, famine, persecution, natural disasters, or poverty, has been a major political problem domestically in many countries and a major diplomatic challenge internationally. Diasporas represent both a domestic element in the changing demographic composition of the citizens of a country, and a foreign policy complication if troubles from home country are imported. Examples of this abound: Tamils in Canada and Sri Lanka, Sikhs in Canada, Jews in most Western countries and the Middle East conflict, Iraqi exiles in the lead-up to the 2003 invasions of Iraq, and Cubans in Florida.

0.1.3 Globalization

National frontiers are becoming less relevant in determining the flow of ideas, information, goods, services, capital, labour, and technology. The speed of modern communications makes borders increasingly permeable, while the volume of cross-border flows threatens to overwhelm the capacity of states to manage them. Far from diminishing, complex interdependence and globalization have increased the scope and volume of negotiations, especially in multilateral forums. The growth in the number of participants taking part in the negotiations, the number of issues that are now the subject of international negotiations, the diversity of negotiating styles of officials coming from vastly different political cultures and levels of development, and the technical complexity of the subject matters up for negotiation have combined to make the process of negotiation more elaborate, highly technical, and more protracted. This has been obvious in this century already with respect to climate change in the effort to move beyond the Kyoto Protocol at major international conferences in Bali (2008), Copenhagen (2009), Cancun (2010), and Durban (2011); in the drawn out and immobilized Doha Round of trade talks; in the failures of the NPT Review conference in 2005 and of the Conference on Disarmament in Geneva; and in the largely failed, if with a few rosebuds of consolation prizes, effort of the UN reform summit in 2005.

0.1.4 The Apparatus of Foreign Relations and Diplomacy

Civil servants are the permanent custodians of permanent interests and permanent problems. A foreign service officer represents a depth of judgement based on experience accumulated over time and aggregated across the different parts and functions of the department. Generalist and specialist skills are often combined.

Reflecting the growing importance of trade promotion in diplomacy, in the 1980s Australia, Canada, and New Zealand reorganized their foreign ministries by integrating trade with classical foreign policy. Somewhat paradoxically, New Zealand concluded a far-reaching free trade agreement with Australia in the 1980s more to avoid foreign policy damage to its most important bilateral relationship resulting from endless bickering over relatively trivial trade disputes, than for calculations of trade benefits.[51]

Not all foreign ministries have adapted equally well to the changing requirements of modern diplomacy. An internal report on the British Foreign and Commonwealth Office (FCO) concluded that the FCO was excessively risk-averse and timid, incapable of defending itself within the British bureaucracy, and prone to promote mediocrity over talent so that the route to career success was in never making any mistakes.[52]

At about the same time, coincidentally, an independent high-powered panel scrutinized Australia's foreign ministry and came to equally unflattering conclusions. The number of foreign service officers had fallen by one-fifth since 1996 and their language skills were deteriorating. The budget of Australia's Department of Foreign Affairs and Trade was just one-twentieth the size of the Department of Defence, pointing to an imbalance in the distribution of resources between the two primary tools of foreign and defence policy for the pursuit of Australian interests in a world made more complex and demanding by the forces of globalization.[53]

Using modern travel and communications, not only can presidents, prime ministers, and foreign ministers go over the ambassador's head directly to their counterparts in other countries; often so can business executives, trade union leaders, journalists, and NGOs. The bigger departments from the home country's bureaucracy, better staffed and resourced, often place their own personnel in overseas embassies: not just defence, but also agriculture, education, and so on. Not only is diplomacy no longer the exclusive preserve of foreign ministries; it is no longer the exclusive preserve of foreign ministers. The crowded international diplomatic calendar includes meetings of non-foreign ministers, for example the G7 finance ministers or the various environment ministers. If the tasks of modern diplomacy cut across swathes of governmental business spread among many different departments, there is the risk that lots of small solutions will be produced to big problems.

The foreign ministry and minister have lost influence to other government departments, to centralizing prime ministers who assert direct control over affairs of state, and to international and non-governmental organizations. Another potential difficulty is that the close involvement of prime ministers and their offices can mean that calculations of politics override the demands of government. The US presidential system of government has hollowed out its own foreign policy capacity by outsourcing development, security, and diplomatic tasks to private contractors.[54] In what respects have alternate roles and influence accreted to them?

The resident mission abroad in foreign capitals remains a vital cog in the diplomatic machinery, but often a large proportion of its work can be devoted to multilateral diplomacy. For example, the search for the elusive second resolution authorizing war on Saddam Hussein was conducted in national capitals; only the outcome would be determined in the UN Security Council. The failure to get the resolution was the failure of bilateral diplomacy in parallel in countries who were members of the Security Council in 2003, albeit in a multilateral context and for a multilateral enterprise. Conversely, lacking the resources to establish resident embassies in all the world's countries, many smaller and poorer countries take advantage of permanent missions to the major international organizations, especially the United Nations, to engage in bilateral diplomacy with the counterpart heads of other missions to the UN.

Diplomats posted abroad must learn as much—and as quickly as possible—about the host country's culture, politics, policies, and personalities. They must cultivate friends and interlocutors and earn their respect, trust, and confidence. They must do so while avoiding falling prey to the dreaded disease of 'localitis' where their understanding of and sympathy for the host country's policy overrides or undermines their own country's interests and policies. Foreign postings are necessary to understand foreign countries. Postings back to one's own capital are just as necessary so as not to lose touch with one's own nation, society, and government.

When, under what circumstances, and to whom, may and should a diplomat speak out or reveal internal information? Craig Murray, the British ambassador to Uzbekistan, was replaced in 2004 when he complained about torture committed in that country. Canadian diplomat Richard Colvin wrote several anxious memoranda while serving in the embassy in Kabul expressing concern about the possibility that prisoners being handed over by Canadian forces to Afghan authorities could face torture. When the Parliament of Canada began investigating possible Canadian complicity in torture, Colvin agreed to testify. Although the government mounted a PR attack on him, legal experts argued that according to the country's highest court, Canada's civil servants owe loyalty to the Crown, not to any governing party.[55] The difficult element in this case is that international law imposes an obligation on Canada to have made sure that the transferred prisoners would not be subjected to torture. The incident recalled the insistence by Britain's Chief of Defence Staff that, to avoid his soldiers being charged with war crimes, he needed unequivocal advice from the Attorney General on the legality of the 2003 Iraq war before he would agree to send any troops there. That is, advances in international humanitarian law are starting to affect relations between diplomats and home governments.

Some diplomatic services have had a tradition of ambassadors sending a valedictory despatch at the end of their overseas tours to their home capital, in which they offered candid personal assessments of the country in which they had been living. Such letters written by British ambassadors, disclosed to the BBC under Freedom of Information laws, show that some of them thought Canadians easily impressed by mediocrity; Nicaraguans to be dishonest, unreliable, violent, and alcoholic; Nigerians to be maddeningly prone to choose self-damaging courses of action; Africans in general to regard cutting off their nose to spite their face as a triumph of cosmetic surgery; and Thais to be generally licentious.[56]

The boundary between domestic and foreign policy is often blurred, for example in the issue area of terrorism. Often, even those acts of terrorism rooted solely in domestic causes and issues, such as with the Liberation Tigers of Tamil Eelam (LTTE), will have an international dimension in the flow of arms and funds. Just as often, terrorist groups have substantial cross-border links and agendas. The close, mirror relationship between foreign policy and defence is captured in the familiar dictum by Clausewitz that war is the continuation of foreign policy by other means. The phenomenon of international terrorism introduced an additional dimension to this dictum via the requirement for intelligence and the involvement of intelligence agencies. Western countries typically separate foreign and domestic intelligence agencies and agendas. The latter is properly part of the domestic law enforcement machinery. Foreign intelligence agencies, on the other hand, operate in the shadowy world between foreign and defence ministries. The role of Pakistan's Inter-Services Intelligence Directorate (ISI) in setting or sabotaging the country's official foreign policy is especially notorious. The US Secretary for Homeland Security bridges the domestic-foreign divide, but the US National Security

Adviser concentrates almost solely on the foreign policy side of the ledger. But in India the same position straddles the domestic-external responsibilities.[57]

0.1.5 Modes, Types, and Techniques of Diplomacy

In the Middle Ages diplomacy was typically engaged in by kings and princes of neighbouring states directly at summit level.[58] The practice fell out of favour partly because of the inherent risk to the personal safety and security of the royals, and partly owing to the paucity of results. The ease and speed of international travel, combined with an explosion in the range of issues that diplomacy now covers, is responsible for a proliferation of diplomatic summits with a resulting convergence between foreign policy-makers and the practice of diplomacy. The international calendar of summit meetings is surprisingly crowded for the leaders of most countries who are expected to attend the regularly scheduled gatherings of the United Nations, regional and sub-regional organizations like the AU, the Arab League, the Southern African Development Community (SADC), the European Council, ASEAN, the ASEAN Regional Forum (ARF), APEC, and the OAS; organizations like the Nonaligned Movement (NAM), the Commonwealth of Nations, the Francophonie, the OIC, the Shanghai Cooperation Organization, and the North Atlantic Treaty Organization (NATO); the G8 and the new G20; etc. There are also the irregular ad hoc summits, for example the famous meeting between Richard Nixon and Mao Zedong in Beijing in 1972 which recalibrated the cold war world order. While some leaders like these summits for the photo-opportunities, others shy away from them because they offer little else beyond photo-ops. Some summits offer little beyond symbolism, some can make genuine progress on shared global challenges and problems, but in any case summits with their alphabet soup of acronyms are an inescapable feature of the contemporary diplomatic topography.

Shuttle diplomacy, which would not be possible without modern travel, will always be associated most closely with Henry Kissinger, as first President Nixon's National Security Adviser and later his Secretary of State. His conceptual approach to diplomacy was traditional, if not classical, European balance of power. But, guided in part by an abiding distrust of the bureaucracy, he engaged in intensive back-channel diplomacy that saw him shuttling back and forth between Washington and other capitals. Secrecy was maintained not just for the intrinsic confidentiality of highly sensitive discussions, but also to minimize the chances of being sabotaged by the almost guaranteed resistance to radical initiatives that reside in large bureaus with their own institutional memories and standard operating procedures.

The practice of Track Two diplomacy has also grown in intensity and influence in recent times. Track One refers to the standard form of diplomacy involving negotiations between officials of two or more countries. Track Two diplomacy involves unofficial and generally informal interaction between non-governmental actors including NGOs, scholars, humanitarian organizations, and former government officials. The involvement of sub-national units like provincial governments in international affairs directly instead of through national authorities—for example delegations from Quebec in France or visits by Australian and Canadian provincial leaders to China and India in search of trade opportunities, votes (from immigrant communities back home) or to reaffirm cultural links—is described as 'paradiplomacy'.[59] Other examples of paradiplomacy include the use of private actors by states, for example personal representatives or envoys, and the engagement in what would normally be termed diplomacy by stateless nations—or, more accurately, nations in search of statehood—like the African National Congress (ANC), the Palestine Liberation Organization (PLO) before they succeeded in their political ambitions, or the Kurds even today. When the interactions and negotiations are in support of and complement official Track One diplomacy, they too can be described as paradiplomacy or, more commonly, twin-track diplomacy. At other times, Track Two diplomacy can compete with, and even undermine, official diplomacy.

Mark Malloch-Brown, the former UN Deputy Secretary-General and then a Foreign Office Minister in the UK, has written that 'Diplomacy has been multilateralised': Britain's power to influence events depends 'on our ability to orchestrate action in Washington, the UN, the European Union or corporate boards'.[60] Multilateral diplomacy has also brought in its wake new forms of diplomatic activity like public debates, extensive committee work, parliamentary procedures that back in the home country are the provenance of politicians, diplomatic caucusing akin to political caucusing in national parliaments, and forging coalitions and alliances. Many so-called international civil servants are in reality national diplomats seconded to international organizations. Yet while on international duty, they are required to act neutrally and not as agents of their governments or in the interests of their country of nationality. When the newly appointed American UN Under-Secretary-General for Management, Christopher B. Burnham, openly declared that his primary loyalty was to the US,[61] Secretary-General Annan had a quiet word to set him right. Many UN agencies, especially in the human rights, humanitarian, and development fields, prefer to work directly with NGOs than governments in service delivery. That is, the conceptual boundaries of diplomacy are expanding ever outwards in an interdependent and globalizing world.

Multilateral diplomacy also expanded the toolkit of both peaceful and coercive instruments to resolve conflicts and punish rule-breaking or norm-deviating states. These are spelt out in Chapters 6 and 7 of the UN Charter and include mediation, negotiation, arbitration, adjudication, diplomatic pressures, economic sanctions, and, as the ultimate resort, military force as against North Korean and Iraqi aggressions in 1950 and 1990.

The atomic age ushered in its own brand of nuclear diplomacy dealing with questions of deterrence, compellence, non-proliferation, and arms control and disarmament—unilaterally, bilaterally, and multilaterally. The sub-discipline spawned its own highly technical and esoteric literature and vocabulary. 'Smart power' seeks to harness the best of hard and soft power to get other actors to do what one wants.[62] Thus in this conception, soft power is not a substitute for hard power but a complement to it.

Several UN agencies, for example UNICEF and UNHCR, have taken to appointing Hollywood and other celebrities as 'goodwill ambassadors'. This is but one example of a growing trend of celebrity diplomacy, with several others joining to do good deeds like alleviate famine suffering and highlight the harsh humanitarian consequences of anti-personnel landmines.

While celebrities exploit the media-fanned oxygen of publicity, diplomats have to operate much more in the glare of global media scrutiny than was ever the case before. This has heightened the requirement for public diplomacy skills, including live debates with opponents and constant press conferences under the unforgiving lights of television where a gaffe will quickly find its way to YouTube. At the same time, skilful diplomacy will make use of media connections and networks to promote one's own message aggressively. The importance of public diplomacy has grown in the global village and in the age of reality TV. The media can be used to float trial balloons, to mobilize public support, to sustain momentum in negotiations, or to sabotage negotiations by leaking details of concessions contrary to individual preferences.

Conference diplomacy has its antecedents in the Eastern Mediterranean in the 4th century BC, when the Greek city-states and Persia convened eight international political congresses and established a mutually guaranteed territorial status quo along with agreed rules of conduct for regulating international affairs.[63] Universal membership and international legitimacy give today's United Nations an unmatched convening and mobilizing power that has been used to organize a large number of global conferences on a diverse range of topics from women to human rights, from population to social development, and from economic development to environmental conservation. Typically, the conferences have involved all the actors of global governance—states, civil society organizations, and, if to a lesser degree, private sector firms. Where the intergovernmental conferences are the sites for the growth of treaty law, the global conferences have been prime sites for the evolution of norms and 'soft law' which over time begins to exert a binding effect in the form of customary international law. As two scholars of the UN note, generally these conferences 'have been important for articulating new international norms, expanding international law, creating new structures, setting agendas . . . and promoting linkages among the UN, the specialized agencies, NGOs, and governments'.[64] Any large global conference is accompanied by extensive diplomatic activity, sometimes stretching over several years, as countries try to ascertain who the like-minded and therefore likely coalition partners are, to harmonize strategies to advance their own and defeat competing interests and efforts, to mobilize NGO support or blunt NGO dissent, and so on.

Another popular technique in the last half-century or so has been to convene blue-ribbon commissions as the means to transmit ideas for improving global governance to the national and international policy community.[65]

0.2 BEYOND THE NATIONAL INTEREST?

In a globalizing and highly interdependent world, the traditional power-maximizing pursuit of competitive foreign policies may not just be anachronistic, but acutely counterproductive. Instead, what is needed is identification of problems that are common to many if not all actors and the adoption of solutions that require collaboration. A joint Brookings Institution/Center on International Cooperation (New York University) study concluded that governments need to change their frame of analysis, embracing responsible sovereignty, reducing risk, promoting foresight, and strengthening resilience, perhaps with the help of institutions like the Intergovernmental Panel on Climate Change (IPCC) that use technical expertise to mobilize consciousness of mutual interests and of consequences of failure.[66]

In the classic formulation, the overriding goal of foreign policy was the promotion, pursuit, and defence of the national interest. Hans Morgenthau defined diplomacy as 'the art of bringing the different elements of national power to bear with maximum effect upon those points in the international situation which concern the national interest most directly'.[67] But if our analysis of the changing number and types of actors, as well as of the changing content and agenda of diplomacy, is correct, then using the national interest as the dominant analytical framework is not just overly simplistic for comprehending and explaining an increasingly complex set and pattern of diplomatic interactions. It is also misleading, if not false. Even states pursue multiple goals and interests, not just one interest. Different groups and participants who make up the collective entity known as the state have different interests based on their professional occupations, sectarian identities, and individual world views. There are non-state actors who by definition cannot be said to have 'national' interests. There is competition, tension, and even outright conflict between the various clusters of values, goals, and interests being pursued by the diverse actors.

Decision-makers therefore have to strike a balance among the different interests and actors, between domestic demands and international imperatives, between principle and pragmatism, between idealistic values and material interests, between what is the expedient and what is the right thing to do, between the national constituency and the international community, and between the immediate, medium, and long terms. Substituting the word 'a' in 'A balance of interests' for 'the' in 'the national interest' has a triple significance. It indicates that one particular balance is struck from among several possible options; it indicates human agency; and therefore it includes the possibility of human fallibility and the prospect of course corrections. Climate change is one of the best current examples of where the analytical framework of the national interest just does not cut it and is singularly unhelpful, perhaps even an obstacle to diplomacy. Effective programmes for tackling one of the gravest challenges confronting humanity require active partnerships among governments, scientists, economists, NGOs, and industry. The traditional, national value-maximizing paradigm of *the* national interest is simply irrelevant.

0.3 FROM CLUB TO NETWORK DIPLOMACY

Shortly before she moved across from Princeton University to take up the post of Director of Policy Planning at the State Department, Anne-Marie Slaughter penned an article in *Foreign Affairs* in which she argued that the key to successful foreign policy is networked diplomacy and that the US enjoys a competitive edge in this type of new diplomacy. War, business, media, society, even religion are all networked. So is diplomacy: 'managing international crises...requires mobilizing international networks of public and private actors'.[68] NGOs too network to multiply their effectiveness.[69] After her shift to the State department, Slaughter repeated that:

> We envision getting not just a new group of states around a table, but also building networks, coalitions and partnerships of states and nonstate actors to tackle specific problems...To do that, our diplomats are going to need to have skills that are closer to community organizing than traditional reporting and analysis. New connecting technologies will be vital tools in this kind of diplomacy.[70]

Conversely, Daniel Markey of the Council on Foreign Relations, himself a former State Department official, argues that India's soft power infrastructure of its diplomatic service, universities, and think tanks is inadequate to the task of managing the agenda of a major power.[71] The institutions charged with conducting analytical research, formulating, debating, and implementing India's foreign policy are underdeveloped, in decay, or chronically short of resources. The 600-strong Indian Foreign Service is too small (appropriate for a country of Malaysia's size, not for a power with global aspirations, according to an unnamed US diplomat),[72] hobbled by an antiquated selection process, and fails to provide mid-career training. India's universities, poorly funded and overly regulated, do not provide world-class education in subjects dealing with diplomacy. Its think tanks lack access to information and resources necessary for conducting policy-relevant scholarship of the highest quality. And its media and private sector firms are leaders in debating foreign policy issues but are not structured to undertake sustained foreign policy research and training. The net result is that India has a stunted capacity to engage in simultaneous and parallel negotiations on multiple subjects. That is, adapting Markey's critique to our conceptual vocabulary, Indian diplomacy is the less effective for being stuck in the club mode instead of shifting to network diplomacy.

Far from being in danger of becoming an endangered activity—rendered increasingly irrelevant by technological progress—diplomacy has become a critical instrument in an age of complex interdependence and of globalization. This empowerment of diplomacy, however, has meant radical changes to the context, tools, actors, and domain of the trade. These changes spring from the very nature of globalization, from the shifting conceptions of national sovereignty, from the realization that emerging transnational challenges in many areas can only be dealt through collective action, and from the growing interpenetration and interdependence of national societies.

One way of describing how diplomacy is coping with these massive changes is to say that we are witnessing a shift from 'club' to 'network diplomacy'. The former is based on a small number of players, a highly hierarchical structure, based largely on written communication and on low transparency; the latter is based on a much larger number of players (particularly of civil society), a flatter structure, a more significant oral component, and greater transparency.

	No. of Players	Structure	Form	Transparency	Main Purpose
Club Diplomacy	Few	Hierarchical	Mostly written	Low	Sign agreements
Network Diplomacy	Many	Flatter	Mostly oral	High	Increase bilateral flows

FIGURE 0.2. Club and network diplomacy
Source: Heine, 'On the Manner of Practising the New Diplomacy', 6.

As Figure 0.2 shows, the nature of diplomacy in the 21st century revolves around complexity management. Given the involvement of an increasingly diverse cast of actors, diplomats must reach out beyond their peers and tap into civil society. The 21st century diplomat must begin to operate in two different spheres—the traditional 'club', dominated by hierarchy and strict gatekeepers, and the emerging 'network', made up of actors that traditionally were kept out of the inner circles of diplomacy and policy negotiation. This interaction between the club and network defines how diplomats operate today— formal negotiations are often conducted through the club although they are ultimately influenced by various members of the networks. To effectively operate under these circumstances, it is essential to have a grasp of the various factors that come into play.

The club model reflects the traditional model of diplomatic practice. Diplomats restrict their interactions and deal solely with other members of an exclusive club, comprised of governmental officials, fellow diplomats, and, occasionally, members of the business community. In certain cases, diplomats also give occasional speeches to members of the community of their host country. The club model is a closed community of individuals who represent the interests of their respective groups. Yet, particularly in the realm of bilateral diplomacy, but also in other diplomatic modes, the club model has become anachronistic. There has been a severe disconnect between diplomats in many parts of the world and the realities that they are faced with. While it remains integral for the process of international negotiations, it does not take into account a host of important actors and interest groups. In a world where information and communication are becoming increasingly democratized, the club model fails to engage adequately with groups that are ultimately affected by the decisions that are made. The diplomat of the 21st century must manage the complex relationship of the club while also tending this ever-expanding network.

The democratization of information has resulted in a push towards greater accountability and transparency for government officials, including diplomats. Foreign policy decisions command greater attention in a world where short news-cycles and the Internet make discussion of events increasingly available. The club model runs into opposition from proponents of transparency, as decisions are made by small, insulated groups that often appear to be unaccountable. Diplomats now find themselves having to reach beyond their circle of peers towards a much more diversified group of players. In doing so, they take advantage of their position as the representative of their country and communicate the social, cultural, and economic values of their countries while abroad.

The club and network models of diplomacy represent different forms of the same practice. Whereas the club focuses upon relations between the ultimate decision-makers, the network builds on links bringing together various actors with different levels of engagement and interest. Both are essential for forging productive relationships. In isolation, neither fully captures the increasingly complex game of modern diplomacy. Clubs seem to have a permanent position in international relations, though no longer an exclusive one, and even so their 'exclusivity' is under considerable pressure to be more open and relaxed in the admission of new members. In turn, the network notion highlights the myriad factors and actors at play in international interactions, and the need for a very different mindset on the part of the diplomatic practitioner.

While there has been a rediscovery and affirmation of the need for diplomacy, there has also been, in many cases, a dramatic decrease in the resources provided to foreign ministries. Some of the reasons for this relate to the perceived diminished significance of traditional instruments like the mission in an age of summitry and ministerial diplomacy, let alone of instant communications. Yet, this betrays a fundamental misunderstanding of what is happening in the diplomatic field. New modes of diplomatic interaction are part and parcel of the exponential growth of international interactions that we are witnessing as a result of the Third Industrial Revolution. Whereas the US Secretary of State would undertake some twenty yearly official visits abroad in the 1960s, this figure had tripled to some sixty a year in the 1990s. From a few a year in the pre-World War Two years, the United States today signs some 160 treaties and some 3,500 international agreements. Top-level meetings are becoming not just widespread, but routine. However, diplomats and their staff remain a vital resource for ensuring their success. Cutting staff and resources from these missions is counterproductive.

Enfeebling the capacity to maintain these networks deprives government officials of the valuable cultural and social resources provided by diplomatic engagement. Global governance and diplomacy have been treated as two worlds apart. In reality they are intertwined with one another.[73] By bridging the gaps between the club and network models of diplomacy, these perceptions can be overcome.

In the global South, the challenges presented by the changing nature of diplomacy are pressing. Falling behind in the practice of diplomacy can lead to diminishing returns in the field of international negotiations. A traditional diplomatic perspective is insufficient in a world that is becoming increasingly networked. Various networks and constellations of players from the developed and developing world are interacting more frequently. The emergence of the G20 is positive proof of the rise of the global South.[74] In a world where China and India are engaging in new forms of post-imperialist diplomacy and Brazil is asserting its new confidence on the global stage, old verities on the handling of international affairs based on established transatlantic mores and practices no longer hold sway.

The financial crisis has accentuated the rise of emerging powers in club settings. However, the crisis has also demonstrated the salience of networks through the greater prominence of institutions such as the reconfigured Financial Stability Board. This body has expanded not only in terms of its membership in terms of state representation, but also in participation by technical experts of prudential authorities, market regulators, and a variety of other international organizations.

0.4 Conclusion

Proclaiming the end of history proved a tad premature. Over the course of human history, human beings have organized themselves into a great variety of political communities. From ancient times through the present to the distant future, independent political actors will engage in interactions with one another that shift and turn in volume, intensity, rituals, etiquette, and conventions. But the fact of contact and interaction is a constant feature of history. Hence therefore the need for institutions, protocols, and codes of behaviour to provide order, stability, and predictability to international political intercourse. That is the essence of diplomacy. The antecedents and lineage of some diplomatic practices and forms can be traced back several millennia; others are of very recent vintage. Thus there are significant elements of continuity alongside major elements of adaptation and innovation. While some traditional forms of diplomacy retain relevance, newer forms are also gaining prominence.

The marketplace of diplomacy has become increasingly congested with a mutually reinforcing explosion in the number of types of actors and an exponential growth in the number and density of interactions between them; the number of personnel engaged in the interactions; the number and types of issues that are covered; and the levels at which they are engaged. For example, consular officials have always looked after the welfare and interests of fellow-citizens who encounter problems while visiting the countries in which the officials are stationed. But the plummeting costs and growing ease of travel has generated a manifold increase in the numbers of people travelling across borders for tourism, cultural and sports recreation, and migrant workers, and so the sheer volume of consular work has mushroomed even proportionately, not just in aggregate. So this is an example of the same type of diplomatic activity expanding in volume.

Examples of newer types of issues that must be addressed by contemporary diplomats include nuclear proliferation and disarmament and global warming, neither of which would have been in the lexicon of diplomats a century ago. Similarly, the number of state actors has jumped fourfold since the end of the Second World War, starting with the demise of the European colonial empires and the most recent being due to the collapse of the Soviet empire. In addition, though, there are newer types of actors like intergovernmental and non-governmental organizations like the United Nations, Amnesty International, and Greenpeace, as well as epistemic networks like the IPCC, which too have become actors in international affairs as advocates, lobbyists, and participants.

The subject matter of diplomacy has expanded, from the high politics of war and peace to health, environment, development, science and technology, education, law, the arts. Diplomats are engaged in an expanding range of functions, from negotiation, communication, consular, representation, and reporting to observation, merchandise trade and services promotion, cultural exchange, and public relations. At the same time, with more work has come a greater amount of 'bureaucratization' where routine, precedent, and standard operating procedures dominate the daily administrative tasks. Ambassadors are the chief administrative officer as well as the top resident diplomat of their country and require the corresponding managerial skills to run their large offices.

The growing number and diversity of actors engaged in diplomacy, the proliferating number and variety of issues covered by diplomacy, the expanding range of functions served by diplomacy, and the increasingly specialized and technical nature of the discussions and negotiations in turn mean that (1) more personnel are needed to staff foreign ministries; (2) diplomats need to be highly versatile; (3) even the most able and versatile diplomats cannot possess the required expertise to handle all the issues and so experts from outside government must often be brought in as technical advisers and consultants; (4) diplomacy has increasingly become a whole-of-government enterprise with a broad range of government departments involved in and often staffing overseas resident missions—in some cases, officials from outside the foreign ministry, for example from the departments of education, finance, immigration, agriculture, defence, etc., can outnumber the total pool of resident 'diplomats' as such.[75] At the same time, private sector, cultural and educational, etc., diplomacy can supplement but not supplant the traditional state-to-state diplomacy.

The OHMD will serve various audiences including diplomatic academies, new to mid-level diplomats, as well as students and academics interested in the study of diplomacy. By including discussion and analysis of both the theory and practice of modern diplomacy this *Handbook* will be of use to both academics and practitioners. Diplomats and foreign ministries in the global South will be a main beneficiary of this project as it will fill in the existing gaps between the current practice of diplomacy and how this is evolving elsewhere.

With chapters written by contributors from across the world, this volume is intended for a global audience. It underlines the global scope and multilateral nature and solutions for today's most pressing problems. The contributors to this volume include both scholars and practitioners of diplomacy. The various sections highlight the many complex areas at play in modern diplomacy. Chapters are designed to show how the theory and practice of diplomacy is attempting to deal with each specific issue area and to identify changes in the field in relation to the intersection of club and network diplomacy. Through the use of pertinent case studies, it highlights the complex challenges facing the modern practitioner of this ancient profession.

The questions that will be addressed in this volume include the following. (These are not the only questions to be investigated by individual authors in their chapters. Nor is every author expected to respond to all these questions.)

- What is the role and nature of diplomacy in the 21st century?
- What are the key features that have remained constant? What has changed, why, and with what consequences and implications for the theory, practice, and organization of diplomacy?
- How do the increased number of actors involved in diplomacy interact and get things done?
- What are the implications for diplomacy of the dynamic nature of the interactions between bilateral, regional, and multilateral diplomacy, and of the linkages across issue areas?
- How has the growing diversity of international actors challenged the maintenance of common norms of diplomatic discourse? Is the diplomatic culture of the 21st century essentially the same as that of the previous century? If not, what are the new elements of contemporary diplomatic culture?
- In what respects have diplomatic methods and practices adapted to the changing world realities over the last century and what are some of the more important innovations?
- How have the rise of transnational relations among non-governmental actors and trans-governmental relations among different departments of government affected the practice of diplomacy?
- How has the increased tempo of the digital age affected established diplomatic practices and mores?
- How can the tension between the demands of public diplomacy and some of the more cherished values of traditional diplomacy be resolved?
- If indeed the very nature of diplomacy is undergoing transformational changes, how can foreign affairs bureaucracies be restructured and revitalized to fit with the new vision?
- How can information tools be best harnessed to advance national interests and promote national values?
- When, by whom, and for which issue areas might it be better to move beyond 'the national interest'?
- What are the differences between 'club' and 'network' diplomacy and how are these affecting the profession? What are the critical sub-tensions that are at play because of these differences?

Notes

1. David Stringer, 'Letters reveal candid views of British diplomats', *Globe and Mail* (Toronto), 18 October 2009.
2. Standard works on diplomacy include R. P. Barston, *Modern Diplomacy*, 3rd ed. (New York: Longman, 2006); G. R. Berridge, *Diplomacy: Theory and Practice*, 3rd ed. (New York: Palgrave Macmillan, 2005); G. R. Berridge and Alan James, *A Dictionary of Diplomacy*, 2nd ed. (New York: Palgrave Macmillan, 2004); Christer Jönsson and Martin Hall, *Essence*

of Diplomacy (New York: Palgrave Macmillan, 2005); Christer Jönsson and Richard Langhorne (eds), *Diplomacy*. 3 vols. 1: *Theory of Diplomacy*. 2: *History of Diplomacy*. 3: *Problems and Issues in Contemporary Diplomacy* (London: Sage, 2004); Harold Nicolson, *Diplomacy* (New York: Oxford University Press, 1988); and Adam Watson, *Diplomacy: The Dialogue Between States* (New York: Routledge, 2004).

3. Quoted in *The Oxford English Dictionary* (OED), 2nd ed., vol. IV (Oxford: Clarendon Press, 1989), 696.

4. OED, vol. IV, 696.

5. Ivor Roberts (ed.), *Satow's Diplomatic Practice*, 6th ed. (Oxford: Oxford University Press, 2009), 4.

6. The term 'diplomatic body' first emerged in Vienna around the mid-18th century; Roberts, *Satow's Diplomatic Practice*, 5.

7. OED, vol. I, 382.

8. Roberts, *Satow's Diplomatic Practice*, 7.

9. An excellent overview of the history of diplomacy in antiquity is provided in Jean-Robert Leguey-Feilleux, *The Dynamics of Diplomacy* (Boulder: Lynne Rienner, 2009), ch. 2.

10. Leguey-Feilleux, *Dynamics of Diplomacy*, 33.

11. Roger Boesche, *The First Great Political Realist: Kautilya and His Arthashastra* (Lanham, MD: Lexington Books, 2002); L.N. Rangarajan (editor, re-arranger, and translator), *Kautilya: The Arthashastra* (Delhi: Penguin Classics India, 1992).

12. Roberts, *Satow's Diplomatic Practice*, 9.

13. See Matthew S. Anderson, *The Rise of Modern Diplomacy, 1450–1919* (New York: Longman, 1993), and Donald E. Queller, *The Office of Ambassador in the Middle Ages* (Princeton: Princeton University Press, 1967).

14. Raymond Aron, *Peace and War: A Theory of International Relations,* translated from the French by Richard Howard and Annette Baker Fox (New York: Frederick A. Praeger, 1967), 5; emphasis in original.

15. Stephen D. Krasner, *Sovereignty: Organized Hypocrisy* (Princeton: Princeton University Press, 1999).

16. See Ramesh Thakur, *The Responsibility to Protect: Norms, Laws and the Use of Force in International Politics* (London: Routledge, 2011).

17. See Stanley Hoffmann with Frederic Bozo, *Gulliver Unbound: America's Imperial Temptation and the War in Iraq* (Lanham MD: Rowman & Littlefield Publishers, 2005).

18. Quoted in David E. Sanger, 'Deficits may alter U.S. politics and global power', *New York Times*, 2 February 2010.

19. See David Arase and Tsuneo Akaha (eds), *The US-Japan Alliance: Balancing Soft and Hard Power in East Asia* (New York: Routledge, 2009); John Pomfret, 'U.S. concerned about new Japanese premier Hatoyama', *Washington Post*, 29 December 2009; Joseph S. Nye, 'An alliance larger than one issue', *New York Times*, 7 January 2010; Daniel Dombey and Mure Dickie, 'US-Japan relations clouded by Okinawa', *Financial Times*, 19 January 2010; Ramesh Thakur, 'Don't count Japan out of future triangle of Asian power', *Daily Yomiuri*, 3 March 3 2010; and George R. Packard, 'The United States-Japan Security Treaty at 50', *Foreign Affairs* 89:2 (March/April 2010), 92–103.

20. *Yearbook of International Organizations: Guide to global civil society networks 2002–2003 Vol. 5: Statistics, visualizations and patterns* (Munich: K. G. Saur, 2002), 35; *Yearbook of International Organizations 1974* (Brussels: Union of International Associations, 1974), S33.

21. Inis L. Claude, *Swords into Plowshares: The Problems and Progress of International Organization*, 3rd ed. (New York: Random House, 1964), 49.

22. See Ramesh Thakur, 'Multilateral Diplomacy and the United Nations. Global Governance: Venue or Actor?', in James P. Muldoon, JoAnn F. Aviel, Richard Reitano, and Earl Sullivan (eds), *The New Dynamics of Multilateralism: Diplomacy, International Organizations, and Global Governance* (Boulder: Westview, 2010).

23. These questions are addressed in Ramesh Thakur and Thomas G. Weiss, 'United Nations 'Policy': An Argument with Three Illustrations', *International Studies Perspectives* 10:1 (January–April 2009), 18–35.

24. See Simon Chesterman (ed.), *Secretary or General? The UN Secretary-General in World Politics* (Cambridge: Cambridge University Press, 2007); Leon Gordenker, *The UN Secretary-General and Secretariat* (London: Routledge, 2005); and Ramesh Thakur, *The United Nations, Peace and Security: From Collective Security to the Responsibility to Protect* (Cambridge: Cambridge University Press, 2006), ch. 14.

25. Thucydides, *The Peloponnesian War*, quoted in Roberts, *Satow's Diplomatic Practice*, 7.

26. Javier Pérez de Cuéllar, 'The Role of the UN Secretary-General,' in Adam Roberts and Benedict Kingsbury (eds), *United Nations, Divided World: The UN's Role in International Relations* (Oxford: Clarendon, 1988), 61–79.

27. A good illustration of both these advantages is provided by the dispute between New Zealand and France over the sinking of the Greenpeace boat *Rainbow Warrior* in Auckland in July 1985. See Ramesh Thakur, 'A Dispute of Many Colours: France, New Zealand and the "Rainbow Warrior" Affair', *World Today* 42(12) (December 1986), 209–14.

28. See Ramesh Thakur and Luk van Langenhove, 'Enhancing Global Governance Through Regional Integration', *Global Governance* 12:3 (July–September 2006), 233–40.

29. See Michael Edwards, *Civil Society* (Cambridge: Polity Press, 2004).

30. See Mary Kaldor, *Global Civil Society: An Answer to War* (Cambridge: Polity Press, 2003), and John Keane, *Global Civil Society?* (Cambridge: Cambridge University Press, 2003).

31. Thorsten Benner, Wolfgang H. Reinecke, and Jan Martin Witte, *Shaping Globalisation: The role of global public policy networks* (2002), 4; downloadable from: <www.globalpublicpolicy.net>.

32. Jackie Smith, 'Social Movements and Multilateralism', in Edward Newman, Ramesh Thakur, and John Tirman (eds), *Multilateralism under Challenge: Power, International Order, and Structural Change* (Tokyo: UN University Press, 2006).

33. Kofi A. Annan, *Renewing the United Nations: a programme for reform. Report of the Secretary-General* (New York: United Nations, A/51/950, July 14, 1997), para. 212.

34. The ICRC is neither a governmental organization nor an NGO, but a hybrid organization with diplomatic status in most countries where it operates. See David P. Forsythe, *The Humanitarians: The International Committee of the Red Cross* (Cambridge: Cambridge University Press, 2005).

35. *We the peoples: civil society, the United Nations and global governance.* Report of the Panel of Eminent Persons on United Nations-Civil Society Relations (New York: United Nations, document A/58/817, 2004). The chair of the panel was former Brazilian president Fernando Henrique Cardoso.

36. *We the peoples: civil society, the United Nations and global governance*, 7.

37. Hugo Slim, *By What Authority? The Legitimacy and Accountability of Non-governmental Organizations* (Geneva: International Council on Human Rights Policy, 2002), 6. Available at <www.%20ichrp.org>.

38. For an uncompromising statement of this thesis, see Gary Johns, 'Relations with Nongovernmental Organizations: Lessons for the UN', *Seton Hall Journal of Diplomacy and International Relations* 5:2 (Summer/Fall 2004), 51–65.

39. Don D'Cruz, 'Tracking aid dollars', *Canberra Times*, 31 December 2004.

40. David Rieff, 'Tsunamis, accountability and the humanitarian circus', *Humanitarian Exchange* No. 29 (March 2005), 50.

41. See Jorge Heine and Ramesh Thakur (eds), *The Dark Side of Globalization* (Tokyo: United Nations University Press, 2011).

42. See John J. Mearsheimer and Stephen M. Walt, *The Israel Lobby and U.S. Foreign Policy* (New York: Farrar, Strauss and Giroux, 2008).

43. See John Gerard Ruggie, 'global_governance.net: The Global Compact as Learning Network', *Global Governance* 7:4 (2001), 371–8.

44. See Kalevi J. Holsti, *War, the State, and the State of War* (Cambridge: Cambridge University Press, 1996).

45. See Andrew Mack et al., *Human Security Report 2005* (New York: Oxford University Press, 2005).

46. Kofi A. Annan, *In larger freedom: towards development, security and human rights for all*. Report of the Secretary-General (New York: United Nations, document A/59/2005, 21 March 2005).

47. Gro Harlem Brundtland et al., *Our Common Future*, Report of the World Commission on Environment and Development (Oxford: Oxford University Press, 1987).

48. 'Oslo Ministerial Declaration—global health: a pressing foreign policy issue of our time', published online April 2, 2007, <http://www.who.int/trade/events/Oslo_Ministerial_Declaration.pdf>, 1–2; published also in *Lancet*, Issue 369, vol. 9570 (April 21, 2007), 1373–8.

49. Brink Lindsey, *The Age of Abundance: How Prosperity Transformed America's Politics and Culture* (New York: Harper, 2007).

50. Michel Camdessus, 'The IMF at the beginning of the twenty-first century: Can we establish a humanized globalisation?', *Global Governance* 7:4 (October–December 2001), 363–5.

51. See Ramesh Thakur and Hyam Gold, 'The Politics of a New Economic Relationship: Negotiating Free Trade between Australia and New Zealand', *Australian Outlook* 37:2 (August 1983), 82–8.

52. Brian Brady, 'Foreign Office is beset by culture of timidity, say staff', *The Independent*, 22 March 2009.

53. Allan Gyngell (chair of the review panel created by the Lowy Institute in Sydney), 'Rudd erodes diplomacy', *The Australian*, 18 March 2009. The title of the article is misleading: the review had little to do with the new Rudd government.

54. See Allison Stranger, *One Nation Under Contract: The Outsourcing of American Power and the Future of Foreign Policy* (New Haven: Yale University Press, 2009), and Thomas L. Friedman, 'The best allies money can buy', *New York Times*, 4 November 2009.

55. Amir Attaran and Gar Pardy, 'Colvin is just doing his job', *Ottawa Citizen*, 27 November 2009.

56. Stringer, 'Letters reveal candid views of British diplomats'. The practice was discontinued in 2006 after the despatch from Sir Ivor Roberts, the departing British ambassador to Italy, quoted at the start of this chapter, was leaked.

57. See the two-part blog by Siddharth Varadarajan, 'More effective externally than internally', and 'It's strategic culture that counts', *Hindu*, 20 and 22 January 2010, <http://www.the-

hindu.com/opinion/op-ed/article82786.ece> and <http://www.thehindu.com/opinion/columns/siddharth-varadarajan/article87783.ece>.

58. Roberts, *Satow's Diplomatic Practice*, 19.

59. Roberts, *Satow's Diplomatic Practice*, 20.

60. Mark Malloch-Brown, 'How to reform the British Foreign Office', *Financial Times*, 14 January 2010.

61. Quoted in Colum Lynch, 'At the U.N., a growing Republican presence', *Washington Post*, 21 July 2005.

62. Joseph S. Nye, *The Powers to Lead* (New York: Oxford University Press, 2008). This should be read in conjunction with his earlier books *Bound to Lead: The Changing Nature of American Power* (New York: Basic Books, 1990), and *Soft Power: The Means to Success in World Politics* (New York: Public Affairs, 2004).

63. Adam Watson, *Diplomacy: The Dialogue between States* (London: Methuen, 1982), 87.

64. Karen A. Mingst and Margaret P. Karns, *The United Nations in the Twenty-first Century*, 3rd ed. (Boulder: Westview, 2006), 42.

65. See Ramesh Thakur, Andrew F. Cooper, and John English (eds), *International Commissions and the Power of Ideas* (Tokyo: United Nations University Press, 2005).

66. Alex Evans, Bruce Jones, and David Steven, *Confronting the Long Crisis of Globalization: Risk, Resilience and International Order* (Washington DC: Brookings, 2010).

67. Hans J. Morgenthau, *Politics Among Nations: The Struggle for Power and Peace*, 4th ed. (New York: Alfred A. Knopf, 1966), 135.

68. Anne-Marie Slaughter, 'America's Edge', *Foreign Affairs* 88:1 (January/February 2009), 94–113.

69. See Anna Ohanyan, 'Policy Wars for Peace: Network Model of NGO Behavior', *International Studies Review* 11:3 (September 2009), 475–501.

70. In an interview with David Rothkopf, 'It's 3 a.m. Do you know where Hillary Clinton is?', *Washington Post*, 27 August 2009.

71. Daniel Markey, 'Developing India's Foreign Policy "Software"'. Seattle: National Bureau of Asian Research, *Asia Policy* no. 8 (July 2009), 73–96, available at <http://www.nbr.org/Publications/Asia_policy/AP8/AP8_Markey_India.pdf.>.

72. Markey, 'Developing India's Foreign Policy "Software"', 77.

73. See Andrew F. Cooper, Brian Hocking, and William Maley (eds), *Global Governance and Diplomacy: Worlds Apart?* (Houndmills: Palgrave Macmillan, 2008).

74. See Andrew F. Cooper and Ramesh Thakur, *The Group of Twenty (G20)* (London: Routledge, forthcoming).

75. See George F. Kennan, 'Diplomacy without Diplomats', *Foreign Affairs* 76:5 (September–October 1997), 198–212.

PART I

SETTING THE SCENE

CHAPTER 1

....

THE CHANGING NATURE
OF DIPLOMACY

....

ANDREW F. COOPER

1.1 THE ESSENTIAL DUALITY
OF DIPLOMACY—CHANGE
AND CONTINUITY

THE *Oxford Handbook of Modern Diplomacy* (OHMD) is an ambitious and highly nuanced project, with a focus on the institutional foundations, the complex sets of processes, and the wider context and meaning of modern diplomacy. Although embedded in International Relations (IR), diplomacy has its own unique culture, ways of doing things, puzzles and contradictions. Indeed it is this mix of rich tradition and capacity and/or necessity for innovation that makes the analysis of diplomacy so exciting and salient.

At the core of the OHMD is a fundamental sense of intellectual and practical contestation about the requirement and models for change over the hold of continuity.[1] Both in thinking and operations an essential duality jumps out—the 'nothing is or will be different now or in the future' perspective and the enthusiastic search for 'newness' and innovation, the focused concern with foreign ministries with the diverse dimensions taking in the larger state structures as well as the array of societal components, the mix of embedded craft techniques and enhanced speed, tools and multiplied options, and the search for core priorities amid the range of normative demands and mass of technical details on an issue-specific basis.

The scale of endeavour of the OHMD allows us to capture the extent of this essential duality in a unique fashion. We have however attempted to apply a central lens and attendant discipline to the project by using the framework of clubs and networks—concepts that allow us as elaborated upon by Jorge Heine—to encompass much of the duality (and often hybridity, in which continuity and change interact and merge) at the core of the enterprise.[2]

1.2 Centralization Impulses Amid Complexity

Most of the recent scholarly works on the evolution of diplomacy highlight the added complexity in which 'states and other international actors communicate, negotiate and otherwise interact' in the 21st century.[3] Diplomacy has to take into account 'the crazy-quilt nature of modern interdependence'.[4] Decision-making on the international stage involves what has been depicted as 'two level games'[5] or 'double-edged diplomacy'.[6] With accentuated forms of globalization the scope of diplomacy as the 'engine room' of IR has moved beyond the traditional core concerns to encompass a myriad set of issue areas.[7] And the boundaries of participation in diplomacy—and the very definition of diplomats—have broadened as well, albeit in a still contested fashion. In a variety of ways, therefore, not only its methods but also its objectives are far more expansive than ever before.

Yet, while the theme of complexity radiates through the pages of the OHMD, changed circumstances and the stretching of form, scope, and intensity do not only produce fragmentation but centralization in terms of purposive acts. Amid the larger debates about the diversity of principals, agents, and intermediaries, the space in modern diplomacy for leadership by personalities at the apex of power has expanded, not contracted. At odds with the counter-image of horizontal breadth with an open-ended nature, the dynamic of 21st-century diplomacy remains highly vertically oriented and individual-centric.

To showcase this phenomenon, however, is not to suggest ossification. In terms of causation, the dependence on leaders is largely a reaction to complexity. With the shift to multi-party, multi-channel, multi-issue negotiations, with domestic as well as international interests and values in play, leaders are often the only actors who can cut through the complexity and make the necessary trade-offs to allow deadlocks to be broken. In terms of communication and other modes of representation, bringing in leaders differentiates and elevates issues from the bureaucratic arena.

In terms of effect, the primacy of leaders reinforces elements of both club and network diplomacy. In its most visible manifestation via summit diplomacy, the image of club diplomacy explicitly differentiates the status and role of insiders and outsiders and thus the hierarchical nature of diplomacy. Although 'large teams of representatives' are involved in this central form of international practice, it is the 'organized performances' of leaders that possess the most salience.[8] At the same time, though, the galvanizing or catalytic dimension of leader-driven diplomacy provides new avenues and legitimation for network diplomacy, with many decisions of summits being outsourced to actors who did not participate at the summit but possess the technical knowledge, institutional credibility, and resources to enhance results.

Notwithstanding their generalized reputation as talk-shops and/or photo-op vehicles of opportunity, specific forms of summits, notably the G20, bring to the fore the dynamics of change in diplomacy both at the club and the network level. Through the club lens the G20 demonstrates the capacity of diplomacy to reinvent itself—to cater to both the demands of efficiency (an elevated and expanded concert-like approach) and legitimacy (with equality between members from both North and South). Yet the G20 serves also as a classic case of the type of cross pressures that foreign ministries (the traditional institutional preserve and incubator for the guild-craft of diplomacy) face. Unlike in the G8, foreign ministers are not privileged actors, with their own forums. Nor is the role of Sherpas dominated by foreign ministries, but rather by finance officials. If the practices surrounding the G20 as much as the G8 rest on 'collective accomplishments',[9] the patterned relationships on which these successes (or failures) depend are very much altered

The G20 also illustrates at the apex of government how leaders and their advisers are ready and willing to take a hands-on and centrally controlling role on an increasingly diverse set of global issues—making any strict delineation between not only foreign and domestic but high and low issue areas meaningless. Leaders bring a different playbook to diplomacy, with fewer and fewer constraints on them in terms of scope of activity by the 'professional' diplomats. This impulse towards leader-focused diplomacy—combined commonly with adviser-oriented 'parallel' diplomacy—is consolidated via the stretching of presidential/prime ministerial offices with diplomatic ambitions and expertise across complex agenda dossiers.

At the same time, nevertheless, the G20 demonstrates vividly the constraints of club diplomacy. Meeting on an ad hoc basis, with no fixed secretariat and no funds of its own, and with an ongoing need to address its legitimacy gaps as a self-selected group, the G20 has not only delegated a good deal of its delivery capacity through international organizations such as the IMF/World Bank, the Financial Stability Board, and the Basel Committee, but built up a series of interconnected network activities, including a process of interaction with civil society and the establishment of a Business 20.

Looking at the leadership role in an extended fashion, the image of major leaders being everywhere and doing everything in the diplomatic arena is pervasive. Although there continues to be meaningful differences in experience, style, and time, even the most 'stay at home' president/prime minister has the combination of incentives pushing him/her into wider diplomatic engagement—and the means (both in terms of technical expertise and logistical capacity) to do so, not only in traditional security issues but economic and social issues as well. As on the financial issues at the heart of the G20 process, the impulse of leaders to try to deal personally with collective action problems jumps out in a wide number of OHMD contributions, even if there are risks attached to failure. On environmental diplomacy, to give one highly visible illustration, there has been a marked rise in attendance of leaders at major summits. Where the 1972 Stockholm UN environmental conference attracted only two leaders (including the host), the 15th Conference of the Parties (COP) in Copenhagen in December 2009 drew over 100 (including 20 who were involved in face-to-face negotiations on the frantic last day, including the dramatic intervention of US President Barack Obama in the closed-door negotiations with key countries from the global South). The same dynamic comes out, furthermore, in areas such as sports diplomacy, with the winning or losing of the Olympic games or the FIFA World Cup most notably being attributed to the diplomatic brand of leaders: Tony Blair versus Jacques Chirac in which the former 'won' the Olympics for London, Luiz Inácio Lula da Silva versus Barack Obama in which Lula 'won' the Olympics for Rio, and to a lesser extent David Cameron versus Vladimir Putin on the World Cup bid 'won' by Russia.

Leaders also consider commercial functions to be an essential component of their diplomatic role. The ridicule of leaders (as evidenced by the dismissal in 1960 by French President Charles de Gaulle of the Japanese Prime Minister as a 'transistor salesman') has long gone.[10] Leaders have increasingly become lead salesman/women on the diplomatic stage, with massive national 'teams' being sent notably by European countries (including France) to the BRICs and in reverse fashion by the BRIC countries to Africa.[11]

Leaders who face constraints on these sales activities, promoting the products of national champions and/or investment opportunities, have to try harder or fall behind. Chancellor Angela Merkel of Germany and President Nicolas Sarkozy of France have over-compensated for controversies over the Dalai Lama, the Olympic flame, and human rights issues more generally by leading commercial teams to China. Merkel visited China, as well as Russia and energy-rich Kazakhstan in July 2010, accompanied by representatives of twenty-five companies, including the chairmen of Volkswagen, Airbus, Siemens, and Metro the retail chain.[12] Sarkozy, with great visibility as the lead salesman for a variety of French products, has led major missions to China and India.

Timing is also an issue of great importance. President Obama, having cancelled earlier trips to Indonesia because of the exigencies relating to domestic politics, delivered a robust sales message when he eventually did tour the country he lived in as a youth. He did so to reinforce the large trade mission led by the US commerce secretary consisting of American energy, construction, and engineering companies. Although overshadowed by security issues, Obama's visits to Korea, India, and Japan also had major sales dimensions. As Obama summed up the importance of the trip in colloquial language: 'The primary purpose is to take a bunch of US companies and open up markets so that we can sell in Asia, in some of the fastest-growing markets in the world, and we can create jobs here in the United States of America. And a whole bunch of corporate executives are going to be joining us so that I can help them open up those markets and allow them to sell their products.'[13]

UK Prime Minister David Cameron toured the Gulf even amid the process of dynamic change and turmoil in the Middle East, and was severely criticized both for going and for not delivering more results. As a scathing article in the *Financial Times* put it:

> There were no arms deals, just one big energy contract, and plenty of eulogizing on democratic renewal. But this week's tour of the Gulf was perhaps the moment when

David Cameron's mercantilist foreign policy came of age. For the first time the prime minister's near obsession with promoting trade was confronted with one of the awkward dilemmas of statesmanship—the short-term rewards and long-term perils of doing business with authoritarian regimes.[14]

The leaders of BRIC (Brazil, Russia, India, and China) have shown a less constrained ambition in terms of diplomatic outreach efforts toward Africa. Chinese President Hu Jintao has made four tours to Africa since 2003. The latest one occurred in February 2009 and encompassed Mali, Senegal, Tanzania, and Mauritius. President Vladimir Putin of Russia visited South Africa in September 2006—the first trip by a Russian leader to sub-Saharan Africa since the fall of the Soviet Union—with a follow up tour by President Dmitry Medvedev in June 2009. Brazilian President Lula da Silva's diplomatic outreach to Africa went even further, involving nine visits to 25 countries over eight years. In November 2006, Lula co-hosted the first ever African-South American summit in Abuja, Nigeria.[15]

Joining material with symbolic objectives, leaders have become as well the diplomatic brand masters for their countries. Few leaders want to be left out of a major new club or extended network. When President George W. Bush hosted the first G20 at the leaders level in November 2008, all the invitees turned up (the Spanish and Dutch leaders coming in on the diplomatic coat-tails of France) and this dynamic expansion has continued with the logic of the G20 to consult with more leaders as representatives of regional bodies (the African Union, the New Economic Partnership for African Development, the Gulf Cooperation Council, the Association of Southeast Asian Nations as well as the 3G group of small and middle countries). Although there is much talk of an informal G2 (between the US and China) being cultivated via the G20 the most interesting feature of the G20 has become its porous nature. Unlike earlier eras—or in the UN through the P5—there is no explicit big 3 (as at Yalta/Potsdam) or 4 (Paris 1919) or 5 (Vienna in 1814–1815) in these more informal clubs.[16]

Faced with this leader-centric environment, small states face some serious disadvantages. As in the past, populist leaders can gain attention but commonly this does not enhance the brand of the country—at least in terms of winning club membership or hosting activity for major events. Other forms of compensation are needed, with greater attention on resource-abundant and skilled diplomacy. Although the leaders of Singapore and Qatar do not have the access to the hub clubs as leaders of G8 and the BRICs enjoy, these states classically punch above their weight diplomatically, to use a term coined in the UK context but more appropriate for smaller players. Qatar can win the competition to host the 2022 FIFA World Cup without a football profile. Singapore can mobilize the 3G Group as a counterpoint to the G20, and win entry as the only non-European country without a regional constituency. The same push for over-compensation comes out in other diplomatic performances by small countries, as illustrated by the vast number of bilateral free trade agreements negotiated by Chile or the lead role (turning vulnerability to resilience) of Maldives as part of the Alliance of Small Island States on climate change.[17]

1.3 Squeezing the Foreign Policy 'Guild'—But Still Space for Initiatives

What increases the pressure on the foreign policy establishment however is that this process of change is not just a uni-dimensional extension of vertical trends witnessed from the 1970s on (with variations of shuttle diplomacy, parallel diplomacy through special advisers, and two-level games of summitry over a much broader spectrum of issues). The guild is also squeezed by a myriad of pressures emanating horizontally at state level and from outside through various forms of society-craft. As has been well rehearsed in a number of the contributions to the OHMD, foreign ministry personnel are no longer the only parts of the state apparatus with a diplomatic dimension.

Some of these non-foreign ministry activities are far from new, although as in the case of defence or finance diplomacy the form and scope may be fundamentally changed in recent years. Other ministries, notably those dealing with border controls, have moved into the spotlight since 9/11. So have health issues due to concerns about global pandemics. As in a domain such as health, states can accord greater recognition to a multi-dimensional issue area as a diplomatic site. Just to put out one illustration of health as a focused area, of 2,000 US embassy/diplomatic officials in Thailand, one-quarter are estimated to work on health-related issues.[18] Such signs of bureaucratic stretching challenge the image of an entrenched club culture dominating diplomatic life.

Nor do foreign service officers have a monopoly over ambassadorial positions, losing status not only to political appointees (and the occasional academic and cultural icon as in the past) but to trade officials and increasingly officials from other departments including defence and finance. Paralleling the trend towards leader-oriented diplomacy at the apex of power is the phenomenon of individual 'trouble-shooters' to play a major role on a discrete or diffuse basis. Some of these individuals have been classic ins and outers such as Richard Holbrooke in the US system, whose diverse career moved between key diplomatic assignments (notably as a key negotiator of the Dayton Accords and the special adviser on Pakistan and Afghanistan), investment banking, and the role of president and CEO of the Global Business Council on HIV/AIDS.

Still, organizational decline in relative terms does not mean an absolute loss of capacity.[19] On the contrary, it reinforces the sense of duality. The erosion of status on a structural basis goes hand in hand with some marked degree of heightened profile of foreign ministers or foreign ministry officials as diplomatic entrepreneurial and intellectual leaders on specific concepts, issues, and deliverables. In some major 'rising' countries, key state officials from the foreign ministry have played a visible and extended role on international negotiations. A case in point has been the work of He Yafei, the assistant foreign minister who served both as China's G8 Sherpa (substituting for President Hu Jintao in the 'outreach' at the 2009 L'Aquila summit when Hu went home early to deal with domestic issues) and G20 summits as well as the chief negotiator at the 15th COP in Copenhagen.

Pushing back against the tendency to overshadow the activity of personnel from second-ary countries, the OHMD exhibits as well the ability of select foreign ministers to pick niches for innovative middle power diplomacy. Nor is this type of skill-set any longer the exclusive terrain of traditional countries located in this category, as witnessed by recent high-profile initiatives taken on by the foreign minister of Turkey, Ahmet Davutoglu (labelled in *Foreign Policy* magazine's 2010 list of 'Top 100 Global Thinkers' as the 'brains behind Turkey's global reawakening') to give just one illustration from a non-traditional middle power.[20]

To indicate the degree of situational resilience of foreign ministers and foreign minis-tries is not to exaggerate the capacity of these diplomatic actors to act as systemic con-trollers. Their future relevance will depend not on club-style command and control but on a sense of awareness on how to operate in fluid networks. As Ross suggests, to deal with the complexity of the global issues that diplomats are expected to deal with, they must 'promote multiple links at multiple levels between governments', and therefore one dimension to the complexity of global issues is to adopt a complex governance structure that works at multiple and overlapping levels of diplomatic activity.[21]

1.4 THE NEED FOR DEFINITIONAL REFINEMENT

Such diversity complicates the understanding of change in diplomacy, including at the outset the answer to the question, who are the diplomats now?[22] The classic definition of diplomats as 'agents' of the state—and the national interest—would appear to exclude all non-state actors if not an 'all of government' approach. This restrictive view however is not reflective of the academic literature. The seminal work of Bull does, to be sure, start off by defining diplomats as the preserve of state agents. Yet he opens the way for a much broader categorization by adding that diplomacy not only includes the conduct of offi-cial relations by states but 'other entities with standing in world politics'.[23] Barston, in his more recent textbook, is also far more inclusive, arguing that diplomacy is 'concerned with the management of relations between states and other actors'.[24]

Alternatively, a variety of academics—most tellingly some who have had extensive experience with 'official' diplomats—push the boundaries well beyond the definition laid out by Bull. Langhorne and Wallace argue that 'diplomacy has spread to many other entities and across many categories of people.'[25] Wiseman has pushed for the recognition of the concept of 'polylateralism' with respect to diplomacy; an approach that takes into account a wider set of relationships involving not only disparate organizations but indi-viduals 'with global interests'.[26]

Obviously the push to extend the status of diplomat is fraught with contestation. To call oneself a diplomat as in the case of 'citizen diplomacy' is very subjective and argua-bly even flimsy. Nor does asserting that states and their diplomats are 'co-participants' in 'post-territorial diplomacy'[27] break down the contested image of diplomacy, in that it animates a backlash by defenders of orthodox forms of club diplomacy who link entrance to the club with sovereign status.[28]

Still, if the extreme points of definitional expansion are discarded, on the ground movements reveal that the answer to the question 'who are the diplomats now?' is being settled before us. From one angle, this dynamic is associated with a contraction or retreat of the state.[29] Using this framework state diplomacy is opened up to new actors in conjunction with a process of privatization or outsourcing. Sometimes this process is very open, with adverts in *The Economist* by some governments for consular officials in the commercial sector, usually in targeted positions such as New York City. The opening up of the UK's Foreign and Commonwealth Office to entry by NGO representatives, notably from Oxfam, was also given ample publicity in the Tony Blair/Gordon Brown years. In other forms, the broad outlines of this process of commercialization or privatization of diplomacy may be known but not the precise details. This phenomenon of change comes out particularly in the trade area. On a wide number of WTO cases negotiations have been outsourced to private law firms such as Dewey Ballantine.[30] This is particularly so in the case of the US, but illustrations can be located in the EU and Brazil as well. Nor are big countries the only agents of this process. The crux of my book on the Antigua–US WTO dispute over Internet gambling is not only about the lobbying of key US industries (with a coalition of Christian social conservatives and professional sports leagues) but the outsourcing of Antigua diplomacy to sectors of the Internet gambling industry.[31]

While important, this process alone is not a direct challenge to state-based diplomacy. On the contrary, the incorporation of private or non-state based actors on a geographical or functional basis reinforces the subordinate status of these groups. Their inclusion is done very much according to the rules of the game set by the Westphalian system. Non-state actors are vital to the process of commercial or developmental diplomacy, for example, but are not thoroughly recognized as diplomats except by their (temporary) relationship with the state.

The definitional stretching is made more salient where state and 'other entities' have combined in various forms of diplomatic networking activities. In the network approach, other types of actors, including international organizations, non-governmental organizations, transnational corporations, and even significant individuals are given privileged positions. Of these, international organizations are most accepted in terms of the possession of diplomatic standing. This is especially true of the United Nations system, encompassing the UN Secretary-General, the UN secretariat, and the various agencies, funds, and programmes which receive extensive coverage through the OHMD with regard to humanitarian diplomacy, refugee, and disaster diplomacy, to name just a few important issue areas.

Non-state organizations, transnational corporations, and individuals are far more vigorously contested in terms of whether they can be deemed diplomatic actors or not. Few practitioners or analysts, however, dispute whether they are part of the diplomatic process and as such with the status of diplomat's 'relevant others'—those actors with whom a diplomat engages in the conduct of diplomacy.[32] For their part, civil society groupings are ambiguous about this sort of attributional inclusion. If some embrace the diplomatic process (although as advocates rather than stakeholders or lobbyists), others prefer to mobilize in parallel or in opposition to the same process.

There continues to be much contestation about whether individuals such as celebrities from the world of entertainment can be termed diplomats, although some such as Bono, Angelina Jolie, and George Clooney possess the soft power capabilities, the access to decision-makers, and the communication skills worthy of top-flight diplomats.[33] Turning to the private sector, is it realistic to continue to deny a non-state actor such as the Gates Foundation de facto if not de jure diplomatic status? Objectively, the Gates Foundation is now a larger international health donor than all governments, except for the US and the UK.[34] Subjectively, even if they do not represent a polity or state interest, Bill and Melinda Gates are received in a manner worthy of a head of government/state when on an overseas 'mission'. Such recognition has been extended, moreover, into the G20 process with the Gates Foundation being accorded insider status at the November 2011 Cannes summit, complete with the recognition of a Sherpa and the role of Bill Gates around the table with heads of government.

The need to factor such super-sized non-state actors into a category very different from even large NGOs such as Oxfam, CARE, and World Vision is animated further by the move of the Gates Foundation into issue areas beyond health. Most significantly, Bill Gates contributed US$30 million to a new fund for poor farmers. In tandem with the US, Canada, South Korea, and Spain this non-governmental donation brought the total amount of funding through this novel form of public-private partnership up to US$875 million.[35]

Alternatively there can be de facto if not de jure limits placed on state officials who are recognized as diplomats. One of the most ingrained components of the institution of diplomacy—along with the protocol and institutional features of embassies—is the issue of diplomatic immunity. Yet, blurred or even 'murky' activities on the front lines of the 'war on terrorism' provide tests about the future of diplomatic immunity—as played out by the recent case of Raymond Davis, a US official at either the US consulate in Lahore or the US embassy in Islamabad, with allegations that he was a security officer for the CIA who killed two Pakistanis working for the Inter-Services Intelligence. If Davis is judged to be a covert operator using 'diplomatic cover', should he have been released (as he was in March 2011) according to the diplomatic exemption?[36]

1.5   Extending the Debate About Purpose

That being said it is misleading to suggest that such choices about change or continuity relate exclusively to actorness. They are also about the purpose of diplomacy. The core purpose of diplomacy traditionally has been to fulfil state-centric objectives. The guild prides itself on its sense of real politik. And faced with crisis, this remains the first instinct. As Hillary Clinton, the US secretary of state, argued before Congress, in defending her department's budget: 'We're in a competition for influence... let's put aside the moral, humanitarian, do-good side of what we believe in, and let's talk straight real-politik'.[37]

One of the many unanticipated albeit contested conceptually and operationally uneven results about the traumatic events over the past decade has been a push for the return of the state. This is true 'at home' with the expansion of the security state in the post 9/11 context, with foreign ministries being nudged commonly aside by interior/homeland defence/public safety ministries/departments in the reordering of borders, walls, and perimeters. It is also true in the post-financial crisis environment of the erosion of the so-called Washington Consensus, many of the tenets of neo-liberalism, and the concomitant balancing towards re-regulation.

However, ample signs of a similar trend are felt 'abroad', as viewed in its most explicit form via the US embrace of coalitions of the willing and an ethos of securitization in the George W. Bush era but with an extended legacy via pro-consular/defence diplomacy. Even 'softer' forms of activity such as public diplomacy can be interpreted as overtly state-centric, not only in the case of the US (with a mounting volume of literature debating the merits and results of such activities) but via the mechanisms associated with the BRICs (especially China and Russia) and small countries such as Qatar. After all, the essence of these activities akin to public relations is to sell a particular message or brand. Even Al Jazeera's broadcasting is interpreted as being a diplomatic projection by Qatar.[38]

Such a uni-dimensional portrait, nonetheless, continues to be contested both intellectually and operationally. It must be recognized that diplomacy as an area both of study and practice is in many ways increasingly up against the tenets of global governance and the development and application of 'new forms of governing'.[39] Traditionally, it is true, it was the separation between diplomacy and global governance that was the dominant component of their relationship. Diplomacy has been traditionally defined by scholars—as much as by practitioners—as a guild activity, with well-placed insiders distinguished from excluded outsiders. Through this lens, diplomatic skills were taken to be a type of extensive knowledge in the areas of representation, negotiation, and communication possessed by a particular set of professionals handed down by a long apprenticeship.

Global governance, by way of contrast, has been defined in an open-ended manner, with a high degree of inclusiveness about whom and what is included in its machinery and agenda. To be sure, serious disputes existed within the intellectual and NGO/civil society community about the details of this arrangement—for instance, on theory-building versus problem-solving and their own individual/organization location in terms of the arrangement. But an apparent consensus has existed that both the aims and means of global governance removed it from the diplomatic realm. Unlike diplomacy, global governance has not been conditioned by a culture of hierarchy and command and control. It puts the emphasis on doing what is 'right' (with an emphasis on global norms), not on what is possible. It places transparency and emotion over discretion and tact. Even the language of global governance can be contrasted to the language favoured by students and practitioners of diplomacy with the focus on the vocabulary using word and phrases such as deliberation and social relations.[40]

At the extreme ends, there are also fundamentally different interpretations about the 'mystery' of diplomacy. To mainstream students of diplomacy the 'mystery' component

are the craft skills of the guild passed along over the generations in defence of state interests and the system of states.[41] To some advocates of global governance—even before the
concept was fully defined—the 'mystery' has a less benign character as diplomacy is
viewed as being complicit (as for example by Henry Kissinger, the archetypal master of
the craft) in a whole roster of covert and/or malevolent activities beyond the formalized
diplomatic culture of espionage (complete with tit-for-tat exchanges of diplomats
accused/compromised in spying).[42]

The extent of these disconnects should not be discounted. It is increasingly well recognized that being 'a good communicator in media-driven societies is of paramount
importance in network diplomacy'.[43] Yet given the embedded 'mystery' component of
diplomacy, state-based diplomats are structurally inhibited from being good public
communicators.

Neither though should these disconnects be exaggerated. Even the most ardent advocate of global governance acknowledges the logic of diplomacy, even as they push for a
reconfiguration of its objectives and methods. Scholte is a good example of this approach,
concluding that 'the study of diplomacy is anything but obsolete. Redefined to reflect
recent historical changes, the subject has arguably never been as important.' Yet diplomacy must adapt to catch up to the changing forces going on around it: 'Representation
must cover many more actors. Communication must handle faster speeds and larger
volumes of messages delivered through multiple technologies and diverse kinds of audi-
tory and visual signals. Negotiation must address not only a proliferation of parties, but
also a diversification of political identities and life-worlds'.[44]

At the same time, either by design or default, many practitioners of diplomacy have
attempted to either embrace or at least come to terms with global governance. In the
design category are the niche diplomacy or alternative coalitions of the willing (with
mixed state and non-state coalitions) associated with entrepreneurial/intellectual leadership with the responsibility to protect and human security. This template also covers
such initiatives as on landmines and the International Criminal Court, child soldiers,
blood diamonds, and small arms. Such activities redefine the status of the constituent
actors and the sites of engagement.[45]

On some key initiatives of more recent vintage there has been some considerable recognition by proponents of global governance that the design of novel arrangements
must be cast in a more pragmatic guise. Under some conditions engagement with a concrete agenda is appreciated as having value over ambition in terms of accountability and
transparency.[46]

Such a shift comes out on the response to the G20. If cast by some critics as a return to
concert power politics,[47] other observers showcased the fact that G20 contained elements of advances towards a cosmopolitan order, in which countries from most of the
major regions and cultures would obtain representation. Not only could the G20 offer
instrumental delivery, it could do so explicitly as a forum of 'un-like' actors, fully reflective of a diversity of voices. As Held has observed in a recent book, the G20 featured 'an
unprecedented successful attempt by developing countries to extend their participation
in key institutions of global governance'.[48]

In the default category are instances where the issue-specific diplomacy of a country changes by a changed perception of problem-solving as opposed to a normative reorientation. Health diplomacy showcases this phenomenon. Although there is sensitivity in this area, as in other forms of 'problems without passports',[49] health issues bend Westphalia without the same push-back found in other issues placed higher on the hierarchy of national interest. Not only is the capacity of states to limit their exposure to health crises originating outside of their borders greatly reduced because of heightened interdependence resulting from globalization,[50] new mediums of information-exchange have made state-driven public health crises difficult to conceal.[51] As a result, individual states that purposefully undermine transnational efforts to reduce global health threats, or demonstrate an unwillingness to address domestic public health challenges that have the potential to spread beyond territorial borders, open the way to the potential for diplomatic embarrassment and/or greatly diminish their own legitimacy as responsible contributors to global governance.

China—as other countries—learnt a lot from the SARS episode in 2003—that withholding information did it more harm than good in terms of reputation. Information will get out about breakouts—so it might as well be managed effectively. Indeed, the international spread of SARS and the public rebuke of Chinese government actions by the WHO pushed Beijing to eventually publicly embrace transparency of process and the timely sharing of health-related information.[52]

Still, this approach is not static. Although China was taken to task by some observers during the more recent H1N1 crisis, it was for the rigor of its strict quarantine regime, not for trying to cover up a problem.[53] Furthermore, there are some signs that China— akin to the other BRIC countries—is moving outwards by design, not default, in terms of its global health diplomacy. Increasingly it will not be simply a question of upgrading China's health system at home, but measuring the impact of China's global reach in terms of health diplomacy—in the distribution of new supplies of vaccines in Africa for example.

To highlight this larger pattern of engagement between diplomacy and global governance is not to suggest though that all the traditional obstacles in merging the two have disappeared. In some cases the embrace of diverse stakeholders appears to be more show than substance. For instance, in order to build momentum for the Copenhagen conference, an ambitious meeting under the auspices of the UN Global Compact was held between 50 heads of state and government with nearly 200 leaders of global business and civil society organizations. In the end, nonetheless, the result of Copenhagen was determined by classic concert (leaders around the table) diplomacy.

As revealed by Hillary Clinton's remarks noted above, furthermore, global governance has not achieved primacy in the vast majority of policy debates. Approaches that promote global governance are commonly trumped by the power dimension in diplomacy with continuity, not change, winning out.

Ideationally and operationally, as revealed in some depth by the WikiLeaks, there is an internal as well as external tension between the culture of secrecy in the pursuit of intelligence (often portrayed as a fundamental norm of diplomacy) and diplomacy as an important conduit of global governance. Although individual US diplomats emerge as strong advocates of human rights and anti-corruption initiatives, the dominant image of the US diplomatic institutional culture is one that at times of stress puts transparency and accountability in a subordinate position to intelligence-gathering by an array of regularized and covert means.

Despite all, though, the fact that there is even a debate about whether modern diplomacy should include advances towards global governance (by default or design) is still highly significant. 'New diplomacy' in the past focused on method (open diplomacy, most notably, at the time of Paris 1919), not goals.[54] In the 21st century this is no longer enough. But questions abound about whether either foreign ministries or states as a whole can pass the bar as set up by academics, think tanks, or civil society? Not only a sense of inclusion but instrumental benefits will be needed, with global governance (as multilateralism has been reshaped)[55] becoming not only a set of principles but enhanced tools in diplomacy. Only by doing so will the basic instinct of state diplomats to follow the dictates of a narrowly gauged national interest (defined in terms of the security and commercial domain) be modified. State officials need to be convinced that global governance is beneficial not only on normative and value-based grounds but in terms of tangible deliverables, as it can certainly be done in areas such as health and the environment, and arguably beyond.

1.6 OPPORTUNITIES AND RISKS AS DIPLOMACY MOVES TO BECOME MORE 'SERVICE' ORIENTED

A third signal of change is the increased preoccupation of diplomacy with the public, not just for manipulation of opinion 'abroad' (through public diplomacy and projections of soft power) but mobilized support 'at home'. Concretely the lack of a domestic client base has long been a source of weakness for foreign ministries. More generally diplomacy has had a historically awkward relationship with democracy. The culture and skills of a classic diplomat—cosmopolitanism, linguistic ability, and appreciation of foreign cultures and protocol—are often at odds with local-oriented and certainly parochial sentiment. If diplomacy is about a struggle for legitimacy, therefore, there is a need for efficiency in terms of delivery across the board—not just deliverables from the process of messengers, negotiators, and 'objective articulators' on policy-related issues pertaining to the national interest (or for that matter towards global governance),[56] but on tangible issues relating to the well-being of citizens in either their public or private lives.

If attractive, however, a more pronounced focus on instrumental delivery to domestic publics is the other side of public diplomacy towards foreigners—it is full of risks. Building a client base, for instance, through commercially-based transactions in some ways reinforces the traditional culture of secrecy. Neither the terms of possible transactions nor, in some cases, even commentary that transactions are being negotiated can be done in a transparent fashion, with sensitivity increasing not only in areas such as arms sales but in cases such as mining/energy investment.

At the same time, this type of service orientation puts extra burdens on diplomacy as an institution. Transformational diplomacy as laid out by Condoleezza Rice placed a great deal of stress on moving US diplomatic missions to where they were needed, that is to say, in the BRICs or big emerging markets.[57] But this implied a reduction in not only traditional missions in Europe but in some small countries as well. This in turn spins out to include ways to service such countries by other means (one-person missions in a hotel, moving missions from site to site for instance).

Building a client base through delivering support for the wider public is also fraught with risks associated with the 'open' delivery. The extent of these risks can be viewed through the case of consular diplomacy. Although the rescue of citizens has long been an element of diplomacy, the intensity and complexity of this process have certainly increased, due to issues such as diasporas with the allowance of multi-passports and the sheer number of people, types of calamities, and sites involved.

At the same time, success at the rescue of citizens can be recast less as citizen-oriented diplomacy and more as power projection. State officials who can effectively evacuate their nationals from problem situations (whether natural disasters such as the tsunami in 2004 or in political crisis situations such as Libya in 2011) demonstrate to the world that they have this form of global capacity. The US, the UK, and France have traditionally set the bar for this test, which 'rising' states, notably India and China, have moved to emulate. Such tests also, it may be added, differentiate according to a hierarchy of states, but reveal some of the limitations of supra-national diplomacy as projected through the EU and sub-national actors whatever the ambitions or deliverables in other areas.[58]

The burdens of responsibilities are ratcheted up in turn by not only the number of obligations, but also of threats. On top of terrorism there are increasing surveillance and monitoring issues related not only to organized crime but hybrids that blur state and non-state activity as in cyber-threats through so-called Chinese 'patriotic hackers'. Even as a wide number of countries have invested heavily in cyber diplomatic capabilities (with clear successes, as in the facilitation of the Dayton Accords) there are clear vulnerabilities at the state as well as the societal level. Indeed, the tensions between the calls for a more open, accountable, relevant, and even 'insurgent' diplomacy [59] and the fears that these trends hurt national interests become more pronounced. The more diplomats want to be accessible via their client base either in commercial or emergency situations (through the use of lap tops and IPads, etc.), the more there are risks of hacking. As two experts detailed the dangers in the context of an investigation of cyber-spying on numerous diplomatic missions, ministries of foreign affairs, and international organizations: 'While Twitter, Google Groups, Yahoo Mail, and Flickr may make our cyberexperiences much more convenient, interactive, and richly engaging, they also create ... a wide spectrum of new security vulnerabilities and a multiplicity of ever-evolving vectors through which victims can be targeted and attacks mounted.'[60]

1.7 Opening up Themes, Trajectories, and Debates

The themes, trajectories, and debates highlighted as being salient to the changing nature of diplomacy of course provide only some entry points for the OHMD project. Almost everything we talk and write about these dynamics can be interrogated, from the very title 'Modern Diplomacy', with some most probably preferring a more innovative description that emphasizes the extent of change taking place in the 21st century (although 'postmodern' offers an even more contested choice) and others who prefer simply 'Diplomacy', reflecting an ingrained bias towards continuity over change, with acknowledgement that diplomacy has an embedded status as the 'master institution' of international politics that will prevail now and in the future.[61]

Although disappointing to both camps, the only sensible conclusion that can be reached is that the essence of duality stands, although the shape of that duality is in flux. The tight hold of tradition is certainly bending. Intellectually, this reflects the weakening grip of Realism notwithstanding 9/11 and some obvious trends towards securitization. One of the many deficiencies beyond formative figures such as Hans Morgenthau has been that diplomacy was written out of the IR script. This is no longer the case. As recognized by the enthusiasm for the OHMD by so many contributors, diplomacy is where much of the real action in IR is.

The negative attitude towards conceiving and doing diplomacy differently is also eroding at the official level. The embrace of the declaratory language of 'new' diplomacy has continued under Obama and Hillary Clinton.[62] President Hu Jintao told a major gathering of Chinese ambassadors, diplomats, and other officials at a 2009 conference organized by the Ministry of Foreign Affairs and the Party Foreign Affairs Bureau that 'new thinking' was needed in China's international relations, with an emphasis in diplomacy on more political influence; more economic competitiveness; a more positive international image; and greater moral influence.[63]

As in the past, however, the transition of these exhortations will not be robustly revolutionary, with a synchronized shift to a similar 'new' template of doing things diplomatically. Change will continue to be uneven and jagged.

What is changing is that diplomacy has a compelling engagement and salient meaning right across the spectrum of political and 'everyday' life. This engagement—whether by leaders at the apex of power, from officials within the extended diversity of the state bureaucracy, or among the diversity of non-state actors and ordinary citizens—will not manifest itself all the time in every place and on every event. Nor does the meaning convey a buy-in for all the operational tenets of modern diplomacy even as it evolves. Expressions of contestation and even suspicion will continue in unabated fashion.[64] But inexorably diplomacy has seeped beyond the institutions and processes at its traditional core to encompass a more comprehensive intellectual and societal set of debates and multiple searches for not only symbolic but palpable connections and outcomes.

Digging further with regard to the wider driving influences, modalities, and impacts of these complex dynamics goes to the heart of the OHMD.

Notes

1. Literature on both sides of this debate includes Geoffrey Berridge (ed.), *Diplomacy: Theory and Practice*, 3rd ed. (Basingstoke: Palgrave, 2005); Paul Sharp, *Diplomatic Theory of International Relations* (Cambridge: Cambridge University Press, 2009); Shaun Riordan, *The New Diplomacy* (Cambridge: Polity 2003); and Jan Melissen (ed.), *Innovation in Diplomatic Practice* (Houndmills: Macmillan 1999).

2. Jorge Heine, 'On the manner of practising the new diplomacy', in Andrew F. Cooper, Brian Hocking, and William Maley (eds), *Global Governance and Diplomacy: Worlds Apart?* (Houndmills: Palgrave Macmillan, 2008).

3. Jean-Robert Leguey Feilleux, *The Dynamics of Diplomacy* (Boulder: Lynne Rienner, 2009), 1.

4. James N. Rosenau, 'Governance in the Twentieth-First Century', *Global Governance* 1 (Winter 1995), 15.

5. Robert D. Putnam, 'Diplomacy and Domestic Politics: The Logic of Two-Level Games', *International Organization* 42:3 (Summer 1988), 427–60.

6. Robert D. Putnam, Peter B. Evans, and Harold K. Jacobson (eds), *Double-Edged Diplomacy: International Bargaining and Domestic Politics* (Berkeley: University of California Press, 1993).

7. Raymond Cohen, 'Putting Diplomatic Studies on the Map', Diplomatic Studies Program Newsletter (Leicester: Centre for the Study of Diplomacy 1998), 1.

8. Emmanuel Adler and Vincent Pouliot (eds), *International Practices* (Cambridge: Cambridge University Press, 2011), 7–8.

9. Adler and Pouliot, *International Practices*, 9.

10. De Gaulle quoted in G. John Ikenberry and Chung-in Moon (eds), *The United States and Northeast Asia: Debates, Issues, and New Order* (Lanham, MD: Rowman & Littlefield, 2008), 81.

11. On the BRICs see Goldman Sachs, 'Dreaming with BRICS; The Path to 2050', *Global Economics Paper* No. 99 (2003), New York. <www.gs.com/insight/research/reports/99.pdf> and Leslie Elliott Armijo, 'The BRICs Countries (Brazil, Russia, India, and China) as Analytical Category: Mirage or Insight?', *Asian Perspective* 31:4 (2007), 7–42. In the larger context see Alan Alexandroff and Andrew F. Cooper (eds.), *Rising States, Rising Institutions: Challenges for Global Governance* (Washington DC: Brookings Institution Press, 2010).

12. Judy Dempsey, 'German business moves beyond Russia to China', *New York Times*, 13 July 2010.

13. Michael D. Shear, 'Obama Recasts Asia Trip as Jobs Mission', *New York Times*, 5 November 2010<http://thecaucus.blogs.nytimes.com/2010/11/05/obama-recasts-asia-trip-as-jobs-mission/>.

14. Alex Barker, 'Trade route leads Cameron into awkward dilemma', *Financial Times*, 25 February 2011.

15. Timothy M. Shaw, Andrew F. Cooper, and Gregory T. Chin, 'Emerging Powers in/around Africa: implications for/from global governance', *Politikon* 36:1 (April 2009), 27–44.

16. See for example G. John Ikenberry, *After Victory* (Princeton: Princeton University Press, 2001).

17. For the evolution of these pattern see Justin Robertson and Maurice A. East (eds), *Diplomacy and Developing Nations: Post-Cold War Foreign Policy Making Structures and Processes* (London: Routledge, 2005); and Andrew F. Cooper and Timothy M. Shaw (eds), *The Diplomacies of Small States: Between Vulnerability and Resilience* (Houndmills: Palgrave, 2009).

18. Embassy of the United States (2010) profiles of health diplomacy, <bangkok.usembassy. gov/health-diplomacy.html>.

19. See the earlier collection edited by Brian Hocking, *Foreign Ministries: Change and Adaptation* (London: Macmillan 1999).

20. 'Mr. Zero Problems', *Foreign Policy*, 13 March 2012.

21. Carne Ross, *Independent Diplomat: Dispatches From an Unaccountable Elite* (London: Hurst, 2007), 210–11.

22. Richard Langhorne, 'Current Developments in Diplomacy: Who are the Diplomats Now?', *Diplomacy & Statecraft* 8:2 (July 1997), 1–15.

23. Hedley Bull, *The Anarchical Society* (London: Macmillan, 1977), 162.

24. R.P. Barston, *Modern Diplomacy*, 2nd ed. (London and New York: Longman, 1997), 1.

25. Richard Langhorne and William Wallace, 'Diplomacy towards the Twenty-first Century', in Brian Hocking (ed.), *Foreign Ministries: Change and Adaptation* (London: Macmillan, 1999), 21–2.

26. Geoffrey Wiseman, '"Polylateralism" and New Modes of Global Dialogue', Discussion Papers No. 59 (Leicester: Leicester Diplomatic Studies Programme, 1999), 2.

27. Christer Jönsson, 'Global Governance: Challenges to Diplomatic Communication, Representation, and Recognition', in Cooper, Hocking, and Maley (eds), *Global Governance and Diplomacy*, 35.

28. Juergen Kleiner, *Diplomatic Practice: Between Tradition and Innovation* (Singapore: World Scientific, 2009).

29. On this debate see Susan Strange, *The Retreat of the State* (Cambridge: Cambridge University Press, 1996) and Linda Weiss, *The Myth of the Powerless State* (Ithaca: Cornell University Press, 1998); and more recently Andrew Gamble, *The Spectre at the Feast: Capitalist Crisis and the Politics of Recession* (New York: Palgrave, 2009).

30. On this dynamic in the WTO see Gregory C. Shaffer, *Defending Interests: Public-Private Partnerships in WTO Litigation* (Washington DC: Brookings, 2003). On NGO support for small states see Donna Lee, 'Bringing an Elephant into the Room: Small African State Diplomacy in the WTO', in Andrew F. Cooper and Timothy M. Shaw (eds), *The Diplomacies of Small States: Between Vulnerability and Resilience* (Basingstoke: Palgrave, 2009), 195–206.

31. Andrew F. Cooper, *Internet Gambling Offshore: Caribbean Struggles over Casino Capitalism* (Houndmills: Palgrave, 2011).

32. Iver Neumann, 'Gloablisation and Diplomacy', in Cooper, Hocking, and Maley (eds), *Global Governance and Diplomacy*, 25.

33. Andrew F. Cooper, *Celebrity Diplomacy* (Boulder, CO: Palgrave, 2008).

34. D. McCoy, S. Chand, and D. Sridhar, 'Global health funding: how much, where it comes from and where it goes', *Health Policy & Planning* 24: 6 (2009), 407–17.

35. Ewen MacAskill, 'Bill Gates donates £20m to kickstart fund for farmers', *Guardian*, 22 April 22 2010.

36. Sajjad Ashraf, 'The Raymond Davis Affair: A Case for Global Ramifications', *RSIS Commentary*, 33/2011, 3 March 2011.

37. Daniel Dombey, 'US struggling to hold role as global leader, Clinton says', *Financial Times*, 3 March 2011.

38. Dombey, 'US struggling to hold role as global leader, Clinton says'. See also Andrew F. Cooper and Bessma Momani, 'Qatar and expanded contours of Small State Diplomacy', *International Spectator* 46: 2 (June 2011), 127–42.

39. Ole Jacob Sending, Vincent Pouliot, and Iver Neumann, 'The future of diplomacy', *International Journal* 66: 3 (Summer 2011), 536.

40. On these themes see Cooper, Hocking, and Maley (eds), *Global Governance and Diplomacy*.

41. Sharp, *Diplomatic Theory of International Relations*.

42. For an early critique see James Eayrs, 'The Deliquescence Diplomacy', in *Diplomacy and its Discontents* (Toronto: University of Toronto Press, 1971), 77. See also Geoffrey Allan Pigman, *Contemporary Diplomacy* (Cambridge: Polity, 2010), 4.

43. Heine, 'On the manner of practising the new diplomacy', 281–2.

44. Jan Aart Scholte, 'From government to governance: transition to a new diplomacy', in Cooper, Hocking, and Maley (eds), *Global Governance and Diplomacy*, 59.

45. See for example Andrew F. Cooper, John English, and Ramesh Thakur (eds), *Enhancing Global Governance: Towards a New Diplomacy?* (Tokyo: United Nations University Press, 2002).

46. Craig Murphy, 'Global Governance: Poorly Done and Poorly Understood', *International Affairs* 76: 4 (2000), 789–804.

47. Anders Åslund, 'The Group of 20 must be stopped', *Financial Times*, 26 November 2009. See also Andrew F. Cooper, 'The G20 as an improvised crisis committee and/or a contested "steering committee" for the world', *International Affairs* 86: 3 (2010), 741–57.

48. David Held, *Cosmopolitanism: Ideals, Realities and Deficiencies* (Cambridge: Polity, 2110), 204.

49. Kofi Annan, 'What is the International Community? Problems Without Passports', *Foreign Policy* 132 (September/October 2002), 30–1.

50. Michael Stevenson and Andrew F. Cooper, 'Overcoming constraints of state sovereignty: Global health governance in Asia', *Third World Quarterly* 30: 7 (October 2009), 1379–94.

51. David L. Heymann, 'SARS and Emerging Infectious Diseases: A Challenge to Place Global Solidarity above National Sovereignty', *Annals Academy of Medicine* 35: 5 (May 2006), 350–3.

52. Melissa Curley and Nicholas Thomas, 'Human security and public health in Southeast Asia: the SARS outbreak', *Australian Journal of International Affairs* 58: 1 (March 2004), 17–32.

53. Jonathan M. Metzl, 'China's ill-considered response to the H1N1 virus', *LA Times*, 12 July 2009.

54. Harold Nicolson, *Diplomacy* (London: Thornton Butterworth, 1939).

55. Luk Van Langenhove, 'The transformation of multilateralism', *Global Policy* 1:3 (October 2010), 263–70.

56. Sharp, *Diplomatic Theory of International Relations*, 101–5. For a good discussion see Ian Hall, 'The transformation of diplomacy: mysteries, insurgencies and public relations', *International Affairs* 86: 1 (2010), 247–56.

57. Secretary Condoleezza Rice, 'Transformational Diplomacy', Georgetown University, Washington, DC, January 18, 2006. Available at <http://merln.ndu.edu/archivepdf/nss/state/100703.pdf>.

58. Brian Hocking and David Spence (eds), *Foreign Ministries in the European Union: Integrating Diplomats*, revised edition (Basingstoke: Palgrave, 2005).

59. Daryl Copeland, *Guerrilla Diplomacy: Rethinking International Relations* (Boulder, CO: Lynne Rienner, 2009), 210, 230.

60. Quoted in Joseph Brean, 'Cyber-scam snares top NATO official', *National Post* (Toronto), 12 March 2012. For a more detailed examination see Ronald J. Deibert and Rafal Rohozinski, 'Risking Security: Policies and Paradoxes of Cyberspace Security', *International Political Sociology* 4:1 (March 2010), 15–32.

61. Martin Wight, *Power Politics*, revised edition (Harmondsworth: Penguin, 1979), 113. See also R.P. Barston, *Modern Diplomacy* (London: Longman, 1988).

62. Hillary Rodham Clinton, 'Leading by Civilian Power', *Foreign Affairs* 89:6 (November/ December 2010), 13–24.

63. Gregory Chin and Ramesh Thakur, 'Will China Change the Rules of Global Order?', *Washington Quarterly* 33:4 (2011), 121.

64. James Der Derian, *On Diplomacy: A Genealogy of Western Estrangement* (Oxford: Basil Blackwell, 1987); Costas Constantinou, *On the Way to Diplomacy*, Borderlines, vol. 7 (Minneapolis: University of Minnesota Press, 1996).

CHAPTER 2

FROM CLUB TO NETWORK DIPLOMACY

JORGE HEINE

THE WikiLeaks episode, in which thousands of classified US State Department cables were released to the public, has raised questions about the practice of diplomacy in the age of the Internet.[1] If the most powerful country on earth cannot protect the secrecy of its own diplomatic communications, who can? If the diplomatic cable, that most sacrosanct of official instruments, a key tool for foreign embassies in their endeavour to provide to headquarters unvarnished assessments of local developments, is no longer safe from the prying eyes of journalists and NGOs, shouldn't it be abandoned altogether? Yet, wouldn't its abolishment become one of the last nails in the coffin of the resident mission as traditionally conceived? Or should cable writing be changed to a blander, more non-descript genre, making such communications into texts expunged of all controversial material that could in any way cast aspersions on bilateral relations? Is not the very purpose of the diplomatic cable to communicate information beyond what is freely available in the media, of which the most sensitive is precisely the most valuable?

The jury is still out on the effects of WikiLeaks on diplomatic reporting. Yet, the episode, with the extraordinary spectacle of high US officials calling their counterparts abroad to explain that cable writers did not mean what they said, illustrates the changing nature of diplomacy in the information age and the difficulty of keeping government communications under wraps in an era when transparency reigns. It also underscores the need to re-examine some of the premises of traditional diplomatic practices, and to develop a somewhat different conception of the diplomatic craft for the 21st century.

In many ways, the Wikileaks episode is only the tip of the iceberg of broader changes that have affected the theory and practice of diplomacy over the past three decades. At the root of these changes lies the process of globalization unleashed since 1980, when the first PC came on the market and the 24-hour news cycle was born with the launch of Cable News Network (CNN).[2] Information technology and telematics are bringing the world closer together and, in so doing, deterritorializing it. We may not be living at a time of 'the end of history', as Francis Fukuyama argued, but a case can be made that we are moving towards 'the end of geography' as we have known it.[3] The effective cost of a telephone call from Buenos Aires to Brussels is no different from one made from Buenos Aires to Cordoba.

A useful distinction is that between globalism and globalization. Globalism, a prominent feature of our time, involves networks of interdependence at intercontinental distances.[4] It implies multiple flows of products, services, or capital, and signifies the shrinkage of distance on a large scale. It also triggers the emergence of global issues and a global agenda to a degree that we had not seen before. The implications of this for diplomacy and diplomats are momentous.

Globalism poses a severe challenge to the nation state, most dramatically expressed in the global financial crisis of 2008–2009, in which questionable lending practices of a number of US banks ended up enveloping much of the world economy and triggering the greatest financial crisis in eighty years.[5] It was this very crisis that led to the creation of the G20 at leaders' level, the 'steering committee of the world economy', as it became apparent that only collective action could deal with the fallout of the crisis, and attempt to prevent the eruption of new ones.[6]

The challenges, however, are not only economic. In the political sphere, globalization, the process by which globalism becomes increasingly 'thicker', making it 'faster, cheaper, and deeper' than ever before, the increasing number of international interactions, and the rapidly diminishing cost of communications have led to a growing number of actors, both domestic and international: non-governmental organizations (NGOs), private companies, churches, business associations, trade unions, and political parties are all making their presence felt and adding layers of complexity to government decision-making.[7]

For a craft in which such venerable institutions as the resident mission arose in the Italian city-states of the 14th and 15th centuries, and many of whose established conventions and practices came into being in parallel to and as a result of the rise of the nation state in Europe, especially in France and England between the 17th and 19th centuries, this poses severe challenges.[8] In many ways, the whole apparatus of traditional diplomacy is anchored in the nation state. At a time when the nation state's fabric is pulled in different directions from 'above' (that is, from an international environment demanding the surrendering of ever larger portions of national sovereignty), and 'below' (by regionalist movements and by pressures for greater local autonomy from the central government), this puts diplomats in a complex situation. They are torn between the old, established ways of doing things, whose routines provide a semblance of order and comfort in a rapidly changing, unpredictable environment, and the demands of this new setting, which often run counter to some of the most sacred principles of the craft.[9]

The argument developed in this chapter is as follows:

1) Globalization, that is, the sustained increase in trans-border flows of goods, services, capital, images, and data that has taken place with the onset of the Third Industrial Revolution (since 1980) has changed many things in our interaction

with the international environment. This is especially true for diplomacy, an activity that acts as a 'hinge' between 'home' and 'abroad'.

2) These changes are partly (but not exclusively) related to technological changes in communications and transport. But they also are due to the changing nature of the international system under the twin pressures of the compression of time and space created by globalization.

3) The disconnect between these increased international flows and the lack of suitable global governance institutions and mechanisms to deal with the challenges created by them, has added numerous issues to the international agenda, with which often understaffed and underfunded foreign ministries find it increasingly hard to cope.

4) Paradoxically, at a time when these international challenges appear to be especially urgent, foreign ministry budgets are being cut, often on the basis of specious reasoning like, 'given summits and emails, who needs diplomats?', thus making it even more difficult to cope with these challenges.

5) One reason for this is the lack of institutional and behavioural adaptation by foreign ministries and diplomats themselves to this new environment.

6) The main features of 'network diplomacy' are then elaborated on, as are the conditions under which they are especially pertinent.[10]

2.1 THE RISE OF THE NETWORK STATE

The apparent paradox of a diplomatic apparatus under siege at a time of increased international flows—that is, at a moment in which one would expect foreign ministries and diplomats to be thriving, if not basking in the glory of their contribution to ever larger trans-border trade and investment flows—merits an explanation.

As Castells has pointed out, globalization cannot be reduced to internationalization.[11] There have been other historical periods, such as the late 19th century, in which international trade and investment also rose swiftly. What is different about this particular period—the one obtaining since the onset of the Third Industrial Revolution, roughly since 1980—is 'simultaneity'. This is the process in which certain units are able to operate as units in real time on a world scale. The best example is the international financial market. This has been made possible by the emergence of a technological system of information, telecommunications, and transport that has connected the planet in a network of flows that links the strategic units in all ambits of human activity.

This technological revolution is not only altering the material basis of society. It is also linking up national economies around the world, enhancing interdependence, albeit asymmetrically. The logic of flows and of networks has had a double impact on the modern nation state. On the one hand, it has forced the state to give up a measure of its national sovereignty to link up with a variety of supra-national and intergovernmental units that attempt to introduce a measure of coordination among national policies.[12] On the other hand, it has opened the 'black box' of the nation state, as many sub-national units and civil society actors link up with their own peers across the world, giving a further impetus to transnational relations.[13] All of this has led to a growing number of actors, both domestic and international, and the always critical 'foreign policy community' to make their presence felt and to add layers of complexity to government decision-making, foreign policy, and the conduct of diplomacy.[14] In short, the model of an international system based purely on independent states has been replaced by one in which the nation state is still a key component, but by no means the only one.

It has been said that the conduct of multilateral diplomacy differs in such fundamental ways from that of bilateral diplomacy that they almost amount to different crafts, relying, as they do, on radically different tools, means, and objectives.[15] Globalization and the network state have introduced such changes into the dynamics of diplomacy as to make it into something very different from what it was in the past. Jean-Robert Leguey-Feilleux has underlined the acceleration of the diplomatic pace and tempo of our time, driven by technology and by the growing number of actors.[16] It is not only the vastly larger number of actors involved that adds complexity to the management of the new diplomacy. This is also due to its much broader scope (the vast array of public policy issues it now includes) and the many policy levels (local, domestic, national, bilateral, regional, and global) it entails. The effects of this are not just quantitative, there are *qualitative* changes in the theory and practice of an old and established profession—perhaps more set in its venerable ways than most, but still in urgent need to adapt to the imperatives of the new century. It is this shift that we refer to when making the distinction between 'club' and 'network diplomacy', comparable to the change from the analogue to the digital watch. In other words, it is not a question of adding a few more pieces to the old mechanical Swiss watch, but, rather, of approaching the venerable and critical issue of time keeping in a different way.

2.2 THE CHALLENGE OF GLOBAL GOVERNANCE

The rise of the network state goes hand in hand with the emergence of a whole new international agenda. The Third Industrial Revolution and the end of the cold war have brought about a very different set of issues to the fore, issues that demand distinct tools and approaches from nation states and their diplomats.[17]

Much as diplomacy has been anchored in the nation state, it has also been framed by the Westphalian international order, one rooted in the twin principles of hierarchy and anarchy that emerged in the 17th century and reigned for three and a half centuries. The international system was based on a certain structure dependent on 'hard' factors that determined national power—particularly military and naval power, key elements in the rise of imperial domains and colonialism. In the 19th century, the First and Second Industrial Revolutions became key propellants of national power, triggering competition and arms races between 'early' and 'late' industrializers, and eventually leading to the First World War.[18]

Much of the basis of that order came to naught at the turn from the 20th to the 21st century. Globalism and globalization have ushered in a new international order. The model of an international system based on independent states has been replaced by one in which the nation state remains a component, but by no means the only one. The hierarchical principle of the old industrial order based on manufacturing as the reigning economic activity has given way to the much flatter organizing notion of the knowledge society where IT and communications hold sway—of Google rather than of General Motors. If this is true domestically, it is also valid internationally. The networked state goes hand in hand with a networked international society.[19]

From the unitary, centralized state guided by a narrowly conceived notion of the national interest, we have thus moved to a more fragmented entity, in some ways hollowed out from above and from below. As Ramesh Thakur points out in Chapter 3 of this volume, this different incarnation of the nation state, one that finds itself in a more crowded international playing field, must necessarily revisit the very notion of the national interest as its all-purpose guiding principle, and replace it with the more current and serviceable notion of the balance of interests.

The switch from a 'national government' perspective to a 'global governance' one is propelled by the confluence of several factors.[20] The changing nature of the nation state, the increasingly plural character of international society, the growing number of global issues (of which climate change is the most visible one) that demand collective action, and the rapidly growing pace and density of international interactions are among the most significant of them.

For traditional diplomacy, for which the realist paradigm of international relations seemed to fit especially well, this paradigmatic shift, far easier to subsume within the liberal or institutionalist perspectives on the field than within the realist optic, has been problematic. Centuries-old verities have been thrown out the window, with no new conventional wisdoms ready to be picked up off the shelf.[21]

At the core of this challenge lies the need to grasp the implications of the change from 'government' to 'governance'. Much as the former was traditionally based on the principles of top-down administration and command-and-control in a hierarchical organization, the latter relies less on administration and regulation than on coordination of a relatively flat network of a vast array of actors. In the international system, where the very notion of any form of global government remains, if it exists at all, the very distant aspiration of a few (as evidenced by efforts such as those undertaken by the G20 on global economic matters), global governance on a de facto rather than a de jure basis is gaining momentum. This should not be surprising. The exponential growth in transborder flows in a number of areas—of which finance is perhaps the most prominent one—makes it necessary to come up with mechanisms of damage control. In the 1990s, the financial crises that bedevilled countries such as Brazil, Indonesia, Russia, and Thailand, as 'hot money' suddenly flew out of emerging markets, often as quickly as it came in, wrought economic havoc, and, in the process, affected the stability of many other economies, including some far removed from the one originating the crisis. Ten years later, on the occasion of the global financial crisis of 2008–2009, the notion that endless liberalization, deregulation, and relaxation of capital and all border controls (except for labour) is a panacea for endless progress has shown to be delusional. The three Baltic nations that embarked on this course (Estonia, Latvia, and Lithuania), as well as countries like Iceland and Ireland, that followed a similar course, had double-digit negative growth in 2009.[22]

There is a lag, of course. The growth in transnational flows has not been matched by an equivalent growth in global governance tools to regulate them.[23] And yet, the very nature of the structure of globalized networks, which intertwine global actors and interests, ensures that no single power is able to maintain its position within the newly emerging global disorder without making compromises with other global players. In turn, one response to global governance gaps has been regional governance. The transfer of state functions to supranational forms of regional governance is one way to cope with emerging crises and/or with illegal flows.

The broader point is that all these 'solutions' require a mindset and a predisposition that is very different from that of traditional diplomacy, one focused on international affairs as a zero-sum game, where one nation's win is another's loss, as opposed to a more balanced perspective on global public goods. As Castells has put it,

> Nation-states still see the networks of governance as a negotiating table upon which to impose their specific interests. There is a stalemate in the intergovernmental decision-making processes because the culture of cooperation is lacking. The overarching principles are the interests of the nation-state and the domination of the personal/political/social interests in service of each nation-state.[24]

2.3 THE RESILIENCE OF CLUB DIPLOMACY

That said, the current crisis of diplomacy, if it can be called that, presents us with a paradox. One would think that the increases in international trade and foreign direct investment (FDI) flows, and the negotiation of many international agreements to facilitate these flows would lead to a 'golden age of diplomacy' in which the roles of foreign ministries and diplomats would be recognized as vitally important. This would also translate itself into increased budgetary allocations and other, more symbolic expressions. This has largely *not* occurred. In fact, the opposite may be true. Attacks like those of 1992 US presidential candidate Ross Perot ('Embassies are relics of the days of sailing ships') continue to hold sway.

Yet, this posits a puzzle. If one can understand such attacks on the diplomatic establishment from populist politicians, it is less obvious why it should be so from the financial establishment. Still, foreign ministries find themselves among the very first to fall under the chopping block of budgetary cutbacks directed by finance ministries all over the world—with rare exceptions.[25] Given that finance ministries should be especially aware of the increases in international flows of goods, services, and capital, and the enormous benefits to be derived from accessing even a small share of them, something for which foreign ministry headquarters and their 'branches' (i.e. missions) are especially well placed to act on, this is especially enigmatic.

It is my contention that the reason for this apparent paradox is the resilience of the 'club model' of diplomacy. By this I mean what is also referred to as 'classical diplomacy' or 'cabinet diplomacy'. In the 'club model', diplomats meet only with government officials, among themselves, and with the odd businessman or woman, and give an interview or speech here or there. By and large, however, they restrict themselves to fellow members of the club, with whom they also feel most comfortable, and focus their minds on 'negotiating agreements between sovereign states'. By definition, those practising this approach find it difficult to tap into the many trans-border flows of our time, since they regard them as beyond their purview.

This template, originally forged in the Italian city-states of the 14th and 15th centuries was formalized subsequently largely by French and British conceptions and practices. In a highly traditional profession—sometimes referred to as 'the second oldest in the world'—this template provides a ready-made, off-the-shelf manual for many diplomats from African, Asian, and Caribbean countries still in the first decades of independent nationhood and the initial stages of developing a foreign service.[26]

Diplomats today are tasked with helping their own countries navigate the perils of globalization. To some degree, this is done by the ministries of finance and those of trade and industry, but it is also, and very significantly, undertaken by ministries of foreign affairs (MFAs) and their missions abroad. Now, the diplomat's traditional skills of dealing, mostly *in camera*, with a relatively small group of government officials and elite decision-makers are quite different from those needed to engage, often in the open and under the glare of television lights, the many actors that have become relevant in international affairs today.

Yet—and herein lies a great paradox—many young diplomats from young countries today are being socialized into a certain way of practising diplomacy precisely at the time when it is becoming obsolete. Many MFAs and diplomats are still stuck in that mode, failing to understand the imperatives of change, as the world makes the transition to a much more dynamic and less hierarchical 'network diplomacy'.

There are a number of objective reasons why the 'diplomatic establishment' finds itself under siege in the new century. A traditional line of attack on MFAs and the elaborate structure of resident missions, consulates, pomp, protocol, and paraphernalia that goes with it, has been its alleged irrelevance in a world in which presidents and prime ministers meet at summits, instant communications are available, and decisions can be made in real time across many time zones.[27] What purpose is served, or so the reasoning goes, by having diplomats stationed at great expense in distant lands, when deals and agreements could be struck over the phone or by teleconferencing and the text sent anywhere in the world in fractions of a second?

A second source of vulnerability has been democratization and the push for greater transparency. Whereas a few decades ago foreign policy and diplomacy were considered by many to be beyond the grasp of the mass public, this is no longer so. Television and 24-hour news channels have brought the world to one's living room. Citizens can now see quite graphically the effects of their leaders' foreign policy decisions and how diplomats cope with them on the ground—even halfway across the world. We are in a different world from the one in which the ordinary voter could be depicted as 'ignorant, lazy and forgetful regarding the international commitments for which he has assumed responsibility', as Nicolson did in 1938.

Transparency is also at play. The media and the public, quite legitimately, want to know what is happening 'behind Embassy windows', at least in terms of how (and if) their interests are being served and furthered, and the demand for diplomatic accountability, something which would have astounded earlier writers on diplomacy like Francois de Callieres, is very much with us. One way in which this expresses itself is in the many belt-tightening exercises to which MFAs and their missions abroad are subjected. Diplomats are thus no longer sheltered from the political give-and-take, at least not so much as they were in the past, and they must respond to these new demands.

And if these 'external' pressures often put MFAs and their missions abroad against the wall, much the same could be said about 'internal' ones, meaning developments inside government. The across-the-board increase in trans-border flows has meant that more and more ministries and government agencies are 'getting into the act' with their own 'Office of International Affairs', which conducts a parallel diplomacy. In some of the bigger countries, an embassy might have more staff from other ministries than from the MFA—staff over which the head of mission may have little effective control. Often these other ministries have more resources, and many of the more specialized functions, such as trade negotiations, are handled by non-diplomatic experts.

All of this leads to a progressive 'hollowing out' of traditional diplomatic functions, and to the impression of diplomats as mere 'coordinators' of the substantive activities of other agencies. As Peter Ustinov put it a few years ago, 'a diplomat these days is nothing but a headwaiter who is allowed to sit down occasionally'.

Yet, these pressures on cutting back diplomatic budgets and activities must be put in perspective. With some 216-member countries in FIFA (Federation Internationale de Football Associations) and 193 at the United Nations, nobody expects governments to have fully manned missions everywhere, and none does. Micro-states, like some of the English-speaking Caribbean islands or those in the Pacific, have only a few missions, and in most countries the MFA budget is among the smallest. In a country like Chile, widely considered to have an effective diplomacy, with a special emphasis on economic issues, the hard currency yearly budget is around USD 150 million for some 60 embassies, a little over USD 2 million per embassy. For a country that exports USD 80 billion a year, and attracts up to USD 10 billion in FDI on any given year, this does not seem like an extravagant amount. It amounts to 0.3 percent of the fiscal budget and 0.1 percent of GDP. On a good day, an ambassador may attract an FDI project amounting to twenty times the yearly budget of the MFA. This seems hardly an unproductive investment of taxpayer resources.

One reason MFA budgets are under seemingly permanent attack is that they have not developed their constituencies or adapted to the new age of 'network diplomacy'. Ministries with much larger budgets—agriculture, health, education—have no such problem, for obvious reasons. Yet, in a world in which more and more jobs depend on international trade and FDI, it should not be too difficult for top MFA authorities, and diplomats themselves, to be a bit more proactive in making clear to the informed public that international markets do not operate on autopilot, that opening markets for one's country's products is not done by an invisible hand, and that it is a tough competition out there to attract multinational corporations and to sign trade and tax agreements.[28]

One obvious route is to generate direct links between missions and their home state's own regions and localities. This can show that diplomats on the ground actually help to generate jobs, something not always apparent to the average citizen. Headquarters will often not approve, as it will feel left 'out of the loop', but it would do well to consider such a strategy as part of its outreach activities. It is certainly needed to counter the strange (and in many ways perverse) MFA cost-cutting syndrome. This is where the ministry with one of the smallest budgets—whose policies often get the best public opinion approval ratings, and which plays a key role in opening export markets and attracting FDI—finds itself permanently operating on a shoestring, closing missions and cutting to the bone its core activities.

This syndrome is especially damaging since, in today's world, diplomacy, far from becoming redundant, as some would have it, is more significant than ever, since there is so much more at stake in international engagements. And the diplomat, as an intermediary between his or her country and the host nation, is critically positioned to make the most of leveraging the opportunities that come his or her way or that are generated though his or her own wits. However, this demands a certain conception of diplomacy that is very different from the traditional one.

2.4 TOWARDS NETWORK DIPLOMACY

It requires understanding, above all, that it is no longer enough to count on the goodwill of the 'Prince', as ambassadors of yesterday did, to get things done and to keep their job. In the 21st century, to be effective, diplomats must practice 'network diplomacy'. This means engaging a vastly larger number of players in the host country—including many who would have never thought of setting foot in the rarefied atmosphere of the salons and private clubs the diplomats of yesteryear used to frequent. More and more, diplomacy is becoming 'complexity management', to a degree earlier master practitioners like Cardinal Richelieu would not have imagined.

The advent of the network model is due not only to increased democratization and the growing number of relevant actors for policy-making—all of whom must be 'kept in the loop' for 'things to happen'—but also to the growing interpenetration of different societies. With modern communications and travel, societies can easily take up experiences from elsewhere and apply them at home. Ideas travel fast in today's globalized world, but they do so even faster if they are shepherded and guided, especially so if they come from small and middle powers without the vast media machinery of the big powers. Diplomats, in their 'labour in exile' as Callieres put it, are ideally placed to communicate to their host societies the ideas, values, and significant social and cultural projects that are under way in their home countries. In so doing, they bridge the gap between them, which can be quite wide, and thus lay the foundation for cooperation across a wide array of issues.

In media-driven societies like those of the 21st century, this implies a capacity to communicate complex issues in an accessible fashion, orally and in writing.[29] This kind of ability—as opposed to the arcane, convoluted, and stilted way of talking and writing that diplomats are sometimes accused of indulging in—is one of the most critical virtues modern diplomats must develop. To be an effective communicator, the contemporary 'network diplomat' needs both sufficient command of the subject matter at hand, be it nuclear policy or reproductive rights, and an ability to convey it in an easily understandable language. This is the only way to make the case for his or her country, effectively and convincingly. This means abandoning the diffident, *blasé* pose so many diplomats strike as part of their *dramatis persona*. And key instruments to help build the network the contemporary diplomat needs in his host society are the media, which not only help set up the network, but also assist its maintenance, refinement, and expansion.

If this is true within the host country, it is also valid for the home turf, where some of the most difficult battles—for resources, for priorities, for high-level visits—are waged. Here too, and this is especially true for heads of mission, the ability to make one's case persuasively, not just to foreign ministry officials, but also to parliamentarians, business leaders, political parties, and trade unionists, can be crucial for the success of any given initiative.

2.5 HILLAPLOMACY AS THE WAY FORWARD?

In few places was the decline of diplomacy as apparent as in the world's only superpower, the United States, in the 2000–2008 period. Many countries distanced themselves from the United States, in disagreement with the policies emanating from Washington. Yet, this was as much a matter of substance as of style. It is difficult to make friends if you start from the premise that you do not need them. As Charles Krauthammer, a leading columnist and supporter of the administration's policy, put it, 'of course it would be nice if we had more allies rather than fewer. It would also be nice to be able to fly.'[30] This lack of belief in diplomacy was best expressed by US ambassador to the United Nations, John Bolton: 'I don't do carrots.'[31]

Not surprisingly, the State Department found itself in dire straits in early 2009. One quarter of all positions were unfilled. There were more lawyers in the Pentagon than foreign service officers at State, and more musicians in US military bands than diplomats manning the 260 diplomatic missions around the world. Morale in the foreign service was at an all-time low. Even such traditional diplomatic tasks as the management of foreign aid had largely been taken over by the Pentagon, given the State Department's meagre resources.

As if to underscore the enormity of the task Ms Hillary Clinton faced as she took up her position in the State Department, President Barack Obama made himself available for the occasion, something few US presidents ever do, and in itself a potent symbol of the enhanced role diplomacy was supposed to play under his watch.

Nearly a full term since his inauguration, the jury is still out as to how significant a change in US foreign policy President Obama and Secretary Clinton have brought about. But in terms of the significance attached to diplomacy as a tool, there has been a sea change. Not only have all those vacant positions at State been filled, but, at the request of the administration, Congress has approved funds for some 1,100 new positions in the State Department. USAID has doubled its staff, with some 1,200 new foreign service officers.[32] For the first time, a Quadrennial Diplomacy and Development Review (QDDR) took place at State, modelled after similar exercises at the Pentagon. As Clinton herself put it,

> The QDDR endorses a new public diplomacy strategy that makes public engagement every diplomat's duty, through town hall meetings and interviews with the media, organized outreach, events in provincial towns and smaller communities, student exchange programs, and virtual connections that bring together citizens and civic organizations. Indeed, in the twenty first century, a diplomat is as likely to meet with a tribal elder in a rural village as a counterpart in a foreign ministry, and is as likely to wear cargo pants as a pinstriped suit.

And Secretary Clinton has herself led from the front in this matter. In her February 2009 tour of Asia, which led to a *New York Times* story entitled 'Clinton Reshapes Diplomacy by Tossing the Script', she moved seamlessly from meetings with heads of state to TV variety shows and speaking to university students.[33] As she put it, she wanted to make a connection to people 'in a way that is not traditional, not confined by the ministerial greeting and the staged handshake photo'. 'I see our job right now, given where we are in the world and what we've inherited, as repairing relations, not only with governments, but with people.' By connecting with people personally, she is convinced she can help mould public opinion, which, in turn, can influence governments. This is a crucial insight into the nature of diplomacy as it is played today.

Moreover, this has gone hand in hand with an energetic deployment of social media. As Secretary Clinton put it herself, 'Our ambassadors are blogging and tweeting, and every embassy has a social media presence.'[34]

There is only one Hillary Clinton, and few other politicians, let alone diplomats, can match her drawing power and celebrity status. But her approach to her duties as the

United States chief diplomat, unthinkable in any of her predecessors, from Henry Kissinger to Condoleezza Rice, shows a profound understanding of the changing nature of this ancient craft. There is a lesson there, for all those who want to see it.

Is this shift in grasping the demands of modern diplomacy confined to the world's most powerful nation? Do not the enormous resources and privileged access to the world's global media machinery provide Washington with considerable trump cards in the game of today's international politics, cards not available to the middle and small powers that make up for the vast majority of UN member states?

Not by any means. Network diplomacy goes way beyond celebrity diplomacy (a term coined by my colleague Andrew Cooper, one of the co-editors of this volume) and public diplomacy. It reflects a certain *approach* to the conduct of diplomatic business. This is unrelated to the *scale* and to the *scope* of the diplomatic undertaking of any given country—be it France, Finland, or Fiji.

2.6 BEYOND PUBLIC DIPLOMACY

Jan Melissen's chapter in this volume (Chapter 24) elaborates on the notion of public diplomacy, in some ways one of the most dynamic specialities in the field, particularly after 9/11. Public diplomacy has generated special attention in diplomatic studies.[35] Its evolution from its original incarnation as cultural diplomacy to its more differentiated current expression has triggered a rich literature and even a specialized journal.[36] A public diplomacy strategy is part of any attempt at network diplomacy. Yet, network diplomacy is much broader than public diplomacy. It includes such remarkable exercises as that of tweeting foreign ministers and ambassadors, such as Carl Bildt, the foreign minister of Sweden, who has 160,000 followers, and Michael McFaul, the US ambassador to Russia, who has 22,700. The latter, tweeting in Russian, is able to reach a wide audience within the host country bypassing traditional media altogether.[37]

Traditional definitions of diplomatic tasks like Nicolson's ('to represent, to inform, and to negotiate'), the Vienna Convention's ('representing, protecting, negotiating, ascertaining, and promoting'), or Kishan Rana's ('promotion, outreach, feedback, management, and servicing') fail to do justice to the centrality of the task of network diplomacy: the *projection* of the diplomat's country into the host nation.

It is all very well to say that diplomacy is 'the art of negotiating agreements between states'. With more than 200 independent nation states, many agreements are signed on a daily basis. But there is a limit to the number of agreements a country can sign. So, for diplomats in many ways the most critical issue is the signing of agreements that are really worth it, with countries that have something to offer. The real task is getting to the negotiations. One effective way to do so is by *bridging the gap between home and host country*—that is, by bringing the societies closer. And for this, the development of extensive networks around key issues in both countries is critical, and for the diplomat to take his country's case to the public at large, that is, to engage civil society.

Unlike the countries of the North, few developing nations have sufficient resources for international cooperation programmes, whether generous or miserly, to engage in what is sometimes described as 'South-South cooperation'. But what they do have is experience in many public policy areas that can be valuable to other countries in the South—experience that, in some ways, is more relevant, and therefore more valuable, than that of developed societies. The transfer of that experience, however, is by no means a mechanical or straightforward process.

It needs to be researched, systematized, and communicated, a task for which diplomatic missions are ill suited. What diplomats can do, however, is to work with research centres and NGOs of their own countries to bring these experiences to host nations. It is here that the role of diplomacy as 'hinge' enters. The relegation of diplomats to mere coordinators of the activities of other ministries abroad, mentioned in section 2.3, is part and parcel of the ostensible decline of diplomacy in the eyes of many. This is especially true if diplomats have little to say on the unfolding agenda of those dealings. Yet, being a proactive facilitator of experience exchanges is very different from being a passive event organizer. It entails identifying priority issue areas that lend themselves for such exchanges, motivating partners in home and host societies to buy in, mobilizing the necessary resources, bringing about the project and seeing to its final completion. If successful, such projects will then take on a dynamic of their own, at which point the mission can move on to other initiatives.

Generating these networks between societies, networks that will often outlast by many years the duration of any diplomat's posting, is something that goes beyond public relations exercises or efforts at enhancing 'country image'. They reach deep into the heart of any given society.

2.7 FROM TRAINED OBSERVER TO PROACTIVE INITIATOR AND MODERN ORATOR

In his classic book, *Diplomacy*, Sir Harold Nicolson refers to the change that took place at some point from the 'orator' diplomat of the Greek city-states to the 'trained observer' of the 19th and 20th centuries, one who sent dispatches reporting to the minister about developments in distant lands. In today's globalized world, the role of diplomats is in some ways even more crucial than before, but the tasks at hand are somewhat different. Increasing trans-border flows, growing interactions between nations, and a far higher number of actors, including many non-state ones, have changed the nature of diplomacy while also raising the stakes of international engagement. If a country manages to find its proper niche in the world economy, as Singapore has, or, to a smaller degree, Chile, it is in business. If it does not, as is the case with many Central and West African countries, it is marginalized and left behind.

With today's communications revolution, many details and analyses of current events happening in the host country are available almost instantaneously at home headquarters. There is thus no need to engage in the extensive reporting about them that was so popular in the diplomatic dispatches of yesteryear. The key, of course, is to identify the major developments that do need an informed opinion, as well as those of significance for the bilateral relationship.

In the traditional model of diplomacy, the functions of a diplomat are to represent, to inform, and to negotiate, with national sovereignty as the bedrock upon which the whole system rests. Its attitude is best summarized in Charles Maurice de Talleyrand's recommendation to all diplomats, and heeded, in more ways than one, to this day: '*et surtout, pas trop de zele*'. This model, based on what worked best in the 18th-century French court, is no longer relevant.

This somewhat contrived diffident pose, combined with the intense cultivation of a few key players, so characteristic of 'club diplomacy', is being replaced by 'network diplomacy'. The latter is based on a much more extensive set of contacts at home and abroad, built around critical 'issue areas' pertinent to the mission. These issue areas flow from what the head of mission identifies at the beginning of his or her tenure as the 'central problem' of the bilateral relationship. This may overlap with, but does not necessarily mirror, the goals defined in the head of mission's instructions—an exercise that needs careful reappraisal after a few months in situ. If properly tended to and nurtured, this network feeds on itself.

In this new model, which demands a radical change in the self-image diplomats have of themselves and their job, negotiation is still present, albeit in a diminished fashion, but the other traditional functions of the craft are superseded by newer variants. For 'representation', with its somewhat old-fashioned, slightly passive connotation (one represents by being rather than by doing), one needs to substitute 'projection'. This means conveying what the diplomat's home country is all about and transmitting it to the host society and government. And 'information' needs to be replaced by 'analysis and influence'—that is, ways by which a diplomat can make a difference for the better in the host society, reflecting the increased interpenetration and interdependence of the 21st century.

In other words, the 'trained observer', no longer suited to a 24/7 world of business process outsourcing and knowledge process off-shoring, needs to become a 'proactive initiator' and 'modern orator'. Twenty-first century diplomats must actively engage the society in which they reside, not just the government to which they are accredited. They must look for ways to project their own nation upon the one they are posted to, and try to make a difference. They ought to reclaim the tradition of the Greek city-states' orators and walk once again into the modern-day equivalent of the *agora*—the modern mass media—and speak out. This has its perils. Yet, it is arguably a crucial step for the world's second oldest profession to arrest the decline which seems to bedevil it.

NOTES

1. On the Wikileaks episode, see Chapter 25, this volume.
2. On globalization, see David Held, Anthony McGrew, David Goldblatt, and Jonathan Perraton, *Global Transformations: Politics Economics and Culture* (Stanford: Stanford University Press, 1999).
3. Francis Fukuyama, *The End of History and the Last Man* (New York: The Free Press, 1992).
4. See Robert O. Keohane and Joseph S. Nye, 'Introduction', in Joseph S. Nye and John D. Donahue (eds), *Governance in a Globalizing World* (Washington DC: Brookings Institution Press, 2000).
5. See Eric Helleiner, Stefano Pagliari, and Hubert Zimmerman (eds), *Global Finance in Crisis: The Politics of Regulatory Change* (New York: Routledge, 2009).
6. See Alan S. Alexandroff and Andrew F. Cooper (eds), *Rising States, Rising Institutions: Challenges to Global Governance* (Washington DC: The Brookings Institution Press, 2010).
7. See Richard Langhorne, 'The Diplomacy of Non-State Actors', *Diplomacy and Statecraft* 16 (2005), 331–9, and Geoffrey Allen Pigman, 'Making Room at the Negotiating Table: The Growth of Diplomacy between Nation-State Governments and Non-State Economic Entities', *Diplomacy and Statecraft* 16 (2005), 385–401.
8. See Garrett Mattingly, 'The First Resident Embassies: Medieval Italian Origins of Modern Diplomacy', *Speculum* 12:4 (1937), 423–39. For 16th-century and early modern diplomacy, see his *Renaissance Diplomacy* (Baltimore: Penguin, 1964), 105–256.
9. See Daryl Copeland, *Guerrilla Diplomacy: Rethinking International Relations* (Boulder; Lynne Rienner, 2009).
10. This chapter builds on and expands on my earlier work on this subject. See my 'On the Manner of Practising the New Diplomacy', in Andrew F. Cooper, Brian Hocking, and William Maley (eds), *Global Governance and Diplomacy: Worlds Apart?* (Basingstoke: Palgrave Macmillan, 2008).
11. Manuel Castells, *The Rise of the Network Society* (London: Blackwell, 1996).
12. The classic example of this is the European Union. On how this has impacted on the conduct of diplomacy, see David Spence, 'Taking Stock: 50 Years of European Diplomacy', *The Hague Journal of Diplomacy* 4 (2009), 235–59; and Knud Erik Jorgensen, 'The European Union in Multilateral Diplomacy', *The Hague Journal of Diplomacy* 4 (2009), 189–209.
13. See Noe Carnago, 'On the Normalization of Sub-State Diplomacy', *The Hague Journal of Diplomacy* 5 (2010), 11–36.
14. See James W. St G. Walker and Andrew S. Thompson (eds), *Critical Mass: The Emergence of Global Civil Society* (Waterloo: Wilfrid Laurier University Press, 2008).
15. On multilateralism, see Edward Newman, Ramesh Thakur, and John Tirman, *Multilateralism Under Challenge: Power International Order and Structural Change* (Tokyo: United Nations University Press, 2006).
16. Jean-Robert Leguey-Feilleux, *The Dynamics of Diplomacy* (Boulder: Westview, 2009), ch. 6.
17. See Iver B. Neumann, 'Globalisation and Diplomacy', in Cooper, Hocking, and Maley (eds), *Global Governance and Diplomacy*.
18. For an incisive analysis of the relationship between military force and diplomacy in that period and into the first two-thirds of the 20th century, see Paul Gordon Lauren, Gordon A. Craig, and Alexander L. George, *Force and Statecraft: Diplomatic Challenges of our Time*, 4th edition (New York: Oxford University Press, 2007).
19. See Volumes II and III of the Castells trilogy on *The Information Age: The Power of Identity*, 1997, and *End of Millennium*, 1998 (London: Blackwell, 1998).

20. See Alan F. Alexandroff (ed.), *Can the World Be Governed? Possibilities for Effective Multileralism* (Waterloo: Wilfrid Laurier University Press, 2008); and Andrew F. Cooper and Agata Antkiewicz (eds), *Emerging Powers in Global Governance: Lessons from the Heiligendamm Process* (Waterloo; Wilfrid Laurier University Press, 2008).

21. For a somewhat different perspective, and the capacity for diplomacy to absorb these changes, see Juergen Kleiner, 'The Inertia of Diplomacy', *Diplomacy and Statecraft* 19 (2008), 321–49.

22. See Jorge Heine and Ramesh Thakur (eds), 'Introduction: Globalization and Uncivil Society', in Heine and Thakur, *The Dark Side of Globalization* (Tokyo: United Nations University Press, 2011).

23. On this, see Thomas G. Weiss and Ramesh Thakur, *Global Governance and the UN: An Unfinished Journey* (Bloomington: Indiana University Press, 2010).

24. Manuel Castells, 'The New Public Sphere: Global Civil Society, Communication Networks and Global Governance', *Annals of the Academy of Political and Social Sciences* 616, (March 2008), 88.

25. Among these exceptions are emerging powers like Brazil, China, Turkey, and India. Brazil increased its number of embassies abroad by 32 between 2003 and 2008, reaching a total of 134 in 2009. A country like the United States had 164 resident embassies in that year.

26. A standard, classical source on the subject is Harold Nicolson, *Diplomacy* (New York: Oxford University Press, 1963). A standard, earlier work is Francois de Callieres, *On the Manner of Negotiating with Princes* (Notre Dame: Indiana, University of Notre Dame Press, 1963). For a commentary on Callieres, see Maurice Keens-Souper, 'Callieres', in G.R. Berridge, Maurice Keens-Souper, and T.G. Otter, *Diplomatic Theory from Machiavelli to Kissinger* (Basingstoke: Palgrave, 2001), 106–24.

27. See Robert Wolfe, '*Still* Lying Abroad? On the Institution of the Resident Ambassador', *Diplomacy and Statecraft* 9:2 (1998), 23–54.

28. See Kishan Rana, *The 21st Century Ambassador: Plenipotentiary to Chief Executive* (New Delhi: Oxford University Press, 2005), 'The Domestic Dimension'.

29. On diplomacy and the media, see Eytan Gilboa, 'Diplomacy in the media age: Three models of uses and effects', *Diplomacy and Statecraft* 12:2 (June 2001), 1–28.

30. Charles Krauthammer, 'Democratic Realism: An American Foreign Policy for a Unipolar World', the Irving Kristol Lecture, American Enterprise Institute, 2004.

31. Cited in *BBC News*, 'Profile: John Bolton', 4 December 2006.

32. For these data, and the subsequent quotation, see Hillary Clinton, 'Leading Through Civilian Power: Redefining Diplomacy and Development', *Foreign Affairs* 89:6 (November–December 2010), 13–24.

33. Marc Landler, 'Clinton Reshapes Diplomacy by Tossing the Script', *The New York Times*, 20 February 2009.

34. Cited in Chrystia Freeland, 'Social media statecraft: A multiplatform outreach strategy', *The Globe and Mail*, Report on Business, 6 April 2012, B2. Carl Bildt, then prime minister of Sweden, and a pioneering user of the Internet, sent the first e-mail from one head of government to another. He seat it to United States President Bill Clinton on 4 February 1994, congratulating him on lifting the U.S. embargo on Vietnam.

35. See, for example, the special issues of the journals *American Behavioral Scientist* 52:5 (January 2009), *Annals of the Academy of Political and Social Science* (March 2008), and *The Hague Journal of Diplomacy* (2007), all on public diplomacy.

36. The journal *Public Diplomacy* is a student-run journal published by the Association of Public Diplomacy Scholars at the University of Southern California, with support from the USC Center on Public Diplomacy and the Annenberg School of Communications.

37. Cited in Freeland, 'Social Media Statecraft'.

CHAPTER 3

··

A BALANCE OF INTERESTS

··

RAMESH THAKUR

In the Obama administration's internal policy debate on Afghanistan there was considerable range and diversity of views among senior officials on most key questions: should there be an increase in troop levels and, if so, by how much and starting and ending when?; should drawdown and exit dates be set and announced?; the reliability of President Hamid Karzai as the main partner in Afghanistan; the double game that Pakistan was playing, with elements within the military–intelligence supporting various factions of the Taliban; and so on.[1] All the principals involved had their individual and bureaucratic-institutional conceptions of the best course of action. All would genuinely have believed their preferred policy option to be in the national interest. They could not all be right. To say that the option finally decided was the one in the national interest is to reduce the concept to a tautology, true by definition. Instead, it seems intuitively accurate to say that faced with competing policy options, identifiable decision-makers concluded that on balance, in the circumstances and given the available knowledge, 'X' was the best course of action.

The same point was made in the context of President Barack Obama's visit to India in November 2010. The 26 November 2008 'Mumbai attack remains a pivotal and delicate issue in relations among the United States, India and Pakistan'. '"*It's a balancing act*", a high-ranking U.S. law enforcement official said.'[2] Obama brought up India's reluctance to criticize the appalling human rights record of the military regime in Myanmar as an example of India not owning up to the responsibilities of being a major power. Yet, 'Like every other democracy, India has to strike a balance between its interests and its values.'[3] In the face of close relations between China and Myanmar and the growing footprint of China in Sri Lanka and Pakistan, India must balance any urge to promote democracy in Myanmar with economic, military, and geopolitical interests in maintaining good relations with the regime in power, just as the Western powers have done with Saudi Arabia. With regard to joining the sanctions against Iran, similarly, 'the pursuit of non-proliferation, Iranian oil and American goodwill are all important for India'. It must therefore strike 'a balance between these interests'.[4] Additional geopolitical reasons underpinning India's efforts to cultivate relations with Iran include access to Central Asia and limiting the influence of Pakistan in Afghanistan by preventing a Taliban comeback.

In 2010, WikiLeaks published 77,000 Afghan war logs and 400,000 documents from the Iraq war, all highly classified. In the ensuing controversy, it became clear that WikiLeaks—even as just a website organization—had to balance decisions on focusing heavily on the US military in Iraq and Afghanistan against the resulting resource-constrained lesser coverage of other exposés, with several of its staff resigning in protest; balance the risk to the lives of informants against the wish to publish all information, with names being revealed in the case of Afghanistan but redacted a few months later in the case of Iraq; and balance the commitment to publish against the threat to the life and liberty of founder Julian Assange. The media had to balance similar considerations against the temptation to publish scoops. The administration had to balance its competing interests in protecting classified information, pursuing those who violate this, the risk of pumping the oxygen of extra publicity with an angry denunciation compared to a nonchalant and low-key response, the right of Americans to maximum information, the risks to its operations, troops, and civilian advisers in war zones with publication, the military and political consequences for allies and friendly governments, and the duty to prosecute those who violate international humanitarian law.

The concept of 'the national interest' is totally inapplicable and irrelevant to WikiLeaks and the United Nations as non-state actors,[5] questionable in the case of globally branded media conglomerates, and limp when applied to the complexities of decision-making by the United States as a state actor. By contrast, 'a balance of interests' covers all groups. Several chapters in this *Handbook*—none better than that by Sir Jeremy Greenstock (Chapter 5)—demonstrate how foreign policy and diplomacy involve a delicate balancing of interests, goals, issues, principles, values, demands, and pressures from a diverse array of actors, domestic and international, governmental and non-governmental. Paul Martin (Chapter 40) argues that in a globalized and interdependent world where national regulatory failings can produce systemic shock and contagion, 'finding the means whereby the great powers can share sovereignty in the global interest becomes essential'. Joseph Nye (Chapter 30) notes that 'states are no longer the only important actors in global affairs, security is not the only major outcome that they seek, and force is not the only or always the best instrument available to achieve those outcomes'. Therefore we need to study and understand the balance of tools, outcomes, and actors.

This chapter will argue that 'a balance of interests' is a more satisfactory descriptor, analytical concept, and policy precept than 'the national interest'. The first two sections describe the dissatisfaction with the national interest, arguing that it is neither 'the', 'national', nor 'interest'. The third section expounds the advantages of 'interests' in the plural, 'balance' instead of 'national', and 'a' rather than 'the'. The final section illustrates the conceptual arguments with selected case studies.

3.1 THE NATIONAL INTEREST

Lord Palmerston famously said that nations have no permanent enemies and allies; they only have permanent interests. This saying is the mantra of the Realist school of International Relations and the gospel of diplomats. But does 'the national interest' exist objectively and independently of the policy-maker and the analyst? It falls into the trap of the logical fallacy of affirming the consequent. That which should be proven by a process of reasoning and evidence-based analysis, is instead asserted to be true. If countries act only in the national interest, then it follows by definition that anything they do is in the national interest. Being axiomatic, this is tautological.

Nor is it a satisfactory guide to policy. It is an exhortation, not a prescription. It leads to the absurd situation where competing policy prescriptions are offered in the name of the same national interest to justify them.

Realist scholars assumed and therefore failed to problematize state interests. Lacking a clear, unambiguous meaning, 'the national interest' is empty of substantive content,[6] used by different theorists and practitioners, in different periods, to justify American isolationism and pacifism, on the one hand, and interventionism and war, on the other. Under hegemonic stability theory, the international interest was conflated with the US national interest, while the latter was broadened to include the expansion of free trade and the maintenance of open sea lanes. Scholars and statesmen alike have differed over whether the national interest should override international law or whether establishing and defending the rule of law in world affairs is itself an important element of the US national interest.

In European history, *raison d'état* gradually displaced religious solidarity as the dominant motive of state behaviour, for example when Catholic France, under Cardinal Richelieu, intervened on the side of the Protestants in the Thirty Years' War in order to contain the increasing power of the Holy Roman Empire. Jean de Silhon defended reason of state as 'a mean between that which conscience permits and affairs require'.[7]

According to Charles Beard and George Smith, 'national interest' entered European political discourse in the 16th century as a substitute for the fading *raison d'état* under the rising sentiment of nationalism.[8] After the Second World War, it became closely associated with the school of Realism.[9] Hans Morgenthau even argued for 'the moral dignity of the national interest'.[10] In a self-help international system, power-maximizing autonomous states must look to their survival and safety as the overarching goal of foreign policy.

The relative de-emphasis of values and principles was always a troubling element in Realism. Appeals to 'the national interest' by itself cannot determine the combination of—or the balance among—a state's interests and values in any given situation. Realism can be reductive, as in the claim that 'the struggle for power is identical with the struggle for survival'.[11] The frequency with which groups of states are engaged in a zero-sum struggle for power is far higher than when their very survival is at stake. The same applies to the claim that the anarchic international 'system forces states to behave according to the dictates of realism, or risk destruction'.[12] States can often behave outside the dictates of Realism without risking outright destruction even though the behaviour might be foolish and damage state interests.

Since the 1970s scholars have introduced alternative concepts, theories, and analytical frameworks to argue that interests are subjective, constructed, and can change in response to shifts in domestic politics and the international milieu. On what basis could the Vietnam war be said to be in the US vital interest when the US homeland was never threatened? Is the South China Sea a vital interest for China simply because Beijing has chosen to redefine it as a 'core interest'? Where do promotion of core political values, ideological principles, a favourable world order, and the long term fit into the scheme?

In a standoff in September 2010 over the captain of a Chinese fishing trawler arrested by Japanese authorities in the disputed Diaoyu/Senkaku islands, Beijing's public denunciations were followed by a halt to the shipment of rare-earth minerals (China controls some 97 per cent of the world's productions of these minerals which are critical to many high-technology items) and the detention of Japanese private sector officials in China. If the national interest paradigm of acquiring power were to be applied, Tokyo should not have backed down. In fact it did and released the captain, in the larger commercial and political interests. One could conclude that Beijing followed the power-maximizing maxim of the national interest paradigm and gained. Certainly the message to all others in Asia—Pacific was to accelerate the shift in respectful attention from Tokyo to Beijing. But this does not include the larger and longer-term costs to China. Japan had been recalibrating relations between traditional protector US and traditional rival China; that was reversed. Coming on the back of a more muscular and assertive China on a slew of issues, the incident also sparked renewed interest among many governments across Asia in ensuring a continued US military presence and role in the region as a strategic counterweight to China. It provoked Australian strategists into reconsidering the balance between China as the main trading partner and the US as the main ally with shared political values.[13] In 2011 Obama announced a major US pivot to the Asia—Pacific. And it led several governments to reappraise the balance between the environmental risks of rare-earth minerals mining and monopolistic market dominance by China of an industrially strategic resource.

3.2 NEITHER 'NATIONAL', NOR 'INTEREST', NOR 'THE'

There are two problems with the word 'national'. In the domestic realm it implies a monolithic actor when in reality there are several competing actors. In international affairs while states remain the primary unit, there are several non-state actors whose role and influence have grown considerably: supranational and intergovernmental organizations

(IGOs), non-governmental organizations (NGOs), uncivil society organizations like terrorist groups, arms and drugs smugglers, and human traffickers,[14] multinational corporations (MNCs), philanthropic foundations, celebrities,[15] transnational professional associations which establish global standards and norms and constitute networked global governance,[16] and individuals like Peter Benenson and Henri Dunant who founded Amnesty International and the Red Cross movement respectively.

Very few countries are homogeneous. The prime determinant of a nation is psychological: the belief that a particular ethno-national group constitutes a distinct, *imagined* political community.[17] The primary definition of a state is juridical: a legal entity endowed with certain rights, privileges, and obligations in international law connoting a territorially-demarcated administrative unit. A convergence between 'nation' and 'state' is exceptional, not the norm. Indeed, 'the national interest' can be employed by the state as a *threat* to nations: the Kosovars in united Serbia, the East Timorese in pre-1999 Indonesia. Similarly, when did it become in the joint national interest of the Czech and Slovak republics to agree to an amicable split of Czechoslovakia? Was the breakup of the Soviet Union in the national interest of the old Soviet Union and/or of Russia and other successor republics? When might a similar situation arise with Canada vis-à-vis Quebec?

3.2.1 Competing Interests and Interest Groups

States are multipurpose organizations pursuing multiple goals simultaneously. When Secretary of State Hillary Clinton insisted that pressing China on human rights 'can't interfere with the global economic crisis, the global climate change crisis and the security crisis', Amnesty International was 'shocked and extremely disappointed'.[18] They should not have been—it is a statement of the obvious.

In most states there will be differences of perspectives, opinions, and preferences among officials and cabinet ministers, reflecting their individual backgrounds, portfolios, and philosophies. There will be just as substantial differences of opinions and policy preferences among the various sector groups, many of whom advocate diametrically opposed policies. Government-owned airlines argue that it is in the national interest to restrict competition in the home market to protect them from foreign carriers whose governments may have deeper pockets, whose own home markets may be protected, whose labour costs may be much lower, or whose access to fuel prices may be significantly advantageous. Airline employees will support continued restrictions in order to protect jobs and service conditions. The resulting restriction of competition and labour market rigidity will push up costs and prices and lower benefits to consumers, which is not in their interest. Thus it is not axiomatic that what is good for General Motors/Air Canada/Air India is also good for the United States, Canada, or India.

Similarly, arms sales may be of commercial benefit to the company making and exporting them, of employment benefit to the workers employed by the firm, to the political benefit of the representatives from the electoral district, and to the security benefit of the exporting country if the recipient country is a critical ally. But it could be damaging to political goals if the recipient country is ruled by an authoritarian regime and the equipment is used to brutalize protesting citizens, as in Libya in 2011; it could be damaging to the global campaign to combat corruption if the deals are finalized through bribes or other blurring of the public–private boundary; it could damage relations with third countries if the weapons are deployed against them; or, over time, if there is a change of regime or circumstances, the recipient country or group could become an enemy and turn their arms, finance, and training on the supplier country.

3.2.2 Subjectivity

If the national interest is whatever governments proclaim it to be, scholars would have to accept at face value that Slobodan Milosevic's atrocities in Bosnia and Kosovo, Saddam Hussein's reign of terror in Iraq, the American and British decision to attack, invade, and occupy Iraq, Iran's pursuit of nuclear weapons, Pakistan's Faustian pact with terrorist groups, India's abuse of human rights in Kashmir, Russia's actions in Chechnya and South Ossetia, North Korea's abduction of Japanese citizens and sinking of a South Korean warship, the Myanmar general's treatment of Aung San Suu Kyi, the decision of the Taliban government to permit Osama bin Laden to set up camp in Afghanistan: these were all in the national interest of the countries concerned because that is what the governments claimed.

Self-evidently, this is absurd. What then is the alternative? If governments can deliberately dress up ulterior motives in the language of the national interest, the possibility is endless for mystical and theological debates over what the 'real' motive was and what would have been the 'real' national interest. How can anyone be confident of who has the right answer? Only decision-makers have access to the relevant facts, even if it may not be all the facts. Outsiders, no matter how skilled and sophisticated, lack access to the facts, thinking, and motives of decision-makers. Their analyses and conclusions are necessarily speculative.

Often, decision-makers will be influenced by the lure of power and/or lucre for themselves individually, family, clan/sect, or political party. They may accept monetary or other forms of inducements from domestic or multinational corporate lobbyists or from foreign governments, to advance commercial or geopolitical interests of others by enriching themselves or denying political office to opponents. Does anyone believe that in an election year, a president's definition of the national interest is never 'contaminated' by electoral calculations? The justificatory rhetoric of the national interest often is invoked to cloak base motives with the mantle of collective legitimacy, since the national interest supposedly represents the social purposes of the political community.

At other times, the language of the national interest will be used conscientiously in the firm belief that the course of action decided on is indeed in the best interests of the collective polity. But, unless political decision-makers possess a measure of absolute infallibility that has eluded even the papacy, there are possibilities for error caused by incomplete or faulty information, or flawed analysis and diagnosis.

Was the Munich Pact in the national interest of Britain and France in 1938? Was it, and the invasion of Poland, in the national interest of Germany? Was the Molotov-Ribbentrop Pact in the national interests of Germany and the Soviet Union? Was it in Japan's national interest to invade Manchuria and attack Pearl Harbor? Were the Soviet invasions of Hungary, Czechoslovakia, and Afghanistan in the national interest of the Soviet Union? Was Argentina's invasion of the Falkland Islands in 1982 initially in its national interest but not after the successful British war to recapture it? Conversely, was the British action to retake the islands by military force in its national interest but would have been contrary to the national interest if Margaret Thatcher had lost the war? Was it in the US national interest for the Pentagon Papers to have been published, as claimed by non-governmental actors, or kept confidential, as argued unsuccessfully by the US government? Who can answer these questions authoritatively and intersubjectively, using what criteria?

It is inherently difficult for outside analysts to judge whether decision-makers themselves believe they are acting in the national interest or are merely camouflaging baser motives, including being bribed, bullied, or blackmailed by foreign corporations and governments. Opinions and judgements change over time to reflect a better understanding of how events actually unfold and factor in the unintended and perverse consequences into the full equation. It seems reasonable to postulate that Washington believed it to be in the US national interest to create, train, arm, and finance, with Saudi help and Pakistani collaboration, the lethally effective Islamist resistance against the Soviet occupation of Afghanistan in the 1980s. By 2012, however, we have a far better understanding of the chain-of-events links that led to the terrorist attacks of 11 September 2001, the Iraq war, and the deepening quagmire in Afghanistan and Pakistan. Would independent analysts still argue and, if so, with how much confidence and agreement among themselves, that the original decision by the Reagan administration was in the US national interest? Similarly, it is possible that in 1973, General Augusto Pinochet and his colleagues genuinely believed their coup against the Marxist regime to be in the national interest. Many contested their narrative at the time. Even for those who supported the military junta in 1973, how will the balance of opinion have shifted since, knowing what we do now of the brutality of the Pinochet regime and the subsequent history of Chile?

Morgenthau accepted that leaders can make mistakes in calculating the state's real interests: an inescapable consequence of believing that the national interest is an objective reality that can be scientifically deduced. Thus 'as disinterested observers we understand his thoughts and actions perhaps better than he, the actor on the political scene, does himself'.[19] Discussing the same dilemma, Reynolds comments that government actions may be said to be in the national interest if they serve the 'real interest' of a community as determined by 'an omniscient observer'. Far from solving the problem, however, he notes, this merely raises additional difficulties, comparable to the problematic elements of Rousseau's 'general will'. It is by no means obvious or certain that any such thing as the 'real' interest exists. And if it does, it is not obvious how it might be identified concretely.[20] A particularly good example of this is US policy on the Middle East and relations with Israel. Successive administrations for decades have maintained inti-mate relations with Israel. Yet two prominent Realist scholars have criticized this as being the result of the excessive influence of the Israel lobby and damaging to the US (and Israeli) national interest.[21] How can we tell who is right?

3.2.3 Non-State Actors

The diplomatic landscape is populated by a growing number, expanding role, and increasing influence of non-state actors. Many MNCs and some NGOs have bigger budgets and greater influence than several states over particular policies and regimes in setting the agenda, establishing norms, and shaping international behaviour. Some have even been engaged in forms of activities associated with states. The Bill and Melinda Gates Foundation, for example, engages in philanthropy that is the equivalent of foreign aid. As David Fidler notes in Chapter 38, the Rockefeller Foundation provided more foreign aid than the US government in the first half of the 20th century. He also draws our attention to how states need to 'balance health protection with trade interests'. Greenpeace, Human Rights Watch, and the International Committee of the Red Cross influence environmental standards, human rights, and international humanitarian law, respectively, more so than many state actors. Humanitarian NGOs work alongside UN humanitarian, peacekeeping, and development actors in the field, often funded by development agencies of governments, in the delivery and provision of emergency relief and assistance, early warning and assessment, and post-conflict reconstruction and peace-building. In addition to WikiLeaks, others like Google, Facebook, and Twitter also have had to balance immediate commercial gains against long-term reputational costs when faced with demands from some governments to censor sites or release information.

The actor-specific limitation is particularly poignant for nations searching for inde-pendent statehood. In the 1970s and 1980s, governments-in-waiting like the Palestine Liberation Organization (PLO) and the African National Congress (ANC) engaged in signing formal agreements with some governments, were given diplomatic accredita-tion in some countries, permitted to address the UN, and engaged in other functions usually associated with states. But 'the national interest' is incapable, *by definition,* of being applied to them.

The United Nations is an international actor both in its own right and as a systemic modifier of state and non-state behaviour.[22] The principal–agent problem notwithstand-ing, the UN system is an actor both institutionally and in the person of its chief execu-tives individually (the Secretary-General, the High Commissioner for Human Rights or Refugees, etc).[23] It has called member states to account for their human rights record against benchmarks set by the organization itself; demanded the adoption of universal health regulations and surveillance systems to check pandemics; overseen the birth of new nations (Namibia); organized and conducted elections to determine governments (Cambodia, Afghanistan); imposed sanctions on countries (Saddam Hussein's Iraq);

authorized war (Kuwait 1990–1991) and the use of force to protect civilians (Libya 2011); intruded into domestic law-making by demanding that certain activities in relation to the financing and support of terrorism be criminalized; and even ordered the arrest and trial of heads of government and state.

Sometimes the UN too must make choices between competing alternatives. Should it renew or terminate the mandates of long-serving peacekeeping missions like the UN Interim Force in Lebanon?[24] Which is more damaging to its credibility, authority, and effectiveness: accepting a measure of ridicule as the price of a long-lived expedient in a conflict-prone region, or withdrawing even at the risk of another war? The debate cannot be couched in the language of the national interest—the conceptual terminology is meaningless in this context. But one could argue that on balance, it would better serve the present and future interests of the UN to persevere or withdraw. Similarly, one could debate whether it has been prudent or harmful for it to have adopted a light footprint strategy in Afghanistan. Even with respect to the UN policies of member states, 'national interest' fails to capture the nuances and complexities. For they must balance calculations of short-term political advantages to their own country against the long-term interest of building the institutional framework, creating the structure of a predictable and stable world order of habitually obeyed rules embedded in universally validated institutions.[25]

The importance of religious orders as powerful and influential actors, historically (the Catholic Church[26]) and today (Islam), is undeniable. The Vatican and the Organization of Islamic Conferences have observer status at the UN. In response to the revelations of the scale and time-span of sexual abuses against children by Catholic clergy, should the Pope be arraigned at the International Criminal Court (ICC)?[27]

MNCs and NGOs, actors in global governance as advocates and participants with identifiable attributes, goals, and policy preferences, also have multiple interests in the plural which they pursue with a variety of means and instruments, in a range of forums, and with uneven effects and degrees of success. Like other actors, they can make mistakes of analysis and policy and may have to compromise on some goals or means in order to maximize the prospects of satisfying core values or interests. Applying the analytical framework of the state-specific national interest to their behaviour is logically nonsensical. The actor-neutral 'balance of interests' is equally applicable to all international actors: states, IGOs, NGOs, and individuals.

3.3 BALANCING MANY INTERESTS

3.3.1 A Balance

Substituting the word 'a' in 'a balance of interests' for 'the' in 'the national interest' has a threefold significance. It indicates that one particular balance is struck from among several possible options; it indicates human agency: individual people make specific decisions in the name of the entity concerned, be it an NGO, MNC, or state; and it includes the possibility of human fallibility and the prospect of course corrections.

The metaphor of the balance scales is accurate also in another important respect. Oftentimes, internal policy debates are the most contentiously fiercest precisely because the opposing arguments and proponents are so finely balanced. It takes just one extra argument, consideration, or policy-maker to tip the scales decisively on one side. 'The national interest' fails to do justice to this tipping effect reality.

3.3.2 Multiple Interests

Many governments prioritize the interests of a particular sector over the broader interests of the taxpayer and the consumer and, when pressed to justify the policy, defend it in the name of the national interest. In July 2009, Ottawa imposed stiff new restrictions on Mexicans entering Canada. The justification was to check fraudulent refugees, asylum seekers, and other violators of Canada's generous entry system for Mexicans. The result was a dramatic fall-off in tourist arrivals from Mexico, considerable bad press there, loss of goodwill among influential media commentators as well as government officials, and the creation of an additional barrier to trade, investment, and academic exchanges.[28]

'The national interest' provides no guidance on how to navigate through competing goals when multiple interests collide; 'a balance of interests' does. Ottawa calculated that the federal and provincial governments would save substantial sums of money on health and welfare costs, the refugee tribunal system, appeals court costs, and the costs of deporting failed claimants.[29] The government estimated that, as a result of the new visa fees and regulations, the number of annual Mexican arrivals would fall from 250,000 to 150,000. In fact they fell to 45,000 in the six months (or 90,000 annualized) after the visa requirement and the C$75.00 processing fee was imposed: 'The costs to the Canadian economy and government from this decline outweigh the savings from fewer refugee claimants. Canada's reputation in Mexico has suffered badly.'[30]

In November 2010, British Prime Minister David Cameron paid an official visit to China and US President Obama to India. Cameron had 'to strike a delicate diplomatic balance in banging the drum for British exporters at the same time as he comes under pressure to signal concern over Beijing's human rights record'.[31] Obama had to perform an intricate and delicate series of balancing acts: to acknowledge India's rising status as a major global player without exaggerating accomplishments or downplaying differences; to avoid being seen to be pandering to India at the cost of relations with Pakistan; and to be mindful of resistance back home to jobs lost to outsourcing in India. His speech to India's two houses of parliament on 8 November tried to strike all the right notes.[32] Did he succeed? Much of the press commentary noted that while the forum was India's parliament, the target audience was Beijing's leadership.[33] Indians were pleased but Pakistan reacted angrily to the endorsement of India's quest for permanent membership of the UN Security Council.[34]

3.3.3 Non-State Actors

The United Nations too must strike several balances: between the realism of power politics and the idealism of Charter principles and values; between current realities and
long-term trends; between the presently powerful and the emerging powers; between
the balance of power and the rule of law; between 'we the peoples' and member state
governments; between the wishes of member states and the corporate interests of the
organization; between the different corporate interests of the General Assembly, the
Security Council, and the Secretariat; between the need to confront the reality of international terrorism and respect for civil liberties and the rule of law; between the humanitarian and security goals of peace operations;[35] between peace, which may require
negotiating with immoral killers as heads of governments or militias, and justice that
seeks their arrest, trial, and punishment; and between sovereignty that as the cornerstone of the interstate system provides order and stability and encroachments into sovereign jurisdictions in the interests of the peoples within those jurisdictions, as well as of
the international community.[36]

Similarly, humanitarian NGOs must try to reconcile competing imperatives and
address the reality of unintended and perverse consequences. Their failure to take into
consideration a wider political context before providing aid results in the paradox that
aid to alleviate suffering often sustains the oppressive action that caused it.[37] Aid agencies must therefore evaluate the ramifications of their aid.[38] And of course the humanitarian community was split between the 'humanitarian hawks' who supported war
against Saddam Hussein in 2003 and others who strongly opposed it, reprising the 1999
debate over NATO intervention in Kosovo.[39]

3.4 Examples

Based on the above analysis, I contend that 'the national interest' should be dropped
from both scholarly and public discourse and replaced by 'a balance of interests'. The
remainder of this chapter demonstrates this with some important contemporary case
studies, starting with selected examples of people actually using the terminology.

In an address to the UN General Assembly on 7 December 1988, Soviet President
Mikhail Gorbachev insisted that 'there is no escaping the need to find a balance of interests within an international framework'.[40] On 25 January 1993, Moscow's Radio-1
reported that the forthcoming visit to India by President Boris Yeltsin was designed to
show that 'Russia is continuing to redress the balance between the Western and Eastern
directions of its policies.'[41]

In 1991, New Zealand Foreign Minister Don McKinnon observed that 'We have to
recognize the totality of our interests [environment, trade, security] and strike a balance
between them.'[42] In the United States, 'Only the president can balance the complex range

of sometimes conflicting U.S. interests that must be taken into account when imposing international sanctions,' wrote Ambassador Stuart E. Eizenstat, the Undersecretary of State for Economic, Business, and Agricultural Affairs.[43]

India's former foreign minister writes that 'The urgent task facing U.S. President Barack Obama is to get American strategy out of its cul-de-sac and move it in a direction that balances its own national interests with those of India, Pakistan and China.'[44] Michael Fullilove comments that 'Beijing needs to strike a new balance between its traditional economic and security concerns and the broader imperatives it must now satisfy, including stable great-power relations, non-proliferation and the development of international prestige.'[45] Patrick Watt of Save the Children writes: 'We...need to have a balanced approach to aid allocation.'[46]

These quotes mark an acknowledgement of the need for a balance among a state's different thematic interests (McKinnon), geographical orientations (Radio Moscow), national and international interests (Fullilove), countries (Singh), or even on one policy tool (Watt).

3.4.1 Iraq War

With most wars—Argentina's invasion of the Falkland Islands, Iraq's of Kuwait, Serbia's violent quest for Greater Serbia, Germany and Japan in the Second World War, Iraq in 2003—it is difficult to impress upon nationalistically inflamed consciousness the great disparity between the goals pursued, means used, and results obtained. Barbara Tuchman famously argued that historical figures made catastrophic decisions contrary to the self-interests of their countries, that were held to be damaging to those interests by contemporaries, and alternative courses of action to which were available at the time.[47] Iraq in 2003 comes into this category. To the principals of the Bush administration, 'For the sake of American prestige and...power, the presiding image of the War on Terror— the burning, smoking towers collapsing into rubble—had to be supplanted by another, of American tanks rumbling proudly down the streets of a vanquished Arab capital.'[48] Going by the writings of many of them since their departure from power, they are like Philip II of Spain, of whom it was said: 'No experience of the failure of his policy could shake his belief in its essential excellence.'[49]

Certainly, Saddam Hussein's brutal regime has been removed. But the balance sheet has to include the substantial and lasting damage caused by the $3 trillion war.[50] Iraq re-legitimized wars of choice as an instrument of unilateral state policy; 4,500 allied soldiers and hundreds of thousands Iraqi civilians are dead; America's reputation for competence, effectiveness, and as human rights champion took a big hit; and US relations with the UN and Europe were strained, with the UN itself losing credibility for not stopping an illegal war by a major power. The credibility of the US media also suffered. All in all, US soft power was badly damaged. As Nye observes in Chapter 30, 'Soft power depends upon credibility' and while it 'may appear less risky than economic or military power', 'it is often hard to use, easy to lose, and costly to re-establish'.

The war caused 'the largest human displacement in the Middle East since 1948'.[51] Two million fled abroad and another two million were displaced internally. Iraq's Christians in particular have left in large numbers.[52] The big strategic victor of the Iraq war was Iran with coffers enriched from the spike in oil prices, US and allied forces entangled in Iraq and Afghanistan, support for overseas military entanglements falling steeply across the Western world, pro-Iranian Shias in firm control of Iraq, and sapped Western and international resolve to go to war yet again to stop another Islamic country from acquiring nuclear weapons. In effect President Bush helped Iran to win its 1980–1988 war with Iraq after a two-decade pause.

The national interest does not even begin to capture the complexities and nuances of the Iraq blunder from the point of view of US interests as a state actor.

A balance of interests is more helpful also in drawing attention to linkages across issues and regions. In Afghanistan and Pakistan there were several additional balances: between securing and stabilizing the country by military means and nation-building led by the civilians; between providing security by foreign troops and building up the Afghan national army and police so ownership could be transferred to the locals; between coalition forces and the UN; between supporting President Karzai and pressing him to end corruption, share power, and democratize; between supporting Pakistan and pressing it to tackle the militants more robustly; between the civilian government and the military and intelligence services of Pakistan; among the various ethnic communities of Afghanistan; among the several regional and extra-regional actors with interests engaged in Afghanistan, including those contributing combat troops to the coalition, plus Russia, China, Japan, India, Pakistan, and Iran. The probable illegality of targeted assassinations by unmanned aircraft,[53] backlash against civilians killed in collateral damage, and suspected informers assassinated by the militants, had to be weighed against the lack of alternative options for taking out the militant leaders, the military necessity to do so, and the risk of being attacked by domestic political opponents for being soft on national security. The risk of re-legitimizing the Taliban and thereby betraying Afghans who reject the Taliban ideology, especially women and girls, as also US human rights, had to be weighed in the balance against the reality of their strength and greater staying power, their permanent interests, their substantial support base among the Pashtuns who comprise the plurality of Afghanistan's ethnic groups, and the need to offer them a deal on power-sharing as a means of bringing the war to a close.

As for Pakistan's 'double dealing' in Afghanistan,[54] after 9/11 Pakistan was subjected to fierce pressure from Washington to cut ties with Islamic militants that it had carefully nurtured as an instrument of state policy in Afghanistan and against India.[55] The stick of sanctions was matched by the carrot of generous aid. Both to keep the billion dollar annual aid flowing and to ease pressure, Pakistan cooperated with the US war in Afghanistan by banning some organizations, hunting some militants to capture or kill them, and launching military assaults on some militant strongholds along its northwestern border. At the same time, the immutable facts of geography ensured that one day all the Western forces would withdraw from Afghanistan but India would remain a troublesome neighbour to the east. Both to control and influence events in Afghanistan post-NATO withdrawal and to use the militants as a strategic asset—and Afghanistan as a strategic sanctuary for them—against India, Pakistan had an interest in preventing their complete destruction and elimination. On balance, therefore, the compromise policy that Pakistan followed—doing enough to appease Washington while still preserving a viable cadre of Islamic militants for future deployment—made eminent strategic, political, and economic sense.

3.4.2 Economic, Legal, and Criminal Justice Tools

Debates over free-trade agreements are usually couched in the language of the national interest. Critics bemoan the loss of policy autonomy and economic sovereignty, warn of the risks to manufacturing and employment from lower-cost partners in the zone, and point to the risks of trade diversion rather than trade creation. Proponents point to the scale economies resulting from an expanded economic integration area, welcome the benefits to consumers as rationalization of production and manufacturing produce efficiency gains and cost reductions, and emphasize productivity gains. Often, governments have to weigh short-term 'creative destruction' of manufacturing and jobs for long-term gain flowing from a more efficient allocation of resources in an integrated market.

Does foreign aid promote development by building capacity or undermine it by fostering dependency? Donors give on a variety of motives and a mix of assessments. They have to balance tied versus untied aid, the benefits of environmental and human and labour rights conditionality, the risks of corruption, and the relative proportions to be channelled multilaterally and bilaterally. Recipient countries might argue that on balance, their needs and interests are better served by an opening of markets—goods, services, and labour—for their products and people. They too have to balance the amounts of aid against the conditionality, onerous and costly reporting requirements, loss of policy autonomy, substantial leakage to high-priced international consultants, and the 'aid' in reality being disguised subsidy to the donor country's internationally uncompetitive industries.

The UN has to balance the desire to punish norm violators through imposition of tough sanctions against the dismal record of sanctions in changing the behaviour of target regimes, enriching and strengthening targeted regimes while imposing harsh punitive measures on their innocent citizens, being caught in a sanctions termination trap even when they are obviously not working as intended, and the damage that they cause to the moral authority and standing of the organization itself because of the hardships inflicted on innocent civilians. In reporting on Iran's compliance with its international obligations, the International Atomic Energy Agency had to balance often inconclusive evidence against considerations of its own credibility, the risks of encouraging pro-war factions in Israel and the US, and the risks of provoking Iran into weaponization.[56]

Nuclear weapons and climate change are particularly good examples of issues on which the pursuit of 'the national interest' risks catastrophic destruction of all planet life,[57] while 'a balance of interest' permits a far better assessment of the diverse actors, short and long-term effects, and different policy options. Agreement on climate change science does not compute into agreement on policy nor trump politics: 'there is still a need to balance benefits and costs of different possible responses with appropriate attention to the uncertainties'.[58] A balance is needed among different domestic goals of development and consumption lifestyles, environmental protection, and resource conservation; among different sectors domestically and different countries globally; among different strategies for combating climate change; between warning policy-makers of the risks inherent in business-as-usual policies and being unjustifiably alarmist; and among different categories of actors including governments, international organizations, environmental activists, energy companies, and scientific communities.

3.5 CONCLUSION

'The national interest' is erroneous as a description of the empirical reality, substitutes tautology for explanation, and is unhelpful as a guide to policy. 'A balance of interests' is superior on all three counts of description, explanation, and prescription. In addition, it captures human agency and allows for human error and multiple balances as weighed by different people reflecting their personal predilections, professional backgrounds, life and career experiences, and institutional interests and perspectives. It is more resistant to being conflated into regime security; 'the national interest' has all too often lent itself to governments delegitimizing difference and dissent as anti-national and harassing, imprisoning, and eliminating critics and opponents.

Even when there is one state there may be several interests. There are also many actors in addition to states interacting, as argued so persuasively by Jorge Heine in Chapter 2, in an increasingly networked web of national and international diplomacy. Governments, international organizations, NGOs, MNCs, and other actors in global governance must all strive for a balance among different sectors and groups domestically and internally, among different nations and groups internationally, and among present and future generations temporally. They must look to balance the interests of consumers, producers, and manufacturers; of importers, exporters, and retailers; between economic growth, resource conservation, and environmental protection within and among nations; between the need to protect vulnerable domestic sectors against powerful global firms and the efficiency and price gains of promoting a competitive economy; between government regulation and the free market; between market and social policy; between the developmental growth priority of poor countries and global labour, human rights, and environmental standards; between the carrot of aid and the stick of sanctions; and so on.

Finally, the examples of military sales, drone missile attacks, landmines, and nuclear weapons show that the choice of tools by itself also has to be weighed in the balance when evaluating alternative goals, the costs, risks, and constraints versus the benefits and advantages of the available tools and instruments in the pursuit of those goals, and the likely consequences in the short, medium, and long term. That is, if policy for all actors—state, international, and non-governmental organizations—is all about priori-tizing, then the use of the appropriate tools has to be part of the exercise of computing a balance of interests.

NOTES

1. Bob Woodward, *Obama's Wars* (New York: Simon and Schuster, 2010).
2. Sebastian Rotella, 'On the trail of Pakistani terror groups' elusive mastermind behind the Mumbai siege', *Washington Post*, 14 November 2010; emphasis added.
3. Timothy Garton Ash, 'Burma's future will depend on a democratic great power. Guess which one', *Guardian* (London), 18 November 2010.
4. Manpreet Sethi, 'India's Iran dance', *The Diplomat Blogs*, 13 February 2012, <http://the-dip-lomat.com/flashpoints-blog/2012/02/13/indias-iran-dance>.
5. In large part the conceptual argument of this chapter has its origins in my identity and role as a senior UN official for nine years. On the one hand, I was required to provide policy recommendations to the United Nations which functions both as a site and an actor in glo-bal governance; see Ramesh Thakur, 'Multilateral Diplomacy and the United Nations: Global Governance Venue or Actor?', in J.P. Muldoon, J. Fagot Aviel, R. Reitano, and E. Sullivan (eds), *The New Dynamics of Multilateralism: Diplomacy, International Organizations, and Global Governance* (Boulder: Westview, 2011). On the other hand, I endeavoured to per-suade member states that in the UN context, they should consider reframing national interests to reconcile it with the international interest, that multilateralism means more than the pursuit of national interests in multilateral forums.
6. Scott Burchill, *The National Interest in International Relations Theory* (London: Palgrave Macmillan, 2005).
7. Quoted in W.F. Church, *Richelieu and Reason of State* (Princeton: Princeton University Press, 1973), 168.
8. C.A. Beard and G.H.E. Smith, *The Idea of the National Interest: An Analytical Study in American Foreign Policy* (New York: Macmillan, 1934).
9. Hans J. Morgenthau, *In Defense of the National Interest* (New York: Alfred A. Knopf, 1951). See also Hans J. Morgenthau, *Politics Among Nations: The Struggle for Power and Peace* (New York: Alfred A. Knopf, 1948, 4th ed. 1967); and Joseph Frankel, *National Interest* (London: Macmillan/Pall Mall, 1970).
10. Morgenthau, *In Defense of the National Interest*, 33.
11. Nicholas J. Spykman, *America's Strategy in World Politics: The United States and the Balance of Power* (New Jersey: Transaction, 1942), 18.
12. John J. Mearsheimer, 'A Realist Reply', *International Security* 20:1 (Summer 1995), 91.
13. Paul Dibb, 'If China bullies on the high seas, it may need to be taught a lesson', *Australian*, 8 November 2010.
14. Jorge Heine and Ramesh Thakur (eds), *The Dark Side of Globalization* (Tokyo: United Nations University Press, 2011).
15. Andrew F. Cooper, *Celebrity Diplomacy* (Boulder: Paradigm Publishers, 2007).
16. Anne-Marie Slaughter, *A New World Order* (Princeton: Princeton University Press, 2005).
17. Benedict Anderson, *Imagined Communities: Reflections on the Origin and Spread of Nationalism* (London: Verso, 1983); Jim MacLaughlin, *Reimagining the Nation-State: The Contested Terrains of Nation-Building* (London: Pluto Press, 2001).

18. Michael Gerson, 'A cold shoulder to liberty', *Washington Post*, 23 September 2009.

19. Morgenthau, *Politics Among Nations*, 5.

20. P.A. Reynolds, *An Introduction to International Relations*, 3rd ed. (London: Longman, 1994), 41–2.

21. John Mearsheimer and Stephen Walt, *The Israel Lobby and U.S. Foreign Policy* (New York: Farrar, Straus, and Giroux, 2007).

22. Charles Pentland, 'International Organizations', in J.N. Rosenau, K.W. Thompson, and G. Boyd (eds), *World Politics: An Introduction* (New York: Free Press, 1976).

23. Ramesh Thakur and Thomas G. Weiss, 'United Nations 'Policy': An Argument with Three Illustrations', *International Studies Perspectives* 10:1 (January–April 2009), 18–35.

24. Jean-Marc Coicaud, *Beyond the National Interest: The Future of UN Peacekeeping and Multilateralism in an Era of U.S. Primacy* (Washington: US Institute of Peace, 2007).

25. Gareth Evans argues for 'good international citizenship' as the third pillar of foreign policy in addition to security and trade: 'Foreign Policy and Good International Citizenship', Address delivered in Canberra, 6 March 1990, <http://www.gevans.org/speeches/old/1990/060390_fm_fpandgoodinternationalcitizen.pdf>.

26. Eric O. Hanson, *The Catholic Church in World Politics* (Princeton: Princeton University Press, 1990).

27. Geoffrey Robertson, *The Case of the Pope: Vatican Accountability for Human Rights Abuse* (London: Penguin, 2010).

28. Andrés Rozental, 'A Mexican Perspective', in F.O. Hampson and P. Heinbecker (eds), *Canada Among Nations 2009–2010: As Others See Us* (Kingston, Ontario: McGill-Queen's University Press, 2010), 79–80.

29. Campbell Clark, 'Ottawa admits visa policy will hurt tourism', *Globe and Mail*, 10 August 2009.

30. Jeffrey Simpson, 'While Mexicans fume, Canada's reputation and revenues take a hit', *Globe and Mail*, 2 February 2010.

31. Nigel Morris, 'Cameron to play balancing act with trade and human rights', *Independent* (London), 8 November 2010.

32. <http://www.thehindu.com/news/national/article874394.ece?homepage=true>.

33. 'UN Security Council offer is Obama's veiled message to China', editorial, *Daily News and Analysis* (Mumbai), 9 November 2010; S.G. Stolberg, and J. Yardley, 'Countering China, Obama Backs India for UN Council', *New York Times*, 8 November 2010; Tom Friedman, 'Containment-lite', *New York Times*, 10 November 2010.

34. PTI, 'Pak slams U.S. for backing India's UNSC bid', *Hindu* (Chennai), 10 November 2010.

35. Xan Rice, 'UN-backed Congo military offensive a "humanitarian disaster"', *Guardian*, 14 October 2009.

36. Ramesh Thakur, *The United Nations, Peace and Security: From Collective Security to the Responsibility to Protect* (Cambridge: Cambridge University Press, 2006).

37. Fiona Terry, *Condemned to Repeat? The Paradox of Humanitarian Action* (Ithaca: Cornell University Press, 2002).

38. M.B. Anderson, *Do No Harm: How Aid Can Support Peace—or War* (Boulder: Lynne Rienner, 1999); David Rieff, *A Bed for the Night: Humanitarianism in Crisis* (New York: Simon and Schuster, 2003); M. Barnett and T.G. Weiss (eds), *Humanitarianism in Question: Politics, Power, Ethics* (Ithaca: Cornell University Press, 2008).

39. Albrecht Schnabel and Ramesh Thakur (eds), *Kosovo and the Challenge of Humanitarian Intervention* (Tokyo: UN University Press, 2000).

40. UN General Assembly Doc. A/43/PV. 72, 8 December 1988, 11.

41. BBC, *Summary of World Broadcasts,* SU/1596 i, 26 January 1993.

42. Don McKinnon, 'Changing Global Alliances and Their Impact on New Zealand in the World', *Dunedin*, 8 August 1991, 10.

43. *Foreign Affairs* 78:3 (May/June 1999), 155.

44. Jaswant Singh, 'March of folly into Afghanistan's cul-de-sac', *Japan Times*, 24 August 2010.

45. Michael Fullilove, *The Stakeholder Spectrum: China and the United Nations* (Sydney: Lowy Institute for International Policy, December 2010), 15. See also Yan Xuetong, *Analysis of China's National Interests*, tr. by Monte Bullard (2006, original Chinese publication 1997), <http://rwxy.tsinghua.edu.cn/xi-suo/institute/english/production/yxt/book/interests%20analysis/cover.htm>.

46. Nicholas Watt, 'Anger as billions in aid is diverted to war zone', *Guardian*, 20 October 2010.

47. Barbara Tuchman, *The March of Folly: From Troy to Vietnam* (New York: Random House, 1984).

48. Mark Danner, *Stripping Bare the Body: Politics, Violence, War* (New York: Nation Books, 2009), 557.

49. Quoted in Tuchman, *March of Folly*, 7.

50. J.E. Stiglitz and L.J. Bilmes, *The Three Trillion Dollar War: The True Cost of the Iraq Conflict* (New York: W. W. Norton, 2008).

51. Alisa Roth and Hugh Eakin, 'They fled from our war', *New York Review of Books*, 13 May 2010, 26; Deborah Amos, *Eclipse of the Sunnis: Power, Exile, and Upheaval in the Middle East* (New York: Public Affairs, 2010).

52. William Dalrymple, 'Iraq's disappearing Christians are Bush and Blair's legacy', *Guardian*, 13 November 2010; Robert Fisk, 'Exodus: The changing map of the Middle East', *Independent*, 26 October 2010.

53. Philip Alston, *Report of the Special Rapporteur on extrajudicial, summary or arbitrary executions, addendum, Study on targeted killings* (Geneva: OHCHR, A/HRC/14/24/Add.6, 28 May 2010), 22, para. 73.

54. Rangin Dadfar Spanta (Afghanistan's national security adviser), 'Pakistan is the Afghan war's real aggressor', *Washington Post*, 23 August 2010.

55. Sumit Ganguly and S. Paul Kapur, 'The Sorcerer's Apprentice: Islamist Militancy in South Asia', *Washington Quarterly* 33:1 (January 2010), 47–59; Ramesh Thakur, 'Delinking Destiny from Geography: The Changing Balance of India—Pakistan Relations', *India Quarterly* 67:3 (September 2011), 197–212.

56. Ramesh Thakur, 'To stop Iran getting the bomb, must we learn to live with its nuclear capability?', *Strategic Analysis* 36:2 (March 2012), 326–32.

57. On the nuclear challenge, not covered in this chapter, see Ramesh Thakur, 'If You Want the Peace of the Dead, Prepare for Nuclear War', *UN Chronicle* 48:4 (December 2011), 26–9.

58. Carolyn Kousky, Olga Rostapshova, Michael Toman, and Richard Zeckhauser, *Responding to Threats of Climate Change Mega-Catastrophes* (19 October 2009), p. i, <http://www.hks.harvard.edu/fs/rzeckhau/CCCats.pdf>.

PART II
THE MAIN ACTORS

CHAPTER 4

THE POLITICAL ACTORS: PRESIDENT, PRIME MINISTER, AND MINISTER OF FOREIGN AFFAIRS

LLOYD AXWORTHY

As a former foreign minister, I routinely refer to my role as that of a plumber. I was always fixing leaks, responding and reacting to whatever new crisis I was presented with. I soon recognized that when the leaks occur too frequently then there must be something wrong with the architecture. That was in 1996 when I took on the Canadian Foreign Affairs portfolio. In the post-cold war world of international affairs the architecture was clearly in need of a change; fragile states were falling apart at the seams and internal conflict was becoming the dominant threat to civilian lives. Old notions of national security and staunch sovereignty suddenly made little sense when faced with the complex global issues that had arisen. The old paradigm of nation-state supremacy seemed inappropriate, and the alliance system of the cold war did not provide a relevant basis for global cooperation. Even the multilateral system, centred on the UN, was rooted in post-Second World War thinking and did not encompass new forms of governance to address these new security threats or to engage productively with new international actors and centres of influence. By the mid-1990s, it became evident that we were in need of improved solutions. The old game of diplomacy was changing.

It was at this time that a conscious effort was made by the Canadian government to address these changes and focus its foreign policy towards the building of new international structures to provide preventative means of global protection, to shift scarce budget resources towards peace-building tasks, and to turn our diplomatic efforts to building global partnerships of like-minded nations and non-governmental organizations (NGOs) to promote global cooperation on an initiative we called Human Security. There was a need to change strategies regarding the means and processes of diplomacy.

Efforts were made to develop new partnerships and engage and participate with the emerging civil entities that were now becoming significant forces in setting opinion, defining the diplomatic agenda around human rights, environmental and development issues. The old processes of diplomacy now had to encounter, indeed *embrace*, the growing influence of civil society both nationally and internationally. Equally, transnational institutions, both private corporations and public organizations like the Red Cross, were now becoming power centres of increasing weight and presence. They often commanded resources exceeding those of many nation states or occupied strategic positions such as first responders to calamity and natural disasters. The Rolodex of a foreign minister became far thicker and more diverse than in the days of classic diplomacy.

Even more transformative was the new information technology and its capacity for instantaneous connection. I recall vividly during my time as Foreign Minister how I was at the hub of an amazing information network. Twenty-four hours a day, voluminous intelligence flowed in from around the world through the closed-circuit communications system called SIGNET, all analysed by skilled officers. Depending on the urgency, next morning responses could be sent, outlining actions to be initiated or requesting further information if required. It was a privilege to have that kind of first-class electronic reach, coupled with expert filtering and assessment, and it led to serious discussion about how the new information technology could and should be used as a tool of foreign policy. Information technologies have progressed so much since that short time ago that the power of the Internet has become even more of an imperative in defining the new diplomacy.

Recent WikiLeaks releases of confidential transactions usher in a further complication in diplomatic practice, as the demand for transparency becomes more easily obtained. This alters the way of doing business and makes the old notion of diplomacy as a closed shop problematic. The advent of even more emphasis on public diplomacy may, in fact, be a healthy development. Equally the Arab Spring has demonstrated the power of social media to mobilize populations and instil new young and popular leaders that are social-network- and media-savvy.

Even with all these new factors the reality remains that the nation state is still the central player in the international system, and it will be national governments that are the primary drivers. Making foreign policy decisions ultimately rests with the head of government, either the prime minister or the president, and with their senior members of cabinet, primarily their foreign minister or, in the American case, the secretary of state. The roles set out for these actors have a long history of evolutionary change as determined by their constitutions or custom. But diplomacy is now going through a challenge to conventional precepts. Adapting to the changing dynamics of the international system became all that more relevant at the end of the last century and continues today. New pockets of influence have opened up, but there are also increasingly more players to contend with, with over 190 states to recognize—each with its own agenda, history, and resources from which to draw upon, as well as individual leaders with their own personal objectives in mind vying for a place at the table in an increasingly crowded diplomatic atmosphere.

To be successful at diplomacy, one must have influence and persuade others to help you in meeting your own ends, and the key ingredient in doing so is power. As another contributor to this volume, Joseph Nye, has stated elsewhere 'Power is the ability to attain the outcomes one wants'.[1] Traditionally this was translated through arms, wealth, and territorial holdings. While these remain the same today, they are not the entire picture. Power and influence in international affairs today are multifaceted, malleable, and contextual. There is an increasingly powerful sphere of influence nested within the public, the media, and a growing number of new regional and international partnerships. Diplomacy today requires expanding networks of communication and forging new kinds of partnerships. I am referring to the rise of soft power and the growing influence of civil society groups in foreign affairs. 'Soft power' is the ability to obtain objectives in diplomacy through communication, agenda-setting, framing conversations, and shaping others' preferences in order to make the anticipated outcome the most attractive.[2] It is something that Canada has normally excelled at, particularly regarding the setting of new agreements on norms and standards governing cross-border issues such as the Ottawa Process that led to the convention to ban anti-personnel landmines (discussed separately by John English in Chapter 44, this volume).

The present chapter addresses the changes that heads of government face when determining their foreign policy objectives and, in turn, the challenges and opportunities that these new changes present in fulfilling agendas. Section 4.1 introduces the actors and the political institutions that frame their roles and determine the extent of their powers. Drawing on my personal experience as a Canadian foreign minister, the changing diplomatic contexts at the end of the last century and into the 21st century are evaluated. Given the roles that individuals play in the practice of diplomacy, section 4.2 introduces some of the changes that have occurred since the end of the cold war, which can be viewed as both constraints and also as opportunities to open up pockets of influence within which foreign actors are able to press their issues. These changes are the rise of civil society and the idea of public diplomacy, expanding communications technologies (exemplified most specifically by WikiLeaks), and the prominence of new state powers and summit diplomacy.

4.1 POWER AND INFLUENCE FROM THE TOP

The heads of government in both Canada and the US act as the key decision-makers regarding the diplomatic ends of their given state. As elected representatives, they are beholden to their constitutionally given powers and, ultimately, the desires of their electorate and the pressures of the various lobbying and interest groups that seek economic or political advantage. Along with the other general duties of statecraft, the necessity to interact with other states to secure domestic interests has not changed all that much since the modern state was born in the Peace of Westphalia in 1648. Generally speaking, any given state's foreign policy is either limited or enhanced given the global context. History, geographical location, resource base, demographics, economic largesse, military capacity, etc., remain influencing factors. Diplomatic strategies are therefore woven into the existing tapestry of historical reality and emerging norms in international relations.

4.1.1 President

In the US, it is the president who traditionally determines the direction of foreign policy and, as such, he or she is generally in a unique position in the world. The US is the most powerful economic and military state, which affords the country a very unique stance in matters of diplomacy and gives the US president a significantly different perspective to that of any other leader. With its abundant supply of hard power, as well as the influence of American culture gaining favour throughout the world, the US president holds a unique vantage point. Given the political climate and the historical context of the time, the president's foreign policy objectives can benefit from the mood of the American people at the time, either more or less isolationist or interventionist or just plain mad as we see with the Tea Partiers.

Recent history, from the second half of the last century into this one, has heavily supported the militarization of US diplomatic efforts. The cold war acted as a guidepost by marking a clear enemy to the freedoms and democratic values of the American people and decisively shaping interstate relations. But by the mid-1990s, a decided shift was taking place in the perceptions and calculations arising out of the vacuum left by the end of the cold war. There were fond hopes of a new era of prosperity based on the liberalization of markets, deregulation, and the global movement of capital. But the tide bringing in such optimism was quick to recede. President George H.W. Bush's bold claims for an emerging system of security based on international cooperation—the 'New World Order'—had run aground early in Somalia and Bosnia. The United States, the world's sole superpower, was increasingly shy of exerting direct leadership in the security requirements of an era of messy internal ethnic conflicts and the United Nations (UN) was discredited by its inaction in Rwanda. There was a definite void in defining security needs and responses. This was especially so in scoping out answers to the dark side of globalization—the increasing threats from international terrorists, human trafficking, and a growing understanding of the severity of climate change.[3]

Generally, presidents hold more weight in foreign policy decision-making than domestic policy. However, they can be constrained by Congress and public opinion. The serious test is in shaping the issue to fit US objectives and to ensure the president will not face any serious backlash on an issue. This is particularly difficult regarding international agreements and treaties. Regarding the Rome Statute that led to the establishment of the International Criminal Court (ICC), the US under President Bill Clinton had been one of its most ardent backers. Once into the negotiations, however, the administration found itself bracketed by opposition from the US military, who were concerned about US soldiers being prosecuted, and from conservative members of Congress. With Republicans in control of the senate, the chairman of the Foreign Relations Committee,

Senator Jesse Helms, exploited his power to hold up appointments and determine budgets in order to blackmail the administration on crucial issues, especially multilateral ones. To Helms, the idea of a UN based criminal court was anathema.

During several discussions with Secretary of State Madeleine Albright, herself a strong supporter of the court, I agreed that we would make every effort to meet US concerns. In particular, we advanced the need for safeguards in the role of the prosecutor, ensuring against frivolous investigations by requiring a panel of court judges to approve any inquiry. Some demands, however, simply could not be met without violating the integrity of the Court. We could not accept an exemption for US servicemen, for example, even though their own court system would have prime jurisdiction, nor could we accept a court that would be limited to cases referred by the Security Council.

In the final days of the Rome meeting, Canadian Philippe Kirsch made a bold decision to forgo the normal UN practice of working from a bracketed text that delegations could haggle over and presented instead a take-it-or-leave-it package that addressed a number of reservations coming from recalcitrant delegations. My job as befits a politician was to help sell this package to the NGOs and governments that had reservations. Sitting in a hallway a few hours before the vote, I reached Secretary Albright on a mobile phone to tell her of the package approach. It was stressed that it met many of the American concerns and that there existed a strong movement of support. It was her role to hear me out, but she ultimately reported that the package would fail. Realizing the likely results of the vote, the US found itself in a very small bloc of opposition, in the company of Libya, Iraq, and Cuba in opposing the cause of stronger humanitarian law and practice. Although President Clinton eventually signed the Rome treaty, he did so as one of his last acts before leaving office when it was far too late to expect Senate ratification on his watch.

Despite a growing global interdependence at the end of the 20th century, the collapse of the Soviet Union had confirmed the dominance of American power and influence as the reality of the global system, fundamentally influencing its foreign policy objectives. With this came increasing US claims that its dominant position carried special responsibilities and therefore prerogatives to act unilaterally. Following the terrorist attacks on 11 September 2001 in New York and Washington, the American people could not help but express confusion and fear at the consciousness of their vulnerability to outside forces. With President George W. Bush at the helm, US interests abroad quickly took on a more aggressive and specifically anti-terrorist approach heavy with suspicion and accusations. The American people identify with the fact that their state has a divine right of exceptionalism and it is accepted that its democracy, with its US-style rights and freedoms, should be defended at all costs.

Time and again President Bush undermined efforts underway at the UN and elsewhere to gain consensus on shared global challenges like climate change, nuclear proliferation, and the international food crisis. One of his earliest decisions was to rescind America's signature to the Rome Statute of the ICC, the most important new institution of the 20th century designed to advance human rights and international justice. And he stood by while Canada and other like-minded countries worked to establish an international agreement on the doctrine of the 'Responsibility to Protect' (R2P) that Thomas G. Weiss discusses in Chapter 42 of this volume, which declares that the international community has a responsibility to step in when governments prove unable or unwilling to protect their citizens from situations of mass atrocity.[4]

With the elections in 2008, there was hope that this aggressive, unilateral international stance would shift. The apparent willingness of the incoming Obama administration to employ smart diplomacy was a welcome sign that consolidated global efforts to address these issues may regain momentum. The endorsement of the UN concept of the R2P was even referenced in Obama's National Security Strategy.[5] Such promise was demonstrated when he was awarded a Nobel Peace prize just nine short months into his presidency, in acknowledgement of the changing attitudes towards the US and his interest in acting more cooperatively. Obama's successes in negotiating further nuclear treaties with Russia should be praised and demonstrates the much more internationally conscious efforts of the current administration. With a Republican majority in Congress, Obama has faced similar challenges as Clinton in the 1990s, making progress on issues of international interest, such as climate change, immigration, and arms control that much more difficult.

Presidents are not solitary actors in their efforts. They are also given the responsibility of selecting a secretary of state, who acts as the chief foreign policy adviser. And through the National Security Council, there is a separate core of advisers who often compete in views with the state department. There is also the vast web of intelligence apparatus which had a notable budget of $80.1 billion for 2010,[6] and of even more weight is the vast military constellation of the US which through its system of international commands has a budget and concomitant influence that dwarfs that of the State Department. As has already been mentioned, it can be observed that US foreign policy is one driven by its military imperative and untouchable privileges as seen by both the public and Congress. But, as Nicholas Kristof has discussed previously, there remains an ongoing debate within the US around the enormous amount spent annually on military power and far, far less in diplomacy, education, and other social programmes which also generate positive international and local outcomes in the name of protecting American citizens.[7] What is frustrating is that neither party seems willing to question the huge allocations of resources to the military and intelligence world. The Republicans seem to believe that these investments reduce American vulnerability, while Democrats are afraid that if they dissent, voters will see the party as weak.

While the president is subject to the whims of the voting public when his foreign policy comes up for review, the secretary of state is at more of an arm's length relationship to the elected. As the 'face' of the US in diplomatic circles, they are appointed by the president, and have little occasion to meet directly with the public. Their main line of public accountability is through congressional hearings which are a filtered reading that does not necessarily reflect public sentiment. I was fortunate enough, during my time as Minister of Foreign Affairs, to have a respectable and even amicable working relationship with Secretary Albright. Once over dinner we discussed the vagaries of our respective jobs and she expressed an admiration for our system where the minister was compelled by survival instincts to return regularly to his or her electoral riding to tend to ordinary constituency activities and therefore gain a direct insight into a slice of public views, instead of being captive inside the beltway.

4.1.2 Prime Minister

As my conversation with Secretary Albright shows, Canada differs significantly from the American foreign policy system. As they are the most politically, militarily, and economically powerful state, they have the ability to decide on their diplomatic efforts based primarily on what serves the American interest at the time. We in Canada do not have the same exceptionalist role and therefore must be more balanced and certainly more adroit and dexterous in our diplomatic handlings. Much like the president, the prime minister is tasked with determining the direction of foreign policy and handing out a mandate to the Minister of Foreign Affairs, which determines the work of the bureaucracy and foreign service officers. Unlike the president, the prime minister (generally) is less constrained by the whims of parliament (should they be fortunate enough to hold a majority in government).

The extent to which prime ministers involve themselves in diplomatic affairs can vary depending on the historical period and the personal interests of the given leader. The era of Lester B. Pearson and his awarding of the Nobel Peace prize is generally considered to be the 'golden era' in Canadian influence and persuasion in global affairs. Brian Mulroney exercised a strong role, especially in relation to Canada–US relations and in the anti-apartheid efforts of that time. Jean Chrétien took a leadership role in certain key areas such as trade and relations with China and was certainly supportive and active in human security initiatives. In the more contemporary context, Stephen Harper dominates the international efforts of the present government.

Just like the president, the prime minister must contend with political realities of the state. Traditionally, the prime minister of Canada did not feel the same kind of overwhelming military pressures pushing for hard-power solutions. That began to change in the post-9/11 world and the combined elements of US pressure to join in the antiterrorist movement, especially as they affected border security and the emergence of a much more aggressive military presence in Ottawa. While Canada resisted being a part of the Iraq invasion, under Prime Minister Paul Martin and the hard power stance of the Chief of Defence Staff General Rick Hillier Canada became deeply involved in the Afghanistan conflict and it is still the determinant of much of foreign policy. That has become accentuated under Stephen Harper, where there remains a clear preference for military strategies and a downgrading of the Foreign Affairs department. In the aftermath of that event Canadians may have been surprised and more than a little dismayed to know just how deeply many of our own basic values have been affected and our policies altered. The impact of the 9/11 attack and the shock it created among Canadians led to a major shift in Canadian thinking on security, wiping out efforts that were underway to establish a distinctive Canadian approach based on human security principles.

Depending on the interests of the prime minister, a central figure in the governmental matrix is the Minister of Foreign Affairs. Ultimately, a Foreign Minister must serve one master, the prime minister, and the relationship that is established, whether close or distant, trusting or indifferent, determines to a substantial degree the effectiveness of the minister. This, in turn, makes a difference in the outcome, harmony of purpose, and consistency of foreign policy overall. It was well known, for example, that Prime Minister Brian Mulroney and his Foreign Minister for much of his government, Joe Clark, struggled to agree on an approach and Mulroney took over management of key files, especially Canada–US relations, without much consultation. Prime Minister Chrétien's style for the most part was to give his ministers a fair degree of latitude. He certainly gave me a good deal of space. We had, I believe, a relationship of mutual respect.

Every minister's tenure begins with a mandate letter from the prime minister which sets out responsibilities and indicating special areas of activity and attention. What is particularly significant about the mandate letter is that it asserts the prime minister's prerogative to be the major player in the foreign field if so desired, to take on independent initiatives on which the Foreign Minister may or may not be informed, and to share or take over key departmental decisions such as the choice of ambassadors, placement of embassies, and organization of major international meetings in Canada. Prime Minister Chrétien had entrusted me with giving direction to Canada's international role and I had charge of formidable, if somewhat circumscribed, resources. It was up to me to put those assets to work.

There were, of course, certain prime ministerial lines that one did not cross without a great deal of care and some trepidation, relations with China being a prime example. The prime minister took a special interest in establishing good ties with the Chinese regime, for he saw China as a major opportunity to advance our trade interests. I, on the other hand, wanted to push on human rights issues. Eventually we agreed on a policy of direct bilateral engagement. I was given the go-ahead to travel to China, initiate a human rights dialogue, and provide legal assistance and training. It did not please the human rights organizations, as they wanted open denunciation of Chinese practices in Tibet and condemnation of the jailing of political dissidents. It did, however, provide the template for a policy of engagement on human rights that extended to many countries, including Cuba and Indonesia. In general, the prime minister focused on trade-related matters, especially the Team Canada initiative, and gave me the political space to work more on human rights and democratic development.

The space I was given to pursue what I understood to be pressing issues of the times (in the best interest of the Canadian people of course), was instrumental in the initiatives that the government at the time was able to accomplish. One of them being the Ottawa Treaty, which Jean Chrétien and I both worked on seeing through to success. This working relationship is determined by the prime minister. We have witnessed with the current Harper government that there is more of a sense of control from the top. In the current government, there have been four ministers of foreign affairs in as many years.

Another tangible benefit in my view of the parliamentary system is the opportunity to develop ideas and notions in a public crucible. In our parliamentary system you are on the firing line every day, having to defend positions and respond to criticism both in the verbal workout known as Question Period and in the media scrum. Your views have to bear open, often unremitting scrutiny. Often when hosting a lunch for a visiting foreign dignitary, I would have to excuse myself just before 2 pm to go to Question Period in the House of Parliament. Many of my guests were horrified and at the same time fascinated that there would be this daily rendering of accountability by a minister, and by the prime minister, secretly wondering what strange form of masochism the Canadian parliamentary system induced. The great advantage of Canadian democracy is that you cannot hide your beliefs or views for long. It is a test of transparency.

4.2 CHALLENGES AND OPPORTUNITIES

For the primary political actors in the diplomatic process, the heads of government and their members of cabinet, the political structures and resources at hand will define and limit the influence and ability any state has to pursue their international interests. In addition to these limits that remain more-or-less constant, or change slowly over time, there is a growing outside influence of actors, access to information, as well as the changing landscape of international affairs. Where diplomacy was traditionally the domain of discreet, high-level meetings, the forum for international negotiation is beginning to open up. The most relevant and pressing issues for political leaders to contend with and adapt to are the influence of civil society groups, increased access to information due to the spread and accessibility of information technologies, and the increased relevance of developing states in formerly exclusive diplomatic circles.

4.2.1 Civil Society

Through personal experience I can attest to the ability of civil society groups to not only advocate for change at the international level, but also to set the agenda, frame arguments, and successfully use their power of networking to spread a message and exert pressure at high-level meetings. The 1990s was a boon decade for civil society groups and also help to welcome in the post-cold war era of soft power. In a globalized and increasingly integrated world, traditional military and economic might, while still important, do not hold the overwhelming pre-eminence they once did. Communication, negotiating, mobilizing opinion, working within multilateral bodies, and promoting international initiatives are increasingly effective ways to achieve international outcomes. These several changes explain the ability of civil society actors to participate. The experience of the Ottawa Process that led to the landmark treaty to ban anti-personnel landmines was an exemplary case of how both civilian interest groups and state actors could work together on common objectives with significant outcomes.[8] Credit must be given to the small group of NGOs who first initiated the International Campaign to Ban

Landmines (ICBL), ultimately the recipients of the Nobel Peace Prize and remains today a global network of over ninety countries.

Canada had been an ideal candidate to take on a leadership role in this effort as the landmines campaign fit squarely with our efforts to draw attention to human security. We were prepared to lend our support, but for an international treaty to work there needs to be significant and real buy-in by all signing parties for it to be anything other than simple words on paper. In addition to the ICBL appealing to their networks and to the general population, our role in the Canadian government was to apply traditional tools of diplomacy. I wrote to every foreign minister I could and made appeals to other notable and sympathetic advocates such as Princess Diana of the United Kingdom. At every bilateral and multilateral meeting I attended, I was constantly lobbying my counterparts from other states, feeling out their interest, and pressing them to consider the possible outcome. Canadian diplomats did what they do best: lobbying governments both formally and informally at international meetings and spreading the message. Prime Minister Chrétien played an important role by speaking with the heads of states, most notably President Clinton who was supportive of the ban. Each level of government had a hand in spreading the message and appealing to the interests of like-minded states.

The success of the Ottawa Process was not due to the hard power wielded by its members, but to their collective skills in mobilizing opinion and negotiating an effective convention. Ultimately, the signing of the convention was the culmination of intensive campaigning by civil society groups and national governments. It is an example of a unique coalition of governments, civil society, and international groups working closely together to bring about a significant change. Lobbying by civil society groups is not new, but what was different in this context was that governments and civil society worked together as members of a team with a common objective. In fourteen short months the treaty moved from the initial proposal for a convention banning anti-personnel mines outright to a formal signature by 122 countries—a number that exceeded the most optimistic forecasts at the start of the process. The swift manner through which it all came together was due in large part to the committed and hardscrabble work of ICBL which acted as a pioneer in the lengthy effort to raise awareness and break down artificial divisions among the humanitarian, development, and disarmament aspects of the issue.

In this case, traditional hard power approaches would not have permitted the international community to address effectively the aggression against civilians that was part of the very nature of this weapon. But soft power cannot always work: the harsh realities of living in a tough, global neighbourhood sometimes require forceful measures. But using human security as a concept and soft power as a tool kit had produced a treaty that set out global norms for the protection of people. Above all, the Ottawa Process was an act of exploration in a dramatically altered global landscape—searching for a new pathway to save lives. Before the Ottawa Treaty, circumventing traditional diplomatic channels was not a viable option. This was an opportunity to forge a new path, one which included the unique expertise and abilities of civil society groups. Civil society representatives were the ones who eventually yanked politicians and officials out of their comfortable chairs and forced them into stride. Focusing on the humanitarian impact of what had hitherto been strictly seen as a disarmament issue helped give the campaign the emotional force that it needed.[9] And this was done by the power of people working in a global network.

The momentum created by the Ottawa Process led to further state and civil society partnerships. The build up to the signing of the Rome Statute that established the ICC is another example where non-state actors used their influence to push ahead an agenda. The Coalition for the International Criminal Court (CICC) remains active in the affairs of the court. Today civil society groups form complex networks, aided by the spread and increased accessibility to information brought about by communication technologies. Clearly, states and civil society groups do not see eye-to-eye on a number of issues. The relationship can be quite tumultuous or even confrontational but there is real power in cooperation when the issue demands it. These groups can act as watchdogs, acting as the eyes and ears of international actors on the ground.

4.2.2 Information Technology

One of the most important trends that is affecting all means of interaction between states, businesses, civil society groups, all the way to families and friends is the ever-evolving communications technology. The Internet, mobile phones, and video teleconferencing abilities simply were not the norm even a mere twenty years ago. The rapid free-flow of information and ideas is a game-changer in every domain, diplomacy included. State leaders experienced the power of groups to organize through new communications technologies during the World Trade Organization (WTO) Ministerial Meetings in Seattle in 1999. With little hierarchical organization, a mass of 40,000 or more people were able to halt negotiations and attract the world's attention. In 2010, a number of countries, including Saudi Arabia and India expressed concern around access to private messages sent via Research in Motion's (RIM) Blackberry phone. The content of that information was of such a concern for governments, that RIM was forced to negotiate a precedent-setting agreement around communications when Saudi Arabia threatened to ban the phones from the country.[10] The gates of information have burst wide open—so shifting the relationship between civilians and government.

With greater access to the interactions between state-players, recorded history will rely less on interpretation of outcomes and more on the revelation of intention. The notoriety of WikiLeaks is a product of our times. This is an age of information and a window peering into the secretive domain of foreign service officers and high-ranking political officials has been thrown wide open, revealing communiqués formerly considered confidential. As recently mentioned in the *New York Times Magazine*, 'for most of history, government has enjoyed an easy superiority in adjusting the ebb and flow of information. Now the rules of the contest have changed.'[11] While there may be concerns from those in the upper echelons of the US government that too much information revealed will also unveil vulnerabilities, it is also true that the public will have a better understanding of the terrorist threat that they are often warned could be coming but have been kept completely in the dark about. This is an example where buy-in by the greater public may actually benefit the state's efforts.

But how will it affect the day-to-day operations of diplomatic actors? We can assume that there will be more awareness of what is communicated and in what manner. There may be some heightened tension between the likes of the US and its contacts around the world. This too will blow over. What state governments everywhere should recognize is that the game is changing and that instead of retreating into their shells, it is time for governments to embrace the new technologies, the ease of movement of information, and utilize it to their advantage. To date, governments have been behind the curve in keeping up to the opportunity that these new information technologies offer. To quote Anne-Marie Slaughter, 'In this world, the measure of power is connectedness.'[12] If we are to take her argument for truth, diplomacy must plug into this network, where relationships of influence occur not only between states, but also 'above the state, below the state, and through the state.'[13] Joseph Nye recently noted that the US currently spends about 500 times more on its military than it does on broadcasting and exchange programmes.[14] Instead of focusing on disseminating information more broadly and garnering public support for US efforts abroad, the traditional approach of most states has been tight-lipped, high-level communications intentionally kept out of the public realm.

There are signs of change. Barack Obama utilized social networking to his own benefit during the 2008 presidential election. Using new media allowed him to tap into an emerging demographic of new voters who will have grown up hardly remembering a time when the Internet did not exist, and who will respond to communication in a format they are familiar with and is part of their everyday lives. Additionally, current Secretary of State Hillary Clinton has promoted a new direction in American diplomacy, one focused on 'civilian power'.[15] The idea is to shift away from a defence-only approach to foreign policy and recognize that there are multiple locations and actors through which diplomacy can take place. This includes not only expanding the reach of the foreign service, but also utilizing new technologies to engage with the public. Secretary Clinton cites the example of using mobile phones in situations of crisis and the provision of aid.

4.2.3 Multipolarity Expanded

All this talk of diplomacy through networks and using 'smart power' brings to mind a new approach about which I have written with Dan Hurley elsewhere.[16] This is the idea of network governance. It is a tool that recognizes and allows all stakeholders to be part of the decision-making process. It supports collaboration across national boundaries, promotes multinational use of best management practices, as well as adoption of successful protocols developed by the world's best experts. It is an approach to diplomacy, state–civil society relations, and international governance that has real potential for application in a world where borders are still significant, but where the challenges facing states require novel solutions that will benefit through collaboration. It is a governance model formed by a new constellation of actors who share ideas and resources to mobilize change. These actors include governments, to be sure, but also civil society groups, and international bodies who are using modern network theory to affect such change and compelling or driving compliance with cross-border norms and standards.

This type of governance has already begun to take shape in the Arctic, starting with the creation of the Arctic Council in 1996. It is already a prototype for collaborative governance. It was the first multilateral institution to have indigenous peoples at the table, along with all circumpolar countries. It sponsored the first major study on the impacts of climate change and it has engaged in expanding scientific and social data, involving working groups from all circumpolar states.

Finally, and of great note, while we still live in a world with a singular superpower, making distinctions between other states and their ability to influence regionally and internationally is becoming increasingly more difficult. Nothing speaks more to this than the emergence of the G20 and its bid to take over where the exclusive club of the G8 left off in an attempt to address the economic challenges of our times. It was questioned in *Maclean's* as Canada was hosting the G20 summit whether or not it may dilute Canada's influence internationally.[17] Being in a club with the likes of South Africa and Turkey may seem less appealing than hanging out with the big boys from London and Washington, but summit events such as the G20 (discussed in Chapter 40, this volume, by former Prime Minister Paul Martin) represent a trend in foreign affairs—one where there will be a growing number of influential state players.

The reality is that there are simply more players to contend with. Few can deny the increasing importance of the BRIC (Brazil, Russia, India, China) countries both internationally and also regionally. With more players vying for key positions, it is imperative that heads of government, who want recognition, play along and work collaboratively with others and within international organizations. One recent example occurred with Canada's bid for a seat on the Security Council. Under Stephen Harper's leadership, Canada's reputation as an ally in cooperative efforts had been lost and our network of connections had been severely cut back by a combination of a fixation on Afghanistan, a re-allocation of foreign aid to a few select governments, and policies of limited support in the climate change debate. The bid failed. Decision-making within any group is notoriously difficult and with state interests muddying the water, even more so. And it demands even more of any government's foreign service and heads of government.

As a foreign minister, I understood that the increase in summitry has resulted in a proliferation of occasions for personal diplomacy, demanding a constant and excruciating requirement to update and juggle the time-slots to gain maximum advantage, all the while balancing the demands of parliament, cabinet, etc. One year I clocked twenty-seven trips abroad, covering more than half a million miles. The calendar, which includes an ever-growing number of set international meetings as well as required regional visits and bilateral engagements, unexpected funerals, inaugurations, and special missions, imposes an unforgiving discipline. But it is important to do so, as each engagement is an opportunity to glean information, advance an argument, stake out a position, establish a rapport. For example, after the funeral of Princess Diana, Britain's Prime Minister Tony Blair held a luncheon that included then-US First Lady Hillary Clinton and our conversation opened up a chance to talk about landmines. Similarly, on the margin of a G8 meeting, US Secretary of State Madeleine Albright and I had the chance to talk about the Pacific Coast salmon dispute between our countries. This does not even include addressing the agenda of the day, which may be focusing on climate change, treaty negotiations, coordination on security issues, or eliminating poverty.

Ultimately, while each of these provide their own challenges to heads of government, particularly in the hectic day-to-day work of running the state, official, state-led diplomacy will remain the means through which international governance plays out. But it is also worth considering that perhaps these new actors and the more public forums from which they have emerged will also bring with them new and exciting opportunities. Heads of government and senior members of the cabinet are entrusted to promote the national interest and secure the best outcomes for their electorate while cultivating positive, productive relationships with both state and non-state actors. Their approach to foreign policy will guide the foreign service and the bureaucratic reach of their administration. If they are unable, or unwilling, to adapt to new constellations of actors and networks and the new norms and responsibilities in this 'new diplomacy', then they will be left behind.

From the top of the heap, the president or prime minister are among the few actors who have the ability to foster new networks of governance, to align themselves with like-minded states, and to advocate and sign international agreements that promote human rights and security, such as the responsibility to protect. The go-it-alone approach is no longer sufficient in a networked world. The international challenges of this new century—climate change, terrorism, human trafficking, etc.—are the products of a world where borders hold less weight and states are threatened by common enemies instead of each other. This is an early phase in the exploration of new pathways to move forward in this landscape of uncertainty and to forge ahead with innovative solutions.

The time has come to reset the diplomatic paradigms and begin teaching, researching, and conversing on the guideposts for change. I still believe that human security and the R2P concepts are important ideas that can help shape the reset. And, it may well be that the rise of people power in the Middle East, dashing the conventional wisdoms of the last half century, is just the catalyst needed to alter the practice of diplomacy.

NOTES

1. Joseph S. Nye, 'The Future of American Power: Dominance and Decline in Perspective', *Foreign Affairs* 89:6 (November/December 2010), 2–12 at 2.
2. Joseph S. Nye, 'Get Smart', *Foreign Affairs* 88:4 (July/August 2009), 160–3. For more see Chapters 29 and 30, this volume.

3. See Jorge Heine and Ramesh Thakur (eds), *The Dark Side of Globalization* (Tokyo: United Nations University Press, 2011).

4. See Gareth Evans, *The Responsibility to Protect: Halting Mass Atrocity Crimes Once and For All* (Washington, DC: Brookings Institution Press, 2008); and Ramesh Thakur, *The Responsibility to Protect: Norms, Laws and the Use of Force in International Politics* (London: Routledge, 2011).

5. United States Government, *National Security Strategy*, 10 May 2010, at 48.

6. Ken Dilanian, 'Overall U.S. Intelligence Budget Tops $80 Billion', *Los Angeles Times*, 28 October 2010.

7. Nicholas D. Kristof, 'The Big (Military) Taboo', *New York Times*, 25 December 2010.

8. Lloyd Axworthy and Sarah Taylor, 'A Ban for All Seasons: The Landmines Convention and its Implications for Canadian Politics', *International Journal* 53 (Spring 1998), 189–203.

9. See Ramesh Thakur and William Maley, 'The Ottawa Convention on Landmines: A Landmark Humanitarian Treaty in Arms Control?', *Global Governance* 5:3 (July–September 1999), 273–302.

10. Omar El Akkad, 'Détente with Saudis Buoys Hope for RIM's Future in Arab World', *The Globe and Mail*, 8 August 2010.

11. Misha Glenny, 'The Gift of Information', *New York Times Magazine*, 5 December 2010, 166.

12. Anne-Marie Slaughter, 'America's Edge: Power in the Networked Century', *Foreign Affairs* 88:1 (January/February 2009), 94–113 at 94.

13. Slaughter, 'America's Edge', 95.

14. Nye, 'Get Smart', 162.

15. Hillary Rodham Clinton, 'Leading Through Civilian Power', *Foreign Affairs* 89:6 (November/December 2010), 13–24.

16. Lloyd Axworthy and Dan Hurley, 'Networks and the Future of the Arctic', *Global Brief*, Spring/Summer 2010, 24–9.

17. 'Who Gets to Rule the World', *Maclean's*, 1 July 2010.

CHAPTER 5

....

THE BUREAUCRACY: MINISTRY OF FOREIGN AFFAIRS, FOREIGN SERVICE, AND OTHER GOVERNMENT DEPARTMENTS

....

SIR JEREMY GREENSTOCK

DIPLOMACY is the activity and set of professional skills serving a national power centre's relationships with other power centres. It involves representation, communication and receipt of messages, information gathering and analysis, negotiation, and the exercising of influence on external decisions and developments. Its evolution and history, as explained elsewhere in this *Handbook*, stemmed from the statecraft of absolute rulers, served by a court. Diplomats were, and are, the extension of a ruler's reach across his border.

As international interactions and government structures became more complex in the 19th and 20th centuries, foreign policy practitioners engaged with events and with one another not just in capitals but wherever international competition sprouted. At the most senior level, they carried the authority to commit their principals to courses of action that could only be disowned at a cost. Accordingly, the mechanism for coordinating their instructions and responding to their reports had to be increasingly sophisticated. Foreign ministries grew from just a secretariat serving the minister (the origin of 'secretary' in diplomatic titles) into a many-layered department. Overseas missions multiplied. The foreign minister, acting on issues beyond the direct observation of domestic constituencies but affecting national interests, often carried a quasi-independent authority within the ranks of government. He might also, in states with a long history of overseas involvement, come to preside over a growing range of interconnected government activities as different specializations merged into a single coordinating department. The United Kingdom's Foreign and Commonwealth Office, for instance, was the eventual amalgamation of seven specialist offices: the Foreign Office, the Dominions Office, the India Office, the Colonial Office, the Commonwealth Office, the Levant Service, and the Consular Service.

As Daryl Copeland describes in Chapter 25 of this volume, during the later stages of the 20th century and into the new millennium, travel times shrank, communication became instantaneous, and sources of information mushroomed. With the spread of freedom after the end of the colonial era and of the cold war, the capacity to exercise choice of action in an international context expanded to many new sovereign territories and to areas way beyond the reach of governments, all the way down to individuals. Open, powerful media and social communications networks dispensed information and comment and galvanized public opinion. Globalization became transparent.

With this exponential growth in the complexity of human exchange, two major developments hit the protected world of the diplomat: the entry into intergovernmental business of most other government departments (and some non-governmental ones); and the heightening of the short-term political sensitivity of overseas business. Both these factors have brought the head of government into closer daily control of foreign affairs and subtracted from the foreign ministry's exclusivity. The requirement for knowledge of abroad has risen dramatically. Professional diplomats, reporting to the foreign minister, no longer find it possible to coordinate the total interface with other states' representatives or to claim a monopoly on the handling or interpreting of external factors in their country's set of interests.

In keeping with the trajectory of this volume, this chapter therefore needs to examine not just the standard structures of foreign ministries, but also how relevant diplomacy is to modern international transactions, where diplomacy ends and technical intergovernmental interface begins, how foreign ministries are responding to the need for cross-government teamwork, and what 21st-century systems are being devised, under political direction, as the best ways to coordinate the very complicated set of foreign policy requirements that a nation state confronts. In doing so, it will point out how carefully governments must plan their investment in foreign policy and diplomatic capability and how necessary it is for systems to adapt to global change.

5.1 MINISTRY OF FOREIGN AFFAIRS

In spite of the pressure on foreign offices to merge their work with other parts of government conducting overseas business, virtually all government systems retain a foreign minister. A head of government needs a colleague to coordinate the state's relationships with other states and to maintain the skills needed to interact with and interpret foreigners. Citizens require help with their private and corporate activities overseas and expect the state to serve them in this respect. The logic of having a separate department to serve the minister responsible for managing these aspects of national interest has not diminished with a changed global environment.

Nor has the relevance of professional diplomatic skills disappeared with the expansion of the competition in information gathering, analysis, and direct communication. The explosion of interactions in a multipolar world has put a premium on judgement of what to expect from, and how to influence, external developments. Multilateral negotiations on common problems have become increasingly intricate as a greater number of states make nationally oriented decisions on their international interests, and as the linkages between political, economic, security, and social pressures multiply and intensify. Meanwhile the international institutions, established to take responsibility for shared areas of national interest between states, are finding it hard, given the polarizing effect of global competition between national identities and ambitions, to pursue supranational work on global public goods in such a complex environment. Constant, hard, well-prepared negotiation between capitals and within international forums remains a compelling requirement; and a state's interests depend on the skill with which this is performed.

In a typical foreign ministry, whether in the advanced or the developing world, the minister is served by an outer office organizing the immediate requirements of the role, by a senior group of diplomats/civil servants overseeing the bureaucracy, and by a set of departments handling the various categories of a state's overseas interests. Some of these departments subdivide the world's political geography into manageable units, while others handle cross-cutting themes such as economic affairs, trade policy, security, the environment, human rights, law, public diplomacy, and services to citizens abroad. Certain governments include the promotion of development assistance, commerce, or culture within the foreign ministry, while others reserve these functions for separate ministries. The coordination between themes and geographical relationships is managed by senior staff, often with an element of debate and competition (consider the interplay, for instance, between bilateral relationships and human rights standards) that leaves room for strong personalities to exercise a marked influence.

The ministry also administrates and directs the overseas activity of the nation's foreign service (see section 5.2), which involves a more diverse set of budget decisions, staffing requirements, and working conditions than in the home civil service. Since most of the front-line personnel of the ministry spend the greater part of their career outside the country, their familiarity with the domestic scene tends to be less extensive than that of their non-diplomatic counterparts. This can affect the amount of weight that a foreign ministry carries in the political and public opinion environment of the home capital. Conversely, as international interdependence grows, the foreign service is better informed on the affairs of allies and neighbours, whose decisions exercise an increasing influence on domestic interests. Perhaps this division of functional expertise should be more readily acknowledged.

In a more transparent and informed world, a Ministry of Foreign Affairs has to take account of the wealth of information on international issues available to the media, to the academic and think-tank field, and to individual citizens. A capacity to handle the public sphere and stay up to date with comment, opinion, and enquiry there is essential. It is equally important not to be swamped by it and to maintain an ability to form judgements on developments and underlying trends that balance management of short-term pressures with longer-term strategic objectives. The quality of the professional diplomatic input into the construction of this balance is a genuine government resource, because the immediacy of the pressures in the public arena can distort the search for choices and decisions that best suit the national strategic interest. It is the ministry at home that has to ensure that the skills and practices necessary for managing the public interface are instilled and nurtured in their professional staffs. The ministry is also responsible for creating, justifying, and administrating systems to preserve the confidentiality of those parts of the business of diplomacy which have to be kept from the public eye, whether to protect sources or to avoid damage to negotiating positions and relationships (see section 5.7).

Given the amount and political importance of international activity, the foreign minister may be supported by lower-ranking ministers, each taking responsibility for an area of work, and by political advisers keeping an eye on the cross-currents between foreign policy and national politics. To a degree greater than in departments dealing with domestic business, where politicians and civil servants tend to have more extensive experience of cooperating, these reinforcements can have difficulty in coming to terms with professional diplomats, and vice versa. But public support for foreign policy decisions, even in non-democracies, is crucial in an increasingly open and informed world; and the more successful foreign ministries have normally worked out a *modus vivendi* between these two groups, the political and the professional. Much depends on personal chemistry and competence, giving rise to the aphorism 'diplomacy begins at home'. Indeed, the networks that career diplomats need to develop most sensibly start with the contacts and friendships that can give them a solid domestic base.

5.2 THE FOREIGN SERVICE

Foreign ministries have to be distinguished from a country's foreign or diplomatic service. The ministry may have a number of employees, usually at a more junior level, who never serve overseas; while with few exceptions a diplomat is committed to accept a posting either at home or in a mission abroad. The majority of foreign service officers spend between a half and two-thirds of their career in overseas postings. The preparedness to live and work in a series of changing environments, normally with a family, marks the career as different from that of a public servant at home and most countries have established a distinct cadre, with its own conditions of service and training, for this purpose. The growing tendency of other government departments to construct a capability to interface with other governments has blurred this distinction, sometimes to the point of tension between the departments involved or with the managers and funders of the civil service as a whole. But so far nearly all governments have retained a foreign service to staff the majority of posts in their offices abroad, because this recognizes the value of diplomatic practice, facilitates the maintenance of the professional and language skills required, and provides an experienced point of coordination, the head of the overseas mission, for managing the spectrum of government business with another country.

In Chapter 6 of this *Handbook*, David Malone goes into greater detail on the nature of a diplomat's overseas work, but the relationship between a foreign ministry and its overseas posts and other operations deserves some comment here. The ministry controls. This is done, implicitly or often explicitly, in the name of the minister as the person with the political authority for foreign policy decision-making. A second secretary in a political department at home can, with suitable cover, instruct an ambassador abroad, however many ranks senior, because the former is closer to that authority and to the factors across government that may have played a part in formulating policy. In some foreign service systems, 'instructions' are the foundation of a mission's actions overseas and they are often conveyed in writing through the foreign ministry even if other government actors have been instrumental in creating them. In other systems, especially those with high information technology skills, the increasing use of email, telephone calls, and casual meetings produces a set of informal channels of communication, often unrecorded, through which authority is transmitted for action overseas. The ministry at home must provide clear guidelines to its entire staff on what constitutes instructions, whatever the channels available.

In an era when the real utility of diplomats has been questioned and the distinctiveness of their work has been blurred, the size and spread of a country's representation abroad has in recent years been scrutinized very carefully when economic pressures make themselves felt. The tasks to be done at home to service ministers' responsibilities can appear to hit an irreducible minimum; and many diplomatic services have been squeezed on overseas staffing in the budgetary cuts that have followed the 2008-onwards financial and economic crisis. This loss of capability abroad comes at a time when an increasing number of states are taking decisions on international issues based on their independent assessment of national interest, rather than relying on the work of a few leading powers, or of the international institutions, to set and implement a sensible global agenda. This ought to bear on a country's decisions on overseas representation, because the capacity to understand and influence other national approaches is taking on a greater, not a reduced, importance as global change accelerates. Where universal coverage is out of the question, mini-missions with only one or two staff, or posts with responsibility for a connected region, are better than no representation at all.

This is an important factor for countries that are only now being included at the world's top tables to take into account as they come to terms with their greater weight in the global arena. China, India, and Brazil, to refer to the three most regularly mentioned examples of the emerging economies (Russia is also part of the BRIC acronym, but has been playing a prominent and proactive role in power diplomacy for longer than the others), are managing this evolution in different ways. They are finding that the rapidly growing size of their economies and consumer markets and the political influence which stems from their economic progress multiply the approaches they receive from other governments and the responses they need to formulate.

China, with its ability to plan strategically over the long life of a government, has invested in an expanded presence overseas in both diplomatic and business terms and its diplomats are rapidly acquiring the skills to mix with the best of their counterparts anywhere. It may have some way to go in developing the language, literally and metaphorically, of easy communication with other cultures; and the state is facing problems in judging how connected it wants its citizens to be when an open society brings awkward political connotations. But it is a focused player in the new era.

India is better placed than China to connect globally in terms of language, mentality, and communications technology, but has a bureaucracy at home and a diplomatic representation overseas which are some way below the staffing and training levels to cope with the exponential rise in business coming its way. Nor has India developed the sense of driving purpose that appears to underlie the Chinese approach.

Brazil possesses an experienced team of diplomats with skills to engage in high-level exchange and negotiation, particularly in multilateral forums, but appears to be taking time to decide where to apply its weight and which partners to choose in the burgeoning competition for influence in setting the global agenda.

All three countries, and many others in a similar stage of development, have internal problems—unsurprisingly, given the speed with which change is taking place—with poverty, social order, education, and cohesion. Nevertheless, all are aware that international developments and relationships bear heavily on their national interests. They need, as states competing in the first rank of modern powers, to organize their diplomatic instruments in a deliberate and resourceful manner; and this should be within their capability in resource terms, since a diplomatic service rarely absorbs a high proportion of the overall government budget. Indeed, no country of whatever size or sophistication can afford to ignore the degree to which its interests can be enhanced by investing in a certain quantitative and qualitative level of diplomatic representation.

5.3 Services to the Public Overseas

Every foreign ministry is tasked to look after the interests of its nationals abroad. Some governments organize their consular and visa services separately from the mainstream diplomatic career; others provide assistance to the corporate sector through a different office. An overseas mission, nevertheless, and especially the head of mission, is bound to have to spend time and effort responding to the requirements of private citizens; and the ministry at home can face media and parliamentary scrutiny if these are not given adequate attention. In the case of some countries, large expatriate communities have come to expect that almost the first priority of an overseas mission is to serve that local community, whose leaders' influence with parts of the media or the political class at home will be brought to bear if they are disappointed. Businessmen need advice on how to access new markets and assistance in dealing with difficulties they may encounter with local laws and officials. Tourists get into trouble from time to time or have to be helped when transport systems break down or natural disasters occur. Any head of mission must preserve a capability to deal with an emergency and expects the ministry at home to back him up.

Yet these duties cannot be allowed to displace front-line diplomacy. The bureaucracy in the capital needs to ensure that there is clarity in the minds of both political decision-makers at home and heads of mission abroad as to what the priorities are. Taxpayers expect government services just as much abroad as at home; and there is no doubt that in an interconnected world a nation can benefit from maximizing the ability of its citizens to pursue business and enjoy travel overseas with as few problems and as great an understanding of the environment as possible. Heads of mission must be able, in terms of training and resources, to build these considerations into the management of their teams. At the same time, diplomats must be left with time and energy to spend on the compelling requirements of their profession. It is up to the ministry to set the balance, defend it or amend it if criticised, and give their overseas staff the guidance and resources to implement it effectively.

5.4 The Head of Government

Heads of state and government are at the apex of the power system that the diplomat serves. They bear the ultimate responsibility for setting the national strategy and, in an age when the number of international contacts and meetings is inexorably rising, frequently have to settle issues in person with their opposite numbers. Almost all heads of government retain a permanent office of foreign and defence policy advisers to work exclusively for them and an even broader mechanism to coordinate external policy across the departments of government. The history of the relationship between the State Department and the National Security Council in the United States illustrates the tension, sometimes creative, sometimes damaging, between these two parts of the machinery. It is an exceptionally difficult task for a head of government both to ensure that top-quality professional advice is fed into decision-making and to drive forward decisions on a timing that cuts through layers of bureaucracy and bears on events to the best national advantage. It normally helps, however, for heads to include on their advisory staff one or more individuals with professional foreign policy experience.

Because so little escapes public reporting and comment nowadays and because domestic issues are so entwined with external ones across the whole field of government, the personal input of the head of government into foreign policy, whatever the nature of a state's constitutional arrangements, easily becomes a political necessity. This diminishes the capacity of a foreign minister to play an independent role even on tactics, let alone strategy. The degree of political and personal understanding between a head and a foreign minister is a significant feature of the effectiveness of a nation's interventions on the international stage, especially in those capitals whose interests require a very broad, perhaps a global, promotion. This understanding is made easier by a daily interaction between their staffs that takes account of all the political, as well as the circumstantial, factors bearing on decisions.

5.5 SPECIAL REPRESENTATIVES

The appointment of special envoys or representatives has become more common as the practice of establishing specialist areas of negotiation on cross-border issues has grown, most often under the auspices of the United Nations or a regional organization. Climate change and human rights are familiar examples. Such appointments may be made formally in the name of the head of state, the head of government, or the foreign minister and they can at times carry a personal responsibility to report to their principal and no one else. They usually involve the assignment of a serving or recently retired diplomat, or perhaps a specialist from another profession relevant to the subject matter, to a job within the normal workings of the foreign affairs bureaucracy, but with a job description that protects them from having to contribute to any other task. They may also imply specially arranged conditions of service.

With this instrument at his disposal, the head of government or minister can portray his personal interest in a subject of immediate or public importance outside the foreign affairs routine, or underline the expectation that he will pay particular attention to an issue of sensitivity. When the Group of Seven industrialized nations (G7) began to meet informally from the mid-1970s onwards at the level of heads of state and government, to create an opportunity for heads to discuss informally and personally between them the most pressing issues of international economic policy, they each appointed personal representatives, who quickly became known as Sherpas, to carry the load of preparation for these summits. As the list grew of UN special conferences, on the environment, on disarmament, against racism, on women's rights, and on several other areas (discussed by A.J.R. Groom in Chapter 14 of this *Handbook*), many capitals chose special envoys to handle the precise business. While such appointments stand just outside the norm of organized diplomacy, they serve a very useful purpose and indeed reflect the origin of diplomacy itself in the extension of a ruler's reach through his chosen representative. A foreign ministry nevertheless has to find the flexibility and sometimes the tolerance to fit these single-issue supernumeraries into their organizational structures, because tensions can arise when there is a balance to be struck with wider considerations and because they will inevitably require services and back-up from the mainstream departments.

5.6 PUBLIC DIPLOMACY

How a policy, or the decisions which implement it, are explained in public, whether to a domestic or an international audience, makes a greater difference to its success the more open the information environment. Later chapters will explain in fuller detail the role of the media (specifically Chapter 11 by Shawn Powers) and of public diplomacy (see

Chapter 24) in the modern era. It is enough to say at this point that every foreign policy bureaucracy, and not just its political leadership, has to take account of public opinion within its working mainstream. The formation of a policy, even if it begins in the lower reaches of a specialist section, must include a conscious effort to assess its sustainability in the implementation phase. A well-organized foreign ministry will have relationships with think tanks, journalists, academics, and civil society which sharpen its sense of where and how outside opinion will bear on its decisions and activities. It will need the confidence in its intellectual and operational strengths to gauge when public opinion should be the guide and when it should be shaped in a new direction. It is one of the necessary skills of a diplomat, at home or abroad, to test the weather in this area and understand how to use his instruments for influencing it. A bureaucracy that is capable of delivering recommendations to a minister that contain the lowest possible risk of unnecessary public controversy is enlarging the capacity of the foreign policy machine to achieve results.

5.7 CONFIDENTIALITY

The debate over the transparency of government activity has intensified with the growth of the power of actors outside government to investigate. It is often assumed that public opinion is more likely to be supportive of policy if it is regularly given all the facts. Even in the case of domestic policy this assumption needs to be examined. There is no doubt that an open approach to describing and explaining decisions is normally sensible, but for governments to be able to function effectively some protection is needed for the way those decisions are reached and implemented. The process is rarely a straight line; and governments, just as much as businesses or individuals, need the opportunity to test, steer sideways, or retreat without being interrogated publicly at each point. The case is stronger in the field of foreign policy because consulting or negotiating with other governments requires discretion when different governments follow different practices in public disclosure. The public interest may lie more strongly in efficient systems and the right results than in open government for its own sake.

That said, it is useful for ministers and senior officials to develop the kind of relationship with professional journalists and other serious commentators on public sector activity that explains the trend of events on a restricted basis. This enables published comment to remain reasonably accurate without the detail being endlessly revealed and dissected with distorted emphasis. A balance in the management of this area also makes it less likely that constant leaks will disrupt the efficiency of government work. While it will usually be the responsibility of ministers to set the norm of public disclosure, a foreign ministry will need to make judgements within the bureaucracy on how to get this balance right. Diplomatic practice has always involved a degree of confidentiality and there is no reason to suppose that global developments have changed this. But excessive secrecy is less wise nowadays when its purpose is to cover an undeclared strategy or to hide action that may be criticized. It has become just too hard to sustain it.

5.8 SECRET INTELLIGENCE

The protection of sources becomes especially important when the diplomatic and intelligence services interact. Most overseas intelligence agencies have a remit to collect information on specific subjects related to national objectives, whether in foreign policy or in security, defence or other fields. Yet it is not necessarily their sole responsibility to interpret the meaning or weight of the intelligence gathered, which may be only one of a number of sources of information on a particular topic. Arrangements are necessary, agreed and managed in the home capital under the overall authority of the head of government or the foreign minister, for the careful handling of intelligence material, for the coordination of intelligence requirements, and for the presentation of processed intelligence to ministers in parallel with other inputs on the issue in hand. Counter-terrorism is one area nowadays where well-designed and efficient channels between different government sectors are needed. Overseas missions, normally heads of missions themselves, need to be aware of intelligence operations on their turf because there are often political factors that have to be aligned with them. Foreign ministries will therefore need to have systems in place which deal with secret activities and material with all the proper safeguards and which link smoothly with the work of other parts of government.

5.9 OTHER GOVERNMENT DEPARTMENTS

Most ministries of foreign affairs have a well-established relationship with certain other ministries with functions that involve international connections, typically those concerned with defence, trade, overseas development, and international economics. As globalization has intensified, more and more business from the domestic arena has spawned international connections and influences, ranging from energy and the environment to agriculture, transport, education, health, and others. Indeed it is hard to think of a department that has no cross-border factors affecting it in today's world. This makes a 'whole of government' approach to organizing international business essential in the 21st century. Countries that belong to active regional organizations devote quite extensive sections of their government machinery to regional cooperation; and in the case of members of the European Union (EU), the most sophisticated and wide-ranging of all the regional institutions, a significant proportion of government work is organized under treaty arrangements for the collective approach of the EU.

No foreign ministry can hope to control or even heavily influence all these complex, often specialist, transactions. A capable one will attempt to keep track of the main themes and will be involved in major negotiations of new formal agreements or other significant changes. Many capitals have evolved coordinating mechanisms outside the foreign ministry which may have their own ministerial direction and which report to the head of government rather than to the foreign minister. Just because the transactions are with foreigners is not an automatic reason to classify them as acts of diplomacy, even if they involve negotiation, language skills, and the collection of information on external factors. A huge amount of technical business is done in specialist areas between government representatives about which foreign offices need to know nothing at all for the national interest to be met.

Effective ambassadors in overseas posts will be informed about the range of issues that are currently under discussion between their capitals and their host government and be in a position, if asked, to add analysis or influence to win a point or unravel a problem if direct exchanges come unstuck for some reason. This can be done without the foreign ministry at home becoming involved or even knowing about it. It is part of the diplomatic skill to help find ways round a problem between governments in a technical area by adding the procedural or contact-making expertise in one mind to the substantive knowledge in another. The foreign ministry itself need be concerned no further than to allow and promote the teamwork within the overall government machine that enables this to happen without fuss. This may usefully include exchanges and secondments between the foreign ministry and other government departments.

There are nevertheless limits to which even pragmatic coordination can be taken. Intergovernmental interactions are too numerous and too frequent for the linkages between them to be monitored, assessed, and refined so effectively in real time that inconsistencies in policy approaches are ironed out or the most productive route to the right result devised. All government activity has a tendency to incompetence built into it and it would be a waste of effort, resources, and professional skills to attempt to reduce that to an improbable minimum. Yet a well-managed system, including in recently emerging states, may be capable of appointing leaders to teams working on international business who have the training and the imagination to be conscious of factors beyond their immediate range of vision and the scope to link in to diplomatic colleagues when complications loom. For this to happen in the middle of negotiations away from home requires relationships and structures at home which share the process of policy-making and create channels for cross-information. While this may be beyond the capacity of some government mechanisms, it needs to be realized that those governments that generate a capability in this respect have a built-in advantage in the international arena. In the context of this *Handbook*, it is enough to point out that diplomatic skills are a resource that can be made available across a wide range of government activity even when trained diplomats are not part of the substantive input into the subject matter.

5.10 THE INVOLVEMENT OF THE LEGISLATURE

In democratic systems, and increasingly in others, it is usually necessary to take account of the views of the congress or parliament on foreign affairs, especially where it exercises a tight control of budgets or where select committees play an influential role. Parliament is also one of several routes (in the modern age these routes are multiplying) to ensuring that public opinion is not going to run contrary to an overseas policy initiative. Ministries of foreign affairs are wise to pay attention to their relationship with the legislature even during a period of low controversy on foreign business.

This raises a dilemma for the government machine over the sharing of information. Parliaments are public bodies; and even where there are arrangements for the handling of confidential information leaks can easily occur. On the other hand, effective supervision of the foreign affairs field, which is healthy for democracy, requires parliamentarians to be well informed. As so often in diplomatic business, the right approach can be an informal one, where good personal relationships and practices between leading players can make up for deficiencies in the formal procedures. Care spent on this area can save trouble later in the process.

5.11 NON-GOVERNMENTAL ACTORS

Global awareness and information technology broaden the field of people interested and active in foreign affairs. Policy-makers and practitioners can benefit from interaction with think tanks, academics, and civil society both in devising the right approach and in delivering it. The better non-governmental organizations (NGOs) are now achieving excellent results in their fields of expertise, especially in their activities in the developing world, and they are well worth bringing on board at the right time. Yet there has to be a limit. Over-importunate NGOs and insular government departments are both unwelcome. As with the media, a foreign ministry must find the mean between constant consultation and a closed door: the government system has to be able to cut through discussion and act when the national interest requires it, but on the basis of good information, advice, and partnerships. Encouraging younger diplomats to develop the habit of interacting with the private sector and civil society brings returns later. Indeed, the scope for the non-governmental sector as a whole, as it expands its capacity to act and interact overseas, to work in cooperation with government departments and contribute to the achievement of national objectives is enormous. This area needs to be part of the networking territory that is constantly expanding in the practice of a competent diplomat.

5.12 THE APPLICATION OF NORMS AND PRINCIPLES

Every power centre that retains a modicum of conscience about international standards, above all in the human rights field, struggles with the trade-off between expediency and principle. The media enjoy poking between the cracks of this dilemma, on whichever side they see the fault as lying, and foreign policy teams can make fools of themselves either if they trumpet their commitment to principle or if they ignore it.

In the UK, the incoming Labour government in 1997 laid out an approach that claimed to establish a foreign policy with an ethical dimension. It was seen as a deliberate attempt by ministers to distinguish their policies from what they regarded as the real-politik tendencies of their predecessors. This was quickly branded by the media as 'ethical foreign policy' and every opportunity was taken to point out when government decisions appeared more expedient than principled. The fact that the foreign secretary's speech setting out the approach had carefully stated the limits on a purely ethical dimension was ignored. In due course the policy emphasis on ethics became diluted, as it normally is, but the point had been made and the attempt to serve good principles was recognized.

In the 21st-century environment it seems that the importance of moral authority, a major element in the application of 'soft power', will increase. As the number of power centres with a capacity for independent action rises, the advantages of pursuing national or subjective interests through military or even economic superiority will diminish. People with freedom of choice and a capacity to exercise it have to be persuaded rather than coerced to follow a certain course of action. While the United Nations Charter and the Universal Declaration of Human Rights are regularly breached by a whole variety of governments, the fact that they and a number of other valuable conventions and charters can be invoked sets a standard of acceptable behaviour which it can be damaging to ignore. International courts with authority to judge these areas, such as the European Court of Human Rights and the International Criminal Court, may come to exercise a growing influence as the century proceeds. This 'shrinking moral universe', as a leading emerging country politician (Indian Congress Party President Sonia Gandhi, in a speech on 19 November 2010) has called it, heightens the influence on the evolution of events of the opinions of people across borders, as the weight of their support for or opposition to a line of policy bears on those taking the decisions. This makes it wise for a foreign affairs ministry, or a government system more generally, to organize its approach to policy formation in a way which gives due weight to international norms and commitments.

5.13 MULTILATERAL DIPLOMACY

It is important for the machinery in capitals to create capacity for diplomatic engagement with other capitals as events and processes unfold. Rarely can a single capital bring the necessary weight to bear on an international issue to achieve its national objective on its own. Working with (in particular) the like-minded amongst other governments, not least with partners in regional organizations or alliances, requires the development of habits and processes to make sure this is done effectively and in real time. A growing example is conflict resolution or stability work in a disturbed area overseas, which requires not only close coordination within a single government's approach, usually involving the foreign, defence, and development departments as a minimum, but also detailed intergovernmental and institutional cooperation. Foreign ministries normally carry primary responsibility for the complex interaction necessary.

Capitals need to be aware that, increasingly in 21st-century diplomacy, in which national prerogatives tend to prevail over supranational ones, collective policy-making frequently follows an ad hoc course. The UN and the other international institutions can be effective in performing familiar tasks in their areas of expertise, but are finding it hard to adapt to global political trends or to deal with more complex or divisive issues. The biggest challenges, such as regional security, climate change, or proliferation of weapons of mass destruction, may not respond to multilateral treatment unless the nations with the largest stake in the issue engage with each other outside institutional channels. This places a premium on the ability in capitals to devise and execute the right tactics for the specific issue, to analyse the likely responses of the relevant inter-locutors, and to exercise influence precisely where it is needed. Again, the advantage goes to governments that maintain an effective and broad overseas representation, which prepare their approaches in depth and which coordinate their decision-making and implementation at home.

The way in which work at the United Nations and other major international institutions is directed and organized from the capital forms an important part of a foreign ministry's make-up. Almost every foreign office has a department dealing with international organizations; and its staffing levels and impact within the ministry will reflect the relative significance of multilateral diplomacy in the government's list of priorities. Smaller and less rich nations, unable to afford a broad spread of overseas missions, rely on the UN and elsewhere to provide opportunities for bilateral and small-group exchanges, often with a concentration on their regional organization's agenda. Some capitals cover quite a large proportion of their diplomatic interactions in this way. They also take care to appoint diplomats to such posts who have a high capacity to handle volumes of complex business. The degree to which a very capable and articulate ambassador at the UN can enlarge the impact of a small member state is not to be underestimated.

Conversely, while it can also be true that an under-qualified UN representative can diminish the punch and weight of a larger country, the powers with a wide spread of interests, relationships, and representations do not depend so heavily on a high-grade performance at the UN. They have networks, alliances, and partnerships elsewhere which carry their main business and absorb their politicians' attention. The International Monetary Fund and the World Trade Organization, or for some developed countries the EU and the North Atlantic Treaty Organization, are more likely to catch the attention of a head of government than the regular issues in front of the UN Security Council. The points worth making here are first, that the capital's focus on the international institutions needs to be staffed and led in a way that accurately reflects the true international interests of the state; and second, that those interests will increasingly include maintaining relationships with and making an impression on a wider range of other governments than in previous eras when the views of the majority of states did not matter so much. Today, persuasion is a more important instrument and international legitimacy a more powerful ally than they were in a less equal world; and this gives smaller states more of a voice in ongoing business. A clear illustration is the final phase of the 2009 Climate Change Conference in Copenhagen, when at one point the objections of small island states affected by rising sea levels stopped the major powers in their tracks.

5.14 THE CHANGING NATURE OF POWER

Diplomacy interprets power, and if the nature of power is changing in the modern age then the practice of diplomacy must adapt to those changes or lose its relevance. The events and experiences of the first decade of the new century suggest that power is shifting from the familiar centres of the second half of the 20th century, mainly Western capitals, in two new directions. First, the emergence of new economies capable of realizing the more open opportunities of a globalized market has redistributed relative weight and influence from the West and North towards the East and South. Countries with large populations or with access to valuable raw materials have, by comparison with the era when industrial capability significantly tilted the balance, a more natural advantage. Second, freedom of choice and action has spread not just to new nations but also to subnational groups, local areas, and individuals. If part of the job of a foreign ministry is to explain and predict to ministers what is going to happen internationally, its staff have to be in a position to understand a multidimensional mix of influences on events, including the popular voice.

All foreign ministries have to make choices, because it is beyond the capacity of a single system, or of any national budget, to cover everything globally that might bear on a state's interests. Attempts to prioritize and simplify have to be made. Yet a judgement is also needed on what ministers really require as background and as advice before they enter an arena of negotiation or make a policy decision. Within the European Union, for instance, confidence in the handling by Brussels of a growing number of issues has led to decisions by national governments to downsize their missions in each others' capitals because bilateral-type diplomacy appears to be less essential. Many states with tight pressures on their resources make arrangements to use their missions at the United Nations to handle bilateral issues with governments in whose capitals they have no permanent representation. But in both cases they leave themselves without access to specific, time-sensitive reporting and analysis that a bilateral mission would provide. Foreign ministries need to understand that the network they run overseas has to adapt to the way in which power is exercised in a changing environment, and that this may mean moving forward from, or even breaking with, the familiar structure of the previous era.

5.15 Conclusions

The pressure on foreign ministries to reflect the implications of massive global change in their structures and practices is growing. The tendency to think that the enormous power of open communications networks offers opportunities for slimming diplomatic representation and tapping a wider variety of open sources is partly misplaced. These networks have a value both for accessing particular facts and trends and for understanding the global environment, but they cannot replace professional diplomatic capability in providing precise judgements on decision-making, negotiation, fault-lines, and power shifts within, between, and among governments.

International affairs bureaucracies therefore have to be staffed, trained, and resourced to cope with the real life impact of power distribution, globalized economics, cultural fragmentation, and modern technology. The capacity to absorb the complexity of a multipolar world, to understand the main linkages between the different influences and actors, and to handle unconventional situations can give a state a marked advantage in realizing its interests.

With this has to come recognition that there are limits. No government system can take into account all the factors weighing on global developments or stay in control of them. Even the most powerful countries are obliged to go with the flow of events to some extent. This places a premium on engaging people of high quality, on constant three-dimensional analysis, and on nourishing a capacity both to adapt and to learn lessons from the external shocks and internal errors that afflict every foreign policy machine. Diplomats, who at their best are trained and practised in handling complexity, can play a central role in these processes if given the right strategic direction and resources within an effective foreign policy bureaucracy.

CHAPTER 6

THE MODERN DIPLOMATIC MISSION

DAVID M. MALONE

WHILE hunting and gathering societies, in a world where harsh climates, disease, and food scarcity kept human numbers under control, may not have required complex relationships among early communities of *Homo sapiens*, with the advent of agricultural cultivation and more ambitious human settlement inevitably came the need for accommodation, and hence communication and negotiation between communities. Units of exchange, of one sort or another, including mutually beneficial marriage—that great standby of later diplomacy—emerged as a favoured technique in ancient international relations.

Early emissaries often enjoyed a very limited remit from their masters and ran serious risks. An offending message could elicit the response of the lifeless head of the go-between. To guard against such outcomes, which tended to discourage volunteers, notions of immunity for the envoy (and, generally also his suite) soon took hold, as did a brisk trade in interception of diplomatic communication, subornment of envoys, and other underhanded tactics that still hold sway today, both among nations and more widely. Thus, on the whole, rulers preferred to 'hear the message rather than eat the messenger'.[1]

The motivations, instruments, and desired outcomes of negotiation in antiquity are readily recognizable to denizens of today's standing diplomatic mission—the embassy, consulate, permanent delegation (to an international organization), and variations thereof.[2] The earlier form of temporary diplomatic mission, often with a single purpose of communication or negotiation, developed into a more permanent, resident arrangement in the 15th century among Italy's many, often intensely commercially-minded, polities, spreading north thereafter.[3]

It was the quest for a balance of powers and a related constant search for advantage that led to the rapid spread of resident ambassadors, information being the key to the achievement of incrementally accrued power.

Diplomacy as we know it throughout the world today is largely an outcome of the Westphalian system of 1648 that codified the role of the state within a defined, sovereign territory as the key actor in international relations.[4] Ludwik Dembinski noted in 1988 that 'as the modern territorial state emerged in Europe in the sixteenth and seventeenth centuries, resident diplomatic and consular missions began taking forms which ... they have kept until now'.[5] To bring order to a growing number of diplomatic actors and interactions, the Congress of Vienna (1815) codified issues of rank among the practitioners.

After 1945, international society was swelled by a large number of new sovereign countries, enfranchised by decolonization, dispatching and receiving diplomatic missions, and also by many new resident missions at international organizations (IOs) such as the United Nations (UN) and regional and more narrowly functional institutions. This greatly expanded the business of diplomacy and, in the process, inevitably somewhat diluted and devalued the stature if not the status of ambassadors and the missions they led.

While the Paris 1919 conference marked a high point of summit diplomacy in extended conference form, and the Second World War gave rise to several highly operational war-planning summit meetings of critical importance among leading Allied powers, it is only in recent decades that summit-level diplomacy—facilitated by electronic communication for accelerated advanced planning and faster modes of transportation—has brought about another major change in the nature of embassies.[6] As a result, today's ambassadors spend a great deal of their time preparing more senior people from within their own governments to interact with those of others.

6.1 THE DIPLOMATIC MISSION—SOME DISTINCTIONS

Diplomatic missions today fall under several headings. In bilateral relations, embassies and consulates (or consulates-general) predominate, although trade offices and other variations on the consulate exist as well. Embassies are led by an ambassador; but between incumbents, and sometimes for reasons of tense relations or worse, they are headed up by a Chargé d'Affaires, *ad interim*. Embassies and consulates can be as small as two or three office staff but conversely can also number in the hundreds and, in rare cases, well over a thousand. In some embassies, for example the US Embassy in Kabul at the time of writing, a half-dozen ambassador-grade officials work together, with only one of them designated as *the* ambassador.

Staff within embassies fall under three broad headings: diplomatic staff, nearly always from the sending country and with a range of designations; support or administrative staff, also not nationals of the country in which the embassy is established; and support staff who are nationals of the country of accreditation, known as local (or locally-engaged) staff.[7] Much more than is widely recognized, the local staff, even when cleaving to more than one loyalty, often are responsible for a large degree of whatever success embassies can claim, knowing their own countries and how to get things done much better than do most of the diplomatic staff.

A rough distinction between embassies and consulates is that the latter are primarily preoccupied with trade and other economic matters, as well as the welfare of citizens of the sending country. They are provided *exequatur* by the receiving state within geographically defined limits, often several provinces or states of a country. They are generally to be found in major commercial centres, such as Hong Kong, Shanghai, or Guangzhou. Their importance should not be discounted; where they are located in major financial and trade centres, for example, Toronto, Sydney, or São Paolo, they can be, for the sending state, of equal significance as the embassy established in a nearby administrative capital (Ottawa, Canberra, Brasília).

Embassies, however, enjoy a wider formal remit, responsible for state-to-state relationships, with accreditation covering the whole country and often engaged in a wide range of activities detailed further on. Non-resident ambassadors (and their staff) possess broadly the same formal prerogatives, but in practice often show up only once to present their credentials or, when their travel budgets allow, several times a year, briefly, mostly to 'wave the flag'.

Resident representation at international organizations (styled as permanent missions or permanent delegations) has vastly increased since the Second World War, generally headed by an ambassador, with wide formal authority for their governments in the international microcosm involved.[8] (In practice, however, experts from capitals often conduct the most sensitive negotiations.)

The web of multilateral organizations grew spectacularly over the same period. Soon, a new form of semi-diplomatic resident representation emerged: that of one IO to another. Thus, the World Bank is represented at UN headquarters alongside the European Union (EU) and Arab League (with distinctly different mandates from their member states), each of the latter carrying ambassadorial designation. Furthermore, generally in connection with political and security crises, the UN and other bodies—such as the North Atlantic Treaty Organization (NATO) and regional organizations—nowadays frequently dispatch senior figures often with a significant entourage, as special representatives or envoys, entrusted with varying and evolving mandates, who often find themselves on the ground for years on end. These figures can be more important in practice to the host government than all but the most powerful local embassy or two.

6.2 FUNCTION OF THE EMBASSY

Beyond its symbolic role as a concrete representation of the importance attached to a bilateral relationship, the functions of an embassy are largely dictated by the nature and scale of the actual bilateral links involved. There was a time, in the heyday of decolonization (from roughly the late 1950s to the mid-1960s) when countries believed it advisable to open embassies in many of the newly independent states as a matter of solidarity, rather than because a meaningful relationship existed. Many of these new embassies soon found a vocation primarily in the aid field.

6.2.1 Political Relations

The ambassador, theoretically accredited to the head of state, in practice deals with the foreign ministry along with some others, including trade, finance, and defence, as do his team. Between two countries of modest scale and having little in common, primarily low-level actors engage each other with inconsequential chat. For those with more at stake, the relationship often warrants reciprocal visits at a political level, consultation on positions to be adopted in regional or international organizations, lobbying for electoral support in relation to candidacies in such organizations, and so forth. (Many smaller countries quite sensibly conduct the bulk of their international relations through multi-lateral institutions, where issues such as candidacies take on great immediacy, and forego the pretence and expense of bilateral embassy-level representation.)

Where the scope of the relationship encourages wider engagement, an embassy (and consulate) in all but totalitarian, or extremely authoritarian, states can engage widely with various actors, for example, with parliamentarians, analysts, and the media. Professionally meaningful relationships between significant ambassadors and ministers of the host government (often in a wide array of portfolios) are not uncommon. The purpose of such engagement is to be in a position to advance one's own country's interests and to gain a better perspective on events and opinions in the country of accreditation for interpretation back to one's own government.

Diplomatic reporting back home (often copied to other bilateral and multilateral diplomatic posts of the diplomatic network involved) was recently, in part, demystified by the 'WikiLeaks' release of an avalanche of US diplomatic documents in late 2010 and in 2011.[9] Very few diplomatic dispatches amount to works of literary or analytical genius, but the WikiLeaks trove—alongside national archives and some diplomatic diaries—reveal a number of diplomatic writers as deeply thoughtful, incisive, elegant, and convincing. While each of today's foreign services harbour a few brilliant writers, able to bring to life for their limited readership the intrigues, scandals, aspirations, and disappointments of distant lands, most of their communications are driven by operational requirements of the relationship. Other than conveying information relating to niche national interests, one successful ambassador notes: 'There's no point competing with *The Economist*!'[10] Likewise, embassy analysts are hard pressed to improve on the analytical reports of such research and advocacy organizations as the International Crisis Group on far-flung, often conflict-prone countries.

Access to information legislation in many countries has proved increasingly inhibiting for many embassy report writers. In Canada, for example, often heavily redacted but nevertheless embarrassing information was divulged by the government at the insistence of a parliamentary committee on its activities in, and views on, Afghanistan in recent years.[11] This did not help the bilateral relationship or ties to allies.

At least as damaging, although less publicly so, is the herd instinct of diplomatic operatives serving up conventional wisdom picked up on the proverbial cocktail circuit. Such
was the case of most diplomatic reporting from Iran in the 1960s, when foreign envoys
and international organizations convinced one another (and were cleverly encouraged
by the Iranian government to believe) that the country's forced march towards Western-
style modernization was proving successful. Save for a few perceptive anthropologists
and sociologists publishing in obscure journals, *bien pensant* international observers of
Iran failed to exercise much analytical acuity. Another risk for diplomats, and a characteristic much derided in sending capitals, is of the envoy or an entire embassy 'going
local', in effect representing their country of accreditation to their own capital more than
the other way around.

6.2.2 Creating Goodwill

G.R. Berridge suggests that the aim of diplomacy, and thus of an embassy, includes
'engendering goodwill'.[12] In literature and in the popular imagination, this involves
mainly the offer of agreeable hospitality to well-dressed local elites. Today, with important people busier than ever, more targeted hospitality remains extremely useful: securing the ear and sharing the analysis of leading personalities over lunch or dinner rather
than during an often hurried and inconvenient office meeting, with note-takers hovering, often yields greater dividends. Large receptions, while often encouraged by local
expectations and protocol, are generally only moderately useful. Key players are too
busy to attend. But a reputation for hosting genuinely enjoyable, interesting, and stylish
smaller events does burnish the image of an envoy and of his or her country. The hospitality expenses required generally amount to little more than 10–20 per cent of the
envoy's remuneration (hardly the princely add-on most imaginations would fancy).
And, without 'walking around money' for outreach and relationship-building, diplomatic missions are largely useless.

Other opportunities for advocacy and the promotion of goodwill include public
speaking, but this requires specific skills if an audience is to be impressed and many diplomatic services do not provide any training therefore. Serious public platforms in leading capitals invite only very few ambassadors—of great powers or those of notorious
personal distinction—to compete on their schedules with more widely known personalities. And in countries with excitable media, public speaking can involve the risk of
being innocently or deliberately misrepresented. Political actors wish to be at the centre
of media attention, and generally do not thank diplomats for casting themselves in
this role.

Cultural links can generate considerable interest and goodwill, particularly when they
are widely reviewed and broadcast. Examples include a leading film festival prize, the
visit by a noted author, or a concert by world-famous artists—all of which can help.[13]
Some cost real money, an increasingly uncomfortable fact for foreign ministries
being instructed at the political level, decade after decade, to 'do more with less'. Further,

political paymasters are sometimes sceptical of 'public diplomacy', viewing it as a costly addendum to negotiation or trade promotion. That said, much of the 'soft power' projected by countries comes at no cost to governments and can greatly help a bilateral relationship.[14]

Sporting events can play an important role in diplomacy, as is sometimes the case in South Asia with cricket. This was most famously the case with table tennis (ping pong) in publicly thawing US–Chinese relations in 1971.[15]

How countries project 'soft power' varies. India plays on its civilizational pull, the magnificence of its monuments, and the majesty of its landscapes, supplementing these with occasional artistic performances. The US has been successful in laying the emphasis on its own vibrant democracy (with all of its flaws revealed alongside its glories) and vigorous national debates refracted through its own and the international media. Further, American popular culture serves as a 'global *lingua franca*' for many.[16] US cultural production has been a huge magnet for audiences the world over. Similarly, Bollywood's more exotic charms have proved exportable to many countries and facilitated an early diplomatic thaw with Moscow in 1953.[17] More recently, a Bollywood comedy became a cult classic among Chinese students.[18]

6.2.3   Economic Interests and Trade

Business is the business of business. Yet governments believe they can successfully promote it and skittish companies, especially when entering markets new to them, tend to agree. Diplomatic representation in distant and culturally alien foreign markets can help introduce and reassure compatriots exploring local opportunities. Governmental export credit and insurance schemes have played an important role in the expansion of international trade. The latter are sometimes represented within embassies in key markets abroad.

However, often, the best that governments can do, through tortured processes of reciprocal concession, is to dismantle the barriers to trade and investment they are so wont to erect. After protectionist policies greatly aggravated the great depression of the 1930s and lessons were learned from these mistakes, the 20th century proved a good one for global economic and trade liberalization, in part through the innovation of multilateral trade negotiations, first under the General Agreement on Trade and Tariffs (GATT) and later within the framework of the World Trade Organization (WTO).

Multilateral trade diplomacy is today somewhat becalmed after a crisis in Doha Round negotiations in Geneva in 2008, but remains much in evidence through efforts to achieve myriad bilateral and regional free trade agreements (or less ambitious economic framework agreements, and preferential trade agreements), even though these are unlikely to provide the widely-shared gains of universal liberalization accords. Meanwhile, in the second half of the 20th century investment flows across borders have arguably greatly exceeded trade flows in their positive effects and have often proved larger than trade flows in goods and services.

6.2.4 Finance Diplomacy

In spite of efforts by several prominent central bankers and some treasury officials to avert the worst of the great depression of the 1930s, by and large, until quite recently, capitals developed and implemented their financial policies without much regard for those of others. The post-Second World War era financial arrangements for a time proved stabilizing.

However, after the demise of the gold standard in 1971, the final quarter of the 20th century brought about profound change, triggering increasingly frequent and severe financial and other economic crises that were globally interlinked. For example, the decision of a number of oil-producing countries in 1973, in the wake of war in the Middle East, to radically raise oil prices, provoked recession elsewhere. In response to this and subsequent crises since then, a variety of powerful consultative groups and caucuses emerged, starting with the Group of Five Finance Ministers in 1974. Consequently, 'finance diplomacy' (also generally involving central banks and sometimes multilateral secretariats), often extending well beyond immediate firefighting requirements, has become a pillar of international relations, from which foreign ministries often find themselves excluded. It is mostly conducted away from the glare of publicity, given the volatility of financial markets. Summit meetings, for example, those of the G8 and G20, to a degree bring together finance diplomacy with the more politically and security-oriented diplomacy generally staffed by foreign ministries. However, many finance and foreign ministries entertain towards each other only faintly veiled contempt. Foreign ministries believe that diplomacy should be left to them, while finance ministries hold (with a degree of justification) that foreign ministries only rarely develop the knowledge and skills necessary for productive international engagement on often technically quite complex issues.

In recent decades, finance ministries of major and aspiring economic capitals assigned to their embassies in other such capitals their own officials to handle their business (and that of central banks). This was often resisted in foreign ministries, but without success. Several key central bankers and finance ministry officials have served in these positions, honing their international skills before rising to senior appointments.

6.2.5 Trade Promotion and Policy

Quite often, as in Canada and Australia, trade and other aspects of diplomacy are managed in the same ministry. While the advantages of this arrangement are obvious, the rivalries between those with predominantly trade interests and those with greater inclination towards political relations can be as sharp as if they served in separate offices of state. In practice, political, trade, and economic officers cooperate more willingly and effectively when assigned together in embassies abroad, within which, under strong leadership, a clear sense of common purpose is more readily established.

In earlier eras, during which largely closed economies only allowed their markets to be pried open through state-to-state negotiations, embassies played an important role in promoting economic ties. Today, with many economies more open to trade and foreign investment, trade-related work in the embassy is often of a more promotional variety. Embassy trade officers can effect introductions (thus opening doors), help with appointments, and brief on local conditions. In foreign environments with strong characteristics of their own, all of this can be useful. But, in spite of tremendous support at the political level for trade as the number one priority in bilateral relations with countries such as China, India, and Brazil, the results of diplomatic trade promotion activity are uneven.

Political leaders, while sometimes reluctant to be seen as shilling for their own country's business interests, know that their domestic constituents want them to grow their economies. Nowadays, this can only be done through international engagement, even for countries with huge domestic markets. Consequently, often oversized and over-hyped 'trade missions' have proliferated, headed up by a national leader or trade minister, which sometimes take on the trappings of a flying circus. To the extent that they generate benefits, it is often for medium-sized and smaller businesses that can take advantage of the trade fair dimension of such itinerant missions. Large businesses have other ways of relating to each other and to meaningful centres of power in potential market countries. For the host authorities (and the host embassy), overblown trade extravaganzas can be a nightmare.[19]

Multilateral and important bilateral trade negotiations are managed primarily by senior trade officials travelling to negotiations from their own capitals, although these teams are often supported by resident diplomats or resident negotiators accredited to the WTO in Geneva (or, for example, the EU headquarters in Brussels) with a good sense of the local terrain and preoccupations.

6.2.6 Development Assistance

In the heyday of development assistance (which, in global volume terms, may well have peaked in 2009–2010), the deployment of large numbers of government staff to 'the field' in order to oversee and administer development programming was a growth industry. It caused Western embassies, notably in Africa, to swell considerably. In many countries, ambassadors were themselves development experts rather than drawn from other fields of diplomacy. Fashion has waxed and waned on mass deployment of aid ministry staff to the field—an expensive proposition. In spite of signal advances of developing continents in literacy, agricultural productivity, local health systems, and the fight against some contagious diseases, the exact correlation with development assistance (which clearly often played some role therein) is difficult to establish. 'Aid effectiveness' and other slogans succeed each other, always in search of demonstrable and preferably spectacular results. But where large sums are expended, as today in Afghanistan, the West Bank, and Sudan, the concerns of taxpayers over the depredations of local corruption and inefficiency often conflict with high-minded principles committing to local control over aid disbursement, advanced in such donor statements as The Paris Declaration (2005) and Accra Agenda (2008).

It is not yet clear what long-term implications the financial and economic crisis of 2008–2009 (during which economic growth performance of developing countries far outstripped that of donor countries) will have for the 'development biz'. It may well be that official development assistance is now fated to drop, in view both of the growing success of different development models in the global South, but also because such assistance patently had very little to do with the recent 'emergence' as global and regional economic powerhouses, of China, India, Brazil, and South Africa. The future of aid may, increasingly, be humanitarian in goal, or of the temporary stabilizing sort offered by the International Monetary Fund. Bilateral donors may increasingly be tempted to divest themselves of aid ministries, channelling remaining assistance through such implementing agencies as the Red Cross system and the World Bank.

6.2.7 Migration and Visas

While often seen as primarily a consular function, the issuance of visas, including those eventually leading to permanent resettlement, is for many countries both politically sensitive and economically important. With terrorism a growing concern internationally and documentary fraud both rampant and highly accomplished in some countries, the work involved can require a high degree of expertise and sharp judgement. For countries encouraging immigration, such as the US, UK, Australia, and Canada, with an eye to boosting their economies, the processing of a single immigration file can be an immensely painstaking task, sometimes requiring several years. Thus, immigration and visa staff can be surprisingly large. For example in New Delhi, Canada's High Commission in 2011 numbered 122 immigration and visa staff out of a total number of 407 staff, including 28 out of its 62 Canadian staff.[20] Visitor visas (often more rapidly issued) can also absorb a great deal of effort (and generate a lot of frustration at the level of applicants). While growing numbers of countries have been able to shift to tourism visas 'on arrival' for some, in recent years there has been a counter-trend, with borders 'thickening' in the wake of the events of 11 September 2001 and with economies under stress in the West.

6.2.8 Consular Relations

Consular duties revolve mostly around documentation and fair local treatment for citizens of the consul's nationality (notarization, registration of births for nationality purposes, liaison with those facing criminal or other charges by local authorities, etc.). Mostly routine, consular duties can prove politically sensitive where public opinion becomes inflamed in either country involved. Western publics tend to assume that any compatriot in trouble abroad must be innocent. The standards of prisons in some parts of the world do not equate to those elsewhere. Nor, in many cases, is adherence to due process and the prevalence of the rule of law deeply entrenched. In cases where opinion in the home country of a detainee, often spurred by sensationalist media coverage, is aroused, parliaments and ministers are soon under pressure to relieve, somehow, the plight of their compatriot. Naturally, the country where the charges have been laid may look at the matter somewhat differently, leading to bilateral tensions requiring careful management.

The 'honorary consul' is normally a citizen of the country in which she or he works, often a prominent business leader with the local connections and the competence necessary to be of assistance to citizens (and economic actors) from the countries appointing them. In many countries, they can be the sole form of diplomatic representation of another state. Although enjoying limited privileges and immunities (being resident in their own countries), they derive some prestige from the role.

Consular relations can require deft skills at times and involvement by ambassadors to secure outcomes seen back home as tolerable, if not good, for their nationals.

6.2.9 Security and Intelligence

Among the diplomatic staff of embassies going back many decades, one reliable standby is the military attaché, dispatched to entertain relations with the host country's defence ministry and armed forces (and to provide information back home on its strengths and vulnerabilities). In some respects the institution is anachronistic (and, when seen en masse, the corps of military attachés can look ideally outfitted for service in a Gilbert and Sullivan *opera bouffe*, many bedecked in extravagant uniforms).[21] Nevertheless, in reality it can be important, given the weight of military procurement decisions in overall global trade and the saliency of geostrategic factors in some regions of the world. These officials of military rank often hold themselves aloof from other members of the embassy staff.

For different reasons, so, often, do intelligence liaison officials. Rather like their military counterparts, they relate to the intelligence authorities of the host state, whose relevant institutions are sometimes numerous and frequently opaque. The notion in popular fiction, particularly prevalent during the cold war, of espionage rings being run out of embassies by covert intelligence operatives, a reality then for several of the great powers and some others, is now less convincing with electronic espionage more the flavour of the day. That said, 'human intelligence' remains a vital link in sensitive information gathering, thus a degree of espionage is also present in the activities of some modern embassies. The professional activities of the incumbents are usually concealed by anodyne diplomatic designations.[22] But, very often, informed observers figure out which diplomats are entrusted with intelligence responsibilities.[23] The presence of intelligence officers, with their own lines of communication to their own authorities at home can arouse discomfort within some embassies, where ambassadors have 'had to learn to live with colleagues whose...very presence in their missions may compromise their relations with host governments'.[24]

As well, non-intelligence related security liaison can be important. Several national police forces the world over assign to their embassies, in the capitals of important nations facing criminal problems interlocking with their own, a police liaison unit often charged with evidence-sharing and cooperation on prosecutions.

6.2.10 Other, Specialized Economic Functions within Embassies

In vital markets, in order better to overcome trade barriers and also master local phytosanitary measures, some countries assign diplomats designated to work primarily or exclusively on agricultural matters. Elsewhere, sectors relating to natural resources and health might merit their own counsellor, secretary, or attaché within an embassy.

6.3 PERMANENT REPRESENTATION TO AND OF INTERNATIONAL ORGANIZATIONS

Permanent missions and delegations to international organizations (or standing conferences) take on many roles similar to those of embassies, although, within IOs, the ambassadors represent shareholders as well as stakeholders. Ambassadors are correspondingly more powerful locally (albeit within a much smaller bubble).

Certain IOs play critical roles. The Security Council of the UN, the Executive Boards of the international financial institutions, and the Council of NATO are all genuinely meaningful bodies. In some cases, regional organizations can be both credible and effective. Such is mostly the case of the EU, sometimes of the Organization of American States (OAS), and at times of the Economic Community of West African States (ECOWAS) and its military 'monitoring' group, ECOMOG, which has mounted several impressive military interventions. The representatives of key states within these bodies play a vital role. But the contemporary sprawl of the multilateral system is alarming, with new institutions frequently created without others being abolished. Much of it displays ineffectiveness. At times, it can seem like a self-interested conspiracy to talk and talk at inflated rates of pay.

The secretariats of IOs and related personnel are often central to effective firefighting, damage-limitation, urgent humanitarian, and other such functions. The individuals involved in mediation, conflict prevention and resolution or urgent field activities can rise well above the formal mandates of their positions, as demonstrated by Dag Hammarskjöld and Kofi Annan in the office of UN Secretary-General. The contrast

between talented, dynamic leadership of a UN peacekeeping or peace-building operation and a less energetic and committed approach can make the difference between unh-
eralded success and failure with dramatic results. Indeed, the difference that individuals
can make within large, faceless international bureaucracies can be striking, and the same
is true in bilateral embassies.[25]

6.4 Proliferation of Diplomatic Missions and Designations

Most members of the public have little reason to think about foreign services and the
diplomatic missions that dot various capitals. Brussels, with bilateral embassies, permanent delegations to NATO, and permanent missions to the EU, as well as significant
bureaucracies of the latter two organizations, perhaps takes the prize for density of
diplomatic representation. Yet Vienna, with bilateral embassies and separate missions
to the Organization for Security and Co-operation in Europe (OSCE) and a wide
range of UN agencies; Geneva, with the WTO as well as a multitude of UN agencies
and programmes; Nairobi, as an African hub with many bilateral missions and also
the headquarters of the UN Environment Programme (UNEP); and perhaps above all
Washington, where all countries wish to have bilateral representation (although North
Korea and Iran are currently denied it), together with the OAS, and the international
financial institutions (on a fairly vast scale), do very well out of the economic spin-offs
of the institutional underpinnings of international relations.

Were all of this not so expensive, the overlapping mandates of institutions and missions might attract little attention. But with the cost of an 'international' employee running often three to four times higher than that of a national one at home, international
diplomatic and IO representation today seems considerably overextended and at risk.
For example, the EU, with its own complicated machinery involving courts, tribunals, a
parliament, a very large executive agency (in the form of the Commission), and now its
own diplomatic service, overlaps with the diplomatic representation of member states,
including in each other's capitals. Rationalization of one sort or another seems likely in
decades ahead, no matter how loath states are to give up or share the symbols of their
sovereignty across the globe.

Former Nigerian foreign minister Ibrahim Gambari argues that many items of diplomatic business and relationship-building can be carried out it in multilateral organizations such as the UN and the African Union. And because leaders and ministers carry
forward the critical files in direct communication with each other, the deployment, size,
and expense of diplomatic missions everywhere is bound to come under greater scrutiny as budgets continue to tighten in most countries around the world. 'The choices of
capitals for establishing and maintaining embassies as well as [how to staff them] must
be more rigorous and cost effective.'[26]

6.5 Innovative Approaches
to Cost Sharing

Given the very high costs of maintaining a network of embassies globally, sometimes in countries either of little account or where few bilateral interests exist, one might have expected foreign ministries to pursue more energetically the possibility of fielding joint embassies. Several European countries have done so, but often not to the extent of all the member states doing so in a given country, and never in major capitals. Australia and Canada gingerly experimented with the concept, with one of them taking on the responsibility to represent a range of interests of the other in certain countries; but even capitals as close as these have not perservered energetically with the experiment.

Financial constraints on foreign ministries as well as the process of European integration may, ultimately, produce further efforts of this sort. The emergence of new countries, such as South Sudan, should make such joint operations tempting; but, in its capital, Juba, where a joint aid representation involving a number of countries was launched and proved at least moderately successful over several years, powers viewing themselves as 'great', or that cultivate local ambitions, opt to operate solo.

Another means of saving on cost is to appoint non-resident ambassadors living in the sending country and sallying back and forth to countries of accreditation only as often as bilateral interests dictate. Norway experimented with this model several decades ago and Singapore has adopted it with some success in recent years (appointing citizens of notable distinction to these positions).

Notions of national prestige have long driven decisions, even by very poor countries, to fund more embassies than seems required or affordable. Brazil, as part of its process of global 'emergence', embarked early in the new century on an ambitious expansion of its impressive diplomatic network of resident missions, seeing its growing number of embassies and other forms of diplomatic representation (seventy new missions, of which approximately forty were embassies) as a tangible manifestation of its new international weight and influence.[27] The Indian government also recently secured from its parliament authority to expand its talented but overworked and surprisingly small foreign service.[28] Meanwhile, powers whose relative weight was declining only reluctantly junked a few small missions to propitiate irate treasuries and parliaments determined that diplomacy should not trump domestic needs. The UK Foreign Office came face to face with the exigencies of cost-cutting throughout the twenty years preceding 2010, when a serious fiscal deficit forced London greatly to increase and accelerate cuts (while some domestically-oriented ministries faced even greater ones).

Still, none of the public, media, parliament, or government in most countries seized the opportunity of a fiscal crisis to rethink fundamentally either the nature or global deployment of its resident diplomatic representation. Dire fiscal exigencies may yet dictate such change; but as of early 2012, 'efficiency savings' were still more the mantra than structural change.

6.6 How is the Role of Diplomatic Missions Changing?

In the postcolonial era diplomatic missions proliferated, thus dispelling their mystique. Furthermore, a diplomatic assignment is rarely nowadays exotic in the way it might have been a century ago. The skills required are different: foreign languages, while very useful, are no longer vital in much diplomacy, given the increasing prevalence of English as the language of global exchange (although in Latin America, Spanish continues to hold its own, as does French in francophone Africa, and knowledge of Arabic can be an asset in the Middle East). While writing skills are still useful, indeed important, within a foreign service, the relative decline of the market at home for 'old order' diplomatic reports, briefing notes, cabinet memoranda, and such, makes exceptional drafting abilities seem like a luxury. On the other hand, a sense of history and its influence on contemporary developments and future ones, economic literacy, an interest in the social underpinnings of a country and in the interaction between various economic and social groups within a nation, are all still vital.

Diplomats are no longer widely seen as essential actors, even when they are. Those at headquarters are often impatient with colleagues serving on distant postings and vice versa (although rotation between capital and field and back helps with this syndrome). Neither believes they entirely need the other. Only the most important, skilled, and engaging diplomats stand out in crowded capitals.

An air of superfluity hangs over diplomats for a further reason: a great deal of information, well beyond that on offer in the media and from the academic world, is now available to anyone with a computer or even a mobile phone. The latter category contains more than 650 million Chinese and an equivalent number of Indians. Much of the information available on the Web contains errors and conceals agendas, but the value of high-quality information is less prized today amidst such quantities on offer, mostly free of charge. Well-trained foreign service personnel are much better equipped to seek out and interpret information relevant to their country or IO of accreditation than is the average mobile phone owner, but this may not be widely prized. And while an effective ambassador may be able to generate much greater local interest in and access for a visiting minister or CEO than would otherwise be the case, the value of this intuitively attractive proposition is hard to demonstrate to cost-cutters.

6.7 The Role and Disposition of the Successful Envoy

Pierre Schori, a contributor to this volume and a very successful Swedish politician, ambassador, and UN envoy, lays emphasis on the need for 'a mix of diplomacy, politics, social and media skills'.[29] In truth, with the proliferation of diplomatic missions, many of those called upon to lead them lack some or all of these qualities. In one recent case, a European capital decided to leave in place a patently inept ambassador after its election to the UN Security Council, counting on his talented deputy to do the running, for reasons that seemed related to political loyalty and patronage considerations back home.

In canvassing a number of the most successful ambassadors and foreign ministers of our age for this chapter, several themes recurred. A successful envoy is one who telegraphs empathy for the country or situation of interlocutors. In the words of John McCarthy, a former Australian envoy, 'you must travel and above all demonstrate you are interested in your host country. People know when you are not.'[30] In the absence of such interest, all the indicators of diplomatic success—access, knowledge, the ability to make a case in terms that might find local favour, capacity to keep one's own business, political, and other constituencies happy—will evaporate.

A surprising number of ambassadors project an air of either mindless superiority or of being on automatic pilot—no way to impress others. Making friends is a key requirement of the job in order to accumulate a capital of personal goodwill that will generate dividends when hard negotiations are required or negative circumstances develop. In multilateral negotiations, generally the most successful delegates are those who cultivate others and who give as well as take. Maximalist posturing may briefly impress the gallery at home but is unlikely to produce happy results over time at the international level.

The single characteristic of diplomacy that came up most often in my survey was the 'human factor'. Former Indian Foreign Secretary Shyam Saran writes of the need to nurture 'the network of human relationships' that drives ties between states.[31] Thus, while the interests of states may appear immutable (although subject to varying interpretations), a variable factor in diplomacy is the human capacity for creativity in the search for compromise and an ability to transcend zero-sum calculations. In trying to deconstruct Saran's success as his country's envoy to several Asian nations, some of them entertaining tense relations with New Delhi, I concluded that, beyond his intellectual qualities, it was his empathy that allowed him to overcome well-honed local reservations about his country. He writes:

> Cross cultural communication for me is not merely tolerance for ways of life or patterns of thinking different from our own. It is, rather, the willingness to understand and to appreciate what lies behind those differences. The exploration of another culture is like reading a book in which each page you turn holds the key to another hundred.[32]

But this is so only for those with a natural disposition towards engagement.

Another factor in the successful envoy is an ability to focus on the one, two, or three issues that matter in the bilateral relationship. At times, in some places, and for some countries, high diplomacy of a geostrategic nature lies at its heart. But in other circumstances, mundane if vital issues connected with international migration, a controversial consular case, or a key commercial contract may be more germane. Having a clear sense of one's own capital and its concerns is key, and this is difficult for envoys who move seamlessly from one foreign capital to another for years on end without returning to live at home for periods in between. Perhaps with this in mind, former Swiss ambassador Jenö Staehelin highlights the 'increasing need for diplomats with specialist knowledge instead of generalists and all-rounders'.[33]

The talented French Arabist and media specialist Charles Henri d'Aragon, a popular and successful envoy to several countries, notes that embassies have an important role to play in dispelling enduring stereotypes that both host and sending countries can nurture of each other and that can undermine their mutual interest in cooperation of various sorts.[34] This is indeed vital in relations between Western and Middle Eastern capitals.

An important distinction needs to qualify the lines above. The characteristics of a locally important foreign ambassador will be studied (even over-interpreted) to a much greater extent than those of one who does not much matter. In that sense, it is doubtless more challenging to serve as American ambassador to Egypt than as Canadian envoy to Ruritania.

6.8 Are Embassies Necessary
in the 21st Century?

Wegger Strommen, Norway's accomplished ambassador in Washington, points out that an embassy 'is still, for many states, in particular smaller ones, a symbol of sovereignty, a sign of life'.[35] As well, embassies serve as forward logistical bases for political-level interactions, where they are warranted. But they are not always. Mexican policy expert and former UN ambassador Enrique Berruga argues that very limited operations may be as successful as full service missions in many places.[36] Other than engaging in the major capitals of the world, it is neighbours who most need to work on understanding each other. Thus, a Peruvian embassy in Ecuador may be as important as its mission in Washington or at the EU.

Strommen speculates that, while the number of diplomats is bound to fall as government finances tighten and information technology picks up some of the slack, the diplomatic mission in important capitals is safe—governments require confidentiality for some sensitive information and capitals wish to know that they have trusted, knowledgeable individuals on the ground capable of doing their bidding against stiff competition.

Even as ambassadors become less prominent, paradoxically they may need to be more accomplished. Thomas Pickering, a much admired former US ambassador and Washington senior veteran, suggests that those 'who serve in embassies will need to be better educated, prepared and trained . . . in a world in which interaction between states and peoples is growing rapidly. They will need to deal much more with groups outside of the government sphere', including the private sector, media, academics, and NGOs, 'in hundreds of different areas of life and work'. Arguing that diplomats will need to be even more successful as knowledge brokers between societies, he concludes that 'good diplomacy requires serious long term effort and deep commitment'.[37] Another, less delicate, way of describing the growing challenge for envoys today is that the dilettantism that sometimes served as a substitute for professionalism in past decades no longer passes muster.

The emergence of powerful new information technologies might suggest that public diplomacy can now be handled electronically. John Dauth, Australia's High Commissioner in London, notes that while social networks present opportunities for vastly expanded communication, decisions on what and how to communicate require more skill and thought than classic media relations used to; the cost of mistakes as well as the rewards for success are much greater.

Thus, while social networks will allow for much greater outreach, personal contact and targeted, individualized messaging will remain vital on sensitive matters affecting national interests. Face-to-face as opposed to electronic communication remains vital, as anybody prominent in the private sector, media, wider government, and civil society worlds knows all too well. This comes through particularly strongly in the personal experience of leading figures of the global South, including South Africa's dynamic Dumisani Kumalo.[38]

Indeed, the need for more public diplomacy of varying sorts in this age of accelerated global interaction is one of the major challenges facing foreign ministries in straitened fiscal circumstances and their missions in the field. Derek Burney, a former Canadian ambassador to the US, makes the point that in important bilateral relationships with significant economic interests at play, advocacy will become more rather than less important.[39]

Thus, the form of diplomacy, and its most visible symbol, the diplomatic mission, is open to considerable change as it adapts to a fast-moving 21st century. And it has competition. Carne Ross, a former British diplomat several years ago founded Independent Diplomat, an institution created to advocate internationally on behalf of those beyond the drawbridge of formal diplomacy, something the institution did very well on behalf of South Sudan in the run-up to its referendum on independence in January 2011. Ross writes: 'The reality of the world is that channels of communication are becoming more diverse and diffuse, and the...funnelling of data entailed by routing them through an embassy runs counter to this trend.'[40] If Ross is right, and I think he is, embassies need to make themselves more accessible to a wider range of interlocutors on a wider range of issues.

6.9 ENVOI

Jean-David Levitte, foreign policy adviser to two of France's presidents and a superb envoy, asserts that the central purpose of the modern diplomat remains that of working to develop human relationships, with the word as primary tool. What is his advice?

Above all, 'listen and then think' before speaking.[41] On one level, this may appear elementary, but the dynamics of contemporary society militate against listening, reflection, and learning, not least as social media and electronic communication (through blogging and otherwise) have unleashed a torrent of self-expression not always matched by eagerness to learn. Further, politicians score immediate points for placing the views and interests of their constituents first, not necessarily for appearing thoughtful on the international stage.

Akin to Saran's analysis, Levitte advocates entering into the 'reasoning and form of thought and expression' of interlocutors, in order to more readily attract them into one's own. A willingness and capacity for compromise is also vital, but not in terms of establishing a mid-point in a disagreement. Rather, with the human imagination being such a rich instrument, a savvy negotiator may well not only deliver on key national objectives, but also leave the other side feeling it has achieved more than it has given up.[42]

Thus, while technological change both enhances and undermines classic diplomacy, little has changed in the central functions of an ambassador with a serious (rather than mainly representational) mandate. Early in the new millennium, her or his key tasks and the winning elements of diplomatic style would immediately be familiar to Benjamin Franklin, Thomas Jefferson, Viscount Granville, or Charles Maurice de Talleyrand-Périgord—practitioners of the profession over two centuries ago.

Notes

1. Keith Hamilton and Richard Langhorne, *The Practice of Diplomacy: Its evolution, theory and administration*, 2nd ed. (Abingdon, UK and New York, NY: Routledge, 2011), 7.
2. Countries of the Commonwealth exchange high commissioners rather than ambassadors (who hold equal rank in diplomatic protocol).
3. See Riccardo Fubini, 'Diplomacy and government in the Italian city-states of the fifteenth century (Florence and Venice)', in Daniela Frigo (ed.), *Politics and Diplomacy in Early Modern Italy* (Cambridge: Cambridge University Press, 2011), 25–48.
4. See Geoffrey Allen Pigman, *Contemporary Diplomacy* (Cambridge: Polity Press, 2010), 19–20; see also Sir Ivor Roberts (ed.), *Satow's Diplomatic Practice*, 6th ed. (New York: Oxford University Press, 2009), 10–11; and G.R. Berridge, *Diplomacy: Theory and Practice* (New York, NY: Palgrave, 2002), 5.
5. Ludwik Dembinski, *The Modern Law of Diplomacy: External missions of states and international organizations* (Dordrecht: Martinus Nijhoff, 1988), 3.
6. See Margaret MacMillan, *Paris 1919: Six Months That Changed the World* (New York: Random House, 2002).
7. This distinction between foreign staff with diplomatic designations and administrative staff without has, in many cases, now fallen into disuse as many countries for reasons of equity, security, and immunity provide diplomatic designation to all of their nationals serving in diplomatic and consular missions.
8. In these multilateral missions, particularly those at the UN in New York, countries sometimes field more than one ambassador—although only ever one permanent representative—leading to a profusion of delegates viewed, at least by themselves, as being of some importance.

9. Sharp judgement and foresight aplenty by US diplomats were among the less discussed but nevertheless principal revelations of the WikiLeaks episode, confounding both cynics and reflexive critics of the US. Some of these reports played a role in discrediting the regimes in Cairo and in Tunis before their fall in early 2011.

10. Confidential correspondence, January 2011.

11. For a sophisticated discussion of the impact of both Freedom of Information legislation and WikiLeaks on modern diplomacy, see John McCarthy, 'Wikileaks [sec = unclassified]', *Asialink* 3:1 (2011), available at: <http://www.asialink.unimelb.edu.au/publications/the_asialink_essays/WikiLeaks_SECUNCLASSIFIED>.

12. Berridge, *Diplomacy*, 1.

13. In India, much of the country's political elite, from Sonia Gandhi on down, would turn out to hear visiting classical artists from Pakistan whose fan base in India was considerable.

14. See David M. Malone, 'Canada and India: Distant Solitudes?', *Literary Review of Canada* (April 2011), 11.

15. Henry Kissinger, *White House Years* (Toronto: Little, Brown and Company, 1979), 708–10.

16. Todd Gitlin, 'World Leaders: Mickey et al.', *New York Times*, 3 May 1992.

17. Tom Wright, 'Medvedev Rekindles Russia's Cold War Bollywood Affair', *The Wall Street Journal*, 22 December 2010.

18. Ananth Krishnan, 'For China's stressed-out students, all is not well', *The Hindu*, 30 January 2011.

19. Some years ago, Mexicans privately complained bitterly after the event about Canadian political show-boating in leading an oversized 'Team Canada' trade mission to Mexico that accomplished little while completely exhausting both official and private sector hosts.

20. Figures provided by the Canadian High Commission in India in January 2011.

21. Lawrence Durrell, beyond his novels, such as those of the Alexandria Quartet, was sharp and quite amusing on military attachés and other diplomatic types in his three collections of 'Antrobus' short stories, derived from his diplomatic experience in Belgrade from 1948 to 1952.

22. One of my UK colleagues in Jordan, a quiet but very accomplished one, attracted little attention to himself. He later became the head of the UK's external intelligence service, MI6, in part due to the then secret intelligence successes he scored while serving under diplomatic cover in Amman.

23. As was the case during my years of service in Cairo for the local CIA station chiefs.

24. Hamilton and Langhorne, *The Practice of Diplomacy*, 196.

25. Galvanizing leadership of UN peace missions by the likes of Lakhdar Brahimi, Sergio Vieira de Mello, and Ian Martin stands in contrast to the humdrum atmosphere pertaining elsewhere. Further, top-flight international operators of their ilk also attract the best staffs, so their mere participation at the head of a mission accrues side-benefits near-automatically.

26. Correspondence, 14 February 2011.

27. The website of Brazil's foreign ministry indicates that during President Lula da Silva's two-term eight-year presidency (2003–2010), sixty-eight new missions were opened.

28. See David M. Malone, *Does the Elephant dance? Contemporary Indian Foreign Policy* (Oxford: Oxford University Press, 2011), 7–8.

29. Correspondence, 24 January 2011.

30. Correspondence, 27 January 2011.

31. Correspondence, 23 January 2011.

32. See Shyam Saran, 'On Cross-Cultural Conversations: Ruminations of a Diplomat', available at <http://www.manushi.in/articles.php?articleId=1492>.

33. Correspondence, 31 January 2011.

34. Correspondence, 11 February 2011.

35. Correspondence, 29 January 2011.

36. Correspondence, 14 February 2011.

37. Correspondence, 1 February 2011.

38. Correspondence, 30 January 2011.

39. Correspondence, 24 January 2011.

40. Correspondence, 14 February 2011.

41. Remarks by Jean-David Levitte to the Institut de France, 17 January 2011.

42. Correspondence, 25 January 2011.

CHAPTER 7

....

INTERNATIONAL ORGANIZATIONS AND DIPLOMACY

....

MARGARET P. KARNS AND KAREN A. MINGST

In the 20th and 21st centuries, international organizations (IOs) and particularly international intergovernmental organizations (IGOs) have become major arenas for diplomacy and decision-making. They are key pieces of global governance, providing cooperative problem-solving arrangements and activities to address international problems. They are also independent actors engaging in diplomatic activities to galvanize international attention, carry out their mandates, work directly with governments, non-governmental organizations (NGOs), and other IGOs. The universe of international organizations includes IGOs, but also less formal IOs such as the Group of Seven/Eight (G7/8) and Group of Twenty (G20), as well as NGOs. It is IGOs and diplomacy that form the focus of this chapter.

7.1 THE WORLD OF IGOS

....

IGOs are organizations whose members include at least three states, that have activities in several states, and which are created through a formal intergovernmental agreement (treaty, charter, statute). The *Yearbook of International Organizations* identifies about 240 IGOs. IGOs range in size from 3 members (North American Free Trade Agreement (NAFTA)) to 193 members plus observers (United Nations (UN)). Their members come from primarily one geographic region (Organization of American States (OAS)), more than one region (Organization of the Islamic Conference (OIC)), or from all regions (World Bank). Although some IGOs are designed to achieve a single purpose (Organization of Petroleum Exporting Countries (OPEC)), others have been developed for multiple tasks (Association of Southeast Asian States (ASEAN)). Most are not global in membership, but regional, sub-regional, or specialized where common interests motivate states to cooperate. Indeed, most regions have multiple formal organizations with overlapping memberships as well as informal partnerships and regular summits. Europe has the densest concentration of IGOs with Asia, especially Southeast and East Asia, showing the most rapid growth since the cold war's end.

Major power wars (the First and Second World Wars), economic development, technological innovation, and the growth of the state system in the 20th century provided impetus for creating many IGOs. Since the 1960s, there has also been a growing phenomenon of IGOs creating other IGOs. Since the mid-1980s, IGO growth has slowed, however, and the death rates of IGOs remain low.[1]

The growing agenda of international problems from climate change to terrorism has contributed to the increased role of IGOs and expansion of various global governance mechanisms. Thus, more international diplomacy takes place in and through IGOs. The parallel proliferation in the number and types of other actors in world affairs has required IGOs to adapt to more complex forms of network diplomacy involving NGOs, corporations, and other IGOs.

IGOs serve a variety of functions, from collecting and analysing information and monitoring trends (United Nations Environment Programme (UNEP)), delivering services and aid (United Nations High Commissioner for Refugees (UNHCR)), to providing forums for intergovernmental decision-making (European Parliament), establishing norms and rules (UN General Assembly (UNGA)), and adjudicating disputes (International Court of Justice (ICJ)).[2] By helping states form stable habits of cooperation through regular meetings and dispute settlement, IGOs also 'construct the social world in which cooperation and choice take place'.[3]

How IGOs serve various functions varies across organizations as they differ in membership, scope of their agendas and rules, resources, level and degree of bureaucratization, and effectiveness. Regional organizations, in particular, vary widely in their organizational structures, the obligations they impose on member states, their resources, and the scope of activities. Likewise, multilateral diplomacy within them ranges from the formality and legalism of the European Union (EU) or the quasi-parliamentary coalition diplomacy of the UNGA to the loose, informal concertization of policies found in Asia-Pacific Economic Cooperation (APEC) and ASEAN. The EU's authority to represent member states in international trade negotiations, for example, requires extensive diplomacy within the Union among the members and with the Commission.

7.1.1 The Evolution of Diplomacy in IGOs

Diplomacy in IGOs is predominantly multilateral although states will frequently use IGO meetings to conduct bilateral diplomacy and IGO secretariats engage in bilateral diplomacy with member states, other IGOs, and NGOs. Since the early 20th century, multilateral negotiations have become key 'management tools in international politics'.[4]

Understanding the nature of multilateral diplomacy is, therefore, important to understanding how IGOs function, how NGOs have become involved in governance processes, and how different kinds of outcomes come about.[5]

IGOs have played a major role in the elaboration and evolution of multilateral diplomacy. During the 19th century, a number of international river commissions and public international unions such as the Universal Postal Union were created to address practical problems. At the same time, the Concert of Europe organized a series of periodic gatherings of great (European) powers. Both established precedents for later international organizations and multilateral diplomacy. For example, the concert idea of mutual consultations was the foundation for the UN Security Council and can be seen also in the G7/8 and G20. The public international unions introduced the practice of involving specialists from outside ministries of foreign affairs as well as private interest groups.

From the creation of the League of Nations at the end of the First World War to the United Nations and the creation of many regional and specialized organizations following the Second World War, there was an accelerated trend from bilateral to multilateral diplomacy. Because the UN is the only IGO with global scope and nearly universal membership whose agenda encompasses the broadest range of governance issues, it has become the central site for multilateral diplomacy. As Ramesh Thakur notes, 'the United Nations is an essential arena in which states actually codify norms in the form of resolutions and declarations (soft law) as well as conventions and treaties (hard law).'[6] Yet the proliferation of international and regional organizations as well as various 'Gs', ad hoc conferences, and summits has created other arenas for multilateral diplomacy.

Hence, multilateralism in the 21st century is far more complex than multilateralism at the end of the Second World War. It is also multilevel, involving sub-national, national, transnational, and international arenas as well as hundreds of participants. Where IGO diplomacy in the past was almost exclusively club diplomacy, today it is a mix of club and network diplomacy.

Greater numbers of players (and coalitions of players) mean multiple interests, rules, issues, and hierarchies that are constantly changing. These all complicate the processes of finding common ground for reaching agreements. Managing complexity has become a key challenge, therefore, for participants in multilateral diplomacy. For example, UN-sponsored intergovernmental global conferences typically have several thousand delegates from 193 countries, speaking through interpreters in English, French, Russian, Chinese, Spanish, and Arabic. There are also likely to be hundreds of NGOs and citizens from civil society. As one veteran noted, 'They are all interested in the subject matter under discussion, all want to be kept informed of every detail, and all have the possibility of being present at almost all of the sessions.'[7]

NGOs are active in UN conferences, regular sessions of many UN bodies, and in other IGOs. They are also key actors with UN agencies, for example, in dealing with humanitarian crises, delivering development assistance, and contributing to post-conflict peace-building missions, all of which require extensive diplomacy. A central issue for many IGOs is how to better incorporate non-state actors in their deliberative and decision-making processes—in short, into IGO diplomacy.[8]

7.1.2 Multilateral Diplomacy and IGO Decision Processes

Many of the techniques used within IGOs have been borrowed from national parliaments, referred to as 'parliamentary diplomacy'. Where voting is used, decisions are often made on the basis of one-state/one-vote either by simple or qualified majority such as two-thirds of those present and voting on an 'important' question in the UN General Assembly. An alternative principle uses weighted voting to give greater weight to some states on the basis of population or wealth. In the International Monetary Fund (IMF) and World Bank, for example, votes are weighted according to financial contribution. The UN Security Council illustrates another form of qualified majority voting with the five permanent members each possessing a veto requiring all to concur (or not object) for decisions taken. The International Labour Organization (ILO) exemplifies yet another type of decision-making with each member state represented by two government officials and one representative each from labour and management, all with individual votes. Both the nature of the IGO and the decision-making process will affect diplomacy within the organization.

Since the 1980s, much of the decision-making in the UN General Assembly, Security Council, the World Trade Organization (WTO), regional organizations such as ASEAN, and many other multilateral settings has taken the form of consensus. Consensus does not require unanimity; it depends on states deciding not to block action and it often means that outcomes represent the least common denominator, i.e. more general wording and fewer tough demands on states.

Whether building consensus in an IGO or trying to put together a winning majority, various types of skills associated with multilateral diplomacy are required: leadership; small, formal negotiating groups; economic or military resources or ability to serve as a broker; informal contacts among actors; and personal attributes such as intelligence, patience, reputation, negotiating skills, and linguistic versatility. Actual negotiating styles vary considerably and the culture within an IGO can be an important variable. ASEAN, for example, is noted for the 'ASEAN Way'—consensual decision-making through discussion, consultation, and mutual adjustment in which open disagreement and controversy are avoided. By contrast, the UN was marked for years by the North–South conflict and the Group of 77's use of its two-thirds majority to dominate the proceedings.

7.1.3 States, IGOs, and Diplomacy

IGOs exist only because states create them through a formal agreement that grants authority to the IGO and outlines its functions. Explicitly or implicitly, states have the power to revoke that authority. IGOs depend on states for funding and operational capabilities.

Different international relations theories provide varying views on the relationship between states and IGOs. States may join IGOs and utilize them to further their national interests, as realists posit. Or, as liberal institutionalism and functionalism assert, IGOs provide arenas for solving practical problems such as coordinating telecommunications or transportation. States may depend on IGOs to provide public goods such as public health and protection of the global commons, as collective goods theorists suggest. Or, states may utilize IGOs to assure others that their own actions and commitments are credible, as neo-liberal institutionalists posit.

Principal–agent theorists have long viewed IGOs as agents of their member states (principals) since they are formed by states and states grant IGOs responsibilities and authority. Yet, few IGOs are direct agents of individual states. Even the US now has decreasing ability to use any particular IGO as its agent.

Rather than one principal/state exerting power over an IGO/agent, more likely is the presence of collective principals, a small group of dominant states which make IGOs their effective agents through control of finances and personnel. For example, the United States, Japan, Canada, and European countries have long jointly commanded more than 60 per cent of the votes in the IMF's weighted voting system. When collective principals disagree, in fact, more power may flow to individuals in the IGO making that organization more independent from states. And, with the rise of China, India, Brazil, and Turkey, power and votes are shifting in the IMF and many other IGOs.[9]

Recent variations on principal–agent theory combined with constructivism have yielded valuable insights on IGO autonomy showing how they are not just tools of states, but are purposive actors that have power and authority. Barnett and Finnemore argue, 'The authority of IOs, and bureaucracies generally, therefore, lies in their ability to present themselves as impersonal and neutral—as not exercising power but instead serving others.'[10] The need to be seen in this way is crucial, for example, to the UN Secretariat, the World Food Programme (WFP), and the EU Commission's credibility. And, with multiple sources of funding available for some IGO activities, Thakur notes 'that the "agents" can go "principal shopping" in order to evade or dilute control by a particular principal'.[11]

Because all IGOs are not alike, the diplomacy within them can vary significantly. We turn, therefore, to examine how such variations affect diplomacy.

7.2 DIPLOMACY IN DIFFERENT TYPES OF IGOS

Robert Cox and Harold Jacobson identified two broad categories—forum organizations and service organizations.[12] The distinctions are not always sharply drawn, however, as all IGOs serve as arenas or forums for diplomatic interactions to some degree. Most IGOs also have become involved in the ongoing management of different types of international problems. Drawing on that categorization, we examine the distinctions between diplomacy in forum and service organizations.

7.2.1 IGOs as Forums

Forum IGOs serve a variety of purposes and provide arenas for different types of multi-lateral diplomacy, including agenda-setting, coalition-building, norm creation, delegate socialization, and bilateral diplomacy. As a result, diplomats serving in these arenas must master a variety of skills and procedures not associated with traditional diplomacy and 'contend with a greater range of cultural differences, work habits, and diplomatic styles'.[13]

IGO forums include regular meetings of an assembly where the participants are dip-lomatic representatives of all member states; they can also include summit meetings of heads of state and government as is the custom in the African Union (AU) and ASEAN. The UNGA convened the World Summit in 2005 to consider issues of terrorism, nuclear proliferation, and UN Charter reform among others. Organizations such as ASEAN and the EU have regular meetings of foreign, finance, and environmental ministers. In addi-tion, the UN has convened many global conferences since the late 1960s.

7.2.1.1 *The Diplomacy of Agenda-Setting*

Forum IGOs are particularly useful for introducing new agenda topics. The UN General Assembly serves that purpose because delegates can consider any matter within the pur-view of the Charter (Article 10). During its annual fall meetings, each beginning with a general debate period, new topics are introduced, ideas endorsed or condemned, and actions taken or rejected. This can be especially valuable for small or developing states. For example, India in 1946 first introduced the issue of South Africa's apartheid as a vio-lation of human rights and Malta in 1967 introduced the principle that the high seas and deep seabed were part of the 'common heritage of mankind', setting the agenda for rene-gotiation of the law of the sea.

In many IGOs, agendas have a tendency to become overloaded, diverting attention from critical issues, usurping resources, and consuming valuable time. So a diplomatic balancing act involves both sufficient flexibility to accommodate new issues and the interests of member states and some strategic sense of what issues need attention.

7.2.1.2 *Coalition-Building*

Because forum IGOs often operate like legislative bodies, especially where decisions are reached by voting, there is a strong impetus for states to build coalitions to put together a voting majority and obtain better outcomes than they can achieve on their own. The diplomacy of coalition-building is likely to be both bilateral and multilateral. It involves negotiating a common position, then maintaining cohesion and preventing defections to rival coalitions, as well as choosing representatives to bargain with others. In other words, there is a both intra-bloc diplomacy and interaction with other blocs, the secre-tariat of the organization and committee chairs or the president of the General Assembly in the case of the UN.[14] In addition, coalition-building and activity requires communi-cation with the governments of coalition members—i.e. diplomats negotiating with their own governments to secure agreement to bloc positions.

In the UN, regional groups were formed very early to elect non-permanent representatives to the Security Council and Economic and Social Council (ECOSOC) as well as justices for the ICJ. The cold war produced competing groups under the leadership of the Soviet Union and United States, plus the Non-Aligned Movement. Decolonization and the creation of the UN Conference on Trade and Development (UNCTAD) in 1964 led to the formation of the G77 by Latin American, African, and Asian states, marking the divide between North and South. Since the 1960s, group diplomacy has been pervasive throughout much of the UN system, as well as in many regional organizations and the WTO.

Failure to find a basis of agreement or failing to identify what is acceptable politically to a large group of states impedes the success of multilateral diplomacy in an IGO forum. Cross-cutting coalitions may be needed to reach broader agreement on a resolution or course of action and to create a winning majority or consensus. Often representatives of small states or middle powers exercise key bridging roles, taking initiatives on their own authority. The diplomacy within forum organizations lends itself to such types of individual leadership to solve problems.

7.2.1.3 *The Role of Committee Chairs*

Because most forum IGOs establish permanent and/or ad hoc committees to share the workload, persons elected as committee chairs exercise significant influence over diplomacy within committees. As committee chairs, they must take on non-national, impartial roles. They are expected to facilitate committee work rather than promoting their own state's interests. They structure the agenda; work with the IGO bureaucracy; push member states to produce resolutions; suspend proceedings to allow blocs more time to negotiate; help broker an agreement; and sometimes create a single negotiating text to push talks along.[15] Although committee chairs may be constrained by the IGO's rules of decision-making and the design of the chairship, they can influence negotiations by having privileged access to information, control over negotiation procedures, and the ability to sequence the negotiation process.[16] Individual diplomats elected to serve as heads of annual meetings, such as the president of the UNGA, function in a similar way to committee chairs but with far broader leadership responsibility.

In short, there is considerable diplomacy involved in running meetings of forum organizations and managing the diplomatic processes. The modes of such diplomacy, however, are affected by the institutional framework as not all forum IGOs are alike.

7.2.1.4 *Characteristics of the Forum Matter*

Size is a critical variable. Those forums with a large number of members have a greater need to set agendas in advance, operate under formal procedures, and delegate work to committees. Smaller membership IGOs can operate more informally with looser agendas and less need for coalition-building, especially when members are like-minded states.

Whether an IGO operates in public view or not is another variable affecting diplomacy. Public, on-the-record sessions mean delegates may be speaking to several different audiences which may complicate the diplomacy of coalition-building. Without a public record, there is more latitude for delegates to alter their views and proceedings are clearly less transparent.[17] The UN Security Council, for example, has adopted the practice of informal consultations where the fifteen members meet without convening a formal session until they have agreed on action to be taken, or a member state has requested it.

Both the multiplicity of IGOs and the variations among forum IGOs in particular mean that states and others can often choose where to take certain issues—a diplomatic practice labelled forum-shopping. Although some issues logically belong only within a particular organization, the interrelatedness of many issues makes neat compartmentalization outdated. For European countries interested in labour issues, for example, the ILO, WTO, and EU are all possibilities. Environmental issues may find sympathetic reception in UNEP, the World Bank, or the UN Commission on Sustainable Development.

In general, states and other actors select IGO forums where they believe they will get the best reception. For example, in the past African states sought solutions from within the region. Yet, some African states have preferred the UN rather than the AU or a subregional organization because of the dearth of regional resources and the anticipation of a more favourable diplomatic outcome. For intellectual property issues, the United States has generally preferred the WTO rather than the World Intellectual Property Organization (WIPO). In the WTO, intellectual property issues are linked to trade and the WTO has the power to punish rule breakers. The existence of so many IGO forums makes forum-shopping a standard diplomatic activity.

7.2.1.5 *The Diplomacy of Norm Creation*

As a forum IGO, the UN has been the progenitor of numerous ideas. With its universal membership, Thakur notes, the UNGA in particular 'is the custodian of the world's conscience'.[18] This makes it the unique forum of choice for articulating global values and norms and the arena in which contested norms can be debated and reconciled. Repeated resolutions and declarations adopted over time delegitimized colonialism, racism, apartheid, and nuclear weapon proliferation and endorsed human rights for all, preventive diplomacy, the responsibility to protect individuals, environmentally sustainable development, human development, and the Millennium Development Goals (MDGs). Many of these ideas and norms have now been catalogued in the UN Intellectual History Project.[19]

The UN may be the ideal forum IGO for building consensus on new norms, but it can also be 'a maddening forum because dissent by powerful states or even coalitions of less powerful ones means either no action or agreement only on a lowest common denominator'.[20] The diplomacy of norm creation involves all the skills of agenda-setting and building and maintaining coalitions on resolutions and declarations during repeated sessions. It can often involve extensive multilateral as well as bilateral diplomatic interactions in and around the UN and other IGOs, consultations with governments, secretariat members, and NGOs. There may well be added diplomatic and intellectual impetus from an independent commission such as the International Commission on State Sovereignty and Intervention that pushed the new norm of responsibility to protect,[21] or the Brundtland Commission of the late 1980s that promoted the norm of sustainable development.

Although forum IGOs are most closely associated with multilateral diplomacy, there is usually extensive bilateral diplomacy between member state representatives, between the secretariat and individual member states, between committee chairs and particular state representatives, and between representatives of coalitions.

7.2.1.6 *The Socializing Effects of Forum Diplomacy*

IGO forums help to socialize individual representatives and states themselves into the practices of multilateral diplomacy. Research on individual policy-makers and on states that have been candidate members for EU membership has shown that when these norms become internalized, actors' identities can be transformed and individual and state interests changed.[22] Similarly, research on Chinese foreign policy has shown distinct changes since the late 1970s when China began to take participation in international organizations more seriously.[23]

Diplomats are socialized into a UN culture of language, politeness, euphemisms, and stock phrases with agreed-on meanings. Although that culture is often criticized, the absence of decorum and shared understandings along with rules of procedure can create havoc. Yet, despite socialization, differences in values, mannerisms, and types of verbal and non-verbal communication and understandings of status can have a negative effect on diplomatic outcomes in IGOs.

By contrast, diplomacy in non-forum organizations differs both in who is involved and the specialized or technical nature of the work. Member state representatives as well as secretariat staff typically will have specialized or technical training such as in nuclear engineering, public health, air transport, maritime safety, or refugee services, and are less likely to come from foreign ministries.

7.2.2 Service, Technical, and Regulatory IGOs

We find it useful to categorize non-forum IGOs as service, regulatory, or technical. Let us look, then, at some of the variations among these different types of organizations.

7.2.2.1 *Service Organizations*

Many IGOs are service organizations that are authorized by states to provide services that states themselves are either unwilling or unable to provide. Technical assistance programmes run by UN agencies such as the Food and Agriculture Organization (FAO) and UN Development Programme (UNDP) constitute IGO services. The Global Maritime Distress and Safety System run by the International Maritime Organization (IMO) is a service to all maritime states. The diplomacy in these organizations concerns decisions on budgets, programmes, and priorities.

The UNHCR and WFP are examples of service organizations with considerable independent power on the ground. Although UNHCR's mandate is to protect refugees until given asylum or they can return home, it, like many service organizations, has developed operational capacities beyond its original mandate.[24] For UNHCR this means addressing the needs of internally displaced persons, helping them to resettle, reintegrate, and rehabilitate in their home country. In remote locations, its staff enjoy considerable latitude to negotiate with local governments, other IGOs (such as the WHO and WFP), and humanitarian NGOs such as the International Committee of the Red Cross, Oxfam, and Doctors Without Borders. This diplomacy is focused on securing the necessary supplies, logistical support, and assistance for those in need.[25]

Thus, service organization staff, operating far from the hallways of any IGOs, set agendas, negotiate with various other actors, and forge the necessary coalitions to provide needed services. With that authority, Barnett and Finnemore note, not only can the UNHCR 'shape how the world understands refugees and their circumstances', but it can also, potentially, 'control their lives and determine their fates'.[26]

The World Food Programme displays similar independence of action. It must engage in bilateral diplomacy with both donors (to get funding) and recipients (to get access to vulnerable groups). Those bilateral contacts are multilevel, with government ministries and local authorities. The WFP secretariat also employs public diplomacy extensively, including YouTube, press conferences, testimony to legislatures, blogs, meetings with civil society, and media interviews to call attention to famine and hunger and to influence the decisions of governments.[27]

Diplomacy in technical and regulatory organizations differs in focus (more technical issues and problems) and in the types of constituencies concerned with the organization's work (fewer local governments and needy populations, more corporate, governmental, and other actors).

7.2.2.2 *Technical Organizations*

Specialized knowledge and expertise have become increasingly critical to global governance efforts. Understanding the science behind environmental problems such as climate change or declining fisheries is critical for choosing policy options. Cost-effective alternatives have to be developed for fuels that emit carbon dioxide and ozone-depleting chlorofluorocarbons if there is going to be political support for making policy changes and new rules. Specialized training is also needed for issues ranging from public, food supply, and nuclear energy to trade and finance. Thus, the secretariats of those IGOs whose work is more technical tend to be made up of experts; these include all of the UN's specialized agencies.

IGOs manned by individuals possessing complex knowledge have a greater probability of being independent actors since understanding technical issues requires a specialized vocabulary and a shared framework to assess information. The diplomacy in such IGOs is likely to be marked by significant involvement of secretariat experts who may form formal or informal groups, caucuses or networks with experts from key governments. If there is a need to negotiate treaty text, more traditional diplomats from member states may also be involved. The IAEA and IMO exemplify technical IGOs with other responsibilities and functions as well.

Generally, the more technical expertise an IGO secretariat has, the greater its independence to conduct the diplomacy necessary to fulfilling its mandate. On less technical issues, such IGOs function more as forums where the diplomacy resembles that of other forum IGOs.

7.2.2.3 *Regulatory Organizations*

Some IGOs are empowered by member states to create binding rules and regulations which member states agree to follow. The International Telecommunications Union (ITU), for example, regulates areas of communications, setting standards for infrastructure and equipment, adopting uniform instruments and Internet protocols.[28] The IMO maintains a comprehensive set of regulations for shipping ranging from safety and ship design to maritime security. The IAEA's safeguard system and standards for handling radioactive materials safely make it also a regulatory IGO.[29] The diplomacy surrounding the creation of such regulations involves the experts in the ITU, IMO, and IAEA secretariats, experts from member states as well as from other IGOs and NGOs.

Thus, the nature of diplomacy varies across different types of IGOs but the distinctions are not always clear-cut. The IAEA, for example, has seen more forum-style diplomacy in recent years when dealing with the non-compliance of North Korea and Iran. Forum IGOs tend to be viewed more as agents of their member states while service, technical, and regulatory organizations may be perceived as independent actors. Experience has shown, however, that the executive heads and secretariats of all types of IGOs have the potential to function as independent actors, active in various types of diplomatic interactions and influencing outcomes.

7.3 DIPLOMACY AND IGOS AS INDEPENDENT ACTORS

As Inis Claude noted many years ago, the secretariat of an IGO '*is* the organization'.[30] It is a symbol of the organization itself and its executive head is its chief representative. Although realist theory has always seen IGOs as either tools of their member states or merely arenas for states to pursue their interests, we noted earlier that recent variations on principal–agent theory and constructivism have led to closer examination of IGOs as independent actors. Understanding how autonomous interests of international bureaucracies may be formed is central to these endeavours, as well as understanding variations in the behaviour of different bureaucracies, how some bureaucracies become independent actors, and some do not.[31] International secretariats can take initiatives on many issues and are not just civil servants carrying out the mandate of the members.

When we speak of IGOs as actors, then, we are often referring to IGO executive heads or other senior secretariat members who, as international civil servants, play key but often invisible roles in persuading states to act, coordinating the efforts of different groups, securing agreements, and ensuring the effectiveness of programmes.[32] The balance between the forum and service activities affects decision-making and influences patterns in IGOs. These variations influence the nature of diplomacy. We turn, therefore, to examine how IGO executive heads and bureaucracies often are independent diplomatic actors.

7.3.1 Executive Heads

Executive heads include the UN secretary-general and his or her under- and assistant secretaries-general as well as special representatives; the directors-general of UN specialized agencies such as the WHO, FAO, and IAEA; the UN High Commissioners for Refugees and Human Rights; the president of the World Bank; the managing director of the IMF; the president of the European Commission; and the secretaries-general or directors-general of regional organizations. The very nature of their positions means that much of the activity in which they engage will be diplomatic, involving communications with state representatives and governments, coalition leaders, committee chairs, and non-state actors. They may broker agreements, break deadlocks, cajole states into providing troops for peacekeeping or funding for development aid, or mediate a ceasefire.

IGO heads and other senior officials often do much more than their member states may have intended. It is they who must turn vague mandates from bodies such as the UNGA into procedures and actions. If the organization is to remain relevant, they must respond to new challenges and crises, provide policy options for member states, change their own missions, and formulate new tasks and procedures. UN secretaries-general, for example, have been a key factor in the emergence of the UN itself as an autonomous actor in world politics. Since 1945, successive secretaries-general have taken advantage of opportunities for initiatives, applied flexible interpretations of charter provisions, and sought mandates from UN policy organs. They have developed their own political roles as well as the role of the institution. A number of secretaries-general have served as norm entrepreneurs.[33] Their personalities and interpretation of the charter, as well as world events, have combined to increase the power, resources, and importance of the position. As Cox remarked, through the secretary-general's leadership, 'an international organization is transformed from being a forum of multilateral diplomacy into something which is more than the sum of its inputs . . . and make[s] more decisions on behalf of the whole community of nation-states'.[34]

Dag Hammarskjöld, the second UN secretary-general during 1953–1961, for example, articulated principles for UN peacekeeping and successfully negotiated the release of US airmen held by China after the armistice in the Korean War. Kofi Annan, the seventh secretary-general, used his position and convening power to promote initiatives on HIV/AIDs, the Millennium Development Goals, the Global Compact on Corporate

Responsibility, and the emerging responsibility to protect norm. As he commented, 'I know some people have accused me of using diplomacy. That's my job.'[35]

The degree to which executive heads play a role as independent diplomats, however, depends greatly on individual personality. Not all UN secretaries-general have chosen to act independently or been effective in doing so. Others, particularly during the cold war years, often found themselves constrained by one or more of the major powers.

Since the late 1980s, with the UN far more active in conflict management, it has become common for secretaries-general to appoint special representatives to conduct international mediation, manage post-conflict peacekeeping and peace-building missions, and to focus attention on issues such as children and armed conflict. Sergio Vieira de Mello, the special representative successively in Lebanon, Kosovo, East Timor, and Iraq, was the epitome of a diplomat who came to represent the organization, both in life and death.[36] Being in the field, charged with carrying out the Security Council's mandate for a mission on behalf of the secretary-general, requires extensive, multilevel diplomacy with parties to a conflict as well as with commanders of military and paramilitary forces, and various UN agencies and NGOs involved in humanitarian aid and peace-building activities. Special representatives, then, are what Leguey-Feilleux refers to as 'diplomats in non-national roles'.[37] Their diplomacy of implementation also involves other members of IGO secretariats and contributes to the broader role of those bureaucracies as independent actors.

7.3.2 International Bureaucracies

Over time, IGO secretariats or bureaucracies tend to develop power, expertise, and autonomy. As a member of the secretariat of the UN Convention on Biological Diversity said, 'As a national delegate it was my highest ambition to change at least one word in the text of the decision, as part of the secretariat I can influence the whole text.'[38]

Barnett and Finnemore argue that international organizations 'help define the interests that states and other actors come to hold and do so in ways compatible with liberalism and a liberal global order. These are important exercises of power.'[39] They add, 'IOs can, indeed, be autonomous actors with power to influence world events.' These same authors, however, note the irony: that the bureaucrats' authority actually rests in 'their ability to present themselves as impersonal and neutral—as not exercising power but instead serving others'.[40]

International secretariats may engage in extensive diplomatic activity with member states, other IGOs, and NGOs not only to carry out a mandate such as for a UN peacekeeping operation or humanitarian emergency, but also to help create international regimes by driving a negotiation process such as that for global climate change.[41] They may also be charged with verifying whether states are fulfilling their obligations, just as treaty review committees do in the UN human rights system, and in that process engage in extensive communications and negotiations with governments over reports.

The more technical the IGO bureaucracy, the more it is charged with regulatory activities, or the more it provides essential services, the more it has the possibility of being an independent actor. Likewise, the larger the size of the bureaucracy, the more initiatives it may take and the greater the need for extensive diplomatic interactions with member states. For example, the World Bank has about 10,000 employees and the IMF about 4,000, the vast majority of whom are economists trained in Western countries and in the liberal economic tradition. Both bureaucracies have strong organizational cultures and an ideology characterized as 'an apolitical, technocratic, and economic rationality'.[42] Their size, expertise, and organizational cultures provide sources of autonomous power and their missions require extensive diplomatic interaction with governments in developing proposals and monitoring and evaluating their effectiveness.

7.4 IGOs and Network Diplomacy

Increasingly IGOs operate within broader networks, as Jacobson realized over thirty years ago when he titled his book *Networks of Interdependence*.[43] More recently, Ohanyan has noted that policy networks 'mediate among the goals, priorities, and preferences of IGOs and often alter the policy objectives of IGOs as ultimately implemented by NGOs'.[44]

The participants in these networks operate on the basis of a degree of shared normative and conceptual frameworks and the awareness that shared goals cannot be achieved by individual actors. Often there is a linking-pin organization which mobilizes coalitions on particular issues or controls the negotiations. Such organizations have seldom been delegated such authority, but are able to legitimize their actions in specific issue areas.[45] Increasingly, such networks have emerged for a variety of issues and problems at the heart of global efforts to address the governance challenges of climate change, HIV/AIDS, and other issues.

It is possible to identify three types of IGO-related networks. The first are networks that link IGOs and governments. The second are networks of IGOs. The third are networks of non-official outsiders and their interactions with either the political bodies of IGOs such as the UNGA or the secretariats. The 'outsiders' constitute what Weiss, Carayannis, and Jolly refer to as the 'third UN'.[46] They include NGOs, academics, consultants, experts, independent commissions, and other groups of individuals that 'routinely engage with the first and the second UN [or other IGO] and thereby influence UN thinking, policies, priorities, and actions. The key characteristic for this third sphere is its independence from governments and UN secretariats.'[47]

Network relationships among IGOs, even among agencies within the UN system note Brinkman and Hyder 'display many of the characteristics of full-blown international diplomacy, including a willingness to work toward common goals and a reluctance to give up particular interests'.[48] The UN Joint Programme on HIV/AIDS (UNAIDS), for example, started as a network of UN agencies. When HIV/AIDS was first identified in the mid-1980s, it was defined as a health problem and the World Health Organization took the lead. Gradually, however, the understanding of HIV/AIDS and its impact shifted so that other UN agencies became involved. Then, UNAIDS was formed in 1996 by five agencies (UN Children's Fund (UNICEF), UNDP, UN Fund for Population Activities (UNFPA), UN Educational, Scientific, and Cultural Organization (UNESCO), WHO, and the World Bank); two others (ILO and UN Drug Control Programme (UNDCP)) joined subsequently.

Today, UNAIDS illustrates an even broader type of network approach as its partnerships include not only seven UN agencies, but also national governments, corporations, religious organizations, NGOs, MNCs, and private foundations. The Global Fund to Fight AIDS, Tuberculosis, and Malaria that was established in 2002 includes local, national, and international stakeholders with representatives from WHO, UNAIDS, and World Bank serving in an advisory role.

The third type of IGO-related network of 'outsiders' (including persons who move between being 'inside' and 'outside' IGOs and governments) is well illustrated by a variety of independent commissions composed of 'eminent persons' and by the UN's Intergovernmental Panel on Climate Change (IPCC).[49] The latter was formed in 1988 at the urging of bureaucrats in the World Meteorological Organization (WMO) and UNEP. Designed as a network of 2,000–3,000 leading climate experts, its purpose was to evaluate the state of scientific knowledge on climate change and to present policy alternatives for official intergovernmental negotiations. Its primary work involves interpretation of peer-reviewed reports as it does not carry out its own research or monitor actual data collection. The IPCC also illustrates what have been called 'epistemic communities' and 'knowledge networks'.[50]

In short, an important innovation in IGO-related diplomacy is networked diplomacy—the diplomacy of mobilizing international networks of both public and private actors to address issues. That diplomacy involves managing the complexity of a diverse, fluid cast of actors. IGOs and especially the UN and its various agencies and programmes are still at the heart of many networks. The diplomatic activity within these various networks coexists and overlaps with the more traditional 'club' diplomacy involving government officials and diplomats. Even 'club' diplomacy, however, is no longer just the domain of a narrow set of official diplomats as trans-governmental networks of judges, legislators, and officials in regulatory agencies and various government ministries have increasingly interacted with counterparts in other countries.[51] These changes contribute to the conceptualization of IOs as pieces of and actors in global governance—pieces that provide arenas and mechanisms for diplomacy to take place and actors that often play key roles in addressing issues and problems.

NOTES

1. Richard Cupitt, Rodney Whitlock, and Lynn Williams Whitlock, 'The (Im)mortality of International Governmental Organizations', in Paul F. Diehl (ed.), *The Politics of Global*

Governance: International Organizations in an Interdependent World (Boulder, CO: Lynne Rienner, 1997), 16.

2. Margaret P. Karns and Karen A. Mingst, *International Organizations. The Politics and Processes of Global Governance*, 2nd ed. (Boulder: Lynne Rienner, 2010).

3. Michael Barnett and Martha Finnemore, 'The Power of Liberal International Organizations', in Michael Barnett and Raymond Duvall (eds), *Power in Global Governance* (New York: Cambridge University Press, 2005), 162.

4. Fen Osler Hampson, with Michael Hart, *Multilateral Negotiations: Lessons from Arms Control, Trade, and the Environment* (Baltimore: The Johns Hopkins University Press, 1995), 6.

5. In this volume, see Chapter 17 on diplomacy by Fen Hampson et al. and Chapter 13 on multilateral diplomacy by Kishore Mahbubani.

6. Ramesh Thakur, 'Multilateral Diplomacy and the United Nations: Global Governance Venue or Actor', in James Muldoon, Jr., JoAnn Fagot Aviel, Richard Reitano, and Earl Sullivan (eds), *The New Dynamics of Multilateralism. Diplomacy, International Organizations, and Global Governance* (Boulder: Westview, 2011), 259–60.

7. John W. McDonald, 'International Conference Diplomacy: Four Principles', excerpted from J.D. Sandole and Hugo van der Werwe (eds), *Conflict Resolution Theory and Practice: Integration and Application* (New York: Manchester University Press, 1993), 249; In this volume, see Chapter 14 on conference diplomacy by A.J.R. Groom and Chapter 47 on climate change diplomacy by Lorraine Elliot for illustrations of the variety of actors.

8. In this volume, see Chapter 9 on civil society by Kathryn Hochstetler.

9. In this volume, see Chapter 49 on rising power diplomacy by Gregory Chin.

10. Michael Barnett and Martha Finnemore, *Rules for the World: International Organizations in Global Politics* (Ithaca: Cornell University Press, 2004), 21.

11. Thakur, 'Multilateral Diplomacy and the United Nations', 251.

12. Robert W. Cox and Harold K. Jacobson, *The Anatomy of Influence. Decision Making in International Organization* (New Haven: Yale University Press, 1973).

13. Jean-Robert Leguey-Feilleux, *The Dynamics of Diplomacy* (Boulder: Lynne Rienner, 2009), 218.

14. In this volume, see Chapter 45 on the permanent extension of the NPT by Jayantha Dhanapala and Chapter 47 on climate change diplomacy by Lorraine Elliot for illustrations of bloc diplomacy.

15. Jonas Tallberg, 'The Power of the Chair: Formal leadership in International Cooperation', *International Studies Quarterly* 54:1 (March 2010), 241–65 at 242–3; Leguey-Feilleux, *The Dynamics of Diplomacy*, 231.

16. Tallberg, 'The Power of the Chair', 245–6.

17. Leguey-Feilleux, *The Dynamics of Diplomacy*, 220–2.

18. Thakur, 'Multilateral Diplomacy and the United Nations', 255.

19. The project was launched in 1999 as an independent research endeavour based at the Ralph Bunche Institute for International Studies of the City University of New York. Led by Richard Jolly, Louis Emmerij, and Thomas G. Weiss, the project includes a large oral history and twelve books on major ideas that have emerged from the UN's work.

20. Thakur, 'Multilateral Diplomacy and the United Nations', 261.

21. In this volume, see Chapter 42 on the responsibility to protect by Thomas G. Weiss.

22. Jeffrey T. Checkel, 'International Institutions and Socialization in Europe: Introduction and Framework', *International Organization* 59:4 (Fall 2005), 801–26.

23. Ann Kent, *Beyond Compliance: China, International Organizations, and Global Security* (Stanford: Stanford University Press, 2007), 57.

24. In this volume, see Chapter 37 on refugees by William Maley.

25. In this volume, see Chapter 19 on disaster diplomacy by Jan Egeland.

26. Barnett and Finnemore, *Rules for the World*, 120.

27. Henk-Jan Brinkman and Masood Hyder, 'The Diplomacy of Specialized Agencies: High Food Prices and the World Food Program', in James Muldoon Jr., JoAnn Fagot Aviel, Richard Reitano, and Earl Sullivan (eds), *The New Dynamics of Multilateralism. Diplomacy, International Organizations, and Global Governance* (Boulder: Westview, 2011).

28. Thomas G. Weiss and Ramesh Thakur, *Global Governance and the UN. An Unfinished Journey* (Bloomington: Indiana University Press, 2010), 183–4.

29. In this volume, see Chapter 8 on regulators and monitors by Eric Helleiner.

30. Inis L. Claude, Jr. *Swords into Plowshares: The Problems and Progress of International Organization*, 3rd ed. (New York: Random House, 1964), 174.

31. Steffen Bauer et al., 'Understanding International Bureaucracies: Taking Stock', in Frank Biermann and Bernd Siebenhuner (eds), *Managers of Global Change. The Influence of International Environmental Bureaucracies* (Cambridge: The MIT Press, 2009), 26–7.

32. John Mathiason, *Invisible Governance: International Secretariats in Global Politics* (Bloomfield, CT: Kumarian, 2007).

33. Ramesh Thakur, *The United Nations, Peace and Security* (New York: Cambridge University Press, 2006); Simon Chesterman (ed.), *Secretary or General? The UN Secretary-General in World Politics* (New York: Cambridge University Press, 2007).

34. Robert Cox, 'The Executive Head: An Essay on Leadership in International Organization', *International Organization* 23:12 (Spring 1969), 205–30 at 207.

35. Quoted in Barbara Crossette, 'Kofi Annan Unsettles People, as he Believes U.N. Should Do', *New York Times*, 31 December 1999, A1–A8 at A8.

36. Samantha Power, *Chasing the Flame. One Man's Fight to Save the World* (New York: Penguin, 2008).

37. Leguey-Feilleux, *The Dynamics of Diplomacy*.

38. Quoted in Frank Biermann and Bernd Siebenhuner, 'The Influence of International Bureaucracies in World Politics: Findings from the MANUS Research Program', in Frank Biermann and Bernd Siebenhuner (eds), *Managers of Global Change. The Influence of International Environmental Bureaucracies* (Cambridge: The MIT Press, 2009), 322.

39. Barnett and Finnemore, *Rules for the World*, 162.

40. Barnett and Finnemore, *Rules for the World*, 21.

41. In this volume, see, for example, Chapter 47 on climate change diplomacy by Lorraine Elliott.

42. Catherine E. Weaver, 'The World's Bank and the Bank's World', *Global Governance* 13:4 (October–December 2007), 493–512 at 504.

43. Harold K. Jacobson, *Networks of Interdependence. International Organizations and the Global Political System*, 2nd ed. (New York: Alfred A. Knopf, 1984).

44. Anna Ohanyan, *NGOs, IGOs, and the Network Mechanisms of Post-Conflict Global Governance in Microfinance* (New York: Palgrave Macmillan, 2008), 3.

45. Christer Jönsson, 'Interorganization Theory and International Organization', *International Studies Quarterly* 30:1 (1986), 39–57.

46. Thomas G. Weiss, Tatiana Carayannis, and Richard Jolly, 'The "Third" United Nations', *Global Governance* 15:1 (January–March 2009), 123–42.

47. Weiss, et al., 'The "Third" United Nations', 127.

48. Brinkman and Hyder, 'The Diplomacy of Specialized Agencies', 273.

49. In this volume, see Chapter 15 on commission diplomacy by Gareth Evans.

50. Emmanuel Adler and Peter M. Haas, 'Epistemic Communities, World Order and the Creation of a Reflective Research Program', *International Organization* 46:1 (1992), 367–90; Diane Stone, *Global Knowledge Networks and International Development* (London: Routledge, 2005).

51. Anne-Marie Slaughter, *A New World Order* (Princeton: Princeton University Press, 2004).

CHAPTER 8

FINANCIAL OFFICIALS AS DIPLOMATS: EVOLVING ISSUES, ACTORS, AND TECHNIQUES SINCE THE 1920S

ERIC HELLEINER

FINANCIAL officials have long assumed an important place in international diplomacy. This chapter analyses their evolving diplomatic role over the past century. Section 8.1 examines their diplomatic activities from the end of the First World War to the early 1930s, an era in which financial officials—particularly central bankers—cooperated to rebuild the pre-war international gold standard. Section 8.2 explores how the diplomatic role of financial officials changed during the age of the Bretton Woods system in three ways: the scope of issues addressed, the actors involved, and the techniques of diplomacy employed. Section 8.3 analyses how the more recent 'age of financial globalization' has generated yet further changes in the diplomatic functions of financial officials across these three areas. The conclusion (section 8.4) not only summarizes the changing nature of the diplomatic work of financial officials over this hundred-year period but also highlights the distinct culture of financial diplomats as one important continuity.

8.1 FINANCIAL DIPLOMATS DURING THE LONG DECADE OF THE 1920S

Many of the modern diplomatic roles of financial officials can traced back to the 'long decade' of the 1920s, a period that lasted from the end of the First World War until the international financial crisis of the early 1930s. Financial diplomacy in this era began

with the convening of a major international conference in Brussels in 1920 whose goal—
like that of the Bretton Woods conference two and half decades later—was to set out a
vision for rebuilding the international monetary system after the economic disruption
caused by war.[1] At the conference, representatives of thirty-nine countries endorsed the
restoration of the pre-war international gold standard as well as various national policies that would support this goal such as balanced budgets, the abolition of exchange
controls, and the creation of independent central banks.

Although its resolutions were non-binding, the conference had considerable political
weight not just because it was one of the first to be held by the new League of Nations but
also because it was backed by powerful officials and bankers in the leading financial
powers of the US and UK. The Brussels conference objectives were then reiterated at a
1922 conference in Genoa and many countries subsequently introduced gold-based currency stabilization programmes based on these principles, often assisted by loans from
the Bank of England, the Federal Reserve Bank of New York (FRBNY), and private
bankers in New York and London. By the end of the decade, an international gold standard had been successfully reconstructed.[2]

The long decade of the 1920s also witnessed the strengthening of cooperation among
central banks, a goal backed explicitly by the 1922 Genoa conference and strongly supported by the most powerful central bankers of the age: the Bank of England's governor
Montague Norman and the FRBNY's president Benjamin Strong. In addition to supporting foreign efforts to restore gold-based currencies, central bankers in these and
other financial powers developed new mechanisms for providing emergency financial
support to their foreign counterparts when the latter were facing financial crises. Before
1914, leading central banks had sometimes extended short-term loans of this kind to
each other on an ad hoc and bilateral basis. But this practice became more widespread
after the war and was institutionalized in a multilateral way with the creation of a new
international financial institution in 1930: the Bank for International Settlements (BIS)
located in Basel, Switzerland.[3]

Central bankers also embraced the notion that the international gold standard operated according to informal 'rules of the game' in this era.[4] When countries experienced
balance of payments deficits (surpluses), they were expected to raise (lower) interest
rates in a mechanical fashion in order to support automatic market adjustment processes. First put forward by the British Cunliffe committee right after the war, this vision
of the proper functioning of the international gold standard was accepted by virtually all
the delegates at the Genoa conference.[5] It represented an early commitment to monetary
policy coordination, although officials at the time saw interest rate adjustments as
simply reinforcing self-equilibrating market-led developments. Classical economic
liberalism—rather than more modern conceptions of discretionary macroeconomic
management—ruled the day.

Another diplomatic role that financial officials assumed during the 1920s was that of
providing financial advice to foreign governments, particularly those in poorer countries that were experiencing monetary or financial problems. The advice of these foreign
'money doctors' was usually very orthodox, reinforcing the kinds of policies that the

Brussels and Genoa conferences had backed (and, in some respects, echoing the IMF`s advice in the 1980s and 1990s). Financial advisory missions of this kind had taken place before the war but they were often associated with colonial or quasi-colonial situations. In the post-1918 world, such missions went to a much wider range of countries, and some of them were now coordinated by the League of Nations.[6] Many of the countries receiving these missions also now welcomed them as a mechanism that could help to attract foreign investment and/or to resolve domestic political struggles over monetary and financial reform.[7]

One of the key reforms backed by foreign money doctors in this era involved the creation of central banks themselves. For central bank cooperation to take place, it was necessary for every country to have a central bank. Before 1914, many did not and the Brussels and Genoa conferences had urged countries to create central banks where they did not yet exist. Norman played a particularly active role in encouraging the creation of central banks abroad, developing key principles for modern central banking and even refusing to visit countries that did not have a central bank.[8] By the end of the interwar period, most independent countries had central banks and Norman had played a key role in the creation of many of them. As one influential financial journalist put it in 1932, 'just as President Wilson will be remembered as the creator of the League of Nations, so Mr. Montague Norman will be remembered as the originator of the League of Central Banks'.[9]

A final diplomatic role of financial officials during the 1920s involved international debt negotiations. Before 1914, debt defaults by poorer countries had sometimes been met with military intervention from more powerful states whose citizens were the main creditors. After the First World War, this kind of gunboat diplomacy was increasingly seen as a 'thing of the past' and diplomacy assumed a larger role in the resolution of debt problems.[10] During the 1920s, the debt negotiations that were most politically prominent at the international level involved Germany's reparations payments. After defaulting in 1923, Germany resumed payments the next year under an international negotiated plan: the 1924 Dawes Plan. The latter was subsequently replaced by the Young Plan five years later, a plan which first recommended the creation of the BIS as a body that could help facilitate reparations payments.[11]

8.1.1 Who Were the Financial Diplomats of the 1920s?

What kinds of financial officials were involved in these various aspects of financial diplomacy during this period? Finance ministry officials played some role, but the key officials in many of the activities were central bankers. Because many central banks—including the all-important Bank of England—were privately owned institutions in this period, there is some ambiguity in describing their employees as 'public officials'. Even in the countries with publicly owned central banks, most central bank officials operated with considerable independence from the national government. Indeed, it was this very independence that helped to explain the ability of central banks to engage in cooperative activities relatively free from domestic political constraints.

Alongside finance ministry and central bank officials, a new kind of financial diplomat emerged in this period that had no precedent in the pre-1914 world: employees of international institutions such as the League of Nations and BIS. Their role should not be overstated; the League's staff working on economic and financial issues was tiny, as was that of the BIS. But they laid the groundwork for the expansion of the diplomatic role of international financial officials in the post-1945 years. This was true not just in terms of practices they pioneered but even in terms of specific personnel. Some of the staff members of the League and BIS during the interwar years went on to play important roles within the IMF after the war. For example, after working for the League throughout the 1930s, Louis Rasminsky played a key role at the Bretton Woods conference as a Canadian delegate and subsequently served as Canada's executive director in the Fund from 1946 to 1962. The Dutchman Jacques Polak followed his League employment during the late 1930s and early 1940s with a six decade-long career with the IMF in which he served in a number of prominent staff positions. Per Jacobsson from Sweden became the IMF's Managing Director during 1956–1963 after a career with both the League during the 1920s and the BIS during the 1930s.[12]

In their diplomatic roles, national and international financial officials engaged actively with private financiers. From the Medicis to the Rothchilds, private bankers have long played an important role in the diplomatic world. During the long decade of the 1920s, British and especially American financiers were particularly prominent as their loans helped support debt settlements, such as the Dawes Plan, as well as the various international currency stabilization initiatives of the 1920s. Indeed, historians argue that the powerful American firm J. P. Morgan and Company often played a more important role in coordinating those stabilization initiatives than the League of Nations itself.[13]

The prominence of US financiers resulted not just from their country's new-found creditor power after the First World War. It was also a product of the reluctance of the US government to join the League of Nations and engage with other forms of international political cooperation in this era. Because they faced domestic political opposition to such engagement, internationally-minded US policy-makers encouraged US private financiers to take up the mantle that they could not.[14] For the same reason, they were also supportive of prominent international financial advisory role of Edwin Kemmerer, a Princeton economics professor who was employed as a money doctor by countries across Latin America as well as countries such as China, Poland, South Africa, and Turkey.[15]

While private financiers played a prominent role in financial diplomacy, other societal groups generally did not. This pattern was set at the 1920 Brussels conference that was dominated by bankers and orthodox economists. Contemporary observers noted the marked contrast with the International Labour Organization's (ILO) conference the previous year where labour representatives played a major role; as one reporter noted at the time, 'we are getting, so far, too much finance and too little humanity'.[16] The pattern of representation was not accidental. Many supporters of the Brussels conference saw the restoration of the gold standard and cooperation among independent central banks as a means of containing growing populist political pressures for more activist monetary policies after the war. As one influential banker, Henry Strakosch, put it in 1925, 'the trend of political evolution the world over...is in a direction which makes it less safe to entrust governments with the management of currencies than it may have been in pre-war days'.[17] This kind of sentiment, and the concomitant nostalgia for pre-1914 classical economic liberal ideas, infused much of financial diplomacy throughout the long decade of the 1920s.

At the same time, the shared purpose of national financial officials engaged in diplomacy during the 1920s should not be overstated. They were, after all, still diplomats representing their respective countries' differing interests. At the same time that they cooperated to rebuild the international gold standard, American and British financial officials competed with each other to expand their respective country's influence with the global financial system. Their struggles often appeared inspired much more by power politics than classical economic liberalism. Financial officials in less powerful states often deeply resented the power of British and/or American finance and fought hard to carve out greater national independence. Indeed, domestic support for the creation of central banks in this period often stemmed at least in part from this goal.[18]

8.2 BRETTON WOODS AND THE AGE OF EMBEDDED LIBERALISM

The collapse of the international gold standard and international financial markets during the momentous financial crisis of the early 1930s was accompanied by a transformation of the pattern of financial diplomacy that had been established during the 1920s. While financial diplomacy had previously been dominated by private financiers and central bankers, finance ministry officials now began to assume a more prominent role. The shift reflected domestic political developments within many countries in the wake of the crisis. As Borio and Toniolo put it, 'with the Great Depression central banks everywhere lost prestige, as public opinion associated "bankers and financiers" with the debacle. Responsibility for monetary policy shifted to the treasuries'.[19]

This shift was reflected well in the negotiations that generated the 1944 Bretton Woods agreements, which created a kind of formal constitution for the post-war international financial order. The negotiations were dominated by representatives of the British and US Treasuries, most notably John Maynard Keynes and Harry Dexter White.[20] White's superior, US Treasury Secretary Henry Morgenthau, even highlighted very explicitly that the Bretton Woods agreements were designed to lock in this changing of the guard. As he put it, the objective was 'to move the financial center of the world from London and Wall Street to the United States Treasury and to create a new concept between nations in international finance'.[21] The antipathy towards the old order was also reflected in the passage of a resolution at the Bretton Woods conference that called for the liquidation of the BIS 'at the earliest possible moment'.[22]

In place of the BIS, the Bretton Woods agreements created two new international financial institutions whose membership was comprised not of central banks but of national governments: the IMF and International Bank for Reconstruction and Development (IBRD; subsequently known as the World Bank). Their purposes were also much wider than that of the BIS. Indeed, in developing his initial drafts of the Bank, White had highlighted the ambitions nature of his thinking with a suggestion that all members should have to subscribe to 'a bill of rights of the peoples of the United Nations' in order to highlight that 'these new instrumentalities which are being developed go far beyond usual commercial considerations and considerations of economic self-interest'. He continued: 'They would be evidence of the beginning of a truly new order in the realm where it has hitherto been most lacking—international finance.'[23]

Although this specific proposal of White's was dropped, the commitment to building international financial institutions to serve a wider purpose remained. Like the BIS, the IMF was given a capacity to extend short-term credit to governments facing balance of payments crises, but its loans were more explicitly designed to provide countries with more policy autonomy than they had had under the pre-1930s international gold standard. The greater priority assigned to national policy autonomy reflected the new commitment to discretionary national macroeconomic management which had emerged in the wake of the Great Depression.[24] The IBRD was even more innovative. For the first time in human history, a public international financial institution was created to provide long-term loans designed for post-war reconstruction and development, tasks that the private financiers were no longer fully trusted to perform well. Support for the new 'development' function of the IBRD was particularly strong among non-industrialized countries which made up well over half of the forty-four countries represented at the 1944 conference.[25]

The Bretton Woods agreements also empowered national governments to take on a more conscious and active role in managing external imbalances than they had under the gold standard. Although countries agreed to peg their currencies to the dollar (which in turn was tied to gold), this was to be an 'adjustable-peg' exchange rate system that enabled national governments to substitute exchange-rate devaluations for harsh domestic deflations which they experienced under the gold standard when confronting payments deficits. Similarly, countries were given the right to control all capital movements in order to prevent speculative and 'disequilibrating' private financial flows from disrupting national economic policy autonomy.[26]

In contrast to the delegates to the 1920 Brussels conference who sought to resurrect a pre-war international monetary order, the Bretton Woods negotiators thus explicitly sought to turn their backs on the past. In place of classical economic liberal ideas, they embraced what Ruggie has called an 'embedded liberal' vision that sought to reconcile the rebuilding of an open liberal international economic system with the larger state role within economic life that had become popular across the world after the early 1930s.[27] Even when many specific provisions of the Bretton Woods agreements were not immediately implemented at the war's end, this underlying normative vision was influential in financial diplomacy. For example, although the IMF and World Bank played very limited roles before the late 1950s, other bodies—such as the US government and the European Payments Union—provided the kind of balance of payments support and loans for reconstruction and development that the Bretton Woods architects had endorsed. A new generation of US financial advisers also promoted embedded liberal ideals in various part of the world during the 1940s and 1950s.[28]

Embedded liberal ideology changed the content of financial diplomacy. As already noted, many of the diplomatic roles that had been assumed by financial officials during the 1920s—such as constructing an international monetary order, providing emergency financial assistance, coordinating macroeconomic policies, financial advising—now took on a different character. The age of embedded liberalism also led financial officials to widen the scope of the issues they addressed, taking on new diplomatic tasks such as the promotion of long-term development lending and the discussion of policy tools to actively manage external imbalances such as exchange rate adjustments and the use of capital controls.

As in the 1920s, shared transnational ideas did not preclude national financial officials pursuing hard-headed state interests as well. These were apparent at the Bretton Woods conference itself, where clashes between US and British negotiators reflected their different positions as creditors and debtors in the world economy. With the onset of the cold war in the late 1940s, national strategic objectives assumed an even greater priority in financial diplomacy.

The techniques of financial diplomacy also changed in the Bretton Woods era. The resolutions of the Brussels and Genoa conferences after the First World War were not binding, and policy-makers during the 1920s followed informal 'rules of the game'. By contrast, the Bretton Woods agreements were formal international monetary treaties that were ratified by national legislatures.[29] The IMF and IBRD also had much greater authority delegated to them and they were assigned much more substantial staff and financial resources than the League of Nations' economic and financial section ever had. These changes partly reflected the greater determination of policy-makers to protect global monetary and financial stability in the wake of the 1930s experience. American policy-makers also backed stronger international financial rules and institutions because they saw economic cooperation as a key tool for strengthening political ties: the Bretton Woods conference was seen as a key foundation for the broader global security system of United Nations.

The formal rules-based multilateralism of the Bretton Woods era should not be overstated. The onset of the cold war prompted the US policy-makers to implement the Marshall Plan under which the Bretton Woods institutions played little role, and bilateral and regional arrangements were key. Even after European currencies were made convertible in 1958 and the Bretton Woods system became more fully operational, financial diplomacy evolved in directions that had not been anticipated by the Bretton Woods architects. As the US experienced growing balance of payments problems during the 1960s, the US defended the dollar with a number of ad hoc measures, including bilateral arrangements with key allies to discourage the selling of dollar reserves. To offset speculative pressures against various currencies during the 1960s, leading central banks also arranged credits and swaps among themselves, reviving the kinds of central bank coop-eration that had flourished in the 1920s. Even more striking was the fact that this coop-eration was centred in the BIS which had escaped abolition after the Bretton Woods conference by proving its worth in facilitating intra-European payments under the Marshall plan.[30]

8.3 THE AGE OF FINANCIAL GLOBALIZATION

The collapse of the Bretton Woods monetary system was ushered in by the US decision to end the dollar convertibility into gold in 1971 and the generalized move to floating exchanges in 1973. Initially, observers found it difficult to describe its successor, not least because international negotiations to create a new international monetary system dur-ing 1972–1974 failed to produce a clear outcome. From the early 1980s onwards, however, the post-Bretton Woods era increasingly came to be defined by one key trend: the glo-balization of financial markets.

Unlike the international gold standard of the 1920s and the Bretton Woods system, the age of financial globalization was not ushered in by any major international confer-ence. It was instead a product of various unilateral financial liberalization and deregula-tion decisions taken by governments from the 1970s onwards, as well as technological and market pressures. Between 1995 and 1997, there was a brief diplomatic effort to lock in the new order by revising the IMF's Articles of Agreement to give the institution a stronger liberalization mandate with respect to capital movements. Even then, however, the initiative failed to gain enough support to be approved by IMF members.[31]

Financial globalization has prompted financial officials to widen the scope of their diplomatic activities. As heightened international capital mobility has imposed new constraints on national policy autonomy, policy-makers have responded by engaging in deeper forms of macroeconomic coordination. European policy-makers have been the most ambitious with their initiative to create a full monetary union at the regional level. At the global level, macroeconomic coordination has been more episodic, usually coin-ciding with periods when large payments imbalances emerged between the major eco-nomic powers such as during the mid-1980s and after the middle of the first decade of the 21st century. At these moments, financial officials have found themselves engaged in heated diplomatic debates on issues ranging from fiscal and monetary policies to exchange rate and domestic savings practices. During the mid-1980s, these debates gen-erated the Plaza agreement and Louvre Accord that helped to engineer a large deprecia-tion of the US dollar.[32] In the current period, a new Mutual Assessment Process (MAP) was created in 2009 to identify and address persistently large imbalances.

Contrary to the hopes of the Bretton Woods architects, the IMF has not been the main forum in which these diplomatic initiatives to address imbalances have taken place. During the mid-1980s, the action was centred in the G5 and G7 forums that had been created a decade earlier to bring together the leading Western industrialized countries.

In the current era, the MAP has been created by the G20, a grouping involving the largest developed and developing economies and which emerged first at the level of finance officials in 1999 and then the leaders' level in 2008. In contrast to the supranational character of the IMF, these 'G' groupings consist simply of informal trans-governmental networks without even a permanent secretariat to support their activities. The commitments they make are non-binding, soft-law communiqués rather than the kind of formal legal commitments that were embodied in the Bretton Woods agreements.

This more informal networked style of financial governance is more reminiscent of the 1920s. Its supporters argue that it allows for more flexibility in an era of rapid global change.[33] To the extent that this informal networked form of financial governance is effective, it works through persuasion, information exchange, trust-building, and the cultivation of shared knowledge and world views. These processes can take place among leaders through the annual summits of the G7 and G20, for which these groupings are best known among the general public. But the more important work associated with financial cooperation takes place in more frequent meetings of financial officials, ranging from finance ministers and heads of central banks down through their various deputies and officials. In those settings, analysts have also noted that the discussions—particularly among more technocratic officials—are often informed by similar world views based on technical knowledge as well as the kind of 'neo-liberal' thinking that became more prominent globally after the 1970s.[34]

Networked governance has become an even more prominent feature of financial diplomacy in the regulatory field. During the interwar and Bretton Woods eras, financial officials discussed regulatory issues only in the context of controls on cross-border financial flows. As those controls were progressively eliminated in many countries from the 1970s onwards, a new issue was placed on the agenda of financial diplomacy: the need for more coordinated regulation and supervision of globalizing financial markets. This activity has brought a whole new set of actors—financial regulators and supervisors—into the world of international financial diplomacy.

The construction of international financial standards has taken place in an incremental fashion in response to various international financial crises since the 1970s.[35] In the wake of a 1974 banking crisis, bank supervisors from the leading financial markets created the Basel Committee on Banking Supervision (BCBS) within the BIS which negotiated the 1975 Basel Concordat to resolve ambiguities surrounding their international responsibilities. In the wake of the international debt crisis of the early 1980s, BCBS members then negotiated the 1988 Basel Accord to set minimum capital standards for international banks (subsequently updated into the Basel II accord during 1998–2004 and Basel III after the 2008 financial crisis).

International financial crises involving Mexico in 1994 and East Asia in 1997–1998 then generated an even more ambitious G7-led initiative to develop a much wider set of international standards concerning issues such as securities regulation, insurance supervision, accounting, auditing, payments systems, and corporate governance. These standards were developed by a number of international standard setting bodies (SSBs) such as the International Organization of Securities Commissions, the International

Association of Insurance Supervisors, International Accounting Standards Board, and the Committee on Payment and Settlement Systems. Most of these SSBs were newly created and, like the BCBS, they are institutions with little formal power and designed primarily just to facilitate loose networked forms of cooperation.

In 1999, the G7 also created a new body, the Financial Stability Forum, to coordinate international financial standard setting by pulling together in one place for the first time all the key SSBs, representatives of other relevant international bodies (such as the IMF, World Bank, OECD, and BIS), as well as representatives from the central bank, finance ministry, and supervisory authority of each G7 country. This body was then transformed into the Financial Stability Board (FSB) in 2009 by the G20 leaders, who took over from the G7 the task of guiding the reform of international financial standards in the wake of the 2007–2008 global financial crisis. The FSB was assigned a slightly larger secretariat, a strengthened mandate (which now includes peer reviews, early warning exercises, the setting of its own standards, and strategic reviews of the work of the SSBs), and a wider membership including all G20 countries as well as Hong Kong, the Netherlands, Singapore, Spain, and Switzerland.[36]

These changes have led some, such as US Treasury Secretary Tim Geithner, to describe the FSB as a new 'fourth pillar' of global economic governance alongside the IMF, World Bank, and WTO.[37] But it is a very different kind of pillar than the others. It has a very small staff, no formal power, and has not been ratified by any national legislature. Its primary role is simply to facilitate informal cooperation and the development and promotion of soft law international standards. In these roles, it acts more like a 'network of networks' than a supranational institutions in the mould of the IMF, World Bank, or WTO.[38]

In addition to their roles in macroeconomic and regulatory diplomacy, financial officials have been actively involved in managing financial crises, whose number and severity have grown in this age of financial globalization. The IMF has emerged as the most prominent international crisis manager in this period. In addition to providing emergency financial assistance to countries, it has assumed a lead role as international 'money doctor', offering advice to poor countries in financial difficulties. Officials from finance ministries of leading financial powers—the US Treasury in particular—have also played an important role in resolving international debt crises in this period as well as being involved in renegotiating the terms of various bilateral official debts of developing countries through a body called the Paris Club. As in the 1920s and 1960s, central bankers—often working through the BIS—have also played a key role in crisis management by offering rapid short-term financing to countries in distress. While these funds have usually served the purpose of providing balance of payments support, the US Federal Reserve offered swaps during the 2007–2008 crisis that were also designed to help foreign central banks provide adequate dollar liquidity to domestic firms.

Alongside these various roles played by financial officials, non-state actors have also emerged as important players in the world of financial diplomacy in this era of financial globalization. As in the 1920s, private financiers have become major actors in international financial negotiations ranging from crisis management to international regulatory initiatives. They have also enhanced their international diplomatic clout through the creation of various international industry associations, such as the Institute of International Finance (which represents hundreds of the world's largest international banks).[39]

In contrast to the 1920s, civil society organizations representing wider social interests have also become involved in financial diplomacy. Prominent non-governmental organizations involved in development work, such as Oxfam, have become active in international debates concerning the IMF and World Bank's policies towards developing countries from the 1980s onwards. NGOs such as the Jubilee 2000 movement and DATA also emerged after the mid-1990s as major players in the negotiation of debt relief for low-income countries. Celebrities associated with the international debt relief movement, such as rock singer Bono, have even been invited to G8 summits to present their views. Other transnational civil society organizations such as ATTAC (Association for the Taxation of financial Transactions and Aid to Citizens) or the New Rules for Global Finance have also become involved in international regulatory debates, promoting causes such as the Tobin tax.[40]

In the wake of the 2008 financial crisis, another group of actors has become more prominent in financial diplomacy: financial officials from emerging market countries. The crisis highlighted the growing influence of these countries, as many American and European banks scrambled to raise funds from their investors and financial institutions. These same investors and financial firms have also taken advantage of the troubles of their American and European counterparts to expand their influence in global markets. More generally, the US government's dependence on foreign borrowing from countries such as China was also revealed starkly by the crisis.

The growing influence of these new centres of wealth has prompted important changes to the world of financial diplomacy. In addition to the creation of the G20 leaders forum and the FSB, the membership of some of the key SSBs—such as the BCBS, the International Organization of Securities Commissions' Technical Committee, and the Committee on Payment and Settlement Systems—was widened in 2009 to include emerging market countries.[41] New efforts have been launched after the crisis to increase the voice of these countries within the IMF and World Bank. Investors and financial institutions from emerging market countries have also become more influential players in various international financial debates. The fact that some of these entities are state-owned—such as sovereign wealth funds, central banks holding large foreign reserves, or state-owned Chinese banks—has only enhanced their diplomatic significance.[42]

The changing geography of financial power in the wake of the crisis has encouraged speculation that the US-led multilateral order may increasingly fragment, encouraging greater resort to bilateral and regional techniques of financial diplomacy. Certainly, some of the key emerging financial powers—such as China and Brazil—are increasingly extending various kinds of bilateral financial assistance to economic partners. Regional financial support arrangements have also been strengthened in the wake of the 2008 financial crisis, such as East Asia's Chiang Mai Initiative (first created in 2000) and Europe's new financial rescue mechanisms created in 2010.[43] But the 'fragmentation' scenario is easily overstated since the multilateral order has simultaneously been strengthened in the wake of the crisis. In addition to the initiatives mentioned above, IMF's resources were dramatically boosted in the wake of the crisis and the IMF has been assigned a key role both by the Chiang Mai Initiative and Europe's rescue mechanisms.

8.4 Conclusion: Change and Continuity

The diplomatic role of financial officials has changed considerably since the 1920s in three respects. To begin with, the scope of the issues addressed has steadily widened. In the 1920s, financial officials already addressed a considerable number of issues in their diplomatic work: designing an international monetary regime, providing emergency financial support, engaging in limited forms of macroeconomic management, international financing advising, and negotiating international debts. During the Bretton Woods era, they added new tasks such as the provision of long-term public international loans and more active management of international imbalances. In the age of financial globalization, financial officials widened the issues they addressed further to include deeper forms of macroeconomic coordination and regulatory coordination.

Second, the types of financial officials involved in international diplomacy have also evolved since the 1920s. Central bankers were the most important national financial diplomats during the 1920s, while finance ministry officials took over that role by the time of Bretton Woods. From the 1960s onwards, central bankers re-emerged alongside finance ministry officials in prominent diplomatic roles once again and they were joined by financial regulators and supervisors for the first time. In country terms, British and American officials dominated international financial diplomacy across the three periods examined in this chapter, but emerging market countries have begun to assume a more prominent role very recently. Looking beyond the role of national officials, the diplomatic significance of financial officials employed by international organizations has also grown steadily from the age of the League and BIS, through the creation of the Bretton Woods institutions, to the more recent addition of the FSF/B, the SSBs, and various regional financial institutions. In their diplomatic roles, financial officials—both national and international—have also engaged to different degrees with non-state actors across the time periods. Involvement with private financiers has been particularly strong in eras when global markets have been powerful, such as during the 1920s and the recent age of financial globalization. The most recent era has also seen civil society organizations engage much more actively with the world of international financial diplomacy.

Finally, the techniques of diplomacy have also changed over the past one hundred years. During the 1920s, financial diplomacy was dominated by loose networks of private and public officials guided by non-binding soft laws and informal 'rules of the game'. At Bretton Woods, governments endorsed a more formal intergovernmental diplomatic model backed by binding rules and supranational institutions. In practice, however, financial diplomacy during the Bretton Woods era also involved many ad hoc bilateral and regional arrangements and, by the 1960s, informal central bank cooperation. In the age of financial globalization, the formal intergovernmentalism at Bretton Woods has coexisted with the more informal trans-governmental networked diplomacy of the G7/G20, the FSB, and SSBs, and central bank cooperation as well as with various bilateral and regional practices.

While the diplomatic role of financial officials has changed in many ways since the 1920s, there has been one important continuity. Across this time period, financial officials have shared with their counterparts a strong intellectual bond based on common technical knowledge about international finacial issues. Because many international financial issues are difficult for other policy-makers to understand fully, financial diplomats have often seen themselves, in the words of Paul Volcker, as similar to 'high priests, or perhaps stateless princes' who are 'schooled in arts with which few are familiar, arts that required both a certain amount of secrecy and mutual confidence'.[44] He also notes that central bankers in particular 'are almost uniquely able to deal with each other on a basis of close understanding and frankness', a fact he attributes to their common 'experience, tenure and training'.[45]

This transnational culture of financial officials has provided them some autonomy in their diplomatic work, an autonomy that has been further reinforced in the case of some central banks and regulatory officials by their formal institutional independence from other branches of government at home. It has also encouraged shared world views that foster cooperation. As we have seen, these shared world views are not static; financial officials shifted from embracing classical economic liberalism during the 1920s to 'embedded liberal' thinking in the Bretton Woods era to more neo-liberal ideas after the 1970s. The influence of these world views should not be overstated since national financial officials, like other diplomats, must ultimately serve the interests of their home state. Still, this unique culture of financial officials has certainly had an impact on global financial governance in the past and it is likely to continue to do so in the future, regardless of what other changes financial officials may experience in their diplomatic role.

NOTES

1. This was not the first major international monetary conference. Others had been held in the pre-1914 period—most notably those in 1867, 1878, 1881, and 1892—but their influence in the creation of the international gold standard of that era is questionable. Although the first did endorse the gold standard, the last three were called to discuss an alternative international bimetallic order. For contrasting views on this issue, see Guillio Gallarotti, *The Anatomy of an International Monetary Regime* (New York: Oxford University Press, 1995) and Stephen Reti, *Silver and Gold: The Political Economy of International Monetary Conferences, 1867–1892* (Greenport: Greenwood Press, 1998).

2. See for example Frank Costigliola, *Awkward Dominion: American Political, Economic, and Cultural Relations with Europe, 1919–1933* (Ithaca: Cornell University Press, 1984); Melvyn P. Leffler, *The Elusive Quest: America's Pursuit of European Stability and French Security, 1919–1933* (Chapel Hill: University of North Carolina Press, 1979); Michael J. Hogan,

Informal Entente: The Private Structure of Cooperation in Anglo-American Economic Diplomacy, 1918–1928 (Columbia, MO: Imprint, 1977).

3. See also Frank Costigliola, 'The other side of isolationism: the establishment of the first World Bank 1929–30', *Journal of American History* 59 (1972), 602–20; Stephen Clarke, *Central Bank Cooperation 1924–31* (New York: Federal Reserve Bank of New York, 1967).

4. See for example Barry Eichengreen, *Golden Fetters* (Oxford: Oxford University Press, 1992).

5. Stephen Clarke, *The Reconstruction of the International Monetary System: The Attempts of 1922 and 1933*, Princeton Studies in International Finance, no. 33 (Princeton: Princeton University, Dept. of Economics, International Finance Section, 1973), 11.

6. Louis Pauly, *Who Elected the Bankers?* (Ithaca: Cornell University Press, 1997); Marc Flandreau (ed.), *Money Doctoring: The Experience of International Financial Advising 1850–2000* (London: Routledge, 2003); Emily Rosenberg, *Financial Missionaries to the World: The Politics and Culture of Dollar Diplomacy 1900–30* (Cambridge, MA: Harvard University Press, 1999). Countries receiving League financial missions in the 1920s included Albania, Austria, Bulgaria, Danzig, Estonia, Greece, and Hungary. According to Paul Einzig, *Montague Norman* (London: Kegan Paul, Trench, Trubner, and Co., 1932), 78, Montague Norman played a key role behind the scenes in many of the League missions.

7. See for example Paul Drake, *The Money Doctor in the Andes: The Kemmerer Missions 1923–1933* (Durham: Duke University Press, 1989).

8. R.S. Sayers, *The Bank of England 1891–1944* (Cambridge: Cambridge University Press, 1976), 159.

9. Einzig, *Montague Norman*, 85.

10. Quote from Michael Tomz, *Reputation and International Cooperation: Sovereign Debt Across Three Centuries* (Princeton: Princeton University Press, 2007), 117. Changing attitudes had been reinforced by the 1907 Hague Convention which prohibited the use of force to collect debts unless the debtor state had refused to accept arbitration.

11. See for example William McNeil, *American Money and the Weimar Republic* (New York: Columbia University Press, 1986).

12. Pauly, *Who Elected the Bankers?*.

13. See for example Mark Metzler, *Lever of Empire: The International Gold Standard and the Crisis of Liberalism in Prewar Japan* (Berkeley: University of California Press, 2006), 303.

14. Hogan, *Informal Entente*.

15. Barry Eichengreen, 'House Calls of the Money Doctor: The Kemmerer Missions to Latin America 1917–31', in Paul Drake (ed.), *Money Doctors, Foreign Debts, and Economic Reforms in Latin America* (Willingminton: Scholarly Resource Inc., 1994); Drake, *The Money Doctor*.

16. Quoted in *The Conference Forum*, no. 3, October 2, 1920, p.23, Bank of England archives, C40/1035.

17. Henry Strakosch to Basil Blackett, October 17, 1925, p.3, Public Records Office, British National Archives, T176/25B. For these broader politics of the gold standard during the 1920s, see Barry Eichengreen, *Golden Fetters* (Oxford: Oxford University Press, 1992).

18. See for example Eric Helleiner, *The Making of National Money* (Ithaca: Cornell University Press, 2003), ch. 7.

19. Claudio Borio and Gianni Toniolo, 'One Hundred and Thirty Years of Central Bank Cooperation: A BIS Perspective', in Claudio Borrio, Gianni Toniolo, and Piet Clement (eds.), *Past and Future of Central Bank Cooperation* (Cambridge: Cambridge University Press, 2006), 25.

20. Eric Helleiner, *States and the Reemergence of Global Finance* (Ithaca: Cornell University Press, 2004), ch. 2.

21. Quoted in Richard Gardner, *Sterling-Dollar Diplomacy in Current Perspective* (New York: Columbia University Press, 1980), 76.

22. Quoted in Helleiner, *States and the Reemergence of Global Finance*, 17.

23. Quoted in Robert W. Oliver, *International Economic Co-operation and the World Bank* (London: Macmillan, 1975), 319.

24. John Ruggie, 'International Regimes, Transactions and Change: Embedded Liberalism in the Postwar Economic Order', *International Organization* 36:2 (1982), 379–405.

25. Eric Helleiner, 'The Development Mandate of International Institutions: Where Did It Come From?', *Studies in Comparative International Development* 44:3 (2009), 189–211.

26. Ruggie, 'International Regimes'; Helleiner, *States and the Reemergence of Global Finance*, ch. 2.

27. Ruggie, 'International Regimes'.

28. Helleiner, *States and the Reemergence of Global Finance*, ch. 3; Helleiner, *The Making of National Money*, ch. 9; Eric Helleiner, 'Central Bankers as Good Neighbors: US Money Doctors in Latin America During the 1940s', *Financial History Review* 16:1 (2009), 1–21.

29. Miles Kahler, 'Bretton Woods and its competitors', in David Andrews, C. Randall Henning, and Louis Pauly (eds), *Governing the World's Money* (Ithaca: Cornell University Press, 2002).

30. Helleiner, *States and the Reemergence of Global Finance*, chs 3–4.

31. For histories of financial globalization, see Helleiner, *States and the Reemergence of Global Finance*; Rawi Abdelal, *Capital Rules* (Cambridge, MA: Harvard University Press, 2009).

32. Yoichi Funabashi, *Managing the Dollar* (Washington: Institute for International Economics, 1988).

33. See for example Anne-Marie Slaughter, *A New World Order* (Princeton: Princeton University Press, 2005).

34. See for example Andrew Baker, *The Group of Seven: Finance Ministries, Central Banks and Global Financial Governance* (New York: Routledge, 2006).

35. For an overview, see Howard Davies and David Green, *Global Financial Regulation: The Essential Guide* (Cambridge, MA: Polity, 2008).

36. Membership in the FSF had already been expanded before the FSB's creation to include Singapore, Hong Kong, Australia, Switzerland, and the Netherlands. See Eric Helleiner, 'What Role for the New Financial Stability Board? The Politics of International Standards After the Crisis', *Global Policy* 1:3 (2010), 282–90.

37. Quoted in Helleiner, 'What Role?', 285.

38. Tony Porter, 'Compromises of embedded knowledge', in Stephen Bernstein and Louis Pauly (eds), *Global liberalism and political order* (Albany: State University of New York Press, 2007), used this phrase to describe its predecessor, the FSF.

39. Tony Porter, *Globalization and Finance* (Oxford: Polity, 2005).

40. Jan Aart Scholte and Albrecht Schnabel (eds), *Civil Society and Global Finance* (London: Routledge, 2002); Porter, *Globalization and Finance*, ch. 9; Andrew F. Cooper, *Celebrity Diplomacy* (Boulder, CO: Paradigm Publishers, 2007).

41. Eric Helleiner, Stefano Pagliari, and Hubert Zimmermann (eds), *Global Finance in Crisis: The Politics of International Regulatory Change* (London: Routledge, 2010).

42. Eric Helleiner and Stefano Pagliari, 'The End of an Era in International Financial Regulation? A Post-Crisis Research Agenda', *International Organization* 65 (2011), 169–200.

43. Greg Chin, 'Remaking the Architecture: the Emerging Powers, Self-insuring and Regional Insulation', *International Affairs* 86:3 (2010), 693–715.
44. Paul Volcker and Toyoo Gyohten, *Changing Fortunes* (New York: Times Books, 1992), 99. In this passage, Volcker is describing the sentiments of financial officials working within the OECD's Working Party Three in the 1960s.
45. Volcker and Gyohten, *Changing Fortunes*, 201. See also Ethan Kapstein, 'Between Power and Purpose', *International Organization* 46 (1992), 265–87.

CHAPTER 9

....

CIVIL SOCIETY

....

KATHRYN HOCHSTETLER

CLASSIC definitions of diplomacy, characterizing it as peaceful interactions among state actors, leave civil society outside the concept.[1] The rise of civil society's participation in global governance in the 20th century is thus transformative, making diplomacy less an exclusive club than a complex network of relationships only partially controllable by traditional diplomats. This chapter aims to find patterns in the influence of these comparatively new actors. After defining civil society and tracing its historical emergence, I argue that civil society organizations are most important at the beginnings and ends of global diplomatic efforts. At the beginning, they are critical for putting new issues on the agenda and shaping the ways those issues are understood. At the end, they help to implement global accords, with their wide presence and loose networking an asset for taking global agreements to the local level. They are less central in the classic stages of diplomatic negotiations between governmental representatives, but their strong presence in other roles now transforms negotiations as well.

9.1 CIVIL SOCIETY: DEFINING AN ELUSIVE CONCEPT

....

Compared to most major diplomatic actors, 'civil society' has an unusually rich conceptual history and an uncommonly varied set of empirical referents.[2] Indeed, the private sector and some international monitors, which are counted as separate actors in this *Handbook*, are often viewed as part of civil society. The fact that actors of civil society are frequently identified by negative terms—e.g. *non*-governmental organizations (NGOs)—contributes to the elusiveness of the concept. The United Nations (UN) contributed the NGOs label to the debate, including any non-state actor in the category, but many other definitions seek more empirical specificity. In this section, I set out an empirical delimiting of my own scope.

Civil society is a sphere of social life that is analytically distinct from the state and market spheres, even as it is closely interrelated with them. The parts of civil society that are most consistently important for diplomacy are the self-organized associations that engage in collective action that crosses state boundaries. Among these, the most prominent are the principled advocacy groups that mobilize in support 'of what they deem the wider public interest'.[3] Willetts' label for NGOs at the UN— 'the conscience of the world' — is typical of this understanding of civil society.[4] Scholars often emphasize the principled character of civil society in order to separate it from the for-profit sphere of the private market sector. As will be discussed in more detail later, this set of civil society organizations is especially active in the normative and agenda-setting dimensions of global diplomacy and governance. Consequently they can both enhance and diminish the broader legitimacy of global state-based action.

While principled advocacy groups are important components of civil society, the definition used here is more expansive in two ways. First, it includes collective actors who participate in global politics on other bases, including the ability to provide expertise or services.[5] The former are especially important on topics where expert knowledge is critical, including environment and health issues, while the latter are vital implementers of global commitments. Both also speak for the wider public interest, but tend to understand it in technical rather than normative terms, such as techniques of standardization or vaccination strategies. Concretely, this expansion means scientists, relief agencies, electoral observers, and the like are also part of civil society and important additions to the world of diplomats.

Second, the focus on principled advocacy groups often smuggles in implicit normative commitments, with the label reserved for 'good' groups. The term *civil* society itself implies an opposite of *uncivil* society, understood as groups pursuing unpalatable ends.[6] In the Western academic literature, for example, research on civil society in diplomacy is heavily focused on a few topics that follow liberal Western norms, including human rights, gender equality, environmental protection, and democracy-promotion. The literature is more divided on its assessments of organizations associated with the liberal economic order.[7] In this chapter, I endeavour to keep such normative limits out of the concept of civil society—even though many civil society groups themselves try to place such limits, as both feminist and traditional Catholic/Islamist groups did at the Fourth World Conference on Women in Beijing.[8] The one substantive limit I draw in this chapter is that groups for whom overthrowing the state is a primary aim or whose tactics include frequent and intentional uses of violence against people are excluded from my discussion. Such groups invoke such different responses from state actors and diplomats that they form a separate piece of the non-state world.

Throughout this definitional section, I have used words like 'groups', 'organizations', and the like routinely, since many of the empirical referents of civil society are in fact established groups. Civil society is a realm of association and collective action, and that often takes an institutionalized form. On the other hand, not all civil society participants are actually fixed organizations. 'Association' is a more flexible term, meaning generally 'attachments we choose for specific purposes,' and the attachments may be thick—as they are in organizations—or thin.[9] One of the hallmarks of global associations is that attachments are often thinner than in similar domestic associations, given distances of geography, language, and lived experience. Much research on civil society at the global level speaks of networks to try to capture the observation that the nature of the connections between actors may be as important as the actors themselves.[10]

9.2 A Historical Overview of the Rise of Civil Society in Diplomacy

Data on civil society association at the international level is sketchy, reflecting the ephemeral quality of many of these actors. Historical studies have relied on the *Yearbook of International Organizations*, whose data support the claim that 25,000 international civil society organizations were created between 1850 and 1988. These are international organizations in both membership and structure. Early growth was small and steady, with really striking expansion appearing only after the Second World War.[11] Of the organizations on which there was detailed information, 17.8 per cent of them were actually industry and trade groups, so outside the definition of civil society used here. Another 14.9 per cent focused on health care, while scientific (11.6 per cent), sports (8.0 per cent), and technical and infrastructure (7.4 per cent) groups made up the rest of the top five categories, totalling nearly 60 per cent of all organizations. The advocacy organizations that gain so much academic attention total about 12 per cent of international non-state organizations.[12]

Many of these organizations rarely directly engage in international diplomacy, although they form part of the civil society backdrop for those that do. Only 511 international organizations currently have full or associate consultative status with the Economic and Social Council (ECOSOC) of the United Nations, for example—although that number has risen since the 418 that did in 1993.[13] On the other hand, many organizations that are not structurally international, having membership and organization in only one country, *do* participate in global diplomacy. The number of organizations attending the activities around the United Nations-sponsored environment conferences grew exponentially from under 300 at the 1972 Stockholm Conference on the Human Environment to the 15,000 who were part of the Johannesburg World Summit on Sustainable Development thirty years later. Tens of thousands more came to South Africa to take part in informal side events.[14]

The count of individual civil society participants in diplomacy is probably in the hundreds of thousands, especially when one includes occasional participants. They can overwhelm diplomatic spaces, as when registered participants for the COP-15 Climate Change conference in 2009 reached 30,123 (NGO observers were 20,611 of these)—for a space that only held 15,000.[15] Government responses to the rise in numbers have ranged from good-faith efforts to accommodate all potential participants, to grumbling about their presence and resorting to various ruses to geographically separate NGO and government participants.[16] In extreme cases, diplomats have chosen to meet in locations where NGOs cannot easily follow, such as the G7 meetings at the Gleneagles golf course in Scotland and the Canadian Arctic territory of Nunavut. At the other extreme, former UN Secretary-General Kofi Annan asked a high-level panel to study ways for the UN to overcome the 'democratic deficit' of global governance. After extensive consultations, the panel's 2004 report, *We the Peoples: Civil Society, the UN and Global Governance*, provided immediate guidance for a more effective response to the Indian Ocean tsunami, although much work remains for full implementation.[17]

Whatever the preferences of states and the exact numbers of participants, it is certainly the case that 'by the Rio conference in 1992, states had to understand that calling a global conference among states also issued a shadow invitation to a plethora of non-state actors' who would appear to pursue their own aims and agendas.[18] Planning for their presence is one of the major challenges of modern diplomacy.

9.3 Diplomacy and Beyond: The Roles of Civil Society in Global Politics

The introduction to this *Handbook* lists roles that civil society can play in diplomacy: 'research; outreach education; advocacy and norm promotion; agenda-setting; lobbying governments and intergovernmental organizations to adopt and police laws, policies, and courses of action; implementing programmes and delivering services and humanitarian assistance; monitoring implementation of international commitments; and direct action'.[19] Here I discuss the roles in more detail, presenting them in their order in the policy process. I first show how civil society helps to raise issues for diplomatic attention—agenda-setting and framing. Second, I examine the roles civil society may play as issues come under active treatment by diplomats. Finally, I discuss how civil society organizations help with the implementation of international agreements. In each of these stages, only some of the activities of civil society directly intersect with formal diplomacy, but even indirect engagement can affect the outcome of diplomatic efforts.

9.3.1 Setting the Agenda

The idea that civil society helps to set the global political agenda is broadly accepted. In a realm of *voluntary* association, civil society's collective actors only come into being when preferences are intense, usually because participants have a direct stake in the outcome or a personal ideological or expertise commitment. Civil society actors tend to specialize in these areas of intense preference, fighting for global attention to the topic and exhorting states to action. They readily form associations around topics that reflect consensual positions. One of their more unusual and important qualities, however, is to often be ahead of popular opinion in the causes they espouse. Early transnational campaigns grounded in civil society activism challenged unreflective societal acceptance of practices like economic slavery or foot binding of women in China.[20] More recently, civil society organizations have insisted on introducing human rights protections in authoritarian regimes in the Southern Cone of South America, when many governments and other parts of society hesitated to take those on. The fact that civil society stands somewhat separate from power structures of state and economy allows it to be the location of critical voices.[21]

Civil society actors also bring issues to the global agenda from their lived experience. The increased density of civil society networking has helped identify shared experiences that are felt locally, but form part of global patterns. The movement between 'tribal 'and 'global villages' by Latin American indigenous populations is a good example; Brysk chooses the word 'collision' to describe the impact. While both human rights and indigenous populations had been on the global agenda before, the emergence and participation of indigenous civil society activists themselves at the global level in the 1990s has transformed all sides.[22] Grassroots groups, including women, sometimes find the world of global diplomacy to be a place where they can be heard more clearly than they can at home.[23] In addition to challenging the ways their governments speak for them internationally, grassroots activists also sometimes challenge the formulations and agenda priorities of principled advocacy organizations.[24]

Actors in civil society bring additional issues to the global agenda as a result of their formal expertise. Experts are especially critical for identifying potential problems that are beyond immediate lived experience. One prominent example is the role of scientists who discovered the hole in the ozone layer over Antarctica, successfully argued that chloroflourocarbon (CFC) and halon consumption were responsible, and helped marshal the international diplomatic response, the Montreal Protocol. Routine scientific research also generated findings that raised the acid rain and climate change issues to the global agenda.[25] In addition to problem identification, experts also play crucial roles in narrowing the range of uncertainty about how to respond. One of the most prominent examples is again from the environmental issue area, where the Intergovernmental Panel on Climate Change (IPCC) has had the ongoing task of assessing expert knowledge on climate change.[26] The simple fact of claimed expertise does not put an issue on the agenda, of course, and scientific expertise has not convinced governments to act on climate issues.[27]

Whatever the means by which an item comes to the civil society agenda, activists tend to use similar strategies to prod governments to act. The most common is some form of generating public awareness. In one well-known example, Rachel Carson's book *Silent Spring* is frequently credited for helping to start the environmental movement in the United States and then elsewhere.[28] The media alternatives have greatly expanded over time, offering civil society many new opportunities for spreading information while making it increasingly hard to actually gain public and diplomatic attention. The networks that increasingly link civil society actors around the world have the same effect.

Disasters often help to concentrate attention in this information-dense context.[29] Barring these kinds of events, activists may make their own news events through protests and other acts designed to draw public attention. Public arousal is often most influential for national governments, who then carry the issue to the intergovernmental agenda.

Civil society actors also engage in activities designed to influence governments more directly. They may lobby their own governments or governments gathered collectively. Civil society groups commonly identify key governments that are likely to be supportive of their agendas, and try to persuade them to bring their concerns into the actual negotiation agenda. For example, peace activists found the German government comparatively receptive to their arguments about the need to change the global security model in the final days of the cold war, and that government in turn pushed a corresponding new diplomatic agenda.[30] Similarly, sixty developing countries took advocacy NGOs' preferred stance on intellectual property and AIDS drugs into the 2001 meeting of the World Trade Organization (WTO), and managed to push much of it through.[31]

The single most important contribution of civil society organizations to global diplomacy is through the way they help to shape public understandings of particular issues, a process known as 'issue framing'. They may have an important framing role even if they do not themselves place an issue on the agenda. Issue framing takes basic facts and shapes a meaning and narrative around them that the framers hope will compel diplomatic action. While the framing is usually done with some basis in the group's own principles and expertise, successful civil society organizations are also typically experts in strategic framing that resonates with the understandings of the actors they are seeking to influence. When states and other targets respond positively, they do so for a range of reasons that fall somewhere on a spectrum between coerced and instrumental reasons (e.g. foreign aid may depend on it) to persuasion and full conversion to the issue as framed.[32]

One example of an act of strategic framing was the successful effort to rebrand debt relief for poor countries through the Jubilee 2000 campaign that made it a quasi-religious act of 'millennial forgiveness'. With this framing, 'Bono made Jesse Helms cry' and that conservative US senator/gatekeeper opened the way for the United States and then the rest of the G7 to put debt relief on the diplomatic agenda in 1999 and negotiate an agreement by 2005.[33] Another common framing pattern finds civil society actors offering opposing accounts of the same issue, as when both industry and NGO networks made humanitarian arguments for their respective positions on intellectual property rights. Industry largely won the debate in the trade negotiations themselves, but NGOs managed to reopen the issue in their favour over HIV/AIDS drugs.[34] As they put issues on the diplomatic agenda, then, civil society actors are critical for framing not just the importance of an issue, but what it is seen to be.

There is no doubt that the greater involvement of civil society in diplomacy has widened the diplomatic agenda. Civil society actors bring the perspectives of *society*, those of ordinary citizens rather than the political elite who by definition make up the world's governments and much of its diplomatic corps. As such, many of their concerns are closely related to ordinary life conditions and needs. This is a role that is especially criti-cal in circumstances where national governments may not represent the aspirations and needs of their populations well. The human rights and humanitarian issue areas are two where civil society has played an expansive role that has increased the international sys-tem's responsiveness to the needs of its most vulnerable citizens. For these reasons, some authors see the activities of civil society in setting the global agenda as probably democ-racy-enhancing.[35]

What is less remarked is that an agenda set by civil society is not necessarily either complete or well oriented. Unequal relations of power, resources, and information may distort the civil society agenda in much the same ways as they do the governmental one. Even principled actors act in concrete environments where they struggle to match their sense of identity to rapidly changing needs and more prosaic competition for resources and support. As Michael Barnett notes with regards to humanitarian organizations, agenda evolution through activism is not necessarily progressive.[36] The same networks and debates that generate activism can also shut it down. Charli Carpenter shows that a combination of buck-passing, too many veto players, and framing disagreements kept human rights activists from taking up the problem of children born of wartime rape—even while the activists worked together on trying to reduce the number of child sol-diers.[37] These considerations raise questions about how democratic the civil society sphere itself is likely to be[38]—although the addition of civil society does not evidently make the diplomatic world *less* democratic than a government-only diplomacy would be. Instead, the diplomatic agenda should include consideration of how to make civil society participation more inclusive.

Finally, citizens as well as elites may be short-sighted in important ways. Human beings often process risk in ways that overemphasize particular kinds while overlooking others.[39] Studies on the psychology of risk associated with climate change, for example, support the general conclusion that 'people are likely to act on decisions derived from affective feelings and personal experience but not on decisions from statistical descrip-tions of risks'.[40] Similarly, conservation organizations feature mammals and birds in their publications (rather than invertebrate, fish, amphibian, reptile, or plant species) because of the greater appeal of these more 'charismatic' species,[41] even though they may objectively be less important. For these reasons, the fact of widespread attention and activism—or its absence—should not become a final arbiter of the global agenda.

This section of the chapter has argued that civil society plays a critical role in helping to decide what issues are and are not on the global diplomatic agenda. They do so both by influencing the public perception of what deserves global attention and by persuad-ing states directly to take up new issues. As they place issues on the agenda, their ability to frame the way the issue is perceived is both a condition of their success and itself changes the way the issue will be addressed diplomatically. Whether civil society agenda-setting enhances global democracy is a subject of some debate. Finally, putting an issue on the diplomatic agenda—and even framing the issue in ways that limit the range of options for diplomats—is not the same as actually achieving a global agreement for action. The next section investigates how civil society might be involved in that step.

9.3.2 A Voice in Negotiations

Diplomatic interaction includes many activities. My discussion here focuses more specifically on the role of civil society in diplomacy-cum-negotiation, since civil society is much more present in these activities than in diplomacy-cum-coercion. In addition, summit and shuttle versions of diplomatic negotiation have little room for civil society, so the main attention is to fairly formal multilateral negotiations.[42] So, then, how is civil society present in diplomatic negotiations? Who sets the rules for that participation, and how has it varied over time and across issue areas? Does civil society participation enhance the democracy and legitimacy of negotiations?

The first two questions must be answered together: while members of civil society are now frequently present in negotiations, states continue to negotiate every time the kind of access civil society will have. A few global organizations stand nearly alone at one end of the spectrum, with civil society organizations as equal partners with governments. The International Labour Organization makes labour and business equal partners with state representatives in all its negotiations on labour issues. Similarly, the International Union for the Conservation of Nature (IUCN) calls itself 'a democratic membership union', with government, NGO, and scientist members as equals.[43]

The exclusive end of the spectrum is much more crowded; it includes not only much of diplomatic history before the 1970s, but continues to characterize many negotiations on economic and security issues. Human rights organizations are often unable to influence states in conflict situations, failing to persuade the US to close the Guantanamo prison, for example.[44] Near the exclusive end, we also find openings that are, as one participant in the civil society forums associated with the negotiations of a Free Trade Agreement of the Americas characterized them, 'at best a *buzón* [a mailbox] and at worst a *lata de basura* [a trash can]'.[45] It is not a coincidence that the habitually closed economic negotiations often find themselves the target of large and hostile civil society mobilizations, as the streets are the primary location from which advocacy efforts can seek to influence the negotiations.[46]

In between these extremes we find diplomatic negotiations on environment, food, health, human rights, women's rights, and many more topics that offer civil society some set of limited opportunities to participate.[47] In Pamela Chasek's summary of eleven major cases of environmental negotiations, civil society was frequently present in agenda-setting, with scientists brought in at an early stage to help identify and evaluate possible alternatives for action. In negotiations themselves, the fullest civil society participation came historically early, when the hybrid IUCN set out to draft an international convention on species conservation back in 1963, not even offering the document to governments until the third draft. The IUCN continues to help implement and update the resulting Convention on International Trade in Endangered Species (CITES). Some NGOs also helped to draft the Montreal Protocol on ozone at its second session in 1987 and civil society was also quite active in these negotiations.[48] These experiences remain a high point of participation, as negotiations since have focused on documents drafted by governments or intergovernmental organizations like the United Nations.

Beginning in the 1980s, ever larger numbers of NGOs also began to come to negotiations as observers, where they sought to lobby government negotiators as the deliberations unfolded. The rise in numbers of civil society participant-observers in global diplomacy followed the explosion in numbers of civil society organizations themselves in the 1990s. It was accompanied by a diversification of types of civil society present. In early years, participating NGOs had tended to be organizations with a great deal of experience in international negotiations, well schooled in diplomatic courtesies. The 1990s brought many more advocacy and grassroots organizations to what had formerly been the province of expertise-based and professionalized advocacy organizations. These quantitative and qualitative transitions were perhaps most evident in the issue conferences that the UN sponsored across the 1990s and 2000s, where tens of thousands of civil society participant-observers began to gather thanks to new registration procedures.

Civil society organizations and their state supporters had to fight a battle to be present before every negotiating process.[49] Their increasing numbers brought consternation to many governments, who debated at the beginning of every new conference process whether civil society should be present and in what forms. Especially Asian and African governments regularly argued against allowing civil society attendance, and wanted to limit the forms of access and participation. Developing countries have worried that NGOs, whose most influential organizations are Western, exacerbate an international power imbalance that already favours North over South. The very flexibility and grassroots scale of civil society organizations, an advantage in other ways, makes them able to penetrate into domestic jurisdictions in ways even states cannot; this is acknowledged by the preference of many Northern governments and development agencies to funnel funds through NGOs rather than states. When joined with thoughtless comments like Colin Powell's that NGOs are 'force multipliers' of US efforts in Afghanistan and elsewhere, the concerns are understandable.[50]

The large numbers of organizations challenged long-time civil society participants as well. Those long-time participants tried to coordinate and channel civil society participation in order to make it more effective in the negotiations—and not derail the efforts of the original civil society participants. During the PrepComs of the 1992 Rio Conference on Environment and Development, NGOs began to hold daily strategy sessions to inform each other on the negotiations and coordinate the day's lobbying. They circulated civil society newspapers like the new *Earth Negotiations Bulletin*, which has become a critical source of information for many government delegations as well as for civil society. They set up working groups to accompany each part of the governmental negotiations and to draft proposals for language revisions and plan specific influence strategies. All of these strategies became part of the repertoire that civil society actors have used in subsequent negotiations on many issues.[51]

Notwithstanding an occasional plenary session, civil society influence in negotiations has mostly consisted of these off-stage efforts to lobby governments. They have been further limited in their lobbying efforts by states' efforts to limit their access to serious negotiations. Writing about the UN conferences of the 1990s, Friedman, Hochstetler, and Clark identified what they called the '4th PrepCom phenomenon': as states progressed into the multi-year preparatory process of writing an international agreement and began to negotiate issues of real dissension, they tended to retreat into less formal sessions behind closed doors.[52] Even more open government delegations, which held regular briefing sessions for national civil society groups, held back information about the state of affairs. Left out of the negotiations, civil society groups combed through trash cans for documents, used mobile phones to call friendly delegates, and produced their own suggested language even if they could not be present to hear it discussed.

While NGOs decried their exclusion, evidence from other negotiations shows that civil society actors do not have to actually be present to influence outcomes. The massive protests at the Seattle meeting of the WTO in 1999 were instrumental in derailing that session (delegates could not even reach the negotiation space at first), which activists cheered. Two years later, in a meeting moved to Doha where NGOs could not easily travel and the government disallowed all protests, the history of the Seattle protests and public attention to earlier claims about intellectual property as a threat to public health (through the cost of anti-AIDS drugs) made the United States and other northern countries accept terms they did not want.[53]

Civil society organizations themselves often display mixed opinions about the value of their participation in governmental negotiations. During the 1990s UN conferences, for example, civil society attendees split between 'lobbyers' and 'networkers'. The former applied for state certification and attended the governmental sessions to lobby for concrete changes in the conference documents. The always-more-numerous networkers came to the negotiation location primarily to interact with other civil society actors, often dismissing the governmental negotiations as missing key agenda items or unable to get beyond state-based solutions.[54] Other negotiations, like those around a Free Trade Agreement of the Americas, saw civil society similarly split between 'insider' and 'outsider' strategies, again dividing on whether they saw governmental negotiations as able to reach an acceptable outcome. In this case, insiders aimed to improve the Free Trade Agreement through lobbying, while outsiders wanted to derail it altogether with their protests.[55]

Similar kinds of calculations affect whether civil society organizations show up at all. Jackie Smith has identified a gradual move by civil society groups concerned with economic justice away from UN negotiations altogether. Seeing the comparatively open UN diplomacy as toothless and unable to address tough economic dilemmas while the same are debated in closed WTO sessions, these activists increasingly went to where they were not welcome rather than to where their participation could not have the impact they wanted.[56] One of the untold stories of the rise of civil society in diplomacy is how often activists choose to stay home. Except for some business and labour organizations, for example, the Mercosur free trade area no longer engages activists, as they have concluded it is not generating outcomes with much impact.[57] Different understandings of economic priorities—and access issues—send business leaders to the annual World Economic Forum in Davos, while leftist civil society activists head south to the World Social Forum.

As this section shows, it is hard to generalize about civil society influence in negotiations. Their impact ranges from major (CITES) to negligible (too many to mention). While civil society organizations have developed many strategies to try to influence governments, a number of governments do not even want them present. Their access must constantly be renegotiated, and even friendly states agree to close them out at contentious stages or on contentious issues. Much civil society influence in negotiations comes in a form that is hard to track and harder to generalize, in the influence of civil society actors on particular national diplomatic delegations.[58] Civil society organizations themselves show considerable ambiguity about their participation in global negotiations. They are often divided between those who find the diplomatic processes important and useful and those who see few positive outcomes from diplomacy and so mobilize in parallel or in order to derail the diplomacy altogether. And sometimes they stay home.

9.3.3 Implementing Diplomatic Agreements

Civil society organizations perform some of their most important functions in the final stage of diplomacy, which is the implementation of diplomatic agreements. Implementation, which depends on many coordinated actions, is a good match for the mutable scale and many types of civil society organizations. While there is no one-to-one correlation between civil society types and implementation roles, there is an elective affinity among them. Thus, when implementation involves establishing a new international institution that requires national reports and the development of standards, experts and some service civil society organizations will have roles to play. Advocacy organizations are critical when national implementation requires the creation of new national legislation and institutions. They also prod and shame governments and others into living up to their international commitments. Finally, grassroots and service organizations are important for enabling the many small activities that bring international agreements into daily practice. This section briefly discusses each of these roles, and then concludes with a final way that civil society groups may step in to implement international aims where governments cannot.

A final step in the negotiation of most international accords is the decision of whether to create a new institution to oversee the accord's implementation or rely on existing institutions and governmental reports for implementation. Civil society actors, who tend to participate because of the intensity of their commitment to an issue, push the creation of new institutions, especially if they can carve out new roles for themselves. Human rights activists successfully insisted on a High Commissioner on Human Rights, and have gained procedures that allow them to present formal complaints that the Human Rights Council will investigate. The High Commissioner also depends on several councils and boards of experts to evaluate human rights complaints, and any part of civil society may bring a complaint. Environmental activists also successfully argued for a new Commission on Sustainable Development. Civil society organizations are active participants in its annual meetings, with most participants coming from scientific or more formal advocacy organizations. They are included in dialogues with governmental representatives and bring statements of their policy recommendations.[59] These examples could be multiplied among the diplomatic accords that include formal international oversight.

At the national level, many international agreements require domestic legislative changes to make laws consistent or to carry out the new accord. Civil society organizations may accelerate this process by pressuring their national governments at home and/or by helping to create a national consensus on the new international plan. International accords are almost inherently imperfect matches for particular national understandings and legal frameworks, so advocacy groups and others play a critical role in 'reversing transnationalism' and translating international agreements into language and institutions that are compelling in the national context.[60] They do this through framing activities and agenda-setting that are quite similar to such activities at the international level. Civil society groups also monitor how well their governments are doing in translating their international commitments into domestic action and report back to the international level. In a variety of ways, the civil society groups are trying to merge the two audiences of diplomats, preventing them from taking positions abroad that they would prefer not to defend at home and making the two-level game of diplomacy increasingly a single-level game.[61]

Ultimately, implementation of most international agreements depends on changes in daily behaviour. This part of implementation frequently relies on the work of grassroots and service organizations of civil society as they are closest to daily life. Large governmental ambitions like the Millennium Development Goals, for example, depend on a myriad of civil society organizations that will organize health clinics, carry out literacy campaigns, and develop new community water systems. Governments will supply many of the funds and resources for these, but civil society groups will be the ones who figure out exactly how to do them. In some cases, it is even the civil society organizations that do the visioning and coordinating of projects that may help to implement governmental goals. This is especially the case with the large foundations that have agendas of their own to address basic diseases like malaria or to formulate policy alternatives on topics from migration to environmental sustainability.[62]

Finally, one virtue of civil society organizations is that they can sometimes act when and where governments cannot, providing a replacement for governmental diplomacy. This role is especially critical in conflict situations where outside governments are mistrusted, including in situations of high conflict. The International Committee of the Red Cross and the Red Crescent Movement have carved out roles of this kind, providing direct care for the victims of conflict and being allowed in as an external observer under the broad orientations of the Geneva Convention.[63] Their explicitly apolitical orientation has historically allowed them access to victims of violence and even to leaders perpetrating violence who they may try to influence on behalf of victims, although participants and observers agree that this positioning requires increasingly tricky negotiations.[64] As humanitarian NGOs have been included in global policy-making debates, the line between them and classic diplomatic actors is also blurred.[65] Yet these roles may have a dark side: as absent states and their challengers take advantage of the presence of NGOs, humanitarian assistance can enable governments to abdicate from their own responsibilities and even prolong conflict.[66]

9.4 Conclusion

This chapter shows that civil society is present in many domains of modern diplomacy. Civil society organizations have placed new concerns on the diplomatic agenda, framing them in ways that move people to action and offer particular resolutions of global problems. In their ability to shape agendas and then follow negotiations closely, they have complicated global diplomacy with new ideas and voices. On the other hand, this 'complication' has also contributed to the potential legitimacy of diplomatic agreements, by building in greater responsiveness to citizen concerns. The process is imperfect, not least because civil society itself is a space of many divisions and power dynamics. At the other end of the negotiation process, civil society appears in a central implementation role for international agreements. The large numbers, diversity, and geographic spread of civil society actors increase the capillary reach of governmental accords, ensuring that they are implemented over both time and space. Civil society is perhaps least important in the classic moment of diplomacy, of direct negotiations among governmental representatives. However, that moment is strongly shaped by the fact that civil society is known to be paying attention, and has changed both the agenda of the diplomatic negotiations and the odds that negotiated agreements will actually lead to the agreed behaviour.

Notes

1. See the editors' introduction, this volume.
2. Jean L. Cohen and Andrew Arato, *Civil Society and Political Theory* (Cambridge: MIT Press, 1992); Elisabeth Jay Friedman, Kathryn Hochstetler, and Ann Marie Clark, *Sovereignty, Democracy, and Global Civil Society: State-Society Relations at UN Issue Conferences* (Albany, NY: State University of New York Press, 2005); John A. Hall, *Civil Society: Theory, History, Comparison* (Cambridge, MA: Blackwell and Cambridge, UK: Polity, 1995); Richard Price, 'Transnational Civil Society and Advocacy in World Politics' (Review Essay), *World Politics* 55:4 (2003), 579–606.
3. Price, 'Transnational Civil Society', 580; Margaret E. Keck and Kathryn Sikkink, *Activists Beyond Borders: Advocacy Networks in International Politics* (Ithaca: Cornell University Press, 1998).
4. Peter Willetts (ed.), *'The Conscience of the World': The Influence of Non-Governmental Organisations in the U.N. System* (Washington DC: Brookings Institution Press, 1996).
5. Anna Vakil, 'Confronting the Classification Problem: Towards a Taxonomy of NGOs', *World Development* 25:12 (December 1997), 2057–70; Peter Haas (ed.), special issue of

International Organization on epistemic communities, 46:1 (Winter 1992); Radoslav S. Dimitrov, 'Knowledge, Power, and Interests in Environmental Regime Formation', *International Studies Quarterly* 47:1 (March 2003), 123–50; Thomas Weiss (ed.), *Beyond UN Subcontracting: Task-Sharing with Regional Security Arrangements and Service-Providing NGOs* (New York: St. Martin's Press, 1998).

6. Jorge Heine and Ramesh Thakur (eds), *The Dark Side of Globalization* (Tokyo: United Nations University Press, 2011).

7. Compare Jackie Smith, *Social Movements for Global Democracy* (Baltimore: Johns Hopkins University Press, 2008); Glen Biglaiser and Karl DeRouen Jr., 'Sovereign Bond Ratings and Neoliberalism in Latin America', *International Studies Quarterly* 51:1 (2007), 121–38; and Benjamin Cashore, 'Legitimacy and the Privatization of Governance: How Non-State Market-Drive (NSMD) Governance Systems Gain Rule-Making Authority', *Governance* 15:4 (2002), 503–29.

8. Friedman, Hochstetler, Clark, *Sovereignty, Democracy, and Global Civil Society*, 91.

9. Mark E. Warren, *Democracy and Association* (Princeton: Princeton University Press, 2001), 39.

10. Keck and Sikkink, *Activists Beyond Borders*; Miles Kahler (eds), *Networked Politics: Agency, Power, and Governance* (Ithaca: Cornell University Press, 2009).

11. John Boli and George M. Thomas, 'World Culture in the World Polity: A Century of International Non-Governmental Organization', *American Sociological Review* 62:2 (April 1997), 174–6.

12. Boli and Thomas, 'World Culture', 183.

13. The 1993 number is from Friedman, Hochstetler, Clark, *Sovereignty, Democracy, and Global Civil Society*, 27. The current 2012 figure is from <http://www.ngocongo.org/membership/ecosoc-and-ngo-consultative-status/>.

14. The 1972 number is from Friedman, Hochstetler, Clark, *Sovereignty, Democracy, and Global Civil Society*, 36. The Johannesburg figures are from the newsletter of the World Federation of United Nations Associations, *UN Connections*, Issue 11, August 2002, online at <www.wfuna.org>.

15. Dana R. Fisher, 'COP-15 in Copenhagen: How the Merging of Movements Left Civil Society Out in the Cold', *Global Environmental Politics* 10:2 (May 2010), 12–14.

16. Friedman, Hochstetler, Clark, *Sovereignty, Democracy, and Global Civil Society*, ch. 2.

17. Thomas G. Weiss and Ramesh Thakur, *Global Governance and the UN: An Unfinished Journey* (Bloomington: Indiana University Press, 2010), 43–5.

18. Friedman, Hochstetler, Clark, *Sovereignty, Democracy, and Global Civil Society*, 157.

19. Editors' introduction. See also P. J. Simmons, 'Learning to Live with NGOs', *Foreign Policy* 112 (Autumn, 1998), 82–96.

20. Keck and Sikkink, *Activists Beyond Borders*, ch. 2.

21. Enrique Peruzzotti, 'Representation, Accountability, and Civil Society', in Lisa Jordan and Peter Van Tujil (eds), *NGO Accountability: Politics, Principles, and Innovation* (London: Earthscan, 2006). Of course, civil society activists may also be or become part of power structures themselves. See Michael Barnett, 'Evolution Without Progress? Humanitarianism in a World of Hurt', *International Organization* 63:4 (Fall 2009), 621–63; Shareen Hertel, *Unexpected Power: Conflict and Change Among Transnational Activists* (Ithaca: Cornell University Press, 2006).

22. Alison Brysk, *From Tribal Village to Global Village: Indian Rights and International Relations in Latin America* (Stanford: Stanford University Press, 2000).

23. Eva Friedlander (ed.), *Look at the World Through Women's Eyes: Plenary Speeches from the NGO Forum on Women, Beijing '95* (New York: Women, Ink and the NGO Forum on Women, Beijing '95, Inc, 1996).

24. Hertel, *Unexpected Power*, 2–3.

25. Pamela S. Chasek, *Earth Negotiations: Analyzing Thirty Years of Environmental Diplomacy* (Tokyo: United Nations University Press, 2001).

26. Chapter 47, this volume.

27. Peter M. Haas, 'When Does Power Listen to Truth? A Constructivist Approach to the Policy Process', *Journal of European Public Policy* 11:4 (August 2004), 569–92.

28. Chasek, *Earth Negotiations*, 17; Rachel Carson, *Silent Spring* (New York: Houghton Mifflin, 1962).

29. Chasek, *Earth Negotiations*, 135.

30. Thomas Risse-Kappen, 'Ideas do not Float Freely: Transnational Coalitions, Domestic Structures, and the End of the Cold War', *International Organization* 48:2 (1994), 185–214.

31. John S. Odell, 'Breaking Deadlocks in International Institutional Negotiations: The WTO, Seattle, and Doha', *International Studies Quarterly* 53 (2009), 2273–99.

32. Joshua William Busby, 'Bono Made Jesse Helms Cry: Jubilee 2000, Debt Relief, and Moral Action in International Politics', *International Studies Quarterly* 51:2 (2007), 247–75; Thomas Risse, Steven Ropp, and Kathryn Sikkink (eds), *The Power of Human Rights: International Norms and Domestic Change* (Cambridge: Cambridge University Press, 1999).

33. Busby, 'Bono Made Jesse Helms Cry', 257.

34. Susan K. Sell and Aseem Prakash, 'Using Ideas Strategically: The Contest Between Business and NGO Networks in Intellectual Property Rights', *International Studies Quarterly* 48:1 (2004), 143–75.

35. Ann Marie Clark, *Diplomacy of Conscience: Amnesty International and Changing Human Rights Norms* (Princeton: Princeton University Press, 2001); Jan Aart Scholte, 'Civil Society and Democracy in Global Governance', *Global Governance* 8:3 (2002), 281–304.

36. Barnett, 'Evolution Without Progress?', 656; Alexander Cooley and James Ron, 'The NGO Scramble: Organizational Insecurity and the Political Economy of Transnational Activism', *International Security* 27:1 (2002), 5–39.

37. Charli R. Carpenter, 'Studying Issue (Non-)Adoption in Transnational Advocacy Networks', *International Organization* 61:3 (Summer 2007), 643–67.

38. Laura MacDonald, 'Globalising Civil Society: Interpreting International NGOs in Central America', *Millennium* 23:2 (1994), 267–85; Mustapha Kamal Pasha and David L. Blaney, 'Elusive Paradise: The Promise and Peril of Global Civil Society', *Alternatives* 23 (1998), 417–50.

39. Cass R. Sunstein, *Laws of Fear: Beyond the Precautionary Principle* (Cambridge: Cambridge University Press, 2005).

40. M. Oppenheimer and A. Todorov, 'Global Warming: The Psychology of Long-Term Risk' (Guest Editorial), *Climactic Change* 77:1–2 (2006), 4. This is the introduction to a special issue on this topic.

41. Barbara Clucas, Katherine McHugh, and Tim Caro, 'Flagship Species on Covers of US Conservation and Nature Magazines', *Biodiversity and Conservation* 17:6 (2008), 1517–28.

42. See the editors' introduction, this volume.

43. <www.iucn.org/about>.

44. See Chapter 36, this volume.

45. William C. Smith and Roberto Patricio Korzeniewicz, 'Insiders, Outsiders, and the Politics of Civil Society', in Jean-Philippe Therien and Paul Haslam (eds), *Governing the Americas: Assessing Multilateral Institutions* (Boulder, CO: Lynne Rienner, 2007), 170.

46. Jackie Smith, 'Globalizing Resistance: The Battle of Seattle and the Future of Social Movements', *Mobilization: An International Journal* 6:1 (2001), 1–19; Smith, *Social Movements*.

47. Chapters 35, 36, and 47, this volume.

48. Chasek, *Earth Negotiations*, 69–75; 103–10.

49. Friedman, Hochstetler, and Clark, *Sovereignty, Democracy, and Global Civil Society*, 162–3.

50. Colin Powell, 'Remarks by Secretary of State Colin L. Powell to the National Foreign Policy Conference For Leaders of Non-Governmental Organizations', 26 October 2001, <http://www.usembassy-israel.org.il/publish/peace/archives/2001/october/102705.html>.

51. Powell, 'Remarks'.

52. Powell, 'Remarks'.

53. Odell, 290.

54. Friedman, Hochstetler, Clark, *Sovereignty, Democracy, and Global Civil Society*, 39–40.

55. Smith and Korzeniewicz, 'Insiders, Outsiders, and the Politics of Civil Society'.

56. Smith, 'Globalizing Resistance'.

57. Kathryn Hochstetler, 'Fading Green: Environmental Politics in the Mercosur Free Trade Agreement', *Latin American Politics and Society* 45:4 (2003), 1–32.

58. Risse-Kappen, 'Ideas do not Float Freely'.

59. Friedman, Hochstetler, Clark, *Sovereignty, Democracy, and Global Civil Society*; Chapter 36, this volume.

60. Elisabeth J. Friedman, 'The Effects of 'Transnationalism Reversed' in Venezuela: Assessing the Impact of UN Global Conferences on the Women's Movement', *International Feminist Journal of Politics* 1:3 (Autumn 1999), 357–81.

61. Robert D. Putnam, 'Diplomacy and Domestic Politics: The Logic of Two-Level Games', *International Organization* 42:3 (1988), 427–60.

62. See Chapter 38.

63. Jonathan Moore (ed.), *Hard Choices: Moral Dilemmas in Humanitarian Intervention* (New York: Rowman and Littlefield, 1998).

64. Moore, *Hard Choices*; Barnett, 'Evolution Without Progress?'.

65. David G. Chandler, 'The Road to Military Humanitarianism: How the Human Rights NGOs Shaped a New Humanitarian Agenda', *Human Rights Quarterly* 23:3 (2001), 678–700.

66. Fiona Terry, *Condemned to Repeat? The Paradox of Humanitarian Action* (Ithaca: Cornell University Press, 2002).

CHAPTER 10

....

THE DIPLOMACY
OF GLOBAL AND
TRANSNATIONAL FIRMS

....

GEOFFREY ALLEN PIGMAN

10.1 INTRODUCTION

This chapter argues that large firms that operate across national borders function increasingly as diplomatic actors in ways analogous to governments of nation states, multilateral institutions, and large civil society organizations (CSOs). As such, firms must engage in the core diplomatic activities of representation and communication by means of standard diplomatic tools such as sending and receiving missions and using public diplomacy. They must negotiate with other diplomatic interlocutors to achieve objectives ranging from gaining access to markets to protecting assets to managing crises. Whilst transnational firms have long participated in diplomacy, the number of firms participating and the extent of their diplomatic engagement is growing steadily and is likely to continue to do so.

10.2 FIRMS AS DIPLOMATIC ACTORS

Ever since the emergence of firms as entities independent of their proprietors in the 16th century, the managers of businesses have had to negotiate with others to achieve their objectives, be they renting a market stall in a *souk* or obtaining an export license from the government for high technology fibre optics technology with possible military uses. Whilst these types of activities occur constantly in businesses large and small, increasingly it has come to make sense to consider a subset of these interactions as more akin to the diplomacy that takes place between governments and between governments and other major non-state actors. Large firms that operate substantially across national borders or even on a global scale must engage with a range of governments, other large firms, multilateral institutions (such as regional development banks), and global civil society organizations (e.g. environmental watchdogs such as Greenpeace) on an ongoing basis as part of the normal course of doing business. The ways in which they do so increasingly resemble the structures and functions of more traditional diplomacy: opening representative offices in national capitals headed by individuals who function as corporate ambassadors, engaging in regular communications and specific negotiations with government and civil society officials, holding 'summit' meetings between CEOs and heads of government, and undertaking public diplomacy strategies intended to inform foreign publics about a firm's policy objectives.

What distinguishes this level of interaction between firms and other actors from those at lower levels is the size and extent of cross-border activity of the firms involved. Smaller businesses and those whose commercial activity lies predominantly within one state find their ability to negotiate with government largely constrained by the political and regulatory structures of the state within which they are incorporated. Hence their use of resources and negotiating skills resembles other forms of interest group lobbying conducted within a domestic politics framework. These firms are ultimately petitioners and the government the decider. But once a firm has crossed a certain threshold of size and cross-border activity, the balance of power between the firm and the government (or other bodies) shifts to the point where each approaches the relationship in general and each set of particular negotiations with objectives to be sought and with assets that can (and must) be offered in exchange. Thus it makes sense to analyse interactions between these larger, more global firms and other interlocutors using the theoretical and historical frame of diplomacy rather than through the lens of domestic political bargaining.

The threshold of size and cross-border activity for firms can be a fuzzy boundary and a moving target, however, governed at least in part by the firm's size in relation to the relevant national (or sub-national) government, multilateral institution, or CSO. A variety of metrics for measuring the size of firms may be relevant: market capitalization (number of shares outstanding multiplied by share price) for publicly traded firms; assets under management (particularly for financial firms); gross revenues; share of the global market for its products. Similarly, there are numerous measures for cross-border activity: number of national markets in which the firm sells; number of countries containing major factories or component sources; international distribution of shareholders; dependence (or lack thereof) upon sales in a single national market. Firms have significantly different structures for operating transnationally or globally, which in turn affect how they conduct business as diplomatic actors. A firm may have its corporate registration and headquarters in one country, or the management functions may be divided. It may manufacture its product in a single country and export around the world; it may produce using a fully integrated global production chain and possess a global distribution chain for final products; or it may produce in many countries for consumption in local markets. A holding company based in one location may serve as an umbrella for subsidiaries in different countries. A firm may license its brand, product, or process for use in different countries by franchisees or other firms. Firms selling services may sell their product electronically to a global market without their staffs ever leaving the home country; alternatively the firm's staff may travel to customers worldwide; or global customers may travel to the point of delivery to consume the service.

Firms that do clear the threshold to qualify as diplomatic actors still differ in important respects from the governments of nation-states, the traditional protagonists of diplomatic interaction. Yet they also share important enough similarities that it makes sense to speak of a diplomatic stage inhabited by different types of nonetheless analogous actors. Whereas the primary mission of a government is to defend and promote the prosperity of a geographical territory and its inhabitants, the primary mission of a firm is to make a profit in the markets in which it operates. Governments operate in a legal diplomatic regime in which formal sovereignty, which bears with it a notion of equality in theory (if not in practice), is conferred through diplomatic recognition by peer states. Firms, by contrast, depend upon no other entities to define their status as interlocutors, relying instead directly upon the power resources at their disposal to negotiate with whom they will to achieve what they can. Governments rely upon military forces, over which their sovereignty is generally acknowledged to grant them a monopoly, to defend the territories under their control. Firms engage private security forces to protect their assets in some circumstances, but often they rely upon the police and military protection afforded to them by the governments of the many territories within which they operate.

These rather evident differences make the similarities between firms and governments all the more striking. Both governments and firms vary enormously in terms of size and power. Both are constrained by their respective size and power in terms of what they are able to achieve through diplomacy. Notwithstanding the notion of formal diplomatic equality conferred by sovereignty upon governments, functional power tends to be the dominant measure of diplomatic achievement. Governments and firms alike have stakeholders and constituencies to whom they must answer and that ultimately confer legitimacy upon them. For governments, stakeholders include voters (in democracies) and populations who inhabit the territories under their control, as well as others who pay taxes to the government, civil society organizations, firms, and other institutions lying within its territories. The stakeholders of firms include its stockholders, customers, employees, and all the suppliers and supporting businesses and communities that exist around where the firm conducts its business, be it manufacturing or production of services. Governments and firms are both accountable to their stakeholders, albeit through different mechanisms that enable managers of firms and governments of states to stay in office. Both have major incentives to act in ways that create and sustain employment and that provide quality goods and services at affordable prices. Even the structures of diplomatic representation and communication employed by firms and governments resemble one another more than it initially might appear. Firms that need to establish ongoing representation in national or regional capitals open representative offices, frequently with titles such as 'Government Relations' or 'Political Communication', which function analogously to the embassies and consulates of governments abroad. Firms and governments alike engage in communication at all levels ranging from routine relationship maintenance of a social character to high-level, high-stakes negotiations to reach agreements or manage crises. Both governments and firms engage in diplomatic summits and 'state' visits, as when Bill Gates visited India in 2004 and announced $400 million in new Microsoft investments at their Indian facilities.[1]

The historical origins of transnational firms at least in part account for their parallel evolution as diplomatic actors in the international system. Transnational firms as entities are as old as the modern nation state, and as long as both have existed they have engaged in diplomatic relations that have reflected their relative, and evolving, powers. When firms and states originated, neither possessed the power over their respective spheres of operation that they have come to do today. Firms initially were limited by the legal liability that their investors bore for the success or failure of the business that they entered. Hence the granting by sovereigns to firms of the legal status of a person separate from its owners or investors, which protected investors by limiting their own liability to the amount invested, was a critical step in the trajectory of their emergence as actors distinct from governments. Contemporary transnational firms originated in commercial ventures that were licensed or chartered by their mediaeval sovereigns to go abroad and engage in trade. These ventures, customarily undertaken by sea, initially were empowered by their sovereigns to act simultaneously as representatives of the sovereign to communicate and negotiate with foreign interlocutors to open and develop commerce. Voyages to the Americas, the East Indies, and Africa encountered societies the governance of which often was organized differently than that of the European polities from which the traders came. Hence leaders of trading missions began to negotiate with local authorities the establishment of zones in which the trading company could conduct business and could enforce European law governing trade and contracts. These zones, of which Calcutta and Hong Kong were amongst the most famous, became in many cases the building blocks of later European colonies throughout the rest of the world.[2]

As early modern European governments began promoting international commerce through their own direct investment and by creating the legal framework for international trade, the first wave of transnational firms found themselves in the business of governance as well as commerce from as early as the 17th century. Parliamentary charters granted by the British and Dutch governments to firms such as the Dutch East India Company, the British East India Company, the Muscovy Company, the Levant Company, the Virginia Company, and the Massachusetts Bay Company granted to these corporations monopoly trading rights over fixed territories. Over time, to varying extents, and under various guises, these firms effectively became the governing authority in the territories in which they operated. The corporate statutes of the Virginia and Massachusetts Bay Companies in turn served as the foundation of the colonial constitutions of Virginia and Massachusetts respectively. This early generation of transnational firms set the legal, political, and economic precedent for the modern firm–government diplomatic relationship, in which the two types of actor were different but analogous, ongoing relations were necessary, and in which outcomes of diplomatic negotiations tended to be a product both of relative distribution of power and the diplomatic skills of the respective representatives.[3]

10.3 CONTEMPORARY FIRM–GOVERNMENT DIPLOMACY

In the contemporary period, the most important diplomatic relationships that transnational and global firms must maintain are with the governments of polities in which they operate. Depending upon the nature of their business, firms may also need to maintain relationships with civil society organizations, multilateral institutions, and other transnational firms (see section 10.5). In each case, however, the organizational structures and skills required for diplomatic representation and communication are much the same. Firms generally maintain an office in their corporate headquarters known as 'Government Relations' or some variant thereof, which is the corporate analogue to a ministry of foreign affairs. The responsibility of the Government Relations department is to manage the firm's relationships with all the governments in countries in which it does business or seeks to do business. The firm may open satellite Government Relations offices in many of the countries in which the firm has substantial operations or major markets, which are analogous to embassies or foreign missions. The heads of these satellites function analogously to a permanent representative or ambassador of the firm to the government of the particular country (or, in some cases, to a sub-national government such as that of a province, state, or major metropolitan area).

The primary diplomatic objectives of firms and governments towards one another are analogous to, even if not the same as, diplomatic objectives of governments with respect to other governments. Diplomatic objectives for most governments are primarily economic and social, but by definition economic and social gains for governments bring political gains that translate into votes (or, in the case of authoritarian governments, social peace and public acquiescence in government rule). Amongst the main objectives of governments are: the creation and maintenance of jobs, particularly well-paying and high value-added jobs; exports that can generate often needed foreign exchange or pay for needed imports; tax revenue and inward investment of capital; transfers of technology; and to ensure that firms operate harmoniously within the nation's social and environmental fabric. All of these goods that firms can provide they can also take away, so another prime goal of government diplomacy is to prevent their loss. In addition, some governments seek to prevent significant repatriation of domestically earned profits abroad. If the government itself or some portion of its citizens own shares in the firm or its local subsidiaries or joint ventures, the government will have an added incentive to act to ensure that the firm prospers and that shareholder interests are protected. For their part firms seek from governments the most favourable investment climate that they can obtain with respect to access to markets, location of production facilities, and, when relevant, repatriation of profits. More specifically, firms want to achieve and maintain the lightest and least onerous burden of compliance with legislative and regulatory restrictions on their business operations. This requires an ongoing effort, because political climates in states can change, sometimes rapidly, and governments can come under pressure from other domestic political interests to change legislative and regulatory environments in ways that can adversely affect firms. One particularly vivid example is the public outcry across many countries following the 2008 global financial crisis for significantly tighter regulation of transnational financial firms.

All that said, much of the diplomacy conducted between firms and governments consists of routine business. Government officials and management and staff of firms get to know and become familiar with one another. There is bilateral information sharing, in the sense that each provides the other with information of mutual interest, which might include government data and data on and analysis of macroeconomic performance, trade and employment, and news of government programmes affecting business. Firms in turn might provide data and colour on in-country operations and plans for new facilities. Each side might request information on an as needed basis, which the other side might or might not be able or willing to give out, at least in full. Firms will want to be briefed on proposed legislative and regulatory changes affecting their business operations and markets, whilst governments may wish to know about prospective mergers and acquisitions that could have an impact upon creation and retention of employment in particular locations. But notwithstanding that these routine interactions constitute the bulk of firm–government diplomacy (as analogous routine interactions constitute the bulk of government–government diplomacy), what tends to be of much greater interest to scholars and students of diplomacy is how firms and governments manage particular situations when they arise: a deal to be done, a significant concern about a regulation or piece of legislation to be addressed, a dispute to be resolved, a crisis to be averted or defused. In situations such as these, the most common way that two sides engage diplomatically is through direct, bilateral communication and, when required, negotiation. However, other diplomatic venues are used routinely as well. Not infrequently disputes between global firms and governments are addressed within the channels of the domestic judicial system of the country in which the dispute occurs (see discussion of the Bhopal disaster in section 10.6.5). In this respect firm–government diplomacy differs from government–government diplomacy, in that in interstate disputes domestic judiciaries can rarely claim jurisdiction.

Judicial systems are not ideal venues for resolving disputes between governments and firms, as judicial processes operate differently from standard political negotiations that diplomats customarily employ. Once begun, judicial processes cannot always be terminated easily at the request of government officials, as the competition law violation ('antitrust') cases brought against Microsoft in the United States in the late 1990s and by the European Union in the early 2000s revealed. In these cases, rival firms of Microsoft such as Netscape, Sun Microsystems, and Oracle sought to take market share from

Microsoft, the dominant player in the global marketplace for operating systems and internet browser software. Shopping for the most effective venue to achieve their desired result, they persuaded attorneys general of several US states, and subsequently the European Commission's competition directorate, to bring antitrust cases against Microsoft seeking to force Microsoft, amongst other things, to 'unbundle' its Explorer internet browser from its Windows operating system. A ruling by US federal judge Thomas Jackson (subsequently overturned) that would have forced the break-up of Microsoft into two separate companies, complicated the diplomatic process in which Microsoft defended politically to the US Congress and the White House the gains it was providing to the US economy.[4]

Yet other venues employed in firm–government diplomacy include multilateral organizations, such as development banks and the World Economic Forum. These bodies provide institutional venues and physical settings in which firms and governments meet and negotiate particular types of business deals, and in some cases they can provide specific types of assistance to facilitate agreements. The Multilateral Investment Guarantee Agency (MIGA), for example, is a unit of the World Bank Group established in 1988 to promote foreign direct investment in developing countries by transnational firms and their financial backers. MIGA provides political risk insurance that can make otherwise risky investments viable.[5] The World Economic Forum, a membership organization whose members are drawn from amongst the 1,000 largest global firms, hosts numerous regional and global 'summit' meetings throughout the year. At Forum meetings, executives of member firms may meet one another as well as senior government officials and representatives of civil society organizations, academics, and the media. The Forum also organizes 'Initiatives' to facilitate the formation of public–private partnerships that bring social and political benefits to governments and civil society, in addition to bringing economic benefits to its member firms. One such initiative involves upgrading classroom technologies for primary and secondary education in developing countries and training teachers to use the new technologies.[6]

Irrespective of which venue a firm and government use to negotiate over an issue, the broad negotiating strategies and specific tactics that each side chooses to use are likely to be drawn from a standard toolkit, which includes some tools shared by both sides and others that are specific to governments or firms. Both firms and governments increasingly use public diplomacy and public relations techniques to rally popular support for their position in a particular conflict. When Microsoft faced US antitrust charges, it joined with other technology firms and business associations to form Americans for Technology Leadership, an organization intended to lobby against onerous government regulation of technology and to catalyze public support for firms like Microsoft. Specific tools at the disposal of governments in negotiating with a firm to make an investment or open a manufacturing facility include offering inexpensive or free access to land and energy, government-funded infrastructure improvements, tax abatements, tariff and trade regulatory concessions, favourable terms for repatriation of profits, and advantageous regulatory suspensions or modifications. In a dispute, governments have the capacity to threaten a firm with imposition of new legislative and regulatory burdens and taxes. As a last resort governments have been known to expel firms from their territory altogether and seize or nationalize their assets.

Tools that firms use include offering to reinvest a substantial portion of profits, as well as to fund local projects with social benefits, such as a medical clinic or community centre. At the same time, a firm seeking the most favourable conditions to make an investment might play two or more national or regional governments against one another. By negotiating with more than one interlocutor simultaneously, with or without the other's knowledge, a firm can attempt to obtain a progressively better deal until either only one bidder remains or else it must choose the best deal. The most powerful firms possess threat of exit: the ability to threaten to move investments and facilities, and even corporate headquarters, from one country to another, in the event of a complete breakdown in relations. At the height of the Microsoft–US Government antitrust dispute, news reports of the provincial governor of British Columbia (Canada) offering a package of incentives to move its corporate headquarters north from Redmond, Washington to B.C. were believed by many to be a compelling threat of exit by Microsoft, even as company officials denied such a threat was being made.[7]

Amidst the various carrots and sticks that governments and firms use in negotiations, what ultimately determines outcomes is similar to that which determines outcomes in diplomatic negotiations between governments. The relative size and distribution of power and assets between any two interlocutors in most cases will play a dominant role in determining the result. Many transnational firms have annual revenue streams that dwarf the annual gross domestic product of numerous developing countries in which they invest, for example. On the other hand, the rapid growth of the economy of the People's Republic of China, already a market of nearly 1.5 billion people, has made it increasingly difficult for very large transnational firms like Google to dictate the terms on which it will do business there (see section 10.6.4). Alongside relative size and distribution of power is the nature of the long-term relationship between the two interlocutors, in terms of the levels of familiarity, trust, and predictability that each side has developed regarding the other. This in turn is often the product of the effective conduct of routine diplomatic business over time, as already noted. Closely related to this are the relative skills of the diplomats involved, both in cultivating the long-term relationship on a daily basis and in doing the actual negotiating when a situation arises. The skills or lack thereof of one side frequently go some distance towards tipping the outcome of negotiations even against otherwise prevailing power distributions. Following the 2010 Macondo oil spill in the Gulf of Mexico, BP plc, which owned the leaking well, was thought to be disadvantaged considerably in its initial crisis negotiations with US federal and local governments by the ineffectiveness at communication of some of its senior executives and other representatives. This contributed to the resignation of BP CEO Tony Hayward.[8]

Notwithstanding their global reach, transnational firms still need to maintain a special diplomatic relationship with the government of the state or states in which they are headquartered. Even firms with extensive transnational operations need to draw upon the legal structures of their primary 'host' states to facilitate raising capital through debt and equity issuance and to enforce contracts. Governments for their part also depend more upon large firms with major operations located in-country, as such firms tend to be providers of larger numbers of jobs and generators of substantial amounts of tax revenue. In general, global firms and host governments each have larger quantities of assets at stake in the relationship than firms do in their relationships with governments of the many other countries in which they do business. This makes it costlier for both sides when diplomacy fails and relations break down, as Microsoft discovered in the late 1990s. Even as the firm had grown rapidly around the world during the 1990s technology boom and courted the governments in New Delhi and Beijing, Microsoft had neglected its diplomatic relationship with Washington, DC, as it discovered to its peril. As late as 1995, Microsoft reportedly only had one permanent representative assigned to Washington to represent the firm's interests before the US federal government.[9]

10.4 A Special Case: Diplomacy between Global Media Firms and Governments

Global and transnational media firms are perhaps a special case, in that media firms function not only as firm-actors in their own right but also as channels for diplomatic communication. The motto on the coat of arms of the British Broadcasting Corporation is 'nation shall speak peace unto nation', which evokes vividly the importance of communication channels to diplomacy. Governments of states must contend with global media firms in the same ways that they must contend with other types of global firms. Yet they also have a special set of relationships with these corporations based upon governments' need for access to channels of communication to disseminate information to global publics in an era in which public diplomacy constitutes an ever greater and more important part of diplomatic activity. Governments also often regulate media activities both in the public interest (ensuring public access to communication channels, protecting against media infringement of privacy rights, etc.) and to prevent particular firms from monopolizing sources of information to the public. Similarly, global media firms must negotiate with governments over all the issues that other global firms do, but they also have special needs that they require governments to provide. Broadcast media firms may need to negotiate for access to government-owned satellites needed for satellite transmission. Broadcast, print, and Internet media firms all have an interest in ensuring that government regulation does not affect adversely their ability to generate revenue.

Diplomacy between governments and global media firms is also conditioned by the particular type of institutional relationship that exists between a given firm and government. These institutional relationships lie along a spectrum that extends from heavy dependence of a media firm upon a particular host government to virtually complete independence from the authority of any single governmental body. Heavy dependence can result from factors that range from full or partial government ownership, sponsorship and/or funding of a media firm to a firm's reliance upon a large country's revenue-rich media market. The British Broadcasting Corporation (BBC), the world's largest broadcaster, is an example of a firm that has a dependent relationship with its host government, that of the United Kingdom. The BBC operates under a Royal charter in the UK (meaning it is owned, in a formal sense, by the Crown as opposed to shareholders) and is licensed by the UK government to provide radio, television, and Internet broadcasting in the public interest. Its UK operations are funded primarily by a 'license fee' or compulsory tax paid by all UK owners of television receivers. This arrangement leaves the BBC obliged to seek to please the UK government and British public, as its license must be renewed at regular intervals. However, the BBC also operates in over 100 countries under the umbrella BBC Worldwide through commercial subsidiaries, such as BBC Asia and BBC America, that generate profits used to support the overall operations of the company.[10] For its part, the UK government relies upon the BBC to facilitate the government's own extensive public diplomacy operations through the BBC's multilingual global radio, television, and Internet channels.

Another example of a dependent firm is Al Jazeera, a global broadcasting firm funded by the government of Qatar with the intention of developing a distinctively Arab perspective on global news and information but whose editorial content is intended to be independent of that of Qatar's government. Al Jazeera's diplomacy with the government of the United States has often been difficult owing to the selection by the non-state actor engaging in terrorist tactics Al-Qa'eda of Al Jazeera as its preferred channel for its own global public diplomacy in the form of audio and video messages by Al-Qa'eda leaders. Al Jazeera's attempts to reach a broader television audience in the United States have been frustrated by the reluctance of many US cable and satellite providers to carry the network's English language service, which is thought by some to be linked to its political unpopularity amongst government officials. Al Jazeera differs from the BBC in that its relationship of dependence is probably greater with respect to the government of the United States, the major global media market that it has the greatest difficulty accessing, rather than with that of Qatar, its host government.[11]

The middle range in the spectrum would include media firms like NBC Universal, jointly owned by US corporate giants Comcast and GE. NBC Universal has extensive global operations through TV outlets such as CNBC, but still depends for much of its revenue upon its home media market, the United States. At the far end of the spectrum from that of the BBC and Al Jazeera lie firms like Thomson Reuters and News Corporation, publicly traded firms with significant media operations, revenue sources, and shareholders in numerous countries. Thomson Reuters is majority Canadian-owned, headquartered in New York, with media and publishing operations in 100 countries and a market capitalization in September 2011 of nearly US $25 billion. News

Corporation, originally incorporated in Australia but since 2004 a US-based firm, owns major broadcast and satellite television, print, and Internet media, sport, and entertainment properties in Australia, China, Israel, the United Kingdom, and the United States, amongst other countries. News Corporation's market capitalization in September 2011 exceeded US $43 billion. The diplomacy of Thomson Reuters and News Corp. differs significantly from that of firms near the other end of the spectrum. As they are less dependent upon particular states' markets and regulatory regimes, and as governments may have even more need of their broad reach as communications channels, the ongoing diplomatic relationship, and specific negotiations when they occur, are more likely to be conducted as between equals.

As in other cases where the interests of global firms and governments conflict, or when issues arise that require negotiation, the relative size of the interlocutors, the relative leverage of each in a given situation, and the negotiating skills of the diplomats involved play the greatest roles in governing outcomes. However, in conflicts and negotiations between governments and global media firms, the role of public opinion is even more significant than it is in situations involving other types of firms. Given the nature of the media's communications function, in such cases often the public must choose which 'side' they trust more: a media firm or a government. Often the public's view is definitive in deciding the outcome. In a well-known conflict between the BBC and the UK government in 2004, criticism of the BBC in the report of a judicial inquiry into the death of Dr David Kelly, a UK Ministry of Defence scientist, resulted in the resignation of BBC Director General Greg Dyke. Kelly was reportedly the source for BBC reports that the Labour government of then-Prime Minister Tony Blair had consciously exaggerated information in a report on Iraq's possession of weapons of mass destruction in order to strengthen the case for the 2003 US–British invasion of Iraq. According to polling following Dyke's resignation, however, British public trust in and support for the BBC was significantly higher than for the government.[12] Another case of government–media firm diplomacy again involving the UK government resulted in a very different outcome, however. In July 2011 the Conservative government of Prime Minister David Cameron ordered a judicial inquiry into allegations that staff of News Corporation publications, including most prominently the Sunday newspaper *News of the World*, had bribed police officials and illegally accessed mobile telephone records of celebrities and crime victims in pursuit of news stories. Release of the allegations precipitated a major UK scandal that resonated as well in other countries with major News Corp. media holdings. Public trust in News Corp. was so damaged that several senior executives resigned, News Corp. CEO Rupert Murdoch apologized publicly before a Parliamentary hearing, and News Corp. took the decision to cease publication of *News of the World* altogether. Despite News Corporation's size and dispersion of operations globally, negative public perceptions of the allegations both in the UK and globally made it necessary for the firm to take responsibility for the problem, make serious concessions to the UK government intended to ensure that it not be repeated (such as replacement of senior management), and make a gesture of public atonement for errors made by closing its most offending publication.

10.5 Diplomacy between Global Firms and Other Non-State Actors

Whilst governments are the most important type of diplomatic actor with which global firms must engage on an ongoing basis, in some circumstances firms have need to develop relationships with other types of non-state diplomatic actor as well, including multilateral organizations and institutions (e.g. the United Nations, the World Bank, etc.), civil society organizations (CSOs) (e.g. Greenpeace, the International Committee of the Red Cross, etc.), and other global firms. Most commonly these relationships tend to focus on a particular area of activity in which the firm has reason to be involved. Many large firms will form partnerships with CSOs and multilateral organizations to undertake charitable projects as part of their corporate social responsibility (CSR) agenda. For example, the global pharmaceutical and chemical firm Merck formed a partnership in 2007 with the World Health Organization (WHO) to distribute its drug Praziquantel to combat the tropical worm disease schistosomiasis, which affects 200 million people in Africa and kills over 200,000 annually. In an effort to aid 27 million severely affected children, Merck is donating the medication and logistical support, whilst the WHO coordinates distribution of the tablets.[13]

Firms' relationships with other global firms are most often, but not always, involved with business deals, which range from joint ventures and partnerships to contracts and subcontracts to sales transactions. Firms that do significant amounts of business with one another must establish and maintain regular channels of communication in much the same ways that firms and governments must do. When firms find themselves in disputes with other firms across national borders, and the dispute cannot be resolved through diplomatic negotiation, often the domestic legal system of one of the countries in which the disputed assets or contract may be involved is engaged. However, this can create ambiguities of jurisdiction that can make dispute resolution difficult and time-consuming. An alternate venue for resolving cross-border disputes between firms is the International Court of Arbitration, which functions under the auspices of the International Chamber of Commerce (ICC), a CSO established to promote the interests of global business and commerce and whose membership consists of domestic business federations.[14]

10.6 Case Studies of the Diplomacy of Global Firms

The concluding section offers a set of examples of diplomacy involving global and transnational firms. These examples are intended to illustrate the range of common situations in which firms find diplomacy necessary, from the most routine (doing deals) to the most extreme (managing crises and disasters).

10.6.1 Doing Deals—Wal-mart and South Africa

The most common type of deal requiring diplomacy between a global firm and a government involves direct investments by global firms, often in the form of a joint venture or acquisition. In 2010 US-based global retailer Wal-mart proposed to acquire 51 per cent of South African retailing firm Massmart for SAR 16.5 billion/US $2.4 billion. The deal, which represented Wal-mart's first major investment in Africa and a significant inward investment in the fast-growing South African economy, was controversial on a number of counts. In an economy still registering 25 per cent unemployment, South African trades unions feared the takeover could lead to job losses at Massmart and a shift by Massmart towards purchasing more imports, which in turn could result in lower demand for domestically produced products and job losses at other domestic firms. The Congress of South African Trades Unions (COSATU), an historically important political ally of the governing African National Congress (ANC), brought pressure on President Jacob Zuma's government to oppose the Wal-mart acquisition. Wal-mart officials negotiated with South Africa's competition authorities, offering to guarantee not to cut any jobs for two years and to honour extant labour agreements for three years. In the negotiations COSATU unsuccessfully sought additional guarantees that Wal-mart would continue to use local suppliers. The South African Competition Tribunal approved Wal-mart's offer in May 2011. Wal-mart officials argued that the deal would create jobs by enabling Massmart to expand into significant African markets such as the Democratic Republic of Congo and Senegal.[15]

10.6.2 Moving Headquarters—HSBC, China, and the United Kingdom

Global firms may decide to move their corporate headquarters from one country to another for a variety of reasons ranging from receiving a better 'offer' from a potential new host government to heightened political risk of remaining in its existing location. The Hong Kong and Shanghai Banking Corporation (HSBC), long headquartered in British Hong Kong, by the 1990s were already a global financial services firm with operations in many countries. In the early 1990s HSBC bought one of the 'Big Four' High Street commercial banks in Britain, Midland Bank. As the scheduled handover of British sovereignty over Hong Kong to the People's Republic of China in 1997 approached, HSBC's management, after negotiating with the British and Chinese governments, took the decision to move the bank's corporate headquarters from Hong Kong to London. HSBC's top managers decided that the legal structures, business climate, and political transparency of Britain were more favourable to the firm and its shareholders than the somewhat less certain environment of Hong Kong under Chinese sovereignty. They did not withdraw their business interests and operations from Hong Kong, but they established a relationship with a different host government. Although the Chinese government in Beijing preferred that HSBC's headquarters remain in Hong Kong, prior to assuming sovereignty over Hong Kong they did not have sufficient leverage over HSBC to dissuade management from their decision.[16]

10.6.3 Power Politics—Gazprom, Russia, Ukraine, and the European Union

A recurring business dispute with significant geopolitical implications beginning in 2006 has pitted Russian natural gas firm Gazprom against the government of Ukraine and its state gas company Naftogaz. The dispute has evolved into an ongoing diplomatic *contretemps* that has drawn in the governments of the Russian Federation and the European Union as well. Gazprom, a publicly traded company that is majority-owned by the Russian Federation government and that is both the largest Russian firm and the world's largest natural gas producer, has repeatedly threatened to cut off gas supplies to Ukraine as a result of Naftogaz's alleged non-payment of its bills to Gazprom. Ukraine withheld payments to Gazprom pending a negotiated resolution of a dispute over how Gazprom adjusted the price charged to Ukraine as a result of changes in global gas prices. The European Union found itself with a material interest in the disagreement, given that in 2008 the EU was buying one quarter of its gas from Gazprom. Most of Gazprom's gas was trans-shipped from Russia to the EU via Ukrainian pipelines, which rendered the EU vulnerable to a Russian cut-off of gas to Ukraine. The negotiations between Gazprom and Naftogaz have been complicated by the involvement of the respective governments behind the two firms, which when they see fit engage in the conflict as the firms' respective champions. The business disagreement has become entangled in the often rocky political relationship between the Russian and Ukrainian governments, and the issue has become a major agenda item for diplomacy between both governments and that of the European Union.[17] In 2010 Russia agreed to a price discount on gas to Ukraine in return for Ukraine's extending Russia's lease of the Ukrainian seaport of Sevastopol for twenty-five years. Ukraine has sought to reduce its dependence on Russian gas, which Gazprom has attempted to prevent through 'take or pay' contracts in which Ukraine must agree to buy a minimum amount of gas annually. The Russian government offered to lower gas prices to the EU if Ukraine agreed to surrender control over its pipeline network. Negotiations and public diplomacy to resolve these ongoing disagreements have regularly involved the Russian and Ukrainian heads of government, making the issue one of the highest profile matters affecting their bilateral relationship.[18]

10.6.4 Asset Protection—Google, China, and the United States

Global firms and governments of major states sometimes clash over in-country assets of potentially substantial value. In 2006 Google, the world's largest Internet search firm, launched a Chinese-language search site in the People's Republic of China, Google.cn. In doing so, Google agreed to adhere to the Beijing government's strict censorship rules preventing access to politically sensitive websites. For following China's censorship rules Google was subjected to considerable global public criticism. Google's decision was viewed as subordinating respect for human rights, such as freedom of access to information, to its desire to participate in the Chinese market of nearly 400 million Internet users. In late 2010 Google accused the Chinese government of 'hacking' into the accounts of Google customers in China, including human rights activists, in order to trace which websites they were viewing and read emails in their 'gmail' accounts. The news provoked a firestorm of criticism of the Chinese government. Speaking for the US government on behalf of a major US-based global firm, US Secretary of State Hillary Rodham Clinton expressed grave concern publicly about the Chinese actions. 'The ability to operate with confidence in cyberspace is critical in a modern society and economy', Clinton commented.[19] In response Google announced that they would cease to censor access to websites through the Google.cn portal and that Google and Chinese government officials would negotiate to determine whether it would be possible for Google to operate an uncensored site in China without violating regulations. Analysts attributed Google's change in policy in part to an assessment that its competitive position in the Chinese-language search market was limited sufficiently by domestic competitors such as Baidu that it could benefit more in terms of global public perception and the credibility of its English-language site Google.com if it were forced to withdraw from the Chinese market altogether owing to Chinese government inflexibility on censorship rules.[20] Two months later Google closed Google.cn and redirected Chinese language searches to its uncensored Hong Kong site, thereby providing unfiltered results to users but leaving the Chinese government with the capacity to filter content to users within China. To outside observers, the clash between China and Google left the Chinese government looking worse and Google better in terms of reputation, whilst not imposing a high business cost upon Google.[21]

10.6.5 Crisis/Disaster Diplomacy—Union Carbide, India, and the United States

When a major crisis or disaster affecting a firm's operations in a country strikes, both the firm and the government have much to lose; consequently, they have a powerful incentive to work together to mitigate the damage. The toxic gas discharge at the Union Carbide facility in Bhopal, India in December 1984 is one of the grimmest examples of such a situation. By some metrics the worst industrial accident ever, the Bhopal gas leak killed 3,800 people immediately and disabled several thousand more. Following the disaster, there was disagreement over whether parent company Union Carbide Corporation (now part of Dow Chemical) or its Indian subsidiary Union Carbide India Ltd. (UCIL) bore responsibility for the accident, and over whether the cause of the disaster was

sabotage caused by terrorists or disaffected employees, as Union Carbide officials contended, or inadequate safety procedures, as coalitions of victims suspected. Claims for
damages were filed rapidly on behalf of the victims in US courts. In March 1985, however, the Indian government passed the Bhopal Gas Leak Disaster Act, which was
intended to deliver speedy and fair compensation to victims by appointing the Indian
government as the sole representative of Bhopal victims in Indian and foreign courts.
This paved the way for the case to be heard in the Indian legal system, and US proceedings were terminated. Union Carbide and the Indian government negotiated a settlement mediated by the Indian Supreme Court, in which Union Carbide accepted moral
responsibility and paid $470 million into a fund for victims. In this case, effective diplo-
macy between the global firm, its Indian subsidiary, and the Indian government facilitated an orderly adjudication of victims' claims by the Indian legal system and a
negotiated settlement. Critics of the settlement contend that it was insufficient, however,
and that more broadly it did not facilitate an improvement in safety standards employed
by transnational chemical firms operating facilities in developing countries like India.[22]

Notes

1. Geoffrey Allen Pigman, *Contemporary Diplomacy* (Cambridge: Polity Press, 2010), 17–18.
2. Niall Ferguson, *Empire: The Rise and Demise of the British World Order and the Lessons for
   Global Power* (New York: Basic Books, 2004), 14–20; John Braithwaite and Peter Drahos,
   Global Business Regulation (Cambridge: Cambridge University Press, 2000), 147–8.
3. Braithwaite and Drahos, *Global Business Regulation*.
4. Richard B. McKenzie, *Trust on Trial* (Cambridge, MA: Perseus Publishing, 2000); Joel
   Brinkley, 'U.S. Judge Declares Microsoft Is a Market-Stifling Monopoly; Gates Retains
   Defiant Stance', *New York Times*, 6 November 1999; Steve Lohr, 'Clear Finding in Blunt
   Language'; Editorial, 'The Microsoft Findings', *New York Times*, 6 November 1999; Steve
   Lohr, 'Microsoft's Horizon', *New York Times*, 7 November 1999; John M. Broder and Joel
   Brinkley, 'U.S. Versus Microsoft: The Strategy; How Microsoft Sought Friends in
   Washington', *New York Times*, 7 November 1999; Joel Brinkley, 'Microsoft's Friends Rue the
   Findings, Its Foes Relish Them', *New York Times*, 7 November 1999; Richard Wolffe and
   Louise Kehoe, 'Response: In defence of domination', *Financial Times*, 8 November 1999;
   Richard Wolffe, Louise Kehoe, and Richard Waters, 'Pressure on Microsoft over antitrust
   case', *Financial Times*, 8 November 1999; Richard Wolffe, 'Outcome: Break-up option',
   Financial Times, 8 November 1999; Leader, 'A case to answer', *Financial Times*, 8 November
   1999.
5. Multilateral Investment Guarantee Agency, Who We Are, <http://www.miga.org/
   whoweare/index.cfm>.
6. Geoffrey Allen Pigman, *The World Economic Forum; A Multi-stakeholder Approach to
   Global Governance* (London: Routledge, 2006).
7. David Willis, 'Canada woos Microsoft', *BBC News*, 2 June 2000, <http://news.bbc.co.uk/2/
   hi/business/774063.stm>; 'Canada Urges Microsoft to Move to British Columbia, BBC
   Says', *Bloomberg newswire*, 2 June 2000.

8. CBS/AP, 'Tony Hayward to Step Down as CEO of BP: Official', 27 July 2010, <http://www.cbsnews.com/stories/2010/07/26/business/main6714516.shtml>.

9. John M. Broder and Joel Brinkley, 'U.S. Versus Microsoft: The Strategy; How Microsoft Sought Friends in Washington', *New York Times*, 7 November 1999; McKenzie, *Trust on Trial*, 169–70; Richard Wolffe, 'Congress welcomes Gates', *The Financial Times FT.com*, 7 April 2000.

10. BBC Worldwide, About BBC Worldwide, <www.bbcworldwide.com>.

11. William A. Rugh, 'Repairing American Public Diplomacy', *Arab Media and Society* 7 (Winter 2009), <http://www.arabmediasociety.com/?article=709>.

12. CNN World, 'Polls: Public backs BBC on Hutton', 30 January 2004, <http://articles.cnn.com/2004-01-30/world/hutton.blair_1_andrew-gilligan-gavyn-davies-bbc?_s=PM:WORLD>.

13. The Merck Group—Responsibility, Society, Praziquantel, <http://www.merckgroup.com/en/responsibility/society/global_responsibility_projects/praziquantel.html>.

14. International Chamber of Commerce, <www.iccwbo.org>.

15. Sikonathi Mantshantsha, 'Wal-Mart's Massmart Takeover Bid Approved, Angering Unions', *Bloomberg*, 31 May 2011, <http://www.bloomberg.com/news/2011-05-31/walmart-s-2-4-billion-bid-for-south-africa-massmart-approved-with-terms.html>; Andrew England and Barney Jopson, 'Walmart given nod for S Africa acquisition', *Financial Times*, 1 June 2011, <http://www.ft.com/intl/cms/s/0/0c3256f0-8bb2-11e0-a725-00144feab49a.html#axzz1YQaoBpr8>.

16. Pigman, *Contemporary Diplomacy*, 78.

17. Roman Olearchyk and Isabel Gorst, 'Ukraine nears Russian gas debt deal', *Financial Times*, 30 December 2008, <http://www.ft.com/intl/cms/s/0/42439a64-d6bb-11dd-9bf7-000077b07658.html#axzz1YQaoBpr8>.

18. Roman Olearchyk and Neil Buckley, 'Ukraine poised to mount Gazprom challenge', *Financial Times*, 31 August 2011, <http://www.ft.com/intl/cms/s/0/ed837292-d3e2-11e0-b7eb-00144feab49a.html#axzz1YQaoBpr8>.

19. US Secretary of State Hillary Rodham Clinton statement, quoted in Alexander Burns, 'Clinton weighs in on Google-China clash', *Politico*, 14 January 2010, <http://www.politico.com/news/stories/0110/31483.html>.

20. Bruce Einhorn, 'In China, Google Declares War on Censorship', *Business Week*, 13 January 2010, <http://www.businessweek.com/stories/2010-01-13/in-china-google-declares-war-on-censorshipbusinessweek-business-news-stock-market-and-financial-advice>.

21. BBC News, 'China condemns decision by Google to lift censorship', 23 March 2010, <http://news.bbc.co.uk/2/hi/8582233.stm>; Miguel Helft and David Barboza, 'Google Shuts China Site in Dispute Over Censorship', *New York Times*, 22 March 22 2010, <http://www.nytimes.com/2010/03/23/technology/23google.html>.

22. Union Carbide Corporation, 'Statement of Union Carbide Corporation Regarding the Bhopal Tragedy' and 'The Incident, Response, and Settlement', <www.unioncarbide.com/bhopal>; AIR 1990 Supreme Court 273, Union Carbide Corpn. vs. India; Edward Broughton, 'The Bhopal disaster and its aftermath: a review', *Environmental Health*, 10 May 2005, <www.ehjournal.net/content/4/1/6>.

CHAPTER 11

....

MEDIA, DIPLOMACY, AND GEOPOLITICS

....

SHAWN POWERS

11.1 INTRODUCTION

In 1995, Irving Goldstein, Chief Executive of the International Telecommunications Satellite Organization predicted that information 'will be for the twenty-first century what oil and gas were for the beginning of the twentieth century'.[1] Thinking about information as a resource is helpful for strategizing what media and emerging communications technologies mean for 21st-century diplomacy. Similar to how every oil well discovered in the 20th century didn't translate into wealth and power, not every dataset of the 21st will result in shifts in power and authority. Strategies are required for translating resources, either oil or information, into power, and those strategies typically require coordination with established actors and organizations. Power will shift, and information technologies will be central to how those shifts occur, but it will be at the margins, and due to savvy, established political actors outsmarting her competitors. Successful diplomats of the 21st century will approach modern technologies as specific means for conveying different types of information, study each medium's particular biases, and strategically apply the most important technologies to achieving her goals. The most important thing to do is understand the communications technologies, understand their strengths, as well as their risks, and evaluate how they can be applied, monitored, or regulated in order to best manage the crucial resource of the 21st century: information.

Media are, of course, central to the evolution of diplomacy from what it was to what it is today. Diplomacy—at its core, a communicative activity—has been altered by the rapid invention and adoption of information technologies and today is confronted with a situation and global context far different from that of previous eras. Yet, diplomats have had to deal with changes in global context before. The advent of modern airplane transportation and wireless telephony transformed how diplomacy was conducted during the 20th century. Today, the World Wide Web and its hardware backbone, the Internet, are transforming how diplomacy is conceived and carried out in the 21st century.

This chapter briefly outlines the technological origins of the modern information age and, in an effort to connect theory to practice, analyses Qatar's Al-Jazeera to demonstrate how communications technologies can be deployed in ways that shift diplomatic practice and geopolitical power.

11.2 THE GENESIS OF THE MODERN INFORMATION AGE

The current evolution in communications technologies and infrastructure stands out from previous advances not simply because it has altered the ways in which societies process information and constitute public opinions, though it certainly has. Rather, the current evolution stands out due to the fact that its ascendance has occurred so quickly that institutions have struggled to try and catch up with the pace and scope of technological change. Many, including US Secretary of State Hillary Clinton, point to the emergence of the Internet as the key to today's changed information ecosystem.[2]

The modern revolution in information technologies was triggered in 1965 when Intelsat I, the first commercial communications satellite, was launched into orbit. Intelsat I was a geostationary satellite, appearing unmoving in the sky from earth, allowing for the adoption of low-cost consumer technology (such as a small satellite dish) able to connect and relay the satellites' transmissions. Followed by Intelsat II and Intelsat III, by 1969 the trio established the world's first complete communications network. Their presence was made known to the world just days after completing the network, on 20 July 1969, when they collectively relayed live coverage of APOLLO 11's moon landing to a half billion people around the world.

The existence of a global satellite communications drove thinking about and the development of the modern World Wide Web. In 1970, a *Popular Science* article quoted Arthur Clark, science fiction author, predicting a single console 'combining the features of a touch-tone (pushbutton) telephone, a television set, a Xerox machine and a small electronic computer. Tuned into a system of synchronous satellites, this console will bring the accumulated knowledge of the world to your fingertips.'[3]

The changing role of information in international politics was clear to stakeholders and policy-makers well before the World Wide Web became a global phenomenon. Former Secretary of State James Baker III recognized the changing role of information on policy-makers, arguing that 'in Iraq, Bosnia, Somalia, Rwanda and Chechnya, among others, the real-time coverage of conflict by the electronic media has served to create a powerful new imperative for prompt action that was not present in less frenetic time.'[4]

Baker's comments were taken as proof of a 'CNN Effect', or the ability of commercial media organizations to drive political agendas and decision-making. Much debated and researched, little solid conclusions came from discussions of the so-called 'CNN Effect', other than the emergence of a consensus that information sovereignty, or the state's capacity to control information flows within its territory, was increasingly challenged by new and emerging communications technologies.

More recently a number of technological prophets such as New York University Professor Clay Shirky[5] and *New York Times'* columnist Thomas Friedman[6] have pointed to non-state actors, such as non-government organizations (NGOs) and multinational corporations as rising players in international politics. In some cases, non-state and non-traditional actors have been able to utilize information technologies as influence multipliers on the global stage, propelling their message to transnational audiences that had been otherwise largely inaccessible. Wikileaks' leaking of evidence of civilian atrocities in Afghanistan and Iraq, for example, was made possible through the savvy use of micro-storage devices (e.g. high-capacity USB drives) and a system of globally interconnected data servers that make up the World Wide Web.

Yet, such technological optimism is quickly dampened as new technologies are successfully embraced and exploited for nefarious and even violent ends. Al-Qaeda's early success in using Internet-based technologies to recruit and train supporters and organize attacks is perhaps the most poignant example.[7] Non-democratic governments have also adjusted to the global information revolution, and, in some cases, have surpassed the new and non-traditional actors in their web-savviness. New America Foundation Fellow Evgeny Morozov argues against the emergence of 'iPod Liberalism', whereby Western diplomats promote Internet connectivity as a means towards democratization, suggesting non-democratic governments can use Internet connectivity to their benefit too.[8] Morozov points to China's '50-cent army', a group of an estimated 50,000 citizens who search out dissident content on the web and then offer rebuttals in support of official state policy, as evidence for how easily the web can amplify traditional sources of political propaganda under the guise of deliberation.[9]

While no single anecdote can capture the complexity of how modern communications technologies are changing the nature of diplomacy, the contested 2009 Iranian Presidential election is certainly instructive. In light of evidence of large-scale voter fraud, millions of Iranians took to the streets to protest the official results of the election. Mobile phones were critical to organizing the protests, and to capture images of large-scale protests, as well as documenting widespread violence used against protestors.[10] As citizen-generated videos and photos made their way to social media applications, some Western journalists took note, often drawing heavily from social media sites like YouTube, Facebook, and Twitter for information. A *New York Times* editorial, 'Dear CNN, Please Check Twitter for News about Iran', criticized the network for being 'shockingly absent from the story'.[11] *The Nation's* Ari Berman concurred, urging readers to 'Forget CNN or any of the major American "news" networks. If you want to get the latest on the opposition protests in Iran, you should be reading blogs, watching YouTube or following Twitter updated from Tehran, minute-by-minute.'[12] Several well-known news organizations, from the *New York Times* to Al-Jazeera English, declared Iran's protests a 'Twitter Revolution'.

Members of the diplomatic core had also taken note, especially in Foggy Bottom. On 16 June, with protests dominating the news, the US State Department contacted the social networking service Twitter urging it to delay a planned system upgrade that would cut service to the website for several hours.[13] Twitter complied, postponing the upgrade in order to 'avoid disrupting service for users in Tehran'.[14] The State Department explained its request, noting, 'Twitter is a medium that all Iranians can use to communicate', adding, 'One of the areas where people are able to get out the word is through Twitter'.[15] Former Deputy National Security Advisor Mark Pfeifle went as far as to call for awarding Twitter the Nobel Peace Prize for 'empowering people to attempt to resolve a domestic showdown with international implications—and enabling the world to stand with them'.[16]

The decision to ask Silicon Valley for help backfired. News of collusion between the State Department and Twitter executives triggered a heavy-handed response by Iranian authorities. According to Morozov, 'the Iranian authorities no longer saw the Internet as an engine of economic growth or as a way to spread the word of the prophet . . . The Web presented an unambiguous threat that Iran's enemies would be sure to exploit. . . . The Iranian authorities embarked on a digital purge of their opponents'.[17] First, the Iranian government argued—compellingly—that Twitter had become an agent of American propaganda, scaring many Iranians from using the service moving forward. Second, they stepped up their online monitoring. Using username and password information gained from incarcerated protesters, the Iranian Republican Guard launched a widespread campaign, tracking down the leaders of the ongoing disobedience via social media networks. Using images and video of the protests posted on the Internet, state security turned to Internet crowd-sourcing to gather the full names and current addresses of protestors who they had not been able to accurately identify themselves. Websites of prominent Iranians in exile were hacked, also by the Iranian Republican Guard, further closing outside access to events in Iran. Within a week, the protests had fizzled, and President Ahmadinejad's authority was firmly re-entrenched.

Since the episode, sober analysis has showed that Twitter turned out to be almost entirely irrelevant to Iranian protestors. *Radio Free Europe*'s Golnaz Esfandiari found that opposition activists primarily utilized text messages, email, and blog posts to organize protests, while 'good old-fashioned word of mouth' was the most influential medium for coordinating opposition. Social media tools like Facebook and Twitter were not ideal for rapid communication among protestors, and were utilized more by observers in other countries. 'Western journalists who couldn't reach—or didn't bother reaching?—people on the ground in Iran simply scrolled through the English-language tweets posted with tag #iranelection'.[18] Rather, social media, and Twitter in particular, was perceived by Westerners as crucial as it was the main means by which experts in the State Department and the mainstream media were following current events in Iran.

Obviously, emerging communications technologies are transforming the ways in which information flows reach new audiences, and how opinions are shaped and policies explained. But, as the Iran example indicates, the changes are far from the 'democratization of information' that so many had hoped for. In order to further explore the nuances of the modern transformation in communications technologies, and how they are shaping the future of diplomatic activity, I analyse Qatar's Al-Jazeera network.

11.2.1 Qatar's Al-Jazeera Network

> The Emir didn't set up Al Jazeera to get a membership card at the press club. It's about power. This has allowed him to, if not checkmate, then at least occasionally check the Saudis. He did it for the same reason he brought Central Command to Qatar. It made him a player in the region and now Al Jazeera English makes him a player on the world stage. (Larry Pintak, CBS Middle East Correspondent)[19]

Launched in 1996, Al-Jazeera has been the subject of much debate. Based in Doha, Qatar, Al-Jazeera is the most important news organization in the Middle East, not only due to its ability to gather large audiences, but also for its ability to mobilize the Arab citizenry perhaps better than any government or political group in the region. Signalling its diplomatic significance, every Arab country has at one time or another protested to the Qatari government about unfavourable content aired on Al-Jazeera. In the West, particularly in the United States, Al-Jazeera is best known as 'Terror TV', or the 'Voice of Osama bin Laden', characterizations that were fuelled by Bush administration officials who publicly decried the organization for its graphic and anti-war coverage in Iraq and Afghanistan.[20]

Having only gained political independence from the United Kingdom in 1971, Qatar was not seen as a geopolitical force until recently. In fact, Al-Jazeera's birth was partly due to fears that other countries in the region—Saudi Arabia in particular, but Iran as well—were plotting encroachments into Qatar in order to access its generous deposits of oil and natural gas.[21] Throughout its operation, the Al-Jazeera network has played an important role in establishing Qatar's reputation in the region and beyond.

Qatar, a constitutional monarchy governed by the Al Thani family, is a small peninsular country in the Persian Gulf sharing its only territorial border with Saudi Arabia. The Al Thani family is, surprisingly for the country's small size, the largest ruling family in the Middle East. It also has a reputation for being the most argumentative: 'Transition from one ruler to another has rarely been smooth and the family's propensity for spilling one another's blood won them the title "the thugs of the Gulf" from one pre-independence British administrator.'[22]

Qatar is geographically small (11,437 square kilometres), roughly the size of the US state of Connecticut. The small emirate gained independence from the United Kingdom on 3 September 1971. It is an archetype of an oil monarchy, in control of the world's third largest remaining natural gas reserve (approximately 14 per cent of the world's total known supply), as well as a small amount of oil (0.4 per cent of global reserves). Like many of the natural gas reserves in the Gulf, some of Qatar's deposits remain in disputed territory with its northern neighbour Bahrain, and its largest deposit, the North Dome, is in the heart of the Persian Gulf, well beyond its protected maritime borders.[23]

Qatar's modern history really begins in 1995, when Amir Hamad bin Khalifa Al Thani came to power after ousting his father, Sheikh Khalifa, in a bloodless coup. As a result, tensions rose between the newly established Qatari government and Saudi Arabia and Egypt, neither of which initially supported the new Emir. As Sakr notes, after the Gulf War, 'Gulf states felt vulnerable to both Saudi Arabia and Iran and always had the Iraqi invasion of Kuwait on their minds. Qatar, in particular, felt it might face a similar invasion like that of Kuwait, but the aggressor this time would be either Saudi Arabia or Iran.'[24] After the deposed Emir and some of his supporters received a warm welcoming in Egypt and Saudi Arabia, 'the Qatari elite felt that Saudi Arabia and Egypt were trying to bring the deposed Emir back'.[25] It is out of this insecurity that Al-Jazeera was born.

At the beginning of Amir Hamad's reign, Qatar was often described as a 'discrete satellite of Saudi Arabia'.[26] But the Sandhurst Military Academy (UK) educated leader was keen to put Qatar on the modern geopolitical map. In the 1970s, Saudi Arabia had exerted its influence as the default protectorate of the emirates and 'forced Kuwait and Bahrain to put an end to their parliamentary experiments', suggesting that such forms of governance were antithetical to the Wahhabi principles of Islam.[27] With this in mind, in his first year of power, Amir Hamad announced an ambitious set of liberal reforms, which included an end to press censorship, as well as municipal and parliamentary elections where women could both vote and be elected. The reforms were bold for the Gulf, including the abolishment of the Ministry of Information. The Saudis saw the move as a clear act of defiance by the young leader.

The liberal reforms, along with a significant grant from the Qatari government, provided space and resources for establishing the first 24-hour Arab news channel, Al-Jazeera. By taking a principled stand for freedom of information, Al-Jazeera allowed for Qatar to stand out from other Gulf Cooperation Council (GCC) and Arab countries, particularly as it was keen to air dissenting views of existing regimes that had long been suppressed throughout the region. 'Qatar's high-profile in uncensored satellite television, conducted via Al-Jazeera, was undertaken at the behest of the Qatari emir as part of a top-down campaign of carving out a distinctive niche for its tiny state.'[28]

Al-Jazeera was founded by royal decree on 8 February 1996. While part of Qatar's commitment to Western reforms, Al-Jazeera was launched also as 'a response to regime vulnerabilities on the Islamic front as well as a means of legitimizing Qatar's military and economic pact with the United States in the [eyes] of angry Arab audiences'.[29] While 'the new regime was vulnerable...it created a media equivalent of a super-gun under the name of Al-Jazeera to keep Iran, Saudi Arabia and Egypt on the defensive, or at the very least to respond to attacks appearing in the Egyptian and Saudi Arabian media'.[30] Ensuring that Saudi Arabia took notice, Qatar's Al-Jazeera hired roughly 120 journalists from a BBC Arabic team that had been disbanded due to its highly critical reporting of Saudi Arabia. Thus, not only did Al-Jazeera have the resources to produce high-quality programming, it also had the talent—trained by the BBC—to produce good journalism.[31]

This is not to take away from the democratic impact that Al-Jazeera has had on the Arab media scene. The news network quickly made a reputation for itself by exposing corruption among Arab governments and initiating political discussions on topics that had previously been taboo.[32] But due to Qatar's small size and tiny regional presence, viewers were rarely concerned by the broadcaster's outward focus. By focusing its provocative coverage towards the region's established centres of power, Al-Jazeera created breathing space for Qatar's young leader to solidify his authority and mastermind a foreign policy that would include a military alliance with the United States, trade relations with the Israelis, and close political and financial ties with Palestinian and Iranian political leaders.

Al-Jazeera's early success caused waves in Arab politics, and Arab citizens and governments quickly took note. Up until the launching of Al-Jazeera, almost all media, particularly the broadcast media, were state-controlled. Newspapers and TV news featured information that helped maintain the political status quo; governments only allowed stories that were critical of political enemies and regional rivals. Thus, when Al-Jazeera hit the airwaves, it was the first broadcast news network indigenous to the region that was highly critical of standing Arab governments. It mirrored CNN in quality, but was distinctly 'Arab', featuring Arab journalists and stories told from a pan-Arab perspective. Al-Jazeera became a source of pride for an Arab citizenry that for so long had struggled with a collective shame of humiliation due to a long history of colonial and corrupt governance.[33]

Conversations regarding the rights of women in Islam, widespread government corruption, and even homosexuality were introduced on Al-Jazeera's highly intense talk shows. Josh Rushing, a former Public Affairs Officer for the Marines, describes the change as such: 'Al Jazeera changed the way Arabs thought about the news in the same way Henry Ford changed the way Americans thought about travel.'[34] Critical to Al-Jazeera's success was its ability to be seen as credible in the eyes of its viewers. Having grown accustomed to being inundated with state-controlled news flows, both Arab and Western, Arab audiences have learned to be naturally sceptical of broadcast news. Yet, Al-Jazeera's news agenda seemed to operate independent from any particular government's interests. In this regard, Qatar's relative obscurity in the Arab world and politics was essential to Al-Jazeera's strength. Had one of the more powerful governments in the region launched a similar news organization—Egypt, Iran, or Saudi Arabia, for instance—viewers would have been more suspicious. At the time, Saudi Arabia was seen by many as Qatar's protector, and thus Al-Jazeera's highly critical coverage of Saudi affairs and influence only added to the network's credibility.[35]

As a result, Arabs believed the news Al-Jazeera reported. Polls showed that 89 per cent of Bahrainis, 93 per cent of Egyptians, 96 per cent of Jordanians, 95 per cent of Kuwaitis, 90 per cent of Moroccans, 94 per cent of Saudi Arabians, 93 per cent of Tunisians, and 96 per cent of Emiratis found Al-Jazeera's programming trustworthy.[36] Despite the growth of a hyper-competitive and oversaturated news media environment, Al-Jazeera remains the most watched source of news. A 2009 poll conducted by University of Maryland with Zogby International found that 55 per cent of participants surveyed in Egypt,

Jordan, Lebanon, the UAE, Saudi Arabia, and Morocco said that when they tuned in to international news they chose Al-Jazeera most often, up from 53 per cent in 2008.[37]

By 1998, Al-Jazeera was available to almost anyone with a satellite dish. The network had found its stride and was broadcasting original content twenty-four hours a day. Soon thereafter, 'the network was recognized as a thorn in the side of regimes that had grown accustomed to controlling the news flow'.[38] Saudi Arabia and Kuwait were among the most critical of the network and leaders in both countries organized a financial boycott of any company that advertised on Al-Jazeera, effectively making it impossible for the network to generate any revenue.

For Qatar, the network dominated its diplomatic discussions. One of the network's earliest controversies took place in November 1998. Al-Jazeera's most popular show, *The Opposite Direction*, featured a debate between a former Jordanian foreign minister and a Syrian critic that resulted in a series of accusations tying Jordan to an Israeli plot to eradicate the Palestinian territories. The day after the show, the Jordanian Minister of Information shut down Al-Jazeera's bureau in Amman, declaring that the show's moderator, Dr Faisal al-Qasim, was conducting an 'intentional and repeated campaign against Jordan'.[39]

Criticisms and condemnations of Al-Jazeera's news were featured prominently in the widely distributed Saudi press, which de facto represented the royal family's opinion. In an article titled 'Arabsat and Another Kind of Pornography', the Saudi Press analogized Al-Jazeera to a form of entertainment pornography, arguing that it should be regulated and banned in a fashion similar to that of traditional pornography.[40] The severity of Arab criticism of the network increased considerably after its coverage of the America-led Operation Desert Fox, where Al-Jazeera covered the 70-hour bombing campaign focusing on a devastated civilian infrastructure, while relying on Iraqi officials to frame the events. Saudi Arabia, the Kurds, and Kuwait all opposed the coverage, calling it 'unacceptable propaganda' used to 'rehabilitate the Iraqi regime'.[41]

Saudi Arabia was especially rattled as the coverage included a focus on the use of Saudi airbases for the attacks on Iraq, thus turning attention towards the Kingdom's complicity with the military attack on another Arab country. As a result, Saudi Crown Prince Abdullah accused Al-Jazeera of being a 'disgrace to the [Gulf Cooperation Council] countries, of defaming the members of the Saudi royal family, of threatening the stability of the Arab world and of encouraging terrorism'.[42] Other members of the Saudi government have similarly criticized Al-Jazeera for its coverage of deaths relating to Arab pilgrimages in Saudi Arabia, calling it 'a dagger in the flank of the Arab nation'. Saudi mosques followed the government's lead, criticizing the organization and issuing a 'political fatwa forbidding Saudis from appearing on the Station's shows'.[43] The Kingdom went as far as to prohibit watching satellite television in coffee shops in an effort to restrict the network's reach.

Kuwait's criticisms of Al-Jazeera similarly escalated in response to a talk show that featured a discussion of women's rights that was critical of the Kuwaiti Amir Sheikh Jaber al-Ahmad Al-Sabah. Kuwaiti authorities were so outraged that they banned the network's journalists from operating in its jurisdiction for 'violating the ethics of the profession and harming the State of Kuwait'.[44] While Kuwait and Saudi Arabia were the two most pronounced critics of Al-Jazeera in the Arab world, every government in the region—save Saddam Hussein's Iraq—had at one time or another lodged formal criticisms against the network or taken action to restrict Al-Jazeera's ability to gather or distribute the news (see Figure 11.1). Libya 'permanently withdrew' its ambassador from Qatar in response to Al-Jazeera's airing of a discussion that included one guest who called Muammar Al Qadhafi a 'dictator'. Morocco also withdrew its ambassador, accusing the network of leading 'a campaign against...its democratic revolution', and Tunisia severed diplomatic ties with Qatar after a programme aired views of members of the Islamic opposition that were critical of human rights conditions in Tunisia.[45]

The Egyptian and Algerian governments accused the network of supporting the cause of Islamic extremists by offering ideological and extremist group leaders access to the mass media airwaves. Algeria went as far as to cut the power to several major cities in the middle of an episode of *The Opposite Direction* that featured blunt criticisms of the government's human rights abuses during the country's civil war.[46] Bahrain banned Al-Jazeera from covering its 2002 elections, arguing that the network had been 'penetrated by Zionists'.[47] Iraq shut down Al-Jazeera's bureau in Baghdad because, according to interim Prime Minister Ayad Allawi, the network was an advocate of violence, 'hatred and problems and racial tension'.[48] All in all, according to Faisal AI-Qasim, moderator of Al-Jazeera's most popular talk show, *The Opposite Direction*, 'six countries—Jordan, Saudi Arabia, Kuwait, Tunisia, Libya, and Morocco—withdrew their ambassadors from Doha because of my program'.[49] Having failed to curtail the network's critical journalism through public criticisms and pressure on the Qatari government, an unnamed Gulf state went as far as to offer Qatari foreign minister $5 billion simply to close down the station.[50]

Al-Jazeera was introduced to most in the West during the US-led invasion of Afghanistan, when it became the go-to channel for news about the conflict. When the US-led coalition first attacked Afghanistan, Al-Jazeera was the only international news organization with a bureau in Kabul. As a result, audiences worldwide depended on Al-Jazeera for timely footage of the conflict. Western news organizations such as CNN, ABC, NBC, and Fox News quickly made agreements with Al-Jazeera to purchase their high-quality and proprietary footage, and American audiences became familiar with its very foreign, 'Arab looking' logo spinning at the bottom of their television screens.[51]

In 2003, with the onset of the war in Iraq, Al-Jazeera began making headlines in the American press as the Bush administration repeatedly decried Al-Jazeera for its one-sided coverage of the conflict. US Deputy Defense Secretary Paul Wolfowitz went as far as to suggest that Al-Jazeera's coverage was 'inciting violence' and 'endangering the lives of American troops' in Iraq.[52] Secretary of Defense Rumsfeld (2004) followed up by accusing the network's coverage of the war on terror as being 'vicious, inaccurate, and inexcusable', arguing that Al-Jazeera had repeatedly cooperated with the insurgents in Iraq to portray US soldiers as 'randomly killing innocent civilians'. Secretary of State Colin Powell contended that the network showed videotapes from terrorists 'for the purpose of inflaming the world and appealing to the basest instincts in the region'.[53] Powell concluded a meeting with visiting Qatari foreign minister by declaring that Al-Jazeera had 'intruded on relations' between the US and Qatar.[54] Hostility towards the

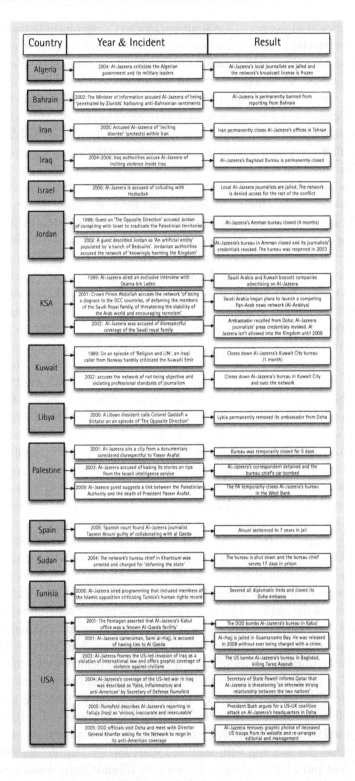

Country	Year & Incident	Result
Algeria	2004: Al-Jazeera criticizes the Algerian government and its military leaders	Al-Jazeera's local journalists are jailed and the network's broadcast license is frozen
Bahrain	2002: The Minister of Information accused Al-Jazeera of being 'penetrated by Zionists' harboring anti-Bahrainian sentiments	Al-Jazeera is permanently banned from reporting from Bahrain
Iran	2005: Accused Al-Jazeera of 'inciting disorder' (protests) within Iran	Iran permanently closes Al-Jazeera's offices in Tehran
Iraq	2004-2006: Iraq authorities accuse Al-Jazeera of inciting violence inside Iraq	Al-Jazeera's Baghdad Bureau is permanently closed
Israel	2006: Al-Jazeera is accused of colluding with Hezbollah	Local Al-Jazeera journalists are jailed; The network is denied access for the rest of the conflict
Jordan	1998: Guest on 'The Opposite Direction' accused Jordan of conspiring with Israel to eradicate the Palestinian territories	Al-Jazeera's Amman bureau closed (4 months)
Jordan	2002: A guest described Jordan as 'An artificial entity' populated by 'a bunch of Bedouins'. Jordanian authorities accused the network of 'knowingly harming the Kingdom'	Al-Jazeera's bureau in Amman closed and its journalists' credentials revoked. The bureau was reopened in 2003
KSA	1999: Al-Jazeera aired an exclusive interview with Osama bin Laden	Saudi Arabia and Kuwait boycott companies advertising on Al-Jazeera
KSA	2001: Crown Prince Abdullah accuses the network 'of being a disgrace to the GCC countries, of defaming the members of the Saudi Royal family, of threatening the stability of the Arab world and encouraging terrorism'	Saudi Arabia began plans to launch a competing Pan-Arab news network (Al-Arabiya)
KSA	2002: Al-Jazeera was accused of disrespectful coverage of the Saudi royal family	Ambassador recalled from Doha; Al-Jazeera journalists' press credentials revoked. Al Jazeera isn't allowed into the Kingdom until 2008
Kuwait	1999: On an episode of 'Religion and Life', an Iraqi caller from Norway harshly criticized the Kuwaiti Emir	Closes down Al-Jazeera's Kuwait City bureau (1 month)
Kuwait	2002: accuses the network of not being objective and violating professional standards of journalism	Closes down Al-Jazeera's bureau in Kuwait City and sues the network
Libya	2000: A Libyan dissident calls Colonel Qaddafi a dictator on an episode of 'The Opposite Direction'	Lybia permanently removed its ambassador from Doha
Palestine	2001: Al-Jazeera airs a clip from a documentary considered disrespectful to Yasser Arafat	Bureau was temporarily closed for 5 days
Palestine	2003: Al-Jazeera accused of basing its stories on tips from the Israeli intelligence service	Al-Jazeera's correspondent detained and the bureau chief's car bombed
Palestine	2009: Al-Jazeera guest suggests a link between the Palestinian Authority and the death of President Yasser Arafat.	The PA temporarily closes Al-Jazeera's bureau in the West Bank
Spain	2005: Spanish court found Al-Jazeera journalist Tayseer Alouni guilty of collaborating with al Qaeda	Alouni sentenced to 7 years in jail
Sudan	2004: The network's bureau chief in Khartoum was arrested and charged for 'defaming the state'	The bureau is shut down and the bureau chief serves 17 days in prison
Tunisia	2006: Al-Jazeera aired programming that included members of the Islamic opposition criticizing Tunisia's human rights record	Severed all diplomatic ties and closed its Doha embassy
USA	2001: The Pentagon asserted that Al-Jazeera's Kabul office was a 'known Al-Qaeda facility'	The DOD bombs Al-Jazeera's bureau in Kabul
USA	2001: Al-Jazeera cameraman, Sami al-Hajj, is accused of having ties to Al Qaeda	Al-Hajj is jailed in Guantanamo Bay. He was released in 2008 without ever being charged with a crime.
USA	2003: Al-Jazeera frames the US-led invasion of Iraq as a violation of international law and offers graphic coverage of violence against civilians	The US bombs Al-Jazeera's bureau in Baghdad, killing Tareq Ayyoub
USA	2004: Al-Jazeera's coverage of the US-led war in Iraq was described as 'false, inflammatory and anti-American' by Secretary of Defense Rumsfeld	Secretary of State Powell informs Qatar that Al-Jazeera is threatening 'an otherwise strong relationship between the two nations'
USA	2005: Rumsfeld describes Al-Jazeera's reporting in Falluja (Iraq) as 'vicious, inaccurate and inexcusable'	President Bush argues for a US-UK coalition attack on Al-Jazeera's headquarters in Doha
USA	2005: DOD officials visit Doha and meet with Director General Khanfar asking for the Network to reign in its anti-American coverage	Al-Jazeera removes graphic photos of deceased US troops from its website and re-arranges editorial and management

FIGURE 11.1. Al-Jazeera's diplomacy, 1998–2009

network finally reached a pinnacle in 2004, when President Bush himself took time out of his State of the Union address to describe Al-Jazeera's coverage of the war in Iraq as 'hateful propaganda', a comment that only further ignited rumours that he had at one point suggested to Prime Minister Blair that the Western coalition add Al-Jazeera's headquarters in Doha to a list of the coalition's military targets in the war on terror.[55]

What started out as an effort to help Qatar step out from under the shadow of Saudi Arabia has since become the fifth most recognized brand in the world.[56] 'Al Jazeera has become the symbol of the emirate as well as the source of its fame. In a sense, Al Jazeera is for Qatar what the casinos are for Monaco.'[57] Egyptian-Canadian academic Adel Iskander argues that Al-Jazeera 'sets the agenda in the Arab world', adding, 'In many countries where there is no official opposition party, Al Jazeera became the opposition party.'[58] Larry Pintak, former Director of American University of Cairo's Kamal Adham Center for Journalism, Training, and Research argues that Al-Jazeera has done for the Arab world what Watergate did to a young generation of journalists in America: 'young Arab journalists see the possibility of changing things and they see the role that their profession can play in doing that. That is a direct response to the presence of Al Jazeera.'[59] Miles describes the organization as 'the most powerful, non-state actor in the Arab world today', arguing that if Al-Jazeera were a political party it would give Hamas or Muslim Brotherhood a run for their money.[60] Tunisian-born academic Mohamed Zayani explains, by 'tapping into the Arab identity during times marked by Arab disunity, Al Jazeera has emerged as a key opinion maker.'[61] Poniewozik agrees arguing, 'Among all the major influences on Arab public opinion—the mosque, the press, the schools—the newest and perhaps most revolutionary is Al Jazeera.'[62]

Al-Jazeera's ability to set the public's agenda, frame the news, and shake up geopolitics was on display during the 2011 Arab Spring. Its non-stop and one-sided coverage in support of protestors in Tunisia, Egypt, Libya, and Syria triggered what Harvard political scientist Samuel Huntington calls 'a demonstration effect', whereby coverage of successful protest movements in one country spill over to neighbouring countries, and vice versa, sparking continued pressure on unpopular governments in the region. At times, Al-Jazeera worked hand in hand with political dissidents to facilitate continued pressure on autocratic leaders like Hosni Mubarak and Zine El Abidine Ben Ali.[63] For example, Rached Ghannouchi, Chairman of the Islamist Ennahda party, victors in Tunisia's first democratic elections since the fall of President Ben Ali, described the network as a 'partner in the Arab revolutions'.[64] Mostefa Souag, Al-Jazeera's Director of News noted, 'In Libya, and in Egypt, when the local mobile phone networks were shutdown and the Internet slowed to a halt, we were the only place where protestors could tune in and find out where and when the next protest would be.'[65]

The government of Qatar has seized on its increased visibility and popularity. In 2008, 'the tiny Gulf state emerged ... at the forefront of regional diplomacy, successfully shepherding the negotiations between feuding Lebanese factions to end months of political turmoil and violence.'[66] The Qatari Emir succeeded at negotiating a settlement after Arab and Western leaders had failed. Qatar is also mediating between the Sudanese government and rebel factions in Darfur, with a measure of success. A recent deal between

Sudan and Chad was signed in Doha under Qatar's tutelage. Moreover, Qatar has also been critical in efforts to bring an end to the al-Houthi rebellion in the north of Yemen. 'They're recognized as just about the only player that seems to be able to make any difference.'[67] While these achievements may seem minor to some, they are significant in the context of the current geopolitical realities of the region: 'The reaction of Egypt and Saudi Arabia is partly explained by the fact that these nations have thus far not been able to prove themselves successful solvers of these [regional] conflicts, whereas the Qataris have on occasion. They are needled by that.'[68]

Qatar has managed to strike a balance in its diplomatic relationships, maintaining strong ties with the West, while also being friendly with Iran, Syria, Hamas, and Hezbollah.

> Qatar has close ties with Iran, yet it also is host to one of the world's biggest American air bases. It is home to Israeli officials and to political Islamists who advocate Israel's destruction; to Al Jazeera, the controversial satellite TV station; and (at least until recently) to Saddam Hussein's widow. Saudi Arabia is a trusted ally, but so is Saudi Arabia's nemesis Syria, whose president, Bashar al-Assad, received an Airbus as a personal gift from the Qatari emir this year.[69]

While the traditional Arab powers—Egypt and Saudi Arabia—resent much of Qatar's diplomatic reach, it has also garnered the small emirate a certain level of respect. 'Despite occasional diplomatic problems and frequent complaints, Qatar's policy seems to have worked, catapulting the country to new levels of recognition around the globe.'[70] Al-Jazeera has allowed Qatar to 'punch above its weight'.[71] Egyptian analyst Amr Choubaki argues, 'Qatar is acting as a mediator . . . and it is using Al Jazeera for this purpose. Qatar created Al Jazeera, but now Al Jazeera is creating Qatar.'[72]

The origins of Al-Jazeera—regime insecurity—and Qatar's investment in the network to increase its diplomatic capital represent a significant case study in advancing our understanding as to how emerging media are altering how power is negotiated and authority legitimated in international politics. Qatar's rise in geopolitical leverage, which included diplomatically isolating each of its neighbouring states, dis-investing in its military, and embracing a path of political reform unfamiliar to its citizens and the region certainly stands out as being non-traditional. Yet, through using a news network, it challenged the authority of existing centres of power—Saudi Arabia, Egypt, Central Command, Tunisia's Ben Ali, Egypt's Mubarak, and Libya's Gadhafi, to name a few—resulting in significant changes in the region's balance of power.

The communications technology central to Al-Jazeera's rise was the existence of a privately owned, geostationary satellite network whereby its programming could be broadcast direct to home, by-passing state licensing and regulators throughout the region. Other communications technologies, such as high-quality mobile video recording cameras, widespread Internet connections facilitating audience-generated content, and advanced World Wide Web interfaces engaging sophisticated audiences from around the world, have also been important for Al-Jazeera's continued success. But, at first, it was its satellite presence in the Middle East that allowed for the network to cultivate substantial audiences and challenge existing regimes of information sovereignty. Importantly, had the Middle East's information infrastructure developed slightly differently, Al-Jazeera could have been much more easily thwarted. For example, had the satellite systems been developed and operated by state entities rather than commercial enterprises, or had the cable systems that dominate the American television market taken hold in the region, the network's broadcasts could have been shut off with much greater ease.

11.3 CONCLUSION

In Jorge Heine's 'From Club to Network Diplomacy' (Chapter 2, this volume), he cites Sir Harold Nicolson's historical observation that the role of the diplomat changed from the 'orator' diplomat of the Greek city-states to the 'trained observer' of the 19th and 20th centuries, 'one who sent dispatches reporting to the minister about developments in distant lands'. What is striking about Al-Jazeera is its ability to do both, playing the role of the Greek orator (particularly through its mastering of the use of the Aristotelian enthymeme) while simultaneously observing, framing, and initiating news from foreign countries. Rather than disseminate Qatari world views to Arab audiences keen to tune out government propaganda, Al-Jazeera tells the story of other governments' corruption or abuse of power, oftentimes broadcasting voices—reporters—local to and familiar with the controversy. Returning to Heine, rather than 'conveying what the diplomat's home country is all about and transmitting it to the host society and government'—Al Jazeera projects an idealized Arab public sphere, where deliberation is valued and politics is democratic. Moreover, rather than merely being a 'trained observer', conveying information back to the homeland, a reporter provides 'analysis and influence', and is a 'proactive initiator', narrating compelling stories and debates that shape opinions among audiences from around the region.

Qatar's Al-Jazeera thus exists at the intersection of what Heine describes as club and networked diplomacy. Dependent on government resources for its operations, and connected directly to the Qatari royal family through its Board of Directors and Managing Director, the network is firmly connected to traditional notions of statecraft and geopolitics. Yet, due to its editorial independence in covering issues outside of the Arab Gulf, and to its diverse team of dedicated journalists from around the region, Al-Jazeera can be simultaneously networked to foreign opinion leaders as well as traditional state actors. Importantly, as Al-Jazeera expands to broadcast in English, Swahili, Turkish, Urdu, and Bosnian/Croatian, its capacity to project idealized democratic values while engaging foreign audiences will grow, as will Qatar's geopolitical muscle.

Al-Jazeera's role in initiating and driving the events culminating in the 2011 Arab Spring provides more than ample evidence of its ability to work at the intersection of club and networked diplomacy. In the case of Egypt, a long-standing nemesis of the Qatari Amir, the network played a crucial role in driving the crisis of Mubarak's legitimacy, keeping a mass mediated spotlight on protesters for weeks until the pressure eventually overwhelmed the standing Egyptian government. Al-Jazeera's ability to deploy and draw from a robust team of Egyptians, many of whom had been ostracized or exiled by President Mubarak, provided the network the credibility and expertise needed to capture audiences, while at the same time furthering a long-held goal of the Qatari government: the removal of Hosni Mubarak from power. In Libya, Al-Jazeera's constant coverage of rebel forces fighting Gadhafi loyalists coincided with Qatar's material support—through training and military equipment—of rebel efforts. Finally, its coverage of Tunisia's popular uprising demonstrates its strength as a networked diplomat, drawing on the extensive social media contacts that its Tunisian journalists had maintained with the homeland to access and broadcast mobile and real-time reports of the uprising.

In short, when institutions adapt to modern communications technologies, and use them to challenge existing centres of power, as Qatar's Al-Jazeera has done, power can shift from one actor to another. The most effective diplomats of the 21st century will be those that understand how technologies work, their strengths and weaknesses, while maintaining focus on what matters most: telling compelling stories to target audiences abroad, as well as at home.

NOTES

1. Cited in Alvin Snyder, *US Foreign Affairs in the Information Age* (Washington, DC: The Annenberg Washington Program in Communications Policy Studies, 1995).
2. For example, see Hillary Clinton, 'Remarks on Internet Freedom', 21 January 2010 <http://www.state.gov/secretary/rm/2010/01/135519.htm.>
3. Wernher von Braun, 'TV Broadcast Satellite', *Popular Science* (May 1970), 65–6.
4. James Baker, *The Politics of Diplomacy* (New York: G.P. Putnam's Sons, 1995), 103.
5. Clay Shirky, *Here Comes Everybody: The Power of Organizing Without Organizations* (New York: Penguin USA, 2008).
6. Thomas Friedman, *The World is Flat* (New York: Farrar, Straus and Giroux, 2005).
7. See A.N. Awan, 'Virtual Jihadist media: Function, legitimacy, and radicalising efficacy', *European Journal of Cultural Studies* 10:3 (2007), 389–408; A.N. Awan, *Radicalization on the Internet? The Virtual Propagation of Jihadist Media and its Effects*, Journal of the Royal United Services Institute 152:3 (2007); A.N. Awan, 'Virtual Jihadist media', in F. Peter (ed.), *Manual of Islamic Movements* (Casa Arabe: Madrid, 2009); Brynjar Lia, 'Al-Qaeda online: understanding jihadist internet infrastructure', *Janes Intelligence Review*, 2 December 2 2005, <http://articles.janes.com/articles/Janes-Intelligence-Review-2006/Al-Qaeda-online-understanding-jihadist-internet-infrastructure.html>.
8. Evgeny Morozov, *The Net Delusion: The Dark Side of Internet Freedom* (Cambridge, MA: Public Affairs, 2011).
9. See Mike Elgan, 'How China's "50 Cent Army" Could Wreck Web 2.0', *Datamation*, 8 January 2009, <http://itmanagement.earthweb.com/netsys/article.php/3795091/How-Chinas-50-Cent-Army-Could-Wreck-Web-20.htm>.

10. Yahya R. Kamalipour, *Media, Power, and Politics in the Digital Age: The 2009 Presidential Election Uprising in Iran* (Lanham: Rowman & Littlefield, 2010).

11. Marshall Kirkpatrick, 'Dear CNN, Please Check Twitter for News about Iran', *The New York Times*, 14 June 2009.

12. Ari Berman, 'Iran's Twitter Revolution', *The Nation*, 15 June 2009, <http://www.thenation.com/blog/irans-twitter-revolution>.

13. Sue Plemming, 'U.S. State Department speaks to Twitter over Iran', *Reuters*, 16 June 2009.

14. Mike Musgrove, 'Twitter is a Player in Iran's Drama', *Washington Post*, 17 June 2009.

15. Musgrove, 'Twitter is a Player'.

16. Mark Pfeifle, 'A Nobel Peace Prize for Twitter', *The Christian Science Monitor*, 6 July 2009.

17. Morozov, *Net Delusion*, 10.

18. Golnaz Esfandiari, 'The Twitter Devolution', *Foreign Policy*, 7 June 2010, <http://www.foreignpolicy.com/articles/2010/06/07/the_twitter_revolution_that_wasnt>.

19. Josh Rushing, *Mission Al-Jazeera* (New York: Palgrave Macmillan, 2007), 134–5.

20. Hugh Miles, *Al Jazeera: The Inside Story of the Arab News Channel that is Challenging the West* (London, UK: Grove, 2006).

21. Mamoun Fandy, *(Un)Civil War of Words: Media and Politics in the Arab World* (London: Praeger Security International, 2007).

22. Miles, *Al Jazeera: The Inside Story*, 13.

23. Territorial disputes have always been a critical point of conflict throughout the Persian Gulf, particularly for the smaller Gulf states like Qatar. Most of the current borders were determined by colonial powers, and they include miles of desolate desert that are difficult to discern. Border disputes are not only common, but they have also proven very difficult to resolve. Adding to the problem is the ubiquity of oil and natural gas deposits in the region, underneath the ground, often crossing over existing political boundaries. Arguably the most significant of the recent border conflicts was Iraq's invasion of Kuwait in 1991. The two nations are separated by a border that was first codified in 1919, during a period of colonial governance. Because many other borders in the region were similarly created at the same time, this invasion sparked a renewed concern about other possible territorial conflicts in the region. See Anthony Cordesman, *Bahrain, Oman, Qatar, and the UAE: Challenges of Security* (Boulder, CO: Westview Press, 1997); Christopher M. Blanchard, *Qatar: Background and U.S. Relations* (Washington, DC: Congressional Research Service Report RL31718, 2008); Hooshang Amirahmadi, *Small Islands, Big Politics* (New York: Palgrave Macmillan, 1996).

24. Naomi Sakr, *Satellite Realms: Transnational Television, Globalization and the Middle East* (London and New York: I.B. Tauris Publishers, 2001), 48.

25. Fandy, *(Un)Civil War of Words*, 46.

26. Olivier Da Lage, 'The Politics of Al Jazeera or the Diplomacy of Doha', in Mohamed Zayani (ed.), *The Al Jazeera Phenomenon: Critical Perspectives on New Arab Media* (London: Pluto Press, 2007), 50.

27. Da Lage, *The Politics of Al Jazeera*, 56.

28. Sakr, *Satellite Realms*, 64.

29. Fandy, *(Un)Civil War of Words*, 47.

30. Fandy, *(Un)Civil War of Words*, 46.

31. Rushing, *Mission Al-Jazeera*.

32. Mohammed El-Nawawy and Adel Iskandar, *Al-Jazeera: The Story of the Network That is Rattling Governments and Redefining Modern Journalism* (Boulder, CO: Basic Books, 2003).

33. Miles, *Al Jazeera: The Inside Story*.

34. Rushing, *Mission Al-Jazeera*, 128.

35. Fandy, *(Un)Civil War of Words*.

36. Mark Rhodes and Rola Abdul-Latif, *Al-Jazeera and Al-Arabiya: A Comparative Study* (Washington DC: Intermedia Research, 2005).

37. Shibley Telhami, '2009 Annual Arab Public Opinion Survey', *University of Maryland with Zogby International* (2009), 1–59; Shibley Telhami, *Reflections of Hearts and Minds: Media, Opinion and Identity in the Arab World* (Washington, DC: Brookings Institution, 2005).

38. Shawn Powers and Eytna Gilboa, 'The Public Diplomacy of Al Jazeera', in Phil Seib (ed.), *New Media and the New Middle East* (New York: Palgrave Macmillan, 2007), 63; Moahmmed El-Nawawy and Shawn Powers, 'Al-Jazeera English: A Conciliatory Medium in a Conflict-Driven Environment?', *Global Media and Communication* 6:1 (2010), 1–24.

39. Miles, *Al Jazeera: The Inside Story*, 45.

40. Miles, *Al Jazeera: The Inside Story*, 46.

41. Miles, *Al Jazeera: The Inside Story*, 54.

42. Habib Trabelsi, 'Crise larvée entre Ryad et Doha', *Agence France Presse*, 24 July 2002.

43. Miles, *Al Jazeera: The Inside Story*, 53.

44. Miles, *Al Jazeera: The Inside Story*, 54.

45. Ian Urbina, 'Al Jazeera: Hits, Misses and Ricochets', *Asia Times*, 25 December 25, 2002.

46. Davan Maharaj, 'How Tiny Qatar Jars Arab Media', *The Times*, 7 May 2001.

47. 'Bahrain bans Al Jazeera TV', *British Broadcasting Corporation*, 10 May 2002.

48. 'Iraq shuts al-Jazeera's Baghdad office', *Associated Press*, 7 August 2004.

49. Interview with author, March 2008 (Doha, Qatar).

50. Urbina, 'Al Jazeera: Hits, Misses and Ricochets'.

51. Khalil Rinnawi, *Instant Nationalism: Mcarabism, Al-Jazeera and Transnational Media in the Arab World* (New York: University Press of America, Inc, 2006).

52. Robert Fisk, 'The US Moves to Close Down Al Jazeera TV: Wolfowitz the Censor', *The Independent*, 1 August 2003.

53. E.A. Torriero, 'US, Media at Odds Over Iraq Coverage', *Chicago Tribune*, 1 August 2003.

54. Paul Richter, 'U.S. Airs Critical Views of Arab TV', *Los Angeles Times*, 28 April 2004.

55. Neil Mackay, 'Wartime Secrets: Did President Bush want to bomb television station?', *The Sunday Herald*, 27 November 2005.

56. Stephen Brook, 'Al-Jazeera is world's fifth top brand', *The Guardian*, 1 February 2005, <http://www.guardian.co.uk/media/2005/feb/01/marketingandpr.broadcasting>.

57. Da Lage, *The Politics of Al Jazeera*, 55.

58. Cited in Rushing, *Mission Al-Jazeera*, 135.

59. Cited in Rushing, *Mission Al-Jazeera*, 141.

60. Hugh Miles, 'Arab Television News and Al Jazeera', The Frontline Club, London, 2 March 2005, <http://www.tbsjournal.com/Archives/Spring05/frontlinetranscript.html>.

61. Zayani, *The Al Jazeera Phenomenon*, 8.

62. James Poniewozik, 'The Battle for the Hearts and Minds: Even before bin Laden's Tape, the US Was Losing the Propaganda War in the Arab World', *Time Magazine*, 22 October 2001, 65.

63. K. Hroub, 'Qatar's Source of Arab Springs', *Project Syndicate*, 18 October 2011, <http://www.project-syndicate.org/commentary/hroub2/English>; H. Edwards, 'Former Al Jazeera Head on Quitting, the Arab Spring, and Qatar's Role', *The Atlantic*, 30 September 2011.

64. F. Baatout, 'Arab Sprog Champion Al Jazeera Marks 15th Year', *Agence France Presse*, 2 November 2011.

65. Interview with author, November 2011 (Doha, Qatar).

66. Nicholas Blanford, 'Why Qatar is emerging as Middle East peacemaker', *The Christian Science Monitor*, 23 May 2008, <http://www.csmonitor.com/2008/0523/p06s02-wome. html>.

67. Dominic Moran, 'Qatar Steps Into the Breach', *ISN Security Watch*, 24 March 2009.

68. Moran, 'Qatar Steps Into the Breach'.

69. Robert F. Worth, 'Al Jazeera No Longer Nips at Saudis', *The New York Times*, 4 January 2008; Robert F. Worth, 'Qatar, Playing All Sides, is a Nonstop Mediator', *The New York Times*, 9 July 2008.

70. Worth, 'Qatar, Playing All Sides, is a Nonstop Mediator'.

71. Vivian Salama, 'Qatar Draws Skepticism Over Darfur', *The National*, 29 March 2009.

72. Jeffrey Fleishman and Noha El-Hennawy, 'Qatar's Ambitions Roil Middle East', *Los Angeles Times*, 21 April 2009.

PART III

MODES OF PRACTICE

CHAPTER 12

....

BILATERAL DIPLOMACY

....

ANDRÉS ROZENTAL AND

ALICIA BUENROSTRO[*]

BILATERAL diplomacy is the basic building block for relations among states. This ancient craft belongs to the domain of empirical knowledge. It is transmitted through mentors and a set of rules, many unwritten. Nations interact with each other because of the nation state's vulnerability, the search for dominance over others, extant common interests, and the powerful incentives of international trade. Diplomacy seeks to build relationships that promote the survival and security of the nation state. It encourages the construction of alliances and the defence of its own interests. Finally, it transforms a bilateral relationship into a strategic one. Politics is thus the cornerstone of relations among nations.

Diplomacy is based on crafting ways to enhance these relations. Bilateral diplomacy determines when, where, and how a specific country-to-country relationship will become more relevant. Likewise, diplomats are expected to prevent bilateral agendas from being overwhelmed by a single issue. In the case of the Mexico–US relationship, the Mexican foreign ministry has tried to keep sensitive matters such as immigration and drug trafficking from affecting the rest of the agenda. It has also aimed to institutionalize the latter by creating a set of working groups and committees to deal with each issue. The ministry has also engaged in the established practice of lobbying Washington in various ways, to deal with the pressing challenge of immigration.

A nation's security will always be its highest priority. Since a country's security is largely determined by its vicinity, geographical proximity may lead to collaboration and/or confrontation across borders. A nation state's relations with others fall into two major categories: strategic and peripheral. Other kinds of associations can be based on shared interests or values. Fortuitous or created circumstances may result in new areas of opportunity. Cultivating political links is at the core of what ministries of foreign affairs and their networks of missions do. Foreign ministries execute foreign policy and instruct and evaluate the work of missions abroad. The latter perform their tasks through a team of professional and local employees as well as a physical and administrative infrastructure. To carry out their duties, diplomats need to understand the power structure in the host country, establish a wide network of contacts, and develop suitable social skills. To reach specific goals, the chief of mission and his/her staff follow standard methods for cultivating political, economic, social, and cultural relations.

12.1 New Contents, Lines of Action, and Tools in Bilateral Diplomacy

Harold Nicolson defined representing, informing, and negotiating as the main activities of bilateral diplomacy. This has changed. Diplomats no longer have the monopoly of representation. Neither is reporting back home about local developments the same anymore. Officials at headquarters have instantaneous access to international media. Thus the content of diplomatic cables has to be original and complementary to available reporting. Likewise, international negotiations have become a technical discipline beyond the purview of diplomats.

Promotion and protection are key to today's bilateral diplomacy. The growing movement of people from one country to another demands more services and attention from diplomatic missions than ever before. Mexico—which has around 12 million nationals living outside its borders—has established the world's largest system of consulates and consular officers across the US (fifty-one), so as to give the special support and protection which migrants require when they travel, work, or live abroad. A significant majority of Mexico's foreign service personnel is dedicated to consular tasks.[1] The fees collected at Mexican consulates in the United States represent around one-fourth of the whole budget of the Ministry of Foreign Affairs (MFA).[2]

Traditional structures in place at many foreign ministries are inadequate for contemporary diplomacy requirements. Many have a shortage of experts in disciplines not traditionally associated with it, such as economics, anthropology, sociology, or marketing. Most suffer from chronic shortfalls in human and material resources because of budgetary constraints and unwillingness by younger professionals to keep constantly on the move. This has led governments to expand their international activity through non-diplomatic channels, reshaping the role of foreign offices.

Some question the usefulness of diplomacy, pointing to the diminishing leadership role of MFAs. Yet, if technology, instant communications, and the new players are adequately deployed, the diplomatic profession can be enhanced. Bilateral diplomacy, through ministries of foreign affairs and their embassies and consulates, remains the best tool to advance a country's interests. It can be deployed to promote trade and investment, to build up a country's image, to project a nation's culture, to communicate with *diaspora* communities, to kick-start negotiations, and to buttress summit diplomacy.

Tapping into these opportunities requires networks of friends and allies to build coalitions and supporting groups. The Vienna Convention of 1961 continues to be the framework for diplomatic work (see Chapter 28, this volume). But the scope of diplomatic action has expanded. Parliaments are now essential allies of diplomats, making lobbying a significant part of their job. New skills and techniques are also essential in an interdependent world that faces similar yet less tangible threats than in the past, but that also offers great opportunities to the fittest. One of them is the persuasiveness required when dealing with decision-makers and leading actors in the host country,[3] as well as the ability to influence key groups in that society.

Promoting one's country in every sphere is now a key task in bilateral diplomacy. This includes a wide range of areas such as trade, investment, and tourism, as well as cultural affairs. Other tasks include 'customer service', that is, services provided to the public. This leads to a new way of managing diplomatic resources, more in line with business standards. Pressed to deliver results, many foreign ministries have fine-tuned their recruitment, personnel evaluation systems, and their approach to encouraging and rewarding their staff.

12.2 New Tasks in the Construction of Bilateral Relations

12.2.1 Public Diplomacy vs Traditional Bilateral Diplomacy

In the past, diplomacy was bound by national sovereignty and the state. The *art* of diplomacy was exercised by a single player, the nation state, with defined rules. Bilateral diplomacy was based on representation and people-to-people intercourse. It was known for its discretion, for its quasi-monopoly on restricted information, and for the relentless pursuit of national influence. Results were measured by the number of agreements signed, the number of conflicts avoided or resolved, and the number of contacts between diplomats and host country players.

Modern *bilateral diplomacy* is practised through networks and publics.[4] Public diplomacy then is more horizontal, and, by definition, more transparent. It deploys new methods, new directions, new approaches, and a new vocabulary.[5]

Parag Khanna defines 'megadiplomacy' as the new form of exercising the diplomatic profession and the only one that can confront today's global interconnected chaos. Megadiplomacy, he argues, promotes the creation of alliances and collaboration between governments and stakeholders. Its building block is an action-oriented network, with inclusion, decentralization, and accountability as its core values. Coordination is achieved by setting goals, pursuing harmonization without imposing control. Solutions are promoted at a local level.[6]

12.2.2 From the Envoy Extraordinary and Plenipotentiary... to the Dynamic Promoter

The shrinking of the state has led to a perceived loss in the influence of diplomats. Gone are the days when foreign envoys would hold court, receiving visitors from different sectors of society by appointment in finely furnished quarters. Imbued with *plenipotentiary* powers, traditional diplomats managed bilateral relations between their governments and the host country in almost exclusive contact with the local ministry of foreign affairs or other government departments, often with little or no guidance from home.

In the past, a key task for diplomats was to report on events in the host country. Much of the information was gleaned from local media, other diplomats, and the occasional meeting with senior local officials. Though based mostly on open sources, diplomatic reporting was treated as confidential and cloaked in a halo of pseudo-secrecy. Those reports were the stock-in-trade of the well-dressed, savvy diplomats of yesteryear. They frequented cocktail parties and dinners, were consummate listeners, and had the type of education and background that allowed them to interpret current events on the spot, without missing a beat. Yet, the IT and communications technology revolution did away with the old-school foreign service officer's role as a provider of inside information. Events abroad are now interpreted by the media, rather than by government officials. News reporting and analysis by professional journalists, unconstrained by diplomatic rules, is much more valuable to headquarters than the wordy—and often untimely—reports generated by diplomats. This is not to say that diplomats do not have access to information and intelligence that is not available to the media, especially those posted to smaller, more distant countries that do not generate much international news, or to closed societies with a controlled press. But even in open societies, the real challenge for the modern diplomat is not so much to convey the broad contours of particular events in the host country, but to dissect the implication of those events for bilateral ties—be it on trade, investment, immigration flows, or regional politics.

Globalization has imposed a new order in which hegemony and pre-eminence are no longer territorial, ideological, or military. Technology and financial resources have become real factors of power. Fierce business competition to attract trade and investment is here to stay. Attractiveness as an investment destination, quality of physical and digital infrastructure, level of economic growth, nature of the business climate, and the country brand are all at play. To describe the modern bilateral diplomat as a glorified salesman, peddling his wares not just to business, but also, with some variation, to NGOs, think tanks, and the media, is not far off the mark.

12.2.3 Diplomacy or Public Relations (PR)?

Diplomats are expected to be socially skilled and to promote their countries' interests aggressively. In diplomacy there is no room for the timid. From the profession's very beginnings, diplomats were often courtiers—or at least worldly individuals able to link up in the host society and navigate its idiosyncrasies. In the past, it sufficed to interact with the governing elite, the diplomatic corps, and a few influential individuals. Today this is not enough, and the network of contacts should include major personalities, actors and sports figures, musicians and artists, lobbying groups, public relations agencies, opinion-makers, and trade union leaders among others.

The sheer amount of information available is such that a key ability is to be able to sift through it all, analyse contrasting views, retain the essentials, and come to solid conclusions. It is not enough to mingle with the 'usual suspects' in the host nation's capital. To reach out to regions and provinces, where much of the economic activity often takes place, is now imperative. Public opinion is mainly driven by the media, and the negative publicity it can generate may alter the perception people have of a country. Yet, the best way to counter it and to build up a good image is not necessarily to respond directly to critics, but to convey positive events and features to the media. Diplomats need to understand the medium: what is news and what is not, how to influence what is written and said about their home country, and who the more influential commentators and opinion-shapers are. This skill is often confused with the role of public relations (PR) firms or lobbyists, paid to spread positive news about countries or to openly attempt to influence policy-makers, something quickly perceived by the target publics as propaganda. Diplomats must be able to communicate, promote, and offer honest, credible interpretations of what takes place back home, not by hiding the truth or painting a rosy picture, but by finding a balance between being seen as a realist, willing to accept the good with the bad, and an idealist who finds fault with anyone who speaks ill of his government. A diplomat is a spokesperson for his government, yet one willing to accept constructive criticism.

12.2.4 The Art of Negotiation

Negotiation is a key instrument in the diplomatic toolkit. While a diplomat does not necessarily have to be a born negotiator, individuals who are able to identify core national interests with respect to any given issue and to forcefully stand up for them are at a premium. These qualities can be developed through training and experience. The ability to conciliate and bridge differences has always been one of the main attributes of a diplomat, but success depends on being able to gauge the limits under which one's counterpart acts as well as how far to push. A good negotiator always puts himself in the shoes of his opposite party. To understand at what point the person sitting across the table is no longer in a position to make further concessions is critical. Compromise is key in diplomacy. Yet, negotiating in the bilateral arena is becoming less common for diplomats. There are now technocrats from specialized government departments entrusted with negotiating agreements on many subjects. The diplomat's role has been reduced to that of a coordinator and, in the best of cases, an overseer to ensure that the political aspects of a relationship are not undermined by technical considerations. Moreover, diplomats still play a key role in *getting* countries to the very point of negotiating an agreement.

12.2.5 Diplomacy and Economics

Although traditional bilateral diplomacy was mostly about politics, commercial interests were very much at the core of the origins of diplomacy. However, diplomats have been generally trained in the social sciences, law, or international relations. Only recently has economics come to play at least as important a part in international relations as the latter. Trade promotion, attracting foreign investment, financial know-how, and business facilitation are now critical competencies of contemporary diplomats. More and more economists are entering the profession. Yet, being a trained economist doesn't necessarily make a successful promoter. Although it helps to understand the essentials of how and why business decisions are made, it is more important to know regulatory frameworks, potential joint venture partners, or national competitive advantages. Nations compete for a limited number of economic opportunities. Success comes to those able to convey and sell the specific attributes and advantages of their countries.

The detachment of diplomacy from trade promotion is not a good idea. In the case of Mexico, a new trade and investment agency, *ProMexico*, was created in 2007. Unfortunately this new entity is not part of the foreign ministry, with a knock-on effect on the training of new professionals specialized in trade promotion, and the overall coordination of the country's positioning abroad.

12.2.6 The Effective Communicator

Diplomacy has always depended on communications, from the hand-carried message to the telegraph, from the telephone to the Internet. Traditional diplomats used French, but today's diplomats must be able to communicate in many languages. English, as the universal language of diplomacy, business, and cyberspace, is a *sine qua non*. A command of spoken and written English is essential to any diplomat's life and work outside the home country and needs to be the highest priority in the training curricula of any foreign ministry.[7]

The media legitimizes and empowers the art of modern diplomacy and to a large extent determines its success or failure. State visits are a good example. Beyond the number of bilateral agreements signed and the dollar value of business deals struck (and the avoidance of *faux pas*) a standard way to measure the success (or lack thereof) of any presidential or prime ministerial visit abroad is media coverage. This is a hard task for the diplomats of smaller and medium-sized countries posted in some of the leading capitals, whose press is reluctant to pay much attention to foreign visits. A key challenge for diplomats is thus how to obtain media presence for one's country and its officials and the ability to convey messages in the spin-driven world of sound bites. Participation in radio and TV programmes, as well as in public events of various kinds, and an effective use of the Internet are central elements in this. Online social networks such as Facebook and Twitter, with their hundreds of millions of users, embody even deeper changes. These new tools are being used, often with great success, by an increasing number of government officials because they respond to society's demand for openness and transparency in government, business, and social relations.[8]

12.2.7 Showcasing Culture and the Use of Soft Power

A nation's image frames its international interactions. A country principally known for endemic violence or persistent human rights violations will find it much harder to establish and maintain people-to-people relations, than one without such a reputation. In turn, culture is an invaluable tool for positioning a country's image. Cultural manifestations that transcend national borders play a huge role in projecting a national image. As a significant element of soft power, culture is one of the most effective and noblest instruments of diplomacy. 'Splendors of Thirty Centuries', one of the largest Mexican art exhibitions ever, was organized by the Mexican government and presented at the Metropolitan Museum in New York in 1990–1991. It covered 3,000 years of Mexican history, showcasing artistic expression throughout that period, including Pre-Columbian cultures, the Viceroy-era, 19th- and 20th-century pieces, muralists, and the overall search for a national identity. It marked a turning point for Mexico's image in the United States and Canada.[9]

Its broad reach and high penetration makes cultural diplomacy central. The visit of a single, well-known artist can do more, if well-managed and handled, to boost the image and standing of a nation abroad than the visits of myriad cabinet ministers or captains of industry. Yet, the low budget assigned to the cultural department in most MFAs shows the limited awareness governments have of this fact. In those ministries large enough to be able to post cultural attachés abroad, the question arises as to whether these should be career diplomats, with some background and training in arts management, or artists in their own right who by sheer force of their own talent are able to make an impact in the host country. While there are pros and cons on both sides of the argument, the reality of limited (and, in many cases, non-existent) budgets for cultural promotion abroad tends to overshadow these finer points in the exercise of cultural diplomacy. In Latin America, there is a long tradition of noted writers posted abroad as diplomats, sometimes as career foreign service officers, in others as political appointees. Novelists and poets like Carlos Fuentes, Pablo Neruda, and Octavio Paz played a role in elevating their countries' image abroad when they served as ambassadors.[10]

12.2.8 Diplomacy and Academia

Modern diplomats can no longer afford to be mere observers. Active involvement is now mandatory. Public speaking is a *sine qua non*. Engaging the academic community, as lecturers or panellists in roundtables, participating in conferences and workshops, and sponsoring publications of various kinds, are now part of a diplomat's job description. By doing so, they are able to shape opinion and take part in the national discourse of the host country. Sometimes these activities appear to be antithetical to traditional diplomacy and are frowned upon by old-school foreign service officers. If the premise is that a diplomat is always a diplomat (especially in the case of heads of mission), no disclaimer will obviate the fact that when he or she speaks in public it will be on behalf of a government. And it can be difficult to hold an audience and to say interesting things when forced to speak in the staid, somewhat forced language of officialdom. To navigate the waters of academia—which puts a premium on transgression and heterodoxy—while at the same time not forgetting the diplomat's essential loyalty to the government he represents and embodies, is one of the trickier challenges of modern diplomacy. Yet, in a world that thrives on ideas, diplomats cannot ignore them.

Universities, research centres, and think tanks are key generators of ideas. They can also be strong allies in the cause of promoting a better understanding between societies. Specialized centres focused on the study of a single country, staffed by experts on specific regions of the world, are becoming common. Such centres can be invaluable partners for the development of a deeper understanding between host and home societies.[11] World affairs councils and similar organizations allow diplomats to network with individuals who are interested in foreign relations and can be natural recipients of information about other countries. The Mexican Council on Foreign Relations (COMEXI), established in 2001, is the first national think tank fully dedicated to the analysis of Mexico's foreign policy and its role in the world. One of COMEXI's key undertakings has been a joint venture with the Mexican Centre for Economic Research and Development (CIDE) to establish a biennial national survey on Mexicans' opinions about the world.

12.2.9 The Social Interlocutor

Today new actors on the diplomatic stage are as—or more—important to a diplomat than the traditional official government interlocutor. Since public diplomacy is about relationships more than about individuals, today's well-rounded diplomat will find ways of partnering with as many of these as possible. Bilateral diplomacy also reserves an important role for diaspora communities in those cases where the origin or nationality of significant numbers of their members is that of the diplomat's home country. Although often assimilated into the recipient nation's culture and society, the links these communities maintain in their country of origin can be a useful tool in strengthening bilateral ties. The many millions of Hispanics in the United States have become significant for Latin American diplomats by virtue of their sheer numbers, growing political influence, and cultural impact. Immigration issues between Mexico and the US constitute an unprecedented case in the world. No other country has a diaspora of such proportions (more than 30 million people of Mexican origin), creating a dynamic engine of influence and power with widespread consequences in the political, economic, and social spheres of American society.

12.3 POLICY DEVELOPMENT
AND IMPLEMENTATION BY MINISTRIES
AND MISSIONS

12.3.1 The Diplomatic Infrastructure: Foreign Ministries, Embassies, and Consulates

Diplomacy has become more complex, as it encompasses a broader dialogue between a larger number of stakeholders and specialized experts. This has eroded many of the professional competencies of foreign affairs ministries. Yet it has also highlighted the relevance of specific activities such as those related to the promotion of trade and investment. Likewise MFAs have given up certain responsibilities to other agencies, such as development financing and cooperation initiatives, essential in the fostering of a country's influence.

An excessive workload and having to do more with less, together with the need to react almost instantaneously to events happening around the globe on a 24/7 basis, has affected foreign ministries. In many cases, absent timely instructions from home, embassies or consulates are often pushed to formulate interim policy on a specific issue without the benefit of a view from headquarters. This sometimes leads to disconnects between the mission and the MFAs.

Thus today's diplomats need to be trained in many more specialized disciplines in order to equip them with the technical knowledge and tools associated with the policy-setting agenda. The diplomat has to be intimately involved in the process of formulating a policy that responds to the situation on the ground. While modern technology is designed to enable real-time consultation, if foreign ministries don't adapt to these realities, they end up as mere logistics coordinators of other, more specialized government institutions.[12] MFAs, in particular those in developing countries, have been slow in their adaptation to the new methods and techniques associated with integral and results-oriented diplomacy. Canada and Australia, on the other hand, have been quick to adjust and position themselves ahead of the curve.

The efficient management of MFAs has also become a priority. The corporate approach increasingly prevails in services provided by government departments, including those of the foreign ministries. Some argue that the administration and measurement of results at the ministry and its network of missions are not that different from those at private companies. 'Good governance' and 'best practices' are now an important part of the diplomatic *milieu*. In the same way that governance of public services has become a global issue, a results-based diplomacy is also gaining strength. This is not easy. Evaluating and measuring the efficiency of a diplomat's job is a challenging, sometimes even impossible task. Ambassadors, as representatives of the head of state, reject any kind of scrutiny.

However, the daily tasks of professionals need to be quantifiable and his or her promotion linked to results, just as in the business world. Any new ambassador or consul should receive clear and precise instructions from his/her headquarters which sets down measurable objectives to reach in a bilateral relation, including those in the areas of trade, investments, media exposure, cultural initiatives, and political contacts, with a schedule and timeline. Productivity levels can be measured and evaluated.

Some MFAs have come up with systems designed to monitor productivity levels, salaries, and staff morale. In some cases, the position of 'general inspector' has been created, including the establishment of quantifiable goals in order to measure the efficiency of a diplomat's performance. Yearly goals linked to compensation are part of this. These initiatives evaluate regularly the status of a bilateral relationship, including changes in the balance of trade, investment flows, resource management, and customer satisfaction with public services.

12.3.2 Hierarchy vs Horizontality

The bureaucratic rigidities prevailing in MFAs often lead to an ineffective diplomacy. A hierarchical, vertical structure centralizes decision-making and inhibits spontaneity, creativity, and the free expression of ideas, especially from diplomats serving abroad. In today's complex world, effective diplomacy can only be exercised with flexibility, openness, long-term vision, and by taking into account the opinions of those abroad. Rigid structures often stand in the way of individual diplomats' capabilities, aptitudes, and merits.[13]

Likewise, a foreign service career starting at the bottom of the pyramid can be a daunting exercise in slow progress through the ranks. Seniority, used in many ministries as the main criterion for promotions and assignments, can stifle creativity and the expression of new ideas, and result in a loss of motivation. Several governments have experimented with fast-track systems that allow lateral entry and rapid promotions for those deemed to deserve to move up the hierarchical ladder more quickly than others. Though interesting, these mechanisms often prove demoralizing to those left behind. In countries where temporary political appointments coexist with career professionals, there are always tensions between career and non-career diplomats. The best solution for a professional foreign service is to ensure that its diplomats are politically sensitive and sufficiently specialized so as not to need political appointees.

12.4 GEOGRAPHIC AND FUNCTIONAL APPROACHES

MFAs need to prioritize regions and issues in order to best advance their bilateral interests. A state aspiring to adopt a global leadership role—such as any one of the permanent members of the United Nations Security Council—has to maintain ties with almost all countries and regions, while middle and smaller powers must prioritize their objectives and diplomatic resources. The geographical approach so often used by foreign offices is no longer useful because it is based on the idea that there should be as many posts as there are major countries and regions. This can waste valuable physical and human resources that could otherwise be deployed more effectively on specific thematic issues.

The traditional approach was that a country's influence was directly proportional to the number of missions it kept abroad. In today's hyper-communicated world this no longer holds true. With scarce human and financial diplomatic resources—even in the richest of the developed countries—the need today is to adjust foreign policy structures according to specific objectives and thematic priorities. Countries that are immediate neighbours are usually first on the list, since these relationships tend to be extremely dynamic and often fraught with problems. Mexico and the United States are linked asymmetrically. Over 80 per cent of Mexico's international trade, more than 70 per cent of foreign investment, and up to 90 per cent of foreign tourists come from the United States. The country is relevant to the US not only as a trading partner, but also on issues such as immigration, border security, and transnational crime. Becoming part of the rich industrialized North American region has been at the centre of Mexico's strategy to position itself successfully in a globalized world.[14]

Other priorities may relate to the geographic region to which a country belongs, political and ideological affinities, cultural and linguistic similarities, trade, investment and monetary flows, and common international objectives, to name a few. This can often mean an increased presence in countries that are geographically distant but share certain attributes, such as commodity producers, technologically advanced societies, or specific political systems.

The trend towards (sub)regional groupings—as in the case of the European Union where a single diplomatic service has been established—will eventually reduce the need for each individual country to maintain a separate diplomatic mission abroad. Mexico, Colombia, and Venezuela experimented with several such joint embassies in the late 1980's in order to maximize their presence in Africa, Asia, and the Caribbean, but changes in government policy and a lack of understanding of what this meant in the host countries ended the practice shortly after it began.

Finally, the emergence of more and more groupings that identify common interests among geographically, politically, and economically diverse countries have led to the creation of thematic divisions within foreign ministries. Examples of this are climate change, human rights, national security issues, alternative energy, and humanitarian law, among others. Many ministries now have roving envoys based at home, tasked with coordinating each of these particular issue areas.

12.4.1 The Real vs the Desirable Function of the Desk Officer

The traditional geographical approach has raised other problems. Today's desk officers are generally responsible for a number of countries, which doesn't allow them to specialize. The speed with which global events unfold often only leaves time for reactive diplomacy and an inability to keep track of (let alone analyse) developments in the countries they are responsible for. Nor are they in a position to prepare appropriate medium or long-term responses. This is often referred to as the firefighting nature of foreign ministry work. Urgent tasks tend to overshadow and displace the important ones. This leads ministries to spend much of their time in a defensive response-mode, rather than in thinking about what policy *should* be. Not surprisingly, many desk officers thus become mere paper pushers, overwhelmed by the numerous demands they face.

The contrast and growing divergence between the work of a desk officer and the day-to-day responsibility of a head of mission and personnel abroad, which are more directly faced with the transformation of diplomatic activity, are increasingly evident. On a normal day at work, ambassadors and consuls find that the schedules of visiting government officials are frequently decided, without consulting them, by very junior ministry officials, or even in extreme cases, by public relations firms. Officials from the home country often arrive with agendas and meetings already set up directly by their own ministries, requesting from the mission nothing more than an interpreter, a note-taker, or a driver. In addition, diplomats now face situations as new and diverse as the publication of private conversations, an art exhibition organized directly by a private entity, or the complaints from citizens who feel they have been mistreated by their country's representatives abroad. Instructions by foreign ministries (specifically by desk officers) to their officials abroad will thus often come late, if at all.

12.4.2 Budgetary Limitations

Budgetary cutbacks have become the bane of foreign ministries, even in the richest countries. Lack of funding has led to improvisation and less emphasis on policy planning. It has also prevented innovation and issue-specific studies, discouraged professionalism, affected salaries and promotions, and contributed to job insecurity. Many foreign offices have become stuck in a holding mode, devoted to coping with cutbacks and discontented officers, rather than to advancing their primary tasks. Perversely, the impact of budget cuts is especially evident in those areas that are most needed to adapt to current international challenges, such as the planning units that identify extant international trends and their impact on the national interest. Other areas that are frequent targets of budget cuts are those dealing with the recruitment and training of new diplomats, the MFAs relations with legislators, civil society, and cultural diplomacy.

Some foreign services have merged their diplomatic and consular activities. The upside of this is that it offers all officers the opportunity for a more well-rounded and comprehensive work experience. The downside is that in countries with large *diaspora* populations, where an endless demand for protection services exists, consular work tends to absorb enormous amounts on human and material resources, to the detriment of strategic and long-term policy-planning tasks.[15]

12.5 TRAINING THE 21ST-CENTURY BILATERAL DIPLOMAT

12.5.1 Is Diplomacy an Art, or Merely a Profession?

For centuries, the diplomatic tradition was handed down from one generation to the next. This tradition was made up of skills and practices that do not necessarily lend themselves to codification. They are experiences transmitted in the course of day-to-day activity and by word of mouth, and cover aspects ranging from the writing style for official documents, to courtesy and social norms. Writing used to be an important part of a diplomat's training. Today the emphasis is much more on oral communication, language ability, and interaction with the media, leading to a decline in a diplomat's written skills, often considered an *art* in itself. In spite of the advent of mass media, effective writing should remain an essential part of any diplomat's toolkit. The ability to synthesize, analyse, and convey vast amounts of information on critical issues of the day distinguishes the diplomat from other professionals.

Another element of diplomacy is *savoir faire*. While no specific training for it exists, diplomats develop certain sensitivities to dialogue and interpersonal relations that enable them to detect other people's strengths and weaknesses. Much like a critical virtue of the banking profession is the ability to judge a person's character and creditworthiness, a diplomat has to be able to pass sound judgement on an interlocutor's credibility and reliability. This is an activity in which much depends on deals struck with a mere handshake. The final signing of formal agreements is preceded by long and elaborate minuets in which both parties carefully calibrate the *demarches* they undertake to keep the diplomatic momentum going. Unless there is a measure of trust in the respective counterpart, that will not happen, or will do so very slowly and inefficiently. This *savoir faire* is partly fuelled by training in matters of protocol, which in the world of jet travel have acquired a heavy component of logistics, and the ability to deal with many types of situations, no matter how complex or unforeseen. Again, state visits provide a good template to test a diplomat's capacity to improvise and respond to unexpected situations, precisely because there is so much at stake and so much of it takes place in the full glare of the media. The paradox, of course, is that traditional diplomatic training did not include dealing with the media, now one of the most important diplomatic skills, nor with business and finance, trade and investment issues, or civil society, all of which are part and parcel of contemporary diplomacy.

Knowledge is the universal tool that provides a starting point for conversation and dialogue and opens the way to achieving specific goals, which means that a diplomat needs an ample reservoir of knowledge on many diverse matters.[16] The traditional diplomat was referred to as being broadly cultured, a person who, despite differences imposed by local disparities, was able to overcome and even gain advantage from such contrasts owing to a well-rounded education. Only relatively recently did the discipline of international relations appear in university curricula. Unlike in the past, when the law and social sciences were the main training grounds for an aspiring diplomat, now there are career paths in areas as specialized as nuclear non-proliferation, environmental negotiation, and international migration flows, which empower the modern diplomat to deploy his/her skills in a more focused manner.

While traditional training continues to be important for the aspiring diplomat, a multidisciplinary education is now a necessity. The curricula of most diplomatic academies has been enriched with the growing number of functions that new officers are expected to perform. In addition to courses in world history, philosophy, political science, and international law, the teaching of economics, crisis management, psychology, human rights, lobbying, and media management are now part of a diplomat's education.

12.5.2 Secondments

Given the proliferation of crosscutting international issues, the number of government entities involved in foreign affairs has multiplied. This has made the coordinating role of MFAs more complex. It has also often led to their loss of influence, as MFAs are perceived as either too conservative, unqualified to deal with technical issues, or as downright dysfunctional. These views are particularly widespread in ministries within the finance and economic sector, which is unfortunate since they control the budgets. As the main function of MFAs is to ensure the coordination and coherence of a country's international policies, one of the ways to increase their influence is to have diplomatic personnel seconded in greater numbers to other ministries and government offices. In countries with weak or non-existent civil services this is even more important because there is little or no movement between departments. After their secondment, diplomats can return to the foreign ministry to better use their acquired knowledge and become useful *liaisons* between government departments. The personal relationships established during these periods can also be very useful in the course of a diplomatic career. They also provide other public servants with a better grasp of diplomacy's role and importance.

12.5.3 Continuing Education

In the past, a basic university degree was sufficient for most diplomats. In addition to graduate degrees in business administration, finance, or political science, continuing education programmes that provide further training in technology, economics, and other disciplines are essential. Such training should be a prerequisite for promotion and assignments to positions of greater responsibility, as well as for strengthening and developing skills in short supply within foreign offices. It needs to cover languages, IT, communication, negotiating skills, lobbying, and media relations. This new vision of a diplomat's role makes communication skills particularly relevant. Faced with an increasingly inquisitive and critical press, there is no area more sensitive and demanding than that related to interaction with the media. Traditional diplomats were not trained in this field because they operated behind closed doors. The public nature of today's diplomacy makes it indispensable to be properly conversant in how to manage the delicate balance between the public's right to know and the discretion required by effective diplomacy.

Training also needs to emphasise capacity building for developing alliances between the public and private sectors. Modern diplomats need to understand economic and business principles. They are often called upon to support their country's business community and to facilitate trade and investment flows. Examples include the organization of discussion forums to analyse issues relevant to the state and its relationship with the private sector such as the corporate social responsibility practices of multinationals or collaborating with private foundations to promote education designed for immigrant communities.

12.5.4 Sabbatical Year for Specialized Training

A few diplomatic services are now offering sabbatical leaves as a way for mid-career professionals to expand their expertise, engage in specific projects that will enhance their knowledge of a country, region, or issue, or simply allow them to undertake an activity for which time is normally not available. The sabbatical can also take the form of a *secondment* to a think tank or to another non-governmental entity. Abilities acquired during the sabbatical year should be demonstrated through mid-career examinations and case resolution. After evaluating the acquired skills there should be the possibility of being promoted and/or assigned new responsibilities commensurate with the training received.

12.5.5 Motivation and Mobility in the Diplomatic Career

As a rule, a diplomat's career no longer culminates in an ambassadorial appointment; so alternative career paths need to be established. As in any other organization, foreign services have a limited number of openings for the appointment of heads of mission. However, this does not inhibit the development of *parallel careers* within the diplomatic profession. The cultural, trade, labour, tourism media, and other thematic *attachés* are a vital part of any diplomatic mission and should have career paths of their own, moving from smaller to larger missions, and from lesser to greater responsibilities. Mobility within a foreign affairs ministry hierarchy, consistent with a diplomat's profile and abilities, will always be an important motivation. Another is financial compensation, which needs to match the level of responsibility in any given posting, the individual characteristics of the country and city involved, and the size of the diplomat's family. Foreign ministries must recognize their officers' merits. Results-based economic incentives are one way of doing that. Valuable examples can be drawn from the private sector in regard to stimulating and rewarding employees. The business world operates in a culture of motivating talent and innovative capacity and in this regard foreign ministries can learn a great deal from private sector practices.

12.6 Bilateral Diplomacy in Service to the State and the New Architecture of Global Governance

12.6.1 New Bilateral Diplomacy and Public Policy

A diplomacy ready to face the challenges of the new millennium and a foreign affairs ministry with the capacity to identify and analyse international trends and able to design strategies and formulate plans of action, are key for sound national public policies. Throughout history individual diplomats have, on different occasions, embodied the aspirations and goals of their state. Metternich, Bismarck, Talleyrand, Franklin, Eden, and Kissinger were all distinguished diplomats who contributed to their countries' interests and foreign policy objectives. They all understood that to build, consolidate, and make a nation prosperous requires an active foreign policy. They also grasped that there is an indivisible link between domestic and foreign affairs.[17]

A developed country with a solid democratic system such as the United States, which seeks to have influence beyond its borders, will design a foreign policy aimed at achieving that goal. Other nations, where democracy is still young and social changes have prompted the restructuring of the state, have at certain times in their history tried to have their foreign policy promote changes on their domestic front in order to fulfil national goals and interests.[18] Small-country diplomacy can be just as successful, as long as it has a *vision of state*; a sense of knowing what is the best for their country at any given moment.[19] Policies that illustrate this were undertaken in the early 1990s to expand Mexico's international presence. During this period, unprecedented efforts were deployed by Mexican diplomacy, including the North America Free Trade Agreement (NAFTA) with the US and Canada, accession to the OECD, and the creation of the Ibero-American Summit, all of which radically transformed Mexico's image beyond its borders.[20] More recently, former foreign minister Jorge G. Castañeda (2000–2003), changed Mexico's attitudes on human rights and democracy as core values in its foreign policy. He also led the country to become a member of the U.N. Security Council in order to enhance Mexico's international status. Likewise, as part of its efforts to promote a more fluent exchange of ideas within the region, the Mexican government designated an ambassador-at-large as a facilitator during the peace dialogue between the government of Colombia and its guerrilla movement.

12.6.2 The International Image-Builder

In the past, a country's territory, population, armed forces, and defence capabilities were the key determinants of a nation's place in the international arena. To these, today we add political stability, democratic maturity, business climate, cultural vigour, and respect for generally accepted values. Countries unable to project these qualities are outliers on the global stage. Bilateral diplomacy helps construct a country's positive image when it is professional, well rounded, highly focused, and non-intrusive. Though one of the duties of diplomats is to change prejudices and stereotypes about their countries, they also have to recognize that no nation is perfect or has all the answers. A diplomat who blindly insists that nothing is wrong back home loses credibility and does his country a disservice. Equally harmful to his nation is the envoy who consistently finds fault with the host country and constantly criticizes its customs and its people, something far more prevalent than one would think.

One of the most important facets of a diplomat's life is the recognition that he or she is the prism through which the host perceives the sending nation. A diplomat can never lose sight of the fact that private aspects of one's life inevitably reflect on the public nature of a government official's behaviour. As with other public officials, diplomats lose the right to an entirely private life and must be careful about what they say and do, even in the 'privacy' of their offices or residences, because they are never sure whether they are being 'listened' to by foreign intelligence services.

12.7 CONCLUSION

While new technologies and the growing number of stakeholders have reduced the scope and functions of foreign ministries and their missions, these changes also embody an enormous potential. A mission will always be the best source of information about a host country, in real time and with a well-rounded perspective. If it deploys these new tools adequately and proactively, it will remain as the only entity capable of building a successful bilateral relation. If not, embassies may well go, paraphrasing Ross Perot, the way of sailing ships.

NOTES

* The authors are indebted to Ernesto Sosa, Career Counsellor at the Mexican embassy in Madrid for his invaluable support in the research of this study.

1. The Mexican foreign service has made it mandatory for its members to work in at least one consulate in order to be eligible for promotion.

2. The authorized annual budget for the foreign ministry in 2012 amounted to approximately 470 million US dollars. The fees collected at Mexican consulates in the US represent around one-fourth of the ministry's whole budget, about 120 million US dollars.

3. Some authors refer to a 'Top 100' list that includes renowned and influential people in the show business, philanthropic, sports, and scientific spheres, in addition to those in the traditional political, business, and cultural worlds.

4. The British Foreign Minister, William Hague, during the announcement of the UK's international new priorities in 2010, stated: 'Today, influence increasingly depends on fluid and dynamic networks, alliances and often informal links that require new forms of commitment.' The new priorities of the Foreign Office are emphasized as a result of Great Britain's unbreakable alliance with Washington, its pragmatism and, undoubtedly, its history as an empire. The new premises are based on the recognition that power and economic opportunities are shifting towards Eastern and Southern countries, such as Brazil, India, and China, the fact that the world's decision-making process is constantly enlarged, and the evolving nature of conflict (in which organized groups of people confront each other as

opposed to states). Speech given at the Foreign and Commonwealth Office (FCO) 'Britain's Foreign Policy in a Networked World', 1 July 2010.

5. Nicholas Cull, director of the master's programme in public diplomacy at the University of Southern California. New public diplomacy refers to: a new context (more voices); new players (NGOs and more powerful individuals); new methods (Internet); new directions (horizontal); new challenges (one world); new vocabulary (branding); new limits (partnerships); new theory (soft power). In public diplomacy, openness matters (open systems are attractive); time matters; image matters; stories matter (the power of example); diasporas matter (individuals carry messages), partnerships matter (no one can go alone); information matters (others will fill the world); success matters (many are hurt by the failure of one). Some of public diplomacy's components are: listening; advocacy; and cultural diplomacy. Public diplomacy is about relationships. Conference given at the annual gathering of Mexican ambassadors and consuls, Mexico City, 6–7 January 2011.

6. See Parag Khanna, *How to Run the World: Charting a Course to the Next Renaissance* (New York: Random House, 2011), 33.

7. The fact that English has become the indisputable global language (followed by Spanish, whose growing number of speakers will soon make the US home to the second-largest Spanish-speaking community in the world) may be perceived as a threat to linguistic diversity. This is not the first time in history that a *lingua franca* exists. Acadian, Greek, Latin, Spanish, and French prevailed during different periods of history.

8. Presidents, foreign ministers, ambassadors, and legislators are increasingly using these new communications tools in an effort to reach their constituencies. One South American foreign minister is even referred to as 'Twitterman' because of his over-extensive use of the 140-word social networking messaging system.

9. The exhibition was inaugurated in October 1990 by President Carlos Salinas in conjunction with a strong political and media campaign.

10. Nobel Laureate Octavio Paz and Carlos Fuentes, who served as Mexico's ambassadors to India in the 1960s and France in the late 1970s respectively, boosted Mexico's image abroad in different ways. While the experience in India heavily influenced Paz's literary work, especially in the field of poetry and essay (see *Vislumbres de la India* (Barcelona: Seix Barral, 1995), 220), Carlos Fuentes was renowned in Paris for his wide array of high-level contacts both in government as well as in the social and cultural French *milieu*.

11. 'Mexicanists' from American and British universities have produced excellent research on political and social issues, fostering priority areas of the country's foreign affairs policies. The work of Dr Demetrios Papademetriou, a former collaborator of the Washington-based Carnegie Endowment for International Peace made great contributions to the study of Mexico–US migration. See Demetrios Papademetriou and A. Hamilton Kimberly, 'El acertijo de la migración: migración de mexicanos a Estados Unidos', *Letras Libres México, Editorial Vuelta* 6: 64 (abril 2004), 75–6.

12. Evan Potter (ed.), *Cyber-Diplomacy: Managing Foreign Policy in the 21st Century* (Montreal/ Kingston: McGill-Queen's University Press, 2002).

13. On these constraints and possible innovative solutions see Andrew F. Cooper, 'Vertical Limits: A Foreign Ministry of the Future', *Journal of Canadian Studies* 35: 4 (winter 2001), 111–29.

14. NAFTA has contributed significantly to the expansion of trilateral trade and investment flows with Canada and the US. It represented a fundamental part of a government's strategy

to modernize and liberalize the country's economy. For further information on the Mexico—U.N. relationship, see Robert Pastor and Jorge Castañeda, *Límites en la Amistad México-Estados Unidos* (México: Joaquín Mortiz/Planeta, 1989), 312.

15. There are fifty-one Mexican consulates across the United States, covering practically all of its territory. On average, consulates located in regions with an elevated concentration of people of Mexican origin (California, Texas, Illinois, and New York) can serve around 500 'customers' daily.

16. The importance of having a vast general culture for diplomats is perhaps the reason many writers, including Octavio Paz and Carlos Fuentes as well as Paul Claudel and Saint-John Perse, were also outstanding diplomats.

17. Another example of a very skilful diplomat was that of Dominique de Villepin, who defended long-standing French foreign policy tradition at the height of the invasion of Iraq. See Dominique de Villepin, 'Ministre des Affaires Etrangères de France, discours dans le Conseil de Sécurité', New York, 14 February 2003.

18. With a bold vision, Jorge Castañeda, sought agreements with the US to grant legal status and documentation to millions of Mexicans living in the US and promoted a 'NAFTA Plus' to further integrate Mexico within North America.

19. On the problems and opportunities for the diplomacy of small states see Justin Robertson and Maurice A. East (eds), *Diplomacy and Developing Nations: Post-Cold War Foreign Policy Making Structures and Processes* (London: Routledge, 2005); and Andrew F. Cooper and Timothy M. Shaw, *The Diplomacies of Small States: Between Vulnerability and Resilience* (London: Palgrave Macmillan, 2009).

20. Andrés Rozental, *La política exterior de México en la era de la modernidad* (México: Fondo de Cultura Económica, 1993).

CHAPTER 13

MULTILATERAL DIPLOMACY

KISHORE MAHBUBANI

MULTILATERAL diplomacy is a sunrise industry. The acceleration of globalization and the consequential shrinking of the globe has led to the literal, not metaphorical, creation of a global village. Every village needs its councils. All the processes of multilateral diplomacy serve to fulfil the functions of these global village councils. For the purposes of this chapter, 'multilateral diplomacy' will be defined as the practice of involving more than two nations or parties in achieving diplomatic solutions to supranational problems. As former UN Secretary-General Kofi Annan has said, 'diplomacy has expanded its remit, moving far beyond bilateral political relations between states into a multilateral, multi-faceted enterprise encompassing almost every realm of human endeavour'.[1]

Several key themes will run through this chapter on multilateral diplomacy. One key theme is the theme of diversity. Since multilateral diplomacy is a rapid growth industry, new forms are emerging constantly, making it difficult to provide a comprehensive description of all types. A second key theme is the constant tension between justice and power in all the multilateral processes. In theory, multilateral diplomacy is guided by some key principles of the international order. Also, in theory, international organizations have been set up, by agreements reached in multilateral diplomacy, to perform certain functions and deliver certain global goods for the benefits of all—in other words, provide global governance in their relevant fields—and not to act as a means to the major powers' ends. In practice, however, power usually trumps principles and ideals. A third key theme is the tension between universal organizations such as the United Nations which represent all of humanity and often enjoy great legitimacy, and several smaller and more informal groups or coalitions (like the G8 and G20) which also try to address key global challenges.

This chapter will first begin by describing the many functions performed by multilateral diplomacy. Section 13.2 will describe the many forms that multilateral diplomacy takes. Section 13.3 will discuss the constant political stresses and tensions that run through multilateral diplomacy. Finally, Section 13.4 will suggest some solutions for the future to resolve these tensions.

13.1 FUNCTIONS OF MULTILATERAL DIPLOMACY

Multilateral diplomacy serves multiple functions, perhaps too many to document in a short chapter. At the apex, it serves as the 'Parliament of Man'. The only way to find out what the 7 billion people of our planet think on any global challenge is to hear the voices of their national representatives in universal forums, like the UN General Assembly (UNGA) or universal conferences, like the Copenhagen conference on climate change. When disagreements surface, as they did at Copenhagen, they simultaneously reflect, like national parliaments do, the different views of the global population and can provide a safety valve.

A second, related function, especially for the 'Parliament of Man' after discerning the urgent needs of the global village, is to set aspirational goals for humanity. Hence, the UN Millennium Summit of 2000 set the Millennium Development Goals (MDGs) for 2015. Many MDGs will not be met but they have nonetheless inspired action on several fronts to improve the living conditions of the very poor on our planet. Without universal organizations like the UN, such agreements would be more difficult.

A third and also related function is norm creation. The world has essentially become a more civilized place since the Second World War through the steady accretion of civilizing norms. For example, the adoption of the Universal Declaration of Human Rights by UNGA in 1948 represented a great leap forward. It delegitimized heinous practices like slavery and torture. More recently the adoption by UNGA of two significant initiatives of banning landmines and cluster weapons indicate clearly how the norm creation function of multilateral diplomacy can serve to make the world a more civilized place. Similarly, UN conventions on children and women have significantly improved norms in these areas. Another significant breakthrough came when the UN Summit of 2005 endorsed the concept of 'Responsibility to Protect' (R2P).[2] Of course one central tension remains when creating norms within institutions such as the UN, where there still exists a contradiction between the sovereign members and the need to reach decisions that these sovereign members are compelled to follow. For the moment, the only way to handle this is through 'consensus'.

Multilateral diplomacy is also the means to negotiate international treaties that improve the state of the world. Two examples stand out. The Nuclear Non-Proliferation Treaty (NPT), adopted on 1 July 1968, in force since 5 March 1970, and renewed indefinitely on 11 May 1995,[3] prohibits the development or transfer of nuclear weapons or related technologies by and to non-weapon holding states. The only non-signers today are Israel, India, and Pakistan. It has succeeded (with minor exceptions) in preventing nuclear proliferation and delegitimizing nuclear weapons. Sadly, the main violators of the NPT as a group have been the nuclear-weapon states, which have not moved quickly to fulfil their obligations to get rid of their horrific nuclear weapons. Similarly, the UN Convention on the Law of the Sea has created a common set of rules for the use of the world's oceans, which cover 70 per cent of the earth's surface. The Convention, concluded in 1982, came into force in 1994 and 159 countries and the European Union have joined the treaty. The US, despite being one of the bigger beneficiaries of the treaty, has not ratified it, although it has largely adhered to its principles and rules.

All these processes of norm creation and treaty negotiation have served to lay down and strengthen international law. Just as the adherence to the rule of law domestically has generated social and political stability, greater adherence to international law has progressively reduced wars since the Second World War. Indeed the number of people dying from wars has reached historic lows. This one statistic alone should make the sceptics of multilateral diplomacy think twice before rubbishing it. Avoidance of war has improved the human condition.

Against this backdrop, the United States, the most powerful actor on the world stage, made a strategic error when it made a concerted effort to delegitimize UNGA as representing the voice of humanity. This decision was driven in part by the powerful pro-Israel lobby in Washington which was concerned over the anti-Israel resolutions passed by the UNGA. The American decision served neither the long-term interests of Israel nor those of the US. Indeed, the view advocated by the American right that the US should forget about the UN and work with the Community of Democracies was easily refuted by Anne-Marie Slaughter who pointed out that many of the opponents of the US war on Iraq belonged to this Community of Democracies. In short, a new American strategic approach is required if multilateral diplomacy is to serve well its key function as the 'Parliament of Man'.

In theory, UNGA also has a role to play in conflict resolution and peace-building. In practice, especially since the end of the cold war, the UN Security Council (UNSC) has played the key role in this area, but its record on this is chequered. While it solved many long-standing problems in Guatemala, Namibia, Cambodia, and the former Yugoslav Republic of Macedonia, and oversaw the inauguration of new national governments following the resolution of conflicts in El Salvador and Mozambique, the UNSC failed woefully in the Balkans, failed to prevent genocide in Rwanda, and has been remarkably ineffective on the Israel–Palestine issue.

Both problem-solving and furtherance of international cooperation is also carried out by the multilateral diplomacy processes of the many specialized agencies that have emerged since the Second World War (including the World Trade Organization (WTO), World Health Organization (WHO), International Atomic Energy Agency (IAEA), International Labour Organization (ILO), UN Environment Programme (UNEP), to mention only a few). Overall, the WTO and its predecessor the General Agreement on Tariffs and Trade, have been spectacularly successful, with world trade growing three times faster than world output growth, from $296 billion in 1950 to over $8 trillion in 2005, thereby improving human welfare, increasing international interdependence, and creating a powerful vested interest in preserving global stability. Trade now accounts for almost one-fifth of the world's total GDP, up from only five per cent in 1950.[4] Even though the latest Doha Development Round is in trouble, all the previous trading rounds succeeded even if the negotiations had been long and protracted. Equally importantly, there has also been no significant backsliding into trade protectionism, even in the world financial crisis of 2007–2009.

On a smaller scale (in terms of the number of countries involved in multilateral diplomacy but not in terms of impact) the G20 Summits of November 2008 and April 2009 played a critical role in saving the world from going over a financial precipice.[5] These institutions and processors of multilateral diplomacy have so far passed the 'critical stress tests' surviving great crises, although of course the G20 could be made more inclusive, transparent, and participatory by periodic issue-wide inclusion of other stakeholders, as espoused by the 'Global Governance Group' in New York.

Kick-started by the global financial crisis, banking regulation will become an increasingly important challenge for ensuring the stability and sustainability of our world economic system; this is yet another area in which the tools of multilateral diplomacy can be put into action. The Basel Committee, made up of representatives of all G20 major economies plus a few others,[6] is a good example of multilateralism at work. Advocates of the second and third Basel Accords have called for the strengthening of international standards to reduce the risks faced by financial institutions, and for the creation of 'buffer' funds that will allow financial institutions to better withstand future periods of stress. Multilateral diplomacy enabled Basel to succeed.

The many and multiple functions performed by multilateral diplomacy demonstrate the importance of understanding how multilateral diplomacy works. More recently, this importance has been further demonstrated by how much of it is now done at the leaders' level. Leaders today consider it an essential part of their job description to travel overseas and attend summit meetings. By contrast, Sir Edward Grey never once travelled abroad during his long tenure as Britain's foreign secretary from 1905 to 1916. How times have changed!

13.2 FORMS OF MULTILATERAL DIPLOMACY

Multilateral meetings that take place in a year have taken on so many forms, and at so many different levels, that it would be difficult to measure all of them. However, even a cursory attempt at counting them will show that since the creation of the UN and the Bretton Woods Institutions (BWI) in 1945, multilateral meetings have exploded, especially in the last two decades.

Any attempt to classify all the multilateral meetings will also face serious difficulties. Nevertheless, if one were to look for a few conceptual baskets to capture most of them, these conceptual baskets could be entitled as (1) universal, (2) functional/specialized, (3) regional, (4) ad hoc.

The creation of the UN and the BWI spawned the industry of universal gatherings and conferences which tried to get all of humanity represented. These universal gatherings have grown from the regular annual meetings of UNGA, the International Monetary Fund (IMF), and World Bank to now include all kinds of global conferences, from the UN Conference on the Law of the Sea to conferences on population, women, and the global environment.

After the failure of Copenhagen, there is now a new pessimism about the future of such global conferences. The new conventional wisdom is that such universal meetings are unworkable as they try to reconcile too many different interests. Yet, even in a small village, it would be folly to ignore the wishes of even a significant minority. True global solutions in a global village require the 'inclusion' of all members of the village in a solution. A dispassionate analysis of Copenhagen will show that it failed for many reasons, including the incompetence of the Danish chairmanship, the shift of power away from the West, the inability of President Barack Obama to persuade the US Congress to impose limits on American greenhouse gas emissions, and the need for China and India to maintain their economic growth rates to sustain their poverty alleviation efforts. In short, multilateral diplomacy exercises are inherently complex and success in them requires skilful leadership, like the kind provided by Ambassador Tommy Koh of Singapore when he ably steered the UN Convention of the Law of the Sea to a successful conclusion despite the many contradictions between groups like the 'Landlocked and Geographically Disadvantaged States' and the 'Continental Shelf' countries. Hence, when universal conferences fail, we should not blame the format. We should blame the lack of skill of the participants and the inherent contradictions of individual states' interests.

The UN family has also created a variety of specialized agencies with their own intergovernmental annual conferences and governing councils that provide direction and guidance on the basis of decisions reached through multilateral diplomacy. While some of their annual conferences and governing councils have also been derailed by political differences, which hamper their ability to provide good global leadership and governance in their respective fields, their track record shows that whenever a common danger is faced, the global community has been able to come together. This is especially true of the reaction to pandemics that do not respect national borders. Hence, it is useful to observe how multilateral diplomacy works well in specialized organizations like WHO to understand how humanity can come together and work together in universal multilateral conferences.

Multilateral diplomacy is growing very rapidly at the regional level. The most successful example of regional cooperation is provided by the European Union (EU). While most laud the economic achievements of the EU, its most striking achievement is not just that there are no wars, but that there is also zero prospect of war between any two EU member states. This is the gold standard of regional cooperation that all other regions should try to emulate. Sadly, no other region comes close.

Nevertheless, one untold story of the world has been how this European gold standard has gradually infected other regional organizations. I can speak with personal experience on what is possibly the second most successful regional organization, namely the Association of Southeast Asian Nations (ASEAN). When I first attended ASEAN meetings in the early 1970s, you could feel the distrust and suspicion among the five founding members. Yet two decades later, when I led the Singapore senior official delegation to ASEAN meetings, there was a much more relaxed and trusting atmosphere for concluding business. Two decades of regional multilateral diplomacy had changed the chemistry of ASEAN meetings and improved trust.

When people come together and interact frequently, over time, they develop a sense of community. This in turn reduces the prospects for conflict and enhances the prospects for cooperation. This is why after practising multilateral diplomacy for over three decades in many different forums, universal and regional, I am a strong believer in its value. The fact that no two ASEAN states have gone to war with each other (despite some close shaves) since ASEAN's creation provides clear and powerful proof of the value of multilateral diplomacy.

Multilateral diplomacy at the regional level has also become a major sunrise industry. ASEAN, for example, has succeeded not just in enhancing cooperation between its ten members but also in providing an essential geopolitical platform for other Asian powers to meet and confer on neutral ground. It began with ASEAN inviting China, Japan, and Korea to join them at the famous ASEAN + 3 meetings. These meetings demonstrated their value quickly. When bilateral relations worsened between China and Japan and their leaders could not meet bilaterally, they could meet each other without losing face in the multilateral setting provided by ASEAN + 3 meetings. The meetings have now effectively expanded to ASEAN + 8 with India, Australia, New Zealand, Russia, and US joining the East Asia Summit meetings.

Relative to the EU, ASEAN is a latecomer. Hence, as the world moves ever more firmly into the Asian century, it would have been natural for the EU to undertake the bold initiative of proposing Asia–Europe cooperation. Instead, the EU remained passive and ASEAN took the lead. Prime Minister Goh Chok Tong of Singapore proposed an Asia–Europe Meeting (ASEM) in 1994.

Fortunately, the EU embraced his proposal readily. I know this from first-hand experience as I travelled to several EU capitals to promote Prime Minister Goh's idea. The first ASEM Summit in Bangkok in March 1996 was an unqualified success. Unfortunately, the Asian Financial Crisis erupted soon after. This gave EU countries a valuable opportunity to demonstrate that they were not 'fair weather' friends of Asia. Sadly, the EU failed this test, demonstrating once again that European policy-makers' judgements are clouded by short-term thinking. With the recovery of Asia, the ASEM process is back on track. Ironically, Europe got into trouble a decade later. Fortunately, the Asian states are showing wiser judgement by not walking away from Europe in its hour of travails.

The success of multilateral diplomacy in Asia has profound implications for the global order as we move into a completely new era of world history marked by the end of Western domination and the return of Asia. It is vital to remember that from the year 1 to 1820, China and India consistently provided the world's largest economies. Hence, by 2050, when they return to their natural places in the global hierarchy of nations, the centre of gravity of world history will also shift to Asia.

Therefore, what Asia does will drive world history. It would not have been inconceivable for the rising Asian powers to reject the Western-based principles that provided the foundations for the 1945 rules-based order created by the US and Europe. Fortunately, the rising Asian powers have decided to embrace rather than reject these Western principles. Ironically, the big question the world faces today is whether the Western states will respect their own principles of global order. Under international law, the use of force is justified only if it is an act of self-defence or authorized by the UN Security Council. The invasion of Iraq in March 2003 did not meet either criterion. Hence, as Kofi Annan declared, the Iraq war was illegal.[7] If the Western states would like rising Asian powers to respect the key Western principles that underpin our global order, they must lead by example. This is why American attitudes towards multilateral diplomacy are critical.

The success of multilateral diplomacy is also demonstrated by the creation of various ad hoc diplomatic gatherings. The most famous and most powerful ad hoc group today is the G20. It saved the world from an economic meltdown in early 2009. Unlike established universal and regional groupings, like the UN or EU, the G20 has no headquarters or even rules of procedure. It is still truly ad hoc. But despite this, its ability to deliver results also shows the value of multilateral diplomacy. The success of a club is shown when outsiders clamour to get in and no insiders want to leave it. This is certainly true of the G20.

Other ad hoc forms of multilateral diplomacy have also emerged, with varying degrees of legitimacy and success. The initiatives against landmines and cluster bombs, despite initial opposition from established powers like the US, Russia, and China, found significant international momentum and were subsequently legitimized when both were endorsed by UNGA. A less successful example of ad hoc multilateral diplomacy is provided by the Proliferation Security Initiative (PSI) launched by the US. Its goal is to allow the interdiction of third-country ships suspected of carrying nuclear weapons in the high seas. Even though it has over 90 states supporting it, it is still opposed by several countries, including China which disputes its legality, and has therefore not yet been endorsed by the UN system.

13.3 INHERENT TENSIONS OF MULTILATERAL DIPLOMACY

International negotiations are supposedly conducted by reasonable men and women sitting around a table to arrive at a mutually beneficial agreement. This practice is deemed to be a significant advance in human civilization as we are seen to have moved away from the 'primitive' world when men made decisions by using their clubs and weapons, not reason. There is no doubt that the voice of 'Reason' has played a role in international negotiations and multilateral diplomacy.

My three decades of experience with multilateral diplomacy (in all its forms) have taught me that when I walk into a multilateral setting, I will encounter three voices: reason, power, and charm. The voice of charm has been underestimated. One simple story will illustrate how it works. In 1981 the UNSC was totally deadlocked over the selection of the next secretary-general. Fortunately, a young Ugandan diplomat (representing an extremely weak country just recovering from Idi Amin's excesses) named Olara Otunnu was elected as the president of the UNSC in December 1981. Using his charm and persuasiveness, he found a solution to the deadlock. Similarly, the legendary Singapore diplomat, Tommy Koh, was also able to use his considerable charm to persuade diplomats from over one hundred countries to agree to a solution in the law of the sea negotiations. Charm works in multilateral diplomacy as in other areas of life.

But neither reason nor charm can override the voice of power, which remains the single strongest factor in multilateral diplomacy and international relations. My two years in the UNSC in 2001–2002 taught me that we have not travelled far from the 'primitive' world order when brute strength and power drove human decision-makings. The five permanent members (P5) would use the power of the veto formally and, more often, informally to distort the decision-making procedures of UNSC, with the result that instead of the UNSC fulfilling its charter obligations of 'preserving international peace and security', it was used to further the national interests and positions of the P5.

The biggest distortion has occurred on the Israel–Palestine issue. There is now a near-universal consensus in the international community that we need to have a two-state solution and that the forty-five-year illegal Israeli occupation of Palestinian land has to end. Any kind of global democratic voting will show there are over six billion people who will vote for a two-state solution. However, the views of six billion people are being thwarted by six million Israelis who have managed to dominate American decision-making. This global distortion could ultimately lead to a long-term tragedy for Israel when the new correlation of forces begins to constrain American power significantly in the 21st century.

To rescue the UN and strengthen multilateral diplomacy, we have to quickly resolve the Israel–Palestinian issue because it has generated more international political poison than any other issue. It has caused the double delegitimization of the UN: delegitimization of the UN in the eyes of the American public because the American media has highlighted its anti-Israel positions in UNGA and delegitimization of the UN in the eyes of 1.6 billion Muslims who notice the pro-Israel positions of the UNSC. Hence, until the Israel–Palestine issue is resolved, the UN will be effectively crippled and multilateral diplomacy will be consequently constrained.

The insistence of the P5 in putting 'national interests' ahead of 'global interests' has led to many other distortions in UNSC decision-making. The Clinton Administration blocked an effective international response to prevent genocide in Rwanda by refusing to allow the word 'genocide' in a UNSC resolution. Similarly, the Bush Administration distorted the role of the UNSC when it used its considerable 'unipolar' power to get the UNSC to go beyond its legitimate role and interfere in a 'judicial' decision by granting immunity to American troops from the International Criminal Court. Similarly, Russia prevented the UNSC from responding in Kosovo in 1999. Similar examples can be found for the other three permanent members.

Power, however, is not static. Having served as Singapore's ambassador to the UN in two different historical phases, I saw at first hand how multilateral diplomacy is conditioned by the international geopolitical order. In the mid-1980s, when the Cold War was still on, the UNSC was paralysed by the gridlock between the USA and USSR. Hence,

UNGA was the main focus of attention. It performed credibly in condemning both the illegal Soviet invasion of Afghanistan and the illegal American invasion of Grenada. When I returned to the UN in 1998, UNGA was completely ignored and all the attention and focus was on the work of the UNSC.

Multilateral diplomacy is now going to face the biggest test of its ability to adapt to a new geopolitical order with the impending biggest shift of geopolitical power we have seen in several centuries. As indicated earlier, we are reaching the end of the era of Western domination of world history (but not, of course, the end of the West) and the return of Asian countries, especially China and India, to their natural position of providing the biggest economies of the world. There is no doubt that the world will have to make massive adjustments to adapt to these huge shifts in power. Multilateral diplomacy will have to do the same.

This will be an extremely complex and difficult exercise. In the current multilateral order, the language, concepts, and definitions of legitimate and illegitimate international behaviour are primarily Western in origin. Indeed, today's international system of states, international organizations, and multinational corporations finds its roots in the Peace of Westphalia, a series of treaties signed in 1648 between European rulers who sought to establish the territorial integrity of their states. Since the Peace of Westphalia, there has not been an occasion when the international community adopted a different view from that of Westphalian state sovereignty and one of the greatest difficulties facing us today is a tension between individual state sovereignty and a need for global solutions to global problems. On the one hand, the United Nations is a collection of sovereign states, and its mission is, to some degree, to protect their sovereignty. On the other hand, global problems demand a united global strategy which may transcend individual states' sovereignty.

However, there have been minor but revolutionary changes. Consider, for example, the latest concept in international relations: the 'Responsibility to Protect' adopted by UNGA in 2005. In theory, this concept overrides national sovereignty. What the leaders agreed to in the outcome document was therefore a landmark decision for international law. The enormous importance of this decision has not quite sunk in yet but it will in time to come. This was the result of a Canadian initiative. Will such concepts be retained or rejected when the West no longer dominates the multilateral order?

One critical, underestimated problem here is that most Western policy-makers and public intellectuals believe that the international behaviour of most Western states has been 'responsible' and 'legitimate'. That is why American leaders can, with a straight face, call on China to emerge as a 'responsible stakeholder' in the international order. Yet, the West only provides less than 12 per cent of the world population. A vast majority of the 88 per cent of the world population that lives outside of the West increasingly questions the 'responsibility' and 'legitimacy' of the West as they are acutely aware of the duplicity and double-standards prevalent in Western international behaviour. The West must learn to listen to the voices of the majority of the world's population or else we may face sad consequences. The story of the invasion of Iraq shows what can go wrong when the West ignores global opinion.

This huge shift in global history could also provide multilateral diplomacy its biggest opportunity to demonstrate its new relevance. Its primary function, as indicated in section 13.1 of this chapter, is to serve as the 'Parliament of Man'. Hence, instead of trying to delegitimize and derail UNGA, the Western powers, especially the US, should try to revive UNGA's early critical role in providing a forum for hearing the voices of the newly-active members of the global community. The strong speeches of India's Jawaharlal Nehru and Egypt's Gamel Abdel Nasser, Indonesia's Sukarno, and Cuba's Fidel Castro in the 1950s and 1960s provided the world with an understanding of what the newly-independent nations aspired to immediately after Western decolonization.

Today, we are witnessing a similar re-emergence of long-dormant civilizations and societies. New voices are emerging, by the billions. The world needs to find an arena to allow these voices to express themselves. Fortunately, we do not have to reinvent the wheel. UNGA already exists. However, in the complex new world order we have, UNGA must capture the complexity of our new world order. In their introduction to this *Handbook*, Cooper, Heine, and Thakur highlight the new actors on the world stage. They quote appropriately Anne-Marie Slaughter, who says:

> We envision getting not just a new group of states around a table, but also building networks, coalitions and partnerships of states and nonstate actors to tackle specific problems... To do that, our diplomats are going to need to have skills that are closer to community organizing than traditional reporting and analysis. New connecting technologies will be vital tools in this kind of diplomacy.[8]

Hitherto, most of these non-state actors have been powerful Western NGOs (like Amnesty International or Greenpeace) or inspired by Western ideas (like the Club of Democracies). This traditional Western domination in the world of non-state actors is also coming to an end. This is why the story of the Turkish flotilla that attempted to reach Gaza in May 2010 provided a powerful harbinger of the world that is coming. Similarly, the pictures of young Chinese students in Western capitals demonstrating against the Western demonstrators who were blocking the passage of the Olympics torch showed that young people all over the world are becoming politically aroused. Given the huge demographic bulge of youth in the developing world, their voices must also be heard. The new UNGA must strive to become an accurate mirror of the views of 7 billion people on our planet.

The arrival of new non-state actors, however, does not mean that some of the previous traditional tensions have disappeared. The failure of the Copenhagen Conference in December 2009 provides a wonderful case study of what can go wrong in contemporary multilateral diplomacy. On the one hand, virtually all the NGOs in Copenhagen, both from the developing and developed countries, argued in favour of stronger global action against global warming. Their voices were best captured by the United Nations Intergovernmental Panel on Climate Change (IPCC), which, unlike Western NGOs, has a global collection of representatives. Yet, all their moral force failed against the traditional dynamic of negotiations among government representatives.

Obama's hands were tied when he arrived in Copenhagen because the US Congress refused to pass any legislation that would restrict American greenhouse gas emissions. If the then-largest emitter in the world would not cooperate, it was obviously absurd to expect the two new emerging powers, China and India, to make any compromises. The Indian PM, Manmohan Singh, put it well when he said he could not deprive the Indian people of electricity: 'Our energy needs are bound to grow. We will be failing in the duty to our nation and to posterity if we do not look ahead and take steps for not just today and tomorrow but for future generations.'[9] More than 400 million Indians lack electricity and supply falls short of peak demand by more than 16 per cent, according to the World Bank. At the end of the day, all the leaders, including Obama, Singh, Brazil's Luiz Inácio Lula da Silva, and China's Wen Jiabao, could not override their domestic national interests in favour of global interests.

The Copenhagen Conference also showed how a new geopolitical order was emerging. In the final meeting, the EU was not even represented in the room, showing what a geopolitical dwarf the EU had become. Apart from the US, China and India were the key players. Despite their bilateral differences, China and India cooperated for a common cause. Brazil and South Africa also demonstrated the importance of newly-emerging economies. In short, a thorough case study of the Copenhagen Conference will draw out many lessons on the complexities of contemporary multilateral diplomacy. This conference also showed how urgently new thinking is needed if the world is going to succeed in global cooperation.

Fortunately, some failures of multilateral diplomacy at the global level are being compensated by successes at the regional level. In most regions of the world, regional cooperation is growing rather than receding. Apart from the well-known success stories of the EU and ASEAN, all regions see the value of working together. In most regions of the world (with the exception of South Asia which is bedevilled by India–Pakistan differences), intra-regional trade is growing. Intra-regional trade in East Asia, for example, accounted for only about 9 per cent of trade in the whole region in 1990. By 2010 it had grown to over 50 per cent, a spectacular increase by any measure. The volume of intra-regional trade in Africa has increased by almost 20 per cent in the first decade of the 21st century and a similar story is true in Central and South America. However, even more important than the economic benefits, the general decline of wars globally can also be attributed to greater regional cooperation.

Having participated in several meetings between ASEAN and EU officials, I have become acutely aware that the culture and mores of regional multilateral diplomacy vary significantly from region to region. In Europe, there is a strong legalistic emphasis with most of the time taken up by long arguments over the draft document. Success is measured by the quality of the written document. In East Asia, most of the focus is on building trust and understanding among the participants. The document is a secondary product. The more important result is the unspoken trust that has developed. I am deliberately exaggerating the differences to draw out the distinctions. But my experience with ASEAN and EU also taught me that new generations of multilateral diplomats must learn to develop deeper cultural sensitivities.

13.4 SOLUTIONS

Looking at the future of multilateral diplomacy, the world's leading policy-makers, including key world leaders, face an acute dilemma in dealing with it. With the shrinking of the globe, the demand for multilateral diplomacy is increasing dramatically. On the other hand, as section 13.3 has documented, the supply is beset with many inherent problems. To resolve this dilemma the world needs to take a step-by-step approach to ensure that the processes of multilateral diplomacy will be available when the world needs them to resolve acute global and regional problems, as I explain in my new book, The Great Convergence: Asia, the West, and the Logic of One World.[10]

The first step is to change our mindset about world order. We need to acknowledge that we live literally, not metaphorically, in a global village. Hence, right now, our primary global contradiction is painfully obvious: the biggest challenges of governance are global in origin, but all the politics that respond to them are local. There are many wise leaders around the world, but there is not enough global leadership.

The first decade of the 21st century has only accelerated the emergence of such global challenges. The era began with 9/11, when a plot hatched by Osama bin Laden while living in Afghanistan brought down the Twin Towers in Manhattan. In 2003 SARS jumped simultaneously from a village in China to two cities on opposite sides of the world—Singapore and Toronto. Barely six years later, H1N1 haunted the globe. The speed and ferocity of the Lehman Brothers crisis brought the world to the brink of a meltdown.

The biggest challenge of all is evolving more slowly than the financial crisis. But climate change is the perfect example of just how ineffective our current leadership structures are. The solution to global warming is quite simple: we have to increase the economic price of greenhouse-gas emissions equitably, with rich countries paying more and poorer nations paying less, but with all countries paying some price. Yet someone has to make the first move. America—whose population is only 5 per cent of the world but consumes 25 per cent of the world's gasoline—is the obvious candidate. If the price of a gallon of gasoline in the US were to be raised by $1 (and that would still make an American gallon cheaper than a European or Singaporean gallon), the change in driving habits would dramatically cut emissions. And American leadership, by example, would likely change attitudes in other nations.

In many ways, the US is the wisest country in the world. It certainly remains the most successful, despite its recent travails. Yet in this land of wisdom and success, not one American politician would dare advocate a $1 solution to save the world. It would mean immediate political suicide. Herein lies the nub of the problem. Politicians are elected in local constituencies to take care of local concerns. Those who try to save the world will not last long.

This is why humanity needs a wake-up call. We can develop good domestic governance, from New Zealand to the Netherlands, from Singapore to Sweden. But good national leaders can only mitigate the shocks of global challenges, not solve them. Solutions have to be tackled through global organizations like the United Nations and the IMF, or global coalitions like the G20.

In theory, everyone agrees that we need to strengthen and open up these institutions. In practice, however, global organizations and coalitions are controlled by a few powerful national governments that put their interests ahead of the world's. This is the ultimate global paradox. Great powers want to use their status to dominate global organizations—see how the US and Europe still control the leadership of the World Bank and the IMF. But the more they control and distort the agenda of those institutions, the more they weaken them. And if these organizations are weak, solutions to global problems will simply not emerge.

The only way around this is to develop a strong, new international consensus, among citizens as well as governments, that the world needs more global governance (not global government).[11] Only then will the mightiest nations think of the greater good and allow institutions—from the G20 to the UN, from the IMF to the WTO—to be revitalized. Indeed, a cooperative solution should provide each stakeholder with a better outcome than a solution reached by individual stakeholders. Yes, these bodies are imperfect. But in the world of politics, it is easier to reform existing institutions than to create perfect new ones.

The second step needs to be taken by the world's greatest power. Ever since the strong leadership of Dag Hammarskjöld (1953–1961), the US has decided (and during the cold war, in complete agreement with the Soviet Union) that its national interest was best served by a weaker UN leadership and weak processes of multilateral diplomacy. Hence, all international organizations, treaties, and laws were seen by American policy-makers as constraints on American power. This policy may have made sense if America could have guaranteed that it would remain in perpetuity as the world's sole superpower (although I would argue that it would not have made sense even then). However, with China about to overtake the US as the world's greatest economic power shortly, it is timely for the US to reconsider its old policies of keeping multilateral institutions and processes weak. If America persists with these policies, there will be fewer constraints on China as it emerges as a great power.

Several beneficial practical consequences will emerge for multilateral diplomacy if the US decides to change its policy. First, the performance of international organizations would improve if the best possible candidates are chosen to run them rather than the weakest acceptable candidates. A UN, for example, with a secretary-general of the calibre of a Kofi Annan rather than a Kurt Waldheim would be a more effective organization. A secretary-general with a strong moral voice would be perceived by the world as a secular Pope who could provide both moral and political leadership in bringing the world together to find strong collective solutions to the rapidly increasing 'global commons' problems we are facing. For this to happen, however, the P5, who wield a power to veto any candidate for the post, will need to overcome their desire to have more of a secretary than a general leading the UN bureaucracy. Indeed, even Kofi Annan was reported to have said that the 'S' and 'G' in his title stood for 'scapegoat'—a reference to the tendency of Western powers to blame the UN or its agencies for their own failures, making the UN the biggest convenient scapegoat.

Second, international organizations should be given the resources they need to meet growing global challenges in many areas. The IAEA Commission of Eminent Persons, led by former Mexican President Ernesto Zedillo, recommended that the IAEA recruit and retain more nuclear-weapons inspectors in response to growing threats of nuclear proliferation. The US should go beyond lifting the Bush Administration's zero-growth budget policies towards international organizations to work with other developed partners to galvanize the necessary support for these organizations, all the while holding them accountable in terms of performance and efficient use of resources.

Third, the improved abilities, resources, and morale of international organizations would in turn increase their standing and prestige globally. The Western media, for example, would start looking to them for solutions to problems rather than portraying them as the problem. A reversal of the Western policy of delegitimizing international organizations would significantly improve their ability to perform better, which in turn would make multilateral diplomacy more attractive for capable young foreign service professionals. I can say this with great conviction because, as a young foreign service officer, I was actually discouraged from going into multilateral diplomacy. A senior Singaporean minister told me: 'Kishore, your job there is only to go to the UN and weep for the world. Don't expect to achieve anything concrete in the UN.' Equally, we should promote the recruiting of experts in areas such as finance or the global environment into the multilateral area, as well as encourage the brightest foreign service officers to focus on global multilateral challenges in their careers.

My own life experience has taught me that the most successful organizations are those able to recruit the best and the brightest, whether the organization is Harvard or McKinsey, Bain, or Goldman Sachs. Over the years, with the steady demoralization of most international organizations, fewer and fewer countries send their best diplomats to multilateral diplomacy. Instead, countries have sent their best diplomats to bilateral diplomacy. This has been a major strategic error as multilateral diplomacy has become more important for the world than bilateral diplomacy. Therefore, the branding and image of multilateral diplomacy must change in our brand-consumed world if it is to succeed in its mission.

It is vital to emphasise that different international organizations face different problems. The IMF and World Bank have been relatively well funded since they are profit-making institutions clearly controlled by the West. However, because they are perceived to be serving Western rather than global interests, their prestige and standing, especially in Asia, diminished significantly after the Asian financial crisis. For the IMF and World Bank to remain relevant in the 21st century, the West must give up its controlling share of both organizations and allow their heads to be selected on merit rather than be the exclusive preserve of the US and Europe.

In short, multilateral diplomacy can be revived and strengthened with some clear practical steps including those mentioned in this chapter. However, these practical steps can only be taken after a new political consensus has emerged in key capitals, both in the established powers and in the newly emerging powers, that the processes of multilateral diplomacy need to be strengthened, rather than weakened. The creation of this new political consensus will in turn require a concerted effort involving both key state and non-state actors.

NOTES

1. 'Address by Secretary-General Kofi Annan to the American Academy of Diplomacy upon receiving the Academy's "Excellence in Diplomacy" Award in Washington, DC, on November 28', United Nations Press Release, 30 November 2001.

2. See Chapter 42, this volume.

3. See Chapter 45, this volume.

4. 'World exports and world GDP, 1870–2005', *World Trade Report 2007*, World Trade Organization, 244. Available at: <http://www.wto.org/english/res_e/booksp_e/anrep_e/wtr07-ob_e.pdf>.

5. See Chapter 40, this volume.

6. As of October 2010, members include: Argentina, Australia, Belgium, Brazil, Canada, China, France, Germany, Hong Kong SAR, India, Indonesia, Italy, Japan, Korea, Luxembourg, Mexico, the Netherlands, Russia, Saudi Arabia, Singapore, South Africa, Spain, Sweden, Switzerland, Turkey, the United Kingdom, and the United States.

7. See for example, 'Iraq war illegal, says Annan', *BBC News*, 16 September 2004. Available at: <http://news.bbc.co.uk/2/hi/3661134.stm>.

8. In an interview with David Rothpokf, 'It's 3 a.m. Do you know where Hillary Clinton is?', *Washington Post*, 27 August 2009.

9. 'Nuclear energy essential for India: Manmohan Singh', *Thaidian News*, 24 March 2008.

10. Kishore Mahbubani, *The Great Convergence: Asia, the West, and the Logic of One World*, New York: Public Affairs, 2012.

11. See Thomas G. Weiss and Ramesh Thakur, *Global Governance and the UN: An Unfinished Journey* (Bloomington: Indiana University Press, 2010).

CHAPTER 14

....

CONFERENCE DIPLOMACY

....

A.J.R. GROOM

In his celebrated essay *Diplomacy*, Sir Harold Nicolson remarked that:

> Diplomacy, in the sense of the ordered contact of relations between one group of human beings and another group alien to themselves, is far older than history. The theorists of the sixteenth century contended that the first diplomatists were angels, in that they served as 'angeloi' or messengers between heaven and earth.

Nicolson then commented tartly that this was not a view that would be held by modern historians.[1] Conference diplomacy, too, has its ancient antecedents, but it is more common to refer to such events as the Peace of Westphalia in 1648 and similar gatherings usually at an end of a war, when a new world order was in the making, as the onset of modern conference diplomacy.

We shall pursue Nicolson's 'angeloi' firstly in historical context during the long 19th century 1815–1920 when conference diplomacy developed in embryonic form before scouring the literature for helpful definitions of the phenomenon. The tempo quickens as global problems give rise to global conferences which begin to constitute a new element in the UN system. How do such conferences come into being and conduct their business, and to what effect?

14.1 CONFERENCE DIPLOMACY IN THE LONG 19TH CENTURY

....

In the 19th century the tempo quickened as the powers gathered in 1815 for the famous Congress of Vienna, which was the beginning of a system of congresses which were held by heads of state and government, or conferences which were usually at the ministerial level. These were held on demand by mutual agreement throughout the 19th century and into the 20th century and began to accrue the attributes of being a system of global governance, albeit for a Eurocentric world. In the calling of such congresses, the place where it was held was of some importance because the host usually provided both the chairperson and the secretary of the conference. Such meetings were normally called at the end of a war to draw up a peace treaty, because of an emergency, or sometimes to deal more generally with a topic that had become ripe for the attention of the powers throughout Europe, and especially the great powers.[2]

The powers themselves—especially Russia, Austria, Prussia, and Britain—acknowledged that they were in the process of creating a system when they agreed in the Treaty of Alliance and Friendship known as the Quadruple Alliance, on 20 November 1815 to meet at fixed periods for consultations on matters of common interest and 'for the repose and prosperity of Nations and for the maintenance of the peace of Europe.'[3]

Much of the work in the Congress of Vienna that followed the final defeat of Napoleon has a modern air to it, in the sense that the Conference was in essence run by the Big Four with an active role also played by France, and lesser roles by Spain, Portugal, and Sweden, in the form of ten separate committees.[4]

The immediate outcome was a set of congresses between the leading victorious powers, and increasingly with France, the vanquished power, playing a role, which dealt with a number of issues of a systemic nature. However, the marriage of convenience to defeat Napoleon split in short order after the war. Looked at in longer perspective, the reason for this was the clash when the movement towards 'democratic republicanism is introduced into a social system composed of dynastic states.'[5] A particular issue concerned the degree to which conservative dynastic powers could intervene within the internal workings of states in order to quell any potential revolutionary movement. The Holy Alliance of Austria, Prussia, and Russia argued that the international system should be geared to upholding the principle of legitimacy, in the sense of the hereditary rights of rulers and their thrones against revolutionary forces within their own countries, or their colonial possessions.[6] For Britain and France, on the other hand, the Holy Alliance was, in Castlereagh's terminology, sublime mysticism and nonsense. Given this ideological and practical disagreement there can be little surprise that the Congress system collapsed, since it was based on the need for a unanimity that was lacking.

This falling apart was only temporary, since the need for global governance at the level of the European global system was evident, and the question which led to its revival in the form of the conference system was that of Belgium independence which was discussed by ambassadors in the 1830–1839 period. This saw a final solution which met with the wishes of the Belgian provinces of the Netherlands and the surrounding great powers, namely, France, Prussia, and Britain. Moreover, throughout the 19th century conferences were held, some of great moment such as the one in Berlin, carving up Africa. Their frequency was quite remarkable, bearing in mind the difficulties of transport and communication at the time. Indeed, the average was one conference every three years, although, of course, they met only on demand. The growth of railways and reliable means of communication, which were swift, secure, and economical, greatly changed the tempo of diplomatic activity. The extent of the progress that had been made could be seen in the conferences at the turn of the 20th century, and especially the Hague Peace Conference of 1899.

This was called to deal with the general question of disarmament and the associated issue of the peaceful settlement of disputes. Twenty-six states attended, including the United States and Mexico. In 1907 a second Hague Peace Conference was held with forty-four participants, including sixteen from Latin America: the 'first conference to have some resemblance to an international legislature'.[7] At the same time, international secretariats began to be established to support the Permanent Court of Arbitration in 1904, as well as a growing range of functional agencies, particularly those concerned with communications and transport, which had periodic conferences, some form of managing committee of a permanent nature, and a small permanent staff.

Outside the halls of diplomatic practice public opinion was beginning to exercise itself in support of the idea of some form of League of Nations, which would aspire to be universal in membership, be supported by a permanent secretariat, and would concern itself with all manner of international relations, including both political and security questions, and go beyond that into functional ties of an economic, social, and cultural nature. The time was rapidly approaching to move from an ad hoc system of conferences to an institutionalized organization dealing with questions that constituted an agenda for global governance. Global society was ahead of the politicians, with the exception of a powerful advocate in the shape of US President Woodrow Wilson, who enjoined his colleagues to adopt the idea of the establishment of such an international body.

What had been the diplomacy of ad hoc conferences was about to become parliamentary diplomacy in terms of the League of Nations. An indication of the magnitude of the change was given by Sir Maurice Hankey, who reported that he had attended 488 international meetings between 1914 and 1920, so that 'it can hardly be doubted that diplomacy by conferences has come to stay'.[8] Nicolson stated the advantages of diplomacy by conference were 'self-evident', since 'it enables those who are responsible for framing policy to conduct negotiation'.[9] This saves time and also enables friendship materially to contribute to the success of diplomacy by allowing absolute frankness of discussion. Yet, Nicolson also found it necessary to warn of the dangers, that as well as friendship, antipathy could develop and the rapidity of discussion could lead to imprecision, misunderstanding, leakage, and indiscretion.[10] Nevertheless, the new world of parliamentary diplomacy within the confines of the League of Nations was here to stay, supplemented by conference diplomacy on ad hoc issues.

The absence of the United States, and initially that of the Soviet Union and Germany, from the League made conference diplomacy a necessity for matters which also concerned those powers. Hence there were discussions on matters such as naval disarmament and the economic reconstruction of Europe and, on occasion, individual countries wished to settle their disputes outside the framework of the League, as for example in the case of Mussolini and the question of the murder of an Italian officer engaged in demarcating the border between Greece and Albania. In the economic sphere there were conferences on financial questions in Brussels in 1920, an economic conference in Geneva in 1927, and the London Monetary and Economic Conference in 1933. Likewise, there were disarmament conferences. At the same time parliamentary diplomacy continued without abatement in the context of the League, even though the League found itself increasingly challenged by the Japanese, then the Italians, and finally Nazi Germany. On the other hand, it had its successes in the expansion of functional cooperation, which was assessed by the Bruce Committee in 1939 in very favourable terms, while at the same time the International Labour Organization was successfully establishing itself to the extent that it continued its work without interruption after the Second World War. The pattern was set with the League on the one hand, and specific conferences on the other hand, and it continued after the Second World War as the United Nations was established to replace the League.

14.2 Definitions

Johan Kaufmann distinguishes between multilateral diplomacy, parliamentary diplomacy, and conference diplomacy.[11] He takes the now conventional formula that multilateral diplomacy

> involves contact among three or more states, but is not necessarily conducted in the framework of an intergovernmental conference. Parliamentary diplomacy, a term derived from a certain similarity between international conferences and national parliaments, overlaps largely with conference diplomacy…parliamentary diplomacy is a narrower concept than conference diplomacy because the latter covers not only public meetings, but also private, often informal meetings held before, during and after international conferences.[12]

Another definition of conference diplomacy cited in the literature with approval is that of Peter Willetts: 'A conference convened on a non-routine basis, under the auspices of the United Nations, with all countries eligible to attend.'[13]

This is a useful broad-based definition since it encompasses Special Sessions of the General Assembly, as well as sequences of global conferences, such as those on the environment. What it does not embrace is the now familiar large-scale contribution of civil society actors, both NGOs and also multinational corporations, in UN-sponsored global conferences. We shall argue later that this large-scale intervention by global civil society in many different forms, especially with the conferences on particular themes, such as the environment, habitat, and the like, is now an integral part of the phenomenon. As such, a coach and horses has been driven through the notions behind Article 71 and a new branch of the UN activity has coalesced over the last half century into a significant development of the Charter.

14.3 The Growth of the New Phenomenon

The realization of the nature and the import of global problems became more acute during the 1960s and 1970s, once the immediate effects of the Second World War had been overcome. To be sure there had always been global problems, but they now featured as an integral part of the process of globalization, in a manner that had not been realized previously. A global problem is one which necessarily involves everybody and from which there is no escape. For example, the Second World War certainly touched every continent of the globe, but an indigenous person in the Brazilian rainforest would not have been affected by the Second World War as of necessity. If, however, there is nuclear war anywhere in the world, then such indigenous people will be affected through fallout, nuclear winter, and the like. They may not realize what is happening, they may not understand what is happening, but it will certainly affect them. Likewise there are other problems of a similar nature, such as resource depletion, environmental degradation, as well as positive global assets such as the development and implementation of human rights on a global scale. What is characteristic of all of these is that whereas some actors may for a while be able to mitigate the effects of a global problem, they cannot escape them entirely in the longer term. What is more, for their management it requires that everybody, certainly all the major actors in a particular functional dimension, be able and willing to take part in the process by which the global problem is identified, managed, and appropriate policies chosen and implemented in order to combat its negative effects.

Such global problems used to be treated essentially, if at all, through the frameworks of worldwide empires, but such empires no longer exist and they have given rise to new states which have their own agendas. The stage was therefore set for an easy recognition of global problems and also a need for an institutional framework to broach such problems. Global conferences were therefore the natural development of this need to recognize, define, and manage problems on a global scale, rather than through the competitive solutions of empires.

The UN system—its principal organs, specialized agencies, and programmes—was not well suited to broaching such issues, even if it could reasonably claim that it now had universality, having gone from 51 member states in 1945 to 192 at the beginning of the new century. The problem with the UN system was that it was weak in its systemic capacities. There was no organizing brain in the system and it was difficult to broach a global problem in a holistic manner. There was a slow recognition within the UN system that it was ill fitted to deal with global problems. At best it made piecemeal efforts over a period of time, until through the holding of global conferences and follow-up conferences a new organic element in the system began to develop. This was able to overcome the rigidity in the system, the failure of ECOSOC, and the lack of an organizing brain. What in fact emerged was a series of functional global-issue assemblies which went beyond the member states of the UN system, and included substantial elements from global civil society, although these tended to be Western in form and orientation, rather than truly global. Nevertheless, civil society increasingly demanded its say, as it had in the 19th century when there was a surprising number of conferences involving bourgeois elements in society calling for a League of Nations or working class revolutionaries looking towards a working class international. Now, they were able once again to make their voice heard because of the improvement in the technology of communications and of travel. Only in 1960 did more people cross the Atlantic by air than by sea, and it was the advent of rapid communications through radio initially, as well as telephone and telex, combined with cheap air travel, that enabled the world community to come together. This then developed through fax, email, and the like, as well as twenty-four-hour news coverage, into a community which was not controlled from any centre, but was nevertheless sufficiently informed and aware of the nature of global problems that it wanted to have its say. As Paul Taylor puts it, there was 'a critical interaction between concern and knowledge'.[14]

There are many purposes that global conferences have been used to serve. Perhaps the most important one is a commitment to normative development of standards of conduct and their monitoring. Where there is a consensus on a norm emerging from a global conference, this is a prelude to it becoming part of soft law, and eventually, perhaps, entering into the full rigour of international law. Not only is it a matter of setting out standards, there is also the question of their implementation. This normally takes the form of an action plan which is agreed upon at the conference and is thereafter reviewed often after a period of five or ten years. The review conferences create a momentum so that the process becomes cumulative, but at the same time there is a danger that it may become routinized. However, by holding such conferences somewhat outside of the normal system of the General Assembly and the UN in general, these elements of routinization can be kept within reasonable bounds while conferences do introduce new issues and approaches into the UN's bloodstream.

One of the great functions of global conferences is to respond to the need to identify and manage new issue areas, such as the environment. The environment as an issue for general consideration among governments, NGOs, and individuals emerged through the 1950s and 1960s and is typified by a best-selling book by Rachel Carson called *Silent Spring* (1962),[15] which made a big impact in the English-speaking world and beyond. This was a wakening call which led eventually to the proposal by the Swedish government to hold the first environmental conference in 1972 in Stockholm. Rio, Kyoto, Copenhagen, and Cancun are the names of towns which are all evocative of a concern with the global problem of environmental degradation. However, global conferences are not only the result of a lookout which points to a growing problem on the horizon. The function of global conferences is also to respond to new developments in older issue areas. Such developments may not be best broached through existing institutions and require a new look, a new impetus, a new knowledge, all of which are more likely to be fostered in the context of a global conference, than in routine meetings in the General Assembly or the specialized agencies. This exemplifies the need to go beyond the archives in the search for new answers. Typically when a question arises in a well-established organization, the attitude of many delegates is to look at what they did last time and to see whether they need to change, rather than to look at a particular problem from a new angle or with a new perception. In short, they are victim of the tyranny of the archives, and one of the purposes of global conferences is to go beyond the archives in the search for new answers to create a non-routine climate of interest, and above all to have a holistic approach to an issue area which is not covered comfortably at the present time by the specialized agencies and programmes.

The conference can make recommendations to government and others such as international organizations and the institutions of civil society, or it may go even further to take decisions to create treaty obligations, which are binding upon governments. In so doing it may change the priorities on the international agenda, and in the outcome there is often the creation of a new institution which embodies the normative framework, the agreed recommendations, and possibly decisions which are written into treaties. If we leave aside, as Willetts suggests,[16] pledging conferences, commodity conferences, and regional conferences, we are in the midst of a process of learning to hang together for fear that we shall hang separately if we do not do so.

14.4 THE PROCESS OF CONFERENCE DIPLOMACY[17]

Conference diplomacy has come a long way since Friedrich von Gentz was called the First Secretary of Europe for the role he played in the Vienna Congress of 1815. He was a Prussian working at the request of the Austrians and his tasks were both administrative and, to some degree, political, although the main function of von Gentz was to service the conference. Nowadays the process invariably begins when a country, or a group of countries, persuades the General Assembly or ECOSOC that a conference is needed. The Assembly then looks into the matter of securing a host country, if one has not put itself forward, and setting up a preparatory committee (PrepCom). The timetable is established which will give usually one or two years for the PrepCom to establish itself and work through a rough agenda, the date will already have been fixed for the conference itself, which normally lasts anything from one week to three weeks. At the same time, a conference budget is set and the UN secretary-general appoints a secretary-general for the conference, who has usually had experience with an appropriate UN body. The organic structure at this point consists of a chair, usually the host country, then a Plenary Meeting of the Whole, which has the formal decision-making power, and below that is a Committee of the Whole, next down the hierarchy is a bifurcation between a Committee of the Whole on the Declaration and a Committee of the Whole which is concerned with the Programme of Action, which may have various sub-committees of the whole on special items. Such is the formal structure but as negotiations progress informal ad hoc groupings proliferate to address specific issues either on the text itself or of procedure.

It is in the PrepCom that much of the work is done which will ensure the success or otherwise of the subsequent conference. The PrepCom agrees on the agenda or the themes of the conference, often through regional preparatory meetings, and the secretary-general usually produces a first draft. Various caucusing groups tend to load this text with all their concerns and then the process is one of shedding particular items through a process of bargaining. Eventually a document is produced which is normally littered with square brackets around phrases or sentences that have not been approved by the PrepCom Committee of the Whole. The function of the final conference, at which ministers may be present, is to remove the square brackets through a process of definition and compromise. Since this can only be done by major political figures, countries tend to save their concessions until such ministers are there, so that they have something to offer in the final maelstrom of confusion, as the sand in the hourglass is slipping away. Indeed, in some instances it is necessary to stop the clock so that the business can be achieved before the official deadline. On one occasion in the EU, when agreement was not achieved by the midnight deadline and the British were in the chair, it was decided to respect the deadline by simply taking British time rather than Brussels time, to give the delegates the extra hour they needed to complete their work!

The PrepCom has much work to do, and this is why it needs a significant period of time to achieve consensus. Consensus is a requirement if both the normative part of the work and the action programme are to be effective. This consensus may be a matter of reluctance for some actors, but they do not wish to stop the whole movement forward towards a declaration and action programme. It is a matter of grave political concern if one player wrecks the whole process and retribution from the others is to be expected.

In all of this process the conference secretary-general and the chair are not the same—the chair being a state. The secretary-general is usually a senior UN official, knowledgeable about the substance of the conference. Both the chair and secretary-general have not only to make all the necessary administrative arrangements, but also to exercise political leadership. They therefore need a great deal of experience, to be able to command respect, a clear grasp of procedure, and the ability to cooperate with the Secretariat and other officials at the conference.[18] They need to stay in touch informally with a large number of actors, not only governments, but also actors from civil society. In a sense, they become denationalized, because they serve the whole, rather than their particular country. They are often aided by a group of 'Friends of the Chair', who tender both support and advice, and if necessary, build bridges between the chair, secretary-general, and recognized groups—a most important function.

Individual delegations to a conference are often staffed by high-flyers, and indeed, generally speaking for a diplomat to spend part, or a considerable part, of his or her career in a situation of multilateral diplomacy, including conference diplomacy, is a sign of a good career in the making. Normally a delegation has a mixture of experts on the institutionalized process of a particular conference, and experts on its substance. Each has a contribution to make and that of the element from the mission to the UN brings information about the caucus structure, individual personalities, vote trading situations in general, previous discussion, how the organizational milieu works, including the role of the secretariat, and like matters in order to be able to operate effectively. On the other hand, the experts on substance are able to use the knowledge about process in order to achieve the policy goals on the substance of the conference, be it the environment, women, or whatever. The mission will normally have instructions and ideally these include firm general political backing from their home government, the delineation of strategic goals to be achieved, but also the freedom to exercise tactical flexibility in their achievement. Small countries tend to have a limited number of specific goals and act to achieve them in the decision-making process, whereas large countries tend to consider the full range of the agenda as set out in the PrepCom. Groups of states will want to have their 'traditional' concerns registered in the text irrespective of the conference's actual substance.

In the UK case, when a conference is on the horizon, bids are invited to be the lead department, and then a consultative process is set up in support of that lead department. In fact the lead department normally 'picks itself' because of the subject matter, whether it likes it or not. Usually the Foreign Office does the process elements of meetings and the interdepartmental committee will manage the substance. A British delegation to a conference will normally include ten to fifteen specialists, who have an onerous task, particularly when the conference is held over a period of one to three weeks. The day can often start at 6 am with meetings of the UK delegation, and then there are consultations with NGOs and coordination within the European Union. Meetings of the Whole, and other meetings on the text, may begin at 8.00 or 9.00 am and often lunch is spent again with other members of the EU and with the EU Commission. Since conferences are often not held in UN premises, delegations have to procure meeting and office facilities in embassies, consulates, or hotels. 'Hand-held' and laptop technology are much used but this creates problems in keeping communications secure and protected. In all of this the EU is central. In the evening there are social events, such as receptions, and there are also meetings of UN official groups, such as the Western European and Other Group or the EU. The day ends in the early hours, while, towards the end of the conference, nego-tiations might go right through the night with individuals in a state of utter exhaustion.

There is a range of types of meeting, going from the formal to the formal-informal, to the informal, or even 'informal informals'! There are also papers and non-papers. In this wide range of process, not only are there government actors, but there are also delega-tions from international organizations, and a host of NGOs. NGOs are important, because they are an element of civil society, although hardly representative of global civil society, since they tend to be organizations that come from developed countries, which are adept at acting in a Westernized decision-making process. Increasingly, however, national NGOs, which are often from the 'South', are playing a role. This still leaves out many organizations, which, nevertheless, are capable of generating the movement of goods, services, ideas, and people, as was seen when, to the astonishment of some, it proved very difficult to track electronically financial dealings in the pursuit of terrorist organizations, since they were operating in a different cultural milieu. Nevertheless, despite this obvious bias, the role of NGOs is to provide information and resources. They are adept at fact-finding and have a role as a moral witness, especially in the implemen-tation of an action plan. They produce conference newspapers which have a great influ-ence and provide a large amount of information for small delegations. They also organize parallel events, and indeed, global society has its own institutions for conference diplo-macy, such as the Global Social Forum and the Davos Meetings. They take themselves very seriously and see themselves as equal with states in terms of legitimacy, which pro-vokes a state backlash that is becoming increasingly evident.

At the end, there is, in a successful outcome, a clear normative declaration of principles and an action plan with an agreement about how it might be implemented. To follow this up, there is then a review conference, which may be held five or ten years after the initial conference and the process for that will start two years before the review conference. There is, therefore, a process of routinization, and this can be seen clearly in the sequence of conferences concerned with the environment, beginning with the Stockholm Conference in 1972 and continuing through to the conference in Rio + 20 in 2012. This routinization has the benefit of being able to build on the past, but it has the drawback that it no longer brings the shock of the new. There are now files, ideas, friendships, groups, and animosities from previous meetings. Thus there is an advantage that a problem may have become clearer, even if the way of managing it still eludes agreement. What counts in the end is a formal treaty and its review process.

14.5 Winham on Negotiations

In a seminal article Gilbert Winham not only surveyed the literature on negotiation as a management process, but also drew on his own research, particularly with trade negotiations.[19] Examining Winham's insights we can see a pattern of negotiations which, in essence, boils down to three major elements. The first is to agree upon a definition of the problem. The second is to find a solution to that problem, and the third is to sell it back to major stakeholders who have not taken part in the process.

It is not always easy to agree upon a definition of what the situation is. Indeed, negotiations frequently start before the parties to the negotiation have a clear idea of the complexity of the issue, be it the long process to negotiate a new law of the sea, or to negotiate a trade round. The initial process lies in the governments of the participating states, as the various ministries and pressure groups come together to light upon an initial position. The various governments then, in their turn, come together and it may take a matter of years before they finally agree on the nature of the problem about which they will negotiate. To a limited degree, the most important point is not whether their interpretation is correct, but that they have agreed on the nature of a problem.

Finding a solution is again a matter of years, when there are periods of intense negotiation and then periods when no negotiation takes place, but there is reflection on the progress achieved and the problems yet to be resolved. Finally, an agreement is made about an appropriate way of dealing with the problem, and the third question comes to light, which is selling it back to the principals.

Because the process may have taken several years, clearly the actors have changed and so have the negotiators. Whereas in the beginning they may be the representative of the states who are negotiating together, as they go through a long sustained process and develop expectations, interpretations, and common subjectivities, they may become more agents of the process, rather than agents of the state. Thus an ambassador might start off as the ambassador of country A, but end up the ambassador of the process to his or her own country, selling the nature of the problem and solution they have found back to his or her own home government. But in the meantime the government may have moved, and indeed gone through several iterations, so that the ambassador risks losing contact with his or her principals. It is for this reason that in global conferences it is often necessary to have ministers and indeed, heads of government, in at the final last minute chaos or confusion, when positions are changed, important principles modified, and the general lemming instinct to find a solution prevails. Otherwise the final result will be rejected by the principal governments.

Winham brings out this process well. He begins by arguing that the traditional view of diplomacy was one in which 'skill, cunning, and craft' predominated: 'Negotiation is considered to be the management of people through guile, and we recognize guile as the trademark of the profession.'[20] He then suggests that there has been 'a meshing of great systems', since, 'Unquestionably, modern negotiation continues to be a contest of will and wit, but the emphasis has shifted. The principal problem for most contemporary negotiators is not to outwit their adversaries, but rather to create a structure out of a large mass of information wherein it is possible to apply human wit.' He goes on to point out that 'Most modern negotiations are carried on between teams that represent bureaucracies, and in large negotiations the teams themselves approach the status of small bureaucracies.'[21]

Winham observes that the motivation for undertaking negotiations include 'reducing uncertainty'.[22] He comments that the negotiation process 'involves a search for acceptable solutions' where unattractive solutions can be kept off the table and 'the development of common perceptions becomes more important to the negotiating process than the exchange of concessions'. Consequently, 'theories of how people develop common perceptions of complex information are more likely to be useful than theories of how people outwit others in bargaining contests'.[23]

Winham insists upon the trial and error nature of negotiations owing to governments' tendency to delay serious engagement with an issue until after negotiations have begun and also because 'what is acceptable is a function of what is available, and that is only demonstrated in the act of negotiation'.[24]

He stresses that the reality of negotiations is tedium, not glamour, not the least because the obstacles to agreement are political rather than intellectual. However,

> Where conflict is resolved, the issue is put aside and is usually not raised again. As the area of agreement widens, the parties develop a greater stake in the negotiation, and this creates a positive momentum toward a final, overall agreement. If in this process parties are unable to agree, they will drop the issue and hence postpone the conflict. The issue in question will be moved up for consideration at a higher level in the negotiating bureaucracy. The same procedure will be used; hence, the most difficult and conflictual issues will be put off until the end of the negotiation.[25]

Eventually the pressure to arrive at some form of agreement mounts, both within the negotiating process itself and also from the principals. Lack of agreement is beginning to hold up other processes. In a situation where a time limit becomes necessary, 'There is ample evidence that the last-minute decisions in a large scale negotiation are taken amid great confusion.'[26] Ample evidence of this proposition could be seen in the agreements made at Cancun on the environment in December 2010. Positions that have been defended valiantly for many months may be pushed aside for the greater need to have an agreement. In some senses the individual notion of self-interest becomes overwhelmed by the collective need for a common interest, which is some form of agreement that all can live with, albeit a much interpreted and possibly fudged final agreement, but one which, nevertheless, has the potential, at least for substance, in the form of an action policy. The devil still remains in the detail. Negotiations about that are still to come, but there is a great sense that a Rubicon has been crossed. The possibilities of misunderstanding are very clear, some of which must be put down to differences of culture. If the language of discourse were, for example, Japanese or German, instead of English, then the processes of negotiation would be likely to be quite different, and when speakers of languages other than English return to their home negotiation framework and culture, then the translation of what has been agreed may be difficult to undertake. To get a taste of these difficulties, which cannot be explored in a chapter of this scale, the work of Raymond Cohen[27] and that of Karen Mingst and Craig Warkentin can be recommended as insightful and knowledgeable.[28] We must, however, not be complacent since some high-profile negotiations fail. Seattle and Copenhagen are recent examples. But the momentum is maintained by those who perceive that they may be blamed or punished if they fail.

14.6 CONCLUSIONS

This chapter began with an account of how conference diplomacy emerged from the pursuit of state interests by the great powers, in particular, in an international setting. This framework was largely predominant until 1970, but thereafter there has been a change of tone, whereby conference diplomacy has been much more concerned with the search for common interests in a multilateral and multilevel setting. The reason for this is primarily the growth of global problems, which are, themselves, exacerbated by the process of globalization. In turn global conferences have extended the UN system to enfranchise new actors, but also to take a fresh look at old problems. Schechter quotes the Chilean diplomat Juan Somavia, who chaired the PrepComs for the World Summit for Social Development, to the effect that 'they are the only common response of the world community to a disorderly process of globalization that runs the risk of spinning out of control'.[29]

In short, there has been a gradual recognition in the UN system that global problems must be tackled, in terms of the common interest, in a holistic manner. Hitherto, specialized agencies had somewhat inhibited this recognition, but the success and frequency of such conferences has overcome these reticencies. However, the process is partially 'imprisoned' by state sovereignty.[30] This takes the form of consensus. Any attempt at broaching a global problem will have veto holders, who are those without whom a global solution is not possible, or those without whom such a solution would be severely inhibited. We have seen such dragging of the feet by the attitude of the United States towards the Kyoto Protocol.

While no one conceived of global conferences as a systemic institutional factor, this is what they have become, and their cumulative effect has been to add a new dimension to the UN system. It is a major reform in the system, which had not been foreseen in the Charter, and one that is now clearly here to stay.[31] Global conferences are not just the result of growing awareness of one-world problems; they are also an occasion for opportunities in which actors can do together that which they cannot do separately.

Such actors include NGOs, who not only have information and resources but can also act as a watchdog with a big bark, if a rather a small bite. Global conferences are an essential element towards the enfranchisement of relevant non-state actors which can provide a useful input into the decision-making process. Such non-state actors are not without their drawbacks in that they tend to engage in turf wars and are reluctant to think and act in a holistic or systemic manner, since they may fear that such cooperation could put at risk their very being, or at least their financial and ideological basis.[32]

We can now identify three periods of global conferences. The first period was the 1970s and 1980s which was one of expansion. In the 1980s there was a slowing or stabilization of the process whereas from the 1990s until the present we can see a systematic institutionalization as part of the UN system. There are relatively few new topics, since many important ones have already been broached and are covered by developments in review conferences. So an attempted moratorium on new conferences led by the United States which declined to finance them has de facto failed or led to their replacement by summit diplomacy, for example the G20. But implementation of G20 decisions still requires the engagement of the UN system.

A more recent assessment of global conferences is that of Thomas Weiss and Ramesh Thakur, whose summary of the positive and debit sides of the ledger many would agree with. On the positive side of the ledger they cite the following achievements:

> they have synthesized existing knowledge; they have changed discourses, priorities, and policies, they have established or endorsed global norms and international standards, principles, and guidelines; they have mobilized governments, NGOs, and global public opinion; they have catalyzed resources, institutions, national institutional infrastructures (e.g., for reporting on human rights, health, and gender equality indicators); and they have legitimized and empowered national ministries and bureaucracies and transnational social movements and networks.[33]

On the debit side they state that:

> Most important, such conferences rarely result in legally binding conventions and treaties. Not setting measurable targets and benchmarks leaves conferences with symbolic rather than substantive accomplishments. Setting targets but not monitoring and achieving them undermines the conference as well as the legitimacy of the United Nations as the convening authority. However, 'failure' would be too strong and misleading. A conference might be said to have failed if there is no agreed final

document, if the final document is a formula to mask substantive disagreement, or if the final document expresses aspirations and endorses principles but does not contain binding and measurable commitments, benchmarks, and targets. Yet none of this would give us a true indication of the global and long-term impact of the conference in raising a new issue, reframing an existing issue, or even focusing more international attention on an issue so that the existing consensus could be shifted and the boundaries of possible action could be expanded.[34]

Perhaps we should also add, on the positive side, that not only have actors from global civil society been enfranchised, but that they have indeed formed their own unofficial global conferences beyond the setting of the official ones, and these are attended, not only by global society actors, but also by governments and international governmental organizations; Davos and the Global Social Forum are examples of such conferences.

Is it going too far to argue that global conferences have become an intermittent and weak functional parliament that goes beyond the state system? If that is indeed the case, or at least the tendency, then David Mitrany will be smiling in his grave. Perhaps we are, at last, on a road towards a working peace system, where the secrecy of traditional diplomacy until the 20th century has given way as a basic norm, in some aspects, to the notion of transparency.

Notes

1. Sir Harold Nicolson, *Diplomacy*, 2nd ed. (London: Oxford University Press, 1958), 17.
2. F.S. Northedge, *The League of Nations* (Leicester: Leicester University Press, 1988), 6.
3. Quoted in Northedge, *League of Nations*, 8.
4. Nicolson, *Diplomacy*, 145.
5. Hudson Meadwell, 'The long nineteenth century in Europe', *Review of International Studies* 27 (December 2001), 165.
6. Northedge, *League of Nations*, 8.
7. Northedge, *League of Nations*, 10.
8. Quoted in Nicolson, *Diplomacy*, 155.
9. Nicolson, *Diplomacy*, 157.
10. Nicolson, *Diplomacy*, 158.
11. Johan Kaufmann, *Conference Diplomacy*, 2nd ed. (Dordrecht: Martinus Nijhoff, 1988), 1–2.
12. Kaufmann, *Conference Diplomacy*, 2–3.
13. Quoted in Michael Schechter, *UN Global Conferences* (London: Routledge, 2005), 12.
14. Paul Taylor and A.J.R. Groom (eds), *Global Issues in the UN Nations Framework* (Houndmills: Macmillan, 1989), 13.
15. Rachel Carson, *Silent Spring* (London: Penguin Classics, 2000).
16. Peter Willetts, 'The Pattern of Conferences', in Taylor and Groom (eds), *Global Issues*, 39.
17. I am grateful to members of the UK Foreign and Commonwealth Office for advice on the process.
18. For an account by the president of a conference, see Chapter 45, this volume, on the 1995 Nuclear Nonproliferation Treaty Review and Extension Conference.
19. Gilbert Winham, 'Negotiation as a Management Process', *World Politics* 30:1 (October 1977), 86–113.

20. Winham, 'Negotiation as a Management Process', 87.
21. Winham, 'Negotiation as a Management Process', 91.
22. Winham, 'Negotiation as a Management Process', 96.
23. Winham, 'Negotiation as a Management Process', 97.
24. Winham, 'Negotiation as a Management Process', 99.
25. Winham, 'Negotiation as a Management Process', 103–4.
26. Winham, 'Negotiation as a Management Process', 109.
27. Raymond Cohen, 'Meaning, Interpretation and International Negotiation', *Global Society* 14:3 (2000), 317–35.
28. Karen A. Mingst and Craig P. Warkentin, 'What difference does culture make in multilateral negotiation?', *Global Governance* 2:2 (1996), 169–88.
29. Schechter, *UN Global Conferences*, 195.
30. Ann Marie Clark, Elisabeth J. Friedman, and Kathryn Hochstetler, 'The Sovereign Limits of Global Civil Society', *World Politics* 51:1 (October 1998), 35.
31. Taylor and Groom (eds), *Global Issues*, 292.
32. Taylor and Groom (eds), *Global Issues*, 294–5.
33. Thomas G. Weiss and Ramesh Thakur, *Global Governance and the UN: An Unfinished Journey* (Bloomington: Indiana University Press, 2010), 224.
34. Weiss and Thakur, *Global Governance and the UN*, 225.

CHAPTER 15

....

COMMISSION DIPLOMACY

....

GARETH EVANS

HIGH-LEVEL panels and commissions of the global great and good, delivering them-selves of weighty reports on matters of international policy moment, were almost unknown until the later cold war years but have become in recent decades a very busy second-track diplomatic industry. Lester Pearson's *Partners in Development* report in 1969 was an early foretaste of what was to come, but the pace was really set by Willy Brandt's Independent Commission on International Development Issues report, *North-South: A Programme for Survival*, in 1980, followed shortly thereafter by major reports from Olaf Palme's Independent Commission on Disarmament and Security Issues in 1982 and Gro Harlem Brundtland's World Commission on Environment and Development in 1987.

Since then more than another thirty such commissions have come and gone, harness-ing the collective talents of over five hundred individual commissioners and panellists to report on issues across the security, development, and general governance spectrum (see Table 15.1).[1] And three more have been announced while this chapter was in prepa-ration—on the death penalty, drug policy, and elections, chaired respectively by Federico Mayor, Fernando Henrique Cardoso, and Kofi Annan.[2]

The distinctive characteristics of these commissions and panels are that they are con-vened to address particular international policy problems (albeit often extremely broadly defined); the problems they address are global rather than country-specific or regional in scope;[3] their advice, though formally sought by a particular international organization, government, or combination of sponsors, is directed to the broader international com-munity; their membership is international; they are independent in character, with their members appointed in their personal capacity rather than as representatives of their states or organizations, even if holding executive office at the time; and they have a finite rather than ongoing lifespan (most commonly two to three years).

The impact of the commissions and panels under review has varied enormously. Some have fundamentally changed the terms of international policy debate—the Brundtland Commission's introduction of the concept of 'sustainable development' being the clearest and best-known example—but a number of others, perhaps too many for comfort given the resources and energy invested in them, have sunk utterly without trace. The discussion which follows will seek to evaluate the utility and significance of 'commission diplomacy' overall, and to explain—at least from one insider's perspective[4]—why some commissions are successful and others are not.

15.1 THE CONTRIBUTION OF COMMISSION DIPLOMACY

The necessary threshold question is what counts as success. Is it operational: achieving specific policy action—or at least clarifying and setting action agendas which are embraced by the relevant players? Is it normative: changing the terms of the policy debate on some issue in a way which is better likely to produce consensus over time, if not immediately? Is it enough that a commission simply raises the profile of an issue or problem which has been neglected, if nothing else changes? Or that the commission can reasonably claim to have added to the general store of knowledge?

The short answer is that an ideally successful commission would touch every one of these bases: add knowledge, raise the global profile of an issue, find new and more consensual ways of debating it, set a credible policy agenda with measurable milestones, and directly influence specific policy actions which are widely seen as beneficial in terms of helping to reduce deadly conflict, improve the quality of human life, better protect the environment, or make for better global or national governance.

15.1.1 Operational Impact

There are fewer clear examples than one might expect of commission reports generating directly attributable executive action. While the commissions chaired by Jeffrey Sachs (on Macroeconomics and Health in 2001, and the UN Millennium Project in 2005), for instance, have generated a vast number of specific practical recommendations on the implementation of the Millennium Development Goals (MDGs), the take-up rate to date has been quite low. The Pearson Commission (1969)—strongly supported by the Brandt Commission (1980)—can reasonably claim original authorship of the 0.7 per cent of GDP target for Overseas Development Assistance now universally accepted as at least an aspirational goal.[5] The Brandt Commission itself can reasonably claim to have had a catalytic effect on the 1981 North–South Summit in Cancun, which can in turn be viewed as an important precursor to the 2000 UN Millennium Summit which advanced the MDGs.[6] But the most directly influential of all the development-focused reports to date—not only in its normative but its operational impact—has probably been the Brundtland Commission (1987). It directly generated the Rio Earth Summit in 1992, the then largest ever meeting of world leaders, which in turn led to the Kyoto Agreements on climate, the Biodiversity Convention, and Agenda 21, as well as helping the establishment of thewO-

Table 15.1. International policy commissions and panels 1960–2010[7]

A. Security Focused

Name	Initiating or Major Sponsoring Government/ Organization	Chair	Report	Year
Independent Commission on Disarmament and Security Issues	Austria et al.	Olof Palme + 15 commissioners	Common Security: A Programme for Disarmament (London: Pan Books, 1982)	1982
Independent Commission on International Humanitarian Issues	Switzerland et al.	Sadruddin Aga Khan, Prince Hassan bin Talal + 26 commissioners	Winning the Human Race? (London: Zed Books, 1998)	1988
Canberra Commission on the Elimination of Nuclear Weapons	Australia	Richard Butler + 16 commissioners	Report of the Canberra Commission on the Elimination of Nuclear Weapons, <http://www.dfat.gov.au/publications/security/canberra-commission-report/index.html>	1996
Carnegie Commission on Preventing Deadly Conflict	Carnegie Corporation of New York	David A. Hamburg, Cyrus R. Vance + 14 commissioners	Preventing Deadly Conflict: Final Report (New York: Carnegie Corporation of New York, 1997)	1997
Independent International Commission on Kosovo	Sweden et al.	Justice Richard Goldstone, Carl Tham + 11 commissioners	The Kosovo Report (Oxford: Oxford University Press, 2000)	2000
			Why Conditional Independence?, <http://heimat.de/home/illyria/kosovocommission.org_report_english_2001.pdf>	2001

A. Security Focused

Name	Initiating or Major Sponsoring Government/ Organization	Chair	Report	Year
Panel on United Nations Peace Operations	United Nations	Lakhdar Brahimi + 9 panellists	Report of the Panel On United Nations Peace Operations, <http://www.un.org/peace/ reports/peace_operations/>	2000
International Commission on Intervention and State Sovereignty (ICISS)	Canada	Gareth Evans, Mohamed Sahnoun + 10 commissioners	The Responsibility to Protect, <http://www. globalr2p.org/media/pdf/ICISS_Report.pdf>	2001
Commission on Human Security	Japan	Sadako Ogata, Amartya Sen + 10 commissioners	Human Security Now, <http://www. humansecurity-chs.org/finalreport/index. html>	2003
High-Level Panel on Threats, Challenges, and Change	United Nations	Anand Panyarachun + 15 panellists	A More Secure World: Our Shared Responsibility, <http://www.un.org/ secureworld/>	2004
Weapons of Mass Destruction Commission	Sweden	Hans Blix + 13 commissioners	Weapons of Terror, <http://www. wmdcommission.org/files/ Weapons_of_Terror.pdf>	2006
Independent Commission on the Role of the IAEA to 2020 and Beyond	IAEA	Ernesto Zedillo + 17 commissioners	Reinforcing the Global Nuclear Order for Peace and Prosperity: The Role of the IAEA to 2020 and Beyond, <http:// www.iaea.org/NewsCenter/News/ PDF/2020report0508.pdf>	2007

(continued)

Table 15.1. (Continued)

A. Security Focused

Name	Initiating or Major Sponsoring Government/Organization	Chair	Report	Year
International Commission on Nuclear Non-Proliferation and Disarmament (ICNND)	Australia, Japan	Gareth Evans, Yoriko Kawaguchi + 13 commissioners	Eliminating Nuclear Threats: A Practical Agenda for Global Policymakers, <http://www.icnnd.org/reference/reports/ent/default.html>	2009

B. Development Focused

Commission on International Development	World Bank	Lester Pearson + 8 commissioners	Partners in Development (New York: Praeger, 1969)	1969
Independent Commission on International Development Issues	Netherlands et al.	Willy Brandt + 17 commissioners	North–South: A Programme for Survival (Cambridge, MA: MIT Press, 1980)	1980
			Common Crisis: North–South Cooperation for World Recovery (Cambridge, MA: MIT Press, 1983)	1983
World Commission on Environment and Development	United Nations	Gro Harlem Brundtland + 20 commissioners	Our Common Future: The World Commission on Environment and Development (Oxford: Oxford University Press, 1987), <http://www.un-documents.net/wced-ocf.htm>	1987
The South Commission	Malaysia	Julius Nyerere + 26 commissioners	The Challenge to the South (Oxford: Oxford University Press, 1990)	1990

B. Development Focused

Name	Initiating or Major Sponsoring Government/ Organization	Chair	Report	Year
International Commission on Peace and Food	United Nations	M.S. Swaminathan + 24 commissioners	*Uncommon Opportunities: An Agenda for Peace and Equitable Development* (London: Zed Books, 1994), <http://www.icpd.org/UncommonOpp/inde.htm>	1994
World Commission on Culture and Development	UNESCO	Javier Peres de Cuellar + 13	*Our Creative Diversity*, <http://unesdoc.unesco.org/images/0010/001016/101651e.pdf>	1995
Independent Commission on Population and Quality of Life	UNESCO et al.	Maria de Lourdes Pomtasilgo + 18 commissioners	*Caring for the Future: Making the Next Decades Provide a Life Worth Living* (Oxford: Oxford University Press, 1996)	1996
World Commission on Dams	World Bank, IUCN-The World Conservation Union	Kader Asmal + 11 commissioners	Dams & Development: A New Framework for Decision-Making, <http://hqweb.unep.org/dams/WCD/report/WCD_DAMS%20report.pdf>	2001
High-Level Panel on Financing for Development	United Nations	Ernesto Zedillo + 10 panellists	Financing for Development, <http://www.un.org/reports/financing/>	2001
Commission on Macroeconomics and Health	World Health Organization	Jeffrey Sachs + 17 commissioners	Macroeconomics and Health: Investing in Health for Economic Development, <http://whqlibdoc.who.int/publications/2001/924154550x.pdf>	2001

(continued)

Table 15.1. (Continued)

B. Development Focused

Name	Initiating or Major Sponsoring Government/ Organization	Chair	Report	Year
Commission on Private Sector and Development	United Nations	Paul Martin, Ernesto Zedillo + 15 commissioners	Unleashing Entrepreneurship. Making Business Work for the Poor, <http://www.undp.org/cpsd/documents/report/english/fullreport.pdf>	2004
World Commission on the Social Dimension of Globalization	International Labour Organization	Tarja Halonen, Benjamin Mkapa + 19 commissioners	A Fair Globalisation: Creating Opportunities for All, <http://www.ilo.org/fairglobalization/report/lang--en/index.htm>	2004
Global Commission on International Migration	United Nations	Jan Karlsson, Mamphela Ramphele + 18 commissioners	Migration in an Interconnected World: New Directions for Action, <http://www.gcim.org>	2005
Global Commission on Social Determinants of Health	World Health Organization	Michael Marmot + 18 commissioners	Closing the Gap in a Generation: Health Equity through Action on the Social Determinants of Health, <http://www.who.int/social_determinants/thecommission/en/>	2008
UN Millennium Project	United Nations	Jeffrey Sachs + 25 task force coordinators	Investing in Development: A Practical Plan to Achieve the Millennium Development Goals, <http://www.unmillenniumproject.org/reports/fullreport.htm>	2005
Commission on Growth and Development	Australia, Netherlands, Sweden, UK, Hewlett Foundation, World Bank	Michael Spence + 21 commissioners	The Growth Report: Strategies for Sustained Growth and Inclusive Development, <http://www.growthcommission.org/index.php?Itemid=169&tid=96&toption=com_content&task=view>	2008

B. Development Focused

Name	Initiating or Major Sponsoring Government/ Organization	Chair	Report	Year
Commission on Legal Empowerment of the Poor	United Nations	Madeleine Albright, Hernando de Soto + 22 commissioners	Making the Law Work for Everyone, <http://www.undp.org/legalempowerment/reports/concept2action.html>	2008

C. Governance Focused

Name	Initiating or Major Sponsoring Government/ Organization	Chair	Report	Year
Independent Advisory Group on UN Financing	Ford Foundation	Shijuro Ogata Paul Volcker + 9 members	Financing an Effective United Nations (New York: Ford Foundation, 1993)	1993
Independent Working Group on the Future of the United Nations	Ford Foundation	Moeen Qureshi Richard von Wiezacker + 10 members	The United Nations in the Second Half-Century, <http://www.library.yale.edu/un/unhome.htm>	1995
Commission on Global Governance	Sweden, Netherlands, Norway et al.	Ingvar Carlsson, Shridath Ramphal + 26 commissioners	Our Global Neighbourhood (Oxford: Oxford University Press, 2005)	1995
Panel of Eminent Persons on United Nations–Civil Society Relations	United Nations	Fernando Henrique Cardoso + 11 panelists	Report of the Panel of Eminent Persons on United Nations–Civil Society Relations, <http://www.un.org/reform/civilsociety/panel.shtml>	2004

(continued)

Table 15.1. (Continued)

C. Governance Focused

Name	Initiating or Major Sponsoring Government/ Organization	Chair	Report	Year
High-Level Panel on United Nations System-Wide Coherence	United Nations	Shaukat Aziz, Luisa Dias Diogo, Jens Stoltenberg + 12 panelists	Delivering as One: Report of the High-Level Panel on UN System-Wide Coherence in the Areas of Development, Humanitarian Assistance and the Environment, <http://www.un.org/events/panel/>	2006
International Taskforce on Global Public Goods	France, Sweden	Ernesto Zedillo, Tidjane Thiam + 15 members	*Meeting Global Challenges: International Cooperation in the National Interest* (ITFG/Swedish Foreign Ministry, 2006), <http://www.ycsg.yale.edu/activities/collabora-tions_taskforce.html>	2006
High-Level Commission on Modernizing the Governance of the World Bank Group	World Bank	Ernesto Zedillo + 10 members	Repowering the World Bank for the 21st Century, <http://siteresources.worldbank.org/NEWS/Resources/WBGovernanceCOMMISSIONREPORT.pdf>	2009

zone Layer Protocol and stimulating a multitude of other ongoing international, regional, national, and local initiatives.[8]

On the security side, Lakhdar Brahimi's Panel on United Nations Peace Operations (2000) produced a number of important changes to peacekeeping practice in the aftermath of the debacles in the 1990s in Srebrenica and elsewhere, when blue helmeted soldiers found themselves without the mandate or capacity to protect civilians under threat of deadly violence. More recently, the military interventions in Libya and to some extent Côte d'Ivoire in early 2011 were based on direct invocation by the UN Security Council of the 'responsibility to protect' concept championed by the International Commission on Intervention and State Sovereignty (ICISS) in 2001 and the High-Level Panel on Threats, Challenges, and Change (2004), and subsequently embraced by the UN General Assembly at the 2005 World Summit. No such consensus had been previously possible around the 'right of humanitarian intervention' in the even more conscience-shocking mass atrocity crime situations that erupted in Rwanda and the Balkans in the 1990s, and it is reasonable to attribute the change directly to the work of these commissions.

A number of commissions, in the security as well as development areas, have played a significant role, if not in generating clear-cut specific executive action, at least in clarifying and setting *agendas* for action which have been widely seen as useful by policy-makers. The report of the International Commission on Nuclear Non-Proliferation and Disarmament (2009) had only a limited direct impact on the language of the 2010 Nuclear Non-Proliferation Treaty (NPT) Review Conference, but its systematic crafting of very detailed action agendas, with identified benchmarks along the way, for the short term to 2012, the medium term to 2025, and the longer term thereafter was seen by many participating states as an important guide to future priorities which would have a lasting impact.

Commissions focusing on governance issues have had varying operational impacts, with the most ambitious generally being the least visibly successful. The Carlsson–Ramphal Commission on Global Governance (1995) produced a hugely wide-ranging set of recommendations, many of which (like reform of the structure of the Security Council) have stimulated debate and remain on the international agenda, but only a handful—for example, that business recognize its responsibility to and contribute more to good global governance, translated by Kofi Annan at the World Economic Forum in 1999 into the 'Global Compact'—have borne much fruit. Some commission recommendations which did have almost immediate effect were those of the Cardoso Panel on UN–Civil Society Relations (2004) relating to multi-constituency processes and partnerships, which were implemented shortly thereafter in response to the Indian Ocean tsunami of that year.[9]

15.1.2 Normative Impact

Perhaps the greatest of all contributions that global commissions are capable of making—and have made in a number of notable instances—is generating potentially game-changing *ideas*: new ways of thinking about unresolved policy issues with which policy-makers have long wrestled. The overwhelming contribution of the Brundtland Commission in 1987 was to establish a new normative point of departure for virtually all environmental policy since, one which changed both the language and substance of international (and often national) discourse, by identifying 'sustainable development' as conceptual ground that could be commonly shared between one-dimensional pro-growth supporters and environmental protectionists.[10]

No other development-focused commission can claim the same kind of success, although a reasonable argument can be made that the Brandt Commission (1980) was simply ahead of its time in identifying the interdependence and need for solidarity between the global North and South, ideas which have come more into their own in the Bretton Woods institutions and elsewhere in recent years with the accelerated pace of globalization.[11] On the wider governance front Sonny Ramphal makes the not unreasonable claim that the concept of 'governance' itself—as distinct from 'government'—only became common parlance with publication of the Commission on Global Governance's report in 1995.[12]

It is in the security area that the normative impact of commission reports has been most visible, perhaps nowhere more so than in the recent ICISS and High-Level Panel-led emergence, as noted already, of the 'responsibility to protect': an evidently game-changing bridge, in the context of mass atrocity crimes within states, between previously irreconcilable defenders of 'the right to intervene' on the one hand and staunch defenders of more or less absolute state sovereignty on the other. It remains to be seen whether the Security Council-authorized interventions in Libya and Côte d'Ivoire in early 2011 set a new benchmark for more intense international engagement in these atrocity crime situations in the future, or will prove to be the high watermark from which the tide will recede. But the normative shift which has manifestly occurred at the time of writing will be, if sustained, one of the most substantial and fastest ever to occur.[13] An associated normative development over the last two decades has been an increasingly intense commitment by government policy-makers and international organizations—albeit still more evident in their rhetoric than their commitment of resources—to a 'culture of conflict prevention', a commitment strongly encouraged by the very active and resource intensive Carnegie Commission on the Prevention of Deadly Conflict (1997), led by David Hamburg and Cyrus Vance.

The Palme Commission's embrace in 1982 of the concept of 'common security'—that states should seek to find their security with others, rather than against them—was expressly designed to offer an alternative to nuclear deterrence and an endless competitive arms race. The concept did not win much traction among Western policy-makers at the time, but unquestionably (with Commission member Georgi Arbatov playing an important linking role) had a major influence on Mikhail Gorbachev's thinking—in particular his articulation of the notion of a 'common European home'—and as such played its part in ending the cold war. And it has continued to resonate in international strategic debate ever since.[14] So too has the centrepiece of the report of the Canberra Commission on the Elimination of Nuclear Weapons (1996), its simple mantra—that so long as any countries have nuclear weapons others will want them; so long as anyone has them they are bound one day to be used, by accident or design; and any such use would be catastrophic—which has been repeated in the reports of the Blix Weapons of Mass Destruction Commission (1986) and the International Commission on Nuclear Non-Proliferation and Disarmament (2009) and innumerable other contributions to the ongoing debate.[15]

15.1.3 Other Impacts

The role of commissions and panels in raising the profile of previously neglected issues or policy approaches—at least putting them on the radar screens of policy-makers and publics—should not be underestimated. The Pearson (1969) and Brandt (1980) Commissions, although less successful than they hoped in changing government behaviour, gave development issues until then unprecedented publicity, as did the intensely media-focused commissions chaired by Jeffrey Sachs in 2001 and 2005. The Brundtland Commission (1987) may not have initiated international institutional and public commitment to the environment—the initial big step forward came with the Stockholm Conference of 1972 and the establishment of the UN Environment Programme (UNEP)—but it gave those movements dramatic new momentum. Both the Palme (1982) and Canberra (1996) commissions, ahead of their time though they may have been and achieving much less public prominence than the Brundtland Commission, nonetheless unquestionably focused intellectual, activist, and significant policy-maker attention on the possibility of a much more optimistic approach to achieving national security in the nuclear age, and their influence has been lasting.

It is also important to acknowledge that, whatever else they may have achieved in terms of operational or normative impact, a number of commissions have added significantly to the store of knowledge on particular global issues. That is particularly true of those which have sponsored the publication of a major series of associated publications accompanying their main report. The Carnegie Commission (1997) was a standout in this respect, generating ten books and over thirty other substantial reports and papers, as were the Sachs commissions (2001, 2005) on development issues, each producing a shelf-full of working papers and associated publications. The ICISS *Responsibility to Protect* report (2001) was accompanied by a 400-page supplementary volume of research essays, bibliography, and other background material which has become itself an indispensable scholarly resource for all those working in the field of response to mass atrocities.

15.2 WHAT MAKES FOR SUCCESSFUL COMMISSIONS?

The most relevant factors in determining whether a commission or panel makes any kind of useful contribution, or is destined to be consigned directly to bookshelves or hard drives and forever thereafter unread and unremembered, fall into three broad categories: task definition, process, and context. Defining the commission's objectives with clarity—being clear about its target audiences and what they might be expected to do with the fruits of the commission's labours—is absolutely crucial: without this focus from the very outset a meandering product is almost inevitable. Process is equally critical: the way the commission operates in terms of leadership, size, and composition of membership, staffing, available resources, consultative process, the branding and packaging of its report and recommendations, and the quantity and quality of its advocacy and general follow-up.

And then there is simply the context in which the commission's report is produced: whether it is permissive or prohibitive. One element here may be its ownership: whether the government or organization sponsoring a particular commission is perceived as a help or hindrance to its wider embrace, or simply a neutral facilitator. But a more obvious one is timing: whether, given whatever else is going on right then, the world is going to be receptive to innovative or challenging thinking on a particular issue.

15.2.1 Clarity of Objectives

The terms of reference for a global commission or panel, which will usually be defined by its sponsoring government or organization rather than the commission itself, are crucially important. If there is not a well-crafted set of objectives, based on careful prior thought as to what exactly is the issue or problem to be addressed by the commission's report, who constitutes its target audiences, and whether those audiences are likely to perceive any utility in whatever analysis and recommendations the commission comes up with, the enterprise is destined from the outset to founder.[16]

That fate has afflicted more than one commission with which the present author has been associated. France and Sweden no doubt thought it a good idea at the time to establish the International Task Force on Global Public Goods (2006), given the familiar problems of achieving cooperative, collective action on a variety of global problems ranging from health to the environment, financial stability, weapons of mass destruction, and knowledge availability. But the commission struggled from the outset in meeting its assigned tasks of defining 'global public goods' in a way which would both satisfy economists and be understandable to anyone else, prioritizing them, and recommending future action that did not just cover the familiar ground of more specifically subject-focused reports. It was never entirely clear who would be likely to read the report or what value added would be seen in it, and as academically interesting as the final product may have been, it had little or no discernible impact.

The breadth of a commission's mission is, as often as not, the enemy of its impact. The Carlsson–Ramphal Commission on Global Governance (1994) was conceived of as having something to say on almost everything, and duly delivered, but is not now remembered for much more than its ambition. The Ogata–Sen Human Security Commission (2003) and the World Commission on the Social Dimension of Globalization (2004) fared not much better. The Human Security Report faced the problem that its centrepiece is a concept about which there is both not very much and yet everything to say: once the very important insight has been communicated and accepted that issues must be looked at through the lens of *human* and not just *state* security (a task essentially accomplished before this report, through the advocacy of the United Nations, the Canadian government, and many others), it is very hard to maintain a sharp focus thereafter because almost every international problem has such a dimension.[17]

Similarly with the Carnegie Commission on Preventing Deadly Conflict (1997), whose core mission was to raise the profile of *prevention* as compared with after-the-event *reaction*. Crucially important as this mission was and still is—and as much as the commission can claim to have consolidated a previously lacking 'culture of prevention' (although even there the really attention-grabbing work was Secretary-General Boutros Boutros-Ghali's *Agenda for Peace* in 1992)—the devil is in detailed implementation across a vast programme area, and it is not clear that this commission, even with its very large resources and output, was ever going to be focused enough to make an operational, as distinct from normative, impact.

15.2.2 Leadership

It is difficult to overstate the importance of the role played by committee or panel chairs in both creating and selling reports. It is true that if they have a mandate that is simply too wide, too vapid, or too indifferent to the needs and interests of any known influential target audience, even the most dedicated, knowledgeable, relentlessly focused and tough-minded individuals are going to have difficulty making a silk purse out of a sow's ear, as Ernesto Zedillo found with the Task Force on Global Public Goods discussed in section 15.2.1. But in most cases they can make a huge difference in insisting that the commission's consultative process is credible, its analysis and recommendations taut and sharp, its report as a whole clearly structured and accessible, its language readable—and that during the post-publication advocacy phase, its message is actually heard.

Many of these functions can be performed by a highly competent and professional commission staff, or—in this author's experience—by two or three members whose energy, commitment, and willingness to push debate to the limits can make up for a certain elegant lassitude at the top. But a role that cannot readily be delegated to, or assumed by, anyone else is adjudicating the differences of opinion that are bound to arise if a commission's membership reflects, as it should, a real-world diversity of views. It is very tempting for chairs to retreat quickly to the kind of lowest common denominator fudge language that is so beloved by multilateral diplomats. But that urge should be resisted as long as humanly possible, on the principle that if a small group of highly experienced individuals committed to a solution cannot reach agreement on meaningful recommendations on a sensitive subject, then no such agreement is ever likely to be reached in the wider international community.

Many of the chairs whose names remain indistinguishable from their commission or panel reports—Pearson, Palme, Brandt, Brundtland, and Brahimi, to mention just a few—seem to have played this variety of leadership roles to the full. But, as usual, recognition does not fully reflect reality. There are many examples both of strongly personalized commissions where the chairs have in fact exercised weak, erratic, or counterproductively strong leadership, and those which have remained more anonymous where the contrary is the case.

Similarly, while a leader with the credentials of a head of government or major international organization can be a major asset in selling a report at the post-publication advocacy stage, as was for example Hans Blix for the Weapons of Mass Destruction Commission (2006), this is neither a necessary nor sufficient condition for effective impact. Commissions led by technical experts (like the Canberra Commission of 1996 or the Sachs commissions of 2001 and 2005) or less exalted former ministers have often made their mark, while a number led by household-name former presidents and prime ministers have fallen flat. What matters more than the name at the masthead is the quality and timeliness of the product, and the energy and creativity with which it is marketed by the chair or co-chairs, preferably with the active help of at least one or two other commissioners.

A separate issue is whether there is advantage in having joint or multiple chairs, rather than a single leader, as has been the case with more than a third of the commissions here reviewed. North–South co-chairs—as with the Carlsson–Ramphal (1995), Evans–Sahnoun (2001), Halonen–Mkapa (2004), and Karlsson–Ramphele (2005)—have become common for commissions addressing issues which have generated controversy across this divide. Whether there is more than mere optical advantage in such arrangements will depend on the personal chemistry and complementarity of approach that the individuals in question bring to the enterprise. Joint management of any process or institution can on occasion be testing, but it is both the impression and direct experience of the present author that in this context it has generally worked well.

15.2.3 Membership

The optimal size for a deliberative commission is twelve to fifteen members—beyond that it is difficult to generate and sustain a group dynamic of strong common commitment. But it is also important that a commission's composition be, and be seen to be, sensitively weighted in terms of geography, gender, expertise, experience, and—desirably—political outlook. And meeting these criteria while maintaining a manageable size overall can be extraordinarily difficult, although well-constructed associated advisory boards and very thorough consultative processes may help to satisfy at least some of the inevitable demand for complete representative inclusiveness.

A major criticism of many past commissions has been their Northern or Western-centric membership and orientation: no global commission, whatever its subject focus, could these days be credible without redressing that imbalance. Gender balance remains, for familiar historical and cultural reasons, much harder to achieve: earlier commissions have largely escaped criticism on this ground, but no present-day commission or panel constructed with less than at least one-third of women members could expect the same easy ride. Past commissions have also neglected representation from civil society organizations to an extent that would neither be sensible nor acceptable today.

The point has been well made that since an ad hoc commission or panel, unlike a think tank or other ongoing institution, cannot build its standing over time but has just one shot at achieving recognition and impact, it is asking a lot for the inherent quality of its report to bear the whole of that burden: 'the commission...cannot depend exclusively on that report to secure interest for its activities. In order to be able to carry out its activities it has to be interesting in itself.'[18] Which is why commissions have overwhelmingly been constituted by individuals who have occupied impressively high positions in governments and international organizations, with generally high name-recognition to match.[19]

But in commission diplomacy, as in show business, all-star casts do not necessarily guarantee long runs. One recurring critique is that the casts in question have too often been too homogeneous—like-minded liberal internationalists marching in unison to tunes they all knew before even commencing their deliberations—and that this has significantly limited their capacity to win attention and affection from more conservative or insular constituencies. There is some truth in this. Surrounding oneself with like-minded colleagues can certainly make for more congenial meetings, and much easier agreement on final text, but may make it harder for the final product to win converts. The former head of the United Nations Association of the USA, Edward Luck, has made this point particularly strongly in describing the reaction of the US Congress to the Carnegie Commission (1997) and a number of reports addressing UN reform.[20]

An interesting contrast in this respect is between the Canberra Commission on the Elimination of Nuclear Weapons (1997) which was deliberately constructed to include those who had long been professionally sceptical not only about the possibility but desirability of such elimination—on the principle already mentioned that a commission which cannot itself bridge disagreement is unlikely to persuade anyone else to do so[21]— and the Blix Weapons of Mass Destruction Commission (2006). The latter was far more obviously like-minded from the outset but, perhaps at least partially for this reason, has not had a comparable impact.

One recurring characteristic of commissions past and present is the frequency with which many names recur as chairs or members, with Brahimi, Brundtland, Cardoso, Ogata, Ramphal, Zedillo—and the present author—being among the more addicted in this respect. While it is easy to paint this critically as 'old boys club' diplomacy—and certainly there is much to be said for leavening commission memberships with at least some individuals whose futures, and capacity for exercising influence, lie ahead of, rather than behind, them[22]—there would seem to be real advantage in the continuity, cross-pollination, and application of lessons learned that this kind of networking-through-overlapping-membership allows. One example involving the present author may make the point: whatever claim to attention on its merits the 'responsibility to protect' concept might have had, the ICISS report he co-chaired in 2001 would almost certainly have sunk without trace without his fortuitous appointment to the High-Level Panel of 2004, which enabled insider proselytization of the concept in the crucial lead up to the 2005 World Summit.

The point might also be made, reinforcing that made earlier about the virtue of avoiding lowest-common-denominator conclusions and recommendations, that well-socialized commission hands tend also to be better able than newcomers to read the play when it comes to distinguishing between positions of fellow members that are going to be pushed tooth and nail to the point of possible dissent unless accommodated, and those which, having been stated for the record, are not likely to stand in the way of consensus.

15.2.4 Staffing and Resources

The Brandt (1980), Palme (1982), and Brundtland (1987) Commissions between them set the pattern for the future not only in their composition and leadership, but in having highly qualified full-time secretariats managing a well-resourced process involving substantial commissioned research, extensive consultative outreach including through multiple country visits, and a substantial programme of follow-up advocacy.[23]

Money alone cannot buy a good commission product and even the finest staff cannot do a commission's job for it if its leading members lack a strong and unified view of what it wants to achieve. But, equally, commissions will not get very far without staff of real professional quality and funding appropriate for the task. What counts as appropriate or necessary resourcing will obviously depend on the scale and complexity of the task being attempted. But for all but the most ambitiously sprawling mandates—which are probably best avoided anyway, as unlikely to have an impact even beginning to match their cost—a two-year period, with resources to match, should be more than enough time once a commission is established (which itself can take up to three months) to generate the necessary research, conduct the necessary consultations, produce and publish a report, and effectively sell its message.

That, at least, was the experience of the present author with both the ICISS (2001) and ICNND (2009) commissions, each of which was able to complete a substantial report (100 pages plus 400-page supplementary research volume, and 300 pages, respectively) within not much more than a year, notwithstanding very intensive worldwide outreach programmes (involving five full commission meetings and eleven regional roundtables, with both government and non-governmental participants, in the case of ICISS; and four commission meetings, four major regional meetings, and other major industry and civil society consultations in the case of ICNND).

15.2.5 Consultation

Consultation of this extent and intensity has become almost the norm. The Brandt Commission focused primarily on high-level talks with government and intergovernmental organization leaders, but the Palme and Brundtland Commissions shortly thereafter set the pattern for very extensive NGO consultations as well, the latter going so far as to collect over 500 submissions—involving more than 10,000 pages of material—in the course of nearly three years of worldwide public hearings.

The most successful consultations with both official and non-government interlocutors, in the present author's experience with both ICISS and ICNND, involve not so much formal submissions as interactive roundtable exchanges—preferably with not more than twenty or thirty non-commission participants—in which those being consulted are given sufficient advance indication of the commission's preliminary thinking on key issues to be able to challenge and respond directly to what is on the table as well as introduce new perspectives of their own. It is crucial that commissions go out of their way not just to seek reinforcing evidence and argument, but to understand the nature and extent of likely opposing views. Sceptics who suggest that this kind of intense focus on interaction with global NGOs is a way of establishing legitimacy and authority for a North government sponsored commission, which might otherwise lack it, miss the point. Non-governmental organizations now play such a crucial policy-influencing and delivery role that any commission which ignored or patronized their input would run the risk of producing both an ill-informed and unsaleable product.[24]

15.2.6 Recommendations

In crafting its recommendations, every commission faces the dilemma of how far to push the envelope: should it stay within readily achievable comfort zones, set targets which are beyond the current horizon, or spell out big ideas which are bound to be seen by at least some policy-makers as not only over the horizon but out to space? The short answer is that the best-received reports are those perceived to be both adventurous *and* practical. Articulating visions as to what ought to be will often be an important contribution, helping set the direction of longer term debate. But unless accompanied by sharply-focused proposals reflecting a clear understanding of political and institutional realities and capable of implementation within a reasonable time frame, a report is likely to fall flat.

The Commission on Global Governance (1995) generated a mass of recommendations that were both adventurous and specific, but so many of them were beyond what the market was capable of bearing for the foreseeable future that its report became almost a byword for wishful thinking. Even the global NGO community was 'passive in responding' to the recommendations—for a UN-based Forum of Civil Society, and a Right of Petition—for which they were the major intended beneficiaries.[25] The Carnegie Commission on Preventing Deadly Conflict (1997) was seen as less successful than it might have been for a rather different reason: essentially because its recommendations were seen as taking a long time to state the fairly self-evident—that prevention beats reaction every time—and insufficiently focused on currently controversial issues like how to build consensus for effective protective action in the Balkans.

Also in the security area, the Blix Commission (2006) generated less traction with policy-makers than its important analysis of the threats posed by weapons of mass destruction deserved, essentially because its many recommendations were seen more as an anodyne wish-list than an immediately graspable agenda. The ICNND (2009) learned from that experience: all its recommendations (many of them identical with Blix's) were shaped into prioritized short-, medium-, and long-term action agendas, and found a more receptive international audience as a result.

15.2.7 Branding and Packaging

Commission reports whose major themes can be encapsulated on a bumper sticker—'common security' (Palme, 1982), and 'responsibility to protect' (ICISS, 2001)—have some inherent advantages, both in initial take-up and longevity, over those which cannot. But this should not be overstated. Equally plausible encapsulations like 'our global neighbourhood' (Carlsson–Ramphal, 1995), 'a culture of prevention' (Carnegie, 1997), and 'human security' (Ogata–Sen, 2003) failed to generate much or any discernible buzz in the media or among policy-makers, while there have been plenty of reports lacking such a badge—the Canberra Commission (1996) just one among them—which are generally seen as successes.[26]

The presentation of reports in other ways can make a difference. A report which is written in clear and lively prose and logically and accessibly constructed—with a good executive summary or synopsis and a comprehensive user-friendly index—has a big head-start over competitors for the attention of busy policy-makers which are turgid and impenetrable. Media analysts have short deadlines, often even shorter attention spans, and need the most newsworthy and comment-worthy material packaged for them in a way that they will find both attractive and accessible.

15.2.8 Advocacy and Follow-Up

As Gro Harlem Brundtland has put it, 'A good report is not the end but the beginning.'[27] Operationally this means, as Ed Luck has expressed it succinctly, 'In terms of getting high-level and/or sustained attention, nothing counts like follow up, follow up, and follow up. The release of a "final" report should be around the mid-point of a project, not its culmination.'[28]

Few commissions follow this prescription as completely as they should, but one recent example is the ICNND (2009), one of whose co-chairs visited some forty NPT member countries in the six months between the publication of its report, *Eliminating Nuclear Threats* and the commencement of the 2010 NPT Review Conference, making both public and private pitches to advance its recommendations. A great deal of effort has also gone into trying to build institutional frameworks to help maintain momentum on the commission's recommended action agendas, including regional networks of political leaders in Europe and the Asia Pacific, and a centre designed to produce a regular 'state of play' report on how well, or badly, the world is doing both against official and commission-identified benchmarks.

Not only commission chairs but individual members can and do make hugely important contributions to this kind of follow-up advocacy. To take another example from the nuclear security area, no one was more important in keeping the findings of the Canberra Commission (1996) alive before the international policy community—and in circumstances where a change of government in Australia had led to the effective disowning of the report—than General Lee Butler, former commander-in-chief of the US Strategic Air Command, a sceptic of nuclear abolition for whom his commission membership had been a transformative experience.[29]

15.2.9 Ownership

As will be evident from Table 15.1, commissions and panels come with a multitude of different provenances—initiated, sponsored, or both by individual governments like Sweden, Australia, Canada, and Japan; groups of like-minded governments; the United Nations, through the secretary-general himself or any one of a dozen agencies, programmes, or institutions within the broader UN family (from the UNDP and UNESCO to the World Bank, ILO, and IAEA); and private foundations like Carnegie and Ford. It is occasionally suggested that this contextual factor must play some part, institutionally, ideologically, or nationally, in determining either the nature or quality of the product, or the likelihood of its general acceptance.[30]

Although it is the case that, with the exception of UN-related sponsors, there is a relentlessly Northern cast to this list which has inevitably generated some criticism—and motivated the occasional effort to build primarily developing-country based counterparts, most notably the South Commission (1990)—it is not clear that the 'ownership' factor has significantly influenced either the way that commissions and panels have gone about their business, or the reception of their reports: they stand or fall on the merits of the tune produced, not who is paying the piper.

In the present author's experience, having worked in every one of the different sponsorship contexts just described, commissions take very seriously their independence, and for all practical purposes conduct themselves in essentially the same way. Many factors, as already discussed, will contribute to the stylistic and substantive output of a particular commission, and its perceived overall success or failure, but ownership as such is not one of them. All this may not work very well in theory, but it seems to in practice.

It is worth making the point that many commission activities do have a lot in common with middle power diplomacy. But that is not directly a function of so many commissions being actually sponsored by familiar middle powers—Australia, Canada, and the Nordics prominent among them—so much as it reflects the reality that commissions are operating within the same set of constraints. A middle power that wants to influence global policy has, by definition, neither the economic clout nor military might that would demand that its voice be heard: it must seek to make its way essentially through the power of persuasion, relying on the creative force of its ideas and the energy and stamina with which it pursues them. And it is effectively confined to 'niche' diplomacy, concentrating resources in specific areas best able to generate returns worth having, rather than trying to cover the field.[31] So too with commissions and panels, whoever 'owns' them.

15.2.10 Timing

A much more influential contextual factor in determining success or failure of commissions is the age that gives them birth, and accidents of timing that occur during their life. It has been much remarked that it was during a hopelessly unpropitious period of cold war tension and neoconservative ideological ascendancy that the Brandt Commission (1980) sought to redefine North–South relations, and the Palme Commission (1982) to redefine approaches to military security: while both, and particularly Palme, can reasonably claim to have had longer-term influence on global thinking, the effort produced nothing at the time.

By contrast the much more visibly successful Brundtland Commission (1987) was not only able to extract some of the benefit from the loosening of that old straitjacketing order towards the end of its term, but also drew momentum from a series of high-profile crises and disasters that occurred while it was at work, including drought in the Sahel, the Union Carbide Bhopal tragedy, and the Chernobyl nuclear catastrophe. Nor did it hurt that Gro Harlem Brundtland again became her country's prime minister, with all the additional profile and prestige that comes with that position, in the commission's last year.[32]

The International Commission on Intervention and State Sovereignty (2001) was both the beneficiary and victim of timing: the former because the issue of humanitarian intervention with which it wrestled was about as ripe as it could be after the successive horrors of Rwanda, Bosnia, and Kosovo, and the international community's incapacity to respond to them on any kind of consensual basis had become universally apparent during the 1990s; the latter because the occurrence of 9/11 just before the report was released comprehensively diverted international attention from the issue. Other dynamics, already described, kept the 'responsibility to protect' theme in play up until its endorsement by the 2005 World Summit, but it was a close-run thing—not least when this concept was sought to be used, quite inappropriately, in support of the coalition invasion of Iraq in 2003.

15.3 Commissions in the Future

There is no sign that the attractiveness of commission diplomacy is palling. New commissions and panels continue to be established, by the same kinds of governments, international institutions, and foundations that have been initiating them for the past half-century, and with the same kinds of hopes and expectations that they will come up with new kinds of conceptual and practical solutions to problems that have eluded policy-makers. On the evidence of the past decades, only a relatively small handful of those hopes and expectations are likely to be satisfied, but that does not seem to be a disincentive to commission creation so long as there is at least some prospect of value being added to the policy debate.

Occasionally commissions are created simply in response to the familiar political imperative to be seen to be doing something, but this is far more common in domestic than international political contexts, and the primary motivation for establishing commissions and panels of the kind reviewed here is overwhelmingly likely to remain genuine concern for good policy, and institutional effectiveness in making and delivering it. One of the great attractions of the commission format is that it enables systematic attention to be focused on problems which are important but not necessarily urgent, and which in the rush of daily events never get properly addressed by policy-makers in national governments or intergovernmental organizations.

The question arises as to whether commissions in the future are in fact likely to add more value than most of those in the past. Much will depend on whether the lessons learned from hard experience about what works and what does not, as sketched in this chapter, will in fact be absorbed and applied. The present author is inclined, from his own experience, to believe that this is occurring, although probably neither as quickly nor as comprehensively as one might prefer. Certainly one area in which it is difficult to imagine any backward step being taken is consultation with civil society. The burgeoning universe of significant non-governmental actors, and of new ways of communicating with them through social media, will make it impossible for commissions and panels to do most of their work behind closed doors, impervious to these currents of opinion.

Not that commissions ever really *have* worked this way. They do certainly have some 'club' characteristics—as the editors of this *Handbook* have defined these—not least in the relatively small numbers of players involved, the well-established positions in various national and international hierarchies enjoyed by most commission members, and the primacy traditionally given to written communication in researching and settling the text of reports. But their mode of operation has also—by contrast with formal governmental process—always had 'network' characteristics, with much wider participation in deliberations than the usual multilateral diplomatic suspects, and relatively fluid internal and external communication patterns.

Commissions of the future are certainly ever more likely to acquire modern network characteristics, with broader-based memberships becoming more common, a greater commitment to consultative outreach becoming ever more evident, and electronic communication ever more dramatically speeding and opening up information and idea sharing. Provided they learn how to harness, and not be overwhelmed by, the general cacophony of the modern electronic universe, and do remain sharply focused on producing useful analysis, deliverable outcomes, and compelling advocacy, their future as reasonably prominent features of the diplomatic landscape seems assured.

Notes

1 Citations for each commission report referred to in this chapter appear in Table 15.1. Although there is much writing about major individual commissions and panels, their role and significance generally has not generated a large literature. The most useful reviews are Unto Vesa (ed.), *Global Commissions Assessed* (Helsinki: Ministry for Foreign Affairs, 2005), and Ramesh Thakur, Andrew F. Cooper, and John English (eds), *International Commissions and the Power of Ideas* (Tokyo: United Nations University Press, 2005). Many of the more important commissions are discussed in Richard Jolly, Louis Emmerij, and Thomas G. Weiss, *UN Ideas that Changed the World* (Bloomington: Indiana University Press, 2009), and there is a useful compilation of data in Frederic Lapeyre, 'The outcome and impact of the main international commissions on development issues', Working Paper No. 20, World Commission on the Social Dimension of Globalization, ILO, 2004, at<http://www.uclouvain.be/cps/ucl/doc/dvlp/documents/lapeyre_wp30.pdf>.

2. International Commision against the Death Penalty, initiated by Spain, October 2010, <http://www.icomdp.org>; Global Commission on Drug Policy, initiated by the International Drug Policy Consortium, January 2011, <http://www.globalcommissionon-drugs.org>; Global Commission on Elections, Democracy and Security, initiated by International IDEA and Kofi Annan Foundation, March 2011, <http://www.uclouvain.be/cps/ucl/doc/dvlp/documents/lapeyre_wp30.pdf>.

3. Regionally-focused commissions and their reports not treated here include, for example, the Commission for Africa, chaired by Tony Blair (2005, 2010), the Partnership for the Americas Commission, chaired by Ernesto Zedillo and Thomas Pickering (2008), and the Latin American Commission on Drugs and Democracy, chaired by Cesar Gaviria, Ernesto Zedillo, and Fernando Henrique Cardoso (2009). The Kosovo Commission (2000, 2001) might be thought an exception to the 'not country specific' rule, but it is included here as making an important contribution to the global debate on humanitarian intervention and proper guidelines for the use of military force; see Richard J. Goldstone and Nicole Fritz, 'Fair Assessment: The Independent International Commission on Kosovo', in Thakur, Cooper, and English (eds), *International Commissions*.

4. The author has been directly involved in six of the commissions and panels discussed in this chapter: assembling one for a sponsoring government (the Canberra Commission on the Elimination of Nuclear Weapons), co-chairing two (the International Commission on Intervention and State Sovereignty, and International Commission on Nuclear Non-Proliferation and Disarmament), and being a member of three others (the Carnegie Commission on Preventing Deadly Conflict; the UN Secretary-General's High-Level Panel on Threats, Challenges and Change; and the International Task Force on Global Public Goods). Most of his experience has been with commissions in the peace and security area, and the examples given in the discussion which follows will for the most part reflect that.

5. See Thomas G. Weiss and Ramesh Thakur, *Global Governance and the UN: An Unfinished Journey* (Bloomington: Indiana University Press, 2010), 170–1.

6. On the Millennium Development Goals, see Weiss and Thakur, *Global Governance*, 184–91.

7. This table seeks to be a comprehensive list of all the commissions and panels reporting during this period that satisfy the criteria in the text, but paucity of accessible data for the earlier years and issues of definition at the margin are bound to have resulted in both real and perceived omissions. The author is indebted to Gloria Martinez and Ben Parr for research assistance in its compilation.

8. See Vesa (ed.), *Global Commissions*, 31; Jolly, Emmerji, and Weiss, *UN Ideas*, 152–4.

9. On the Global Compact see Thakur, Cooper, and English (eds), *International Commissions*, 41–2, and on the application of the Cardoso report Weiss and Thakur, *Global Governance*, 44–5.

10. See Weiss and Thakur, *Global Governance*, 208–14.

11. See Thakur, Cooper, and English (eds), *International Commissions*, 41–2.

12. Quoted in Vesa (ed.), *Global Commissions*, 90.

13. See Gareth Evans, *The Responsibilty to Protect: Ending Mass Atrocity Crimes Once and For All* (Washington DC: Brookings Institution Press, 2008); Weiss and Thakur, *Global Governance*, ch. 10.

14. See David Cortright, 'Making the Case for Disarmament: An Analysis of the Palme and Canberra Commissions', in Vesa (ed.), *Global Commissions*, 61; also Geoffrey Wiseman, 'The Palme Commission: New thinking about security', in Thakur, Cooper, and English (eds), *International Commissions*.

15. See on the Canberra Commission Marianne Hanson in Thakur, Cooper, and English (eds), *International Commissions*, 123–41.

16. 'This would seem obvious, but it is remarkable how many policy projects are launched on the equivalent of a wish and a prayer. Enthusiasts, in particular, should be encouraged to stop and ask themselves candidly a) whether a market exists for the product they intend to produce and b) whether their commission or study will truly bring added value to the subject', Edward C. Luck, 'The UN Reform Commissions: Is anyone listening?', in Thakur, Cooper, English (eds), *International Commissions*, 279.

17. Michael Barnett makes an even tougher assessment in Vesa (ed.), *Global Commissions*, 52–3.

18. Jon Pederson, 'Ideas, think-tanks, commissions and global politics', in Thakur, Cooper, and English (eds), *International Commissions*, 272.

19. The Sachs commissions (2001, 2005) are probably the most prominent exceptions to this rule, with compositions very largely reflecting technical and 'technocrat' expertise: probably appropriate given the focus at the time on specific strategies to implement the already agreed aspirational targets constituted by the Millennium Development Goals; see Helge Hveem in Vesa (ed.), *Global Commissions*, 20.

20. Luck, 'UN Reform Commissions', 277–87.

21. On the membership of the Canberra Commission—which included former US Strategic Air Command General Lee Butler and Defence Secretary Robert McNamara, UK Field Marshall Michael Carver, and French Prime Minister Michel Rocard—and the dynamics which produced consensus recommendations from them, see Cortright in Vesa (ed.), *Global Commissions*, 64–5.

22. Cortright in Vesa (ed.), *Global Commissions*, 280.

23. See Vesa (ed.), *Global Commissions*, 122–7.

24. Compare Pedersen in Thakur, Cooper, and English (eds), *International Commissions*, 274.

25. Barry Carin, 'An Analysis of the Commission on Global Governance', in Vesa (ed.), *Global Commissions*, 96.

26. See Thakur, Cooper, and English (eds), *International Commissions*, 20–1.

27. Quoted by Helge Hveem in Vesa (ed.), *Global Commissions*, 30.

28. Luck, 'UN Reform Commissions', 279.

29. See Cortright in Vesa (ed.), *Global Commissions*, 65; Hanson in Thakur, Cooper, and English (eds), *International Commissions*, 138.

30. For a fuller account of the issues here see Cooper and English, 'International commissions and the mind of global governance', in Thakur, Cooper, and English (eds), *International Commissions*, 12–17.

31. See, for example, Gareth Evans and Bruce Grant, *Australia's Foreign Relations* (Melbourne: Melbourne University Press, 2nd ed. 1995), 344–8.

32. See Cooper and English in Thakur, Cooper, and English (eds), *International Commissions*, 8–10; Hveem in Vesa (ed.), *Global Commissions*, 29–30.

CHAPTER 16

···

INSTITUTIONALIZED
SUMMITRY

···

RICHARD FEINBERG[*]

[A Group of 20 leaders meeting] should get political leaders doing what they alone can do—making tough choices among competing interests and priorities. (Paul Martin, former prime minister of Canada)[1]

GATHERINGS at the maximum level of political authority, summits are—potentially— the powerhouse of modern diplomacy. By definition, summits refer to official meetings among heads of state and government—meetings among leaders at the apex of state power.[2] In earlier eras, summits were often between just two rulers and occurred on an irregular, ad hoc basis, for example the sometimes dramatic encounters during the cold war between the leaders of the United States and the Soviet Union.[3] These summits advanced stability between the two dominant nuclear powers and may have helped to bring a peaceful end to the cold war; whereas the 1961 Geneva summit between the young US president, John F. Kennedy, and the Soviet leader Nikita Khruschev stoked personal misunderstandings that may have contributed to the miscalculations leading to the 1962 Cuba missile crisis, bringing the world to the brink of nuclear annihilation, a crisis thankfully resolved by the same two leaders albeit via diplomatic channels rather than face-to-face meetings. Summit conferences have also been convened to herald the end of a period of conflict and to lay the foundations for future order; the 1919 Paris Peace conference was summoned to settle the First World War and, it was imagined at the time, to design a formula for enduring peace.[4]

This chapter, however, will focus not on dyadic summits or one-off conferences but rather on the newer yet increasingly common form of summitry that emerged only in the second half of the 20th century which we label 'institutionalized multilateral summitry' or in abbreviated form simply institutionalized summitry. Institutionalized multilateral summitry is characterized by official meetings (1) of heads of state and government, (2) attended by at least several leaders and generally many more, (3) that convene repeatedly (as opposed to ad hoc, one-off events), and (4) that are underpinned by one or another form of institutionalized bureaucratic structure that facilitates preparation and continuity between leaders' meetings.

This chapter will explore the drivers behind the rise of this institutionalized summitry as it occurs in its various global and regional embodiments. Next we will assess the strengths and weaknesses of gatherings of political chiefs and their senior ministers: are summits mere photo-ops for the egos and public relations of leaders or are they important forums where leaders set strategic directions for global governance? Further, what can be done to minimize the inherent drawbacks to gatherings of super-charged egos and maximize their value-added to managing the many challenges that globalization presents to nation states? The chapter will also elaborate upon the varying degrees of institutionalization exhibited by summits and the key variables that define institutional robustness. Among the new elements of modern summitry is the increasing participation of non-state actors, including business leaders and representatives of non-governmental organizations (NGOs)—potentially adding depth and legitimacy to summitry. Finally, it will be noted that so common have summits become that they crowd the calendars of leaders, begging for a more rational ordering.

16.1 Modern Diplomacy and Summitry

Institutionalized summits are creatures of the modern era. Summits depend upon the facilities of air travel, not only to fly in leaders but also to gather the staffs to the many, often hectic, preparatory bargaining sessions. Modern summits also require telecommunications to facilitate preparation of communiqués and the rapid arrangement of complicated logistics, including security for the leaders and their often huge delegations. Air travel and telecommunications have facilitated three other ancillary components of modern summitry: the active participation of civil society and the private sector, the massive presence of media representatives and, in some cases, the highly visible petitions of pop superstars and the antics of protestors and counter-summits.

Summits are also the offspring of the ever-increasing interdependence among nations and markets and the complexities and interconnectedness among issues that cut across ministries and responsibilities—all of which cry out for collective management at the highest levels. International finance and trade, pandemics and terrorism, poverty in Africa and climate change worldwide, all spill across national boundaries and defy local treatment. Nevertheless, one may ask, can't these global issues be handled at slightly lower levels, either by ministers or by well-equipped permanent international agencies? Why the emergence of leaders' meetings?

There are a number of drivers that have made summits commonplace in modern diplomacy, beyond the technical advances in transportation and communications. First, populations do not want critical issues that determine the quality of their political and economic lives left to obscure ministers or faceless bureaucrats. Rather, they want the highest political authorities making the big decisions. Populations want to see decisions made by leaders who are, at least in electoral democracies, directly accountable to popular opinion.

Summits transmit the message that the assembled leaders are in control of events. However much of an illusion, this is a message that most people very much want to hear. Especially in periods of uncertainty and instability, populations want to believe that their tribal chiefs have the steering wheels of history firmly in their grasps.

Second, the increasingly evident interconnectedness among global issues that cut across ministries—for example environmental sustainability and poverty alleviation—requires decision-making by those authorities that can set priorities and that can seek solutions promoting synergies and minimizing adverse consequences across issue areas. Only presidents and prime ministers who chair their national cabinets can sort out the inherent tensions among ministries burdened by their parochial responsibilities.

Third, leaders themselves want to be seen by their respective populations as taking the big decisions that make history. To project an image of authority, the leaders must be present where and when important agreements are being negotiated among nations. Perhaps the swift streams of history rather than vain individuals are in the driver's seat; but political authorities still want to project the illusion of control. Nor do leaders want to be brushed aside by their ministers, even less by career officials. Rather, leaders beckon their ministers and staff to accompany them to summits, where they will be button-holed into positions clearly subordinate to their masters.

Fourth, in an era of multipolarity, states want to participate in global governance—in perception and fact. For example, the Group of Seven (G7), now the Group of Twenty (G20), evolved in part, first, to give Europe and Japan, and now to bestow upon the larger emerging market economies, seats at the table. From the perspective of the United States, power-sharing also has its advantages. It spreads the costs of global governance, beckons other nations to shoulder responsibilities, and cloaks a more pluralistic, even democratic, mantle on international diplomacy.

Once established, summits often generate their own inertia. National delegations vie to host future meetings for the prestige and glory that will accrue to the leader-as-host and to the host city, for many summits are forever associated with the town in which they were held. Where supportive bureaucracies have been established, they quickly develop a strong vested interest in maintaining summit momentum. Official agencies and non-governmental groups that are engaged by summit initiatives also grow stakes in summit continuity. Once initiated, summits are habit-forming and can be hard to suppress.

The agenda and membership of some summits have a global reach, such as the G20 which tackles global macroeconomic cooperation, but many summits limit themselves to promoting regional cooperation and integration. Regionalism is a major force in contemporary diplomacy, as geographically proximate nations simultaneously seek collective management of common problems and to work together to construct local responses to powerful global forces. Many summits form part of regional integration initiatives, such as the European Council, Asia Pacific Economic Cooperation (APEC), Summits of the Americas, Association of Southeast Asian Nations (ASEAN), African Union (AU), and the Arab League Summit. Some regional summits are in competition with each other; for example, the Brazilian-led Summit of Latin American Nations appears as a competitor to the Summit of the Americas (and the ministerial-level Organization of American States), just as the Chinese-led East Asia Summit looks to many to be a competitor to APEC which was driven in its early years by Japan, Australia, and the United States.[5] Lurking behind these competitions among summits are competitions among nations for regional leadership.

Summits, then, are made possible by modern technology, made necessary by globalization and regionalism, are considered useful by jealous and ambitious political authorities and by both rising and declining nation states, and over time tend to gain a certain autonomous momentum of their own.

16.2 THE VALUE ADDED OF SUMMITRY

Summits may capture the headlines as the media focus on celebrities and pageantry, but do summits really matter? In the international relations (IR) literature, summits are understudied. IR specialists prefer to study systemic structures and broad historical trends, downplaying the roles of personalities and, often, of ideas. It is the broad shifts in military power, economic prowess, and demographic trends that capture the imaginations of most scholars. History viewed from 30,000 feet diminishes the labours of individuals, however high and mighty.

The debates over the value and import of summits have been overly polarized between the boosters (often participating officials) and the sceptics (often media and academics).[6] Are summits fully orchestrated and pre-cooked by lower-ranking officials or are they forums where leaders engage in substantive discussions? Are summits more oriented toward the domestic political calculations of politicians (which national leaders are, by definition) or do the leaders focus their attentions on matters of international cooperation? Do summits serve primarily as platforms where national interests are advocated or are they forums for forging public goods and advancing the welfare of the community of nations? The best answers to these binary questions: both are possible and it depends—the relative weights between the superficial and the substantive, the choreographed and the spontaneous, the domestic and international, the parochial and the global, vary from summit to summit, from one group of leaders to another, depending upon the thoroughness of preparation, the opportunities and demands of the moment, and the quality of individual leaders and the chemistries among them.

16.2.1 Potential Pay-Offs

The presence of heads of state and government brings potentially huge pay-offs as well as entailing serious risks. Let us first consider the potential leverage that summitry brings to contemporary multilateral diplomacy, including the abilities of heads of state to oversee the broad agenda and interrelationships across issues and domains, domestic and international, political and economic, governments and markets; their leaders' capacities to focus the attention of underlings and force decisions; their authority to bargain across issues and to cut deals; and to bring legitimacy to and mobilize resources and public opinion behind an international agenda.

Leaders enjoy a vantage point not available to ordinary mortals.[7] Ministers have more narrowly defined responsibilities and even foreign ministers, who transit the globe, are focused more on diplomacy and security than, say, on macroeconomics or social welfare. From the pinnacles of power, only the top-echelon leaders have unbounded horizons that scan all issue areas. Potentially, therefore, leaders can best capture the interrelatedness of issues, grasping how they impinge upon one another, often with unintended consequences, for good or evil. With their broad responsibilities, leaders can best weigh priorities and seek to balance interests across competing goals. For example, in the preparations for the 1994 Summit of the Americas, the Brazilian career diplomats wanted to highlight the primacy of political democracy but Argentine President Carlos Menem personally weighed in with his US counterpart to propose that the forthcoming summit focus on a far bolder regional free trade vision.[8] Menem's personal correspondence carried great weight with US President Bill Clinton.[9] Whereas the summit communiqué gave pride of place to political democracy, the centrepiece of the summit itself—and the initiative for which that summit is best remembered—became the launch of negotiations on Menem's proposed free trade area of the Americas.

Leaders are also well placed to grasp the complex interplay between governments and markets; e.g. between ministries of finance and regulatory agencies on the one hand, and private banks and investment houses on the other. In the wake of the 2008 global financial crisis, French President Nicolas Sarkozy proposed elevating the G20 meetings of finance ministers and central bankers to leaders' summits, elevating political leaders to direct the process of reform of the international financial system. It was painfully obvious that the G20 ministers had failed to foresee or forestall the worse financial crisis since the Great Depression, so it behoved the supreme political authorities to seize the reigns and construct a more stable and resilient international system.

The summit preparatory process focuses attention of multiple layers of decision-making. The summit secretariats are temporarily lifted from their day-to-day administrative chores and return to the strategic purposes for which they were created in the first place. Within the executive branches of governments, and among interested non-governmental constituencies in civil society, meetings are convened to address the summit agenda, and ambitious policy entrepreneurs recognize an opportunity to advance new ideas and overcome the many veto points and other obstacles to policy innovation, or to press for more energetic implementation of previously approved mandates. The looming deadline of the summit speeds the pace of diplomats preparing the summit agenda itself, limiting debate and forcing agreement on contentious matters. Thus, in the aftermath of the 1997–1998 Asian financial crisis, the approach of the G7 summit provided the necessary incentive for squabbling finance ministers to resolve their differences; the heads gave their authority to what the finance ministers had agreed.[10] According to an observer of summits of the North Atlantic Treaty Organization (NATO), 'the very fact of an impending summit both feeds into and drives the alliance policy process—this last, indeed, is identified as perhaps the primary utility of NATO summits'.[11]

And not least, the leaders themselves are required to focus on the summit's international agenda and to turn their attention to the summit's longer-term issues normally lost amidst the pressures of *crises du jour*. To be on an equal footing with their counterparts, the leaders will want to master their briefs on the range of foreign policy issues.

Having focused attention, the summit deadline can drive decisions, compelling both national bureaucracies and international negotiators to resolve thorny issues. The looming date of a summit concentrates the minds of those responsible for summit success—and all involved are well aware that leaders expect summits to be perceived as successes. Knowing that leaders will be present and will want an attention-grabbing agenda (with visible 'deliverables'), the summit preparatory process is under pressure to resolve rather than to deter tough but vital issues. At their best, summits 'rescue multilateralism from its inherent bureaucracy and caution'.[12]

At the summits, leaders are best placed to hammer out agreements on issues not resolved by more junior officials during the preparatory negotiations. Since leaders are the ultimate decision-makers, there is no need to cable back to capitals for multiple clearances. At summits, there is no principal–agent gap, as the principals and agents are identical. If the leaders so wish, deals can be closed instantly and sealed with their handshakes (although some initiatives may ultimately require approval by national legislatures). 'Never underestimate the power of peer pressure in getting to yes,' former Canadian Prime Minister Paul Martin reminds us.[13]

Initiatives approved at the summit immediately enjoy the legitimacy conferred by the seals of ultimate political authority. More than any other assemblage, the leaders represent the aggregate of their nations' interests. This is especially the case where leaders have gained power through democratic, constitutional procedures. Only at the top political level can a history-making accord as grandiose as the Maastricht Treaty of European Union receive its proper political blessing.[14]

In addition, summits have several other advantages over meetings of more minor officials:

- Leaders can commit to mobilizing resources to implement initiatives and can command their finance ministers to make room in national budgets (albeit often subject to legislative action). Their governments are more likely to deliver on their leader's promises (although with the passage of time other priorities and budgetary pressures may intervene). At the 2005 Gleaneagles summit, the G8 leaders pledged substantive increases in international assistance to sub-Saharan Africa, some of which were eventually honoured, some less so.

- With their superior visibility, leaders can use their media access to address the broader public, to educate their populations about the realities and opportunities of international affairs and why many contemporary problems require multilateral solutions. Media-savvy leaders can immediately build public support for summit initiatives.
- In light of their frequent attendance at other summits and international meetings, leaders are well positioned to promote convergence among the agendas and goals of other diffuse and disconnected multilateral venues. Leaders can combat siloing and promote synergies in an increasingly crowded diplomatic galaxy.

Paradoxically, multilateral summits are also efficient mechanisms for promoting bilateral diplomacy. At the margins of summits, leaders make good use of their time to hold face-to-face meetings with each other where they can review issues of bilateral interest. Escaping the protocol and pageantry of official state visits, these ad hoc meetings also economize on travel time, reducing the transactions costs of diplomacy.

16.3 RISKS OF SUMMITRY

In earlier eras, professional diplomats disliked summits, typically of the bilateral type.[15] They feared that princes and politicians were often uninformed about international affairs and were amateurs at diplomacy. Especially to be avoided was actual substantive negotiations by ignorant, impulsive political chiefs. 'Summitry is more likely to produce mistaken and misleading impressions than a clear meeting of minds,' opined veteran US diplomat George Ball.[16] The bilateral summit in 1961 in Vienna between Kennedy and Khrushchev, where the Soviet leader badly misjudged Kennedy's toughness, epitomized the dangers of one-off dyad summits among politicians.[17]

On the other hand, face-to-face meetings among leaders can sometimes reduce misunderstandings and correct misinformation, building trust and confidence—critical foundations for international cooperation. Among leaders, summit agreements can lead to diffuse reciprocity: not tit-for-tat bargaining but rather a general atmosphere where the interests of counterparts are taken carefully into account across a range of issues. In this healthy atmosphere, expectations are more stable—another important gain for diplomacy.

In any case, today's institutionalized summitry sharply reduces the dangers associated with exceptional diplomatic encounters. Today's summits are generally well-orchestrated affairs where leaders are rooted in large bureaucratic networks. Moreover, as game theory demonstrates, the serial meetings of institutionalized summitry provide incentives for courteous, constructive behaviour.

Nevertheless, institutionalized summits still carry certain risks. For a start, some leaders are more informed, competent, and conscientious than others. Political leaders have their own personal agendas and their own political calendars and these distractions may not contribute to constructive summitry. And politicians will want to posture for their national press corps who have accompanied them from back home. To ostentatiously display his power and wealth, Zaire's president Sese Seko Mobutu's entourage at African summits was consistently larger and more obvious than those of the other delegations.[18] At their wrap-up press conferences, self-centred leaders may stress their personal triumphs rather than the consensus results.

Perhaps the greatest quandary with summits of national leaders is the tension between the leaders' inherent nationalism and the very purpose of summits—collective management. Leaders, more than ministers and certainly more than international civil servants, embody the national interest, however aggregated and contested and, ultimately, partial. Therein lies the supreme challenge to diplomacy: the capacity to find common ground among disparate national interests. In the context of the European Union, the European Council of leaders has sought to reassert national influence against the supranational commission; yet, paradoxically, the Council's actions, guided by leaders infused with the Europeanist vision, have further empowered the Brussels bureaucrats.

In the worst case, leaders will use a summit platform to air old grievances against other nations sitting around the table, to demonstrate 'toughness', and to affirm national pride in the face of historic rivals or distrusted neighbours. At the 2004 special Summit of the Americas in Monterrey, Mexico, Bolivian President Evo Morales denounced neighbouring Chile's 19th-century conquests while Argentine President Nestor Kirchner seized the opportunity to excoriate the IMF in the presence of US president George W. Bush—and Kirchner immediately and proudly informed the media that he had done so. At the 2009 Summit of the Americas in Trinidad and Tobago, Nicaraguan President Daniel Ortega fired off a detailed denunciation of the history of US policies in Latin America. Politicians whose personal governing style is confrontational and purposefully polarizing may display those attitudes at summits, as when Venezuelan President Hugo Chavez openly insulted the Spanish representatives at an Ibero-American Summit in Santiago, Chile in 2007. Rejectionist, revolutionary states may seek to disrupt the existing institutional architecture and deny accepted international norms.

With their high-profile visibility, summits raise expectations and attract attention. The dangers of failure, therefore, are amplified. In the run-up to the G20 meeting in South Korea in 2010, the Obama administration had created the expectation that a bilateral trade accord would be signed at the summit; the failure of negotiators to reach closure in time tarnished the entire summit and the rest of Obama's Asia trip. Similarly, in the run-up to the 2005 Summit of the Americas at Mar del Plata, Argentina, when preparatory meetings failed to find consensus language on the central issue of the day—the proposed free trade area of the Americas—leaders fell to squabbling among themselves and several presidents opposing the trade pact actually joined in anti-summit street protests. Finally, pledges made at summits that go unfulfilled make ready, high-profile targets for critics, whether their purpose is to decry their political opponents or multi-lateralism and/or globalization more generally.[19]

There is yet one more summit trap. When leaders themselves forge agreements that have not been fully filtered by specialized and authoritative bureaucracies, agreements quickly forged in the glare of the media spotlight, the risk of principal–agent slippage arises during the implementation phase. This danger of non-compliance is especially acute when accords have been driven by transient personalities who will not be present to monitor outcomes.

How best to minimize these multiple risks? Meetings can be timed around political calendars so that leaders can better focus on the summit agenda rather than on personal ambitions. Preparations can be made with great care by the professional diplomats labouring hard to resolve contentious issues before the leaders assemble. The fatal inability of negotiators to arrive at consensus language on the hot issue of free trade prior to the 2005 Summit of the Americas in Mar del Plata opened the gates to that boisterous display of disunity and summit failure. In briefing the media, spokespersons can seek to set reasonable expectations, and explain how summits are less about dramatic breakthroughs than about an on-going process of managing complex problems. Most importantly, summits can embed themselves in institutions that reduce risk and promote summit success.

16.4 INDICES OF INSTITUTIONALIZATION

Around the world, summits exhibit varying degrees of institutionalization. National leaders and ministries may hesitate to approve institutional structures which if they were to gain some degree of autonomy might allow the summit process to slip from the tight controls of national governments. Popular opinion may fear supranational forces apparently beyond their control. Yet, these hesitations to build institutional frameworks for summitry prejudice the aims that nations, in their own interests, may hope to accomplish. Summits are not immune to this common dilemma of multilateralism. Over time, the forces of collective action sometimes gain traction and surmount these fears, gradually adding building blocks to better institutionalize a summit process.

Inevitably, within summitries, there are tensions among member states. As happens in international institutions more generally, pre-existing national rivalries quickly make themselves manifest. The stronger powers continue to jockey among themselves for leadership, while weaker states will fear domination by the more powerful and will select among the available strategies—from solicitous bandwagoning to antagonistic balancing—for managing their debilities. At the same time, stronger powers may fear that lesser states will join forces and gang up on them, tying their hands, paralysing procedures, or forcing concessions.

The depth of summit institutionalization, therefore, is an expression of the balance between these clashing hopes and fears.

In measuring the depth of institutionalization, these seven variables count:

1) *Mission statement.* Some summits are firmly embedded in founding charters or treaties of which summitry is one instrumentality (the European Council, North Atlantic Treaty Organization or NATO, ASEAN, the Southern Cone's Mercosur, the Central American Integration System or SICA, the Gulf Cooperation Council); some constituent documents, such as the European Union's Lisbon Treaty, explicitly enumerate the purposes and powers of leaders' conclaves. Other summits have morphed gradually over time, generally from meetings of senior ministers, gaining their missions from successive summit communiqués, however non-binding. For example, APEC began at the ministerial level and its core regional integration goal—freer trade and investment flows throughout the Asia Pacific—surfaced at a summit meeting in Bogor, Indonesia, and hence became known as the Bogor goals.[20] Similarly, the G20 grew out of meetings of finance ministers and central banker governors and although its agenda has expanded in response to new international challenges its core competency remains international financial coordination (even as it lacks a ratified charter).[21] The Summit of the Americas process, absent a charter or even a core consensus goal once the free trade area of the Americas receded, has only its periodic communiqués to guide it.

2) *Meeting periodicity.* The Lisbon Treaty mandates that the leaders of the European Union meet four times a year whereas the Central American and ASEAN leaders twice annually. The tempo of other summits is less intense, with annual meetings being most common, as is the case with APEC, the South Asian Association for Regional Cooperation (SAARC), the Arab League Summit, the Gulf Cooperation Council, and the African Union. The Ibero-American summits are held every eighteen months, the Commonwealth Heads of Government Meeting (CHOGM) every two years. The Summits of the Americas have gathered five times since the first Miami summit in 1994. Allowances are typically made for special or emergency sessions as well.

More regular meetings have obvious advantages: institutional memory will be stronger; decisions are more likely to be consistent and coherent; the same leaders are more likely to be in office from one meeting to the next, going beyond meet-and-greet to foster a rapport among themselves conducive to serious business; such leaders are more likely to feel some responsibility for insisting on implementation of announced texts; and momentum behind initiatives may build from meeting to meeting.

3) *Control over agenda-setting.* Summit agenda are typically hammered out during a prior negotiating process among the member nations. These negotiations may occur in a highly structured format of meetings among ministry officials, as occurs with the quarterly meetings of APEC senior officials (SOMs); or by appointed 'sherpas' that gather with increasing intensity as the summit date approaches, as is the case with the Group of Twenty.[22] Or summit agendas may be heavily influenced by a permanent secretariat, as tends to be the case with

ASEAN. In the case of the Summits of the Americas,[23] agenda-setting has gradually shifted to a pre-existing regional organization, the Organization of American States (OAS) and its permanent ambassadors who report to their respective foreign ministries. For some summitry processes, the host nation has considerable sway in preparing the summit agenda, especially its headline slogans, as is the case in the Summits of the Americas and, to a lesser but still not insignificant degree, in APEC and the European Council. Summit leaders themselves sometimes play a role in driving the agenda, most likely where summits have a clear and agreed-upon mission and sense of purpose, as is the case with the European Council; the leader chairing the European Council normally makes a tour of capitals in the weeks preceding Council meetings to clarify positions, test possible solutions, or suggest a form of words for the final communiqué.[24]

Heads of state chafe under a highly structured agenda and a choreographed summit that leaves them little room for personal input or fruitful conversations among their peers. In response, some summits, such as the European Council, APEC, and the Ibero-American Summits, now allow for private, 'heads only' colloquies (each leader possibly accompanied by one minister or a sherpa but who remain silent). At these exclusive retreats, the agenda may be narrowed to just a few high-level issues and formal speeches are discouraged in favour of a genuine exchange of views. Occasionally, new initiatives may be born from these exclusive councils, as occurred in Genoa in 2001 when G7 leaders decided to launch a new anti-poverty initiative for Africa.[25]

4) *Secretariats*. Intergovernmental bureaucracies have come under scrutiny and even ridicule in some circles, yet the success of summits is significantly correlated to their robustness. The European Council, which is assisted by the General Secretariat of the Council of the European Union (EU), is further bolstered by ministries of foreign affairs as assembled in their own council. The leaders' European Council, now meeting in Brussels, sits above the massive structures of the Brussels-based European Commission, well equipped to implement its mandates. The President of the European Commission has a seat on the European Council, making explicit this close working relationship. For its part, APEC leaders have identified its minimalist secretariat in Singapore as a weakness and have begun to bolster its capacities, albeit slowly in the face of foot dragging by some members that are not enthusiastic about a stronger APEC.

Other summit processes rely heavily on pre-existing multilateral institutions, whether to help prepare their agendas or to implement their mandates. The OAS now negotiates the Summit of the Americas communiqués and its Summit Implementation Review Group (SIRG) is tasked with overseeing implementation.[26] The G20 relies on the host government to organize and coordinates its meetings, with assistance from past and future hosts (the troika system), preferring a 'virtual' secretariat for coordinating agenda items and paper flow across a distributed network.[27] The G20 turns to the well-staffed and resource-rich International Monetary Fund (IMF) and World Bank to help implement and monitor its accords on international economic matters. Secretariats with permanent executive secretaries, such as ASEAN and SICA, the European Council with its stable, full-time president, and now APEC, benefit from recognized leaders who can push forward the goals of the summit process.

5) *Financial resources.* A major drawback of summits is that they typically lack their own financial resources with which to fund the mandates they so readily approve, so summits must turn to other institutions for budgets. In some cases, robust summit networks readily lead to financial resources; for example, the G20 is prepared by sherpas and sub-sherpas one of whom is located in ministries of finance—the very same ministries that oversee their nations' participation in the resource-rich IMF and World Bank. But APEC has suffered from the refusal of the Asian Development Bank to consider itself to be an implementing arm; as compensation, a few APEC members have allocated modest sums for dispersal on behalf of APEC initiatives, placed under the aegis of the Singapore-based secretariat. An intermediate case is the Summit of the Americas which has turned to the wealthy Inter-American Development Bank; yet the IDB has maintained that its board and membership include nations not present at the regional summits and hence the Bank refuses direction from the Americas summits even as it has published reports demonstrating that its programmes are generally aligned with summit goals.[28]

6) *Ministerial forums.* Summit leaders are by nature generalists who convene for one or two days and issue high-level communiqués. In many cases, ministerial-level meetings, in their respective areas of functional expertise, prepare language for the leaders to incorporate and bless in their final texts. Ministers often accompany their leaders to summits, particularly if their issue area is high on the summit agenda, and frequently hold parallel meetings among themselves, either just prior to or during the leaders' summit. Ministers may convene again after the summit to pursue implementation of summit-authorized mandates entrusted to them. Indeed, these standing ministerials may take on a life of their own, generating new initiatives for themselves and future summits.[29] Further, summits or ministerials may create more specialized working groups and task forces to elaborate specific initiatives and may include additional experts sometimes drawn from civil society and the private sector. As an example, the 2009 Summit of the Americas gave birth to three follow-on ministerial-level forums, led by the United States, in the areas of energy efficiency, micro-enterprise, and poverty alleviation; following the model sometimes dubbed 'coalitions of the willing' or 'variable geometry', countries were invited to participate on a voluntary basis.

7) *Reporting and evaluation mechanisms.* A robust institution routinely evaluates itself and proposes corrective measures to improve performance. National leaders are notoriously reluctant to submit to external scrutiny, so that it is not surprising that summit processes typically escape self-evaluation. The Summit of the Americas has attempted to monitor implementation of its many mandates, but the mechanism of national self-reporting has proven defective and many

governments have simply refused to participate. To garner greater credibility for its communiqués, the G20 has asked the IMF to help monitor national implementation of its collective commitments.[30] APEC has taken stock of its progress towards its Bogor goals of free and open trade and investment flows.[31]

Based on these seven variables, summits can be located on a spectrum of institutionalization, ranging from strong to weak. Strong institutionalization would be characterized by a formal, inspiring mission statement, a frequent and regular meetings schedule, a proactive agenda-setting process capable of overcoming bureaucratic inertia and excessive caution, a well-staffed and well-led secretariat, purposeful ministerial and other expert forums, access to financial resources, and credible monitoring and feedback mechanisms. In such ideal cases, the summits are well embedded in a rich constellation of mechanisms that constitute a continuous summitry process. Examples of robust institutionality are most often found at the regional level, e.g. the ASEAN Summit and the European Council (further empowered most recently by the European Union's Lisbon Treaty), where member states share a common vision.

Conversely, weak summit institutionalization would be characterized by the absence of a cogent mission statement, infrequent, irregularly meetings, a stolid bureaucratized agenda-setting process, a weak or non-existent secretariat, ministerial meetings lacking leadership and direction, difficulty accessing financial resources, and no evaluation mechanisms. The Summit of the Americas process exhibits many of these characteristics, hobbled as it is by the deeply rooted distrust between the United States and some Latin American nations and multiple rivalries among the Latin American and Caribbean nations themselves.

Summits can gradually evolve over time, progressing along this spectrum from relatively weak to relatively strong. This positive evolution may occur when governments gain increasing confidence in the summitry process and find common purpose in shared goals. The G20 process may be making this journey. However, where mutual suspicions and national rivalries remain strong, or where purposes are ill defined, diffuse, or appear beyond reach, governments are less likely to want to empower summit institutions.

16.5 Proliferation of Summits

As globalization accelerates and the range of problems requiring cross-border management expands, summits are proliferating. Furthermore, launching your own summit carries cachet, a sign of enhanced stature. Regional powers, such as Brazil, China, South Africa, India, and Saudi Arabia all boast of leading their own regional summits, sometimes in competition with other regional contenders, sometimes going head-to-head with global powers. Summit agendas increasingly overlap as mission creep tends to expand each summit's issue scope. Summits also tend to gradually increase the number of participants, as countries gravitate to new centres of perceived power and summits seek wider representation and legitimacy.

With the steady proliferation of global, regional, and functional summits, the travel calendar of many leaders has become increasingly crowded. Truth be told, many leaders welcome the opportunities to slip away from their domestic travails to bask in the pageantries of summitry. Leaders also relish gripping among themselves about intrusive, trivializing media, the unreasonable expectations of ungrateful publics, and the intractability of complex issues. Summits provide a psychological support group for these 21st-century grandees.

Nevertheless, the punishing travel schedules and overlapping agendas among summits are cause for concern, giving rise to accusations of 'summit fatigue'. To reduce transactions costs of summit travel, some summits may be held back-to-back, as occurred with the G20 and APEC Leaders Meeting held in late 2010 in South Korea and Japan, respectively. Over time, a healthy competition among summits may cause some to disappear or be absorbed into other summit processes.

More could be done to maximize the value added by the universe of summits. Already, some summits act as caucuses which seek to stimulate action in more universal bodies such as the United Nations, the Bretton Woods twins, and the World Trade Organization (WTO). Leaders who fly from summit to summit can carry the same messages to each and every forum, promoting a trans-forum consistency and complementarity. Summit secretariats could make greater efforts to communicate among themselves, establishing points of contact and periodic workshops for inter-summitry information exchanges. Within their executive branches, governments can also open offices or inter-agency committees where officials segregated into their regional and functional domains can keep abreast of the multiple summit agendas and exchange best practices.

A new form of international diplomacy, institutionalized multilateral diplomacy, is very much a work-in-progress. Over the coming decades, continual institutional innovations will build on the achieved strengths and seek to overcome the many evident shortcomings. Those summits that build more robust institutional structures are more likely to endure. What is clear is that summitry as a vital feature of modern diplomacy is here to stay.

NOTES

*   The author would like to thank Ane Elisabeth Lykke Nielsen for her valuable research assistance.
1. Paul Martin, 'A Global Answer to Global Problems: The Case for a New Leaders' Forum', *Foreign Affairs* 84:6 (May/June, 2005), 6.
2. For a discussion of the definition of summits, see David H. Dunn, 'What is Summitry?', in David H. Dunn (ed.), *Diplomacy at the Highest Level: The Evolution of International Summitry* (London: MacMillan Press, 1996).
3. There is an extensive literature on the cold war summits. For a recent treatment, see David Reynolds, *Summits: Six Meetings that Shaped the Twentieth Century* (New York: Basic Books, 2007).
4. Margaret MacMillan, *Paris 1919: Six Months That Changed the World* (New York: Random House, 2001).

5. Y. Funabashi, *Asia Pacific fusion: Japan's role in APEC* (Washington, DC: Institute for International Economics, 1995). On APEC, see Richard Feinberg, 'Voluntary multilateralism and institutional Modification: The first two decades of Asia Pacific Economic Cooperation (APEC)', *Review of International Organizations*, Winter (2008), 239–258; Richard Feinberg (ed.), *APEC as an Institution: Multilateral governance in the Asia-Pacific* (Singapore: Institute of Southeast Asian Studies, 2003); John Ravenhill, *APEC and the construction of Pacific rim regionalism* (Cambridge: Cambridge University Press, 2001).

6. Two summaries of some of the pros and cons of summits are: David H. Dunn, *Diplomacy at the Highest Level: The Evolution of International Summitry*, especially ch. 15; and G.R. Berridge, *Diplomacy: Theory and Practice*, 4th edition (New York: Palgrave Macmillan, 2010), ch. 10. For a methodology for assessing the performance of individual summits, see Nicholas Bayne, *Staying Together: The G8 Summit Confronts the 21st Century* (Aldershot, England: Ashgate Publishing Company, 2005), 3–15.

7. The classic work on the presidential vantage point, in the US political context, is Richard Neustadt, *Presidential Power and the Modern Presidents: The Politics of Leadership* (New York: John Wiley, 1960).

8. Richard Feinberg, *Summitry in the Americas* (Washington, DC: Institute for International Economics, 1997), 65.

9. Author's personal observation, when serving on President Bill Clinton's National Security Council.

10. Bayne, *Staying Together: The G8 Summit Confronts the 21st Century*, 202.

11. Bill Park, 'NATO Summits', in Dunn (ed.), *Diplomacy at the Highest Level: The Evolution of International Summitry*, 88–9.

12. Former Canadian Prime Minister Joe Clark, as quoted in Peter I. Hajnal, *The G8 System and the G20: Evolution, Role and Documentation* (Hampshire, England: Ashgate Publishing, 2007), 31.

13. Martin, 'A Global Answer to Global Problems', 3.

14. John Redmond, 'From "European Community Summit" to "European Council": The Development and Role of Summitry in the European Union', in Dunn (ed.), *Diplomacy at the Highest Level: The Evolution of International Summitry*, 63.

15. See Harold Nicolson, *The Evolution of Diplomatic Method* (London: Constable, 1954); and George Ball, *Diplomacy for a Crowded World* (Boston: Little, Brown and Company, 1976).

16. Ball, *Diplomacy for a Crowded World*, 32.

17. David Reynolds, *Summits: Six Meetings that Shaped the Twentieth Century*, ch. 4, 163–221.

18. Richard Hodder-Williams, 'African Summitry', in Dunn (ed.), *Diplomacy at the Highest Level: The Evolution of International Summitry*, 137.

19. Jeffery Sachs, 'The Unaccountable G-8', *The International Economy*, Summer (2010), 42–3.

20. For example, APEC trade ministers, 'A mid-term stocktake of progress toward the Bogor goals', 17th APEC Ministerial Meeting, Busan, Korea, 15–16 November 2005.

21. On the Group of Twenty, see Hajnal, 'The G8 System and the G20: Evolution, Role and Documentation'; and the website of the Brookings Institution's project on the G20, <http://www.brookings.edu/topics/g20-summit.aspx>. On earlier G7/8 meetings, see Bayne, 'Staying Together: The G8 Summit Confronts the 21st Century'. For a sceptical view, see John Williamson, 'The Role of International Organizations in Creating a More Stable World Economy', Peterson Institute for International Economics, lecture delivered at the Emirates Center for Strategic Studies and Research, Abu Dhabi, 30 November 2010.

22. 'Sherpas' refers to the local bearers who assist mountaineers in the Himalayas. It was a name which entered the diplomatic lexicon at the same time as 'summits' as a result of the publicity surrounding the first successful ascent of Everest in 1953.

23. On summits in the Americas, see Feinberg, *Summitry in the Americas: A Progress Report*; and Carlos Jarque et al. (eds), *America Latina y la Diplomacia de Cumbres* (Madrid: Secretaría General Iberoamericana, 2009).

24. Philippe de Schoutheete, 'The European Council', in John Peterson and Michael Shackleton (eds), *The Institutions of the European Union* (New York: Oxford University Press, 2006).

25. Bayne, *Staying Together: The G8 Summit Confronts the 21st Century*, 217.

26. The SIRG's web site is <http://www.summit-americas.org/sirg.html>.

27. Stewart Patrick, *The G20 and the United States: Opportunities for More Effective Multilateralism* (New York: The Century Foundation, 2010), 41–3.

28. See Carlos M. Jacque, *Summit of the Americas: the IDB Agenda to Support the Mandates of the Summits of Quebec and Nuevo Leon* (Washington, DC: IDB, 2005).

29. Bayne, *Staying Together: The G8 Summit Confronts the 21st Century*, 191–212.

30. See The G20 Seoul Summit Leaders' Declaration, 11–12 November 2010. Available at <http://www.imf.org/external/np/g20/pdf/111210.pdf>.

31. APEC, *A mid-term stocktake of progress toward the Bogor goals*. 17th APEC Ministerial Meeting, Busan, Korea, 15–16 November 2005.

CHAPTER 17

....

NEGOTIATION

....

FEN OSLER HAMPSON, CHESTER A. CROCKER, AND PAMELA AALL

SIMPLY put, 'negotiation is getting something by giving something, and it is the search for solutions when there are conflicts of interest between countries that meet the foreign policy goals of one country while giving enough to another to motivate it to keep its promises'.[1]

The modern state system was born out of the negotiated treaties of the so-called Peace of Westphalia, enshrined in the Osnabrück and Munster Treaties of 1648, which not only ended the religious wars of Europe and formalized the principle of sovereignty,[2] but also sought to guarantee for religious minorities the right to practice their own religion with the understanding that all parties to the Treaty would respect these rights in exchange for territorial (i.e. sovereign) control.[3] Since its founding, negotiation has thus been both the body and soul of the modern state system. It is the preferred instrument for resolving disputes between and among nations, although its failure can and does lead to war. This chapter explores three questions: (1) why has negotiation increasingly become the preferred instrument for resolving disputes in the late 20th and early 21st centuries?; (2) what are some of the different approaches to the study of negotiation?; and (3) what are some of the new issues for research in the study of negotiation and diplomacy?

17.1 THE APPEAL OF NEGOTIATION

....

The preference for negotiation in today's world is one that has taken place against a backdrop of globalization, which has brought states and the societies that inhabit them into increasingly close proximity—a proximity characterized by a growing density of interactions that cross the economic, commercial, social, cultural, and political divide.[4] As the frequency and depth of these interactions has grown, so too has the potential for conflicts of interest, beliefs, and values, which can only be resolved through processes of dialogue and negotiation. Frequently, such dialogue is directed at identifying new norms, rules, and procedures to govern future interactions while lowering transactions costs.[5] Dialogue is also premised on an understanding of the processes of interest-based negotiations, a method of structuring negotiations towards a 'win-win' solution in which both parties reach a satisfactory agreement on issues critical to each.[6]

The rapid growth in the number of international institutions in the 20th century, which accelerated after the Second World War with the founding of the United Nations and a host of regional and sub-regional institutions and arrangements, also gave further impetus to international negotiation processes, especially multi-party and multi-issue negotiations which take place within the formal multilateral and rule-bound settings of these institutions.[7] The obvious importance states attach to these bargaining processes is reflected in the sizeable cadre of professional international negotiators who are to be found not just in foreign ministries, but also in the many different functional departments and agencies of national governments that deal with cross-border issues.

Although adjudication, arbitration, and various judicial means are occasionally used to deal with interstate disputes,[8] as well as disputes between private actors that cross international boundaries, the continued importance that states attach to their sovereignty in international affairs has meant that the opportunities for judicial recourse are generally limited. Bargaining and negotiation are thus the default option when disputes arise. This is because states are often reluctant to let themselves be governed by extranational legal institutions even if they have formally agreed to submit themselves to the legal rules and norms of those institutions. This is especially true for those great powers that see themselves as independent actors in the international system.

Negotiation emerged as the preferred means for managing deep-rooted ideological rivalries during the cold war. There are a number of reasons for this, not least of which is the advent of nuclear weapons technology. As many scholars and commentators have pointed out, the advent of nuclear weapons had a progressively sobering effect on the way the two superpowers managed their strategic and ideological rivalries during the cold war.[9] Nuclear brinksmanship, which reach its highest and most dangerous point during the Cuban missile crisis, eventually yielded to a more business-like relationship characterized by regular summits between the leaders of the United States and the Soviet Union and negotiations on arms control, troop deployments, and other kinds of confidence-measures directed at reducing tensions and the risks of escalation in crisis situations. The leaders of the West, but especially the United States, also invested diplomatic political capital and energy in negotiating a relatively smooth and trouble-free transition when the Soviet Union collapsed and the Berlin Wall fell.

It was not just technology and the costs of war that influenced the strategic calculus of negotiation. Realist theories of international relations stress that the prospects for diplomacy and negotiation in international relations are conditioned by the balance of power, the presence or absence of military stalemate, and domestic political pressures.[10] All of these variables have salience in recent international relations, including the management of superpower relations during the cold war.

Liberal theories of international relations point to another set of factors that help to explain why negotiation is the preferred option for managing interstate relations. An important body of scholarship argues that there is a strong correlation between democracy and peace. Following the writings of Immanuel Kant, liberals argue that democratic states have an overwhelming tendency to resolve their differences via peaceful, i.e. diplomatic, as opposed to violent means.[11] However, there are some important exceptions to this rule. Weak democracies have a tendency to exhibit both illiberal and belligerent tendencies, which suggests that the 'democratic peace' thesis should not be taken at face value, interpreted and applied simplistically.[12] Nevertheless, the spread of pluralist values throughout the world with the rise in the number of democratic states—what Samuel Huntington refers to as the 'third wave of democracy'[13]—has buttressed a preference for diplomacy and negotiation in international relations, a trend that is likely to continue if democracy is consolidated in those states where liberal norms are shaky or weak. This proposition will likely be tested anew as the Arab awakening continues to unfold across diverse societies and sectarian alignments.

The continued importance that states attach to sovereignty[14] itself has generally tended to act as a brake on temptations to challenge the status quo or to try to redraw state boundaries through the use of force. The normative appeal of Westphalian principles remains strong in international affairs, although, in some respects, the 'pillars' of this system are crumbling with the emergence of new normative principles that are centred on the concept of human security.[15] Sovereignty has come under challenge when there are violations of human rights and governments fail to protect or respect the basic rights and freedoms of their citizens. International interventions in Bosnia, Kosovo, East Timor, the DRC, Libya, and elsewhere were carried out in the name of higher humanitarian principles.[16] But even the strongest champions of humanitarian intervention believe that the international community should only use force as a last resort after all other peaceful means, including the negotiation option, have been exhausted.[17]

In the case of intra-state conflicts,[18] the embrace of the negotiation option by the parties to these conflicts is also apparent. As the PRIO/University of Uppsala Data Set,[19] Mack,[20] and others have documented, there was a steady rise in the frequency and magnitude of civil wars during the cold war up until the late 1980s–early 1990s when the trend reversed itself and intra-state conflicts experienced a steady decline. However, unlike civil wars in the past the majority in more recent decades ended in a negotiated settlement, usually mediated by one or more third parties

The rise in mediated settlements, in which third parties help disputants secure a negotiated outcome, is one of the notable trends of the late 20th and early 21st century. Determining how many intra-state conflict negotiations are assisted by third parties is a difficult task, as many of these attempts occur in secrecy or are not acknowledged publicly by the parties. However, the fact that the United Nations has a special envoy for most ongoing conflicts around the world and that many states, large and small, as well as regional and non-governmental organizations have made similar appointments, points to an explosion in the available supply of third parties. At the same time, the numbers of conflicts that have ended with negotiated agreements (roughly a third) also point to an increased interest among combatants in engaging in peace talks.

One explanation for this rise in third-party assistance to negotiated settlements can be traced to the post-cold war transformation of the international system. At least initially, the United Nations suddenly assumed greater relevance as the great powers looked to international institutions to play a greater role in conflict management processes, including the mediation and negotiation of international disputes.[21] The same is true of regional and sub-regional organizations, which expanded their roles in conflict management in their own neighbourhoods, sometimes a trend that has continued into the 21st century.[22] The reasons behind greater international involvement in peacemaking are many, but include a strengthening international commitment to protecting civilians from war, bad governance, human rights abuses, and humanitarian crises related to conflict.

During the past two decades, a wide variety of small-state and non-state actors also began to offer their services in conflict management and resolution processes. For example, small and medium-sized powers, like Australia, New Zealand, Norway, Sweden, Switzerland, Turkey, and Qatar which had long been active in international peacekeeping operations, began to actively market their negotiation and intermediary services to warring parties.[23] From the Middle East to Central America to Africa and the Asia-Pacific region, these countries played key roles in instigating negotiations between warring sides, backstopping negotiations once they got underway, and ensuring that the parties remained committed to the peace process once a negotiated settlement was concluded. Prominent international non-governmental organizations, like the Community of Sant'Egidio—a Catholic lay organization that has been active as a mediator in Mozambique, Algeria, and Kosovo[24]—have also played key roles in bringing parties to the negotiating table and creating much-needed forums for dialogue, discussion, and negotiation, especially at the inter-communal and societal levels.

Another explanation for why many of these conflicts ended in a negotiated settlement is that they fall into the category of what Roy Licklider refers to as 'long civil wars'. At Licklider observes, 'We have some evidence that long civil wars are disproportionately likely to be ended with negotiated settlements rather than military victory. This is plausible since a long civil war means that neither side has been able to achieve a military victory.'[25] The logic of this process is spelled out by Robert Harrison Wagner. He notes

> that a military stalemate merely transforms a counterforce duel into a contest in punishment, in which war becomes indistinguishable from bargaining. Thus in deciding whether to accept some proposed settlement, there are two ways in which a party to a stalemate might expect to do better if it continued fighting instead: it might be able to overcome the stalemate and achieve a military advantage, or its opponents might, after further suffering, decide to settle for less. A negotiated settlement therefore requires that all parties to the conflict prefer the terms of the settlement to the expected outcome both of further fighting and of further bargaining.[26]

Parties to the conflict do not necessarily recognize that they are in a stalemate, however, and herein lies an important contribution of third parties in sharpening the parties' perceptions of stalemate and of the benefits of settlement.[27]

The parallel ending of many of these civil conflicts with the end of the cold war also suggests that broader, systemic forces may have been at play. Many conflicts in the third world during the cold war were aided and propelled by the two superpowers who were busy arming insurgents (or governments) in order to strengthen and expand their respective spheres of influence. The desire to end these so-called 'proxy wars' as the cold war wound down encouraged the two superpowers to pursue negotiated solutions so that they could gracefully exit from their regional commitments, which had also become very costly.[28] Nowhere was this desire for a negotiated 'exit' to their difficulties more evident than in the case of Cambodia.[29] Negotiation efforts, which were led by the five permanent members of the Security Council, were tied to a wider exit strategy so that China, Russia, Vietnam, and the United States could disengage from their military commitments in the region and move towards the normalization of relations. Similarly, in Southern Africa, US efforts to negotiate a peaceful termination to the conflict in Namibia were tied more broadly to a negotiated withdrawal of Cuban troops from Angola, which became the cornerstone of the US policy of 'constructive engagement' in the region.[30]

Although the end of the cold war had its positive effects in some regions, it is important not to stack the historical deck. The bipolar system arguably checked many conflicts or prevented them from breaking out, and the Soviet collapse followed by US disengagement coincided with a number of 1990s conflicts that might never have occurred in cold war times, including wars in Somalia, Sudan, the Democratic Republic of the Congo, Liberia (and its neighbours), Afghanistan (between the Mujahadeen and Taliban), Aceh/Moluccas/Timor, Tajikistan, Nagorno-Karabakh, Georgia, Moldova, and the Balkans. In this regard, it is worth noting that as US and NATO forces are withdraw from in Iraq and Afghanistan respectively, negotiations will play a critical role in rebuilding state institutions and engaging opposition elements in new political structures; in short, in preventing a resurgence of conflict.

17.2 APPROACHES TO STUDY OF INTERNATIONAL NEGOTIATION

Contemporary international negotiation is a complex phenomenon. It takes place between collective groups (nations, states, bureaucracies, civil society) even though it is individuals who do the bargaining. Each of the perspectives discussed below offers a different insight on how we should view the negotiation process in modern diplomacy and how the negotiation process works. Each perspective is also rooted in a different set of assumptions about the sources of individual behaviour. Some assume utility maximizing behaviour on the part of negotiators, such that negotiated outcomes are defined through instrumental goals. Others suggest that we need to pay much more attention to the psychological, relational, and even emotive aspects of negotiation and the ways dialogue can help change ingrained attitudes, behaviours, and values.

There are obviously different ways to classify the literature on negotiation and all schemes are somewhat arbitrary. A threefold categorization of the different approaches to international negotiation is offered here: 'structural analysis' defined as power-oriented explanations of international negotiation; 'decisional analysis' or approaches which rely on formal, i.e. utility maximization, models of decision-making; and 'communications-based approaches' which address the context of international negotiation and how it affects actors' choices and decision-making. Each approach offers different insights into the nature of the bargaining process and the factors and forces which may promote (or conversely hinder) agreement.

17.3 STRUCTURAL THEORIES AND THEIR CRITICS

Structural approaches typically treat international bargaining problems in terms of the power resources and capabilities of the parties to the negotiation. In the international relations literature, this approach is most commonly identified with the realist and neo-realist schools, which emphasise the impact of the international distribution of power on the behaviour of states (i.e. military capabilities, economic wealth, and the size of national economies) in political outcomes including those that take place at the bargaining table.[31]

Realists argue that strong states prevail at the bargaining table because they can use their superior resources in any given issue area to coerce and cajole weaker parties into submission. The outcome of international negotiations—bilateral or multilateral—will thus represent the preferences of the more powerful actors in the international system, i.e. bargaining outcomes are predetermined.

To the extent that weaker actors do become involved in negotiations with more powerful ones, as in negotiations between advanced-industrial states and developing countries on development and environmental issues, they will motivated by a desire to change the rules of the game in favour of regimes that augment their own wealth and power. Such efforts, however, will be thwarted by more powerful states, unless redistributive measures are seen to be in their own long-term interest.[32] From a realist standpoint, therefore, international negotiation is not considered to be an especially interesting phenomenon or worthy of special study because it is merely a reflection of broader, systemic processes and the exercise of structural power in international politics.

In contrast to the realist school, some students of international negotiation argue that weaker parties can overcome structural impediments and asymmetries in power capabilities to achieve bargaining outcomes that are favourable to themselves.[33] These approaches start with the observation that the strong do not always necessarily prevail over the weak and that international politics is more often like Jonathan Swift's tale of Gulliver and the Lilliputians. Instead of viewing power capabilities and resources as immutable, these approaches identify ways weaker parties can manipulate bargaining situations to their advantage even when the initial power balance works against them.[34]

In these approaches, bargaining and negotiation are important intervening variables between structural power and outcome in international politics. Weaker actors will react to asymmetries in structural power by adopting bargaining tactics and strategies that change the status quo and raise their own security points. For example, weak parties will seek more formal negotiating forums to strengthen their hand in negotiations (especially if decisions are based on majority voting rules). Weak states may also resort to erratic or irresponsible behaviour to strengthen their moral claims. Weaker parties may also refuse to make concessions or make unreasonably high demands at the outset of negotiations until they are convinced that the stronger party is willing to make concessions.[35]

By manipulating deadlines, asking for mediators, withholding signatures, splitting coalitions, and pairing demands with more powerful actors, weak states can also increase their bargaining leverage. Effective use of linkage strategies and bargaining tactics across different issues can also be a source of power for the weak. However, some studies suggest that parties do best in negotiation when they feel equal and when both sides can exercise a veto over the other's unilateral achievement of goals.[36] It is argued that symmetry (or the perception of it) can be crucial to negotiation success. Parties intent on negotiation may be advised to wait until such symmetry has emerged.

Coalition behaviour can also affect bargaining strategies and outcomes. A coalition of the weak can affect regime-creation if it stays unified and develops a bargaining strategy appropriate to the context of the decision.[37] Understanding the countervailing sources of the group's negotiating power, and the importance of placing inter-group needs for agreement ahead of intra-group needs for unity, are accordingly important ingredients for successful bargaining. As Zartman notes, structural analysis has moved away from its 'initial post hoc formulation that outcomes are determined by the power position of the parties' towards a 'tactical analysis' based on a definition of power as 'a way of exercising a causal relation'.[38] Tactical analysis thus treats power as a responsive or situational characteristic of negotiations where outcomes depend not just on absolute capabilities but also bargaining skills and knowledge and the way such resources are organized and utilized.

There are, however, a number of problems with structural analysis as a theoretical tool and in its application to international negotiation. First, although structural analysis is essential to understanding the basic form of any political relationship, the concept of power defined as resources, skill, knowledge, and so forth, is notoriously ambiguous and highly context specific. As Bercovitch notes, 'qualities which are valuable in one bargaining setting may have contrary value in others and we therefore need better tools— concepts, ideas, and propositions—to examine real-life situations of bargaining and negotiation'.[39]

Second, structural analysis is more amenable to cases of bilateral negotiation where questions about symmetry or asymmetry can be posed than it is to multilateral negotiations where encounters are more likely to be rule-oriented than power-oriented because of the number of parties that are involved. Although some multilateral negotiations are, in essence, bilateral dealings between two large coalitions or blocs, e.g. North–South negotiations within the UNCTAD (United Nations Conference on Trade, Aid, and Development), parties are likely to form shifting alliances for bargaining purposes and there may well be more than two camps as other coalitions form during the negotiation process.

Third, to the extent that non-governmental actors, international organizations, and trans-governmental coalitions or groupings are directly or indirectly involved in international negotiation, as they were, for example, in negotiations leading to Montreal Protocol for the protection of the ozone layer or the Basel Convention on hazardous wastes, structural approaches which focus on state actors and their capabilities may be deficient in explaining the fundamental nature of bargaining processes and outcomes of international negotiation. They may overlook the importance of non-governmental organizations and transnational social movements in mobilizing public opinion, setting the agenda, and pressuring governments to reach an agreement.[40] Moreover, as noted by Putnam, international negotiations are typically two-level games involving domestic constituencies and coalitions and the controlled exchange of partial information.[41] The emergence of 'win-win' sets in international negotiation may therefore depend crucially on the compatible and overlapping interests of supportive domestic constituencies within states. This is because two-level game possibilities create opportunities for negotiators to break deadlocks by linking issues in order to create winning coalitions.

Structural analysis may therefore present an overly reified and simplistic image of international bargaining and negotiation processes, especially in complex, international settings.

17.4 DECISIONAL ANALYSIS

In contrast to structural analysis, which emphasises the role of power in bargaining relationships, formal decisional analysis treats bargaining as a preference revelation problem among parties with competing interests where, once relative linkages and trade-offs are recognized, Pareto-optimal and other bargaining solutions can be assembled. These models assume that all individuals are utility maximizers and that bargaining pay-offs are quantifiable and amenable to formal analysis. These approaches also seek to prescribe the best course of action and best outcome for each party in a distributive bargaining relationship.

In game theoretic approaches, bargaining situations are distinguished by (a) the number of parties involved; (b) whether the conflicts are zero-sum or non-zero-sum; (c) whether the game is iterated or not; and (d) whether there are multiple equilibria or not.[42] The concept of strategic rationality is central to game theory because it recognizes that no egoistic rational actor can pursue its own interests independently of the choices of other actors. Actors' choices/preferences may result in different kinds of games, e.g. Chicken versus Prisoners' Dilemma in simple 2 x 2 games. Iteration may change not only the outcome of the game but also the structure of the situation. The prospect of cooperation is thus enhanced, or diminished, in different kinds of iterated games.[43]

In large N-person games, preference revelation problems are compounded by the large number of actors and strategic complexity. Game-theoretic approaches have dealt with complexity in terms of a number of simplifying assumptions.[44] When N is very large, it is assumed that each actor's actions will go unnoticed and therefore each actor will behave on the assumption that other actors will not react hence the problem of collective action and free riders. In smaller groupings, when actors can monitor each other's behaviour, strategic relations between actors are generally assumed to be symmetric. Public goods provision models, for example, work on this assumption—although some models do allow for asymmetry. It is also assumed that actors can pursue discriminatory policies towards other actors thus linking good behaviour with rewards and bad or undesirable behaviour with sanctions.

In some models, N-person games are treated as essentially linked two-person games thus allowing for the evolution of cooperative relationships even when N is large.[45] Others deal with complexity by assuming that issues are unidimensional and that alternatives can be arrayed in a continuum, i.e. some alternatives are valued more highly than others. Still other approaches deal with complexity in multi-party games through coalition analysis focusing on the strategic problems players may face in deciding whether to join particular coalitions and how to share different units of reward.[46] However, the simplifying assumptions that are often called for to model coalitional behaviour are difficult to sustain when the number of players that are involved is large, coalitions do not have a monolithic structure, and non-economic and non-objective trade-offs are involved between different issues.

In one sense, game-theoretic approaches are useful to understanding the structural problems associated with cooperation in large numbers and the mechanisms that can diminish transaction and information costs. These approaches underscore the importance of reducing large multilateral negotiations to smaller numbers (i.e. through coalitions), although strategies to reduce the number of players will impose costs on third parties and reduce the overall magnitude of the gains from cooperation. Game theory is also useful for identifying pay-off structures in different kinds of games and the kinds of strategies that will elicit cooperative versus non-cooperative behaviour among players.[47] However, the virtues of parsimony and elegance prove to be its principal weaknesses in trying to explain negotiation processes in complex international settings when multiple actors and interests are involved and a large number of diverse values, interests, and perceptions have to be accommodated.

Many of the assumptions upon which game-theoretic models are based are also either untested or unproved. These include such assumptions as the following: that all actors are utility maximizers and enjoy perfect or close to perfect information concerning their opponents' preferences; that the rules of interaction are fixed; that the actors are single players representing only themselves. Although game-theoretic approaches are useful for identifying different trade-offs and Pareto-optimal packages, they have relatively little to say about actual bargaining processes and how actors will negotiate to arrive at an outcome. It is simply assumed that once actors identify the relevant pay-off structure they will automatically seek the optimal solution even though there is little direct evidence to support this contention.

17.5 COMMUNICATION-BASED APPROACHES

Communication-based approaches typically stress the importance of negotiation as vehicle or means for changing parties' perceptions in a conflict so that they learn to trust each other to the point where they are prepared to engage in a reciprocal exchange of concessions. Trust is developed by bringing the parties into direct contact with each other in forums that encourage dialogue, discussion, the building of relationships, and ultimately negotiation[48] and generally involves the engagement of an impartial third party in the process. The negotiation/mediation process is therefore defined essentially as a relationship- and trust-building activity that facilitates communication by tapping into the deeply rooted needs of the parties and elicits empathic responses in the way they view the needs of their negotiating partners.

In the communication frame of reference, negotiation is also a learning process wherein the parties progressively redefine their own perceptions about their own needs, which are met by eschewing violence as the 'preferred' option. The establishment of a dialogue, of a pattern of informal as well as formal exchanges and contacts between and among official parties or other influential representatives, helps set the stage for cooperation and the search for more lasting negotiated political solutions to their differences. A key to this process is often the involvement in the dialogue not just of the principal political authorities, but also a wider group of civil and opinion leaders whose support is essential for the long-term sustainability of the peace process.

In communications-based approaches, an important assumption is that although parties identify specific issues as the causes of conflict, conflict also reflects subjective, phenomenological, and social fractures and, consequently, analysing 'interests' can be less important than identifying the underlying needs that govern each party's perception of the conflict.[49] Because much of human conflict is anchored in conflicting perceptions, identity and status demands, and in misperception, negotiation processes must be directed at changing the perceptions, attitudes, values, and behaviours of the parties.[50] Accordingly, the negotiation process should begin with an informal dialogue—sometimes referred to as a pre-negotiation—that allows conflict parties to develop personal relationships before they actually begin to discuss the different dimensions of their conflict. These relationships are critical to building a basis for trust that will eventually help to sustain the negotiation process. Informal dialogue or pre-negotiation may be organized by an official mediator or by semi- or non-official entities working to develop an environment conducive to negotiations.

Attitudinal change is promoted through a variety of instruments, including, for example, consultative meetings, problem-solving workshops, training in conflict resolution at the communal level, and/or third-party assistance in developing and designing other kinds of dispute resolution systems, which are compatible with local culture and norms and are directed at elites at different levels within society.

The problem-solving workshop is directed at communication and creating more open channels of communication which allow the participants to see their respective intentions more clearly and to be more fully aware of their own reactions to the conflict.[51] Workshops are aimed at cultivating respect and objectivity so that the parties develop a mutual commitment to cooperative exchanges in their relationship. Based on findings that show that individuals are more disposed to cooperative behaviour in small, informal, inter-group activities, the problem-solving workshop establishes relations among significant players who may be in a position to influence the parties to the conflict and, in so doing, to contribute to the de-escalation of conflict. The approach seems to work best if individuals are middle-range elites such as academics, advisers, ex-officials, or retired politicians who continue to have access to those in power.

A somewhat different kind of pre-negotiation activity is third-party assisted dialogue, undertaken by both official and non-governmental structures. This activity is directed at ethnic, racial, or religious groups who are in a hostile or adversarial relationship.[52] Like 'circum-negotiation', this dialogue occurs at a quasi-official level around or prior to the formal peace process.[53] Dialogue is directed at both officials and civic leaders, including heads of local non-governmental organizations, community developers, health officials, refugee camp leaders, ethnic/religious leaders, intellectuals, and academics. This dialogue process can be assisted by specialized training programmes that are directed at exploring ways of establishing and building relationships, furthering proficiency in facilitation, mediation, and brokering, data collection, fact-finding, and other kinds of cooperative decision-making. As Kriesberg notes, much of this activity is directed at developing 'constituency support for peace efforts'.[54]

As noted above, the practice of dialogue and communication is not limited to the non-governmental sector, but in fact underlies the approach of regional organizations in promoting dialogue and confidence-building pre-negotiations. Lacking in some instances the resources of individual states or the UN and in other instances reluctant to use the resources they have, regional organizations have used consultation, problem-solving, dialogue, and a kind of moral example to shift perceptions and change attitudes among conflict parties.[55]

Communications-based approaches stress the importance of third-party interveners in establishing communication channels between different groups in society, initiating discussions of framework solutions to problems of mutual concern, identifying steps for breaking impasses, developing new norms, and creating an understanding of the kinds of decision-making processes that can lead parties out of conflict. In these kinds of activities, third parties are supposed to play a neutral and essentially facilitating role, enabling and encouraging a mutual learning process rather than guiding or still less influencing and directing the parties to mutually acceptable approaches to problem-solving. Their involvement is based on their expert and/or reputational authority or on their ability to represent a normative or real community to which the combatants aspire. However, if such third parties are successful in promoting dialogue, their importance as conveners will diminish over time as the parties to the dispute take ownership of their dialogue and learn to manage the negotiation process by themselves.

17.6 New Issues for Research

Agency and Culture. Recent studies of international negotiation and bargaining processes stress the role of agency in bargaining processes, suggesting that there is an important relationship between agency and structure because actors themselves must develop ways to overcome the numerous barriers (structural, positional, and even cultural) that stand in the way of cooperation. Some of these studies argue that international actors will take on specialized roles and resort to specific bargaining strategies and techniques that reduce complexity and organize interests and issues such that the probability of agreement is enhanced. Many of these studies, in particular, stress the importance of personal leadership and other 'non-tangible' qualities of the actors/parties doing the negotiating.[56] Although some scholars dispute the importance of leadership,[57] most studies do not. There is growing recognition that different kinds of leadership qualities (structural, entrepreneurial, intellectual) are required for different kinds of situations and the presence/absence of certain kinds of leadership can aid and abet the negotiation process.

There is also a renewed interest in the meaning and importance of culture in negotiation. Political scientists, economists, and even sociologists and psychologists have traditionally tended to discount the importance of culture to negotiation. This is because they have considered culture to be too vague and elusive to define and difficult to operationalize in the form of testable hypotheses. But it is increasingly recognized that culture, defined as communication styles, various spoken and unspoken beliefs about social systems, and institutionalized norms and hierarchies of social behaviour, can thwart the negotiation process either because the parties see their own value systems as being superior, or because they are not attuned to the special patterns of communication and decision-making of their negotiating partner. New studies on culture and negotiation stress the importance of understanding the cultural cognitive frames of reference in cross-cultural negotiations and of devising way to help parties (either through language training or cultural sensitivity training) adjust to cultural differences and different national or sub-national negotiating styles.[58]

Justice. The problem of how to deal with issues of justice in international negotiation is also a matter of growing interest.[59] This is especially true of problems involving the 'global commons' such as the environment. Virtually all environmental problems raise ethical dilemmas. The issue of whose preferences should receive attention or of whose rights should have priority in negotiating 'just' solutions to pressing global, environmental problems are questions not easily addressed. What does 'fairness' mean in negotiating and dividing responsibilities between rich and poor nations regarding problems like global warming, whose causes are debated and whose consequences may not be experienced for decades to come? How should negotiating procedures for addressing these ethical issues be structured? Some studies argue that concepts of social justice rooted in traditional liberal theory are not adequate for addressing the kinds of competing moral claims that have arisen over environmental issues.[60] The interests of disenfranchised majorities—like the world's poor who live at or below the subsistence level, or those unborn generations—are problematic from the point of view of theories which start with the assumption that individual preferences are equal and should simply be taken at face value. This stance is too passive when it comes to the environment, not only because some parties are not represented at the bargaining table (e.g. the unborn who will experience the direct costs of global warming), but because the pattern of preferences of those who are represented are often at the root of the problem.

17.7 COMPARING APPROACHES

There are clearly a number of different theoretical approaches to the study of international negotiation, all of which contain important theoretical insights into the negotiation process. No single approach is inherently superior to the other although there are clear trade-offs between the level of generality and the degree of empirical relevance or historical accuracy of each model. Process-oriented models of negotiation seek to move beyond the restrictive assumptions about rationality inherent in game-theoretic and other formal models of decision-making. They allow for greater empirical richness and consideration of a wider array of variables in international negotiation processes. Given the complexity of international negotiation processes, and the fact that such negotiations are not particularly amenable to formal decisional analysis, unless a number of highly simplifying assumptions are introduced, inductive as opposed to deductive methods of analysis may prove more useful in understanding the processes and methods of reaching international agreements. At the same time, these approaches seek to explain why decision-makers do not always pursue Pareto-optimal strategies in bargaining situations, why they forego key windows of opportunity, or accept an agreement later that they could have had much earlier. Unlike formal models of negotiation, process models do not treat actors as monoliths or unitary actors. Actors are multidimensional and decision-making will have an internal or domestic component as well as an external one.

These approaches also stress the integrative (versus distributive) aspects of negotiation and the construction of positive-sum agreements around a formula that will guide the implementation process.[61] In order to resolve divergent interests and positions, leadership, imagination, and incremental or 'trial-and-error' methods of negotiation are often called for. Mediators may also play a crucial role acting as go-betweens and bringing parties and issues together.

Although much of the negotiation literature assumes utility maximizing behaviour on the part of negotiators such that negotiated outcomes are defined through instrumental goals, there is growing interest in the cognitive and relational aspects of international negotiation and the processes whereby attitudes, behaviours, and values are changed through negotiation and coalition-building and third-party assisted processes. As noted above, much of this work stresses that international negotiation is both a coalition-building and a social learning enterpr ise, involving not just states but a large variety of non-state actors, experts, and international organizations. Leadership, negotiating strategies and tactics, and formulas are directed at and related to the process of building coalitions (both transnational and trans-governmental) and fostering knowledge-based networks and the kind of public policy consensus that will allow the negotiation process to move forward.

Notes

1. Fen Osler Hampson and William I. Zartman, *The Global Power of Talk: Negotiating America's Interests* (Boulder, CO: Paradigm Publishers, 2012), 3.
2. The doctrine of sovereign inviolability dates to the Peace of Augsburg in 1555, which formalized the principle of *cuius regio, eius religio* (the ruler decides his country's religion). This was subsequently reaffirmed and modified in the negotiated Peace of Westphalia, which marked the end of the Thirty Years War.
3. Stephen Krasner, *Sovereignty: Organized Hypocrisy* (Princeton: Princeton University Press, 1999).
4. David Held et al., *Global Transformations* (Cambridge: Polity Press, 1999); Paul Battersby and Joseph M. Siracusa, *Globalization and Human Security* (Lanham, MD: Rowman and Littlefield, 2009).
5. Robert O. Keohane, *After Hegemony: Cooperation and Discord in the World Political Economy* (Princeton: Princeton University Press, 1984).
6. Roger Fisher, William Ury, and Bill Patton, *Getting to Yes: Negotiating Agreements Without Giving In*, 2nd edn (New York: Penguin, 1991).
7. Fen Osler Hampson, *Multilateral Negotiations: Lessons From Arms Control, Trade, and the Environment* (Baltimore: The Johns Hopkins University Press, 1995); Victor A. Kremenyuk (ed.), *International Negotiation: Analysis, Approaches, Issues* (San Francisco: Jossey-Bass, 1991).
8. Richard B. Bilder, 'Adjudication: International Tribunals and Courts', in Jacob Bercovitch (ed.), *Resolving International Conflicts: The Theory and Practice of Mediation* (Boulder: Lynne Rienner, 1997), 155–90.
9. Alexander L. George, Philip J. Farley, and Alexander Dallin (eds), *U.S.-Soviet Security Cooperation: Achievement, Lessons, Failures* (New York: Oxford University Press, 1988).
10. A.K.F. Organski, *World Politics*, 2nd edn (New York: Random House, 1968); Arthur Stein, *Why Nations Cooperate: Circumstances and Choice in International Relations* (Ithaca: Cornell University Press, 1990).

11. Bruce Russett, *Grasping the Democratic Peace: Principles for a Post-Cold War World* (Princeton: Princeton University Press, 1993).

12. Edward Mansfield and Jack Snyder, 'Democratization and the Danger of War', *International Security* 20:1 (1995), 5–38.

13. Samuel P. Huntington, *The Third Wave: Democratization in the late Twentieth Century* (Tulsa: University of Oklahoma Press, 1993).

14. Abram Chayes and Antonia Handler Chayes, *The New Sovereignty: Compliance with International Regulatory Agreements* (Cambridge, MA: Harvard University Press, 1995); Krasner, *Sovereignty*.

15. Mary Kaldor, *Human Security* (Cambridge: Polity Press, 2007); Neil S. MacFarlane and Yuen Foon Khong, *Human Security and the UN: A Critical History* (Bloomington: Indiana University Press, 2006).

16. International Commission on Intervention and State Sovereignty (ICISS), *The Responsibility to Protect* (Ottawa: International Development Research Centre, 2001).

17. Samantha Power, *A Problem from Hell: America and the Age of Genocide* (New York: Harper Perennial, 2003).

18. The term should not be taken too literally as many so-called intra-state conflicts have a tendency to spill over into their neighbourhoods and regions, simultaneously engaging a wider range of external state and non-state actors from other parts of the globe.

19. <http://www.prio.no/CSCW/Datasets/Armed-Conflict/UCDP-PRIO>.

20. Andrew Mack, *Human Security Report: War and Peace in the 21st Century* (New York: Oxford University Press, 2005); Andrew Mack, *Human Security Report 2009/2010: The Causes of Peace and the Shrinking Costs of War* (New York: Oxford University Press, 2011).

21. Fen Osler Hampson, *Nurturing Peace: Why Peace Settlements Succeed or Fail* (Washington, DC: United States Institute of Peace Press, 1996); Stephen John Stedman, Donald Rothchild, and Elizabeth Cousens (eds), *Ending Civil Wars: The Implementation of Peace Agreements* (Boulder: Lynne Rienner, 2003); Mack, *Human Security Report 2009/2010*.

22. Chester A. Crocker, Fen Osler Hampson, and Pamela Aall, *Taming Intractable Conflicts: Mediation in the Hardest Cases* (Washington, DC: United States Institute of Peace Press, 2004).

23. See Crocker, Hampson, Aall, *Taming Intractable Conflicts*; Chester A. Crocker, Fen Osler Hampson, and Pamela Aall, *Grasping the Nettle: Analyzing Cases of Intractable Conflict* (Washington, DC: United States Institute of Peace Press, 2005); Thomas Princen, 'Camp David: Problem Solving or Power Politics as Usual?', *Journal of Peace Research* 28:1 (1991), 57–69; Thomas Princen, 'Mediation by a Transnational Organization: The Case of the Vatican', in Jacob Bercovitch and Jeffrey Rubin (eds), *Mediation in International Relations: Multiple Approaches to Conflict Management* (New York: St. Martin's Press, 1992); Thomas Princen, *Intermediaries in International Conflict* (Princeton University Press, 1992).

24. Andrea Bartoli, 'Mediating Peace in Mozambique: The Role of the Community of Sant'Egidio', in Chester A. Crocker, Fen Osler Hampson, and Pamela Aall (eds), *Herding Cats: Multiparty Mediation in a Complex World* (Washington, DC: United States Institute of Peace Press, 1999).

25. Roy Licklider, 'Comparative Studies of Long Wars', in Chester A. Crocker, Fen Osler Hampson, and Pamela Aall (eds), *Grasping the Nettle: Analyzing Cases of Intractability* (Washington, DC: United States Institute of Peace Press, 2005), 39.

26. R. Harrison Wagner, 'The Causes of Peace', in Roy Licklider (ed.), *Stopping the Killing: How Civil Wars End* (New York: New York University Press, 1993), 260.

27. I. William Zartman, 'Justice in Negotiation', in Peter Berton, Hiroshi Kimura, and I. William Zartman (eds), *International Negotiation: Actors, Structure/Process, Values* (New York: St. Martin's Press, 1999).

28. Thomas G. Weiss, *The United Nations and Civil Wars* (Boulder: Lynne Reinner, 1996).

29. Richard H. Solomon, *Exiting Indochina: U.S. Leadership of the Cambodia Settlement and Normalization with Vietnam* (Washington, DC: United States Institute of Peace Press, 2000).

30. Chester A. Crocker, *High Noon in Southern Africa: Making Peace in a Rough Neighborhood* (New York: W.W. Norton, 1992).

31. See Hans J. Morgenthau, *Politics among Nations: The Struggle for Power and Peace* (New York: Alfred A. Knopf, 1985); Kenneth Waltz, 'Structural Realism after the Cold War', *International Security* 25:1 (2000), 5–41.

32. Stephen D. Krasner, *Structural Conflict: The Third World Against Global Capitalism* (Berkeley: University of California Press, 1985).

33. Samuel B. Bacharach and Edward J. Lawler, 'Power Dependence and Power Paradox in Bargaining', *Negotiation Journal* 2:2 (1986): 167–74.

34. Bacharach and Lawler, 'Power Dependence'; Zartman, I. William, *Positive Sum: Improving North-South Negotiations* (New Brunswick: Transaction Books, 1987).

35. I. William Zartman and Maureen R. Berman, *The Practical Negotiator* (New Haven: Yale University Press, 1982), 205–7.

36. Hampson, *Multilateral Negotiations*.

37. Robert L. Rothstein, 'Regime-Creation by a Coalition of the Weak: Lessons from the NIEO and the Integrated Program for Commodities', *International Studies Quarterly* 28:3 (1984), 307–28.

38. I. William Zartman, 'Common Elements in the Analysis of the Negotiation Process', *Negotiation Journal* 4:1 (1988), 31–43 at 33.

39. Jacob Bercovitch, *Social Conflicts and Third Parties: Strategies of Conflict Resolution* (Boulder: Westview Press, 1984), 134.

40. Robert O. Keohane and Joseph S. Nye Jr., *Power and Interdependence*, 3rd edn (New York: Longman, 2000); Peter M. Haas, 'Do Regimes Matter? Epistemic Communities and Mediterranean Pollution Control', *International Organization* 43:3 (1989), 377–404; Ernst B. Haas, *When Knowledge Is Power: Three Models of Change in International Organization* (Berkeley: University of California Press, 1990); Peter M. Haas, *Saving the Mediterranean: The Politics of International Environmental Cooperation* (New York: Columbia University Press, 1990); Peyton H. Young (ed.), *Negotiation Analysis* (Ann Arbor: University of Michigan Press, 1991).

41. Robert D. Putnam, 'Diplomacy and Domestic Politics: The Logic of Two-Level Games', *International Organization* 42:3 (1988), 427–60.

42. Daniel Druckman, 'Negotiation Models and Applications', in Rudolf Avenhaus and I. William Zartman (eds), *Diplomacy Games: Formal Models and International Negotiation* (Berlin: Springer Verlag, 2010).

43. See Rudolf Avenhaus and I. William Zartman (eds), *Diplomacy Games: Formal Models and International Negotiation* (Berlin: Springer Verlag, 2010); Duncan Snidal, 'The Game Theory of International Politics', in Kenneth A. Oye (ed.), *Cooperation Under Anarchy* (Princeton: Princeton University Press, 1986); Robert Axelrod, *The Evolution of Cooperation* (New York: Basic Books, 1984); Steven J. Brams, *Negotiation Games: Applying Game Theory to Bargaining and Arbitration* (New York: Routledge, 1990); Oran R. Young (ed.),

Bargaining: Formal Theories of Negotiation (Urbana: University of Illinois Press, 1975); Frank C. Zagare and Marc D. Kilgour, *Perfect Deterrence* (Cambridge: Cambridge University Press, 2000).

44. See Bruce Buena de Mesquita, 'Multilateral Negotiations: A Spatial Analysis of the Arab-Israeli Dispute', *International Organization* 44:3 (Summer 1990), 317–40.

45. Axelrod, *Evolution of Cooperation*; Snidal, 'Game Theory of International Politics'.

46. William Riker, *The Theory of Political Coalitions* (New Haven: Yale University Press, 1962); Howard Raiffa, *The Art and Science of Negotiation* (Cambridge, MA: Harvard University Press, 1982), 257–74.

47. See, for example, David A. Lake and Robert Powell (eds), *Strategic Choice and International Relations* (Princeton: Princeton University Press, 1999).

48. Harold H. Saunders, *Politics is about Relationship: A Blueprint for the Citizens' Century* (New York: Palgrave Macmillan, 2005).

49. L.W. Doob, *Intervention: Guides and Perils* (New Haven: Yale University Press, 1993); John Paul Lederach, *Building Peace: Sustainable Reconciliation in Divided Societies* (Washington, DC: United States Institute of Peace Press, 1995).

50. Louis Kriesberg, 'Preventing and Resolving Destructive Communal Conflicts', in David Carment and P. James (eds), *The International Politics of Ethnic Conflict: Theory and Evidence* (University of Pittsburgh Press, 1997); Louis Kriesberg, *International Conflict Resolution: The U.S.-USSR and Middle East Cases* (New Haven: Yale University Press, 1992).

51. Herbert C. Kelman, 'Social-Psychological Dimensions of International Conflict', in I. William Zartman and J. Lewis Rasmussen (eds), *Peacemaking in International Conflict: Methods and Techniques* (Washington, DC: United States Institute of Peace Press, 1997); Herbert C. Kelman, 'The Interactive Problem-Solving Approach', in Chester A. Crocker and Fen Osler Hampson with Pamela Aall (eds), *Managing Global Chaos: Sources of and Responses to International Conflict* (Washington, DC: United States Institute of Peace Press, 1996).

52. Paul Wehr and John Paul Lederach, 'Mediating Conflict in Central America', in Jacob Bercovitch (ed.), *Resolving International Conflicts: The Theory and Practice of Mediation* (Boulder, CO: Lynne Rienner Publishers, 1996).

53. Harold H. Saunders, 'Prenegotiation and Circum-negotiation: Arenas of the Peace Process', in Chester A. Crocker and Fen Osler Hampson with Pamela Aall (eds), *Managing Global Chaos: Sources of and Responses to International Conflict* (Washington, DC: United States Institute of Peace Press, 1996).

54. Louis Kriesberg, 'Varieties of Mediating Activities and of Mediators', in Bercovitch (ed.), Resolving International Conflicts, 228; Harold H. Saunders, 'Interactive Conflict Resolution: A View for Policy Makers on Making and Building Peace', in Paul C. Stern and Daniel Druckman (eds), *International Conflict Resolution after the Cold War* (Washington, DC: National Academy of Sciences, 2000); Nadim N. Rouhana, 'Interactive Conflict Resolution: Issues in Theory, Methodology and Evaluation', in Paul C. Stern and Daniel Druckman (eds), *International Conflict Resolution after the Cold War* (Washington, DC: National Academy of Sciences, 2000).

55. Chester A. Crocker, Fen Osler Hampson, and Pamela Aall, *Rewiring Regional Security in a Fragmented World* (Washington, DC: United States Institute of Peace Press, 2011).

56. Hampson, *Multilateral Negotiations*; I. William Zartman, *International Multilateral Negotiation: Approaches to the Management of Complexity* (San Francisco: Jossey-Bass, 1994).

57. Andrew Moravcsik, 'A New Statecraft? Supranational Entrepreneurs and International Cooperation', *International Organization* 53:2 (1999), 117–46.
58. Raymond Cohen, *Negotiating Across Cultures: International Communication in an Interdependent World* (Washington, DC: United States Institute of Peace Press, 1997).
59. See Ceclia Albin, 'Justice, Fairness, and Negotiation: Theory and Reality', in Peter Berton, Hiroshi Kimura, and I. William Zartman (eds), *International Negotiation: Actors, Structure/ Process, Values* (New York: St. Martin's Press, 1999); Ceclia Albin, *Justice and Fairness in International Negotiation* (Cambridge: Cambridge University Press, 2001); Fen Osler Hampson and Judith Reppy, *Earthly Goods: Environmental Change and Social Justice* (Ithaca: Cornell University Press, 1996); Young, *Negotiation Analysis*; Zartman, 'Justice in Negotiation'.
60. Hampson and Reppy, *Earthly Goods*.
61. Terrence P. Hopmann, 'Two Paradigms of Negotiation: Bargaining and Problem Solving', *The Annals of the American Academy of Political and Social Science* 542 (November 1995), 24–47.

CHAPTER 18

···

MEDIATION

···

MARTTI AHTISAARI WITH
KRISTIINA RINTAKOSKI

ONE of the central functions of international diplomacy is to contribute to peaceful settlement of disputes between states and other actors. Therefore, it is not surprising that mediation has been a part of the 'tool box' of diplomats from the beginning. Already the official envoys sent for example by the rulers of Greece, Persia, India, or China in ancient times mediated in disputes between neighbouring sovereigns.

Peace negotiations and mediation long remained the domain of state actors. Negotiators and mediators were predominantly diplomats and senior statesmen. Classical diplomacy was conceived and practised as an elites-only club. The decisions of war and peace were made behind closed doors.

While the last thirty years have seen a significant growth in the use and recognition of mediation in both the domestic and international spheres, the changes in international relations that influence the whole world of diplomacy have also altered considerably how mediation is practiced. The shift from 'club' to 'network' diplomacy is clearly visible in the field of mediation.

Globalization, advances in information technology and communications are influencing political, social, and cultural relations across international boundaries. In conflicts and their resolution we cannot ignore the increasing relevance of non-state actors, particularly their ability to build networks of interrelationships for conflict or collaboration outside the framework of the state. The complexity of the international environment is such that states can no longer facilitate the pursuit of peace alone. Consequently, we have witnessed a phenomenal growth in the number of international and transnational organizations, all of which may affect issues of war and peace. These organizations have become, in some cases, more important providers of services than states. They have also become, in the modern international system, very active participants in the search for mechanisms and procedures conducive to peacemaking and conflict resolution. And indeed, today, peace mediation is an increasingly crowded and unregulated field, characterized by multiple and varied initiatives, sometimes competing ones.

At the same time, the causes generating and sustaining violent conflict remain plentiful: there is a large number of fragile states with weak institutions and a limited capacity to carry out basic state functions in the areas of security, inclusive and responsive governance, and civil administration; there is growing social inequality within states and globally between states and regions; and there is an increasing capacity of criminal and terrorist networks and other non-state actors to utilize the instruments of globalization to undermine peace and security.[1] As a result, we witness the persistence of both domestic and international conflicts such as those in the Horn of Africa, South Asia, and most notably the Middle East, which challenge the international community and its capacity for conflict resolution.

In this chapter I focus on mediation as an instrument for international diplomacy and conflict resolution reflecting the experiences gained through my involvement as a mediator in the peace processes in Namibia, Kosovo, and Aceh, Indonesia.

18.1 Mediation and Mediators Today

Mediation is one of the available methods of peaceful settlement of international conflicts listed in Article 33 of the UN Charter, which requests that the 'parties to any dispute, the continuance of which is likely to endanger the maintenance of international peace and security, shall, first of all, seek a solution by negotiation, inquiry, mediation, conciliation, arbitration, judicial settlement, resort to regional agencies or arrangements, or other peaceful means of their choice'.

Mediation is here defined as a process of conflict resolution, related to but distinct from the parties' own negotiations, where those in conflict seek the assistance of, or accept an offer of help from, an outsider (whether an individual, organization, group, or state) to change their perceptions or behaviour, and to do so without resorting to physical force or invoking the authority of law.[2]

Third-party mediation is often called upon when opposing parties, countries, or internal parties within a country have agreed to discuss their differences within an agreed framework in order to find a satisfactory solution to their demands, but are unable to overcome a deadlock or reach such a solution. The participation of mediators is based on the trust of all of the conflict parties. Mediators do not choose the conflicts they become involved in—the conflict parties choose the mediator.

Ever since its creation, the United Nations has been a principal actor in the peacemaking scene. In the United Nations, the act of mediation describes the political skills utilized in efforts carried out by the Secretary-General or his representatives, through the exercise of the Secretary-General's 'Good Offices', without the use of force and in keeping with the principles of the Charter. As a mediator, the United Nations has two clear advantages. Most obviously, it is the world's only global organization with unparalleled legitimacy. Though this legitimacy may be strained at times and be different in different parts of the world, there still is no substitute for the moral authority and convening power of the UN. A second advantage is the very extent of the UN system. The UN system, though unwieldy and lacking any real command and control system, is still linked in many ways with the UN Secretariat and the various agencies, funds, and programmes involved in almost every conceivable issue. The fact remains that only the UN can mediate start-up and manage a peacekeeping operation, raise funds and deliver humanitarian assistance, and lead a process for longer-term reconstruction and development.

Relatively little has changed over the years in how the world body engages in mediation. The 'Good Offices' continue to be a key form of action. Only during the past few years, however, has a dedicated UN mediation capacity and expertise been developed: the Mediation Support Unit within the political department of the UN Secretariat.[3] The bigger shift has happened around the UN and the way it engages with partners in mediation has been redefined. It works on mediation with member states but also with regional organizations and private diplomacy and mediation NGOs.

In addition to the UN a wide range of actors—international and regional organizations, non-governmental organizations, eminent individuals, as well as states, large and small—have become involved in preventing conflicts and ending wars through dialogue and mediation. Multiple actors help if the effort is managed, which is not the case at the moment. Good intentions of competing mediators can have serious counterproductive effects on a peace process.

In this new world of multiple mediators, the UN is the only actor that can effectively regulate the mediation market by standards, codes of conduct, and basic principles of good mediation practice. But in operational mediation the space for UN mediation has shrunk and it is not the primary actor and perhaps should not be.

Regional organizations, such as the European Union,[4] the African Union, the Organization for Security Cooperation in Europe (OSCE), or the Association of Southeast Asian Nations (ASEAN) are also increasingly active in peacemaking and mediation. This is a positive development and will strengthen the overall capacity of the international community to solve conflicts and hopefully engage in preventive diplomacy much more effectively. However, there is a need to enhance mutual cooperation on plans, resources, and even capacities between the UN and regional organizations.

States continue to be major actors in mediation and often find themselves having to mediate a conflict that may otherwise threaten their own interests. States, both large and small, frequently have reason or motive to mediate in conflicts, especially when these are in their region or where they may have some interests to promote or protect. Whether it is Switzerland, Norway, or Turkey, states find themselves very often at the forefront of mediation activities. For small states an active role in peace mediation serves as a public diplomacy instrument. A country can become known, admired, and also rewarded for its peace efforts, which increases prestige and influence.

The terms 'Track I' and 'Track II' (also referred to as unofficial mediation or private diplomacy) are often used to distinguish between governmental and non-governmental diplomacy. They also serve to acknowledge that mediation and dialogue should not be the sole domain of elites, but should take place at varying levels of society.

The importance of Track II diplomacy in resolving conflicts has increased in past years due to the increased ability of different organizations and individuals to reach out to communities affected by conflict. Track II is less public and therefore open to a larger degree of movement. Track II organizations have more political freedom than their official counterparts carry and can thus be more effective, for instance in providing networking capabilities among parts of societies that are 'off limits' to most government personnel. Track II processes target influential actors within civil society, including business, institutional, academic, and religious leaders. Unofficial processes can ensure that grassroots participants are involved and notified of the advancements in the negotiation process. These actors are positioned to provide advice to government officials, as well as to amplify the concerns of grassroots communities. Track II processes often provide feedback on proposals, suggest agenda items overlooked by political leaders, or test innovative approaches before they are introduced at the Track I level. When official negotiations stall, organizations with vertical and horizontal reach into society—such as women's groups, religious networks, and business associations—may continue with dialogues so that the momentum for peace can move forward.

There are also limits to the involvement of Track II actors. Sometimes civil society actors start processes that are beyond their skills and abilities to complete. They may also be too small, too isolated, or lack the capacity to work with each other. The legitimacy of NGOs as actors is sometimes questioned.[5] However, the fact that civil society organizations can be perceived by many conflict parties as powerless may increase their attractiveness to the antagonists: if the attempt to open the dialogue fails the parties lose little by way of reputation or potential inducements to settle.

18.2 THE DESIGN OF A MEDIATION PROCESS

Peace processes, including the mediation phase, are often complex, multilayered efforts that involve a host of actors at different levels of society. Mediation is most effective when seen and practised as a part of a wider peace process and coordinated with other instruments, such as confidence-building, dialogue, and peace-building. Thus, mediation activities must be strategically designed, well supported, and skilfully implemented. The mediator has a key role in understanding the overall process and bringing together the necessary political support, both locally and internationally, relevant thematic expertise, logistical support, as well as designing the conduct of negotiations.

Of crucial importance for the mediator and the team is a 'feasibility study'. A thorough analysis of the conflict situation, the parties, and their incentives for war and peace should be carried out as the first priority. It is a part of the professional conduct of a mediator and can sometimes even lead to their withdrawal from the process. This conflict analysis influences the whole process design and mediation strategy: at what level to engage, how to gain leverage, and on whom to focus efforts. At this phase one should identify states that are able and willing to serve as guarantors of a peace settlement as well as what sources of support they can bring to make a settlement more attractive and help with its implementation. Also, the roles that international and regional organizations could play in the process should be considered. In this section, some key elements of designing a mediation process are discussed in more detail based on practical experience.

18.2.1 The Role and Mandate of the Mediator

The task of the mediator is to help the parties to open difficult issues and nudge them forward in the peace process. Mediators can play different roles. They can serve as hosts, observers, facilitators, formulators, educators, manipulators, or advocates. At least I have served in all of those roles in the different phases of peace processes. The mediator's role combines those of a ship's pilot, consulting medical doctor, midwife, and teacher. A mediator has to be able to evaluate the setting and to adopt the role that is the most suitable for that particular setting. Being a mediator is a particular skill, and it is not for everybody working in diplomacy and international relations.

Practitioners and researchers alike have made an effort to describe different styles of mediation. In general, one can distinguish between the following approaches: facilitative, evaluative, and transformative mediation. Facilitative mediation is the 'original' style of mediation. The facilitative mediator does not make recommendations to the parties, give his or her own advice or opinion as to the outcome of the case, or predict what a court would do in the case. The mediator is in charge of the process, while the parties are in charge of the outcome. In evaluative mediation the mediator has a much greater level of participation and interaction in the process to ensure that the disputing parties reach a settlement. An evaluative mediator might make formal or informal recommendations to the parties as to the outcome of the issues. Transformative mediation, finally, is based on the idea that mediation can potentially generate transformative effects, and that these effects are highly valuable for the parties and for society. Transformative mediation stresses the concepts of empowerment and recognition. Empowerment refers to enabling the parties to understand the variety of options available to them and allowing them to realize that there are choices to be made and that they have control over these choices.[6]

Different mediation styles and approaches are appropriate in different situations depending on the conflict situation and the profile and experience of the mediator. Facilitative mediation is what is commonly understood to be mediation, but I have never been able to identify myself completely with that definition or approach. I believe my mediation style is a combination of all three approaches.

My experience is that peace negotiations need to have a clear goal. The mediator needs to know rather well where to take the process, even if they are just there to help the parties. Without a clear objective it is easy to have long talks with few or no results.

In conventional thinking about mediation, third-party mediators are assumed to be neutral. So much so that many definitions of mediation include the term neutrality or impartiality. This universal principle is often presented in such a way that it does not tell us much about the mediator, or about how mediation is conducted.

I have not myself been neutral or impartial with regard to the issues or content of a peace process. When speaking of neutrality and impartiality it is important to distinguish between the issues on the one hand, and the parties involved on the other. It is very possible to take a clear stand on certain issues, but at the same time not to side with the parties. The Norwegian mediators in Sri Lanka provide a good example of this. While their basic position was to stay neutral and to aim towards a balanced process with respect to the parties, there were issues, such as children's rights, which they pressed for in negotiations.

Absolute neutrality in a peace process might render the role of mediators as protectors of peace meaningless. The mediator has, through their actions, an influence over the outcome of negotiations. If the mediator had no influence in guiding the process, then they would not be needed.

My experience and practice have thus made me sensitive towards the terms 'impartiality' and 'neutrality'. I much prefer the term 'honest broker'. For me it is important that the negotiating parties know who I am, what I stand for, and where I draw the red lines. This way I can honestly and openly work with the parties towards finding a solution to the conflict. The more mediators hide their influence, the more they actually increase their chance of being seen as manipulative.

In order to generate the appropriate strategies, mediation initiatives need clear mandates. The underlying purpose of the mandate may be to resolve a conflict, to contain it so as to maintain regional stability, or to freeze it until anticipated contextual changes occur. Sometimes the goal of mediation is merely to create political cover; a state may send an envoy to a conflict zone so as to be seen to be doing something, but the conflict may actually receive little attention. Strategies that exceed mandates are unlikely to find political support.

Some mediators have a high profile and the full backing of major powers or international organizations. They engage official representatives of conflict parties and may have considerable resources at their disposal. Others will have a much lower public profile but may nonetheless function with important political support and significant resources. By contrast, non-governmental or religious organizations have little political power of their own. That weakness, however, is a strength in that it grants them greater flexibility. Unencumbered by a perceived political interest or official protocol, Track II mediators can conduct their activities with greater operational dexterity than governmental mediators and can more easily gain the confidence of opposing sides as they are perceived as less threatening.[7]

The mediation processes that I have been involved in have had different mandates. In the Namibia and Kosovo peace negotiations, I was serving under a UN mandate. In the Aceh peace process, on the other hand, I acted as a representative of my non-governmental organization, which had been accepted to serve as a mediator by the conflict parties.

In Namibia, my mandate derived from being the Special Representative of the Secretary-General (SRSG) specified in UN Security Council resolutions 431 and 435 (1978). According to the resolutions, the key task of the SRSG was to supervise and control the process leading to the independence of Namibia through free elections. The Western five (France, United Kingdom, United States, Germany, and Canada), led by the United States had a key role in ensuring South Africa's acceptance of the process. Ultimately, the post of SRSG derived its power, influence, and authority from its political credibility. The SRSG represented the will of the international community as expressed by the UN Secretary-General and Security Council. This tacit authority, as well as the active political support expressed by the international community, is what provided the SRSG with political capital.

From the beginning it was clear to us in the United Nations Transition Assistance Group (UNTAG) that the operation needed to be linked to and supported by broader political mechanisms, at the Security Council and beyond, that reinforced its political role and brought weight and authority to bear on UN messages. The complexity of the operation and the intense interest it aroused led the Secretary-General to establish at Headquarters in New York a high-level Namibia Task Force, which met daily under his chairmanship, to coordinate the Secretariat's role and to provide policy guidance and maximum support to the SRSG in the field. The Task Force helped to maintain adequate political engagement and ensured continued consensus around mission objectives.

In a very different fashion, the mandate for the Aceh peace negotiations in 2005 came from the conflict parties themselves. The government of Indonesia requested my assistance in facilitating their discussions with the Free Aceh Movement (GAM) to end the thirty-year war in Aceh province. The government's non-negotiable position in terms of Indonesia's integrity meant that peace had to be built on an agreement that was based on some form of autonomy for Aceh within Indonesia; the government offered special autonomous status for the province. I met with GAM in January 2005 to obtain assurances of their seriousness and willingness to talk. My assessment was that special autonomous status was the best offer GAM would get from the government. I told them that I would be available to facilitate their talks with the government if they wanted to explore what special autonomous status would mean in practice and whether it would meet their key demands.[8] GAM agreed to this within the timeframe we had agreed in the January meeting.

This 'mandate' and process gained strength and credibility from the firm backing of the international community. The Aceh peace agreement would not have been possible without the combined efforts of many different actors: the EU and ASEAN, several supporting governments (including Sweden), local civil society, research organizations, and international NGOs (Olof Palme Centre, Centre for Humanitarian Dialogue, etc.) whose expertise Crisis Management Initiative (CMI) used in several occasions. The official, Track I diplomacy, while not in the forefront of the negotiation process, provided invaluable support during the negotiations, and emerged as the leading track during the peace implementation phase. Barbara Kemper's study of the two mediation processes conducted in Aceh by non-governmental actors—the Centre for Humanitarian Dialogue and the CMI—points out the importance of the leverage that a non-governmental mediator needs to have on hand for mediation to be successful. Given the necessary support official authorities can provide in cases when non-governmental personnel appear to be the better-suited mediator, this study emphasises the need for the further constructive development of communication and cooperation between international actors and interveners to a conflict on all levels of society.[9]

On the future status of Kosovo, I was approached by UN Secretary-General Kofi Annan in November 2005. Acting on the basis of the conclusions of the Security Council that the situation in Kosovo was no longer sustainable, he asked me to lead the political process to determine Kosovo's future status. As his Special Envoy and as per my terms of reference I was given maximum leeway in order to undertake my task and I was to report directly to him.

The work of the UN Office of the Special Envoy for Kosovo was carried out in close consultation with the Contact Group (France, Germany, Italy, Russia, the United Kingdom, and the United States) that together formulated a set of guiding principles, which provided a political framework for the negotiating parties. One of the guiding principles, in particular, proved to be of central importance:

> The Settlement of Kosovo's status should strengthen regional security and stability. Thus, it will ensure that Kosovo does not return to pre-March 1999 situation. Any solution that is unilateral or results from the use of force would be unacceptable. There will be no changes in the current territory of Kosovo, i.e. no partition of Kosovo and no union of Kosovo with any country or part of any country. The territorial integrity and internal stability of regional neighbours will be fully respected.

I made my first trip to the region in November 2005 and told the leadership in Belgrade that I interpreted the above-mentioned guiding principle so that Kosovo will not revert to Serbian control. My hosts, especially the prime minister, did not share this interpretation. Furthermore, during these initial visits to Belgrade and Pristina, it became apparent that the positions and perceptions of the status were deeply entrenched and so widely contradictory, that any immediate attempt to narrow these differences would have led nowhere.

In January 2006 the Contact Group met on ministerial level in London. At this meeting it was suggested that the Contact Group members would individually deliver a set of private messages to the Kosovo Status Process parties, highlighting that a return of Kosovo to Serbian rule was not a viable option and calling the parties to compromise to allow for a sustainable multi-ethnic society in Kosovo, with effective constitutional guarantees mechanisms to protect the human rights of all citizens of Kosovo.[10]

All but Russia delivered these private messages in February–March 2006 to Belgrade, Pristina, and the Kosovar Serbs. All members of the Contact Group, including Russia, agreed in the Ministerial Statement of January 2006 that the settlement needs to be acceptable to the people of Kosovo. Many, including the international media, believed at that time that Russia would in the end follow the line adopted in the Contact Group.[11]

18.2.2 Engaging the Conflict Parties

There often tends to be too much focus on the mediators that disempowers the conflict parties and creates the false impression that peace comes from the outside. It is the negotiators who matter, not the mediators—but in some cases mediators can help. The only people who can make peace are the conflict parties themselves, and just as they are responsible for the conflict and its consequences, so too should they be given responsibility and recognition for peace.

It is essential to have negotiators with real power, who act in the name of the parties, who are in a position to implement any agreement. Mediation cannot succeed unless the right people are at the negotiating table. Negotiation with representatives that do not represent the constituency they purport to represent is seldom worthwhile. If a group has no legitimate leader, there is no point in mediating until one can be established.

Questions related to having the right parties at the table have become increasingly complex with the rising number of internal conflicts with multiple groups fighting against each other and the government. The mediator needs to think about and strike a balance between inclusivity and progress: whether the mediator should strive to include all conflict parties in negotiations or whether the mediator should focus on making progress with those willing to participate.

Mediation may not be the right answer when the parties do not demonstrate serious intent to explore a political solution. In such circumstances, the mediator needs to test parties' motives and avoid pleading for the engagement. The mediator should be cautious about engaging when mediation may play into the hands of a dominant party, legitimizing actions by the parties that may cross the line of acceptable conduct.

Rather than starting the negotiations when the situation is not 'ripe', other activities might take the process further. Engagement in the pre-negotiation phase should enhance the conditions or skills needed for successful negotiations between the adversarial polities. Parties may have limited capacity to formulate or carry out agreements or may need to gain consensus, even within their own communities, about what issues are in dispute. Institutions, agencies, or processes may need to be established or enhanced to facilitate fair negotiations. Preparing a political environment for official negotiations might include establishing dialogue at unofficial levels, assisting civil society voices, or removing barriers to peace talks.

There is a strong recognition of the need to increase the role of women in peace talks. This is not about formal participation to ensure a gender-sensitive process, as this reduces gender concerns to little more than a box-ticking exercise. The particular challenge in many contexts is that women are not in such positions in government, political parties, and rebel groups, or even in communities, that they would be seen as legitimate representatives of these groups in peace talks. A mediator cannot bring in women just to address the gender balance if they do not have the support of a constituency. A mediation process, let alone a mediator, cannot change the society overnight. However, while acknowledging this, ways to bring women into peace processes at different levels need to be devised. One such way would be to show an example through the mediator's team and other international engagements. For example, during the Kosovo process I met women's organizations from both sides every time I visited the region. These meetings provided them with a channel to raise their concerns and also to gain recognition as important actors even if not included in the formal process.

18.2.3 Reaching Out Beyond the Negotiating Table

Constituents are less likely to accept an agreement reached if they have not been involved in the process enough to understand why the agreement was designed as it was and why it is the best alternative available. Lasting trust between the parties typically needs to be re-established at multiple levels of society for agreements to be successfully negotiated and implemented.

Reaching beyond the negotiation table is vital. My experience is that the combined effort of different actors in different tracks often yields the best results. A good conflict resolution strategy has to be multilevel and needs to include the official process of mediation, possible quasi-official processes promoted by unofficial groups, public peace processes aiming at sustained dialogue, and the various activities of civil society. At its best, a multilevel conflict resolution strategy gains entry at different stages, opens new avenues for dialogue, creates leverage, and shares costs and risks.

I believe we were particularly successful in Namibia in reaching out. In order to establish UNTAG as a legitimate authority with all Namibians our strategy was to have the staff of the forty-two districts and regional offices to interact as much as possible with the local population. The widely distributed field presence allowed for creativity and flexibility on the part of the staff in seeking contact with the Namibians. We also wanted to raise public awareness of what UNTAG was doing and why through an information programme that was an integral part of the operation. In retrospect, I believe that we managed relatively well in engaging the local population and creating local ownership of the transition process.

Local structures for traditional dispute resolution, reconciliation, and administration should be given the means to reconstitute themselves as they can have an important role to play in local dispute resolution and reconciliation that will be necessary in order for a sustainable peace to prevail.

The greatest source of risk often comes from spoilers—leaders and parties who believe that peace emerging from negotiations threatens their power, world view, and interests, and use violence to try and undermine the process. This is another reason why multi-track approaches are important—namely to reach out inclusively and to allow the reframing of issues so that all will see the benefits of a sustainable peace. Spoilers do not automatically get a seat at the negotiation table, but they must be listened to.

In general, diaspora communities have not been formally engaged as a constituency in official negotiations to resolve conflicts in their home country. However, there is increasing acknowledgement of the ways in which diaspora communities are directly affected by and impact conflict dynamics back home. Recognizing their stake in and influence on the political negotiations would be an important factor when attempting to solve a conflict. The mediator needs to know what the diaspora is thinking so that they do not become an obstacle to the peace process.

18.2.4 Regional Actors

Perhaps the complexity of international peace mediation lies in its 'surroundings'. For example, the role and engagement of regional actors is vital, as they can either support or undermine peacemaking efforts. It would be unwise to launch any process without serious consideration on how to work with regional actors in parallel to the peace talks. Namibia is an excellent example of the constructive role international and regional actors can play in a peace process. Looking back, it seems almost unbelievable that we managed to get all the principal actors—the Western five, the five permanent members of the Security Council (P5), Organization for African Unity, Frontline States, the South African government, and all political parties in Namibia including the Southwest African People's Organization (SWAPO), to work towards a shared goal. The Joint Commission consisting of South Africa, the US, Angola, Cuba, and Soviet Union had an important trouble-shooting role. The role of the UN and the successive US governments changed during the long peace process. During the negotiation process leading to the implementation of the Security Council resolution, there were times when the UN was needed and at times it was operating more in the background. The cooperation of the P5 was and is crucial.

In the Aceh peace talks, the neighbouring countries had a limited but constructive role. The deployment of monitors from five ASEAN countries as part of the EU–ASEAN Aceh Monitoring Mission increased the credibility and acceptability of the operation.

In the Kosovo process the neighbouring countries supported the process fully. However, the European Union was divided over the Kosovo status, which limited its role and influence. Even today, Spain, Greece, Romania, Slovakia, and Cyprus have not recognized Kosovo's independence. The international community—primarily the EU and the UN—could perhaps have handled the Kosovo status process better. The divergent position of Russia vis-à-vis the EU and the US has made the world question the authority of the UN Security Council.

18.2.5 Issues to be included on the Negotiation Agenda

The list of potential issues to be discussed in peace negotiations is long: disarmament, demobilization and reintegration, gender issues, relations with civil society, constitution-building, and power-sharing. Peace agreements cannot solve all problems. At best, they can create a democratic institutional and political framework that enables the parties to continue working together on the issues agreed upon. However, there is only a limited amount of research and debate on what issues can or should be productively included or excluded from a negotiation or mediation process. The parties and the mediator ultimately decide on themes and agenda points.

Yet, when we think about multidimensional conflicts, such as the one in Aceh, the challenge for the mediator is how to balance between past, present, and future. The list of issues was long: the political status of Aceh needed to be defined, natural resource ownership allocated, disarmament specified, a plan for a new role for the Indonesian military had to be agreed, and both sides knew they would have to face the difficult issue of whether to allow internationally monitored disarmament, and, if so, its terms. The economic agenda on the table varied from auditing systems of provincial revenues to taxation issues and centre–province allocation of finances. And, somehow, the ghastly human rights past—and present—that loomed over the talks would also have to be addressed. During the Aceh peace talks we had space for discussing the past but at some stage this had to stop. In order to move on and to achieve jointly agreed goals, it was necessary to shift the focus towards the future, instead of trying to solve all the past wrongdoings around the negotiation table.

In the Kosovo process we started by addressing the so called 'technical aspects' of status: rights of communities and their members: decentralization; religious and cultural heritage; economic provisions and property. Technical agreements or at least rapprochements were thought to serve as building blocks for the resolution of the status question. While technical talks yielded some agreements in a number of areas—including the protection of cultural heritage, community rights, and decentralization—parties remained intransigent on the status issue. Belgrade insisted that Kosovo should remain an autonomous province within Serbia, while Pristina insisted on independence. I had hoped, and would very much have preferred, that this process would have led to a negotiated agreement. Instead the process left no doubt that the parties' respective positions on Kosovo's status did not contain any common ground for such an agreement. I concluded that no amount of additional negotiations would change that. The potential for negotiations was exhausted.

In recent years, transitional justice and dealing with the past have been one of the widely debated issues within international conflict resolution, for justice is the cornerstone of lasting peace. When a mediator gets involved with a peace process, there are two main concerns, firstly to prevent the recurrence of the problem that caused the conflict in the first place and secondly to lay the foundations for reconciliation and start building a well-functioning, reliable, and independent legal system. Many peace agreements fail to be sustainable and revert to violence within a few years. Some of this is due to the fact that collective memories and suffering are so strong that unless they are addressed in one way or the other there is little potential for a peaceful future.

In the context of the Aceh peace talks I have been both blamed for not addressing the issue of justice adequately,[12] and praised for being able to ensure that the agreement included provisions for human rights and transitional justice.[13]

Sometimes insisting on the inclusion of transitional justice mechanisms brings several associated risks. Conflict parties may not want to deal with mediators who are going to force the inclusion of human rights provisions, investigations of possible war crimes, and subsequent justice into the peace process. Likewise, institutions such as the EU might find it problematic to engage with actors who refuse to consider addressing massive human rights abuses and other crimes committed during the conflict. However, the inclusion of transitional justice measures need not be as black and white as a stark choice between either prosecutions for war criminals or broad amnesty. A broad range of both judicial and non-judicial measures exist, including truth seeking and truth and reconciliation commissions, institutional reforms, providing reparations to victims, advance community reconciliation, and memorials.

A peace agreement is not the end, it is the beginning. The implementation of the treaty and resulting democratic changes within the society are the true test of the agreement and will take several years. Post-agreement implementation activities are designed to ensure that successful negotiations bear fruit. Development aid may be used to quickly establish technical committees that provide logistical support, monitoring, and institutional mechanisms for implementing and sustaining new cooperative relationships. Timely support for agreement implementation can help reassure uncertain parties, build trust, and show results of peace. These activities may include their own processes for addressing disputes associated with implementing negotiated changes.

While mediated agreements are unlikely to be transformational on their own, they do have the potential to lay the foundation for a successful transition to peace. It is absolutely vital that the linkages between peacemaking and peace-building be tightened and the gaps, which hamper so many recovery processes, be narrowed. Every society recovering from conflict needs a long-term development plan closely interlinked to the peace process itself. Even a successful peacemaking phase can fail if it is followed by peace-building and state-building efforts that are detached from the society and the peace process.

18.3 Mediation as Part of Diplomatic Practice Today

The old techniques of power and deterrence seem increasingly less relevant to deal with the problems and conflicts confronting us. Mediation may well offer the most coherent and effective response to these issues. To ensure that it can also be successful, we need to develop a better understanding of the process and offer consistent guidelines to the many actors involved in mediation.

There are elements of both continuity and change in the conduct of mediation as part of 21st-century diplomacy. As discussed, leverage, which often comes from the political and other support from states and intergovernmental organizations, continues to be one of the key factors for a successful outcome in peace mediation.

Networks have become a vital tool for a mediator. Actors include transnational non-governmental organizations, multinational corporations, international organizations, and regional organizations. Engaging a considerable number of players at different levels of diplomacy and exploiting their comparative advantages while being able to manage the complexity for the benefit of the peace process, form a part of a mediation process design. Often the potential of several tracks of diplomacy is under-utilized owing to different reasons. Sometimes the necessary will or networks do not exist. Sometimes the time and resources available do not allow this to happen. This is a clear indication of the need to expand the conception of diplomacy in such a way that it takes into cognizance the complex nature of the modern international system and the adaptation of diplomatic practice to accommodate this new reality. The inclusiveness of peace processes is something that needs continued improvement in the interest of sustained peace.

NOTES

1. See Jorge Heine and Ramesh Thakur (eds), *The Dark Side of Globalization* (Tokyo: United Nations University Press, 2011).
2. Jacob Bercovitch and Ayse Kadayifci, 'Exploring the relevance and contribution of mediation to peace-building', *Peace and Conflict Studies* 9:2 (December 2002), 21–40.
3. See Thant Myint-U, *The UN as Conflict Mediator: First Amongst Equals or the Last Resort?* (Geneva: Center for Humanitarian Dialogue, 2006).
4. On the EU's role in peace mediation, see further <http://www.initiativeforpeacebuilding.eu/mediation.php>.
5. For the role of NGOs in contemporary diplomacy, see Chapter 9, this volume.
6. On mediation styles, see further Sarah Bolger, Brenda Daly, and Noelle Higgins, 'International Peace Mediators and Codes of Conduct: An Analysis', *Journal of Humanitarian Assistance* (August 2010), 13–25.
7. Amy L. Smith and David R. Smock, *Managing a Mediation Process* (Washington: United States Institute of Peace, 2008).
8. Thus, independence was not on the table in the negotiations, but GAM did not demand autonomy during the negotiations. Nothing being agreed before everything was agreed, GAM could see the 'whole package', for instance what the government of Indonesia would offer inside the framework of autonomy, and then decide if that was enough for them to give up independence.
9. See Barbara Kemper, *Mediation in Intrastate Conflicts: The Contribution of Track-Two Mediation Activities to Prevent Violence in the Aceh Conflict* (Duisburg: Institute for Development and Peace and University of Duisburg-Essen, 2007).
10. The private messages were:
    - The unconstitutional abolition of Kosovo's autonomy in 1989 and the ensuing tragic events resulting in the international administration of Kosovo have led to a situation in which a return of Kosovo to Belgrade's rule was not a viable option.
    - While today's democratic leadership of Serbia cannot be held accountable for the policies of the Milosevic regime, leaders in Belgrade and Pristina must come to terms with its legacy and have important responsibilities.
    - The leaders of Serbia and Kosovo have a responsibility to participate constructively in the status negotiations and prepare their publics for the inevitable and necessary compromises. The status process must result in a secure, multi-ethnic Kosovo that meets the highest standards of human rights, democracy, and rule of law; it should result in better living conditions for all citizens and communities in Kosovo.
    - The leadership of Serbia's priority must be to help secure the ethnic Serb community's future in Kosovo. It must focus on sustainable multi-ethnicity in Kosovo, with effective

constitutional guarantees and appropriate mechanisms to protect the human rights of all citizens of Kosovo. The Kosovo Serb community has an essential role to play in shaping Kosovo's future and should participate actively in the status process and in the Kosovo Government, Assembly, and working groups.

- The leadership of Kosovo's priority must be to accelerate standards implementation and focus on conforming with democratic values and meeting European standards. In this context, we attach particular importance to the issues of decentralization; minority rights; establishment of conditions facilitating the return of refugees and displaced persons; mechanisms to allow the participation of all Kosovo communities in government, both on the central and local level; and specific safeguards for the protection of the cultural and religious heritage of Kosovo.

- The international community will establish a post-settlement international civilian and military presence that will exercise appropriate supervision and control of compliance of the provisions of the settlement.

- In this context, the international community reiterates its commitment to the people of Serbia and Kosovo to support their goal of living in prosperity, freedom, and security and of realizing their Euro-Atlantic aspirations. We reiterate the importance of full cooperation with the International Criminal Tribunal for the Former Yugoslavia (ICTY), in particular bringing to justice all those indicted by the tribunal.

- We look forward to concluding the final status process in the course of 2006.

11. See Guy Dinmore and Daniel Dombey, 'Russia and China "pledge not to block new Kosovo"', *Financial Times*, 14 March 2006.

12. 'Despite the deep involvement of international actors in both phases, three main factors limited both their ability and their willingness to promote a justice agenda more forcefully. The first two factors concern the political context in which the peace process occurred: first, the relative bargaining power that one of the negotiating parties—the Indonesian government—had in the negotiations and its hostility toward extensive international role and, second, the limited time horizon for international involvement set by the context of the Indian Ocean tsunami. These two factors in turn shaped the third factor, which was the tactics used during the negotiations by the mediator, President Ahtisaari. His decision to move very rapidly to a final negotiated agreement, which would by necessity be a rather minimalist document, had a lasting impact on the subsequent implementation of the peace process and therefore deserves separate consideration in its own right.' Aspinall, Edward, *Peace without justice? The Helsinki Peace Process in Aceh* (Geneva: Center for Humanitarian Dialogue, April 2008), 12.

13. 'In practice, mediators have managed to get agreement on the inclusion of human rights issues in peace agreement. For example, in the case of the mediation process between the GAM and the Indonesian government, the mediator, Ahtisaari, was successful in getting the agreement from the parties to include provisions on human rights and transitional justice in the final draft of the peace agreement. Article 2 of the Memorandum of Understanding deals with human rights and the establishment of a Human Rights Court and a Commission for Truth and Reconciliation. The third section covers Amnesty and Reintegration into Society, whereby the government of Indonesia agree to grant amnesty to all persons who have engaged in GAM activities and agree to release all political prisoners and detainees.' Bolger, Daly, and Higgins, 'International Peace Mediators and Codes of Conduct', 13–25.

CHAPTER 19

··

HUMANITARIAN DIPLOMACY

··

JAN EGELAND

THERE are situations of conflict, crisis, and chaos where traditional diplomacy has given up or there simply are no governments or organizations able or willing to invest the time and resources needed to find a political solution. There is, however, in our age of information, advocacy, and non-governmental activism no place with widespread suffering where there is no humanitarian diplomacy and action.

In certain protracted conflicts, from Colombia to Burma and Somalia, states and organizations are at times inactive in terms of finding political solutions, but they cannot refrain from efforts to save the lives and limit the suffering of vulnerable individuals and communities. When political and military envoys give up, but also when they are in full swing the UN, major capitals, and leading international organizations at least agree on one seemingly apolitical and uncontroversial thing: send the humanitarians! From North Korea to Libya and from Afghanistan to eastern Congo, emergency relief thus represents a minimum default version of diplomatic activity and international relations when everything else fails.

Humanitarian affairs have grown in scope, size, and quality and are primarily undertaken by the UN system, the Red Cross and Red Crescent Movement, some governmental international assistance agencies, and a growing number of local, national, and international non-governmental relief groups. Within these broad categories of organizations there are today several hundred bigger and thousands of smaller humanitarian groups, agencies, and organizations, with a total recorded spending of USD 13.3 billion in 2010.[1]

Local and international humanitarian workers struggle every day to reach civilians in more than thirty armed conflicts and the affected population in more than a hundred natural disasters that unfold at any given time. Much has been done to improve the effectiveness, efficiency, coordination, and security of humanitarian operations. Because humanitarian work has become so widespread and visible, peoples all over the world now seem to expect that, when conflict or disasters strike, the needy will get immediate relief.

All major religions, ideologies, and humanistic philosophies prescribe that the sick, the suffering, and the starving should be helped irrespective of race, creed, or culture. But this expectation, shared by heads of state and the public at large, that humanitarians will rush to the neediest irrespective of circumstances, is often not backed by a correspondingly unconditional political and military support for the basic humanitarian principles that are a precondition for secure and unrestricted access by impartial humanitarian workers. Hence, there is a need for the so-called 'humanitarian community' to invest in a corresponding increase in humanitarian diplomacy.

As the UN Emergency Relief Coordinator and UN Under-Secretary-General for Humanitarian Affairs I saw how unhindered humanitarian action, or lack of such, is measured in human lives. I witnessed the strengths and weakness of contemporary international diplomacy, international politics, and compassion on our watch. It was my job to mobilize attention, gather resources, and try to promote positive change when disasters and conflicts occurred. Coordinating humanitarian action within the United Nations, and between the UN and other governmental and non-governmental humanitarian organizations, meant that I had access to all the actors, good and bad, but could not order anyone to do anything unless they were convinced it was right.[2]

In this period (2003–2006), we coordinated through the United Nations massive, life-saving international relief in the Indian Ocean tsunami, the South Asian earthquake, the Horn of Africa, Southern Africa, the Lebanon war, and the Darfur crisis. In several of these overwhelming emergencies, tens of thousands of lives were predicted to perish. The sombre predictions were averted because humanitarian action, building on local capacities, can today be greatly more effective than it was a generation ago.

At times humanitarian affairs, diplomacy's ground zero, become an alibi for the inaction of donors and international institutions that cannot or will not invest what it may take to solve the crisis. Blankets and food rations are provided when inadequate political and security measures fail to address the root causes of the crisis. Life-saving relief is neither more nor less than a temporary band-aid and an expression of solidarity and compassion with those who suffer at humanity's frontlines.

The inherent limitation of humanitarian aid is that it administers and ameliorates the crisis, but does not solve it. From Darfur to Somalia and Gaza the effectiveness of UN agencies, the Red Cross and Red Crescent, and non-governmental groups is keeping people alive, but not giving them a durable and stable outcome that can bring development and peace.[3]

This chapter will first look at some definitions of humanitarian diplomacy. I will then draw on personal experience to discuss humanitarian action in times of natural disaster and war before reflecting on some enduring challenges facing humanitarian actors and drawing lessons for reforming humanitarian diplomacy.

19.1 WHAT IS HUMANITARIAN DIPLOMACY?

Definitions of the term 'humanitarian diplomacy' constitute several sub-sections of the initially presented definitions of general 'diplomacy' in earlier chapters of this *Handbook*. Definitions vary slightly according to the main area of interest of the humanitarian actors in question. In their current web-posted policy paper on 'Humanitarian Diplomacy Policy', the International Federation of the Red Cross and Red Crescent Societies provides the following definition: 'Humanitarian diplomacy is persuading decision makers and opinion leaders to act, at all times, in the interests of vulnerable people, and with full respect for fundamental humanitarian principles.'[4]

The Red Cross and Red Crescent societies work mostly in peace, natural disasters, and with social and rescue work, whereas the original International Committee of the Red Cross (ICRC), since its foundation in Geneva in 1863, has concentrated its work on assisting non-combatants in armed conflicts. In an academic paper by one of their own lawyers we find the following definition: 'The ICRC's humanitarian diplomacy is a strategy for influencing the parties to armed conflicts and others—States, non-State actors and members of civil society. Its purpose is purely humanitarian and it is carried out through a network of sustained relationships—bilateral and multilateral, official and informal.'[5]

An important and difficult part of humanitarian diplomacy is humanitarian negotiations with armed groups. In the UN we defined humanitarian negotiations as 'those negotiations undertaken by civilians engaged in managing, coordinating and providing humanitarian assistance and protection for the purposes of: (i) ensuring the provision of protection and humanitarian assistance to vulnerable populations; (ii) preserving humanitarian space; and (iii) promoting better respect for international law.'[6]

Modern humanitarian action, as initiated by ICRC founder Henry Dunant, has been inspired by some 'fundamental humanitarian principles' that were finally agreed to be the following seven by the International Conference of the Red Cross and Red Crescent in 1965: humanity, impartiality, neutrality, independence, voluntary service, unity, and universality.[7]

Effective humanitarian action *inter arma*—between and among armed groups—requires that the armed actors respect the impartiality and independence of relief work, which again requires that the humanitarian group successfully seeks and gets the acceptance of the parties to a conflict. Such an acceptance approach is defined as 'Actively building and cultivating good relations and consent as part of a security management strategy with local communities, parties to the conflict, and other relevant stakeholders and obtaining their acceptance and consent for the humanitarian organization's presence and its work.'[8]

A related method of humanitarian diplomacy in conflict is 'deconfliction':

> The exchange of information and planning advisories by humanitarian actors with military actors in order to prevent or resolve conflicts between the two sets [sic]

objectives, remove obstacles to humanitarian action, and avoid potential hazards for humanitarian personnel. This may include the negotiation of military pauses, temporary cessation of hostilities or ceasefires, or safe corridors for aid delivery.[9]

19.2 THE 2004 INDIAN OCEAN TSUNAMI

With hundreds of humanitarian organizations, thousands of relief workers, and billions of dollars of material supplies and services involved, the coordination of humanitarian operations is becoming increasingly important. Humanitarian diplomacy is, to a large extent, the art of facilitating the optimal relief, reaching through the best channels and actors, without delay and waste, to those in greatest need. All the coordination work to avoid bottlenecks and bureaucratic and political impediments and all the needed consultation with and for the actual beneficiaries must take place while the chaotic and confusing real-time circumstances play out.

The massive Indian Ocean tsunami of December 2004 was such a situation—and I was the UN Emergency Relief Coordinator at the time.

The operational Geneva office of the UN Office for the Coordination of Humanitarian Affairs (OCHA) had been alerted at around 2 am Geneva time on 26 December, minutes after a massive earthquake west of the northern tip of the huge Indonesian island of Sumatra. The duty officer had awakened a number of colleagues and the system had clanked into action. Some started to piece together a first situation report, others began alerting our stand-by personnel for immediate deployment to the field, and still others started to answer press enquires, draft the first press statement, and phone the diplomatic missions of the affected countries in Geneva, the world's 'humanitarian capital', to offer UN support and expertise. When I was called at 6 am New York time, the first team was already on its way to Sri Lanka and the Geneva colleagues had offered all the affected nations UN assistance and coordination, which the Maldives and Sri Lanka had already requested.

The same early morning a cell of relief coordinators became active also in New York. From both cities we linked up with our UN country teams in the affected countries, but nearly all of the UN resident and humanitarian coordinators were on home leave over New Year and as always in large, sudden-onset disasters the biggest immediate problem was the lack of reliable information. Bad news were trickling in from our acting UN country heads in an increasing number of countries during the first hours and days. The tsunami had travelled at a speed of 500 km per hour. It had reached Sumatra in twenty minutes, and had taken about one and a half hours to reach Sri Lanka and Thailand, a couple of hours to reach India, three hours to the Maldives, and several hours later as far as the eastern coast of Africa. No organized warning or evacuation had taken place anywhere. There was complete confusion in all the affected countries. It was impossible for the governments even to formulate what assistance they needed from us.

The first day of the emergency I sent, as principal for humanitarian relief with the Administrator of the UN Development Programme (UNDP), the following instruction to the chief UN representatives in the affected countries:

> We do trust that you have already convened crisis meetings with your UN Country Team (UNCT), or are in the process of doing so. We depend on you to be fully updated on the situation in your respective country, on the action of the UNCT, on how you are mobilizing the existing resources of the UNCT, and what resources are required to immediately enable you to provide assistance to the Governments. You are requested to continue the contacts established during today Sunday with OCHA to discuss further assistance that may be required from OCHA. This information, as well as any request for additional support from the respective agencies, should be relayed to the respective headquarters as soon as possible. In addition, the Emergency Relief Coordinator is mobilizing reinforcements to all Country Teams through the deployment of relief personnel. Contact with each office will be established for this purpose.

19.2.1 Who Should Be in Charge?

Two days later, when the local, national, and international relief operations were beginning to take shape, US President George W. Bush called a press conference where he promised huge military resources, including transport aircrafts, marine expeditionary units, and the aircraft carrier *USS Abraham Lincoln* with lots of helicopters. In contrast with politically charged armed conflicts, military assets are usually very beneficial in 'apolitical' natural disasters. Local infrastructure, transport, and communications are usually non-functional when they are most needed and there are no corresponding civilian logistical capacities at those times.

In the same press conference, President Bush also made a potentially worrying announcement: 'The United States has established a regional core group with India, Japan and Australia to help coordinate relief efforts. I'm confident more nations will join this core group in short order.' The rest of that day we tried to find out what this odd group would actually do, given the fact that the US and the other 'core' countries had already given the UN and my office the mandate to coordinate relief efforts. We spoke to contacts in Washington and with diplomats from the other core countries, none of whom understood the rationale behind such a group. On the contrary, all the diplomats, including the Americans, were highly appreciative of the rapid UN deployment to the field, our briefings to diplomats, agencies, and affected countries, and our continuous advocacy for a coherent international response coordinated with local and national governments. Humanitarian diplomacy in this case seemed to be a case of public politics: the US administration needed to communicate to its own public that they were playing a key role in responding to the tsunami which was the number one news item in America and the rest of the world.

During the following days we tried to build the widest possible coalition of donor governments, civilian and military assistance efforts, and private corporations for tsunami relief and early recovery efforts. The several hundred projects that we managed to specify in the 'Flash Appeal', which Secretary-General Kofi Annan launched at a conference in Jakarta on 6 January, included forty partner organizations asking for $977 million for the next six months. Within a week of the appeal's launch, it was almost fully funded as part of the incredible $4 billion that were pledged by private individuals, corporations, and governments. The Jakarta conference was hastily convened by Indonesia's president in cooperation with Sri Lanka, Thailand, and the other hard-hit countries.

I watched the outcomes of the Jakarta conference from New York where we had a dozen daily meetings, conferences, and videoconferences with humanitarian partners in the affected regions. Perhaps the clearest sign that we had proven that the UN can provide the needed leadership in crisis was that the 'core group' announced that it had dissolved itself after only eight days, to fold into the overall coordination of the United Nations. The conference reaffirmed that the UN would be firmly in charge of international relief coordination.

19.2.2 Political Challenges

As logistical bottlenecks were overcome, political problems surfaced. Muslim groups in Aceh were campaigning to impose deadlines for the Western military and civilian presence. The government agreed that the foreign military forces should stay only a few weeks and hinted that they might limit the number of Western organizations and expatriate relief workers. The first notion I rejected publicly, on behalf of the UN, as a bad idea. This was not the time to do anything but welcome the military contributions which brought crucial water purification plants, field hospitals, helicopters, landing crafts, and airport handling crews. The idea of limiting the number of aid groups was something we understood they wanted to discuss, but we cautioned that it is not easy to block some groups and allow others to start work.

Nearly all of the approximately 200 international relief organizations coming to Aceh were bringing in generous funding, but perhaps too many amateurs were setting up shop in a field of action where the difference between high- and low-quality action is measured in human lives. At many live phone-in shows with BBC, CNN, and other major outlets the large UN was often contrasted with the small, 'un-bureaucratic', non-governmental aid groups that without administrative overheads and red tape can go straight to the needy with their relief. Journalists instinctively love small groups and idealists and are sceptical of large agencies and organizations.

I chose to praise the undisputed idealism and speed of action of the smaller NGOs but tried to warn of the effects of hundreds of groups not being coordinated with one another or with the national authorities as they chase worthy emergency projects. In retrospect, I should have taken the unpopular view that groups with no previous contact with Sri Lanka or Indonesia should stay home and send their money to organizations with a track record of providing humanitarian assistance in these countries.

19.2.3 Reconciliation in Times of Crisis

Another worrying development was the resurgence of old political and military divides in Sri Lanka. Sri Lanka does not have anti-Western lobbies as does Indonesia, but its political leaders lacked the Indonesian government's ability to view the national tragedy as an opportunity for peace with the armed opposition. Whereas the peace talks with the Acehnese armed opposition group GAM were intensified and led to a cease-fire and ultimately a successful peace agreement,[10] the initial cooperation between the Sri Lankan army and Tamil Tigers in assisting casualties and retrieving and exchanging the wounded and sick was soon overtaken by old and bad political antipathies.

The first sign that Sri Lanka's president was neither able nor willing to seize the opportunity for peace came when Kofi Annan during his visit was not allowed to visit the Tamil Tiger-held areas of northern Sri Lanka where the devastation was as bad as on the government-controlled eastern and southern shores. Not even a personal appeal from Annan himself, when arriving in Colombo after the visits to Jakarta and Aceh, moved President Chandrika Kumaratunga. 'We concluded it was not worth for the world's topmost diplomat to go. The talks with the Tamil Tigers would be embarrassing for the government', the president told Annan in her presidential palace. Thus a great opportunity for bridge-building was lost. Relief officials and relief consignments got access, but the peace process was not advanced and Sri Lanka would pay a great price for the government's intransigence.

Two weeks after the tsunami struck I chaired a large international donors' conference in Geneva. With a few New York and Geneva colleagues we finalized our main power point presentation on needs and plans for the next six months five minutes before going on the podium to open the event that had drawn 250 high-ranking delegates from nearly 100 nations.

It took nearly ten months before I was able to visit the tsunami stricken communities in Sri Lanka and Aceh to see for myself what went right and what went wrong. And there were indeed many lessons to be drawn. I was pleased to hear from Sri Lankans and Indonesians alike that they appreciated the strong initial response from the UN, the early relief and the early teams of relief workers, and our strong advocacy for action, funds, and coordination.

I was disappointed to see, in October 2005, so many, especially in Aceh, still sitting passively in the same tents that they were provided with in the first weeks after the tsunami struck. In Sri Lanka many prefabricated temporary housing units had been produced, but there also permanent housing had not come to most of the hundreds of thousands of homeless, in part due to the government's slow allocation of land where new and safe housing could be built. On the first anniversary of the tsunami, tens of thousands were still in tents and without any livelihood. At the second anniversary, nearly all had solid roof and had been helped into old or new livelihoods.

19.2.4 Lessons Learned

My own observations are very much in line with the conclusions of the huge set of evaluation reports undertaken by independent experts and published under the name of the Tsunami Evaluation Coalition. We had from OCHA, along with forty donor governments and UN and non-UN organizations, helped initiate and coordinate the thousands of pages of lessons learned. The evaluation confirmed that

> generous relief provided affected populations with the security they needed to begin planning what to do next. Large amounts of funding allowed rapid initial recovery activities... Within a few months there was palpable evidence of recovery. In all countries, children were back in school quickly and health facilities and services were partly restored and, in some cases, much improved... The international response was most effective when enabling, facilitating and supporting (local and national) actors, and when accountable to them. Overall, international relief personnel were less successful in their recovery and risk reduction activities than they were in the relief phase.[11]

The tsunami aftermath saw the most rapidly and generously funded disaster response in history. The global total of $13.5 billion represent an astonishing $7,100 for every affected person, as opposed to only $3 per head actually spent on someone affected by floods in Bangladesh in 2004.

Sadly, in key areas the evaluators found the colossal tsunami effort a 'missed opportunity', as summed up in a key recommendation: 'The international humanitarian community needs a fundamental reorientation from supplying aid to supporting and facilitating communities' own relief and recovery priorities.'

19.3 LEBANON 2006: A WAR WITH MORE DEAD CHILDREN THAN ARMED MEN

In the intensely politicized atmosphere of armed conflict the work of the humanitarian envoy is even more sensitive than in times of natural disasters. During the war in Lebanon between Hezbollah and Israel an intensive humanitarian diplomacy was employed.

Hezbollah militants first attacked an army post in northern Israel and the Israelis retaliated with air strikes and later with troops across the border. Soon, the world and even the parties themselves were shocked by the uncontrolled escalation of hostilities. Hezbollah launched hundreds of rockets from Lebanon on civilians in northern Israel. Israel started massive bombing of Lebanese infrastructure as well as residential areas that might harbour Hezbollah and its missiles.

After a few days of war I was sent by Secretary-General Annan to Lebanon and Israel to assess the situation, launch the humanitarian operations, and meet the parties as a humanitarian envoy. Tens of thousands were fleeing every day from southern Lebanon when we were flown into Beirut in a British military helicopter. Hundreds were wounded and dozens died every day. Lebanese and international humanitarian organizations were trying to come to the relief of as many as possible. Every day UN and Red Cross truck convoys painstakingly made their way on some of the roads that were still usable.

In letters to the Israeli and Lebanese governments and through press conferences I announced that we would establish humanitarian corridors for emergency relief supplies by land from Syria at the northern border and by sea from Cyprus to Beirut. We also set up a notification system agreed with the High Command of the Israeli Defence Forces (IDF). This ensured safe passage for our increasing number of convoys from our hubs in Beirut, going down south and inland where the situation was increasingly desperate for hundreds of thousands.

After meeting the Lebanese and Israeli governments and launching an appeal for humanitarian funding with links from Beirut to diplomats gathered in Geneva and New York, I returned to New York to consult with Annan and seek his approval for the following proposal to the UN Security Council: a seventy-two-hour humanitarian truce that implored the parties to cease fire in order to permit a major operation where the UN and partner organizations, as well as the International Red Cross and the Lebanese Red Cross, would be able to move freely in the combat areas and do four things:

- Relocate the children, the wounded, the disabled, and the elderly who had not been able to escape the fighting in the worst war zones;
- Resupply hospitals and health centres with emergency medical relief items and fuel for generators to avoid a complete breakdown of public health facilities caring for the thousands of wounded;
- Provide water and sanitation facilities, food, and other basic supplies to the tens of thousands of displaced who were seeking shelter in public buildings in the conflict zones; and
- Establish an emergency communications system to vulnerable communities allowing us to address acute needs urgently where and when they arose.

With Annan's approval, I launched the proposal in the Security Council only hours after my return from the conflict areas: 'Mr. President, the Middle East is at a crossroads', I began the briefing. 'My fear is that more violence, more missiles, more terror, and more destruction creates more anger, more hatred and more disillusioned youths, and ultimately leads to less security throughout the region.'

I described the effects of the war in some detail and our efforts to alleviate the suffering through the convoys that now benefitted from us having already embedded a former US military officer as our UN representative in the IDF High Command.

> Yet, Mr. President, it must be clear to all, the parties to the conflict and the members of the Security Council, that the limited and carefully controlled assistance we will be able to provide through this notification system with the IDF is not enough to prevent the excessive suffering of the civilian population. We need an immediate

cessation of hostilities, followed by a cease-fire agreement, the deployment of a security force, and the political settlement of the conflict. As a first step, I am recommending to the Secretary-General and through him to you, a humanitarian truce. We need at least 72 hours of tranquilities for the sake of the children of Lebanon and northern Israel who, I believe, we all agree are the innocent victims of this escalating conflict.

All the ambassadors exercised their right to speak after I was done. None was negative, most were strongly supportive of my call for an immediate end to the fighting. I wish I had had the same engagement and support from the Arab and Islamic ambassadors, as well as from the Western powers, in the Darfur discussions.

The humanitarian truce proposal got the traction we had hoped for. NGOs, diplomats, humanitarian colleagues, and the media pick up on the idea. That evening CNN's 'Situation Room' lead with: 'Up first this hour, a new and dramatic call for a pause, a pause in the warfare here in the Middle East. The United Nations Emergency Relief Coordinator is asking for a 72-hour cease-fire to allow relief workers and humanitarian aid to get into crucial combat areas in Lebanon. Jan Egeland says this, "There's something wrong with a war where there are more dead children than armed men."'

The Israeli government at first was not willing to accept a humanitarian truce, but we got a green light for most of our convoys which were bringing in increasing supplies for expanding humanitarian programmes under the leadership of a humanitarian coordinator in Beirut whom we redeployed from Jerusalem. When the Russians said that they would table the truce proposal in the Security Council if there was no progress on a general ceasefire, the US intensified diplomatic efforts for a UN force that could enter southern Lebanon as the Israelis left and created conditions for a cessation of hostilities.

After a difficult start, the UN's political diplomacy under Kofi Annan's leadership worked exactly as it should. We helped to coordinate a growing humanitarian operation, we got agreement for a greatly expanded and empowered UN Interim Force in Lebanon (UNIFIL), and we recruited in record time the required number of troop contributors. The senseless war ended with the UN-brokered ceasefire on 14 August (Security Council Resolution 1701, 2006).

19.4 PROGRESS ON OUR WATCH, INJUSTICE IN OUR TIME

The long and global trends are that global diplomacy, including humanitarian diplomacy, is contributing to progress for most human rights and for most of human kind. The world is, in spite of all the setbacks, the recent international economic recession, and numerous political crises, getting steadily better for the majority of us. There is more peace and more children get education and health care than when the cold war ended. Fewer children die, even in a growing world population. The UNDP's annual Human

Development Reports show that due to more effective disaster risk reduction and more and better humanitarian organizations fewer people die each year, not only from armed conflict, but also from the growing number of natural disasters.

In the United Nations as well as in government and NGO service, I also witnessed, first-hand, how effective multilateral action with local and regional partners has helped to build progress and peace. Wars ended and hope was provided in Liberia and Sierra Leone, Angola and Burundi, south Sudan and northern Uganda, Guatemala and El Salvador, Kosovo and Bosnia, East Timor and Nepal. The number of armed conflicts has fallen from more than fifty to fewer than forty since the early 1990s. There is a marked increase in life expectancy on all continents and in all but a handful of nations. There are many more democracies, fewer military coups, and less genocide than a generation ago.

But there is also a darker side to globalization: the world is more socially unjust than in previous generations.[12] The distance between the top and the bottom billion has increased dramatically as the world economy has grown. The affluent nations and the richest within nations have become rich beyond the wildest imaginations of our forefathers. But the poorest two billion live in the same abject misery as before and on less than two dollars a day.[13]

While fewer civilians are killed in conflict now than twenty years ago, the brutality of armed actors and the suffering of the defenceless remain at medieval depths in a small number of countries. There is a pattern to the violence and atrocities that I saw in Afghanistan, Iraq, Gaza, the Congo, Ivory Coast, Kosovo, Darfur, Chad, Colombia, and Chechnya because the fighting takes place amidst and often against the civilian population. I saw, time and again, how in our time and age, it is more dangerous to be a woman or a child in these battlefields than armed adult male soldiers.

19.4.1 Westernized Humanitarianism

There is a near-consensus across the political, cultural, and religious spectra that we need to protect and promote effective assistance to the most vulnerable in times of crisis and conflict. All world religions promote ideals of compassion, justice, and respect for the dignity of life. No religion condones or approves the killing of innocents. But all major religions have been exploited to justify violence and intolerance by extremist groups. In the present generation, this is especially so on the fringes of some Islamic groups and sects.

The danger is that humanitarianism, a universal imperative and shared inter-cultural system of principles, become so Westernized in its funding, staffing, organizational structure, and political profile, that it risks long-term adversity in many non-Western settings. On top of that we often see the wrong countries push the right causes and thus undermine the effectiveness of action. In both Afghanistan and Libya the UN resolutions authorizing the use of force had near-universal backing in 2001 and 2011 respectively. But the real international operations end up as US or NATO-led military action that is increasingly controversial and which has directly negative consequences for the humanitarian actors, with their Western face and funding. When Burma's military rulers block life-saving aid to their own people, it should immediately fall upon China, India, and the Association of Southeast Asian Nations (ASEAN) to take the lead, as neighbours, in convincing the regime to provide access for international relief. The ball falls in their court because these Asian economic powers have real leverage, as opposed to the West that ends up with the only visible action and condemnation.

Similarly when we tried in 2003–2006 to mobilize against the atrocities in Darfur, there was little help or interest among Sudan's Asian or Arab trading partners. That neglect became fateful, because they might have made an impact in Khartoum—as opposed to the Westerners who failed during this period. Once, when I protested before government high officials the massive rape of women in Darfur, they counterattacked: 'we see your criticism in Western media, but we also see who support you: the same nations that tear apart Iraq and betray the Palestinians—and you want us to take moral lessons from them?'. The history of international solidarity has been paved by examples of wrong countries pushing right causes, while the potentially influential ones become passive bystanders.

19.4.2 Humanitarians in Danger

The so-called 'access negotiation' is a classical task of a humanitarian envoy. In reality, humanitarian action is often under attack, but neither governments, parties to armed conflicts, nor other influential actors are willing or able to guarantee safe and unimpeded access for relief groups to those in need. On the contrary, those who control territory, funding, or simply the closest guns often harass, politicize, militarize, and undermine humanitarian action with impunity. The last ten years represent one of the worst decades ever in terms of attacks on humanitarian workers and lack of humanitarian access. More than a hundred humanitarian workers have been killed each year in the new millennium.[14]

I spent a long night during 2–3 July 2004 with the foreign minister of Sudan negotiating the first breakthrough agreement on access for humanitarian organizations to Darfur. President Omar al-Bashir and Secretary-General Annan announced this Moratorium on Restrictions at the end of our first high-level visit. It meant the opening for what was to be one of the largest humanitarian operations ever. Since then new walls of administrative obstacles strangling operations has slowly been rebuilt and reversed humanitarian gains in both Khartoum and Darfur. A quicksand of endless bureaucratic obstacles has often consumed the time of humanitarian relief managers.

Some NGOs have half their staff paralysed due to the lack of travel, work, or residence permits alongside any number of other obstacles. The same is true for journalists who tried to report back to the donor community on humanitarian activities. Two American journalists were prevented from travelling with me to Darfur. This is part of a wide effort by the government to restrict access and reporting on Darfur. Journalists have been detained, threatened with expulsion, and harassed by a multitude of government authorities, particularly national security.

The ability to obtain and maintain access to populations in need is the key prerequisite for national and international humanitarian agencies. Without access they cannot deliver humanitarian assistance nor provide protection to vulnerable populations. While most countries remain safe for relief work, an increasing number of conflict zones are becoming progressively more dangerous.

On an early Saturday morning in August 2010, the bullet-riddled bodies of ten relief workers—three of them women—were found along a road in the Badakshan province of eastern Afghanistan. 'Before their travel we warned them not to tour near jungles in Nuristan but they said they were doctors and no one was going to hurt them', the local Afghan police chief told Reuters.[15] These execution-style killings of unarmed, civilian humanitarian workers are a stark reminder of how humanitarian action struggles to survive in the political and literal cross-fires of our time and age. It also graphically shows the nature and challenges of current relief work—how globalized, politicized, exposed, and vulnerable relief operations have become.

The majority of attacks on aid workers in the past decade have occurred in Afghanistan, Chad, Iraq, Pakistan, Somalia, Sri Lanka, and Sudan. In particular, it is national staff of UN agencies and NGOs who bear the brunt of this risk. Moreover, perceptions of affiliations with political and military agendas have eroded acceptance of humanitarian actors. The core humanitarian principles of impartiality, neutrality, humanity, and independence are not honoured. The protective natures of the emblems of the United Nations, the Red Cross and Red Crescent, and of humanitarian organizations have been dangerously undermined.[16]

Much can be done through humanitarian as well as traditional diplomacy to break the vicious cycle where humanitarians are attacked and blocked and victims in wars and disasters suffer unassisted. Those who attack or hinder the right to assist needy people must be held accountable for their breaches of international law. Humanitarian organizations must become more professional, more disciplined, and more principled in how they act and how they enforce principles and standards in high-risk circumstances. The UN and all non-UN humanitarian leaderships must more vigorously defend their right of humanitarian initiative and access and the security of their frontline staff. And humanitarian organizations that are willing to become tools for political agendas and compromise fundamental and inherited humanitarian principles for easy money must face greater peer pressure.

19.5 Humanitarian Reform

In 2005, as global Emergency Relief Coordinator, I initiated an ambitious humanitarian reform process. More than anything this effort of change management was triggered by the initially weak UN and NGO response to the humanitarian needs in Darfur in 2004. In OCHAs we felt we had ample proof that our old systems for funding, preparedness, and coordination did not work as they should. We were simply too slow to come to the rescue of the one million displaced in western Sudan, even after June 2004 when our pressure succeeded in lifting many of the Sudanese government's restrictions on our access. Even with the so-called 'CNN effect' working on our side and ministers and diplomats flocking to our briefings and fundraisers, during several long months we got too few experienced logisticians, water engineers, camp managers, and protection experts inside Darfur.

Knowing that it is usually easier to get forgiveness than permission, I decided to start up the reform process with humanitarian colleagues immediately and ask for formal approvals later. A humanitarian response review was undertaken by experienced experts interviewing operational organizations and field workers. With UN agencies and NGOs we reached agreement that the reform should boost our humanitarian muscles by ensuring predictability, accountability, and partnership: reaching more beneficiaries with more comprehensive needs-based relief and protection, in a more effective and timely manner.

The humanitarian reform programme was launched at the end of 2005 with several key pillars. First, we agreed through the standing humanitarian Inter-Agency Committee (consisting of the UN agencies, three large NGO federations, and the Red Cross and Red Crescent Movement) to make the response capacity stronger and more predictable in the areas of apparent gaps. Concretely, we agreed to establish a series of functional and operational partnerships, which we called the 'cluster' approach. These clusters have since been set up in most large emergencies to ensure effective coordinated action in such areas as water and sanitation, emergency health, logistics, shelter, and protection of the civilian population. We asked individual operational agencies to take the lead in each of these clusters and ensure that materials and expertise are planned, mobilized, and applied to good effect.[17]

When we started the reform efforts, our response capacity varied hugely from one area and population to the other. More often than not food was effectively provided through the World Food Programme (WFP), but tons of corn or lentils are of no use to a mother if her child is dying from lack of clean water. It was therefore important that the UN Children's Fund (UNICEF), partnering with NGOs, took responsibility for providing water supplies and latrines in a more predictable manner, while other agencies concentrated on other gap areas. The cluster approach is slowly but surely having the effect of providing more predictable assistance for more people in more emergencies.

Second, we needed more predictable funding for this improved response capacity; not so much for the media-exposed emergencies like the Indian Ocean tsunami, Darfur, and the Lebanon war in 2006, but for forgotten or neglected emergencies far removed from public attention. Annan agreed to propose that the 2005 UN General Assembly summit agree to set up a new and greatly expanded Central Emergency Response Fund (CERF) aiming at $500 million in voluntary contributions from UN member states. We secured important support from the governments of the UK, Sweden, Norway, and Luxemburg, who were willing to invest in and campaign for a fund that could guarantee that we had 'water in our hose when a fire was detected', to quote UK Development Minister Hilary Benn.

When the proposal to establish the new Emergency Fund came before the General Assembly in late 2005 it was already an uncontroversial fait accompli and the first element of the whole UN reform package to be agreed on. All regional groups had been consulted, donors had promised sufficient money to get going, and humanitarian organizations had been included in the planning process. Only four months later the CERF was launched with impressive initial contributions from 48 governments and private sector groups. Since its launch in 2006, CERF has committed over $1.8 billion from as many as 122 countries to 1,700 projects in some 80 countries.[18]

There will be neither operational clusters nor efficient use of funding if there is no guarantee of effective leadership on the ground. The third element of the humanitarian reform therefore was a systematic effort to recruit and train a stand-by pool of highly qualified humanitarian coordinators for emergency relief operations. The work of these key 'Field Marshals' has varied in terms of leadership and creativeness. Too often UN resident coordinators had continued business as usual when they were also given humanitarian emergency responsibilities. The number of trained and experienced candidates from inside and outside the UN system has been steadily expanded in recent years and can now be deployed promptly to major disaster or conflict zones.

Third and finally, we started a process of broadening partnerships by trying to be less 'UN-centric' and less 'Northern'. The UN system is engaged in larger and more numerous relief and recovery operations than ever before, but its relative share of the total humanitarian response is shrinking. The UN is needed for standard-setting, coordination, facilitation, and ensuring that political, security, and humanitarian efforts come together in a coherent whole. Most of the actual delivery of assistance on the ground is, however, undertaken by the growing number of NGOs and civil society movements from the North and increasingly from the South.

Time and again we see that more lives are saved in earthquakes, floods, and tsunamis by local groups than by expensive airborne fire brigades. Similarly, it is usually local and regional actors who make or break peace-building efforts and reconciliation. Recognizing the need to discuss a new deal in forging effective partnerships beyond borders and artificial organizational barriers, we called a first meeting of executive leaders of leading humanitarian organizations from the North and the South and from UN and non-UN agencies to form a 'Global Humanitarian Platform' in Geneva in 2006. This work is continuing and expanding.

The growth in high-quality civil society movements, especially within third-world societies, is probably the single most important trend in global efforts to combat poverty and conflict. They are more important than governments and inter-governmental organizations.

19.6 CONCLUSION

Man walked on the moon more than a generation ago, but we are still far away from securing even an absolute minimum of predictable international relief and protection for women, children, and civilians at large in many of the conflicts and crises of our time.

Too many communities are neither a strategic concern nor a media or public priority. I have been a humanitarian worker, researcher, and activist for more than thirty years. More often than not I have felt that whether our appeals on behalf of people in desperate need are heard is decided by a bizarre lottery for international attention rather than by the objective needs of the affected and the global resources at hand.

If you are African, non-English speaking, and affected by a slow onset natural disaster or one of the protracted ongoing conflicts you will lose out in Western media, and in Washington, London, and the Scandinavian capitals which are best able to place humanitarian priorities on the international agenda. The emerging and de facto economic powers outside of the Western hemisphere must be engaged to promote and protect humanitarian operations. Today, the net short-term outcome of deliberations among the powers is too often funding for a minimum of blankets and band aids to keep people alive, but not the comprehensive investment in development, security, justice, and political solutions which could help people out of their vicious circle of misery and vulnerability.

These criticisms and qualifications must be seen in perspective. Over the years I have witnessed how the international community, in spite of often half-hearted investment by the powerful and the rich, has succeeded in providing life-saving assistance and protection to those in greatest need. Through the United Nations and other international organizations I have seen how we can organize, against all odds, tremendous processes of change when we have the requisite political support from the most powerful capitals and a sufficient minimum of resources from the richest nations. So there is, in spite of all the troubles and threats, hope for humanitarian action.

Notes

1. <http://www.globalhumanitarianassistance.org/record-humanitarian-appeal-for-2011-1906.html/total-humanitarian-funding-2>.
2. See Jan Egeland, *A Billion Lives: An Eyewitness Report from the Frontlines of Humanity* (New York: Simon & Shuster, 2008).
3. See Michael Barnett and Thomas G. Weiss, *Humanitarianism Contested: Where Angels Fear to Tread* (London: Routledge, 2011).
4. <www.ifrc.org/Global/Governance/Policies/Humanitarian_Diplomacy_Policy.pdf>, p. 2.
5. Marion Harroff-Tavel, 'The Humanitarian Diplomacy of the International Committee of the Red Cross', 1. Available at: <www.icrc.org/eng/assets/files/other/humanitarian-diplomacy-icrc.pdf>. This is an English translation of an article originally published in French: 'La diplomatie humanitaire du Comité international de la Croix Rouge', *Relations Internationales* 121 (January–March 2005), 72–89.
6. Gerard McHugh and Manuel Bessler, *Humanitarian Negotiations with Armed Groups: A Manual for Practitioners* (New York: United Nations, 2006), 1. Available at: <http://ochaonline.un.org/humanitariannegotiations/index.html>.
7. International Federation of Red Cross and Red Crescent Societies, 'The seven Fundamental Principles', <http://www.ifrc.org/en/who-we-are/vision-and-mission/the-seven-fundamental-principles>.

8. Jan Egeland, Adele Harmer, and Aby Stoddard, *To Stay and Deliver: Good practice for humanitarians in complex security environments* (New York: United Nations OCHA, 2011), xiv. Available at <http://ochanet.unocha.org/p/Documents/Stay_and_Deliver.pdf>.

9. Egeland et al., *To Stay and Deliver*, xiv.

10. See Chapter 18, this volume.

11. See John Telford and John Cosgrave, with Rachel Houghton, *Joint Evaluation of the International Response to the Indian Ocean Tsunami: Synthesis Report* (London: Tsunami Evaluation Coalition, July 2006), available at: <http://www.alnap.org/pool/files/889.pdf>.

12. See Jorge Heine and Ramesh Thakur (eds), *The Dark Side of Globalization* (Tokyo: United Nations University Press, 2011).

13. See the Millennium Development Goal Indicators, at: <http://unstats.un.org>.

14. Egeland, Harmer, and Stoddard, *To Stay and Deliver*, 1.

15. Green, Matthew, 'Christian group denies converting Afghans', *Financial Times*, 8 August 2010, <http://www.ft.com/cms/s/0/1e7ae4e0-a309-11df-8cf4-00144feabdc0.html#axzz1 SQCTutp1>.

16. 'Providing aid in insecure environments: 2009 Update', HPG Policy Brief 34, Overseas Development Institute, April 2009.

17. See <www.humanitarianreform.org>.

18. <http://ochaonline.un.org/Default.aspx?alias=ochaonline.un.org/cerf>.

CHAPTER 20

DEFENCE DIPLOMACY

JUAN EMILIO CHEYRE

AT first sight, the notion of defence diplomacy may sound like a contradiction in terms—after all, military force has traditionally been the *ultima ratio*, the last recourse to be deployed by the defence apparatus of any given country, that is, the armed forces, when diplomacy has failed to keep the peace and such force is needed to preserve the nation state's territorial integrity or otherwise stand up for its national interest.

In fact, far from being an oxymoron of sorts, in the post-cold war era defence diplomacy has emerged as a not insignificant instrument of state policy. Defined as the 'employment, without duress, in time of peace of the resources of Defence to achieve specific national goals, primarily through relationships with others',[1] it has come to play an important role as part and parcel of the shift from 'club' to 'network' diplomacy that is such a prominent feature of this era.

In the recent past, the concept of defence diplomacy resurfaced because of the needs of the states of the Western Balkans and Central and Eastern Europe, was subsequently used elsewhere, and ended up being conceptualized and refined in Great Britain, a country that 'was an early champion of defence diplomacy, first mentioning the concept in its Strategic Defence Review of 1998 and addressing the role of the attaché in this regard'.[2]

In some ways, of course, diplomacy and military force have been joined at the hip from the beginning of time—the latter lurking always in the background of the former, and this link being embodied by the great military leaders in the Peloponnesian wars as well as by the Roman empire's powerful military representatives. In the modern era, the practice of what we know as defence diplomacy came into being during the Thirty Year War in the 17th century, as the Duke of Richelieu posted military officers abroad to liaise with the allied powers, monitor developments in the field, and gather intelligence information. By the 18th century, the practice of assigning defence attachés to embassies was initiated.[3]

It was Napoleon Bonaparte who formalized the appointment of military officers assigned to collect information and analyse it for the benefit of political leaders. This had already been recommended by Nicolo Machiavelli in *The Prince*,[4] who recommended that the latter always be accompanied by military officers to gather information about the different places he visited. Napoleon appointed a number of generals as his ambassadors abroad and, in 1806, appointed a military officer as second secretary at the French Legation in Vienna, in what is considered to be the first time a military man was designated in an ongoing advisory capacity at a diplomatic mission.

Among the first instances of that was the practice that emerged in Europe in the middle of the 19th century of assigning military officers to overseas missions and delegations. Designated as *military attachés*, they were given diplomatic status in 1857. Qualified with a thorough knowledge of at least one country, *attachés* were originally prepared for positions as commanders or team leaders.[5] By the late 19th century, they were fully incorporated into foreign missions, held official military representation among the powers of the time, and carried important roles in the dialogue and exchanges among delegations.

During the cold war, the United States understood very well the significance of military attachés. This was formalized in 1965 with the Attaché System within the Pentagon, and their postings to US embassies abroad. The military attaché thus became the principal adviser to the head of mission and serves as the single point of contact for intelligence for the Secretary of Defense and the Joint Chiefs of Staff of the United States.[6] In 1961, the Vienna Convention (see Chapter 28, this volume) established that defence attachés have the same privileges and immunities as diplomats.

Perhaps no one embodies better a certain conception of the role of the military in diplomacy at the height of the cold war than retired general Alexander Haig, appointed by President Ronald Reagan as his first Secretary of State, and thus as US diplomat-in-chief. Haig's elevation to such a position reflected one view of how US strategy in confronting the Soviet Union should unfold, relying on a former general, known for his rather bellicose views, to head US diplomacy. It could well be posited that during this period, the notion of 'defence diplomacy' relied solely on hard power as a bargaining factor to be deployed in the management of international tensions.

Yet, with the end of the cold war, things changed. Suddenly, the military were to be deployed well beyond the area of their traditional, specific competencies to achieve a variety of goals in the complex game of international power politics. The original role of the military attaché thus came to an end. President Bill Clinton's National Security Strategy of Engagement and Enlargement acknowledged the need to ditch the containment of communism as the guiding principle of US foreign policy and replace it with a forward strategy led by the leading market democracies. The latter was aimed at engaging international partners on military matters and at establishing a credible presence abroad, thus leveraging a strong interaction between the military and the diplomatic spheres.

> Such overseas presence demonstrates our commitment to allies and friends, underwrites regional stability, ensures familiarity with overseas operating environments, promotes combined training among the forces of friendly countries, and provides timely initial response capabilities... U.S. engagement is indispensable to the forging of stable political relations and open trade to advance our interests. Included in engagement are issues such as supporting democracy, providing economic assistance, and increasing interactions between U.S. and other militaries around the world.[7]

This indicates precisely what defence diplomacy stands for in our time. Associated with it is the defence support of public information, defined as 'the ability to understand, engage, influence and reform key foreign audiences through words and actions to foster understanding of US policy and advance US interests, and to collaboratively shape the operational environment'.[8] This capability includes public information activities as well as information operations to reach foreign audiences through websites, radio, press, and television.

This reformulation of defence diplomacy is by no means limited to the United States and Europe. Latin America, though the region with the lowest levels of interstate conflict, was by no means alien to cross-border tensions and centrifugal forces—as was the case of the differences that almost led to a war between Chile and Argentina in 1978 and an actual shooting war between Peru and Ecuador in 1995.[9] Thus, the duties of military attachés and the main purpose of international defence initiatives in the region throughout most of the 20th century were maintaining ties between the armed forces, managing an agenda of various types of exchanges, and scheduling mutual visits of different sorts. It was often suspected that a key purpose of these representatives abroad was to seek out information about the defence capabilities of the host nation.

We should also keep in mind that from the 1960s to the 1990s, many Latin American nations were under military rule. The armed forces thus came to exercise a de facto political leadership within many foreign ministries, replacing traditional policy-makers and high officials from the foreign service. The conduct of foreign relations acquired, accordingly, the imprint of the military government of the day. Professional diplomacy was often substituted by ideologically-driven, doctrinaire approaches, which left little room for the contribution of political, economic, and social actors, and where the military monopolized the definition, management, and implementation of foreign relations. At the time, many Latin American states had weak ties with multilateral bodies, as the representativeness and very legitimacy of these military regimes was questioned in many UN agencies. These governments did not share any kind of comprehensive regional vision and it was impossible to establish or further the development of regional integration mechanisms.

After the region's transition to democracy in the 1980s, this changed dramatically. As of this writing, in 2012, only Cuba retains an undemocratic regime. In countries like Argentina, Brazil, Chile, Colombia, Peru, and Uruguay, among others, relations between elected officials and the military have been fully normalized, and the armed forces are subordinated to civilian control. Though not without problems, democracy has re-established itself in Latin America like never before.

Under these circumstances, military interference in diplomacy is no more. The conduct of foreign policy has devolved to the exclusive authority of the president, who exercises it mostly through the foreign ministry. Regional integration has acquired a new impetus. Strategies to strengthen cooperation across the hemisphere through a variety of agreements have gained momentum, leading to the application of confidence-building measures, and new security schemes built around bodies such as MERCOSUR (Southern Common Market) and the South American Union of Nations (UNASUR).

Arguably, 'this conception favours integration through sub-regional economic blocs primarily, without discarding the link with large blocs such as the North American Free Trade Agreement (NAFTA) and the European Union (EU)'.[10]

A multidimensional, much more nuanced notion of what security is all about has also emerged, formalized in the Declaration of Security in the Americas:

> agreed at the Special Conference on Security in Mexico City, on October 28, 2003, unanimously declaring shared values and common approaches to a new concept of hemispheric security that gives it the character of 'multidimensional' and that includes traditional threats and new threats, seeking to engage the States in building peace, integral development, social justice based on democratic values, as well as the respect, promotion and defence of human rights, solidarity, cooperation and respect for national sovereignty.[11]

In such a framework, defence diplomacy in its new incarnation finds many areas where it can be deployed to bring together the political, economic, and social sectors of each state in the fulfilment of this new notion of hemispheric security.

Before dwelling on the emerging trends in defence diplomacy, however, it is important to situate them within their proper context.

20.1 NATIONAL DEFENCE AND COMPLEX INTERDEPENDENCE

For too long, military thinkers and analysts have been caught up in the realist perspective on international relations, one that assigns to raw military power and to a somewhat mechanical, undifferentiated promotion of the national interest the pre-eminent place in the conduct of foreign affairs. The work of Hans Morgenthau played a key role in this regard, something that was especially valid at the height of the cold war, in the 1950s and 1960s. Yet, with the end of the cold war and the onset of globalization, the prescient work of Keohane and Nye[12] on complex interdependence acquired particular relevance, illustrating the very different role to be played by the instruments of national defence in this new setting.

On the one hand, we have witnessed a gradual decline of the nation state as the sole wielder of power and influence on the world stage. This is due, among other things, to the emergence of a large number of new actors—transnational corporations, non-governmental organizations (NGOs), trade unions, and the media, to name but a few, acquiring an ever higher profile. On the other hand, the steadily ever more important trans-border flows that reflect what globalization is all about mean that many key decisions, with an impact on matters as critical as foreign investment and job creation, fall beyond the purview of government officials.

Under these conditions, the old-fashioned notion of the state as an all-powerful Leviathan, behind whom lurked its military arsenal, one that would have the final say in case traditional diplomacy was unable to hold sway, has become obsolete. As Keohane and Nye point out, in a world in which war between developed nations is simply too expensive a proposition to be given serious consideration, there are other tools that must come into play to sort out the differences, however serious, between them. And while their proposition does not necessarily hold for nations from the developing world, there is little doubt that the changing nature of power on the international scene is a phenomenon by no means limited to the countries bordering the North Atlantic, and has implications well beyond them.

According to the realist definition, hard power is the ability to compel another to act in a certain way. Hard-power strategies focus on military intervention, coercive diplomacy, and economic sanctions to further the national interest. Joseph S. Nye (see Chapter 30, this volume), who coined the term 'soft power' in 1990, contends that this relies instead on the ability to persuade (as opposed to cajole) others to do something, in other words, as the ability to get what you want through attraction and persuasion over force.[13] In turn, the most recent literature has introduced the term 'smart power'. Ernest Wilson defines it as 'an actor's ability to combine elements of hard and soft power mutually reinforcing them, making the actor's purposes more effective and efficient'.[14] Wilson indicates that the use of smart power implies knowing well the attributes of oneself and of one's counterpart. Understanding of one's goals and capabilities is critical, as is the proper selection of tools and the timing to deploy them.

With this perspective in mind, we must realize that within the state apparatus the various agencies have had their own institutional culture, thus often making cooperation difficult. For the sake of simplification, it could be argued that traditionally, the foreign ministry has embodied something more akin to the exercise of soft power, whereas the defence ministry and armed forces, almost by definition, have done the same with the exercise of hard power. Yet, given the complexities of today's international environment, this will no longer do. What is needed is a much more integrated approach to the conduct of foreign relations, one that ends this compartmentalized, silo-like division and is able to assemble the various pieces of the complex foreign policy puzzle in a seamless fashion.

The key term here becomes that of 'public diplomacy' (see Chapter 24, this volume). Unlike classical, traditional diplomacy, public diplomacy involves a much larger group of people both on the sending and the receiving end, and involves broader interests than those strictly of the government of the day. It is based on the premise that the image and reputation of a country are public goods that can create either positive or negative environments for furthering any given nation's objectives.

Delivering the message about the image of the country has three dimensions: a political/military one, an economic one, and a socio-cultural one.[15] What I am positing is that defence diplomacy in its new, post-cold war incarnation, falls at least partly within the broader umbrella of public diplomacy, as well as more broadly within the *portmanteau* of network diplomacy (see Chapter 2, this volume) and can play a key role in furthering the state's foreign policy goals. To do so, however, it must be fully integrated.

20.2 DEFENCE DIPLOMACY IN
THE NEW CENTURY

Defence diplomacy's origins lie in the classic military diplomacy extant since ancient times and revived in the Napoleonic era. Its evolution, until the end of the cold war, witnessed no major changes, being focused on military relations and thus limited to the classic military field. In the 1990s, the dawn of a new era in international affairs, the steady rise of complex interdependence, the growing rise of new actors on the global scene, as well the emergence of public diplomacy, all made room for a new conception of defence diplomacy.

This new conception implies that military attachés have developed a broader horizon, to encompass issue areas like the following:

- Coordinate with governments and international organizations (IOs) support for peacekeeping operations (PKOs) in which the sending country is participating.
- Ascertain the nature of the changes taking place within the armed forces in countries around the world—not just in neighbouring ones, but also among the major powers, where these changes often initiate major international trends in the defence and security sectors. Some of these changes will relate to the use of military force, but others will be in the areas of military administration, military justice, or logistics.
- Establish the sort of military equipment that is available for sale by the local armed forces, something that became especially apparent in Europe in the 1990s, when many countries had to dispose of vast amounts of material, from guns to fighter planes.
- Identify broader defence systems technology to be deployed at home.
- Exchange information on the so-called non-traditional threats, in which terrorist groups and internationally organized crime have become especially active in the post-cold war era.

In that perspective, defence diplomacy is a component of public diplomacy that seeks, through specific actions, to secure peace, maintain the territorial integrity of the state, and cooperate in the international tasks aimed at avoiding the emergence of conflict, particularly through the United Nations. Generating trust between the armed forces of neighbouring countries and those of specific regions is another goal. This entails directing and managing military exchanges aimed at strengthening operational interaction in education, logistics, and personnel, and otherwise deepening links between the armed forces of different countries. Providing advice to political authorities on security and defence matters that affect foreign policy and the conduct of diplomacy through the suitable governmental and constitutional channels is another important function of defence diplomacy.

Defence diplomacy is deployed through the defence ministry and the armed forces as the executing agency. The defence attachés are part of that structure. To them we must add personnel assigned to PKOs abroad, units set up to support educational and training tasks with other armed forces, as well as those related to the fields of science and technology. It is part and parcel of the foreign policy state apparatus and must be considered as such, being guided by the directives and guidelines that inform that policy, which will set the tasks and objectives to be met by the defence ministry and the armed forces. The latter must thus comply with the established requirements as well as seek coordination with other agencies and entities that participate in the foreign policy realm. Needless to say, it must be discharged in full compliance with international law, international human rights law, and international humanitarian law.

Within these broad guidelines, defence diplomacy today manifests itself in the following areas.

20.2.1 The Organization of the Armed Forces to Implement It

Once given the appropriate missions by the defence ministry, the armed forces must plan their implementation. To this effect, they develop, at general staff level, advisory bodies at each of the service branches to deal with international issues, though sometimes this is handled by the directorate of operations of the armed forces. Thus, the ministry of defence and each of the services initiate international activities aimed at enhancing cooperation with other armed forces, IOs, and agencies of other states. In addition, the military must develop the advisory capacities needed to provide the foreign and defence ministries with the inputs required to analyse particular strategic *conjunctures*.

In many states, advisory bodies in which the heads of each of the services and the defence minister are joined by other high-level officials and governmental authorities such as the ministers of finance and economic affairs and the chairs of the relevant committees in parliament, also play a role in periodically evaluating the international situation and its implications for the security of the state and its citizens. This facilitates the anticipation of emerging threats and the prompt reaction to them.

20.2.2 The Deployment of Defence Attachés

These attachés are posted at their countries' embassies throughout the world, be it in particular countries or at different IOs. Until recently, their duties were largely limited to maintaining links with the host country's armed forces. Today, their brief has been extended, as that of advisers to the head of mission on how best to pursue defence cooperation with the host country. The same goes for their enhanced role as coordinators of the many more international defence exchanges that take place in the new century, in training, operations, joint exercises, bilateral control, thematic conferences, logistics, and even PKO, where joint, bi-, or multinational units are becoming more common.

This has gone hand in hand with an expansion of the sheer numbers of defence attachés. Until 1990, the established pattern for most countries around the world was that they would solely post defence attachés to the neighbouring countries and to the Great Powers. Twenty years later, that is no longer the case. A review of the deployment of defence attachés from countries as different as Italy, Spain, Argentina, and Chile shows that they all have defence attachés in Russia, India, South Africa, Turkey, China, Republic of Korea, Australia, and Israel—states at great geographic distance from most of these four nations, but whose geopolitical, economic, or technological significance makes it imperative to establish defence links with them.

The study cited above of the Geneva Centre for the Democratic Control of the armed forces indicates that the main roles of a defence attaché at present are the following:

1) Is an advocate for his/her country's military and security interests;
2) Represents his/her country's military authorities and liaises with those of the host country;
3) Provides a security-policy and military network capable of operating even in times of troubled or reduced bilateral relations;
4) Acts as a military and/or security advisor to his/her ambassador and embassy staff;
5) Observes conditions in the host country with a bearing on security and reports on them to home country authorities;
6) Oversees and manages activities in the area of military outreach, defence diplomacy and security cooperation, both in bilateral exchanges and through multilateral programmes such as NATO's Partnership for Peace;
7) Promotes, in some instances, the home country armaments industry; and
8) May play a role in spearheading emergency response and relief efforts when crises arise.[16]

Many of these duties are no longer just performed in post at missions accredited to other nation states, but also when posted to IOs or military alliances, such as the UN, NATO, the European Union, the Organization of American States, or the Economic Community of West African States.

20.2.3 United Nations Peacekeeping Operations

PKOs have become another key area for the deployment of defence diplomacy. With the rise of PKOs in the post-cold war era as a result of the eruption of civil wars and other forms of internal conflicts, the United Nations has been forced to step in—mostly in Africa and in Asia, but also in Europe, and even in the Americas, as in the case of Haiti. In many ways, this is an imperative of globalization. The programme 'An Agenda for Peace' led by UN Secretary-General Boutros Boutros-Ghali laid the foundations for preventive diplomacy, peacemaking, peace-keeping, and post-conflict peace-building. These concepts were placed in a regulatory framework that defined state actions under the mandates of the UN Charter.

There has been a dramatic rise in the number of PKOs in the past two decades, leading to a situation in which, as of this writing, some 100,000 troops from 120 UN member states take part in them, supervised by the UN Department of Peacekeeping Operations (DPKO) (see Chapter 43, this volume). Countries choose to participate in PKOs for different reasons. For some, it is a way of subsidizing at least part of the armed forces' payroll. For others, particularly those countries that have not been involved in interstate wars in the recent past, it is a way to let their men and women in uniform acquire real life combat experience, in a manner that cannot be duplicated in any training exercises, no matter how tough. For all participating states, however, PKOs represent an extraordinary opportunity to link up and share experiences, on the ground, with other armed forces, and to develop valuable networks. This is particularly true for the military from the developing world, as the armed forces from the NATO member countries participate less and less in PKOs, being absorbed by wars such as those in Iraq and Afghanistan. Mainly, however, by participating in PKOs UN member states communicate that they take their international civic duties seriously, by putting their soldiers in harm's way for the sake of international peace.

There are few instances indicating in such clear-cut fashion the significance of PKO as a tool of defence diplomacy (and the latter's rising importance within a country's overall foreign policy system) as that of Chile and its participation in the Multinational Interim Force for Haiti (MIFH) in 2004, first, and in the United Nations Mission for the Stabilization of Haiti (MINUSTAH), from 2004 onwards, later.

The case of Chile is an especially interesting one because of its foreign policy profile and the role it took on in international affairs in the 1990s and early 2000s. In this period Chile became an active player in a variety of UN forums and agencies. It took a leading role in the setting up of the UN Social Summit held in Copenhagen in 1995, was twice elected to a non-permanent seat in the UN Security Council (1996–1997 and 2002–2003), was a member of the coalition of 'like-minded' countries that took up a number of key international initiatives in this period, including that of the Ottawa treaty to ban landmines (discussed in Chapter 44, this volume) and the Rome Statute that led to the establishment of the International Criminal Court (ICC) (see Chapter 41, this volume). It was also a member of the Human Security Network, a loose coalition of mostly North Atlantic countries that propounded a variety of measures to put the security of individuals (as opposed to solely that of states) as a prime concern on the international agenda.

All of this contributed to raising Chile's profile in multilateral affairs in general and within the UN system in particular. Yet, as argued elsewhere,[17] Chile's participation in UNPKO until as recently as the year 2000 had been quite limited. Between 1935 and 1960, only 20 members of the Chilean army participated in these operations. From 1990 to 2000, the number increased to 186, a still quite modest number in relation to the size of the Chilean army, as well as in comparison to the number of troops deployed by other South American countries in UNPKO. Yet, from 2001 to 2006 this number increased dramatically to 2,057 troops.

The key turning point here was Haiti, where Chile was the only Latin American country to go in (together with the United States, Canada, and France) as a part of MIFH first, and later—this time in partnership with other countries from the region—as part of MINUSTAH, with two Chilean former foreign ministers (Juan Gabriel Valdes during 2004–2006, and Mariano Fernandez from 2011 onwards) as the UN secretary-general's special representative, and thus as heads of the UN mission there. In a scarce seventy-two hours after the UN Security Council approved Resolution 1529 which authorized the deployment of MIFH, Chile sent in 300 men in uniform to Haiti, and has been there with a significant contingent of some 600 men and women from all three service branches and of Chile's national police, the *Carabineros*, ever since.

Why was this significant?

First of all, it moved Chile from a position where it had previously participated only with limited forces—originally as military observers and later with contingents of no more than fifty—to one in which it plays an active role in UN initiatives involving Chapter VII. For Chile, this was a real turning point in the deployment of its military abroad. It also aligned its policy on UNPKO with the thrust of its foreign policy—until then, Chile had talked a good game on multilateralism and international civic duties, but had not really put its money where its mouth was—that is, had not sent any significant number of troops to UN missions. In Haiti, Chile crossed the Rubicon, as it were, and has not looked back since, in a classic display of defence diplomacy that contributes to the achievement of important foreign policy goals.

But Chile's participation as the only regional power in MIFH, together with the United States, Canada, and France, had another, roll-on, effect. It gave regional legitimacy to the UN presence in Haiti, and facilitated the subsequent formation of MINUSTAH, which was to become the first UNPKO formed by a majority of Latin American troops, with as many as nine Latin American nations providing a little over half the contingent, that reached some 12,000 by 2012. Revealingly, Brazil was invited to join MIFH, but refused to do so, asking for a three-month period to evaluate the evolving situation in Haiti.

And, as a good illustration of the positive results a well-calibrated defence diplomacy can have, in Latin America today government of different political persuasions have similar views on UNPKOs in a multicultural context. PKOs also provide the forces with the opportunity to interact and cooperate, which builds trust even when they come from countries with a history of border differences, such as Peru and Ecuador and Chile and Argentina.

20.2.4 Educational Exchanges

As mentioned in section 20.2.2, the rise of defence diplomacy in the post-cold war era has gone hand in hand with a much greater diversification of links between the armed forces of various countries—well beyond the traditional ones with the neighbours and the Great Powers, which had been the established pattern until then. Given that this is also the age of information, it should not be surprising that education and training have been at the forefront of these linkages.

Much as the armed forces of developing nations seek to establish contact with those of the newly emerging powers of the 21st century so as to be better prepared to face their own challenges in the defence realm, they are also keen to upgrade the skills of their officer corps and allow it to come to terms with current threats. In the case of Latin American armed forces, this has often meant upgrading military forces equipped with 1950s technology, to smaller and more compact, but high-tech, forces. Chile made the transition from a territorially defined army to a functional, interoperative one, with rapid action forces, equipped to NATO standards, as well as with up-to-date electronic communications and modern anti-aircraft artillery. In so doing, the Chilean army also undertook an ambitious post-graduate education programme for its officers that sought the best centres in the world to train them at the doctoral and master's level in materials science and technology, among many other fields. In 2006, 150 Chilean army officers were studying at foreign universities and military institutes. That same year, 122 foreign army and non-commission officers took courses of one sort or another in Chile, including from countries as far away as Britain, France, Germany, South Africa, Spain, Turkey, and the United States, in addition to those from Latin American ones like Argentina, Brazil, Ecuador, Uruguay, and Venezuela.[18]

20.2.5 International Conferences

Network diplomacy thrives on international conferences and the defence realm is no exception. There is thus a steadily expanding programme of meetings, some of them regional, and others of a more global reach. A dense network of summits, thematic gatherings, and high-level seminars to discuss issues of strategic, political, or operational significance makes for a packed yearly agenda for senior government officials and military officers responsible for defence diplomacy. These meetings will often pave the ground for the signing of bilateral or multilateral agreements aimed at building mutual trust and/or at sharing information and undertaking joint projects in areas such as training, military doctrine, and equipment to tackle common challenges.

At the ministerial level, there is a hemisphere-wide Conference of Defence Ministers of the Americas. One long-standing entity is the Board of Commanders-in-Chief of the Army, Navy, and Air Force of the Americas. As part of it, the Conference of American Armies meets annually to discuss regional issues of common interest. In Central America, the Conference of Central American armed forces (CFAC) was established in 1997. The new regionalism that has emerged in Latin America, and particularly in South America, in the 2000s, has arguably made the need for a proactive defence diplomacy especially apparent. Shortly after the establishment of UNASUR in 2008, the South American Defence Council came into being, with its first chair being the defence minister of Ecuador. In turn, the Pacific Armies Chief Conference, in which Chile participates since 2005, and the Pacific Armies Management Seminar, are interesting instances of entities that bring together armies as far away as those in South America with those in Southeast Asia.

NATO, of course, as befits a military alliance that has among its members some of the most industrialized countries in the world, has developed the art and science of these international defence meetings to a high degree, making them into very elaborate and sophisticated events. Thus, the April 2009 NATO Strasbourg summit reviewed the strategic concept that had been in place since 1999, in an exchange led by NATO Secretary-General Anders Rasmussen and a group of experts. The proposals coming out of those deliberations were discussed at a follow-up meeting held in Lisbon in November 2010. The outcome of those exchanges would seem to underscore the validity of the argument developed in this chapter in terms of the changing nature of defence diplomacy. As the said review concluded, 'strategic concepts had to change their format and become more of a public diplomacy tool, than a tool for military planning and conduction'.[19]

As far as international conferences go, the ones of the London-based International Institute for Strategic Studies (IISS) are especially significant, bringing together government, the armed forces, business, and research centres. The IISS hosts three major conferences a year designed to promote exchanges on security and defence topics in certain specific regions. These are: The Shangri-La Dialogue[20] (Singapore), The Manama Dialogue (Dubai), and The Global Strategic Review (Geneva). Participants will include current or former heads of state or government, foreign and defence ministers, heads of the armed forces, and CEOs of top companies in the defence sector, in addition to leading IR and defence analysts.

20.2.6 Business and Logistics

Activities related to weapons and military equipment purchases, to the development of defence industries, to science and technology exchanges, to the search for partners in joint production ventures, and to logistics and supply systems to the armed forces are another key component of defence diplomacy. In this regard, two situations are of interest.

- The first is represented by those countries with a high level of scientific and technological development, that are in the business of exporting know-how and products. They include nations such as the United States, the United Kingdom, France, Israel, Spain, Brazil, and Turkey. The defence attachés in their missions are extremely active on this front. Often the activities of the regular attachés will be complemented by special missions of a temporary or permanent nature, tasked exclusively with this responsibility.
- The second is embodied by those nations whose armed forces are undergoing transformation and modernization. The latter aim to identify trends that will help them to manage these changes. They thus rely on a variety of means to acquire the information needed for their adaptation to the new challenges of our time.

20.3 Conclusion

Perhaps paradoxically, defence diplomacy has emerged as a key component within the 21st-century diplomatic toolkit. An expression of network diplomacy, of which public diplomacy is such an important part, it links the implementation of foreign policy objectives to those of the defence sector. If managed properly, it can be an invaluable instrument of statecraft, by bringing to bear the manifold dimensions of both soft and hard power on any given issue. UN peacekeeping operations, which have undergone a dramatic increase in the post-cold war era are one of the best expressions of this, but, as outlined in this chapter, there are many others.

Notes

1. F. Sanz Roldán, 'La diplomacia de defensa: una aproximación desde España', *Revista Arbor, CLXV* 651 (2000), 519–27.
2. Geneva Centre for the Democratic Control of Armed Forces (DECAF), *Defence Attachés*. DCAF Backgrounder, 2007.
3. DECAF, *Defence Attachés*.
4. Niccolò Machiavelli, *El príncipe. comentado por Napoleón Bonaparte; traducción de Eli Leonetti Jungl* (Barcelona: Espasa, 2010).
5. A. Vagst, *Defence and Diplomacy* (New York: King's Crown Press, 1956).
6. G. A. D'Angelo, *The contemporary role of the military attache and problems relating to the attainment of a quality corps* (Texas: Graduate Faculty of Texas Tech University, 1972).
7. W. J. Clinton, *A national Security Strategy of Engagement and Enlargement* (The White House, 1996), 17.
8. D.S. Reveron, 'Shaping and Military Diplomacy', *The 2007 Annual Meeting of the American Political Science Association*, 30 August–2 September 2007, 7. 'Joint Capability Areas Tier 1 and Supporting Tier 2 Lexicon, Post August 24, 2006 JROC', available at <http://www.mors.org/UserFiles/file/meetings/06bar/luke.pdf>.
9. J. E. Cheyre,. 'Chile y su circunstancia geopolítica estratégica', in R. Lagos and R. Lagos (eds), *Cien años de luces y sombra* (Santiago: Taurus, 2010).
10. J. Griffiths, 'Cooperación en el plano de la defensa. Una visión desde la perspectiva de Chile en el ámbito vecinal', in F. Kernic and T. Chuaqui (eds), *Seguridad y Cooperación: Aspectos de la seguridad y las relaciones entre la Unión Europea y América Latina* (Santiago: Academia Nacional de Defensa Austriaca y la Pontificia Universidad Católica de Chile, 2006).
11. OAS, *Declaración sobre seguridad en las Américas* (Ciudad de México: Departamento de Coordinación de Políticas y Programas Secretaría de Seguridad Multidimensional, 2003).
12. R. Keohane and J. Nye, *Poder e Interdependencia. La política mundial en transición* (Buenos Aires: Grupo Editor Latinoamericano, 1977).
13. J. Nye, *Soft power: The Means to Success in World Politics* (New York: Public Affairs, 2004).
14. E. Wilson, 'Hard Power, Soft Power, Smart Power', *The Annals of the American Academy of Political and Social Science* 110:616 (2008), 110–24.
15. M. Leonard, 'Public Diplomacy', *The Foreign Policy Center* (2002), 1–101.
16. DECAF, *Defence Attachés*.

17. See Juan Emilio Cheyre, 'UNPKO and the Latin American forces', in Jorge Heine and Andrew S. Thompson (eds), *Fixing Haiti: MINUSTAH and Beyond* (Tokyo: United Nations University Press, 2011).

18. Ejército de Chile, *Memoria* (Santiago: Instituto Geográfico Militar, 2006).

19. Grupo de Trabajo sobre el Concepto Estratégico de la OTAN del Real Instituto Elcano. (26 de noviembre de 2010). El Concepto Estratégico de la Alianza Atlántica y los intereses nacionales: propuestas para la cumbre de la OTAN en Lisboa. *Real Instituto Elcano.*

20. International Institute for Strategic Studies, *The Shangri-La Dialogue* (London: Hastings Printing, 2011).

PART IV

TOOLS AND INSTRUMENTS

CHAPTER 21

··

ECONOMIC DIPLOMACY

··

STEPHEN WOOLCOCK AND NICHOLAS BAYNE[*]

21.1 INTRODUCTION

··

THIS chapter introduces the topic of economic diplomacy. It first discusses how economic diplomacy might be seen as a distinct component in diplomacy in general and how the approach to decision-making and negotiation on mainstream economic topics may diverge from more overtly political diplomacy. The chapter then makes the case that economic diplomacy has become more important with increased international economic interdependence or globalization and the greater need to find negotiated solutions to challenges, such as stable financial systems, open trade and investment, or climate change, in order to achieve domestic policy objectives. The chapter rests on the view that states remain the main actors in economic diplomacy, despite the relative increase in the importance of non-state actors and the fact that markets must be treated as endogenous to the policy process. It therefore discusses the distinctive characteristics of the conduct of economic diplomacy by governments. To illustrate the points made, the chapter then discusses the cases of international investment policy and economic summitry, before concluding with an assessment of the trends in economic diplomacy.

21.2 WHAT IS ECONOMIC DIPLOMACY?

··

The first question to be addressed is what is economic diplomacy and are there grounds for differentiating between economic diplomacy and diplomacy in general given the relative increase in the economic content of international relations and thus of diplomacy? The brief definition used here for economic diplomacy is decision-making and negotiation in core issues affecting international economic relations. In practice, this means international financial arrangements and coordination, negotiation of trade and investment, development and international environmental policies (although there are, of course, many sub-categories of these core issues and other issues that touch on international economic relations). Economic diplomacy is therefore concerned with the processes of decision-making and negotiation on policy or questions relating to international economic relations in these core topics. This decision-making will clearly involve the state and therefore state (or regional or international level) institutions. But the club of core decision-makers will reach beyond key players in the executive and legislative branches of the state to include those in quasi-governmental bodies or national regulatory agencies and even private, non-state actors. So the emphasis is on the process of decision-making and negotiation rather than the substance of the policy issues, which might be better covered by the term foreign economic policy.

Diplomacy has been defined as the '(reconciliation) of the assertion of the political will of independent (state) activities'.[1] Economic diplomacy differs in that it is about reconciling domestic and international policy objectives in an increasingly interdependent if not global economy. As mentioned already domestic policy objectives cannot be achieved independently of what is happening in the global economy or of the policies of other countries. The degree of interdependence can and does of course fluctuate over time, but there can be little doubt of its importance today. The stability of financial markets around the world depends on actions taken elsewhere or on cooperation between national authorities. With higher levels of trade dependence due to the fact that growth of trade and especially investment has consistently outpaced output for decades, economic growth and employment depend on an open trade and investment system. Environmental challenges, such as climate change, and a range of other less high-profile issues, cannot be resolved by individual national policies. In other words, economic diplomacy has become an essential instrument in the pursuit of domestic policy objectives. Economic diplomats in a range of different guises must seek to reconcile both the domestic and international policy aims if they are to be successful.

The popular image of diplomacy is often viewed as maintaining good relations between states, which when combined with the conventional view of the anarchic nature of international relations suggests non-binding or voluntary relations. Economic diplomacy consists of both voluntary and binding relations between states. Indeed, in the economic sphere there is arguably a denser network of international organizations and regimes than is the case for general political or strategic relations, even if many economic regimes are of a technical nature. These range from the G20 summits, IMF, and World Trade Organization or multilateral environment agreements (MEAs) at the political or heads of state and government level to the technical but arguably equally important standard-setting bodies, such as the Basel Committee on Banking Supervision for capital adequacy rules or the Codex Alimentarius for regulatory standards for the use of bio-technology in food and agriculture, and many others. Economic diplomacy therefore also encompasses the decision-making and negotiation that goes on in these international bodies, which may be multilateral, plurilateral (i.e. consisting of like-minded states or states that share common norms and values), regional (as in the European Union or other regional groups), or bilateral (as in the case of many recent trade and investment initiatives). Such negotiations can result in voluntary cooperation, peer reviewed standards, or binding commitments, which when broken can lead to financial penalties or to treaty-backed rights to retaliate.

Before suggesting some ways in which economic diplomacy could be seen as a distinct branch of diplomacy it is helpful to limit the scope of the term by saying what it is not. Our definition of economic diplomacy does not include the use of economic leverage, either in the form of sanctions or inducement, in the pursuit of specific political or strategic goals. This we would define as sanctions or perhaps economic statecraft.[2] Economic diplomacy is about the creation and distribution of the economic benefits from international economic relations. Clearly political and strategic interests will be a factor in economic negotiations, whether in terms of promoting a liberal, capitalist world order or in choosing negotiating partners for trade agreements. The conclusion of a trade or economic agreement can be seen as a means of promoting economic stability, growth, and employment and thus political stability in a country, such as in the countries of North Africa that have undergone reform since the spring of 2011. But the means remain the economic agreement, the substance of which will be shaped by a range of domestic sectoral and other interests. In other words, political objectives will not infrequently be a factor in decisions to initiate negotiations, but the concrete agenda, content, and conduct of the negotiations will be largely determined by economic factors and interests. We include international environment negotiations in our definition of economic diplomacy because of the close interdependence between economic and environmental objectives. By extension we also see economic diplomacy as an integrated part of a grand strategy combining political, military, and economic relations.

Nor does our definition of economic diplomacy include the promotion of exports or investment, whether outward or inward. While governments have always intervened to promote their national industries, there has been a trend towards more active involvement of foreign services or even diplomatic services in seeking markets for national companies in recent decades.[3] This differs from more traditional industrial policy or mercantilist trade policies. As traditional forms of intervention such as tariffs, subsidies, and other instruments that used to promote national champions have been disciplined by WTO and other trade regimes, governments have used diplomatic links, trade fairs, or visits of heads of state to promote commercial interests. Such activities are better captured by the term commercial diplomacy, which contrasts with economic diplomacy; the latter facilitates trade and investment by establishing the framework of rules and disciplines within which markets and such commercial diplomacy function.[4]

21.3 Economic Diplomacy has Gained in Significance

The principal reason why economic diplomacy has become more important is that international economic relations have themselves become more important relative to political/security relations, as globalization replaced more arms-length interdependence.

Globalization has reduced the ability of individual states or even coalitions or groups of states to shape outcomes. Before globalization and the emergence of challenges such as global warming it was possible to make more of a distinction between domestic economic objectives and international developments. Today it has become increasingly difficult for governments to satisfy domestic economic demands without engaging in extensive international negotiation.

The old (arguably artificial) distinction between the high politics of international security and the low politics of commerce has lost all significance since the end of the cold war. This has led to a widening of the definition of security to include such things as the stability of the international financial system or the need for development in order to ensure collective security. The financial crisis of 2007–2008 and the continuing instability have left no doubt as to the systemic nature of financial markets and the need for coordinated responses. With regard to the latter, underdevelopment has, especially since the early 2000s, been seen as a source of political instability, which can in turn result in destabilizing migration or failed states that facilitate terrorism.

The increased importance of economic diplomacy has also come about as a result of the emergence of a multipolar world economy. The point here is similar to that already made, in that the stability of the international or global economy now requires negotiated solutions that include the emerging powers and perhaps some developing countries. In the immediate post-1945 era the United States was an economic hegemon and could shape the Western international market economy. The rest of the 'Western world', which meant primarily the broader transatlantic community plus Japan, then followed the US lead. In the field of economics US hegemony, with the exception of international monetary policy at least until recently, was replaced in the 1970s and 1980s by a 'club' of the OECD countries under US leadership.[5] This club was then able to both provide leadership, thanks to its share of world GDP, and develop the norms or provide the model for other countries, seeking to engage in the 'multilateral' system of the West, to follow. Today this OECD club no longer has the credibility to provide this sort of leadership. The emergence of major new economies, such as China, India, and Brazil, with real economic power and views that do not always coincide with those of the like-minded members of the OECD club, means that continued cooperation requires a more inclusive system. This in turn means a need for more negotiation as a more fluid pattern of coalitions and interests has come to replace the old OECD club model. The contrast with foreign policy or security diplomacy is that the US has retained a hegemonic role in terms of military capability.

21.4 Is Economic Diplomacy Conducted Differently?

Economic diplomacy, like other forms of diplomacy, is conducted on two levels. An efficient process of domestic decision-making is essential to prepare for and support international negotiation. Once the negotiations are concluded, the domestic level is still required for ratification and implementation of the international agreement reached. Thus the two levels interact with each other constantly.

21.4.1 Domestic Decision-Making

This chapter has already stressed the growing penetration of external factors into domestic policy-making on economic issues, which has intensified with the advance of globalization. A distinctive feature of economic diplomacy therefore is that the foreign ministry is usually not in the lead in driving the decision-making process. More often it is the home-based ministry responsible for the subject in question—finance, environment, transport—that is the lead department. That department therefore takes responsibility for producing a common government position, defends this in the legislature, bears any costs on its budget, and heads the delegation for international negotiations.

In most subjects of economic diplomacy the foreign ministry is in second place and sometimes has to struggle to make its voice heard. There are exceptions to this rule, however. Where the international economic dealings have a very high political content, the foreign ministry will lead; this happened with East/West economic relations during the cold war. The foreign ministry may also coordinate policy when negotiations cover a very wide range of economic issues, with none predominating; this has been the practice in preparing the G7/G8 economic summits. More generally, the foreign ministry is more likely to lead on economic diplomacy in developing countries that have only recently become internationally active. But as their economic interdependence increases, foreign ministries often lose the predominance and have to exert their influence in other ways.

The treatment of international trade negotiations is instructive in this respect, as countries try to reconcile domestic and external factors in a variety of ways. Some give trade negotiations to a separate agency, as in the United States, or a dedicated trade ministry, as in China. Some allocate them to the ministries for economics (as in Germany), for finance (as in France), or even development (as in the UK for a time). Japan gives the foreign ministry the lead, which risks friction with the powerful trade and economics ministry. Brazil has been very successful in making its foreign ministry, the Itamaraty, also responsible for external economic issues. Other countries increasingly favour integrated ministries of foreign affairs and trade, both large ones like Australia and Canada and smaller ones like Kenya and Mauritius. This diversity in trade contrasts with financial diplomacy, where finance ministries are always in the lead and usually limit consultation to central banks and regulators.

A second distinctive feature of economic diplomacy, as compared with other forms, is the greater involvement of private sector bodies, since they, rather than the government itself, may be the direct beneficiaries of successful strategies. Government officials routinely consult business interests in the course of deciding policy and devising negotiating strategies and each department will have its preferred contacts. Industrial firms and confederations will deal with economics ministries, banking associations with finance ministries, farming lobbies with agriculture ministries. The departments will often rely on the private sector bodies for guidance on negotiating objectives, but must be careful not to become 'captured' by these special interests. Ministries often offset business pressure by consulting more widely with academic experts, who may be more neutral, and civil society think tanks and advocacy groups, who can provide an alternative perspective.

Decision-making in economic diplomacy is therefore a complex process, even in small or low-income countries.[6] A range of ministries are involved, each with its own objectives. Every ministry will engage in external consultation with their preferred business groups, NGOs, or technical experts. Other public bodies outside central government will also be involved: central banks, financial supervisors, environmental and food safety regulators. In federations or other highly decentralized countries sub-national bodies, like provincial authorities, may also have to take part. For example, international investment policy will generally need to include state or provincial governments as these seek to attract inward investment by means of tax or other incentives. Most governments have put in place machinery for reconciling all these different pressures, because they know that they cannot negotiate effectively if their internal divisions are manifest to their negotiating partners. Even so, this complexity increases the risk that domestic obstacles will frustrate international agreement. In the European Union this risk is often aggravated by the need to agree in advance a negotiating mandate that reconciles the views of all the member states.[7]

21.4.2 International Negotiation

Internationally, the most ambitious aspect of economic diplomacy is the negotiation of multilateral agreements that are binding on the participating governments. This is most conspicuous in international trade, where the Uruguay Round agreements that entered into force in 1995 brought all forms of trade—industrial goods, agriculture, and services—under multilateral rules and launched the World Trade Organization (WTO), with almost worldwide membership. WTO commitments can be enforced through a dispute settlement mechanism that sanctions members in breach. A comparable process was also launched in the global environment during the 1990s, with the conclusion of multilateral treaties on the ozone layer, climate change, and biodiversity. But though these issues require to be treated globally, so that all countries are covered, it has proved harder to agree common rules and there are no dispute settlement provisions. In finance, the IMF is the dominant multilateral institution, but it rarely conducts binding negotiations. The exchange rate regime has been very fluid since floating rates became prevalent in the 1970s. There are few constraints on members, except that any country seeking to make large drawings on the resources of the Fund has to meet conditions set by the Fund staff. Since the crisis brought about by the collapse of Lehman Brothers in 2008, stricter disciplines have been drawn up to assure financial stability, but these are applied nationally rather than collectively, as explained in what follows.

While multilateral regimes are the most ambitious, economic diplomacy is pursued through other levels too. A country like the United States will belong to plurilateral groups of like-minded states, such as the OECD; be a member of a regional grouping like NAFTA; conclude bilateral trade and investment agreements, for example with Chile and Singapore; and introduce unilateral measures, for example in monetary policy, that have widespread international impact. This *multilevel* economic diplomacy will include both formal agreements, at bilateral and regional level, and voluntary cooperation, as in the OECD, where undertakings do not have legal force but are sustained by common interest and peer pressure.

Multilevel economic diplomacy of this kind provides the opportunity to shift between levels, depending on the prospects of success. In some cases plurilateral understandings at the OECD, for example on trade in services, will be used as the basis for multilateral regimes.[8] Conversely, when multilateral rules are too weak, for example on investment, stronger commitments will be pursued at bilateral or regional level. Strong countries, like the United States, have used the threat of unilateral action to bring others to the negotiating table. But small, weak countries have obtained redress even against the US and the EU through the WTO dispute settlement mechanism.

21.5 ILLUSTRATIONS OF ECONOMIC DIPLOMACY AT WORK

This section illustrates the general points made above with reference to the two key policy areas of trade and investment and finance.

21.5.1 International Trade and Investment

The field of trade and investment illustrates how progressive policy decisions over the post-1947 period have led to a steady increase in economic interdependence. This has been facilitated by negotiated as well as unilateral liberalization. The advances in trade liberalization have not been linear. In between major advances there have been periods when there was limited progress in multilateral negotiations, such as during the 1950s, the 1970, and the 2000s. Nevertheless advances in liberalization together with the fact that commitments under the GATT/WTO are binding, meaning they are only reversible at some considerable cost to any party wishing to revert to more closure, have meant a progressive increase in trade and investment interdependence.

The coverage of trade and investment agreements has also been steadily extended to cover more and more topics. Starting with tariffs, the scope was extended to non-tariff measures in the 1980s to encompass industrial subsidies, technical barriers to trade, and government procurement,[9] and to regulatory issues in the 1990s to encompass sanitary and phytosanitary measures, services, trade-related intellectual property rights, and trade-related investment measures. This meant that trade policy encroached first onto national industrial policies and then onto how key services sectors were regulated and how national governments went about establishing national environmental and health/ food safety standards. The, by now well documented, effect of this was to alert many more interests to the impact and importance of trade diplomacy. As a result trade policy ceased to be an activity conducted by a relatively small policy elite made up of officials and the private sector representatives and trade unions in those sectors of the economy most affected and became an activity in which there were many more actors. This expansion in the number of actors concerned with trade policy took place at the beginning of the 1990s in the middle of the Uruguay Round of GATT negotiations. Environmental NGOs in North America led in highlighting the impact of the trade regime on environmental policy objectives and were followed by development NGOs that stressed the need for all policies including trade to take account of the needs of developing countries. In the case of international investment the policy community involved had been even smaller than trade, with policy shaped by a few key officials and lawyers in some of the major companies that engaged in significant foreign investment. A wider awareness of the impact of investment negotiations came after the end of the Uruguay Round negotiations when civil society NGOs focused on the negotiations on a Multilateral Investment Agreement (MAI) that began in the late 1990s. The MAI sought to strengthen the investment regime that had been developed over the previous thirty years within the OECD club and use it as the model for a wider multilateral regime.

The emergence of more extensive regimes that intruded further into national competence had implications for trade diplomacy. The expansion of issues meant that more ministries had to be included in decision-making. It also meant that decision-makers had to reach out to civil society as well as regulatory bodies, from financial market regulators to standards-making agencies. As civil society NGOs also operated via public advocacy rather than the quiet technical consultations used by private sector interests, trade policy also had to be conducted in a more public fashion. The advance of globalization, as interdependence came to be termed in the mid-1990s, also meant that trade and investment diplomacy became more important in achieving domestic policy objectives. The distinction between external policies and domestic policies, which had never been very clear, became even less distinct.

Trade also illustrates how economic diplomacy has become multipolar. This means that trade diplomacy today requires the negotiation of more inclusive agreements, whereas in the past it was possible for the dominant OECD economies to shape outcomes. When the GATT was established the US was a hegemon able to shape both the norms on which it was based and to a large extent the outcome of negotiations. When US hegemony began to wane, which could be put as early as the 1970s, the international trading system was shaped by the OECD.[10] This OECD Club, which continued under US leadership during the lifetime of the GATT, was then able to determine the multilateral trade regime. Norms or rules were developed in the OECD and then introduced into GATT negotiations. There was also a core of OECD countries that effectively negotiated the GATT rounds and presented the results to the rest of the world. This was made possible by the two-tier nature of the GATT system in which developing countries were granted special and differential treatment, which meant they effectively opted out of the full GATT commitments but also of full membership of the GATT club.

This has now changed. At the end of the Uruguay Round of trade negotiations, which transformed the GATT into the WTO, all members were obliged to adopt the Single Undertaking and thus the full set of trade rules. This raised expectation on the part of developing countries that they would have an equal say when it came to drafting the rules, though differentiation remained in practice. More important, however, has been the emergence of new trade powers in the shape of China especially, since it joined the WTO in 2001, but also India and Brazil. Their relatively rapid growth, combined with relatively protected markets, at least in terms of binding commitments to liberalization, means that these WTO members now have real economic power, which they are willing to use. These leading trade powers, grouped together in the G20 trade coalition, are no longer willing to accept an agenda shaped by the US and EU or outcomes that suit the interests of the developed countries but not their own. This then has finally brought an end to an approach to trade shaped by hegemonic leadership of a club of developed countries. From now on it will be necessary to get the support of such WTO members.

Trade and investment also illustrates how economic diplomacy has come to be more concerned with and shaped by an ever denser network of international regimes or organizations. In the early post-1945 period the main regimes were the GATT and the OECD. The GATT was a flexible negotiating forum. Provided governments did not openly flaunt the basic principles of non-discrimination, there was considerable 'policy space'. The OECD had few if any binding rules at the beginning and voluntary codes or norms were implemented by means of peer review only. In time, however, the degree of binding, rule-based regimes in the field of trade and investment increased. The Uruguay Round resulted in a significantly more rule-based regime and a more legalistic system of dispute settlement in the shape of the WTO Understanding on Dispute Settlement. In addition to the multilateral (or global) level there has also been a growth in regimes at the plurilateral level, such as in the shape of such agreements as the Information Technology Agreement (ITA), the Government Procurement Agreement (GPA), or within the OECD agreements on export credits, competition, or investment. Perhaps more striking has been the growth of bilateral agreements. In the field of investment there has been a significant growth in bilateral investment treaties (BITs). In trade there has been an equally striking growth in bilateral agreements since around the middle of the 1990s. In recent years these have also begun to include investment in comprehensive trade and investment agreements.

In addition to increasing the number of actors involved in trade diplomacy, globalization has also placed the market more at the centre of policy-making. The steady growth of interdependence has meant that the costs of protection for individual countries have increased. With more and more liberal trade and investment flows the role of national policy has shifted from supporting national industries in international competition to one of seeking to attract investment and thus economic activity. The emergence of global supply chains in which the various stages of production are spread across different countries and sometimes different regions has accentuated this trend. This competition between locations is most pronounced in investment, where states increasingly compete to attract investment and thus economic activity, jobs, and tax revenue. In other words, markets have become more endogenous to the policy process. In the case of trade and investment this is perhaps less pronounced than in financial markets. The conclusion of binding trade or investment agreements is seen as a commitment to stable policies or non-intervention. This is the case for the WTO, as well as regional or bilateral trade or investment agreements. In practice the picture is rather more complex with market size, proximity, the importance of sunk costs, and a range of other factors influencing decisions on the location of any investment.

21.6 INTERNATIONAL FINANCE AND ECONOMIC SUMMITRY

The world monetary and financial system is still sustained by the International Monetary Fund created at the end of the Second World War. At the outset, the IMF embodied an exchange rate system based on fixed parities, but this broke down in 1971 and since then most countries have adopted floating rates. Some, however, still tie their currencies to others' formally or informally; in particular, China has linked the renminbi to the dollar. In addition, the members of the European Community (EC), later European Union (EU), progressively tightened the links between their exchange rates until most of them could adopt a common currency, the euro. The eurozone is the only significant regional monetary arrangement still in force.

The IMF's original remit also provided for loans to countries unable to meet their financial obligations and this became its principal activity once the fixed parity regime ended. The governance structure provided for rich countries, who would lend resources to the Fund, to have more votes than poor countries, who would need to borrow to cover their debts. Rich countries also have more seats on the executive board and the ministerial committees that meet twice yearly. This weighting in favour of rich countries has dominated financial diplomacy until very recently.

In the 1970s the world economy was shaken by the tripling of oil prices provoked by OPEC. Oil-importing countries faced lower growth, higher inflation, and widening external deficits. The IMF struggled to agree a response to the crisis, so that the leading economies began meeting in small informal groups to move things forward: first the G5 finance ministers (US, Japan, Germany, France, UK) meeting in secret; then the public G7 summits of heads of governments, to which Italy, Canada, and the EC were added. Any agreements at G5 or G7 level only amounted to voluntary cooperation, and needed to be endorsed by all the IMF members to have worldwide effect. But the early summits of the 1970s proved very successful in agreeing a new exchange rate regime (still in force today), reviving economic growth, easing the pressure on the energy market, and promoting the conclusion of multilateral trade negotiations. This was enough to establish the G7 summit as an institution. Its performance fell away in the Reagan administration and the finance ministers regained some of their earlier power. But the need to help countries escaping from communism, as the cold war ended, gave the summit a new lease of life and in due course Russia joined, to make it G8. By then the G7/G8 format was widely copied. Other economic institutions regularly met at head of government level, from the European Council of the EU to the annual Asia-Pacific Economic Cooperation (APEC) summit.

Economic summit diplomacy has been a policy domain in which ministries of foreign affairs have been able to hold their own. Such diplomacy depends on the careful preparation carried out by the heads' personal representatives, called sherpas, supported by two 'sous-sherpas', one each from the foreign and finance ministries. This team can invoke the authority of the head of government to galvanize the rest of the bureaucracy and reach agreements blocked at lower levels. Sometimes the agreements are tied up even before the heads meet, which explains why summit communiqués can be largely written in advance. But on more difficult and sensitive issues it requires personal contact and persuasion among the heads to clinch the final deal. For example, British Prime Minister Blair himself won over Bush (US), Koizumi (Japan), and Schroeder (Germany) to support the aid package for Africa agreed at the 2005 Gleneagles summit. But the summit does not have its own machinery for implementation and follow-up. By a process of multilevel diplomacy, this is passed on to other institutions to ensure global application. In aid issues, debt relief, and other financial matters this means the IMF and World Bank; some of these required treatment over many decades and still remain relevant today.

21.6.1 Debt Relief for Middle-Income and Poor Countries

One measure promoted by the G5 finance ministers and the IMF after the first oil crisis was intended to help oil-importing developing countries. With IMF backing, private banks holding funds deposited by rich oil-exporters were encouraged to lend these on to middle-income oil-importing countries that had access to the markets. G5 governments in parallel made concessional loans to poor oil importers. At first developing countries could service these loans, thanks to healthy growth; but in the world recession of the early 1980s their debt burdens became intolerable. Middle-income countries threatened to default, which would have rendered Western banks insolvent. The G7 finance ministers (enlarged from G5) and the IMF spent a decade in negotiating agreements to reschedule these debts, obliging the debtor countries to accept strict economic policies which held back their development. But Western governments treated the lending banks more leniently, only obliging them to write down their debts once they had replenished their reserves.

Relief for poor countries on their debts to governments took even longer to resolve. Finance ministers took little interest, as they were not economically significant. But at the Toronto G7 summit of 1987 the UK, France, and Canada convinced the other heads of government to act, using moral and political arguments. From this beginning it took another seventeen years to complete the process at Gleneagles in 2005, when heavily indebted poor countries became entitled to 100 per cent relief on their debts both to governments and international institutions. The protagonists won over the sceptics in the G7 one by one—first the US, then Germany, then Japan. Having persuaded governments, the next stage was to convince the IMF and World Bank themselves to forgive their debts. The UK and Canada regularly used multilevel diplomacy, winning support in the plurilateral Commonwealth before putting initiatives to the summit or the wider IMF. An articulate coalition of charities, faith groups, and other NGOs kept up steady pressure on the governments to act.

21.6.2 Private Sector Financial Crises

As already noted the end of the cold war and the advance of globalization in the 1990s greatly increased the flow of international private investment, especially to developing countries with access to the market. This stimulated very strong growth performance in East Asian countries, especially as they pursued prudent macroeconomic policies. But their financial supervision was less strict and they tolerated dangerous levels of foreign currency borrowing. An unforeseen strengthening of the dollar in 1997 caused a sudden outrush of capital. Thailand, Indonesia, and South Korea faced financial disaster. All the regional economies suffered, except heavily protected China, while contagion later spread to Russia and Brazil, as well as to a big US hedge fund. It was the first financial crisis clearly attributable to the private sector and illustrates how financial markets had become endogenous to the policy process.

Once again the G7 countries and the IMF mobilized funds to rescue those in trouble. But as before the Western governments were most concerned to protect their own banks and investors, rather than help the stricken economies. They supported the IMF's usual prescription of stringent fiscal and monetary policies, though this was in fact the wrong strategy. The countries of the region resented this treatment and took steps never to have to call in the IMF again. They piled up vast currency reserves, creating persistent payments imbalances between their surpluses and the deficits of the US and most other Western countries.

The G8 summits of 1998 and 1999 endorsed 'new financial architecture' prepared by their finance ministers to prevent a recurrence. These measures were adopted by the entire membership of the IMF and World Bank. In an example of how financial diplomacy had become more inclusive, the G7 finance ministers co-opted other 'systemically important' countries, like Brazil, China, and India, in a new G20 grouping. A Financial Stability Forum was created, bringing together governments, central banks, and supervisory agencies from the G7 and a few other centres, to review and improve standards of financial regulation. This was supplemented by a new Financial Stability Action Programme, where the IMF staff provided guidance for its members. These actions indicated a trend towards the promotion of more uniform standards of financial regulation. The initial results of the 'new architecture' were benign. Apart from a crisis in Argentina that did not prove contagious the world economy entered a period of calm, with strong growth and low inflation everywhere. It appeared that the private financial markets could satisfy everyone. The IMF had less and less to do, while the G8 summit turned its attention to other issues.

In this deceptive calm, banks and other financial operators in Western economies progressively built up unsustainable levels of debt, in opaque and complex instruments that concealed the risks. Regulators trusted the wisdom of the markets, governments welcomed growing tax revenues, and consumers happily borrowed to sustain their life-styles. Anxiety gradually crept in from the international impact of troubles in the US sub-prime housing market. But the true extent of the danger was only revealed when the bankruptcy of Lehman Brothers, in September 2008, threatened the collapse of the entire financial system. Governments and central banks in the US and Europe suddenly had to intervene on a scale not seen before outside wartime, pouring in liquidity, rescuing and even taking over insolvent banks and acting to neutralize toxic assets that had lost all their value.

21.6.3 The Emergence of the G20

In this crisis the G8 summit was seen as inadequate. Its members were gravely hit by the crisis, while the prudent policies of the emerging economies had left them largely untouched. A solution to the imbalances in the international economy required an approach that went beyond the G8. In November 2008 the G20, which hitherto had only met at finance minister level, held its first summit in Washington, thus engaging the emerging powers on equal terms. The G20 summit rapidly emerged as an institution, with four more summits held by the end of 2010. Under the pressure of the crisis the G20 summits agreed on principles for economic stimulus, to check the recession caused by the financial collapse; on a programme of regulatory reform to avert any recurrence of the crisis; and on both massive replenishments of the resources of the IMF and reforms to its governance. As the crisis eased, the G20 sought to coordinate macroeconomic policies to correct the payments imbalances that had provoked the crisis.

Though the G20 summit, with its wider membership, superseded the G8 as the 'premier forum for economic cooperation', it preserved many of its methods of work. The country hosting the summit retained responsibility for organizing and preparing the event. After an initial period when the G7 members appeared to monopolize this process, a rational sequence emerged, with the chair rotating regionally and giving full scope to non-G7 members. Detailed preparations remained in the hands of the leaders' sherpas, though these were normally drawn from and supported by finance ministries. This continued the practice developed among the G20 finance ministers who now regularly met in advance of the summits. Foreign ministries were less involved in the G20, though they retained their place in the surviving G8 summit, from which finance ministries largely withdrew.

From the outset the G20 summit pursued multilevel diplomacy. It revived close links with the IMF, from which the G8 had become detached. The non-G7 members overcame their initial distrust of the Fund and agreed to expand its resources, in return for pledges to reform IMF governance. This reform was agreed at the Seoul G20 summit in November 2010. It expanded the quotas, and thus voting rights of many emerging countries, led by China, India, Brazil, and Russia, while the Europeans gave up two of the eight seats they normally occupied in the IMF executive board. The G20 also charged the IMF to develop methods to coordinate policies designed to reduce imbalances, but this has proved much harder. In addition, the G20 summit, for the first time, gave clear instructions to the renamed Financial Stability Board (FSB) and the Basel Committee on Banking Supervision (BCBS). The G20 enlarged the membership of both institutions, in line with its own. It made clear the coverage of financial reform it wished to see and kept up the pressure for results. As a result the BCBS announced new rules on capital levels for international banks in time for the Seoul G20 summit and these were followed by measures agreed in the FSB. While previously both institutions were strongly influenced by the private banks and other operators, now the regulators were determined to establish their own authority.

In contrast to the formal bilateral, regional, or multilateral treaties negotiated in the trade field, international financial diplomacy proceeds more often by voluntary cooperation, through the summits, or through informal understandings that can only be enforced by the IMF where it is making loans with conditions attached. Even the regulatory reforms agreed in the FSB and the BCBS do not have mandatory impact, but rely on national measures for their implementation. This opens the risk of inconsistency, with no more than peer pressure to keep countries in line. The position is rather different in the European Union. In regulatory reform, the EU has introduced new supervisory institutions and prepared its own measures for applying the new BCBS rules in all its member states. Where governments in the eurozone, like Greece, Ireland, and Portugal were unable to service their debts, the eurozone has created its own rescue mechanism, providing loans subject to policy conditions. But this process has revealed severe tensions. Electorates in creditor countries were reluctant to back the rescue operations, while in debtor countries they resented harsh corrective measures imposed from outside. Many European banks became dangerously exposed to the debts of vulnerable governments and also needed to be rescued. Thus the sovereign debt crisis generated full-blown macroeconomic and banking crises, to which the eurozone has responded by moving towards a fiscal and banking union.

21.7 TRENDS IN ECONOMIC DIPLOMACY

The economic and financial crisis unleashed by the collapse of Lehman Brothers in 2008 produced a major upheaval in economic diplomacy. Four years later, this crisis is still far from over. The immediate response was to stimulate economies worldwide, in order to check and reverse the recession. But in many Western countries that was only achieved at the cost of a dangerous increase in public debt, as banks and consumers tried to reduce their excessive levels of private debt. Many governments have therefore introduced corrective measures to bring down public deficits, but this has slowed down growth performance after the initial climb out of recession. The debate on the policy response has been particularly acute in the United States, being aggravated by the electoral timetable, and in the eurozone, because of the persistent sovereign debt crisis. There are wider uncertainties about inflation prospects, energy prices, and exchange rate policy. So it is harder than usual to pick out lasting trends.

One unmistakable feature of 21st-century economic diplomacy is the growing power and influence of the emerging economies, led by China and with Brazil, India, and others in support. During the last decade these countries grew at impressive rates, steadily catching up with the mature industrial states, so that China is now the largest economy after the US. Most of them survived the financial crisis with only a short hesitation in growth, thanks to their cautious policies, while the imprudence of the Western countries led them into a deep recession from which they are only slowly recovering. In these conditions, the emerging economies have rightly taken their place on equal terms with Western countries and no major decisions can be taken without their full involvement. The establishment of the G20 summit is clear evidence of this.

This trend reconciles political structures with economic performance, but has not made it easier to reach agreement on the key issues of economic diplomacy. China and the others are not rejecting the open economic system that encouraged their rapid growth. But they are insisting on putting their own stamp on any agreements reached. After the crisis, the emerging powers readily agreed on emergency measures in the G20 summit, which suited them well. But they have not agreed on the coordination of measures to reduce payments imbalances. In the WTO's Doha negotiations on agriculture, a group of developing countries led by Brazil (also called the G20) have proved tough and demanding negotiators. In climate change, the final deals that emerged from the 2009 Copenhagen and 2011 Durban conference depended on input from the 'BASIC' countries (Brazil, South Africa, India, and China). Many emerging countries, especially China, are ready to take helpful economic or environmental measures on a national basis. But they are reluctant to integrate these into international agreements and resist external pressure to do so.

This approach reflects a more widespread attitude in economic diplomacy around the world. Growing domestic pressure on governments, as globalization penetrates national economic activity, makes it harder for them to accept the obligations of formal multilateral treaties. Worldwide negotiations on trade, investment, and the environment therefore mark time. Instead, governments favour agreements on a regional or bilateral level, where they can more easily control the outcome. They resort to voluntary cooperation arrangements, from which they can withdraw if conditions turn adverse. They adopt unilateral economic measures which have international impact but do not depend on international partners. This approach to economic diplomacy was regarded as tolerable in the early 2000s, when the undisturbed operation of the markets seemed to deliver steady growth with low inflation. But faith in markets and market operators was badly shaken by the abrupt outbreak of the financial crisis and the recession that followed. Stronger regulation of financial markets is inevitable from now on and regulatory tightening may spread to other areas. Regulatory reform may be agreed internationally, as is happening in financial stability, but the actual measures will be adopted and enforced nationally.

In a globalized world, binding multilateral regimes, which apply equally to all, are the best way of promoting and protecting economic public goods and ensuring that poor and vulnerable countries are not marginalized. It is therefore worrying that, under domestic pressures, governments are favouring regional and bilateral approaches over multilateralism and voluntary cooperation or national action over rule-based systems. To reverse the trend and promote successful economic diplomacy over the coming decades, it is essential that countries engaged in international negotiation are better able to understand and influence the domestic decision-making processes in their partners. If they wait to act at the negotiating table, it will be too late. This strategy requires greater transparency in policy-making and a readiness to invest time and effort in understanding how other countries' systems work. It puts a premium on the traditional skills exercised by diplomatic missions resident in foreign capitals. If followed, it could lead to a revival of the role of foreign ministries, who staff these missions, and compensate for any loss of their influence in decision-making in economic diplomacy at home.

NOTES

* This chapter draws on a decade of running a masters option at the LSE on the topic of economic diplomacy that has drawn on contributions from academics as well as practitioners. A more extensive treatment of the topic can be found in N. Bayne and S. Woolcock, *The New Economic Diplomacy: Decision Making and Negotiation in International Economic Relations*, 3rd edition (Farnham: Ashgate, 2011).

1. A. Watson quoted in D. Lee and D. Hudson, 'The Old and New Significance of Political Economy in Diplomacy', *Review of International Studies* 30 (2004), 343–60.

2. J.-M.F. Blanchard and N.M. Ripsman, 'A Political Theory of Economic Statecraft', *Foreign Policy Analysis* 4 (2008), 371–98. For a more detailed discussion of the definition of economic diplomacy that broadly corresponds with our definition here see M. Okano-Heijmans, 'Conceptualizing Economic Diplomacy', in P.A.G. van Bergeijk, M. Okano-Heijmans, and J. Melissen (eds), *Economic Diplomacy: Economic and Political Perspectives* (Leiden: Martinus Nijhoff, 2011); and Lee and Hudson, 'The Old and New'.

3. K. Rana, 'Serving the Private Sector: India's Experience in Context', in Bayne and Woolcock (eds), *The New Economic Diplomacy*; van Bergeijk, Okano-Heijmans, and Melissen (eds), *Economic Diplomacy*.

4. Economic diplomacy would therefore include negotiations to establish agreed international rules on the provision of export credit, such as the OECD Code of Conduct, while commercial diplomacy covers the use by governments of such support to gain contracts.

5. The use of the term 'club' here is as in the description of the post US-hegemonic economic system as being one led by a club of developed OECD countries in economic forums such as the OECD, the IMF, the G7, and the GATT.

6. T. Soobramanien, 'Economic Diplomacy for Small and Low Income Countries', in Bayne and Woolcock (eds), *The New Economic Diplomacy*.

7. S. Woolcock, *European Union Economic Diplomacy* (Farnham: Ashgate, 2012).

8. K. Heydon, 'The OECD: lessons from investment and services', in Bayne and Woolcock (eds), *The New Economic Diplomacy*.

9. These issues were covered by qualified most-favoured nation codes. This meant in effect that only the OECD countries signed them.

10. It is not possible to give a precise date when the US lost its hegemony in the trading system. The first US trade deficit was in 1973. Thereafter the US shifted from the position of a benign hegemon in trade using its large market as the basis for the GATT to a policy less tolerant of free riding. In the early 1980s the US was unable to persuade its OECD partners to start a new round of trade negotiations, so that the Uruguay Round did not begin till 1986. But it was at the end of the 1990s and beginning of the 2000s that the US appeared to give up any desire to lead the multilateral trading system.

CHAPTER 22

....

TRADE AND INVESTMENT
PROMOTION

....

GREG MILLS

THE Ugandan Minister of Planning stood up at the end of the panel session at the 2010 Confederation of Indian Industries 'Partnership Summit' in the southern Indian city of Chennai (formerly Madras). He commented that such events did not deliver the goods they needed, and asked of the 1,300 people present at the conference: 'What are you doing for South–South relations?'

Over lunch, I queried the minister. What had he meant by his statement? Surely, I asked, he should come to India with some goals in mind, and a means to achieve them—not wait for them to be delivered by others. He replied in (surprisingly) good humour that the problem was they did everything that the world asked for—better policy, better governance, and the incentives that investors wanted—but the results were not forthcoming. I sympathized, but his position contrasted markedly with the whole tone of the event until that point. The Maldives' President Mohamed Nasheed, the first to be elected by a multi-party democracy in his islands-state who would later be ousted by a coup, had given a very uncompromising and inspirational opening address, decrying the corruption and bureaucratic maladministration of his predecessor's thirty-year rule. A journalist and former political prisoner, the boyish Nasheed, then just forty-two, outlined the 'unprecedented market-based reforms' on the islands. The economic reforms, he explained, involved the need for financial prudence and long-term stability; a radical policy of privatization and public–private partnerships; and cutting red tape and reducing government bureaucracy wherever possible. Stressing that the state cannot and should not play the role of business, Nasheed said 'for three decades, the dynamism of the Maldivian economy was hindered by the suffocating regulations of a meddlesome state'.[1] He said his goal was to rebalance the relationship between the public and the private sectors, adding that a 'government's rightful place' was to correct market failure, and also to provide a safety net for the most vulnerable people in society.[2]

His address came after the deputy chief minister of Tamil Nadu state—the inappropriately named MK Stalin—had given a very strong sales pitch on why investors should come to his province. Instead of shying away from comparisons, all his benchmarks were on the basis of what the other twenty-seven Indian states had achieved and where Tamil Nadu ranked in terms of production capacity and foreign investment. There was no beating around the bush. He proudly listed multinational companies which had established factories in his state, which read like a who's who of international business including Microsoft, Caterpillar, Dell, BMW, Hyundai, Motorola, Nokia, Renault-Nissan, Michelin, Toshiba, Komatsu, and Samsung. No wonder, then, was Tamil Nadu the third-largest Indian state for FDI, attracting around $8–9 billion each year. With nearly 22,000 factories in ninety-one special economic zones, and the largest producer of cars in India, no wonder Mr Stalin appeared confident in his words 'of taking this to the next level'.

Nasheed was followed, over lunch, by the Malaysian trade minister, Dato Sri Mustapa Mohamed, who carefully ran the assembled audience through his country's investment advantages and the various incentives that had been established to bring in foreign money and expertise. The head of the Malaysian one-stop investor shop, the Malaysian Industrial Development Authority, was on hand to answer specific questions, while her staff went around the packed gathering handing out leaflets encouraging foreigners to invest in second homes in Malaysia under the 'MM2H' scheme. It was Malaysia's professed multiculturalism in action.

The Ugandans, not to mention the large (in more ways than one) Zimbabwean delegation in attendance, were comparatively clueless. They were willing to attend the event, yet did not apparently have a plan when they got there. Yet the process itself had become the benchmark by which many African leaders judged their value. From the myriad of groups (all the way from G2 through the G8 and G20 to the UN itself, the G192), including specialist agencies and the African Union, the international agenda was cluttered with a full and demanding menu of conference choices.

Ironically, given the Chennai exchange, a luxury convention facility near Kampala reminded me six months earlier of the scale of the enterprise and its tautological nature. A National Seminar on Managing Oil Revenue in Uganda ran alongside an event on public health in East Africa. While expensive suits strutted their important stuff through the five-star venue, officials noisily discussed over breakfast the scale of their per diems in between the declining fortunes of the UN Development Programme in Somalia.

Forget that Uganda has no oil revenues, at least not yet, or that there is no development process imaginable for the UN in Somalia—this is not the point. Such participation is at least as much about showing the flag as about flagging, although seldom resolving, issues.

When leaders cannot decide on something, they apparently call a summit.[3] If they cannot decide on even that, they establish a roundtable. When they cannot agree on issues, they call for an investigation or a commission of inquiry. And when they agree not to agree, they conclude a memorandum of understanding or make a pledge—the only understanding being that no binding agreement is possible. The purpose of such actions is ostensibly to kick the problem down the road to be solved another day. But this runs the danger that such events are, from the outset, the overall aim of such engagements. And there is the omnipresent danger of short-term tactical politicization overshadowing any strategic considerations.

The contemporary era of globalization suggests one in which sovereignty does not carry the same meaning as it did when defined by the Treaty of Westphalia in the 17th century. The state no longer has untrammelled power and jurisdiction in domestic or foreign affairs. Independence on local issues is bound by the nature of global norms and values along with a host of international political, economic, and security agreements, as well as by participation in international and supranational organizations. There is too increasingly an overlap between foreign and domestic policy, particularly with the growing dependence of economies on foreign trade and investment, and the need to address transnational problems (crime, drugs, the environment, energy, transport, and so on) on the global stage. Put simply, domestic goals now mostly have to be pursued internationally, which places a huge responsibility on foreign representatives, and focuses attention on their capabilities, resources, and the relationships that they enjoy with a range of increasingly active and important non-governmental global players and interest groups, especially business. Modern diplomacy can thus be summed up as entailing:[4]

- The conduct of foreign policy in the national interest, including trade, finance, politics, culture, and tourism matters.[5]
- The conduct and management of international relations by negotiation. A diplomat is said to be 'disarming when his or her country is not'.
- The apparatus for managing international relations, including consular, cultural, sporting, legal, investment, and trade relations.
- The manner and skill with which international relations are managed, including the 'reconciliation of diverse foreign policy priorities'.[6]

This chapter examines the way in which the relationship between business and government is structured, with a special emphasis on trade and investment promotion, noting the experiences of a number of case studies including Costa Rica and Singapore in considering both general principles and making specific recommendations about the relationship. It posits that the ways in which business and diplomacy interact depends on a combination of economic systems and traditions. In much of the Western world, by comparison, government and business maintain a healthy division, one carefully regulated and legally ordained. This division is less clear throughout much of the developing world. In China, for example, the state and business are usually inseparable. In Africa, with few exceptions, the relationship is usually uncomfortably close or outright hostile. A similar pattern is discernible in other regions where elite interests drive policy choices. Such patterns are a product of history, circumstance, pragmatism, and culture.

22.1 Reshaping Diplomacy

As intimated already, the veteran British diplomat Peter Marshall highlighted a series of 'invasions' which have impacted on the management of international relations, including:

The increasing importance of economic affairs in a rapidly integrating and interdependent world. With regional integration, external policies have become a most crucial determinant of domestic politics rather than the other way around—take the role of the European Union for example, particularly for the smaller countries. Given, too, the importance of global trade and investment for economic development prospects, foreign policy has become more, not less, concerned with foreign economic relations. This highlights the need for a better and more constructive business–government nexus in foreign policy, and for a different focus (and skills) on the part of diplomats with greater finances and personnel dedicated to trade and investment matters.

The increasing number of state and non-state actors. As a result, and coupled with the media revolution, public affairs have become a key concern in the creation and conduct of foreign policy. This has demanded a flow of explanation and information to parliament and its bodies, the media, academia, and other elements of civil society. In a related respect, decolonization not only expanded the number of states, but also served to make the right of self-determination a permanent concern of the international community, who question both the nature of the post-colonial state and the role of such states as equal partners in a multilateral order. To these demands can be added the burgeoning importance of the multilateral environment in the conduct of foreign policy, though it is apparent that this supplements rather than supplants the bilateral relationship. (It should be noted that the role that some developed world NGOs play in some regions, in particular in Africa, is often quite dismaying, including in moulding positions for developing countries at World Trade Organization summits.)

The media revolution.[7] The pace of the information revolution which has blurred the distinction between the process and substance of foreign policy, has (or, at least, should have) changed the way in which diplomacy is conducted, both in a technical and a conceptual sense. Public interest has made diplomacy everybody's interest, and the business of many more people than are employed by the state. In this environment, substance and process are inextricably linked—where, as Marshall terms it, 'how to do it may determine to a very great extent what to do.'[8] Traditional diplomatic channels are no longer sufficient in reaching an international audience if one of the goals of diplomacy (and foreign policy) today is to create and strengthen international understanding. This involves better use of communications in addition to those instruments (government information, news, development, and cultural agencies such as the BBC, Voice of America, Deutsche Welle, Goethe Institut, British Council, Alliance Française, US Information Agency, etc.) traditionally employed by governments for this purpose. Yet, paradoxically, the barrage of electronic information and the prospect of miscommunication and misunderstanding arising from it emphasises more than ever the importance of the human aspect.

Technology shifts. With the technological and policy innovations of the late 20th century, transportation and communication costs lowered significantly, markets became integrated de facto, and international trade became more important than it used to be. This is one of the key drivers as to why trade and investment issues and mechanisms prevail today over the traditional concerns of foreign affairs, and why the inelegant characters (technocrats, not diplomats) and hybrid institutions (like investment promotion efforts) of trade now usurp the traditional diplomatic realm.

The emergence of so-called 'new issues'. The promotion of ethics and values such as human rights and democracy, humanitarian situations, drug abuse and trafficking, the spread of HIV/AIDS, the need to combat terrorism, and the safeguarding of the environment are issues that must now be factored into the diplomatic calculation. The last of these issues sparks concerns about the management not only of resources, but also of the potential contradiction between sustainable development and the tensions it could give rise to in developing countries and across the North–South axis. Indeed, perhaps the greatest recent shift in international affairs—and derivatively of diplomacy—is that from the primacy of national interests as the *fons et origo* of foreign policy towards the adoption of a set of 'global norms', against which national policy and practice are putatively to be measured. Of course there are issues that are purely concerns of the North and that somehow are very easy to sell in the South. For instance, Africa has strongly embraced the European anti-GMO concerns, even though the real motivation appears to be a European issue (that European farmers cannot compete against GMO from the Americas), and despite the huge potential contribution of GMOs to the challenge of feeding Africa.

In sum, to reiterate, sovereign states no longer control international relations. The expansion in the number of actors has two major implications: First, this greatly complicates the management of foreign policy, where more is expected of a foreign service (often with diminished capacity and resources) in an age where there is greater external and domestic scrutiny and interaction. The concept of international relations no longer means the same as traditional diplomacy, epitomized by 'intergovernmental' or 'interstate' relations, and has implications for the type and quality of personnel recruited and trained for a foreign service. Second, it presents enormous new opportunities.

What do these implications portend for the conduct of diplomacy in practice? No longer is the state the only, or perhaps even the most important, actor in modern diplomacy. Globalization has expanded the role of non-state entities, in particular business and civil networks. For inclusive government is not only, as the then UN Secretary-General Kofi Annan termed it, the best 'guarantor against internal violent conflicts' where 'democracy is a non-violent form of internal conflict management',[9] but it also spawns civil society institutions with similar value structures, interacting in what are termed 'global public policy networks'. The range of issues faced by government and intergovernmental organizations is too wide to be dealt with by them alone, particularly in developing countries. Moreover, many policy issues are transnational by nature, demanding global action where the active participation of non-state actors is critical in developing policy outcomes.[10]

These institutions do not exist for their own sake, however. The complexities of running a modern economy and the wide range of international actions required cannot be met by the state alone. Diplomacy can no longer be confined, as Marshall has noted, 'to sovereigns, ministers and professional diplomats'.

Here, the development of an effective foreign service and policy is critical in both getting views across to the international community and in creating the opportunities domestically that will enable states to prosper. To do so, they will have to understand their position, the needs of the global order, and the importance of domestic coordination in their response. Indeed, the modern diplomat has to be something akin to what Jack Spence has described as a 'polymath', capable of dealing with the wide range of new issues and multiplicity of actors in international relations today: economic management, human rights concerns, and information technology management, as well as a raft of new threats to security including terrorism, pollution, and health hazards.

The decentralization of authority away from foreign services impacts not only on the extra- but also the inter-departmental relationship. Extraneous governmental forces include other departments, agencies, and parliamentary committees in, as George Kennan put it, 'a turgid sea of constantly changing parochial and competing domestic interests'.[11] This stresses the need for an effective machinery of government for the efficient conduct of foreign policy. Given that policy-making does not occur in an emotional vacuum, and that the role of human personalities may inevitably distort objectivity, it is also critical that the policy-makers and the bureaucracy interact to establish a process, whatever the tensions that result.

The series of invasions of the traditional terrain of diplomacy by other actors raises concerns about both people and policy: about the focus of diplomacy and about the type of people and structures necessary to carry out these tasks. While much focus is on diplomacy as the interface with the world outside of government, their actions—and their success—are dependent on policy which they do not themselves set.

22.2 Relaunching Trade Promotion?

Whatever the arguments about the value of the multilateral environment, there are a number of clear international trends as we face a world in which the 'dizzying pace of the transformations brought on by globalisation' has deprived countries of their 'traditional landmarks'.[12]

First, there is a need for better coordination of the activities of diplomatic interests of trade and foreign affairs divisions. In the Canadian (1985), New Zealand (1989), and Australian (1987) cases, this has involved the amalgamation of the two departments concerned—what one Australian diplomat referred to as a 'shotgun marriage, but ultimately well worth it'. Stuart Harris, then the Secretary of the Australian Foreign Affairs

Department, likened the experience to Dean Acheson's description of reorganizing the State Department as being like performing an appendectomy on a man carrying a piano up a flight of stairs, but in the Australian case with someone trying to play the piano as well![13] As Harris argued, this amalgamation reflected the greater integration of politics and economics internationally, the growing priority of economic as against political issues with the passing of the cold war, growing global interdependence, and the continued growth in the linkage between domestic and foreign policies. Critically, this illustrated the need to stop seeing strategic relationships as distinct from the economic relationships simply because of bureaucratic convenience or corporate cultures.[14]

Second, there is a need for the allocation of more diplomatic resources to trade and investment issues. Of the eight 'Business Lines' of Canada's DFAIT (International Business Development, Trade and Economic Policy, International Security and Cooperation, Assistance to Canadians Abroad, Public Diplomacy, Corporate Services, Services to Other Government Departments, and Passport Services) in 1995–1996, the first two areas, which were both directly concerned with trade/investment issues, consumed one-quarter of its budget.[15] As a result, more than half of the DFAIT's staff abroad were said to be 'dedicated to the delivery of trade, economic and investment programs'.[16]

Third, there is a tendency to isolate geographical areas within this focus. In the Australian case

> [t]he national interest does not change with a change of government. The priority accorded to the Asia Pacific, and especially to the countries of East Asia, the forging of close relationships with the United States, Japan, Indonesia and China, the commitment to further trade liberalisation, and strong support for the World Trade Organisation (WTO) and APEC are among the important elements of continuity in the government's policy framework.[17]

Consequently, its trade strategies focused

> on bilateral efforts, APEC, and the WTO. Each has a contribution to make to increasing Australia's standard of living through expanded trade and investment. None offers the only way ahead, and all three will be needed if Australia is to improve its trade performance. Other practical steps, such as closer links between CER (Australia's economic relations agreement with New Zealand) and the ASEAN Free Trade Area (AFTA), will also be pursued.[18]

Fourth, this translates also into a need to place missions where there is the greatest potential benefit, for example:[19]

- At major multilateral centres in New York, Washington, Brussels, Vienna, or Geneva.
- In countries where there are strong economic, political, cultural, or military ties— main trade and investment partners plus those identified as areas of potential benefit, especially those with large populations and growing economies.
- At regional centres such as Brussels or Addis Ababa.
- In capitals and major cities of neighbouring states.

And, fifth, this stresses the importance of improving the relationship between government and civil society, especially business.[20]

22.3 RECASTING THE GOVERNMENT–BUSINESS–CIVIL SOCIETY NEXUS

In the mid-1990s, the Canadian government recognized that it was operating in a globalized economy 'in which companies must export to survive, grow and prosper' and where there was thus a need to compete with other countries to 'maintain and expand market share for goods, services and inward investment flows'. To meet these challenges, it pinpointed the need for working with the private sector, particularly small- and medium-sized businesses, on improving the number of exporters; and also for building market share in priority and fast-growing markets, while expanding the country's share of global foreign investment.[21] For its Commonwealth cousin, Australia, its

> [e]conomic well-being depends on domestic and international factors, especially the competitiveness and flexibility of the Australian economy, and the strength of international markets and their openness to our exports and investment. Australian interests therefore require action on all these fronts.

Indeed, it is clear that business–government foreign policy consultation is central in dealing with the developmental problems faced by states. There is also the related need to make government aware of the specific role, benefits, and difficulties of business. From this stems the imperative to create strategies for business–government dialogue, through which solutions can be generated. The development of synergy and networks between government–business and civil society could thus involve the following:

Sharing professional expertise and experience. Most movement between the public and private sectors occurs when senior government officials resign or retire permanently and join a corporation. Alternative and potentially important sharing of personnel could include the appointment of a very senior and well-known business leader as a 'special advisor' or 'deputy' to the foreign minister; secondment opportunities for 'rising corporate and government stars' for two or three years of line counterpart experience; use of business people to augment commercial functions at embassies; adding corporate representation in delegations to bilateral meetings and also to sub-regional, continental, and special or annual meetings of multilateral financial organizations and specialized agencies whose mandates could affect national business interests. Naturally, ways will have to be found to prevent corporations which lend expertise to government from engaging in 'insider trading'.

Information sharing. Imperatives of government security and service to broader national interests will limit business access, just as corporations remain sensitive to sharing proprietary or other information that could help competitors. But much more could be done to exchange intelligence about local economic and political conditions, especially in countries of growing economic interest. Some have even suggested that the economic reporting of diplomats should be reduced. 'We've got this huge private sector that spends zillions of dollars doing just that, and they do it better than the State Department is ever going to do it. Just buy everyone a Bloomberg.'[22] Corporate and government representatives could also help each other to understand better the role of third-country competitors and partners, as well as that of multilateral donors and agencies.

Policy Planning and Advice. Established corporate councils advising government have proven valuable in industrial democracies. When deciding whether and how to apply or adhere to sanctions regimes, such bodies can be of critical importance. Increasingly, the UN and international financial institutions make use of such regular consultative mechanisms. Joint government/corporate efforts should be made to ensure national representation on such bodies, and that information gathered is shared with stakeholders at home. Special events may also require rapid consultations. Delegations to promote stronger and more comprehensive bilateral ties with key countries (as well as bi-national commissions and other mechanisms) could also benefit from corporate participation. Adding a government representative to business delegations could work positively in reverse.

Promoting Social Responsibility and Civil Society. Government and business share an interest in assisting the development of civil society and the rule of law in countries where long-term partnerships are envisioned. This practice of 'corporatism' involves bringing civil organizations into decision-making and consultation processes in return for government having 'privileged access'.

This 'third leg' of democracy is particularly weak in many developing countries. Finding affordable, cost-effective, and politically acceptable ways to assist the development of civil society (including trade unions and labour rights organizations) is a long, difficult, and problem-prone process, but it is one which can only benefit from effective communication and collaboration between corporate, labour, and government sectors. This extends to the development of academic institutions as well. All governments, particularly those stretched for resources as in Africa, will be poorer if they rely solely on their bureaucracy for ideas, analysis, and management; and the continent will be poorer still if the external debate is dominated by external, non-African civil society institutions.

These considerations point the way to a demand for better analysis of the global economy and its challenges. Although there has been an explosion of information through the Internet and the media, analysis is sometimes less clear, given that 'there's more to understand and the information is coming at us from every direction'.[23] It is important for government and businesses to devote greater resources to understanding the way in which the world works.

Developing Human Capital: Cooperation between business and government to facilitate the training of young and mid-career private, public, and civil society leaders can be a mainspring to long-term bilateral partnerships and business advantage.

*

How then should the increasing and seemingly unstoppable link between trade and foreign affairs be best managed?

22.4 Economic Diplomacy I: At Home

Success abroad at promoting international trade and investment, the 'stuff' of business–government collaboration, depends on having the right macro- and micro-economic policies to promote, as well as conditions of political stability or, at least, political and policy predictability.

If policy (and investor predictability thereof) is a necessary foundation for success, the next level up concerns the methods of communication, institutional or otherwise, between the private sector and business. Put differently, if building growth coalitions is key, how might this occur?

Take Africa, where the relationship of business to government has been, as already noted, often predatory or too close. The institutional relationship between business and government has not progressed much from the formula of Chambers of Commerce meeting infrequently (if at all) with government, with little apparent direct impact on policy. Only South Africa is the exception to this model, as befits a highly-developed industrial and mining sector and a sensitized civil society, with a plethora of business–government bodies, divided (even c.2011) to an extent on racial (and size) lines: Business Unity South Africa (BUSA) is the overarching organization, which includes membership of Chambers of Commerce (including the SA Chamber of Commerce and Industry, the National African Chambers of Commerce, and the Afrikaner Handelsinstituut), corporate organizations (such as Business Leadership SA), and professional and sectoral bodies. Parallel to these bodies exists NEDLAC (the National Economic Development and Labour Council) which establishes a dialogue on policy matters is established between business, government, and labour, and the Millennium Labour Council, a bilateral, by-invitation labour–business organization. The Business Trust was established as a bridging body between business and government in the initial post-apartheid period, from which emerged the Big Business Working Group, which engaged the Mbeki government (1999–2008) on critical issues. It was the South African government's intention, in 2011, to create a similar body for economic policy discussions. However, as with many initiatives in South Africa—and indeed, across the continent—government's approach has largely been top-down and about setting policy to which organizations have to sign up, and not listening, a style 'rich in process and thin', in the words of one business person, 'in detail'.[24]

At the continental level, attempts to create pan-African institutions have met with limited success. The NEPAD Business Group and Foundation, aimed at promoting the objectives of the New Partnership for Africa's Development through envisaging 'an African powerhouse that utilizes all its resources to generate innovative economic growth that engenders socio-political stability and sustainable livelihood for all its people on par with global standards'.[25] It has, however, gone into obscurity, partly given its (too) close association with former South African president Thabo Mbeki and NEPAD's envelopment by the African Union, and partly because it operates 'too closely in the government ambit, and its reach to the private sector is not that strong'.[26] The AU also established an Economic, Social, and Cultural Council (ECOSOCC) in 2008, an advisory organ composed of different social and professional groups of member states, that regularly stages various business summits both sector- and country-specific. The website of the AU, however, under 'partnerships' in 'economic affairs' says 'Coming Soon'.[27] The lack of hard results in these areas overall reflects the AU's problems of a lack of political will, teeth, and cash.[28] This may help to explain why, aside from hosting meetings, the AU Commission has changed track in trying to play to its multilateral strengths in promoting business interests. The AU's January 2011 summit adopted a public service charter aimed at establishing best practice in improving civil service policy and bureaucratic efficiencies, thereby lowering the transaction costs for business.

*

If domestic success demands an international dimension, what are the bureaucratic, institutional methods that might best promote national interests externally?

22.5 Economic Diplomacy II: Abroad

Today, the only way a country can suffer real injustice at the hands of the global economy is by being excluded from it. How might it pursue these ambitions? Take two examples—Singapore and Costa Rica.

At independence in 1963, Singapore had a GNP per capita of less than US$320. Infrastructure was poor, there was little capital, and the handful of industries produced only for domestic consumption. Low-end commerce was the mainstay of the economy, and there was little or no direct foreign investment. Massive unemployment and labour unrest following the withdrawal of the British troops from the island meant that creating jobs was the priority. This translated into creating labour-intensive industries. But this required, first, an environment conducive to industrial development.

Thus Jurong Industrial Estate was born in a swampy area along the west coast of the island. In 1961, the Singapore government created a public–private development board, the Economic Development Board (EDB), comprising key members of government and foreign and local business people. This reflects the critical imperative for institutional expertise and memory to keep the growth process on a single, integrated track. It also relates to the need for a holistic, 'national' approach to attract investment, where provinces or local geographic areas do not bid against each other. In fulfilling its motto that 'There is always an EDB near you', today the agency employs 500 people (300 of whom are graduates) in nineteen offices worldwide, including six in the US and five in the European Union.[29] Another agency, the government International Enterprise (IE), is similarly tasked with promoting Singapore's companies outside the country, again through 465 staff (of which 100 are abroad), by taking 100 overseas missions annually and through its thirty offices worldwide. With both IE and the EDB, their budgets ($40 million and $120 million respectively) are dependent on how well they perform. In essence, the Singapore state has 'corporatized' its development process and interests.

With the challenge for Singapore to develop export-oriented industries, the EDB opened its first overseas centres, in Hong Kong and New York, with the aim of wooing foreign investors.[30] By the 1970s, the EDB was marketing Singapore as a quick operations 'start-up' location where factories were built in advance of demand, and a highly skilled workforce was readily available. More EDB offices were set up in Europe, USA and Asia. As Singapore's industrial base widened, this led to new investments, particularly in electronics, and product diversification which greatly enhanced export performance, and increased R&D activities by multinational companies. Between 1971 and 1976, EDB offices were opened in Zurich, Paris, Osaka, and Houston. By the mid-1970s, in spite of a global recession, the EDB pushed for more industrial projects and manufacturing became the largest sector in the economy, surpassing trade. The 1980s saw Singapore embarking on a 'Second Industrial Revolution', a move into knowledge-intensive activities such as R&D, engineering design, and computer software services. To meet these needs, EDB established institutions of technology jointly with the governments of Japan, Germany, and France, training Singaporeans in electronics and engineering. EDB also took on the task of administering the Skills Development Fund to encourage the right kind of manpower training.

To promote local enterprises and improve competitiveness, in 1986 the EDB set up the Small Enterprise Bureau. By 1990, EDB had sixteen investment promotion centres worldwide. Its role had broadened into that of a business architect helping companies configure and design activities through strategic planning partnerships. Today some 7,000 multinational companies operate in Singapore, with about half having regional operations. Fundamentally, the Singapore government promotes a pro-business environment that continues to encourage MNCs and local companies to invest and expand in Singapore. The government is able to anticipate problems and come up with effective solutions. The role of the EDB in this success is, at its core, to make Singapore's environment conducive and competitive for global business.

*

Elsewhere, Costa Rica has shown what can be achieved in going from an agricultural to a high-tech and services base—from coffee and bananas to computer chips, medical equipment, and high quality services. Exports in goods and services rose 10 per cent per annum, from $870 million in the early 1980s to over $14 billion in 2010—extraordinary for an economy of four million people. This was built on openness to trade and capital, by 'Ticos' using their heads and good policy as the principal tools. Costa Rica also showed how collaboration with experienced business people was crucial in creating a supportive and mutually reinforcing business environment.

The Costa Rican success story is about using incentives to attract manufacturing and services industries, especially from North America, creating over 50,000 direct jobs in the last decade through export-led growth. Roberto Artavia, the former head of the INCAE business school, observed about Costa Rica,[31] 'Our commitment to free and compulsory education in 1871 accounts for much of our success, the rest is down to our nature.' Or as Bill Merrigan, head of Proctor and Gamble's Americas' back-office, a 1,300-employee-strong operation based in Costa Rica, said, 'If you ask for a miracle, the joke goes here, the Costa Ricans say "when do you want it delivered?". They work so hard and are so driven.'[32] There has been widespread use of consistently applied tax holidays. Yet Intel's signal 1997 investment in Costa Rica had, however, generated $2.5 in personal income tax for every $1 of tax relief. Of course, policy is not enough without the protection offered to investors by sound domestic, democratic institutions. And Costa Rica established a specialist institution, run on not-for-profit grounds, to promote investment and exports. From the Costa Rica Investment Promotion Agency (CINA) to Colombia's Proexport, the professionalism and energy of their staffers was impressive—usually young, foreign educated, multilingual, and equally as comfortable with the private sector as government. They were, according to their business clients, 'responsive and proactive on everything from visas to after-care'.

The Costa Rican Investment Promotion Agency (CINDE)[33] was established in 1985 as a private, non-profit, and non-political organization. This board relies on $2 million in annual income, 80 per cent of which is sourced from an endowment, the remainder from grants. The thirty-strong body relies on ten investment specialists, and two small overseas offices. CINDE, an NGO, works hand-in-glove with other institutions: COMEX (the Ministry for Trade), and PROCOMER (the export promotion agency, similar to El Salvador's PROESA or Ireland's IDA) which is 'a public institution ran under the private sector legal regime'. PROCOMER's board is presided by the COMEX Minister, but four of the other seven members are Business Chamber representatives. CINDE's board is fully private, but also receives financial support from PROCOMER. All three coordinate closely, the people in charge play musical chairs between them. All three have much more influence over presidential decisions than foreign affairs ever did.

CINDE has attracted more than 200 companies to Costa Rica, including worldwide leaders such as Intel, Procter and Gamble, Hospira, Baxter, St Jude Medical, Western Union, and many others. CINDE is small (its budget around $1.5 million; its staff comprising twenty professionals and six administrators), but is very motivated. It sees its role as mainly providing information and guidance (a company that invests today and leaves next year because they were in the wrong place is good to nobody). It continues partnering with the companies after they are installed, not only during their decision process. It focuses on re-investment efforts (expansions by existing companies and deepening of their activities) as much as new investments. It always has excellent communication with the presidency and with COMEX. It does not respond to business chambers (who are more focused on lobbying the issue of the day) but rather to leaders and long-term initiatives. As much as it tries to communicate to potential investors the good they will find in Costa Rica, much of its role is to research and communicate to government what is wrong with the place, to then lobby and follow up on the implementation of solutions. It sits in the National Competitiveness Board. The bulk of the job is done at home—expensive offices abroad are a waste of money (with just one staffer abroad who works out of her home in New York; for the rest, it is felt easier to send an officer from San José to the US or Europe than to keep an office in either place). Expensive advertisement is also, in the opinion of CINDE, 'a vulgar waste of money' (and there is a well-developed industry that takes advantage of newly appointed officers inexperience, or their desire to see themselves in print, to extract resources to useless forms of marketing). Of the 2011 $1.5 million in budget, PROCOMER contributed one-quarter, and the many businesses that benefit from investment (construction developers, lawyers, industrial parks, employment consultants, etc.) voluntarily contribute another 25 per cent.[34]

22.6 CONCLUSION

A range of developing country experiences suggest the following general rules to expedite policy implementation (as distinct from policy formulation):

– First, bureaucratic capacity is key to development—and is generally a long-term project, starting with the education system along with the recruitment and retention of suitable skilled personnel. Civil services are in many cases the engine that moves the first waves of human capital creation. That is at least the case in Singapore and Costa Rica, where in the 1960s and 1970s (in some professions, even today), the reason to go to college was largely to be in the civil service, and civil service was perceived as a badge of honour. Much has changed, but only after tens of thousands had staffed the state.

– Second, specialist agencies should be structured along functional lines. Where possible, they should also be self-funding. For example, the Singapore Economic Development Board became a key agency in shaping development policy and building internal and external constituencies; the Costa Rican Investment Promotion Agency has become a critical body in the delivery of nearly $2 billion in annual inflows. The involvement of line-function ministries in such inter-ministerial boards is important, however. (These examples are further examined below.)

– Third, priorities have to be set as to where to place capacity. In Costa Rica's case, for example, this was first education and institutions, financial stability, investment, and trade later.

– Fourth, most successful systems in the world usually have one format for all ministries, involving a top political appointee (minister), a second political appointee that also plays the role of 'boss of the administration' (assistant ministers, or vice ministers), and then a structure of semi-permanent, non-politically appointed, professional civil servants. The few ministries that deviate from the model have good justification for it. In general, too many chiefs is a bad idea, especially when institutions are talent- and resource-starved already.

– Fifth, the establishment of 'growth coalitions' is important in realizing the private sector's potential to be a driving force for social good.

In diplomatic terms, the tasks of statesmen or women remain in many respects the same as they were centuries ago: to create and maintain an orderly international system. Yet the nature of the actors and the abilities of states to affect this system have both changed substantially with the advent of globalization. As Tom Friedman has argued,[35] globalization is constructed around three balances: the traditional balance between nation states now dominated by the United States; that between nation states and global markets, where the 'bond' is as powerful as the 'bomb' (if not more so); and that between individuals and nation states, where technology has empowered the individual investor, activist, and terrorist alike. In this world, the distinction between national, local, and international has become increasingly blurred,[36] with implications for bureaucracies and the practice of diplomacy. As the Australian 1997 foreign policy White Paper *In the National Interest* noted:[37]

> Globalisation offers huge opportunities for internationally competitive economies, but also brings in its wake challenges for political and economic management. It has profound implications for trade policy. It blurs the division between foreign and domestic policy, increases competitive pressures in markets, and makes globally based trade rules and disciplines even more important.

One of the features of the globalized world is, therefore, that the concept of the 'national interest' becomes much harder to define, as numerous actors pursue their different interests across state frontiers; while it is important to recognize that other actors (such as business or NGOs) have their own 'foreign policies' which they can (and have to) follow with as much dexterity as do states.

In the past, the conduct of diplomacy was seen as political, elitist, and 'far from the madding crowd'.[38] It was exclusive rather than inclusive, and often its executive conduct was centred on unelected elites, notably, royalty—sometimes described as 'outdoor relief for the upper classes'. It was overwhelmingly concerned with patterns of influence and the maintenance and exercise of power. Whereas diplomacy was unavoidably linked with geography and states, globalization and the technology revolution in combination have altered the meaning of sovereign status, and the reach and role of state structures.

Today this environment has changed, and so has diplomacy. It is no longer bound by territorial concerns, or by traditional political questions. It is, as Marshall observes, populist rather than elitist, absorbed by economic issues as well as questions of democracy, the environment, and human rights. It is a subject of wide and intense public debate and interest in which 'the auditorium is as important as the stage'.[39] This may be an overstatement, given that much of the content of diplomatic exchanges does not enter the public domain, but it indicates the extent to which diplomats are now forced to operate under the glare of public scrutiny.

Diplomacy still remains a first line of defence *against* and engagement *with* the challenges facing states in this world. But new ways have had to be found to interact with an environment where the customs, norms, and perceived national needs to which diplomacy was geared have shifted. We live in a fast-changing world, where information technology has altered fundamentally the way in which companies conduct business, and a multiplicity of non-state actors has emerged on the international scene.

NOTES

1. '"Unprecedented" economic reforms in the Maldives—President Nasheed', *Miadhu*, 24 January 2010, <http://www.miadhu.com/2010/01/local-news/%E2%80%9Cunprecedente d%E2%80%9D-economic-reforms-in-the-maldives-%E2%80%93-president-nasheed/>.
2. At <http://www.miadhu.com/2010/01/local-news/%E2%80%9Cunprecedented%E2%80% 9D-economic-reforms-in-the-maldives-%E2%80%93-president-nasheed/>.
3. For more on summits, see Chapter 16 in this volume.
4. See Peter Marshall, *Positive Diplomacy* (London: Macmillan, 1997), 7.
5. The UK's former Foreign Secretary, Douglas Hurd, has said that there are three functions of diplomacy: the accumulation and analysis of information; negotiation; and the promotion of national interests—including trade, finance, politics, culture, and tourism. See Douglas Hurd, *The Search for Peace: A Century of Peace Diplomacy* (London: Warner, 1997), 5.
6. Multilateral Branch, SA Department of Foreign Affairs, *Introductory notes and policy considerations concerning the issue of trade and environment* (Pretoria: DFA, October 1996), 3.
7. For more on this topic, see Chapters 11 and 25 in this volume.
8. Marshall, *Positive Diplomacy*, 1.
9. See *Report of the Secretary-General on the Work of the Organisation* (New York: United Nations, 1999), 5.
10. These arguments explain, for example, the rise of studies on the role and function of public–private–civil society partnerships, such as 'Visioning the UN Project', at <http://www.globalpublicpolicy.net>.
11. George F. Kennan, 'Diplomacy Without Diplomats?', *Foreign Affairs*, September/October, 1997.
12. Lloyd Axworthy, 'Between globalisation and multipolarity: The case for a global, humane Canadian foreign policy', *Revue Études internationales* XXVIII:1 (March 1997), at <http://www.dfait-maeci.gc.ca/english/foreignp/humane.htm>.
13. See, for example, Stuart Harris, 'The Amalgamation of the Department of Foreign Affairs and Trade' and Richard Woolcott, 'The Amalgamation of the Department of Foreign Affairs and Trade', *Managing Australia's Diplomacy: Three Views from the Top* (Melbourne: Australian Institute of International Affairs (Victoria Branch)/School of Social Sciences, Deakin University Occasional Paper Number 2, 1989), 18–31 and 31–40. The comments were made by an Australian diplomat in the course of my conducting research on this issue in Canberra, Australia, December 1997.
14. See Harris, 'The Amalgamation of the Department of Foreign Affairs and Trade', and Woolcott, 'The Amalgamation of the Department of Foreign Affairs and Trade'. These comments were also made in an interview at Australian National University, Canberra, January 1998. For additional information, see John Halligan, 'Reorganising Australian Government Departments, 1987', *Canberra Bulletin of Public Administration*, 40–7; Stuart Harris, 'Change in the Department of Foreign Affairs and Trade: Experience and Observations', paper given to the *National Organisation Change Conference*, Royal Institute

of Public Administration and the Public Service Commission, Canberra, 28–29 November 1988.

15. Canada, Department of Foreign Affairs and International Trade, *Annual Report 1995–1996*, (Ottawa: 1996), 16.

16. André Ouellet, 'Notes for an address before the Standing Committee on Foreign Affairs and International Trade', *DFAIT*, Statement 95/31, May 16, 1995, 2. Cited in Jean-Francois Rioux and Robin Hay, 'Canadian Foreign Policy: From Internationalism to Isolationism?', *International Journal* LIV:1 (Winter 1998–1999), 57–75.

17. Commonwealth of Australia, *In the National Interest: Australia's Foreign and Trade Policy (White Paper)*, 1997, <http://www.australianpolitics.com/foreign/elements/whitepaper.pdf>, iii.

18. <http://www.australianpolitics.com/foreign/elements/whitepaper.pdf>, vii.

19. See Marshall, *Positive Diplomacy*, 143.

20. For more on civil society, see Chapter 9 in this volume; for business, see Chapter 21 in this volume.

21. Canada, Department of Foreign Affairs and International Trade, *Annual Report 1995–1996*, 17.

22. Cited in 'Reinventing Diplomacy in the Information Age', *CSIS Draft Paper*, 9 October 1998, 101.

23. Marshall, *Positive Diplomacy*, 8.

24. Interview, Johannesburg, 1 February 2011.

25. See NEPAD Business Foundation, <http://www.nepadbusinessfoundation.org>.

26. Discussion, African Union Commission official, 1 February 2011.

27. At <http://au.int/en/dp/ea/partnerships>.

28. See 'The African Union: Short of Cash and Teeth', *The Economist*, 27 January 2011, at <http://www.economist.com/node/18014076>.

29. With three in China, two in Japan, one in India, and one in Indonesia.

30. This section draws from two research trips to Singapore in 2008 and 2009, and also from information sourced at <http://www.sedb.com/edb/sg/en_uk/index/about_edb/our_history/the_1960s.html>.

31. This was said at a Brenthurst Foundation-led study-trip to Costa Rica in August 2008.

32. Ibid. See also Greg Mills and Michael Spicer, 'A Latin American Growth Formula?', *The Somaliland Times*, Issue 377, <http://www.somalilandtimes.net/sl/2009/377/37.shtml>.

33. See <http://www.cinde.org/>.

34. I am grateful to my colleague, Alberto Trejos, the former Costa Rican Minister of Trade and Chairman of the CINDE board, for his input into this and other sections of the chapter.

35. Thomas Friedman, *The Lexus and the Olive Tree* (London: Harper Collins, 1999), 11–12.

36. Multilateral Branch, SA Department of Foreign Affairs, *Introductory notes and policy considerations concerning the issue of trade and environment*, 3.

37. See Commonwealth of Australia, *In the National Interest: Australia's Foreign and Trade Policy (White Paper)*, 1997, <http://www.australianpolitics.com/foreign/elements/whitepaper.pdf>.

38. Marshall, *Positive Diplomacy*, 9.

39. Marshall, *Positive Diplomacy*, 9.

CHAPTER 23

....

CULTURAL DIPLOMACY

....

PATRICIA M. GOFF

THERE are certain actors and activities that immediately come to mind when we think of diplomacy. The ambassador, the diplomatic mission, and the consulate are good examples. It is difficult even to imagine the conduct of diplomacy in the absence of these things. The same cannot be said for cultural diplomacy. Scholars have given cultural diplomacy little sustained attention.[1] Governments have experimented with cultural diplomacy, but their commitment to it tends to be uneven.[2] Cultural diplomacy is not typically the first avenue that officials pursue. Yet in this era characterized by globalization, the information society, and network diplomacy, cultural diplomacy is an important tool.

Of course, to assert that cultural diplomacy can be an effective tool is somewhat abstract. In more concrete terms, what are the specific practices that comprise cultural diplomacy? Under what conditions might they be effective? Answers to these questions are more complicated because they are multiple. There is no single formula for what works. Different cultural diplomacy approaches work in different places at different times. What works in a major capital may not work in a smaller city. What works with a close ally may not work where ties are more tenuous. What worked twenty years ago may not work now. Cultural diplomacy is, by its very nature, contingent and ad hoc. This chapter seeks to shed some light on the nature and usefulness of cultural diplomacy. In particular, I argue that cultural diplomacy can be helpful in bridging difference and in opening new avenues of communication. It cannot change outcomes where policies are entrenched, but it can soften, clarify, complicate, and provide expanded opportunities for connection in the hands of an adept diplomat.

Cultural diplomacy springs from two premises: first, that good relations can take root in the fertile ground of understanding and respect. These latter two do not always flow from official policy exchanges; they need to be cultivated. As Cavaliero puts it, 'human exchanges are recognized as being the most effective solvent of prejudice or disinformation'.[3] Cultural diplomacy can facilitate such exchanges. Second, cultural diplomacy rests on the assumption that art, language, and education are among the most significant

entry points into a culture. They are fundamental and distinctive for individual societies. Yet there is also a universal aspect that can transcend and neutralize polarizing
political elements. Culture and education can draw people closer and accentuate commonalities whereas official policy can appear adversarial or accentuate differences.

There is a cultural component to many policies that governments undertake, but not
all policies with a cultural component count as cultural diplomacy. While it is relatively
easy to generate examples of cultural diplomacy, it seems much more difficult to arrive
at an uncontested definition of the concept. As Mark puts it,

> there is no general agreement among scholars about cultural diplomacy's relation-
> ship to the practice of diplomacy, its objectives, practitioners, activities, timeframe,
> or whether the practice is reciprocal or not. Some regard cultural diplomacy as a
> synonym for public diplomacy, others for international cultural relations, or a state's
> foreign cultural mission, and others regard these as distinct practices.[4]

Cultural diplomacy sits on a spectrum of ideational approaches to diplomacy. Alongside
it on this spectrum one can locate soft power, branding, propaganda, and public diplomacy. Cultural diplomacy is on the soft power side of the hard power–soft power equation since it functions by attraction and not coercion in Joseph Nye's famous distinction.[5]
Although cultural diplomacy predates public diplomacy, it has in some significant ways
been eclipsed by it. Public diplomacy shows up as a hot button term in many government policy statements. Academics have also been drawn to public diplomacy. Yet
cultural diplomacy is distinctive in ways that I explore in greater depth in this chapter.

Perhaps the most oft-cited definition comes from Milton Cummings, who argues that
cultural diplomacy is 'the exchange of ideas, information, art and other aspects of culture among nations and their peoples to foster mutual understanding'.[6] In a similar vein,
Laqueur characterizes cultural diplomacy as 'the use of creative expression and
exchanges of ideas, information, and people to increase mutual understanding'.[7] Mark
offers a more overtly political view:

> Despite the semantic confusion, it is nevertheless possible to conceive of cultural
> diplomacy as a diplomatic practice of governments, carried out in support of a gov-
> ernment's foreign policy goals or its diplomacy (or both), usually involving directly
> or indirectly the government's foreign ministry, involving a wide range of manifes-
> tations of the culture of the state which the government represents, targeted at a
> wider population as well as elites.[8]

Mark's definition is emblematic of the challenges associated with gaining consensus on
cultural diplomacy. This excerpt from his discussion suggests that cultural diplomacy is
simultaneously 'this and that'. The foreign ministry may be involved directly or indirectly. Efforts may be directed at elites or the general population. This resistance to easy
categorization may be a strength of cultural diplomacy. To be sure, language instruction,
academic exchange, and tours by artists are the hallmarks of cultural diplomacy.
However, an effective cultural diplomacy need not be constrained by these traditional
parameters.

Cultural diplomacy is first and foremost about bridging differences and facilitating mutual understanding. Cultural diplomacy can tell another story about a country (or province or state or regional grouping). This may be a story that differs from what official policy would imply. It may be a story that counters what opponents are recounting. In so doing, cultural diplomacy can offset negative, stereotypical, or overly simplistic impressions arising from policy choices or from hostile portrayals. It may also fill a void where no stories of any kind exist.

Cultural diplomacy can explain aspects of a culture that might otherwise be difficult to grasp for foreign populations. Student exchanges provide one-on-one opportunities for transmission of this type of deeper knowledge about why a particular society favours certain practices or espouses certain beliefs. Cultural diplomacy can also reach constituencies that might not otherwise be engaged by traditional diplomatic activity. There may be no official relations between two governments, but artists can communicate with each other and forge meaningful ties. The United States and Cuba have been involved in artist exchanges—many high profile—including the New York Philharmonic, the New York City Ballet, and the Jazz at Lincoln Center musicians, despite chilly official diplomatic relations between the two governments. These exchanges arguably create fertile ground for traditional diplomacy; maintain links when official relations are imperilled; and remind citizens of the two countries that they have things in common despite official policy to the contrary.

Cultural diplomacy can provide context for policy decisions or official actions. It can humanize. Official lines of communication can transmit a one-dimensional message. Cultural diplomacy opens up other lines of communication that can supplement and complicate the official message or the prevailing image. One common example of this is travel by American jazz musicians to the Soviet Union during the cold war. Soviet officials and citizens had a reductionist understanding of the United States. However, encountering African-American musicians who spoke openly and critically of the racial history of the United States, while simultaneously celebrating a quintessentially American musical form and expressing their pride as Americans, complicated the Soviet view of the United States. Another recent example is a carefully-timed loan by the Vatican to the Victoria and Albert museum in London. On the occasion of a papal visit to Great Britain, amidst controversies over church policies, the Vatican loaned 16th-century tapestries depicting scenes from the Acts of the Apostles. These priceless works of art, rarely seen outside of the Vatican, tell another story about the Catholic Church, thus complicating its image, and provoking engagement through a less politically charged medium of exchange.

What is the relationship between cultural diplomacy and public diplomacy? To be sure, there are many similarities and overlaps. Each shares a fundamental ideational essence. Each targets audiences beyond official diplomatic circles. A report commissioned by the US Department of State calls cultural diplomacy 'the linchpin of public diplomacy; for it is in cultural activities that a nation's idea of itself is best represented'. The report goes on, 'the values embedded in our artistic and intellectual traditions form a bulwark against the forces of darkness…Cultural diplomacy reveals the soul of a nation.' Cultural diplomacy helps create a 'foundation of trust' with other peoples, which policy makers can build on to reach political, economic, and military agreements...demonstrates our values...creates relationships with peoples, which endure beyond changes in government; can reach influential members of foreign societies who cannot be reached through traditional embassy functions; provides a positive agenda for cooperation in spite of policy differences; creates a neutral platform for people-to-people contact; serves as a flexible, universally acceptable vehicle for rapprochement with countries where diplomatic relations have been strained or are absent;...counterbalances misunderstanding, hatred, and terrorism.[9]

Cultural diplomacy is also distinguished by the fact that it is not unidirectional. Public diplomacy and branding tend to involve the outward projection of one's message. As Berger puts it,

> the difference in approach between public and cultural diplomacy: while public diplomacy is unilateral with an emphasis on explaining one's policies to the others, cultural diplomacy takes a bi- or multilateral approach with an emphasis on mutual recognition. Cultural diplomacy is therefore explicitly not meant to be the promotion of a national culture. Cultural diplomacy focuses on common ground, and the condition thereto is that one needs to know what makes the other tick.[10]

From this perspective, listening to others' messages with an eye to understanding their views is integral to cultural diplomacy. 'This cultural policy demands that one enters a relationship on the basis of equality and reciprocity. It also demands a genuine interest in the other: where does it stand, what does it think, and why does it think that way?'[11]

Therefore, sending French academics on exchange to Arab countries is cultural diplomacy. But so is the *Institut du monde arabe* in Paris, which seeks to familiarize the French with Arab history and culture on French soil. Similarly, Katzenstein argues that postwar Japanese cultural diplomacy, which relied mostly on high culture and language teaching abroad, focused on ' "explaining" to others the unique features of the Japanese polity that foreigners simply cannot grasp'.[12] However, it soon evolved to include the importation of ideas. 'Haltingly in the 1980s and more rapidly in the 1990s gaining a better understanding of and respect for foreign cultures became part of the government's official cultural diplomacy.'[13] Such examples evoke the definitions offered at the beginning of this chapter that emphasise mutual understanding. While many experienced diplomats may know the importance of listening and learning, these components of diplomatic practice receive less attention in descriptions of public diplomacy. Yet they are central to effective cultural diplomacy.

23.1 THE CONTEXT OF CULTURAL DIPLOMACY

It is a cliché to note that we have entered the era of the information society. Global media outlets among other components of globalization ensure that we have more information about each other than ever before. What we think about each other and the meanings that we attach to actors, practices, etc., is a crucial determinant of support for or opposition to policies and policy-makers. The Internet democratizes the sharing of information in new ways. Intellectual property occupies an important role in the economies and societies of countries at all levels of development. All of these arguably emerge from the fact that information flows so much more freely across borders.

These phenomena have an impact on the world of diplomacy. Partly this manifests itself in what Heine describes in Chapter 2 of this volume: 'globalism, a prominent feature of our time, involves networks of interdependence at intercontinental distances. It implies multiple flows of products, services, or capital, and signifies the shrinkage of distance on a large scale. It also triggers the emergence of global issues and a global agenda to a degree that we had not seen before.' It also affects the exercise of power. As Tardif puts it,

> power, rivalries and conflicts are no longer played out within the framework of a physical territory as they were when the main concern was the control of natural resources. Power is now tied to the ability to manipulate symbols in the mediatised global space.... Culture (values, symbols, world representation, language, art...) and its modes of expression structure relationships between humans and societies at every level of human activity, including the global level.[14]

Ironically, we have more information about each other, but we may not know more about each other. Traditional notions of cultural diplomacy presume an ability to project a distinct and distinctive national culture. But this is increasingly difficult to do, if indeed it ever was possible. There is no singular cultural message emanating from countries. Today, the nearly constant flow of ideas and images through media and popular culture complicates matters. These flows, which are largely outside the hands of diplomats, provide a resource and a foil that cannot be ignored. Multiple depictions—some accurate and some not, some well intentioned and some not—have an authoritative veneer. Cultural diplomacy can provide a welcome corrective, 'sharpening the picture where you think the picture may be blurred, fuzzy, or wrong'.[15]

In this era of globalization, the cultural flashpoints of global politics have also shifted. Today, the global landscape is characterized by rising powers like India and China, as well as perceived civilizational encounters between and across multiple Wests[16] and the so-called Muslim world, among others. The challenges and the possibilities of cultural diplomacy in this context are great. In some ways, the advent of globalization and the redistribution of power signify great change. But there is also continuity. If September 11 is a defining referent of the current diplomatic era, the cold war provided the backdrop for the previous one. Both conflicts played—or are playing—out on military *and* ideational battlegrounds, making cultural diplomacy relevant to both. If winning 'hearts and minds' was the goal of cold war cultural diplomacy, reaching Thomas Friedman's 'Arab Street' is one aspect of contemporary cultural diplomacy. As Laqueur notes, traditional diplomacy is of little use in the face of the new, post-cold war, 'anti-Western onslaughts' while 'cultural diplomacy, in the widest sense, has increased importance'.[17]

The contemporary era of globalization also gives unrivalled prominence to popular culture. Traditional cultural diplomacy rested on high culture as a foundational pillar. Thus, simultaneously exploiting the possibilities of popular culture while ensuring that one's preferred message is heard above the din is a new challenge for cultural diplomats. Schneider goes so far as to argue that 'popular culture is the greatest untapped resource in the cultural diplomacy arsenal'.[18] She is speaking about the United States in her statement since, as she notes, 'products of popular culture—films, TV, music—are America's largest export'.[19] It is true that Americans can most urgently benefit from reflection on how to incorporate popular culture into an effective cultural diplomacy strategy. But they are not alone. Japan, India, Brazil, and France are just some of the countries that export cultural products in great number and, thus, have the potential to use popular culture to their advantage. To be sure, it is not immediately evident how popular culture might be harnessed. As Schneider observes, there are obstacles to diplomats making effective use of popular culture. Why? As she puts it, 'distributed according to the rules of the marketplace, popular culture does not make the best ambassador'.[20]

The fact that popular culture is a thriving private sector activity complicates its contribution to cultural diplomacy. Popular culture can be a double-edged sword. On the one hand, it can transmit an image of a place where one might otherwise not be forthcoming or where a prevailing image can be opaque or negative. Japan is a good example of this. The export of Japanese popular culture, including Manga graphic stories, Animé video, and the acclaimed works of Japanese filmmakers has created access points to a culture that might otherwise be inaccessible to many. Popular culture can also reach audiences that might otherwise not be reached. While a symphony or a classical ballet company has wide appeal, it may not draw youth in the same numbers that a hip hop artist might. Malone reports in Chapter 6 of this volume that, 'Bollywood's more exotic charms have proved exportable to many countries, and facilitated an early diplomatic thaw with Moscow in 1953. More recently, the Bollywood comedy, "Three Idiots" is reported to have become a cult classic among Chinese students.'

While there seems to be enormous potential for products of popular culture to enter the cultural diplomacy conversation, the fact remains that popular culture is, at bottom, a commercial enterprise. This can be promising in a moment when diplomatic budgets generally, and cultural diplomacy budgets specifically, are decreasing. Popular culture offers resources that will be produced and likely made available to international audiences regardless of whether foreign ministries decide that they are valuable. On the other hand, popular culture can circulate images that are undesirable or that may need to be counteracted. For example, American Hollywood blockbusters that reach all corners of the globe often carry with them violent images or gender stereotypes that do not accurately portray the average American's experience.

The implication of recent studies, including this one, is that the use of popular culture for the purposes of cultural diplomacy is nascent at best. However, it is worth pointing out that broadcasting, which might justifiably be included in the popular culture category, has been a mainstay of soft power (though perhaps not cultural diplomacy) for some time. Governments have used broadcasting to their advantage, deploying state-run entities like Voice of America or the US-run Arab language television station, Al Hurra. Arms-length public broadcasting systems, like the BBC or France Info, have also served important soft-power roles. More recently, the broadcasting landscape has been complicated by the appearance of powerful commercially-minded actors with global reach. CNN, Al Jazeera, and the China Xinhua News Network Corp are just three variants on this model. Thakur notes that India may be an exception. 'In its desperation to control information, news and analyses, the Indian government has effectively aborted the rise of independent news services with the authority and credibility to command a global following.... The net result is that India does indeed lack a key agent of international influence and a crucial ingredient of soft power in the modern networked world.'[21]

On the other hand, the so-called twenty-four-hour news cycle makes cultural diplomacy difficult and necessary. Media coverage supplies many of the visual images that people have of a place and they are widely circulated in some instances. For example, the State Department study of cultural diplomacy confirms the dominance of media images in shaping perceptions.

> The idea of an American ideal is drowned out by Arab media coverage of the Israeli-Palestinian impasse and the war in Iraq; the fallout from the Abu Ghraib prison scandal—the photographs, broadcast repeatedly and circulated continuously on the Web, of hooded prisoners attached to electrodes, of leering American soldiers and so on—would long haunt the image of the United States.[22]

The 'CNN effect', then, adds another dimension at the intersection of cultural diplomacy and popular culture.

Much of this analysis implies that cultural diplomacy in an era of globalization still implicates national cultures primarily. But this is incomplete. Cultural diplomacy has since the Second World War included a multilateral dimension whereby states work through intergovernmental organizations like UNESCO. More recently, cultural diplomacy is refracted through regional and civilizational lenses. Cultural diplomacy has been deployed with great effect as a tool to cultivate mutual understanding and a sense of belonging among the members of the European Union. In addition, the United Nations Alliance of Civilizations seeks to facilitate dialogue across religions and cultures, all the while transcending national borders.

23.2 The Role of Governments in Cultural Diplomacy

Diplomacy has traditionally been the preserve of the state. By definition, diplomats are representatives of governments and their work is intended to advance the interests of a particular state.[23] A deeper look problematizes the role of the state in the conduct of diplomacy. Must state representatives be directly involved for diplomacy to be taking place? In the introduction to this volume, Cooper, Heine, and Thakur acknowledge this ambiguity by defining diplomacy as 'the conduct of business, using peaceful means, and among international actors, *at least one of whom is usually governmental*' (emphasis added). Harold Nicolson goes even further, defining diplomacy as 'an ordered conduct of relations between one group of human beings and another group alien to themselves'.[24] Among the major changes that have occurred in the world of diplomacy and diplomats, Thakur cites 'the rapidly expanding *numbers and types of actors*, from governments to national private sector firms, multinational corporations, NGOs and regional and international organisations' (emphasis in original).[25] The debate over the role of the state and of official state representatives in diplomacy is nowhere more trenchant than in cultural diplomacy.

Some analysts are unwilling to conceive of cultural diplomacy in the absence of state involvement. For example, Haigh defines cultural diplomacy as 'the activities of governments in the sphere—traditionally left to private enterprise—of international cultural relations'.[26] Similarly, Arndt posits that cultural diplomacy 'can only be said to take place when formal diplomats, serving national governments, try to shape and channel this natural flow to advance national interests'.[27] Mark seems to corroborate this view, arguing that

> cultural diplomacy is a diplomatic practice of governments—mostly single governments, but also groups of governments such as the European Union and sub-national governments, such as the government of the Canadian province of Québec... Cultural diplomacy is carried out in support of a government's foreign policy goals or its diplomacy, or both. Because of its connection to foreign policy or diplomacy, cultural diplomacy usually involves directly or indirectly the government's foreign ministry, or, in the case of governments representing parts of a federation, that ministry responsible for international engagement... Naturally, cultural diplomacy's connection to a government's foreign policy goals, to its diplomacy, and to its foreign ministry varies between states, but the absence of any such link precludes an activity from being deemed cultural diplomacy.[28]

If the government must play a role, then what is the nature of that role? Must a government representative carry out cultural diplomacy programmes herself? Or is it sufficient for a government to provide funding or to serve as a catalyst that gets a particular programme in motion? Examples of all levels of government involvement exist. Britain, France, Germany, Spain, and China all operate what might be considered traditional mainstays of cultural diplomacy: the British Council, the Alliance française, the Goethe Institute, the Cervantes Institute, and the Confucian Institutes, respectively. These longstanding and effective initiatives function with varying degrees of input from their governments. The British Council and the Goethe Institutes are para-public entities operating at arm's length from the governments of Britain and Germany. The Alliances française are independent of the French government. The Confucian Institutes involve relatively greater state involvement. Each of these instances of varying degrees of state involvement would qualify as cultural diplomacy. Debate ensues, however, in cases where some feel government is—or should be—absent.

One aspect of this debate maps onto a distinction between official and unofficial activity. When academics travel abroad as part of the Fulbright Program, they are considered to be cultural diplomats. When these same academics go abroad independent of this government programme, have they relinquished their potential as cultural diplomats? When have we crossed the line from cultural diplomacy into quotidian cross-border relations? Is it useful to distinguish between official and unofficial cultural diplomacy or formal and informal cultural diplomacy? This line of questioning is not irrelevant to the discussion of popular culture in the previous section. Simply because messages and messengers that could promote mutual understanding are not doing so as part of an official programme in cultural diplomacy, does it mean that their contribution should be ignored?

An interesting example concerns the role of private philanthropists. Just a few years ago, Shelley and Donald Rubin founded the Rubin Museum of Art in New York City.[29] Long-time collectors of Himalayan art, they exhibit their own collection. But the museum also runs extensive educational programming on Himalayan art, culture, and regional religions, among other things. The governments of Bhutan or Nepal, for example, had no formal role in the founding of the museum. Arguably, those governments would not be able to achieve what the Rubins have achieved, insulated from the politics of promoting national culture. The museum's very existence in a major world arts centre means that people who would not otherwise come into contact with Himalayan culture can develop a deeper understanding of it. How should Shelley and Donald Rubin be situated in a discussion of cultural diplomacy? As is the case for Bill Gates in discussions of development aid, globalized network diplomacy may necessitate new categories.

Perhaps most complicated in this debate is the concern that government involvement of any kind can interfere with the artistic, educational, or cultural mission. As Channick puts it,

> there is a fundamental difference between the official approach to cultural diplomacy—where the emphasis is on the diplomacy, and culture is merely a tool or, worse, a weapon—and the approach taken by artists. Artists engage in cross-cultural exchange not to proselytize about their own values but rather to understand different cultural traditions, to find new sources of imaginative inspiration, to discover other methods and ways of working and to exchange ideas with people whose worldviews differ from their own. They want to be influenced rather than to influence.[30]

Some instruments need distance from a government to be effective. There is a risk that the credibility of an agent and/or a patron of cultural diplomacy can be jeopardized if there is a clear affiliation with a government.[31] Kennedy provides an interesting example of this. The photographic exhibition *After September 11: Images from Ground Zero* was launched in February 2002 by then US Secretary of State Colin Powell. Kennedy explains that the exhibition featured images by the only photographer given full access to Ground Zero from 13 September 2001 onward to build an archive of photos. Not only did the State Department support the exhibition, but American embassies and consulates in over sixty countries promoted it.

US Under Secretary of State for Public Diplomacy and Public Affairs, Charlotte Beers, explains the value of an exhibition like *After September 11*.

> As time has passed since last September, we found that we needed to give people a visceral reminder of the devastation and death in New York. We needed to depict—not in words, but in pictures—the loss, the pain, but also the strength and resolve of New York, of Americans, of the world community to recover and rebuild on the site of the World Trade Center... A message that—without words—documents that the World Trade Center was not a collection of buildings or a set of businesses—but a community, a way of life, a symbol, a place of the living and, now also, the dead. How do you do that? How do you tell such a sad, grim, shocking, and ultimately uplifting story? You do that in pictures.[32]

Kennedy notes that the cities where the exhibition would be shown were chosen with care. Most were in the Middle East and North Africa; fewer in Europe and South America. The exhibition was intended to show the emotional side of the American experience of September 11, but also to transcend this to touch a more universal empathy about human suffering. As Kennedy puts it, 'this later exhibit has been more overtly designed as propaganda, yet it also carries the cachet of "culture" (most obviously, via the signature of a renowned photographer) and is intended to transmit a universal message that transcends the politics of difference.'[33] Some responses to the exhibit were quite negative, precisely because it was received as a calculated attempt on the part of the US government to elicit sympathy. A similar response would be unlikely had the exhibit had no ties to official circles.

Huygens captures a widely-held view about the appropriate relationship between government and agents of cultural diplomacy.

> If arts—or a deliberate selection or combination of artworks—are made instrumental to goals other than artistic expression, they can no longer fulfill their distinctive role and merely reflect the official policy of a country or other cultural entity... It is especially its distance to power and issues of the day that makes art valuable in our understanding of societies and in international relations. It is the independence of arts that cultural diplomacy should cherish and support.[34]

Perhaps most radically, Berger maintains that cultural diplomacy encompasses not only those activities that governments execute or support—though it may include these—but activities that

> focus on understanding the other by looking at the variety of ways that the other expresses itself.... Evading the trap of cultural relativism and remaining in dialogue with the other party while at the same time not abandoning one's principles, *that* is why cultural diplomacy is called 'diplomacy.' Not because it is the work that diplomats should do, but because it is an interaction that requires diplomatic skills on a human level.[35]

Much of the preceding discussion captures the difficulty of navigating the intersection of art and power at the site of reception. If a participant in a cultural activity perceives close government involvement, she may experience it differently than art with none of these political or instrumental ties. Nonetheless, challenges can also emerge at earlier stages in the process, precisely because artists and government officials have different agendas and goals.

Even artists who consciously and voluntarily take part in official cultural diplomacy programmes may bump up against the ideological commitments of a ruling party or prevailing views on the role of art in society. Artists who challenge prevailing values or academics who stake out radical positions may not be embraced by a sitting government. Artists' peer review selection processes may conflict with what local embassy or consulate staff might have chosen to fulfil their mandate.[36] Ultimately, cultural diplomacy's position at the intersection of government and the cultural world is both a source of strength and challenge.

23.3 Club and Network Diplomacy

As this volume demonstrates, the evolution from club to network diplomacy is one of the central shifts in modern diplomacy. As Thakur explains it, 'the four core tasks of the diplomat were to represent his country's interests, protect his country's citizens visiting or residing in his accredited country, inform his own and host government and people about each other, and negotiate with the host country. This was conducted in a world of "club diplomacy".'[37] Network diplomacy, on the other hand, 'has more players than club diplomacy, is flat rather than hierarchical, engages in multiple forms of communication beyond merely the written, is more transparent than confidential, and its "consummation" takes the form of increased bilateral flows instead of formal signing ceremonies.'[38]

The fact that cultural diplomacy is 'people-to-people diplomacy' suggests that it has a natural resonance with network diplomacy. The synergies seem even more clear in light of Thakur's assertion that, 'in attempting to navigate the shoals while exploiting the opportunities of a globalised and networked world, the diplomat must cultivate all manner of constituencies in home, host, and sometimes even third countries. That is the key to network diplomacy: cultivating all relevant constituencies.'[39]

To be sure, cultural diplomacy is an effective way for ambassadors to connect with each other and to build relationships. As David Malone argues in Chapter 6 of this volume, 'targeted hospitality remains extremely useful: securing the ear and sharing the analysis of leading personalities over lunch or dinner rather than during an often hurried and inconvenient office meeting, with note-takers hovering, often yields dividends'. Nonetheless, Malone also notes that 'important people [are] busier than ever', with numerous demands on their time. Cultural events of any kind have the potential to cut through the list of invitations and have an unmatched appeal. Nonetheless, cultural diplomacy also provides a means to reach constituencies beyond elite, ambassadorial types.

As Heine puts it in Chapter 2 of this volume,

in the 'club model', diplomats meet only with government officials, among themselves and with the odd businessman or woman, and give an interview or speech here or there. By and large, however, they restrict themselves to fellow members of the club, with whom they also feel most comfortable, and focus their minds on 'negotiating agreements between sovereign states'. By definition, those practising this approach find it difficult to tap into the many trans-border flows of our time, since they regard them as beyond their purview.

He continues, arguing that network diplomacy 'means engaging a vastly larger number of players in the host country—including many who would have never thought of setting foot in the rarefied atmosphere of the salons and private clubs the diplomats of yesteryear used to frequent'. Cultural diplomacy can very effectively connect diplomats under the 'club' model. But it also easily transitions to the network diplomacy age.

23.4 THE 'HOW TO' GUIDE

To suggest that there is one right way to engage in cultural diplomacy would be unwise. Indeed, depending on the cultural resources available to a given actor, as well as the goals and objectives of that actor in a particular place at a particular time, there may be as many ways of practising cultural diplomacy as there are diplomats and governments. One useful distinction is between the official cultural diplomacy framework policies that are put in place by a central government on the one hand, and the cultural diplomacy efforts that are undertaken by a given staff in a consulate or embassy, on the other. The former is more enduring, more consistent over time and space, evolving with a change of government. It can be quite costly. The latter is more contingent, ad hoc, the product of individual creativity. It is reactive and dynamic and can be effective on a shoe string. With this in mind, some strategies present themselves.

Connection. The effective diplomat is always looking for ways to connect and culture can provide an effective mode for doing so, especially if the diplomat has listened and internalized the areas of interest and points of resonance that are meaningful to her interlocutors. As one former Canadian High Commissioner to India recounts, he realized early on that exposure to what Canadians perceive to be their great artists was not of paramount interest to many of his Indian contacts. However, drawing on the Indo-Canadian artistic community, as well as the links between Bollywood and the Toronto International Film Festival, afforded valuable opportunities to connect across cultural, linguistic, religious, and other differences.[40] Such an approach is arguably more likely in this era of globalization, characterized in part by flows of people across borders. Diaspora communities can offer unique opportunities for connection.

A former Chilean ambassador to South Africa tells a similar story. Finding himself faced with South African interlocutors with little knowledge of Chile, he built an event around the Chilean writer, Ariel Dorfman. Many South Africans were familiar with Dorfman, but unaware of his Chilean roots. A bridge was created, accentuating what

Chileans and South Africans shared in common.[41] Similarly, Canada's former ambassador to Bhutan describes a film festival held in the capital. Embassy staff knew that a film set in Bhutan had been screened at the Banff Mountain Film Festival. The staff arranged an event around this film, in the process bridging difference, creating an opportunity for dialogue and deeper mutual understanding.

These are stories of success. It is reasonable to assume that the outcome will not always be as auspicious. There may not be a resonant cultural bridge or a good faith effort may fail. Nonetheless, the savvy diplomat will get to know both his or her home and host cultural communities well and be on the lookout for opportunities to connect. These diplomats were able to create successes because they were intimately aware of what was going on in their home and host countries. As Canada's former ambassador to Bhutan puts it, 'know what your assets are and capitalize on them. Don't spend all your time with other ambassadors. Embrace a society and figure out what they need.'[42]

Consistency. It would appear that many perceive cultural diplomacy to be most useful when more traditional or official channels are unsuccessful or unavailable. It is clear that cultural diplomacy can fill a void. Even when relations are at their worst, a cultural exchange can take place. In 2008, at a low point in US—North Korea relations because of the North Korean nuclear programme, the New York Philharmonic accepted an invitation to travel to Pyongyang. They closed their programme with a beloved Korean folk song, leaving the audience and the musicians deeply moved.[43] This is the strength of cultural diplomacy, the possibility of human connection even where official relations are strained. However, the fact that cultural diplomacy is perceived by some as being most useful as a last resort means that it does not always get the consistent support that it deserves. It is more commonly the case that, in moments of crisis, the cultural diplomacy machine is activated. This was apparent following September 11 when the American government quickly put in motion an attempt to connect with the Muslim world. By all accounts, these efforts were, at best, only partially successful, in part because they were seen to be an emergency measure and not a genuine effort to cultivate mutual understanding. Interestingly, a subsequent State Department fact-finding mission discovered that, to the degree that constituencies in the Middle East sought to engage with the United States in a cultural diplomacy exchange, they welcomed training and equipment—exchanges of technicians, directors, animators, web designers, special effects, and music preservation consultants—that would allow their own cultural communities to thrive.[44]

This and other experiences of this kind suggest that it is important to have a cultural diplomacy framework in place at all times. A more consistent commitment must be made so that the fruits of cultural diplomacy are in place when crisis hits. It is in those moments when people are exposed to negative images, policies, and impressions that one hopes that they have also encountered at some point more positive, sympathetic ones. It is upon the release of the images from Abu Ghraib prison that one hopes that people in the Arab world have met that sympathetic Fulbright scholar or benefitted from the heritage preservation fund or had the opportunity to study in the United States. These latter experiences can provide a bulwark against an otherwise wholesale indictment of the American government, its policies, and its way of life. Cultural diplomacy is an insurance policy of sorts. There is no point in activating one's policy after a car accident. Instead, one is grateful to have paid one's premiums in full as one watches the car be towed away.

Innovation. While language, education, and the arts arguably still lie at the heart of cultural diplomacy, they cannot be mobilized in exactly the same way that they were in previous historical periods. Language provides a good example. In the past, language instruction provided an entry point into cultural understanding. Learning a language allowed people to understand cultural products hitherto inaccessible to them. Also, contact with native speakers afforded opportunities to learn about the values, beliefs, and practices of the language teacher and learner. These activities can still be very powerful. Nonetheless, globalization has led to the elevation of some languages for commercial purposes and the downgrading of others. How, then, might language be used to make a culture accessible if foreigners are not interested in acquiring your language? Some studies suggest that translation may be one answer. 'Translation is an inexpensive form of exchange, the fruits of which—the dissemination of information and ideas, the inculcation of nuanced views of foreign cultures, increased empathy and understanding, the recognition of our common humanity—will be on display for a very long time.'[45] Yet translation is not an automatic reflex in many countries. The 2002 UN Arab Human Development Report reports that

> translation is one of the most important channels for the dissemination of information and communication with the rest of the world. The translation movement in the Arab world, however, remains static and chaotic. On average, only 4.4 translated books per million were published in the first five years of the 1980s (less than one book per million people per year), while the corresponding rate in Hungary was 519 books per one million people and in Spain 920 books.[46]

The point of this discussion is not to establish that translation is a panacea for cultural diplomacy. Rather, it is to suggest that the context of cultural diplomacy is evolving and one cannot cling to old instruments that may have lost their edge. The same goals can be achieved through different means.

23.5 THE LIMITS OF CULTURAL DIPLOMACY

As I have argued in this chapter, cultural diplomacy can achieve many things. But it is neither unambiguously effective nor necessarily a force for good. It has its limits. First, cultural diplomacy requires a long-term commitment. The dividends of cultural diplomacy may not be paid for a decade or two.[47] As Laqueur notes with regard to public diplomacy—and the same applies to cultural diplomacy—'the bureaucratic queries about tangible achievement that can be measured at the end of the budgetary year simply do not apply'.[48] Cultural diplomacy plants a seed. As such, it may take root over time. It is possible that cultural diplomacy efforts will yield no fruit whatsoever.

Assessing whether cultural diplomacy has had any sort of effect is similarly challenging. 'No metric or language exists by which to gauge the success of a cultural initiative. As Milton Cummings notes, "a certain degree of faith is involved in cultural diplomacy".'[49] It is certainly possible to track the number of people who attend a music performance or participate in a student exchange programme. But it is extremely difficult to determine what effect, if any, the experience has had on the participant. You cannot control the reception of a piece of art or the quality of human interaction. While you may hope that the experience of a particular event will evoke a certain reaction, you can never be sure.

Cultural diplomacy cannot work magic. It cannot change policy outcomes or compensate for their harmful or negative consequences. It can, however, help to (re)build relationships or to foster understanding.[50] In some instances, cultural diplomacy cannot even get out of the starting gate. Cultural diplomacy functions best when people can move easily across borders. But security concerns can make academic exchanges and tourism, both contributors to cultural diplomacy, more challenging in certain moments.

Nonetheless, cultural diplomacy may be essential to the work of the diplomat. Heine notes in Chapter 2 of this volume that some perceive the art of negotiating agreements to be the stock in trade of diplomats. But he counters that 'the real task is getting to the negotiations. One effective way to do so is by *bridging the gap between home and host country*—that is, by bringing the societies closer' (emphasis in original). Cultural diplomacy's purpose is exactly this.

NOTES

1. Simon Mark, *A Comparative Study of the Cultural Diplomacy of Canada, New Zealand and India*. Thesis submitted for the degree of Doctor of Philosophy in Political Studies, The University of Auckland, 2008, 5.
2. US Department of State, *Cultural Diplomacy: The Linchpin of Public Diplomacy* (Report of the Advisory Committee on Cultural Diplomacy, September 2005).
3. R.E. Cavaliero, 'Cultural Diplomacy: The Diplomacy of Influence', *The Round Table* 298 (1986), 139–44 at 143.
4. Mark, *A Comparative Study of the Cultural Diplomacy of Canada, New Zealand and India*, 39.
5. Joseph Nye, 'The Decline of America's Soft Power', *Foreign Affairs* 83:3 (May–June 2004), 16–20.
6. Milton Cummings, 'Cultural Diplomacy and the United States Government: A Survey', *Center for Arts and Culture* (2003), 1.
7. Walter Laqueur, 'Save Public Diplomacy: Broadcasting America's Message Matters', *Foreign Affairs* 73:5 (September–October 1994), 19–24 at 20.
8. Mark, *A Comparative Study of the Cultural Diplomacy of Canada, New Zealand and India*, 3.
9. US Department of State, *Cultural Diplomacy: The Linchpin of Public Diplomacy*, 1.
10. Maurits Berger, 'Introduction', *Bridge the Gap, or Mind the Gap? Culture in Western-Arab Relations* (January 2008), Netherlands Institute of International Relations 'Clingendael', 3–7 at 3. Available at <http://www.clingendael.nl/publications/2008/20080100_cdsp_paper_berger.pdf>.

11. Berger, 'Introduction', 6.
12. Peter Katzenstein, 'Open Regionalism: Cultural Diplomacy and Popular Culture in Europe and Asia', paper prepared for the Annual Meeting of the American Political Science Association, August 2002. Available at <http://ics-www.leeds.ac.uk/papers/pmt/exhib-its/1133/Katzenstei.pdf>.
13. Katzenstein, 'Open Regionalism: Cultural Diplomacy and Popular Culture in Europe and Asia', 17.
14. Jean Tardif, 'Globalization and Culture', *Permanent Forum on Cultural Pluralism* (July 2004), <http://www.planetagora.org/english/theme1_note.html>, 1.
15. Former Canadian Ambassador to Bhutan, personal interview, 23 May 2011.
16. Peter Katzenstein (ed.), *Civilizations in World Politics: Plural and Pluralist Perspectives* (New York: Routledge, 2010).
17. Laqueur, 'Save Public Diplomacy: Broadcasting America's Message Matters', 20.
18. Cynthia Schneider, 'Diplomacy that Works: "Best Practices" in Cultural Diplomacy', Cultural Diplomacy Research Series, Center for Arts and Culture (2003), 14.
19. Schneider, 'Diplomacy that Works', 14.
20. Schneider, 'Diplomacy that Works', 14.
21. Ramesh Thakur, 'Asia-Pacific Challenges for Diplomacy', revised paper of keynote lecture 'Diplomacy in the Asia-Pacific: Changes and Challenges', delivered at Diplomatic Update 2006, Asia-Pacific College of Diplomacy, Australian National University, Canberra, Australia, 12–14 November, 7.
22. US Department of State, *Cultural Diplomacy: The Linchpin of Public Diplomacy*, 11.
23. See Chapter 3, this volume.
24. Harold Nicolson, *Diplomacy* (London: Oxford University Press, 1939), 17.
25. Thakur, 'Asia-Pacific Challenges for Diplomacy', 1.
26. A. Haigh, *Cultural Diplomacy in Europe* (Strasbourg: Council for Cultural Cooperation, 1974), 28.
27. Cited in Ramin Asgard, 'U.S.-Iran Cultural Diplomacy: A Historical Perspective', *Al Nakhlah* (Fletcher School, Tufts University, Spring 2010). Available at <http://mashregh-news.ir/Images/News/AtachFile/8-3-1390/FILE634422673069531250.pdf>.
28. Mark, *A Comparative Study of the Cultural Diplomacy of Canada, New Zealand and India*, 43.
29. I am grateful to Lucie Edwards for this example.
30. J. Channick, 'The Artist as Cultural Diplomat', *American Theater Magazine* (May–June 2005), 1.
31. See Harvey Fiegenbaum, 'Globalization and Cultural Diplomacy', Art, Culture and the National Agenda Project, Center for Arts and Culture (2001), 31 and US Department of State, *Cultural Diplomacy: The Linchpin of Public Diplomacy*.
32. Liam Kennedy, 'Remembering September 11: Photography as Cultural Diplomacy', *International Affairs* 79:2 (2003), 315–26 at 318.
33. Kennedy, 'Remembering September 11: Photography as Cultural Diplomacy', 323.
34. C. Huygens, 'The Art of Diplomacy, the Diplomacy of Art', *Bridge the Gap, or Mind the Gap? Culture in Western-Arab Relations* (January 2008), Netherlands Institute of International Relations 'Clingendael', 17–29 at 18. Available at <http://www.clingendael.nl/publications/2008/20080100_cdsp_paper_berger.pdf>. See also Cavaliero, 'Cultural Diplomacy: The Diplomacy of Influence'.
35. Berger, 'Introduction', 4.
36. I am grateful to Lucie Edwards for pointing this out.

37. Thakur, 'Asia-Pacific Challenges for Diplomacy', 1.
38. Thakur, 'Asia-Pacific Challenges for Diplomacy', 1.
39. Thakur, 'Asia-Pacific Challenges for Diplomacy', 2.
40. Former Canadian High Commissioner to India, personal interview, 14 March 2011.
41. Former Chilean ambassador to South Africa, intervention, 14 March 2011.
42. Former Canadian ambassador to Bhutan, personal interview, 23 May 2011.
43. Daniel J. Wakin, 'North Koreans Welcome Symphonic Diplomacy', *New York Times* (27 February 2008). Available at <http://www.nytimes.com/2008/02/27/world/asia/27symphony.html>.
44. US Department of State, *Cultural Diplomacy: The Linchpin of Public Diplomacy*.
45. US Department of State, *Cultural Diplomacy: The Linchpin of Public Diplomacy*.
46. Cited in US Department of State, *Cultural Diplomacy: The Linchpin of Public Diplomacy*, 12.
47. Richard Arndt, 'Cultural Diplomacy and the Public Agenda', paper prepared for the Center for Arts and Culture, p. 9, cited in Harvey B. Feigenbaum, 'Globalization and Cultural Diplomacy', Center for Arts and Culture, Issue Paper, November 2001. Available at <http://ics-www.leeds.ac.uk/papers/pmt/exhibits/159/culdip.pdf>, p. 27.
48. Laqueur, 'Save Public Diplomacy: Broadcasting America's Message Matters', 22.
49. US Department of State, *Cultural Diplomacy: The Linchpin of Public Diplomacy*, 14.
50. Schneider, 'Diplomacy that Works', 15.

CHAPTER 24

....

PUBLIC DIPLOMACY

....

JAN MELISSEN

24.1 INTRODUCTION

THE debate on public diplomacy now dominates research agendas in diplomatic studies. With many newcomers from a variety of disciplines joining this niche sub-field, public diplomacy has become diplomatic studies' best export, as shown by a flurry of public and private advisory reports, books, and articles. The launch of a number of specialized journals makes one wonder how far this market of ideas on public diplomacy can be stretched.[1] With e-bulletins, blogs, and other Internet-based resources, public diplomacy is an activity that seems more at home in the global communications' realm than other modes of diplomacy. A growing number of foreign ministers have their personal blogs or write daily tweets for their 'followers'. Policy dialogues with members of the public are becoming more common as a result of the spread of social media. Diplomacy today is evolving at a much faster rate than in the second half of the 20th century. It is no longer a stiff waltz among states alone, but a jazzy dance of colourful coalitions, and public diplomacy is at the heart of its current rebooting.[2] While traditional diplomatic practice is associated with actors involved in largely invisible processes of international relations, public diplomacy is about diplomatic engagement with people.[3] It has been instrumental in opening up the traditionally closed domain of accredited practitioners and made diplomats more visible than they have ever been.

Public diplomacy is, then, 'an instrument used by states, associations of states, and some sub-state and non-state actors to understand cultures, attitudes, and behaviour; build and manage relationships; and influence thoughts and mobilize actions to advance their interests and values'.[4] It is therefore in a sense a metaphor for the democratization of diplomacy, with multiple actors playing a role in what was once an area restricted to a few. Importantly, collaborating with those outside government and operating in the field is fast becoming a necessary condition of success in diplomacy. Governments realize that developing their country's overseas attractiveness requires reaching out to transnational civil society, and academics quickly understood that they could have a say in this. It is important to stress, however, that the comprehensive knowledge network in which modern diplomacy and public diplomacy are debated extends well beyond academia.[5] Scholar-diplomats, and others familiar with diplomatic practice as well as the world of organized learning, have made a particularly distinctive contribution by articulating the importance of 'soft power' and its implications for contemporary statecraft.[6]

'Theory' followed practice in public diplomacy studies. Just as the end of the cold war took international relations students by surprise, the perceived need for public outreach that preoccupied foreign policy practitioners preceded scholarly interest in the subject. As long as foreign ministries did not pay much attention to public diplomacy, neither did those who studied them. Think tanks such as the Center for Security and International Studies (CSIS) in Washington DC and the Foreign Policy Centre in London were among the first to stake a claim, questioning the changing nature of diplomatic practice in the communication age. Some of their early insights have stood the test of time.[7] Permeating this work was the consensus that public diplomacy offered opportunities for expanding and updating the repertoire of diplomatic tools. The difficulty was—and remains—how to move forward in this field. Some countries started seeing public diplomacy as a first (and cheap) line of defence, associating it with short-term political agendas that tended to undermine public diplomacy's external legitimacy. For many observers the best example of how *not* to proceed was US public diplomacy under George W. Bush's administration, infused with corporate advertising and marketing approaches that were applied to the rather more complex world of transnational relations. Other governments—particularly nations in transition such as the Central European powers, which desired association with organizations like the EU and NATO—were quick to incorporate public diplomacy in their foreign policy planning, viewing it as instrumental in achieving their strategic purposes and interests.

This chapter aims to help both students and practitioners think about public diplomacy's characteristics and modernization more clearly. It first outlines criticisms levelled against public diplomacy, as well as some conceptual implications of such criticisms. It then reviews some of the different states' practices, and points out that the juxtaposition of traditional approaches and the 'new public diplomacy' stifles thinking on its evolution. The chapter examines the public diplomacy of different types of actors, and how their perspective has a bearing on their working relationship with states, so as to point in directions where governments may be able to enhance their public diplomacy potential. It takes the view that public diplomacy flourishes in a 'polylateral' world of multiple actors[8] in which the state remains highly relevant in increasingly diverse international networks (see Box 24.1). Meanwhile, it recognizes that in day-to-day practice, the role of government may be both crucial and problematic. Finally, this chapter's advice to practitioners and trainers is that much can be learnt outside their comfort zone from how public diplomacy is practised in distinct organizational and cultural settings.

Box 24.1. Polylateralism: Diplomacy's third dimension

Geoffrey Wiseman[9] argues that the 20th-century evolution of diplomatic practice has resulted in a third dimension in the conduct of international relations, next to the familiar bilateral and multilateral diplomacy. Polylateral diplomacy, or state–non-state diplomacy, is equivalent to governments' diplomatic cooperation with transnational civil society actors. Wiseman defines polylateralism as the 'conduct of relations between official entities (such as a state, several states acting together, or a state-based international organization) and at least one unofficial, non-state entity in which there is a reasonable expectation of systematic relationships, involving some form of reporting, communication, negotiation and representation, but not involving mutual recognition as sovereign, equivalent entities'.[10] This development should not, however, be read as part of a supposed decline of the state in international relations. One should not underestimate the innovative capacity of state-based diplomacy. A number of factors contribute to state–non-state diplomacy. For example, strong democracies are more likely than (semi-)authoritarian states to accommodate transnational civil society. Transnationalism on low politics is more probable than on high political issues such as security, and long-term transnational relations are more likely to produce success in diplomacy than short-term campaigns.

24.2 CRITIQUE VERSUS ACCEPTANCE

Most governments today embrace public diplomacy, at least publicly. Few, if any, see it as a threat to more traditional diplomatic methods. Diplomats after 1945 became more accustomed to diplomacy opening up to society and, in the words of Harold Nicolson referring to political leaders, 'the fascination it exercises upon the amateur'.[11] In their reminiscences, diplomats heavily criticized the proliferation of summit meetings between political leaders in the second half of the 20th century,[12] but public diplomacy's recent rise did not encounter similar resistance from practitioners. Overt opposition might indeed have a boomerang effect as public diplomacy empowers the public, at least in the democratic world. At a time of growing civil discontent with government, official opinion seemingly designed to curb the voice of the people would not go down well. Lip-service to public diplomacy is thus *de rigueur*. Non-democratic countries, however, are a special category. One might assume that they have more centralized control over the image they want to project, yet the difficulty for authoritarian governments lies in persuading foreign publics of something that their own domestic public may not believe. Where unleashed public *opinion* is seen as a threat to governmental control, public *diplomacy* is bound to meet scepticism (see Box 24.2).

Political correctness and professional survival instincts are silencing most professional critics, who even tend to stay silent after retirement, as seen from the absence of critiques in diplomatic memoirs. It is mostly in conversation, sometimes in conference settings, and only rarely in writing that one finds practitioners who refuse to distinguish between propaganda and public diplomacy. The dismissal of public diplomacy can

Box 24.2. The 'Old School' critique of public diplomacy

Sceptics among diplomatic practitioners see public diplomacy as interfering with 'the real job'. They coincide with a small cohort of traditionalists in diplomatic studies who prefer to stick to the tried and tested methods of diplomacy. Traditionalists see public diplomacy as a modern name for white propaganda—that is, propaganda admitting its source, and directed mainly at foreign publics, but also at the domestic constituency. Because this 'fashionable practice' is not really diplomacy in their view, traditionalists consider public diplomacy a misnomer and a largely overrated or misunderstood activity.[13] In their assessment, diplomats and their political masters know best how to conduct international affairs and therefore 'the public ought to occupy a position peripheral to diplomacy'.[14] Such authors show no interest in public diplomacy's historical pedigree, or in forecasting the salience of this activity in future international relations. Yet one annoying reality for traditionalists is that the same foreign ministries that are at the centre of their conception of diplomacy *do* regard public diplomacy as part of their toolbox.

rather be observed by it being ignored in places where it should, arguably, be debated. 'Old School' diplomats see it as a form of political advertising. They do have a case, although only partly, when they mention that a host of bilateral relationships leaves relatively little room for engagement with civil society, as in authoritarian states.

The challenge of Western outreach to the Muslim world is squarely confronted with the difficulty of making public diplomacy work in a public environment that is not congenial to exchange and engagement of the wider public.[15] The recent uprisings in Northern Africa and the Middle East are presenting other governments with new, and equally daunting, public diplomacy challenges. Theory and practice are sometimes worlds apart in the world of public diplomacy. It is not always clear, even in the closest bilateral relationships, when ambassadors' actions become an infringement upon the host country's domestic affairs, thus violating the Westphalian principle underpinning the society of states. Outside the democratic world it is easier to find common appreciation of such limits than, for instance, in Europe. The European Union has become a true laboratory for public diplomacy experimentation, constantly pressing the boundaries of what is acceptable diplomatic behaviour. Among EU member states, walking the fine, invisible, and undefined line between the acceptable and the unacceptable may nevertheless be problematic, as governments encourage ambassadors to engage in public debates in their host society. Examples abound of ambassadors who have run into trouble with their own foreign ministry, although many such incidents remain hidden from the public. *Plus ça change* in diplomacy.

Criticism of public diplomacy is a healthy antidote in a field in which it is seen to act as a force for good. First, the critique serves as a reminder that its acceptance is not universal, although most academic writers sign up to a broad 'public diplomacy consensus'. Enough governments and individual practitioners remain, however, that see public diplomacy as intrusive, threatening, and undermining their country's stability. Second, the critique invites broader reflection on how diplomacy is changing and how public

diplomacy is an expression of the changing relationship between the diplomatic establishment and wider society, both at home and abroad.

24.3 'NEW' VERSUS 'OLD' PRACTICE—AND BEYOND

The terrorist attacks of September 11, 2001 were the main trigger for the global debate on
public diplomacy. Students of public diplomacy were ready for a fresh start, but had too
little patience to learn from history, and a sense that contemporary challenges in the global communication sphere had little in common with the cold war experience.[16] Without
doing justice to post-war experience, as reflected in some of the literature,[17] public diplomacy revisionists were quick to incorporate existing best practices in a 'new public
diplomacy' model. Neither public diplomacy nor propaganda were strangers to the
post-1945 ideological stand-off between East and West, the basic difference between the
two being that—unlike public diplomacy—propaganda is generally uninterested in dialogue or any meaningful form of relationship-building. In the West, the US government
developed a great deal of public diplomacy expertise between the 1950s and late 1990s
through the work of the United States Information Agency (USIA), while European
countries such as Germany and the United Kingdom channelled part of their public
diplomacy work through cultural institutions like the Goethe Institut and the British
Council. In the context of a new Europe, Germany saw an immediate need to develop its
public diplomacy after the Federal Republic's foundation, despite it being practised
under another name; its relations with neighbouring countries like France and the
Netherlands foreshadowed the later importance of public diplomacy in the European
Union. Late 20th-century Europe showed much variety in public diplomacy practices,
serving a range of economic, social, and political purposes. As distinct from lobbying,
which is focused on policy-making circles, public diplomacy aimed to influence broader
opinion in foreign societies. Some public diplomacy was defensive in nature, but countries also took advantage of this tool to support their rise. The Netherlands, for instance,
started focusing on ethical issues such as euthanasia, or liberal policies on soft drugs and
homosexuality that, in the eyes of many foreigners, were hallmarks of its overly permissive society, while Spain, after its transition to democracy, started engaging foreign publics with its supposed modernity.

Post-September 11, the normative call for a 'new public diplomacy'[18] was mostly based
on a forward-looking analysis of evolving practices in avant-garde countries in the
transatlantic world. It was also, however, a response to the political climate in which US
diplomacy and public diplomacy became traumatized by the 'war on terror' and dominated by considerations of national security. The need for updated public diplomacy
practices was generally based on a more liberal view of international relations and a
reaction to the United States' approach, which was dominated by security concerns and

corporate practices. Outside North America, it was much less common to view public diplomacy mainly in the context of the threat of terrorism. Many practitioners saw public diplomacy's rise as a window to modernizing their profession. Inside government, advocates of the 'new public diplomacy' saw the whole debate, and new approach, as a way to help change a largely risk-averse and inward-looking diplomatic culture when it came to dealings with the public. They criticized existing government practices that conceived of 'PD' as mere information work characterized by one-way communication to foreign publics and relatively little leeway for embassies in their contacts with the foreign press. In academia, meanwhile, a new generation of public diplomacy scholars, with credentials in disciplines like history, politics, communication studies, and public relations, anticipated and proposed new forms of diplomatic engagement in which contacts with foreign societies were no longer at the periphery of diplomatic affairs. Outside government, meanwhile, the same think tank researchers, academics, and consultants who had initially been surprised by public diplomacy's rise started acting as advisers to practitioners who, in their view, needed to be enlightened about what was happening to their profession. In North America and Europe, foreign ministries produced public diplomacy manuals guiding their staff at overseas embassies through the practicalities of public diplomacy work. Including references to public diplomacy strategy, issues such as the question of prioritization, 'lessons learned', and evaluation of policy, such documents have proven useful tools for public diplomacy training and a reality check for advocates of the 'new public diplomacy'.[19] Parallel to such in-house initiatives, practitioners' seminars on public diplomacy hosted by foreign ministries or other institutions became opportunities for policy-sharing among countries. With their gradually widening focus, they also contributed to broader reflection on the modernization of diplomacy per se.[20]

In the literature, interest in innovation or 'newness' in public diplomacy did not bring much conceptual clarity to the debate. It did, however, remind practitioners and policymakers that public diplomacy today is increasingly based on listening to 'the other', that it is about dialogue rather than monologue, and is not just aimed at short-term policy objectives but also at long-term relationship-building. A flood of books and articles conveyed a growing consensus that governments' legitimacy and credibility in an increasingly transnational environment required a greater role for social actors, and that public diplomacy was not just in the national interest but also in the common interest.[21] In Europe, which was much less affected by the anti-terrorist leitmotiv than the United States, public diplomacy focused on a variety of social concerns, including immigration and integration, ethical issues, and cross-border environmental and public health matters. Most initiatives were government-driven, but public diplomacy in Western Europe did wake up to the importance of contributions from civil society to strengthen such initiatives' legitimacy. Increasingly turning around transnational issues and debates, public diplomacy thus started moving beyond the notion of being an interstate beauty contest. The idea of public diplomacy as a form of country promotion and brand projection nevertheless survives today, mainly in countries with limited experience and capacity in this field, as well as the trade promotion and tourism sectors of most governments, but, perhaps surprisingly, also in some advanced countries.[22] The Swedish government, for instance, conceives of public diplomacy as a sustained effort to develop Sweden's brand identity, 'Brand Sweden', which featured some remarkable innovations—notably the creation of virtual meeting places—but is also based on a competitive conception of the national interest that is still largely defined in economic terms.[23]

The civil society dimension that is conspicuously present in state-of-the-art public diplomacy in Europe and North America is traditionally less visible outside the West, where public diplomacy is largely conceived in terms of governmental national strategy. East Asia is particularly fascinated with soft power and the question of how public diplomacy can help the national image keep up with economic growth, counterbalance existing historical rivalries, and contribute to international regional community-building.[24] China finds it hard to parade a storyline that is as powerful with Western publics as the democracy/rule of law/human rights triad that is a major soft-power resource for democratic states.[25] China's centralized public diplomacy style sits rather uneasily with the evolving concept of public diplomacy in Europe and North America, although it is less constrained by such considerations in international relationships in the developing world, where foreign aid and public diplomacy go hand in hand (see Box 24.3).

Lessons from public diplomacy as it unfolds in East Asia and other cultural settings can only enrich an academic debate that has been largely centred on Western traditions and practices. Academics and diplomats are well advised to take advice from China's experiences and those of other Asian countries—just as Asians have learned, and are still learning, a great deal from the West.

24.4 States and International Regions

It is hard to generalize about the public diplomacy of states, even in the seemingly homogenizing European Union. In public diplomacy terms, the United Kingdom and France, for instance, have professional cultures that show as many differences as similarities. Also in Europe are (at the end of the queue) Kosovo, and modern but fractured states like Belgium and Spain, with powerful sub-state regions practising their own assertive public diplomacy. Practices vary a great deal among countries, and can often be labelled as fairly traditional communication and information. Old-style messaging, promotion activities, nation-branding efforts based on corporate sector techniques, and highly centralized public diplomacy practices, however, do not exclude governments from learning from the more enlightened principles of the 'new public diplomacy'. The challenges facing many young states, or those that have gone through radical political and economic change, have taught governments of such states that dealing with foreign publics is not as easy as it seems and requires a degree of agreement of opinion at home. The experiences of Central European states like Poland or the Slovak Republic, for example, show how important a precondition of public diplomacy it is to have a broad domestic consensus about national identity.[26] When different political factions have

Box 24.3. A case study with learning points from East Asian public diplomacy*

Three features of East Asian public diplomacy deserve attention in the West.

- First, there appears to be a more *strategic perspective* on public diplomacy than has been observable in the West. This is probably part of an intrinsically Asian approach that attaches more importance to the long haul than to correcting short-term damage to national reputations. Second, a number of East Asian countries also recognize the merits of a *public diplomacy with a regional dimension*. The importance of more diffuse communication and socialization processes in East Asia should not be underestimated, and public diplomacy may have the capacity to assist in regional community-building and cooperation. Democratic countries such as Japan, South Korea and Indonesia have public diplomacy strategies based on shared values and a preference for multilateralism. Public diplomacy may therefore have potential beyond national image and reputation. Finally, countries like China and Indonesia, for instance, acknowledge that public diplomacy has a distinctly introspective dimension, and that a nation's soft power is related to its self-perceptions and confidence in its own institutions.

The experiences of individual East Asian countries are noteworthy for practitioners elsewhere:

- Particularly hard for China is parading a storyline that is as powerful with foreign, particularly Western, publics as the democracy/rule of law/human rights triad that is a major soft-power resource for non-authoritarian states. In a world of ever-growing transnational relations, China's centralized public diplomacy style sits rather uneasily with the evolving concept of public diplomacy.
- The Achilles' tendon of Tokyo's soft power in East Asia remains its wartime history, and in recent decades Japan's public diplomacy has been troubled by a process of soul-searching about its identity that reflected insecurity about its place in the world. At the same time, it has become clear that Japan's dedication to a distinctly liberal, values-based public diplomacy helped Tokyo to tackle Japan's soft-power predicament.
- A 'middle power' like South Korea and emerging powers such as Indonesia need public diplomacy to help tackle their lack of self-confidence in relatively young democratic institutions. The Indonesian example shows how countries in transition can be effective in developing a public diplomacy that supports strategic policy objectives overseas, while underlining the appositeness of public diplomacy in one's own civil society for purposes of national cohesion.
- The case of Taiwan shows the demonstrative potential of its democratic political system. State-based public diplomacy can be ruled out in cross-Strait relations, but a range of social actors that engage with China do enhance Taiwan's soft power on the Chinese mainland.

* Extract from Jan Melissen, 'Concluding Reflections on Soft Power and Public Diplomacy in East Asia', in S.J. Lee and J. Melissen (eds), *Public Diplomacy and Soft Power in East Asia* (Basingstoke: Palgrave Macmillan, 2011).

their own reading of a country's social and political history, the past can be an obstacle to framing a future-oriented public diplomacy.

In the first decade of the 21st century, governments have made noticeable progress by constructing a 'self-learning' national public diplomacy system, in which best practices are shared and the level of expertise is upgraded by trial and error. The effects of public diplomacy projects in some 'PD' avant-garde countries, such as Canada, the United States, and the United Kingdom, are also constantly measured. Nonetheless, evaluation issues remain public diplomacy's Achilles' heel,[27] and it is important to bear in mind that meagre results have made the past decade a sobering experience for many. The case of the United States' popularity ratings going from bad to worse in Pew Research Center polls is well known. Europeans have also learned the lesson that the requirements of success go beyond the last word in public outreach, modern management techniques, and recalibrated administrative procedures. Countries that have gone through image crises (the Netherlands and Denmark), that have been severely affected by severe financial and economic downturns (Ireland, Greece, Italy, Portugal, and Spain), or that have suffered serious reputational damage to their body politic (Italy and some of the Balkan EU members) understand that progress in public diplomacy is only made in small steps. In recent years most governments have nevertheless increased their public diplomacy budget, yet often lacking clear-cut proof that it has been working and in competition with other areas of policy that usually have a stronger constituency. Expenses for public diplomacy are modest in comparison with anything else in the foreign affairs budget, not to speak of defence and intelligence budgets. The US State Department's expenditure on public diplomacy of 1 per cent of its total budget perfectly illustrates how governments find it hard to put their money where their mouth is—and the US percentage compares favourably with other countries.

Where does all this leave public diplomacy within wider diplomatic practice? Contributions to the study of public diplomacy from a number of disciplines outside diplomatic studies do not assess public diplomacy in the wider context of the conduct of international relations, of which it is an inalienable part. One could take the view that public diplomacy and diplomacy are merging into something new, as opposed to the conventional view that each is driven by a different logic.[28] In such an inclusive type of diplomatic praxis, in which diplomacy and public diplomacy blend, public diplomacy becomes epiphenomenal—that is, accompanying broader developments in a morphed diplomacy. Traditionalist authors do not accept that the increasing linkages between diplomatic institutions and domestic and foreign societies contribute to diplomacy's transmutation into a more 'societized' form of diplomacy. Ironically, however, such a change is a palpable development in the day-to-day experience of people working inside foreign ministries. Advocates of the 'new public diplomacy' have contributed to our understanding of the practice by emphasising and dissecting the novel techniques of diplomatic relations with 'others'. In the final analysis, the revisionist juxtaposition of traditional and 'new' public diplomacy remains unsatisfactory, however, as it fails to analyse its subject in the context of overall change in diplomacy or conceptualizes public diplomacy as the exclusive practice of states, linked to the 'club' model of diplomacy.

This *Handbook*'s editors maintain that, in a networked diplomacy model, the public variant of diplomacy is not the prerogative of states, although states arguably remain the principal actors in international society. It is hard to generalize about the public outreach of states. On the European subcontinent alone, the likes of Liechtenstein, Norway, and Belarus share the same social space, as do Germany, France, Montenegro, and the Holy See. The public diplomacy of states can serve many specific purposes. It may stem from their desire to be noticed by other countries (or remain unnoticed for the darker side of their social reality) to spreading universal values to others; from pressing economic concerns in a climate of enhanced global competition to the ambition to deliver global public goods; from building a line of defence against foreign criticism to considerations of national strategy. Rising economic powers outside the West see public diplomacy as a tool to help them move upwards on the global league tables.[29] In an international environment of tectonic power shifts, the intense interest in public diplomacy by the BRICs (Brazil, Russia, India, and China), the MIKTs (Mexico, Indonesia, South Korea and Turkey), and other emerging economies in Latin America, Asia, and Africa can indeed be seen as an expression of the impatience of the 'rising Rest'.

Public diplomacy's rise outside the Western world throws up intriguing questions, including how, apart from states, the international regions of which states are members have entered the sphere of soft power. The public diplomacy dynamics of regions in Latin America, East Asia, or the Middle East are sometimes strikingly different from those in North America and Europe. Little comparative public diplomacy research has been undertaken on such regions outside the Western world. One matter of dispute in many of the world's regions is that they have not yet sorted out their common historical legacy in the way that Western Europe did after the Second World War. The extent to which, for instance, France and Germany have locked themselves into a common destiny and even educated their youth with the same history books is a distant prospect for most other countries in the world. Elsewhere, past differences tend to cast long shadows over bilateral relations, reinforcing the tendency for political controversies to be played out by 'megaphone diplomacy'. East Asia retains the issue of public hypersensitivity of historical enemies Japan, South Korea, and China. In the Western hemisphere, economic risers such as Brazil and Mexico are frustrated that overseas publics see only the divisions in their societies rather than their economic successes. One stark difference between East Asia and Latin America is that public diplomacy in the Americas is more overtly competitive and political. An encouraging development in East Asia, meanwhile, is a growing sense that, in the absence of well-established multilateral structures, the potential for public diplomacy to contribute to regional community-building is recognized. Such developments in different parts of the world reveal how national public diplomacy strategies can be tied up with regional power relations in ways that contribute to international stability and transparency, a perspective that deserves further scrutiny by practitioners and academics.

Apart from looking at public diplomacy in terms of its potential for cooperation between states, public diplomacy coordination within states has the potential to become a bone of contention between different departmental interests. Governments like to speak with one voice, but national coordination in public diplomacy is easier on governmental drawing boards than in the reality of day-to-day bureaucratic infighting. Administrative arrangements designed for coordination purposes rarely produce the desired results. Public diplomacy strategy boards come and go, advisory councils tend to lead a relatively marginal existence in the hands-on world of diplomacy, and government departments' rival interests make it hard to deliver the paper reality of a 'joined-up' approach, as experienced even by countries with a sophisticated public diplomacy, such as the United Kingdom and United States. For starters, the public diplomacy perspective of foreign ministries, defence departments, and the ministry of economics, respectively, tends to vary significantly.

Domestic coordination problems also complicate the informal synchronization of countries' public diplomacy. One example of such international collaboration can be found in the streamlining of Western policies towards the Islamic world in the interests of stimulating counter-narratives that are meant to replace radical Islamist discourses. Yet structural harmonization of public diplomacy policies is hard for individuals and governments with mental maps that tend to contrast national interests.

Finally, an interesting public diplomacy variant is that democratic governments sometimes undertake public diplomacy on behalf of autocrats craving international support. Western European leaders like Tony Blair, Gerhard Schröder, and Jacques Chirac, who all paid tribute to Libyan leader Muammar Gaddafi, must have realized they did just that when they visited Tripoli's eccentric dictator. In a similar vein, US President Obama's historic 2009 speech in Cairo on relations between the West and the Islamic world was read as a tacit tribute to Hosni Mubarak, Egypt's 'last Pharaoh'. Today's massive political changes in Libya and Egypt do not, of course, bring an end to Western public diplomacy in Northern Africa and the Middle East. Rather, Western public diplomacy will have to address the greater challenge of working with a turbulent civil society instead of the countries' former leaders.

24.5 COLLABORATION BEYOND THE STATE

The processes and purposes of international organizations' public diplomacy are different from those undertaken by the states that comprise them. National public diplomacy depends largely on the work of embassies, but most international organizations see public diplomacy more as a centrally directed communication effort. Some have ambitious communication units, such as the North Atlantic Treaty Organization's Public Diplomacy Division at NATO's Brussels headquarters. Other international organizations have woken up to their public diplomacy mission more recently, sometimes as a result of reorientation of their mission, or have just started looking beyond the circle of their traditional institutional stakeholders, such as the Organization for the Prevention of Chemical Weapons (OPCW) in The Hague.

Some of the larger organizations with regional membership, such as NATO or the EU, now see public diplomacy as an existential necessity. They focus a great deal of their public outreach, however—indeed the lion's share of their communication work—on internal audiences. NATO's outreach to its treaty area electorates aims to muster support for its revamped organization and missions, while an important EU focus is promoting an EU identity and inculcating EU citizens in the rather distant objective of Union citizenship. Beyond their membership, NATO's and the EU's public diplomacy efforts are aimed at demonstrating their coherence as an international actor, as well as their contribution as global norm entrepreneurs. In addition, the EU has developed some collaborative public diplomacy initiatives that are breaking new ground: one is the so-called EUNIC scheme, which aims to overcome the diminishing returns of parallel national programmes and aims at cooperation among several European countries' cultural institutes, such as the Alliance Française, the Instituto Cervantes, and the British Council; the other is the highly ambitious European External Action Service (EEAS), the EU's own diplomatic service to spread the Union's influence through a wide network of 'embassies' called external delegations. These are early examples of a kind of supranational collaborative public diplomacy that is likely to develop gradually during the 21st century, as long as it serves greater efficiency without eroding the national profile of member states.

The question of cooperation between states and different types of sub-state actors, especially cities and regions, is of an entirely different nature. Cities increasingly stress their own representative interests and concerns about image and reputation. They are open to coordinating their public relations activities with states when there is a mutually perceived need. Typically, such coordination is an extension of joint lobbying in favour of common objectives, as is the case with joint bidding for milestone events such as the Olympic Games or World Expo, or when trying to attract the headquarters of international organizations or major non-governmental organizations (NGOs). By contrast, the independent foreign projects and activities of cities in fields such as overseas development, post-conflict reconstruction, or collaboration with their immigrant populations' countries of origin are more likely to interfere with the national government's foreign policy. What also stands in the way of such state–sub-state collaboration is the clash of professional cultures. Local civil servants may be worldly-wise, but usually operate in circles that are markedly different from the specific habitat of diplomats hovering around national, foreign, and diplomatic spheres. Still, overlapping interests between national and local governments, in particular big cities, suggest that there is sufficient scope for cooperation. Foreign ministries would be wise to see the advantages of informal international networks that are cultivated by local governments.[30] Moreover, individual contacts—the proverbial 'last three feet'—in local communities will reinforce outreach to a level of society that is less familiar ground for those operating in national circles.

Public diplomacy collaboration between states and regions is an entirely different story. In federal states, regions with special competences in economic, cultural, and educational fields are investing heavily in public diplomacy. Some, such as Quebec in

Canada or Catalonia in Spain, have been active in cultural and public diplomacy for decades. In the absence of the trappings of statehood, regions striving for international recognition attach exceptional importance to public diplomacy. Regional public diplomacy is often about identity and 'nation-building', and the domestic dimension of such regions' public diplomacy is well developed. Manifestations of sub-state regional public diplomacy can also be found in authoritarian countries like Russia and China, which, paradoxically, give carefully controlled leeway in foreign affairs to regional authorities to help strengthen the reputation and legitimacy of the central government.[31]

In the tug of war between regional and national governments in parts of the Western world, public diplomacy has become a complex affair. Some federal states find it hard to harmonize regional and national public diplomacy narratives into one seamless whole. Public diplomacy collaboration between sub-state regional and national governments is not necessarily politically sensitive, as can be seen in federal states like Mexico or Australia, but examples also point in a contrary direction. One would, for instance, expect the priority capital cities to be targeted by Scotland's and Catalonia's public diplomacy to be London and Madrid, but this does not wash with these two regions' political elites. In many other places, emotions do not tend to run so high, but the public diplomacy of regions seems overall to be more supplementary than complementary to that of the state. In the knowledge that they are usually better known at home than abroad, regions have to navigate between public diplomacy cooperation with the national government and presenting an alternative to it. The fact that the countries of which they are a component part are more visible on the international stage, and that some of the more powerful regions feel purposefully neglected by 'club' diplomacy, has no doubt prompted their often zealous commitment to an independent regional public diplomacy.

Comparisons of best practices and policy transfers on public diplomacy are nowadays widespread and traverse different levels of governance, but actual cooperation among international organizations, national governments, and regional and local authorities encounters various kinds of resistance. Coordination difficulties and differences in organizational culture are evident, and progress in this field is therefore likely to be slow. This can be contrasted with public–private cooperation between national governments and NGOs, or government and international business. State–NGO collaboration in the field of public diplomacy has been well researched. A variety of cases, including those leading to the Ottawa Treaty[32] and the creation of the International Criminal Court (ICC), are well documented. Mobilizing international support in such coalitions generally takes place in a short-term campaign that bears little resemblance to conventional multilateral diplomacy. Contacts between some governments and a number of reputable NGOs have even turned into structural exchange relationships. With the rising number of NGOs and fast-growing transnational links, a dynamic form of collaborative diplomacy is emerging that stands in contrast with the rather more stale ministry of foreign affairs aim of official policy coordination. In the small but growing number of countries where such practices are becoming common, the initiative is by no means reserved to governments. Non-state actors' public diplomacy in multiple transnational networks is taking this further, with civil society organizations and citizens as participants at the centre of events. This type of public diplomacy has surfaced in European relations with the Middle East, where the absence of success with more conventional approaches has led governments to risk experimenting by keeping government officials in the background.

Finally, three forms of public diplomacy that require a brief mention are: public–private partnerships between government and business; citizen diplomacy; and the domestic dimension of public diplomacy. All three push the boundaries of public diplomacy's traditional conception. Governments can learn a great deal from corporate sector practices in areas such as marketing, public relations, and branding. International business relations now deserve more attention from practitioners in the context of public diplomacy. Large companies, employers' organizations, and international chambers of commerce have become more conscious of the importance of national image and the cultivation of nations' economic brands. A series of Western countries that suffered from image crises has seen business willingly step up to the plate in this matter. Second, voluntary public diplomacy in the guise of (more or less) independent citizens' contributions to international understanding[33] seems far removed from the contributions made by business. Both cases, however, reflect a belief that private initiatives can assist in developing a kind of public diplomacy that is not only less government-driven, but ultimately also more effective. A more conceptual question for continuing debate is whether it is appropriate to refer to such private forms of international engagement as 'diplomacy' (see Box 24.4). Third, the same applies to the assumption that governmental engagement with the domestic public is part of a nation's overall public diplomacy effort, as it employs similar communication techniques and its public outreach activities have much in common with those of classical public diplomacy aimed at foreign publics. Building on the asset of an active civil society, the domestic dimension of public diplomacy is not just an attractive proposition, but in the eyes of governments in, for example, neighbouring Australia and Indonesia already a fact of modern diplomatic life.

Box 24.4. Domestic publics and the case for a holistic public diplomacy

The difference between public diplomacy aimed at overseas public opinion and at domestic outreach is defined by the public, but their separation can be questioned in an interconnected, online, and highly mobile world of global citizens, diasporas, and expatriates. The domestic body of citizens becomes increasingly heterogeneous, with more connections to key segments of other countries' populations. Citizen diplomacy and public diplomacy's domestic dimension have a people-to-people approach in common, but the state's role and the link to foreign policy content are more prominent in domestic public diplomacy. Domestic groups and citizens are seen as the government's potential partners. In such a conception, the support of 'at home' citizens for international policy choices is a precondition for effective public diplomacy abroad. International messages must resonate at home, and a society's projected image must be embedded in its identity to be credible to foreign publics.

24.6 CONCLUSION

From the perspective of diplomatic studies, one premise of this analysis is that public diplomacy can only be understood if analysed in the context of change in the wider process of diplomatic practice. One interesting observation here in the recent evolution of public diplomacy is that public diplomacy is becoming less national, not only in terms of the actors involved but even when considering the themes that states pick to tell 'their story'. National governments always have their own interests in mind but, when practising public diplomacy, they increasingly emphasise common interests as well as global public goods. Meanwhile, non-state and particularly non-official actors play an increasingly large role in public diplomacy. In practice as it is unfolding now, non-state actors can acquire the capacity to act as initiators of public diplomacy, but even 'new public diplomacy', or a morphed variant of diplomacy that includes public diplomacy, does not do away with the role of government. Interestingly, public diplomacy at the beginning of the 21st century is moving away from a straightforward promotional perspective. Governments perceive public diplomacy more as a form of diplomatic engagement as well as part of a broader collaboration with other actors, although working with some is easier than synchronizing aims and activities with others.

The discussion in this chapter suggests that among a variety of actors, across cultures, and regardless of the extant political structures, public diplomacy has been accepted to such a degree that one could speak of a global 'public diplomacy consensus'. Head-on critiques of public diplomacy are rare in public diplomacy studies, and are seldom voiced openly by practitioners. Yet critiques should be welcomed, by academics and also by trainers who want to simulate real-life situations. Similarly, one should keep in mind that the 'old' and the 'new' coexist. Patterns of post-modern evolution in certain parts of the world cannot be extrapolated mechanically to places and actors that are trying to familiarize themselves with the basics. Many states are indeed still struggling to get their public diplomacy act together, in spite of the fact that exceptional individual talents can be found anywhere. It would also be rash to overlook the fact that there are still numerous governments and individuals around that regard the public diplomacy activities of others as an intrusion in their domestic affairs. These diplomats or politicians would do well to accept and embrace public diplomacy as inevitable in international relations, before learning about it the hard way.

More systematic comparative analysis between actors and across cultures would highlight the different objectives that public diplomacy serves and provide an opportunity to look more carefully at the nexus between power and public diplomacy. Research on its practice in different regions around the world might yield interesting results for practitioners who would benefit from thinking harder about public diplomacy in collaborative instead of strictly competitive terms. Moreover, comparing different types of actors in public diplomacy would be instructive for forward-looking diplomats. Recent practice shows more evidence than previously of not-state-initiated public diplomacy.

This chapter proposes the idea that public diplomacy collaboration between states and non-official actors is probably more flexible and results-oriented than states and official non-state entities working independently. This could be seen as a symptom of a rising collaborative public diplomacy, boiling down to more official cooperation with non-state actors and greater involvement by civil society. Such a development presupposes the acceptance of less governmental control in public diplomacy. Recent trends in this field do in fact bid farewell to the 'club' model of diplomacy, on the assumption that meaningful 'connections to others' in a network of international relationships will ultimately bear more fruit.

NOTES

1. Three journals focusing on public diplomacy are *Place Branding and Public Diplomacy*, *Public Diplomacy Magazine*, and *Exchange: The Journal of Public Diplomacy*, while an academic journal like *The Hague Journal of Diplomacy*, which is dedicated to the study of diplomacy in general, has experienced a surge in articles on public diplomacy.

2. P. Khanna, *How to Run the World: Charting a Course to the Next Renaissance* (New York: Random House, 2011), 22.

3. J. Welsh and D. Fearn (eds), *Engagement: Public Diplomacy in a Globalized World* (London: Foreign and Commonwealth Office, 2008).

4. B. Gregory, 'American Public Diplomacy: Enduring Characteristics, Elusive Transformation', *The Hague Journal of Diplomacy* 6:3/4 (2011), 353.

5. J. Melissen and Ana Mar Fernández (eds), *Consular Affairs and Diplomacy* (Boston MA and Leiden: Martinus Nijhoff, 2011).

6. J.S. Nye, Jr, *The Future of Power* (New York: Basic Books, 2011).

7. See R. Burt and O. Robinson, *Reinventing Diplomacy in the Information Age: A Report of the CSIS Advisory Panel on Diplomacy in the Information Age* (Washington DC: CSIS, 1998); M. Leonard and V. Alakeson, *Going Public: Diplomacy for the Information Society* (London: The Foreign Policy Centre, 2000); M. Leonard, with C. Stead and C. Smewing, *Public Diplomacy* (London: The Foreign Policy Centre, 2002).

8. G. Wiseman, ' "Polylateralism": Diplomacy's Third Dimension', *Public Diplomacy Magazine* 1 (Summer 2010), 24–39.

9. Wiseman, 'Polylateralism'.

10. Wiseman, 'Polylateralism', 27.

11. Cited in G. Craig, 'The Professional Diplomat and His Problems, 1919–1939', *World Politics* 4:2 (1952), 154–8 at 146.

12. J. Melissen, *The New Public Diplomacy: Soft Power in International Relations* (Basingstoke: Palgrave Macmillan, 2005).

13. G.R. Berridge, *Diplomacy: Theory and Practice* (Basingstoke: Palgrave Macmillan, 2010), 179 and 183.

14. P. Sharp, *Diplomatic Theory of International Relations* (Cambridge: Cambridge University Press, 2009), 271.

15. R. Van Doeveren, 'Publicizing the New Public Diplomacy', The Hague: Netherlands Institute of International Relations 'Clingendael', unpublished manuscript, 2011.

16. N.J. Cull, *Public Diplomacy: Lessons from the Past*, CPD Perspectives on Public Diplomacy (Los Angeles, CA: Figueroa Press, 2009).

17. G.D. Malone, *Organizing the Nation's Public Diplomacy* (University Press of America, 1988); H. Tuch, *Communicating with the World: US Public Diplomacy Overseas* (New York: St Martin's Press, 1990); J. Manheim, *Strategic Public Diplomacy and American Foreign Policy: The Evolution of Influence* (New York and Oxford: Oxford University Press, 1994).

18. Melissen, *The New Public Diplomacy*.

19. Netherlands Ministry of Foreign Affairs, *Public Diplomacy Manual* (The Hague: Ministry of Foreign Affairs, 2011).

20. Wilton Park, 'Public Diplomacy: Moving from Policy to Practice' (2010), available at <www.wiltonpark.org.uk/en/reports/?view=Report&id=22859434>.

21. Melissen, *The New Public Diplomacy*; *Annals of the American Academy of Social and Political Science* 616 (March 2008); N. Snow and P.M. Taylor, *The Routledge Handbook of Public Diplomacy* (Abingdon: Routledge, 2009).

22. S. Anholt, *Competitive Identity: The New Brand Management for Nations, Cities and Regions*, (Basingstoke: Palgrave Macmillan, 2007); P. Van Ham, 'Place Branding: The State of the Art', *Annals of the American Academy of Social and Political Science* 616 (March 2008), 126–49.

23. J. Pamment, *The Limits of the New Public Diplomacy: Strategic Communication and Evaluation at the US State Department, Foreign and Commonwealth Office, British Council, Swedish Foreign Ministry and Swedish Institute*, PhD thesis, Stockholm University (2011), 175–218; J. Pamment, 'Innovations in Public Diplomacy and Nation Brands: Inside the House of Sweden', *Place Branding and Public Diplomacy* 7:2 (2011), 127–35.

24. S.J. Lee and J. Melissen (eds), *Public Diplomacy and Soft Power in East Asia* (Basingstoke: Palgrave Macmillan, 2011).

25. I. d'Hooghe, 'The Limits of China's Soft Power in Europe: Beijing's Public Diplomacy Puzzle', in Jian Wang (ed.), *Soft Power in China: Public Diplomacy through Communication* (New York: Palgrave Macmillan, 2011); I. d'Hooghe, 'The Rise of China's Public Diplomacy', in Sook Jong Lee and Jan Melissen (eds), *Public Diplomacy and Soft Power in East Asia* (New York: Palgrave Macmillan, 2011).

26. G. Szondi, 'Central and Eastern European Public Diplomacy: A Transitional Perspective on National Reputation Management', in Snow and Taylor (eds), *The Routledge Handbook of Public Diplomacy* (New York: Routledge, 2009).

27. Pamment, *Limits of New Diplomacy*; P.C. Pahlavi, 'Evaluating Public Diplomacy Programmes', *The Hague Journal of Diplomacy* 2:3 (2007), 255–81.

28. J. Melissen, 'Public Diplomacy', in P. Kerr and G. Wiseman (eds), *Diplomacy in a Globalizing World* (New York: Oxford University Press, 2012).

29. E. Gilboa, 'The Public Diplomacy of Middle Powers', *PD Magazine* 2 (2009), 22–8; Andrew F. Cooper, 'Middle Powers: Squeezed Out or Adaptive?', *Public Diplomacy Magazine* 2 (2009), 29–34.

30. J. Wang, 'Localizing Public Diplomacy: The Role of Sub-National Actors in Nation-Branding', *Place Branding* 2:1 (January 2006), 32–42.

31. E. Albina, 'The External Relations of Tatarstan: In Pursuit of Playing Sovereignty or Playing the Sub-Nationalist Card', *The Hague Journal of Diplomacy* 5:1/2 (2010), 99–124; Z. Chen, J. Jian, and D. Chen, 'The Provinces of China's Multi-Layered Diplomacy: The Cases of GMS and Africa', *The Hague Journal of Diplomacy* 5:4 (2010), 331–56.

32. J. Williams, M. Wareham, and S. Goose (eds), *Banning Landmines: Disarmament, Citizen Diplomacy, and Human Security* (New York: Rowman & Littlefield, 2008).

33. P. Sharp, 'Making Sense of Citizen Diplomats: The People of Duluth, Minnesota, as International Actors', *International Studies Perspectives* 2 (2001), 131–50; S. Mueller, 'Professional Exchanges, Citizen Diplomacy, and Credibility', in William P. Kiehl (ed.), *America's Dialogue with the World* (Washington DC: Public Diplomacy Council, 2006).

CHAPTER 25

DIGITAL TECHNOLOGY

DARYL COPELAND

OVER the past decade, much has been said and written about the changing nature of diplomacy and the associated need for reform of foreign ministries and foreign services.[1] A large part of the discussion about the *new diplomacy* has been driven by the adoption, within diplomatic institutions and government more generally, of digitally-based systems of data creation, transmission, and storage using the Internet, social media platforms, computers, and a variety of wireless electronic devices. While the application of digital technologies has finally become widespread within foreign ministries, this chapter will focus on the use of these facilities by diplomats in the discharge of their reporting, analytical and problem-solving responsibilities, and in their efforts to connect digitally and collaborate with diverse audiences and online communities abroad through public diplomacy, or PD.[2]

In the information-saturated 21st century, the party with the best story, the most compelling narrative, is most likely to win the day. International political conversations, often involving large numbers of participants, are taking place across cyberspace. Foreign ministries need to get in on that exchange.

The challenge is steep. Foreign ministries are amongst the oldest parts of the apparatus of state. They are typically conservative and change resistant. The habits of interstate relations conducted primarily by designated envoys die hard—centuries of abiding by tradition—and the reflex of acting according to convention have made diplomats hesitant to embrace the unconventional. For these reasons and more, in a decreasingly state-centric world foreign ministries have been struggling to adapt.

Still, there are now indications of change, and a determination to evolve; initial resistance within diplomatic institutions to exploring the full potential of the new media is fading.[3] Foreign ministries and individual diplomatic missions most everywhere maintain web sites. Some host blogs, some feature wikis, others offer a variety of RSS feeds. A growing number are turning to popular social media platforms, enjoining cyber-visitors to follow them on Twitter or Tumblr, join their Facebook group, or see them on YouTube or Flickr. Embassies and consulates are conducting research and formulating strategies for e-engagement,[4] while communications bureaus at ministry headquarters are hiring tech-savvy employees to work the new media, not just by pushing material out, but by responding to incoming messages and engaging in continuing dialogue, often in multiple languages. Similarly, diplomats in the field use satellite-enabled mobile phones, laptops, and various hand-held appliances not just to relay and receive messages, but to bridge the divide between the challenges they confront on the ground and the search for possible solutions.

In the 21st century, diplomats are not only spending more of their time in cyberspace, they are also, of necessity, conducting an ever-increasing amount of their business outside the chancery, often in conditions of substantial insecurity or serious underdevelopment. Whether in providing advice on matters of public health and disease control, bringing information on the impact of climate change or commodity price swings directly to subsistence cultivators, or acting as cultural interpreters in conflict zones, the old diplomatic stereotypes of pin stripes and pearls are gradually giving way. In a world in which so many front-line issues are rooted in science and driven by technology—climate change, diminishing biodiversity, food and water insecurity, genomics—diplomats must master the techniques required to engage the issues.

25.1 INTERNET RULES

Much of what is new in diplomatic practice may in one way or another be attributed to the emergence of the Internet, which over the space of about twenty years has displaced other venues as the principal medium for global information exchange and interaction. As more and more people look to the Web as a primary source of information and communication, including e-mail, social networking, video conferencing, and telephony, and as higher transmission speeds and greater bandwidth expand audio and visual streaming possibilities, communications media are converging.[5] In recent years the Internet has edged out newspapers, TV, radio, and conventional telephones as the primary communications medium. Current applications, featuring an emphasis on networks, interactivity, file sharing, and downloadable 'podcasts', in contrast to the simple presentation of information, promise to further accelerate this trend.[6]

Today, anyone with a mobile phone or digital camera and uplink can become a reporter—think of the first images of 9/11 in 2001; the Indian Ocean tsunami in 2004; the 2007 pro-democracy uprising in Burma; the anti-Chinese rioting in Llahsa, Tibet, in 2008; suicide bombings in Iraq and Afghanistan, or; the unrest throughout the Greater Middle East in 2011. Almost none of that initial content was provided by journalists employed by corporate news organizations such as Al Jazeera, CNN, or the BBC. Most of it was unmediated. And almost none of it could be effectively suppressed by local authorities.

The elemental qualities of immediacy and interactivity that characterize Internet-based communications are particularly evident in the explosive growth of blogs and blogging. While not quite the equivalent of face-to-face contact, blogs represent something much closer to 'live' conditions than the publication of documents posted on static web sites. These attributes make blogs especially effective at breaking down cultural barriers. Bloggers from Libya, Afghanistan, Iraq, and elsewhere in the Middle East[7] have brought the human toll of those conflicts to desktops around the globe: executions have been streamed live on anti-occupation sites, and the Abu Ghraib prison pictures spread faster than Seymour Hersh's writing in *The New Yorker* could ever be distributed.[8] Those images effectively branded the US presence in Iraq, and turned Bush-era public diplomacy into something akin to mission impossible.[9] In the wake of developments such as these, it is not entirely surprising that Rand Corporation analysts recommended that the US military try Madison Avenue Internet marketing techniques to win hearts and minds in Iraq and Afghanistan.[10]

The most innovative, technologically sophisticated public diplomacy, however, will never be enough to compensate for failed policy. What a country does will always have more impact than what it says, and when those two dimensions diverge, the resulting 'say–do gap'[11] can have a devastating impact on international credibility, reputation, and influence.[12]

25.2 Big Picture in Transition

Diplomats—and journalists—are today only two sources that feed into an increasingly crowded infosphere. In both cases their long-standing advantages over the sourcing and control of information have disappeared. In the age of mass travel and communications and the exponential growth of Internet use, more people are able to exchange more data and ideas with increasing speed. A substantial share of all the world's accumulated knowledge is for the first time available to anyone with an Internet connection. Among other things, this is having the effect of breaking down barriers, of blurring borders of every kind, and of creating a kind of shared consciousness, a form of universal and collective intelligence.[13]

The line between diplomacy, journalism, and other forms of international communication has become especially indistinct with the publication, both online and in print, of over 250,000 US-origin classified diplomatic cables by the WikiLeaks web site, founded by Julian Assange.[14] The implications associated with this affair, not least as an illustration of the double-edged quality of science and technology in the era of globalization, will endure long after the story has been exhausted.

25.3 Public Diplomacy and the New Media

Traditional diplomacy is all about international problem-solving and conflict resolution through political and cross-cultural communication, negotiation, complex balancing, and compromise. It is intimately related to the pursuit of national interests, and is conducted by accredited diplomats, ministers, and heads of state. Although it occupies a shrinking space in the diplomatic tableau, it is not about to disappear. In places where civil society actors are scarce, where insecurity or underdevelopment limit the options for public diplomacy, or where host governments are especially sensitive about representatives of foreign governments dealing directly with their citizens, traditional diplomacy may be the only means available for transacting business between national governments.

Public diplomacy, in contrast, is based on persuasion, influence, and what Joseph S. Nye (see Chapter 30, this volume) has famously termed *soft power*, or the power of attraction.[15] PD involves a sophisticated form of triangulation: diplomats from sending states use dialogue, partnerships, image projection, and reputation management to appeal directly to foreign populations—opinion leaders, NGO representatives, business people, journalists, and others—in order to galvanize support and advance objectives with host governments.[16] Influence on policy and decision-making in receiving states may be indirect, but it can be highly effective.[17] In many respects, public diplomacy has become the *new* diplomacy, and for some states PD is now the diplomatic business model of choice. Simply put, it produces results, especially as regards the management of international relations within and between OECD countries, where PD techniques face few limitations.[18]

Using both traditional, state-to-state methods, as well as more popular means involving joint ventures and the identification of shared values and interests as a basis for making common cause with elements of civil society in receiving countries (PD), diplomats can be great generators of knowledge and intelligence. Foreign ministries represent the institutional repositories for such information, and that, in combination with a close connection to *place* conferred by the maintenance of a network of missions and staff abroad, is the basis of their comparative advantage vis-à-vis other government departments. These qualities, in conjunction with rigorous entry requirements and the sophisticated use of ICTs, should suffice to position foreign ministries favourably within government.

25.4 STRUGGLING INSTITUTIONS

In practice, however, neither diplomats nor foreign ministries have adjusted easily or well to the challenges of the globalization age, and in many countries diplomacy is facing a protracted resource and performance deficit in an ever more competitive environment.[19] Compared to the military, or to business and civil society actors, diplomats have been late adapters, slow off the mark and sluggish on the technological uptake. In part as a result, effectiveness has suffered and the financial and political support accorded diplomacy has stagnated or shrank.[20]

As the sources of power and influence become more diffuse and decentralized and public finances remain constrained or diminished, governments have been looking for better ways to cope. In response to this crisis, and in part because it fits so well with the

PD approach, managers, analysts, and diplomatic studies scholars have been pondering how to adapt the use of the new media to diplomacy for over a decade.[21] Some foreign ministries have begun to experiment, and several are migrating an increasing proportion of their activities towards the Web.

25.5 LEADERSHIP AND BEST PRACTICES

In the second half of the 1990s, city-states Singapore and Hong Kong were out in front of the pack in establishing Web-based international identities. As foreign ministries go, the Canadian Department of Foreign Affairs (DFAIT) for almost a decade was in the forefront of the race to use new media to advance diplomatic objectives. That advantage was forsaken when a change of government abruptly ended the practice of Canadian PD in 2006–2007.[22] Since then, the US and UK have become leaders in the field, and many more countries are scrambling to join the fray.[23]

After a very slow start, the US State Department[24] is now the world's most active practitioner of e-PD and the source of many best practices in digital diplomacy.[25] It operates an official blog called DipNote,[26] and actively services Twitter accounts in Arabic, Farsi, Russian, Spanish, Hindi, and French, as well as English.[27] This new business line—'Twiplomacy' in the increasingly popular idiom—is growing fast, with more and more U.S. diplomatic missions and practitioners joining the fray. The Department has created an Office of e-Diplomacy, responsible for knowledge management, e-collaboration, and ICT decision-making. That division has created a network of virtual presence posts,[28] hosts, and a wiki-like intranet application called *Diplopedia*, and manages a variety of highly innovative programmes ranging from employee inreach and community formation to a 'virtual student foreign service'.[29] Secretary of State Hillary Clinton has a content-rich Web page[30] and she speaks frequently on the necessity of diplomatic engagement through the new media.[31]

In 2010 an extensive array of the State Department's digital diplomatic activities were gathered under the rubric of *21st Century Statecraft*, which is defined as 'complementing traditional foreign policy tools with newly innovated and adapted instruments of statecraft that fully leverage the networks, technologies, and demographics of our interconnected world'.[32] Stated policy objectives, which some critics have called into question, include support for freedom of expression on the Internet, and a concomitant end to censorship in cyberspace.[33] By providing practical support to efforts intended to keep the Internet open and by defending the 'freedom to connect', US officials hope that civil society and online democratic activism will flourish.[34]

The UK's Foreign and Commonwealth Office (FCO) also run a highly interactive web site,[35] featuring bloggers and links to YouTube, Facebook, Flickr, Foursqare, and specialized resources such as a commissioned volume on public diplomacy.[36] Foreign Secretary William Hague is on Facebook.[37] In 2008 the FCO began actively recruiting 'digital diplomats',[38] and recently established a distinct site devoted to the practice of 'digital diplomacy'.[39]

25.6 The Virtues of Virtuality

Given the overheads associated with conventional government communications, not to mention the cost of putting personnel on the ground, an increasing reliance upon Web-based and wireless media can make for enormous efficiencies. It is also the most practical way to reach the profusion of non-state actors whose support for diplomatic initiatives is often crucial.[40] Not least, in terms of demonstrating value for money, the results of digital diplomacy, especially as regards its impact on public opinion, can also be measured on Web analytics facilities such as Klout. [41]

Benefits include:

Effectiveness: in an increasingly network-centric world, foreign ministries can better connect and communicate with new players in international society—NGOs, business, think tanks, universities, journalists, and individuals—some of whom might otherwise be attracted to radical religion or extremist politics.[42]

Efficiency: digital diplomacy can capture scale economies, reach much larger audiences, and capture a range of related benefits associated with the move from bricks to clicks.

Leverage: as a key component in any strategy to maximize comparative advantage in a competitive environment, foreign ministries can use the new media to play to the strengths of national image and reputation while minimizing the constraints associated with capacity or security limitations.

Diplomats have begun to understand the potential of the new media as a force multiplier which allows them to connect directly with foreign populations; finding better, more creative ways to do this is now one of diplomacy's new frontiers. Moreover, the Internet can play a crucial role in helping diplomats overcome the often severe restrictions on face-to-face contact imposed by personal safety considerations in an increasing number of locales.

25.7 Obstacles, Constraints ... and Opportunities

Still, the use of the Internet for public engagement, let alone the more far-reaching applications of e-diplomacy, remains in many foreign ministries somewhat of an untested, even suspect concept.[43] The *blogosphere* is exploding with content of interest to diplomats, but it is largely unmonitored by foreign ministries.[44] Because the norms of the new media favour the immediate and most traffic is unmediated, there can be a cultural clash with the management mores and conventions of traditional diplomacy. Some senior officials are suspicious because the pace is so fast-moving and the public input unpredictable. Others just don't get the revolutionary significance of the new media per se. Lateral communications networks are inherently more open and democratic and are by nature subversive of hierarchy and authority. This can cause acute discomfort. Many governments are not yet ready to cede centralized control over communications and policy development.

The result is a paradox. For the very reasons that the Internet is so popular with youth and the non-governmental organization community, its role and place in the foreign ministry—as a PD and branding tool? Policy instrument? Communications vehicle? Technical service?—remain unsettled. As a result, the full potential of the Internet has yet to be realized.[45] But in the foreign ministry's quest for greater relevance, it will fall upon e-diplomats to overcome resistance, to tap into the emerging global political economy of knowledge, and to find their way to the leading edge of practice, even if there are a few harrowing corners, dead ends, and false turns along the way.[46]

Considerable work could be done to enlarge further our understanding of digital diplomacy's potential. Don Tapscott, for example, argues convincingly that the active sharing of intellectual property can stimulate mass collaboration in a way that produces the desired results more effectively and efficiently than could ever be achieved through conventional corporate or bureaucratic secrecy and competition.[47] His research carries fascinating implications for international policy and public administrative problem-solving, as well as for the creation and maintenance of wiki-style briefing materials on ministerial, bilateral, and global issues. Some governments have recently moved to implement novel forms of e-collaboration such as crowdsourcing, but relative to the potential, not least for democratizing policy development, it is a modest start.

With the lines between the real and the *virtual* worlds becoming increasingly indistinct, the scope for diplomatic experimentation with the new media will continue to grow. The technological hardware and software available for transnational interaction and advocacy has already become so powerful[48] that scepticism has diminished in recent years. There is today ample room for attempting to accomplish objectives in cyberspace which would be difficult or impossible to achieve on this side of the screen.[49]

The scope for innovation continues to grow.[50] Were the full potential of ICTs within foreign ministries to be exploited, a catalogue of candidate applications might look something like this:

25.7.1 Outward Focused

- public diplomacy, advocacy, and dialogue
- strategic communications, branding, and PR campaigns
- collaborative intelligence, innovation, and problem-solving
- trade and investment promotion
- contact development, relationship building, and network formation/maintenance
- outreach and constituency-building
- travel advice and consular information
- representation in virtual worlds

25.7.2 Inward Focused

- knowledge access, generation, and accumulation
- development of ideas, analysis, projects
- international policy formulation
- information sharing and internal publishing
- telework, distance learning, language training and simulations
- employee in-reach and internal communications
- channels for reform, dissent, and criticism
- institutional memory

Several of the possible modalities, such as wikis, blogging, chat rooms, and online communities, or virtual missions, teams and desks, would be suitable for both inward and outward deployment. Similarly, there is great scope for the conduct of meetings and presentations via live audio/video links, perhaps eventually using holography. Whatever the specific needs, most foreign ministries would benefit from the creation of a focal point for ICT-driven initiatives of all sorts. As suggested by the US and UK examples, this could translate into the creation of a corporate home for both e-diplomacy and internal online interaction.

25.8 LOOKING BEYOND

Pushed to its furthest extent, the possibilities attached to digital diplomacy extend well beyond the construction of electronic hubs and otherwise accommodating the operational needs of foreign ministries. One particularly intriguing area of research brings together elements of globalization, diplomacy, and grand strategy, and is rooted in a body of thought elaborating the concept of the *noosphere* and developed by French theologian Pierre Teilhard de Chardin in the 1950s.[51] Teilhard detected the emergence of an integrated, trans-human sphere of awareness, which he believed to be the final evolutionary stage in a progression from the inanimate (geosphere) to the animate (biosphere) to the collectively cognitive (*noosphere*). He conceived of a global mind or shared world of interacting ideas, which in many ways prefigured the notion of the Internet, the infosphere, and the contemporary flight into cyberspace.

Some of the more practical implications of Teilhard's thinking, particularly in relation to soft power and public diplomacy, have been developed by John Arquilla and David Ronfeldt into the notion of *noopolitik*.[52] Arquilla and Ronfeldt maintain that any analysis of the strategic role that information plays in international relations cannot be confined to a narrow technical discussion about platforms and process but must also take into account the role played by values, identities, and practices in the context of nascent global networks. New technology has made possible the creation of, and access to, a common life of the mind, a 'web of living thought' more or less equivalent to Teilhard's *noosphere*.

Arquilla and Ronfeldt demonstrate that when the *noosphere* becomes instrumental, which is to say when a network, its connections, and content can be applied internationally in the pursuit of specified goals and interests, states and foreign ministries become implicated. Put another way, when developments in the *noosphere* start to impact upon the world of power and politics among and between nations, diplomats become—or should become—engaged.

Of course, observing the potential of the *noosphere* is one thing; making use of it in terms of projecting values, advocating policies and pursuing interests, and harnessing access to the 'web of living thought' in service of diplomatic objectives, is quite another. When that Rubicon is crossed, the availability of human and financial resources, as well the span of decision-making authority vested in individual diplomatic agents, become critical issues. In that respect, and in any consideration of the reform of foreign ministries more generically, issues of capacity and empowerment will be crucial in determining outcomes.

25.9 WikiLeaks/Cablegate

The WikiLeaks phenomenon, like digital diplomacy, is a product of globalization. Yet 'Cablegate' is an example not of technology *in* diplomacy, but rather of diplomacy *in* technology. To evaluate the implications of the disclosures, it is appropriate to construct something of a ledger. With the publication on the WikiLeaks web site of hundreds of thousands of US-origin diplomatic cables between November 2010 and September 2011, the small diplomatic studies section of the Noosphere received a giant infusion of new material. The cables were produced between December 1966 and February 2010 by 274 American diplomatic missions worldwide.[53] The classification of the messages varies from unclassified to secret, and they cover a vast array of subjects. The volume and content of the WikiLeaks/Cablegate release has provided an unprecedented amount of information about, and insights into, the workings of contemporary diplomacy.

25.10 Negative Impacts: A Setback for Serving Envoys

Continuing casualties. The disclosures have caused some collateral damage, including the expulsion of the US ambassador to Ecuador, the resignation of the US ambassador to Mexico, and—ironically—the firing of the director general of Al Jazeera News.[54] More worrisome still, despite the considerable effort to remove names and other possible identifiers on the part of the large media organizations whom initially partnered with WikiLeaks and Mr Assange in the release of the cables, the entire unredacted trove was released on 1 September 2011, leading to acrimonious exchanges over who was to blame.[55] As a result, some sensitive, vulnerable sources have undoubtedly been exposed.[56] At time of writing the consequences of this dangerous and irresponsible action remain unclear, but they could yet prove tragic.[57]

Suffering tradecraft. By undermining the confidence, trust, and respect upon which diplomatic exchange is based, the revelations have introduced somewhat of a chill into diplomatic practice. Privacy has been invaded, and confidentially betrayed, both on a grand scale. New sources may hesitate to come forward. There have been reports of diplomats being excluded from high-level political meetings for fear that private conversations may end up on the front pages.[58] The result is damage to networks, contacts, relationships. Keeping envoys isolated in their offices, out in the corridor, or on the other side of closed doors will necessarily affect the quality of reporting and analysis.

Rebounding secrecy. Concerns over confidentiality will almost certainly lead to higher levels of classification, to less information sharing, and to a return to bureaucratic stovepipes and silos. Sensitive conversations are likely to go 'off paper', to secure telephony and face-to-face encounters. Fewer records of such exchanges will be made or retained. This will diminish transparency, harm accountability, and impoverish the historical record.

In short, both the craft of diplomacy and the quality of public administration and governance are likely to suffer. That said, the business of government goes on, and the need to transact that business through international political communications endures. When it comes to the conduct of relations between states, there is often no alternative to direct contact. The means will evolve, and work-arounds will be found, but the diplomatic process will continue.

25.11 POSITIVE IMPACTS: LARGELY UNRECOGNIZED

Although most assessments of the larger implications for diplomacy of the 'Cablegate' imbroglio have been negative, there is an upside. It illustrates, among other things, the law of unintended consequences.

Forcing governments to be more honest, consistent, and transparent. Disclosures of this sort are becoming more frequent. As a result of the increased civic awareness and media oversight which has been engendered by such releases, governments are likely to be more careful to ensure that public statements align with facts gathered and actions taken.

Upping international affairs content in journalism. At a time of diminishing foreign and international coverage in the mainstream media,[59] the simple existence of this type of story has had a tonic effect on the quality of the news mix. By injecting a large dose of international content, and bolstering its prominence, the usual preoccupation with local news, domestic issues and personalities has been leavened. In the age of infotainment, this rebalancing—however fleeting—can only be beneficial to the health of the body politic.

A scholarly bonanza for students of diplomacy and internal relations. Publication of the quarter million plus 'Cablegate' messages has added substantially to an ever-growing e-collection of previously protected government documents. Elaborate screening mechanisms and protracted wait times—typically twenty-five to fifty years for documents of this classification—have been circumvented. This new archive represents a fabulous new resource for journalists and scholars, one which offers telling, and highly contemporary insights into the nature of power and the exercise of influence. The advent of universal, free access to a research trove of this exceptional nature is unprecedented.

Protecting information. The magnitude of the breach may result in some technical and procedural improvements to communications security and innovations in the handling, storage, and distribution of classified material.[60] In the case of genuinely sensitive content or sources, reforms of this variety can likely be justified, especially if not overzealously or inappropriately applied.[61]

Burnishing the diplomatic brand. All of the possible benefits elaborated above may pale in comparison to the effect upon the diplomatic brand. Diplomacy suffers from a negative image. The mainstream view of diplomats and diplomacy is probably not far from a composite characterization which I have constructed based upon several years of informal focus group testing with cabbies in London, England. Their view? Diplomats are dithering dandies, lost hopelessly in a haze of irrelevance, stumbling blindly between protocol and alcohol.

The publication of hundreds of thousands of cables has severely subverted that corrosive caricature, and in so doing has burnished diplomacy's badly tarnished reputation. How so? By illuminating the day-to-day reality of a very busy profession, and in so doing undercutting the notion of envoys snoozing away their afternoons after long, well-lubricated lunches, or breezing around as privileged passengers in embassy limos, or drifting aimlessly through elegant receptions or lavish dinner parties.[62] To the contrary, the 'Cablegate' dispatches show diplomats, time and again, working hard at their jobs, pursuing interests, projecting values, and advocating policies. Many will find those values, policies, and interests disagreeable, and in some cases extremely so. But the overwhelming picture which emerges is that of dedicated employees with their noses to the grindstone.

In the US, this counter-cultural characterization has changed the minds of more than a few opinion leaders about the role played and value added by the State Department.[63] That alone could pay dividends at a time of increasing competition for scarce resources. Moreover, the sheer volume of reportage on WikiLeaks/Cablegate has had the effect of helping to bring diplomats and diplomacy from the farthest reaches of popular consciousness into something approximating the cultural mainstream. This de-mystification can only have beneficial implications as regards diplomacy's brand vis-à-vis its international policy rivals, and may also augur well for recruiting efforts and departmental performance during the annual budgetary auction.

25.12 A MIXED BALANCE

Distilled to its essence, it is by no means clear that the 'Cablegate' disclosures were intended to support freedom of information, transparency, probity in government, or defence of the public interest. Instead of serving as a conduit for the transmission of vital knowledge out of the shadows and into the light, this affair seems more about personal self-aggrandisement and the commoditization of information. In the US, UK, Canada, Peru, Australia, India, Holland, and elsewhere, releases have been carefully timed and targeted, designed to produce maximum publicity for the source. This is closer to classic muck-raking and entrepreneurship than journalism, heroism, or principled support for good governance. Some scepticism is clearly warranted regarding Mr Assange's claims that the 'Cablegate' revelations played a major role in encouraging of the Arab Spring.[64] While there was quite possibly some influence on the margins, it is also likely that few of those who participated in the uprisings had any idea of the content of the cables which reported on corruption, nepotism, and various other unsavoury practices in Tunisia and Egypt.

'Cablegate' may not have changed the world, but it has nonetheless produced a 'Napster moment' for governments, and may yet prove pivotal for international relations writ large. Just as the emergence of the music file sharing site Napster in the mid 1990s transformed the music retailing industry forever, the emergence of WikiLeaks, and the similar sites that are popping up all over cyberspace, looks very much like a game changer. Think culture shift, with the Web emerging as a new political centre. The classified information monopoly once enjoyed by governments is over, and for those inclined towards secrecy and information control, life will never be the same again.[65]

Finally, when viewed as a whole the 'Cablegate' collection offers some compelling insights into machinations of US foreign policy. While it is impossible to know what percentage of total US diplomatic communications is represented by this sample, in the most contemporary messages, dated 2008–2010, clear reporting priorities, such as the global financial crisis, climate change, or the implications of power shifting to the Asia Pacific are not much in evidence. Viewed in aggregate, these reports suggest the antithesis of American grand strategy. Rather than providing a portrait of an empire at the top of its game, the impression is one of a rather dishevelled Uncle Sam bumping along into the imperial darkness, desperately trying to plug cracks in an increasing number of failing dykes, worldwide. For those conspiracy theorists who see the dark side of American power behind everything that goes wrong in the world, this record offers little solace. Indeed, the content of the 'Cablegate' archive will more likely be interpreted by the declinist school as indicative of America's ebbing place in the world.

25.13 BY WAY OF CONCLUSION

Transparency in government is important, and most information generated by civil servants has been financed by taxpayers and should therefore be in the public domain. Still, not all information needs to be freed. To give just one example, publication early on in the 'Cablegate' affair of the US government's estimate of the world's most vulnerable critical infrastructure sites surely did not serve the general interest.[66] Even if the details on such locations were otherwise available, an estimate of the American government's foremost concerns was not. In any event, why make high-grade research material available to those who might use it to do harm?

In a similar vein, why risk the exposure of sensitive contacts, such as democracy activists in Burma or human rights campaigners in China? And how many future sources of valuable intelligence will not now come forward for fear of being revealed and punished?

The 'Cablegate' episode has happened not so much because it *should*—to repeat, there is little evidence of probity or the public interest in play as motives—but because it *could*. The issues and key drivers seem to have more to do with personal ambition, digital capacity, and technological possibility than with morals or ethics.

To conclude: though the effects have been mixed, it is not on balance clear that the world needs more 'Cablegates'. Contemporary international relations, however, and in particular the prospects for development and security, would benefit from more and better diplomacy. Conflicts persist in Iraq, Afghanistan, Libya, and elsewhere, and political violence—civil wars, terrorism—if decreasing slightly overall, remains all too pervasive.[67] The *Global War On Terror*, by whatever name, has so militarized international policy that non-violent alternatives have been sidelined and marginalized.

The costs are mounting. The dispatch of an expeditionary force will not permit governments to occupy the alternatives to the carbon economy. The most lethally equipped military cannot defend borders against attacks by infectious disease. Air strikes are ineffective in the battle to reverse climate change.

Today, defence expenditures dominate, but in the case of universal threats to humanity, armed force is not the treatment required. If the most profound challenges which imperil the planet are to be addressed, then more supple, subtle, and comprehensive approaches will be needed.

In the rapidly evolving world of virtuality and e-communications, developments are so fast-breaking that much of what I have written here will inevitably be out of date by the time it is read. That said, the sophisticated use of new media by foreign ministries holds much promise, and the practice of digital diplomacy has already begun to make a demonstrable difference. To build on these gains, relentless innovation, sufficient resources, and a fundamental shift in international policy direction will be required.

NOTES

1. See, for example, Shaun Riordan, *The New Diplomacy* (London: Polity, 2003); Jan Melissen (ed.), *The New Public Diplomacy: Soft Power in International Relations* (Basingstoke: Palgrave, 2006); Daryl Copeland, *Guerrilla Diplomacy: Rethinking International Relations* (Boulder: Lynne Rienner Publishers, 2009).

2. A prefatory note on terms is essential. In the ever-expanding literature on what will be referred to in this chapter as *digital* diplomacy, the related terms *virtual, cyber, e-*, and *i-* are used more of less interchangeably. For a useful explanation of the current state of terminological play, see the note on the usage of *virtual* in *The Free Dictionary*, <http://www.thefreedictionary.com/virtual>.

3. In November 2004 I attended a conference on *Diplomacy and the Web* organized in London by the Oxford Internet Institute. The majority of the senior officials who participated regarded the Internet—with some suspicion—as just another broadcast medium which would have to be 'managed'.

4. For one example launched by the Dutch Consulate General in San Francisco, see Carolijn Van Noort, *Social Media Strategy: Bringing Public Diplomacy 2.0 to the next level* (2011). Available at: <http://dl.dropbox.com/u/1574605/Blog/Public%20Diplomacy%202.0%20 Research,%20Carolijn%20van%20Noort.pdf>.

5. Jon Husband has coined the term *wirearchy*, by which he refers to 'an emergent organizing principle based on interactivity and listening to the voices of people connected by on-line capabilities and social media'. See <http://www.wirearchy.com/>.

6. Parts of the following discussion of the impact of new and digital media on the operations of foreign ministries are set out in Daryl Copeland, 'Virtuality, Diplomacy and the Foreign Ministry', *Canadian Foreign Policy* 15:2 (Summer 2009), 1–15.

7. See, for instance, <http://www.dahrjamailiraq.com/>.

8. See Seymour Hersh, 'Torture at Abu Ghraib', *The New Yorker*, 10 May 2004. Available at: <http://www.newyorker.com/archive/2004/05/10/040510fa_fact>.

9. A succession of Undersecretaries of State for Public Diplomacy—Charlotte Beers, Margaret Tutwiler, Karen Hughes, James Glassman—were unable to reverse the impact of US foreign policy, especially the Iraq invasion and occupation. On the failure of 'listening tours', satellite broadcast efforts, and related PD initiatives undertaken by the Bush administration post-9/11, see R.S. Zaharna, *Battles to Bridges: U.S. Strategic Communication and Public Diplomacy after 9/11* (Basingstoke: Palgrave, 2010), 11–65. See also Ilana Ozernoy, 'Ears Wide Shut', *The Atlantic* November 2006. Available at: <http://www.theatlantic.com/magazine/archive/2006/11/ears-wide-shut/5271/>.

10. See Todd Helmus et al., 'Enlisting Madison Avenue: The Marketing Approach to Earning popular Support in Theaters of Operation', *Rand* (2007). Available at: <http://www.rand.org/pubs/monographs/2007/RAND_MG607.pdf>.

11. See Daryl Copeland, 'PD's most formidable adversary: The *say-do* gap', *USC/CPD Blog*, 16 June 2009. Available at: <http://uscpublicdiplomacy.org/index.php/newswire/cpdblog_main/author/Daryl_Copeland/P5/>.

12. On the extent of the post-9/11 damage to the American brand, which in most of the Arab and Islamic world has persisted or worsened under President Obama, see Pew Global Attitudes Project, <http://www.pewglobal.org/category/survey-reports/>.

13. I have referred to this phenomenon elsewhere in terms of the emergence of a *global political economy of knowledge*. Science, technology, and ICT savvy also play a central role in my conception of *guerrilla diplomacy*. See Copeland, *Guerrilla Diplomacy*.

14. See WikiLeaks, 'Secret US Embassy Cables', <http://wikileaks.org/cablegate.html>.

15. See Joseph S. Nye, *Soft Power: the Means to Success in World Politics* (New York: Public Affairs, 2004).

16. The literature on, and general interest in, PD is exploding. A comprehensive bibliography on PD is maintained by the Netherlands Institute of International Relations (Clingendael): <http://www.clingendael.nl/library/literature/public_diplomacy.pdf>. Bruce Gregory of George Washington University produces an excellent research survey: <http://publicdiplomacy.wikia.com/wiki/Bruce_Gregory%27s_Reading_List>. John Brown publishes a current review of broadly-based PD materials: <http://publicdiplomacypressandblogreview.blogspot.com/>.

17. PD, soft power, and human security were effectively combined during 1996–2000 by Canadian Foreign Minister Lloyd Axworthy. With major initiatives on land mines, child soldiers, and blood diamonds, as well as the creation of the International Criminal Court and the articulation the Responsibility to Protect doctrine, he rang up an impressive string of achievements which came to be known as the Human Security Agenda. See Robert McRae and Don Hubert, *Human Security and the New Diplomacy* (Montreal: McGill Queen's, 2001); Daryl Copeland, 'The Axworthy years: Canadian foreign policy in the era of diminished capability', in Fen Hampson, Norman Hillmer, and Maureen Molot (eds), *Canada Among Nations* (Toronto: Oxford University Press, 2001). Canada was an early leader in PD, but it has slipped subsequently to the back of the pack.

18. On the possibilities associated with networks and influence, see Ali Fisher, 'Music for the Jilted Generation: Open-Source Public Diplomacy', *The Hague Journal of Diplomacy* 3 (2008), 1–24; Ali Fisher, 'Looking at the Man in the Mirror: Understanding Power and Influence in Public Diplomacy', in Ali Fisher and Scott Lucas (eds), *The Trials of Engagement* (Leiden: Brill, 2011). For a critique of PD, see Daryl Copeland, 'The Seven Paradoxes of Public Diplomacy', in Ali Fisher and Scott Lucas (eds), *The Trials of Engagement* (Leiden: Brill, 2011).

19. Contemporary Australia provides a particularly poignant example, notwithstanding that the foreign minister, Kevin Rudd, is a former diplomat and prime minister. See Alex Oliver and Andrew Shearer, *Diplomatic disrepair: rebuilding Australia's international policy infrastructure* (Sydney: Lowy Institute, 2011). Available at: <http://122.252.12.194/Publication. asp?pid=1673>; Lowy Institute, *Australia's Diplomatic Deficit*, 2009. Available at: <http://www.lowyinstitute.org/publications/australias-diplomatic-deficit>.

20. By way of the Canadian example, see Bill Robinson, 'Canadian Military Spending 2010–11', *Foreign Policy Series*, Canadian Centre for Policy Alternatives, March 2011, <http://www.policyalternatives.ca/sites/default/files/uploads/publications/National%20Office/2011/03/Canadian%20Military%20Spending%202010.pdf>; Michelle Collins, 'Foreign Affairs Hit with $639 Million in Cuts', *Embassy*, 18 March 2009. Available at: <http://www.embassymag.ca/page/view/foreign_affairs_cuts-3-18-2009>; Daryl Copeland, 'Old Rabbits, New Hats: International policy and Canada's foreign service in an era of reduced diplomatic resources', *International Journal* 60:3 (2005), 743–62.

21. There has been a proliferation of recent studies and the literature on diplomacy and the new media is becoming rich. For a sampling, see, for instance, Nicholas Cull, 'WikiLeaks, public diplomacy 2.0 and the state of digital public diplomacy', *Place Branding and Public Diplomacy*, 2011. Available at: <http://www.palgrave-journals.com/pb/journal/v7/n1/full/pb20112a.html>; Sam Dupont, 'Digital Diplomacy', *Foreign* Policy, 3 August 2010.

Available at: <http://www.foreignpolicy.com/articles/2010/08/03/digital_diplomacy>; Jozef Bàtora, *Foreign Ministries and the Information Revolution* (Leiden, NL: Martinus Nijhoff Publishers, 2008); Evan Potter, 'Web 2.0 and the New Public Diplomacy: Impact and Opportunities', *Engagement: Public Diplomacy in a Globalised World* (London: Foreign and Commonwealth Office, 2008); Evan Potter (ed.), *Cyber-Diplomacy* (Montreal: McGill-Queen's University Press, 2002). Excellent early surveys are offered by Center for Strategic and International Studies (CSIS), 'Re-inventing diplomacy in the information age', 9 October 1998. Available at: <www.csis.org>, and David Bollier, 'The Rise of Netpolitik: How the Internet is Changing International Politics and Diplomacy', *Aspen Institute*, 2003. Available at: <http://www.ciaonet.org/wps/bod05/bod05.html>. The US Institute of Peace published a path-finding series of papers under the heading *Virtual Diplomacy*. See: <http://www.usip.org/events/virtual-diplomacy-global-communications-revolution-and-international-conflict-management>. Some excellent PD web sites include those hosted by the University of Southern California (<http://uscpublicdiplomacy.com/index.php>) and George Washington University (<http://pdi.gwu.edu/>).

22. Personal observations by the author, who served in various capacities as a DFAIT executive during this period. Examples of early initiatives at the intersection of diplomacy and ICTs include the proposed Canadian International Information Strategy (1997); creation of the PD Resource Site (1998); the Canada.Cool.Connected branding campaign (2000); the online *Foreign Policy Dialogue* (2003); Policy e-discussions (2004). See Daryl Copeland, 'Virtuality, Diplomacy and the Foreign Ministry', *Canadian Foreign Policy* 15:2 (Summer 2009), 1–15.

23. For example, in April 2011 DiploFoundation organized a workshop on e-diplomacy for African diplomats based in Addis Ababa. See: <http://edip.diplomacy.edu/addis_workshop>. India's Department of External Relations has been very keen on exploring the potential of e-PD over the last few years. See Abhisbek Baxi, 'Government of India's Digital Diplomacy', *Techie Buzz*, 11 September 2011. Available at: <http://techie-buzz.com/technews/government-of-indias-digital-diplomacy.html>.

24. See <http://www.state.gov/>.

25. US digital diplomacy has in a few short years become so mainstream that it is being covered by the likes of *Time* magazine. See Sam Gustin, 'Digital Diplomacy', *Time*, 2 September 2011. Available at: <http://www.time.com/time/specials/packages/article/0,28804,2091589_2091591_2091592,00.html>.

26. See <http://blogs.state.gov/>.

27. See Alex Howard, 'Empowering digital diplomacy at the edge of the network', *O'Reilly Radar*, 1 March 2011. Available at: <http://radar.oreilly.com/2011/03/state-department-twitter.html>.

28. See, for example, <http://canada.usembassy.gov/canada-us-relations/the-arctic/canada-north-virtual-presence-post.html>.

29. See <http://www.state.gov/m/irm/ediplomacy/>.

30. See <http://www.state.gov/secretary/>.

31. The US Embassy in Jakarta, by way of example, has launched a variety of digital campaigns; their Facebook page boasts over 300,000 registered viewers. See <http://www.facebook.com/jakarta.usembassy>.

32. See US Department of State, <http://www.state.gov/statecraft/index.htm>. Links to Secretary Clinton's key public addresses on e-diplomacy and Internet freedom, as well as the Quadrennial diplomacy and Development Review are available there. A useful summary of this US effort is offered by Tori Horton, 'United States Wages 21st Century Statecraft', *USC/CPD Blog*, 25 July 2011. Available at: <http://uscpublicdiplomacy.org/index.php/newswire/cpdblog_detail/united_states_wages_21st_century_statecraft_part_i_what_does_this_actually_/>. A more detailed treatment of the workings of US digital diplomacy is found in J. Lichtenstein, 'Digital Diplomacy', *New York Times Magazine*, 16 July 2010. Available at: <http://www.nytimes.com/2010/07/18/magazine/18web2-0-t.html>.

33. On the political power of social media, see Clay Shirky, 'The Political Power of Social Media', *Foreign Affairs*, January/February 2011, 28–41. Available at: <http://www.foreignaffairs.com/articles/67038/clay-shirky/the-political-power-of-social-media>. For alternative views, see Malcolm Gladwell, 'Small Change', *The New Yorker*, 4 October 2010. Available at: <http://www.newyorker.com/reporting/2010/10/04/101004fa_fact_gladwell?currentPage=all>; Evgeny Morozov, *The Net Delusion: The Dark Side of Internet Freedom* (New York: Public Affairs, 2011); Daniel Drezner, 'Weighing the Scales: The Internet's Effect on State-Society Relations', *The Brown Journal of World Affairs* 16:2 (Spring/Summer 2010). Available at: <http://www.bjwa.org/article.php?id=gk5HI7zD9NmuIYGSd66jz8H4robHlSafn3QOVVgS>.

34. For a summary of the US strategy on International Cyber Diplomacy, see <http://www.state.gov/documents/organization/168901.pdf>. In some cases the American investment in e-PD, such as the post-9/11 launch of Arabic-language satellite television (Alhurra) and radio (Radio Sawa) networks, has not yielded the expected dividends. See, for example, Dafna Linzer, 'Ahurra Targeted for Review by State Dept. Inspector General', *Pro Publica*, 17 September 2009. Available at: <http://www.propublica.org/article/alhurra-targeted-for-review-by-state-dept.-inspector-general-917>.

35. See <http://www.fco.gov.uk/en/>.

36. See <http://www.fco.gov.uk/resources/en/pdf/pd-engagement-jul-08>.

37. See <http://www.facebook.com/williamjhague>.

38. See <http://webarchive.nationalarchives.gov.uk/20110108023357/blogs.fco.gov.uk/roller/hale/entry/becoming_a_digital_diplomat>.

39. See <http://digitaldiplomacy.fco.gov.uk/en/>.

40. PD and ICTs can also be used offensively. In this context, the US State Department in 2011 established the Center for Strategic Counterterrorism Communications, which works to undermine extremism by countering its ideological basis.

41. See Brian Fung, 'Klout and the evolution of digital diplomacy', *Washington Post*, 22 August 2011. Available at: <http://www.washingtonpost.com/national/on-innovations/how-klout-could-change-americas-image-abroad/2011/08/22/gIQAsooNWJ_story.html>.

42. Again, the US, who at one point believed that they were losing the online PR battle for hearts and minds, has lately been in the forefront in adapting digital diplomacy for counter-terrorism purposes in the context of a broader 'smart power' strategy. See Hillary Clinton, 'Smart Power approach to Counterterrorism', *Remarks*, US Department of State, 9 September 2011, <http://www.state.gov/secretary/rm/2011/09/172034.htm>.

43. With a few exceptions, led by Singapore and Taiwan, significant diplomatic players in East Asia, Latin America, and Africa have not kept pace with the US, UK, and Europe.

44. The blogosphere had its tenth anniversary in 2008; that this rich domain is not systematically monitored and assessed, or even regularly surveyed by most foreign ministries, is a major shortcoming. The unrealized potential here is enormous. See <http://technorati.com/> which is unsurpassed on the growing importance of the blogosphere.

45. For some further thinking on possibilities for use of the new media, see Mark Mayberry, 'Trends in New Media', in Alan Heil (ed.), *Local Voices/Global Perspectives* (Washington: Public Diplomacy Council, 2008).

46. Not all e-diplomats will be young, but many will be part of a demographic that has grown up with the new media. For members of this cohort, the full interactive potential of the medium, and the applications related to PD and branding, will seem second nature. On the Internet generation, see Don Tapscott, *Grown Up Digital: How the Net Generation is Changing Your World* (New York: McGraw-Hill, 2008).

47. See Don Tapscott and Anthony Williams, *Wikinomics* (Toronto: Portfolio, 2006).

48. How blurred have the lines become and how powerful is the technology? See material posted on the TED web site, <http://www.ted.com/>, especially the 'jaw-dropping' category; see also the amazing work of Johnny Chung Lee at <http://www.cs.cmu.edu/~johnny/>.

49. Such experiments are occurring. See <http://secondlife.com/>.

50. Ron Diebert at the Munk Centre's *Citizen Lab* project is doing some very interesting work (see <http://www.citizenlab.org/>); see also James Der Derian's research on networks at <http://www.watsoninstitute.org/contacts_detail.cfm?id=24>.

51. See Pierre Teilhard de Chardin, *The Phenomenon of Man*, trans. B. Wall (New York: Harper and Row, 1965). For theorizing about the Internet per se, see Manuel Castells, *The Rise of the Network Society, The Information Age: Economy, Society and Culture*, vol. 1, 2nd edition (Oxford: Blackwell, 2000); Manuel Castells, *The Power of Identity: The Information Age—Economy, Society and Culture*, vol. 2, 2nd edition (Oxford: Blackwell, 2000); Manuel Castells, *The End of the Millennium, The Information Age: Economy, Society and Culture*, vol. 3, 2nd edition (Oxford: Blackwell, 2000).

52. See John Aquilla and David Ronfeldt, *The Emergence of Noopolitik* (Santa Monica: Rand, 1999). Available at: <www.rand.org/pubs/monograph_reports/MR1033/index.html>; John Aquilla and David Ronfeldt, *Networks and Netwars* (Santa Monica: Rand, 2002); John Aquilla and David Ronfeldt, 'The Promise of Noopolitik', *First Monday* 12:8 (2007). Available at: <http://firstmonday.org/issues/issue12_8/ronfeldt/indext.html>.

53. See WikiLeaks, <http://www.wikileaks.ch/cablegate.html>. A single batch of 251,287 unedited diplomatic cables and related messages is beyond the capacity of most individuals to review and process. It must be mediated. This is probably why WikiLeaks founder Julian Assange turned initially to five of the largest news organizations in the world—*The New York Times, The Guardian, El País, Der Spiegel*, and *Le Monde* to handle the job. Although not the subject of this analysis, recall that the 'Cablegate' message onslaught came on top of the previous WikiLeaks release of 392,000 military reports on Iraq, 92,000 on Afghanistan, and more recently, 792 on Guantanamo. *The Guardian* has been highly comprehensive and proficient in covering all aspects of the WikiLeaks story. See <http://www.guardian.co.uk/media/wikileaks>. Book-length treatments are offered, among others, by Micah Sifry and Andrew Rasiej, *WikiLeaks and the Age of Transparency* (Berkeley: Counterpoint, 2011); David Leigh and Luke Harding, *WikiLeaks: Inside Julian Assange's*

War on Secrecy (New York: Public Affairs, 2011); Greg Mitchell, *The Age of Wikileaks: From Collateral Murder to Cablegate (and Beyond)* (Sinclair Books/Amazon Digital Services, 2011). My initial assessment of the Wikileaks/Cablegate episode, some of which is expanded upon in this treatment, appears in Daryl Copeland, 'Taking Stock of Wikileaks and Cablegate', *USC PDIN Monitor*, 2:1, January 2011. Available at: <http://uscpublicdiplomacy. org/index.php/pdin-monitor/article/taking_stock_of_wikileaks_and_cablegate_a_napster_ moment_for_government/>.

54. Wadah Khanfar was allegedly fired because of his susceptibility to US editorial influence as described in a number of cables released by WikiLeaks in September 2011. For an assessment of these US lobbying efforts, see Maximilian Forte, 'What WikiLeaks' U.S. Embassy Cables Reveal about U.S. Pressure and Propaganda', *ZNet*, 25 September 2011. Available at: <http://www.zcommunications.org/what-wikileaks-u-s-embassy-cables-reveal-about-u-s-pressure-and-propaganda-by-maximilian-forte>.

55. The relationship between WikiLeaks and *The Guardian* has been ruptured over this issue. See, for instance, Jaqui Cheng, 'WikiLeaks: unredacted cable release is guardian's fault', *Law and Disorder*, 1 September 2011. Available at: <http://arstechnica.com/tech-policy/ news/2011/09/wikileaks-unredacted-cable-release-is-guardians-fault.ars>.

56. See Scott Shane, 'WikiLeaks Leaves Names of Diplomatic Sources in Cables', New York Times, 29 August 2011. Available at: <http://www.nytimes.com/2011/08/30/us/30wikileaks. html?_r=1&hpw>.

57. One Ethiopian journalist, whose name appeared as a confidential contact in one of the cables, has reportedly fled Addis Ababa, fearing for his personal safety. See Committee to Protect Journalists, 'Ethiopian journalist ID'd in WikiLeaks cable flees country' (2011). Available at: <http://www.cpj.org/2011/09/ethiopian-journalist-idd-in-wikileaks-cable-flees.php>.

58. Verified by the author through personal and confidential communications with serving diplomats.

59. This is a result of cost-cutting media fragmentation and reader migration to new sources of information on the Web. See, for example, Jodi Enda, 'Retreating from the World', *American Journalism Review*, December/January 2011. Available at: <http://www.ajr.org/article. asp?id=4985>.

60. As a result of the *9/11 Report* criticism regarding inadequate information sharing, the State Department made its confidential reporting accessible to some 500,000 US government employees worldwide through a facility called SIPRnet.

61. Cyber security has already become a growth industry, in part because of the increasing incidence of cyber spying. See, for example, Ryan Charkow, 'Cyber spying is the new face of espionage', *CBC News*, 21 September 2011. Available at: <http://www.cbc.ca/news/canada/story/2011/09/20/f-cyber-espionage.html>.

62. There is legitimate representational work to be done in social settings. In most places, however, not least due to cost pressures, this sort of activity occupies an ever smaller proportion of a long work day.

63. Private conversations over the past year with politicians, academics, and journalists have revealed a pattern of consistent admiration for the quality of the 'Cablegate' reporting, and several admitted that their views of diplomacy have been changed.

64. Mr Assange's parody of a Mastercard commercial, designed to draw attention to the banking blockade against donations to WikiLeaks, is nonetheless brilliant. See <http://www. youtube.com/watch?v=jzMN2c24Y1s>.

65. This lesson may take some time to sink in. The US government, for example, has ordered its employees to refrain from accessing web sites hosting the WikiLeaks cables. This has produced some Kafkaesque situations. See, for example, Peter Van Buren, 'Freedom Isn't Free at the State Department', *TomDispatch*, 27 September 2011. Available at: <http://www.tomdispatch.com/post/175446/tomgram%3A_peter_van_buren%2C_wikileaked_at_the_state_department/#more>.

66. See, for instance, Norman Spector, 'Wikileaks mad attack on Canada', *The Globe and Mail*, 6 December 2010. Available at: <http://www.theglobeandmail.com/news/politics/second-reading/spector-vision/wikileakss-mad-attack-on-canada/article1826060/>.

67. See Human Security Report Project, *Human Security Report 2009–10* (2010). Available at: <http://www.humansecuritygateway.com/>.

CHAPTER 26

CONSULAR AFFAIRS[*]

MAAIKE OKANO-HEIJMANS

CONSULAR affairs have long been regarded by foreign ministries as a matter of necessity. This is hardly surprising as they are of a practical nature, largely dealing with assistance and commercial concerns of citizens and the private sector, rather than with national interests that constitute core government concerns. Similarly, the diplomatic studies tradition has on the whole been preoccupied with high politics, staying within the traditional realm of narrowly defined notions of diplomacy even as attention for the widening scope of actors grew. Both perceptions are up for substantial revision. As citizens became more assertive, news reporting more international, and public—private interaction more diverse, points of contact as well as links between diplomats and the public have increased. Indeed, almost two decades ago a British study on the Foreign Office already found that '[a]s far as most British people are concerned, the Foreign Office is the Consular Service'.[1]

In recent years, relatively low-priority service tasks of the foreign ministry moved up the agenda and gained a distinctly diplomatic character. Consular and other citizen services were extensively discussed in a high-level meeting of secretaries-general from twenty-two countries' foreign ministries in 2011, discussing challenges and opportunities for the 'Foreign Ministry of the Future'.[2] The trend towards greater attention for service tasks is prevalent in the various functions of the consular institution—that is, in the assistance, representational, and mercantile dimensions—and occurs as a result of distinct although related developments in each field. In the process of consular affairs' return to the limelight in recent years, the role and responsibilities of the state expanded, while an increasingly diverse group of organizations assists it in (consular) governance. The consular institution thereby contributes to the growing network of (diplomatic) actors, while the distinction between consular affairs and diplomacy is increasingly blurred. The rise of attention and status for consular affairs in recent years has also raised stress levels of consular officials and diplomats working in the field, whose every (perceived) mistake is amplified. At a more general level, this renewed attention to consular affairs raises critical questions about the tension between securing broad, long-term national interests and the narrow interests of individual citizens. As two Dutch diplomats working in the consular field put it: '[h]ow far must we go?'.[3] This difficult question is increasingly heard, but practitioners and academics alike leave the issue largely unaddressed.

While recent (semi-)government publications on consular affairs tend to deal with consular affairs in the narrow sense of assistance to citizens in distress abroad,[4] the actual work of a consul—especially at a consulate general—is much broader and includes also commercial, representational, judicial, and public diplomacy tasks. Informed by such a practical context, this chapter addresses the questions how the consular institution changed over time, how different consular functions relate to diplomacy, what the purposes of consular affairs are, and what the role of the state is. While the motivation of the consul to help citizens has remained fundamentally unaltered throughout the centuries, substantial changes in the type of person that is assisted and the context in which services are delivered necessitate a qualification of assumptions about the relationship between consular affairs and diplomacy. A closer look at the evolving relationship between the state and its citizens, as well as changes in the foreign ministry and in diplomacy, exposes the challenges that governments need to address in these changing circumstances.

A practical problem that needs to be addressed stems from the essential nature of consular protection: when is consular assistance an issue of maintaining or returning to 'life as usual' for an individual or corporate actor, and when is it the subject of national and, at times, even international (consular) governance and policy? The main argument here is that while not *all* consular activities *always* involve a degree of diplomacy or international, high politics, the consular institution as a whole has been—and continues to be—constitutive of commercial and economic diplomacy, consular diplomacy, visa diplomacy, and, to a lesser extent, even political and public diplomacy. It is time to take stock of developments in these fields—both separately and in relation to one another—and to rethink governments' consular activities in relation to the balance of national (i.e. government) and individual (i.e. citizen) interests.[5]

This chapter is structured as follows. Section 26.1 briefly reviews change in the consular institution throughout the centuries and considers its core concepts and context. This is followed, in section 26.2, by an analysis of the interrelationship between consular functions and diplomacy. Building on these findings, section 26.3 on consular governance and politics considers foreign and domestic goals of consular affairs and discusses the changing role of the state. The chapter concludes (section 26.4) with observations on the consular institution in relation to the theory and practice of diplomacy, arguing that foreign ministries in the years ahead need a forward-looking strategy to balance the tension between securing broad national interests and protecting the narrow interests of individual citizens—travelling, living, or doing business abroad.

26.1 CONSULAR AFFAIRS THROUGHOUT THE CENTURIES

The consular institution is in constant flux. That is to say, while the essence of consular affairs as 'assistance to individuals'—often limited to 'protection of citizens'—in foreign lands remains the same, fundamental changes occur in the character of the 'individual' and of 'assistance', as well as in the environment in which consular services are delivered. The scope of consular activities varies in accordance with the requirements of time and place, making for variations in the relative emphasis on the mercantile, judicial, assistance and protection, political and representative functions. For example, throughout the past centuries the focus of assistance shifted from representing traders' interests to responding to the interests of leisure travellers and the general public. Also, the legal and practical context of service delivery changed substantially as marine traffic was largely replaced by air travel. And as international exchanges grew, so did the challenges relating to international marriages, dual citizenship, and child abduction across borders.

Consuls existed long before the state and the diplomatic institution appeared in its current form. In the Greek civilization of the 6th to 4th centuries BC, consuls were at work in Alexandria protecting the interests of the Greek community in Egypt, which also employed them.[6] The Middle Ages and the modern era saw the birth and gradual affirmation of the consular institution as it is known today. The British government, for example, tussled with the London-based Levant Company over influence and money with regard to the post in Constantinople from the 16th century until the company was dissolved in 1825.[7] Indeed, it was not until the 17th and 18th centuries, that the consular institution was brought under state control, while standardization of the consular services began in earnest only in the 19th century.[8]

The height of the powers of consuls, consular roles, and the number of consular posts is said to have been in the long 19th century—lasting from 1800 until 1914.[9] The surge in consular activity at that time resulted from the progressive triumph of liberal ideas and the extension to continental Europe of England's Industrial Revolution, which brought with them an intensification of international trade.[10] Mercantile functions had primacy, as is illustrated by the Spanish definition of the consul as 'commercial administrative agent of the Nation', who also has judicial and notarial powers.[11] Even during the institution's heyday, however, consular activities did not earn the consul much respect among colleagues in the foreign ministry. The 19th century was a period in which social class was openly at the forefront of public affairs, and a strict distinction existed between the consul and the diplomat, and between consular and diplomatic functions. The distinction was marked in uniforms—the consular one embroidered with silver, the diplomatic with gold; formal salutes—a consul-general was entitled to no more than the salute given to a British factory (trading station) abroad, while a consul was given even less than the nine-gun salute; and hierarchy—consuls-general of whatever seniority rated in precedence after the most junior diplomats.[12]

In the following decades the 'commercial attaché' emerged, who challenged the dominance of the consul in practising the mercantile function. This led to a system wherein commercial tasks were performed by specialized commercial attachés or trade diplomats in larger representational offices (embassies or trade offices), while the consul remained in charge in those places where (s)he was the sole representative of a country. In this process, consular services in many countries were merged with the rest of the foreign service.[13]

The Vienna Convention on Consular Relations of 1963 was the first multilateral agreement to govern consular relations, privileges, and immunities. But in comparison with its predecessor, the 1961 Vienna Convention on Diplomatic Relations, the Consular Convention was 'less a codification of long-established rules' while 'the régime it sets out is less uniformly applied'.[14] Indeed, the breadth and depth of consular and commercial assistance varies between countries nowadays, and the same can be said of the extent to which governments call upon the help of private actors to assist in providing services. Not surprisingly, the lack of an international (legal) framework for consular affairs can seriously hamper problem-solving of consular issues between governments. It is therefore not surprising that calls are now heard to 'create joint, collaborative solutions', including the creation of common consular standards.[15] Earlier efforts towards this aim by the European Union illustrate, however, that this is by no means an easy task since governments may be unwilling even to share data that can be used, for example, for consular process metrics. That governments are hesitant to openly discuss consular affairs even within a like-minded group suggests that the harmonization of consular standards among an even larger number of countries is an immense diplomatic challenge indeed.

Importantly, and as codified in the Consular Convention, no entity other than the state has the (legal) capacity to manage or deal with the core of consular issues. That is to say, citizens in distress in foreign lands can turn to the state of their nationality for protection and— certain limits notwithstanding—consular officials have the legal right to have access to and communicate with such citizens, even when they are in prison, custody, or detention.[16] Not least due to juridical and judicial tensions reality can often be much more complex than this seems to suggest, however. This is illustrated in the case study on consular affairs and international law based on the Humberto Leal Garcia case, presented in Box 26.1.

The Vienna Convention on Consular Relations provides that consent to diplomatic relations implies—unless otherwise stated—consent to consular relations. It adds, however, that the severance of diplomatic relations shall not ipso facto involve the severance of consular relations.[17] In other words, it is possible—although unusual—for a state to launch or maintain consular relations without also having agreed upon the establishment of diplomatic relations. Herein lies the representational function of the consular institution in relations between countries; in special circumstances, it may be useful to preserve some degree of communication by resident means when resident diplomatic missions cannot be maintained.[18] The United Kingdom and Argentina, for example, resumed consular relations several years after the Falklands war in 1982 as an interim

Box 26.1. Case study on consular affairs and law

On 7 July 2011 Humberto Leal Garcia, a Mexican national, was executed via lethal injection in the state of Texas. This case brings into sharp relief the relationship between consular affairs on the one hand and diplomacy and society on the other. It also illustrates the tensions that may arise in consular practice between international and domestic law, between the federal and state governments, and the executive and the judiciary.

As a Mexican national, Leal was never appraised of his right—stipulated in the 1963 Vienna Convention on Consular Relations—that foreign nationals who are arrested or detained abroad may have access to their embassies or consulates. Critics of the decision to execute Leal argue that the subpar legal assistance that he received during his trial as a consequence of this may have cost him his life. Moreover, requests by the White House and State Department, Mexican authorities, top judges, senior military officers, and the United Nations to halt the execution on the grounds that this fact be taken into consideration and that the capital punishment could jeopardize American citizens arrested abroad, as well as US diplomatic interests, were in vain. At the time of his arrest, Leal did not reveal his Mexican citizenship, however, and the issue of consular access was not raised during the trial.

This was not the first time that the state of Texas acted against the explicit requests made by (inter)national authorities. An earlier case had led in 2004 to a decision of the International Court of Justice (ICJ) in The Hague that Leal and about fifty other Mexican inmates had been denied their rights under the Vienna Convention, ordering the United States to comply with its obligations. Besides, other countries also have raised objections against US handling of similar cases wherein citizens' consular rights have been violated. In 2008, the Supreme Court acknowledged that the ICJ ruling was binding but said that the president acting alone could not compel states to comply with it and that the enforcement mechanism specified in the treaty was for Congress to enact legislation. The US Supreme Court and the Texas governor rejected the appeal of the US government and let the execution proceed.

step towards the resumption of full diplomatic relations. A state can also perform consular services on behalf of another state. The 'Group of Five' Commonwealth countries have coordinated consular services for many years, for example, while the Swedish embassy in Pyongyang acts as the United States' interim protecting power and provides basic consular services to US citizens travelling in North Korea.

As this very brief history shows, great disparity persists throughout the ages and between countries in the assigned functions, status, and organization of consuls and consular activities. This continuously changing reality and the resulting difficulty in defining the scope of consular functions, explains why most efforts at codification have omitted any enumeration.[19] Even today, most foreign ministries refrain from defining the arguably most essential concepts of consular affairs—the individual and assistance— for example in their guidelines on assistance to citizens in distress abroad. Such ambiguity may be understandable from a practical viewpoint, as it facilitates the case-by-case interpretation that is often required in the highly disparate consular assistance activities. More surprising is the fact that the consul and the consular institution are similarly underexplored in the literature, despite their long and diverse history and the fact that the development of the consular institution is in a sense constitutive of the emergence of the European system of sovereign states; consuls indeed preceded resident ambassadors.[20] The underlying attempt to unravel the consular institution and the evolving link between consular affairs and diplomacy throughout the centuries therefore continues with closer scrutiny of the core concepts of consular affairs and the context in which they relate.

26.1.1 Individuals and Assistance

The assistance and protection functions of the consular institution involve an inward and outbound expression. That is to say, services are provided to a state's own citizens abroad—and, when necessary, their family or other designated contacts at home—and to foreign individuals residing in or wanting to enter the country. The latter is about immigration matters including visa and residence permits. With regard to inward consular services to citizens travelling abroad, most governments implicitly or explicitly distinguish three kinds: documentary services, individual assistance, and assistance at times of crisis in foreign lands. The inward and outbound dimensions of consular assistance can be regarded as two sides of the same coin. However, they involve distinctive legal frameworks, different government and partner organizations, and diverging interests for the foreign ministry.

The more substantial political challenges to the foreign ministry originate in changes in individual and crisis assistance to citizens abroad in distress. As the two case studies (Box 26.1 and Box 26.2) show, developments in these fields illustrate how changes in society, diplomacy, and consular affairs relate to and reinforce one another. What is really new and thereby the main challenge in this field nowadays is the expanding role of the media and of politicians—which cannot be seen separate from the increase in expectations. Assertive citizens nowadays demand high quality and quantity of services and—when necessary—find their way to the media or parliamentarians to make their voices heard by government. The case study on international crisis assistance illustrates this (Box 26.2).

The mercantile function of the consular institution is also about assistance—here, to representatives of the private sector. Further to the division between services to own citizens and foreign individuals, a conceptual and practical distinction thus needs to be made in the character of the individual that asks for assistance; that is, between a request for assistance by a person in a private capacity (usually a tourist or a citizen residing abroad) and a business representative. The types of services provided to these individuals differ vastly: while the former may require a new passport or help in dealing with local police authorities, the latter may desire knowledge about or a personal introduction to a foreign (state-owned) company. 'Consular assistance'—that is, assistance to a private person—thus needs to be distinguished from 'commercial assistance'—services to business representatives or the mercantile function.

Box 26.2. Case study on consular affairs and international crises

Changing patterns of international tourism, cross-border crime, international terrorism, and natural disasters account for a surge in consular challenges. The terrorist attacks of September 2001, the Asian tsunami of December 2004, and the Lebanon crisis and evacuation of July 2006, have for instance served as eye-openers for the US, Sweden, and the European Commission. In March 2011 China was forced to organize its biggest-ever evacuation for more than 30,000 nationals stranded in the conflict zone of Libya. These large-scale emergencies triggered considerable attention for improved consular assistance in the respective countries and illustrate how consular affairs evolve rather reactively—during and after the crises.

The political risk of being ill prepared is illustrated by the faltering Swedish response to the Asian tsunami. Consular officials were severely criticized for adhering all too strictly to the 2003 *Financial Assistance to Swedish Citizens Abroad Act*, which propagates 'help with self-help', and the domestic backlash led to an in-depth investigation by the Swedish Tsunami Commission. Partly as a result of such experiences, limits to assistance in many countries are now easily stretched as a result of media pressure. A distinct political logic seems to apply to consular affairs: the bigger the crisis, the bigger the exception.

MFAs continually monitor their representation abroad and periodically shift resources to meet citizens' needs of speedy on-the-spot assistance in case of consular emergencies. At home, a growing number of MFAs have established professional crisis centres, which operate a 24/7 service to assist citizens in distress. Moreover, 'rapid reaction forces' are trained to step in when a consular emergency occurs in places where consular and diplomatic staff can be easily stretched. International cooperation is sought, but formalization may be hampered by practical obstacles. In the case of the European Union, for example, larger member states are wary that institutionalized cooperation can be at the expense of speed and visibility of consular service, thereby increasing the risk of criticism from domestic constituencies.

International consular crises—such as large-scale evacuations from emergency and conflict zones in Lebanon and the Middle East—also bring the cost issue to the fore. While many governments are stretched in their financial resources, most are hesitant to engage in a public discussion on the financial burden of ad hoc international crisis response. Rather, they invest in targeted 'safe travel' campaigns, calling on travellers to be properly prepared and insured.

As alluded to earlier, while representation of traders' interests may be called the origin of the consular institution, this function is *not* what foreign ministries refer to when they speak of 'consular assistance' these days. The assistance function of consular affairs is at the core of foreign ministries' consular departments, while the mercantile function is nowadays largely overseen by economic ministries and performed by (quasi-)government agencies. Although both may be responsibilities/tasks of a consul residing at a consulate (general) abroad, the two are generally performed by different individuals at embassies and overseen by different departments at home: respectively the Ministry of Foreign Affairs (MFA) and line ministries, including the ministry for economy (and trade), the ministry of agriculture, and the ministry of transport.

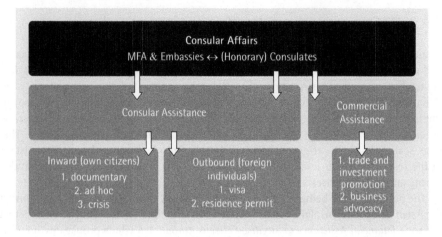

FIGURE 26.1. Consular affairs in the broadest sense: actors and activities

This blurring of the relationship between mercantile services and consular affairs stems, at least in part, from the fact that (honorary) consuls are not the sole executors of the commercial function and most likely also no longer the primary actors in this regard. Trade and investment promotion—an important element of commercial diplomacy—may be a task of both consuls and (commercial) diplomats, while the responsibility for trade diplomacy—for example negotiations in the World Trade Organization or on bilateral trade disputes—lies solely with (trade) diplomats rather than with consuls. Thus, while professional and honorary consuls perform both the consular and commercial assistance function,[21] embassies and MFA headquarters generally distinguish between 'commercial and trade diplomats' (or attachés)—carrying out mercantile, primarily trade and investment promotion, functions—and 'consular officials'—engaging in assistance and judicial functions to travelling citizens and to individuals residing in the host country. Figure 26.1 illustrates schematically the various actors and activities of the consular institution.

26.1.2 Context

In the early days of the consular institution, the assistance and commercial functions by and large overlapped. Importantly, the businessmen that were recipients of government services themselves also had a strong interest in maintaining friendly relations with the countries they visited or in which they resided. This is hardly the case for the hordes of tourists who travel the world nowadays on short visits. As citizens travel across borders in increasingly large numbers and become more willing and able to make their voice heard—including through the press and politicians—consular challenges have surged. The recent upgrading of consular services and the narrowing link between consular assistance and diplomacy can be seen to stem largely from these developments.

Governments in various countries—especially the developed economies in the West—are under direct pressure from the public and politicians at home—calling for improved consular and commercial assistance—and feel a growing desire and need to win the hearts and minds of foreign publics with distinct backgrounds—by broadening and diversifying presence. It is thus no coincidence that foreign ministries strive to professionalize consular services and that the sites of consular activity are shifting. This includes the opening of consular posts that cater to targeted audiences, particularly in large countries where diplomatic presence in the capital alone does not suffice. Due to the large number of Mexican Americans residing in the United States, for example, Mexico has no less than fifty consulates in that country. Other examples of consular posts established for political and commercial reasons include the Canadian consulate in Chandigarh, India, which is perceived to cater to the Sikh population that forms an important voting bloc in Canada, and the representative offices that many countries are opening in Western China to support commercial activities in that region.

At a general level, travellers' 'moral hazard' and a possible vicious spiral in government intervention provide a challenge for consular officers and government officials. The problem of moral hazard plays out in the consular assistance function, as a result of the situation that travelling citizens commonly feel little responsibility for the consequences of their acts, which increases the likelihood that they are willing to take risks that would otherwise not have been taken. This can be illustrated with reference to travel insurance, which grants an individual more leeway to act because the insured person knows assistance will be extended in emergency situations. While this is a sensible and essentially desirable way of facilitating travel,[22] it is not often recognized that the logic behind and coverage of travel insurance does not extend to the diplomatic arena. Governments therefore need to inform the public not only about physical hazards—as they do proactively and increasingly through 'safe travel' campaigns. A next step in public outreach could be aimed at improving awareness of the political interests that are involved in relations between countries—that is, of the broader picture of the balance of national interests of the home country in the global arena and the way in which consular cases may interfere with these concerns.

Developments in the commercial assistance function of consular affairs cannot be seen separate from growing government interventionism in the economy, resulting from the rise of newly emerging countries and shifting mindsets in industrialized nations. For example, the rise of China's influence—and of other countries where the separation between public and private is relatively more blurred—and the Lehman shock of 2008 gave a strong rationale for restoring government intervention.[23] This trend is prevalent in countries as diverse as Japan and the Netherlands and leads to a reappraisal of the commercial function of the diplomatic and the consular institution. Advanced economies that propagated free market fundamentalism earlier should be careful not to throw out the baby with the bathwater, however; acceptance in principle of the advantages of commercial assistance does not negate the need to limit certain aspects of it.

These are, obviously, not easy tasks and questions, nor do they imply that national, long-term interests should always precede interests of individual citizens. Rather, they are a call for deeper consideration of the tensions inherent in present-day consular and commercial assistance—between the interest of the individual traveller and the balance of national interests, and of short-term and long-term commercial interests. Moreover, it is to point to the responsibility of governments as well as individual consuls and diplomats to address these issues directly and proactively. The mutually constitutive processes and interests involved in new consular challenges and diplomacy need to be clearly delineated, lest we misunderstand their consequences.

26.2 Consular Affairs and Diplomacy

That consular affairs and diplomacy are inherently related is shown by the fact that the function of consul came about before that of the resident ambassador and can in a sense even be regarded as its forerunner. Even so, certain writings on the emergence of diplomacy do not mention consuls at all, while others see them as precursors of diplomacy and yet a third approach is to see the diplomat and the consul as personae that have evolved in parallel.[24] The common distinction between consular affairs and diplomacy is shifting nowadays, however. This is illustrated by the observation of a former foreign service officer of the United States that '[i]n the twenty-first century, the US State Department's overseas presence has moved well beyond the traditional diplomatic/consular dichotomy into a much more complex environment where functions overlap'.[25]

Thinking on the overlap between consular affairs and diplomacy is directly related to one's interpretation of what the consular institution is about. As discussed, the assistance function of consular affairs that is at the core of foreign ministries' consular departments today is much narrower than the daily activities of the consul; while consular officers at MFA headquarters deal with consular assistance, consuls may serve a variety of consular and diplomatic functions. If consular affairs are narrowly interpreted as inward and outbound consular assistance, their diplomatic dimension is referred to as consular diplomacy and visa diplomacy, respectively. Where it concerns commercial assistance or political and representational functions, consular affairs involve commercial and public and political diplomacy, respectively. Figure 26.2 illustrates this schematically.

Consular affairs in the broadest sense of the word change diplomacy by making it more visible to domestic and foreign publics and, in certain countries, more accessible and open to potential partners in service delivery. Furthermore, although consular affairs certainly do not always involve a degree of diplomacy or high politics, substantial developments since the late 1990s necessitate a qualification of assumptions about the relationship between consular affairs and diplomacy.

As the number of highly mediatized consular cases increases and internationally coordinated attempts to bring consular services to a higher level grow, consular assistance increasingly involves a degree of 'consular diplomacy'.[26] Two types of 'consular diplomacy'

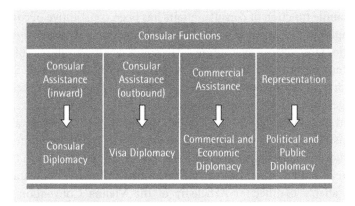

FIGURE 26.2. Consular functions and diplomacy

can be distinguished: the negotiation of preventive, practical arrangements of inward consular assistance between states, and high-profile assistance that is under close scrutiny from the media and politicians. In recent years, a growing number of bilateral negotiations have been pursued and signed to improve international cooperation and extend protection, as multilateral agreements are deemed inappropriate for current circumstances and are not signed by all countries.[27] At the same time, calls grow for a new multilateral treaty as well as coordinated attempts between like-minded countries to bring consular services to a higher level, for example within the European Union (EU).[28] Inward consular assistance obviously does not always involve a degree of diplomacy or international, high politics. Rather, the growing number of cases that do, pose challenges for foreign ministries that need to be addressed within the wider conduct of international affairs.

When considering the visa dimension of consular affairs, the use of visa issuance or denial at an individual, group, and interstate level, to influence another state's policies has been referred to as visa diplomacy. This practice is very political and only consular in its implementation.[29] Control of visitor flows has become a critical diplomatic instrument to facilitate cooperation and signal recognition between countries, while non-issuance signals protest or non-recognition.[30] Visa diplomacy is yet another consequence of the ease with which individuals—amongst them suspected terrorists or *persona non grata*, and some potentially carrying infectious diseases—travel across borders. It also explains why managing the influx of people into one's country at a group level has been referred to as 'the first line of defense'[31]—meaning that it constitutes the defence of one's country far beyond its physical borders by preventing terrorists, transnational criminals, and others intending to do harm from reaching the country. At the individual level, visa diplomacy is usually a matter of high politics and diplomacy. Exemplary of this is the politics behind visa requirements for Taiwanese citizens travelling to countries (such as the EU, the US, and Japan) in relation to China, which views Taiwan as a renegade province. In this regard, visits of serving and former Taiwanese presidents to the United States and Japan in particular have aroused controversy.

The mercantile function of consular affairs has been constitutive of commercial and economic diplomacy—even if, as seen before, this function is increasingly performed by actors outside of the consular institution.[32] The commercial (as well as public diplomacy) function gains in importance in the daily work of the (honorary) consul. Small outposts in various parts of a host country are perceived as cost-effective and necessary complements to large embassies in foreign capitals.

As alluded to earlier, political and public diplomacy[33] activities may also be undertaken by consular officials. Under special circumstances and with the agreement of the receiving state, consulates may be empowered to conduct diplomacy in the absence of diplomatic relations and/or embassies.[34] This follows from the representation function of consular affairs, codified in Article 17 of the Vienna Convention on Consular Relations. For example, a study of the British consulate-general in Hanoi shows how this post remained active throughout the Vietnam war and 'undertook a significant political function that would normally have been ascribed to a resident embassy'.[35] Diplomatic functions performed by the consulate-general included political reporting, support for and involvement in incoming missions, even if the post did not have direct access to the leadership of the host country. More recently, WikiLeaks revealed that the US consulate in Istanbul, Turkey performed similar functions of intelligence gathering and political reporting. Cables sent by this consulate contained, for example, Turkish and foreign historians' comments on the Turkish government's policy of denying the Armenian genocide, as well as on Iranian issues such as the health of religious leader Ayatollah Khamenei.[36]

Small outposts spread around the host country are also perceived as cost-effective and necessary complements to large embassies in foreign capitals—facilitating prompt, personal consular and commercial assistance and serving the political intelligence function of the sending state as well as the public diplomacy effort towards the foreign public. A former US official, for example, recalls that in a country like India, consulates-general 'functioning in districts as large as most European countries, operate in many respects as little embassies, largely on their own'.[37] This is more an exception than regular practice, however, and host countries generally do not like consular officers taking up political tasks.

26.3 Consular Governance and Politics

Consular affairs are not merely a domain of diplomacy but can also be an instrument in their own right. That is to say, while consular affairs are one area of government activity, they can also directly relate to foreign policy goals. This constitutes the difference between consular affairs as 'low politics'—involving the majority of consular activity—and as a 'high issue' of foreign policy—sometimes referred to as consular, visa, or economic diplomacy. As will be shown, the former has become an example of 'network diplomacy', as a growing number of actors became involved in the upgrading of consular services.[38] Consular affairs as 'high politics', however, is still largely a matter of 'club diplomacy', where actors other than representatives of government may be an object but are not a subject or undertaker.

26.3.1 Goals and a Balance of National Interests

The diversity in consular functions implies that consular affairs involve a variety of foreign and domestic goals. These are best assessed by looking at each function individually. Beginning with the mercantile dimension, motivations to provide assistance range from enhancing the country's (economic) prosperity to increasing the political stability of the nation.[39] As noted earlier, while support to the private sector other than through activities of trade and investment promotion offices was off limits for many countries in the 1990s, more recently so-called industrial policy or industry-specific policy is on the rise. A significant part of this change, which involves a rearrangement and deepening of the links between the public and private sectors, occurs outside of the consular institution. Even so, the effects of this trend herald a reappraisal of commercial assistance, which at the end of the day also entails an upgrading of the mercantile function of consular posts. Renewed attention for honorary consuls as cost-effective and commercially viable is an early example of this.[40]

The upgrading of consular assistance that began in the 1990s was motivated by defensive as well as offensive reasons. Foreign ministries aim to meet the growing demands of citizens and—as a consequence and extension of this—of politicians and high-ranking government officials.[41] Managing practical as well as accountability expectations, foreign ministries guard themselves against criticism from citizens. At the same time they recognize the potential marketing value of consular affairs. If properly dealt with, the foreign ministry can boost its image among the public through communication with citizens about consular protection in general and individual consular assistance in particular. Developments in consular affairs are thus part of a trend towards diplomacy's increased dealings with the general public and of 'network diplomacy'. Proactive efforts by foreign ministries and the European Commission to engage the public are one aspect of this.[42] Overall, however, foreign ministries are on the defensive side, with their media exposure growing as consular issues take the limelight in daily papers, television, and on the Internet. The consular institution thereby directly relates also to the domestic side of public diplomacy.[43]

As for the representation function, the goals of the consular institution lie in their very existence: the consular post is employed as a complement to the work of embassies in an outer area of the host country or for conducting diplomacy in the absence of diplomatic relations. This is particularly useful in large, emerging countries where it is important to be present in places other than the capital and where an active and visible consul also performs a permanent public diplomacy function. As argued earlier, this role and responsibility of the consular institution continues to grow in importance.

26.3.2 Changing Role of the State

Developments in consular affairs need to be considered within the broader development of changing relations in the last decade between the state and citizens, whereby the state takes up corporate standards and the citizen increasingly comes to be seen as a consumer who wants 'value for money'. Adding to this are new complications that have arisen with modern globalization and its new complexities, such as dual citizenship, multiple passports, and the responsibilities expected from a state. These challenges obviously go beyond the West, as illustrated by the fact that also China and India have redefined their relationship with overseas populations.

Notwithstanding the fact that continuous change is a constant feature of the consular institution, a relatively new development stems from the changing role of the state and the subsequently narrowing link between consular affairs and diplomacy. These developments are part of the 'normalization' of diplomatic practice at large, which changes consular affairs by making them (1) no longer by and between elites, but involving a growing number of actors (network diplomacy); (2) increasingly involve service tasks that gain a diplomatic dimension (consular diplomacy); and (3) more accountable to domestic and foreign publics (addressed through public diplomacy).

The trend towards 'network diplomacy' in consular affairs is part of the broader development wherein the boundaries of the state evolve horizontally—to include for example the private sector and non-governmental organizations[44]—and vertically—the sub-national, supra-national, and global levels. Foreign ministries call upon travel agencies, insurers, and non-governmental organizations to improve consular services and feel the need for international cooperation to address differences in consular standards and to enhance the efficiency of cooperation between countries. This is a typical example where 'the content and practice of diplomacy is shaped by the changing nature of sovereign political actors'.[45]

The evolving boundaries of the state contribute to the shift in statecraft from govern*ment* to gover*nance* and, ultimately, a decline in strategic capacity.[46] Against this background the essential nature of consular protection presents a practical problem, alluded to earlier: when is consular assistance an issue of maintaining or returning to 'life as usual' for an individual or corporate actor and when is it the subject of national and, where necessary, even international (consular) governance and policy? The problem of distinguishing between everyday consular work and regulatory policy, on the one hand, and high-profile consular cases, on the other hand, is exacerbated by the fact that consular work is often a matter of 'trial and error', requiring quick decisions by officers on the ground.

Views about consular governance and how far government assistance should go in specific cases is inseparable from the issue of how the relationship between government, citizens, and the balance of (national) interests is perceived, capitalized, and dealt with. When does an issue of consular and commercial assistance impact on the balance of (national) interests? Various factors influence individual perceptions, which determine whether these issues are given greater or lesser priority and placed on the political agenda or removed from it. These include events or crisis experiences such as the Asian tsunami of December 2004 and the Lebanon crisis and evacuation of July 2006 (see Box

26.2), the influence of public opinion (calling for greater assistance to prisoners detained abroad and for specific visa sanctions policy, for example), identity and sovereignty (including cases of abduction of a child of dual nationality by a parent), and the political and institutional contexts that shape ideas on the desirable level of government interference in the economy.[47]

Also challenging the ability to prioritize specific consular tasks as part of a long-term strategy is the fact that different political parties prioritize different elements of consular and commercial assistance to various degrees. In the Netherlands, for example, labour and democratic parties of the centre left tend to emphasise assistance to individuals in distress abroad—they are the chief proponents of improved assistance to citizens detained in foreign lands and to parents of murdered children—while centre right liberal parties emphasise the need for enhanced assistance to the private sector—or the professionalization of economic diplomacy. The observation of a Canadian consul that 'we have been busy like children, handling cases, but now we need to become adults'[48] can be traced back directly to this political context: while political parties have managed to place a variety of consular activities high on the agenda, the accumulated effort has not seriously been placed against required investments and trade-offs—in financial and personnel terms, or in diplomatic terms. Indeed, it needs to be recognized that the broadening of consular assistance not only amplifies the relatively straightforward delivery of consular services, but also enhances the diplomatic dimension of the consular institution.

Even if political agenda-setting is viewed primarily in elitist terms, there is little denying that the political agenda reflects those issues that key decision-makers wish to focus on at a particular moment, influenced by actors outside of government including parliamentarians and the media. As consular issues increasingly take the limelight—in other words, become politicized—this has important consequences for diplomatic practice. With the risk of a consular case grabbing the attention of media and politicians, diplomats of all ranks need to be prepared to engage the public and the media. Practical examples include the case of Joshua French and Tjostolv Moland, former soldiers in the Norwegian Armed Forces who were sentenced to death in Congo for murdering their driver and whose case became both a domestic and a bilateral diplomatic high-profile issue; the disastrous experience for the Swedish government of the Asian tsunami in 2004 that led to the creation of the position of director-general for consular affairs in the Swedish foreign minister's office in late 2005; and China's arrest of four Japanese nationals/businessmen in September 2010, against the backdrop of diplomatic disputes[49]—a sign of Beijing's willingness to make a political/economic dispute also a consular issue.

The point is that while globalization has induced new limits on the power of central governments, it has at the same time enlarged their responsibility for conflict management and the well-being of citizens and, on certain occasions, private sector interests. Different from the challenge of (conter-)terrorism, which gives the state in general and diplomats in particular a formidable test that requires long-term and profound interaction with a foreign public, the consular challenge is mostly practical and involves a large domestic dimension. It involves consular governance—that is, providing direction to society through a process of steering and coordination[50] of an increasingly large number of actors. While the majority of consular activities involve standardized procedures, interference of domestic and international politics has the potential to make consular acts a diplomatic concern. Domestic politics is even readily prioritized above effectiveness—both in terms of finance and cooperation—which is an important reason why certain EU member states with extensive diplomatic networks are hesitant about or resist far-going, formalized cooperation at the EU level.

All this strengthens the argument that foreign ministries will be unable to address today's consular challenges without a new strategy that reflects the evolving balance of national interests, including the interests of individual citizens. While the consular workload of many governments has grown, the resources of governments at large, including foreign ministries, have not been increased accordingly—inevitably resulting in a diversion of resources away from other diplomatic tasks.[51] The same scenario can be predicted for the mercantile function—wherein challenges also grow, as power balances continue to shift.

26.4 CONCLUSION

Overwhelmed by simultaneously occurring events and developments in the consular institution that are apparently unrelated, but have in common the somewhat paradoxical effect of politicizing service tasks, governments risk losing sight of the forest for the trees. As consular challenges grow, foreign ministries in the years ahead need a forward-looking consular and diplomacy strategy to balance the tension between securing 'high' national interests and protecting the narrow interests of individual citizens—whether travelling, living, or doing business abroad. While consular activities involve a growing network of actors, the sphere of governance of the state is broadening. Taken together, this leads to a blurring of the distinction between consular affairs and diplomacy. Consular activities do not always involve a degree of diplomacy or international, high politics, but the consular institution as a whole has been and continues to be constitutive of commercial and economic diplomacy, consular diplomacy, visa diplomacy, and even political and public diplomacy. This has important ramifications for the role and position of the consular institution within the diplomatic studies tradition. As these processes unfold, this understudied subfield within the diplomatic studies tradition is worthy of attention from students and practitioners alike.

NOTES

*   This paper owes much to earlier collaboration and joint publication with Jan Melissen of the Netherlands Institute of International Relations 'Clingendael'. The author wishes to thank him for his creative inspiration then and now, and for his (in)direct support for this chapter.

1. Ruth Dudley Edwards, *True Brits: Inside the Foreign Office* (London: BBC Books, 1994), 182.

2. The Foreign Ministry at a Tipping Point, unpublished Post-Conference Report of The Foreign Ministry of the Future Conference, Brussels, 10–11 July 2011.

3. Renée Jones-Bos and Monique van Daalen, 'Trends and Developments in Consular Services: The Dutch Experience', *The Hague Journal of Diplomacy* 3:1 (2008), 92.

4. For example, the Canadian Ministry of Foreign Affairs and International Trade published an internal review in November 2004 (*Review of Consular Affairs—Final Report*); the National Audit Office in the United Kingdom presented a report in November 2005 (*The Foreign and Commonwealth Office: Consular Services to British Nationals*); the Dutch government commissioned a confidential review in 2006 (Maaike Heijmans and Jan Melissen, *Consulaire Zaken en Diplomatie: Buitenlandse Zaken met Binnenlandse Prioriteiten*); and the European Commission launched a public debate on diplomatic and consular protection in 2006 (*Green Paper: Diplomatic and Consular Protection of Union Citizens in Third Countries*).

5. For more on the concept of 'a balance of (national) interests', see Chapter 3, this volume.

6. John Dickie, *The British Consul: Heir to a Great Tradition* (London: Hurst & Company, 2007), 5.

7. G.R. Berridge, 'British Ambassadors and their Families in Constantinople', in *The Counter-Revolution in Diplomacy—and other essays* (Basingstoke: Palgrave Macmillan, 2011), especially 120.

8. Halvard Leira and Iver B. Neumann, 'The Many Past Lives of the Consul', in Jan Melissen and Ana Mar Fernández (eds), *Consular Affairs and Diplomacy* (Leiden/Boston: Martinus Nijhoff Publishers, 2011), especially 243.

9. Jörg Ulbert and Lukian Prijac (eds), *Consulship in the 19th Century* (Hamburg: DOBU Verlag, 2010), 9.

10. Jesús Núñes Hernández, 'The History of the Spanish Consular Service: An Institution in its Own Right', in Jan Melissen and Ana Mar Fernández (eds), *Consular Affairs and Diplomacy* (Leiden/Boston: Martinus Nijhoff Publishers, 2011), 259.

11. Hernández, 'The History of the Spanish Consular Service', 262.

12. D.C.M. Platt, *The Cinderella Service—British Consuls since 1825* (Hamden, CT: Archon, 1971), 1–2.

13. In the United States, for example, the Foreign Service—created in 1924 by the Rogers Act—combined all consular and diplomatic services into one administrative unit. In the United Kingdom the Eden Reforms of 1943 brought the Consular Service as a whole into the amalgamated Foreign Service, while in the Netherlands the Consular Service, Diplomatic Service, and Translation Service merged into the Foreign Service in 1946.

14. Sir Ivor Roberts (ed.), *Satow's Diplomatic Practice*, sixth edition (Oxford: Oxford University Press, 2009), 251.

15. The Foreign Ministry at a Tipping Point, 15.

16. Article 36 of the Vienna Convention on Consular Relations, 1963. The importance of this provision was highlighted in the clash in 2010 between Australia and China, which had arrested and sentenced an executive with Australian nationality (but of Chinese background) of mining company Rio Tinto without granting Australian consular officials access to the individual—in violation also of a bilateral agreement on consular relations between the two countries. See Frank Ching, 'Did China trash a treaty?', *Japan Times*, 3 April 2010.

17. Article 2 of the Vienna Convention on Consular Relations, 1963.

18. Other than (honorary) consular posts and sections, this may be done through interest sections, representative offices, and front missions, which are all—in contrast to consular

posts and sections—allegedly 'disguised missions'. See G.R. Berridge, *Diplomacy, Theory and Practice*, second edition (New York: Palgrave, 2002), 142. For example, after the Netherlands closed its embassy in Sri Lanka in the 1970s it was represented by an honorary consul general.

19. Article 5 of the Vienna Convention on Consular Relations of 1963, titled 'Consular functions' was a compromise between those in support of a general definition of consular functions and an enumeration of the most important functions. See Luke T. Lee and John Quigley, *Consular Law and Practice*, third edition (Oxford: Oxford University Press, 2008), 107. Cf. the European Convention on Consular Functions of 1967, which remains signed by only eight European member states and ratified by no more than four, and has not yet entered into force.

20. Leira and Neumann, 'The Many Past Lives of the Consul', and Maaike Heijmans and Jan Melissen, 'Foreign Ministries and the Rising Challenge of Consular Affairs: Cinderella in the Limelight', *Foreign Ministries: Managing Diplomatic Networks and Optimizing Value* (Geneva: DiploFoundation, 2007).

21. Professional or career consuls generally contain three classes: consuls-general, consuls, and vice-consuls. A career consul is usually a national of the sending state, but as per the Vienna Convention on Consular Relations consular work may also be carried out by diplomatic staff. Honorary consuls are generally local residents in the receiving state, for which the consular work is not the primary function. Supporting administrative and technical services are carried out by consular employees. A consul-general signifies permanent presence in a particular district, and is only established if the region in question is of special importance to the sending state.

22. For example, Canada, Sweden, the UK, and the Netherlands—to name a few—engage in extensive campaigns, reaching out to the public through travel advice, postcards, public events, television announcements, and social media including Facebook, twitter, and apps for smart phones. It is not uncommon for such outreach to be undertaken in cooperation with well-known and popular third parties including travel guide companies, insurers, and banks.

23. See also Heizō Takenaka, *Speech at the IISS Geo-Economic Strategy Summit*—The Bahrain Global Forum, Manama, 14 May 2010.

24. Leira and Neumann, 'The Many Past Lives of the Consul', 228.

25. Donna Hamilton, 'The Transformation of Consular Affairs in the Twenty-first Century: The United States' Experience', in Jan Melissen and Ana Mar Fernández (eds), *Consular Affairs and Diplomacy* (Leiden/Boston: Martinus Nijhoff Publishers, 2011), 172.

26. For a detailed discussion, see Maaike Okano-Heijmans, 'Changes in Consular Assistance and the Emergence of Consular Diplomacy', in Jan Melissen and Ana Mar Fernández (eds), *Consular Affairs and Diplomacy* (Leiden/Boston: Martinus Nijhoff Publishers, 2011), 21–41.

27. See Gar Pardy, 'Consular and Diplomatic Protection in an Age of Terrorism: Filling the Gaps', in Nicole LaViolette and Craig Forcese (eds), *The Human Rights of Anti-terrorism* (Toronto: IrwinLaw, 2008).

28. The regular consular meetings between EU missions are another indicator of the importance that MFAs attach to consular work.

29. The visa denial practice is sometimes referred to as 'sanctions policy'. Interview with an official of the Dutch MFA, 4 November 2010. On visa diplomacy, see Kevin D. Stinger, 'Visa Diplomacy', *Diplomacy and Statecraft* 15:4 (2004), 655–82, at 656.

30. Donna Lee and Brian Hocking, 'Economic Diplomacy', *International Studies Encyclopedia Online* (Denemark: Robert A. Blackwell Publishing, 2010), Blackwell Reference Online, 18 March.

31. Maura Harty, 'US Visa Policy: Securing Borders and Opening Doors', *Washington Quarterly* 28:2 (2005), 2.

32. On economic diplomacy, see Chapter 21, this volume.

33. On public diplomacy, see Chapter 24, this volume.

34. Berridge, *Diplomacy, Theory and Practice*, 132 and 138–9.

35. Simon Kear, *The political role of consulates: the British consulate-general in Hanoi during the Vietnam war* (Leicester: Centre for the Study of Diplomacy, Leicester University, 1998), 3.

36. Cables sent by the US consulate in Istanbul on 12 July 2004 and in August 2009, released by WikiLeaks in July 2011 and November 2010, respectively. See Chapter 25, this volume, for a discussion of WikiLeaks.

37. Smith Simpson, 'Political Functions of Consuls and Consulates', in Martin F. Herz (ed.), *The Consular Dimension of Diplomacy* (Lanham: University Press of America, 1983), 16.

38. For more on club and network diplomacy, see Chapter 2, this volume.

39. For more on this, see for example Maaike Okano-Heijmans, 'Conceptualizing Economic Diplomacy: The Crossroads of International Relations, Economics, IPE and Diplomatic Studies', *The Hague Journal of Diplomacy* 6:1–2 (2011), 7–36.

40. Kevin Stringer, 'Think Global, Act Local: Honorary Consuls in a Transforming Diplomatic World', *Discussion Papers in Diplomacy*, No. 109 (November) (The Hague: Netherlands Institute of International Relations 'Clingendael', 2007).

41. It should be noted that, although governments have the *responsibility* to protect citizens in distress abroad, most countries do not grant citizens the legal *right* to consular assistance. For further discussion, see Maaike Okano-Heijmans, 'Conceptualizing Economic Diplomacy'; Giorgio Porzio, 'Consular Assistance and Protection: An EU Perspective', *The Hague Journal of Diplomacy* 3:1 (2008), 93–7, at 94, and Ramesh Thakur, 'Governments have a duty to aid citizens caught in a nightmare', *Japan Times*, 5 April 2010. The case of the EU is of particular interest in this regard: with the so-called 'Lisbon Treaty', which entered into force in December 2009, EU-citizens were given 'the right to enjoy, in the territory of a third country in which the Member State of which they are nationals is not represented, the protection of the diplomatic and consular authorities of any Member State on the same conditions as the nationals of that State'. EU member states still differ, however, on the meaning of this clause.

42. See Mattias Sundholm, 'Making the Case for Europe? An Exploratory Study of EU Consular Crisis Management Cooperation as a Means of EU Public Diplomacy', paper presented at the EUSA Eleventh Biennial International Conference Panel, Los Angeles, 23–25 April 2009. Interestingly, the European Commission in its communication with European citizens advertises its role and added value. This stands in stark contrast to the practice of certain MFAs, including the United Kingdom, that wish to circumvent explicit mentioning of their department in safe travel campaigns so as to not arouse suspicion of citizens.

43. Berridge notes that 'the State Department has one major bureau, the Bureau of Public Affairs, devoted almost exclusively to the domestic audience'; Berridge, *Diplomacy, Theory and Practice*, 18.

44. In an attempt to upgrade service levels, cooperation in the consular field is sought with travel operators, insurance companies, and non-governmental organizations—that give

psychological support to imprisoned citizens abroad or their family at home, for example. Furthermore, MFAs may 'outsource' the intake of visas to the private sector (a practice that is coordinated between EU member states in certain countries).

45. See the introduction in this volume by Andrew F. Cooper, Jorge Heine, and Ramesh Thakur, 3.

46. See also Matthew Flinders, 'Public/Private: The Boundaries of the State', in Colin Hay, Michael Lister, and David Marsch (eds), *The State: Theories and Issues* (Basingstoke: Palgrave Macmillan, 2006).

47. This framework, although obviously not the examples, follows Johan Eriksson and Erik Noreen's model to better understand threat image politics. *Setting the Agenda of Threats: An Explanatory Model*, Uppsala Peace Research Paper no. 6 (Uppsala: Uppsala University, Department of Peace and Conflict Research, 2002), <http://www.pcr.uu.se/digitalAssets/18/18591_uprp_no_6.pdf>.

48. Canadian consular official in a personal meeting with the author, The Hague, 19 September 2008.

49. The disputes were with Australian miner Rio Tinto and the Japanese government, respectively. In both cases, China accused the detained foreign nationals/businessmen on suspicion of stealing state secrets and entering a restricted military zone, respectively, apparently attempting to increase the stakes by exerting political pressure.

50. This follows the definition of governance adopted in Jon Pierre and Guy Peters, *Governance, Politics and the State* (Basingstoke: Macmillan Press, 2000), especially 2 and 14.

51. Hugh White, *Looking after Australians overseas* (Sydney: Lowy Institute Policy Brief, 2007), October, <http://www.lowyinstitute.org/publications/looking-after-australians-overseas>.

CHAPTER 27

....

DIPLOMACY AND INTERNATIONAL LAW

....

TOM FARER

DIPLOMACY is conducted for seven generic purposes.[1] The first two are specific to the conditions of intense hostility. One is to communicate the terms on which a belligerent is prepared to suspend coercive activities. The other is to set the long-term framework for normalized relations between the hostile actors.

A third purpose is to persuade other states to join in positive-sum games, that is, an interaction or network of interactions—for example a free-trade regime—that should yield benefits to all which are greater than any could achieve by acting alone. Since states will often be concerned with relative as well as absolute gains, the task of diplomacy here is to illuminate the potential gains for all parties while assuaging concerns about the allocation of those gains.

A fourth purpose is to induce participation in a scheme of reciprocated unilateral actions such as reducing armaments, allowing overflight by commercial airlines, treating diplomatic premises as inviolable, or conducting armed conflict by means consistent with the humanitarian laws of war.

A fifth purpose, important both in conflict-ridden bilateral relations and in the case of insecure allies, is to clarify and reinforce a state's interests and commitments. An exemplary failure of diplomacy in this respect was the 1991 Gulf War. It is unlikely that Saddam Hussein would have invaded Kuwait if the senior US diplomat on the scene had been instructed to tell him that the US would treat an invasion of Kuwait as equivalent to an invasion of the United States. An ongoing illustration of the diplomacy of reassurance is US policy in East Asia where, by maintaining powerful naval and substantial ground forces, the US signals to Japan, South Korea, China, and North Korea alike the strength of its commitment to the security of its allies.

A sixth purpose, one to some degree in contrast to the fifth, is to convey benign intentions to or sympathetic empathy with a potential adversary. One might characterize contemporary American diplomacy towards China as a conscious display of empathy and benignity, hedged, however, by building ties to India and the actions mentioned just above.

Finally, diplomacy is a means for clarifying and confirming the very few prohibitions deemed controlling under all circumstances. They include genocide, other crimes against humanity, and wars to appropriate the resources or territory of other states.

Bearing in mind that the very nature of international law (not merely its substance) is sharply contested, the question this chapter addresses is: what conception of international law best serves diplomacy's purposes?

27.1 INTERNATIONAL LAW

27.1.1 The Mainstream[2]

The generality of lawyers probably still subscribe more-or-less unconsciously to H.L.A. Hart's definition of a legal order as a hierarchical system of authoritative rules: *primary rules* that govern the lives of persons and institutions by allocating rights and responsibilities and declaring the legal consequences of innumerable quotidian activities; and *secondary rules* that set out the means through which the primary rules are 'recognized' as *legally* binding (which distinguishes them from mere moral injunctions, customary courtesies, and transient political understandings), are applied, and are both generated and altered.[3] It is hierarchical in the sense that the system contains an ultimate rule of recognition which enables participants to resolve inconsistencies among primary rules and conflicts among institutions for interpreting and applying them. In a fully developed system of law, according to this view, there is both a supreme rule or set of rules (what we could call the 'constitutional rules') and an apex institution with the authority to apply them. Thus arguably one could say with respect to the legal system of the United States that the ultimate Rule of Recognition is a decision of the Supreme Court applying federal constitutional norms or the rule that the Supreme Court is the unreviewable arbiter of constitutional meanings.

Hart's conception of the legal system makes the international one seem underdeveloped, in that while it has many primary rules that can be analogized to the rules of domestic tort, contract, criminal, administrative, and property law, its secondary rules do not establish autonomous and specialized institutions to generate, alter, and apply the primary rules and do not provide an indisputable apex Rule of Recognition, much less an institution for declaring and applying it to resolve legal conflicts definitively. Indeed, it could be argued, without a centralized procedure for determining whether a given rule has a 'legal' character, international law is more in the nature of a vast network of political arrangements (that assume the form of rules, principles, and institutions) reflecting transient perceptions of national interest.

Today' radical sceptics about the very existence of international law, persons often having links of various strength to the hyper-nationalists of the political right,[4] tend to rely neither on an extrapolation from Hart nor the often cited injunction of the

19th-century English legal scholar John Austin that law consists of orders backed by threats (from which he concluded that international law could not be law since it lacked institutions for predictably enforcing threats of punishment for non-compliance).[5] They rely instead on a conception of sovereignty that makes every state the sole judge of the propriety or necessity of its behaviour. So even if, for instance, a head of state agrees to accept, on the basis of reciprocity, some limitation on the state's freedom of action (for instance, to develop nuclear weapons), she and her successors remain free to change their minds (ostensibly on behalf of the state) at any time without being subject to the claim that in doing so, they have violated a legal obligation.

But what is the practical difference between violating a legal obligation and violating the natural expectation that promises concluded with some measure of formality after arduous negotiations will be kept? The answer at least of an American sceptic like John Bolton, the former US Permanent Representative to the United Nations, would presumably be that the beneficiaries of the promise have no complaint.[6] For like the first to renege, they too have had the right to change their minds. And precisely because the discretion of a sovereign state's government to choose whatever means it believes will advance the state's interests is indefeasible, all parties to any agreement ought to know that consent to be bound can be withdrawn at any point. So even if in the intercourse of individuals, the failure of one to comply with promises made to another might be deemed morally culpable, such culpability does not attend breach of promise in the intercourse of states. After all, an individual speaks for herself when making a promise, while a political leader speaks only as the transient personification of the state and therefore lacks the authority to suspend indefinitely its freedom of action. By this sort of argument radical nationalists hope to gain traction against more cosmopolitan political leaders in domestic debates over foreign policy by stripping international law of any aura of moral compulsion.

Mainstream scholars and practitioners reply to radical sceptics approximately along the following lines. The structure of a society's legal order is a function of its political arrangements. Since it has a radically decentralized political structure, a structure populated by entities that reciprocally attribute to one another a broad (but not unlimited) measure of discretion in defining and pursuing their interests, international society's legal order must have a very different character and structure than the legal order of an independent state. Hart's analysis is not, therefore, irrelevant but it must be applied loosely.

Political sovereignty, as it has come to be understood over the past four centuries, precludes the imposition of norms on dissenting states even by very large majorities except for a very few norms (*jus cogens* in the idiom of international lawyers) regarded by most states as expressing peculiarly important shared values and interests. Even in a refined democratic society laws can in theory—and sometimes in fact—be imposed by small majorities on large and bitterly dissenting minorities. But in the society of sovereign states, other than for the exception noted above, norms become obligatory for each society member only after it consents to be bound. Consent (explicit or implied) is, therefore, the touchstone of validity, the Rule of Recognition.[7]

The theoretical conundrum associated with this mainstream description of the international legal order is plain even to the laity and has, of course, been endlessly debated. If sovereignty is the defining feature of the contemporary international order,[8] and if, as far as law-making is concerned, consent as a condition of legal obligation is deemed a corollary of sovereignty, the claim that consent cannot be withdrawn at will seems inconsistent with the very nature of sovereignty (as radical nationalists continue to argue).

Mainstream scholars,[9] backed by practitioners, have offered several answers to that claim. Approaching it first conceptually: the supposedly logical (i.e. that is definitional) impossibility of being sovereign and at the same time being debarred by a previous exercise of will from exercising it again to evade the earlier commitment is a misunderstanding arising from an ahistorical definition of sovereignty. Sovereignty was never untrammelled authority to do whatever the state authorities wished within the territorial boundaries attributed to them by other states. In practice it always was a bundle of rights and obligations recognized by and owed to other sovereigns the contents of which, like the immunities of diplomats, changed over time. Moreover, mainstream scholars add, even if you were to treat sovereignty as unrestrained will, the conclusion that the sovereign could not bind itself would concede a constraint on the sovereign's will.[10] Thus the a priori argument ties itself in knots.

The principal answer, however, rests on the observable fact that in dealing with one another, political leaders and state officials act as if once they consent to be bound by a norm, their withdrawal of consent simply on the grounds of shifting perceptions of interest is illegitimate and will, moreover, incur the cost of making them appear unusually unreliable. Presumably being so perceived will be an obstacle to future cooperation. Conversely, where norms are declared in ways (such as most if not all General Assembly resolutions)[11] not regarded as capable of creating legal obligation, states can deviate from their original position without comparable costs.

Perhaps the best evidence of this belief in a hierarchy of norms—with some being deemed 'legal' or 'binding' while, for reasons at least partially associated with the process of their articulation, others are not—is the bureaucratic time, energy, and political capital states invest in the process of negotiating international agreements, generally regarded by officials as the principal source of legal norms. As a prelude, political actors in each state must negotiate a single negotiating position. The costs of those internal negotiations in terms of time, energy, acrimony, and political risk may exceed the costs associated with the ensuing interstate negotiation.[12] Why would officials and political leaders bear the cumulative costs of internal and then external negotiations, mainstream scholars ask rhetorically, and why would states so fiercely debate the language of an agreement, why would they in some cases pay diplomatic costs by refusing to sign agreements or attaching contentious interpretations and reservations to them as they sign, if it were understood by all the participants that states were not really committing themselves to anything other than compliance with the negotiated terms *until their ongoing calculations of self-interest turned negative*? Moreover, why would states bother to specify in certain instances that an agreement, for example the Helsinki Accords negotiated at the apex of cold war détente with great care and effort, is not intended to create 'legal' obligations, if there were not an inter-subjective consensus about a qualitative difference between legal and other, less compelling, norms?

Furthermore, the mainstream can fairly argue,[13] how can one plausibly deny this distinction in the face of the widespread educational and professional infrastructure operating under the name of international 'law': courses, degrees, professorships, examinations, offices, private firms, contracts, fees, briefs, and courts dedicated to the acquisition of knowledge about and the identification, application, elaboration, and alteration of principles and rules deemed authoritative, in the sense of having what the great legal scholar Tom Franck called 'compliance pull'.[14] As an epistemological matter, an emperor who to the jaundiced eye of ambassador Bolton appears naked yet is seen by thousands of attendants and courtiers and, more importantly, by other emperors as clothed, even if flimsily, probably is clothed.

Mainstream scholars have treated Article 38 of the Statute of the International Court of Justice as an authoritative statement of how to find the rules of international law.[15] The article lists three as principal sources: international conventions, international custom ('as evidence of a general practice accepted as law'), and 'the general principles of law recognized by civilized nations'. The first of these principal sources, 'international conventions', is plainly consistent with the view that consent is international law's touchstone of validity. In order to make 'custom' consistent with this view, scholars, practitioners, and courts have generally, but to a considerable degree nominally, insisted that whenever claimants invoke custom as evidence of a rule's status as law, they cannot simply show that state practice is consistent with the alleged rule (for example, a rule specifying a certain limit to the territorial sea); in addition those who invoke custom need to show that behavioural consistency with the rule stemmed from a sense of legal obligation to comply (the *opinion juris*).

Not surprisingly, this strategy for aligning custom as a source of law with the touchstone of consent has generated ceaseless unease among international law's mainstream theoreticians. For if a state must consent, expressly or implicitly, in order to be bound by any rule, why would a state feel a legal obligation to adopt a particular position, if it had not *previously* manifested consent?

Scholars have found various ways of breaking out of this apparent circularity.[16] Initially, no doubt, a number of states will adopt a certain practice because it seems consistent with their interests and capabilities or, occasionally, with moral norms that have strong domestic constituencies. Perhaps they do so by informal agreement which may come after some period in which divergent practice proves inconvenient and does not reflect important and conflicting national interests. Particularly where a certain practice is adopted by powerful states, weaker ones may follow suit to avoid conflict. Although the decision to harmonize practice may well be taken without any sense of legal obligation, over time compliance with the iterated standard will tend to be naturalized in the minds of officials and thus become subjectively experienced as part of the corpus of general international law. Naturalization could develop around domestic legislation or executive-branch regulations or judicial decisions impelled by the need to find some rule for resolving a private dispute.

Whatever its conceptual problems, the *opinio juris* requirement has not proven to be a disabling impediment to the invocation of custom in diplomatic discourse and in practice before international tribunals. Where advocates can cite widespread and sustained conformity with a certain behavioural norm and some specific claims that the behaviour in question is required by international law, a state suddenly denying the status of law to the customary practice will naturally bear a considerable burden of persuasion. It will have to question the sufficiency of duration, repetition, continuity, and generality or it will have to show that it had dissented as the custom was forming.[17]

As for justifying the treatment of general principles found in *national* legal systems as a source of international legal norms, perhaps all that can usefully be said is that in the relatively few cases where they are invoked, states have not objected to treating a fundamental principle of their own legal systems as a measure of their legal obligations to one another in the absence of governing conventions or custom.

For mainstream scholars, perhaps the most unsatisfactory feature of their conception of the international legal order is its provision for normative change. In the case of rules adopted through interstate agreements,[18] change is not problematic as long as all parties to the agreement concur in changing it. The most recent iteration will prevail. Where only some parties agree, the matter is no more problematical, as long as the parties concurring in changes to the original agreement accept that vis-à-vis the non-concurring parties, the original terms remain controlling.

With respect to rules stemming from custom, however, the process of change is conceptually messy.[19] Theoretically, once a rule evolving through the conforming practice of states has achieved recognition by diplomats in their discourse among themselves and by scholars in their writings as a rule of law, it is as binding as a rule embodied in an agreement. But it stands to reason that, if all states became convinced at some point in this evolutionary process that a certain rule better expressed their individual interests than any alternative, they would embody the rule in an agreement. So it could be argued that the continuing absence of an agreement long after a custom has allegedly crystallized implies a measure of doubt among some states about the advantages of the rule, or at least of their recognizing it as a rule of *law*. Moreover, by the time there is sufficient conformity of practice to support a claim that a rule has ripened into law, the balance of interests that prompted certain states at an early point in this process of evolution to behave in a way consistent with the rule may have shifted. And so at the very moment of crystallization, those states for which the rule is no longer beneficial may begin to deviate from its injunctions. If, over time, deviance becomes widespread and uniform in character, eventually a different rule could be seen as having crystallized. In theory, however, the initial precedents for rule change will be illegal acts.

In practice, the change process is likely to be marked by debatable evasion of rather than confrontation with a crystallized rule. One evades by distinguishing one's case from those the rule was allegedly intended to cover. For instance, in 1945 the United States affirmed its right to resources on and under the continental shelf. Although under navigable albeit shallow ocean water, the shelf, the US argued, was properly seen as an extension of the landmass of the United States. At the same time the US insisted that the assertion of national jurisdiction over the resources of the shelf did not amount to an extension of the territorial sea beyond the three-mile limit embodied in customary international law. In the view then urged by the US, the three-mile rule was concerned with navigation on the sea and not with resources under it.[20]

Using this to illustrate 'evasion' may well be unfair. Arguably it is simply a reasonable interpretation of a rule the ambiguity of which became apparent once technology had advanced to the point of allowing the extraction of natural resources from land covered by the sea. As a sign of its good faith in asserting jurisdiction over the shelf, the US said it would recognize a comparable assertion of jurisdiction by any other state that was the beneficiary of the same geographical condition, namely submerged land that sloped very gradually off a country's coast before finally, far out to sea, dropping off sharply to great depth.[21]

Good faith or not, rapidly in the wake of the US claim a number of Latin American countries that did not enjoy such a shelf, much less one believed to contain substantial petroleum resources, but did have rich fishing grounds off their coast, asserted national jurisdiction over the living resources in the seas up to a distance from their coasts roughly equivalent to the breadth of the US continental shelf. Implicitly they were saying that the real issue raised by the unilateral US act was control of coastal resources. Some advanced this interest by declaring resource zones. Others seemed to be asserting an extension of the territorial sea.[22] A resulting period of acerbic diplomatic dialogue and acrimonious incidents culminated in the decade-long Law of the Sea Conference which, among other things, produced a new consensus on the breadth of the territorial sea and on the right of countries to assert jurisdiction over their continental shelves, if they had one.

The history of the law of the sea case suggests why conventional rules can be the locus of controversy about their content or application *in a given context* just as easily as customary ones. To be sure, in the case of conventions there is a text. But whether a rule is laid down at one time and place by a text or evolves over time through acts both rhetorical and material, the technological, political, social, and ideological conditions that undergirded the shared identity of perceived interest in having such a rule will not remain constant. And those changes will generate scenarios in which literal application of the rule would lead to outcomes inconsistent with the policy preferences of a few—or possibly many—of the states that supported the rule in the first place.

Consider, for example, the UN Charter, the text that is the starting point of mainstream lawyers for assessing the legality of the use of force across national frontiers. In article 2(4), the Charter states that 'all states shall refrain in their international relations from the threat or use of force against the territorial integrity or political independence of any state, or in any other manner inconsistent with the Purposes of the United Nations'. To the distinguished British international legal scholar Ian Brownlie, those words, adopted in 1945 when the human rights movement was nascent, plainly preclude armed intervention even for the Good-Samaritan purpose of ending crimes against humanity, unless the intervention is authorized by the Security Council.[23]

What was plain to him, however, was by no means plain to every other scholar. In opposition to Brownlie's position, some argued that a brief intervention for the limited purpose of ending genocidal slaughter should not be construed as violating territorial integrity or political independence and, moreover, was clearly consistent with one of the stated purposes of the United Nations, namely 'promoting and encouraging respect for human rights'.[24] Or, if among those threatened with slaughter were nationals of the intervening state, one could argue that intervention to rescue them was an act of self-defence, in that a state consists not only of a territory with defined boundaries but also the people associated with that territory.

A well-ordered national society possesses independent judicial institutions to resolve the ambiguities stemming from the virtually infinite variety of factual settings in which various rules can be invoked. In the society of nations, lacking courts of general and compulsory jurisdiction, the decision stream stems largely from the parties themselves in the form of diplomatic claims and counterclaims and attendant acts and omissions. All that said, it does not follow that rules are incapable of expressing a consensus on what constitutes permissible behaviour in the plainly envisioned standard case. If they suffered from that incapacity then, as noted earlier, it seems unlikely that either private sector actors or states would make the investments they continuously do in finding language to express their desires and expectations.

27.1.2 Against the Mainstream

27.1.2.1 *Policy-Oriented Jurisprudence*

Not long after the Second World War two brilliant academicians at Yale University, the lawyer Myres McDougal and the political scientist Harold Lasswell, fashioned an intellectually impressive challenge to the mainstream description of international law.[25] Often described as 'policy-oriented jurisprudence' or simply as 'The Yale School', it was in part a response to the fact just noted, namely that in the decentralized international authority structure, the legislators and interpreters of the law were the same as its subjects and law was therefore necessarily embedded in the stream of decisions—the claims and counterclaims and attendant acts and omissions—issuing from them in their official capacities as decision-makers in the policy hierarchy of each state.

According to Lasswell and McDougal (and their many acolytes), by expressing the law in the form of more-or-less contextless rules and principles, mainstream writers misrepresent the nature of law and correspondingly ignore the epistemological needs of their addressees which are not courts, but rather authoritative decision-makers confronting all sorts of political, economic, and strategic issues, each in its complex context constituting a distinctive policy challenge. Claims in the language of mainstream law, that is, claims invoking texts and allegedly binding customs, are part of the context surrounding the particular instance of some policy issue that relevant decision-makers face at any given moment, but only one among many dimensions of the decisional problem. These decision-makers are not judges. They are not called upon to decide what is or is not legally permissible by reference to texts or summaries of past decisions made in different and insufficiently specified contexts. Their task is to make judgements that advance some policy. McDougal and Lasswell recommended that the policy goal be a world order characterized by the optimal realization of human dignity.

Two members of the Yale School characteristically distinguish mainstream scholarship as follows:

> The jurisprudence of positivism provides the counter-image to [our] empirical, dynamic conception of law. Its common focus on 'existing' rules, emanating solely from entities deemed equally 'sovereign', does not properly reflect the reality of how law is made, applied, and changed. Positivism remains fixated on the past, trying to reap from words laid down, irrespective of the context in which they were written, the solution to a problem that arises today or tomorrow in very different circumstances. Without identifying the conditioning factors of the past decisions they rely on—such as the personality, political inclinations, gender and cultural background of the decision makers, as well as the mood of the times, and other societal factors—positivists try hard, in an ultimately futile quest for 'certainty' of law, to predict future decisions. But, as they do not take into account changing and changed contexts (e.g. different legislators, judges, shifts in public opinion), their predictions are unlikely to be precise; they may even be inaccurate. Moreover, positivists gain no help from their theory when asked what the law 'should' be.[26]

Although they do not rely exclusively on texts, mainstream scholars are 'positivists' in the sense that they prove the existence of law by reference to evidence that states, through the declarations or acquiescence of their representatives or through operational acts or significant failures to act, have positively manifested consent to be bound in their future actions by certain norms.[27] Their positivism does not preclude, as Yale School acolytes suggest, taking some account of social context. Indeed they cannot avoid doing so when trying to determine what in fact states were consenting to when, for instance, they ratified a particular convention. Since no two settings for the application of a rule are identical and since the creators of a legal rule normally have a two-layered intention—addressing in precise detail some issue of immediate concern but doing it in a way consistent with some broader value or policy goal—the mainstream analyst cannot do justice to the intentions of the signatories or custom-creators without considering the social and political context at the time a rule was negotiated or crystallized. And if they ignored context at the time of a rule's invocation, they would risk applying it in a way that tended to thwart rather than advance the broad purposes of its creators. But if they too take context into account, how do they differ from the Yale School?

To begin with, adherents of the Yale School relentlessly disparage the capacity of rules ('texts') to shape and constrain decision (the 'futile quest for certainty'). Rules are 'fixated on the past'; they are mere 'summaries of past decisions' made in different contexts; they cannot 'predict future decisions'. *For mainstream scholars texts provide an anchor to what could otherwise be a boundless enquiry into context.* Without that anchor, the vast heaps of contextual facts littering the historical ground around any flow of decisions can be appropriated by interested parties and assembled into convenient rationalizations for whatever powerful actors want to do. Moreover, for mainstream lawyers the function of rules is not simply to 'predict the future' behaviour of decision-makers. Rules also function as a metric for assessing proposed and contemporary behaviour and anticipating the reactions of other actors. Changing circumstances will doubtless produce changing interpretations or, more precisely, will alter perceptions of the similarity of a new case's pattern of facts to a previously decided one, to the extent that a different rule of decision will seem best suited to advance the purposes of the original text. But for mainstream analysts, texts or crystallized customs (illuminated in legal texts published by positivist scholars, in semi-official restatements of the law or in diplomatic notes and other official communications) tend to stabilize interpretation, to reduce the advocate's capacity for distinguishing previous cases on the grounds of changed circumstances or an insufficient grasp of the racing 'flow of decisions' in which the formal agreement was only a single landmark among many noted in passing.

Positivists, Yale School acolytes allege, 'gain no help from their theory when asked what the law 'should be'. This seems both to misunderstand the mainstream and to underline another difference between the two conceptions of law. For the mainstream what the law should be is a restraint on the arbitrary or whimsical exercise of power. Of course no rule that does not serve the interests of governing elites in powerful states can aspire to the status of law. But neither can it come to be acknowledged as law if it does not coincidentally promise better outcomes for the less powerful than a condition in which there is no agreed rule of behaviour sufficiently precise to set some limits to interpretation. In laying claim to the resources of its continental shelf, the United States felt it could disarm potential resistance by acknowledging the legal force of similar claims by all similarly situated states regardless of their place in the pecking order of national power.

27.1.2.2 *The Jurisprudence of Rational Choice*

Rational choice legal scholars apply to international law the insights and premises of the law-and-economics intellectual movement that has achieved considerable prominence in US law schools over the past several decades largely as a way of analysing domestic legal issues. Its premise 'is that international law emerges from states acting rationally to maximize their interests, given their perceptions of the interests of other states and the distribution of state power'.[28] They do not track realists like Hans Morganthau in assuming that a state's interests are limited to security and wealth. And they recognize that what passes for state interests can be the result of complex processes of internal contestation among diverse groups and that governments can sometimes behave in irrational ways. Nevertheless, they believe that there is, over time, a broad consistency in the perception of interest that states acquire and, they imply, that in general states act rationally to advance those ends.

Law, they acknowledge, particularly in the form of international agreements, is an important servant of national interest in that such agreements, and presumably the whole process of negotiating and maintaining them, are instrumental in the many circumstances where it is in the interest of states to coordinate and to cooperate. What principally distinguishes rational choice theory from mainstream scholarship is its premise that international law as such does not have a compliance pull or, to put it in rational choice terms, a preference for compliance with international law *because it is 'law'* is not one of the elements that factor into state preferences.

> [Even] if there were a preference among citizens and leaders for international law compliance, the strength of that preference would depend on what citizens and leaders are willing to pay in terms of the other things that they care about, such as security or economic growth. We think that citizens and leaders care about these latter goods more intensely than they do about international law compliance; that preferences for international law compliance tend to depend on whether such compliance will bring security, economic growth and related goods; and that citizens and leaders are willing to forgo international law compliance when such compliance comes at the cost of these other goods.[29]

Since they do not refer to it, presumably they reject the view that through the incorporation of a rule of international law in domestic legislation, or through long-term compliance with a rule and parallel compliance by most other states, or through the continuous invocation of that rule in explaining and justifying the state's behaviour, the rule will come to be seen by officials as the presumptive expression of the national interest; it will have, in other words, a kind of inertial force. In that event, a considerable burden of persuasion would fall on persons insisting at a certain juncture that non-compliance will better advance the national interest. The location of the burden of persuasion can be decisive in shaping the outcome of political no less than legal debates. So on my suggested hypothesis about how compliance induced initially by calculations of interest (exclusive of international law) could come to be seen as integral to the realization of substantive interests, one could coherently claim that international law does have an independent capacity to induce continuing compliance.

Politically conservative rational choice theorists reject not only the proposition that to some significant degree states do in fact comply with international law *because it is law*, but also the proposition that states *should* tend to comply for that reason and that international lawyers should use their influence to encourage compliance for the sake of compliance:

> [W]e cannot condemn a state merely for violating international law...[because the institution of international law] can exert no moral force comparable to the moral force of domestic law [since it] has no democratic pedigree or epistemic authority; it reflects what states have been doing in the recent past and does not necessarily reflect the moral judgment or interests or needs of individuals.[30]

27.1.2.3 *The 'Newstream' Counter-Narratives: Feminist, Third-World, and 'Critical' Perspectives*

Of course there are important differences among these approaches to international law but, for the purpose of this chapter, it is the overlap in their critique of the mainstream and their perceptions of international law that bears on the subject of international law and diplomacy. All three elements of the newstream find mainstream writing about international law to be deeply flawed.[31]

One flaw is conveying the impression that the development of international law is a narrative of progress in advancing the ideals of justice, when in fact it has been an exercise in the rationalization and institutionalization of injustice. The actual methods and substance of international law, newstream scholars contend, have been exclusionary.[32] Until recently, feminist[33] and third-world scholars,[34] NGOs and civil society organizations have not been able to participate in the shaping of international law. Not surprisingly, then, until very recently international law (as described by mainstream scholars and invoked by diplomats) has been unresponsive to the interests of women and, from the newstream perspective, hostile to the aspirations, interests, and values of peoples in the global South.

The third-world stream of scholarship contends, not unpersuasively, that the 19th-century elaboration and spread of international law among the states of the West as a way of talking about international relations was inspired by the necessities of that century's ebullient colonialism: the need (a) to sort out territorial claims, (b) to rationalize and justify the subjugation of indigenous peoples and the concurrent eradication of indigenous political authority (in part by differentiating between 'civilized' states and the 'uncivilized' regimes that had to be swept away or reduced to satellite status, particularly in Africa), and (c) to make the semi-independent world on the fringes of the West secure for private capital investment. Western governments invoked international law to support the gunboats and marines sent to protect the interests of Western bondholders well into the 20th century and continue to invoke it to support economic coercion of governments in the global South expropriating foreign investments. What follows from this historical record, scholars in the third-world stream argue, is that mainstream international law's claim to universality, and to the virtue associated with the idea of the rule of law as the vehicle in any society for equal treatment and respect, is hollow.

The vision of law as a means of institutionalizing and concealing rather than gentling the operation of power in society was a salient theme of the critical legal studies movement that began to acquire a firm footing in US law schools in the 1970s as an outgrowth of the 1960s fierce civil rights and anti-war challenges to the American policy-making elite and in general the long-established order of things. Domestic legal and institutional arrangements were the initial targets of movement scholars, but their broad vision seems reflected to varying degrees in many tributaries of the so-called 'newstream' of international legal scholarship. All of them share with feminist and third-world scholarship a vision of law as rationalizing, naturalizing, and concealing the ruthless operation of power differentials and all have plainly been influenced by the broader postmodern stream of scholarship initially associated more with literature and philosophy, to the extent that its raging currents can be so neatly categorized.[35]

In the process of deconstructing, in the sense of revealing the deep and problematical intellectual and moral structures of, familiar ideas, social practices, and explanatory narratives, postmodernism has problematized the communicative capacity of language and loosened the ties between language and the material realities and social relationships mainstream thought has historically assumed it can and does express.[36] The influence of postmodernism in the field of international law can be seen in the suggestion of some newstream scholars that the use of international law in the course of international relations can most accurately be seen as a language game, in which the players invoke rules and principles, but those rules and principles have no inherent capacity to dictate an outcome in the material world. In short, the whole enterprise of international law is an epiphenomenal cosmetic rhetoric. Meanwhile power veiled by that rhetoric has its way.

Although most postmodern scholars reside on the left of the political spectrum, those who endorse the language-game view of international law are de facto allies of right-wing nationalists like John Bolton and conservative rational choice scholars like Jack Goldstone. After all, if you believe that international law in all its parts is little more than a language game, the claim that states should comply with international law because it is law has neither moral nor prudential force.

27.2 CONCLUSION: DIPLOMACY AND INTERNATIONAL LAW

Millennial hopes for the rule of law in international relations are not needed to support the claim that law, roughly as described in the mainstream narrative, is a useful instrument of diplomacy, just as diplomacy is a means for the development of international law.

In the first place, the principles and rules of international law as ordered and sharpened by leading scholars, by the legally-based claims and counter-claims of governments, and by the legal discourse of intergovernmental institutions and NGOs constitute a specialized, generally understood idiom which can facilitate diplomatic communication. One illustration of the idiom's utility is President John F. Kennedy's decision to call the partial blockade of Cuba during the 1962 missile crisis (see Chapter 46, this volume) a 'quarantine'. His advisers had doubtless informed him that according to leading writers on international law, a 'blockade' constitutes an act of war.[37] Thus employing that word to describe US intentions could have been construed by the Soviet Union and other countries as evidence of US determination to exploit the crisis for the purpose of overthrowing the regime of Fidel Castro or, at the very least, humiliating Moscow to the greatest extent possible. Conversely, the choice of 'quarantine' implied a narrower objective, an implication consistent with other signals being sent to Soviet Premier Nikita Khrushchev.

Secondly, principles and rules provide a relatively stable framework for quotidian decision-making by government and non-governmental actors dealing with transnational issues. A ship owner can plan routes knowing that commercial vessels enjoy free passage through straits and territorial seas. The owners of new commercial airlines know the procedures that will enable them to overfly the territory of most countries. Diplomats can rely on immunity from the criminal law of the countries where they operate. And governments can enter into complex schemes of cooperation and coordinated unilateral measures with the expectation that cooperation and coordination will endure in the face of ever-changing circumstances which could, at one point or another, transiently or marginally affect in unanticipated ways the perceptions of national interest which initially drove the project. Governments do not—and as a practical matter cannot—recalculate the national interest every day in order to decide whether to adhere to normative arrangements and practices. Until circumstances change conspicuously, they tend to comply with rules and principles perceived as law *because formal agreements intended by the parties to constitute 'legal' arrangements and long-established and broadly recognized customary rules embody calculations of self-interest made with great deliberation.* Goldsmith and Posner acknowledge much the same point when they write that 'when states coordinate with each other or cooperate, they need to establish *a point of coordination*. For this purpose, interpretive techniques [peculiar to the legal profession] are helpful.'[38]

But why call them and the texts and customs they construe legal? If like Goldsmith and Posner and Bolton, one believes that agreements and custom do not create legal obligations that should be deemed like their domestic law counterparts as binding *because they are law*, then one could instead refer to those techniques, indeed to the whole complex of activities and materials that in diplomacy parade under the banner of the legal, as a 'special kind of politics, one that relies heavily on precedent, tradition, interpretation, and other practices and concepts familiar from domestic law'.[39]

If that is an option, it is plainly one that has been ignored over the centuries and continues to be ignored. It is not only lawyers and law professors who cling to the idea that there is a qualitative difference between political understandings, no matter how detailed, and understandings intended by the parties to create obligations similar in character to the obligations of citizens stemming from domestic law. State elites also cling to this view, even though it results in a constraint on the exercise of discretion by potentially increasing the costs of non-compliance beyond those they would experience if all agreements among them were seen as mere products of transient political convenience.

Goldsmith and his intellectual associates overlook a third way in which international law as 'law' facilitates diplomacy in general and, in particular, its central task in a nuclear-armed, tightly-integrated world, namely that of minimizing the peculiarly dangerous interstate conflicts that are driven more by nationalist passions than material interests, like conflicts over slivers of territory made by nationalist demagogues to appear as part of the living flesh of every citizen in each concerned country. The evocative idea of the 'rule of law' can assist prudent political leaders and their diplomats in containing the demagogues. Legal norms help to delimit and detoxify disputes, as can the availability of an international court and long-established precedents for international arbitration.

The sum of the matter, then, is this. Governing elites have long concluded that imputing the character of law to certain norms and using legal texts as a focal point for diplomatic discourse facilitates the pursuit of national interests. In this judgement they are joined by the officials of intergovernmental organizations and NGOs and by private-sector actors who necessarily rely on a stable framework of norms to protect trade and investments. It would be presumptuous, if not absurd, to disregard this vast confluence of convictions about the peculiar nature and substantial utility of international law in the practice of diplomacy.

Notes

1. On the nature and purposes of diplomacy, see Adam Watson, *Diplomacy* (Philadelphia: Institute for the Study of Human Issues, 1983); Harold Nicholson, *Diplomacy* (Oxford: Oxford University Press, 1950); James Der Derian, *On Diplomacy* (Oxford: Basil Blackwell, 1987); and Garrett Mattingly, *Renaissance Diplomacy* (London: Jonathan Cape, 1955).

2. For the broad distinction between 'mainstream' and 'newstream', see in particular Deborah Cass, 'Navigating the Newstream: Recent Critical Scholarship in International Law', *Nordic Journal of International Law* 65 (1996), 341–83.

3. H.L.A. Hart, *The Concept of Law* (Oxford: Clarendon Press, 1994).

4. See, for instance, Charles Krauthammer, 'The Curse of Legalism', *The New Republic*, 6 November 1989, 44–50.

5. John Austin, *The Province of Jurisprudence Determined and The Uses of the Study of Jurisprudence* (London: Weidenfelt and Nicolson, 1954).

6. John H. Bolton, 'Is There Really 'Law' in International Affairs', *Transnational Law & Contemporary Problems* 10 (2000), 1–48.

7. See Hersh Lauterpacht's eighth edition of L. Oppenheim, *International Law: A Treatise*, vol. 1 (Philadelphia: David McKay, 1963), 817. This treatise is a classical expression of the Mainstream (or 'Positivist') conception of international law.

8. On sovereignty generally see Ian Brownlie, *Principles of Public International Law*, 5th ed. (Oxford: Oxford University Press, 1998), 289–99.

9. Among whom the author includes himself.

10. Brownlie, *Principles of Public International Law*, 290, quoting the ruling of the Permanent Court of International Justice in the *Wimbledon* case: 'the right of entering into international engagements is an attribute of State sovereignty' (1923), PCIJ, Ser. A, no. 1, p. 25.

11. Very occasionally the General Assembly emits 'Declarations' that purport to clarify the implications of existing international legal norms of a general character. See, for instance, The Declaration on the Granting of Independence to Colonial Countries and Peoples (Resolution 1514–XV, 1960) which declared the right to self-determination of all non-self-governing peoples within colonial boundaries which were implicitly deemed to be the frontiers of the envisioned decolonized states. For positivist scholars the evidentiary value of such declarations in establishing norms of international law is a function of the depth and breadth of their support in the Assembly.

12. I write from personal experience early in my career at the US Department of Defense where, in 1962, I was involved in a minor way in the sale of Polaris missiles to Britain and the negotiation and ratification of the Limited Test Ban Treaty of 1963.

13. One of the most respected instances of such argument is Louis Henkin's *How Nations Behave* (New York: Columbia University Press, 1979).

14. Thomas Franck, 'Legitimacy in the International System', *American Journal of International Law* 82 (1988), 708.

15. See *Restatement of the Law Third: The Foreign Relations Law of the United States*, Volume 1, Sections 102 and 103 (St. Paul: American Law Institute Publishers, 1986), 24–39.

16. For a particularly lucid discussion of customary law, see Anthony D'Amato, *The Concept of Custom in International Law* (Ithaca, NY: Cornell University Press, 1971).

17. An example would be Saudi Arabia's and South Africa's abstentions (an abstention in this context being a polite 'no' vote) when, in 1948, the General Assembly adopted almost unanimously the Universal Declaration on Human Rights.

18. The rules governing the creation, interpretation, modification, and termination of treaties are set out in the Vienna Convention on the Law of Treaties (1969), UN Treaty Series, Vol. 1155, p. 331 (2005).

19. See D'Amato, *Concept of Custom in International Law*; Brownlie, *Principles of Public International Law*, 4–11.

20. See Tom Farer, 'United States Policy on the Law of the Sea', in Ralph Zacklin (ed.), *Western Hemisphere Perspectives on the Law of the Sea* (Amsterdam: Sijhtoff, 1974).

21. Presidential Proclamation No. 2667, concerning the Policy of the United States with respect to the Natural Resources of the Subsoil and Sea Bed of the Continental Shelf, *Department of State Bulletin* 13 (1945), 485–6.

22. See F.V. Garcia-Amador, 'The Latin American Contribution to the Development of the Law of the Sea', *American Journal of International Law* 68 (1974), 33–50.

23. Ian Brownlie, 'Humanitarian Intervention', in J.N. Moore (ed.), *Law and Civil War in the Modern World* (Baltimore: Johns Hopkins Press, 1974), 217.

24. Jane Stromseth, 'Rethinking Humanitarian Intervention', in J.L. Holzgrefe and Robert Keohane (eds), *Humanitarian Intervention* (Cambridge: Cambridge University Press, 2003), 237.

25. See M.S. McDougal & Associates, *Studies in World Public Order* (New Haven: Yale University Press, 1960); M.S. McDougal, *Law and Minimum World Order* (New Haven: Yale University Press, 1961); and M.S. McDougal and Gray Dorsey, 'Agora: McDougal-Lasswell Redux', *American Journal of International Law* 82 (1988), 41–57.

26. Siegfried Wiessner and Andrew Willard, 'Policy-Oriented Jurisprudence and Human Rights Abuses in Internal Conflict: Toward a World Public Order of Human Dignity', in Steven Ratner and Anne-Marie Slaughter (eds), *The Methods of International Law* (Washington, DC: American Society of International Law, 2004), 52–3.

27. On positivism, see, Bruno Simma and Andreas Paulus, 'The Responsibility of Individuals for Human Rights Abuses in Internal Conflicts: A Positivist View', in Ratner and Slaughter (eds), *Methods of International Law*.

28. Jack L. Goldsmith and Eric A. Posner, *The Limits of International Law* (Oxford: Oxford University Press, 2005), 3.

29. Goldsmith and Posner, *The Limits of International Law*, 9.

30. Goldsmith and Posner, *The Limits of International Law*, 199.

31. Residing both within and above the Newstream in the form of brilliantly illuminating expositions of the historical development and enduring problems of international law are the abundant works of Martti Koskenniemi, in particular, *The Gentle Civilizer of Nations: The Rise and Fall of International Law 1870–1960* (Cambridge: Cambridge University Press, 2005) and *From Apology to Utopia* (Cambridge: Cambridge University Press, 2005).

32. See Cass, 'Navigating the Newstream'; David Kennedy, 'A New Stream of International Law Scholarship', *Wisconsin International Law Journal* 7 (1988), 1–49.

33. For a brief but lucid summary, see Hillary Charlesworth, 'Feminist Methods in International Law', in Ratner and Slaughter (eds), *Methods of International Law*: 'Feminist methods seek to expose and question the limited bases of international law's claim to objectivity and impartiality.' See also Hillary Charlesworth, Christine Chinkin, and Shelley Wright, 'Feminist Approaches to International Law', *American Journal of International Law* 85 (1991), 613–45.

34. See Anthony Angie, *Imperialism, Sovereignty, and the Making of International Law* (Cambridge: Cambridge University Press, 2005).

35. See Nigel Purvis, 'Critical Legal Studies in Public International Law', *Harvard International Law Journal* 32:1 (1991), 81–128.

36. For a helpful overview of postmodern thought, see John Paul Jones III, Wolfgang Natter, and Theodore Schatzki, *Postmodern Contentions: Epochs, Politics, Space* (New York: Guilford Press, 1993).

37. See Oppenheim, *International Law*.

38. Goldsmith and Posner, *Limits of International Law*, 202–3.

39. Goldsmith and Posner, *Limits of International Law*, 202.

CHAPTER 28

THE VIENNA CONVENTIONS ON DIPLOMATIC AND CONSULAR RELATIONS

JAN WOUTERS, SANDERIJN DUQUET,
AND KATRIEN MEUWISSEN

28.1 INTRODUCTION

THE 1961 Vienna Convention on Diplomatic Relations (hereinafter 'VCDR')[1] and the 1963 Vienna Convention on Consular Relations (hereinafter 'VCCR')[2] form the core of international diplomatic and consular law. To a large extent, the VCDR codified customary rules on bilateral diplomatic relations between states.[3] Meanwhile, its provisions have largely become part of general international law themselves.[4] With 187 state parties, its application is truly global.[5] The VCCR equally found its origins in the United Nations' striving for the codification of international law. Contrary to its diplomatic counterpart, which was also concluded at the Neue Hofburg in Vienna, agreement had to be found among delegates on a greater number of disputed issues in consular law than had been the case for diplomatic law in 1961.[6] It was therefore not considered to be a simple codification of customary law,[7] although its main provisions have acquired customary status over time[8] and 173 states have ratified the Convention. The VCCR embodies a general framework of minimum standards and both recognizes the validity of other agreements, bilateral or regional, which had been in existence before the VCCR came into force and the conclusion of agreements supplementing, extending, or amplifying provisions of the VCCR.[9]

This chapter aims to examine, without striving for completeness: the establishment of diplomatic and consular relations (section 28.2), the diplomatic and consular functions (section 28.3), and the application of privileges, immunities, and inviolability in recent case law (section 28.4).

28.2 ESTABLISHMENT OF DIPLOMATIC AND CONSULAR RELATIONS

Under international law, the recognition of a state, the establishment of diplomatic or consular relations, and the establishment of a permanent mission have to be distinguished.[10] The establishment of diplomatic relations is distinct from but can precede the establishment of a diplomatic representation, often referred to as a diplomatic mission.[11] The establishment of diplomatic and consular relations and missions is carried out by mutual consent (Art. 2 VCDR and Art. 2, §1 VCCR). According to the VCDR, the establishment process commences via a formal request made by the ministry of foreign affairs of the sending state to the receiving state's authorities. The actual decision on the opening of a diplomatic mission is taken by the head of state or government.[12] States deciding to establish diplomatic relations herewith concurrently imply the establishment of consular relations, unless stated otherwise.[13] Consular relations can also be established regardless of the existence of diplomatic relations;[14] the termination of diplomatic relations does therefore not *ipso facto* involve the severance of consular relations.[15]

International diplomatic law governs the formal accreditation process of diplomatic agents.[16] A diplomatic representative is appointed by the head of the sending state whereupon his name is submitted to the government of the host state.[17] The appointment of an ambassador is announced in a 'Letter of Credence' signed by the head of the sending state and addressed to the head of the receiving state, in order to receive *agrément*.[18] However, since the essence of the *agrément* procedure is its informality, the VCDR does not prescribe a form or method to be used.[19] The ministry of foreign affairs of the receiving state is notified of the details of the appointment of members of the mission.[20] The head of a diplomatic mission is considered as having taken up his functions in the receiving state either when he has presented his credentials or when he has notified his arrival and a true copy of his credentials has been presented to the ministry of foreign affairs of the receiving state.[21] Similarly, the sending state will request the receiving state to grant an '*exequatur*' to enable the commissioned head of a consular post[22] to be admitted to the exercise of his functions.[23] The VCCR does not spell out any formal requirements for the consular exequatur, but does require the receiving state to immediately notify the competent authorities of the consular district of its authorization and admittance of a head of a consular post, even provisionally to the exercise of his functions.[24] The Conventions do not compel a receiving state to motivate its decision not to grant the necessary authorization to a foreign diplomat or consul.[25]

28.3 Diplomatic and Consular Functions

28.3.1 Diplomatic Functions

28.3.1.1 *The Vienna Convention on Diplomatic Relations*

Article 3, §1 of the Convention on Diplomatic Relations enumerates the functions of a diplomatic mission: (a) representing the sending state in the receiving state, (b) protecting the interests of the sending state and its nationals in the receiving state, (c) negotiating with the government of the receiving state, (d) ascertaining the conditions and developments in the receiving state and reporting thereon to the sending state, (e) promoting friendly relations between the sending state and the receiving state, and developing their economic, cultural, and scientific relations. The first function of representation is often overlooked or naively minimized according to Berridge,[26] although it embraces all functions subsequently listed in Art. 3 VCDR.[27] Three subsidiary functions can be distinguished as being part of the representational function: protection, negotiation, and observation.[28] The list contained in Article 3 VCDR is not exhaustive.[29]

Article 3, §2 VCDR stipulates that the performance of consular functions by a diplomatic mission should not be prevented.[30] The legal framework for the performance of all consular functions by diplomats is the VCCR rather than the VCDR.[31] A diplomat performing consular tasks nevertheless is granted diplomatic immunity according to the provisions of the latter Convention, since he is acting within his official functions.[32] Members of a diplomatic mission assigned to the consular section or charged with the performance of consular functions do not have to request a consular 'exequatur',[33] although their names will be submitted to the ministry of foreign affairs of the receiving state.[34] The realization of the functions described in Article 3 VCCR[35] by diplomatic agents will differ depending on the various circumstances in the receiving state and bilateral agreements between states.[36]

28.3.1.2 *Diplomatic Functions in the 21st century*

The basic functions of diplomats have changed surprisingly little over time.[37] The context of diplomatic practice, on the contrary, did change significantly. Since the introduction of the VCDR, a major shift has been brought about by the process of globalization.[38] Whereas diplomacy used to be an interstate affair, globalization introduced new relevant actors[39] such as international organizations, multinational enterprises, and NGOs.[40] Under influence of new circumstances, the focus, method, and procedures of diplomatic practice have changed.[41] In several cases, the development of political systems other than a classical state have introduced diplomatic relations of sub-state governments,[42] of supranational organizations,[43] and of parliaments.[44]

Furthermore, attention is paid to performance management in order to enhance supervision and transparency of diplomatic missions.[45] Informing and mobilizing civilians is seen as essential to promote friendly relations among states and to influence public opinion in the receiving state ('public diplomacy').[46] The development of new means of communication such as the Internet allows for efficient communication with civilians; setting up a web site of the diplomatic mission is an essential requirement nowadays.[47] Business enterprises also became highly relevant for diplomacy: an important function of a diplomatic mission is indeed to attract foreign investors and to promote bilateral trade between the sending state and the receiving state ('economic diplomacy').[48] Furthermore, there is the growing influence of multilateralism on diplomatic missions: international topics such as climate change, energy policy, and HIV/AIDS, which are discussed at international conferences and international organizations, are important items on the diplomatic agenda. Whereas in the first place ministers of foreign affairs and heads of government represent countries at international summits, diplomatic missions play an important role in respect of the preparation and follow-up of these summits.[49] Diplomatic missions often dispose of experts to focus on a specific international theme.[50] Next to a 'functional specialization', the emergence of multilateralism entails the merging of multiple bilateral diplomatic missions into 'territorial units', extending the sphere of competence of these diplomatic missions while facilitating thematic specialization within these units.[51] Lastly, technological developments, specifically in the area of communication, have an important impact on diplomatic relations.[52] The use of Internet and email allow for international negotiations by diplomats physically situated in multiple countries, an evolution which affects the role of diplomatic missions.[53] This leads to new forms of presence in countries, such as travelling ambassadors for countries where there is no permanent diplomatic representation.[54] The emergence of 'rapid' means of communication also entails the availability of more information, and underlines as such the important function of diplomatic missions to filter out pertinent data. In view of the particular knowledge of diplomatic missions concerning the receiving state, these missions have the expertise to gather useful information on the local situation and to inform the sending state effectively.[55]

28.3.2 Consular Functions

28.3.2.1 *The Vienna Convention on Consular Relations*

One of the major challenges during the 1963 treaty negotiations was to define standards for the consular functions. This resulted in the enumeration in the VCCR of a broad range of tasks for consular agents.[56] According to the non-exhaustive list of Article 5 VCCR, consular functions consist of: (a) protecting the interests of the sending state and of its nationals; (b) furthering the development of commercial, economic, cultural, and scientific relations between the sending and the receiving state; (c) ascertaining conditions and developments in the commercial, economic, cultural, and scientific life of the receiving state; (d) issuing passports and travel documents; (e) helping and assisting nationals; (f) and (g) performing notarial and administrative functions; (h) and (i) safeguarding the interests of minors and other persons lacking full capacity who are nationals of the sending state; (j) transmitting and executing judicial and extrajudicial documents; (k) and (l) exercising rights of supervision and inspection in respect of vessels and aircrafts having the nationality of or which are registered in the sending state and extending assistance to these vessels and aircraft and to their crews. As the final paragraph (m) of Art. 5 VCCR spells out, consular functions are not limited to the foregoing enumeration since consular agents are permitted to perform any other function entrusted to a consular post by the sending state which is not prohibited by the laws of the receiving state. In special circumstances and with the consent of the receiving state, these consular functions can be exercised outside the consular district.[57] Upon notification to the receiving state, a consular post of the sending state may even exercise consular functions in another state[58] or exercise consular functions in the receiving state on behalf of a third state.[59]

In certain prescribed circumstances, consular officers can perform diplomatic acts. Art 17 VCCR distinguishes three conditions that have to be met for a consular officer to be authorized to execute diplomatic functions: (1) the sending state does not have a diplomatic mission of its own in the state concerned nor is represented by a diplomatic mission of a third state, (2) the consular officer has the consent of the receiving state, (3) and this performance of diplomatic functions cannot affect its consular status. These conditions stress the subsidiary role a consular agent is allocated in diplomatic law and the extraordinary character of the performance of a consular agent of acts of a more political nature.[60] The mere exercise of diplomatic functions by a consular agent does not confer upon him any right to claim diplomatic privileges and immunities as foreseen in the VCDR.[61]

Consular functions are also described in the 1967 European Convention on Consular Functions, adopted in the context of the Council of Europe, which recently came into force following the ratification by the Republic of Georgia on 9 June 2011.[62] The European Convention focuses specifically on the consular functions, since the Committee of Governmental Experts that prepared the Convention reasoned that the subject of 'consular privileges, immunities, and relations' was already satisfactorily covered in the VCCR.[63] Articles 2 to 16 of the Strasbourg Convention extend the scope of consular functions and grant new functions to consular officers in those fields where their role was considered most useful,[64] leading to a more detailed and modern codification of consular functions compared to Art. 5 VCCR.[65] Certain elements considered to be inherent to the European consular context also found their way into the Convention.[66] The European Convention does not contain any provision similar to that in Article 70 VCCR, governing the exercise of consular functions by the members of a diplomatic mission.

28.3.2.2 *Consular Assistance and Protection*

Consular functions particularly relevant for individuals are the different forms of consular assistance and protection offered abroad, as foreseen in Art. 5, (a), (e) and (i) VCCR.[67] After a consular officer has established that an individual is a national of the sending state, protection may be offered in different forms: coordination of the repatriation of the individual, settlement of disputes with local authorities or private actors, assistance in case of emergencies and natural disasters, visits to nationals in the hospital or prison, etc.[68] The freedom of communication and contact between a consular agent and a national stipulated in Article 36, § 1, (a) VCCR is a prerequisite for access to consular assistance and, subsequently, the effective fulfilment of other consular functions.[69] Recent developments such as the growing global mobility of individuals have amongst others resulted in an increase in the number of foreigners being charged with criminal offences and thus in need of consular access.[70] The international community in Article 36, § 1, (b) acknowledged the possibility for consuls to support their nationals facing criminal charges in a receiving state, which has evolved into a global practice.[71] The rationale therefore is to oversee that the police and judicial system treats the foreign detainee fairly.[72] However, neither Article 5 nor Article 36 VCCR imposes an obligation on the part of the sending state to exercise consular functions.[73]

Article 36 VCCR is regularly invoked by individuals and states in national and international proceedings on the VCCR.[74] Courts' decisions on the article—especially on the existence of a duty of officials of the receiving state to inform foreigners on their rights to consular access and on the appropriate judicial remedy—vary to a great extent.[75] In 1999, the Inter-American Court on Human Rights issued an advisory opinion in which it recognized that Article 36 creates individual rights.[76] The International Court of Justice on its part addressed the VCCR on the merits in two recent cases of alleged violations of the consular rights under Article 36 VCCR of individuals sentenced to death in the United States: the 2001 *LaGrand* case[77] and the 2004 *Avena and Other Mexican Nationals* case.[78][79] In the first case, concerning two German brothers on death row, the ICJ noted that the language of Article 36, §1, (b) VCCR does not leave room for misinterpretation where it stipulates that 'the said authorities shall inform the person concerned *without delay*[80] of his rights under this subparagraph'.[81] The ICJ in the *LaGrand* case provided a rare instance in which a treaty obligation, namely the right to consular assistance of nationals of the sending state in a receiving states, was recognized to affect both the rights of the sending state (the so-called 'right to consul')[82] and the individual rights of the national concerned,[83] which are moreover both subject to international adjudication.[84] The latter ICJ case concerned fifty-two Mexican nationals convicted to the death penalty in the United States who were unable to communicate with the Mexican consulate in order to get consular assistance.[85] Moreover, the consulate was not given the opportunity to correspond with the prisoners and to arrange for their legal representation. The interdependence of the violation of rights of the individual and those of the sending state under Art. 36 VCCR was expressly confirmed in the 2004 ICJ *Avena* case.[86] The Court further decided that the duty to inform a prisoner 'without delay' of his rights under the VCCR may vary according to circumstances, but should nevertheless take place upon realization 'that the person is a foreign national, or once there are grounds to think that the person is probably a foreign national'.[87] The United States was found to have violated this standard with respect to fifty-one out of the fifty-two Mexican nationals involved.[88]

In the direct aftermath of this case law, the United States withdrew from the Optional Protocol to the Vienna Convention on Consular Relations, concerning the Compulsory Settlement of Disputes, which had formed the basis for ICJ jurisdiction in the discussed

LaGrand and *Avena* cases.[89] To bring the country into compliance with its international legal obligations and to streamline the various approaches taken by American courts in Article 36 cases,[90] the United States intends to find a solution through the proclamation of new legislation.[91]

28.3.2.3 *Administrative and Legal Consular Functions*

The consular agent is also tasked with the performance of more basic administrative, legal, and notarial functions in the receiving state,[92] all of which demand a basic knowledge of the local laws and regulations.[93] The consul is amongst others involved in the issuance of passports, visa, and other travel documents recognized by a sending state;[94] notarial and registration services, such as declarations of adoption or parenthood, the administration of estates, marriage and divorce; depositions, service of process, and the transmittance of judicial and extrajudicial documents. The consul renders these services in the clear interest of the sending state and finds himself therefore instructed by governmental officials performing similar functions at home.[95] On the other hand, the general duty of all consular officers to respect the laws and regulations of the receiving state is of particular importance to consuls exercising public authority.[96] The sometimes delicate balance that has to be found on the one hand in respecting local laws and customs and on the other hand in guidelines from the sending states, has resulted in a variety of practices as to the details of the execution of certain consular functions, such as the role of a consul in regard to marriage, for which the countries have retained control.[97]

28.3.3 Diplomatic vs Consular Functions

The functions of a diplomatic and a consular agent are to be distinguished. Consular functions do not have a representative or political character and are instead of a more commercial, practical, and administrative nature.[98] The absence of the representational function consequently impedes a consular agent to be authorized to bring or defend legal proceedings on behalf of his state in the receiving country, except when expressly mandated to do so.[99] Next to this, the diplomatic functions are mostly carried out interacting with the central government of the receiving state, as opposed to consular functions, which are performed through contacts with local actors such as enterprises, police or prison officers, the cultural sector, and so on.[100]

Granting that there are important differences between the two Conventions, clear intersections are to be observed.[101] First, Lee and Quigley note that, because of the growing interconnectedness of politics and economic and commercial affairs of sending states abroad, in many instances a complete distinction of diplomatic and consular functions is considered unfeasible.[102] Art. 5 (a) VCCR for example tasks the consul to protect all interests of the sending state and of its nationals, both individuals and enterprises, in the receiving state, without further specification. Denza correctly notes that a distinction of the diplomatic and consular functions should be made based on how the function is carried out and the methods used, rather than on a textual reading of Articles 3 VCDR and 5 VCCR.[103] Second, as explained in more detail already, the Conventions foresee the possibility of consular functions being performed by diplomatic agents and diplomatic functions being performed by consular mission respectively. Third, although admittedly the functions listed in Article 5 VCCR are intended to be more detailed and specific in comparison to the broadly formulated functions in Article 3 VCDR, neither article is intended to be exhaustive.

28.4 Privileges, Immunities, and Inviolability

Both the VCDR and the VCCR include provisions on privileges, immunities, and inviolability. However, in neither one of the Conventions these terms are defined. In general,[104] a distinction between the different concepts has to be made as follows. 'Immunity' encompasses immunity from jurisdiction (Art. 31, §1 VCDR; Art. 43 VCCR) and immunity from execution (Art. 31, §3 VCDR; Art. 45, §4 VCCR). 'Inviolability' entails on the one hand a special (positive) duty of protection for the receiving state, and on the other hand a (negative) duty for the latter to abstain from exercising any sovereign right, in particular enforcement rights.[105] 'Privileges', in turn, can be best understood as 'other advantages than immunities and inviolability'.[106] Contrary to immunities, which are procedural in nature, privileges are substantive rights: a privilege denotes an exemption from laws or regulations, whereas an immunity does not imply any exemption from substantive law, but confers procedural protection from the enforcement processes in the receiving state.[107] The rules laid down in the VCDR regarding diplomatic privileges, immunities, and inviolability are mainly based on customary international law and have become international custom themselves.[108] Before the elaboration of the VCCR only very limited consular immunity and inviolability, and no privileges, were accepted as customary international law.[109] However, today, the rules laid down in the VCCR regarding consular privileges, immunities, and inviolability are also generally recognized as international custom.[110]

Diplomatic and consular advantages are justified by a functional need. The Preamble of both the VCDR and the VCCR states that the purpose of privileges and immunities is not to benefit individuals but to ensure the efficient performance of their respective functions.[111] While the ratio for diplomatic and consular immunities is the same, as the content of diplomatic and consular functions differs,[112] the scope of diplomatic/consular immunity varies accordingly. Diplomats carry out more sensitive political work for which guaranteed confidentiality is essential, while consuls do not formally represent the sending sovereign.[113] Consequently, the protection of diplomats has a larger scope than the protection of consuls: whereas diplomats and their missions enjoy personal immunity and absolute inviolability, the protection of consuls is limited to official consular acts and functional inviolability.[114]

Since states have a reciprocal interest in respecting diplomatic and consular law (being both sending and receiving state), immunities, inviolability, and privileges of diplomats and consuls are in general well respected. Moreover, in view of this reciprocity, consuls are sometimes accorded privileges and immunities beyond what is essential for their official functions. In this regard, it should be noted that next to the VCCR, bilateral treaties are governing consular relations between many states. As such, it is important for posts to check whether bilateral consular conventions are applicable to their situation, even when both countries are parties to the VCCR.[115] Lastly, it should be noted that the privileges and immunities accorded to honorary consuls are sometimes more limited than privileges and immunities enjoyed by career consuls.[116] Chapter II of the VCCR applies to consular posts headed by career consuls, while the provisions of Chapter III VCCR govern consular posts headed by honorary consular officers (Art. 1, §2 VCCR). This chapter focuses on the rules applicable for career consuls, while reference is made to the applicable rules for honorary consuls.

28.4.1 Inviolability of Diplomatic and Consular Premises

The inviolability of diplomatic premises (Art. 22 VCDR) is similar to the inviolability of consular premises (Art. 31 VCCR),[117] with some notable differences.[118] The receiving state must take all appropriate steps to protect the diplomatic/consular premises (positive duty), while it is forbidden for agents of the receiving state to enter these premises without due consent (negative duty). The inviolability of diplomatic missions is strictly interpreted: without consent of the head of the mission, the agents of the receiving state may not enter the diplomatic missions (Art. 22, §1 VCDR). Even when the receiving state believes that the inviolability is being abused and the premises are used in a manner 'incompatible with the functions of the mission' (which is prohibited under Art. 41 VCDR), the receiving state does not have a right of entry without the permission of the head of mission.[119] In case illegal activities take place in a diplomatic mission, possible solutions should be found through diplomatic negotiation, or—as *ultimum remedium*—the declaration of *persona non grata* of a diplomatic agent (Art. 9 VCDR) or the termination of diplomatic relations with the sending state (Art. 45 VCDR). The International Court of Justice confirmed this principle in the *US—Iran Hostages Case*.[120]

The protection provided by the VCCR is more limited.[121] The VCCR allows officials of the receiving state to enter consular premises without consent of the head of the post, if the officials secured consent of the designee of the head of the post or of the head of the diplomatic mission. Moreover, the parts of the consular premises which are not exclusively used for the purpose of the work of the consular post (such as a kitchen) can be entered without any consent. Even more, in case of fire or another disaster 'requiring prompt protective action' the consent of the head of the consular post may be assumed. The more limited protection of consular posts under the VCCR can be traced back to the fact that traditionally (i.e. before the VCCR), inviolability of consular posts was not recognized as a rule of customary international law.[122] Article 31, §2 VCCR has been the result of a compromise between states which favoured absolute immunity of consular posts (such as the former Communist states), and states which favoured conditional immunity of consular posts (such as Nigeria, Greece, Japan, and the UK).[123]

Both the VCDR and the VCCR put forward the positive duty for the receiving state to take all appropriate steps to protect diplomatic/consular premises against any intrusion or damage and to prevent any disturbance of the peace of the premises or impairment of their dignity (Art. 22, §2 VCDR; Art. 31, §3 VCCR). The requested protection is not absolute: 'appropriate steps' are to be interpreted as measures which are proportionate in light of the security risk at hand.[124] This obligation may be reflected in special domestic laws, or it may be left to the police in the circumstances of each case. No permanent surveillance can be expected, but when authorities are aware of specific threats, they are obliged to provide an appropriate level of protection.[125] In case the receiving state does not provide the appropriate protection against intrusion of diplomatic/consular premises or the occurrence of damage, it has to make reparation for the injury caused.[126]

A final element of diplomatic inviolability is that the premises of the mission, their furnishings (and other property thereon),[127] and the means of transport of the mission are immune from search, requisition, attachment, or execution (Art. 22, §3 VCDR).[128] The VCCR, in contrast, limits this protection to the immunity from any form of requisition for the purposes of national defence or public utility (Art. 31, §4 VCCR). Expropriation is allowed if it is necessary for these purposes,[129] but all possible steps should be taken to avoid impeding the performance of consular functions, and prompt, adequate, and effective compensation should be paid to the sending state (Art. 31, §4 VCCR).

28.4.2 Privileges and Immunities of Diplomatic/Consular Agents

28.4.2.1 *Immunity*

As already indicated, the VCDR accords more immunities to diplomats than the VCCR to consuls: diplomats enjoy personal immunity (Art. 31 VCDR), whereas consuls only enjoy a functional immunity in relation to official consular acts (Art. 43, §1 VCCR).[130] Diplomatic immunity encompasses criminal, as well as civil and administrative immunity from jurisdiction (Art. 31, §1 VCDR). Diplomatic immunity from criminal jurisdiction is absolute.[131] With regard to civil and administrative jurisdiction, the VCDR states three limitative exceptions concerning: (a) a real action relating to private immovable property, (b) an action relating to succession in which the diplomatic agent is involved in his private capacity, (c) an action relating to any professional or commercial activity exercised by the diplomatic agent in the receiving state outside his official functions (Art. 31, §1 VCDR).[132] The immunity from jurisdiction is broad and encompasses actions performed by a diplomatic agent both in an official and private capacity (e.g.:

divorces or family affairs).[133] A functional approach to immunity, however, is adopted regarding a diplomatic agent who is a national or permanent resident in the receiving state (Art. 38, §1 VCDR).[134] Next to immunity from jurisdiction, diplomats enjoy immunity from execution (Art. 31, §3 VCDR). The three limited exceptions referred to in the field of civil and administrative immunity are also applicable regarding immunity from execution. Diplomatic immunity continues to exist after the termination of the diplomatic function (Art. 39, §2 VCDR). However, for acts not performed by the diplomat in the exercise of his functions, the immunity only continues until he leaves the country or for a 'reasonable period of time in which to do so' (Art. 39, §2 VCDR).[135]

The immunity from jurisdiction of consular officers and consular employees is limited to acts performed in the exercise of their function (Art. 43, §1 VCCR).[136] Article 5 VCCR provides a non-exhaustive list of the most important consular functions.[137] However, as the list of consular functions provided by the VCCR is not exhaustive, the delineation of consular immunity is dependent upon a case-by-case interpretation questioning whether a certain act falls within the scope of consular functions.[138] Consuls do not enjoy immunity in respect of civil action arising out of a contract unless they expressly or impliedly contracted as an agent of the sending state (Art. 43, §2, (a) VCCR). Moreover, regardless whether in the exercise of their function, a consular officer or employee does not enjoy immunity for damage arising from an accident in the receiving state caused by a vehicle, vessel, or aircraft (Art. 43, §2, (b) VCCR). In line with the rules laid down in the VCDR, the immunity for consuls continues to exist after the termination of the consular function (Art. 53, §4 VCCR). Again, for acts not performed by the consul in the exercise of his functions, the immunity only continues until he leaves the country or for a 'reasonable period of time' to do so (Art. 53, §3 VCCR).

28.4.2.2 *Personal Inviolability*

Diplomats enjoy personal inviolability, and will not be liable to any form of arrest or detention (Art. 29 VCDR). The receiving state has to treat the diplomat with due respect and has to take all appropriate steps to prevent any attack on his person, freedom, or dignity (Art. 29 VCDR). The last sentence of Article 29 VCDR is copied in Art. 40 of the VCCR. However, the inviolability of consular officers is more limited than that of diplomats.[139] In case of a 'grave crime'[140] and pursuant to a decision by the competent judicial authority, consuls can be arrested or detained (Art. 41, §1 VCCR). If arrested or detained, the head of post must be notified (Art. 42 VCCR), and proceedings against the consular officer must be instituted with the minimum of delay (Art. 41, §3 VCCR). In case criminal proceedings are instituted against a consular officer, he must appear before the competent authorities, although proceedings have to be conducted with due respect to the position of the consul and in a manner which will hamper his functions as little as possible (Art. 41, §3 VCCR). Also in this situation, the head of post must be notified (Art. 42 VCCR). If a consular officer is found guilty and no appeal is possible against the decision, a consul can be imprisoned (Art. 41, §2 VCCR).

28.4.2.3 *Privileges*

As stated earlier, consular privileges historically did not form part of customary international law. However, the increased merging of consular and diplomatic services after the

Second World War entailed that states became convinced that they would benefit from according consular privileges on a reciprocal basis. Today, privileges accorded to diplomats in the VCDR are similar to privileges given to consular officers by the VCCR.[141] Both diplomats and consuls are given privileges regarding social security (Art. 33 VCDR; Art. 48 VCCR). With some exceptions, diplomats and consuls are exempt from taxes of the receiving state (Art. 34 VCDR; Art. 49 VCCR).[142] And, in view of the frequent travelling of diplomats and consuls, privileges regarding custom duties and baggage search are being given (Art. 36 VCDR; Art. 50 VCCR). Family members and private servants of consuls and diplomats are also accorded privileges, but to a lesser extent (Art. 36 VCDR; Art. 50 VCCR).[143]

28.4.3 Sovereignty, Territoriality, Immunities, and Human Rights

State sovereignty remains a crucial principle in international law.[144] Within its territory the exercise of judicial, legislative, and executive jurisdiction by a state constitutes an essential corollary of that sovereignty.[145] This is an exclusive power, which must be respected by other states.[146] State jurisdiction extends over the whole territory and whoever present there, including non-state subjects. [147] The exercise of jurisdiction is simultaneously limited by international law.[148]

In a diplomatic and consular context, principles of state sovereignty and jurisdiction have a specific purpose. Both Conventions are based on the principle of respect for the territorial sovereignty of the receiving state. Art. 41, § 1, VCDR explicitly stipulates the duty of all persons enjoying privileges and immunities under the Convention 'to respect the laws and regulations of the receiving state' and 'not to interfere in the internal affairs of that state'. An analogous provision (Art. 55, §1 VCCR) demanding respect for the laws and regulations of the receiving state can be found in the VCCR. Both Conventions prohibit the utilization of diplomatic and consular premises respectively in any manner incompatible with the exercise of diplomatic or consular functions.[149]

On the other hand, inviolabilities, privileges, and immunities were laid down in the VCDR and the VCCR, as a result of which the state parties accepted restrictions on the exclusive jurisdiction over their own territory: certain laws and regulations either do not apply (privileges) or cannot be enforced (immunities and inviolability).[150] Today, a certain tension exists between a number of the typical features of diplomatic/consular law and human rights law.[151] With respect to the receiving state this may involve a tension between the obligation under international law to respect on its territory both immunities and inviolabilities as set forth in the VCDR and VCCR and the duty to respect and protect international or national human rights obligations. With respect to the sending state, obligations stemming from international law or domestic human rights law may be at odds with the aforementioned non-interference principle. Particularly concerning the complete immunity of diplomats, the international community has already expressed its interest to limit immunities in case of misuse.[152] Reference can for instance be made to the recommendation of the Parliamentary Assembly of the Council of Europe on 'domestic slavery', in which it recommends member states to 'amend the Vienna Convention in order to waive diplomatic immunity for all offences committed in private life'.[153] Another proposal is to draw up a 'black list' of diplomats who abused their privileges and immunities, in order to be able to limit the privileges of these persons.[154] The matter is somewhat less pressing regarding consular missions, since consular officers and employees are granted a more limited immunity in respect of acts performed in the exercise of consular functions.

28.4.4 Immunity vs Impunity

Immunity is only procedural in nature, and should not be confused with impunity.[155] As said, both consuls and diplomats are obliged to respect the laws and regulations of the receiving state and are not allowed to interfere with the internal affairs of that state (Art. 41, §1 VCDR; Art. 55, §1 VCCR). As consuls only enjoy immunity in the exercise of their consular functions, the receiving state laws are judicially enforceable in all cases except when Article 43 VCCR grants them immunity.[156] In view of the fact that diplomats enjoy complete criminal, civil, and administrative immunity (with some limited exceptions) the domestic laws and regulations of the receiving state cannot be judicially enforced. As Plantey states: *'La sanction de l'abus ou de la faute, n'est pas, à l'étranger, juridictionnelle mais diplomatique.'*[157] In this regard, it is important—particularly for diplomats enjoying a quasi-complete immunity—that actions other than judicial enforcement can be taken vis-à-vis diplomatic or consular agents who commit a crime in the receiving state.[158] Firstly, minor offences may be drawn to the attention of the head of mission/head of the consular post. If the head of mission/head of consular post so decides, he can take appropriate action (e.g. a disciplinary sanction) regarding the diplomat or consul in question. Moreover, it is possible for the receiving state to demand the sending state to waive the immunity of the diplomat or consul (Art. 32 VCDR; Art. 45 VCCR). If immunity is waived, the diplomatic/consular agent can be tried by the competent courts of the receiving state for crimes committed on the territory of the receiving state.[159] Furthermore, the receiving state can withhold certain privileges of the diplomat/consul (e.g. fiscal privileges), when minor offences are committed repeatedly. In last instance, it is possible for the receiving state to declare the diplomat/consul in question *persona non grata*; consequentially the diplomat/consul will be recalled by the sending state, or terminate his functions with the mission/post (Art. 9 VCDR; Art. 23 VCCR).[160]

28.4.5 Inviolability of Diplomatic/Consular Communication and Documents

The protection of archives and documents and the insurance of free communication are essential for the effective functioning of embassies and consular posts. As such, the inviolability of archives and documents has since long been accepted as a rule of customary international law.[161] Also in this line, both the VCDR and VCCR ensure the inviolability of archives and documents (Art. 24 VCDR; Art. 33 VCCR), and protect free communication (Art. 27 VCDR; Art. 35 VCCR). Due to the technological evolution since the introduction of the VCDR and VCCR, communication has changed significantly.[162] The introduction of the Internet and electronic mail (email), for example, have an enormous impact on modern diplomatic and consular practice and on the application of both Conventions.

28.4.5.1 *Inviolability of Archives and Documents*

Both the VCDR and the VCCR state that documents and archives of the mission/consular post 'shall be inviolable at all times and wherever they may be' (Art. 24 VCDR; Art. 33 VCCR).[163] The term 'archives' is not further described in the VCDR. The VCCR, however, does define the term: ' "consular archives" includes all the papers, documents, correspondence, books, films, tapes and registers of the consular post, together with the ciphers and codes, the card-indexes and any article of furniture intended for their protection or safe keeping' (Art. 1,§1,(k) VCCR). By analogy, this wide definition would apply to diplomatic archives, without being exclusive of other methods of information.[164] Moreover, it is accepted that modern forms of storage, such as computer files and diskettes, also fall within the scope of the VCCR and VCDR.[165] The inviolability of diplomatic/consular archives and documents entails that they cannot be opened, searched, or requisitioned without consent, and cannot be used as evidence.[166]

28.4.5.2 *Freedom of Communication*

The Conventions permit the diplomatic mission/consular post free communication with their government (and the other missions and consulates of the sending state) by 'all appropriate means' (Art. 27, §1 VCDR; Art. 35, §1 VCCR).[167] It is accepted that these means include modern means of communication such as (mobile) telecommunication, fax, and email.[168] The receiving state has to permit and protect free communication to the extent that it is used for 'official purposes'. The interception of, or any attempt to become acquainted with, the content of diplomatic/consular communication is not allowed.[169] Missions and posts do not have to ask the receiving state's permission in order to communicate with the sending state; the consent of the receiving state is only imperative for the installation and use of wireless transmitters (Art. 27, §1, *in fine* VCDR; Art. 35, §1, *in fine* VCCR).

28.4.5.3 *Wikileaks: Threat to Secure Communication?*

The development and application of new communication techniques bring about new threats. One could think of challenges to the inviolability of archives and documents of a diplomatic mission or consular post (Art. 24 VCDR; Art. 33 VCCR). The recent publication of diplomatic documents on the secret-sharing web site WikiLeaks[170] clearly showed the risks involved in the (even restricted and secured) access to diplomatic documents through the Internet (or intranet).[171] Initial reactions to the WikiLeaks revelations indicated its disastrousness for diplomacy since diplomatic relations and negotiations are not feasible without guaranteed confidentiality.[172] The consequences of WikiLeaks for diplomacy should, however, not be exaggerated. In practice, the absolute protection of free and safe diplomatic communication can never be guaranteed. In this regard, the case law of the European Court of Human Rights (ECHR) concerning freedom of the press is enlightening. According to the ECHR, 'press freedom assumes even greater importance in circumstances in which state activities and decisions escape democratic or judicial scrutiny on account of their confidential or secret nature'[173]—as is the case for diplomatic (and consular) documents. Several instances are known of breaches of free and safe communication.[174] Of course, the extent to which protection can be guaranteed depends on the means of communication; a letter sent by mail is—even though protected under the VCDR or VCCR—easier to open than a sealed diplomatic/consular bag carried by a courier.[175] Analogously, we can state today that the security of sensitive information sent via electronic mail is very difficult to guarantee. The use of encrypted messages for diplomatic/consular communication over the Internet does enhance the security of diplomatic/consular Internet communication to a certain extent.[176] However, for the exchange of the most sensitive information, the use of a diplomatic/consular bag (Art. 27, §3, VCDR; Art. 35, §3 VCCR) carried by a courier (Art. 27, §§ 5–6; Art. 35, §5–6 VCCR) is the more secure option.

28.4.5.4 *The Diplomatic and Consular Bag*

Diplomatic and consular bags are protected by the Conventions if they bear visible external marks of their character[177] and if they contain documents or articles intended for official use (Art. 27, §4 VCDR; Art. 35, §4 VCCR). In case the diplomatic/consular bag is carried by a courier guarding the bag (Art. 27, §5 VCDR; Art. 35, §5 VCCR), security is even better guaranteed. The VCCR permits competent authorities of the receiving state having serious reason to believe misuse of the consular bag to request an authorized representative of the sending state to open the bag in their presence or to return the bag to its place of origin (Art. 35, §3 VCCR). The VCDR is stricter:[178] it states that the diplomatic bag cannot be opened or detained (Art. 27, §3).

The prohibition to open the diplomatic bag in an absolute manner is (and has been) subject to controversy, as this provision allows potential abuse of a diplomatic bag (e.g. the use of the diplomatic bag to facilitate drug traffic or the smuggling of weapons).[179] Accordingly, several states entered reservations regarding the protection of the diplomatic bag as defined by Article 27 VCDR.[180] By entering a reservation, these countries sought to limit the inviolability of the diplomatic bag, and tried to reserve the right to open or return a diplomatic bag in specific circumstances. Other states objected to these reservations.[181] They argued inter alia that the reservations go against the object and purpose of the VCDR[182] and as such are not valid.[183] Because of the reciprocity in diplomatic relations, conflicts will mostly be solved by a mutual agreement amongst the states concerned.[184] Arguably, whereas the textual difference between the two Conventions concerning the treatment of diplomatic bags and consular bags remains in place, the distinction has blurred in practice.[185]

The difficult balance between the protection of diplomatic communication and the prevention of misuse has resulted in another contemporary area of tension. As indicated a moment ago, Article 27, §3, VCDR protects the diplomatic bag by prohibiting opening of the bag. Today, however, modern screening methods exist allowing the contents of the bag to be detected without opening it. It is argued that the use of such techniques to discover the presence of explosives, metal, drugs, or nuclear substances is permitted under international diplomatic law, since according to Article 27, §4 VCDR diplomatic bags may only contain documents or articles intended for official use.[186] Nevertheless, no unanimity has been found as of yet on the validity and prerequisites regarding detection methods.[187] There is a generally accepted practice for airline authorities to scan diplomatic bags and even to refuse their transport where a threat to aircraft safety is presumed.[188] Harmonized European legislation on standards of aviation security states that the appropriate authority 'may allow a diplomatic bag to be exempted from screening or to be subjected to special security procedures provided that the requirements of the Vienna Convention on Diplomatic Relations are met'.[189] In case the sending state refuses the scan of a diplomatic bag by airline authorities, it will have to search for other means to transport the bag.

28.5 Conclusion: the Vienna Conventions in the 21st Century

The rules laid down in the VCDR and VCCR have shown and continue to show their durability, as evidenced by the broad application in the diplomatic/consular corps around the world and in the general interaction between states. At the same time, international diplomatic and consular law has substantially evolved in practice. A number of these developments have been discussed in this chapter. Due to globalization and technological development, the functions of diplomats and consuls as laid down in the Conventions have been subject to change over the past fifty years. Also, the consular function to provide assistance and protection to nationals abroad has gained importance and entailed a massive body of case law with inter alia recent ICJ cases interpreting Article 36 of the VCCR. The immunities, privileges, and inviolabilities laid down in the Conventions have gained the status of customary international law. These rules are generally well respected. The importance for states to mutually respect the protection awarded to their diplomatic/consular corps accounts for this. It is noteworthy that in the same territory the receiving state has full and exclusive territorial jurisdiction, confers immunities, and has the obligation to respect and protect human rights. This leads to frictions, and it has even been suggested that the VCDR be amended in order to respond to these evolutions. The weight of international human rights has increased remarkably in a period of fifty years. This evolution is contrasted by the conservatism in form and content that characterizes international diplomatic law. Since the drafting of the VCDR, diplomatic communication has also changed drastically: paper mail has been largely replaced by electronic mail, diplomatic negotiations are often conducted using electronic methods, and modern detection techniques undermine the confidentiality of the diplomatic bag and the inviolability of diplomatic documents. The recent leaking of US diplomatic cables via WikiLeaks demonstrates that the confidentiality of diplomatic documents is under pressure. A delicate balance has yet to be found between the protection of diplomatic communications and the protection of certain fundamental rights such as the freedom of speech (and the associated access to information) and the freedom of the press.

It was impossible for the authors of the VCDR or VCCR fifty years ago to foresee these developments. They do require a refinement of the current treaty regime, which in certain cases has already begun via innovative case law.

Notes

1. Vienna Convention on Diplomatic Relations, signed at Vienna on 18 April 1961, entry into force 24 April 1964, *UNTS*, vol. 500, p. 95, no. 310. Two optional protocols were added to the Convention: the Optional Protocol concerning the Acquisition of Nationality, done at Vienna on 18 April 1961, entry into force 24 April 1964, *UNTS*, vol. 500, p. 223, 51 state parties; the Optional Protocol concerning the Compulsory Settlement of Disputes, done at Vienna on 18 April 1961, entry into force 24 April 1964, *UNTS*, vol. 500, p. 223, 66 state parties.

2. Vienna Convention on Consular Relations, signed at Vienna on 24 April 1963, entry into force 19 March 1967, *UNTS*, vol. 596, p. 262, no. 8638, 173 state parties. Two optional protocols were added to the Convention: the Optional Protocol to the Vienna Convention on Consular Relations concerning Acquisition of Nationality, done at Vienna on 24 April 1963, entry into force 19 March 1967, *UNTS*, vol. 596, p. 469, 39 state parties; the Optional Protocol to the Vienna Convention on Consular Relations concerning the Compulsory Settlement of Disputes, done at Vienna on 24 April 1963, entry into force 19 March 1967, *UNTS*, vol. 596, p. 487, 48 state parties.

3. M. Bossuyt and J. Wouters, *Grondlijnen van Internationaal Recht* (Antwerp-Oxford: Intersentia, 2005), 405; G.R. Berridge, *Diplomacy: Theory and Practice*, 4th edition (Basingstoke: Palgrave Macmillan, 2010), 109–10; E. Denza, *Diplomatic Law: A Commentary on the Vienna Convention on Diplomatic Relations* (Oxford: Oxford University Press, 2008), 3–12; R. Langhorne, 'The Regulation of Diplomatic Practice', in C. Jönsson and R. Langhorne (eds), *Diplomacy*, 2nd edition (Cornell, NJ: Sage Library of International Relations, 2006), 316–33; J. Verhoeven, *Droit international public* (Brussels: Larcier, 2000), 106.

4. See ICJ, *Case concerning United States Diplomatic and Consular Staff in Tehran of 24 May 1980* (U.S. v. Iran), *I.C.J. Rep.* 1980, 3, § 62 *in fine*; ICJ, *Case concerning the Arrest Warrant of 11 April 2000* (Democratic Republic of the Congo v. Belgium), 14 February 2002, *I.C.J. Rep.* 2002, 1, § 52.

5. Denza, *Diplomatic Law*, 1; H.P. Hestermeyer, 'Vienna Convention on Diplomatic Relations (1961)', *Max Planck Encyclopedia of Public International Law*, 1, available at <www.mpepil.com>.

6. L.T. Lee and J. Quigley, *Consular Law and Practice*, 3rd edition (Oxford: Oxford University Press, 2008), 21–3.

7. Lee and Quigley, *Consular Law and Practice*, 17–18 and 25; Bossuyt and Wouters, *Grondlijnen van Internationaal Recht*, 420.

8. See ICJ, *Case concerning United States Diplomatic and Consular Staff in Tehran of 24 May 1980* (U.S. v. Iran), *I.C.J. Rep.* 1980, 3, § 62 *in fine*.

9. Art. 73 VCCR.

10. M. Zieck, 'Diplomatiek en Consulair Recht', in Nathalie Horbach, René Lefeber, Olivier Ribbelink (eds), *Handboek Internationaal Recht* (The Hague: T.M.C. Asser Press, 2007), 278; I. Roberts, *Satow's Diplomatic Practice*, 6th edition (Oxford: Oxford University Press, 2009), 71 (hereafter: Satow). Although different legal acts, the distinct steps can take place at the same time.

11. Zieck, 'Diplomatiek en Consulair Recht', 278.

12. B. Sen, *A Diplomat's Handbook of International Law and Practice* (Dordrecht: Kluwer, 1988), 22.

13. Art. 2, § 2 VCCR.

14. Satow, 227.

15. Art. 2, § 3 VCCR. Following the invasion of the Falkland Islands (1982), all diplomatic and consular relations between the United Kingdom and Argentina were severed. In a joint statement of 19 October 1989 the re-establishment of consular relations was announced (Art. 4), a full year before the re-establishment of diplomatic relations; Malcolm Evans, 'Current Developments: Public International Law: The Restoration of Diplomatic Relations Between Argentina and the United Kingdom', *International and Comparative Law Quarterly* 40:2 (1991), 473–82.

16. Denza, *Diplomatic Law*, 49.

17. Sen, *A Diplomat's Handbook of International Law and Practice*, 34; Denza, *Diplomatic Law*, 49; Satow, 84.

18. Sen, *A Diplomat's Handbook of International Law and Practice*, 50; Zieck, 'Diplomatiek en Consulair Recht', 281.

19. Denza, *Diplomatic Law*, 49. Members of a diplomatic mission other than the head of the mission are not subject to the previous agrément of the receiving state (Art. 7 VCDR).

20. Art. 10 VCDR.

21. Art 13, §1 VCDR.

22. In order to be given exequatur in the receiving state, the sending state will provide the head of a consular post with a document, called 'a commission', certifying its capacity and consular rank and class; Art. 11, §1 VCCR. Some governments require by law or regulations that consular officers, other than the head of mission, also receive exequatur, see Art 19, §§ 3–4 VCCR; Satow, 214; Lee and Quigley, *Consular Law and Practice*, 83.

23. Art. 12 VCCR.

24. Art. 12, §§ 1 and 14 VCCR.

25. Art. 4, §2 VCDR and 12, §2 VCCR. The decision of the French government not to grant approval for the opening of a consular post of the Republic of Albania in Caen, and subsequently, its refusal of the necessary exequatur for the Albanese honorary consul, cannot be appealed before the French administrative court system; Administrative Court of Appeal (Cour administrative d'appel), Nantes, France, Rejet, N° de rôle 05333, 2 December 2005, available at <www.lexeek.com/jus-luminum/>, Jurisprudence Jus Luminum n°J185700.

26. G.R. Berridge, *Diplomacy: Theory and Practice*, 4th edition (Basingstoke: Palgrave Macmillan, 2010), 114.

27. Satow, 77.

28. Denza, *Diplomatic Law*, 36

29. Art. 3 VCDR stipulates that the functions of a diplomatic mission inter alia consist in the tasks listed.

30. For an assessment of these consular functions, see *infra*. This can be in the general interest in the absence of consular missions, but is even possible where a sending state does have a consular and a diplomatic mission in a receiving state; Lee and Quigley, *Consular Law and Practice*, 550.

31. Art. 3 VCCR spells out that 'Consular functions are exercised by consular posts. They are also exercised by diplomatic missions in accordance with the provisions of the present Convention'; Art. 70, §1 of the same Convention stipulates: 'The provisions of the present Convention apply also, so far as the context permits, to the exercise of consular functions by a diplomatic mission.' Denza, *Diplomatic Law*, 39; Satow, 78–9.

32. Art. 70, § 4 VCCR; Denza, *Diplomatic Law*, 307; Lee and Quigley, *Consular Law and Practice*, 550. For an assessment and a comparison with consular immunity, see *infra*.

33. See *supra* and Art. 11 VCCR.

34. Art. 70, §2 VCCR; Lee and Quigley, *Consular Law and Practice*, 551.

35. For a more detailed description of these consular functions, see *infra* Section III §2.

36. J. Salmon, *Manuel de Droit Diplomatique* (Brussels: Bruylant, 1994), 526.

37. Denza, *Diplomatic Law*, 35; Satow, 77; R.B. Barston, *Modern Diplomacy*, 3rd edition (Essex: Pearson Education, 2006), 4; S. Sofer, 'Old and New Diplomacy: A Debate Revisited', in Jönsson and Langhorne (eds), *Diplomacy*, 395.

38. A. K. Henrikson, 'Diplomacy's Possible Futures', *The Hague Journal of Diplomacy* 1 (2006), 5; J. Heine, 'On the Manner of Practising the New Diplomacy', *The Centre for International Governance Innovation Working Paper No. 11*, 2006, 3, available at <http://igcc.ucsd.edu/pdf/HeineNewDiplomacy.pdf>; C. Jönsson and M. Hall, 'Communication: An Essential Aspect of Diplomacy', in Jönsson and Langhorne (eds), *Diplomacy*, 410–11.

39. In this regard, Heine refers to an evolution from 'club diplomacy' to 'network diplomacy', 'On the Manner of Practising the New Diplomacy', 3–10.

40. The recent 'Memorandum on the modernization of Dutch diplomacy' describes the change in diplomacy as follows: 'Diplomacy is no longer limited to traditional interstate relations. The network and the tasks of diplomacy have increased dramatically in size, complexity, dynamics and stratification. The current diplomat has to deal with large, established and start-up companies, trade unions, human rights defenders, local authorities, universities, the creative sector, NGOs, media etc.' (Our own translation.) See Dutch ministry of foreign affairs, 'Nota modernisering Nederlandse diplomatie', 8 April 2011, 4, available at <http://www.rijksoverheid.nl/documenten-en-publicaties/notas/2011/04/08/nota-moderniser-ing-nederlandse-diplomatie.html>.

41. Barston, *Modern Diplomacy*, 1–15.

42. See: D. Criekemans (ed.), *Regional Sub-State Diplomacy Today* (Leiden/Boston: Martinus Nijhoff, 2010).

43. See e.g. the European diplomatic network which was made subject to the VCDR through specific agreements with host states. Of the 138 EU delegations, 131 bilateral delegations—including regional delegations—are accredited to nearly 160 countries. Seven delegations are representing the EU in other international organizations. For a detailed assessment, see

J. Wouters and S. Duquet, 'The EU and International Diplomatic Law: New Horizons?', *The Hague Journal of Diplomacy* 7:1 (2012), 31–49.

44. On 'parliamentary diplomacy', see inter alia F.W. Weisglas and G. De Boer, 'Parliamentary Diplomacy', The Hague Journal of Diplomacy 2 (2007), 93–9.

45. K. S. Rana, *21st Century Diplomacy: A Practitioner's Guide* (London: Continuum International Publishing, 2011), 115–29.

46. 'Public diplomacy' is here defined as 'the efforts by the government of one state to influence public or elite opinion of another state for the purpose of persuading these foreign publics to regard favorably its policies, ideals and ideas'; E.H. Potter, 'Canada and the New Public Diplomacy', *Discussion Papers in Diplomacy* no. 81 (The Hague: Clingendael), 3; C. Jönsson and M. Hall, 'Communication: An Essential Aspect of Diplomacy', 406; Heine, 'On the Manner of Practising the New Diplomacy', 9.

47. See Heine, 'On the Manner of Practising the New Diplomacy', 15; Henrikson, 'Diplomacy's Possible Futures', 10; M. Koch, 'Wozu noch Diplomaten?', in *Auswärtiges Amt: Diplomatie als Beruf*, 4th edition (Wiesbaden:VS Verslag Für Sozialwissenschaften, 2005), 358; K. Th. Paschke, *Report on the Special Inspection of 14 German Embassies in the Countries of the European Union* (Berlin: Federal Foreign Office, 2000), also available at <http://grberridge. diplomacy.edu/paschke-report/>.

48. Economic diplomacy is, for example, an important pillar in Dutch diplomatic policy, inter alia because of the importance of energy and resource security for the Dutch economy. An integrated approach to economic diplomacy, human rights, and development policy is therefore promoted as part of a modern approach to diplomacy. The Netherlands will invest 5 million euros by 2015 in the economic function of its network of embassies and consulates. See Dutch ministry of foreign affairs, 'Nota modernisering Nederlandse diplomatie', 8 April 2011, 1910 and 1930, available at <http://www.rijksoverheid.nl/documenten-en-publicaties/ notas/2011/04/08/nota-modernisering-nederlandse-diplomatie.html>. See also N. Bayne and S. Woolcock, *The New Economic Diplomacy: Decision-Making and Negotiation in International Economic Relations* (London: Ashgate, 2005); Berridge, *Diplomacy: Theory and Practice*, 119; Heine, 'On the Manner of Practising the New Diplomacy', 9; Paschke, 'Report on the Special Inspection of 14 German Embassies in the Countries of the European Union', VI, B; S. Strange, 'States, Firms and Diplomacy', *International Affairs* 68:1 (1992), 1–15.

49. In this regard the term 'summit diplomacy' is used; see specifically J. Melissen, 'Summit Diplomacy Coming of Age', *Discussion Papers in Diplomacy* nr. 86, Clingendael, available at http://www.clingendael.nl/publications/2003/20030500_cli_paper_dip_issue86.pdf. See Berridge, *Diplomacy: Theory and Practice*, 115 and ch. 10; Henrikson, 'Diplomacy's Possible Futures', 11; Paschke, 'Report on the Special Inspection of 14 German Embassies in the Countries of the European Union', III.

50. In this regard the term 'functional' or 'thematic diplomacy' is used. Henrikson, 'Diplomacy's Possible Futures', 18; Paschke, 'Report on the Special Inspection of 14 German Embassies in the Countries of the European Union', VII; Rana, 'Foreign Ministries: Change and Reform', 8.

51. Rana, 'Foreign Ministries: Change and Reform', 8; Henrikson, 'Diplomacy's Possible Futures', 10–14.

52. In this regard the term 'e-diplomacy' is used.

53. See G. Haynal, 'Diplomacy on the Ascendant in the Age of Disintermediation', Weatherhead Center for International Affairs, Harvard University, 2002, available at <http://www.wcfia. harvard.edu/fellows/papers/2001-02/haynal.pdf>; Henrikson, 'Diplomacy's Possible Futures', 7–10.

54. The Netherlands, for example, uses 'laptop posts' and 'laptop ambassadors'. See Dutch ministry of foreign affairs, 'Nota modernisering Nederlandse diplomatie', 8 April 2011, 9 and 23, available at <http://www.rijksoverheid.nl/documenten-en-publicaties/notas/2011/04/08/nota-modernization-Dutch-diplomatie.html>.

55. C. Jönsson and M. Hall, 'Communication: an Essential Aspect of Diplomacy', 398–9; Paschke, 'Report on the Special Inspection of 14 German Embassies in the Countries of the European Union', VI, E; Plantey, *Principes de Diplomatie* (Paris: Pédone, 2000), 267; Rana, 'Foreign Ministries: Change and Reform', 6–8 and 21.

56. V. M. Uribe, 'Consuls at work: Universal instruments of human rights and consular protection in the context of criminal justice', *Hous. J. Int'l L.* 19 (1996–1997), 375–424, at 386; Lee and Quigley, *Consular Law and Practice*, 107.

57. Art. 6 VCCR.

58. Art. 7 VCCR. The exercise of functions in a third state is prohibited in case there is express objection by one of the states concerned.

59. Art. 8 VCCR.

60. Salmon, *Manuel de Droit Diplomatique*, 524.

61. Art. 17, § 1 VCCR.

62. European Convention on Consular Functions, CETS No. 061, Paris, 11 December 2011, available at <conventions.coe.int/Treaty/en/Treaties/Html/061.htm>. The five state parties to the Convention are Georgia, Greece, Norway, Portugal, and Spain.

63. General Consideration No. 2, European Convention on Consular Functions—Explanatory Report—[1967] COETSER 4, 11 December 1967, available at <conventions.coe.int/Treaty/en/Reports/Html/061.htm>.

64. General Consideration No. 6, European Convention on Consular Functions—Explanatory Report—[1967] COETSER 4, 11 December 1967, available at <conventions.coe.int/Treaty/en/Reports/Html/061.htm>; Lee and Quigley, *Consular Law and Practice*, 113.

65. For example, in summing up the consular functions, the Strasbourg Convention in its Art. 14 copies the expression 'safeguard the interests of minors' from Art. 5 (h) of the Vienna Convention. The use of this expression in the Strasbourg Convention was however designed to take into account the evolution in the law on protection of minors to go beyond the traditional limits of guardianship and trusteeship. Art. 14, §2 (b) paragraph 2 (b) gives the consular agent the power, if need arises, to present observations or suggestions or to assist the minor or person incapable of looking after his own affairs, in any case where this is permitted by the law of the receiving state. See General Consideration No. 80 Explanatory Report to the Strasbourg Convention.

66. For example, in Art. 2 §2, the expression 'consular co-operation' is used in preference to the word 'consular relations' which, according to the General Consideration 24 of the Explanatory Report, is better suited to a European context.

67. Sir Ivor Roberts calls the function of protection in the broadest sense the most important consular function. See Satow, 259.

68. Satow, 263.

69. M.J. Kadish, 'Article 36 of the Vienna Convention on Consular Relations: A search for the right to consul', *Mich. J. Int'l. L.* 18 (1996–1997), 565–614, at 569.

70. Lee and Quigley, *Consular Law and Practice*, 139.

71. Consular assistance under Article 36 embraces the recommendation of legal representation, explanation of the judicial system and proceedings of the country concerned, and

facilitation of the location of evidence or witnesses; J. Quigley, 'LaGrand: A Challenge to the U.S. Judiciary', *Yale J. Int'l L.* 27 (2002), 435–40, at 435.

72. Uribe, 'Consuls at work', 390; Lee and Quigley, *Consular Law and Practice*, 140. The Canadian Alberta Court of Appeal in R. v. Van Bergen, [2000] A.J. No. 882 (QL), reported 225 W.A.C. 386, agreed with the Canadian Minister of Justice that the purpose of Art. 36 was 'to ensure that foreign detainees receive equal treatment under the local criminal justice system and are not disadvantaged because they are not familiar with and do not understand the proceedings against them'.

73. In a 2003 Dutch case it was decided that pursuant to Article 36 of the VCCR, Dutch nationals in custody solely have the right to request the receiving state to inform representatives of the sending state about their custody; Dutch consulates do not have an obligation to fulfill this request; § 3.9. District Court of The Hague (the Netherlands), Civil Law Section, Kuijt v Minister of Immigration and Integration, Administrative appeal, No. KG 03/137, 18 March 2003, ILDC 149 (NL 2003). In France, the Conseil d'Etat held that there is no obligation for a consular agent to represent a national before the courts of another state. Conseil d'Etat, Section Premier ressort, 29 Janvier 1993, Rejet, N° 111946, 111949, N° de rôle 015, published in Recueil des décisions du Conseil d'État—Lebon 1993.

74. Lee and Quigley, *Consular Law and Practice*, 159–62.

75. Certain national courts considered the non-notification of rights under Article 36 VCCR a violation of an individual right: the German Constitutional Court ruled that non-compliance with Article 36 VCCR, as established in international case law (see the ICJ *LaGrand* and *Avena* case, discussed *infra*) constituted a violation of the complainants' constitutional right to a fair trial. German Consular Notification Case, Joint constitutional complaint, Bundesverfassungsgericht, 2 BvR 2115/01, 19 September 2006, ILDC 668 (DE 2006). See also: Bundesgerichtshof, 5th Zivilsenat, Beschluss, 12 May 2011, Aktenzeichen: V ZB 23/11; Bundesgerichtshof, 5th Zivilsenat, Beschluss, 18 November 2010, Aktenzeichen: V ZB 165/10, and Bundesverfassungsgericht, 2nd Senat, 2nd Kammer, Stattgebender Kammerbeschluss, 8 July 2010, Aktenzeichen: 2 BvR 2485/07, 2 BvR 2513/07, 2 BvR 2548/07 available at <www.juris.de>. In the Netherlands, courts upheld a similar reasoning in e.g. Court of First Instance's-Gravenhage, AWB 08/34834, 9 June 2006. The Dutch Courts however did not always recognize an individual right based on the article; see Court of First Instance Amsterdam, AWB 06/918, 2 June 2006 and Court of First Instance Amsterdam, AWB 06/742, 7 October 2008, all available at <www.rechtspraak.nl>. In certain cases, the national courts did not find any violation of the rights of defence because of an Art. 36 VCCR violation; see Court of Cassation (2nd Chamber.), No. P.00.0788.N, 13 juni 2000 (D.), available at <www.cass.be> (Belgium). In Canada, the statements given by a detainee were considered admissible, even though there was a clear violation of Art. 36 VCCR, Ontario Supreme Court, *R. v. Partak*, 2001 CanLII 28411 (ON SC), 31 October 2001, available at <http://www.canlii.org/en/on/onsc/doc/2001/2001canlii28411/2001canlii28411.html>. Courts in the United States have proven to be even more reluctant to reverse convictions based on Art. 36 violations. District Court for the Western District of North Carolina (USA), *Garcia v. United States*, Decision on motion to vacate, 16 October 2008, ILDC 1216 (US 2008), § 3 Court of Appeals for the Ninth Circuit (USA), *Cornejo v County of San Diego and others*, Appeal Judgment, 504 F3d 853 (9th Cir 2007), 24 September 2007, ILDC 1080 (US 2007). In *Sanchez-Llamas v. Oregon* (2006), it was assumed, without deciding, that the VCCR created rights that were judicially enforceable by individuals (§ 18). The US Supreme Court nevertheless decided that evidence did not have to be excluded solely based

on the fact it was obtained in violation of Article 36 of the VCCR: United States Supreme Court, *Sánchez-Llamas v. Oregon*, 548 U.S. 331 (2006), 28 June 2006 (United States of America), ILDC 697. The VCCR did not provide detained aliens with a private right of action that could be asserted through an action for damages (a novel tort); See § 7, *Mora v New York* (USA), Appeal Judgment, 524 F3d 183 (2d Cir), 24 April 2008, ILDC 1100 (US 2008).

76. § 87 Advisory opinion of the Inter-American Court of Human Rights, OC-16/99, 1 October 1999, Inter-Am. Ct. H.R. (Ser A) No. 16 (1999).

77. ICJ, *LaGrand* (Germany v. United States of America), Judgment of 27 June 2001, I.C.J. Reports 2001, p. 466.

78. ICJ, *Avena and Other Mexican Nationals* (Mexico v. United States of America), Judgment of 31 March 2004, I.C.J. Reports 2004, p. 12.

79. In 1998, the ICJ issued provisional measures calling the United States not to execute a Paraguayan national, Angel Breard, who had not been aware of rights to consular access. Although the US Supreme Court declined the ruling, Paraguay decided to dismiss the case after Breard was executed, and no final ICJ judgement was issued. ICJ, The Vienna Convention on Consular Relations (*Paraguay v. United States of America*), Order of 10 November 1998, I.C.J. Reports 1998, p. 426.

80. In a Dutch case, the Court referred to the authoritative English and French versions of the VCCR—which respectively use the terminology 'without delay' and 'sans retard'—to decide that the term 'without delay' has to be understood as meaning 'instantly'. A delay of ten days to notify consular authorities of an alien's detention constitutes a breach of Art. 36, §1, (b) VCCR, although the Court held that the detention itself was lawful. District Court The Hague (the Netherlands), sitting in Den Bosch, Chamber for Aliens Affairs, *A v Minister of Immigration and Integration*, Administrative appeal, AWB 05/34215 VRWET, 23 August 2005, ILDC 854 (NL 2005).

81. J. Fitzpatrick, 'The unreality of International Law in the United States and the LaGrand Case', *Yale J. Int'l L* 27 (2002), 427–33, at 428.

82. Kadish, 'Article 36 of the Vienna Convention on Consular Relations', 565–614.

83. Article 36 includes three distinctive individual rights. First, nationals of the sending state shall have the same freedom with respect to communication with and access to consular officers of the sending state; second, any communication addressed to the consular post by the person arrested, in prison, custody, or detention shall be forwarded by the said authorities without delay; third, consular officers shall have the right to visit a national of the sending state who is in prison, custody, or detention, to converse and correspond with him and to arrange for his legal representation. See M.J. Kadish, 'Article 36 of the Vienna Convention on Consular Relations: The International Court of Justice in *Mexico v. United States (Avena)* speaks emphatically to the Supreme Court of the United States about fundamental nature of the right to consul', *Geo. J. Int'l L.* 36 (2004–2005), 1–60, 5–6.

84. In the 2001 *LaGrand* case, the ICJ confirmed that Article 36, § 1 VCCR creates individual rights for the national concerned, which may be invoked before the ICJ by the national state of the detained person. The Court also followed Germany in that the failure of the United States to inform the LaGrand brothers of their right to contact the German authorities prevented Germany from exercising its rights under Art. 36 §1 (a) and (c) VCCR and violated the various rights conferred upon the sending state vis-à-vis its nationals in prison, custody, or detention as provided for in Art. 36, §1, (b) VCCR. See §77 and § 125 *LaGrand* Case which concerned two German nationals who were executed by the state of Arizona

following a violation of Article 36 VCCR. For a more detailed assessment of this case, see Quigley, 'LaGrand: A Challenge to the U.S. Judiciary', 435–40 and Fitzpatrick, 'The unreality of International Law in the United States and the LaGrand Case', 427–33.

85. Art. 36 §1, (b) stipulates that if the national so requests, the competent authorities of the receiving state shall, without delay, inform the consular post of the sending state if, within its consular district, a national of that state is arrested or committed to prison or to custody pending trial or is detained in any other manner.

86. § 40 *Avena and Other Mexican Nationals* case: 'It would further observe that violations of the rights of the individual under Article 36 may entail a violation of the rights of the sending state, and that violations of the rights of the latter may entail a violation of the rights of the individual.' See also ICJ, Request for Interpretation of the Judgment of 31 March 2004 in the Case Concerning Avena and Other Mexican Nationals (Mexico v United States of America), 9 January 2009, available at <www.icj-cij.org/docket/files/139/14939.pdf>.

87. § 63, *Avena and Other Mexican Nationals case.*

88. N. Klein, 'Avena and Other Mexican Nationals (Mexico v. United States of America): Case notes', *Austl. Int'l L.J.* 11 (2004), 143–57, at 151.

89. On 7 March 2005, the UN Secretary-General received from the government of the United States of America a communication notifying its withdrawal from the Optional Protocol. As a consequence of this withdrawal, the United States does no longer recognize the jurisdiction of the ICJ reflected in that Protocol, although the Protocol does not expressly provide for a 'denunciation clause'. For a detailed assessment, see J. Quigley, 'The United States' withdrawal form International Court of Justice jurisdiction in consular case: reasons and consequences', *Duke J. Comp. & Int'l L.* 19 (2008–2009), 263–306.

90. Kadish, 'Article 36 of the Vienna Convention on Consular Relations: The International Court of Justice in *Mexico v. United States (Avena)*', 9–17. The *LaGrand* and *Avena and other Mexican Nationals* cases which held that the application of procedural default rules to claims of consular notification violations failed to give 'full effect' to the purposes of the VCCR were not considered binding on US federal courts; § 43 United States Supreme Court, *Sánchez-Llamas v. Oregon*, 548 U.S. 331 (2006), 28 June 2006 (United States of America), ILDC 697. This resulted in courts holding that a violation of the VCCR did not infringe any enforceable individual right; § 6 District Court for the Western District of North Carolina (USA), *Garcia v. United States*, Decision on motion to vacate, 16 October 2008, ILDC 1216 (US 2008), § 3 Court of Appeals for the Ninth Circuit (USA), *Cornejo v County of San Diego and others*, Appeal Judgment, 504 F3d 853 (9th Cir 2007), 24 September 2007, ILDC 1080 (US 2007). Other courts did implement the ICJ's judgement in the *Avena* case; see Oklahoma Court of Criminal Appeals (USA), *Torres v. State of Oklahoma*, Application for post-conviction relief, No PCD-04-442; unpublished opinion (Oklahoma Court of Criminal Appeals), 13 May 2004, ILDC 113 (US 2004). In this case, the court applied the VCCR and Optional Protocol under the Supremacy Clause, noting that the Court was 'bound to give full faith and credit to the Avena decision'. See also: § 18 and 35 Court of Appeals for the Seventh Circuit (USA), *Jogi v Voges and others*, Appeal judgment, 480 F3d 822 (7th Cir 2007), 12 March 2007, ILDC 808 (US 2007) which held that legislative history of the VCCR left little doubt that the Convention concerned separate individual rights of detained nationals.

91. D. Hollis, 'Proposed Legislation Seeks VCCR Compliance by the United States', *Opinio Juris Blog*, 14 June 2011. Scholars have commented on how to bring the US into compliance with the Treaty; see e.g. L.E. Carter, 'Lessons from Avena: The inadequacy of clemency and

judicial proceedings for violations of the Vienna Convention on Consular Relations', *Duke J. Comp. & Int'l L.* 15 (2004–2005), 259–80, at 273.

92. See Art. 5, (d), (f), (g), (i), (j), and (k) VCCR.

93. Satow, 261.

94. French consular agents are granted the authority to effect final decisions on requests to issue visa to enter France. For an application of this authority, see Conseil d'Etat, Premier ressort, Rejet, N° 181092, N° de rôle 136, 27 May 1998, published in Tables du Recueil Lebon.

95. One can think of the assistance offered to immigration officers when issuing travel document; see Lee and Quigley, *Consular Law and Practice*, 215. In Belgium, the diplomatic agent, when performing consular functions, does not have extended powers compared to a registrar in the home country. It follows that when issuing a particular certificate, not listed as falling within the issuance powers of a Belgian registrar and lacking any reference to a positive or negative order of hierarchical authority, the diplomat is acting outside his duties as an officer of civil registration. See Court of Appeals Brussel 24 November 1998, *A.J.T.* (1998–99), 871, note Lambein, K.; *Rev.dr.étr.* 1998, 576.

96. See Art. 55 VCCR. In a Dutch court case, it was decided that Art. 55 VCCR cannot be invoked by Dutch authorities as a ground to refuse the issuance of a visa to a Colombian citizen by the local Dutch consulate. The Dutch minister of foreign affairs had taken the view that by issuing the visa, it would assist a Colombian national to evade the jurisdiction of the receiving state. The Court of First Instance ruled that although the Netherlands must comply and implement Art. 55 VCCR in exercising consular functions, this provision solely is intended to be binding upon contracting state (and their respective consular officers) in the exercise of friendly relations between the contracting parties. The article therefore is not directly applicable and binding on all persons, let alone that the provision in itself may serve as a basis for jurisdiction of a defendant to refuse a passport. Court of First Instance (Rechtbank) 's-Gravenhage, the Netherlands, AWB 10/1219 WET, 8 December 2010, available at <www.rechtspraak.nl>. The Dutch Council of State however decided that Article 5 (f) and (m) VCCR do not require the explicit consent of a receiving state (*in casu* Ghana) for consular officers of the sending state to examine and verify birth certificates issued by the receiving state before legalization of the sending state; Council of State (Raad van state), the Netherlands, AB0572, No. 200001669/1, 20 February 2000, available at <www.rechtspraak.nl>.

97. Satow, 246. In the Netherlands e.g. three conditions must be fulfilled for a foreign consul to be able to perform a marriage: (1) none of the prospective spouses can be a Dutch national; (2) the foreign consular or diplomatic officer has the competence to perform marriages under the law of the sending state, and (3) the sending state allows the Dutch consular or diplomatic officers to perform marriages in its territory (reciprocity requirement). In cases of double citizenship, the Dutch courts did recognize the marriage of a national performed by a foreign consular agent; High Council of the Netherlands (Hoge Raad der Nederlanden) 's-Gravenhage, the Netherlands (Cassation), no. 8919, 13 December 1996, available at <www.rechtspraak.nl>.

98. Salmon, *Manuel de Droit Diplomatique*, 522; Satow, 249 and 260.

99. Salmon, *Manuel de Droit Diplomatique*, 461 and 522.

100. Satow, 79, 249, and 259.

101. Denza, *Diplomatic Law*, 40; Satow, 259. See also Chapter 26, this volume.

102. Lee and Quigley, *Consular Law and Practice*, 541; in the same sense: Satow, 260.

103. Denza, *Diplomatic Law*, 40. For example: both Art. 3 VCDR and Art. 5 VCCR list the protection of nationals as a core function; however, while a diplomat will protect in a more collective, general sense, the consular agent will protect the national in individual cases upon concrete needs; see Satow, 249 and 260.

104. As Satow and Lee and Quigley note, the distinction between the term 'privilege' and the term 'immunity' is not easy to define precisely, and the terms are often used interchangeably. Satow, 121–2; Lee and Quigley, *Consular Law and Practice*, 341.

105. Denza, *Diplomatic Law*, 135–6; Bossuyt and Wouters, *Grondlijnen van Internationaal Recht*, 389; Zieck, 'Diplomatiek en Consulair Recht', 284.

106. Bossuyt and Wouters, *Grondlijnen van Internationaal Recht*, 390; Zieck, 'Diplomatiek en Consulair Recht', 284.

107. Satow, 121–2; Lee and Quigley, *Consular Law and Practice*, 341; Bossuyt and Wouters, *Grondlijnen van Internationaal Recht*, 390–1.

108. ICJ, *Case concerning United States Diplomatic and Consular Staff in Tehran* (V.S./Iran), arrest 24 May 1980, I.C.J. Rep. 1980, 3, § 62 in fine; ICJ, *Case concerning the Arrest Warrant of 11 April 2000* (Democratic Republic Congo/Belgium), 14 February 2002, 2002 I.C.J. Rep. 1, § 52. See also Bossuyt and Wouters, *Grondlijnen van Internationaal Recht*, 405; Berridge, *Diplomacy: Theory and Practice*, 109–10; Denza, *Diplomatic Law*, 3–12; Langhorne, 'The regulation of Diplomatic Practice'; Verhoeven, *Droit international public*, 106.

109. Before the VCCR, only the inviolability of consular archives and the immunity of consuls in regard of their official acts were recognized as customary international law. See W.E. Beckett, 'Consular Immunities', *BYIL* (1944), 34–50; Lee and Quigley, *Consular Law and Practice*, 341; Satow, 265–6.

110. ICJ, *Case concerning United States Diplomatic and Consular Staff in Tehran* (V.S./Iran), arrest 24 May 1980, I.C.J. Rep. 1980, 3, § 62 in fine; ICJ, *Case concerning the Arrest Warrant of 11 April 2000* (Democratic Republic Congo/Belgium), 14 February 2002, 2002 I.C.J. Rep. 1, § 52. See also Bossuyt and Wouters, *Grondlijnen van Internationaal Recht*, 420; Lee and Quigley, *Consular Law and Practice*, 341, C.J. Milhaupt, 'The Scope of Consular Immunity under the Vienna Convention on Consular relations: Towards a Principled Interpretation', *Columbia Law Review* 88 (1988), 841.

111. See in the same vein: Article 25 VCDR obliging the receiving state to 'accord full facilities for the performance of the functions of the mission' and Art. 28 VCCR: 'The receiving state shall accord full facilities for the performance of the functions of the consular post.'

112. See *supra*.

113. See Preamble VCDR: 'Realizing that the purpose of such privileges and immunities is not to benefit individuals but to ensure the efficient performance of the functions of diplomatic missions as representing states', while Preamble VCCR states: 'Realizing that the purpose of such privileges and immunities is not to benefit individuals but to ensure the efficient performance of functions by consular posts on behalf of their respective states.' See *supra*. Also: Satow, 268, §19.16; Lee and Quigley, *Consular Law and Practice*, 341–2; Salmon, *Manuel de Droit Diplomatique*, 521–2, §661–2.

114. See *infra*.

115. As stated by Article 73 VCCR: '§1: The provisions of the present Convention shall not affect other international agreements in force as between state parties to them. §2 Nothing in the present Convention shall preclude states from concluding international agreements confirming or supplementing or extending or amplifying the provisions thereof.' For

more information, see: S. Kho, 'Article 73 of the Vienna Convention on Consular Relations: The Relationship between the Vienna Consular Convention and Other International Consular Agreements', *Chinese (Taiwan) Yearbook of International Law and Affairs* 13 (1994–1995), 235–76; Lee and Quigley, *Consular Law and Practice*, 567–73; Satow, 266–7.

116. Court of 's-Gravenhage, the Netherlands, BK-04/02292, 9 June 2006, available at: <rechtspraak.nl>, notes that substantial differences exist between career consuls and honorary consuls (such as: the status, competences, functions, and wages).

117. Premises of honorary consuls are not inviolable, but must be protected by the receiving state against intrusion, damage, or impairment of dignity; Art. 59 VCCR.

118. Diplomatic premises include the private residence of a diplomatic agent, which enjoys the same inviolability and protection as the premises of the mission (Art. 30, §1 VCDR). The private residence of a consul, in contrast, is not considered as being part of the 'consular premises' and does not enjoy inviolability (Art. 31(1) VCCR: 'Consular premises shall be inviolable to the extent provided in this article'). Therefore, it is important to clearly delineate residences of consuls (and consular staff) if they are located in the same building as the premises used exclusively for the work of the consular post. Concerning a private residence of a diplomatic agent, see Attachment Court (Beslagrechter) Brussels, Belgium, 20 October 2000, nullified by Court of Appeal (Cour d'Appel), Brussels, Belgium, 11 September 2001, R.W. 2002–2003, nr. 38, 1509. The question arose whether a building that appears to be deserted, and is in bad condition, should continue to be regarded as a private residence of a diplomatic agent according to Art. 30 VCDR. According to the Court of Appeal, the interruption of actual inhabitation does not entail the ending of the immunity of the building, when it is unclear whether the building lost its domestic purpose definitively.

119. J. d'Aspremont, 'Premises of Diplomatic Missions', *Max Planck Encyclopedia of Public International Law*, §15 available at: <www.mpepil.com>; Denza, *Diplomatic Law*, 150; Salmon, *Manuel de Droit Diplomatique*, 198–9; Satow, 102.

120. ICJ, *Case concerning United States Diplomatic and Consular Staff in Tehran* (U.S./Iran), Judgment 24 May 1980, I.C.J. Rep. 1980, 3, §§ 83–87. Moreover, the Eritrea–Ethiopia Claims Commission recently concluded that Ethiopia had breached Article 22 VCDR by sealing off the Eritrean embassy on the basis of suspicion of criminal activity taking place in the embassy, without the consent of Eritrea. The Claims Commission underlined that 'Ethiopia was not defenseless in the face of alleged criminal activity', as 'Ethiopia was at all times free to terminate diplomatic relations with Eritrea and hence to close its mission.' See: Eritrea–Ethiopia Claims Commission, Partial Award: *Diplomatic Claim—Eritrea's Claim 20* (Eritrea/Ethiopia), decision 19 December 2005, *Report of International Arbitral Awards*, vol. XXVI 381, §§ 46–7. For a more detailed analysis, see Bossuyt and Wouters, *Grondlijnen van Internationaal Recht*, 409–11; Denza, *Diplomatic Law*, 147–50; Salmon, *Manuel de Droit Diplomatique*, 194–207; Satow, 102–3 and 268.

121. Art. 31, §2 VCCR: 'The authorities of the receiving state shall not enter that part of the consular premises which is used exclusively for the purpose of the work of the consular post except with the consent of the head of the consular post or of his designee or of the head of the diplomatic mission of the sending state. The consent of the head of the consular post may, however, be assumed in case of fire or other disaster requiring prompt protective action.'

122. Only consular archives were protected under the former customary international law. See Beckett, 'Consular Immunities'.

123. For an elaborate overview of the negotiations on the inviolability of consular premises, see Lee and Quigley, *Consular Law and Practice*, 356–9.

124. See for example, Constitutional Court Latvia, Assemblies Case, *Agesins and ors v Parliament of Latvia* (Saeima), Constitutional Review, Case No 2006-03-0106, *ILDC* 1062 (LV 2006), 23 November 2006, available at Oxford Reports on International Law in Domestic Courts. The Court decided that neither the VCCR (Art. 31, §3), nor the VCDR (Art. 22, §2), nor customary international law requires Latvia to prohibit peaceful assembly within fifty metres of embassies and consular posts.

125. Recently, the UN Security Council condemned attacks against embassies in Damascus which resulted in damage to embassy premises and injuries to diplomatic personnel. It recalled 'the fundamental principle of the inviolability of diplomatic missions and the obligations on host Governments, including under the 1961 Vienna Convention on Diplomatic Relations, to take all appropriate steps to protect embassy premises'. See UN Security Council, 'Security Press statement on Embassy Attacks in Damascus', SC/10321, 12 July 2011, available at: <http://www.un.org/News/Press/docs/2011/sc10321.doc.htm>. See also ICJ, Armed Activities on the Territory of the Congo (DRC/Uganda), Judgment 19 December 2005, I.C.J Rep. 2005, 31, §342; ICJ, *Case concerning United States Diplomatic and Consular Staff in Tehran* (U.S./Iran), Judgment 24 May 1980, I.C.J. Rep. 1980, 3, $, pp. 30–2, §§ 61–7. d'Aspremont, 'Premises of Diplomatic Missions', §29; Denza, *Diplomatic Law*, 166; Hestermeyer, 'Vienna Convention on Diplomatic Relations (1961)', §25; Lee and Quigley, *Consular Law and Practice*, 373–9; S.D. Murphy, 'Protection of Embassy Properties as a Discretionary Function', *American Journal of International Law* 95:4 (2001), 873–4, at 873; J.-P. Pancracio, *Droit et institutions diplomatiques* (Paris: Pédone, 2007), 239–41; Satow, 104; Salmon, *Manuel de Droit Diplomatique*, 240.

126. ICJ, *Case concerning United States Diplomatic and Consular Staff in Tehran* (U.S./Iran), arrest 24 May 1980, *I.C.J. Rep.* 1980, §95.5.

127. Discussion has emerged regarding the question whether bank accounts are covered by Article 22 VCDR, as they are not held on the mission's premises as required by the wording of the article. Nowadays a functional interpretation has been accepted: as bank accounts serve the functioning of an embassy, they cannot be made subject to attachment or execution. See Court of Appeal (Cour d'Appel), Brussels, Belgium, 4 October 2002 (J.T. 2003, 318, CASES). The Court found that there is a (rebuttable) assumption that money on the account of an embassy is intended for sovereign purposes. Therefore, it enjoys the protection of the VCDR. See Bossuyt and Wouters, *Grondlijnen van Internationaal Recht*, 410–11; Verhoeven, *Droit international public*, 115; Denza, *Diplomatic Law*, 156–9; J.-P. Pancracio, *Droit et institutions diplomatiques*, 233–4; Salmon, *Manuel de Droit Diplomatique*, 202–6; Satow, 103–4; Zieck, 'Diplomatiek en Consulair Recht', 289.

128. Court of Appeal (Cour d'Appel), Brussels, Belgium (8th chamber), 11 September 2001, *R.W.* 2002-2003, 1509: The immunity from requisition of diplomatic premises cannot only be deduced from the Vienna Convention 18 April 1961 on Diplomatic Relations, but is also laid down in international customary law. See also Court of Appeal (Gerechtshof) 's-Gravenhage, the Netherlands (1st civil chamber), preliminary judgment, no. 200.020.729/01, 19 May 2009, §3.4., confirmed by the High Council of the Netherlands (Hoge Raad der Nederlanden) 's-Gravenhage, the Netherlands (Cassation), no. 09/03236, 24 September 2010, both available at: <www.rechtspraak.nl>: The requisition of

diplomatic premises of the ambassador of Columbia breaches (the purpose of) the VCDR; Court of First Instance (Rechtbank) 's-Gravenhage, the Netherlands, AWB 07/5555 GEMWT, 7 October 2008, available at: <http://jure.nl>: decision to tolerate an illegal garage behind the Iranian embassy, in view of Article 22 VCDR. As the head of the Iranian mission expressed his unwillingness to cooperate in order to make an end to the illegal situation, no executorial measures could resort effect. See also District Court, District of Columbia, U.S.A., *AF-CAP, INC.v. DRC*, 326 F. Supp. 2d 128, No. CIV.A.03-1963 JR, 23 July 2004: The US District Court found that the Congolese embassy in the US is immune from attachment in view of Art. 22 VCDR.

129. Lee and Quigley note that requisition and expropriation are often used interchangeably. However, whereas in case of requisition, the property will be returned to its owner, expropriation is permanent (this is in line with the UK interpretation of the terms). See Lee and Quigley, *Consular Law and Practice*, 362.

130. The same goes for honorary consuls: Art. 58, §2 VCCR. See Court of Cassation (Cour de cassation), Belgium, AR P.01.0531.N, 10 September 2002, *Arr.Cass.* 2002, vol. 9, 1774, available at: <http://www.cass.be>: the displacement of an honorary consul to the consulate in order to discuss something with a consular employee was not accepted as 'an act performed in the exercise of his consular functions'.

131. The ICJ stressed the importance of criminal immunity in the *Iran Hostages Case*: 'the Court considers it necessary here and now to stress that, if the intention to submit the hostages to any form of criminal trial or investigation were to be put into effect, that would constitute a grave breach by Iran of its obligations under Article 31, paragraph 1 of the 1961 Vienna Convention'. ICJ, *Case concerning United States Diplomatic and Consular Staff in Tehran* (U.S./Iran), judgment 24 May 1980, I.C.J. Rep. 1980, 3, § 79.

132. Recent American cases: US District Court of Columbia, *Gonzales Paredes v Vila*, 479 F. Supp. 2d 187, 29 March 2007; US District Court of Columbia, *Sabbithi v Al Saleh*, 605 F. Supp. 2d 122, 20 March 2009: 'When examined in context, the term 'commercial activity' [as used in the Vienna Convention on Diplomatic Relations] does not have so broad a meaning as to include occasional service contracts as [plaintiff] contends, but rather relates only to trade or business activity engaged in for personal profit.' For a more detailed analysis of these exceptions, see Denza, *Diplomatic Law*, 289–308; Pancracio, *Droit et institutions diplomatiques*, 217–18; Salmon, *Manuel de Droit Diplomatique*, 309–16; Satow, 130–2.

133. Court of First Instance (Vredegerecht) St.-Pieters-Woluwe, Belgium, 14 May 2007, *J.T.* 2007, 727: confirms that the immunity of diplomatic agents abroad is not limited to actions performed in an official capacity, but encompasses actions performed in a private capacity, with the limitative exceptions of Art. 31 VCDR.

134. Court of Cassation (Cour de Cassation), France (criminal), no. 09-88675, 8 April 2010, *Bull. Crim.*: Applicant (the Permanent Representative of Angola to UNESCO) was a French national. As the criminal facts took place before applicant was hired as a diplomatic agent, the criminal facts are not to be conceived as 'official acts performed in the exercise of his functions' (Art. 38, §1 VCDR).

135. A recent American case *Swarna v. Al-Awadi* confirms: 'while residual diplomatic immunity applies to the acts performed by such a person in the exercise of his functions as a member of the mission, it does not apply to actions that pertain to his household or personal life and that may provide, at best, an indirect rather than a direct benefit to diplomatic functions'. Court of Appeals, New York, U.S.A. (Second Circuit), 622 F. 3d 123, 77

Fed.R.Serv.3d 785, 24 September 2010. The judge can consider the facts of the case to determine the scope of diplomatic protection, notwithstanding cases where immunity is raised *in limine litis*. See e.g.: Supreme Court, New York, U.S.A., *Reinoso v. Bragg*, 2010 WL 3607482, 14 September 2010: Plaintiff sought to recover for personal injuries allegedly sustained in a motor vehicle accident; defendant, conducting the motor vehicle, claims diplomatic immunity through the diplomatic status of his wife, a UN diplomatic agent. As the accident occurred three days before the appointment of the defendant's wife as diplomatic agent, the New York Supreme Court found that diplomatic immunity does not automatically entail the incompetence of the judicial system.

136. Court of Cassation (Cour de cassation), Belgium, AR P.00.0401.N, 30 October 2001, *Arr. Cass.* 2001, vol. 9, 1811, available at: <http://www.cass.be> (21 December 2001): when a criminal process is initiated against a consular agent, it is the consular agent who needs to deliver factual proof indicating that the acts for which he is prosecuted, were performed in the exercise of his consular functions. The criminal judge then assesses this defence, with application of the rules concerning the burden of proof in criminal matters. According to these rules, the public prosecutor can then prove that the consul's defence is faulty. Police Court (Politierechtbank) Ghent, Belgium, 14 April 2000, *T.G.R.* 2000, 264: the public prosecutor needs to prove that the consular agent was not acting in the exercise of his consular functions in order to prevent that immunity (Art. 43, §1 VCCR) applies. In casu, the public prosecutor failed to do so.

137. See *supra*, part 28.3.2.1.

138. Milhaupt describes several possible conflicting interpretations: broad interpretations (based on an extensive interpretation of Art. 5 and 43 VCCR), narrow interpretations (e.g. based on an extensive interpretation of Art. 55 VCCR), alternative interpretations (e.g. a political solution to the problem), interpretations according to functional necessity (balancing the interests of the sending state and the receiving state). See M.J. Milhaupt, 'The Scope of Consular Immunity under the Vienna Convention on Consular relations: Towards a Principled Interpretation,' *Columbia Law Review* 88 (1988), 845–57. See also Lee and Quigley, *Consular Law and Practice*, 448–51. For example: Court of Appeal (Oberlandesgericht) Düsseldorf 2, Germany, 3 May 1996, available at: <juris.de>: the VCCR does not prevent the prosecution of a consular agent for an offence committed during a private holiday with a motor vehicle. Even if the vehicle carries an official consular badge, the trip with the motor vehicle cannot be considered as a consular activity; United States District Court, No. 10-10524., 2010 WL 4791436 (E.D. Mich.), 13 October 2010: issuing or refusing visa does fall within the functions of a consul, therefore he enjoys immunity in this regard.

139. Honorary consuls do not enjoy inviolability, but the receiving state is under a duty to accord to an honorary consular officer such protection as may be required by reason of his official position (Art. 64 VCCR).

140. As Satow notes, the term 'grave crime' is not defined in the VCCR, but is defined in the law of a number of state parties to the Convention, including the UK Consular Relations Act 1968 (c18). See Satow, 271, footnote 14.

141. For privileges of honorary consuls see: Art. 62 VCCR (exemption from customs duties); Art. 66 VCCR (exemption from taxation); Art. 67 VCCR (exemption from personal services and contributions).

142. On fiscal privileges for diplomats: Constitutional Court (Arbitragehof), Belgium, (preliminary question), no. 149/2005, 28 September 2005, *A.A.* 2005, vol. 4, 1913, §B4; available

at: <www.const-court.be>; on fiscal privileges for consuls: Court of Antwerp, Belgium, 9 September 1997, *Fisc. Act.* 1997, vol. 35, 2; Administrative Court of Appeal (Cour Administrative d'Appel) Lyon, France, 2nd chamber, 01LY00201, 7 February 2002, available at: <http://legimobile.fr/fr/jp/a/caa/69123/2002/2/7/01LY00201/>.

143. For example: United States Court of Appeals, Second Circuit, *The City of New York v. The Permanent Mission of India to the United Nations*, 618 F. 3d 172, 10 March 2010: The District Court addressed the Missions' claimed tax exemption under the applicable Conventions: Article 32 of the Vienna Convention on Consular Relations and 23 VCDR. The District Court held that 'the plain language of the VCCR and the VCDR unequivocally supports the City's (New York) position' that the portions of the missions used to house employees and their families are not tax exempt.

144. Cf. Art. 2(1) United Nations Charter. The second recital of the VCDR's preamble refers to the principle of sovereign equality of state as laid down in the Charter.

145. I. Brownlie, *Principles of Public International Law*, 7th edition (Oxford: Oxford University Press, 2008), 299.

146. D. Carreau, *Droit International*, 10th edition (Paris: Pédone, 2009), 336–8.

147. A. Aust, *Handbook of International Law*, 2nd edition (Cambridge: Cambridge University Press, 2010), 43.

148. Aust, *Handbook of International Law*.

149. In Art. 41, §3 VCDR and Art. 55, § 2 VCCR respectively.

150. For a more detailed analysis, see section 28.4.

151. J. Salmon, 'Les immunités diplomatiques dans la tourmente', *Liber Amicorum Jean-Pierre Cot. Le Procès International* (Brussels: Bruylant, 2009), 215; A. Plantey, *Principes de Diplomatie*, p. 24, § 66; F.O. Vicuna, 'Diplomatic and Consular Immunities and Human Rights', *I.C.L.Q.* (1991), 35. Also Chapter 36, this volume.

152. See inter alia L. Sh. Farhangi, 'Insuring Against Abuse of Diplomatic Immunity', *Stanford Law Review* (1986), 1517–50; R. Higgins, 'The Abuse of Diplomatic Privileges and Immunities: Recent United Kingdom Experience' *A.J.I.L.79* (1985), 641–51; M.B. McDonough, 'Privileged Outlaws: Diplomats, Crime and Immunity', *Suffolk Transnational Law Review* 20 (1997), 475–97; W.G. Morris, 'Constitutional Solutions to the Problem of Diplomatic Crime and Immunity', *Hofstra Law Review* 36:2 (2007), 60136.

153. Parliamentary Assembly of the Council of Europe, Recommendation 1523 (2001), Eur. Parl. Ass. Deb. (18th Sess.), 26 June 2001, Art. 10 (iv).

154. Salmon, 'Les immunités diplomatiques dans la tourmente', 216.

155. The ICJ underlined in the *Arrest Warrant Case*: 'Immunity from criminal jurisdiction and individual criminal responsibility are quite separate concepts. While jurisdictional immunity is procedural in nature, criminal responsibility is a question of substantive law. Jurisdictional immunity may well bar prosecution for a certain period or for certain offences; it cannot exonerate the person whom it applies from all criminal responsibility.' See: ICJ, *Case concerning the Arrest Warrant of 11 April 2000* (DRC/Belgium), 14 February 2002, 2002 *ICJ Rep.* 1, § 60; M.A. Summers, 'Diplomatic Immunity Ratione Personae: Did The International Court of Justice Create a New Customary Law Rule in *Congo v Belgium*?', *Michigan State Journal of International Law* 459 (2007–2008), 461–5.

156. Milhaupt, 'The Scope of Consular Immunity under the Vienna Convention on Consular relations', 843–4; Lee and Quigley, *Consular Law and Practice*, 74–7; Satow, 270.

157. 'The sanctioning of abuse or misconduct committed abroad is not legal but diplomatic.' Plantey, *Principes de Diplomatie*, p. 287, § 1095.

158. See amongst others: Higgins, 'The Abuse of Diplomatic Privileges and Immunities', 649–51; Lee and Quigley, *Consular Law and Practice*, 467; Plantey, *Principes de Diplomatie*, 287; Salmon, 'Les immunités diplomatiques dans la tourmente', 216; Satow, 128–40.

159. Recently: District Court, District of Columbia, U.S.A, *Great Socialist People's Libyan Arab Jamahiriya v Miski*, 638 F. Supp. 2d 1 DDC, 25 January 2010: Diplomatic immunity, like sovereign immunity, can be waived. The Libyan ambassador's invocation of his diplomatic immunity to avoid testifying in Libyan government's action alleging, inter alia, violation of its trademark rights, did not require dismissal of the action, where defendant would not be prejudiced if Libyan government chose not to call the ambassador as a witness at trial; there were other officials employed by the Libyan embassy who had personal knowledge of the facts underlying the complaint. Supreme Court of the Russian Federation (Appeal Judgment), *O. v. L.*, N 5-GO5-1, 1 February 2005, ILDC 959 (RU 2005): A Russian diplomat in Ukraine was sentenced by a local court to pay alimony for his minor child. His former wife demanded the execution of the Ukrainian court's decision in Russia. In the following Russian appeal procedure, the Supreme Court found that the diplomatic immunities determined by the VCDR preclude the jurisdiction of Ukrainian authorities to hear the case. The applicant should have brought the case before Russian courts. For a detailed discussion on waiver of immunity, see Denza, *Diplomatic Law*, 330–48; Salmon, *Manuel de Droit Diplomatique*, 328–45; Satow, 35–137.

160. Federal Court of Appeal, Ottawa, Canada, *Copello v Canada (Minister of Foreign Affairs)*, 2003 FCA 295 (Can LII), 3 July 2003, § 21, available at: <www.canlii.org/en/ca/fca/doc/2003/2003fca295/2003fca295.html>: Appeal against a declaration of persona non grata: it was found that the declaration of persona non grata is not a legal issue and remains in the political arena. Therefore, it was found that the decision was not justifiable. For a more elaborate analysis of the declaration of 'persona non grata', see J. d'Aspremont, 'Persona Non Grata', *Max Planck Encyclopedia of Public International Law*, available at: <www.mpepil.com>; Denza, *Diplomatic Law*, 73–87; Salmon, *Manuel de Droit Diplomatique*, 348; Satow, 206–15.

161. See Beckett, 'Consular Immunities'; see also Lee and Quigley, *Consular Law and Practice*, 389 who refer to the Harvard Research Draft which considered it 'the most universally recognized of all consular immunities'; Denza, *Diplomatic Law*, 189–92.

162. See Chapter 25, this volume.

163. The consular archives and documents of a consular post headed by an honorary consular officer are inviolable, provided that they are kept separate from other papers and documents (Art. 61 VCCR).

164. Satow, 113; Salmon, *o.c.*, 209, §317; Denza, *Diplomatic Law*, 195.

165. Satow, 113; W.-M. Choi, 'Diplomatic and Consular Law in the Internet Age', *Singapore Yearbook of International Law* 10 (2006), 117–32, at 123.

166. Salmon, *Manuel de Droit Diplomatique*, 210, §318; Satow, 113; Choi, 'Diplomatic and Consular Law in the Internet Age', 123.

167. For communication of consuls with nationals of the sending state (Art. 36 VCCR) see above. The right of consuls to communicate with the receiving state is a qualitative right (Article 38). See Lee and Quigley, *Consular Law and Practice*, 405.

168. Satow, 115; Hestermeyer, 'Vienna Convention on Diplomatic Relations (1961)', §28; Choi, 'Diplomatic and Consular Law in the Internet Age', 125.

169. In practice, however, surveillance operations do take place. A recent example is the 2003 surveillance operation ordered by the US National Security Agency against the

delegations in New York of members of the Security Council during the diplomatic efforts to obtain a resolution explicitly authorizing the use of force against Iraq. This information was leaked in *The Observer* of 2 March 2003, available at <www.guardian.co.uk/world/2003/mar/02/usa.iraq>. See Denza, *Diplomatic Law*, 222. Lee and Quigley also note that the emergence of electronic correspondence has opened new avenues of interference with communications, and refer to an example of 2007, when Estonia experienced a flood of incoming messages, emanating apparently from Russia. Lee and Quigley, *Consular Law and Practice*, 402.

170. For more on WikiLeaks and related phenomena, see Chapter 25, this volume.

171. In March 2011, the US ambassador to Mexico resigned over a leaked cable in which he had stated the failure of the Mexican government's anti-crime strategy. This appears to be the biggest fallout yet from thousands of sensitive US diplomatic cables from around the world released by WikiLeaks. *The Guardian,* 'US ambassador to Mexico resigns over WikiLeaks embassy cables', 20 March 2011; T*he Washington Post*, 'U.S. ambassador to Mexico resigns after WikiLeaks revelations', 19 March 2011.

172. *The Telegraph*, 'WikiLeaks sparks worldwide diplomatic crisis', 28 November 2010; Opinio Juris Blog, P. Spiro, 'Latest WikiLeaks Dump: Swan Song for the Diplomatic Cable?', 28 November 2010; DiploFoundation Blog, J. Kurbalija, 'How will WikiLeaks affect diplomacy?', 30 November 2010.

173. ECHR, *Stoll v. Switzerland*, 10 December 2007, no. 69698/01, § 110.

174. Denza, *Diplomatic Law*, 211–27; Lee and Quigley, *Consular Law and Practice*, 402; Pancracio, *Droit et institutions diplomatiques*, 248; Plantey, *Principes de Diplomatie*, 293; Salmon, *Manuel de Droit Diplomatique*, 250; Satow, 114–16.

175. See in this regard Satow, 116: 'in practice this inviolability cannot be guaranteed if the letters are sent through the public post rather than through a sealed diplomatic bag, this provision is seldom relied on or publicly invoked'.

176. Hestermeyer, 'Vienna Convention on Diplomatic Relations (1961)', §43; Plantey, *Principes de Diplomatie*, 293–4.

177. See e.g. Court of First Instance (Rechtbank) Haarlem, the Netherlands (criminal), no. 15/500349-06, 23 June 2006, available at: <www.rechtspraak.nl>. It concerned a case where cocaine was transported in an allegedly diplomatic bag. As the bag was only sealed, and did not bear visible external marks of its character (Art. 27, §4, VCDR), the bag did not meet the requirements to be conceived as a diplomatic bag.

178. The regulation adopted by the VCDR is also stricter than the customary law that applied prior to the entry into force of the VCDR. The international customary rule allowed—as the VCCR does—to return the diplomatic bag or request to open the diplomatic bag in case of suspicion of abuse. See M.J.F. Addicott, 'The Status of the Diplomatic Bag: A Proposed United States Position', *Houston Journal of International Law* 13:2 (1991), 221–57, at 224–5; d'Aspremont, 'Diplomatic Courier and Bag', *Max Planck Encyclopedia of Public International Law*, §8, available at: <www.mpepil.com>; Denza, *Diplomatic Law*, 227; Satow, 116.

179. d'Aspremont, 'Diplomatic Courier and Bag'; Denza, *Diplomatic Law*, 227; Salmon, *Manuel de Droit Diplomatique*, 247–9; Satow, 116; A. Zeidman, 'The abuse of the diplomatic bag: a proposed solution', *Cardozo Law Review* 11 (1989), 427.

180. Amongst others, Bahrain, Qatar, Kuwait, Libya, and Saudi-Arabia entered such reservations. For an overview of all reservations, see UN Treaty Collection, available at: <http://

treaties.un.org/Pages/ViewDetails.aspx?src=TREATY&mtdsg_no=III-3&chapter=3&lang=en>.

181. See e.g. the objections of Australia, France, the UK, Ireland, and the US, <http://treaties. un.org/Pages/ViewDetails.aspx?src=TREATY&mtdsg_no=III-3&chapter=3&lang=en>.

182. See e.g. the objections of Mongolia, Poland, and the Soviet Union, <http://treaties.un.org/ Pages/ViewDetails.aspx?src=TREATY&mtdsg_no=III-3&chapter=3&lang=en>.

183. See Art. 19c Vienna Convention on the Law of Treaties, signed at Vienna on 23 May 1969, entry into force 27 January 1980, *UNTS*, vol. 1155, p. 331, nr. 18232. According to this article, no reservation can be made that goes against the object or purpose of the treaty in question.

184. The objection of the Netherlands against the reservation of Bahrain concerning the diplomatic bag exemplifies this: 'The Kingdom of the Netherlands does not accept the declaration by the State of Bahrain concerning Article 27, paragraph 3 of the Convention. It takes the view that this provision remains in force in relations between it and the State of Bahrain in accordance with international customary law. The Kingdom of the Netherlands is nevertheless prepared to agree to the following arrangement on a basis of reciprocity: If the authorities of the receiving State have serious grounds for supposing that the diplomatic bag contains something which pursuant to Article 27, paragraph 4 of the Convention may not be sent in the diplomatic bag, they may demand that the bag be opened in the presence of the representative of the diplomat mission concerned. If the authorities of the sending State refuse to comply with such a request, the diplomatic bag shall be sent back to the place of origin.'

185. Lee and Quigley, *Consular Law and Practice*, 412–13; Satow, 269.

186. See Denza, *Diplomatic Law*, 241; Satow, 117; these authors argue to allow sniffer dogs and other techniques which allow external control of diplomatic bags.

187. Unlike e.g. New Zealand which did not allow scanning, Austria permitted it to the extent that the scanning was practised on a non-discriminatory basis, while Kuwait scanned diplomatic bags systematically. See Denza, *Diplomatic Law*, 239–40; Salmon, *Manuel de Droit Diplomatique*, 248–9. Relevant is the report of the ILC on the subject, which recommends states to organize an international conference to further codify international rules on the application of diplomatic bags and couriers, and putting forward a proposal for a uniform solution to the problem (prohibiting the opening of diplomatic bags and the scanning of these bags, but allowing control of the diplomatic bags in line with the provisions of the VCCR). ILC, 'Status of the Diplomatic Courier and the Diplomatic Bag not Accompanied by Diplomatic Courier', *ILC Yearbook 1989*, vol. II, session 41, 1989.

188. Addicott, 'The Status of the Diplomatic Bag', 236–7; d'Aspremont, 'Diplomatic Courier and Bag'; Denza, *Diplomatic Law*, 242; Satow, 117.

189. Commission Regulation (EU) No 185/2010 of 4 March 2010 laying down detailed measures for the implementation of the common basic standards on aviation security, OJ. 2010, L 55/1, Annex, 4.1.2.11.

CHAPTER 29

SOFT POWER

SU CHANGHE

> There are but two powers in the world, the sword and the mind; in the long run, the sword is always beaten by the mind. Napoleon

IN contemporary diplomacy and international relations, there is probably no concept more widely accepted among policy-makers and students of international relations than that of soft power. Soft power was originally coined as a phrase by Joseph Nye during the debate on whether the US was declining in the late 1980s. It refers, according to Nye, to 'the ability to get what you want through attraction rather than coercion or payments. It arises from the attractiveness of a country's culture, political ideals, and policies. When our policies are seen as legitimate in the eyes of others, our soft power is enhanced.'[1] Building on his original notion of soft power, as a means of persuasion, Nye elaborated on the concept in 2006 with a focus on soft power as the ability to alter the behaviour of others to get what you want by attraction and co-optation as opposed to coercion.[2] Since the emergence of the concept of soft power, it has quickly become accepted by a wide range of statesmen and intellectuals and become thoroughly embedded in the conversation about international diplomacy. Certainly it has been given a great deal of attention and has been applied deeply through public diplomacy by successive US administrations, especially since 9/11. Equally important, it has moved beyond the confines of the United States. In a report delivered to the 17th Communist Party Congress, the Chinese President Hu Jintao notably used this concept and spoke of the need to increase China's soft power in foreign relations.

As a form of cultural power, of course, soft power existed long before it was put forward as a concept within the framework of International Relations. As Fernand Braudel has shown, Spain as a centre of civilizational diffusion in the 17th century had generated great cultural attraction in Europe, especially in the court life in France; the elite group in France fully embracing Spain fashion and generally Cervantes novels in particular.[3]

In 1825 the Russian Decembrist, most of them influenced by Voltaire and Rousseau's Enlightenment thought during their military expedition in Paris, generated an uprising to challenge the rule of tsars. These illustrations exemplify the use of soft power in the historical dissemination of ideas. As a cultural condition, traditional Confucianism wisdom particularly emphasises the importance of governance by kindness, generosity, and virtue, whether in domestic governance or in foreign relations. It reflects the importance of soft use of power in the art of state and was a key factor in assuring the effectiveness of the Chinese hierarchical international system in the East Asian world order. In current terminology, this way of governance could be labelled as soft power.

The mind is mightier than the sword; this is why the notion of soft power attracts so much attention in the world. With this importance in mind, this chapter begins with a discussion about power as a relationship among actors. Moving away from traditional definitions of power, it defines power in the context of connectedness. Section 29.2 explains why soft power becomes more and more significant for diplomacy and international relations. Section 29.3 alternatively explores the ways in which soft power is produced; it pays special attention to the roles of knowledge and education in this process. Section 29.4 suggests some indicators for evaluating the scope of soft power, though soft power is actually very hard to measure. Cultural promotion and public diplomacy as means to increase soft power are then explored in section 29.5. Lastly, section 29.6 surveys the ongoing trajectory of soft power, particularly in the global manifestations of local cultural attributes.

29.1 POWER AS A RELATION AMONG ACTORS

People or states live in a setting of multiple relations, and their behaviours are mostly determined by the nature of those relations. If relations are dominated or defined by the threat of violence or military pressure, then the strong side can exert power over the weak side. The traditional definition of power, as Robert Dahl defines, is more or less based on confronting coercive relations among actors. Power, for Robert Dahl, is a matter of A getting B to do what A wants, or of A forcing B not to do what B wants to do. 'A has power over B to the extent that he can get B to do something that B would not otherwise do.'[4] In this case, power heavily depends on the amount of material resources possessed by the stronger side; power is to some extent equal to influence. The will and choice of one side is to be altered by the other's coercive power. In such cases, more power means an actor should maintain and develop its material elements of power, such as territorial size, number of population, economic quality, and military technology. According to Nye, this kind of power should be called 'hard power'.

Power would also naturally emerge if the particular relation is located in a asymmetrical setting of interdependence. In an influential book on power and interdependence, Robert Keohane and Joseph Nye put forward two concepts of vulnerability and sensibility to understand power as a relation among actors. The sensibility 'involves degrees of responsiveness within a policy framework—how quickly do changes in one country bring costly changes in another, and how great are the costly effects'; the vulnerability can be defined as 'an actor's liability to suffer costs imposed by external events after policies have been altered.'[5] Put simply, in a world of growing interdependence, the more resources, instruments, or policy choice used by a country, the greater the power it can exert over another country. Therefore, the asymmetrical nature of relations is one source of power. On the other hand, the role of power may be diminished or even disappear if relations are more equal or *mutually* dependent. Suppose two countries live in an ideal condition of *equal* interdependence; each country's power over the other will be offset by mutual capability. A familiar example for us is the balance of terror in a nuclear era; once both countries possess the ability of the second strike, no side can exert its nuclear power over the other as a means to achieve its goals.

Obviously, not all relations among actors must be defined in terms of material resources; in fact, relations can also be determined by rules and norms. The origin of power could also be based on the consent of the actors. If relations reflect more equal contracts between government and people, then the government's power, to some large extent, is diminished and constrained, while the legitimacy of government is maintained. Most governments are organized and run under this principle in modern society. That is to say, democratic government has been promoted as common model all over the world, although some countries may disagree with the idea that there is a single model of democracy. Be that as it may, government's power is largely grounded in people's consent; its power over people is limited, while it is also effective when it is given by consent of the people. To be concise, in this form of relationship contractual relation, rules, and norms matter, and power has been transferred from monopoly actor to third-party institutions, such as government or the legislative body. Applying this logic to international relations, international institutions, as one kind of third-party institution, and multilateralism would be quite important for constructing contractual relations among countries. Countries that have an intimate knowledge of institutions will be proficient in using the contractual relations with other countries; this will in turn definitely create soft power for them.

The nature of social relations could also be defined in terms of common knowledge. Any social relation will be fragile if it operates as a one-off action, while the relation will be strong and reciprocal when it is associated with more extensive forms of interaction. Common knowledge is of great help in creating trust, identity, and collective action in a society. When Nye talks about 'co-optive power', i.e. 'the ability of a country to structure a situation so that other countries develop preferences or define interests in ways consistent with its own',[6] he is stressing the importance of a country's common knowledge in shaping the beliefs and behaviour of another country. This is why common knowledge is so important for a country's accumulation of soft power.

The societal nature of power enables us to better understand the widely non-coercive use of power in domestic and international politics. However, it is still necessary for us to appreciate some of the criticisms made of the notion of relational power. The societal aspect of power, as well as the material aspect of power, has been frequently criticized by postmodernist schools. Michel Foucault, one of the masters in contemporary philosophy, shows us how modern society has become penal and coercive in nature, and criticizes the discipline and punitive mechanism involved in shaping citizens' thinking and behaviour. He emphasises the factor of the distorted relation, as a symbol of the prison, in constructing and institutionalizing a complex discourse of power networks. Power is in turn displayed as a hidden and punitive power everywhere; people have no chance of making their own individual decisions.[7] Another influential cultural critic has been Edward Said. In his research on Western/occidental discourse, he aims to show how one's identity is more or less determined by one's relationship with the Other (the third world) through cultural enterprise. In Said's eyes, therefore, *soft power* is another form of cultural hegemony; the use of soft power is actually motivated by the particular desire for cultural hegemony.[8] Postmodernism and cultural relativism have exercised extensive influence over the world; as we know, soft power assumes that there are universal values and norms which could be valid and applicable everywhere. The two schools, cultural universalism and relativism, are fundamentally in contradiction. When we discuss the notion of soft power, therefore, we should bear their distinctive claims in mind, even if neither school turns out to prevail over the other in the future.

29.2 SOFT POWER MATTERS

Soft power has become increasingly important and it is used strategically in many countries. At least three factors contribute to soft power's increasing role in current diplomacy and international relations.

The most important factor is the appearance of nuclear weapons, which makes a major war unlikely and unacceptable among great powers. With the appearance of the ultimate weapon, human beings profoundly experienced the horror of wars, and states realized that it is increasingly difficult to achieve political goals exclusively through the use (or threat of use) of military power. This doesn't mean that military power no longer has any effect, but the fact is that its effects are really reduced and undermined in current international relations. Furthermore, even though a country can perhaps in select cases easily conquer and occupy another country through the use of military force, it is obvious that ruling over the occupied country successfully is a formidable challenge. Additionally, the prevailing ethos of non-violence across the world also reduces the possibility of using military force or hard power in achieving goals. Finally, in terms of costs, the economic and cultural means of achieving what a country wants seems to be more effective and viable than the way of coercive action; therefore, states prefer the use of soft over hard power.

The second factor is the popularization of advanced education, which creates favourable conditions for the use of soft power. With the extension of advanced education and the rise of literacy rates across the world, it is easier for select publics and not just elites to access information. In a traditional society, information and knowledge are more or less monopolized and controlled by small groups. But the progress of advanced education and information technology fundamentally destroys the information monopoly machines. It is no exaggeration to select publics are becoming more attentive. People with advanced education are more inclined to accept rational knowledge through their own judgement process. Akin to rational consumers in the supermarket, their ability to discriminate between suitable and unsuitable knowledge enables them to accept more reasonable values, institutions, and ways of life. This doesn't mean that through their own exercise of judgement select publics always make the best choices or lead the best lives, but it is desirable nevertheless for them to be allowed to search themselves for better order and a better life. More importantly, with the worldwide democratization movement and the relaxation of political systems, it is very likely that domestic audiences, through their voting power, transform their vision into political reality, forcing governments to behave in accordance with international norms. The promotion of advanced education, the increasing number of educated people, and the loosening of social structures therefore makes it possible for the pen to be mightier than the sword.

The third and related factor is the strong, penetrating power of information and knowledge, particular in the Internet era. During the Middle Ages it was said that a man or woman could be promoted to professor just because of his or her exclusive monopoly of a book, while in 2010 in China alone seven billion books have been published. Information and knowledge undoubtedly flow more easily and quickly than guns, and people's ways of thinking and acting are ultimately influenced by the information and knowledge to which they have access. A country may exclude the physical way of influence, such as coercive intervention and trade quotas, but it is highly unlikely to reject the spread and penetration of public information. This is one reason why the media and information industry have so much power of influence in current society.

Among the mediators of information and knowledge, global television and Internet are two of the most effective means that each country prefers to use to promote proper ideas and norms. Both means are essential to the use of soft power. The BBC and CNN are definitely the two most influential TV stations in the current global media order. The bipolar media system, however, is more or less challenged by emerging mediators from developing countries, for example, the Qatar-based Al-Jazeera satellite television and China's CCTV International Channel. Significantly, the president of Chinese Xinhua News Agency published an article in *The Wall Street Journal* calling for a 'FAIR' world media order.[9]

In an age of growing globalization, as Nye argues, a country's capacity to organize information and effective communication may prove more relevant for its accumulation of soft power.[10] The world appears to be 'flat' rather than a hierarchical bureaucracy.[11] Structural power based on a hierarchy system has become largely ineffective with the rapid horizontal diffusion of knowledge and information. Moreover, the social organizational structure has been forced to adapt to the flat situation, which makes the use of penetrating soft power easier than that of physical hard power.

29.3 THE WAYS OF SOFT POWER'S PRODUCTION

Knowledge is an asset and a source of power for all of countries. A country's soft power is highly dependent on its ability to provide thinking and knowledge to its people and the rest in the world. Historically, the centre of knowledge production is also the centre of diffusion of soft power. However, not all knowledge could be diffused and ultimately accepted by others; local knowledge is seen to be as useful in a small community.[12] Knowledge that is based on particularism or relativism will be hard to be accepted and shared by other society until it is first upgraded and transformed into common knowledge. Common knowledge is applicable in other societies; it binds people together politically, it economically improves living conditions and creates wealth, and it facilitates harmonious order socially and morally. The movement of globalization makes sense of common knowledge for managing the public issues facing the world. Some natures are usually considered as necessary prerequisites that should be satisfied for the possible promotion of common knowledge. Firstly, the knowledge should give reasonable answers to fundamental problems facing human beings; secondly, it should be commensurable among divergent societies; thirdly, it should be effective. Therefore, for example, the form(s) of government by the people, of the people, and for the people has been widely seen and accepted as the competitive domestic governance model around the world. It undoubtedly originated in modern Western political practice. We could in many instances assert that common knowledge about responsible democratic government is a kind of soft power, and is very important knowledge capital for governing public affairs.

Along this logic, suppose a country is a pioneer in generating a new low-carbon model of economics; undoubtedly, this country would gain great soft power by providing a new way of living to the rest of the world. Another example is the social business model, which has been a subject of intense speculation recently. Self-interested-oriented business models have been criticized, especially during financial crises; as these models are seen to be an unsustainable and zero-sum approach. The business model based on the coordination of profits and social responsibility in turn has become increasingly desirable for any society. In overall terms, the attraction of soft power is based on the capacity of a country in knowledge innovation, whether in the area of political systems, social organization, or business models. The country with strong innovative capabilities will play the role of a purposeful guide in the international society. In this sense, it is true that the U.S.'s power of innovation in the high-tech area (e.g. the creation of the Internet) contributes greatly to its soft power resources in attracting people all over the world to follow its technology model.

The production of soft power is also highly related to opinion leaders. Opinion leaders' power originates from their credibility, reliability, and resolution for public affairs. Opinion leaders in current society are now scattered around issue areas. In traditional societies, religious leaders, as well as the monarchy, had great power in affecting people's thinking and behaviour. However, the opinion leaders of today are quite fragmented; no one could claim that he or she had absolute resources to attract all kinds of people in all issue areas to follow them. As we know, a lot of people have been great admirers of Steve Jobs because of his innovative ability in designing computers, while other people prefer to follow the actions of Greenpeace in trying to protect the environment. Opinion leaders may also be authoritative content providers, such as Disney World/Land in the entertainment industry, Google in search technology and information gathering, and other media giants. Therefore, the carrier of soft power is not monolithic; it has been diffused from government to non-government actors.

Education may be seen as the most effective way to produce and promote soft power. A good education system by itself is the dynamic of innovation; it contributes to producing new knowledge, which is an indispensable requirement for soft power. The modern graduate education originated in Germany, and it has direct connection with the Humboldt idea of a university. In current international education, the U.S. is endowed with a world-class tertiary educational system second to none. It has attracted a large number of international students to study at its universities. There is no implication that these students must take pro-American attitudes when they graduate and return to their homelands, but they are really a force which must not be ignored in the process of promoting the U.S. cultures.

Last but not least, the popularization of a particular language is generally considered to be a highly favourable factor for accumulation of soft power. Spanish was extremely useful in Europe as a language of commerce; French has all along been as international law language; while in current international communications, English has been as 'globish' language for commerce and negotiation. It is estimated that more than forty-five countries' official language is English, and one-third of the world's population speaks English. Therefore, it is no exaggeration to say that English is the lingua franca of the world. At present, more than 1.4 billion people, approximately one-fifth of the world's population, speak Chinese as their mother tongue. However, the majority of Chinese speakers live in China, so the internationalization of the Chinese language does not in fact compare to that of English, or even French. Obviously, language and soft power mutually reinforce one another. They exist in a cause-and-effect relationship. But this does not mean that language is a necessary and sufficient condition for the production of soft power; the lower internationalization of a native language does not in fact translate into weaker soft power in the world. The point is only that the popularization of language is very beneficial to the extension of soft power.

The above points are quite related to the general production of soft power. In terms of diplomacy and international relations, based on the contractual relations among countries, soft power mostly depends on a country's ability to build institutions. Since the end of the Second World War, multilateral international institutions have been valued by more and more countries as a mechanism of the rule of law for maintaining the stability of the international system. In his 1990 book, Nye put forward a point about institutional power, to the effect that a country could achieve soft power through designing institutions, agenda-setting, and the establishment of coalitional willingness.[13] In more detail, the soft power of a country in terms of international institutions depends on the following factors. Firstly, the country should be acquainted with the rules and norms of international institutions. Although some international institutions are criticized for being unequal and unfair, most of them are still indispensible factors for the operation of international communications. Secondly, the country should learn to set agendas not merely for its own interests, but also for the public interests, since only the agenda which represents the greater number of public interests is likely to gain support. The agenda-setting to some extent reflects a kind of discourse power; however, it also requires a country to have strong communication skills to create consensus in a group with divergent views. Thirdly, the successful design solution for a tough issue created by a country could also attract other countries to follow it, thus increasing its soft power. For example, Chinese Premier Zhou Enlai's constructive role in the Bandung Conference in 1955, particularly his principle of seeking common ground while reserving differences to meetings of participants, was one key factor in making the conference successful, and therefore expanded the reputation and influence of China in the third world. There are lots of similar examples in diplomatic history, such as the role of Jimmy Carter in the Middle East peace progress mediation. Fourthly, credibility-saving is also critical to a country's soft power in international institutions. Put simply, the national image is an important element of soft power; the more a country complies with international rules and norms, the more reputation and social capital it can create in the international society. Lastly, a country's actions based on inclusive interests rather than self-interests increases its soft power; conversely, narrow nationalism is, to a great extent, a disadvantage in the accumulation of soft power. In the case of China's influence in Africa, it was said that African countries had an authentic attraction for China, the reason being that Africans never forgot China's timely and disinterested aid to them during the 1960s. However, China's soft power in Africa is very likely to be drained due to some of its entrepreneurial activities guided by narrow self-interest.

29.4 MEASURING SOFT POWER

To some extent, soft power is a kind of social capital.[14] Akin to social capital, measurement of soft power is difficult. Some indicators are normally used to measure the size of hard power, such as geographical resources, economic size, and military capability. Compared with the relatively feasible measures of hard power, soft power, just like love and feeling, is hard to measure. Nye speaks of aspects of soft power, such as cultural and ideological attraction, as well as rules and institutions of international regimes.[15] But it seems that nobody could tell us *how much* soft power a country possesses in international relations. In a soft power survey in East Asian countries, the Chicago Council on Global Affairs shows that the U.S. has much more soft power than China in East Asia; China's soft power, in some indices, is even weaker than that of South Korea and Japan.[16] In a recent Chinese National Image of Global Survey by Shanghai Jiaotong University nearly 40.6 per cent of those polled said that China has a rich cultural heritage, and 72.5

per cent don't think China has attractive popular cultures; 55 per cent of those polled believe that China's political institutions could satisfy public demand, and 80 per cent believe that China's global influence will rise in the future.[17]

Thanks to the progress of census-data processing technology, the evaluation of a country's soft power might be feasible. Some indicators used in such exercises for evaluating the scope of soft power are worth of mentioning here.[18]

1. Politics: responsible democratic system; level of rule of law; equality and efficiency of governmental actions; corruption index; protection of human rights; governmental capability in addressing public bads; citizens' happiness feeling; flexibility of institutions in resource mobilization.

2. Economics: the recognized degree of business model; reliable and credible rating agencies; numbers of corporate name brands; innovation capability of economic organization; healthy financing system; contribution ratio to world economy; the openness of economic system; quality of products; likelihood of buying foreign products.

3. Social and Cultures: tolerance of racial and religious difference; the mobility of social ladder; inclusiveness of divergent cultures; the contribution of innovative knowledge to the world; level of influence of popular culture; the degree of internationalization of its native language; number of registered patents, the quoted frequencies of articles in science and social sciences; the export number of books, magazines, and films; number of international medias; textbooks accepted by foreign universities; enrolled number of international students; number of leading scholars in science and social sciences; effectiveness in cultural promotion institutes; sensitivity to foreign culture; attractiveness as tourist destination; number of international non-profit organizations.

4. Diplomacy and international relations: overall national image; the 'we-ness' consciousness of internationalism; scope of like-minded coalition; low frequency in using military force in achieving goals; accepted number of initiating agenda; size of foreign aid; emphasis of social responsibility of MNCs in other countries; leadership in designing international institutions; high-level positions in international public administrations; attitude to multilateralism; compliance record in international institutions; number of popular opinion leaders; effectiveness in resolving global public issues; effectiveness of agenda-setting; discourses quoted in international society; number of international lawyers; supply of public goods like ideas, welfare, and security for other countries.

To be sure, it is not likely that a country will possess comprehensive soft power in all above areas. In fact, soft power is not proportionately distributed in each area. For example, the U.S. is quite rich in social organizations, which enable it to have strong social networks around the world. Also, the American multinational corporations can play roles in promoting the American style of business culture in the world; another thing that should not be neglected is America's universities and research institutes, whose strong innovation power makes it possible for America to set the trend. In diplomacy and international relations, however, the US's vacillating attitude to multilateralism may decrease its soft power in addressing global public issues.

If we go beyond the way of state-centric thinking, soft power may be increasingly diffused to an array of different actors, some of the loyalties of which may not necessarily be consistent with that of the state. This is partly a consequence of global fragmentation, and increases our difficulties in evaluating a specific country's soft power. In short, then, soft power is not monolithic. If hard power is largely monopolized and mobilized by hierarchical forces, soft power is more or less increasingly distributed among different actors and issue areas.

29.5 THE SOFT USE OF POWER AND DIPLOMACY

Soft power is a useful component of foreign policy. It can be used in all areas and different levels in diplomacy. The state can achieve its goals by resorting to coercive or co-optive means; however, the coercive use of power by government has not been encouraged and has even been restrained greatly whether at the level of domestic political culture or at the level of international norms and rules. This prompts governments to use soft power to achieve what they want.

In interstate relations and diplomacy, the soft means a country could use to increase its power are most manifest in the following two aspects. Firstly, the primary goal of a country's diplomacy should be focused on making friends and cultivating a culture of friendship rather than creating enemies and military alliance. As the old Chinese saying goes, 'virtue is not left to stand alone; he who practices it will have neighbours'.[19] A man of virtue can never be isolated; he is sure to have like-minded companions.

Therefore, a just cause enjoys abundant support while an unjust cause finds little. It is similar to interstate relations. Alexander Wendt discusses the importance of a culture of friendship enmeshed in the Kantian culture of maintaining international order.[20] It is a pity, however, that he magnifies the community of homogeneous states, but neglects the necessities for seeking a peaceful coexistence among heterogeneous states. In other words, the means to accommodate divergent views and cultures and make all kinds of friends is more necessary and important than promoting consistency and uniformity in international society. Strategy, which traditionally meant physically eliminating the enemy, should be concentrated on how to turn enemies and strangers into friends. Secondly, financing ability is also a form of soft use of power, particularly in economic diplomacy. The traditional, widely accepted economic orientation in diplomacy is to try to alter a country's behaviour through coercive economic sanctions. As critics suggest, however, it is not always effective in case of direct economic sanctions. Another form of economic measure encouraged by the international society since the Second World War is official development foreign aid. The most important of aspect of this approach is reflected in international economic institutions where a country could try to use its economic resources as soft power tools. The U.S. has traditionally played a leading role in this area and it did gain much soft power through institutional arrangement frame-works,[21] although some of its soft power and financing ability in international institutions may be eroded by its serious and huge fiscal deficits after the financial crisis in 2008.

However, the most effective method, consistent with the cultural definition of soft power, is to conduct public diplomacy, defined as 'the ways in which both governments and private individuals and groups influence directly or indirectly these public attitudes and opinions which bear directly on other governments' foreign policy decisions.'[22] Traditional public diplomacy is heavily focused on improving the national image or changing other people's image through cultural communication; it looks more or less like cultural promotion. Contemporary public diplomacy gives special attention to mutual understanding and dialogue among different civilizations. From this perspective, a country with rich resources in culture would be likely to create attractiveness of its culture for other people, if it has well-established cultural promotion institutes, such as media, content data base, and universities. Currently, more and more governments have established special public diplomacy offices, such as the U.S., France, and China. But public diplomacy reaches far beyond the governmental sphere; it is by itself mostly motivated by non-governmental organizations. People-to-people contacts, such as human resources training, education exchange, cultural dialogue, and joint research programmes, would be more important than traditional intergovernmental communications. Although these kinds of interaction don't necessarily lead to the reduction of misperception and mutual fears among countries, it is generally acknowledged that they do contribute to better understanding and cultivation of 'we-ness' consciousness among people from different countries.

29.6 SOFT POWER IN FRAGMENTATION?

The notion of soft power has become increasingly accepted as a new and useful form of power for countries. However, important questions remain which deserve attention and discussion.

When applied improperly, the soft use of power may stir antagonistic feelings in other countries, with severe forms of backlash. Since soft power's resources are mostly concentrated in the cultural area, the promotion of a culture easily risks being described as cultural chauvinism, or as the revival of cultural colonialism, as the postmodernists and nationalists have criticized. Furthermore, culturally, since the end of Second World War, there is an irresistible trend of rising cultural awareness in developing countries. Cultural self-consciousness and social awakening may ultimately, however, downgrade the role of other cultures in developing countries. The confrontation and debate between cultural relativism or particularism and cultural universalism will continue for the foreseeable future. Politically, people of each country are entitled to choose independently the social system and road to development suited to their national conditions and their own way of life. Economically, the waves of democratization reinforce the attraction of democratic systems in the rest of the Western world. However, the goal of development is prompting developing countries to seek a suitable development model. In the view of nationalist and anti-globalization groups, the attempt to let one set of values and one culture dominate the world and negate the unique traditions and independent choices of individual countries goes against the trend of the diversification of international society.

If it is correct to say that mind is mightier than sword, maybe it is also right that the widely self-conscious mind is much more uncertainty both for domestic and global politics. It is the reason why we often ask ourselves that why they hate us. To varying degrees, nearly all great powers (e.g. America, China, France, and Russia) face this situation in their relationships to middle or small countries. In fact, in a shifting world, it seems to us that great powers' images in the world are not quite positive and promising; even their investment in soft power has been dramatically increased. It is frequently reported that China's image in Africa, compared with its image there thirty years ago, is quite mixed. China greatly increased its official aid to some African countries, but its image is more or less damaged by some Chinese companies' profits-before-everything activities there. Another example is the US. As Nye shows, anti-Americanism has increased in recent years, and the U.S.'s soft power—its ability to attract others by the legitimacy of U.S. policies and the values that underlie them—is consequently in decline. According to Gallup International polls, majorities in twenty-nine countries say that Washington's policies have had a negative effect on their view of the United States. A European barometer poll found that a majority of Europeans believe that Washington has hindered efforts to fight global poverty, protect the environment, and maintain peace.[23] The soft use of power may be a way to address this problem. After all, it reminds us that some principles, such as tolerance, equality, dialogue, and mutual respect, need to be maintained when public diplomacy is conducted.

Another factor that may contribute to reinforce cultural self-consciousness in some countries is language. It is quite related to the role of English. Nicholas Ostler has recently even predicted the ultimate decline of English in the future. The first reason for this is that the world movements towards democratization in politics or equality in society will undermine the status of elites, who are the major users of non-native English. The language may therefore slowly retreat to its native-speaking territories. Secondly, the rise of states like Brazil, Russia, India, and China will challenge the dominance of native-English-speaking nations, and therefore reduce the international preference for English. Morever, the progress of new technologies and instant translation among major languages is enhancing the status of mother tongues and lessening the necessity for any future lingua franca.[24] Without doubt, English is and will continue to be the most widely spoken language for the foreseeable future. However, suppose its dominance comes to be challenged by other competing languages, what are its implications for the current soft power configuration?

All of this remind us that we should give special attention to the fact of diffusion of loyalties among different actors. On the one hand, it highlights the importance of soft power in achieving goals in the plural international society. On the other hand, it also increases the difficulties of soft use of power, concerning the global emergence of cultural relativism. Perhaps this is a paradox of soft power in a globalized world. At any rate, cultural dialogue rather than cultural confrontation is quite urgent for public diplomacy, as well as soft power building. A well-known Chinese social anthropologist, Fei Xiaotong, the student of former British anthropologist Bronislaw Malinowski, once spoke of some maxims for guiding cultural dialogue. Here I quote and it may be useful for us to think of the notion of soft power: 'Every form of beauty has its own uniqueness; precious is to appreciate other forms of beauty with openness; if beauty represents itself with diversity and integrity, the world will be blessed with harmony and unity.'

29.7 What's About China's Soft Power?

Although it may be improper in the present *Handbook* to explore a specific country's soft power, Chinese understanding and motivation of soft power is nevertheless attracting wide international attention.

One of the most frequently used political and social concepts over the last decade in China is that of soft power. A mayor of a small-size city in China advocates improving his or her city's soft power when they talk about their city's future development agenda. One of the major reasons for China's easy acceptance of soft power is that soft use of power has a strong cultural foundation in traditional Chinese foreign relations. A renowned historian in China in the early of 20th century, who received his PhD in the U.S. and then taught at Nankai university, summarizes that traditional China has a rich military-free culture, which mostly contributes to China's use of cultural power in its foreign relations.[25] The recent revival of material and then cultural power prompts China to easily find an echo in the concept of soft power. Nearly all Chinese people are proud of their cultural history. Given that soft power is highly related to culture, it is natural that China should stress the importance and use of cultural and soft power concerning its competitive cultural advantage in international society. Moreover, to most Chinese elites, the factor of civilization plays a key role in shaping future world order. In the eye of Chinese officials and scholars, the way civilizations shape world order is not through *clashes*, as Samuel Huntington implausibly claims, but through *dialogue* between them. This belief in civilization also reinforces China's emphasis on soft power. Another reason for it is that Chinese society is fundamentally a relations-based society. Social power originated mostly, though not entirely, from the density of relational networks. Social power should be used for strengthening rather than disrupting the balance of social relations. This particular understanding of power is also consistent with the nature of soft power.

Some principles relating to Chinese use of soft power in foreign relations could be briefly summarized as follows. First of all, at the cultural level, people from different civilizations should be mutually appreciated through communication. Diplomacy is thus seen by China to be a useful means to reduce tensions among civilizations. Secondly, at the economic level, China prefers to use persuasive rather than coercive means to address political disputes. In many cases, China insists that disputes can't easily and simply be resolved through economic sanctions. Thirdly, at the societal level, soft power building should help to establish mutual social assistance systems in international areas. This is why China highlights the importance of transnational societal linkage in a globalized world.

Most Chinese officials and scholars are fully aware of the great gap in terms of soft power capacity between China and the U.S. Zi Zhongyun, former director of the American Studies Institute at the Chinese Academy of Social Sciences and a famous expert on China, said in a meeting that when the long line at the America embassy visa application window in Beijing starts to get shorter, this may well mean that the soft power gap between China and the U.S. has become more balanced. Through the opposite lens, with the growing wave of China-craze and businessmen's rush to China, is it correct to say that China is facing an unprecedented opportunity to upgrade its soft power? Instead of placing weight only on the economy and material resources, for the application of soft power, the future of China's soft power will depend on what kinds of ideas China can contribute to the world, especially under the current uncertain international conditions.

NOTES

1. See Joseph Nye, *Soft Power: The Means to Success in World Politics* (New York: Public Affairs, 2004), x.
2. See Joseph Nye, 'Soft Power', *Bound to Lead: the Changing Nature of American Power* (New York: Basic Books, 1991), preface; Joseph Nye, 'Soft Power', in *Foreign Policy* 80 (Autumn 1990), 153–71; Joseph Nye, 'Think Again: Soft Power', in *Foreign Policy* 152 (February 2006), web exclusive at <http://www.foreignpolicy.com/story/cms.php?story_id=3393>.
3. Fernand Braudel, trans. Sian Reynolds, *The Mediterranean and the Mediterranean World in the Age of the Phillip II*, Volume II (University of California Press, 1996), 833–5.
4. Robert Dahl, 'The Concept of Power', in *Behavioral Science* 2:3 (July 1957), 201–3. This definition is also discussed in Robert Dahl, *Modern Political Analysis* (New York: Prentice Hall, 2002).
5. Robert Keohane and Joseph Nye, *Power and Interdependence* (London: Longman, 2008), 10–11.
6. Nye, 'Soft Power', 168.
7. See Michel Foucault, *Power: The Essential Works of Foucault (1954–1984)* (New Press, 2001). On power, see especially Michel Foucault, *Discipline and Punish: The Birth of the Prison*, trans. Alan Sheridan (New York: Vintage Books, 1977).
8. Edward Said, *Orientalism* (New York: Vintage, 1979); Edward Said, *Culture and Imperialism* (New York: Vintage, 1993).
9. Li Congjun, 'Toward a New World Media Order', *The Wall Street Journal*, 1 June 2011. 'FAIR' stands for 'Fairness, All-win, Inclusive, and Responsibility'.
10. Nye, 'Soft Power', 164.

11. See Thomas Friedman, *The World is Flat: A Brief History of the 21st Century* (New York: Farrar, Straus and Giroux, 2006).

12. On common knowledge and local knowledge, see Clifford Geertz, *Local Knowledge: Further Essays in Interpretive Anthropology* (New York: Basic Books, 1985). In international relations theory see also Alexander Wendt, *Social Theory of International Politics* (Cambridge: Cambridge University Press, 1999). On the importance of overlapping consensus in achieving common knowledge, see John Rawls, *Political Liberalism* (New York: Columbia University Press, 2005), 150–4.

13. See Nye, *Bound to Lead*.

14. On social capital, see Robert Putnam, *Making Democracy Work* (New Jersey: Princeton University Press, 1994).

15. Nye, 'Soft Power', 168.

16. See Christopher Whitney and David Shambaugh, *Soft Power in Asia: Results of a 2008 Multinational Survey of Public Opinion*, Chicago Council on Global Affairs web site, <www.thechicagocouncil.org>.

17. See <http://news.cntv.cn/20110222/108200.shtml>.

18. The following indicators are mentioned in Whitney and Shambaugh, *Soft Power in Asia*, 15.

19. The Analects of Confucius, translated by James Legge, in Book VI Le Jin; see <http://ebooks.adelaide.edu.au/c/confucius/c748a/book4.html>.

20. Wendt, *Social Theory of International Politics*, 297–307.

21. On importance of institutional arrangements for sustainable order, see especially John Ikenberry, *After Victory: Institutions, Strategic Restraint, and the Rebuilding of the Order After Major Wars* (New Jersey: Princeton University Press, 2001).

22. Arthur Hoffman (ed.), *International Communication and the New Diplomacy* (Bloomington: Indiana University Press, 1968), 30.

23. See Joseph Nye, 'The Decline of American Soft Power', *Foreign Affairs* 83 (May/June 2004), 16–20.

24. See Nicholas Ostler, *The Last Lingua Franca: English Until the Return of Babel* (London: Penguin, 2010).

25. Lei Haizong, *Chinese Culture and Chinese Soldiers in History (Zhongguo Wenhua Yu Zhongguo De Bing)* (Beijing: Commercial Press, 2001).

CHAPTER 30

....

HARD, SOFT, AND SMART POWER

....

JOSEPH S. NYE, JR

30.1 DEFINING POWER

....

PEOPLE's choice of definition of power reflects their interests and values. Some define power as the ability to make or resist change. Others say it is the ability to get what we want.[1] This broad definition includes power over nature as well as over other people. The dictionary tells us that power is the capacity to do things, but for our interest in policies and diplomacy, we are interested in the ability to affect others to get the outcomes we want. Some people call this influence, and distinguish power from influence, but that can be confusing because the dictionary defines the two terms interchangeably.

Power implies causation and is like the word 'cause'. When we speak of causation, we choose to pick out the relation between two items in a long and complex chain of events because we are interested in them more than the myriad other things that we might focus upon. We do not say in the abstract that 'an event causes' without specifying what it causes.

In the same way, there are many factors that affect our ability to get what we want. We live in a web of inherited social forces, some of which are visible and others of which are indirect and sometimes called 'structural'. We tend to identify and focus on some of these constraints and forces rather than others depending on our interests.

While structural social forces are important, for policy and diplomacy, we want to understand what actors or agents can do within certain situations. As John Harsanyi put it, 'one of the main purposes for which social scientists use the concept of A's power over B is for the description of the policy possibilities open to A'.[2]

When we focus on particular agents or actors, we cannot say that an actor 'has power' without specifying power 'to do what'.[3] One must specify *who* is involved in the power relationship (the scope of power) as well as *what* topics are involved (the domain of power.) For example, the Pope has power over some Christians, but not others (such as Protestants.) And even among Catholics he may wish to have power over all their moral decisions, but some adherents may reject his power on some issues (such as birth control or marriage outside the church). Thus to say that the Pope has power requires us to specify the context (scope and domain) of the relationship. In terms of behaviour, a policy-oriented concept of power depends upon a specified context to tell us *who* gets *what, how, where*, and *when*.[4]

Behavioural definitions judge power by outcomes which are 'ex post' (after the fact) rather than 'ex ante' (before the fact). Policy-makers and diplomats want predictions about the future to help guide their actions. Thus they frequently define power simply in terms of the resources that can produce outcomes. By this second definition of power as resources, a country is powerful if it has a relatively large population, territory, natural resources, economic strength, military force, and social stability. The virtue of this second definition is that it makes power appear to be concrete, measurable, and predictable—a guide to action. Power in this sense is like holding the high cards in a card game. But this definition has major problems. It helps ex ante, but is sometimes wrong ex post. When people define power as synonymous with the resources that (may) produce outcomes, they often encounter the paradox that those best endowed with power do not always get the outcomes they want.

This is not to deny the importance of power resources. Power is conveyed through resources, whether tangible or intangible. People notice resources. If you show the highest cards in a poker game, others are likely to fold their hands rather than challenge you. But power resources that win in one game may not help at all in another. Holding a strong poker hand does not win if the game is bridge. Even if the game is poker, if you play your high hand poorly, or fall victim to bluff and deception, you can still lose. Power conversion—getting from resources to behavioural outcomes—is a crucial intervening variable. Having power resources does not guarantee that you will always get the outcome you want. Strategy and diplomacy make a difference. For example, in terms of resources, the United States was far more powerful than Vietnam, yet lost the war. Converting resources into realized power in the sense of obtaining desired outcomes requires well-designed strategies and skilful leadership—what I will later call smart power. Yet strategies are often inadequate and leaders frequently misjudge—witness Japan and Germany in 1941 or Saddam Hussein in 1990.

Nonetheless, defining power in terms of resources is a shortcut that policy-makers find useful. In general, a country that is well endowed with power resources is more likely to affect a weaker country and be less dependent upon an optimal strategy than vice versa. Smaller countries may sometimes obtain preferred outcomes because they pick smaller fights or focus selectively on a few issues. On average, and in direct conflicts, one would not expect Sweden or Georgia to prevail over Russia. As a first step in any card game, it helps to start by figuring out who is holding the high cards and how many chips they have. Equally important, however, is that policy-makers have the contextual intelligence to understand what game they are playing. Which resources provide the best basis for power behaviour in a particular context? In traditional views of international diplomacy, war was the ultimate game in which the cards of international politics were played. When all the cards were on the table, estimates of relative power were proven and disproven. But over the centuries, as technologies evolved, the sources of strength for war often changed, and war is not always the ultimate arbiter in the 21st century, for example on important issues like financial stability, trade disputes, climate change, and pandemics.

Because of this, some analysts reject the traditional 'elements of national power' approach as misleading and inferior to the behavioural or relational approach that became dominant among social science analysis in the latter half of the 20th century. Strictly speaking, the sceptics are correct. Power resources are simply the tangible and intangible raw materials or vehicles that underlie power relationships, and whether a given set of resources produce preferred outcomes or not depends upon behaviour in context. The vehicle is not the power relationship.[5] Knowing the horsepower and mileage of a vehicle does not tell us whether it will get to the preferred destination.

Even though predictions based on resources alone can be misleading, policy-makers and diplomats turn to resource-based definitions because they are measurable, can be quickly grasped, and provide at least a first approximation at the probabilities of outcomes. Thus they are willing to risk using the shorthand definition of power as resources. In practice, discussions of power and diplomacy involve both definitions.[6] So long as that is the case, it is important to make clear whether we are speaking of behavioural or resource-based definitions of power and to be aware of the imperfect relation between them. For example, when people speak of the rising power of China or India, they tend to point to the large populations and increased economic or military resources of those countries. But whether the capacity that those resources imply can actually be converted into preferred outcomes will depend upon the contexts and the countries' skill in converting resources into strategies that will produce preferred outcomes.

In the end, since it is outcomes, not resources, that we care about, we must pay close attention to contexts and strategies. Power conversion strategies turn out to be a critical variable that does not receive enough attention. Strategies relate means to ends, and those that combine hard and soft power resources successfully in different contexts are the key to smart power.

30.2 21ST-CENTURY CONTEXTS

Power always depends on context. The child who dominates on the playground may become a laggard when the recess bell rings and the context changes to a well-ordered classroom. In the middle of the 20th century, Josef Stalin scornfully asked how many divisions the Pope had, but in the context of ideas, five decades later the Papacy was still intact while Stalin's empire had collapsed.

Today, power in the world is distributed in a pattern that resembles a complex three-dimensional chess game. On the top chessboard, military power is largely unipolar and the United States is likely to remain supreme for some time. But on the middle chessboard, economic power has been multipolar for at least two decades, with the US, Europe, Japan, and China as the major players, and others gaining in importance. On this board, unlike the top board, Europe often acts as an entity, and Europe's economy is larger than America's. The bottom chessboard is the realm of transnational relations that cross borders outside of government control, and it includes non-state actors as diverse as bankers electronically transferring sums larger than most national budgets at one extreme, and terrorists transferring weapons, or hackers threatening cyber-security at the other. It also includes new challenges like pandemics and climate change. On this bottom board, power is widely diffused, and it makes no sense to speak of unipolarity, multipolarity, hegemony, or any other such term.

In transnational politics—the bottom chessboard—the information revolution is dramatically reducing the costs of computing and communication. Forty years ago, instantaneous global communication was possible but costly, and restricted to governments and corporations. Today it is virtually free to anyone with the means to enter an Internet cafe. The barriers to entry into world politics have been lowered, and non-state actors now crowd the stage. In 2001, a non-state group killed more Americans than the government of Japan killed at Pearl Harbor. A pandemic spread by birds or travellers on jet aircraft could kill more people than perished in the First or the Second World War. And increasingly, power will be exercised in the diffuse domain of cyber interactions. Diplomats will have to cope with everything from cyber attacks on infrastructure to massive disclosure of their confidential communications such as WikiLeaks caused in 2010. This is a new world politics with which we have less experience.

The problem for all states in the 21st century is that there are more and more things outside the control of even the most powerful states, because of the diffusion of power from states to non-state actors. Although the United States has more power resources than any other state, and does well on military measures, there is increasingly more going on in the world that those measures fail to capture. Under the influence of the information revolution and globalization, world politics is changing in a way that means Americans cannot achieve all their international goals acting alone. For example, international financial stability is vital to the prosperity of Americans, but the United States needs the cooperation of others to ensure it. Global climate change too will affect the quality of life, but the United States cannot manage the problem alone. And in a world where borders are becoming more porous than ever to everything from drugs to infectious diseases to terrorism, nations must mobilize international coalitions and build institutions to address shared threats and challenges. In this sense, power becomes a positive sum game. It is not enough to think in terms of power *over* others. One must also think in terms of power *to* accomplish goals which involves power *with* others.[7] On many transnational issues, empowering others can help us to accomplish our own goals. In this world, networks and connectedness become an important source of relevant power.

Contextual intelligence will become a crucial skill in enabling leaders to convert power resources into successful strategies. We will need contextual intelligence if we are to understand the problems of power and diplomacy in the 21st century. Various forms of multilateral diplomacy become more important parts of the mix. Even the largest country cannot achieve its aims without the help of others. That will require a deeper understanding of power, how it is changing, and how to construct smart power strategies.

30.3 Realism and the Types of Power Behaviour

The dominant classical approach to international affairs has been called 'realism', and its lineage stretches back to such great thinkers as Thucydides and Machiavelli. Realism assumes that in the anarchic conditions of world politics, where there is no higher international government authority above states, they must rely on their own devices to preserve their independence, and that when push comes to shove, the ultima ratio is the use of force. Realism portrays the world in terms of sovereign states aiming to preserve their security with military force as their ultimate instrument. Realists come in many sizes and shapes, but all tend to argue that global politics is power politics. In this they are right, but some limit their understanding by conceiving of power too narrowly. A pragmatic or common-sense realist takes into account the full spectrum of power resources including ideas, persuasion, and attraction. In behavioural terms, one can obtain preferred outcomes in three major ways: threats of coercion (sticks), payment (carrots), or attraction and persuasion (soft power). Many classical realists of the past understood the role of soft power better than some of their modern followers.

Realism represents a good first cut at portraying some aspects of international relations. But as we have seen, states are no longer the only important actors in global affairs; security is not the only major outcome that they seek, and force is not the only or always the best instrument available to achieve those outcomes. Indeed, these conditions of complex interdependence are typical of relations among advanced post-industrial countries such as the US, Canada, Europe, Australia, and Japan. Mutual democracy, liberal culture, and a deep network of transnational ties mean that anarchy has very different effects than realism predicts. In such conditions, a smart power strategy has a much higher mixture of the soft power that is described in what follows.

It is not solely in relations among advanced countries, however, that soft power plays an important role. In an information age, communications strategies become more important and outcomes are shaped not merely by whose army wins, but also by whose story wins. In combating terrorism, for example, it is essential to have a narrative that appeals to the mainstream and prevents their recruitment by the radicals. In battling insurgencies, the hard power of military force must be accompanied by soft power instruments that help to win over the hearts and minds (shape the preferences) of the majority of the population.

Smart strategies must have an information and communications component. States struggle over the power to define norms and framing of issues grows in importance. For instance, while CNN and the BBC framed the issues of the first Gulf War in 1991, by 2003, Al Jazeera played a large role in shaping the narrative in the Iraq War. Such framing is more than mere propaganda. In describing events in March 2003, one could say that American troops 'entered Iraq', or that American troops 'invaded Iraq'. Both statements are true, but they have very different effects in terms of power to shape preferences. Similarly, if one thinks of international institutions, it makes a difference if agendas are set in a Group of 8 with a few invited guests or a Group of 20 equal invitees.

The spectrum of power behaviours is represented below:

Hard   *Soft*
   Command> *Coerce Threat Pay Sanction Frame Persuade Attract* <Co-opt

In general, the types of resources that are associated with hard power include tangibles like force and money, while the resources that are associated with soft power often include intangible factors like institutions, ideas, values, culture, and perceived legitimacy of policies. But the relationship is not perfect. Intangible resources like patriotism, morale, and legitimacy strongly affect the capacity to fight and win. And threats to use force are intangible, but a dimension of hard power.[8] Many of the terms that we use daily such as 'military power' and 'economic power' are hybrids that combine both resources and behaviours.

If one remembers the distinction between power resources and power behaviour, one realizes that resources often associated with hard power behaviour can produce soft power behaviour depending on the context and how they are used. Command power can create resources that can create soft power at a later phase, for example, institutions that will provide soft power resources in the future. Similarly, co-optive behaviour can be used to generate hard power resources in the form of military alliance or economic aid. A tangible hard power resource like a military unit can produce both command behaviour (by winning a battle) and co-optive behaviour (attraction) depending on how it is used. And since attraction depends upon the minds of the perceiver, the subject's perceptions play a significant role in whether given resources produce hard or soft power behaviour.

For example, naval forces can be used to win battles (hard power) or win hearts and minds (soft power) depending on who the target and what the issue is. The American navy's help in providing relief to Indonesia after the 2004 Indian Ocean tsunami had a strong effect on increasing their attraction towards the United States, and the Navy's 2007 Maritime Strategy refers not only to war-fighting but 'additionally maritime forces will be employed to build confidence and trust among nations'. [9] Similarly, as we will see later, successful economic performance such as that of the European Union or China can produce both the hard power of sanctions and restricted market access as well as the soft power of attraction and emulation of success.

Some critics complain that the definition of soft power has become fuzzy through expansion 'to include both economic statecraft—used as both a carrot and as a stick— and even military power.... Soft power now seems to mean everything'.[10] But these critics are mistaken because they confuse the actions of a state seeking to achieve desired outcomes with the resources used to produce them. Many types of *resources* can contribute to soft power, but that does not mean that soft power is any type of *behaviour*. The use of force and payment (and some agenda-setting based on them) I call hard power. Agenda-setting that is regarded as legitimate by the target, positive attraction, and persuasion are the parts of the spectrum of behaviours I include in soft power. Hard power is push; soft power is pull. Fully defined, soft power is the ability to affect others to obtain preferred outcomes by the co-optive means of framing the agenda, persuasion, and positive attraction.

30.4 Soft Power and Smart Power

I used the term 'smart power' in 2003 to counter the misperception that soft power alone can produce effective foreign policy. I defined it as the ability to combine hard and soft power resources into effective strategies.[11] Unlike soft power, it is an evaluative concept as well as a descriptive concept. Soft power can be good or bad from a normative perspective, depending on how it is used. Smart power has the evaluation built into the definition. Critics who say 'smart power—which can be dubbed Soft Power 2.0—has superseded Soft Power 1.0 in the US foreign policy lexicon' are mistaken.[12] A more accurate criticism is that because the concept (unlike soft power) has a normative dimension, it often lends itself to slogans, though that need not be the case.

Smart power, defined as strategies that successfully combine hard and soft power resources in differing contexts, is available to all states (and non-state actors), not just large states, though a recent index of soft power ranks France, Britain, the USA, Germany, and Switzerland as the five states with the greatest soft power in 2010.[13] Small states have often developed smart power strategies. Norway, with 5 million people, has enhanced its attractiveness with legitimizing policies in peacemaking and development assistance that enhance its soft power. And at the other extreme in terms of population size, China, a rising power in hard economic and military resources, has deliberately decided to invest massively in soft power resources so as to make its hard power look less threatening to its neighbours.

Smart power goes to the heart of the problem of power conversion. As we saw earlier, some countries and actors may be endowed with greater power resources than others, yet not be very effective in converting the full range of their power resources into strategies that produce the outcomes they seek. Some argue that with its inefficient 18th-century governmental structure, the United States is weak in power conversion. Others respond that much of American soft power is generated outside of government by its open economy and civil society—with everything from Hollywood to Harvard playing a role. And it may be that power conversion is easier when a country is large enough to have a surplus of assets and can afford to absorb the costs of mistakes. The first step to smart power and effective power conversion strategies is an understanding of the full range of power resources and the problems of combining them effectively in various contexts.

Hard and soft power sometimes reinforce and sometimes undercut each other, and good contextual intelligence is important in distinguishing how they interact in different situations. But it is a mistake to think of information campaigns in terms that misunderstand the essence of soft power. 'The military has to understand that soft power is more challenging to wield in terms of the application of military force—particularly if what that force is doing is not seen as attractive.'[14] If the other levers of soft power are not pulling in the same direction, then the military cannot create favourable conditions on its own. Except at the tactical level, the military options for the use of soft power have to been seen in a larger policy context.

Though the concept of soft power only goes back to 1990, the behaviour it denotes is as old as human history. In 18th-century Europe, the spread of French language and culture enhanced French power. During the American Civil War, some British statesmen considered supporting the South, but despite their obvious commercial and strategic interests, British elites were constrained by popular opposition to slavery and attraction to the cause of the North. Before the First World War, when the United States wrestled with the choice between Germany and Britain, 'Germany's primary disadvantage in 1914 was not its record in American opinion, but the absence of a record. So little existed to counteract the natural pull toward Britain.... which dominated the channels of transatlantic communication.'[15] Contrary to the views of some sceptics, soft power has often had very real effects in history, including on the movement of armies.

Some analysts have misinterpreted soft power as a synonym for culture and then gone on to downgrade its importance. For example, Niall Ferguson described soft power as 'non-traditional forces such as cultural and commercial goods', and then dismissed it on the grounds that 'it's, well, soft'.[16] Of course eating at McDonalds or wearing a Michael Jackson shirt does not automatically indicate soft power. Militias can perpetrate atrocities or fight Americans while wearing Nikes and drinking coke. But this criticism confuses the resources that may produce behaviour with the behaviour itself. As we saw earlier, whether the possession of power resources actually produces favourable behaviour depends upon the context and the skills of the agent in converting the resources into behavioural outcomes. But this is not unique to soft power resources. In terms of hard power resources, having a larger tank army may produce victory if a battle is fought in the desert, but not if it is fought in a swamp. Similarly, a nice smile can be a soft power resource and you may be more inclined to do something for me if I smile whenever we meet, but if I smile at your mother's funeral it may destroy soft power rather than create it.

The soft power of a country rests heavily on three basic resources: its culture (in places where it is attractive to others), its political values (when it lives up to them at home and abroad), and its foreign policies (when others see them as legitimate and having moral authority). The parenthetical conditions are the key in determining whether soft power resources translate into the behaviour of attraction that can influence others towards favourable outcomes. With soft power, what the target thinks is particularly important and the targets matter as much as the agents. Attraction and persuasion are socially constructed. Soft power is a dance that requires partners.

In some contexts, culture can be an important power resource. Culture is the pattern of social behaviours by which groups transmit knowledge and values, and it exists at multiple levels.[17] Some aspects of human culture are universal; some national; others are particular to social classes or small groups. Culture is never static, and different cultures interact in different ways. More research needs to be done on the connection between culture and power behaviour. For example, can Western cultural attraction reduce current extremist appeals in Muslim societies? Some see an unbridgeable cultural divide. But consider the Islamic state of Iran. Western music and videos are anathema to the ruling mullahs, but attractive to many of the younger generation.

Culture, values, and policies are not the only resources that produce soft power. We saw earlier that military resources can produce soft as well as hard power behaviour. The same is true of economic resources which can be used to attract as well as coerce. A successful economy is an important source of attraction, as Japan and China have each discovered. At the same time, it can provide resources that can be used as hard power inducements in the form of aid as well as coercive sanctions. Sometimes in real world situations, it is difficult to distinguish what part of an economic relationship is comprised of hard and soft power. European leaders describe the desire by other countries to accede to the European Union as a sign of Europe's soft power.[18] But how much are the changes the result of the economic inducement of market access and how much is the result of attraction to Europe's successful economic and political system? The situation is one of mixed motives and different actors in a country may see the mix in different ways. Journalists and historians must trace particular processes in detail to disentangle causation.

A number of observers see China's soft power increasing in Asia and other parts of the developing world, particularly after the 2008 global financial crisis that started in the United States.[19] According the *The People's Daily*, 'soft power has become a key word...there is great potential for the development of China's soft power'.[20] The so-called 'Beijing Consensus' on authoritarian government plus a successful market economy has become more popular than the previously dominant 'Washington Consensus' of liberal market economics with democratic government in parts of the developing world. But to what extent are Venezuelans and Zimbabweans attracted to the Beijing consensus, or admire China's tripling of its GDP over three decades, or are induced by the prospect of access to a large and growing market? Moreover, even if the authoritarian growth model produces soft power for China in authoritarian countries, it does not produce attraction in democratic countries. What attracts in Caracas may repel in Paris.[21]

Some realist critics argue that the difference between hard and soft power is a contrast between realism and idealism. To them, 'soft power is nothing more than a catchy term for the bundle of liberal international policies that have driven US foreign policy since World War II and which are rooted in the Wilsonian tradition'.[22] But they are mistaken. There is no contradiction between realism and soft power. Soft power is not a form of idealism or liberalism. It is a simply a form of power, one way of getting desired outcomes. Legitimacy is a power reality. Competitive struggles over legitimacy are part of enhancing or depriving actors of soft power.

And not just states are involved. Diplomacy now includes a variety of non-state actors. Corporations, institutions, NGOs, and transnational terrorist networks often have soft power of their own. Even individual celebrities are able to use their soft power 'by making ideas, palatable, acceptable, colorful. Or as the singer Bono put it . . . his function is to bring applause when people get it right, and make their lives a misery when they don't.'[23] In 2007, in the run up to the Beijing Olympics, Steven Spielberg sent an open letter to President Hu Jintao asking China to use its influence to push Sudan to accept a UN peacekeeping force in Darfur. 'China soon dispatched Mr. Zhai to Darfur, a turnaround that served as a classic study of how a pressure campaign, aimed to strike Beijing in a vulnerable spot at a vulnerable time, could accomplish what years of governmental diplomacy could not.'[24]

30.5 WIELDING SOFT POWER

Incorporating soft power into a government strategy is more difficult than may first appear. For one thing, as just mentioned, success in terms of outcomes is more in the control of the subject than is often the case with hard power. A second problem is that the results often take a long time and most politicians and publics are impatient to see a prompt return on their investments. Third, the instruments of soft power are not fully under the control of governments. While governments control policy, culture and values are embedded in civil societies. Soft power may appear less risky than economic or military power, but it is often hard to use, easy to lose, and costly to re-establish.

Soft power depends upon credibility and when governments are perceived as manipulative and information is seen as propaganda, credibility is destroyed. One critic argues that if governments eschew imposition or manipulation they are not really exercising soft power, but mere dialogue.[25] While governments face a difficult task in maintaining credibility, this criticism underestimates the importance of pull rather than push in soft power interactions.

Of course, it is important not to exaggerate the impact of soft (or any other form of) power. There are some situations where soft power provides very little leverage. It is difficult, for example, to see how soft power would solve the dispute over North Korea's nuclear weapons. Some critics make the mistake of assuming that because soft power is often insufficient, it is not a form of power. But that problem is true of all forms of power. On the other hand, when a government is concerned about structural milieu goals or general value objectives, such as promotion of democracy, human rights, and freedom, it is often the case that soft power turns out to be superior to hard power.

Soft power is difficult for governments to wield. Sustained attraction—being a 'city on a hill'—requires consistency of practice with values. Going further to project attraction, frame agendas, and persuade others is even more difficult. The causal paths are often indirect, the effects often take time to ripen, some of the general goals to which it is directed are diffuse, and governments are rarely in full control of all the instruments.

To be credible, efforts to project soft power will have to avoid the dangers of an over-militarized and state-centric approach. Power becomes less hierarchical in an information age and social networks become more important. To succeed in a networked world requires leaders to think in terms of attraction and co-option rather than command. Leaders need to think of themselves as being in a circle rather than atop a mountain. That means that two-way communications are more effective than commands. As a young Czech participant at a Salzberg Seminar observed 'this is the best propaganda because it's not propaganda'.[26] Interactive discourse fits with empowering choices. It involves recognition that the sharing of values can be interactive and binding on the home state as well as others.

One of the major ways that governments attempt to wield soft power is through public diplomacy. Classical diplomacy, sometimes called cabinet diplomacy, involved messages sent from one ruler to another, often in confidential communications. But governments also found it useful to communicate with the publics of other countries in an effort to influence other governments indirectly. That indirect form of diplomacy became known as public diplomacy. The diffusion of power away from states has made public diplomacy more complex. The lines of communication are no longer a straight bar between two governments, but more like a star that includes lines between governments, publics, society to society, and non-governmental organizations (NGOs).

In such a world, actors other than governments are well placed to use soft power. Government A will try to influence the public in society B, but transnational organizations in society B will also wage information campaigns to influence government A as well as government B. They use campaigns of naming and shaming to influence other governments as well as to put pressure on other non-governmental actors such as large corporations. Sometimes they will also work through intergovernmental organizations. The result is a new set of mixed coalitions of governmental, intergovernmental, and non-governmental actors, each using public diplomacy for its own goals. For example, the International Campaign to Ban Landmines allied smaller governments like Canada and Norway, along with networks created by an activist in Vermont, and the public fame of Princes Diana to defeat the strongest bureaucracy (the Pentagon) in the world's only superpower.

Governments trying to utilize public diplomacy to wield soft power face new problems in the cyber age. Promoting attractive images of one's country is not new, but the conditions for trying to create soft power have changed dramatically in recent years. For one thing, nearly half the countries in the world are now democracies. In such circumstances, diplomacy aimed at public opinion can become as important to outcomes as the traditional classified diplomatic communications among leaders. Information creates power and today a much larger part of the world's population has access to that power. Technological advances have led to dramatic reduction in the cost of processing and transmitting information. The result is an explosion of information, and that has produced a 'paradox of plenty'.[27] Plentiful information leads to scarcity of attention. When people are overwhelmed with the volume of information confronting them, it is hard to know what to focus on. Attention rather than information becomes the scarce resource and those who can distinguish valuable information from background clutter gain power. Cue-givers become more in demand, and this is a source of power for those who can tell us where to focus our attention.

Among editors and cue-givers, credibility is the crucial resource and an important source of soft power. Reputation becomes even more important than in the past and political struggles occur over the creation and destruction of credibility. Governments compete for credibility not only with other governments, but with a broad range of alternatives including news media, corporations, NGOs, intergovernmental organizations, and networks of scientific communities. Politics has become a contest of competitive credibility. The world of traditional power politics is typically about whose military or economy wins. As we noted earlier, politics in an information age 'may ultimately be about whose story wins'. [28]

Narratives become the currency of soft power. Governments compete with each other and with other organizations to enhance their own credibility and weaken that of their opponents. Witness the struggle between Serbia and NATO to frame the interpretation of events in 1999 in which broadcasts and the Internet played a key role, or the contest between the government and protesters after the Iranian elections in 2009 in which the Internet and Twitter played important roles in transnational communication. Sceptics who treat the term 'public diplomacy' as a mere euphemism for propaganda miss this point. Simple propaganda is counterproductive as public diplomacy. Nor is public diplomacy merely public relations campaigns. Conveying information and selling a positive image is part of it, but public diplomacy also involves building long-term relationships that create an enabling environment for government policies.[29]

The mix of direct government information to long-term cultural relationships varies with three concentric circles or stages of public diplomacy, and all three are important.[30] The first and most immediate circle is daily communications, which involves explaining the context of domestic and foreign policy decisions. The first dimension must also involve preparation for dealing with crises. In today's information age, many actors will rush in to fill any vacuum in information that might occur after an event. A rapid response capability in public diplomacy means that false charges or misleading information can be answered immediately. This circle is measured in terms of hours, days, and weeks.

The second dimension or concentric circle is strategic communication, which develops a set of simple themes much as a political or advertising campaign does. While the first dimension is measured in hours and days, the second occurs over weeks, months, and even years. Special events like the Shanghai Exposition of 2010 or the World Cup in South Africa fit this description. The campaign plans symbolic events and communications over the course of the next year to reinforce the central themes, or to advance a particular government policy. Special themes focus on particular policy initiatives. For example, when the Reagan administration decided to deploy missiles while negotiating to remove existing Soviet intermediate range missiles, former Secretary of State George Schultz later concluded, 'I don't think we could have pulled it off if it hadn't been for a very active program of public diplomacy.'[31]

The third and broadest circle of public diplomacy is the development of lasting relationships with key individuals over many years or even decades through scholarships, exchanges, training, seminars, conferences, and access to media channels. Over time, about 700,000 people have participated in American cultural and academic exchanges, and these exchanges helped to educate world leaders like Anwar Sadat, Helmut Schmidt, and Margaret Thatcher. Other countries have similar programmes. For example, Japan has developed an exchange programme bringing 6,000 young foreigners each year from forty countries to teach their languages in Japanese schools, with an alumni association to maintain the bonds of friendship that are developed.[32] These programmes develop what Edward R. Murrow once called the crucial 'last three feet'—face-to-face communications which are a two-way process with the enhanced credibility that reciprocity creates.

Each of these three dimensions of public diplomacy plays an important role in helping governments to create an attractive image of a country that can improve its prospects for obtaining its desired outcomes. But even the best advertising cannot sell an unpopular product. A communications strategy cannot work if it cuts against the grain of policy. Actions speak louder than words, and public diplomacy that appears to be mere window dressing for hard power projection is unlikely to succeed. The treatment of prisoners at Abu Ghraib and Guantanamo in a manner inconsistent with American values led to perceptions of hypocrisy that could not be reversed by broadcasting pictures of Muslims living well in America. In fact, the slick production values of the American satellite television station Al Hurrah did not make it competitive in the Middle East, where it was widely regarded as an instrument of government propaganda. Former ambassador John Bolton dismissed fears that an attack on Iran would rally support around the regime, saying that 'all that would be needed is an accompanying public diplomacy campaign.'[33] Under the new conditions of the information age, more than ever, the soft sell may prove more effective than the hard sell. Without underlying national credibility, the instruments of public diplomacy cannot translate cultural resources into the soft power of attraction.

The centralized mass media approach to public diplomacy still plays an important role. Governments need to correct daily misrepresentations of their policies as well as to try to convey a longer term strategic message. The main strength of the mass media approach is its audience reach and ability to generate public awareness and set the agenda. But the inability to influence how the message is perceived in different cultural settings is its weak point. The sender knows what she says, but not always what the target(s) hear. Cultural barriers are apt to distort what is heard. Networked communications, on the other hand, can take advantage of two-way communications and peer-to-peer relations to overcome cultural differences.

The greater flexibility of NGOs in using networks has given rise to what some call 'the new public diplomacy', which is 'no longer confined to messaging, promotion campaigns, or even direct governmental contacts with foreign publics serving foreign policy purposes. It is also about building relationships with civil society actors in other countries and about facilitating networks between non-governmental parties at home and abroad.'[34] In this approach to public diplomacy, government policy is aimed at promoting and participating in rather than controlling such networks across borders. Indeed, too much government control or even the appearance thereof, can undercut the credibility that such networks are designed to engender. The evolution of public diplomacy from one-way communications to a two-way dialogue model treats publics as peer-to-peer co-creators of meaning and communication.[35]

For governments to succeed in the networked world of the new public diplomacy they are going to have to learn to relinquish a good deal of their control, and this runs the risk that non-governmental civil society actors are often not aligned in their goals with government policies or even objectives. Wielding soft power is important, but it is not always easy, particularly in the diplomatic conditions of a cyber age. And combining it with hard power into smart power strategies makes the diplomat's task doubly difficult. But as the American Secretary of State Hillary Clinton described the diplomacy of the 21st century: 'America cannot solve the most pressing problems on our own, and the world cannot solve them without America. We must use what has been called "smart power", the full range of tools at our disposal.'[36]

Notes

1. Kenneth E. Boulding uses both in *Three Faces of Power* (London: Sage, 1989), 15.
2. John Harsanyi, 'The Dimension and Measurement of Social Power', reprinted in K.W. Rothschild, *Power in Economics* (Harmondsworth: Penguin Books, 1971), 80.
3. Jack Nagel, *The Descriptive Analysis of Power* (New Haven: Yale University Press, 1975), 14.
4. Harold Lasswell and Abraham Kaplan, *Power and Society: A Framework for Political Inquiry* (New Haven: Yale University Press, 1950).
5. Philosophers such as Anthony Kenny and Peter Morriss argue that reducing power to resources constitutes the 'vehicle fallacy', but Keith Dowding contends that 'the vehicle fallacy is not a fallacy if resources are measured relationally, for example, the power of money is relative to its distribution. It follows that strategic considerations must enter into the very essence of the concept of power.' See Keith Dowding, 'Power, Capability and Ableness: The Fallacy of the Vehicle Fallacy', *Contemporary Political Theory* 7 (2008), 238–58.
6. David A. Baldwin contests my statement, but does not offer compelling evidence that would make me change it. See 'Power and International Relations', in Walter Carlsnaes, Thomas Risse, and Beth A. Simmons (eds), *Handbook of International Relations* (London: Sage, 2002), 185–6. In my experience in government, policy-makers do tend to focus on resources.
7. Peter Morriss, *Power: A Philosophical Analysis*, 2nd ed. (Manchester, Manchester University Press, 2002), 33–5.
8. Baldwin and others have criticized my earlier discussion of tangibility. I should have made clearer that intangibility is not a *necessary* condition for soft power. I define soft power in behavioural terms as the ability to affect others to obtain preferred outcomes by co-option

and attraction rather than coercion or payment, and I was careful to use language that suggested an imperfect relationship ('tend to be associated, are usually associated') between soft power behaviour and the intangibility of the resources that can produce it. But the criticism is justified and that explains this restatement.

9. Chief of Naval Operations, *A Cooperative Strategy for 21st Century Seapower* (Washington: 2007), 3.

10. Leslie Gelb, *Power Rules* (New York: Harper Collins, 2009), 69.

11. See Joseph S. Nye, *Soft Power: The Means to Success in World Politics* (New York: Public Affairs, 2004), at 32 and 147. I am grateful to Fen Hampson for the term. Suzanne Nossel also deserves credit for using the term in 'Smart Power', *Foreign Affairs* 83:2 (March/April 2004), 131–42, but I was not aware of this until later.

12. Christopher Layne, 'The Unbearable Lightness of Soft Power', in Inderjeet Parmar and Michael Cox (eds), *Soft Power and US Foreign Policy: Theoretical, Historical and Contemporary Perspectives* (London: Routledge, 2010), 67ff.

13. Jonathan McClory, *The New Persuaders: An International Ranking of Soft Power* (London: Institute for Government, 2010), 5.

14. Angus Taverner, 'The Military Use of Soft Power—Information Campaigns: the Challenge of Applications, Their Audiences and Effects', in Parmar and Cox (eds), *Soft Power and US Foreign Policy*, 149.

15. Robert H. Wiebe, *The Search for Order, 1877–1920* (New York: Hill and Wang, 1967), 264.

16. Niall Ferguson, 'Think Again: Power', *Foreign Policy* 134 (January–February 2003), 18–22.

17. Clifford Geertz defines culture as 'an historically transmitted pattern of meanings embodied in symbols, a system of inherited conceptions expressed in symbolic forms by means of which men communicate, perpetuate, and develop their knowledge about and attitudes toward life'. *The Interpretation of Cultures* (New York: Basic Books, 1973), 89.

18. Martin Wolf, 'Soft Power: The EU's Greatest Gift', *Financial Times*, 2 February 2005.

19. Yanzhong Huang and Bates Gill, 'Sources and Limits of Chinese "Soft Power" ', *Survival* 48:2 (June 2006), 17–36. See also Sheng Ding, *The Dragon's Hidden Wings: How China Rises with Its Soft Power* (Lanham: Lexington Books, 2008).

20. People's Daily Online, 'How to Improve China's Soft Power?', 11 March 2010, <http://english.people.com.cn/90001/90785/6916487.html>.

21. Ingrid d'Hooghe, *The Limits of China's Soft Power in Europe: Beijing's Public Diplomacy Puzzle*, Clingendael Diplomacy Papers No. 25, Netherlands Institute of International Relations, Clingandel, 2010.

22. Layne, 'The Unbearable Lightness of Soft Power', 73.

23. Alan Cowell, 'Power of Celebrity at work in Davos', *International Herald Tribune*, 29 January 2005.

24. Helene Cooper, 'Darfur Collides with Olympics, and China Yields', *New York Times*, 13 April 2010.

25. John S. Dryzek, *Deliberative Global Politics: Discourse and Democracy in a Divided World* (Cambridge: Polity Press, 2006), 82.

26. Inderjeet Parmar, 'Challenging Elite anti-Americanism in the Cold War', in Parmar and Cox (eds), *Soft Power and US Foreign Policy*, 115.

27. Herbert A. Simon, 'Information 101: It's Not What You Know, It's How You Know It', *The Journal for Quality and Participation* (July–August 1998), 30–3.

28. J. Arquila and D. Ronfeldt, *The Emergence of Noopolitik: Toward an American Information Strategy* (Santa Monica: RAND, 1999).

29. For a thorough survey of American public diplomacy, see Kennon Nakamura and Matthew Weed, *U.S. Public Diplomacy: Background and Current Issues* (Washington: Congressional Research Service, 2009).

30. Mark Leonard, *Public Diplomacy* (London: Foreign Policy Center, 2002).

31. Hans N. Tuch, *Communicating with the World: U.S. Public Diplomacy Overseas* (New York: St. Martin's Press, 1990), ch. 12.

32. See Watanabe Yashushi and David L. McConnell (eds), *Soft Power Superpowers: Cultural and National Assets of Japan and the United States* (London: M. E. Sharpe, 2008).

33. Ambassador John Bolton interviewed on Fox News, 24 December 2009. See Ben Armbruster, 'Bolton: Strike on Iran Is No Problem as Long as It's Accompanied by a "Campaign of Public Diplomacy"', Think Progress (Blog), 23 December 2009, <http://thinkprogress.org/2009/12/23/bolton-iran-public-diplomacy>.

34. Jan Melissen (ed.), *The New Public Diplomacy: Soft Power in International Relations* (London: Palgrave McMillan, 2005), 22–3.

35. Kathy R. Fitzpatrick, 'Advancing the New Public Diplomacy: A Public Relations Perspective', *The Hague Journal of Diplomacy* 2 (2007), 203.

36. National Public Radio, 'Transcript of Clinton's Confirmation Hearing', 13 January 2009, <www.npr.org/templates/story/story.php?storyId=99290981>.

PART V

ISSUE AREAS

CHAPTER 31

THE DIPLOMACY OF SECURITY

K. J. HOLSTI

SINCE human beings began living in settled communities, they have sought to protect themselves against a variety of military threats to life and livelihood. Archaeological records indicate that security was a main consideration in the design and construction of villages and towns. Palisades, moats, walls, turrets, and the like are the hallmarks of early community architecture throughout the world.

The ancients did not bother with arcane discussions of security as a concept. They knew only too well from experience what the consequences of war were likely to be. The purposes of war varied from pillage, slave capture, and territory, to access to resources, revenge, abduction of women (the Trojan wars), strategic routes, honour and prestige, empire building, and dreams of glory. Those settlements and polities that lost wars faced draconian consequences. Wars typically ended with the slaughter of the surviving male population, pillage, and the capture of youth and women as slaves. Towns and villages were burnt and laid waste, as in the case of the second Punic war, when the Romans, having defeated the Phoenicians at Carthage, destroyed the city and salted it so it could never rise again. Leniency was not a hallmark of the victors of ancient wars.

The record of war since ancient times indicates that peace and security for many communities and polities have been scarce. Short periods of 'tranquillity' (as European diplomats referred to peace in the 18th century) were punctuated by frequent outbreaks of war: the constant expansion of the Persian Empire by armed force in the 6th century BC, the Greek—Persian wars (492–77 BC), the Peloponnesian war (431–404 BC), the Period of Warring States in China (403–221 BC), the multiple wars of the Roman Empire, the major crusades in the medieval era, Mongolian conquests stretching from the Middle East to Vietnam, the Thirty Years' War (1618–1648) which reduced Germany's population between 20 and 60 per cent, the Napoleonic Wars (1795–1814), and the two great World Wars of the 20th century. These are the best known, but they represent only a small fraction of the total number of wars recorded in history.

31.1 The Clausewitzian Revolution and its Demise: War and Security in the Modern States System

If war throughout most of history was characterized by extreme ferocity and savagery limited only by primitive weaponry, there were also eras where war was constrained by norms, conventions, and notions of honour. In feudal Japan, the warrior's code of honour (*bushido*) helped provide some sense of security for innocent civilians, if not for their rulers. In 18th century Europe, there was a sense of restraint in the conduct of war. This was summarized theoretically in Karl von Clausewitz' famous text *On War*[1] which reflected a highly rationalistic perspective on organized violence. In his view, war features three main characteristics: (1) it is an instrument of statecraft, used cautiously and deliberately for (2) known political ends. It is (3) the ultimate instrument used only when diplomacy has failed.

Each suggests limits. In the 18th century, purposes were usually limited: a tract of territory, a claim to a crown, reprisals, fighting over colonies or fishing rights, and the like. The strategic goal of armed combat was to force the surrender of the opponent, not to annihilate it or to massacre civilian populations. There were strict rules of engagement, etiquette associated with the breaching of city walls, and formalities of surrender and negotiating peace. While states were engaged in war, commerce and travel for the most part went on as in peacetime. According to the Prussian ruler Frederick the Great, the ideal war was a contest between armed forces of which ordinary subjects or citizens were hardly aware.[2]

Warfare in the 20th century effectively destroyed the ever-increasing body of rules, regulations, and norms designed to protect civilians from harm. The First World War was fought mostly away from cities and other population centres, but long-range weaponry, Britain's naval blockade of Germany, submarine attacks, and air power increasingly targeted civilians.

The Second World War completed the demolition of measures designed to provide security for both the territorial integrity of states and for civilian populations in wartime. The list of atrocities is sufficiently lengthy to put into question those who believe that societies move in a progressive and more humane direction. Hitler's attacks on Poland and the Soviet Union (1939 and 1941) were designed specifically to destroy or render into slavery the occupied populations. The 'Final Solution' to the Jewish 'problem' resulted in approximately 6 million murders. About 3 million Russian prisoners of war in Nazi hands were worked to death or otherwise killed in captivity. Japanese armed forces brutalized, raped, and killed about 175,000 civilians in two weeks of mayhem in Nanking, in 1937. In 1941–1942 the Japanese Imperial Army killed by armed force and germ warfare an estimated 4 million Chinese civilians in a massive assault in the north of the country.[3] Allied incendiary bombing raids on Hamburg, Dresden, and Tokyo killed hundreds of thousands. They were designed to kill the maximum numbers of civilians, not to hit military targets. The two atomic bombs dropped on Hiroshima and Nagasaki in August 1945 are far better known, but the numbers immediately killed were not significantly higher than those who perished from conventional fire bombs. While many Nazi and Japanese leaders were captured, tried, convicted, and hanged for war crimes and crimes against humanity, victorious Soviet, British, and American architects of atrocity escaped similar fates. Of the approximately 74 million casualties in the Second World War, about 60 per cent were civilians.[4]

In the 20th century, security became the most prominent value sought by governments. The funds expended to achieve it and the amount of time and money diplomats spend negotiating security arrangements are the measure of this commitment. Contemporary states typically spend vastly more for defence against known and anticipated enemies or threats than they do on education, housing, and other domestic priorities. Security is what people make of it[5] and in our era, protecting states, their territories, and their populations from real or imagined external threats has become a *Grundnorm* of all policy-makers.

31.2 Unilateral Reponses to Security Threats

If threats to life and livelihood have been throughout history the greatest problems rulers and peoples have faced, what have they done about it? While classical tyrants may not have worried much about the fate of peoples over whom they ruled, they were at least concerned about their own lives. For those rulers with more highly developed conceptions of governance, they also had to worry about the fate of the towns and villages over which they ruled.

The most common response to perceived security threats is to build defences. The remaining walls, moats, bastions, towers in the world today are testimony to these efforts. Many were reasonably successful in offering a modicum of security to a polity's populations. Sieges and assaults were often unsuccessful, although we have no statistical evidence to allow an estimation of failure.

The processes of building defences required resources including manpower and money. Rulers had to extract these either in the forms of slave labour or taxes or some combination of them. The history of the modern state is intimately connected with the provision of security. Canons rendered mediaeval castles and walled towns and cities obsolete as units of defence. The king of France in the 17th century could not protect his domains by building walls around them. He needed a large army instead, and it and its associated weaponry cost a great deal. This required the royal figures to centralize power at the expense of local lords, to extract taxes, to sell political offices, and to hire or conscript an armed force and navy. All of this required government administration, new classes of bureaucrats and tax collectors, and commercial enterprises that could help fund the defensive and state-building projects. While it is an oversimplification and while state-building went in many different directions, with differing consequences, Tilly's aphorism contains substantial truth: 'war made the state and the state made war'.[6]

Political philosophers understood that the fundamental normative purpose of state-making is safety and security. Hobbes, among others, insisted that security is a social and political condition necessary for the happy life.[7] It is not a question of calamities caused by nature (e.g. floods, earthquakes), but threats to the 'happy life' posed by others, meaning both domestic rebels and foreign aggressors. The state—the Leviathan—is the sovereign ruler who acquires the 'sword of justice' or the 'right of punishing' to ensure domestic peace and the 'sword of war' or the right to 'compel citizens to take up arms' to ensure national defence.[8]

State formation and building defences are thus intimately connected. The actual resources devoted today to security range from a low of less than 1 per cent of GNP in some small states to more than 20 per cent of GNP for countries such as North Korea. These reflect the varying degrees of insecurity (both domestic and externally generated) in different countries, but what is telling is that with the exception of Iceland, Costa Rica, and a few small island states that have contracted out to others for their security, every country in the world possesses armed forces. They are an insurance policy against future uncertainties in their immediate neighbourhoods.

Most state-building efforts have been designed to help *fight* wars, either through defence or offensive moves. Some states have also emphasised *deterrence* as a means of increasing security. This is supposedly the main function of nuclear weapons. They are designed and deployed in such a way that any aggressor would know that an attack would result in nuclear retaliation. During the cold war, the theory of 'mutual assured destruction' guided American nuclear planning and to a much lesser extent, the nuclear doctrines and deployments of the Soviet Union. According to this theory, security can be enhanced if two or more parties know that any attack will result in immediate retaliation, meaning national destruction. Few would debate whether the theory might operate according to expectations in the event of a nuclear attack. Much less certain are whether nuclear retaliation would be ordered in the event of a conventional war or where the adversary attacked an ally. Nuclear weapons were irrelevant in the outcome of most cold war crises, but the crisis over the emplacement of Soviet missiles in Cuba in 1962 proved that there are immense incentives to resolve a crisis peacefully when confronted with the possibility of nuclear war. Since the end of the cold war, nuclear deterrence has receded significantly as a national priority. The kinds of wars and security threats of the 21st century make nuclear weapons mostly irrelevant. One cannot, for example, deter terrorist plots or Taliban attacks by threatening to use nuclear weapons.

31.3 BILATERAL STRATEGIES FOR SECURITY

Most polities have not attempted to provide for their security solely by self-help means. They have also sought the help and cooperation of others. This has been done primarily through bilateral alliances negotiated by diplomats and their ancient counterparts.

Alliances, however, have had a chequered history as a means of augmenting security. Commitments are easy to make; they are more difficult to meet when the costs are too high. The famous Melian dialogue (415 BC) when Athenian forces threatened to invade the island of Milos during the Peloponnesian war offers a succinct summary of the dilemma of alliances. Faced with conquest, the neutral Melians tried to dissuade the Athenians by stating that the gods and Athens' enemy, Sparta, would come to save them. The Athenians replied that hypothetical friends, whether divine or secular, are weak reeds to lean on when it comes to security. In the event, the Spartans did not come to the aid of the Melians and they suffered Athenian conquest. A more contemporary alliance failure is the case of the Franco—Czechoslovakian 1924 treaty, which committed France to the defence of the Czechs. At the Munich Conference in 1938, the French abandoned the Czechs under Hitler's threats. Alliances, moreover, help spread the geographic scope of war and, finally, there is significant evidence that alliances, rather than deterring, are one of several steps that lead to war.[9] Both diplomacy and alliances are uncertain remedies for the weak, vulnerable, and threatened.

31.4 MULTILATERAL SECURITY PLANS AND PROJECTS

As polities historically came increasingly in contact with each other through trade, diplomacy, and war, it became apparent that unilateral and bilateral security strategies were often insufficient. Regional or universal security arrangements offered alternatives. During the Warring States period in China (403–221 BC) security was sought increasingly through multilateral 'leagues' (alliances) and local balances of power. The peace settlement of Westphalia (1648) that formally ended the ruinous Thirty Years War sought to create a continent-wide security system. It did this primarily through three means: a formula for religious tolerance (*cuius regio, eius regio*: 'whose realm, his religion') that settled the main issue surrounding the war, (2) a rough territorial balance of power, and (3) creating two guarantors of the peace, Sweden and France. The formula helped prevent another pan-European war for half a century, but collapsed under the military assaults of Louis XIV at the turn of the 18th century. The main guarantor of Westphalia had become a predator and the second guarantor, Sweden, did not have the military capacity unilaterally to enforce the settlement.

Like the Thirty Years War, the Napoleonic wars were a great learning experience. The peace settlement at the Congress of Vienna (1814–1815) was designed not just to deal with specific issues such as territorial exchanges, but sought to create a multilateral security system for the entire continent. The most significant feature was the delegitimization of military conquest. Borrowing from the French revolutionaries who formally renounced conquest (and inscribed that renunciation in the 1791 constitution), the Vienna Final Act declared that sovereignty could no longer be acquired by conquest, nor could it be transferred to the conqueror without the consent of the vanquished. This was one of the most revolutionary acts in the history of diplomacy and presaged the formal renunciation of conquest in Article 10 of the League of Nations Covenant, the Kellogg—Briand Pact of 1928 and the 1931 Stimson doctrine, whereby the United States refused to recognize as legal any territorial revisions made through the use of arms. This has now become a universal norm of the society of states.

The Congress also established a 'club' of states led by the great powers. They arrogated for themselves the task of monitoring and reviewing all diplomatic settlements in Europe, establishing a territorial balance of power for the continent, and holding periodic summit meetings (Congresses) and foreign ministers meetings (Conferences) to discuss important security issues or looming crises. Throughout the 19th century, the great powers developed a series of norms, protocols, and etiquette designed to prevent diplomatic conflicts from escalating to war. They failed to prevent the Crimean War, the wars of German unification, and the Franco-Prussian war, but the system worked reasonably well in lesser crises so that by the early 20th century most European publics had come to expect peace as the normal state of affairs on the continent.[10]

The First World War destroyed the *fin de siècle* optimism about peace. More than 4 per cent of France's population perished in the war. The figure for the Ottoman Empire was an astounding 14 per cent.[11] Those who wrote the Versailles peace settlement in 1919 were determined to prevent a repeat of this catastrophe. They recognized that balances of power and alliances of the 19th-century format had failed to provide lasting security and, indeed, they commonly denounced them, believing that they had caused the war. The architects of peace therefore attempted to create new multilateral diplomatic machinery. The League of Nations was based on four major assumptions: (1) the security of any single state depends upon the security of all, (2) the international community, through the League, has a responsibility to prevent wars (thus overturning the concept of neutrality), (3) wars are most commonly caused by poor communication and misperceptions, and (4) territorial conquest is no longer permissible. The main purpose of the League of Nations was to provide security for individual states by making mediation and conciliation mandatory in diplomatic disputes, promoting disarmament, and providing collective help for victims of aggression.

While these formulas helped to contain several crises among small states in the 1920s and 1930s, they were useless against the aggressions of Imperial Japan, Nazi Germany, Fascist Italy, and the Soviet Union. By the mid-1930s it was clear that the assumptions underlying the concept of collective security were flawed, that no one was prepared to disarm in a world of increasing menace, and that aggressors would simply ignore mandatory mediation.

The United Nations was created in 1945 to prevent the recurrence of the second great catastrophe of the century. The sense of urgency evident in 1919 was now even greater, but the formulas for security were not significantly different from the earlier model and the assumptions on which it was based. The Charter makes some form of mediation compulsory and it promotes disarmament. Under Chapter VII, it can impose mandatory sanctions, including the use of force, against a 'threat to the peace', a 'breach of the peace', or in response to 'an act of aggression'. The most radical departure from the League of Nations model was the provision to create a permanent international army, navy, and air force to assist victims of aggression. After years of negotiations and posturing, the plans for creating a permanent United Nations armed force have come to nothing.

Knowing that the theory of collective security did not work under the League regime, the drafters of the United Nations Charter insisted that member states should be free to make alliances outside of the UN system. This was essential because the great powers held a veto in the Security Council and thus a collective response to a crisis situation could never be fashioned against the interests of one or more of them. For most of the cold war crises—Berlin in 1958 and 1961, Cuba in 1962, Vietnam in the 1960s—the UN was at best a peripheral player. Only in the case of the attack on South Korea in 1950 and Iraq's invasion of Kuwait in 1990 did the organization operate roughly as the authors of the 1945 document had envisaged.[12] During the cold war era, security was established primarily through the great powers' nuclear deterrents and through multilateral alliances such as NATO and the Warsaw Pact. These arrangements were negotiated through the traditional means typical of 'club' diplomacy.

For most of the post-1945 period, the security agenda revolved around the Soviet—US confrontation. But during the era there were other wars, such as those fought between India and China over territory in the Himalayas (1962), two wars between India and Pakistan (1965, 1971), the brief war between England and Argentina over the Falkland/Malvinas islands (1982), and the long and deadly war between Iran and Iraq (1980–1988). Three wars between Israel and its Arab neighbours also stand out. There were also nineteen armed conflicts ('wars of national liberation') that ended colonialism. Most of these traditional-type wars and wars of national liberation ended with the military defeat of one of the parties. Others, such as the India—China border dispute, have never been formally settled and remain on the agenda. Multilateral institutions helped to end most of these wars, but they could not prevent them.

So, security since 1945 appears as scarce as it ever was; indeed, compared to relatively peaceful 19th-century Europe, the world in our era has been littered with more crises and armed conflicts. But three major historical changes must be noted. First, there has been no great power war since 1945.[13] This breaks a pattern of almost chronic great power warfare in Europe since the 15th century. Second, although the main area of warfare in the world since medieval times had been Europe, since 1945 Europe has become a zone of peace[14] and the probabilities of this situation changing are remote. And, finally, there has been a dramatic overall decline in the incidence of interstate war so that in this realm the world begins to approximate 19th-century Europe. Put in terms of probabilities, the chance of a state currently becoming involved in war with another state in any year is less than one in one hundred. In the 1930s it was about one in three.[15]

Wars have also become significantly less deadly since the 1950s. The battle death rate in the 1990s and into the present century was only one-third that of the 1970s. Perhaps the best single indicator of the declining deadliness of wars is the average number of battle deaths per conflict per year. In the 1950s the average interstate war resulted in about

21,000 annual deaths. In the 1990s, the figure declined to approximately 5,000, and in the first decade of the new millennium average annual fatalities declined further to less than 3,000.[16]

Explanations for these three dramatic changes in the security environment are numerous and in some cases contradictory. According to John Mueller[17] human beings have learned through two tragic world wars to deal with conflicts in more peaceful ways. War is a human institution, and just like slavery and duelling, human beings can change institutions. Following the opinion of many commentators prior to the First World War, he suggests the costs of war have so far outweighed any possible benefits that the military option to achieve objectives or to defend independence and territorial integrity no longer makes sense. This is particularly true in the case of nuclear war. Others would argue that American hegemony has helped preserve the peace, and there is the view that territory—a major cause of international conflict in the modern era—has lost its significance and value. Today, trade and the expansion of markets matter more than land. As Mueller has argued, 'Free trade furnishes economic advantages of conquest without the unpleasantness of invasion and the sticky responsibility of imperial control.'[18] Other candidates for explanatory power include the hypothesis that democracies do not use military force against each other,[19] the effectiveness of the non-conquest norm, the balance of power, the end of the cold war, the lack of conquest dreamers like Hitler and Mussolini, and the overall economic well-being of the world since the great post-1945 recovery.[20] Finally, the UN and various regional organizations have played a significant role in promoting the peaceful settlement of disputes and crises and in helping to terminate wars.

Traditional types of security problems—threats to state sovereignty, independence, and territorial integrity—have not disappeared, however. Despite the dramatic decline in interstate warfare, the world is not secure for all. Since 1945, there have been seven cases of aggression, starting with the British—French—Israeli attack on Egypt in 1956, and ending most recently with the American attack on Iraq in 2003 and the Georgian and Russian invasion of Abkhazia in the summer of 2008.

There are also areas of chronic instability and enduring rivalries. The conflict between Israel and its neighbours gave rise to three wars since 1948 and as the Israelis continue their colonizing activities in lands claimed by the Palestinians, the central issue of an independent and viable state of Palestine remains unsettled. China presents all sorts of uncertainties for both regional and global security. It is a revisionist state with twenty-three territorial claims against Russia, India, Japan (Senkaku Islands), and the disputed islands in the South China Sea. Like Korea, it remains a divided country, claiming that Taiwan is an integral part of the state. Despite all the security problems of Northeast Asia, however, the region has survived without a war since Korea (1950–1953).

This state of affairs illustrates how traditional security rivalries and territorial disputes have been ameliorated by the growing compulsions of economic growth and corresponding development of multilateral diplomatic institutions. T.J. Pempel offers the following explanation for the seeming anomaly between rivalry and cooperation:

Across East Asia as a whole and generally across the Asia-Pacific, there has developed a pervasive conviction that economic growth offers a powerful route through which nations can enhance their power and prestige. The consequence has been a collective backing away from prior conceptualizations of military might and territorial conquest as the principal means of enhancing national influence and a greater focus on individual and collective economic growth as a positive sum approach to enhanced national power.[21]

His comments could very well apply to all of Europe, including Russia, and Latin America and parts of Africa.

31.5 FROM EXTERNAL TO INTERNAL WARS

Since 1950, approximately, the predominant military security problem has arisen in the new states of the world, and especially in South Asia, the Middle East, and Africa. The problem is no longer war between states (although a few, such as the costly Iraq—Iran war of the 1980s are notable), but within states.[22] The wars have involved attempts at secession (e.g. Biafra), attempts to topple governments (revolutions), civil wars, and organized violence between ethnic groups within states. Prominent recent examples include the twenty-five-year attempt of the Tamil Tigers to carve out a Tamil-based state from Sri Lanka, Burma's ongoing ethnic rebellions, starting in the early 1960s, the Taliban assault in Afghanistan, and the multi-party armed conflict in the collapsed state of Somalia. While these and many other armed conflicts continue to make daily headlines, their incidence has, like interstate wars, also declined significantly. Intra-state wars climbed steadily between the end of the Second World War and 1992, after which there has been a notable decline.[23] But their incidence remains significantly higher than interstate wars. For example, Pakistan, Afghanistan, Somalia, and the Congo remain areas of chronic internal armed strife.

The correlates of these intra-state wars include a colonial legacy, multi-ethnic societies, political repression of ethnic and/or religious groups, government corruption and lack of legitimacy, weak state institutions and infrastructure, and foreign involvement. Other sources include conflicts over resources, the small arms trade, environmental degradation, feelings of relative deprivation, and stagnant or lowering incomes.[24] Collapsed states (e.g. Somalia, Congo) create security vacuums quickly filled by local militias, warlords, and extreme religious movements. In many cases of these wars, the line separating armed conflict and organized crime is blurred. The hallmarks of these kinds of conflicts include unknown or vague political objectives, pillage, the mobilization and impressments of child soldiers, targeting of civilians, mass rape and theft, lack of military discipline, in short, war that challenges all the significant conservative elements of war outlined by Clausewitz.[25] Recent or contemporary examples include armed conflicts in Sierra Leone, Liberia, Somalia, Chad, Darfur, and the depredations of the Lord's Resistance Army in Uganda.

31.6 HOBBES REVERSED: THE STATE AS SECURITY THREAT

According to the 17th-century political philosopher, Thomas Hobbes, men (generically speaking) in a state of nature are in a state of war, all against all; even the weakest has the capacity to kill the stronger. In this situation, individual security can be gained only by creating government (the state) or, in his terms, the Leviathan. Men symbolically contract with the Leviathan in order to provide domestic security. The main task of the Leviathan is to protect; as Hobbes put it, 'the safety of the people is the supreme law' of the Leviathan.[26] It does this through disarming the society, maintaining a monopoly of the legitimate use of force within society, punishing criminals, and administering the law. The Leviathan also provides protection against external threats.

Hobbes did not foresee the government-tolerated pogroms against Jews in Imperial Russia in the late 19th century. Nor did he have in mind a Leviathan that organized or abetted the massacre of several million Greek and Armenian minorities in the Ottoman Empire between 1915 and 1917. In the 1930s Stalin, Molotov, Beria, and other leaders of the Soviet Union liquidated approximately 11 million Soviet citizens, about 5 million of whom, mostly Ukrainians, were killed by forced starvation. At the same time, the Nazi regime organized campaigns of repression, illegal incarceration, and murder of German Jews, communists, homosexuals, Gypsies, and the mentally deficient. During the war, the SS created 'Einsatzgruppen' attached to regular army units. Their primary task on the eastern front was to round up and kill all Jews, resistance fighters, and captured Soviet officials. The 'Final Solution' to the Jewish 'problem' was to culminate in the transport and murder of all Jews in German-occupied territories in Europe. Contemporary genocides in Kampuchea in the 1970s, Rwanda in 1994, and gendercides in Bosnia in the 1990s are added to the list of mass killings of civilians by Stalin and Mao Zedong and more recent tragedies in the Congo.[27] One report noted that 20th-century inter-state and civil wars resulted in 37 million combatant deaths, while the number of civilians killed by their own governments in the century was 170 million.[28] In our era the Leviathan has occasionally become an industrial mass murderer. This is a problem that traditional diplomatic methods and multilateral institutions could not prevent or remedy.

31.7 RESTORING HOBBES

The architects of the United Nations did not foresee a generation of wars of 'national liberation', regions characterized by weak and collapsing states, genocides, and all the brutalities of domestic wars. Diplomats have had to improvise means of managing these types of conflicts and this has not been an easy road because, among other difficulties, the

Charter clearly stipulates that matters essentially within the domestic jurisdiction of the state (Article 2, par. 4) cannot be the subject of international scrutiny, much less action.

The major means around this problem has been to characterize many domestic situations as a 'threat' to international peace and security (Article VII), and hence amenable to international monitoring and action, including sanctions and the use of force. Numerous peacekeeping forces (often a misnomer since there is usually no peace to keep) have been organized to prevent or ameliorate armed conflicts within Somalia, Lebanon, East Timor (Timor Leste), Darfur, Liberia, Sudan, Kosovo, and the Congo, among others.[29] In most cases, these interventions have been organized with the consent of the state involved, but in a few consent was achieved only after considerable international pressure. Some of the interventions were also jointly organized with regional organizations such as NATO and the Organization for African Unity (OAU).

At the height of the era of domestic wars in the early 1990s, the United Nations had under its direction more than 78,000 troops in the field. In 2008 there were thirty UN and UN-authorized peace operations, the majority including armed components.[30] All of these efforts are adaptive innovations to the problems raised by non-Clausewitzian and anti-Hobbesian domestic wars.

What can the UN do if governments do not consent to some forms of international diplomatic or quasi-military intervention? A partial solution is in an innovative interpretation of the sovereignty doctrine. The idea of the 'responsibility to protect' is a good example of how new actors and non-governmental bodies have come to participate in security issues.[31] The doctrine has been approved by the General Assembly and now constitutes a developing if still contentious norm of international relations.[32] In 2011, the Security Council passed resolution 1973 granting member states (in fact a NATO-led coalition) the task of protecting the Libyan population against threatened massacres by the beleaguered Libyan dictator, Colonel Gaddafi. However, the restoration of Hobbes' concept of sovereignty has come under serious criticism on a number of grounds, not the least of which is that the veto (and superior power) guarantees that the international community could never intervene militarily against a great power that was systematically violating the human rights of its own people.

31.8 TWO NEW SECURITY THREATS

While classical interstate wars, great power wars, and all sorts of domestic wars have declined significantly in the past two decades, two new types of problems have emerged on the international security agenda. Terrorist tactics—the deliberate targeting of innocent civilians for propaganda and other political purposes—have been a regular feature of some wars since ancient times and were prominent in almost all anti-colonial wars. They are typically the tactics of the weak, the parties that could not and cannot mobilize regular armed forces and their armaments to match those of their enemies. In fact, there have been very few wars even of the conventional type where one or more parties did not employ irregular forms of violence against civilians.

But whereas these means were primarily an adjunct to more conventional forms of warfare, in the last two decades various organizations and networks have appeared that have no command of regular military capabilities and seek to achieve their political objectives solely through the use of terror. The international community, through the United Nations, has condemned terrorism as a form of political action (Security Council Resolution 1371, 2001). The High-Level Panel's 2004 report to the Secretary General of the United Nations listed terrorism as the fifth of six main security problems facing the world. The 11 September 2001 attack on the twin towers of Manhattan and on the Pentagon, resulting in more than 3,000 deaths, significantly raised threat perceptions around the world and particularly in the United States which, under President Bush, declared a 'war on terror'.

But 'terrorism' is a highly undifferentiated concept. In today's environment, it can refer to the activities of governments against their own citizens, the tactics used by resistance fighters against occupation (as many Palestinians insist), secessionist movements, politically disgruntled loners, psychopaths, amateur 'jihadists', and any number of misfits, malcontents, and those fighting for causes (e.g. animal rights, the Basque extremists) that appear to make no progress. Clearly, these kinds of actors and activities are not what George Bush or the Security Council had in mind when they condemned terrorism.

The threat refers primarily if not exclusively, to the objectives, purposes, actions, and actors associated with al-Qaeda. These include its acolytes and mimics around the world. How serious is the threat? It depends upon how we classify incidents: who were the perpetrators, who were the victims, and where were the attacks? By far the highest numbers of incidents are attacks by Muslim extremists on fellow Muslims, particularly in Pakistan and Somalia. In the former, there has been an average of 1,000 civilian deaths annually so far in this century.[33] Many of the killings have little to do with the al-Qaeda network. The statistics for Islamist terror attacks on targets in the *West* are low. The 9/11 attack resulted in more than 3,000 deaths, but when we delete this single incident, the average annual fatalities for the 1989–2008 period are 14 deaths and 107 wounded.[34] Compared to people annually killed by gunmen in American shopping malls, schools, and offices, these figures are miniscule. In Europe in 2009 (excluding Britain), there was only one Islamist attack.[35]

Two events in 2011 seriously damaged al-Qaeda's claims to legitimacy and effectiveness. The 'spring revolution' throughout the Middle East demonstrated that the vast majority of Arab Muslims want democratic reforms and the observance of human rights, not the politics of religious fundamentalism. The idea that al-Qaeda could lead a revolution was buried under the drive for democracy. The assassination of al-Qaeda leader Osama bin-Laden by American Special Forces was the second major blow to terrorist aspirations.

It is too early to proclaim that this dimension of the world's security agenda has abated to the point of insignificance. The al-Qaeda network might commit more attacks, but the chances that it could overthrow a government and replace it with a Taliban-resembling theocracy are remote. The consequences of Iran having nuclear weapons might be more dangerous.

The second new security agenda item, then, is proliferation of weapons of mass destruction. Because of the immense destructive power of nuclear weapons, the prevention of their proliferation has become a major goal of security policy among most government, and in particular the great powers. The 1968 Nuclear Non-Proliferation Treaty (NPT) commits non-nuclear signatory states to forego their development, those who possess them to abolish them, and to set in place various inspection protocols to make certain that nuclear facilities designed for peaceful power purposes do not produce weapons-grade fuels.

But the main threat may not be states with nuclear weapons—the international nuclear taboo, a powerful universal norm operates against everyone.[36] The current security nightmare is that terrorist groups will gain control of weapons of mass destruction, however defined. Since such groups or networks cannot easily—if at all—be deterred by conventional or nuclear means, unlike states, they might have no reservations about using them.[37] Their objective, presumably, would be to inflict the most extreme levels of damage to targeted civilians.

31.9 THE EXPANDING SECURITY AGENDA

In the 1990s, scholars and diplomats began to argue that the UN Charter and similar documents of regional organizations are state-centric, defining security only in terms of protecting the sovereignty, independence, and territorial integrity of states. What is crucial, they suggested, is the security of individuals who face an array of threats to their lives and welfare. Human security, the International Commission on Intervention and State Sovereignty declared, includes peoples' 'physical safety, their economic and social well-being, respect for their dignity and worth as human beings, and the protection of their human rights and fundamental freedoms'.[38] It is beyond the scope of this chapter either to debate the advantages or costs of loading the world's diplomats with a 'human security' agenda, or to examine even briefly the many actions and plans that have been developed to deal with them. It may suffice to acknowledge the immense cast of actors who are dealing with these issues.

There are thousands of scientists in the world who address the issue of climate change and dozens of transnational non-governmental organizations devoted to ameliorating the effects of growing greenhouse gases in the atmosphere and lobbying governments to take official actions to deal with the problems. There are both official and non-governmental efforts to control and reduce the incidence of piracy (another item on the new international security agenda), human trafficking, the gigantic international drug trade, child labour, and many other problems. These are dealt with through a combination of local, regional, national, and international networks of activists, government officials, and diplomats at international organizations. Much of the research work that develops knowledge of these problems is undertaken in universities and non-official think tanks. The cast of activist characters involved in various forms of diplomacy—problem-solving across national borders—is immense and constantly growing. All this activity is buttressed by extensive intergovernmental networks operating independently of official cabinet-level control,[39] and working on an incredibly broad security agenda. Scholars, activists, researchers, lobbyists, and publicists all play their advocacy roles, but ultimately it is the diplomats representing their governments that negotiate the agreements and fashion, however weakly or hesitatingly, various solutions. The domain of 'human security' issues is a site of constant 'network' diplomacy

However, the domain of core security concerns such as independence and territorial integrity remains confined primarily to 'club' diplomacy, where governments plan and execute their strategies and tactics of negotiating agreements and tackling both bilateral and multilateral problems and threats. They often rely on technical and academic experts for advice, but it is government agents, not publics, that largely determine outcomes. Why? Because it is only governments that can make the commitments and allocation of resources required for national security. NGOs, experts, and advocacy groups have their say, but they cannot decide for the state. The diplomacy of security remains largely a domain of 'club' diplomacy and is likely to remain as such for the foreseeable future. As Hobbes implied, one cannot address issues such as health, development, human trafficking, and global warming in the absence of state security and international and domestic order. Human fulfilment is dependent upon them.

Notes

1. C. von Clausewitz, *On War*, ed. and trans. Michael Howard and Peter Paret (Princeton: Princeton University Press, 1984).
2. G. Treasure, *The Making of Modern Europe 1648–1780* (London: Methuen, 1985), 207; K.J. Holsti, 'Reversing Rousseau: The Medieval and Modern in Contemporary Wars', in William Bain (ed.), *The Empire of Security and the Safety of the People* (London: Routledge, 2006), 38–41.
3. I. Chang, *The Rape of Nanking* (UK: Penguin Books, 1997).
4. <http://en.wikipedia.org/wiki/World_War_II_casualties#To>.
5. Meaning that security is a question of perception, not a given. See O. Waever, 'Securitization and Descuritization', in R. Lipschutz (ed.), *On Security* (New York: Columbia University Press, 1995).
6. C. Tilly, 'Reflections on the History of European State-Making', in C. Tilly (ed.), *The Formation of National States in Western Europe* (Princeton: Princeton University Press, 1975), 42; see also R.N. Lebow, *A Cultural Theory of International Relations* (Cambridge: Cambridge University Press, 2008), 298–304.
7. W. Bain, 'Introduction', in W. Bain (ed.), *The Empire of Security and the Safety of the People* (London: Routledge, 2006), 1.
8. Quoted in R. Jackson, 'The Safety of the People is the Supreme Law: Beyond Hobbes but not as far as Kant', in Bain (ed.), *The Empire of Security and the Safety of the People*, 21.

9. J. Vasquez, 'Re-examining the Steps to War: New Evidence and Theoretical Insights', in M. Midlarsky (ed.), *Handbook of War Studies II* (Ann Arbor, MI: University of Michigan Press, 2000), 371–406.

10. For discussion of the norms and rules of the Congress system, see K.J. Holsti, 'Governance without Government: Polyarchy in Nineteenth-Century European International Politics', in J. Rosenau and E.-O. Czempiel (eds), *Governance without Government: Order and Change in World Politics*, (Cambridge University Press, 1992).

11. <Http://en.wikipedia.org/wiki/World_War_I_casualties#Cas>.

12. In both cases the Security Council did not, as it could under Chapter VII, compel member states to make forces available to counter an act of aggression or breach of the peace. It invited member states to make voluntary contributions.

13. The Korean War (1950–1953) is a possible exception. Most commentators do not include it as a great power war because the Chinese intervention in 1951 was by 'volunteers' and not formally by the Peoples' Liberation Army. Moreover, China was not then a great power.

14. If we include ex-Yugoslavia and Turkey as parts of Europe, we could not make this statement. The Balkan wars of the 1990s and the enduring rivalry between Greece and Turkey, if counted, mar the otherwise perfect record.

15. K. Holsti, 'The Use of Force in International Politics: Four Revolutions', in W. P. Sidhu and R. Thakur (eds), *Arms Control after Iraq: Normative and Operational Challenges* (New York: United Nations University Press, 2006), 25–6.

16. Human Security Report Project, Simon Fraser University, *Human Security Report 2009/2010: The Causes of Peace and the Shrinking Costs of War* (Oxford: Oxford University Press, 2011), ch. 1.

17. J. Mueller, *Retreat from Doomsday: The Obsolescence of Major War* (New York: Basic Books, 1989).

18. J. Mueller, *Capitalism, Democracy, and Ralph's Pretty Good Grocery* (Princeton: Princeton University Press, 2000), 77.

19. B. Russett and J.R. Oneal, *Triangulating Peace: Democracy, Interdependence, and International Organizations* (Princeton: Princeton University Press, 2001).

20. K.J. Holsti, 'The Decline of Interstate War: Pondering Systemic Explanations', in R. Väyrynen (ed.), *The Waning of Major War: Theories and Debates* (London: Routledge, 2006).

21. T.J. Pempel, 'More Pax, Less Americana in Asia', *International Relations of the Asia-Pacific* 10:3 (2010), 473.

22. K.J. Holsti, *The State, War, and the State of War* (Cambridge: Cambridge University Press, 1996); Human Security Centre, the University of British Columbia, *Human Security Report 2005: War and Peace in the 21st Century* (Oxford: Oxford University Press, 2005).

23. Human Security Report Project, Simon Fraser University.

24. K.J. Holsti, 'The Political Causes of Humanitarian Emergencies', in E.W. Nafziger, Frances Stewart, and Raimo Väyrynen (eds), *War, Hunger and Replacement: The Origins of Humanitarian Emergencies* (Oxford: Oxford University Press, 2000); and W. Navziger and J. Auvinen, 'The Economic Causes of Humanitarian Emergencies' in the same volume. For a critical review of statistical studies of the sources of internal wars, see Human Security Report Project, Simon Fraser University.

25. Holsti, 'Reversing Rousseau'.

26. T. Hobbes, *On the Citizens*, ed. R. Tuck and M. Silverthorne (Cambridge: Cambridge University Press, 1998).

27. For details, see A. Jones, *Genocide: A Comprehensive Introduction*, 2d. ed. (London: Routledge, 2011).

28. *The Economist*, 11 September 1999, 7.

29. See Chapter 43, this volume, on the diplomacy of peacekeeping.

30. *Human Security Report 2009/2010*, ch. 4.

31. See Chapter 42, this volume.

32. R. Thakur, *The United Nations, Peace and Security: From Collective Security to the Responsibility to Protect* (Cambridge: Cambridge University Press, 2006), and G. Evans, *The Responsibility to Protect: Ending Mass Atrocity Crimes Once and for All* (New York: Brookings Institution Press, 2008).

33. South Asian Terrorist Portal, 'Civilian Fatalities in Pakistan', <www.satp.org>.

34. M. Harrow, 'The Effect of the Iraq War on Islamist Terror', *Cooperation and Conflict* 45:3 (2010), 274–93.

35. European Union, Europol, *Te-Sat 2010: European Union Terrorism Situation and Trends Report* (European Union, 2010).

36. Thakur, *United Nations, Peace and Security*, 161–4; see also T.V. Paul, *The Tradition of Non-Use of Nuclear Weapons* (Stanford: Stanford University Press, 2009).

37. A. Lupovici, 'The Emerging Fourth Wave of Deterrence Theory—Toward a New Research Agenda', *International Studies Quarterly* 54:3 (2010), 705–32.

38. International Commission on Intervention and State Sovereignty, *The Responsibility to Protect*, International Development Research Centre (Ottawa), 2001, 15.

39. See S. Hollis, 'The Necessity of Protection: Transgovernmental Networks and EU Security Governance', *Cooperation and Conflict* 45:3 (2010), 312–30.

CHAPTER 32

....

ARMS CONTROL AND DISARMAMENT DIPLOMACY

....

REBECCA JOHNSON

STRATEGIC relations dramatically transformed in the early 1990s, precipitating critical changes in how arms control, disarmament, and diplomacy have come to be perceived and practised. The era of bipolar hegemonies locked in mutually reinforcing rivalries ended as communist governments across the Soviet bloc were toppled by their own citizens. For the dominant American and Soviet state systems, which were simultaneously driven and constrained by their nuclear arsenals and mutual fear of unleashing worldwide nuclear annihilation, arms control was important for maintaining bilateral strategic stability and avoiding nuclear war. The more diverse, multifaceted geostrategic environment that developed at the end of the cold war has given rise to different security assessments, expectations, challenges, and opportunities, for which traditional military capabilities are of diminishing relevance.

The range of formal and informal diplomatic interactions now being employed to enhance security through the restriction and prohibition of certain kinds of military technologies, weapons, and practices[1] goes far beyond the rubric of arms control. 'Disarmament', which has broader meaning and is employed both to describe the process of reducing and eliminating certain weapons systems and the objective or end-state when a specific type of weapon has been abolished, is a more appropriate subject for contemporary analysis than arms control, with recognition that both terms are imbued with contested political connotations and may be employed inconsistently and with competing purposes. Also relevant is the concept of non-proliferation embedded in the 1968 Treaty on the Non-Proliferation of Nuclear Weapons (NPT). The NPT carried into international law a near-universal objective that encompasses preventing the spread of nuclear weapons, controls over weapons-related technologies that also have civilian applications, and disarmament. The treaty became the cornerstone of a regime of interconnecting obligations, norms, rules, and formal and informal arrangements, ranging from the International Atomic Energy Agency (IAEA) to the ad hoc Nuclear Suppliers

Group (NSG), nuclear security summits, and UN Security Council resolutions, including inter alia 1540 (2004) and 1887 (2009). Though not required to adhere to its stringent safeguards regime, in Article VI of the NPT the five defined nuclear-weapon states (NWS—United States, Soviet Union/Russia, United Kingdom, France, and China) undertook reciprocal obligations to end their nuclear arms race, pursue negotiations 'in good faith' on nuclear disarmament, and work with all states parties to achieve 'a treaty on general and complete disarmament under strict and effective international control'. 'Counter-proliferation' and 'anti-proliferation' describe policies advanced by a few, mainly US, policy-makers from the late 1990s. The primary aim was to prevent others from acquiring nuclear materials, technologies, and capabilities without necessarily undertaking reciprocal commitments with regard to their own or allies' nuclear capabilities. Though diplomacy may be necessary to reach agreement among military or political allies that undertake joint counter-proliferation activities such as the US-led Proliferation Security Initiative of 2003, the intent is to bring together 'coalitions of the willing' to police others rather than to engage in mutual limitations or disarmament, and so will not be addressed in this chapter.

The break-up of the Soviet bloc was both consequence and cause of fundamental transformations in the international security environment as the cold war ended, with anti-nuclear movements and disarmament diplomacy playing a small but crucial role during the 1980s. Before the altered 'new world order' had time to develop significantly different attitudes towards arms control and disarmament, the terrorist attacks of 11 September 2001 (9/11)—particularly the military and political responses of the George W. Bush administration (2001–2008)–profoundly affected the objectives and conduct of diplomacy across the international spectrum. Concerns intensified over terrorism, new additions to the nuclear 'club', and the proliferation activities of repressive regimes.[2] Iraq was substantially disarmed in accordance with UN Security Council resolutions after the 1990–1991 Gulf War. Various diplomatic arrangements addressed the safety and security of sensitive materials and technologies, including cooperative threat reduction programmes that focused primarily on the nuclear facilities in Russia and newly independent former Soviet states, financed by private philanthropy as well as government funds.[3]

In addition to the increased value attached to multilateral diplomacy even for weapons possessed by relatively few states, such as nuclear and chemical, disarmament diplomacy has grown far beyond 'diplomats sitting in a conference room negotiating a legally binding agreement'[4] and now encompasses a broad range of approaches, types of weapons, actors, and mechanisms. Though state-centred treaties continue to be a desired objective, particularly for their normative value as shared instruments under international law, different forms of disarmament diplomacy have proved their utility for different purposes, including the necessity in some cases of bypassing political and institutional obstacles. At one end of the spectrum, the 1990–1991 Presidential Nuclear Initiatives undertaken by Presidents George H.W. Bush and Mikhail Gorbachev (later Boris Yeltsin) provided for deep reductions in non-strategic/tactical nuclear forces by means of coordinated unilateral declarations, which provided a timely agreement that bypassed slow and often difficult domestic requirements for treaty ratification.

Negotiated by US and Russian diplomatic teams, these also prompted independent unilateral reductions in tactical nuclear weapons by France and the UK, even though neither had been formally represented in the negotiations.

Though instituted during the cold war, review process negotiations have increased in salience for strengthening and extending existing treaties such as the NPT and the 1972 Biological and Toxin Weapons Convention (BWC). UN diplomacy also benefited from the less rigid political environment. After the 9/11 attacks, the Security Council was used to augment existing treaties' disarmament and security obligations to prevent non-state actors from acquiring the means to make and use weapons of mass destruction (WMD), as illustrated by Security Council resolutions 1373 (2001) and 1540 (2004). Limited to political gesture and rhetoric during the cold war, the UN General Assembly facilitated negotiations to get international agreement on a Programme of Action on Small Arms and Light Weapons (SALW) in 2001, which continues to be taken forward through review meetings, and has also acted as midwife to a proposed Arms Trade Treaty. Most significantly, many of these post-cold-war initiatives built on alliances and strategies forged by civil society actors and governments to negotiate measures to control and limit the use, production, and/or trade in weapons that are characterized as particularly inhumane. Two key treaties—the 1997 Mine Ban Treaty and 2008 Cluster Munitions Convention (CMC)—were made possible only when a group of 'like-minded' governments in conjunction with transnational civil society actors developed ad hoc negotiating forums outside established structures and institutions, bypassing the structural and political impediments of the framework Convention on Certain Conventional Weapons (CCW) and the paralysed Conference on Disarmament (CD).[5]

32.1 From Limitation to Prohibition: Disarmament Diplomacy in Transition

Four kinds of developments have shaped changes in the expectations, objectives, and conduct of modern disarmament diplomacy: transformative advances in networked communications and weapons technologies; transnational criminals who include sensitive materials and weapons procurement among their trafficking activities; broader civil society networks linked transnationally and motivated by humanitarian, environmental, and anti-militarist concerns;[6] and changes in public attitudes towards international security, warfare, and 'acceptable' versus 'unacceptable' means for achieving national and international policy objectives.

Since the 1980s, developments in electronic and space-based technologies have accelerated globalization and led to an unprecedented diffusion of information and exchange through networked communication. Driven in part by military interests, this 'third industrial revolution' advanced capabilities in computing, communications, space-based monitoring, information-collection, and targeting. As the United States forged ahead, they hailed these advances as a 'revolution in military affairs'. As with all revolutions, however, there were losses as well as gains. The growing civil and military dependence on space-based assets and highly sensitive electronic and technological tools has brought new capabilities, but also new threats and challenges. Former Defense Secretary Donald Rumsfeld, for example, explicitly cited vulnerability to a pre-emptive 'Space Pearl Harbor'[7] to justify why the US should expand military capabilities in space, potentially including systems banned under existing treaties, such as the 1972 Anti-Ballistic Missile (ABM) Treaty, which the George W. Bush administration withdrew from in 2002, and the 1967 Outer Space Treaty. As with weapons and military advances from time imme-morial, when one power develops greater capabilities, others will seek to go further, cre-ating destabilizing arms races that drive insecurity until halted by either the carnage of war or commitments to mutual disarmament. In contrast to Rumsfeld's militaristic assumptions, networked communication and responsible uses of space as a protected 'global commons' and 'common good' carry the possibility of increasing global security, with shared advantages for all. From the wide information resources available through Google, Wikipedia, and Wikileaks, to collective action and demonstrations such as brought about the 'Arab Spring' uprisings in 2011, networked communication is ena-bling greater civil society participation in governance and political change, amplifying the growing awareness of shared, global interests, such as environmental protection, disarmament, development, and the responsible production and consumption of energy and scarce resources. This 'end of geography',[8] as noted by Jorge Heine, is influencing profound changes in modern diplomacy, including disarmament issues.

A further relevant development is the way in which the humanitarian impact of weap-ons has become a driving force once more, bypassing the assumptions and premises that narrowed the scope and prospects for disarmament in the cold war. Where diplomatic efforts for the latter half of the 20th century were dominated by technical and military discussions about utility, defence roles, modes of deployments, verification, and criteria for usage and trade restrictions, the diplomatic strategies that succeeded in banning landmines and cluster munitions focused on the human impact, thereby shifting the burden of justification onto those seeking to retain, deploy, manufacture, and trade in these weapons. The Oslo Declaration that launched the process for the 2008 Cluster Munitions Convention epitomized this new approach to 'disarmament as humanitarian action' when its forty-six signatory states explicitly identified their objective as to 'pro-hibit the use, production, transfer and stockpiling of cluster munitions that cause unac-ceptable harm to civilians'.[9] Concerns about the long-term health and environmental effects of nuclear weapons had also framed early nuclear disarmament efforts in moral terms, but were for decades dismissed as irrelevant by nuclear club practitioners steeped in the premises and rituals of realist nuclear doctrines. In the wake of successful strate-gies to ban other inhumane weapons, nuclear diplomacy is increasingly being pushed by non-nuclear governments, in conjunction with civil society networks, using concepts such as 'catastrophic humanitarian consequences' and calling for compliance with Inter-national Humanitarian Law (IHL).[10] After decades of arms control, non-proliferation, and counter-proliferation doing little to dent the military and political value some states attach to nuclear weapons, new strategies based on 'humanitarian action' and delegiti-mizing nuclear deterrence doctrines have begun to be employed to pave the way for multilateral negotiations on a comprehensive treaty or framework of agreements to accomplish the internationally-supported objective of a world free of nuclear weapons.

The context, conduct, and objectives of disarmament diplomacy are determined not only by exogenous events and political relations between states, but by political and philosophi-cal changes in how national and international security are perceived and pursued. Far from being fixed or rational, as portrayed by realist theoreticians, states' interests in negotiations are trade-offs in a complex relationship dynamics between security, disarmament, foreign policy, defence, arms producers, and domestic opinion-shapers; negotiating postures are frequently contested and subject to capture, recapture, and transformation. Weapons that appear useful in one historic era may come to be seen more as problems than assets in a dif-ferent political and security environment. Means of waging war or projecting power that once appeared acceptable, necessary, or inevitable may be reframed over time as unaccept-able, unnecessary, and ripe for elimination. For some—from street gangs to nuclear weapon states—the possession of certain weapons may be framed in terms of defence or deterrence when the underlying drivers have more to do with notions of identity, status, club member-ship, or power projection. Others may perceive those same weapons as destabilizing and threatening, contributing to greater insecurity and arms racing, where a mistake or act of aggression can have fatal—even catastrophic—consequences. While arms control has been a widely accepted tool to promote and underpin security, it may also be a means for main-taining strategic positioning and relationships that block progressive regional or global security developments or, alternatively, it may appear as an insidious mechanism to reduce a country's military advantages and defence capabilities vis-à-vis others. Disarmament, once regarded as the business of governments and their military experts, is driven now by concepts of international and human security, intersecting with globalist perspectives in which governance is assessed by international standards, with value attached to human rights and humanitarian effects that erode the primacy formerly accorded to national secu-rity justifications, military force, and state sovereignty.

Three of the precursors that led to the significant weapons restrictions initiated by the Hague Conferences of 1899 and 1907 have been interestingly echoed in post-cold war developments; dramatic epistemic advances in science and weapons technologies that increased the military options of certain states far beyond what had been previously possible, leading to arms racing and war among major powers; the rise of feminist and anti-militarist perspectives as women became more politically assertive; and changes in public attitudes towards what constituted 'acceptable' and 'unacceptable' weapons and wars. The Hague Conferences of 1899 and 1907 brought together the major powers and social progressives of the time to codify elements of the rules of war, resulting also in the restriction or prohibition of the use of certain weapons, notably dum dum bullets and asphyxiating chemicals, deemed particularly inhumane. Nonetheless, chemical weap-ons such as mustard gas and phosgene were used by both sides in the First World War. After that war, a flurry of diplomatic activity focused on controlling and limiting the technological means and size of military forces usable for future wars. The principal enduring outcome was a framework treaty, the 1925 Geneva Convention on the Arms Trade, which brought in minimum standards of reporting and regulations for the use of certain types of weapons. The Geneva Protocol for the Prohibition of the Use in War of Asphyxiating, Poisonous or other Gases, and of Bacteriological Methods of Warfare was the most significant restriction to be agreed at that time. It prohibited the use of biological and chemical weaponry in warfare, but did not deal with production, deployment, stockpiling, trade or, most importantly, the use of chemicals and asphyxiating gases to kill civilian non-combatants, as occurred during the 1939–1945 war.

The end of the Second World War heralded the beginning of the nuclear age and the bitter military-ideological rivalry between the United States and Soviet Union, which became the dominant military-industrial powers. By detonating atomic weapons on Hiroshima and Nagasaki in 1945, President Harry Truman simultaneously demonstrated US technological and military superiority and forestalled the entry of Soviet forces into the Japanese mainland. As images from the two devastated cities spread round the world, reactions were divided: some wanted to access these powerful weapons of mass annihilation for themselves, while others sought to prohibit and abolish them. When the United Nations was founded, its first General Assembly resolution of 24 January 1946 concerned 'the problems raised by the discovery of atomic energy'. In 1946, the Baruch Plan characterized nuclear disarmament as 'a choice between the quick and the dead'. Such early multilateral efforts to contain atomic weapons technologies failed, and the Soviet Union, United Kingdom, France, and China soon followed the United States in developing, testing, and deploying nuclear arsenals. Nuclear weapons dominated strategic thinking, not only as a greatly-feared tool of mass destruction, but also as a highly-prized currency of power.

From 1945 until the early 1960s, military rivalry and brinkmanship characterized strategic relations between the US and Soviet blocs. The mushroom clouds from atomic and hydrogen bombs tests in the atmosphere provoked public and political pressure to end nuclear testing, organized by women's groups, philosophical and moral leaders, doctors and scientists in Western countries and Japan, with strong support from non-aligned governments led by India, Indonesia, and Sweden. Yet it was not until after the 1962 Cuban Missile Crisis that the dominant powers acted to control nuclear arms. Recognition of how close they had come to nuclear war gave the major powers a shared incentive to prevent the further spread of nuclear weapons but not necessarily to get rid of their own arsenals. The first product was the 1963 Partial Test Ban Treaty (PTBT), negotiated by the United States, Soviet Union, and Britain and then opened for other states to sign and ratify. Though greeted with relief, the PTBT constituted more of a setback than victory for civil society and many non-aligned and middle power governments, which had been advocating a fully comprehensive ban on all nuclear testing.

Following the PTBT, the cold war powers turned their attention to getting a non-proliferation treaty, which had been advocated in slightly different resolutions from Ireland and Sweden to the UN General Assembly in 1961.[11] Though the NPT is generally viewed as a success for multilateral diplomacy, it was designed to protect the strategic interests of the United States and Soviet Union, who maintained overall control of the negotiations by tabling identical treaty drafts and, finally, a joint draft treaty.[12] The non-nuclear members of the Eighteen Nation Disarmament Committee[13] played a significant role in pushing for a disarmament commitment and a right for treaty parties to develop nuclear technologies for non-military (described as 'peaceful') purposes. Even so, the treaty was castigated by some as discriminatory and unequal, due to the weak, watered down language on disarmament that made it into Article VI, and the lack of provisions for monitoring the five nuclear-weapons states defined in the treaty text, in contrast with the stringent obligations and safeguards requirements imposed on all the non-nuclear-weapon states that acceded to the NPT. In consequence, a number of states with nuclear programmes or aspirations (for example, Argentina, Brazil, France, India, and several African states) abstained on the UN resolution recommending adoption of the NPT in June 1968. In a move that was to be echoed twenty-eight years later with the CTBT, India castigated the NPT as discriminatory and publicly declared its refusal to sign.[14]

Soon after the NPT entered into force in 1970, the US and Soviet Union recognized that biological weapons were not a usable military asset and pushed through negotiations on the BWC. Though this was another bilaterally managed treaty in multilateral clothing without multilateral verification or monitoring provisions, the BWC did not seek to emulate the NPT's non-proliferation structure but promulgated a universal prohibition on the production and use of biological and toxin weapons, applicable to all states. During a period of détente, further bilateral treaties were negotiated, primarily to stabilize the US–Soviet strategic relationship and reduce the financial burden of their arms racing. The most important of these was the ABM Treaty, which enshrined the concept of deterrence based on mutual vulnerability, and the SALT I Interim Agreement, the first to limit strategic nuclear weapons. Designed as a package, these entered into force together in 1972. In 1979, a further US–Soviet strategic arms limitation agreement, SALT II, was signed, but was never implemented due to political and electoral shifts in the United States and the deployment of new generations of intermediate-range 'theatre' missiles by the Soviet Union and NATO. Reacting to fears of a new atomic arms race and nuclear war in the European 'theatre', American civic leaders called for a 'freeze' on US and Soviet arsenals, while across Europe a new generation of activists demanded the removal of Soviet SS20s and the US cruise and Pershing missiles from both sides of the Berlin Wall. More than just a re-energizing of earlier peace movements, the new peace activists went far beyond the established anti-nuclear NGOs. Drawing from civil rights, anti-war, feminist, and gay liberation movements of the previous two decades, they were politicized to embrace diversity and use creative non-violent actions. The latest nuclear weapons deployments were framed not only as life threatening, but as a representative tool of patriarchal ideologies of division, coercion, and control. Calling for the dissolution of the NATO–Warsaw Pact blocs as well as the removal of their respective weapons, the 1980s movements engaged new generations of activists across the political and cultural spectrum, integrating feminist and human rights consciousness with emerging green and environmental awareness. Embedded in grassroots campaigns with charismatic 'norm entrepreneurs',[15] Western activists reached across the 'iron curtain' to communicate with women's groups and other religious and political dissidents in the Soviet bloc, seeking new ways to talk about shared concerns such as peace, freedom, and human rights.

The turning point occurred in October 1986, when Soviet President Mikhail Gorbachev and US President Ronald Reagan met in Reykjavik and 'began to outbid each other' in visions of how to remove the nuclear threat through disarmament.[16] Superficially, the diplomatic endgame that resulted in the 1987 Intermediate-Range Nuclear Forces (INF) Treaty may have resembled the bilateral club diplomacy of the 1960s–1970s. Closer analysis, however, shows transitional characteristics associated with the globalist disarmament diplomacy of the early 21st century. The impetus for negotiations was driven by civil society networks acting transnationally. The INF Treaty did not just mandate limitations or reductions in obsolete weapons systems, but required the complete removal of an entire class of ground-based state-of-the-art nuclear missiles. For a few hours, the superpower leaders moved beyond the deterrence equation of mutual threat, and shared visions that they could get rid of all nuclear weapons and make the world a safer place.[17] They failed, due in large part to President Reagan's obdurate attachment to the science-fiction fantasy of an impenetrable missile shield (the so-called Strategic Defense Initiative), as anxious political advisors on both sides scrambled to rein in their presidents' aspirations. Though there were still disarmament opponents in the military and nuclear weapons laboratories that sought to undermine political leaders' visions of what was possible, they did not create the kind of exaggerated verification hurdles of the past.[18] Once the political commitment was made, technical and verification questions were treated as challenges requiring solutions and not as obstacles to derail the INF Treaty objective. Improved access to communication and information about each others' lives, through television and radio as well as people-to-people initiatives, made it possible for civil society to breach the East–West borders from both directions. Gorbachev was a beneficiary of these changes as well as an instigator, and has acknowledged the importance of civil society—notably international organizations of physicians and scientists and the Greenham Common Women's Peace Camp—in convincing him to take risks in proposing deep nuclear disarmament. In dynamic interaction, the political upheavals that led to the Reykjavik Summit also contributed to changing a generation's mindset. The 1980s peace movements reshaped disarmament diplomacy through their actions, analysis, and appeals, thereby influencing and enabling the profound systemic changes that ended the cold war.

As US and Russian leaders reassessed their interests and policies in the post-cold war transition, multilateral diplomacy was able to accomplish two important objectives that had been stuck on the CD's agenda for years: the CWC and CTBT. Concluding these long-sought treaties became possible as power balances shifted and arsenals that could poison or destroy the world lost much of their salience. The negotiations to ban chemical weapons, which concluded in 1992, conformed in many ways to John Ruggie's principles of multilateralism, which he derived from trade negotiations and characterized as diffuse reciprocity, indivisibility (for example, through shared responsibilities and benefits), and non-discrimination.[19] The major players were traditional government elites with advice and input from pharmaceutical and chemical industries.

By contrast, the test ban treaty, which was negotiated over 1994–1996, exhibited more of the hallmarks of modern diplomacy. The nuclear-armed P5 entered the CTBT negotiations intent on normalizing the possession of nuclear weapons by their privileged group, while preventing the rise of additional nuclear-weapon possessors such as non-NPT states India, Pakistan, and Israel.[20] Despite their determined efforts, however, the 'minilateral' P5 negotiations were far from decisive. Epistemic actors, from civil society and scientific institutions, played particularly important roles in shaping states' preferences on scope and verification, bearing out theories that link integrative convergence strategies with the cognitive and ideational roles of civil society, and the recasting of values, norms, and ideas.[21] Exemplifying Thakur's analysis on balance of interests (Chapter 3, this volume), the integrative outcomes on scope and verification were made easier to achieve because competing perceptions of national interest among the P5 led to stalemate regarding permitted activities and verification technologies, creating space for interests to be reframed and traded through input by other actors that would previously have been excluded. The zero-yield decision became possible not only because the P5 were deeply divided over threshold levels, but also because there were competing objectives within the various national positions, most notably among the US agencies. Interests and power were fragmented, with pressure exerted on many sides, including from domestic and trans-governmental alliances between the nuclear scientists and military officials of more than one country. As a consequence, the outcome was determined by three intersecting levels of activity: trans-governmental, involving diplomacy among officials from different states; transnational civil society networking to frame objectives and options and broaden understanding of the negotiations that still largely took place behind closed doors; and cross-level interactions, in which governmental and non-governmental actors from different states collaborated in formal and informal alliances to achieve regime-building objectives.[22]

Multilateral institutions such as the CD, the United Nations (most notably the Security Council), the IAEA, and treaty-based forums were structured to promote and protect the interests of the dominant powers of their time, the nuclear-weapon states, which established for themselves veto powers and special responsibilities. Conducted by professional and technical cadres with special interests as well as expertise, the bilateral (US–Russian) and 'minilateral' P5 talks exemplified club diplomacy at its most elite, with concomitant cultures of secrecy that concealed mistakes and incompetence as well as militarily sensitive information.

32.2 HUMANITARIAN-CENTRED DISARMAMENT AND INTEGRATIVE DIPLOMACY

The growing role of integrative approaches in modern diplomacy reflects the increased importance of civil society and epistemic actors who use cognitive and communications strategies to change how governments view security issues, disarmament objectives, and the achievability of potential solutions and agreements. In contrast to the zero-sum assumptions of distributive negotiations, which often require the key players to be on board before negotiations can begin, integrative diplomacy aims to expand the options and change perceptions of the zones of possible agreement, building support as the disarmament process develops.[23] Treating military and political interests as factors that can be altered, integrative diplomacy may be overtaking traditional arms control by employing a range of tools and techniques that reframe security concepts and objectives and build public and political momentum for disarmament on the basis of norms such as 'unacceptable harm'.

The ending of the cold war created fresh opportunities for millions of people. It also enabled negative developments, as illustrated by the eruption of ethno-nationalist violence in countries from Yugoslavia to Rwanda in the 1990s, and increased trans-border trafficking in weapons, drugs, and human beings, by transnationally networked criminal gangs.[24] Against this background of armed criminality and wars, a growing number of NGOs and governments redoubled efforts to stem the carnage wrought by small arms and the weapons that left their explosive remnants to kill civilians long after the military has departed. After early attempts to address inhumane weapons through the CCW, advocates of a comprehensive ban on landmines concluded that this approach would lead to failure, likely to become tangled up in fruitless years of negotiations on technical, incremental, and partial steps. Impelled to tackle the humanitarian crisis caused by such munitions in several countries, cross-regional networking by civil society and politically significant 'middle power' states have carried through important disarmament initiatives that bypassed the CD and other established institutions. Instead of using the state-centred, military-stability arguments associated with 20th-century arms control, the new approach mobilized support for disarmament action on the grounds of human impact, humanitarian concerns, and international humanitarian law.

The first agreement achieved in this way, the 1997 Mine Ban Convention, gave rise to a new term in diplomacy—the 'Ottawa Process'—as the Treaty was opened for signature in Ottawa, reflecting the prominent role played by Canada.[25] Though there are disagreements about the lessons and broader applicability of the Ottawa Process, the term is generally used to describe strategies to ban certain kinds of weapons through the mobilization of humanitarian arguments by civil society and concerned governments acting in partnership, and the innovative use of ad hoc negotiating forums where necessary to bypass blockages in the diplomatic environment. From Norway to South Africa, Canada to Viet Nam, civil society created awareness and political pressure on behalf of victims and potential victims and engaged with middle power governments to achieve a comprehensive ban on landmines that went much further than the major powers envisaged.[26] Through networked leadership, the basic campaign demands were transmitted to civil society groups throughout the world, who translated them into messages, actions, and on-the-ground political campaigns that forced many reluctant governments to change policy, join in the negotiations, and in most cases sign and ratify the resulting treaty.

The lessons from the Ottawa Process have been transferred and adapted for other weapons systems, from small arms and cluster munitions to nuclear weapons. Building on the success of the International Campaign to Ban Landmines, partnerships among enlightened governments and civil society advocates of gun control from many different countries engaged in diplomatic strategies that brought about the ground-breaking Programme of Action on Small Arms and Light Weapons (SALW) in 2001. Negotiated under UN auspices, this contained a range of measures to be undertaken through national, regional, and global action to 'prevent, combat and eradicate the illicit trade in small arms and light weapons in all its aspects'.[27] Although lacking the formal accoutrements of a treaty, the SALW Programme of Action instituted an ongoing process with biennial meetings, expert groups, and five-yearly conferences to review implementation and take the programme further, providing multiple levels for civil society to undertake and promote SALW disarmament efforts locally, nationally, and internationally. Working on the ground to stem the weapons' use and trafficking, local NGOs have continued to share information and strategies and amplify their effectiveness through a global network constituted as the International Action Network on Small Arms (IANSA), which initiates diplomatic strategies and exerts pressure on local and national governments, regional bodies, and the United Nations. Further initiatives, such as an Arms Trade Treaty, developed as spin-offs from diplomatic work to implement the SALW Programme of Action.

US and NATO actions in Iraq and Afghanistan revived concerns about the unacceptable harm caused by cluster munitions, designed to disperse into multiple bomblets which then continue to explode, fragment, and kill or maim unwary civilians. Children were especially vulnerable, as they were attracted by the toy-like size and colouring of the bomblets. Radicalized by work on landmines and SALW, civil society already had networks that were able to respond when Norway coordinated a group of like-minded governments and provided leadership and resources to coordinate multilateral negotiations and achieve the 2008 Cluster Munitions Convention, despite opposition by a number of significant military powers.

32.3 DISTRIBUTIVE AND INTEGRATIVE TACTICS IN DISARMAMENT DIPLOMACY

The most important shift in diplomatic practice is the growing incorporation of integrative, negotiating strategies and tactics associated with creating 'positive sum' outcomes.[28] Faced with the military-industrial interests of larger states with greater sources of aggregate power and influence, small and middle power states are developing new ways to foster convergence, augmenting their issue-based power through 'like-minded' alliances that were a far cry from the cold war 'group system' that has trapped decision-making in the CD and other UN-based institutions. The tactics described in this section show some of the key differences between distributive and integrative approaches. Integrative tactics draw diplomacy towards mediation and away from the traditional notion of 'war by another means', and are therefore more likely to be constructive than obstructive, whereas distributive tactics seek national or individual advantage and encourage blocking and concealing manoeuvres as well as trade-offs. Integrative strategies and tactics are used to facilitate convergence towards mutually beneficial agreements. Seeking to draw adversaries into recognizing interests outside narrow, nationally-bounded perceptions, integrative approaches are employed to bridge differences and construct new understandings of security interests. If solutions are not possible within currently recognized structures and assumptions, then cognitive strategies are used to reframe the perceived options and expand the zones of possible agreement, where acceptable compromises may be forged.[29]

32.3.1 Delaying Tactics

- Waiting for Godot—interminably delaying for the arrival of some mythical moment when the time is perfectly ripe.
- Quicksand—bogging an initiative down in questions, objections, or demands for definitions or an inquiry.
- Ping-Pong—shunting an issue back and forth between different committees, institutions, or negotiating forums.

32.3.2 Concealment

- Hide and seek—concealing real objectives, for example in high-minded rhetoric or a mass of technical data and extraneous detail.
- Slipstreaming—concealing preferences behind the positions of another state or delegation.
- Fronting—a form of collaborative slipstreaming, in which one delegation adopts a position that is stronger than its own interests would require, enabling others to benefit by coasting in its wake.
- Faking—a two-faced tactic of pretending to support a proposal that you actually oppose or vice versa.

32.3.3 Defection and Linkage Tactics

- Moving the goalposts—whatever is achievable becomes by definition inadequate so that the reachable is perpetually ditched for a more inaccessible position.
- Best versus good—rejecting adequate or useful agreements on the grounds that they do not match up with some grander but less practical or accessible ideal.

- Linkage—tying progress or agreement on one issue with achievement of agreement or gains on another issue.
- All or nothing—a linkage tactic asserting that nothing is agreed until everything is agreed.
- Hostage-taking—coercively presenting a contested point or outcome in your favour as a make or break issue for the whole negotiations.
- Tit for tat—you've done something to thwart or annoy me, so I'll do something to thwart or annoy you back.

32.3.4 Bridging and Trading

- Concession-trading—a bargaining process of trading concessions to facilitate convergence.
- Mediation—when a third party or parties help to promote agreement by enabling antagonists to address underlying causes of disagreement.
- Bridge-building—in which one or more of the antagonistic parties are prepared to concede or modify demands to promote convergence.
- 'Third-party bridging'—by an 'honest broker' (which can comprise officials, states, or civil society) exploring ways to bring antagonistic parties closer together.

Integrative negotiations employ more constructive than blocking tactics:

32.3.5 Regime-Building 'Cognitive' Tactics

- Norm-shaping—stigmatizing the weapon or problem and presenting alternatives and solutions.
- Reframing—recasting hurdles, problems, or solution options in less adversarial terms, offering integrative solutions with mutual gains.
- Step-ladder—deploying new information to enable parties to view problems from a different perspective and so surmount the obstacles impeding agreement.
- Unpacking—in which a problem is disaggregated or separated into its constituent parts to facilitate incremental agreement or progress.

32.3.6 Bypassing the Obstacles

- Bypass operation—can be used to radically redefine the context or, alternatively, to create or adapt an alternative forum for negotiations or adoption of a measure or agreement if the established forum is inadequate or obstructed.

- Leap-frogging—a more dramatic means of avoiding deadlock, such as when a group of like-minded states carry an issue by jumping over a structural or political obstacle.

32.4 Conclusions

As regional, economic, and political upheavals continue to affect the geostrategic environment, so changes in security threats and perceptions have influenced the theory and practice of disarmament diplomacy. Technological advances, networked communications, and globalization have amplified certain threats, including transnational, mass-destructive terrorism. To the global security challenges of climate chaos and other human-induced environmental changes must be added asymmetric and intra-state wars and conflicts, with causes related to declining resources, demographic pressures, perceptions of comparative disadvantage, or ethnic, religious, and nationalist rivalries. While nuclear weapons, missiles, and potential space weaponization remain major targets for disarmament diplomacy, grassroots action will continue on conventional weapons, including small arms. War-fighting technologies will increasingly depend on remotely-controlled drones, missiles, space-based and cyber components, enhanced through nanotechnologies. While offering potentially destabilizing capabilities for extra-judicial execution of adversaries and warfare pursued by militaries keeping a 'safe distance', space-based and remotely-controlled assets may also provide new tools for disarmament and arms control, particularly verification.

Concepts of human and global security are still in the process of being developed and defined, but balancing human needs with addressing the security imperatives of environmental and trans-boundary threats will shape new kinds of networked and multilateral diplomacy. The realist and neo-liberal diplomacies of competing states pursuing national defence interests were capable of delivering some regime benefits, but they have also been responsible for deadlock and sub-optimal agreements. These are more likely to occur when those responsible for managing the endgame fudge complexities, split differences, or concede to the most obstructive parties (generally those with the military capabilities or practices that the rest of the world wants to limit). In such interactions, dominant actors are able to determine or even impose a final settlement, as illustrated in the PTBT and NPT. Such a 'managed convergence' may be acceptable to other actors if they perceive the tangible or regime benefits to be greater than the alternative of getting no agreement,[30] but recent history indicates that such outcomes are overly limited and may even be counterproductive for human and international security.

Four important factors that were largely absent from cold-war arms control are coming to the fore and will influence disarmament diplomacy in the future: human security perspectives; trans-boundary, globalized security challenges, such as industrially-induced environmental and climate changes that cannot be tackled or contained at a national level; positive-sum integrative negotiating approaches; and increasingly significant roles undertaken by non-state actors, whether as terrorist combatants or disarmament experts, grassroots activists, and citizen diplomats in partnership with progressive governments. As economic health rather than military assets will increasingly determine strategic positioning, stability, and the international security environment, the perceived military-industrial interests of economically-weak governments are likely to be of declining influence in diplomacy for the purposes of constraining and prohibiting weapons. Though opposition from nuclear-dependent and heavily-armed powers may weaken the effectiveness of disarmament agreements, their nationally perceived interests are no longer decisive in preventing negotiations from being pursued through to conclusion, legal application, and even entry into force. Other governments and non-governmental actors have demonstrated what can be achieved with a progressive, dynamic approach to negotiations in which disarmament is framed as humanitarian action to protect vulnerable civilians. Even so, progress is unlikely to be quick or smooth. The institutions, expectations, and conduct of arms control and disarmament are slow to change, in large part because many senior governmental and academic practitioners and diplomats continue to prioritize adversarial distributive approaches because these are the forms of diplomacy in which most of them were trained and educated. Despite their resistance, however, new configurations in international security and strategic stability are knocking at the door, requiring more effective theories and strategies for disarmament and diplomacy.

Notes

1. The best sources for tracking these developments are in national and international journals on foreign policy and international relations. For overviews, see Thomas C. Schelling and Morton H. Halperin, *Strategy and Arms Control* (Washington: Pergamon-Brassey's, 1985) and Jeffrey A. Larsen and James J. Wirtz (eds), *Arms Control and Cooperative Security* (Boulder: Lynne Rienner, 2009).

2. In 1998 India and Pakistan conducted nuclear tests and proclaimed themselves 'nuclear-weapon states', while Israel has been assumed to have a significant nuclear arsenal since the late 1970s, camouflaged under a policy of nuclear opacity. In addition to these three additional nuclear-armed states, there have been various actual or potential new proliferators giving concern, including Iraq, Iran, Syria, and North Korea, with connections to the 'Nuclear Walmart' run by Abdul Qadeer Khan, who masterminded Pakistan's nuclear weapons programme in the 1980s and 1990s. See Christopher Clary, 'Dr Khan's Nuclear WalMart', *Disarmament Diplomacy* 76, London, March/April 2004.

3. For example, CNN founder Ted Turner donated millions of dollars for nuclear disarmament which were primarily disbursed by the Nuclear Threat Initiative (NTI), which carried through cooperative threat reduction programmes that had been curtailed due to US funding cuts by the George W. Bush administration and inadequate take-up by the EU countries.

4. Michael Moodie, 'Regional Perspectives on Arms Control', in Larsen and Wirtz (eds), *Arms Control and Cooperative Security*, 170.

5. See Rebecca Johnson, *Unfinished Business: The Negotiation of the CTBT and the End of Nuclear Testing* (Geneva: United Nations, 2009).

6. Ann M. Florini (ed.), *The Third Force: The Rise of Transnational Civil Society* (Washington: Carnegie Endowment for International Peace, 2000). See also Helmut Anheier, Marlies Glasius, and Mary Kaldor (eds), *Global Civil Society* (Oxford: Oxford University Press, 2001).

7. Report of the Commission to Assess United States National Security Space Management and Organisation, Washington DC (Public Law 106–65), 11 January 2001.

8. For more, see Chapter 2, this volume.

9. John Borrie, *Unacceptable Harm: A History of How The Treaty To Ban Cluster Munitions Was Won* (Geneva: United Nations, 2009). Borrie was also involved in developing the concept of 'disarmament as humanitarian action' for the UN Institute for Disarmament Research. See John Borrie and Vanessa Martin Randin (eds), *Disarmament as Humanitarian Action* and *Thinking Outside the Box in Multilateral Disarmament and Arms Control Negotiations* (Geneva: United Nations, 2006).

10. Diplomats from non-nuclear states worked with civil society to incorporate humanitarian concepts in the 2010 NPT Review Conference outcome to pave the way for nuclear abolition and comprehensive treaty approaches: 'The Conference expresses its deep concern at the catastrophic humanitarian consequences of any use of nuclear weapons and reaffirms the need for all States at all times to comply with applicable international law, including international humanitarian law.' Conclusions and recommendations for follow-on actions, 2010 Review Conference of the Parties to the Treaty on the Non-Proliferation of Nuclear Weapons, Final Document, 1.A.v. See Rebecca Johnson, Tim Caughley, and John Borrie, *Decline or Transform: Nuclear disarmament and security beyond the NPT Review Process* (London: Acronym Institute for Disarmament Diplomacy, 2012). <http://www.acronym.org.uk/>.

11. The Irish resolution, A/RES/1665, was adopted unanimously and the Swedish resolution, A/RES/1664, by 58 votes to 10, with 23 abstentions, on 4 December 1961.

12. For a detailed history of the NPT negotiations, see Mohammed Shaker, *The Nuclear Non-Proliferation Treaty: Origin and Implementation, 1959–1979* (New York: Oceana, 1980).

13. The Commission comprised five NATO and five Warsaw Pact and non-aligned countries. France, though invited, did not attend.

14. Four also voted against: Albania, Cuba, Tanzania, and Zambia. Of those who abstained or spoke against the NPT in 1968, all but India have now acceded. Israel, Pakistan, and South Africa voted in favour of the resolution but did not sign at the time. See Alva Myrdal, *The Game of Disarmament: How the United States and Russia Run the Arms Race* (Manchester: Manchester University Press, 1977).

15. See Richard Price, 'Reversing the Gun Sights: Transnational Civil Society Targets Landmines', *International Organization* 53:3 (1998), 613–44; Ethan A. Nadelmann, 'Global prohibition regimes: the evolution of norms in international society', *International Organization* 44:4 (1990), 479–526; and Jody Williams and Stephen D. Goose, 'Citizen Diplomacy and the Ottawa Proces: A Lasting Model?', in Jody Williams, Stephen D. Goose, and Mary Wareham (eds), *Banning Landmines: Disarmament, Citizen Diplomacy and Human Security* (Lanham: Rowman and Littlefield, 2008).

16. Lawrence Freedman, *The Evolution of Nuclear Strategy*, 2nd ed. (London: Macmillan, 1989), 419.

17. Jeffrey W. Knopf, 'Beyond two-level games: domestic-international interaction in the intermediate-range nuclear forces negotiation', *International Organization* 47:4 (1993), 599–628.

18. See Nancy W. Gallagher, *The Politics of Verification* (Baltimore: Johns Hopkins University Press, 1999).

19. John Gerard Ruggie, 'Multilateralism: the Anatomy of an Institution', in J.G. Ruggie (ed.), *Multilateralism Matters* (New York: Columbia University Press, 1993), especially 7–12.

20. Israel's interests as an undeclared nuclear-weapon possessor were largely protected by the United States, since Israel was not a member of the CD when CTBT negotiations opened. See Johnson, *Unfinished Business*.

21. James Sebenius credits Walton and McKersie with coining the term 'integrative bargaining', which they defined as a problem-solving approach that seeks to expand or change the zone of possible agreement and so present a different range of options for convergence than first appear to be on the table. See Richard Walton and Robert McKersie, *A Behavioral Theory of Labour Negotiations* (New York: McGraw-Hill, 1965). It became associated with the negotiation-analytic approach of Duncan Luce, Howard Raiffa, and Thomas C. Schelling, *Games and Decisions* (New York: Wiley, 1957).

22. Johnson, *Unfinished Business*. This analysis also bears out elements of Jeffrey W. Knopf's 'three-and-three analysis' in 'Beyond two-level games'.

23. See Walton and McKersie, *A Behavioral Theory of Labor Negotiations*; Luce, Raiffa, and Schelling, *Games and Decisions*. On integrative bargaining and mixed motive games, see Thomas C. Schelling, *The Strategy of Conflict* (Cambridge, MA: Harvard University Press, 1980). For alternative approaches to mixed motive interactions, see Kenneth A. Oye (ed.), *Cooperation Under Anarchy* (Princeton: Princeton University Press, 1986); Robert Axelrod, *The Evolution of Cooperation* (London: Penguin Books, 1990); Glen H. Snyder and Paul Diesing, *Conflict Among Nations: Bargaining, Decision Making and System Structure in International Crises* (Princeton: Princeton University Press, 1977).

24. See Jorge Heine and Ramesh Thakur (eds), *The Dark Side of Globalization* (Tokyo: United Nations University Press, 2011).

25. See Chapter 44, this volume, and Ramesh Thakur and William Maley, 'The Ottawa Convention on Landmines: A Landmark Humanitarian Treaty in Arms Control?', *Global Governance* 5:3 (July–September 1999), 273–302.

26. Price, 'Reversing the Gun Sights'; Maxwell A. Cameron, Robert J. Lawson, and Brian W. Tomlin (eds), *To Walk Without Fear: The Global Movement to Ban Landmines* (Toronto: Oxford University Press, 1998).

27. UN Document A/CONF.192/15, <http://www.iansa.org/resource/2001/12/un-programme-of-action-poa>.

28. See James K. Sebenius, 'Challenging conventional explanations of international cooperation: negotiation analysis and the case of epistemic communities', in Peter M. Haas (ed.), *Knowledge, Power, and International Policy Coordination* (Columbia SC: University of South Carolina Press, 1992).

29. This list of negotiating tactics was developed by the author. See Johnson, *Unfinished Business*. The list builds on earlier analysis by Johan Kaufmann in *The Diplomacy of International Relations: Selected Writings* (The Hague: Kluwer Law International, 1998), 11–30. On logrolling and bridging tactics, see Dean G. Pruitt, *Negotiation Behaviour* (New York: Academic Press, 1981), 153–5. See also Fen Osler Hampson and Michael Hart, *Multilateral Negotiations: Lessons from Arms Control, Trade and the Environment* (Baltimore: Johns Hopkins University Press, 1995).

30. On alternatives to accepting agreement and no-agreement dilemmas, see Sebenius, 'Challenging conventional explanations of international cooperation', 334–5.

CHAPTER 33

....

PEACE-BUILDING AND
STATE-BUILDING

....

SIMON CHESTERMAN[*]

As the editors note in their introduction to this *Handbook*, the practice of diplomacy assumes the involvement of governmental actors representing a state. That assumption has not always held when the objective of diplomatic activity is preserving or rebuilding precisely such state institutions. In such cases, which increased significantly in the post-cold war 1990s, questions arise as to who represents a state with weak institutions and how relations with other states and international organizations should be managed. The proliferation of actors in these situations—with donors and peacekeepers joined by aid organizations, international and local NGOs, and so on—is suggestive of the shift from club to network diplomacy. Yet since the goal of the interaction is, ostensibly, the joining of the club of states, this shift has been far from smooth or uniform.

For the diplomats involved in such activities—whichever parties they represent—the multiple actors and levels of engagement present strategic and tactical challenges. The formulation of strategy is complicated by the divergent interests at stake and the disparity in resources available to advance those interests: those with the greatest interest in achieving the goal of sustainable and legitimate national governance may often have the least leverage to press for sustained and well-resourced engagement; those with the greatest leverage and resources may have the least interest in remaining engaged beyond an initial period of crisis management. At the tactical level, the sheer number of actors with overlapping mandates—including governmental, intergovernmental, and non-governmental actors—can be a source of frustration and exhaustion.

A further layer of complexity is the role of those who represent bodies such as the United Nations and its various funds and agencies. In the cases described in this chapter, these individuals clearly go beyond the role of 'agents' representing 'principals' in the form of the member states. The UN Secretary-General, his or her special representatives, and many other actors clearly carry out functions analogous to diplomacy (not least in that they enjoy a form of diplomatic immunity), but beyond vague assertions that these international civil servants represent the 'international community' it is often unclear whom they represent or to whom they are accountable.

This chapter considers these issues by looking at the rise of peace-building and state-building as diplomatic practices, some of the problems that have emerged, and the prospects for near-term improvement or at least clarity as to a way forward.

33.1 THE RISE OF PEACE-BUILDING AND STATE-BUILDING

In early 1995, chastened by the failed operation in Somalia, the failing operation in Bosnia and Herzegovina, and inaction in the face of genocide in Rwanda, UN Secretary-General Boutros Boutros-Ghali issued a conservative supplement to his more optimistic 1992 *Agenda for Peace*. The *Supplement* noted that a new breed of intra-state conflicts presented the United Nations with challenges not encountered since the Congo operation of the early 1960s. A feature of these conflicts was the collapse of state institutions, especially the police and judiciary, meaning that international intervention had to extend beyond military and humanitarian tasks to include the 'promotion of national reconciliation and the re-establishment of effective government'. Nevertheless, he expressed caution against the United Nations assuming responsibility for law and order, or attempting to impose state institutions on unwilling combatants.[1] General Sir Michael Rose, then commander of the UN Protection Force in Bosnia (UNPROFOR), termed this form of mission creep crossing 'the Mogadishu line'.[2]

Despite such cautious words, by the end of 1995 the United Nations had assumed responsibility for policing in Bosnia under the Dayton Peace Agreement. The following January, a mission was established with temporary civil governance functions over the last Serb-held region of Croatia in Eastern Slavonia. In June 1999, the Security Council authorized an 'interim' administration in Kosovo to govern part of what remained technically Serbian territory for an indefinite period; four months later a transitional administration was created with effective sovereignty over East Timor until independence. These expanding mandates continued a trend that began with the operations in Namibia in 1989 and Cambodia in 1993, where the United Nations exercised varying degrees of civilian authority in addition to supervising elections.

Efforts to construct or reconstruct institutions of the state from the outside are hardly new: decolonization and military occupation are the estranged ancestors of more recent activities in this area. What was novel about the missions undertaken in Kosovo and East Timor was the amount of executive authority assumed by the United Nations itself, placing it in the position of an occupying power. Though this power was, presumably, understood to be exercised in a benevolent fashion, problems associated with foreign rule repeated themselves with some predictable results in the cases examined here.

Post-conflict reconstruction through the 1990s and 2000s thus saw an increasing trend towards rebuilding governance structures through assuming some or all governmental powers on a temporary basis. Such 'transitional administration' operations can be divided into two broad classes: where state institutions are divided and where they have collapsed. The first class encompasses situations where governance structures were the subject of dispute with different groups claiming power (as in Cambodia or Bosnia and Herzegovina), or ethnic tensions within the structures themselves (such as Kosovo). The second class comprises circumstances where such structures simply did not exist (as in Namibia, East Timor, and Afghanistan). A possible third class is suggested by the Iraq war of 2003, where regime change took place in a territory with far greater human, institutional, and economic resources than any comparable situation in which the United Nations or other actor had exercised civilian administration functions since the Second World War—but with results that were catastrophic.[3]

The term 'nation-building', sometimes used in this context, is a broad, vague, and often pejorative one. In the course of the 2000 US presidential campaign, Governor Bush used it as a dismissive reference to the application of US military resources beyond traditional mandates. The term was also used to conflate the circumstances in which US forces found themselves in conflict with the local population—most notably in Somalia—with complex and time-consuming operations such as those underway in Bosnia, Kosovo, and East Timor. Although it continues to be used in this context, notably within the United States, 'nation-building' also has a more specific meaning in the post-colonial context, referring to efforts by new leaders to rally a population within sometimes arbitrary territorial frontiers. The focus here is on the *state* (that is, the highest institutions of governance in a territory) rather than the *nation* (a people who share common customs, origins, history, and frequently language) as such.[4]

Within the United Nations, 'peace-building' is generally preferred. This has been taken to mean, among other things, 'reforming or strengthening governmental institutions'[5] or 'the creation of structures for the institutionalization of peace'.[6] It tends, however, to embrace a far broader range of activities than those particular operations under consideration here—at times being used to describe virtually all forms of international assistance to countries that have experienced or are at risk of armed conflict.[7]

For present purposes, the term state-building will be used to refer to extended international involvement (primarily, though not exclusively, through the United Nations) that goes beyond traditional peacekeeping and peace-building mandates, and is directed at constructing or reconstructing institutions of governance capable of providing citizens with physical and economic security. This includes quasi-governmental activities such as electoral assistance, human rights and rule of law technical assistance, security sector reform, and certain forms of development assistance. Within this class of operations, 'transitional administration' denotes the less common type of operation in which these ends have been pursued by assuming some or all of the powers of the state on a temporary basis.

It is frequently assumed that the collapse of state structures, whether through defeat by an external power or as a result of internal chaos, leads to a vacuum of political power. This is rarely the case. The mechanisms through which political power are exercised may be less formalized or consistent, but basic questions of how best to ensure the physical and economic security of oneself and one's dependants do not simply disappear when the institutions of the state break down. Non-state actors in such situations may exercise varying degrees of political power over local populations, at times providing basic social services from education to medical care. Even where non-state actors exist as parasites on local populations, political life goes on. How to engage in such an environment is a particular problem for policy-makers and diplomats in intergovernmental organizations and donor governments. But it poses far greater difficulties for the embattled state institutions and the populations of such territories.

International actors, the focus in this chapter, may play a critical role—if only in creating the opportunity for local actors to establish legitimate and sustainable governance. Sometimes creating such opportunities means holding back. Humanitarian and, to some extent, development assistance flows most freely in response to crisis, but it rarely addresses the underlying causes of either poverty or conflict. Such assistance, if not well managed, may in fact undermine more sustainable recovery by establishing relationships of dependence and by distorting the economy with unsustainable allocations of resources.

Until recently, there was little strategy in how international actors approached such problems. Indeed, reflecting Boutros-Ghali's earlier objections there was no agreement that post-conflict reconstruction was something in which the United Nations should become involved. The fact that such operations continue to be managed by the UN Department of Peacekeeping Operations is suggestive of the ad hoc approach that characterized transitional administration. This was evident in the 2000 Report of the Panel on UN Peace Operations, known as the Brahimi Report, which noted the likely demand for such operations as well as the 'evident ambivalence' within governments and the UN Secretariat itself concerning the development of an institutional capacity to undertake them. Because of this ambivalence it was impossible to achieve any consensus on recommendations, so the Department of Peacekeeping Operations continued to play the dominant supporting role.[8]

The creation in December 2005 of a Peace-building Commission, then, was a significant development—even if only as belated recognition that this was an important function of the United Nations. Established by the General Assembly to, among other things, 'propose integrated strategies for post-conflict peace-building',[9] it remains a work in progress. In theory this could be the vehicle that develops and oversees strategic policy in this area, overcoming some of the principal–agent problems that arise. As we will see, however, theory has rarely led practice in the UN experience of peace-building.

33.2 PROBLEMS

Is it even possible to establish the necessary political and economic conditions for legitimate and sustainable national governance through a period of benevolent foreign autocracy under UN auspices? This contradiction between ends and means has plagued recent efforts to govern post-conflict territories in the Balkans, East Timor, Afghanistan,

Iraq, and elsewhere. Such state-building operations combine an unusual mix of idealism and realism: the idealist project that a people can be saved from themselves through education, economic incentives, and the space to develop mature political institutions; the realist basis for that project in what is ultimately military occupation.

Much research has focused on the doctrinal and operational difficulties experienced by such operations.[10] This is a valuable area of research, but may obscure three sets of contradictions between means and ends that undermined such operations: the means are *inconsistent* with the ends, they are frequently *inadequate* for those ends, and in many situations the means are *inappropriate* for the ends.

33.2.1 Inconsistent

Benevolent autocracy is an uncertain foundation for legitimate and sustainable national governance. It is inaccurate and, often, counterproductive to assert that transitional administration depends upon the consent or 'ownership' of the local population.[11] It is inaccurate because if genuine local control were possible then a transitional administration would not be necessary. It is counterproductive because insincere claims of local ownership lead to frustration and suspicion on the part of local actors. *Clarity* is therefore required in recognizing: (i) the strategic objectives; (ii) the relationship between international and local actors and how this will change over time; and (iii) the commitment required of international actors in order to achieve objectives that warrant the temporary assumption of autocratic powers under a benevolent international administration.

In a case like East Timor, the strategic objective—independence—was both clear and uncontroversial. Frustration with the slow pace of reconstruction or the inefficiencies of the UN presence could generally be tempered by reference to the uncontested aim of independence and a timetable within which this was to be achieved. In Kosovo, failure to articulate a position on its final status inhibits the development of a mature political elite and deters foreign investment. The present ambiguity derives from a compromise that was brokered between the United States and Russia at the end of the NATO campaign against the Federal Republic of Yugoslavia in 1999, formalized in Security Council resolution 1244 (1999). Nevertheless, it is the United Nations itself that is now blamed for frustrating the aspirations of Kosovars for self-determination.

Clarity in the relationship between international and local actors raises the question of ownership. This term is often used disingenuously—either to mask the assertion of potentially dictatorial powers by international actors or to carry a psychological rather than political meaning in the area of reconstruction. Ownership in this context is usually not intended to mean control and often does not even imply a direct input into political questions.[12] This is not to suggest that local control is a substitute for international administration: the malevolence or collapse of that political dynamic is precisely the reason that power is arrogated to an international presence in the first place. How much power should be transferred and for how long depends upon the political transition that is required; this in turn is a function of the root causes of the conflict, the local capacity for change, and the degree of international commitment available to assist in bringing about that change.[13] Local ownership, then, must be the end of a transitional administration. But it is not the means.

Clarifying the commitment necessary to bring about fundamental change in a conflict-prone territory is a double-edged sword. It would ensure that political will exists prior to authorizing a transitional administration, but perhaps at the expense of other operations that would not be authorized at all. The mission in Bosnia was always expected to last beyond its nominal twelve-month deadline, but might not have been established if it had been envisaged that troops would remain on the ground for a full decade or more. Donors contemplating Afghanistan in November 2001 balked at early estimates that called for a ten-year, $25 billion commitment to the country. Political considerations already limit the choice of missions: not for lack of opportunity, no major transitional administration has been established in Africa, where the demands are probably greatest. The primary barrier to establishing transitional administration-type operations in areas such as Western Sahara, Somalia, and the Democratic Republic of the Congo has less to do with the difficulty of such operations than with the absence of political will to commit the resources necessary to undertake them.

Resolving the inconsistency between the means and the ends of transitional administration requires a clear-eyed recognition of the role of power. The collapse of formal state structures does not necessarily create a power vacuum; as indicated earlier, political life does not simply cease. Constructive engagement with power on this local level requires both an understanding of culture and history as well as respect for the political aspirations of the population. Clarity will help here also: either the international presence exercises quasi-sovereign powers on a temporary basis or it does not. This clarity must exist at the formal level, but leaves much room for nuance in implementation.

33.2.2 Inadequate

International interest in post-conflict operations tends to be ephemeral, with availability of funds linked to the prominence of a foreign crisis on the domestic agenda of the states that contribute funds and troops. Both have tended to be insufficient. Funds for post-conflict reconstruction are notoriously supply- rather than demand-driven. This leads to multiplication of bureaucracy in the recipient country, inconsistency in disbursement procedures, and a focus on projects that may be more popular with donors than they are necessary in the recipient country. Reluctance to commit funds is surpassed only by reluctance to commit troops: in the absence of security, however, meaningful political change is impossible. This was confirmed in the most brutal way possible with the attacks on UN personnel in Baghdad on 19 August 2003.

The ephemeral nature of international interest in post-conflict operations is, unfortunately, a cliché. When the United States overthrew the Taliban regime in Afghanistan, President Bush likened the commitment to rebuild the devastated country to the Marshall

Plan. Just over twelve months later, in February 2003, the White House apparently forgot to include *any* money for reconstruction in the 2004 budget that it submitted to Congress. Legislators reallocated $300 million in aid to cover the oversight.[14] Such oversights are disturbingly common: much of the aid that is pledged either arrives late or not at all. This demands a measure of artificiality in drafting budgets for reconstruction, which in turn leads to suspicion on the part of donors—sometimes further delaying the disbursement of funds. The problem is not simply one of volume: Bosnia has received more per capita assistance than Europe did under the Marshall Plan, but the incoherence of funding programmes, the lack of a regional approach, and the inadequacy of state and entity institutions have contributed to its remaining in financial crisis.[15]

Many of these problems would be reduced if donors replaced the system of voluntary funding for relief and reconstruction for transitional administrations with assessed contributions, which presently fund peacekeeping operations. The distinction between funds supporting a peacekeeping operation and those providing assistance to a government makes sense when there is some form of indigenous government, but is arbitrary in situations where the peacekeeping operation *is* the government. Given existing strains on the peacekeeping budget, however, such a change is unlikely. A more realistic proposal would be to pool voluntary contributions through a trust fund, ideally coordinated by local actors or a mixed body of local and international personnel, perhaps also drawing upon private sector expertise. At the very least, a monitoring mechanism to track aid flows would help to ensure that money that is promised at the highpoint of international attention to a crisis is in fact delivered and spent. The experience of Afghanistan suggests that there is, perhaps, some learning taking place in this area, though even during one of the greatest outpouring of emergency relief fund in recent history—in response to the tsunami that struck the Indian ocean region on 26 December 2004—Secretary-General Kofi Annan felt compelled to remind donor governments that 'We have often had gaps in the past [between pledges and actual donations] and I hope it is not going to happen in this case.'[16] The use of PricewaterhouseCoopers to track aid flows also points to a new flexibility in using private sector expertise to avoid wastage and corruption.

A key argument in the Brahimi Report was that missions with uncertain mandates or inadequate resources should not be created at all:

> Although presenting and justifying planning estimates according to high operational standards might reduce the likelihood of an operation going forward, Member States must not be led to believe that they are doing something useful for countries in trouble when—by under-resourcing missions—they are more likely agreeing to a waste of human resources, time and money.[17]

This view finds some support in the report of the International Commission on Intervention and State Sovereignty, *The Responsibility to Protect*, which called for the 'responsibility to rebuild' to be seen as an integral part of any intervention. When an intervention is contemplated, a post-intervention strategy is both an operational necessity and an ethical imperative.[18] There is some evidence of this principle now achieving at least rhetorical acceptance—despite his aversion to 'nation-building', President Bush stressed before and during operations in Afghanistan and Iraq that the United States would help in reconstructing the territories in which it had intervened.

More than rhetoric is required. Success in state-building, in addition to clarity of purpose, requires time and money. A lengthy international presence will not ensure success, but an early departure guarantees failure. Similarly, an abundance of resources will not make up for the lack of a coherent strategy—though the fact that Kosovo received twenty-five times more money and fifty times more troops, on a per capita basis, compared with Afghanistan, goes some way towards explaining the modest achievements in developing democratic institutions and the economy.[19]

33.2.3 Inappropriate

The inappropriateness of available means to desired ends presents the opposite problem to that of the inadequacy of resources. While the question of limited resources—money, personnel, and international attention—depresses the standards against which a post-conflict operation can be judged, artificially high international expectations may nevertheless be imposed in certain areas of governance. Particularly when the United Nations itself assumes a governing role, there is a temptation to demand the highest standards of democracy, human rights, the rule of law, and the provision of services.

Balancing these against the need for locally sustainable goals presents difficult problems. A computerized electoral registration system may be manifestly ill suited to a country with a low level of literacy and intermittent electricity, but should an international NGO refrain from opening a world-class medical clinic if such levels of care are unsustainable? An abrupt drop from high levels of care once the crisis and international interest passes would be disruptive, but lowering standards early implies acceptance that people who might otherwise have been treated will suffer.

Although most acute in areas such as health, the issue arises in many aspects of transitional administration. In the best tradition of autocracies, the international missions in Bosnia and Kosovo subscribed to the vast majority of human rights treaties and then discovered *raisons d'état* that required these to be abrogated. Efforts to promote the rule of law tend to focus more on the prosecution of the highest profile crimes of the recent past than on developing institutions to manage criminal law in the near future. Humanitarian and development assistance is notorious for being driven more by supply than demand, with the result that those projects that are funded tend to represent the interests—and, frequently, the products and personnel—of donors rather than recipients.[20] Finally, staging elections in conflict zones has become something of an art form, though semi-regular elections in Bosnia over the past fifteen years have yet to produce a workable government.[21]

The United Nations may never again be called upon to repeat operations comparable to Kosovo and East Timor, where it exercised sovereign powers on a temporary basis. Even so, it is certain that the circumstances that demanded such interventions will recur.

Lessons derived from past experiences of transitional administration will be applicable whenever the United Nations or other international actors engage in complex peace operations that include a policing function, civilian administration, development of the rule of law, establishment of a national economy, the staging of elections, or all of the above. Learning from such lessons has not, however, been one of the strengths of the United Nations.

33.3 Prospects

If there is a single generalizable lesson to be learned from the recent experience of state-building, whether as transitional administration or preventing state failure, it is modesty. The challenges before the United Nations now are not, therefore, to develop grand theories or a revivified trusteeship capacity. Rather, what is required is a set of workable strategies and tactics with which to support institutions of the state before, during, and after conflict.

33.3.1 Strategy

The accepted wisdom within the UN community, articulated most clearly in the Brahimi Report, is that a successful UN peace operation should ideally consist of three sequential stages. First, the political basis for peace must be determined. Then a suitable mandate for a UN mission should be formulated. Finally, that mission should be given all the resources necessary to complete the mandate.[22] The accepted reality is that this often happens in the reverse order: member states determine what resources they are prepared to commit to a problem and a mandate is cobbled together around those resources—often in the hope that a political solution will be forthcoming at some later date.

Strategic failure may affect all levels of an operation. The most common types of failures are at the level of overall mandate, in the interaction between different international actors with competing or inconsistent mandates, and in the relationship between international and national actors on the ground. Kosovo's uncertain final status, for example, severely undermined the ongoing peace operation there, contrasting starkly with the simplicity of East Timor's transition to independence.

A second level at which strategic failure may take place is when different actors have competing or inconsistent mandates. Security actors are a notorious example of this—with the independence of the NATO-led KFOR in Kosovo and the ISAF in Afghanistan at times undermining the authority of the international civilian presence. Ensuring a single chain of command would be desirable, but runs against the received wisdom that the United Nations is incapable of waging war.

Reference to strategy should not be misunderstood as suggesting that there is some template for governance that can be applied across cases. Instead, clarity about the purposes of engagement and the respective responsibilities of international and national actors provides a framework for developing a coherent strategy that takes the state itself as the starting point.

33.3.2 Coordination and the Peace-Building Commission

The High-Level Panel on Threats, Challenges, and Change rightly criticized the UN experience of post-conflict operations as characterized by 'countless ill-coordinated and overlapping bilateral and United Nations programs, with inter-agency competition preventing the best use of scarce resources'.[23] Its key recommendation to remedy this situation was the call for a Peace-Building Commission to be established as a subsidiary organ of the UN Security Council under article 29 of the UN Charter.[24]

The Commission is generally considered to be one of the more positive ideas to come from the High-Level Panel and appeared likely to be adopted by the membership of the United Nations. When the Secretary-General drew upon this to present his own vision of the Peace-Building Commission in his 'In Larger Freedom' report of March 2005, he specifically removed any suggestion of an early warning function—anticipating pressure from governments wary that they might be precisely the ones under scrutiny.[25]

Two essential aspects of how the Commission would function were left unresolved: what its membership would be, and to whom it would report—the Security Council or the Economic and Social Council. These issues ended up paralysing debate on the Commission in the lead up to the September 2005 World Summit and were deferred for later consideration. The World Summit Outcome document broadly endorsed the Secretary-General's view of the Peace-Building Commission as essentially limited to mobilizing resources for post-conflict reconstruction.[26]

The General Assembly formally established the Peace-Building Commission on 30 December 2005. Described as an 'intergovernmental advisory body', its standing members comprise seven members of the Security Council (ambiguously described as 'including permanent members'), seven members of ECOSOC, five of the top providers of assessed and voluntary contributions, five of the top troop contributors, and a further seven elected by the General Assembly for regional balance.[27] Selection of these members was predictably politicized: in particular, the permanent members of the Security Council have all ensured their own membership.

Far from being a new Trusteeship Council, then, the Peace-Building Commission began to look more like a standing pledging conference, one of the most important forms of coordination for donors that currently exists.[28] If it can succeed in sustaining attention on a post-conflict situation beyond the current limits of foreign policy attention deficit disorder, the Commission will have achieved a great deal. It is less clear that this additional layer of coordination will assist in how these new resources are spent.[29]

The cases of Burundi and Sierra Leone were put on the Commission's agenda in 2006, joined by Guinea-Bissau in 2007 and the Central African Republic in 2008. For each of these items, the Commission adopts a distinct 'configuration' with additional members (including intergovernmental organizations such as the World Bank and IMF) and a different chair.[30] It is still too early to evaluate the effectiveness of the Commission, though it has at least served to prevent some of these 'orphaned' conflicts from falling off the UN agenda completely.

33.3.3 Evaluation and Exit Strategies

In his April 2001 report on the closure or transition of complex peacekeeping operations, UN Secretary-General Kofi Annan warned that the embarrassing withdrawal of peacekeepers from Somalia should not be repeated in future operations. 'No Exit Without Strategy', the report was called.[31] For the UN Transitional Administration in East Timor (UNTAET), elections provided the basis for transfer of power to local authorities; they also set in place political processes that would last well beyond the mission and the development assistance that followed. In Kosovo, where the UN operation was determinedly called an 'interim' administration, the absence of an agreed end-state has left the territory in political limbo. Reflection on the absence of an exit strategy from Kosovo, following on the apparently endless operation in Bosnia and Herzegovina, led some ambassadors to the Security Council to turn the Secretary-General's phrase on its head: 'No strategy', the rallying cry went, 'without an exit'.

East Timor presents two contradictory stories in the history of UN peace operations. On the one hand, it is presented as an outstanding success. In two and a half years, a territory that had been reduced to ashes after the 1999 referendum on independence held peaceful elections and celebrated independence. On the other hand, however, East Timor can be seen as a series of missed opportunities and wastage. Of the UN Transitional Administration's annual budget of over $500 million, around one-tenth actually reached the East Timorese. At one point, $27 million was spent annually on bottled water for the international staff—approximately half the budget of the embryonic Timorese government, and money that might have paid for water purification plants to serve both international staff and locals well beyond the life of the mission. More could have been done, or done earlier to reconstruct public facilities. This did not happen in part because of budgetary restrictions on UN peacekeeping operations that, to the Timorese, were not simply absurd but insulting. Such problems were compounded by coordination failures, the displacement of local initiatives by bilateral donor activities, and the lack of any significant private sector investment. When East Timor (now Timor-Leste) became independent, it did so with the dubious honour of becoming the poorest country in Asia.[32] The outbreak of fighting in May 2006 proved to many that warnings of an unduly abrupt withdrawal were well founded.[33]

Clarity about the objectives of an operation may be helpful—even if it requires a retreat from the rhetoric that justifies the expenditure of resources for a peace effort. Often it will not be possible (even if it were desirable) to transform a country over the course of eighteen months into, say, Canada. Instead, perhaps the most that can be hoped for is to create the conditions in which a vulnerable population can start a conversation about what kind of country they want theirs to be.

33.4 CONCLUSION

In his book *In My Father's House*, Kwame Anthony Appiah notes that the apparent ease of colonial administration generated in some of the inheritors of post-colonial nations an illusion that control of the state would allow them to pursue as easily their much more ambitious objectives. Once the state was turned to the tasks of massive developments in infrastructure, however, it was shown wanting: 'When the postcolonial rulers inherited the apparatus of the colonial state, they inherited the reins of power; few noticed, at first, that they were not attached to a bit.'[34]

Given the fraught history of so many of the world's states, it is not remarkable that some states suffer basic crises in their capacity to protect and provide services for a population—on the contrary, it is remarkable that more do not. As indicated earlier, discussion of such institutional crises frequently suggests that, when a state 'fails', power is no longer exercised within the territory. In fact, the control of power becomes more important than ever—even though it may be exercised in an incoherent fashion.

Engagement with such states requires, first and foremost, understanding the local dynamics of power. The much-cited Weberian definition of the state as claimant to a monopoly of the legitimate use of force is less a definition of what the state *is* than what it *does*. The legitimacy and sustainability of local power structures depend, ultimately, upon local actors. Certain policies can help—channelling political power through institutions rather than individuals, and through civilians rather than the military; imposing term limits on heads of state and government; encouraging and regulating political parties—but their implementation depends on the capacity of local leaders to submit themselves to the rule of law, and local populations to hold their leaders to that standard.

For international actors and the diplomats that represent them, a troubling analogy is to compare engagement with weak states to previous models of trusteeship and empire. Current efforts at state-building attempt—at least in part—to reproduce the better effects of empire (inward investment, pacification, and impartial administration) without reproducing its worst features (repression, corruption, and confiscation of local capacity). This is not to suggest nostalgia for empire or that such policies should be resurrected. Only two generations ago, one-third of the world's population lived in territory considered non-self-governing; the end of colonialism was one of the most significant transformations in the international order since the emergence of sovereign states. But the analogy may be helpful if it suggests that a realistic assessment of power is necessary to formulate effective policies rather than effective rhetoric.

Notes

* This work draws upon material discussed at greater length in Simon Chesterman, *You, The People: The United Nations, Transitional Administration, and State-Building* (Oxford: Oxford University Press, 2004) and Simon Chesterman, Michael Ignatieff, and Ramesh Thakur (eds), *Making States Work: State Failure and the Crisis of Governance* (Tokyo: United Nations University Press, 2005). Many of the examples cited draw upon confidential interviews conducted in Dili, Kabul, New York, Phnom Penh, Pristina, and Sarajevo.

1. 'Supplement to An Agenda for Peace: Position Paper of the Secretary-General on the Occasion of the Fiftieth Anniversary of the United Nations', UN Doc A/50/60-S/1995/1 (1995) available at <http://documents.un.org/>, paras 13–14.

2. Michael Rose, 'The Bosnia Experience', in Ramesh Thakur (ed.), *Past Imperfect, Future Uncertain: The United Nations at Fifty* (New York: St Martin's Press, 1998), 139.

3. See generally Chesterman, *You, The People*.

4. Massimo D'Azeglio famously expressed the difference in the context of post-Risorgimento Italy: 'We have made Italy', he declared. 'Now we must make Italians.' On the creation of states generally, see James Crawford, *The Creation of States in International Law* (Oxford: Clarendon Press, 1979). On nation-building, see, e.g. Benedict Anderson, *Imagined Communities: Reflections on the Origin and Spread of Nationalism* (London: Verso, 1983); Ranajit Guha (ed.), *A Subaltern Studies Reader, 1986–1995* (Minneapolis: University of Minnesota Press, 1997); Jim MacLaughlin, *Reimagining the Nation-State: The Contested Terrains of Nation-Building* (London: Pluto Press, 2001).

5. An Agenda for Peace: Preventive Diplomacy, Peacemaking, and Peace-keeping (Report of the Secretary-General pursuant to the statement adopted by the Summit Meeting of the Security Council on 31 January 1992), UN Doc A/47/277-S/24111 (1992) available at <http://documents.un.org>, para. 55.

6. Supplement to An Agenda for Peace: Position Paper of the Secretary-General on the Occasion of the Fiftieth Anniversary of the United Nations, para. 49. From a UN development perspective, peace-building aims 'to build and enable durable peace and sustainable development in post-conflict situations'. See, e.g. Role of UNDP in Crisis and Post-Conflict Situations (Policy Paper Distributed to the Executive Board of the United Nations Development Programme and of the United Nations Population Fund), DP/2001/4 (New York: UNDP, November 27, 2000) available at <http://www.undp.org>, para. 51. The Development Assistance Committee (DAC) of the OECD maintains that peace-building and reconciliation focus 'on long-term support to, and establishment of, viable political and socio-economic and cultural institutions capable of addressing the root causes of conflicts, as well as other initiatives aimed at creating the necessary conditions for sustained peace and stability': OECD, Helping Prevent Violent Conflict, Development Assistance Committee Guidelines (Paris: OECD, 2001) available at <http://www.oecd.org>, 86.

7. Elizabeth M. Cousens, 'Introduction', in Elizabeth M. Cousens and Chetan Kumar (eds), *Peace-Building as Politics* (Boulder, CO: Lynne Rienner, 2001), 5–10.

8. Strengthening of the United Nations: An Agenda for Further Change, UN Doc A/57/150 (2002), para. 126: 'To strengthen further the Secretariat's work in international peace and security, there is a need to bring a sharper definition to the existing lead department policy, which sets out the relationship between the Department of Political Affairs and the Department of Peacekeeping Operations. The Department of Political Affairs will increase its focus in the fields of preventive diplomacy, conflict prevention and peacemaking. The

Department will also intensify its engagement in policy formulation across the full spectrum of the Secretariat's tasks in the domain of international peace and security. It will continue to be the lead department for political and peace-building offices in the field. The Department of Peacekeeping Operations will be the lead department for the planning and management of all peace and security operations in the field, including those in which the majority of personnel are civilians.'

9. GA Res 60/180 (2005), para. 2(a).

10. See, e.g. Roland Paris, *At War's End: Building Peace After Civil Conflict* (Cambridge: Cambridge University Press, 2004); Richard Caplan, *International Governance of War-Torn Territories: Rule and Reconstruction* (Oxford: Oxford University Press, 2005); Ralph Wilde, *International Territorial Administration: How Trusteeship and the Civilizing Mission Never Went Away* (Oxford: Oxford University Press, 2008); Carsten Stahn, *The Law and Practice of International Territorial Administration: Versailles to Iraq and Beyond* (Cambridge: Cambridge University Press, 2008); Eric de Brabandere, *Post-Conflict Administrations in International Law: International Territorial Administration, Transitional Authority and Foreign Occupation in Theory and Practice* (Leiden: Martinus Nijhoff, 2009).

11. See further Simon Chesterman, 'Ownership in Theory and in Practice: Transfer of Authority in UN Statebuilding Operations', *Journal of Intervention and Statebuilding* 1:1 (2007), 3–26.

12. Chesterman, 'Ownership in Theory and in Practice'.

13. Michael W. Doyle, 'War-Making and Peace-Making: The United Nations' Post-Cold War Record', in Chester A. Crocker, Fen Osler Hampson, and Pamela Aall (eds), *Turbulent Peace: The Challenges of Managing International Conflict* (Washington, DC: United States Institute of Peace Press, 2001), 546.

14. Paul Krugman, 'The Martial Plan', *New York Times*, 21 February 2003; James G. Lakely, 'Levin Criticizes Budget for Afghanistan; Says White House Isn't Devoting Enough to Rebuilding', *Washington Times*, 26 February 2003. Aid was later increased further: David Rohde, 'US Said to Plan Bigger Afghan Effort, Stepping Up Aid', *New York Times*, 25 August 2003.

15. See, e.g. Crisis Group, Federation of Bosnia and Herzegovina—A Parallel Crisis (Sarajevo/Istanbul/Brussels: Europe Report No. 209, 28 September 2010) available at <http://www.crisisgroup.org>.

16. Scott Shane and Raymond Bonner, 'Annan Nudges Donors to Make Good on Full Pledges', *New York Times*, 7 January 2005.

17. Report of the Panel on United Nations Peace Operations (Brahimi Report), UN Doc A/55/305-S/2000/809 (2000) available at <http://www.un.org/peace/reports/peace_operations>, para. 59.

18. International Commission on Intervention and State Sovereignty, The Responsibility to Protect (Ottawa: International Development Research Centre, December 2001) available at <www.responsibilitytoprotect.org>, paras 2.32, 5.1–5.6.

19. See James Dobbins et al., *America's Role in Nation-Building: From Germany to Iraq* (Santa Monica, CA: RAND, 2003), 160–6.

20. See generally Shepard Forman and Stewart Patrick (eds), *Good Intentions: Pledges of Aid for Postconflict Recovery* (Boulder, CO: Lynne Rienner, 2000).

21. Crisis Group, Federation of Bosnia and Herzegovina—A Parallel Crisis.

22. Report of the Panel on United Nations Peace Operations (Brahimi Report), paras 9–83.

23. A More Secure World: Our Shared Responsibility (Report of the High-Level Panel on Threats, Challenges, and Change), UN Doc A/59/565 (2004) available at <http://www.un.org/secureworld>, para. 38.

24. A More Secure World, paras 261–5.

25. In Larger Freedom: Towards Development, Security, and Human Rights for All (Report of the Secretary General), UN Doc A/59/2005 (2005) available at <http://www.un.org/larger-freedom>, para. 115.

26. 2005 World Summit Outcome Document, UN Doc A/RES/60/1 (2005) available at <http://www.un.org/summit2005>, para. 98.

27. GA Res 60/180 (30 December 2005), paras 1, 4.

28. See, e.g. Stewart Patrick, 'The Donor Community and the Challenge of Postconflict Recovery', in Shepard Forman and Stewart Patrick (eds), Good Intentions: Pledges of Aid for Postconflict Recovery, 40–1.

29. See further Simon Chesterman, 'From State Failure to State Building: Problems and Prospects of a United Nations Peacebuilding Commission', Journal of International Law and International Relations 2:1 (2005), 155–75.

30. Report of the Peace-Building Commission on Its Third Session, UN Doc A/64/341–S/2009/444 (2009) available at <http://documents.un.org>.

31. No Exit Without Strategy: Security Council Decision-Making and the Closure or Transition of United Nations Peacekeeping Operations (Report of the Secretary-General), UN Doc S/2001/394 (2001).

32. 'Getting Ready for Statehood', Economist (London), 13 April 2002.

33. 'UN Prepares to Start a New Peacekeeping Mission in East Timor', New York Times, 14 June 2006.

34. Kwame Anthony Appiah, In My Father's House: Africa in the Philosophy of Culture (New York: Oxford University Press, 1992), 266.

CHAPTER 34

....

TRADE DIPLOMACY

....

DIANA TUSSIE[*]

Free trade is God's diplomacy. There is no other certain way of uniting people in the bonds of peace. (Richard Cobden, cotton trader, British politician, originator of the Cobden Chevalier Treaty, 1857)

Dieu est mort, l'OMC l'a remplacé! (Demonstrators, WTO headquarters, 1999)

34.1 INTRODUCTION

....

TRADE arouses passions in many directions; is it the reason for going to war or the pillar of peace? Yet traders have always been diplomats. International trade diplomacy is as old as trade itself. What has turned so dramatically since Cobden articulated his vision of free trade as God's diplomacy? The aim of this chapter is to highlight the potential uniqueness of trade, on the one hand and, on the other, the broader transformations in terms of the range of participants and the patterns of interaction they now deploy. I concentrate on specificity, novelty, and change.

Trade allocates economic resources between private interests. It creates winners and losers leading to demands as well as claims for compensation. Trade negotiations are about *who* gets *what* and *how*. Even Cobden's free trade ideal is a political balancing act between higher notions of the public good and the interests of specific constituencies; and even more a question of distribution than optimality. This implies normative choices about who should benefit and who should bear the burdens of adjustment. In this sense, the 'free' trade ideal and the 'protectionist' backwater are constructions at best made in heaven (or hell). Real preferences are pragmatic choices situated along a continuum where neither one ever reigns supreme.

Trade diplomacy as such is concerned with the management of trade regimes as well as the market factors affected by the regime. A distinctive feature of trade and economic diplomacy at large (see Chapter 22, this volume) is that market actors are involved in the push–pull of diplomatic efforts, either at the forefront or the rear guard, either tacitly or explicitly.

Trade diplomacy thus faces tensions between political authorities and markets. Market interests will drive diplomacy but political considerations can also outweigh trade interests. For example, many Muslim majority countries have yet to establish trade relations with Israel and likewise many countries with close ties to Israel have resisted recognizing the State of Palestine. In the opposite direction, in order not to upset trade relations, when the government of Bangladesh allowed the establishment of a private business office from Taiwan, copious diplomatic efforts were deployed to confirm the 'one-China policy' (meaning Taiwan is recognized as part of China).

Today, a significant part of diplomatic work is dedicated to commercial issues. Firms are fervently trying to capture export markets and countries are deepening their cooperation in the master body, the World Trade Organization (WTO), as well as in regional, bilateral, continental, and transcontinental trade agreements. This burst of activity has led to a scenario that is enormously more challenging, complex, and demanding than it has ever been. Economic globalization has turned trade diplomacy into a significant factor in foreign policy. Many foreign offices have merged with trade departments. The Department of Foreign Affairs was changed to Department of Foreign Affairs and Trade in Australia in the late 1980s and in the early 1990s in Argentina and Canada. In Chile the Foreign Ministry gained overall responsibility for trade diplomacy in 1994 (see Chapter 5, this volume).

In many parts of the world, the field of trade diplomacy as such only materialized with the nationalization of industry from the 1950s to the 1970s.[1] Professional diplomats were gradually trained in trade matters to commercialize their country's products. Nowadays, trade and economic affairs have become the midfield of international relations and diplomacy. The bounce represents an appealing turn in the history of diplomacy. Even a couple of decades back, trade diplomacy was conceived as a sort of a 'black hole' by diplomats pursuing a fast-track career, and paled in comparison with political work. Trade diplomacy seen previously as largely inconsequential now looms large on all fronts. The stand-off in the Doha Round is a clear indication of the fundamental change in trade diplomacy.

The global South[2] was a late-comer to this event. But this stage entry has changed the structure as well as the process of negotiation, a theme that remains considerably underrepresented in the literature.[3] The newcomers are now at the cusp of the transformation of trade diplomacy. Recognising the relevance of trade and foreign direct investment in economic development, governments have multiplied their commercial representation in other countries. At the same time they have a new willingness to engage in the WTO and in regional agreements, coming out of the fringes and shedding their defensiveness. Leading global South countries empowered by mastering the rules and practices of reciprocity-based bargaining have posed challenges to the WTO's practices.

This chapter explores the particular and most outstanding manifestations of trade diplomacy in this era. It aims to locate it in a context broader than dominant assumptions and traditional actors. By doing so, it will be highlighted how this space is now shared and shaped in new ways and increasingly occupied by an ample network of dip-lomatic structures working in a number of proliferating sites. It first examines how the governance of global trade has moved away from a single focal point to multiplying sites. Secondly, it explores the challenges that the eruption of civil society has posed to tradi-tional state processes; and finally it looks at how diplomacy has been shaken to its core by the rise of new knowledge-based bargaining strategies in the global South.

34.2 The Tangled Web of Global Trade Governance: From a Single Window to a Spiral of Escalators

As argued by the editors in the introduction to this *Handbook*, international organiza-tions are sites of global governance in which the unfavourable position of the weaker party are offset somewhat, albeit not totally. The WTO and its predecessor, the General Agreement on Tariffs and Trade (GATT), was for a long time the single standard setting body that aimed to ensure rules for market access. It was not seen as a site in which the weaker parties could find refuge. At best it was viewed as lacking transparency and suf-fering a democratic deficit, while able to satisfy one powerful constituency—multina-tional corporations that sought to expand their own exports and investment abroad.[4] Citizens were confronted with a number of *faits accomplis*, making domestic politics easier to manage. From the standpoint of professional diplomats these were welcome features. They could limit the intrusion of domestic politics and hold good working rela-tionships with their colleagues from other countries. As the WTO gained relevance and diverse membership, it became more controversial, as the Seattle demonstrations of November 1999 showed rather loud and clear.

Until the early 1990s most developing countries were hardly integrated into interna-tional trade-and-production networks and remained on the sidelines of trade flows and trade diplomacy. Under the axis of state-led industrialization strategies and the nation-alist creed that characterized the decolonization process, their trade policies focused on the domestic markets and heavy state intervention, and thus ran in the opposite direc-tion to the gradual trade liberalization that took place among Western industrial coun-tries until the rise of an export-oriented strategy in East Asia in the 1960s and 1970s. It became increasingly clear that those developing countries that turned to export-led growth now had a growing interest in a better multilateral organization per se. It also meant that industrial countries now saw them as competitors, and were thus reluctant to open spaces for change.

Decision-making within the GATT was solidly 'pyramidal' in structure in the sense that the major trading partners (US, EU, and Japan) had implicit, yet effective, veto power over the negotiation's overall outcome.[5] Formal equality, in which every country has an equal vote, did not translate into participation in diplomatic construction. Rule-making remained in the hands of a few major industrial countries in the so-called 'green-room process'. The 'green room' was the name given to the traditional method used in the GATT/WTO to expedite consultations. It refers to a real room, the director-general's boardroom but also the closed meetings between the director-general and a small group of members, numbering between twenty-five and thirty and including the major trading countries, both industrial and developing, as well as a number of other countries deemed to be representative. Once a narrowed down consensus was obtained, agreements were passed on to those outside the green room for approval or rejection, thus legitimating negative 'consent'. The composition of the green-room meetings tended to vary by issue, without an objective basis for participation.[6]

The informal system imploded in Seattle when it was realized that this old way of getting business done could not work anymore, because neither civil society organizations nor developing countries could be 'rolled over' as quiet bystanders. As a result of the significant concessions made in the Uruguay Round, developing countries felt entitled to be included in the green-room process. On multiple occasions from that point on they had submitted declarations stating that they would not adhere to any consensus reached without their effective participation. In the run up to the 1999 ministerial meeting, diplomatic activity went into a frenzy. Almost 250 proposals were submitted to the WTO General Council in the preparatory process for the Seattle conference. Developing countries assumed an active role by submitting over half of these proposals. These inaugurated a new diplomatic tone and form, moving away from protest and confrontation to well-founded proposals working within the culture of the WTO.

After the implosion of the 1999 meeting in Seattle, the subsequent ministerial meeting in Doha in 2001 convened right after September 11 was rather tame by comparison. But the turning point was the subsequent ministerial meeting in Cancún in 2003. While ministerial meetings are now fraught with drama and uncertainty, after the 2005 ministerial, the WTO failed to hold another full ministerial in 2007 or 2008, although there is a mandate to hold a ministerial every two years. It would appear that the director-general and the members are reluctant to hold formal ministerial conferences unless there is a possibility for substantive diplomacy in terms of making decisions on new rules or new market access outcomes, unattainable under a mood of widespread unhappiness and even outrage.

By now there is a new vitality in ever-multiplying regional sites of trade diplomacy. Trading rules have always been tolerant of regional associations—a policy not viewed as inconsistent with the purpose of the global freeing of trade. The disintegration of the USSR in 1991 marked an end of the bipolar world and paved the way for the spurting of regional congregations. Earlier regional trade diplomacy had taken place in integration processes involving several member countries, both in Europe (the European Economic Community and the European Free Trade Association) and among developing countries. A slightly later vintage of this type of agreements was the 1983 Australia New Zealand Closer Economic Agreement. In the developing world, the most active regions had been Western and Southern Africa, Latin America, and the Caribbean, but there were also some agreements in the Middle East (the Gulf Cooperation Council), East Asia, and the Pacific. The movement that took off in the 1990s with the creation of NAFTA and led to a veritable proliferation of trade agreements has prompted many to speak of a world of regions.[7] In the 1990s we saw the establishment of NAFTA, MERCOSUR, and AFTA. In the 2000s, the East Asian region became the most intense site of regional trade diplomacy, again led by a few countries, particularly Singapore and, increasingly, Japan and China. Turkey has also turned to regional diplomacy over the past decade. The former members of the USSR became active in the late 1990s, essentially replacing the old trade arrangements of the Soviet era with new agreements among themselves, with Ukraine as the most active country, also involved with other regions (such as countries that made up former Yugoslavia).[8]

Mapping regional activity and discerning its global trends and characteristics presents severe difficulties due to the fast pace and random nature of this rapidly moving 'kaleidoscope'.[9] But some trends stand out. For most countries regional sites are now the centrepiece of their trade diplomacy. Increasingly, these sites have ceased to be geographically bound. There are also North–South and South–South links (tied to the emergence of several major hubs) and cross-regional sites as well. The latter represent the most distinctive feature of the current 'kaleidoscope'. Indeed they connote a shift from the traditional concept of 'regional integration' among neighbours to the emergence of new partnerships and ultimately the creation of new regions across the globe linking, for example, South Korea with Peru, Panama, or Chile or Brazil, Venezuela, and Argentina with the Arab countries.

The case of the Association of South East Asian Nations (ASEAN) is of particular interest since it was the only regional arrangement which was born as a security arrangement from which trade links were forged. It was created in 1967 by five states (Indonesia, Malaysia, Philippines, Singapore, and Thailand) later followed by five others (Brunei, Vietnam, Myanmar, Lao, and Cambodia). In 1992 ASEAN created the ASEAN free trade area (AFTA) which later continued widening by inviting other Asian countries to participate. The ASEAN + 3 initiative was implemented between 1998 and 2006 and is the result of free trade agreements signed with China (2002), Japan (2003), and South Korea (2006). ASEAN stands out among developing country groupings because on various occasions it has successfully presented a unified position at the WTO, especially in matters relating to the information technology agreement to which they were all signatories. Narlikar attributes this to the setting up of a Geneva Committee and the loose nature of this regional arrangement.[10] By avoiding tighter (and classical) forms of integration, countries were able to negotiate on an ad hoc basis and generate common positions at the WTO.

The most interesting aspect of regional trade initiatives is that, while they attempt to inscribe a set of established trade practices onto the regions' pattern of interaction,[11] these practices are both expressions of regional specificity, as well as of regional projection on the global scene. We are essentially back to the complexity of bilateral rules that characterized the 1930s, paradoxically for exactly the opposite reason: competitive liberalization rather than competitive protectionism. Since then, the pace has been continuous and has contributed to multipolarity in a world where it is not the individual states but their regional congregations which seem to make a difference in trade diplomacy. Socio-economic and political interdependence within a region, and the ability of a developed or a fast developing state to apparently control diplomatic endeavours in its region, have contributed to multipolarity. A multipolar structure captures the complexity of the new world and provides an accurate description of the pattern in which economic power is distributed among players.[12] Even the rapid adaptation of trade policies towards China has been the result of the fact that it is now a hub for a wide range of Asian countries and a recognized factor of transformation.

To understand how the proliferation of sites can affect diplomacy, it is worth reflecting on why international institutions are considered to be important in the first place. (See the editors' introduction as well as Chapter 7 in this volume.) The process through which institutions can facilitate cooperation is by creating a common set of rules. According to this approach, international institutions are a key mechanism which enables diplomatic cooperation. By becoming focal points, institutions can bring to light instances when states defect from the agreed rules.

The proliferation of international trade forums makes it more difficult to determine when an actor has actually defected from specific rules. Under a single international regime, it is easier for members to recognize when a partner is deviating from the rules. If there are multiple, conflicting regimes to resolve a particular issue, members can argue that they are complying with the regime that favours their interests the most; even if they are defecting from other regimes. In a world thick with competing sites, the problem is but selecting among a welter of possible sites. Institutional choice is now more than just a starting point. For many issues and/or regions, more than one set of rules can claim competency.

Consider, for example, a trade dispute between the United States and the European Union over genetically modified organisms (GMOs) in food. The US insists that the issue falls under the WTO's purview—because the WTO has embraced rules that require the EU to demonstrate scientific proof that GMOs are unsafe. The EU insists that the issue falls under the 2001 Cartagena Protocol on Biosafety—because that protocol embraces the precautionary principle. The result is a legal stalemate, with the biosafety protocol's precautionary principle flatly contradicting the trade regime's norm of scientific proof of harm and vice versa. Examples of the overlapping of trade rules abound. For instance, when the global financial crisis hit Ecuador, rather than restricting imports from neighbours under the Andean Community rules, the country negotiated a WTO safeguard covering all imports. A divisive row ensued: Andean countries upheld their regional rights and Ecuador its multilateral cover.

Once international regimes are created, they will persist even after the original distributions of power and interest have shifted. True—but stalemates also occur and the modus operandi changes when there is no visible member support for either a bottom-up or top-down redesign of the WTO's institutional structures. The global governance structure of trade has morphed from a single focal point to a web of agreements marked by proliferation and overlapping, from a tightly woven compact to a loose net of variegated sites of diplomacy.

34.3 CIVIL SOCIETY: SPINNING THE WHEELS

While the eruption of regional associations represents a loss of centrality, diplomacy within the WTO has also morphed. After the end of cold war all global institutions had become subject to the piercing scrutiny of non-governmental organizations (NGOs). At the root of the anti-WTO backlash was the democratic deficit of trade diplomacy, not only in taking for granted that what is good for the market is good for society at large, but also presenting outcomes as *faits accomplis*. Ever since the mid 1990s, the participation of NGOs has been gathering momentum, exercising voice, demanding participation, and rejecting prefabricated processes. The number of NGOs represented in ministerial meetings increased with each session. For the Hong Kong session of the ministerial conference in December 2005, the number of accredited NGOs had reached 1065, of which 836 actually attended (see Table 34.1 below).

NGO participation has evolved in two linked phases: first rolling from protest to protest, but gradually becoming suppliers of technical assistance. The power of persuasion with the backing of scientific evidence is seen to carry much more weight than emotional claim-making and mobilizing. By definition, technical assistants work within the established political parameters of an era. They produce evidence to support a particular cause in increasingly contested settings. As suppliers of technical assistance NGOs strive for a compromise between the concerns of policy space and the intellectual power of institutionalized ideas; without the aspiration of throwing the system down they are vigilant and industrious with information, arguments, and perspectives.

Several case studies of NGO influence in trade diplomacy demonstrate that in the two years that passed between Seattle and the Doha ministerial meeting in 2001, large international NGOs had become engaged in negotiations alongside states, present at the table as part of country delegations. The drive to eliminate cotton subsidies illustrates the

Table 34.1. NGO representation at WTO ministerial conferences

	Number of accredited NGOs	NGOs attended
Singapore 1996	159	108
Geneva 1998	153	128
Seattle 1999	776	686
Doha 2001	651	370
Cancún 2003	961	795
Hong Kong 2005	1065	836

Source: Peter Van den Bossche 'A Comparative Perspective on NGO Involvement in the WTO: Is the Glass Half-full or Half-empty?', in Debra Steger (ed.), *Redesigning the WTO for the XXI Century* (Canada: CIGI and Wilfred Laurier University Press, 2010).

point. The success in getting cotton into the Doha agenda as a single separate issue, the creation of the Sub-Committee on Cotton, and the inclusion of the ambition on elimination of cotton subsidies in the Hong Kong ministerial declaration were all the result of the efforts of a transnational alliance between developed-country NGOs, African NGOs, and African member states. The cotton campaign involved close cooperation and collaboration between the Cotton 4, the group of four West African cotton-producing economies (Benin, Chad, Burkina Faso, and Mali), a few international NGOs with technical credentials, and grassroots African organizations of cotton-producing interests. The alliance was characterized by a division of labour and the pooling of resources and capacities. Oxfam ran the media campaign and its Make Trade Fair campaign highlighted the inequities of cotton subsidies. The International Centre for Trade and Sustainable Development hosted Cotton Day at the Hong Kong ministerial and acted as initial facilitator for the alliance to take shape. Enda Tiers Monde produced the White Book on Cotton providing a platform for African voices, and financed travel arrangements for delegates. NGOs provided strategic advice, procedural and scientific information, and conducted a coordinated external media and lobbying campaign.[13]

Likewise, the Consumer Project on Technology, Médecins Sans Frontières, and Oxfam were key drivers of the declaration on trade-related intellectual property (TRIPS) and public health that was agreed by ministers in Doha.[14] The declaration responded to civil society concerns that the intellectual property rules were excessively biased in favour of pharmaceutical interests. The declaration stated that:

> The TRIPS Agreement does not and should not prevent members from taking measures to protect public health. Accordingly, while reiterating our commitment to the TRIPS Agreement, we affirm that the Agreement can and should be interpreted and implemented in a manner supportive of WTO members' right to protect public health and, in particular, to promote access to medicines for all.[15]

In August 2003, an additional WTO agreement was reached to clarify remaining ambiguities from the Doha declaration. In December 2005 the sum of these reforms were finally codified through a permanent amendment to the TRIPS agreement. These events were the culmination of a sustained campaign by global civil society designed to scale back intellectual property restrictions on the production and distribution of generic drugs to the developing world. Global civil society advocates and developing countries wanted as broad a 'public health' exception to TRIPS as possible, covering any and all forms of illness—and got what they wanted in the Doha Declaration.[16]

In this way, NGOs have emerged as strategic actors in global trade negotiations, deploying multiple strategies, making use of political opportunities, framing and steering issues, aligning strategies to state interests, defining problems, setting agendas, and influencing norms and outcomes, sitting with pen and pencil back to back with delegations. Ostry has called them transformational coalitions.[17] Many have access to specific professional expertise and specialized knowledge that facilitates the construction of focal points for resolving coordination problems across multiple issues. Rather than confronting the informational and transaction costs themselves, government diplomats frequently find that cooperation with NGOs can provide effective and efficient assistance to support their cause.

In the process, non-state actors have moved out of the fringes as mere *consumers* of trade diplomacy into the forefront as *producers* of diplomatic outcomes.[18] They provide a wealth of specialized knowledge, resources, and analytical capacity. Indeed, a revolving door has opened between NGOs and governments where collaborative horizontal relationships predominate, and essentially turning the closed preserve of trade diplomats (merely accountable to each other) inside out. This creates a more subtle and nuanced pattern of relationships between state and non-state actors than the conflict stereotype more frequently suggested. Esty and Geradin describe the situation as one of 'co-opetition'—a mix of cooperation and competition both within and across governments and between government and non-governmental actors.[19]

34.4 GOVERNMENTAL COALITIONS: THE BUILDING OF NESTED CIRCLES

If Seattle signalled the entry of civil society, four years later, Cancún signalled the new-found confidence of the global South, marking another turning point in the diplomatic process. The pressure of NGOs and the exponential growth in WTO membership had by then shaken the diplomatic terrain allowing political opportunities for erstwhile bystanders. Today approximately 100 of the WTO's 144 members are developing countries which have strived to increase their leverage articulating their specific interests and building coalitions issue by issue.[20] These coalitions are voluntary—no member of the WTO has to join a coalition, nor does a member undertake vows to remain part of it. But their emergence and indeed proliferation (see Table 34.2 below) has added new substantive issues to the agenda and changed the larger dynamics of building consensus. Coalitions are now important players.

The Recently Acceded Members, the African Group, the Small and Vulnerable Economies (SVEs), G33, G90, and so on, provide their members with an opportunity to learn about issues with fellow travellers and to coordinate positions for WTO meetings. The resistance of the Like-Minded Group (LMG) and the African Group against the exclusionary decision-making procedures had been a factor leading to the breakdown of the ministerial meeting held in Seattle in 1999. Two years later, backed by civil society, two other initiatives had hatched at Doha, the TRIPS and public health coalition,[21] and the Cotton 4.[22] Leaning on these campaigns, governments can manipulate value conflicts, trim proposals, and react with counterproposals. Dealing with asymmetry becomes less of an exercise in helplessness. Instead, it becomes more of an exercise in negotiated accommodation where state and non-state actors interact and feed off each other in a process whereby values become shared, rules gradually codified, and all actors get to reinvent themselves.

Table 34.2. A sample of selected coalitions in the WTO

Common characteristics groups	Agriculture	Non-agricultural market access	Rules	Environment	Services	TRIPS
G90	Offensive coalitions:	NAMA 11	Friends of Fish	Friends of Environmental Goods	G25	African Group
- ACP	- Cotton 4	Friends of MFN	Friends of Anti-dumping Negotiations (FANs)	Friends of the Environmentand Sustainable Development	ASEAN 1	Disclosure Group of Developing Countries
- LDCs	- Tropical and Alternative Products	Friends of Ambition in NAMA			African Group, ACP, LDCs, SVEs	Friends of Geographical Indications
- African Group	- Cairns Group					
Small and Vulnerable Economies (SVEs)	- G20					
Recently Acceded Members (RAMs)	Defensive coalitions:				Real Good	Friends against Extension of Geographical Indications
Small and Vulnerable Coastal States (SVCS)	- G10				Friends of GATS/ Friends of Friends	
Like-Minded Group (LMG)	- G33				Plurilateral 'friends' (promoting specific sectors and modes of delivery)	
	- RAMs					
	- SVEs					

Source: R. Wolfe, 'Adventures in WTO Clubland', Bridges 11:4 (2007), <http://ictsd.org/downloads/bridges/bridges11-4.pdf>.

These were important precedents for developing countries in signalling the relevance of forming new groupings as a means to promote their views on key issues collectively.[23] The Cancún meeting in 2003 catalysed the emergence of at least four new coalitions: the G20,[24] the G33, the Core Group on Singapore Issues, and the Cotton Group—in addition to the activism of others that predated the ministerial, including the African, Caribbean, and Pacific Group, the Least Developed Countries Group, the Africa Group, and the Like-Minded Group. They succeeded in getting three of the four so-called Singapore issues (investment, competition policy, and government procurement) dropped off the negotiating agenda of the Doha Round and led to the impasse at Cancún. Cancún marked a diplomatic turning point. In its aftermath the G33 stepped up its demands for special and differential treatment as a prerequisite for progress in the negotiations, particularly the right to identify special products on which there would be no tariff or quota reduction commitments.

Present-day coalitions differ from their older counterparts and predecessors. They adopt a more prominent and publicly visible diplomatic role, which often involves issuing public declarations, holding press conferences, engaging in media campaigns, creating logos and forms of branding. Another distinctive feature of new coalitions is their engagement with NGOs in the framing of negotiating positions and in the undertaking of public advocacy campaigns. The alignment with NGOs on cotton subsidies and the framing of negotiations of intellectual property as a health issue in the Doha conference illustrate the point. Finally, there is also considerable cooperation between various coalitions which at times can overlap. The resulting openness to other coalitions rather than an 'us versus the rest' antagonism and logrolling that is not completely random but relatively more focused on a smaller set of issues (partly as a result of the analytical support) makes the more recent coalitions considerably evolved, and certainly more evolved than the traditional ideology-driven third worldist demands.

The particular form that is adopted by these coalitions depends largely on the kinds of agendas for which they were created. Coalitions that are built in response to particular threats—which tend to dissipate over time—are formed by 'alliance-type' groups that come together for 'instrumental reasons'. Conversely, coalitions built for the negotiation of a variety of issue areas generally consist of 'bloc-type' groups of like-minded states. In this case, such coalitions rely on identity-related methods,[25] and often develop some kind of formal structure to facilitate analytic burden-sharing in the preparation of proposals. Coalitions provide countries not only weight but also resources (including analysis) to balance the agenda.

Two coalitions stand out in this regard for the hot issue of agriculture: the G33 with defensive interests and the G20 where offensive interests predominate.[26] The G33 emerges from the bottom-up understanding among civil society actors—small-scale farmers, non-governmental organizations (NGOs), academics—that economic liberalization has been negative for food security and rural communities. The G20 is driven by agribusiness, forged in reaction to the inadequacy of the US and the EU proposals to liberalize agriculture on the eve of Cancún.

The G33 relies primarily on the analysis produced by key member countries (e.g. India, Indonesia, Philippines); a multilateral institution, the Food and Agriculture Organization (FAO); an intergovernmental institution, the South Centre; and a handful of NGOs. Its work has primarily been to strategize on the content and timing of negotiating positions, tactics, and public statements. On this basis, a technical group builds its proposal, which is submitted to a periodic meeting of heads of delegations. From there, it goes to capitals for consideration. Heads of delegations then meet to assess reaction from capitals and approve the proposal by consensus. On a day-to-day basis, G33 negotiators in Geneva have the ability to do some research and formulation of positions, but they require back-up in certain situations, especially when specific technical questions arise or they require confidence that their formulations are strong enough. At crucial points the coalition may turn to outside institutions and researchers for help. For example, the International Centre for Trade and Sustainable Development (ICTSD) assisted the G33 in ways to develop the concept of special products and to operationalize it through indicators. As the G33 negotiators then set about to refine the indicators, they sought assistance from other research institutions in Geneva to validate their thinking. When the World Bank added pressure with a paper that suggested the application of special products would actually increase poverty in low-income countries, the coalition requested additional research input from the South Centre and ICTSD to assess the potential impact of special products on South–South trade.[27]

Like the G33, the G20 also turns out substantive research without endowing itself with a collective analytical capacity. Particular countries take the lead on specific issues that are then incorporated as part of the G20 agenda. A de facto division of labour thus emerges as issues roll on. Research initiatives of the G20 have contributed to the substance of the negotiations on formula reductions, on special safeguards for agriculture, and on product-specific caps. This is not grand agenda-setting, but one meant to flesh out proposals and shape counterproposals. Many developing countries have learnt that coalitions are essential in an organization that never takes votes and where nothing is agreed until everything is agreed (the so-called single undertaking). Considerable effort is also expended in government consultations with various domestic groups in each country. That process has served an important function of legitimization—this time, to the domestic audience.

The drive for the formation of the G20 was summed up by the Brazilian Permanent Representative of Brazil to the WTO, Luiz Felipe de Seixas Corrêa, when he asserted that:

> What prompted the creation of this group in the WTO was a recurrent phenomenon that we think has to be changed in order to cope with the new realities of multilateral negotiations. There is the belief or understanding that everything can be solved when the two majors get together and carve out a deal that represents their convergence of interests. And that the rest of the world, being so disunited or being so fragmented or having so many different perspectives, ends up one by one being co-opted into an agreement—for lack of an organizational framework.[28]

Old established processes are now shaken and splintered both by the emergence of significant opportunities elsewhere and by equally significant coalition-building inside.

Part of what the many coalitions in Table 34.2 have done is to create a claim that one of their members should have access to any closed meeting. The strengthening of accountability in countries across the globe has made trade negotiators both more cautious and tougher, as they have constituencies watching for any indication that their interests have not been adequately defended or represented. Government diplomats no longer 'command and control'; instead they negotiate. Governing activity is diffused over various social actors with the state increasingly in the role of facilitator and cooperating partner.[29] The jury is still out on whether coalitions have helped or hindered the Doha round itself, which was still struggling when this chapter was written. But that is not the point here. One way or the other it is safe to assume that coalitions have changed the scene and will remain with us in varying shapes and sizes. In the same way that the proliferation of sites leads to a spiralling system of escalators, coalition formation from within has resulted in a process of nested circles where coalitions and civil society are part of the process. It is not that the master organization has become irrelevant but that ever- multiplying stakeholders within it (as the new sites of activity outside) have churned up the tranquil pools of diplomacy.

34.5 Hierarchy Gives Way to Networking

This chapter has been concerned to raise questions and suggest linkages that emerge from the way that the structure as well as the process of negotiation has been agitated in the last two decades. It allows proposing some conclusions.

With emerging countries asserting themselves in every region of the world, trade diplomacy has become a multifaceted creature. What we have seen is that the club model of diplomacy has burst at the seams. In the club model of diplomacy, diplomats remain limited to interaction with the fellow members of the clubs: themselves and business. Yet it is no longer possible to assume a tightly centralized bureaucracy standing in isolation. In the same manner that the trade scene is changing from a single focal to multiple focal points, there is an overall shift in process from the club model to a networked process, which applies not only to international organizations but to national diplomacy as well.[30] The network model stresses the need for states to develop the capacity to engage with an increasingly diverse range of institutions and actors.[31] The shift from a 'club' model, where the few decide for the many, to a 'network' model, in which the many decide for the many is illustrated in Table 34.3. It presents as ideal types the most outstanding differences of each model.

Newcomers have challenged the 'classic' way of doing business. Nowadays, numbers do make a difference, but so does the intellectual landscape in which newcomers operate and to which they contribute. As contending players grow in strength and stature they have at the same time invested in becoming technically empowered to propose and counterpropose through knowledge, research, and value creation. Diplomacy has become intensely knowledge-driven. Indeed, some participants present the production

Table 34.3. Club and network diplomacy

	Players	Structure	Transparency	Main purpose
Club Diplomacy	Few	Hierarchical	Low	Sign agreements
Network Diplomacy	Many	Flatter	High	Improve process; introduce issues

Source: adapted from J. Heine, 'On the Manner of Practising the New Diplomacy', CIGI Working Paper No. 11 (Waterloo, Ontario: Centre for International Governance Innovation, October 2006).

and exchange of analysis as core functions of the networked diplomacy itself. Knowledge is used to frame or reframe an issue, to define interests, identify policy problems and preferred solutions, and especially to posit causal relationships. Such constructions can matter, not simply because they can provide the substantive content of demands in a trade negotiation, but also because they can serve as an important legitimizing device. This search for legitimacy is at the core of diplomacy; it concerns the ability of governments to frame particular demands and agendas in terms of notions, concepts, or themes that can enhance the imperatives of one position over another, avoiding or softening visibly ideological grounds. In the elusive quest for legitimacy, successful trade diplomacy renders compromises between parties. Without legitimacy, international agreements are hard to make and are often not kept, at least not for long; with legitimacy, states are arguably more easily bound to their commitments. In that way knowledge is played out through a complex and contested process of feedback and adaptation in order to gain trust and ultimately sustain legitimacy.

Indeed, a reaffirmation of the fundamental and intrinsic centrality of diplomacy emerges as a forceful conclusion from this analysis. If the Uruguay Round closed on mixed hope, finger-crossing, and ignorance ('there is no alternative'), in today's world we are called on to navigate a sea of contending perspectives. Knowledge must argue that the world we have is nowhere near as good as the world we could have. In other words, trade negotiations require interest-based knowledge. Agenda-setting, assessment, and the construction of counterproposals involve continuous evaluations and filtering to suggest alternative modes of actions. Knowledge-building matters not simply in providing the substantive content of a country's demands in a trade negotiation, but also because it articulates a different world with fresh options moving the agenda away from the mantras that 'there is no alternative' which is functional to 'the maintenance of order on a hierarchical basis' (as put forth in the editors' introduction to this volume). A diplomat demanding a high level of concessions from the opponent or refusing to make any concessions needs first to challenge universalist claims, and will subsequently be taken more seriously when backed up by detailed studies. There are thus two distinctive, and sometimes mutually exclusive, purposes to knowledge-building in networked diplomacy: the first is to genuinely give shape to a country's negotiating agenda; the second is to somehow legitimize the agenda that has evolved as a result of several other, often political, forces. The distinction between these two purposes of knowledge assumes special importance today.

This is so in a variety of senses, of which one might be highlighted: negotiations require the construction of a maximum aspiration position as well as a reserve position, which will be the lowest acceptable outcome. A negotiating strategy includes a comparison of the potential advantages of a negotiated solution with alternatives available away from the negotiating table. The strategy of walking away should be based on sound analysis of the likelihood of securing a better or more acceptable outcome through negotiations. A negotiating party can develop the strength and availability of what is often called a best alternative to a negotiated agreement (BATNA), while conversely introducing evidence into the negotiating process that threatens the attractiveness of other negotiating parties' BATNAs. Clear analyses of BATNAs are important factors in a successful negotiating strategy because they allow for wise decisions on whether to accept a negotiated agreement. As such, they provide a standard that will prevent a party from accepting terms that are too unfavourable and from rejecting terms it would be better-off accepting. Furthermore, having a good BATNA increases a party's negotiating power and a well-prepared negotiating team will be able to gauge the desire of the other team for an agreement. This will allow for the most effective use of pressure and the most appropriate demands being placed on the other negotiating team.

In the process of negotiation, analyses and integration of different proposals is required. The gap between competing interests is breached when each side gives something to the other side. This is possible through issue linkages; each party makes concessions in different topics so that the balance produces relative satisfaction. Parties must work to develop potential options for such issue linkages and need to have something to offer each other. Negotiators can enlarge the space of agreement by identifying and discussing a range of alternatives, by improving the quality and quantity of information available to the other parties, and by trying to influence their perceptions. Much of trade negotiation involves such integrative bargaining because parties can enlarge the area where their interests overlap by identifying and discussing a range of alternative options and opinions. Facing the demands of complex and perennially moving agendas, negotiators seek analytical support that is usable for a specific place and period of time. Governments may therefore need the capacity not only to absorb and produce their own research, but also to share and contrast findings.

Harnessing cooperation in the 21st century will require such networks to provide context-based knowledge and adaptation to concrete issues. The state now lies at the intersection of a vast array of processes and structures as we witness the reconfiguration of the world trading system into a more fragmented and regionally anchored one and the rapid expansion of transnational social links. With all states pursuing new frames to enhance their strategic interests, trade diplomacy will be less prefabricated in terms of issues, sites, process, and outcomes than we have known it.

No grand narrative in the making, but a complex reality in a state of flux, where knowledge inputs create an enabling environment for trade diplomacy for the sake of wider circles. Neither the hand of God bonding peoples, nor the demon in WTO clothes ready to spread sulphur across the globe.

NOTES

*   The generous and diligent research assistance of Linda Curran is acknowledged with gratitude.

1. H. Rashid, 'Economic Diplomacy in South Asia', Address to the Indian Economy & Business Update, August 2005. Available at <http://www.crawford.anu.edu.au/acde/asarc/pdf/papers/conference/CONF2005_04.pdf>; P. Cerny, 'Embedding Neoliberalism: The Evolution of a Hegemonic Paradigm', *The Journal of International Trade and Diplomacy* 2:1 (2008), 1–46.

2. I use the term 'Global South' somewhat loosely as both geographic metaphor and historical fact to describe a very diverse group of countries, at sharply different stages of development, who see themselves as a bloc of countries with different interests than the Global North—the advanced economies of the globe.

3. J.S. Odell (ed.), *Negotiating Trade: Developing Countries in the WTO and NAFTA* (Cambridge: Cambridge University Press, 2006).

4. R. Keohane and J. Nye, 'The Club Model of Multilateral Cooperation and the World Trade Organization: Problems of Democratic Legitimacy' (2000), available at <www.hks.harvard.edu/visions/publication/keohane_nye.pdf>.

5. G.R. Winham, 'Explanation of Developing Country Behaviour in the GATT Uruguay Round Negotiation', *World Competition* 21:3 (1998), 109–34.

6. G.K. Helleiner, 'Developing Countries in Global Economic Governance and Negotiation Processes', in Deepak Nayyar (ed.), *Governing Globalization: Issues and Institutions*, UNU/WIDER (Oxford: Oxford University Press, 2002); N. Kumar, 'Building a Development-friendly World Trading System', *Bridges* 11:5 (2007), a publication of the International Centre for Trade and Development (ICTSD), 3–5, at 5; United Nations Development Programme (2001), 13–14, 77–8; E. Smythe, 'Assessing the Doha Development Round', in D. Lee and R. Wilkinson (eds), *The WTO after Hong Kong* (Chippenham, UK: Routledge, 2006).

7. A. Acharya, 'Regional Worlds in a Post-hegemonic Era', keynote speech, third GARNET Annual Conference, Bordeaux, 17–20 September 2008, available at <http://www.durkheim.sciencespobordeaux.fr/Cahiers%20de%20SPIRIT_1/Cahiers%20de%20SPIRIT_1_Acharya.pdf>.

8. For a complete list of agreements notified to the GATT/WTO totalling over 200, see <http://rtais.wto.org/UI/PublicAllRTAList.aspx>.

9. R. Fiorentino, L. Verdeja, and C. Toqueboeuf, 'The Changing Landscape of Regional Trade Agreements', 2006 Update, DISCUSSION PAPER NO 12, World Trade Organization, available at <www.wto.org>.

10. A. Narlikar, *International Trade and Developing Countries: Coalitions in the GATT and WTO* (London: Routledge, 2003).

11. L. Fawcett, 'Exploring Regional Domains: A Comparative History of Regionalism', *International Affairs* 80:3 (2004), 429–46.

12. P. Subacchi, 'New power centres and new power brokers: are they shaping a new economic order?', *International Affairs* 84:3 (2008), 485–98.

13. S. Sapra, 'Domestic politics and the search for a new social purpose of governance for the WTO', in Debra Steger (ed.), *Redesigning the WTO for the XXI Century* (Canada: CIGI and Wilfred Laurier University Press, 2010).

14. J.S. Odell and S.K. Sell, 'Reframing the issue: the WTO coalition on intellectual property and public health, 2001', in J.S. Odell (ed.), *Negotiating Trade—Developing Countries in the WTO and NAFTA* (Cambridge: Cambridge University Press, 2006).

15. 'Declaration on the TRIPS Agreement and Public Health', <www.wto.org/english/thewto_e/minist_e/min01_e/mindecl_trips_e.htm>.

16. K. Shadlen, 'Patents and Pills, Power and Procedure: The North-South Politics of Public Health in the WTO', *Stud. In Comp. Int'l Dev.* 39:3 (2004), 76–108. The turn to providers of technical assistance has materialized in the same manner in regional trade diplomacy, except in the case of the European Union. In the Americas nonetheless the Hemispheric Social Alliance managed to bury the Free Trade Area of the Americas (FTAA) with the backing of the Brazilian, Argentinian, and Venezuelan governments in the Mar del Plata Summit in 2005.

17. S. Ostry, 'The Trade Policy-Making Process—Level One of the Two-Level Game: Country Studies in the Western Hemisphere' (Institute for the Integration of Latin America and the Caribbean, INTAL-ITD-STA, Occasional Paper 13 2002), available at <http://idbdocs.iadb.org/wsdocs/getdocument.aspx?docnum=784457>.

18. B. Hocking, 'Changing the terms of trade policy making: from the club to the multistakeholder model?', *World Trade Review* 3:1 (2004), available at <http://www.jhubc.it/ecpr-porto/virtualpaperroom/047.pdf>.

19. D. Esty and D. Geradin, 'Regulatory Co-opetition', *Journal of International Economic Law* 3:2 (2002), 235–55.

20. Odell, *Negotiating Trade*; Narlikar, 'International Trade and Developing Countries'; A. Narlikar, 'Bargaining over the Doha Development Agenda: Coalitions in the World Trade Organization', *Series LATN Papers*, no. 34 (2006), available at <www.latn.org.ar>; Kumar, 'Building a Development-friendly World Trading System'; A. Narlikar and D. Tussie, 'The G20 at the Cancún Ministerial: Developing Countries and their Evolving Coalitions in the WTO', *World Economy* 24:7 (2004), 947–66.

21. Odell and Sell, 'Reframing the Issue'.

22. M. Patel, 'New Faces in the Green Room: Developing Country Coalitions and Decision-Making in the WTO', GEG Working Paper 2007/33, Global Economic Governance Programme, University of Oxford, 2006; available at <www.globaleconomicgovernance.org>.

23. D. Keet, *South-South Strategic Alternatives to the Global Economic System and Power Regime* (Amsterdam: Transnational Institute, 2006), available at <www.tni.org>, at 14.

24. This G20 is different from the finance G20 and is composed of Argentina, Bolivia, Brazil, Chile, China, Colombia, Costa Rica, Cuba, Ecuador, Egypt, El Salvador, Guatemala, India, Indonesia, Mexico, Nigeria, Pakistan, Paraguay, Peru, Philippines, South Africa, Thailand, Tanzania, Uruguay, Venezuela, and Zimbabwe.

25. Narlikar, 'International Trade and Developing Countries'.

26. This G20 is different from the finance G20 and is composed of Argentina, Bolivia, Brazil, Chile, China, Colombia, Costa Rica, Cuba, Ecuador, Egypt, El Salvador, Guatemala, India, Indonesia, Mexico, Nigeria, Pakistan, Paraguay, Peru, Philippines, South Africa, Thailand, Tanzania, Uruguay, Venezuela, and Zimbabwe.

27. Paul Mably, 'Centralized production: The Group of 33', in D. Tussie (ed.), *The Politics of Trade* (Leiden: Martinus Nijhoff/Brill, 2009).

28. Statement at the WTO, 26 January 2005, available at <www.wto.org/english/thewto_e/dg_e/stat_seixas_correa_e.htm>.

29. Susan Strange, *The Retreat Of The State: The Diffusion Of Power In The World Economy* (Cambridge: Cambridge University Press, 1996).

30. Hocking, 'Changing the terms of trade policy making: from the club to the multistakeholder model?'; J. Heine, 'On the Manner of Practising the New Diplomacy', CIGI Working Paper No. 11 (Waterloo, Ontario: Centre for International Governance Innovation, October 2006).

31. A.-M. Slaughter, 'Everyday global governance', *Daedalus* 132:1 (2003), 83–90.

CHAPTER 35

....

FOOD SECURITY

....

JENNIFER CLAPP

35.1 INTRODUCTION

THE food crisis of 2007–2008 highlighted the need for a concerted global effort to tackle hunger and food insecurity. For most of the previous thirty years food prices were generally low and falling due to overproduction and high levels of agricultural subsidies in industrialized countries. The situation was rapidly reversed in 2007–2008 when food prices shot to record high levels, resulting in food riots and rising hunger across the developing world. By early 2009, as a more general economic crisis set in and despite falling food prices by that time, the number of hungry people on the planet stagnated at around 870 million, putting a halt to earlier progress on reducing hunger. The situation was exacerbated by the fact that by 2007 food aid levels had slumped markedly from levels achieved in the 1990s. Since the 2007–2008 crisis, turmoil on world food markets has continued, with prices reaching new record highs in late 2010 and early 2011, directly affecting access to food for the world's poorest people.

International governance arrangements regarding global food security—and food aid in particular—have been both under fire and reinvigorated by this crisis. After years of neglect and absence from the global agenda, food security has been brought back into the spotlight in high-level summits of leaders and in special meetings of those organizations that make up the global food security governance architecture. Yet despite increased diplomatic interactions between various stakeholders through these various governance forums, consensus on the best way forward for food security, and for food aid in particular, is far from secured.

In this chapter, I argue that a key reason for the weakness in the global response to the 2007–2008 food crisis is that the governance of food security at the international level is highly fragmented. Fragmentation in global governance, where distinct institutional and governance arrangements that address specific issue areas are not fully integrated, has been identified as a force that can hinder progress in addressing those issues.[1] Global food security governance organizations and arrangements are present in distinct arenas, reflecting both the complex nature of food insecurity, as well as the particular history of the institutions involved in addressing it. I focus in particular on one area of food security governance that clearly illustrates this fragmentation: food aid. Multiple arrangements and agreements exist for food aid that have separate rules, reporting mechanisms, and norms, yet there is little collaboration or coordination between these arrangements.

The fragmented nature of global food aid governance has existed from early on in the food aid regime. It has, however, become more fragmented over time as new governance arenas have been added and the role of existing ones has changed. This increased fragmentation has resulted in messy diplomatic interactions among stakeholders, where progress on the issue in one arena does not necessarily mean progress in other arenas. Stakeholders, then, must operate in multiple arenas with a variety of different actors in order to advance the same policy objectives. Early on most diplomacy on the issue took place between donor states and between donors and recipient governments. Yet in more recent years a range of actors has been engaged on the issue, including not just the traditional donor and recipient countries but also new donors, development and humanitarian NGOs, and business actors. Accompanying the expansion of actors engaged in food aid diplomacy has been the emergence of new debates about food aid which have only contributed to the weak coordination across the distinct and increasingly fragmented food aid governance arenas.

35.2 THE COMPLEX LANDSCAPE OF FOOD AID GOVERNANCE

Food aid governance arrangements largely centre on donor country commitments to provide aid and policies that facilitate the delivery of that aid through multilateral and bilateral channels. The US is by far the largest donor of food aid, and as such it has an enormous influence on international food aid flows and practices. The US carries significant weight in shaping international norms and rules that govern it. The European Union is also an important player, although its significance as a donor of food aid has diminished over the past few decades. Canada, as a large grain exporter, has historically been and remains an important donor of food aid and it carries considerable clout in the international food aid governance context.

Although donor governments set their own food aid policies within their domestic policy-making settings, they are also bound to some extent by a complex set of international arrangements that seek to govern food aid at the international level. These various governance arrangements all deal directly with food aid, but they serve somewhat different functions, and come out of their own distinct histories. The result is a series of governance arrangements for food aid that each have their own separate rules and are located in distinct institutional cultures and physical locations. The membership of these bodies also varies, with the result that each has a unique diplomatic setting.

35.2.1 Consultative Subcommittee on Surplus Disposal

The earliest international governance arrangement addressing food aid is a voluntary code of conduct, known as the Principles of Surplus Disposal and Consultative Obligations that are overseen by the UN Food and Agriculture Organization (FAO). These principles were adopted in 1954 and they are monitored by the Consultative Subcommittee on Surplus Disposal (CSSD), a subcommittee of the FAO Committee on Commodity Problems. The Principles of Surplus Disposal seek to ensure that food aid, especially surplus food provided by the donor country, does not disrupt domestic production in recipient countries nor displace normal commercial trade from grain exporting countries to food aid recipient countries. Maintaining levels of normal commercial trade also ensures that food aid is actually additional consumption—that is, consumption beyond what would have occurred with normal commercial imports—in recipient countries.[2]

Both donors and recipient countries are members of the FAO's CSSD, and the secretariat of the subcommittee is housed in Washington, DC. When it was established in 1954, there were thirty-seven members of the CSSD, and its role was important given that nearly all food aid at the time was surplus disposal. Today, the CSSD has forty-one members and sixteen observers, and although food aid is not primarily surplus disposal for all donors (as will be explained shortly) donors are still required to report all food aid transactions to the CSSD.[3] In its early days, donors took their reporting to the CSSD seriously, but in the past decade donor reporting to this body has dropped off significantly.[4] Because the focus of the CSSD is on the potential for trade displacement, the diplomatic culture of this committee has been dominated by government trade ministries.

35.2.2 World Food Programme

The World Food Programme (WFP) was established in 1962 as a joint initiative of the United Nations and the FAO. It was established at the encouragement of the US, as a way to facilitate the movement of food surpluses to food-deficit areas and to share the burden of food aid which had to that point become largely placed on North American countries: the United States in particular, and to a lesser extent Canada. As a specialized agency of the UN, the WFP was given the specific task of coordinating donations of food aid for both long-term development needs, as well as for emergencies (both short-term and protracted crises). The WFP is located in Rome, the effective hub of UN-based food agencies such as the FAO and the International Fund for Agricultural Development (IFAD). The WFP accepts contributions from donor countries and provides a multilateral channel for food aid provision in recipient countries.

There have been important changes to the WFP's operations since it was established. In the 1960s when the WFP was young, it handled only around one-tenth of all food aid deliveries (the rest being handled by donor countries in bilateral arrangements). Today it handles some 70 per cent of food aid and feeds 70–90 million people per year. The WFP still relies on donors to provide the bulk of its annual budget, but it gradually took on the lion's share of the logistics of getting food to hungry people. The WFP is one of the largest UN agencies in terms of staff numbers who are located not just in Rome but around the world in seventy recipient countries where it delivers food.[5] The WFP's operations have also shifted from that of providing food aid primarily as a long-term development tool, to one that provides mainly emergency assistance. As a product of this shift, the WFP has acquired specific expertise in responding to humanitarian crises.

The WFP is governed by an executive board that includes representation from both donor and recipient countries.[6] As such, diplomatic exchanges around the WFP's activities take place not just amongst donors, but between donors and recipients. The WFP increasingly relies on NGOs to assist in its delivery operations, and as a result there is also extensive interaction with non-state food organizations. Due to the focus of its work, to deliver food aid, the diplomatic culture of the WFP has a humanitarian and development orientation. Diplomatic interactions between states and the WFP have thus been primarily with government development agencies.

35.2.3 Food Aid Convention

The Food Aid Convention (FAC) came out of a different historical process from that of the WFP. Although its purpose originally was similar to the WFP in that it sought to facilitate international food aid movements and to share the burden of doing so amongst a range of donors, it is not a UN-based arrangement. The FAC is an agreement among major donor countries under which they commit to provide a minimum amount of food aid per year for a number of years. The idea behind minimum commitments is to ensure predictability in donations across a range of donors, a feature that aimed to benefit both donors and recipients by enabling forward planning. First negotiated in 1967, the FAC is updated periodically according to what donor countries feel they can commit in terms of food aid resources.[7]

The FAC was negotiated at the time of the Kennedy Round of the General Agreement on Tariffs and Trade, and was specifically tied to the Wheat Trade Agreement that was negotiated alongside it. Concessions in the Wheat Trade Agreement were given to food-importing wealthy nations, such as Japan and the UK, in return for their agreement to become signatories to the Food Aid Convention, effectively forcing those countries to become regular donors of food aid. In this way, the US was able to share the food aid burden more widely. But because the FAC was closely tied to the Wheat Trade Agreement, which was overseen by the International Grains Council in London, the FAC found its institutional home in London under the IGC secretariat, rather than in Rome under the WFP.[8]

As a result of its origins as a trade-linked treaty amongst donors, rather than a UN treaty, the FAC has a different diplomatic culture. Given its physical distance from the WFP and the fact that it is not a UN arrangement, the FAC has effectively become a donors-only club. In its early decades diplomatic efforts in the FAC were dominated by the trade and surplus disposal dimensions of food aid, engaging government represent-atives from agriculture and trade ministries. The FAC is overseen by the Food Aid Committee, the governing body of the FAC which is made up of donor states. The Food Aid Committee has been relatively un-transparent, providing little access for non-governmental organizations. Recipient countries have occasionally attended FAC meetings as observers, but all decisions are made by the donors when the Food Aid Committee meets biannually alongside meetings of the International Grains Council (IGC). A new Food Assistance Convention was released for signature in 2012.

35.2.4 Agreement on Agriculture of the World Trade Organization

A fourth arena in which food aid is governed is the World Trade Organization (WTO). Agriculture had been exempt from WTO agreements until the Uruguay Round Agreement on Agriculture (URAA) was completed in 1994. Food aid is not strictly disciplined under the URAA, but it is mentioned in the context of encouraging WTO members not to use food aid as a means by which to circumvent commitments to reduce export subsidies. The agreement calls on WTO members to ensure that food aid is not directly or indirectly tied to commercial exports of agricultural products to recipient countries and to ensure that all food aid donations are given in accordance with the FAO Principles of Surplus Disposal and Consultative Obligations.[9] It also encourages members, to the extent possible, to give food aid in fully grant form or on terms that are no less concessional than those outlined in the 1986 Food Aid Convention. WTO members also adopted the Marrakesh Decision as part of the URAA, calling for increased food aid donations in the face of an expected increase in food prices.[10]

Although the URAA provisions on food aid are not strict rules per se, but rather encouragement of members regarding food aid practices, the inclusion of language on food aid in the WTO does carry weight because the WTO's enforcement mechanisms carry legal significance. But at the same time, there is no language requiring coordination between the WTO Committee on Agriculture and the FAC, the CSSD, or the WFP, and there is no clear course of action in cases of non-compliance.[11]

The Doha Round, launched in 2001, has undertaken an overhaul of the URAA, and food aid has been hotly debated in that context, as will be discussed shortly. There is currently a draft text on food aid that is tentatively agreed, and which will likely become part of the final agreement once the Doha Round is completed. The new food aid text makes important changes in member obligations to ensure that food aid does not distort trade.[12] Negotiation on this text has taken place primarily amongst trade negotiators from WTO member states. Donor state trade negotiators, the US and the EU in particular, were especially active in developing the text on food aid. Although some recipient states, including some African countries, did submit texts in the course of the negotiations, the final outcome is largely a compromise between the dominant donor states.

35.3 TRENDS IN FOOD AID DIPLOMACY

An appreciation for the different institutional settings and their diplomatic cultures is important for understanding past and present trends in the diplomatic processes around food aid. Some of the above institutional and governance arrangements for food aid have been more relevant in food aid debates than others at different points in history. Coordination between these arenas has not been strong, illustrating the messy nature of food aid diplomacy in this fragmented governance context.

Early food aid programmes were established in the 1950s and 1960s, with Canada setting up its programme in 1951, the US in 1954, and the European Community in the 1960s. In this early era, most diplomatic interactions on food aid took place among states within the early food aid governance institutions, with little if any input from civil society or business actors. Up until the late 1960s, the CSSD and the WFP were the only arrangements that governed food aid at the international level. Diplomatic discussions over food aid were largely among donors on the one hand and between donors and recipients on the other hand. In its early years, the WFP was somewhat marginal as a player in the governance of food aid because it was dependent on donor governments and delivered only a small fraction of all food aid. The CSSD oversaw a reporting mechanism, as noted earlier, after food aid deals between states were struck.

In this early era of food aid, donors sparred with one another over the management of surplus flows of grain, concerned about whether food aid deliveries made by other donors might have harmful effects on their own commercial food exports to developing countries. The negotiation of the first Food Aid Convention in 1967 was directly in line with this concern. The FAC agreement itself was aimed at ensuring not only a sharing of the burden of food aid deliveries, but also a smooth interface with international grain trading arrangements. This part of food aid diplomacy in these early years was handled mainly by trade departments of governments, rather than their aid agencies. There was also intense diplomatic interaction between donors and recipients in this era, as food aid allocations from donors were made largely on the basis of political considerations. Donors typically chose recipients based on whether they were considered allies or whether they had geopolitical importance in the cold war. These interactions were thus handled by foreign affairs ministries of donor countries as part of the high politics of the cold war. Food aid diplomacy, then, was initially more about trade and politics than it was about development and humanitarian concerns.

Important shifts in food aid diplomacy began to emerge in the 1970s. The 1973–1975 food crisis, a period when food prices rose sharply and rapidly, refocused diplomatic attention to issues of hunger and food security and prompted the UN FAO to hold the first World Food Conference in 1974. Food aid donations fell in the mid-1970s to danger-ously low levels, which prompted calls for food aid to be directed mainly to the neediest countries, and not according to their political persuasion. The World Food Conference adopted a resolution directed at improving food aid policy, calling for better ways to deliver food aid, to be oriented more around recipient needs rather than as a means by which donors manage their grain stocks and seek political favour. The resolution also called for higher minimum amounts of food aid to be given so as to avoid the sharp fluc-tuations in levels according to world food prices, and for more of that aid to be in the form of grants rather than concessional loans, the latter a form of food aid that the United States practised widely.[13]

The 1974 World Food Conference was also important for reorganizing the food aid governance regime in that it established two new institutions to help monitor and coor-dinate food aid. These were the WFP Committee on Food Aid Policies and Programmes (the CFA) which aimed to monitor food aid policies and coordinate them amongst donors, and the FAO Committee on World Food Security, which sought to coordinate food security issues more broadly. Donors were encouraged to channel more of their food aid via the WFP. The FAC was renegotiated by its members in 1980, and the total minimum tonnage commitment was increased from 4.5 to 7.6 million tonnes. This level was still below the 10 million tonnes recommended by the World Food Conference, but higher than it had been previously. Many analysts saw these changes as evidence that the food aid regime had shifted from being one based primarily on donor interest, to one based on recipient need.[14] Indeed, coordination of food aid programmes in this period was improved as a result of these actions. But this did not last long, as international food aid resumed its intensely political clashes, particularly amongst donors, within a few decades.

By the 1980s and 1990s, non-state actors took a greater role in shaping food aid policy and governance. Donors and the WFP began to work more closely with NGOs who actively advocated that food aid maintain a development and needs-oriented focus. In the early 1990s, donors such as the US and Canada increasingly relied on NGOs, includ-ing groups such as CARE and World Vision for the US, and the Canadian Foodgrains bank in Canada, to act as delivery agents for food aid in recipient countries. As a result, these NGOs developed a direct interest in food aid policy and governance, as it had a direct implication for their activities as well as their operating budgets. With changing food production and storage policies in donor countries, food aid became less linked to direct surplus disposal of donor countries at this time. By the 1990s food aid was largely purchased on open markets by donors, giving agribusiness a key interest in food aid policy. In the US, shipping industry also developed a strong interest, as food aid shipments according to US law had to be carried on US flag ships.[15]

In the 1990s the focus of food aid itself began to shift, away from the use of food aid as a development tool, and toward its use in short-term emergency situations. As this focus shifted, a larger share of food aid was channelled multilaterally via the WFP. These changes reflected an increase in crisis situations—from natural disasters to conflict. Food aid became a key part of responding to these emergencies, partly a reflection of widespread media attention on the 1984–1985 Ethiopian Famine and subsequent disasters in which people faced starvation without external food assistance. The CFA that had previously coordinated food aid policies was replaced by the WFP executive board in 1996, as these shifts took place.

By the late 1990s and early 2000s food aid diplomacy was influenced by new debates in new arenas that were deeply political and sparked enormous controversy. It was at this time that food aid became caught up in the wider diplomatic skirmishes over the trade in genetically modified organisms (GMOs). The US and the EU took very different policy directions with respect to GMOs from the late 1990s, resulting in transatlantic political tensions over international trade in GMOs.[16] The European Union took a precautionary stance regarding agricultural biotechnology, and placed a de facto moratorium on the import of GMOs in 1998. The US on the other hand pursued a very permissive policy towards GMOs, seeing them as effectively equivalent to conventional crops.

These tensions between the US and the EU over agricultural biotechnology spilled over into food aid diplomacy, as US food aid contained genetically altered grain.[17] Controversy erupted in 2002–2003 when drought-stricken southern African countries were sent food aid in response to emergency appeals. The food aid that arrived from the US, unsurprisingly, contained GMOs. By this time international debate over the issue had become globalized, with many developing countries as yet unsure of their own policies with regard to agricultural biotechnology. The Cartagena Protocol, an international agreement that established rules regarding the trade in genetically modified organisms, was under negotiation from 1996 to 2001. But prior to the ratification of that agreement in 2003, there was much uncertainty about how trade in GMOs should be handled.[18] Many developing countries lacked the scientific expertise to establish their own biosafety policies and that fact, plus their closer historical ties to Europe, led many African countries to follow the EU's lead regarding the import of GMOs.

Countries in the southern African region began to carefully consider whether to accept the genetically modified food aid. Zambia refused it outright, while other countries in the region—Zimbabwe, Mozambique, Malawi, Swaziland, and Lesotho—said that if the food aid was milled first, which in effect would prevent it from being planted and crossing with their own crops, that they would accept the assistance. A coalition of 126 non-governmental groups from around the world issued a statement of solidarity with the southern African nations in August 2002 to raise awareness of the issue during the World Summit on Sustainable Development which was being held in Johannesburg at that time.[19] Tensions between the US and southern African countries regarding the shipments of GMOs in food aid ran very high at this time. US officials openly accused African leaders of turning their backs on the hungry and accused European countries and environmental groups of egging them on.[20] Throughout the diplomatic disputes over GMO food aid, the WFP and the FAC had little to say. Both lacked rules on the matter and both downplayed the incident, seeking to stay out of the crossfire over the issue.[21]

Further international disputes emerged over food aid just a few years later in a new setting. In 2004–2005, heated debate between donors erupted over questions of whether food aid that was tied to donor production constituted a distortion to trade. Food aid had long been provided to recipient countries out of donor surplus stocks, and there had been little questioning of this practice. A significant portion of the US food aid programme was made up of discount sales of US grains, rather than grants. But by the mid 1990s, the European Union began to shift its own food aid policy towards cash assistance in 100 per cent grant form for local and regional purchase of food. The rationale was that food purchased closer to the area of need in developing countries would not only be more efficient in terms of cost of that food, but also would provide important agricultural incentives in poor countries. But while the EU took this move with its own food aid programme, the US continued with its policy of nearly 100 per cent of its food aid sourced from the US, much of it in the form of loans.

This division in approach to food aid policy between the two largest donors sparked a major controversy, spilling into debates at the FAC and the WFP regarding the practice of tied aid and food aid sales. The debate over these practices, however, played out most clearly at the WTO, where the Agreement on Agriculture was being renegotiated after 2001 as part of the Doha Round. The EU argued that the US practice of tied food aid and food aid sales to developing countries constituted distortions to trade, and demanded that they be eliminated. For the EU, the insistence that the US change its food aid practices was directly linked to its own bargaining position in the WTO talks. It refused to reduce its own export subsidies as part of the deal unless the US changed its food aid policies.

The trade debate over food aid practices included not only traditional diplomatic spats between the US and the EU over agricultural policies, but also drew in NGOs such as the Alliance for Food Aid and business lobby groups, including those from the grain and shipping industries, with great force. The locus of these interactions was the WTO, a relatively new arena for food aid governance. The NGOs and business groups linked up with one another in the United States to shape US food aid policy, which in turn deeply influenced international debates on the issue.[22] Some of these non-state actors had significant interests in maintaining US food aid policies and practices, and sought to lobby the WTO and other international food aid forums to endorse these practices. Other NGOs, however, began to argue for untying food aid, and pressed for the US to follow the suit of other donors, including Australia and Canada in addition to the EU, in untying its food aid. Developing country members of the WTO were also drawn into the debate, largely taking the side of the European Union.

The result was a compromise text, tentatively agreed in late 2008, that specifies the kinds of food aid that are most appropriate and least trade-distorting. One of the key sticking points was whether tied aid could be considered appropriate in emergency situations, and who can determine when an emergency situation exists. In the end, the US was able to secure the right to maintain tied aid practices in emergencies, while the EU was able to secure the elimination of food aid sales.[23] The text makes no mention of the CSSD or the FAC. The WFP is only mentioned in the context of being a recognized agency for determining when food emergencies exist.

Tracing the key trends and debates that have been at the centre of food aid politics over the years show that diplomatic practice regarding this form of aid has changed significantly during this time, although it has retained its fragmented nature by taking place in distinct arenas that are not very well coordinated. In its early days, it was largely a state-to-state affair, with the key interactions between donor and recipient, and amongst donors, with a focus on trade and cold war considerations. The CSSD, WFP, and the FAC were products of this era. As food aid's role in global food security governance changed after the 1970s food crisis, the profile of the WFP was increased with the shift to more multilateral and emergency food aid, and non-state actors gained importance in the diplomatic process, particularly as they had a growing role in food aid programme delivery and advocacy. The advent of agricultural biotechnology and growing concerns about the liberalization of trade also created new tensions over food aid, accompanied by diplomatic spats between the US and African countries, and between the US and the EU, with the WTO becoming a new locus of food aid governance.

As these trends in food aid diplomacy unfolded, food aid gradually became very much a marginal resource compared to decades earlier. Whereas food aid constituted around 25 per cent of overseas development assistance in the early 1970s, by 2005 it had dropped to only 5 per cent.[24] No doubt this drop in significance of food aid in the broader food security governance architecture is a product of declining surpluses on the part of donors, especially since the early 2000s.

35.4 THE 2007–2008 FOOD CRISIS AND THE FUTURE OF FOOD AID DIPLOMACY

The 2007–2008 food crisis galvanized diplomacy on food security, including that of food aid. The crisis itself revealed serious weaknesses in the complex of food aid governance arrangements, shining a bright light on the extent of fragmentation of food aid governance in these various arenas. With the Doha Round not yet concluded, the WTO's food aid rules embodied in the new Agreement on Agriculture have not yet come into place. Since the early 2000s, reporting to the CSSD has dropped to just a few notifications per year, only a small fraction of the food aid delivered. The FAC, though still in place to ensure a minimum commitment in terms of tonnage on the part of food aid donors, maintained a low profile during the crisis, and its existence was barely noticed by the media. The WFP, by contrast, maintained a high profile as a frontline agency responding to rising rates of hunger.

A closer look at the WFP and the FAC in the wake of the food crisis, as the two more active food aid governance arenas for food aid today, highlights the continuation of vastly different diplomatic cultures in different institutional settings, as well as the lack of coordination between food aid governance arenas. This stands in contrast to the wake of the 1970s food crisis, when collaboration between the two governance arenas was enhanced following a period of crisis. Diplomacy in the WFP today is very networked, involving a range of activities and a number of actors: states, intergovernmental organizations, and non-state actors. The WFP's interactions with these various players are highly transparent, and this has given it a high profile in the food crisis. The FAC, however, has remained as strictly a donor's club. Although some non-governmental organizations have attempted to network with the FAC's members regarding its activities and functioning, it has remained largely closed and un-transparent in its activities.

As food prices rose quickly in 2007–2008, the WFP immediately faced a significant budget shortfall, forcing it to make a broad appeal to donor countries to the tune of US$755 million.[25] The largest donor in response to this special appeal was Saudi Arabia, a new donor which stepped up to the plate with a US$500 million donation in the form of un-earmarked cash. The WFP received donations in 2008 from ninety-two governments, including a large number of developing countries such as India, South Africa, and Brazil.[26] This figure is far greater than the eight signatories to the Food Aid Convention, signalling a more inclusive network that goes beyond the traditional donors of food aid to incorporate not just rising states, but also many recipient countries themselves. The WFP also receives donations from a number of private sources.

Also at the height of the crisis, the WFP fully embraced changes in its procurement practices that it had already begun to undertake, in particular the purchase of food from developing countries. This change reflected the broader discourse around food aid effectiveness that academics and some NGOs had been pressing, particularly around tied food aid and the benefits of purchasing it locally, as well as efficiency gains during a time of high food and transportation prices. WFP's high profile both for donations and for local purchase was highlighted in the Statement on Food Security adopted at the G8 Hokkaido Summit in 2008.[27] Despite this higher profile, however, the budget challenges for the WFP remained in 2009–2011, as food prices maintained their high levels, making procurement of food aid that much more expensive.

The food crisis of 2007–2008 also sparked serious rethinking of the Food Aid Convention as part of the broader response to the situation. The 1999 FAC had been due to expire in 2002, but was given a series of one-year extensions on the hopes of the WTO Doha Round being concluded before members took on full renegotiation. It had become increasingly clear, however, that the FAC was in need of updating for the new situation and could not wait for the flagging Doha Round to be completed. Throughout the food price crisis of 2007–2008, the FAC was neglected both in the media and in UN diplomatic initiatives around food security. The reason was clear: despite the existence of an international agreement to provide a minimum tonnage of food aid on an annual basis, the FAC's minimum pledges did not provide an adequate amount of food aid in the face of rising food prices that pushed hundreds of millions more people into short-term hunger. As noted earlier, food aid levels fell sharply at this time just as food prices rose.

The 2010 G8 development ministers' meeting endorsed renegotiation of the FAC in order to give the agreement more legitimacy and profile. The minutes of this meeting were explicit about this: 'Ministers believe in a Food Aid Convention (FAC) for the 21st century that focuses on providing appropriate and effective food assistance to vulnerable populations.'[28] By late 2010, with the end of the Doha Round nowhere in sight and food prices rising again, member countries agreed to take on a full renegotiation of the FAC. Two aspects of the 1999 FAC in particular were in need of revamping: the overall level of commitments as well as the way in which they are counted; and the governance arrangements of the agreement.

In terms of donor commitments, there has been little talk in recent years about major increases to food aid donations, which is a stark contrast to the response to the 1970s food crisis. Today, more attention is focused on increasing food production in developing countries, rather than food aid. This global attitude has reinforced the FAC's low profile on this issue. Indeed, some FAC donors were keen to change the way in which their commitments are counted under the agreement, preferring a switch to measuring donations in monetary form as opposed to tonnes of grain. Moving to a monetary-denominated commitment system, however, would bring its own problems, particularly when food prices rise quickly, because it would shift the burden of volatile food prices from donors to recipients.

The governance arrangements of the FAC also posed challenges. The location of the FAC, in the private International Grains Council in London, distances the Food Aid Committee from coordination with other food aid governance arrangements, particularly the WFP in Rome. This arrangement only reinforces the club nature of the FAC's practices, which exclude civil society and recipient country voices in the decision-making processes. Several proposals were put forward to relocate the FAC in Rome, potentially under the CFS (which itself was reformed in 2008 to include more civil society representation), for better cooperation with other Rome-based food agencies.[29] However, member countries have been deeply resistant to this idea, indicating a preference for maintaining a state-based closed club.

The text for a new Food Assistance Convention was finally released in mid-2012.[30] This text made some important changes over the previous Food Aid Convention. First, it reinforces some of the shifts in food assistance practices and policies in a number of donor countries over the past decade. The change in the name of the treaty—from the Food Aid Convention to the Food Assistance Convention—highlights this shift. The new agreement allows for more kinds of assistance to be counted by donors as part of their commitments, and emphasises the important role of local and regional purchase of food aid provided in grant form. The new agreement also signals a move toward possibly more inclusive and transparent governance of, and participation in, the treaty, by calling for more monitoring and enforcement as well as more openness to wider stakeholder participation, although it is unclear how much this will change in practice. The location of the secretariat remains in London, but the provisions of the agreement allow for this to be changed in the rules of procedure rather than requiring a full renegotiation of the agreement. The treaty also allows for a much more flexible means by which donors can count their commitments, including counting by value rather than tonnes of grain, a development which has raised some concerns because of the burden it places on recipient countries in times of high food prices. Whether these changes will be endorsed by member governments, and whether they indicate a true change in the diplomatic culture of the FAC, remains to be seen.

The very different institutional and diplomatic cultures of the WFP and the FAC through the 2007–2008 food crisis posed challenges for the future of food security governance in this era of higher and more volatile food prices. Better cooperation and collaboration between the two governance arrangements could provide a more secure supply of food aid through the FAC that in turn could allow for better long-term planning and wider operations on the part of the WFP. It is as yet uncertain whether the new FAC will bring about this change. For the moment, the two institutions still remain separated not only by physical distance, but by very different operational cultures and diplomatic practices.

35.5 CONCLUSION

Food aid governance has long been fragmented in different institutional arrangements and arenas. The rules, institutions, and norms that govern food aid via the CSSD, WFP, FAC, and WTO are all products of their distinct histories, and as such each has a vastly different diplomatic culture and set of actors with which it interacts. Since its early days, food aid governance has only become more fragmented, particularly with the adoption of new international arenas in which different aspects of food aid are governed. In its early days, when food aid governance was dominated by the CSSD, the FAC, and to a lesser extent the WFP, food aid diplomacy was largely dominated by state–state interactions. As the importance of the WFP as a provider of food aid has grown, and as the WTO has become a new arena governing food aid, the diplomatic processes around the issue have become increasingly networked with a range of non-state actors. Despite this increase in new actors on the food aid diplomatic scene, more pronounced fragmentation within the complex of food aid governance arrangements has hindered effectively cooperation and forward movement in this issue area. The dispute over GMO food aid, and over the potential trade distortions that might arise from certain forms of food aid, have illustrated the lack of coherent collaboration across the arenas that govern food aid. Indeed, concern over the trade implications of food aid have spawned yet another institutional arrangement for food aid that is itself disconnected from the other already existing food aid governance mechanisms.

The 2007–2008 food crisis brought increased attention to the WFP and the FAC which revealed stark differences in the diplomatic practices between these two governance arrangements in particular. The WFP is more open and networked in terms of its interactions, and has a high profile in forums such as G8. But its high profile and the wide range of actors associated with its activities have not led to significant changes to secure its funding. The FAC, on the other hand, has remained closed and un-transparent in the face of the food crisis, which has given it a very low profile. Although the FAC has been renegotiated as a broader Food Assistance Convention, it remains to be seen if it will be more effective in practice in the current context of volatile food prices. With these diplomatic differences between different governance arrangements for food aid hindering cooperation and coordination, both the FAC and the WFP are at risk of being neglected by donors. Such an outcome would not bode well for the future of food aid and its governance, which is especially troubling at a time of rising food prices accompanied by stubbornly high rates of hunger in the world's poorest countries.

NOTES

1. Frank Biermann, Philipp Pattberg, Harro van Asselt, and Fariborz Zelli, 'The Fragmentation of Global Governance Architectures: A Framework for Analysis', *Global Environmental Politics* 9:4 (2009), 14–40.

2. See Food and Agriculture Organization (FAO), *Reporting Procedures and Consultative Obligations Under the FAO Principles of Surplus Disposal: A Guide for Members of the FAO Consultative Subcommittee on Surplus Disposal* (Rome, Italy: FAO, 2001). Available at: <ftp://ftp.fao.org/docrep/fao/007/y1727e/y1727e00.pdf>, 3.

3. Food and Agriculture Organization of the United Nations (FAO), *The State of Food and Agriculture 2006: Food Aid for Food Security?* (Rome, Italy: FAO, 2007), 17–18.

4. See Food and Agricultural Organization Committee on Commodity Problems, *Consultative Subcommittee on Surplus Disposal (CSSD) Forty-Third Report to the CCP* (2010). Available at: <http://www.fao.org/docrep/meeting/018/K7806E.pdf>.

5. See World Food Programme (WFP), *Food Aid Flows 2007* (Rome, Italy: WFP, 2008). Available at: <http://documents.wfp.org/stellent/groups/public/documents/newsroom/wfp180471.pdf>; Edward Clay, 'Responding to Change: WFP and the Global Food Aid System', *Development Policy Review* 21:5–6 (2003), 697–709.

6. For an excellent history of the WFO see, D. John Shaw, *The UN World Food Programme and the Development of Food Aid* (Basingstoke, UK: Palgrave Macmillan, 2001).

7. The original signatories of the agreement were Argentina, Australia, Canada, Denmark, Finland, Japan, Norway, Sweden, Switzerland, the United Kingdom, the United States, and the European Economic Community and its then member states: Belgium, France, Germany, Italy, Netherlands, and Luxembourg. Today its members are: Argentina, Australia, Canada, The European Union, Japan, Norway, Switzerland, and the United States. On the FAC, see Charlotte Benson, 'The Food Aid Convention: An Effective Safety Net?', in Edward Clay and Olav Stokke (eds), *Food Aid and Human Security* (London: Frank Cass Publishers, 2000), 102–18.

8. John Hoddinott, Marc Cohen, and Christopher Barrett, 'Renegotiating the Food Aid Convention: Background, Context and Issues', *Global Governance* 14:3 (2008), 283–304.

9. Wyatt Thompson, *Food Aid in the Context of the WTO Negotiations on Agriculture* (2001). Available at: <http://www.fao.org/docrep/005/y3733e/y3733e06.htm>.

10. See Sophia Murphy, *Food Aid: What Role for the WTO?* Institute for Agriculture and Trade Policy (2005). Available at: <http://www.iatp.org/iatp/publications.cfm?accountID=451&refID=77567>.

11. Panos Konandreas, 'WTO Negotiations on Agriculture: A Compromise on Food Aid is Possible', in Jamie Morrison and Alexander Sarris (eds), *WTO Rules for Agriculture Compatible with Development* (Rome: Food and Agriculture Organization of the United Nations, 2007), 324.

12. See Christopher Barrett and Daniel Maxwell, 'Towards a Global Food Aid Compact', *Food Policy* 31:2 (2006), 105–18.

13. See D. John Shaw and Edward Clay, *World Food Aid: Experiences of Recipients and Donors* (Rome, Italy: World Food Programme; London: James Currey, 1993); Peter Uvin, 'Regime, Surplus and Self-Interest: The International Politics of Food Aid', *International Studies Quarterly* 36:3 (1992), 293–312.

14. Uvin, 'Regime, Surplus and Self-Interest'; Raymond Hopkins, 'Reform in the International Food Aid Regime: The Role of Consensual Knowledge', *International Organization* 46:1 (1992), 225–64.

15. See Christopher Barrett and Daniel Maxwell, *Food Aid After Fifty Years: Recasting Its Role* (London: Routledge, 2005).

16. Aseem Prakash and Kelly Kollman, 'Biopolitics in the EU and the U.S.: A Race to the Bottom or Convergence to the Top?', *International Studies Quarterly* 47:4 (2003), 617–41; Thomas Bernauer and Erika Meins, 'Technological Revolution Meets Policy and the Market: Explaining Cross-National Differences in Agricultural Biotechnology Regulation', *European Journal of Political Research* 42 (2003), 643–83.

17. See Noah Zerbe, 'Feeding the Famine? American Food Aid and the GMO Debate in Southern Africa', *Food Policy* 29:6 (2004), 593–608; Jennifer Clapp, 'The Political Economy of Food Aid in an Era of Agricultural Biotechnology', *Global Governance* 11:4 (2005), 467–85.

18. See, for example, Aarti Gupta, 'Governing Trade in Genetically Modified Organisms: the Cartagena Protocol on Biosafety', *Environment* 42:4 (2000), 22–33; Robert Falkner, 'International Cooperation Against the Hegemon: the Cartagena Protocol', in Robert Falkner (ed.), *The International Politics of Genetically Modified Food: Diplomacy, Trade and Law* (Basingstoke: Palgrave Macmillan, 2007).

19. This statement is posted at: Norfolk Genetic Information Network, <http://ngin.tripod.com/230802c.htm>.

20. See Robert Paarlberg, 'The Real Threat to GM Crops in Poor Countries: Consumer and Policy Resistance to GM Foods in Rich Countries', *Food Policy* 27 (2002), 247–50.

21. Clapp, 'Political Economy of Food Aid'.

22. Barrett and Maxwell, *Food Aid After 50 Years*.

23. See Jennifer Clapp, *Hunger in the Balance: The New Politics of International Food Aid* (Ithaca: Cornell University Press, 2012).

24. OECD 2005; Clay, 'Responding to Change'.

25. WFP 2008, 1.

26. See <http://www.wfp.org/about/donors/wfp-donors/2008>.

27. Group of Eight, *G8 Leaders Statement on Global Food Security*, Hokkaido Toyako Summit, 8 July 2008. Available at: <http://www.g7.utoronto.ca/summit/2008hokkaido/2008-food.html>.

28. Group of Eight Development Ministers, *G8 Development Ministers' Meeting Chair's Summary* (2010). Available at: <http://www.acdi-cida.gc.ca/acdi-cida/ACDI-CIDA.nsf/eng/ANN-428145532-Q7R>.

29. Oxfam International, *Bridging the Divide: The Reform of Global Food Security Governance*. Oxfam Briefing Note, 16 November 2009. Available at: <http://www.oxfam.org.uk/resources/policy/conflict_disasters/downloads/bn_bridging_the_divide_en_web_111109.pdf>.

30. This text is available at: <http://treaties.un.org/doc/source/signature/2012/CTC_XIX-48.pdf>.

CHAPTER 36

··

HUMAN RIGHTS

··

DAVID P. FORSYTHE

THE United Nations Charter from 1945, which comes close to being an embryonic global constitution, requires all member states to recognize and take action on behalf of human rights. Its article 55 reads: 'with a view to the creation of conditions of stability and well-being which are necessary for peaceful and friendly relations among nations based on respect for the principle of equal rights and self-determination of peoples, the United Nations shall promote:…universal respect for, and observance of, human rights and fundamental freedoms for all without distinction as to race, sex, language, or religion.' Thus in the UN era discussion about human rights in territorial states became internationalized and was no longer protected from international attention by the idea of state sovereignty. Nothing is more sensitive than the relationship between individuals and their government, this latter entity being the voice of the state. But now even this relationship is grist for the diplomatic mill.

The antecedent League of Nations Covenant from 1919 had contained no similar provision on human rights. The segregationist Woodrow Wilson refused to accept a Japanese proposal to write into the Covenant language endorsing racial equality. Having done so, Wilson abandoned his interest (shared by the British) in writing the principle of religious freedom into that document. While the League dealt with 'social' problems such as refugees and slavery, to name just two, League action in such domains was not a response to personal rights. The Nansen office on refugee affairs and the League inquiry into slavery in Liberia reflected voluntary and optional policies which, however important, were not required by the Covenant or any other part of international law. League action did not reflect duties that member states owed to individuals.[1]

But in the UN era, because the founders believed the interwar years of 1919–1939 showed a linkage between gross violations of human rights and international war, respect for human rights became a duty of sovereign states. In international legal theory, individuals had fundamental rights and states were obligated to respect them. This 'Lockean liberalism' of course was an old and well-established view in liberal democracies, but it became a matter of general international law only in 1945. Nations like America and France had proclaimed the universal 'rights of man' in the last quarter of the 18th century, but it was primarily Franklin D. Roosevelt and Harry S. Truman, under the influence of British intellectuals such as H. G. Wells, and aided by others such as Eleanor Roosevelt, who led the way in making universal human rights an international legal reality from 1945.

Much like the US Constitution, the UN Charter did not specify the human rights that were to be protected. And just as Americans added a Bill of Rights (the first ten amendments) to their foundational legal instrument, so in international relations in 1948 interstate diplomacy through the UN Human Rights Commission and General Assembly led to the adoption of the Universal Declaration of Human Rights. The General Assembly resolution, not legally binding at the time of its adoption, listed thirty human rights principles covering civil, political, economic, social, and cultural rights. No state objected (although 8 did abstain at the time, seven of them later disavowing their hesitant stance). The Universal Declaration has achieved iconic status over time and has led states to use their diplomacy to negotiate a flood of human rights treaties, specifying in law and in considerable detail the principles contained in the 1948 resolution. It is clear that many states, including even those who feel it sometimes necessary to adopt harsh and repressive policies, nevertheless wish to be associated with the idea of human rights. The two core Covenants or treaties on human rights, covering in the first instance civil and political rights, and in the second case economic, social, and cultural rights, have been ratified by over 160 out of the more than 190 states.

Formal recognition of the idea of human rights in international law, through primarily consent to treaties and acceptance of the emergence of customary international law, is, however, not to be confused with a genuine effort to protect the rights of persons who necessarily find themselves within a territorial state, or under the control of that state, as either citizen, alien, legal resident, refugee, or stateless person. Lip service to the abstract idea of human rights is definitely not the same as the quotidian respect for human rights in the public policy of states. In fact, it has been often noted that there is a very large gap between, on the one hand, the ratification of human rights treaties and, on the other hand, the harsh repression and oppression of many persons in many places on planet earth in the early 21st century.

It is precisely because of this evident gap between the theory and practice of human rights in the world that we see so much diplomacy for human rights in the continuing UN era. Much diplomacy is directed to the establishment of new human rights norms, either because a much-needed norm has yet to be codified (e.g. protection of gays and lesbians), or because an established norm needs to be refined further in the hopes of securing additional compliance (e.g. the rights of persons with disabilities as a civil right). If one looks back just to the League period ending effectively in 1939 (technically in 1945), it is remarkable how much the contemporary UN age concerns itself with human rights diplomacy. The concept of human rights has proven enormously appealing since its Western origins and early applications in the 17th and 18th centuries. But states and other actors often find themselves in situations where human rights are seen as expendable rather than absolutely required. And it is precisely this condition that gives rise to so much modern diplomacy for human rights. If recognized rights were truly respected, we would not see so much diplomacy related to human rights.

36.1 Actors

36.1.1 States

Despite the existence of the United Nations and other important intergovernmental organizations (IGOs) like the European Union, international relations still constitutes fundamentally a nation-state system—albeit modified by these IGOs and other non-state actors (like advocacy groups or armed factions). Social convention agrees that it is the territorial state that possesses sovereignty, or ultimate legal authority. IGOs exist because sovereign states create them. If true that states have to share the diplomatic chessboard with various non-state actors, from for-profit corporations to various types of militias, in general it is still the territorial state that often has significant power and can command significant loyalty from individuals. There are reasons grounded in power and political psychology explaining why states remain the primary subject of international law. In many respects international relations remain state-centric, albeit less so that in earlier historical eras. In any event states are still seen as sovereign, with the authority to negotiate treaties and pronounce on customary international law.

We have human rights norms in international law because states use their constituent sovereignty to restrict their operational sovereignty. States use their sovereign consent to establish the rules for what should be done. In the case of human rights norms, states agree to restrict their policy option under those norms in order to achieve policy objectives apart from independence. By consenting to the international law of human rights, states expect to achieve objectives such as peace, stability, economic advance through the workings of a protected private right to property, or beneficial ideas through respect for freedom of thought and freedom of speech, etc. States renounce the option, at least formally, to torture, to engage in extra-judicial killings, to deny voting rights, etc. States agree to limit their sovereign authority not simply because morally it is the right thing to do, but also because they expect to gain more than they lose by restricting their absolute freedom of choice. States agree that some governmental action is out of bounds and that all are better off from that condition. This is as true for human rights as for diplomatic immunity or any other part of international law.

States engage in much diplomacy to establish human rights norms either through IGOs or in diplomatic conferences. For example, the two UN basic human rights Covenants mentioned earlier were negotiated through what was then the UN Human Rights Commission (now the UN Human Rights Council). A few human rights treaties were negotiated through other UN agencies. Treaties on labour rights are usually negotiated through the International Labour Organization (ILO). The 1951 refugee convention was negotiated through the UN General Assembly.

By comparison, treaties on international humanitarian law (IHL), sometimes referred to as human rights in armed conflict, are always developed in diplomatic conferences formally apart from the UN system. By tradition, treaty developments in IHL occur in diplomatic conferences called by the Swiss government, with the private International Committee of the Red Cross (ICRC) acting as a drafting secretariat and organizer of pre-conference meetings. This is because of tradition, with the first Geneva Convention for victims of armed conflict evolving in 1864 through this process. This tradition may continue in part because of the hope of sheltering the development of IHL from UN political squabbles, but this hope is probably naive. During 1974–1977 two protocols were added to the 1949 Geneva Conventions arguably for the protection of victims of war in international and internal armed conflicts. (A third protocol was added in 2005–2006.) But many of the same North–South and East–West fissures that characterized UN debates were also found in the Geneva Diplomatic Conference on IHL that ran for four years. In fact, many states sent the same diplomatic personnel to the Geneva diplomatic conference on IHL that had been active in UN bodies.[2]

Whether pertaining to human rights treaties narrowly defined or defined more broadly to include IHL, states use the diplomatic process to advance a variety of interests and values. For example, with regard to 1977 Additional Protocol I pertaining to international armed conflict, a number of states from the global South sought new norms that would affect armed conflicts in which fighting parties were struggling against racist, occupying, or colonial regimes. On the surface this was an effort to extend the coverage of IHL. Disputes that had been seen by colonial powers as internal were henceforth to be internationalized. Beneath the surface, this was a move to give added political status to those taking up arms against: Israel and/or its occupation of Palestinian territories, South Africa under apartheid, and the Portuguese colonies in Angola and Mozambique. The Soviet Union and its communist allies supported that part of the global South pushing for Protocol I as it evolved through the diplomatic process. What happened at the Geneva Diplomatic Conference of the 1970s was not so different from the UN Conference on Human Rights that met in Teheran in 1968. Not only were the same states involved in both, but often the same diplomats were arguing about the same or similar issues. The pariah states at Teheran, namely Israel, South Africa, and colonial Portugal, remained pariah states at Geneva slightly later. In 1968 at Teheran much of the global South sought to put their imprint on internationally recognized human rights and this move continued at the Geneva Diplomatic Conference of 1974–1977.

Diplomacy on human rights internationally is not always different from attention to human rights in domestic politics. In the US Congress, for example, senators who address human rights abroad in their floor speeches may be genuinely interested in the subject because of a broad concern with human dignity. But some of the verbal interventions just happen to address human rights violations in foreign states that are alleged to be taking jobs away from Americans.[3] It seems that some attention to human rights abroad stems from the effort to block trade agreements with certain states which manifest human rights blemishes. Both in domestic politics and in foreign diplomacy, attention to human rights may be a means to various ends.

Famously in the 1970s, certain US senators sought to draw attention to communist repression of Jewish citizens who desired to emigrate from Romania and the USSR. This Senate debate and resulting policy not only showed concern for the human rights (viz.

freedom to travel) of Jews living under European communism, but also was an effort to undermine the Nixon–Kissinger policy of détente, or relaxation of tensions between the US and USSR. Some senators knew full well that focusing on the right to emigrate would add controversy to Soviet–US relations and impede development of stable relations. They wanted to contest the very existence of European communism on moral grounds, not stabilize relations between the NATO countries and the Warsaw bloc.

When noting how non-human rights matters can affect human rights diplomacy by states, one has to face the reality that sometimes state human rights diplomacy is driven primarily by strategic interests rather than an even-handed concern for human dignity. From 2006 the UN Human Rights Council, which replaced the UN Human Rights Commission, adopted the process known as Universal Periodic Review. Each state, starting with members of the Council, had to present a human rights report to the Council concerning human rights in its jurisdiction and then defend the report in the face of questioning. The questioning in the Human Rights Council was done by states—not by independent or uninstructed persons sitting in their personal capacity. So in the UN Human Rights Council state diplomacy on human rights might be motivated by strategic considerations, as enemy or antagonistic states sought to embarrass and dele-gitimize the reporting state. Once again we see that diplomacy on human rights by polit-ical actors, even if within the framework of an IGO, may be driven by considerations at least partially distinct from pure concern with personal rights.

It is normally the case that in the UN Human Rights Council, state members are more likely to publicly criticize their political adversaries than their political friends. It was certainly the case during the cold war that state members of NATO were not hesitant to levy chares of violations of human rights against the communist states making up the Warsaw Pact. For their part, communist members of the Warsaw Pact often criticized NATO members for violations of socio-economic rights, while maintaining silence about the evident violations of civil-political rights by their allies. As the United States moved to restore normal relations between itself and the People's Republic of China, so as to make life more difficult for the Soviet Union, the Carter administration was much more critical of human rights violations by Moscow than by Beijing.

This pattern continues, unfortunately, after the cold war. In the UN Human Rights Council the United States is more prone to criticize human rights violations in Cuba or Iran than in Saudi Arabia or Egypt. The Arab states are more likely to criticize Israel for human rights violations than for those same or worse violations in certain members of the Arab League. The unpleasant fact is that human rights diplomacy can be used as a political weapon to try to delegitimize target governments, rather than to advance the cause of human dignity in a balanced and even-handed process. Many if not most states have used human rights diplomacy for political gain at one time or another. After all, from a diplomat's traditional perspective, how wise is it to publicly criticize one's friends and allies? If the diplomat's primary goal is smooth relations with friendly states, engag-ing in candid public discussion of an ally's human rights defects requires new thinking. This new thinking may seek a balance between protection of personal rights on an even-handed basis, and protection of traditional national interests.

One also has to admit that some apparent human rights diplomacy by states is a matter of public posturing and duplicity. A classic example concerns Henry Kissinger and the Western hemisphere. President Richard Nixon and Kissinger, his principal foreign policy adviser, came under domestic criticism at one point for lack of attention to human rights in foreign policy. The charge was that these realist policy-makers were only interested in balance of power diplomacy mainly focused on the Soviet Union. Hence they were criticized for lacking a moral dimension to their foreign policy. In this criticism, US foreign policy was said to ignore human rights violations in those hemispheric states aligned with the United States in the effort to resist communism. In this context Kissinger gave a speech in the Organization of American States (OAS) reaffirming US interest in democracy and human rights in the hemisphere. But Kissinger then engaged in quiet diplomacy to reassure brutal, authoritarian allies in the region that the speech was for domestic consumption.[4] Here we see state diplomacy on human rights as part of domestic politics, and the effort of a government official to placate domestic critics without making a substantive change in foreign policy.

When negotiating new human rights treaties or extensions of existing ones, state representatives must necessarily consider certain non-human rights matters such as the likelihood of acceptance 'back home'. Diplomats from the foreign ministry usually have an eye on the likelihood of opposition from the military or justice or interior bureaucracies, or from legislators who might be opposed for varying reasons. Most diplomats are concerned about 'sovereignty costs', or whether opposition will arise to the treaty being negotiated because too much discretion in policy-making will be taken away from the state. Since ratification of treaties usually involves at least part of the legislature acting according to the terms of the national constitution, the views of important legislators are usually taken into account and often some legislators are included in the state delegation that negotiates a treaty.

During negotiations modern diplomats, especially from democratic states, are constantly checking with 'home base' about what is likely to prove acceptable or troublesome. Many diplomats from many countries are aware of the famous case of Woodrow Wilson and the Versailles Treaty of 1919. Wilson negotiated the treaty with the other victorious Great Powers of the time, but he failed to give adequate attention to key US senators who would need to give advice and consent in the ratification process under the US constitution. Wilson's narrow-mindedness and rigidity contributed to the defeat of the treaty in the Senate, and thus the failure of the United States to join the League of Nations. In the 1920s many senators were concerned that under the treaty the United States would be obligated to come to the defence of other states militarily and that the Congress would thus lose its authority to declare war. Rightly or wrongly, these senators considered the sovereignty costs (and loss of congressional authority) too high under the Versailles Treaty and associated League of Nations Covenant.

On a more positive note, we should certainly acknowledge that states sometimes do pursue human rights diplomacy for genuine and valid moral reasons. As discussed in Chapter 41 of this *Handbook*, a number of 'like-minded' states did work hard to reach agreement at a Rome diplomatic conference in 1998 in order to create the International

Criminal Court (ICC) to try defendants accused of genocide, crimes against humanity, and war crimes. For many of them, their concern to end impunity for those responsible for these gross violations of human rights resulted in a determination to create the first standing international criminal court, to be brought off the shelf and into play when a relevant state was 'unwilling or unable' to properly act via investigation and prosecution. These like-minded states were committed enough so that opposition to the final document by the United States and certain other important states like China and Russia did not deter them.

Likewise, several states have made up a group of 'friends of the UN Secretary-General', or some other similar grouping, to work for self-determination for Namibia in early 1990, or to end atrocities in El Salvador in the late 1980s. Happily one can note many examples of states using human rights diplomacy to protect the recognized human rights of 'others'.[5] The presence of some expedient political factor as part of a government's calculus does not negate the genuine commitment to human rights that exists. That is to say, a government may want to placate critics or be on the right side of history by cozying up to an emerging elite, but such factors do not erase the genuine interest in human rights that is present. Much state foreign policy is the result of mixed motives. A given policy may reflect varying inputs from different parts of the foreign policy establishment.

36.1.2 IGO Personnel

A defining characteristic of international organizations, more precisely intergovernmental organizations, is a bureaucracy headed by a secretary-general or a director-general. An organization has leadership and administration within a set of rules; a movement or network does not. In the case of the United Nations and similar IGOs like the OAS, European Union, the North Atlantic Treaty Organization (NATO), African Union, Arab League, etc., one can talk about two models of leadership: more active (Albert Thomas) and more passive (Eric Drummond).[6] If we jump to the current UN and other relevant IGOs, with regard to human rights we find that the top secretariat office and various agency heads are expected to undertake appropriate diplomacy, but at the same time they are expected to maintain the support of the member states which comprise the organization. This is either impossible or fraught with peril. It is not for nothing that the job of UN Secretary-General, for example, has been called the most impossible job in the world.

One can recall that the first UN Secretary-General, Trygve Lie of Norway, took a forthright public stand about communist responsibility for the start of the Korean War. By so doing, he became *persona non grata* to the Soviet Union, which subsequently refused to deal with him. Thus he was unable to carry out many of his functions for the UN and felt it necessary to resign before the end of his term. We now fast forward from the 1950s to the 1980s. We find that the top UN human rights official, Theo van Boven from the Netherlands, was very outspoken in his criticisms of the human rights violations by the

Argentine junta, then in the process of executing its 'dirty war' involving the forced disappearance of some 30,000 persons, many of whom were tortured and murdered. The Reagan administration, however, saw the junta as sufficiently anti-communist to merit support. Washington therefore pressured the Secretary-General not to renew the contract of van Boven, which is precisely what transpired. We fast forward again to the early 21st century, and we find that the UN has created the post of High Commissioner for Human Rights. At the time of the first George W. Bush administration, the post is held by Mary Robinson from Ireland. She speaks publicly and with passion about such subjects as Israel's treatment of the Palestinians and US treatment of terror suspects at, among other places, the prison at Guantanamo. Once again, Washington pressures the Secretary-General not to renew the contract of Robinson, which is precisely what transpires.

Leadership for human rights by the heads of IGOs or IGO offices is tricky business. At the time of the 1994 Rwandan genocide, the Office of the UN High Commissioners for Refugees (UNHCR) was headed by Sadako Ogata from Japan. She wound up managing refugee camps in Zaire, and in many of these camps were armed militias made up of Rwandan Hutus who had fled from their project of trying to eliminate the Rwanda Tutsi. She asked the UN Security Council to demilitarize the refugee camps. The Council refused to do so, lacking the political will to confront some very nasty characters. Thus to secure the genuine refugee nature of the camps, she had to turn to some armed forces from what was then Zaire to try to control the militias, a less than fully perfect solution given the lack of full discipline by some of the Zairian troops. In this example, we see dynamic leadership from the UNHCR, lack of proper support from important member states, and persistent creativity by Ogata in trying to do the best possible in a most imperfect situation. And in this case, we see that IGO diplomacy for human rights, in this case refugee rights, is inseparable from management of the IGO, in this case the UNHCR.

All UN Secretaries-General are now expected not only to engage in quiet diplomacy for human rights but also to speak out on rights matters.[7] But at the same time they have to calculate when and how to engage in public diplomacy so as not to push important members too far. The same is true for the UN High Commissioner for Human Rights, the UN High Commissioner for Refugees, the head of the UN Children's Fund (UNICEF), and so on. The head of the OAS and other such organizations face the same tension. So do the special rapporteurs of the UN Human Rights Council who are appointed in their personal capacity to make studies about, and engage in diplomacy about, particular human rights problems. All of these persons have legal independence and are not instructed in their official duties by any state or group of states (after the establishment of their mandate). At the same time, the UN, OAS, NATO, etc., cannot be fully effective if the United States is totally estranged from the organization. UNHCR cannot meet is budgetary needs without the voluntary support of the wealthy liberal democracies who donate to the budget and provide (sometimes) diplomatic support. So IGO personnel walk a tightrope between faithfulness to international standards on human rights and efforts either not to alienate important member states or to engender their positive support. IGO diplomacy on human rights is not for the simple-minded.

The diplomatic game is played slightly differently in treaty monitoring mechanisms. We will use the International Covenant on Civil and Political Rights as an example. The treaty creates the UN Human Rights Committee to monitor the record of states that have ratified the treaty. Each ratifying state must submit a periodic report to the Human Rights Committee about the steps it has taken to implement the treaty and any problems that have arisen. The Committee is authorized to raise questions about the government's report. The government is obligated to send a delegation to the Committee in Geneva to provide answers to questions. The Committee is authorized to make particular and summary statements, as well as to make General Comments about the proper interpretation of the treaty. The Committee is staffed by individuals sitting in their personal capacity and not as state representatives. Sometimes their questions are probing; sometimes their conclusions are not to the liking of states. But having been elected by the states that are parties to the treaty, they cannot be removed before their terms end. The Committee is not a court and its comments and judgements are not immediately legally binding. But the Committee does generate some influence for human rights, especially over time through its General Comments. The UN Human Rights Committee is the scene of formalized multilateral diplomacy on human rights.[8]

Some UN personnel associated with 'special procedures' on human rights will join or network together in seeking maximum effect. We see this pattern, for example, with regard to US treatment of presumed enemy prisoners at the Guantanamo detention facility after the terrorist attacks of 11 September 2001. In 2006 five UN independent persons compiled a report on human rights issues relating to that detention. Given how fragmented the various UN human rights initiatives can be and how easy it is for states to lose an individual comment or report in the vast number of issues in play from UN processes, it is rational for UN officials to utilize this combined or networked approach. In this example, however, there was no clear evidence of short-term positive impact from the well-considered report, the Bush administration manifesting a tendency to dismiss the views of UN officials when critical of US policy.[9]

A number of UN agencies like UNICEF, the World Health Organization (WHO), and the United Nations Development Programme (UNDP) had originally been considered development or specialized agencies. Over time these UN bodies progressively took a human rights approach to their work, or part of their work. That is to say, for example, that UNICEF increasingly over time linked its work for the benefit of children and mothers to the language found in the Convention on the Rights of the Child. The WHO increasingly was active on health and health care as human rights. Even the World Bank, officially part of the UN system, incorporated some human rights diplomacy into its activities (but not to the extent of UNICEF). So at the UN one saw the 'mainstreaming of human rights', or the incorporation of human rights language and diplomacy into activities previously seen as matters of relief or development.[10]

IGO diplomacy for human rights, and here I am speaking only about international civil servants, is a characteristic of contemporary international relations. There is much of this kind of non-state diplomacy. But it is a delicate matter. States often do not take kindly to public commentary on their rights record by IGO personnel. States fund the budget and set the basic rules for the IGO in question, which sometimes seems to bite the hand that feeds it. It is possible on rare occasions for public IGO diplomacy to make a difference. In the winter of 2004–2005, the UN Coordinator for Humanitarian Affairs Jan Egeland (whose own account of the events is given in Chapter 19 of this *Handbook*) publicly rebuked Western states for not being generous in the response to a massive natural disaster in the form of an Asian tsunami or tidal wave. The results of this public commentary were entirely positive, in the sense that the wealthy democracies stepped up their relief efforts. It was officially a matter of humanitarian assistance, but inherently at play were such human rights as the right to life, to adequate nutrition and medical care, and so on.

We should add a word about quiet diplomacy, the eminent practitioner of which is the ICRC. It is usually treated as if it were an IGO, having a headquarters agreement with Switzerland for its main offices in Geneva. It signs similar agreements with states where it sets up delegations. It is given rights and duties in public international law, principally the Geneva Conventions and Protocols for victims of war. On the professional side of the house it has an international secretariat. It has observer status at the United Nations. So here we will treat it as if it were an IGO, even though in Swiss law it is a private, civil society organization.

Particularly with regard to prison visits, whether in international armed conflict, internal armed conflict, or domestic tensions and troubles, the ICRC relies heavily on discreet diplomacy. While it has a right of visitation to all detainees in international armed conflict, whether military or civilian, it still believes that discretion is its preferred means of action. Thus its reports on the conditions of detention and the treatment prisoners receive go only to the detaining power in a discreet process (and to the state of origin if the situation is one of international war). The ICRC believes that quiet diplomacy aids its access, particularly where international law does not give it a right of access, and furthermore promotes trust between it and the detaining authority. In general, unlike such organizations as Amnesty International and Human Rights Watch, the ICRC does not put much faith in the 'naming and shaming game'.

The ICRC, however, reserves the right to engage in public commentary if insufficient humanitarian progress is achieved over time. What is sufficient progress, over what period of time, has never been publicly codified, much less made clear to observers. Nevertheless, on some occasions the ICRC, which has been described by more than one observer as credible and cautious, will suspend or withdraw its delegation from a round of prison visits, sometimes making a public comment about events. It has to be careful about becoming complicit in violations of humanitarian law and relevant human rights norms, without being able to show progress in protecting detainees.

Its archives are open to researchers after forty years and this is another factor in decision-making. We can now research, for example, ICRC diplomacy towards the Greek junta (1967–1974) in its early days and make a judgement about ICRC quiet diplomacy, its vigour and sophistication and impact. Did the diplomacy of the ICRC contest junta abuse of prisoners with appropriate skill and determination, given the factors at play in that situation? The ICRC, being aware of the eventual access to its archives, knows that its reputation will eventually be affected, which is an inducement to appropriate quiet diplomacy on behalf of detainees. Of course the organization believes that its commitment to humanitarian and human rights values will lead it to do the right thing without worrying about future evaluations.

Nevertheless, concern with its reputation over time, based on well-considered diplomacy in complex situations, is a factor not to be totally discounted. The organization is well aware that it was criticized for not manifesting sufficient interest in the fate of Jewish and other civilian 'political' detainees subjected to Nazi persecution and even genocide during the 1930s and 1940s. In fact after the war it eventually apologized primarily for its lack of fully vigorous quiet diplomacy in that situation and made various organizational changes to try to address the underlying causal factors—e.g. forbidding Swiss state officials from simultaneously serving on its governing board, the Assembly.[11] Organizational concern about reputation over time can be an important factor in IGO and even state diplomacy. It certainly often figures in NGO diplomacy, considered next.

36.1.3 NGOs

The ICRC and a few other NGOs such as the Anti-Slavery Society (now named Anti-Slavery International) existed from the 19th century and acted to try to advance human dignity. Some of these private organizations were active in League of Nations debates in the 1930s and 1940s. But it was not until the UN era and especially from the 1960s that one saw the proliferation of what are now called human rights and humanitarian NGOs. Amnesty International got its start in 1961, initially focusing on political prisoners in dictatorial Portugal. Human Rights Watch started as Helsinki Watch in 1978 to monitor state compliance with the 1974 Helsinki Accord—a diplomatic agreement between NATO and Warsaw Pact countries and which included 'basket three' on human rights and humanitarian affairs. These are but two of the more prominent human rights international NGOs active in diplomatic circles in New York, Washington, Geneva, and other diplomatic centres.

While there are thousands of NGOs active in international relations to try to better the condition of individuals, those that link their mandate to internationally recognized human rights are far fewer. And those that have the resources to address many human rights issues in many places are far fewer still. Those international groups that persistently attract the attention of major governments may number only a dozen or so. In addition there are strictly local or community-based organizations, not covered here. In some circles these international human rights NGOs are seen as public-interest lobbies or single-issue pressure groups. The distinction between lobbying on a transnational basis and engaging in diplomacy may be a matter of subjective perception and definition. Be that as it may, the reference to NGO diplomacy for human rights is common or widespread.

It is clear that the more sophisticated human rights NGOs calculate how to maximize their influence. Whatever the details of their representations and whether they seek to get media coverage, meet with governmental officials, mobilize public interest, etc., all of these activities hinge on a foundation of accurate information. Amnesty and Human Rights Watch cannot hope to persuade public officials to make or change public policy if their basic information is found to be incorrect. On occasion Amnesty through one of its branches has taken some public position only to have to renounce it later because of faulty information. If this transpires very often, the reputation of the organization suffers which leads to a loss of credibility and eventually influence.

Amnesty, Human Rights Watch, and other human rights organizations frequently face charges of bias. Governments which are targeted for criticism often dispute the views of these groups and may mobilize their supporters to challenge the veracity of the NGO views. When Amnesty referred to US secret prisons utilized in the 'war on terror' as comprising a 'gulag', there was public controversy about the accuracy of that usage. When Human Rights Watch criticized this or that Israeli policy, there was public controversy about whether it was anti-Israel or even anti-Semitic—despite the fact that the executive director of Human Rights Watch at that time was Jewish. As the ICRC knows well, there is the politics of neutrality and impartiality, meaning there is a calculated struggle to try to maintain the image of and reputation for correct diplomacy based on accurate information presented in the appropriate way. These are political and subjective matters depending on perception, not scientific formula.

For part of its work an organization like Amnesty relies on citizen diplomacy. With regard to its core work to protect what it terms prisoners of conscience or what others sometimes call political prisoners, Amnesty asks its members to write letters to the detaining authority either seeking release or better treatment. For other parts of its work it may utilize traditional diplomacy, with Amnesty officials contacting various public officials to discuss the need for this or that policy or decision. Human Rights Watch, not being a mass membership organization, cannot rely on citizen or membership diplomacy.

There is no doubt that these human rights organizations, singularly or as part of a combined or networked approach, can point to some successes. They helped shape the contents of, and eventually get adopted at the UN, the Convention against Torture and Cruel, Inhumane, and Degrading Treatment. They helped in the creation of the ICC. And so on. In these processes, the NGOs help like-minded states do what they are inclined to do anyway. That means, for example, they may help small developing countries with a small diplomatic corps keep up with events in a large and complicated diplomatic conference. They may help make drafting precise. They do not, in general, have the power to convince antagonistic states to completely change their views.

On the other hand, there is no doubt that they have incurred many disappointments, despite sometimes pooling their efforts. They have called for the closing of the US prison facility at Guantanamo, and the prosecution of those responsible for serious abuse of detainees there and at other US facilities involved in the 'war on terrorism'. They have sought liberalization of the Chinese political system. They have sought decisive action to stop atrocities in places like Sudan, the Democratic Republic of Congo, and against the highly repressive Mugabe regime in Zimbabwe. And so forth.

Given the breadth of their agendas and the long list of various human rights at play in contemporary international relations, no one can possibly calculate precisely the extent of their success or failure. Moreover, the very notion of successful diplomacy is itself a contested concept. It may be considered a success just to get off the ground a reasonable discussion of gay rights in the Islamic world, even if the NGOs are unable to help achieve the passage of progressive legislation on the subject.

There are scholars who believe that the institution or system of NGO human rights diplomacy has made a cumulative difference in international relations and that without the diplomacy of these groups the nature of international relations would be different than what it is. One cannot prove or disprove a counterfactual—viz. what would have happened in the absence of these groups. But it is certainly true that NGO diplomacy for human rights is a feature of the contemporary world. It is also true that public officials often take them seriously—if only to contest NGO views in salient ways, even moving to bar human rights NGOs from a situation. The Kagame government in Rwanda pronounced Alison des Forges of Human Rights Watch *persona non grata* because she demanded balanced attention to Tutsi as well as Hutu violations of human rights. That is perverse tribute to the potential power of human rights NGOs to name and shame and by doing so to embarrass governments who are doing the wrong thing. Whether one can then get those governments to change policy and begin doing the right thing is another question.

36.2 Fundamental Issues and Values

For present purposes, and teasing out some points worth emphasising from section 36.1, one can say that modern diplomacy for human rights may be thought of in two ways, corresponding to political views of desired world order.

36.2.1 Separatist (Pluralist) View

If one believes in the value of the traditional nation-state system of international relations, with strong notions of absolute state sovereignty and a preference for weak IGOs to facilitate exchanges at the margins, then human rights diplomacy will remain largely an afterthought to more important undertakings. In such a system, which existed until 1945 and elements of which certainly remain thereafter, the most important diplomatic initiatives are undertaken to secure the short-term self-interests of states. Above all these interests centre on protecting the physical security of the state from armed attack and advancing economic interests, as pursued by strictly national decisions. Much state diplomacy, even on human rights, is also expended on behalf of petty state advantages, such as placing citizens in offices in IGOs. Concerns about the general welfare and the common good on an international basis are often far down the list of state objectives.[12]

In this view, states may pursue human rights diplomacy when it fits with 'vital' national interests such as traditional security and economics. Thus the United States during the Nixon–Kissinger era came around to supporting the collective human right to self-determination for the people of Zimbabwe, but this was made possible in the leaders' thinking because they were afraid the Soviet Union might expand its influence in southern Africa by exploiting white minority rule as it existed in Southern Rhodesia at the time of the Ian Smith government. Support for majority rule in a new Zimbabwe fit with the US objective of containing Soviet power. At best, states may press for genuine human rights advances in foreign places when they do not have to sacrifice important expedient concerns. Thus Western states can easily criticize human rights violations in Myanmar and even apply sanctions because they do not have important security and economic interests in that small and isolated state.

In this view of world affairs, endorsement of abstract human rights may well occur, but great effort will be made to protect domestic jurisdiction and freedom of national policy-making. Hence human rights treaties will be ratified, but reservations will be added preventing their use in national courts or in other ways carving out great loopholes regarding enforcement. Arab states, for example, accept treaties pertaining to women's equality but then negate that formal commitment through various reservations. The United States does essentially the same on civil and political rights and torture, ratifying the treaties but attaching crippling reservations or using carefully worded implementing legislation so that the object and purpose of the treaty is negated within national jurisdiction. The central objective of such manoeuvres is to associate the state with human rights norms for purposes of public relations, but then ensure freedom of national policy-making at variance with the human rights norms officially accepted. As noted already, the plethora of human rights standards is accompanied by generally weak enforcement measures. This is true especially with regard to UN processes, by comparison to European and inter-American arrangements.

It is well to recall that Bernard Kouchner, former foreign minister in the Sarkozy government in France, despite—or maybe because of—previously being active in human rights and humanitarian circles, said that states could not do (consistent) human rights diplomacy because of national security (and economic) concerns, given the nation-state system of international relations. He regretted advocating a cabinet-level minister for humanitarian affairs. In this view structural realists are correct: given the nation-state system of danger and competition, states are required to use their diplomacy to elevate national security and economic advantage for the national group over the protection of the human rights of foreigners, except perhaps in easy cases.

36.2.2 Solidarist View

In this view, it is the purpose of diplomacy as exercised by state and non-state actors to 'push the envelope' about advancing not just the endorsement but the enforcement of human rights without distinction as to nation, race, gender, or other superficial distinctions. Hence the highest calling for diplomats is to exercise new thinking in order to advance the social solidarity of the planet, finding a progressive balance between traditional state interests and guaranteed human dignity through protection of human rights for all.

It is well to note that since the Second World War states have utilized their diplomacy to create such arrangements as significant regional mechanisms for human rights in Europe and the Americas; a standing international criminal court; various more limited special criminal courts; an authoritative UN Security Council with the right to take binding decisions when human rights violations threaten international peace and security; and so forth. Once created in a political process involving the diplomacy or lobbying of various non-state actors such as human rights NGO and IGO personnel, these arrangements then often feature prosecutors and judges acting as independent persons rather than as state representatives taking instructions from national capitals. The result of this diplomacy has been an uneven, fragile, and still evolving advance in the international protection of internationally recognized human rights. The historical trend is clearly towards the diminution of absolute and broad state sovereignty—especially when governments utilize their position to discriminate, persecute, and murder.

At the United Nations in 2005, states endorsed the notion of R2P, the responsibility to protect. This is sometimes seen as a reformulated and expanded version of the notion of humanitarian intervention. When 'sovereign' states prove unwilling or unable to eliminate atrocities in their national jurisdiction (specifically genocide, crimes against humanity, war crimes, and ethnic cleansing), the international community has the right and duty to intervene to correct the situation. The acceptance of this general norm is noteworthy. At the same time we should recall the difference between abstract endorsement and implementation, as well as the fact that abstract agreement can obscure disagreement on various specifics—such as precisely when is outside intervention justified, who is authorized to execute the intervention, and what form the intervention should take.

36.3 Conclusion

Just as international relations has changed significantly since 1945, so has diplomacy and the diplomat's trade. The system is no longer fully characterized by simply separatist sovereignty. The system is characterized by pockets of pooled sovereignty leading to some supra-national or quasi-supranational institutions. This is certainly true in the domain of human rights. Consequently states diplomats, who actually helped bring about this situation, share the field of diplomacy with various non-state actors, and the objective of some diplomats is not just the advancement of parochial interests and protection of independence of national policy-making. Rather, for some diplomats the name of the game is the transformation of the international political system, in whole or in part, to various aspects of global governance in pursuit of better protection of human rights. Any overview of contemporary diplomacy must acknowledge this tension between separatist and solidarist views. The constantly changing synthesis from this dialectic is not just interesting, but crucial to the future of the planet. After all, diplomacy is a process of communication. But *what* is communicated, meaning the values that guide it, is of utmost importance.

Notes

1. The major exception to this generalization is found in the interwar treaties on minority rights, under which certain states defeated in the First World War were obligated to respect minority rights and were supervised by a League body. Under this special treaty regime individuals had the right of petition about alleged mistreatment. By comparison, under treaties on slavery and the slave trade, states owed duties to other states, but individuals got no rights of action themselves.

2. In 1899 and 1907 the Hague Diplomatic Conferences also produced norms on IHL, also called the law of war. These legal provisions pertaining to prisoners of war, etc., were folded into the Geneva Conventions and Protocols through the actions of states at the Geneva Diplomatic Conference of the 1970s.

3. Ellen A. Cutrone and Benjamin O. Fordham, 'Commerce and Imagination: The Sources of Concern about International Human Rights in the US Congress', *International Studies Quarterly* 54:3 (September 2010), 633–56.

4. See, among other sources, Kathryn Sinkkink, *Mixed Signals: U.S. Human Rights Policy and Latin America* (Ithaca: Cornell University Press, 2004).

5. See further Alison Brysk, *Global Good Samaritans: Human Rights as Foreign Policy* (Oxford: Oxford University Press, 2009).

6. When the development of IGOs began to expand circa 1919, the ILO was headed by the activist Albert Thomas whereas the League of Nations was first headed by the rather passive Sir Eric Drummond.

7. See further Kent Kille (ed.), *The UN Secretary-General and Moral Authority: Ethics & Religion in International Leadership* (Washington: Georgetown University Press, 2007).

8. I do not cover here the processing of private complaints alleging violation of the Covenant, allowed by states accepting the first optional protocol to the treaty.

9. 'Situation of detainees at Guantanamo Bay', E/CN.4/2006/120, Commission on Human Rights, 15 February 2006.

10. See Joel E. Oestreich, *Power and Principle: Human Rights Programming in International Organizations* (Washington: Georgetown University Press, 2007).

11. David P. Forsythe, *The Humanitarians: The International Committee of the Red Cross* (Cambridge: Cambridge University Press, 2005). The Nazis had contingency plans for the invasion of Switzerland. Swiss leaders in Bern did not want to antagonize Berlin. Thus they engaged in such cooperative measures as helping Berlin turn looted resources into hard currency via Swiss banks and turning back German Jewish refugees at the Swiss border. Some Swiss state leaders also sat on the all-Swiss governing board of the ICRC in Geneva. From that position the Swiss state officials and their supporters sought to make sure that ICRC decisions and actions did not antagonize Berlin. The crux of the matter came to a head in the fall of 1942, when the ICRC Assembly debated making a public protest about

various human rights violations including Nazi treatment of German Jews. The Assembly declined to make that public protest. The post-war apology stressed the matter of inadequate discreet diplomacy, not the issue of public diplomacy.

12. See Carne Ross, *Independent Diplomat: Dispatches from an Unaccountable Elite* (Ithaca: Cornell University Press, 2007). Ross was a British diplomat who became disgusted with widespread state diplomacy at the United Nations. See also John Stoessinger, *The United Nations and the Superpowers* (New York: Random House, 1977) who argues that states at the UN take a short-term, self-interested approach to conflict management and are not much interested in general principles of peace, justice, and order.

CHAPTER 37

REFUGEE DIPLOMACY

WILLIAM MALEY

REFUGEES are a major focus of contemporary diplomatic activity. Whether in bilateral engagements between states,[1] at regional forums, or in the course of the annual meeting in Geneva of the Executive Committee of the Office of the United Nations High Commissioner for Refugees, the issues of how refugees are to be treated, how refugee flows are to be managed, and—increasingly—how refugee movements are to be prevented or deterred, figure prominently on international agendas. Refugee diplomacy is striking for two particular reasons. First, time and again, the fear of refugees has surfaced as a domestic political issue, especially in developed countries that see 'border control' as central to the maintenance of sovereignty. Refugee diplomacy sits squarely in the space where domestic and international political challenges meet. Second, the lead role in refugee diplomacy is often, perhaps usually, taken not by career diplomats from foreign ministries, but by politicians and by officials of ministries concerned with border control, immigration, and even internal order. The appearance of such officials rapidly breaks down any notion of a diplomatic 'club' dominating this sphere of diplomacy, although like-minded officials reflecting a shared 'culture of control' sometimes come close to creating a club of their own.

37.1 THE MEANING OF 'REFUGEE'

The word 'refugee' has a number of connotations and these varying connotations to some degree have demarcated different forms of diplomatic engagement. For sixty years, there has been a widely accepted *legal* definition of 'refugee', embodied in Article 1A(2) of the 1951 Convention Relating to the Status of Refugees, which broadly speaking defines a refugee as a person who 'owing to well-founded fear of being persecuted for reasons of race, religion, nationality, membership of a particular social group or political opinion, is outside the country of his nationality and is unable or, owing to such fear, is unwilling to avail himself of the protection of that country'. This can be augmented by regional agreements. For example, Article 1.2 of the 1969 Organization of African Unity (OAU) Convention on the Specific Aspects of Refugee Problems in Africa provides that the term 'refugee' shall 'also apply to every person who, owing to external aggression, occupation, foreign domination or events seriously disturbing public order in either part or the whole of his country of origin or nationality, is compelled to leave his place of habitual residence in order to seek refuge in another place outside his country of origin or nationality'.[2] Similarly, section III.3 of the 1984 Cartagena Declaration on Refugees includes 'persons who have fled their country because their lives, safety or freedom have been threatened by generalized violence, foreign aggression, internal conflicts, massive violation of human rights or other circumstances which have seriously disturbed public order'.

Alongside such legal conceptions are *sociological* conceptions of what it is to be a refugee. Of these, perhaps the most widely cited is that of Andrew Shacknove, for whom a refugee is a person 'whose government fails to protect his basic needs, who has no remaining recourse than to seek international restitution of those needs, and who is so situated that international assistance is possible'.[3] In reaching this conclusion, Shacknove takes as his point of departure the discrepancy between the definitions of the 1951 Convention and the OAU Convention, finding the latter more sensitive to the diverse ways in which the 'normal bond between the citizen and the state can be severed'.[4] A further definition which goes beyond that in the 1951 Convention is offered by Zolberg, Suhrke, and Aguayo: refugees are 'persons whose presence abroad is attributable to a well-founded fear of violence, as might be established by impartial experts with adequate information'.[5]

These sociological definitions of 'refugee' are useful in putting refugee diplomacy in context, for two reasons. First, they arguably come closer to 'ordinary language' understandings of what the word means than can a legal 'term of art'.[6] Second, and more importantly, they better describe many of the millions of indigent, vulnerable people, outside their countries of nationality, who turn to other states and to international organizations[7] for protection and assistance. They may not fear individualized persecution, but life in their home country may truly be 'solitary, poor, nasty, brutish and short'.

This highlights a future challenge that diplomats are likely to have to confront, namely what Alexander Betts has called 'survival migration', a label that refers to 'persons who are outside their country of origin because of an existential threat for which they have no access to a domestic remedy or resolution', typically as a result of 'a combination of environmental disaster, livelihood failure, and state fragility'.[8] While it is still the case that roughly 97 per cent of the world's population is made up of people living within rather than outside their country of nationality,[9] those who face the kinds of problems that Betts highlights are unlikely to be perpetually cowed by the notion that destitution is their natural state and that for the sake of the Westphalian global order, they should sit back and accept the lot in life that the birthright lottery has handed them.

This brings us to a third approach to making sense of the refugee condition, one that can be called *systemic* or *structural*. This flows from the emergence of a global system of demarcated territorial states. Political leaders are understandably inclined to treat 'sovereign states' as part of the natural order of things, but of course they are not. Outlining what he calls an 'assigned responsibility model', philosopher Robert E. Goodin has argued that 'it is the boundaries around people, not the boundaries around territories, that really matter morally. Territorial boundaries are merely useful devices for "matching" one person to one protector. Citizenship is merely a device for fixing special responsibility in some agent for discharging our general duties vis-à-vis each particular person.'[10] But a further consequence flows as well. Emma Haddad reminds us of the need to 'take into account the very structure of the international system within which states act', adding that with its 'insistence on separate territorial states with clearly defined borders and populations, this structure is in large part responsible for the creation of refugees'.[11]

Refugees are the detritus left by a system in which the assignment of responsibility has broken down. One might therefore argue that, to the extent that existing states benefit from the Westphalian order, they owe parallel duties of protection towards those whom the system has failed. Where such egregious examples of failure as genocide are concerned, there indeed has been some notable progress, especially surrounding the idea of a responsibility to protect. However, as we shall see, the robust discharge of protective responsibilities towards refugees has often proved unpalatable for states, and much 'refugee diplomacy' has been concerned with (discreetly) evading responsibility to refugees.

37.2 The Emergence of Refugee Diplomacy

Until the late 19th century, border controls were weak and travel without a passport was relatively easy, but since the number of exiles was small, there was no real question of a need for concerted action by states to address a 'refugee problem'. Two developments in the aftermath of the First World War led to the emergence of what we now see as the challenge of refugees. One was the massive population displacements associated with the Bolshevik revolution of 1917 and the civil war in Russia from 1918 to 1921. The other was the establishment of the League of Nations in 1920. The former created a humanitarian crisis to challenge the conscience of humanity. The latter for the first time provided a multilateral framework within which concerted responses could potentially be crafted. It was the confluence of these two developments that opened the door for modern refugee diplomacy, directed not only at the alleviation of suffering, but at crafting mechanisms within which suffering could be alleviated and the burdens of such alleviation shared between different actors.[12]

The refugee crisis in Russia created new stresses for a Europe that had only just emerged from the most disastrous war that the world had ever seen. Between 1.5 and 2 million Russian refugees made their way to Central and Western Europe, the bulk of them educated professionals.[13] Their position was wretched in the extreme. As Hannah

Arendt put it, 'Once they had left their homeland they remained homeless, once they had left their state they became stateless; once they had been deprived of their human rights they were rightless, the scum of the earth.'[14] It was in the face of this crisis that the League of Nations stepped in, and the approach that it took in some ways provided a template for subsequent activity in this area. It sought the services of a distinguished *individual*—in this case the Norwegian polar explorer Fridtjof Nansen—to serve as its 'High Commissioner' for Russian Refugees in Europe. Dr Nansen's greatest achievement was to develop the so-called 'Nansen passport', the predecessor of the contemporary *titre de voyage*, as a travel document for refugees, and even more remarkably, to persuade a large number of states to recognize it. He was helped, however, by the finite nature of the problem he had been asked to address. From the end of the civil war, the Bolsheviks moved successfully to block emigration from Russia, using mechanisms of coercive border control that later were to prove very effective in sealing off the Soviet Union and then the Eastern Bloc, culminating in the building of the Berlin Wall.[15] This staunched the westward flow of Russian refugees, and left Nansen with the task of assisting those refugees who had already escaped, something he did with great skill. He needed all the skill he could muster, for he had no core relief budget and depended on donations to sustain his programmes. A great deal of his diplomatic activity was thus concerned with fundraising, although his unique standing—he was described by a keen observer as one of the League's 'mightiest personalities'[16]—assisted him in his efforts.

Following Nansen's death in 1930, the weaknesses of the League's approach became apparent. The dominant role played by Nansen as an individual meant that the institutional structures he left behind were relatively underdeveloped. This became all too clear as the major powers found themselves confronted from 1933 by the problem of outflows of Jews from Nazi Germany. Although they were notoriously labelled *Wirtschaftsemigranten* (economic migrants) by Berlin, they fell squarely within the category of 'anticipatory refugees',[17] those who foresee the onset of persecution and manage to leave before the axe falls. An energetic American, James G. McDonald, was appointed as High Commissioner for Refugees Coming from Germany, and served from October 1933 until he resigned in December 1935. Swiftly he came to the conclusion that the problem was one that required a political response, and that 'quiet diplomacy' would not work. This was reflected in his resignation letter where he wrote that when 'domestic politics threaten the demoralization and exile of hundreds of thousands of human beings, considerations of diplomatic correctness must yield to those of common humanity'.[18] Unfortunately, his letter had virtually no impact on the position of the League or its key members, and as the pre-eminent historian of refugee policy in this period put it, 'McDonald has the distinction of being the only refugee administrator in the Inter-war Period to publicly criticize the German government for its treatment of Jews and other "non-Aryans", and to call for international intervention to deal with the root causes of the refugee exodus.'[19]

Faced with the League's inertia, other forms of diplomacy were attempted. In March 1938, President Franklin D. Roosevelt invited a large number of states to send delegations to a conference to address the plight of Jewish refugees from Germany. The conference took place in Evian in France in July 1938 and established a new Intergovernmental Committee on Refugees which the United States was committed to support. But that said, concrete commitments to accept those fleeing Nazism were few and far between and the Australian representative, T. W. White, notoriously remarked that 'as we have no racial problem, we are not desirous of importing one'.[20] Even the US administration saw its scope for action as severely limited, something that became apparent in 1939 with the so-called 'Voyage of the Damned'. The *MS St Louis* sailed from Hamburg for Havana in May of that year with over 900 Jewish refugees on board. Despite the efforts of Captain Gustav Schröder to secure their safe disembarkation, the vast majority were refused entry to Cuba and the US made no provision for their admission either, since its strict system of immigration quotas had no place for them. The *St Louis* ultimately returned to Europe, where the passengers were distributed between United Kingdom, the Netherlands, Belgium, and France. More than a third of those who went to the latter three countries subsequently perished in the Holocaust.[21]

37.3 Institutional and Legal Frameworks for Refugee Diplomacy

The coming of the Second World War saw policy towards refugees subsumed for a while in wider questions of post-war reconstruction in which the position of displaced persons was but one of a range of issues of concern. In November 1943 the United Nations Relief and Rehabilitation Administration was established to provide relief services, but the United States saw it as unduly sympathetic to Soviet concerns and Washington pressed for the establishment of a new body to deal with European refugees. On 1 July 1947, the Preparatory Commission of a new International Refugee Organization took over the responsibilities of both the Intergovernmental Committee on Refugees and United Nations Relief and Rehabilitation Administration. The International Refugee Organization came into existence on 20 August 1948 and continued until 1 March 1952. It was largely a resettlement organization, and between 1 July 1947 and 31 December 1951, it resettled 1,038,750 refugees, of whom 328,851 went to the US, 182,159 to Australia, and 132,109 to Israel.[22] The International Refugee Organization was a specialized agency of the United Nations, but it was always seen as temporary in character, charged (like Nansen in the 1920s) with dealing with a problem that was finite. This was one reason why it did not assume responsibility for Palestinian refugees after the 1948 war in the Middle East; instead, the United Nations General Assembly through Resolution 302 (IV) of 8 December 1949 established the United Nations Relief and Works Agency for Palestine Refugees in the Near East as a subsidiary organ of the General Assembly to provide such support.[23]

The successor to the International Refugee Organization was the Office of the United Nations High Commissioner for Refugees (UNHCR). It was established on 14 December

1950 by Resolution 428 (V) of the General Assembly, to which the 'Statute of the Office of the United Nations High Commissioner for Refugees' was annexed. The Statute provided for the High Commissioner to be elected by the General Assembly on the nomination of the UN Secretary-General, and while it initially provided only for operations until the end of 1953, it now has a continuing mandate and is a very well-established fixture on the international landscape. The key provision in the Statute is Article 8, which defines a clear set of diplomatic roles for the High Commissioner, including promoting 'the conclusion and ratification of international conventions for the protection of refugees', promoting 'the admission of refugees, not excluding those in the most destitute categories, to the territories of States', and keeping 'in close touch with the Governments and inter-governmental organizations concerned'.

The establishment of UNHCR was complemented by the convening of a diplomatic conference in Geneva in July 1951 that adopted the Convention Relating to the Status of Refugees, which finally entered into force on 22 April 1954. Initially confined to those who became refugees as a result of events occurring before 1 January 1951, it was given a general and unconstrained ambit as to both time and place by the 1967 Protocol Relating to the Status of Refugees. The Convention set out a detailed list of refugee rights,[24] most importantly that of non-refoulement in Article 33.1— 'No contracting State shall expel or return ('refouler') a refugee in any manner whatsoever to the frontiers of territories where his life or freedom would be threatened on account of his race, religion, nationality, membership of a particular social group or political opinion.' Some have viewed the post-war refugee regime, embodied in UNHCR and the 1951 Convention, as an instrument of cold war politics, but a recent study undermines this claim, highlighting the diverse aspirations that the different states involved in its creation entertained when they were negotiating its particulars.[25]

Ever since its establishment, UNHCR has been the focus of a great deal of diplomatic activity, much of it highly politicized. This is in part because of the High Commissioner's role as a norm entrepreneur. As UNHCR's most eminent historian has noted,

> Most High Commissioners have realized that in order to have had any impact on the world political arena they had to use the power of their expertise, ideas, strategies and legitimacy to alter the information and value contexts in which states make policy...For most of its history, the office has acted as a 'teacher' of refugee norms. The majority of the UNHCR's tactics have mainly involved persuasion and socialization in order to hold states accountable to their previously stated policies or principles.[26]

But of course, states too are actively involved in shaping UNHCR's behaviour, with some states using diverse diplomatic tools to shield themselves from pressure from the High Commissioner. One venue for vigorous diplomatic engagement is the annual meeting, held around October each year in Geneva, of the UNHCR Executive Committee. Established by the UN General Assembly in November 1957, the Executive Committee brings together more than seventy states and it annually adopts 'Conclusions' on a wide range of issues, which are not formally binding but are widely viewed as a form of 'soft law'. Executive Committee meetings are often preceded by discussions among officials of like-minded member states, directed at knotting out points of agreement. They are also typically accompanied by vigorous lobbying by advocacy groups and other NGOs that recognize the opportunity for shaping international agendas that such meetings offer.

But beyond formal occasions of this kind are ongoing conversations conducted between government representatives and UNHCR officials in bilateral discussion. It is here that the toughest forms of leverage can be applied. Like Nansen in the 1920s, UNHCR is substantially dependent on voluntary contributions to support its activities,[27] and even a veiled threat by a state to withhold or withdraw support can be unsettling. This problem has become even more pressing in the light of UNHCR's role not just in offering protection to refugees narrowly defined, but in providing costly assistance to vast populations displaced by war or civil strife,[28] something that came to a head when UNHCR was given the 'lead agency' role in delivering assistance during the Bosnian conflict.[29] The High Commissioner all too often must walk through political minefields. It is not surprising that some have proved notably better than others at doing so.

Finally, it is important to note that persistent pressures can lead to shifts in organizational culture, to the point where the application of diplomatic pressure is no longer necessary because the organization in point has substantially ceased to resist. Critics of UNHCR have pointed to a drift away from emphasis on protection—which can see UNHCR at odds with some of its key donors—in favour of either emergency assistance, or 'voluntary' repatriation of refugees.[30] It would be simplistic to attribute this to diplomatic pressures alone, since a range of other factors can also shape organizational culture,[31] but it does highlight the importance of recognizing that UNHCR is an inescapably political body, rather than a neutral, technical body guided only by its Statute.

37.4 REFUGEES AS OBJECTS OF INTERNATIONAL AND DOMESTIC POLITICS

A distinctive factor that complicates almost all refugee diplomacy is that refugee movements are frequently matters of controversy in the domestic politics of states. When vast numbers of refugees are on the move—typically from one poor country to another—there may be serious security problems for the receiving state, not just in terms of the maintenance of law and order, but also because of the possibility that people movements may upset delicate ethnic balances and inflame dormant local tensions.[32] At the extreme, states may even seek to generate refugee flows as a way of destabilizing other states.[33] Poor countries, of course, may have very limited capacity to withstand large flows, even if domestic opinion is not especially sympathetic to the new arrivals. Where wealthy developed countries are concerned, the story is rather different. They typically *do* have some capacity to control movement of refugees onto their territory—through visa systems that deny visas to those who are likely to seek asylum, through measures to make life difficult for those who make successful asylum claims, and even through the use of the coercive instrumentalities of the state to prevent physical access to a state's territory.[34] Such measures have contributed directly to the emergence of people-smuggling.

As well as moving to close borders, wealthy countries have increasingly moved to *reframe* the refugee issue: refugees who act on their own, rather than wait for bureaucracies to rescue them, can be depicted as deviant or even criminal.[35] The disposition to close the door to refugees has ballooned in the last two decades and while there is evidence that political leaders have been responding to some extent to demands from mass electorates to keep refugees out, it is also the case that politicians on occasion have deliberately sought to stoke up anti-refugee sentiments as a way of mobilizing political support.[36] This has then been reflected in the diplomatic stances taken by states on refugee issues. A dramatic manifestation of this was the so-called *Tampa* affair in Australia in August 2001, and the election shortly afterwards in which the prime minister proclaimed that 'We will decide who comes to this country and the circumstances in which they come.'[37] One observer bluntly described this as 'race wrapped in the flag',[38] and the 11 September 2001 attacks certainly facilitated the 'securitization' of the refugee issue.[39]

However, there was more to the *Tampa* affair than just a quest for votes and another factor underlying the Australian approach has some broader implications for refugee diplomacy. It is that Australia was and is profoundly hostile to the idea of its becoming a country of *first* asylum, a characteristic which it has shared with other countries with long experience of refugee resettlement. It would prefer to remain a country of resettlement alone, despite its Convention obligations. This gives rise to a serious diplomatic challenge. As a party to the 1951 Convention, Australia has a range of responsibilities towards refugees that are underpinned by the principle of *pacta sunt servanda*, and by the broader norms of reciprocity that allow international law to function as a source of some order. By contrast, its resettlement of refugees through a programme of offshore selection is not a product of any international obligation, but purely of the decision of successive Australian governments to run such a programme. To use the existence of such a programme as a basis for evading responsibilities as a country of first asylum is unlikely to go down well with other states. There are two reasons why this is the case. First, many poor countries experience influxes vastly greater in number than the 13,750 for whom Australia nominally provides annual resettlement places. Second, Australia awards resettlement places not simply on the basis of need. For more than half of the designated places, it is necessary that an applicant have a sponsor in Australia. Applicants can also be rejected on the grounds of ill health. Countries of resettlement can easily be overwhelmed by a sense of their own generosity; to other countries, such 'generosity' can look suspiciously like a cherry-picking exercise in which rich countries resettle the educated and healthy, leaving poor countries to look after the unskilled, the disabled, and the non-literate. To dispel this impression is no easy task, but it is one which the diplomats of developed countries are increasingly charged with performing. This brings us to the vexed question of burden-sharing.

37.5 CHALLENGES FOR REFUGEE DIPLOMACY: BURDEN-SHARING

The greatest challenge for refugee diplomacy is to find ways of distributing the burden of assisting refugees fairly amongst the states that commit to do so. No one could reasonably claim that the current distribution of responsibilities is defensible. A poor country such as Pakistan, which is not even a party to the 1951 Convention, has hosted refugees *in the millions* for more than three decades, while a number of rich countries which are party to the Convention have manifested widespread panic in the face of boat arrivals in numbers that are totally insignificant when compared to the burden that Pakistan has patiently carried. Diplomacy offers some opportunities to advance the cause of burden-sharing, if not to break what seems a particularly vicious circle. Suhrke has remarked that since 'most states at one time and at one level or another must deal with refugees, they have an overriding interest in developing common responses', but adds that 'the incentive to share costs and responsibility is inherently weak'.[40] The risk is that well-off states will make nominal commitments at low levels, doing just enough to satisfy the demand that they do *something*, but not enough to strike at the core of the problem.

What often becomes a trigger for action is the emergence of protracted refugee situations,[41] or what some have called the 'warehousing' of refugees. At a certain point, these can become a source of international embarrassment, creating opportunities for UNHCR to press states to play a role in providing a durable solution through resettlement. As High Commissioner from 1956 to 1960, Auguste Lindt made a concerted effort to bring about the closure of the camps in Europe in which many thousands of displaced persons from the Second World War continued to live. One might offer the same argument in explanation of the recent move to resettle Bhutanese refugees from Nepal, but in this case, the refugees may also have benefited from some darker considerations. As one analyst put it, 'there was a need to find refugee populations that would allow Western countries to fill their resettlement quotas without turning to those populations viewed as potentially dangerous—that is, the Middle East refugees'.[42] The application of moral suasion may also be more effective when the number of refugees in a warehoused population is not large.

A rare case of a collective approach where the numbers *were* large came in the form of the burden-sharing programme for refugees from Vietnam that was adopted in Geneva in 1979.[43] What is of interest from a diplomatic point of view is what factors led to the adoption of the 1979 approach in the first place. Here, Suhrke argues that the scheme was essentially hegemonic: 'One major actor, the United States, was moved by humanitarian and political reasons to put pressure on other states, set the rules for collective action, and took its own "fair share"'.[44] However, even the strength of initial US commitment did not prove sufficient to sustain the approach and it was succeeded in 1989 by the so-called Comprehensive Plan of Action, premised on the need to return to Vietnam those who were not found to be refugees in a process of individual status determination. What led the 1979 approach to unravel was that it offered a rare example of a situation where 'pull factors' genuinely came into play: 'the generous assistance and preferential treatment for Indo-Chinese refugees had a magnet effect, attracting large numbers of people out of the embattled and impoverished countries of Indo-China'.[45] Given the risks of boat travel, not least because of piracy in the South China Sea, this was a matter of real concern. If there is a lesson from this case, it is that refugee diplomacy backed by a powerful hegemon may lead to agreement, but not necessarily to durable solutions to complex problems.

In the light of these experiences, one might well ask whether there is much scope at all for diplomacy to play a creative role in generating cooperation to solve refugee problems. The divergent interests of states might seem to foster talk rather than effective action. Here, recent work by Betts is instructive. On the one hand, his point of departure is more pessimistic than Suhrke's. He sees the asymmetries of power between states in the North and South as leaving the latter in a position 'in which they have few options other than either to take "what is on offer" in terms of limited earmarked contributions of the North or to disengage from negotiations entirely'.[46] What they can do, however, is seek to change the terms of the game, specifically by substantive issue-linkages (sometimes called 'trading across issues'). Betts concludes that where 'Northern states have had linked issues in other issue-areas—notably in migration, security and trade—they have sometimes been prepared to voluntarily contribute to refugee protection in the South'. In these cases, UNHCR has played an important facilitating role, and the mechanisms through which it 'has been able to use cross-issue persuasion to influence states have included institutional design, information provision, playing an epistemic role, and argumentation'.[47]

It is also important to note that in a bilateral context, a simple North–South dichotomization can break down. This was the case with the Tampa affair in 2001, where for domestic political reasons it was desperately important for the Australian government to secure the support of some other state to accept the Tampa refugees, who Prime Minister John Howard had declared would not be allowed to set foot on Australian soil. Since it was quite clear that no developed country that was party to the 1951 Convention would accept more than a token number, the search began for a country in the South that would agree to do so, and Nauru, a vulnerable, failed island-state in the Pacific, became the focus of Australian diplomatic activity. 'The vulnerable and small societies of the Pacific', Fry has argued, 'did not just *happen* to be approached by Australia; they were approached *because* they were vulnerable and dependent upon Australia'.[48] Yet the result was that Australian resources and policies became hostage to the wishes of Nauru, which was able to extract a considerable price for its cooperation. Australia paid over US$1 million towards outstanding hospital accounts for treatment in Australia of Nauruan citizens, a payment that amounted to little more than a bribe to the Nauruan elite whose members were relieved of the burden of private debts. Even more embarrassingly, Australia reportedly lobbied (unsuccessfully) for the lifting of 'countermeasures' against Nauru arising from its being included on the List of Non-Cooperative Countries and Territories maintained by the Organization for Economic Cooperation and Development's Financial Action Task Force on Money Laundering.[49] Here was a case of issue linkage being undertaken by the (ostensibly) stronger state. Cases such as this may be the exception rather than the rule, but they point to the importance of identifying the specific political contexts within which diplomatic bargaining occurs.

37.6 FUTURE CHALLENGES FOR REFUGEE DIPLOMACY

As one looks ahead, there are a number of significant matters that are likely to play a continuing and dominant role in shaping refugee diplomacy. One relates to the substance of protection. While 'protection' is not a precisely defined term, there is much to be said for Helton's view that 'When we speak of "protection", we mean *legal* protection.'[50] Yet in recent times, neither UNHCR nor states have shown a determined interest in promoting or enhancing protection of this kind. As noted earlier, UNHCR has been increasingly drawn into providing mass relief to large displaced populations. For states, the enhancement of refugees' legal rights can easily seem a barrier to the convenient exercise of executive discretion. One consequence has been a heightened role for advocacy groups in lobbying for more attention for protection.[51] Another has been involvement of members of the legal profession, frequently acting *pro bono*, in attempting to use the courts to challenge the decisions of the executive. The efforts of these groups have on occasion met with some success, and it is more than likely that we will see more rather than less of such activity in the future. A striking example came in August 2011, with the unravelling of an attempt by the Australian government to remove asylum seekers to Malaysia, a country which was not a party to the 1951 Convention. On 25 July 2011, the Australian and Malaysian governments had signed a Memorandum of Understanding in which, in exchange for Australia's resettling 4,000 refugees over a four-year period from Malaysia, the latter agreed to accept up to 800 asylum seekers irregularly arriving in Australia by sea—the objective of the exercise being to deter such movements in the first place. The collapse of the initiative came about when lawyers acting *pro bono* for an asylum claimant secured a ruling from the High Court of Australia that the Minister for Immigration and Citizenship lacked the statutory power to remove such a claimant to Malaysia, or indeed to any country which was not a party to the 1951 Convention.[52] In a society in which the rule of law prevails, the executive government does not necessarily have a free hand to give effect to commitments that it makes diplomatically.

At the extreme, governments frustrated by judicial organs might seek to denounce the provisions of the 1951 Convention altogether. This is something which states can do unilaterally, but an avalanche of criticism would likely descend on the state that took the first move, and the argument could well be mounted that in any case, the non-refoulement obligation is now part of customary international law. A greater danger would be an attempt to rewrite or reinterpret key provisions of the 1951 Convention, but is unlikely that the 1951 Convention could easily be amended in ways that would adulterate the responsibilities of these Western states, since under Article 45.2, it is for the UN General Assembly to 'recommend the steps, if any, to be taken' if a party to the Convention requests its revision and the weight of the global South in the General Assembly remains significant. However, that is not to say that states might not launch a diplomatic campaign to revise the Convention, even if only for reasons of domestic consumption.

37.7 Refugee Diplomacy and the Evolution of Diplomacy

The distinction between 'club' and 'network' diplomacy, discussed in the editors' introduction to this *Handbook*, is an extremely useful one in illuminating trends in modern diplomatic practice.[53] In many spheres of activity, the 'club' model is severely outdated. Network diplomacy has a great deal to offer those leaders who wish to pursue positive agendas of change, especially in areas where positive-sum rather than zero-sum outcomes are in prospect. Examples such as Canada's entrepreneurial promotion of the 1997 Ottawa Convention demonstrate that network diplomacy is no mere aspirational utopia: it has the potential to deliver concrete outcomes that can make a real difference to the lives of ordinary people. But that said, in the specific area of international refugee policy, there has been much less progress down this path than in some other issue areas. NGOs abound and are from time to time consulted by agencies of the state, but the relationship is hardly one of partnership. For if forced to choose between the wisdom of an expert NGO or the prejudice of the median voter, political leaders are still more likely to opt for the latter.

To the extent, however, that a 'club' model continues to prevail, it is not necessarily a club of professional *diplomats*, united by a shared professional culture and responsibilities defined at least in part by the 1961 Vienna Convention on Diplomatic Relations. Rather, it is a club largely made up on the one hand of professional politicians and on the other hand of officials from agencies other than a country's foreign ministry. There is nothing particularly novel about this. At the Evian Conference, for example, the British delegation was headed not by the Foreign Secretary, Viscount Halifax, but by the Chancellor of the Duchy of Lancaster, Lord Winterton; just as the Australian delegation was headed not by the minister for external affairs, but by the minister for trade and customs. This has implications for trading across issue areas. Where ministers take the lead, then trading across issue areas may be facilitated: the principal Australian negotiator with Nauru in 2001 was the minister for defence, who had great latitude to meet whatever demands the Nauruans presented. However, where the lead is taken by officials from immigration or border-control bureaucracies, then the scope for trading across issue areas may be severely limited. Such officials may lack the breadth of experience to recognize opportunities to trade, or may lack the authority to pursue trade expeditiously.

That said, the shifting sands of refugee policy mean that the foundations for this 'club' are not stable. As issues are reframed, the identity of state officials who have claims to involvement in addressing them will likely change as well. For example, on 27–28 February 2002, a high-level meeting was held in Bali, Indonesia, to address the issue of people-smuggling. This contributed to the framing of the issue as one of finding means for combating a form of transnational organized crime, rather than as one of enhancing protection for refugees. A consequence, however, was to draw into the process represent-atives of state law enforcement agencies. This then gave a distinct focus to what came to be called the 'Bali Process' and ongoing cooperation between the participants was shaped by this focus. The lesson is that when one moves away from a 'club' made up of career dip-lomats, the clubs that emerge in place are not necessarily of the same character.

37.8 Conclusion

Refugee diplomacy has its own distinctive features. It falls well short of amounting to a manifestation of 'global governance' at work: as Benz and Hasenclever put it, 'States are the gatekeepers and decisive actors within this policy field.'[54] Apart from the annual meeting of the UNHCR Executive Committee, refugee diplomacy largely lacks a struc-tured framework. It is often some perceived regional crisis that brings states together for high-level ad hoc discussions, as one saw in Geneva in 1979, and securing agreement is no easy task, unless there is an energetic hegemon pressing for a particular outcome. It is also complicated by the potentially high salience of issues related to refugee movements in the domestic politics of states, as well as by the cultures of control that often pervade the immigration bureaucracies that have frequently sidelined foreign ministries as key actors in this area. What one can say with confidence, however, is that the need to inter-act diplomatically around the issue is likely to endure. As long as there are repressive or failed states in which ordinary people are exposed to persecution, and indeed, as long as states remain the principal structures for the organization of interests in international society, the phenomenon of the refugee will be with us.

Notes

1. For more on bilateral diplomacy, see Chapter 12, this volume.
2. For detailed discussion of legal definitions, see James C. Hathaway, *The Law of Refugee Status* (Toronto: Butterworths, 1991), 1–27; and Guy S. Goodwin-Gill and Jane McAdam, *The Refugee in International Law* (Oxford: Oxford University Press, 2007), 15–50.
3. Andrew E. Shacknove, 'Who Is a Refugee?', *Ethics* 95:2 (January 1985), 274–84 at 282.
4. Shacknove, 'Who is a Refugee?', 276.
5. Aristide R. Zolberg, Astri Suhrke, and Sergio Aguayo, *Escape from Violence: Conflict and the Refugee Crisis in the Developing World* (New York: Oxford University Press, 1989), 33.
6. Goodwin-Gill and McAdam, *The Refugee in International Law*, 15.

7. See Chapter 7 in this volume for more on how international organizations are involved in diplomatic processes.

8. Alexander Betts, 'Survival Migration: A New Protection Framework', *Global Governance* 16:3 (July–September 2010), 361–82 at 365.

9. Khalid Koser, *International Migration: A Very Short Introduction* (Oxford: Oxford University Press, 2007), 4.

10. Robert E. Goodin, 'What Is So Special about Our Fellow Countrymen?', *Ethics* 98:4 (July 1988), 663–86 at 686.

11. Emma Haddad, *The Refugee in International Society: Between Sovereigns* (Cambridge: Cambridge University Press, 2008), 34.

12. For background, see Gil Loescher, *Beyond Charity: International Cooperation and the Global Refugee Crisis* (New York: Oxford University Press, 1993), 32–40.

13. See Richard Pipes, *Russia under the Bolshevik Regime* (New York: Alfred A. Knopf, 1993), 139.

14. Hannah Arendt, *The Origins of Totalitarianism* (New York: Harcourt Brace Jovanovich, 1973), 267.

15. See Andrea Chandler, *Institutions of Isolation: Border Controls in the Soviet Union and its Successor States 1917–1993* (Montreal and Kingston: McGill-Queen's University Press, 1998).

16. F.S. Northedge, *The League of Nations: Its Life and Times 1920–1946* (Leicester: Leicester University Press, 1988), 77.

17. E.F. Kunz, 'The Refugee in Flight: Kinetic Models and Forms of Displacement', *International Migration Review* 7:2 (Summer 1973), 125–46.

18. Quoted in Claudena M. Skran, *Refugees in Inter-War Europe: The Emergence of a Regime* (Oxford: Oxford University Press, 1995), 235.

19. Skran, *Refugees in Inter-War Europe*, 230.

20. Quoted in Martin Gilbert, *The Holocaust: The Jewish Tragedy* (London: William Collins, 1986), 64.

21. See Sarah A. Ogilvie and Scott Miller, *Refuge Denied: The St. Louis Passengers and the Holocaust* (Madison: University of Wisconsin Press, 2006).

22. Louise W. Holborn, *The International Refugee Organization. A Specialized Agency of the United Nations: Its History and Work 1946–1952* (London: Oxford University Press, 1956), 433.

23. See Benjamin N. Schiff, *Refugees unto the Third Generation: UN Aid to Palestinians* (Syracuse: Syracuse University Press, 1995).

24. For a detailed discussion, see James C. Hathaway, *The Rights of Refugees under International Law* (Cambridge: Cambridge University Press, 2005).

25. Bruce Cronin, *Institutions for the Common Good: International Protection Regimes in International Society* (Cambridge: Cambridge University Press, 2003), 152–84.

26. Gil Loescher, *The UNHCR and World Politics: A Perilous Path* (Oxford: Oxford University Press, 2001), 5.

27. Raimo Väyrynen, 'Funding Dilemmas in Refugee Assistance: Political Interests and Institutional Reforms in the UNHCR', *International Migration Review* 35:1 (Spring 2001), 143–67.

28. See Randolph Kent, 'Emergency Aid: Politics and Priorities', in Gil Loescher and Laila Monahan (eds), *Refugees and International Relations* (Oxford: Oxford University Press, 1989); William Maley, 'A New Tower of Babel? Reappraising the Architecture of Refugee

Protection', in Edward Newman and Joanne Van Selm (eds), *Refugees and Forced Displacement: International Security, Human Vulnerability, and the State* (Tokyo: United Nations University Press, 2003).

29. On the dilemmas to which this role gave rise, see S. Alex Cunliffe and Michael Pugh, 'UNHCR as Leader in Humanitarian Assistance: A Triumph of Politics over Law?', in Frances Nicholson and Patrick Twomey (eds), *Refugee Rights and Realities: Evolving International Concepts and Regimes* (Cambridge: Cambridge University Press, 1999).

30. See Michael Barnett and Martha Finnemore, *Rules for the World: International Organizations in Global Politics* (Ithaca: Cornell University Press, 2004), 73–120.

31. See Mark Walkup, 'Policy Dysfunction in Humanitarian Organizations: The Role of Coping Strategies, Institutions, and Organizational Culture', *Journal of Refugee Studies* 10:1 (March 1997), 37–60.

32. See William Maley, 'Refugees and Forced Migration as a Security Problem', in William T. Tow, Ramesh Thakur, and In Taek Hyun (eds), *Asia's Emerging Regional Order: Reconciling 'Traditional' and 'Human' Security* (Tokyo: United Nations University Press, 2000).

33. See Kelly M. Greenhill, *Weapons of Mass Migration: Forced Displacement, Coercion, and Foreign Policy* (Ithaca: Cornell University Press, 2010). This can be seen as one manifestation of a broader problem, namely the manipulation of refugees for political ends; see Stephen John Stedman and Fred Tanner (eds), *Refugee Manipulation: War, Politics, and the Abuse of Human Suffering* (Washington DC: Brookings Institution Press, 2003).

34. For more detailed discussion of methods of restriction, see Matthew J. Gibney, ' "A Thousand Little Guantanamos": Western States and Measures to Prevent the Arrival of Refugees', in Kate E. Tunstall (ed.), *Displacement, Asylum, Migration: The Oxford Amnesty Lectures 2004* (Oxford: Oxford University Press, 2006); Matthew E. Price, *Rethinking Asylum: History, Purpose, and Limits* (Cambridge: Cambridge University Press, 2009), 207–31; Thomas Gammeltoft-Hansen, *Access to Asylum: International Refugee Law and the Globalisation of Migration Control* (Cambridge: Cambridge University Press, 2011).

35. For discussion of how this happens, see Sharon Pickering, *Refugees and State Crime* (Sydney: The Federation Press, 2005), 22–81; Catherine Dauvergne, *Making People Illegal: What Globalization means for Migration and Law* (Cambridge: Cambridge University Press, 2008), 50–68.

36. See Vicki Squire, *The Exclusionary Politics of Asylum* (Basingstoke: Palgrave Macmillan, 2009).

37. Quoted in Wayne Errington and Peter Van Onselen, *John Winston Howard: The Definitive Biography* (Melbourne: Melbourne University Press, 2008), 309.

38. David Marr and Marian Wilkinson, *Dark Victory* (Sydney: Allen & Unwin, 2003), 176. For further discussion of Australian policy at this time, see Matthew J. Gibney, *The Ethics and Politics of Asylum: Liberal Democracy and the Response to Refugees* (Cambridge: Cambridge University Press, 2004), 166–93; and Anne McNevin, *Contesting Citizenship: Irregular Migrants and New Frontiers of the Political* (New York: Columbia University Press, 2011), 75.

39. Ralf Emmers, 'Securitization', in Alan Collins (ed.), *Contemporary Security Studies* (Oxford: Oxford University Press, 2010), 145–6. The prime minister also sought to depict his actions as ultimately humanitarian; see Danielle Every, 'A Reasonable, Practical and Moderate Humanitarianism: The Co-option of Humanitarianism in the Australian Asylum-Seeker Debates', *Journal of Refugee Studies* 21:2 (June 2008), 210–29.

40. Astri Suhrke, 'Burden-sharing during Refugee Emergencies: The Logic of Collective versus National Action', *Journal of Refugee Studies* 11:4 (December 1998), 396–415 at 398, 401.

41. For an overview, see Gil Loescher, James Milner, Edward Newman, and Gary Troeller (eds), *Protracted Refugee Situations: Political, Human Rights and Security Implications* (Tokyo: United Nations University Press, 2008).

42. Susan Banki, 'Resettlement of the Bhutanese from Nepal: The Durable Solution Discourse', in Howard Adelman (ed.), *Protracted Displacement in Asia: No Place to Call Home* (Aldershot: Ashgate, 2008), 49.

43. See W. Courtland Robinson, *Terms of Refuge: The Indochinese Exodus and the International Response* (London: Zed Books, 1998), 50–8.

44. Suhrke, 'Burden-sharing during Refugee Emergencies', 413.

45. Loescher, *The UNHCR and World Politics*, 208.

46. Alexander Betts, 'International Cooperation in the Refugee Regime', in Alexander Betts and Gil Loescher (eds), *Refugees in International Relations* (Oxford: Oxford University Press, 2011), 61.

47. Betts, 'International Cooperation', 77. For more detailed discussion of these mechanisms, see Alexander Betts, *Protection by Persuasion: International Cooperation in the Refugee Regime* (Ithaca: Cornell University Press, 2009), 179–83.

48. Greg Fry, 'The "Pacific solution"?', in William Maley, Alan Dupont, Jean-Pierre Fonteyne, Greg Fry, James Jupp, and Thuy Do, *Refugees and the Myth of the Borderless World* (Canberra: Keynotes no.2, Department of International Relations, Research School of Pacific and Asian Studies, Australian National University, 2002), 23–31 at 22.

49. See William Maley, 'Asylum-Seekers in Australia's International Relations', *Australian Journal of International Affairs* 57:1 (April 2003), 187–202 at 195.

50. Arthur C. Helton, 'What is Refugee Protection? A Question Revisited', in Niklaus Steiner, Mark Gibney, and Gil Loescher (eds), *Problems of Protection: The UNHCR, Refugees, and Human Rights* (London: Routledge, 2003), 20.

51. See Elizabeth G. Ferris, 'The Role of Non-Governmental Organizations in the International Refugee Regime', in Steiner, Gibney, and Loescher (eds), *Problems of Protection*.

52. *Plaintiff M70/2011* v. *Minister for Immigration and Citizenship* (2011) 244 CLR 144.

53. See Jorge Heine, 'On the Manner of Practising the New Diplomacy', in Andrew F. Cooper, Brian Hocking, and William Maley (eds), *Global Governance and Diplomacy: Worlds Apart?* (Basingstoke: Palgrave Macmillan, 2008).

54. See Sophia Benz and Andreas Hasenclever, ' "Global" Governance of Forced Migration', in Alexander Betts and Gil Loescher (eds), *Refugees in International Relations*, 205.

CHAPTER 38

....

HEALTH DIPLOMACY

....

DAVID P. FIDLER

INTEREST in health diplomacy has grown in the past 10 to 15 years.[1] Although diplomats have addressed health for over 150 years, recent interest in the relationship between diplomacy and health suggests that it now exhibits features that make it distinct from previous periods. This chapter analyses contemporary diplomatic activities concerning health. The analysis reveals an area of diplomatic activities marked by confusion, a range of health threats, a proliferation in the actors, a complex and multiplying set of diplomatic processes, and controversies about what shapes health diplomacy. To capture the texture of contemporary health diplomacy, this chapter examines how health threats, concepts, and mechanisms arise in different diplomatic contexts. The chapter concludes with thoughts on the future of this relationship—a future that will not, in all likelihood, continue the trajectory that has made health an increasingly important issue in diplomatic endeavours.

38.1 CONCEPTUAL AND DEFINITIONAL ISSUES

....

In international politics, health traditionally was a neglected area of political interest, foreign policy, and diplomatic expertise. States routinely engaged in collective action on health threats, such as the cross-border spread of communicable diseases, but health cooperation attracted little interest among foreign policy experts, diplomats, and international relations specialists. This neglect had consequences when, in the past decade, interest in the diplomatic dimensions of health increased. Chief among these consequences was the lack of a common vocabulary and understandings between the foreign and health policy communities. Into this void poured an energetic but cacophonous stream of writings about 'health diplomacy', 'medical diplomacy', and 'global health diplomacy'. Given health's neglect as a diplomatic endeavour, this diversity of perspectives is refreshing despite a paucity of analytical rigour or lack of consensus about what the relationship between health and diplomacy means.

Underneath the diversity of definitions and concepts flow deeper changes that contributed to the wide-open discourse about why and how linkages between health and diplomacy were changing. To begin, globalization forced health experts to realize that the protection of health faced new challenges and opportunities for which health systems were unprepared. This vulnerability, combined with the severity of a mounting number of threats, triggered more domestic and international political concern about, and foreign policy attention on, health problems. From a neglected issue, health started to be discussed as important to the core functions of foreign policy—protecting national security, strengthening national economic well-being, advancing the development of strategic countries and regions, and protecting human dignity.[2] In addition, broad definitions of 'global health' that include not only threats from disease-causing agents but also conditions that contribute to poor health outcomes—the 'social determinants of health'—reinforced the expanding political and foreign policy agendas concerning health. Put another way, domestic and international political processes that shape a country's foreign policies began to reflect broader and deeper concerns about a larger range of intensifying health issues.

These heightened political and foreign policy interests in health translated into more diplomatic activities as states were forced, or chose, to address health threats to their security, economic, development, and human dignity interests. The conduct of diplomacy revealed the importance of non-state actors to global health problems. Negotiations produced ground-breaking agreements,[3] initiatives,[4] and strategies,[5] contributing to a revolution in global health governance in the first decade of the 21st century.[6] These steps fed into the domestic and international politics shaping foreign policies, the foreign policy articulation of national interests in diplomatic settings, the role of non-state actors, and the dynamics of diplomatic action on health concerns.

The complexity of global health's transformation as a foreign policy, diplomatic, and governance[7] issue contributed to the conflation of these developments into simplistic narratives about 'health diplomacy' or 'global health diplomacy', when the changes relate to more than diplomatic processes. This conflation produces confusion because it works against identifying differences between the formulation of foreign policy within countries, the conduct of diplomacy among states, and the functioning of governance mechanisms as instruments of collective action. 'Diplomacy' is not a synonym for all phenomena that make up international relations, and the same is true with respect to the function of diplomacy in health contexts.

The literature on health diplomacy has exhibited little agreement on what the function of diplomacy in global health is. One perspective views health diplomacy through a normative lens by presenting it as a process imbued with the potential to improve health outcomes and, because of the focus on health, to create progressive 'spillover' effects that can improve cooperation in other areas of international politics.[8] This approach elevates health as a transformative political endeavour and subordinates diplomacy to this potential. Another strand in the literature rejects this approach and asserts that a focus on health does not change diplomacy—it remains the traditional process through which states articulate, advance, defend, and negotiate over their national interests in the condition of political anarchy.[9] This perspective rejects 'health' as a basis for international political change and sharpens the focus on what happens in diplomacy—the clash and convergence of interests, influence, and power among states. At a deeper level, these divergent positions reveal no agreement on the meaning of 'health' or 'diplomacy'.

This chapter does not resolve these disagreements. However, in order to analyse this topic, a working definition of 'health diplomacy' is needed. For this purpose, I adopt the definition developed collaboratively through meetings on global health diplomacy in 2009 sponsored by the Rockefeller Foundation and the World Health Organization (WHO), which defined such diplomacy 'as the policy-shaping processes through which States, intergovernmental organizations, and non-State actors negotiate responses to health challenges or utilize health concepts or mechanisms in policy-shaping and negotiation strategies to achieve other political, economic, or social objectives'.

This definition is descriptive and does not adopt the normative approach found in other definitions. It identifies two contexts for diplomatic activity involving health: (1) responding to health challenges, such as communicable diseases; and (2) using health concepts and mechanisms to achieve non-health objectives, such as incorporating health into an overall package for improving relations among countries. The first context represents the classical relationship between health and diplomacy. The second context reflects health as an instrument of 'soft power' or 'smart power' (concepts discussed by Joseph Nye in Chapter 30 of this volume) by states in their pursuit of influence, allies, and competitive advantage in the international system The definition recognizes that diplomacy involves negotiations, has the potential to shape policies of the participants, and includes the participation of states, intergovernmental organizations (IGOs), and non-state actors.

38.2 HEALTH DIPLOMACY: RESPONDING TO SPECIFIC CHALLENGES TO HUMAN HEALTH

The most frequent use of diplomacy in the health context involves states, IGOs, and non-state actors negotiating responses to health threats. This type of health diplomacy began with the first International Sanitary Conference in 1851 that addressed cholera, plague, and yellow fever and continues through the present day. This kind of health diplomacy, and the changes it has undergone, can be analysed by examining the *problems, players, processes,* and *principles* such diplomacy has addressed, involved, utilized, and applied.

38.2.1 Problems

WHO defines 'health' as the complete state of physical, mental, and social well-being, not merely the absence of disease or infirmity.[10] This definition remains controversial because its scope means that every policy sphere potentially has relevance for health. This scope creates a sweeping political geography for health diplomacy. In the diplomatic sphere, the number and diversity of health problems addressed reflect the broad definition of health. Although communicable diseases have long garnered and continue to stimulate significant diplomatic activities, health diplomacy from the latter half of the 19th century until today has addressed a variety of health challenges.

For example, diplomatic activity began in the mid-19th century with the first International Sanitary Conference, which led to conferences addressing communicable diseases.[11] This activity produced governance mechanisms in the form of treaties and health-focused IGOs. In this period, diplomacy also addressed non-communicable disease harms associated with cross-border pollution, trade in alcohol and narcotic drugs, and conditions for labourers—producing agreements and another IGO, the International Labour Organization (ILO), created in 1919.[12] Direct threats to health were also addressed in the development of the laws of war, particularly through rules that sought to reduce the suffering of combatants and non-combatant populations and protect the delivery of medical assistance in war zones.[13]

The range of problems addressed diplomatically expanded vertically and horizontally after WHO's establishment in 1948. Vertical expansion occurred in established areas of diplomatic practice, including communicable diseases, trade, environmental pollution, labour standards, and the laws of war. Within each area, the number and diversity of health issues addressed have increased. Diplomacy on communicable diseases has expanded beyond the initial concerns with cholera, plague, and yellow fever and now includes pandemic influenza, HIV/AIDS, neglected tropical diseases, antimicrobial resistance, and access to vaccines and drugs. Horizontal expansion happened as states, IGOs, and non-state actors addressed threats not previously the focus of diplomatic attention, including tobacco consumption, obesity-related diseases, road traffic injuries, mental illness, health-system capacity, migration of health workers, depletion of the stratospheric ozone layer, climate-change related health challenges, and deteriorating social determinants of health.

Understanding the number of health challenges that appear in diplomatic contexts does not, however, reveal much about diplomacy on any given problem. The challenges involve different scientific, epidemiological, political, and diplomatic aspects that make generalizations foolhardy. Analysing how health diplomacy differs with the various threats requires breaking them down into categories that reveal characteristics observable in practice. The four problem categories are:

- Communicable diseases;
- Non-communicable diseases and health harms;
- Health-system capacity problems; and
- Social determinants of health.

38.2.1.1 *Communicable Diseases*

Communicable diseases have dominated the health diplomacy that addresses specific threats. This kind of diplomacy began with 19th-century European states attempting to

deal with the spread of cholera, plague, and yellow fever and today, we see the dominance of communicable disease problems in the emphasis given to pandemic influenza,
HIV/AIDS, tuberculosis, and malaria. Many cutting-edge developments in global health
governance focus on communicable diseases, including the International Health
Regulations (IHR) (2005),[14] the Global Fund to Fight AIDS, Tuberculosis, and Malaria
(Global Fund), and the International Finance Facility for Immunization. Advocacy for
more diplomatic action on health often identifies other communicable disease challenges that require more collective action, including polio eradication, proliferation of
biological weapons, neglected tropical diseases, spread of dengue fever, antimicrobial
resistance, and the threat of epidemics during humanitarian crises.

The reasons why communicable diseases have dominated health diplomacy are complex, which reflects the diversity of these diseases and the political interests they affect.
However, certain observations can illuminate the priority communicable diseases have
received. First, states generally perceive communicable diseases with the potential to
spread internationally as more threatening to their interests. Pandemic influenza is epi-
demiologically, politically, and economically more dangerous than most, if not all, non-
communicable disease problems. States' incentives to pay attention to acute, mobile
communicable diseases have remained robust over time, even if the intensity of political
interest in them has waxed and waned. These incentives attach to a limited number of
communicable diseases, which means that many communicable diseases have not been
prominent diplomatically (e.g. neglected tropical diseases).

Second, states understand that addressing communicable diseases of transnational
concern needs collective action, especially on sharing information for surveillance of
threatening diseases. Facilitating such sharing has required negotiations from the
International Sanitary Conference of 1851 to the IHR (2005). With these types of communicable diseases, states find themselves in a condition of interdependence—they are
mutually dependent for surveillance concerning communicable diseases of epidemic or
pandemic potential. This interdependence does not extend to communicable diseases
that pose no threat of spreading globally or would have little impact if they did.

Third, technological developments, especially vaccines and antibiotics, have often
given states, IGOs, and non-state actors the means to craft interventions that are scientifically and politically feasible. For example, the availability of vaccines has enabled diplomatic action on the eradication of smallpox (successful), polio (ongoing), and on
childhood immunization in low-income countries. The development of antiretrovirals
in the mid-1990s transformed diplomacy on HIV/AIDS and led to the push for greater
access to antiretrovirals in low-income countries.

Conversely, the development of antimicrobial resistance complicates diplomacy because
it forces intervention strategies to be less technological and more politically controversial
(e.g. isolation or quarantine rather than treatment). Similarly, the lack of technologies for
disease prevention and control, or the lack of access to such technologies, complicates diplomatic endeavours, as seen in controversies experienced in addressing HIV/AIDS prior to
the development of antiretrovirals[15] and in the problems with vaccine and anti-viral access
during outbreaks of avian influenza A (H5N1) and pandemic influenza A (H1N1).[16]

Although communicable diseases have dominated health diplomacy, the diplomacy is often in tension with public health tenets, especially the importance of disease prevention and the need for broad-based health systems that can handle disease prevention and control. Throughout the history of international cooperation on communicable diseases, a pattern has appeared—states engage in diplomatic action in response to communicable disease outbreaks. The diplomacy focuses on the immediate needs of responding to the problem and, typically, does not address the causes of the outbreak to build prevention into the strategies negotiated. Once the crisis passes, foreign policy interest in addressing underlying causes dissipates, and the public health emphasis on prevention remains marginalized in communicable disease diplomacy.

The diplomatic attention communicable diseases have garnered has produced another pattern that runs counter to public health thinking—the proliferation of vertical, disease-specific initiatives that fail to build health-system capacity in low-income countries. The availability of technologies for treatment of infections factors into these disease-specific efforts because diplomacy often focuses on applying the technologies in affected countries. The failure of states, IGOs, and non-state actors to craft serious HIV prevention programmes because of emphasis on antiretroviral treatment illustrates this problem.[17] As examined in what follows, health-system capacity issues have received less attention in health diplomacy, even though such capacity is critical to effective strategies against communicable and other disease threats.

38.2.1.2 *Non-Communicable Diseases and Health Harms*

Health diplomacy has grappled with many non-communicable diseases and health harms across decades. As with communicable diseases, the number and variety of such diseases and harms addressed diplomatically have increased over time. The current period is witnessing a push by WHO and the United Nations (UN) to elevate cardiovascular disease, cancer, chronic lung disease, and diabetes as diplomatic priorities, including through a UN high-level summit on non-communicable diseases in September 2011. Advocates for more foreign policy attention on these and other non-communicable diseases worry about the low level of diplomatic activity and funding these diseases have received despite the disease burden they cause. Emblematic of this mismatch is the lack of targets related to non-communicable diseases in the UN's Millennium Development Goals (MDGs). In terms of funding, data indicate that '[n]oncommunicable diseases receive the least amount of funding compared with other health focus areas'.[18]

Like communicable diseases, non-communicable diseases and health harms include a range of problems that are not easily comparable. Trans-boundary pollution involves non-communicable threats from pollutants, toxic chemicals, or radioactive fallout, but these threats differ from many non-communicable health risks, such as tobacco, obesity, and alcohol. Diplomatic activities have been more frequent with respect to non-communicable disease threats that involve cross-border movement of pollutants and products than with non-communicable diseases associated with individual product-consumption and behaviour (e.g. smoking, inadequate diet and exercise, and drinking).

The cross-border scenarios reveal states operating in contexts of interdependence. In order to address non-communicable disease threats moving across borders, states need to cooperate because no state can unilaterally control emergence of the threats or their cross-border movement. This dynamic has been present in diplomacy on trans-boundary pollution from the late 19th century to the present day and appears in the context of health harms arising out of degradation of global commons resources, such as the ozone layer and the world's climate. This interdependence also informs trade diplomacy, particularly negotiation of rules designed to protect health from toxic or otherwise dangerous ingredients or components in products moving in international commerce.

In terms of non-communicable diseases associated with product consumption and behaviour patterns, these diseases do not reflect interdependence and, thus, do not generate the same reciprocal interests among states. Instead, they reveal interconnectedness among states, which tends to exhibit interest divergence and/or political indifference more than incentives for diplomatic action. The interconnectedness most often arises from trade in health-affecting products—such as tobacco, alcohol, or obesogenic foods and beverages—and the spread of lifestyle patterns that promote consumption of these products. Beyond how international trade law regulates commerce in and advertising of these products, exporting and importing states have weak common interests in whether the importing state prevents or controls these non-communicable diseases.

For example, states that have reduced tobacco consumption, such as the United States, have done so through interventions, such as raising taxes, which require no other state to take action. Health improvements in the United States from reduced tobacco use do not create health, economic, security, or political benefits in other countries, demonstrating that key interests of these countries do not depend on the United States reducing tobacco consumption. The reverse is also true—US security, economic well-being, and health do not depend on whether any other country controls tobacco use. Low- and middle-income countries that require assistance to reduce tobacco consumption are dependent on high-income countries to achieve this goal.[19] Thus, prevention and control of tobacco consumption does not exhibit, or require, reciprocal dependence among states to occur. Further, the main US interest in other countries' tobacco regulations relates to their impact on US tobacco exports, creating a divergence of trade and health interests, which puts emphasis on international trade law rather than health protection per se.

Diplomacy on problems of interconnectedness in the non-communicable disease area occurs in a number of venues, so interconnectedness is not a bar to negotiation of collective action, as evidenced by the adoption of the WHO Global Strategy for the Prevention and Control of Non-Communicable Diseases (2000) and the WHO Framework Convention on Tobacco Control (FCTC) (2003). However, getting problems of interconnectedness in the non-communicable disease area addressed diplomatically in sustainable ways at high political levels has proved difficult. The FCTC was a landmark achievement of health diplomacy, but, in 2009, WHO reported that FCTC implementation was lagging.[20] This pattern of high-level attention followed by anaemic implementation reveals a debilitating elasticity in foreign policy interests that undermines sustainable progress on these kinds of global health problems.

Getting problems of interconnectedness in the non-communicable disease area more prominent foreign policy and diplomatic attention has required WHO and other experts to reframe the threat to include not only the burden of disease but also the economic consequences the growing prevalence of these diseases might have in countries. 'Noncommunicable diseases are a dire threat', declared WHO in December 2010.[21] This strategy attempts to shift the politics and foreign policy interests concerning the biggest non-communicable disease risks onto the development agenda and into the national macroeconomic arena, bringing these risks closer to more prominent political, economic, and foreign policy interests of states.

38.2.1.3 *Health-System Capacity Problems*

A complaint about health diplomacy is its failure to produce and sustain initiatives that help low-income countries build and maintain sufficient health-system capacity to handle the health problems they face. The lack of capacity is, in nearly every area of global health, identified as a critical problem that continues to be inadequately addressed.[22] As noted earlier, experts identify the prevalence of vertical, disease-specific initiatives as a symptom and cause of a lack of interest in health-system capacity building. The building blocks of a robust health system are well understood,[23] so the disconnect is not in technical knowledge or its promulgation to countries.

Diplomatically, health-system incapacity proves difficult to address effectively. Building health-system capacity in low-income countries constitutes a development task, but, as such, the challenge creates political problems and potentially expensive, open-ended financial commitments from donor countries. A functioning health system depends on political, economic, and governance capabilities, such as the rule of law, control of corruption, education and training, and generation of economic resources (e.g. economic growth, tax revenues). Realistically, health-system capacity building has to involve, in addition to the health-specific components, interventions into the politics, economics, and governance of recipient countries.

This agenda is attractive neither to donor nor recipient states, as evidenced by the limited aid spent on health-system strengthening.[24] Diplomatic attention on this issue tends to focus on capacity building as part of more limited issue- or disease-specific strategies. Thus, initiatives on HIV/AIDS or maternal health increasingly include capacity-building elements.[25] The concern is that this piecemeal approach will not generate the capacity needed, especially in light of the growing burden of non-communicable diseases.

38.2.1.4 *Social Determinants of Health*

The last category involves the social determinants of health (SDH). These determinants identify political, economic, and social conditions—such as poverty, access to education, gender inequalities, and environmental degradation—that affect health outcomes of societies and of specific populations, such as women and children.[26] Efforts to improve maternal health have struggled because of gender discrimination.[27] Worsening social determinants that affect the health of women and girls limit what maternal health initiatives can accomplish with technically oriented interventions, such as access to midwives or contraception. Maternal health is, however, just one example of how SDH play major roles in health outcomes globally.

Diplomatically, SDH constitute an even broader agenda than building health-system capacity. The WHO Commission on Social Determinants of Health captured the scale of the challenge by arguing that nothing less than the redistribution of power, money, and resources was required.[28] Many interventions needed to address SDH, such as poverty and gender inequalities, require strategies against political, economic, and social practices far beyond the health sector, meaning sustained, intrusive diplomacy in many areas is necessary. Development strategies make the most logical diplomatic location for such multi-sectoral solutions and the MDGs illustrate that this approach is what has developed. In addition to three specific health goals, the MDGs target four SDH— poverty reduction, education, gender equality, and environmental protection.

As the 2010 UN summit on the MDGs demonstrated, progress on achieving the MDGs by the 2015 target has been inadequate. Although the MDGs continue to receive support, the gap between rhetoric and reality highlights diplomatic problems that limit progress on SDH and on problems, such as maternal health, that depend on improvements in specific determinants. These problems include inadequate funding from donor countries that the UN and others argue is essential for advancing SDH, whether in the context of the MDGs or elsewhere. As noted earlier, donor countries prefer initiatives with more limited scope, meaning that such funding might only have marginal impact on SDH. This dynamic echoes the pattern seen in health-system capacity building, demonstrating that this characteristic is deeply grooved in health diplomacy.

38.2.2 Players

38.2.2.1 *States*

Understanding health diplomacy on specific health challenges requires perspective on the players that participate in, or seek to affect, it. Traditional conceptions of diplomacy view this process as dominated by states, either in their relations with each other or through IGOs. The history of health diplomacy records states as central actors and, in addition to conventional reasons why states play leading roles, the health context reinforces the centrality of states.

The key functions of public health, such as surveillance, are 'public goods', meaning that responsibility for their provision rests with governments rather than the private sector. Disease interventions have to be implemented on a population scale, which makes governments the central actor. The scale of population health activities—including building health-system capacity, improving SDH, and providing development assistance—requires broad-based funding only public taxation systems can provide. Fears that the increased development assistance for health encourages governments to 'free ride' speak to the critical need to have states engaged in their own public health responsibilities, whether at home or in diplomatic forums.

As in other areas of international relations, strong states play an important role in health diplomacy. Their interests weigh heavily in negotiations and funding from high-income countries is necessary for initiatives to bear fruit. Diplomatic activity on health has, over time, risen and fallen in conjunction with the interest the great powers have shown towards health threats. In the mid-19th century, European powers started health diplomacy in response to political fears and economic concerns about epidemics, and the prominence of health in foreign policy and diplomatic venues over the past ten to fifteen years connects to the re-engagement of the great powers, especially the United States and other Group of 8 (G8) countries, with global health.

38.2.2.2 *Intergovernmental Organizations (IGOs)*

Beyond states, other participants, such as IGOs and non-state actors (e.g. multinational corporations, NGOs) affect health diplomacy in important ways. IGOs and non-state actors have shaped foreign policy interests and the trajectories of negotiations. In terms of IGOs, states have created these bodies to facilitate health diplomacy. In the first twenty-five years of the 20th century, countries established the Pan-American Sanitary Bureau (1902), the Office International d'Hygiène Publique (1907), and the Health Organization of the League of Nations (1923). States consolidated them in the WHO in 1948. Other intergovernmental bodies have played roles in health diplomacy, including UN agencies (e.g. the UN Children Fund (UNICEF), UNAIDS, the World Trade Organization (WTO)), regional organizations (e.g. European Union (EU), Association of South-East Asian Nations (ASEAN)), and identity-based entities (e.g. Organization of Islamic Conference (OIC)).[29]

38.2.2.3 *Non-State Actors*

The impact of non-state actors starts at the beginning of health diplomacy. European merchants—upset with the costs they had to bear in dealing with different national quarantine systems—lobbied their governments to negotiate a harmonized approach to quarantine. The nearly century-long series of international sanitary conferences and the sanitary conventions that followed bore the imprint of commercial interests in trade. Early efforts to address trans-boundary pollution and occupational safety and health also involved the private sector. The not-so-invisible hand of corporate interests in health diplomacy continues to this day, as seen in efforts by companies in the pharmaceutical, tobacco, airline, shipping, health services, and food and beverage industries to have their interests taken into account in negotiations. Global health has also been a fertile area for 'celebrity diplomacy',[30] illustrated by the rock star Bono's lobbying of President George W. Bush concerning HIV/AIDS.

NGOs also have long participated in health diplomacy. For example, the ILO, starting in 1919, included union and employer representatives in its governance structure, ensuring a voice for non-state actors in development of standards for occupational safety and health. The WHO Constitution recognized the importance of NGOs by authorizing WHO to consult and cooperate with them. Civil society movements advocating for access to antiretrovirals have affected the diplomacy focused on this problem, as illustrated by the impact these movements had on WTO negotiations that produced the Doha Declaration on the Trade-Related Intellectual Property Rights (TRIPS) Agreement and Public Health. NGOs participate in public–private partnerships, including the Global Fund, that have become venues for health diplomacy.[31]

38.2.2.4 *Philanthropic Foundations*

Philanthropic foundations have had high-profile roles in global health since the early 20th century. From its establishment in 1913 through the Second World War, the Rockefeller Foundation provided more foreign aid than the US government, and the Foundation spent much of this assistance on health.[32] Today, the dominant philanthropic actor in global health is the Bill and Melinda Gates Foundation which disperses almost two billion dollars annually.[33] The scale of the Gates Foundation's commitment makes it a powerful player because it has become integral to negotiations and initiatives, as illustrated by its participation with IGOs in the so-called 'Health 8' coordinating group and its 1.5 billion dollar contribution to the G8's Muskoka Initiative on Maternal, Newborn, and Child Health.

38.2.3 Processes

The comprehensive definition of health, the number of health challenges, and the diversity of players and their interests means that health diplomacy transpires in many contexts, including in security, trade, environmental, development, humanitarian, and human rights settings handled through bilateral, regional, and multilateral processes. A number of factors contribute to the proliferation of diplomatic processes relevant to health. Informed by broad conceptualizations of health, the health agenda tends to expand because so many policy areas potentially affect health. Thus, health diplomacy ranges far and wide—from handling a cholera crisis, to addressing controversies about patented pharmaceuticals and debating strategies for climate change adaptation. State interests can also multiply diplomatic processes through preferences for addressing problems bilaterally, regionally, through 'club diplomacy' (e.g. G8),[34] by diplomatic 'forum shifting', in solidarity groupings (e.g. South–South forums), or creating new processes for new initiatives.

Over time, patterns have developed that reveal strategies to manage the proliferation of diplomatic processes relevant to health. The first pattern is the attempt to consolidate health diplomacy within IGOs, which serve as a 'centre of gravity' for global health work. WHO is the best example of this strategy. However, the last ten to fifteen years have seen an unprecedented proliferation of diplomatic processes addressing health, which have undermined WHO and harmed the ability of low-income countries to participate effectively in health diplomacy.[35] This proliferation and its consequences have led to calls for a new 'architecture' for global health that seeks to reconsolidate diplomatic and governance processes into more streamlined, efficient, and effective mechanisms.

However, in recognition that health is such a multi-sectoral issue, even a reformed or remodelled WHO cannot be the locale for all diplomatic activity on health. To make sure health interests are taken into account in other diplomatic processes, the second pattern involves advocacy for all policy areas to reflect health concerns. The slogan 'health in all policies' captures this approach, as do attempts to argue that health should be at the centre of policy debates and diplomatic negotiations—as in 'health should be at the centre of development thinking'[36] or 'health should be at the centre of climate change policy'.[37] The effectiveness of these arguments is, however, questionable. Despite efforts to make health prominent in these settings, climate change negotiations in Copenhagen in December 2009 failed to reflect health concerns,[38] and the crafting of a development agenda for the Group of 20 (G20) in Seoul in November 2010 did not include health as a plank of this strategy.[39]

38.2.4 Principles

Diplomacy on specific health challenges has witnessed the use of many normative ideas and principles, ranging from the empirical to the ideological. This normative complexity is not surprising given the expansive territory health diplomacy covers. An overarching meme has been an emphasis on the need for policies to reflect scientific principles and empirical evidence. 'Evidence-based policy-making' is a mantra applied to diplomatic negotiations as well as domestic policy. The lack of scientific and epidemiological information can hinder diplomatic negotiations, as evidenced by the failure of 19th-century international sanitary conferences until 'germ theory' clarified how states could balance health protection with trade interests. However, often the problem is not the lack of scientific evidence. Rather, diplomatic problems arise when states' interests resist or reject the policy prescriptions the evidence supports. The empirical case for building resilient health-system capacity is strong; however, as noted earlier, diplomatic action on this need in low-income countries has long been weak.

Health diplomacy is also a setting in which more philosophical concepts frequently appear. Representatives from states, IGOs, and NGOs often argue for or against courses of action in the name of human rights, equity, solidarity, social justice, and humanitarian compassion. The ubiquity of these concepts in global health indicates that this area stimulates deep beliefs about health and its role in societies. However, the use of such normative principles is not unique to health diplomacy because they appear in most, if not all, other areas of diplomatic engagement. Nor is it clear that these principles produce more traction in the health context than in other diplomatic settings. Just as scientific evidence does not determine the nature of health diplomacy, these more philosophical ideas do not control diplomatic practice in this area.

Perhaps recognizing the gossamer qualities of norms, such as equity, in the real world of diplomacy, health and foreign policy experts have, in the last ten to fifteen years, attempted to reframe how states, IGOs, and non-state actors should view global health. In addition to the conventional arguments about human rights, solidarity, social justice, and the humanitarian imperative, health diplomacy has become populated with arguments about the dangers health problems pose to national and international security, economic growth and welfare, and development strategies. These normative reframings aim at the perceived central concerns of states in the formulation of their foreign policies, with the objective of triggering those concerns sufficiently for states to take more decisive diplomatic action on health.

38.2.5 Summary: Diplomacy on Specific Health Challenges

Diplomatic endeavours involving specific health threats has a long, diverse history, but, without question, these endeavours today involve more problems, players, processes, and principles than witnessed in any other period. The proliferation of threats, actors, venues, and norms challenges attempts to bring order to this expansion of diplomatic activities on health. For health advocates, this expansion is a bitter pill—higher diplomatic profile tends to equate with worsening health problems, meaning that prevention of disease and creation of conditions that produce better health outcomes is failing globally.

38.3 Health Diplomacy as 'Soft Power': Using Health to Achieve Other Foreign Policy Objectives

The second context for health diplomacy is controversial because it focuses on how states use health to pursue non-health foreign policy goals. Controversy arises because this use of health conflicts with the ethos that health is an end in itself and should not be manipulated for other purposes. However, use of health as a means to achieve other foreign policy interests is real and needs to be examined as a part of historical and contemporary health diplomacy.

Conceptually, this context involves a state providing health services or assistance and/or engaging in health cooperation with other states as part of an effort to achieve a higher-order foreign policy objective. In these scenarios, health becomes an instrument of a state's 'soft power' or 'smart power', which it uses to increase its leverage and position vis-à-vis rivals. As such, health concepts and mechanisms become part of the arsenal the state deploys in the competition for power, influence, and advantage in international politics. Use of health diplomacy as 'soft power' has occurred in many ways and in diverse contexts, but the most frequent channel is bilateral diplomacy. This pattern helps explain why, despite calls for delivering more development assistance (including for health) through multilateral channels, donor governments prefer to distribute such assistance bilaterally.

Importantly, health diplomacy often involves foreign policy 'double dipping': states provide assistance to other states in order (1) to address a particular health threat of mutual concern, and (2) to strengthen ties with those states in the face of political or economic competition from rivals. Thus, a donor country might provide resources to another nation to build capacity to conduct surveillance on pandemic influenza—a disease the donor country fears and, to protect itself better against it, needs global surveillance capabilities. This assistance also helps the donor state improve relations with the recipient country, which increases the donor country's chances of maintaining or expanding its influence in a strategically important country and region.

Although use of health diplomacy as 'soft power' has recently gained attention, the practice is not new. The use of medicine by European powers as a 'tool of empire' has been studied.[40] During the cold war, the United States and Soviet Union included health assistance in efforts to court friends and allies,[41] and China and Cuba sent thousands of medical personnel to low-income countries to gain influence in the developing world.[42] In the post-cold war period, existing and emerging powers—the United States,[43] Brazil,[44] China, India,[45] Russia,[46] and Cuba—have practised health diplomacy as 'soft power'.

The repeated use of health diplomacy as 'soft power' over time by states of different political orientations indicates that foreign policy-makers find this diplomacy useful. However, this diplomatic pattern might reflect that this approach targets 'low hanging fruit' because bilateral health cooperation does not, typically, threaten to create serious interest divergence between the states involved. Experience also suggests that the potential upside of this kind of health diplomacy is limited because, after the speeches and summits end, health cooperation tends to become a technical enterprise with little potential to create positive 'spillover effects' for more serious political issues in the bilateral relationship.

In addition, whether projects undertaken as health diplomacy as 'soft power' produce effective, sustainable *health* results is not clear, but scepticism is warranted. First, producing such results is not the main point of the strategy. Second, the mounting severity of health problems, the lack of health-system capacity globally, and fears about deteriorating SDH suggest that health diplomacy as 'soft power' after the Second World War has not been a success from a global health perspective.

38.4 CONCLUSION: THE FUTURE OF HEALTH DIPLOMACY

Contemporary health diplomacy exhibits features that make it distinct from such diplomacy in the past, especially in terms of the attention foreign policy-makers pay to health, the amount of funding devoted to global health, and the number of problems, players, processes, and principles in play concerning diplomatic efforts against health challenges. However, the differences between yesteryear and today are perhaps not as radical as recent excitement about the relationship between health and diplomacy might suggest.

In terms of diplomacy on specific health problems, diversity in threats, actors, venues, and norms existed in the decades of diplomacy before the WHO's establishment. One could, in fact, see in the WHO's creation an attempt to address an increasing set of health challenges, a more diverse collection of participants, confusion produced by uncoordinated diplomatic forums, and emergence of new norms. As for health diplomacy as 'soft power', seeing differences between what happens today and what once transpired during the cold war is difficult. Thus, the rise of health diplomacy in international relations over the past ten to fifteen years is an important phenomenon, but perhaps not as astonishing a transformation as some believe.

The future trajectory of health diplomacy depends on whether foreign policy-makers continue to perceive health diplomacy as worth the 'blood and treasure'—human, political, and economic capital—global health now attracts. The emergence of serious problems at home, such as massive fiscal imbalances, and abroad, such as the development of a destabilizing Sino-American balance-of-power dynamic, might push health diplomacy to the margins of foreign policy.

The rate of increase in global health funding is declining after years of increases, which points to a flat-lining of, or reduction in, spending over the next decade. Question marks hang over donor countries, such as the United States and EU countries, because they are struggling with debt and deficit crises that will take years to sort out. Thus, significant influxes of new money from high-income governments look unlikely and emerging powers—such as Brazil, China, and India—do not appear prepared to pick up the funding slack. This scenario might enhance the power of the Gates Foundation, possibly taking its influence beyond the stature the Rockefeller Foundation had in international health in the first half of the 20th century. Geopolitical concerns about the decline of US influence and China's rise are generating worries that this power shift could produce more 'hard power' problems, which might overshadow health as 'soft power' trope that gained more prominence during the post-cold war period of American hegemony.

If these developments come to pass, the latest cycle of the rise and fall of health diplomacy will be complete. However, just as the rise of health diplomacy might not be as spectacular as thought, its fall from its present stature does not presage a diplomatic sunset. Rather, the relationship between health and diplomacy will lose high-level foreign policy traction (except in times of crises) and operate more through functional, technical efforts and confront too many problems, in too many geographical and diplomatic locations, with too little political gravitas, and with not enough resources—a situation previous generations of health experts navigated without losing their abilities and passion for doing good.

Notes

1. See, e.g. formation of the Global Health Diplomacy Network, at <http://www.ghd-net.org/>.

2. David P. Fidler, 'Health as Foreign Policy: Between Principle and Power', *Whitehead Journal of Diplomacy and International Relations* 6 (Summer/Fall 2005), 179–94.

3. See, e.g. World Health Organization (WHO) adoption of the Framework Convention on Tobacco Control (2003) and International Health Regulations (2005).

4. See, e.g. Global Fund to Fight AIDS, Tuberculosis, and Malaria, at <http://www.theglobal-fund.org/en/>.

5. See, e.g. WHO Global Strategy on Diet and Nutrition (2004).

6. David P. Fidler, *The Challenge of Global Health Governance* (New York: Council on Foreign Relations Working Paper, May 2010).

7. For an analysis of health as an issue in global governance, see Thomas G. Weiss and Ramesh Thakur, *Global Governance and the UN: An Unfinished Journey* (Bloomington: Indiana University Press, 2010), ch. 9.

8. See, e.g. Richard Horton, 'Health as a Foreign Policy Instrument', *The Lancet* 369 (2007), 806–7; Ilona Kickbusch et al., 'Global Health Diplomacy: Training Across Disciplines', *Bulletin of the World Health Organization* 85:12 (2007), 971–3.

9. See, e.g. Harley Feldbaum and Joshua Michaud, 'Health Diplomacy and the Enduring Relevance of Foreign Policy Interests', *PLoS Medicine* 7:4 (April 2010), e1000226. doi:10.1371/journal.pmed.1000226.

10. WHO Constitution (1946), preamble.

11. Norman Howard-Jones, *The Scientific Background of the International Sanitary Conferences, 1951–1938* (Geneva: WHO, 1975).

12. David P. Fidler, 'The Globalization of Public Health', *Bulletin of the World Health Organization* 79:9 (2001), 842–8.

13. See, e.g. Hague Convention (IV) Respecting the Laws and Customs of War on Land and Annex: Regulations concerning the Laws and Customs of War on Land (1907).

14. WHO, *International Health Regulations (2005)*, 2nd ed. (Geneva: WHO, 2008).

15. Lawrence O. Gostin, *The AIDS Pandemic* (Chapel Hill: University of North Carolina Press, 2004).

16. David P. Fidler, 'Negotiating Equitable Access to Influenza Vaccines', *PLoS Medicine* 7:5 (2010), e1000247.doi:10.1371/journal.pmed.1000247.

17. Laurie Garrett, 'The Wrong Way to Fight AIDS', *New York Times*, 30 July 2008.

18. Institute for Health Metrics and Evaluation, *Financing Global Health 2010* (Seattle: Institute for Health Metrics and Evaluation, 2010), 9.

19. S. Albuja and Richard A. Daynard, 'The Framework Convention on Tobacco Control (FCTC) and the Adoption of Domestic Tobacco Control Policies: The Ecuadorian Experience', *Tobacco Control* 18 (2009), 18–21.

20. WHO, *Report on the Global Tobacco Epidemic, 2009* (Geneva: WHO, 2009).

21. WHO, <http://www.who.int/en/>.

22. Bruno Marchal, Anna Cavalli, and Guy Kegels, 'Global Health Actors Claim to Support Health System Strengthening—Is This Rhetoric or Reality?', *PLoS Medicine* 6:4 (2009), e1000059. doi:10.1371/journal.pmed.1000059.

23. WHO, *Key Components of a Well-Functioning Health System* (May 2010), at <http://www.who.int/healthsystems/EN_HSSkeycomponents.pdf>.

24. Institute for Health Metrics and Evaluation, *Financing Global Health 2010*, 15.

25. Julio Frenk, Jonathan D. Quick, and Ariel Pablos-Mendez, 'Are the Millennium Development Goals for Health on a Collision Course?', *Huffington Post*, 16 September 2010, at <http://www.huffingtonpost.com/julio-frenk-md-mph-phd/are-the-millennium-develo_b_719904.html>; and UN Secretary-General Ban Ki-moon, *Global Strategy for Women's and Children's Health* (New York: United Nations, September 2010).

26. WHO Commission on Social Determinants of Health, *Closing the Gap in a Generation: Health Equity through Action on the Social Determinants of Health* (Geneva: WHO, 2008).

27. UN Development Fund for Women, *Gender Justice: Key to Achieving the Millennium Development Goals* (New York: UN Development Fund for Women, 2010).

28. WHO Commission, *Closing the Gap in a Generation*, 2.

29. UN General Assembly, *Global Health and Foreign Policy: Strategic Opportunities and Challenges—Note by the Secretary-General*, A/64/365, 23 September 2009.

30. Andrew F. Cooper, *Celebrity Diplomacy* (Boulder, CO: Paradigm Publishers, 2007).

31. Judith Richter, 'Public-Private Partnerships for Health: A Trend with No Alternatives?', *Development* 47:2 (2004), 43–8.

32. Rockefeller Foundation, *Our History—A Powerful Legacy*, at <http://www.rockefeller-foundation.org/who-we-are/our-history>.

33. Institute for Health Metrics and Evaluation, *Financing Global Health 2010*, 24.

34. See Chapter 2, this volume, for analysis of club diplomacy.

35. See, e.g. Devi Sridhar, Sanjeev Khagram, and Tikki Pang, 'Are Existing Governance Structures Equipped to Deal with Today's Global Health Challenges?—Towards Systematic Coherence in Scaling Up', *Global Health Governance* 2:2 (Fall 2008/Spring 2009), at <http://www.ghgj.org/Sridhar%20Khagram%20and%20Pang_Are%20Existing%20Governance.pdf>.

36. Gro Brundtland, WHO Director-General, 'Health at the World Summit on Sustainable Development', Speech to the XXIV World AIDS Conference, Barcelona, 9 July 2002, at <http://www.who.int/director-general/speeches/2002/english/20020709_HealthatworldsummitonSustainableDevelopment.html>.

37. Poonam Khetrapai Singh, Deputy Regional Director, WHO Southeast Asia Regional Office, 'Health at the Centre of Climate Change', *Jakarta Post*, 3 December 2010, at <http://www.thejakartapost.com/news/2010/12/03/human-health-center-climate-change.html>.

38. Laurie Garrett, Council on Foreign Relations Global Health Update, 23 December 2009, 4.

39. G20, *Seoul Development Consensus for Shared Growth and Multi-Year Action Plan on Development*, 12 November 2010, at <http://www.g20.utoronto.ca/2010/g20seoul-consensus.pdf>.

40. See, e.g. Daniel R. Headrick, *The Tools of Empire* (Oxford: Oxford University Press, 1981).

41. See, e.g. Judyth Twigg, 'Russia's Global Health Outlook: Building Capacity to Match Aspirations', in Katherine E. Bliss (ed.), *Key Players in Global Health: How Brazil, Russia, India, China, and South Africa Are Influencing the Game* (Washington, DC: Center for Strategic and International Studies, 2010), 34–40 at 34.

42. On China, see Yanzhong Huang, 'Pursuing Health as Foreign Policy: The Case of China', *Indiana Journal of Global Legal Studies* 17:1 (2010), 105–46. On Cuba, see Julie Feinsilver, 'Cuba's Medical Diplomacy', in Maurico A. Font (ed.), *Changing Cuba/Changing World* (New York: Bildner Center for Western Hemisphere Studies, 2008).

43. Feldbaum and Michaud, 'Health Diplomacy and the Enduring Relevance of Foreign Policy Interests'.

44. Katherine E. Bliss, 'Health in All Policies: Brazil's Approach to Global Health within Foreign Policy and Development Cooperation Initiatives', in Bliss (ed.), *Key Players in Global Health*; and Kelley Lee, Luiz Carlos Chagas, and Thomas E. Novotny, 'Brazil and the Framework Convention on Tobacco Control: Global Health Diplomacy as Soft Power', *PLoS Medicine* 7:4 (April 2010), e1000232. doi:10.1371/journal.pmed.1000232.

45. See, e.g. India-Africa Framework for Cooperation, 8–9 April 2008.

46. Twigg, 'Russia's Global Health Outlook'.

CHAPTER 39

··

SPORT AND DIPLOMACY

··

DAVID BLACK AND BYRON PEACOCK

THE domains of sport and diplomacy have had a long, often fraught, and generally under-appreciated relationship, at least since the emergence of the modern Olympic movement in the late 19th century. Given the unparalleled visibility, popularity, and mobilizing potential of modern sport, accompanied by intense manifestations of identity (national, regional, local, sectarian, ethnic, etc.), it is hardly surprising that sports teams, events, and venues have been viewed as compelling vehicles for the political and diplomatic ambitions of both governments and the range of actors engaged in 'network diplomacy'. Yet particularly in the various societies of the Anglo-American world (including the Commonwealth), a full engagement with the politico-diplomatic possibilities of sport was long inhibited by what Lincoln Allison has termed 'the myth of autonomy'. This is the idea 'that sport was somehow separate from society, that it transcended or had "nothing to do with" politics and social conflict', under-pinned by the paradoxical convictions that it was 'both "above" or "below" the political dimensions of social life'.[1] This myth has proven highly durable, despite much contradictory evidence. The result was that for many governments, there was a deep reluctance to explicitly engage the 'world of sport' as a focus of diplomatic analysis and practice.[2]

Authoritarian regimes of all stripes—fascist, communist, military, etc.—have on the whole been considerably less reticent about embracing sport as a tool of international diplomacy.[3] Here and elsewhere, however, would-be 'users' have encountered another challenge: the limited and erratic fungibility of sport as a diplomatic currency. In short, investments in sport do not reliably generate the anticipated benefits and, in some cases at least, can positively recoil on their users in unanticipated ways. A particularly striking example is the 1988 Seoul Olympics, which rebounded on the country's authoritarian military rulers in ways that decisively advanced the process of liberal democratization.[4] In this respect, there is some real substance to the idea that sport, and the organizations that govern it, has a relatively high degree of autonomy that makes it difficult to control and manipulate with durable political effects.

In this chapter, we will explore the potent yet ambiguous possibilities of sport as it relates to diplomacy. We will survey the range of actors that have engaged in sport diplomacy, and how these have changed—and broadened—in the incomplete transition from 'club' to 'network' diplomacy. In particular, we will highlight the distinctive and often highly influential role of international sports organizations (ISOs), along with state governments, intergovernmental organizations (IGOs), civil society organizations and 'movements', multinational corporations (MNCs), and, in some contexts, urban and regional governments. Throughout the history of modern sport diplomacy, a key theme has been the prevalence of sport as a vehicle for *public diplomacy*—though the objectives of this public diplomacy have evolved substantially in the post-cold war era of globalization. We will analyse these trends and transitions in the sections that follow. First, however, we will introduce some of the distinctive features of ISOs.

39.1 International Sports Organizations as Diplomatic Actors and Forums

The politico-diplomatic nature of international sport is, in part, the result of the formative role of the International Olympic Committee (IOC), the Olympic movement it spearheads, and its social mission—Olympism—in world politics. Though international and transnational sporting engagements were not uncommon prior to the IOC's founding in 1894, Pierre de Coubertin (the reviver of the Olympic Games in the modern era) imbued this resolutely non-governmental organization with the overtly diplomatic aim of promoting a prominent sort of cultural 'internationalism'.[5]

Given the de facto privileges and immunities (e.g. extraterritoriality, legal exemptions, treaty-making and monitoring, etc.) it has consistently enjoyed, the IOC has functional equivalence to an IGO; in fact states respect its decisions and jurisdiction more reliably than many IGOs.[6] In addition, commercialization of the Olympic 'brand' over the past several decades has made the IOC an exorbitantly wealthy NGO, so much so that much of its behaviour, policies, and accounting measures more closely resemble a large MNC. As such, the IOC embodies key elements of three of the four actor types that characterize contemporary network diplomacy (i.e. NGOs, IGOs, and MNCs). This peculiar but powerful role makes the IOC and the Olympic movement singularly relevant to international diplomacy and curious (yet attractive) to those who study and engage it.

The IOC is only one of many international sports organizations (ISOs) however. There is a veritable alphabet soup of organizations that (1) govern essentially all sporting disciplines, (2) regulate legal, media, medical, or other technical matters necessary for international sport, and (3) oversee international sporting events that involve multiple disciplines. Unlike the IOC's driving social purpose, however, many of these ISOs did not necessarily evolve out of (but may have later adapted to) a devotion to Coubertin's brand of internationalism. Rather, these ISOs usually emerged as a response to the rationalizing, bureaucratizing forces that made international and transnational competition possible through standardization, calendar coordination, mediation through due process, and, often, centralized communications and deliberations. The increasing popularity of sports (and particularly spectator sports) at the end of the 19th century made bureaucracies such as the Fédération Internationale de Football Association (FIFA), the International Amateur Athletics Federation (IAAF; changed to the International Association of Athletics Federations in the contemporary, professional era), the Fédération Internationale de Gymnastique (FIG), and other ISOs a virtual necessity. As the complexity of international sport increased throughout the 20th century, second-order organizations emerged to handle the technical matters that proved too specialized, too legally intricate, or too broad-based for any one sports organization to control.

In order to fully understand the significance of sport in international diplomacy, it is necessary to understand the two roles of international sports organizations in the diplomatic order. On the one hand, most ISOs (beginning with the IOC but extending to other ISOs as well) now frequently declare that their bureaucratic structures serve a supremely diplomatic purpose: international peace and tolerance through athletic exchange (or some variant thereof). On the other hand, ISOs also function as multilateral organizations or arenas for diplomatic intercourse in and of themselves.[7] Since universalism is the cardinal norm among ISOs, the individual national members that usually comprise the organization can and often do act as diplomatic delegations representing the interests of their constituent countries or governments. Thus, ISOs are both diplomatic actors in their own right, pursuing social causes in world politics,[8] *and* forums for diplomatic exchange among internal and national units that generally follow the contours of traditional 'club' diplomacy.

The International Olympic Committee provides examples of both types of diplomatic activity. Formally, it has often portrayed itself as the United Nations (or, as Coubertin put it in an earlier era, a 'miniature League of Nations') of global sport.[9] In many ways the IOC has constructed a parallel universe of global power (albeit confined to the world of sport) that shadows the political realities of international diplomacy, but does not mimic them exactly. James Rosenau and Hongying Wang have called the IOC 'virtually a world government unto itself and one whose authority and autonomy have not been seriously challenged'.[10] Like the UN (or some hypothetical 'world government') the organization of the so-called 'Olympic Family' is divided into national units—the National Olympic Committees (NOCs). The Olympic world is also extremely hierarchical, far more so than the 'anarchic' international diplomatic order. Virtually all key decisions are made by the unelected, non-representative IOC and its decisions must be respected by all NOCs (and other Olympic Family members) at the risk of expulsion (which has occurred on numerous occasions).[11] The hierarchy of the Olympic movement defined clear roles and channels of communication between Lausanne and its worldwide Family. Also, not unlike the traditional 'club' diplomacy of the 19th and early

20th centuries, the IOC was for decades (and remains, to a considerable extent) an 'old-boys club', with membership heavily drawn from aristocratic circles and prone to brokering backroom deals through elitist power networks.[12]

As the scope, the number of actors, and the complexity of diplomacy have increased in recent decades however, ISOs have struggled (sometimes belatedly or unsuccessfully, other times adroitly) to adapt. New actors, issues, levels of engagement, and complexities have all changed the substance and delivery of ISO-led diplomacy as well as the diplomatic practices that occur within the organizations. Nowhere is this clearer than in the increasingly competitive and high-stakes processes by which major sporting events (above all the Olympics and the FIFA World Cup) are awarded to host cities and countries—and in the related nexus between ISOs, commercial broadcasters, and privileged corporate sponsors. We will expand on these themes in the next two sections, concerning club diplomacy and network diplomacy respectively.

39.2 Sport in 'Club' Diplomacy

In the predominantly state-centred world of club diplomacy, which also prevailed in the realm of sport until the 1980s, governments and their diplomatic representatives attempted to instrumentalize sport for a variety of public diplomacy purposes. These purposes included propagandistic and prestige-seeking activities; relatively low-cost, high-visibility forms of protest and punishment; precursors and facilitators of improved diplomatic relations; and means of pursuing diplomatic recognition or signalling rehabilitation within the international 'community of nations'.

The pursuit of status or prestige is an under-appreciated objective of much international diplomatic activity.[13] There is no more obvious instance of this than the 'Nazi Olympics' of 1936 in Berlin, which were comprehensively conceived and orchestrated as a vehicle to project the glories of Nazi Germany both to the world and to Germany's own citizens.[14] This example highlights the degree to which sport diplomacy is often a 'two-level game', targeting international and domestic audiences simultaneously. As noted earlier, this objective may be particularly compelling to authoritarian or revolutionary regimes.[15] Yet even in countries that historically adhered to a more apolitical public view of sport, such as the UK, governments have long been mindful of its potential role in 'reflecting and enhancing, as well as diminishing, British prestige at home and abroad'. An example was the decision to carry through with the 1948 London Olympics at a time when Britain was reeling from the impacts of war and reconstruction.[16]

In the context of the cold war, international sport became a proxy for 'hotter' forms of conflict. Indeed, George Orwell's famous remark that international sport was nothing more than 'war minus the shooting' was made in reference to a set of particularly nasty football matches (and fan reactions) played between a Soviet team (FC Dynamo Moscow) and an all-star English team at the very beginning of the cold war.[17] Perhaps the most prominent manifestation of cold war sporting animosity were the tit-for-tat boycotts of the 1980 Moscow Games (in response to the Soviet invasion of Afghanistan) by the US and fifty other countries,[18] and of the 1984 Los Angeles Games by the USSR and thirteen of its allies. Because these boycotts were principally symbolic in their impact, it was hard to assess their 'success': clearly the first was felt as a blow to the prestige of the Moscow organizers, while the latter was arguably counterproductive since it reinforced the orgy of patriotism that accompanied the Los Angeles Games, with US dominance unchallenged by its East bloc rivals. Nevertheless, the fact that the Moscow boycott did not cause the USSR to waver in its occupation of Afghanistan led many to construe it as a failure, and as further evidence of the ineffectualness of the Carter administration's foreign policy. This case illustrates both the tendency toward unanticipated repercussions of diplomatic interventions in sport, and the relative lack of understanding by professional diplomats in the State Department (and elsewhere) of the peculiarities of the world of sport.

Of course, the 'war minus the shooting' paradigm is by no means limited to the cold war. Ryszard Kapuscinski labelled the four-day war between Honduras and El Salvador in 1969 the 'Soccer War' because of the role that a World Cup-qualifying match played in sparking mutual animosities, overheated rhetoric, and nationalist sentiment. Thus, while the match itself saw no bloodshed, it seems to have led directly to the breakdown of diplomacy. Other geopolitical rivalries that have 'played out' in international sport include the 'blood in the water' water polo match between Hungarian and Soviet teams (set against the backdrop of the 1956 Hungarian revolution and Moscow's brutal response) or the more recent eruption of violence between Egyptians and Algerians who, after a contentious set of World Cup-qualifying matches, attacked each others' football teams, embassies, national symbols, and fans. Such riotous incidents test and sometimes rupture the limits of diplomatic deference between countries.[19]

Sports sanctions, such as the Moscow and Los Angeles boycotts, arose regularly in the era of club diplomacy. A more successful example of the use of sport sanctions was the international campaign to isolate apartheid South Africa from international competition. This case is intriguing because it illustrates the hierarchical nature of international sport governance, and the way in which this *can* lead to more enforceable decision-making within its limited domain. In short, once ISOs finally determined that the apartheid regime should be excluded from international competition (a protracted and contentious process), they were able to enforce this decision among their national 'constituents' far more comprehensively than virtually any other sanction against South Africa. Moreover, this case provided an early example of the potential of transnational social movements to affect international diplomatic outcomes. In this instance, anti-apartheid sport activists mobilized around the exiled, shoestring South African Non-Racial Olympic Committee (SANROC) and made common cause with newly independent 'third world' governments to successfully lobby for an enforceable sport boycott. Nevertheless, it took several decades of escalating pressure before the apartheid regime was supplanted, and the role played by the sport boycott in this outcome remains contentious.[20]

In the 'club era', various governments made intermittent use of sport as a form of cultural diplomacy, in an effort to foster goodwill and understanding as the basis for more cooperative international relationships. Precisely because of the myth of autonomy, sport was often viewed as a relatively benign precursor and precedent for improved relations. In addition to the well-known ping-pong diplomacy of the 1970s, 'wrestling diplomacy' between Iran and the United States in the 1990s and 'cricket diplomacy' between India and Pakistan more recently have had a significant, and sometimes a very public influence on political leaders and the societies of these respective countries.[21] Such sporting overtures are, if anything, becoming more frequent.[22] However, as noted earlier in this section, given the fiercely competitive nature of much international sport, the effects of such cultural diplomacy can prove counterproductive. The behaviour of touring Canadian amateur ice hockey teams in Europe in the mid-1960s, for example, was characterized in an official Canadian Department of External Affairs memo as 'brutish' and 'reprehensible'. As goodwill exercises, the Department clearly regarded these tours as failures.[23]

Finally, governments and their representatives have attempted to use sport to secure recognition—both formal and informal—and to signal rehabilitation or 'arrival' as legitimate and/or developed countries in international society. In this, they have been aided and abetted by the desire of ISOs to promote their cardinal norm of universality. For example, the former Axis powers of the Second World War pursued the hosting of Olympic Games with the objective of diplomatic rehabilitation, in 1960 (Rome), 1964 (Tokyo), and 1972 (Munich) respectively. Mexico sought to use the 1968 Summer Olympics and the 1970 FIFA World Cup in an unsuccessful effort to transcend its identity as a developing country, while South Korea was more successful in using the 1988 Summer Games for this purpose, though with unanticipated domestic political consequences.

In addition to the aspirations associated with mega-event hosting, having a recognized NOC or other national sports body (e.g. a football association) can legitimize the very existence of a state or a state-like polity. From the very earliest days of the IOC (when Finns and Czechs wanted separate NOCs from the imperial Russian and Austrian ones), ISO recognition of national sports associations has aided many polities in making de facto claims to diplomatic recognition. During the cold war, the use of sporting recognition to presage diplomatic recognition was particularly noteworthy. The long, persistent, and successful efforts of East Germany (GDR) to be recognized and compete independently of West Germany as well as the decades-long exclusion of the People's Republic of China (PRC) are emblematic. So influential can sporting recognition be that the words and even the letters used to signify various polities elicit heated debate. Israel, for example, tried to insist that the NOC representing Arab Palestinians be called the 'Palestinian Authority' rather than 'Palestine', since the latter might imply sovereignty.[24] The famous solution (known as the 'Olympic Formula') to the long exclusion of the PRC was the inventive tactic of renaming the Republic of China/Taiwanese NOC the 'Chinese Taipei Olympic Committee' (thus implying that Taiwan is under PRC sovereignty but still allowing autonomous participation). Adaptations of the Olympic Formula have been used by non-sporting international organizations as a means of including both polities, and the same rhetorical devices were used when Hong Kong reverted to PRC sovereignty.[25]

Recognition by ISOs (especially the IOC and FIFA) continues to be a fervent goal of many territories with contested, emerging, or otherwise ambiguous sovereignty.[26]

Even polities which do not claim sovereignty use formal sporting recognition or informal participation in sporting events to reinforce cultural, historical, or economic autonomy. Gibraltar has been in a long-running battle to have its football association recognized (over strenuous Spanish objections), and numerous other (mostly small-island) dependencies of the UK, France, and the United States have eagerly embraced independent participation in global sport. More informally, some sub-national groups maintain distinctive teams that are not recognized by ISOs but nevertheless afford diverse ethnicities, language groups, or regions a sense of autonomy. The Catalonia region in Spain, for example, has a 'national football team' that competes in non-tournament matches against FIFA-recognized national teams, or, sometimes, other sub-national teams such as the Basque country or Provence in France. The fact that the Catalan team has employed Johan Cruyff (one of Europe's most successful players and coaches of all time) as its manager is indicative of the seriousness with which Catalonians take their separate football identity.

39.2.1 Club Diplomacy and ISOs

Although it preceded the explosion of civil society and non-governmental influence in diplomatic circles, the IOC has, throughout its history, played a significant role in international diplomacy as an institution with its own diplomatic identity. In order to carve out institutional space for itself, the IOC inhabited the environment of traditional diplomatic practices and norms. For example, early versions of what became the Olympic Charter referred to the ambassadorial precedence that was to be accorded to the Olympic Family during the Games:

> No special [foreign] embassy can be accepted by the organizing country on the occasion of the Games. For the duration of the Games precedence belongs to the members of the International Olympic Committee, the members of the organizing Committee, the presidents of the national Olympic Committees and the presidents of the [ISOs]. They form the Olympic senate.[27]

The space of the Games sites have also been accorded a kind of extraterritoriality or inviolability that resembles the territorial privileges normally enjoyed by foreign embassies, consulates, and missions. In one of the more prominent examples of this, the IOC president during the 1936 Games in Berlin successfully ordered Hitler to remove anti-Semitic signage from highways, stadia, and other venues with the injunction that: 'When the five-circled flag is raised over the stadium, it is no longer Germany. It is Olympia, and we are the masters then.'[28]

Athletes at the Olympic Games form a type of Olympic diplomatic corps. East German officials used to advise their departing competitors, 'you are sports-diplomats in track suits'.[29] Of course, such messages as these from the GDR and other governments were frowned upon by the IOC as 'politicizing' the Games (in this case with Marxist–Leninist ideology), but the mission of Olympism is actually strikingly similar. The IOC's diplomatic efforts have been primarily based at the state level and have involved encouraging decision-makers and enthralled populations alike to come to better know and respect their counterparts in other countries. Olympic athletes, as some of the world's earliest celebrity diplomats, are the fundamental bearers of this mission, which is to be carried out through honourable, meritocratic performance and gracious and reflective winning *and* losing. In one sense, the Eastern bloc's instrumentalization of international sport to promote a Soviet-style political economy was nothing more than an effort to familiarize the world with the normative and cultural features (and ostensible superiority) of their countries. Regardless of the ideology or the context, however, Olympic athletes are in some respects the foreign service officers of the Olympic movement, meant to spread Olympic values that paradoxically include the mutual glorification of national cultures. The primary political level to which these values are addressed is that of the nation state, as reflected in the celebratory 'parade of nations' that initiates each edition of the Games and the stylized national pageants staged by host countries at the opening and closing ceremonies.

Both the formal practices and the substantive diplomatic message of the Olympic movement reflect a time (late 19th and early 20th centuries) and a place (Europe) in which the practice of diplomacy was of the more exclusive 'club' type. Most other ISOs adopted, to a greater or lesser extent, the internationalist-pacifist stance of the IOC, at least rhetorically. Given the inferior prominence, visibility, and popularity of most other events and sports (excepting the FIFA World Cup and occasionally other events such as the Commonwealth Games) however, most ISOs cannot aspire to the de facto diplomatic status and privileges of the IOC.

In addition, most ISOs more closely resemble the UN and other IGOs than does the IOC. FIFA, the IAAF, and most other ISOs such as the Fédération Internationale de Ski or the International Archery Federation have a confederated structure in which membership is open to all national units (duly accredited), each of which has an equal vote on substantive matters. Such a structure frequently produces many of the same dynamics seen in large and inclusive IGOs: bloc and tactical voting, gridlock and a failure to produce sufficient majorities, etc. Despite the ostensibly non-political nature of the matters under consideration and the formal banning of government officials or influence, the isolation of Israeli national federations, the boycotting or expulsion of the Rhodesian and apartheid South African national federations, the support for enemies of enemies, and many other examples highlight how diplomatic dynamics within ISOs reflect the broader diplomatic dynamics of world politics.

Substantively, as diplomatic actors themselves, many ISOs have pursued agendas that can best be described as 'niche diplomacy'. Perhaps most notable in this regard is the International Table Tennis Federation (ITTF). The ITTF has been active in ways expected within traditional diplomacy as well as the more contemporary network diplomacy. For example, the ITTF was central to the ping-pong diplomacy that prepared the ground for Sino–US diplomatic normalization. ITTF President Roy Evans suggested to

Premier Chou En-lai that he invite foreign athletes from Western countries to visit mainland China at the conclusion of the championships in Japan. The ITTF was also 'the prototype for the [ISO apartheid] boycott campaign', becoming the first ISO to expel the racially-exclusive South African Table Tennis Union in favour of the non-racial South African Table Tennis Board, which it continued to recognize throughout the decades of apartheid.[30] Similarly, it was hastier than most ISOs in facilitating the unification of the white and non-racial federations as apartheid was being dismantled.[31]

The ITTF has made a habit of ushering in and training new, newly independent, and contested countries or polities (e.g. Taiwan), thus welcoming them to the elite club of international sport and demanding sporting-diplomatic recognition by existing national federations. Such diplomatic activism is not inconsequential. The ITTF recognized a Kosovar federation in 2003 (five years prior to Kosovo's declaration of independence) and was the first 'international organization' listed as having done so on the public diplomacy website 'Who Recognized Kosova as an Independent State' (at <www.kosovothanksyou.com>). When the Kosovar team encountered visa problems prior to the European championships in Belgrade in 2007, the ITTF retaliated by rejecting Serbia's bid to host the World Table Tennis Championship in 2011. Afghanistan, Iraq, East Timor, and others have all been beneficiaries of the ITTF's proactive diplomatic engagement.

It is clear from these examples that club diplomacy was practised both *within* ISOs and *between* ISOs and the broader realm of interstate diplomacy. Moreover, many of these practices persist even as they have been increasingly accompanied and complicated by features associated with the network era.

39.3 SPORT IN NETWORK DIPLOMACY

It is hard to believe from the vantage of the early 21st century that in the early 1980s the future viability of the Olympic Games—the ultimate sport mega-event—was widely questioned. Reeling from successive boycotts as well as the financially disastrous 1976 Montreal Olympics, it was becoming harder and harder to attract viable hosts. When Los Angeles was awarded the right to host the 1984 Games in 1978, it was the only bidder. Similarly, when Seoul—then the capital of a repressive military regime on the front lines of the cold war as the pro-Western half of a divided state—was awarded the 1988 Games it was regarded as a politically risky choice and a surprise winner over the only other candidate city, Nagoya.[32]

Today, the Games, along with other sport mega-events, are the focus of high-profile, high-stakes competitions among many of the world's great cities and aspiring world cities, strongly supported by regional and national governments and their political leaders. Shuttle diplomacy at the highest political levels (presidents, prime ministers, royalty, and others) is now pervasive at the conferences where hosting decisions are made. In the process, leaders are routinely humbled and/or aggrandized. Many attribute the near-necessity of dispatching a country's highest political officer to win a sport mega-event to

British Prime Minister Tony Blair's vigorous lobbying on behalf of London's successful 2012 Olympic bid. By Blair's own account the Parisian bid, with President Jacques Chirac at its head, was comparatively aloof and did not engage in the same face-to-face lobbying of hundreds of politicians and IOC members in the final days, accounting for the failure of what was perceived by many to be the technically stronger bid.[33] In contrast, the newly sworn-in US President Barack Obama was widely perceived as having been snubbed by the IOC despite his face-to-face advocacy of Chicago's 2016 Olympic bid. It was soundly defeated by the Rio de Janeiro bid, strongly supported by extensive lobbying from an emotional President Lula.[34] Thus, although the lobbying of a country's highest ranking politician may now be a virtual *necessity* for winning the right to stage mega-events, it is no longer *sufficient*. FIFA's choice of Russia over England for the 2018 World Cup despite the vigorous advocacy of both Prime Minister David Cameron and Prince William is further evidence of this reality.[35] These trends in diplomatic activity at the highest political levels reflect the degree to which, in the post-cold war era of neoliberal globalization, international sport and sport mega-events have become coveted prizes in the quest for global visibility and 'marketing power'.[36] Indeed, international sport can be seen as a uniquely apt strategic response to globalization, simultaneously celebrating and promoting values of competitiveness at home while reinforcing constructed national identities for internal and external audiences.

The increasing salience of sport in this distinctive form of public diplomacy has been underpinned by a number of key trends. These include the dramatic increase in the profitability of sport, sport franchises, and sporting events, and the concomitant rise of the 'sport-media complex'. The unique synergy between sport and electronic media heighten the reach, visibility, and influence of sports events, iconic sports teams and rivalries, and individual sporting 'heroes', many of whom have become (as noted earlier) among the most famous celebrity diplomats of the age.[37] Virtually no other form of international communication short of responses to large-scale natural disasters or armed conflicts can command a comparable degree of international attention—although, as always, the opportunities come with risks of very public 'failure' (witness the negative publicity generated by the 1996 Atlanta Olympic Games or the question of whether the venues for the 2010 Delhi Commonwealth Games would be safe and ready in time). Moreover, there is a chronic tendency to exaggerate the potential benefits of international sporting success, whether competitive or organizational. These trends have, in turn, led to the rising salience of many new players in the sport diplomacy arena, even as the old practices of club diplomacy persist.

39.3.1 Network Diplomacy, ISOs, and 'New Actors'

Over time, a plethora of diverse actors have come to occupy the diplomatic space of international sports. As with the broader trend towards non-governmental influence in diplomatic networks, the world of international sport has seen the rise of many NGOs that pursue issue-specific or country-specific mandates. A vibrant and much-discussed community of actors who apply sporting practices to the task of 'international development' has arisen in recent decades; a perusal of the database of organizations maintained by the International Platform on Sport and Development reveals NGOs addressing everything from HIV/AIDS to post-conflict peace-building and reconciliation.[38] Many of these NGOs are financed or sponsored by governments, national sporting bodies or leagues (e.g. the English Football Association or the American National Basketball Association), or private firms (e.g. major sports wear MNCs), thus further complicating the layers of diplomacy and the interests in play. For example, Right to Play—perhaps the most prominent 'sport for development' NGO—receives significant funding from (inter)governmental agencies (e.g. the Canadian International Development Agency and the United Nations Children's Fund), multinationals (e.g. Goldman Sachs), other NGOs (e.g. Save the Children) and sports organizations (e.g. the International Ski Federation and the Chelsea Football Club). The question of diplomatic space becomes dramatically complicated by the fact that Right to Play is, at once, perceived to represent Canadian and Norwegian values as well as the interests of Goldman Sachs, UNICEF, and Chelsea FC.[39]

Within this growing panoply of players, the leading ISOs have adapted and indeed thrived, notwithstanding periodic scandal. They, in turn, have elicited new interest and roles on the part of other non-governmental as well as government actors. Though the IOC was not the first ISO to commercialize its product or to allow professionals into its historically amateur ranks, these decisions had monumental effects upon the entire universe of ISOs. When Juan Antonio Samaranch—a controversial former Falange politician in Franco's Spain and later Spanish ambassador to the USSR—became the IOC president in 1980, the organization was nearly bankrupt.[40] His decision to invite commercial sponsors to bid for the right to associate themselves with the Olympic movement and to raise the stakes significantly for aspiring television broadcasters made the IOC one of the richest NGOs on the planet. It also incorporated MNCs and their interests firmly within the international sporting scene. Many other ISOs and NOCs followed the IOC's example (though few as profitably), and even those who retained amateur features or attracted little commercial interest have benefitted financially because of the distribution of IOC resources throughout the Olympic system. As a consequence, MNCs have become integral to the Olympic movement, notably through exclusive and lucrative sponsorship arrangements that give these privileged corporate 'partners' a major stake in the preservation and propagation of the internationalist image and ideology of Olympism. They have also often influenced or made demands upon Olympic actors, as manifested in the National Broadcasting Corporation's insistence that certain high-profile events be scheduled for primetime viewing in the United States or critics' suspicions that host city selections are at least partially determined by the presence of attractive markets for Olympic sponsors. Corporate sponsors, in turn, have enabled the IOC to attain unprecedented reach and power from its already privileged position. In many ways then, as noted a moment ago, the IOC's decision to market its 'brand' has transformed it into a virtual MNC in its own right.

The ability of the IOC and other ISOs to act as diplomats has been constrained somewhat by the rise of non-governmental actors that limit or oppose their actions. Some of these NGOs have arisen from within the international sports world. The Court of Arbitration for Sport (CAS), for example, serves as a check on the power of ISOs by introducing due process and sound jurisprudential practices to international sport. Athletes, teams, NOCs and other national federations, ISOs, and other relevant actors can (and in many cases are obligated to) bring disputes before a CAS legal panel for arbitration. Sometimes the panels decide against the IOC or other ISOs. Likewise, the World Anti-Doping Agency (WADA) is composed of representatives from the world of international sport and from governments around the world who make decisions about (il) legal substances, prosecution, discipline, national legislation, and other matters related to doping. WADA's hybrid structure allows it some independence from ISOs. Both organizations have become significant actors in the prosecution of international diplomacy through sport. The CAS, for example, has ordered FIFA (on two separate occasions) to allow the application of Gibraltar for an accredited national football (soccer) federation to progress through the normal process, over strenuous objections from the Spanish government and football association.[41]

Other non-sporting NGOs and social movements have begun to play an increasingly significant role in ISO diplomacy as well. In the wake of severe environmental degradation at the 1992 Winter Games in Albertville, France for example, environmental organizations denounced the IOC for allowing such an outcome. Before long this pressure prompted the IOC to declare 'the environment' to be the third 'pillar' of Olympism (in addition to culture and education) and to demand environmental impact studies (based on recommendations from the United Nations Environmental Programme) of future host candidates.[42] Human rights groups have long protested many of the effects of hosting Olympic Games on local populations; such protests nearly overwhelmed the IOC during the global torch relay preceding the Beijing Games in 2008. So widespread were the protests that current IOC President Jacques Rogge conceded that human rights considerations would play a role in future hosting decisions.[43]

One final set of relatively new actors in international sport diplomacy are intergovernmental organizations. Where organizations such as the United Nations Educational, Cultural, and Scientific Organization (UNESCO) were once perceived as rivals and potential threats to the IOC and other ISOs,[44] most UN institutions and other IGOs are now vocal supporters of, and active partners with, sports organizations.[45] The IOC in particular has signed formal partnership agreements with dozens of UN agencies, funds, and programmes to collaborate on areas of mutual interest, to draw upon specialized skill sets, to provide mutual aid, and other such activities. Beginning with Secretary-General Kofi Annan, the UN has even had a senior-level liaison with the international sports world (the Special Adviser to the Secretary-General on Sport for Peace and Development) and the UN flag now flies at all Olympic Games venues. Nowhere has this IGO–ISO nexus become more prominent than in relation to the aforementioned 'Sport for Development and Peace' movement, which has rapidly developed a diverse following among official aid agencies, non-governmental organizations (large and small), and a growing number of celebrity athletes.[46] Other IGOs have also 'hitched their wagon' to international sport however—few more prominently than the (formerly British)

Commonwealth, whose most visible and vital manifestation in its long, slow decline has become the Commonwealth Games. These Games have become a means by which key 'rising states'—first Malaysia and most recently India—have attempted to signal their arrival whilst establishing credibility as potential hosts for larger, 'first order' events.[47]

The dramatic rise in actors involved in international sports diplomacy is no surprise given the rapidly increasing scope of tasks that ISOs are now expected to undertake. In addition to the environmental and human rights considerations mentioned earlier, the IOC alone has had to continually address issues of women's rights, excessive or damaging commercialism, the related issues of corruption and bribery, and terrorism. FIFA has likewise had to address most of these issues, including, very recently, serious allegations of vote-buying bribery as well as systematic complaints about racism and violence in international and transnational football. Given the massive global interest in the FIFA World Cup and similar mega-events, terrorism and security have become particularly acute concerns for ISOs and host governments, ever since the Munich Olympic Games were infiltrated by Palestinian terrorists in 1972.[48] In sum, where once ISOs focused on the limited task of delivering sports events, presuming that regular, international competitions would foster tolerance among nations, the prosecution, promotion, and perpetuation of their particular brand of diplomacy has placed increasingly diverse and onerous demands upon them.

ISOs have also had to move beyond their traditional reliance on national delegations or federations as their only level of engagement. The Olympic Games, for example, are hosted by cities, not countries, and the IOC has accordingly become more intimately involved in municipal and sub-national relations than ever before. As urban concerns intersect with mega-event hosting (including housing rights, pollution control, 'white elephant' venues, land rights, poverty, etc.), residents, activists, and occasionally a global audience have become increasingly sceptical concerning the positive public diplomacy potential touted by ISOs. Conversely, urban and regional (provincial, state) governments have become increasingly active in the international diplomacy of courting ISOs and the events they offer. When their bids are successful, they have attempted to orchestrate sophisticated campaigns designed to secure public support at home, and 'branding' benefits and tourist promotion abroad. Key players in this new diplomacy of sport are powerful organizing committees (LOCOG in London, VANOC in Vancouver, etc.)—public–private partnerships that enjoy extraordinary access, attention, and resources from governments and corporations alike, while being largely shielded from the conventional means of public accountability to which government agencies would be subject.

In the first part of the 21st century, ISOs are increasingly turning to developing countries to host mega-events, including Olympics in Beijing (2008) and Rio de Janeiro (2016) and FIFA World Cups in South Africa (2010), Brazil (2014), and Qatar (2022). This is consistent with ISOs' ongoing pursuit of universalism, and the growing ubiquity of mega-event hosting on the path to 'emerging power' status. The ramifications of this trend for hosts in terms of development, sustainability, and social equity are far from certain given its historic novelty. Similarly, there will likely be increasing criticisms of

ISOs that do not understand or accommodate significant local political and cultural sensibilities.

Besides the new actors working for or against particular ISOs, the bureaucracies of the latter have nearly universally expanded since the beginning of Samaranch's tenure as IOC president. The IOC's administration ballooned from one (particularly infamous) executive director with a small, partially voluntary support team to a professionalized operation with hundreds of employees divided into twelve departments across Lausanne.[49] FIFA has likewise expanded its administrative apparatus at 'FIFA House' in Zurich. Lausanne in particular and Switzerland in general now have thousands of professionals working in bureaucratic capacities for dozens of ISOs. The pace of expansion and specialization reflects the increasing expectations placed upon ISOs in order to fulfil their self-proclaimed diplomatic missions.

The increasing wealth of many ISOs has enabled this expanded in-house capacity and has also provided opportunities for further diplomatic engagements. For example, the IOC regularly hosts conferences on a variety of topics where sports and international relations intersect. Recent examples include environmental sustainability, women's rights, health, and socio-economic development and peace.[50] Such conference diplomacy, like that of many UN agencies, involves government officials, ISO representatives, academics, celebrities/athletes, advocates and activists, and the like.

Smaller ISOs have continued to play niche diplomatic roles in this more complex, networked environment. The ITTF is again exemplary. Since 1999, it has overseen an extensive 'Development Program' that seeks to develop the sport globally, but predominantly in developing countries.[51] Alongside the development and expansion of the game, ITTF has fostered a growing 'Goodwill Fund' that specifically targets areas of humanitarian disaster or dire need. Examples include a girls-only project in rural parts of Egypt, a 'Tsunami Rebuilding' project, and undertakings in Afghanistan, Yemen, and East Timor. Under these two programmes, hundreds of projects are carried out annually, many with funding from the IOC, in all parts of the world.[52] The ITTF has thereby made a name for itself in international diplomatic circles, partnering with multilateral organizations (such as the United Nations High Commissioner for Refugees) and winning awards for its endeavours.

39.4 Conclusion

As with foreign ministries today, ISOs continue to address their diplomatic efforts primarily toward states and/or the accredited national federations and the countries they are supposed to represent. For these organizations, the simplest situation is one in which their objectives and initiatives can be accomplished through the traditional channels of 'club' diplomacy, including internal diplomacy among the national federations. However, the increasing number of actors (both supporters and critics) involved in sports diplomacy, the expanding scope of the practice, the increasing specialization necessary, and the new formats for engagement all make a more networked approach the only feasible way forward.

Meanwhile, for the traditional state-based actors that have long been at the core of international diplomacy, the increased range, complexity, and prominence of sport diplomacy has generated an array of new demands at a time when, as the editors of this *Handbook* note, many traditional foreign ministries are facing a dramatic decrease in resources. Much of the work they must now do is ancillary to the international activities of a range of new actors: bid committees, organizing committees, NOCs and national sports federations, ministries of sport and culture, national sports academies and institutes, etc. Likewise, that work must be focused on facilitating coordination among the complex range of tasks and actors that contemporary sporting venues and events require, from consular, to protocol, to security, to public relations and marketing activities. These functions remain as ubiquitous and essential as they are inconspicuous, underscoring the continued salience of diplomatic functions in a very different diplomatic 'ecosystem'.

NOTES

1. L. Allison, 'The Changing Context of Sporting Life', in L. Allison (ed.), *The Changing Politics of Sport* (Manchester: Manchester University Press, 1993), 5.
2. See, for example, E. Bergbusch, 'Sport and Canadian Foreign Policy', *Behind the Headlines* 45:2 (December 1987).
3. See, for example, P. Arnaud and J. Riordan, *Sport and International Politics: The Impact of Fascism and Communism on Sport* (London: E and FN Spon, 1998).
4. See D. Black and S. Bezanson, 'The Olympic Games, human rights, and democratization: lessons from Seoul and implications for Beijing', *Third World Quarterly* 25: 7 (2004), 1245–61.
5. See J. Hoberman, 'Toward a theory of Olympic internationalism', *Journal of Sport History* 25:1 (1995), 1–37.
6. See, for example, B. Peacock, ' "A Virtual World Government unto Itself": Uncovering the Rational-Legal Authority of the IOC in World Politics', *Olympika: The International Journal of Olympic Studies* XIX (2010), 41–58, especially 44–9.
7. Unlike the IOC, which is composed of individuals that are neither selected on a one-member-per-country basis nor representatives of their countries to the Committee, most ISOs that govern individual sports are administered by a congress of each of the nationally-accredited federations.
8. Indeed, there is a nexus of expanding and related causes. For example, many ISOs explicitly promoted non-racialism in the context of the struggle against apartheid and minority rule; more recently, they have sought to promote environmentalism and international development, albeit with limited and contradictory effects.
9. P. de Coubertin, 'Olympism: Selected Writings', in N. Müller (ed.), *Olympism. Selected Writings of Pierre de Coubertin* (Lausanne: International Olympic Committee, 2000), 209.
10. H. Wang and J. Rosenau, 'Transparency International and Corruption as an Issue of Global Governance', *Global Governance* 7 (2001), 25–49 at 26–7.

11. Recent examples of expelled or suspended NOCs include the Afghan committee under the Taliban and Iraq's post-Saddam suspension because of governmental interference. The expulsion of apartheid South Africa's NOC is perhaps the most prominent.

12. For an account of this type of interaction, see Hoberman, 'Toward a theory of Olympic internationalism'; for more polemical accounts, see A. Jennings and V. Simson, *The Lords of the Rings: Power, Money, and Drugs in the Modern Olympics* (Toronto: Stoddart, 1992); and A. Jennings, *The New Lords of the Rings: Olympic Corruption and How to Buy Gold Medals* (London: Pocket Books, 1996).

13. See L. Allison and T. Monnington, 'Sport, prestige, and international relations', in L. Allison (ed.), *The Global Politics of Sport* (London: Routledge, 2005).

14. There is an extensive literature on these games. For one example, see A. Guttmann, 'The "Nazi Olympics" and the American boycott controversy', in Arnaud and Riordan (eds), *Sport and International Politics*.

15. Cuba is a fascinating case in point. See T. Slack and D. Whitson, 'The place of sport in Cuba's foreign relations', *International Journal*, XLIII:4 (1988), 596–617; and R. Huish, 'Punching Above its Weight: Cuba's use of sport for South-South cooperation', *Third World Quarterly* 32:3 (2011), 417–33.

16. P.J. Beck, '"The most effective means of communication in the modern world"? British sport and national prestige', in R. Levermore and A. Budd (eds), *Sport and International Relations: an Emerging Relationship* (London: Routledge, 2004), 78 and throughout.

17. G. Orwell, 'The Sporting Spirit', *Tribune*, 14 December 1945.

18. Though 50 eligible NOC's of 140 did not attend the Moscow Games, a number of these had never intended to participate. Bergbusch, 'Sport and Canadian Foreign Policy', 6.

19. R. Kapuscinski, *The Soccer War* (London: Granta Books, 1990); H. Araton, 'Raw Emotion and Spilled Blood of '56', *New York Times*, 21 July 1996; M. Slackman, 'This Time, Egyptians Riot over Soccer, Not Bread', *New York Times*, 20 November 2009.

20. On this case, see for example B. Kidd, 'The campaign against sport in South Africa', *International Journal*, XLIII:4 (1988), 643–64; D. Black, '"Not cricket": the impact of the sport boycott', in N. Crawford and A. Klotz (eds), *How Sanctions Work: Lessons from South Africa* (London: Macmillan, 1999); and D. Booth, *The Race Game: Sport and Politics in South Africa* (London: Frank Cass, 1998).

21. 'Old Glory Gets a Cheer as U.S. Team Plays in Iran', *New York Times*, 18 February 1998. For an overview of India–Pakistan 'cricket diplomacy', see 'Timeline: India-Pakistan "Cricket Diplomacy"', *Agence France-Presse*, 30 March 2011.

22. One recent example of the continuing tendency to frame sports contests as steps towards diplomatic *rapprochement* is the 'football diplomacy' that has been widely reported on between Turkey and Armenia. See 'Football diplomacy: Turkish-Armenian Relations', *The Economist*, 3 September 2009.

23. See D. Macintosh and M. Hawes, *Sport and Canadian Diplomacy* (Montreal: McGill-Queen's University Press, 1994), 23–6.

24. L. Cyphers, 'Team Palestine Gets OK Olympic Ruling Hits Israel's Objections', *New York Daily News*, 16 July 1996.

25. See G. Chan, 'From the "Olympic Formula" to the Beijing Games: Towards Greater Integration across the Taiwan Strait?', *Cambridge Review of International Affairs* 15:1 (2002), 141–8; and G. Chan, 'The "Two-Chinas" Problem and the Olympic Formula', *Pacific Affairs* 58:3 (Autumn 1985), 473–90.

26. For a comprehensive review of the use of international sport in diplomatic recognition see B. Peacock, ' "Géographie Sportive": Playing the Olympic Sovereignty Game', MA Thesis, Graduate Institute of International and Development Studies, Geneva, 2009.

27. *Olympic Rules*, Rule 9, 1946.

28. Quoted in E. Cashmore, *Making Sense of Sport* (New York: Routledge, 2010), 504.

29. A. Strenk, 'Diplomats in Track Suits: the Role of Sports in the Foreign Policy of the German Democratic Republic', *Journal of Sport and Social Issues* 4:1 (1980), 34–45.

30. M. Keech and B. Houlihan, 'Sport and the End of Apartheid', *The Round Table* 349 (1999), 109–21, at 112.

31. K. Mbaye, *The International Olympic Committee and South Africa* (Lausanne: International Olympic Committee, 1995), 186.

32. See C. Hill, *Olympic Politics* (Manchester: Manchester University Press, 1996), ch. 7; Black and Bezanson, 'The Olympic Games, human rights, and democratization', 1250.

33. See T. Blair, *A Journey* (London: Hutchinson Random House, 2010).

34. See A. O'Connor and T. Reid, 'Olympic Snub for Obama as Rio beats Chicago in 2016 Bid', *The Times*, 9 October 2009; 'Brazil's Weeping President Luiz Inacio Lula da Silva Revels in 2016 Olympics Vote', *The Telegraph*, 3 October 2009.

35. It should be noted, moreover, that despite Russian Prime Minister Vladimir Putin's widely acclaimed role in securing the 2014 Winter Games for Sochi after a powerful address uncharacteristically delivered in English, he made a very public decision not to engage in shuttle diplomacy before the World Cup vote, ostensibly to avoid tarnishing a process already widely maligned by corruption allegations. See 'Putin not to Attend FIFA Decision over "Smears" ', *BBC News*, 1 December 2010.

36. See, for example, D. Black and J. van der Westhuizen, 'The allure of global games for "semi-peripheral" polities and spaces: a research agenda', *Third World Quarterly* 25:7 (2004), 1195–214; and J. Horne and W. Manzenreiter, *Sports Mega-Events: Social Scientific Analyses of a Global Phenomenon* (Oxford: Blackwell, 2006). See also D. Black, 'Dreaming big: The pursuit of "second order" games as a strategic response to globalization', *Sport in Society* 11:4 (2008), 467–480, at 470–2.

37. See P. Gilchrist, 'Local heroes and global stars', in Allison (ed.), *The Global Politics of Sport*.

38. For one recent discussion see the special issue: Mainstreaming Sport into International Development Studies, *Third World Quarterly*, 32(3), 2011. For the databases of the International Platform on Sport and Development visit <http://www.sportanddev.org/en/connect/>.

39. For a list of Right to Play funders see <http://www.righttoplay.com/International/the-team/Pages/FundersandPartners.aspx>.

40. See M. Payne, *Olympic Turnaround* (New York: Greenwood Publishing Group, 2006).

41. See rulings in M. Reeb, *Digest of CAS Awards III, 2001–2003* (The Hague: Kluwer Law International, 2004).

42. H. Cantelon and M. Letters, 'The Making of the IOC Environmental Policy as the Third Dimension of the Olympic Movement', *International Review for the Sociology of Sport* 35:3 (2000), 294–308.

43. Deutsche Presse-Agentur, 'Rogge to Strengthen Human Rights Aspect in IOC', 2 May 2008.

44. On the potential usurping of the Games by UNESCO see, for example, A.E. Senn, *Power, Politics, and the Olympic Games* (Champaign, IL: Human Kinetics, 1999).

45. See B. Peacock, '"A Secret Instinct of Social Preservation": Legitimacy and the Dynamic (Re)Constitution of Olympic Conceptions of the "Good"', *Third World Quarterly* 32:3 (2011), 477–502.

46. See I. Beutler, 'Sport serving development and peace: Achieving the goals of the United Nations through sport', *Sport in Society* 11:4 (2008), 359–69; and B. Kidd, 'A new social movement: Sport for development and peace', *Sport in Society* 11:4 (2008), 370–80.

47. See G. Smith, 'Worst of times, best of times', *The Globe and Mail* (Toronto), 15 October 2010; and J. van der Westhuizen, 'Marketing Malaysia as a model modern Moslem state: the significance of the 16th Commonwealth Games', *Third World Quarterly* 25:7 (2004), 1277–91.

48. See K. Toohey, 'Terrorism, sport and public policy in the risk society', *Sport in Society* 11:4 (2008), 429–42.

49. See chapter 2 of J.-L. Chappelet, *The International Olympic Committee and the Olympic System* (Florence, KY: Routledge, 2008).

50. To review the scope and types of conferences hosted or subsidized by the IOC, see <http://www.olympic.org/conferences-forums-and-events/documents-reports-studies-publications>.

51. For a sense of the current scope of this 'Development Program', see *ITTF Development Plan 2009–2012* and browse the ITTF's web site under 'Development', both accessible at <http://www.ittf.com/_front_page/ittf4.asp?category=development>.

52. The policy document on the Goodwill Fund can be examined at <http://www.ittf.com/ittf_development/PDF/ITTF_Goodwill_Fund.pdf>.

PART VI

CASE STUDIES

CHAPTER 40

THE G20: FROM GLOBAL CRISIS RESPONDER TO STEERING COMMITTEE

PAUL MARTIN

40.1 INTRODUCTION

THIS chapter begins with a brief history of the 'G' system and its evolution towards the Leaders' G20, when in 2008 it was successful in preventing a 1930s type depression. Since then, it has begun the needed transition from global crisis responder to modern diplomacy's steering committee. The case study addresses some of the issues the G20 must resolve in order to succeed in this latter endeavour.

With the occasional commentary from my own experience, I suggest that the conditions precedent to the G20's success as a global steering committee are to be found in its ability to respond to two challenges: first, can it improve the way globalization works for everyone whether they are at the G20 table or not? Second, can it limit the contagion that appears to be the inevitable consequence of the interdependence of nations? In both instances I believe the answer lies in the G20's ability to demonstrate that the protection of sovereignty in today's world is directly proportional to the degree it is shared, an ability which is best exercised by national government leaders because of their overarching responsibilities and heightened sensitivity to domestic concerns.

40.2 THE ROAD TO THE G20

40.2.1 From the G5 to the G8

Beginning in 1973, at a time of recession, the end of the gold standard, and the first oil crisis, the finance ministers of the United States, the United Kingdom, France, West

Germany, and Japan met informally in the library of the White House to 'review developments of the international monetary system'.[1] These initial meetings of the 'library group' were arranged confidentially so as not to create further pressure on the exchange markets. The Finance Ministers' G5 thus was born.

Later in the decade, two alumni of the Finance Ministers' G5, France's Valéry Giscard D'Estaing and West Germany's Helmut Schmidt, who by then had become the leaders of their respective countries, sought to build upon the experiences of the old library club by elevating it to the highest level. They proposed to hold an informal meeting, comprised of the leaders of France, the United States, the United Kingdom, Germany, and Japan in the autumn of 1975 to discuss the then current monetary crisis. The proposal was well received. President Ford and Secretary of State Henry Kissinger, for example, envisioned the summit as a 'democratic global concert' to stave off democracy's threatened decline.

Before its first meeting in Rambouillet, France, the meeting of the five original countries was enlarged to include Italy (G6). At Rambouillet they decided to follow up with a conference in the United States. The next year, the United States brought in Canada at the San Juan summit (G7) to offset the numerical dominance of Europe.[2]

This configuration of seven nations continued for some twenty-two years until Russia's inclusion in 1998 turned it into the Group of Eight (G8) at the leaders' level. In this context, it is significant to note the different path taken by the G7 Finance Ministers and central bankers ('G7 Finance Ministers') as compared to their leaders. The finance ministers did not admit Russia as a member of the club, but only as an occasional observer.

Over time however, while the G7 Finance Ministers served the developed world's interests effectively, it became clear in the wake of the rise of the emerging economies that it could not deal adequately with the expanding range of global financial issues. In short, the absence of the newly emerging economies at the table began to call into question the ability of the G7 Finance Ministers to perform the role of global economic steering committee which it had assumed. Accordingly, the finance ministers moved ahead of their leaders in 1999 and created a parallel and more broadly based organization—the Finance Ministers' and central bankers' G20 (the Finance Ministers' G20).

40.2.2 The Finance Ministers' G20

The first attempt at creating the Finance Ministers' G20 followed the Mexican financial crisis of 1993–1994. This occurred some months before Canada's 1995 budget which ultimately led to the elimination of its deficit. At the time of the Mexican upheaval, Canada's financial situation was highly suspect and we were badly sideswiped by the crisis. It was then that I suggested to my counterparts in the G7 that a wider grouping was required to prevent the kind of contagion from which Canada and others in similar circumstances were suffering. Not surprisingly, there were no takers.

Two years later, however, another tremor occurred, this time in Asia—and it was much more serious. In the intervening period, there had been vigorous growth in Asia, which in turn triggered massive inflows of short-term capital, or 'hot money', from abroad. However, the lack of depth of Asia's domestic financial systems and excessive reliance on short-term borrowings in foreign currencies left many countries in the region vulnerable to a sudden reversal of confidence, which duly occurred. The domino effect that began in Asia eventually enveloped Brazil, which was forced into a major devaluation of its currency. This, coupled with Russia's default on its debt and the near failure of the giant American hedge fund, Long-Term Capital Management, threatened the stability of the global financial system. The sharp adjustments that followed not only stifled economic growth, but set back much of the social progress gained in vast segments of the developing world over the previous decade. Poverty rates soared, currencies plummeted, output declined, and inflation and unemployment ratcheted up.

Prompted by the G7 Finance Ministers, the IMF responded with solutions born of the Washington Consensus—deep spending cuts, fiscal austerity, and even greater liberalization of financial markets. The response of the emerging economies was swift. They told us that they would not be lectured to by countries that did not understand their reality, let alone countries that did not even include them in the decision-making dialogue.

It was at this point, Canada's deficit issues well behind us, that I raised much more forcefully the earlier suggestion I had made after the Mexican crisis—that of creating the Finance Ministers' G20. I did so first with my American counterpart Treasury Secretary Lawrence Summers and subsequently with Chancellor Gordon Brown of the United Kingdom. Both were supportive. As a result of these initial discussions, I met with Larry Summers and between us we identified the countries that would make up the G20. With his support, without which none of this would have been possible, our officials and I then approached the other finance ministers of the G7 and those of the countries that would eventually make up the Finance Ministers' G20. All were in agreement and not long afterwards I was named inaugural chair, chairing the first meeting held in Berlin in 1999, as well as the second in Montreal in 2000, and then an unplanned meeting in Ottawa in 2001.

The reader will note that there are only nineteen countries in the G20.[3] This occurred because, after Treasury Secretary Summers and I agreed on the list, Indonesia and Nigeria began to suffer major problems of governance which jeopardized their membership. Indonesia resolved its issues and became a member prior to the first meeting; unfortunately Nigeria did not. While it would be hazardous to open the G20's membership to conflicting claims at this stage, there is one exception to the Pandora's Box that could ensue if the existing membership were to be augmented.

With South Africa as its only G20 member, Africa is clearly underrepresented at the table and too often its issues are ignored. At this time, the continent sends the chair of the Heads of State and Government Implementation Committee (HSGIC) of the New Partnership for Africa's Development (NEPAD), the chairperson of the African Union Commission, and the President of the African Development Bank to represent the broader African interest. However, the problem is that the G20 is primarily an organization of countries and thus South Africa can find itself in the anomalous position of being looked to as speaking for a broader constituency. This causes hesitation within Africa and within South Africa as well. For this reason I believe the G20 should be open to a second African nation.

If, however, there is insufficient support at the present time for such a step, which appears to be the case, at a minimum Africa itself should do more to increase its effectiveness within the G20. To begin with, it should create a substantive and permanent internal-secretariat which would work to establish a greater consensus within the continent on G20 issues, at the same time establishing greater links with the bureaucracies of the other G20 members from whom Africa is too often isolated. The importance of the latter point cannot be overestimated.

That being said, the overall legitimacy of the G20 is evident from its membership, which is much more representative of the global reality than is the G8. The criteria agreed to by Larry Summers and myself were that the member countries must be either global economic powers in their own right or of such regional economic importance that they can speak credibly albeit informally about their region. The G20 represents both developed and emerging economies from every region of the globe: 66 per cent of the world's population, 88 per cent of the world's gross domestic product (GDP), and 60 per cent of the world's poor. This ensures the direct participation in discussions of countries whose size or strategic importance gives them a particularly crucial role as global needs are discussed.

Two final points before passing on to the Leaders' G20. First, at the inaugural finance ministers meeting in Berlin in 1999, certain members had some difficulty adjusting to the G7's tradition of informal, unscripted exchanges with all members on an equal footing. Therefore, at the second meeting in Montreal in 2000, after warning both of them beforehand, I opened the discussion by asking Trevor Manuel, South Africa's finance minister, and Larry Summers, to have at it on the issue of agricultural subsidies—an issue that was and remains contentious between the developing and developed worlds. Neither was a shrinking violet, and they performed exactly as one would have hoped, as did the other participants who willingly joined into the debate. In doing so, they not only set the tone for the Montreal meeting, but also established a standard of frank, unscripted discussion for meetings to come. I hope the leaders' version of the G20 is able to maintain this tradition—otherwise much of the benefit will be lost.

The second point speaks to the G20's scope and adaptability. In the aftermath of the terrorist attacks of 11 September 2001, and the increased risk of a follow-up attack elsewhere in the world, the security authorities of national governments everywhere were extremely reluctant to sanction any further high-profile international meetings. The pause lasted two months and would have gone on much longer but for the Finance Ministers' G20. As chair, I called a meeting to confront the issue of terrorist financing, which was beyond the capability of the G7. It was held on 16–17 November 2001 in Ottawa, which was the only capital city acceptable to everyone for security reasons. As a result of that call others soon followed and meetings of the G7 Finance Ministers, the International Monetary and Financial Committee of the IMF, and the Development Committee of the World Bank were held in Ottawa as well and the log jam was broken.

40.3 THE LEADERS' G20

In 2003, when I became prime minister of Canada, it was evident that gridlock was paralysing the international system as a whole. The same lack of representativeness that had prevented the G7 Finance Ministers from speaking for a wider constituency bedevilled the G8 at the leaders' level as well. Issues ranging from agricultural protectionism to global financial imbalances required the emerging economies to be at the table. It was my view that if globalization was going to work, it needed a new steering committee which reflected contemporary multipolar realities.

For this reason, I again approached my counterparts, this time seeking to recreate the G20 at the leaders' level. I first raised the idea with Premier Wen Jiabo of China, who happened to be in Ottawa on the eve of my inauguration as prime minister. Within a matter of months I spoke face-to-face with my counterparts from the United Kingdom, Russia, Brazil, South Africa, Mexico, and France—all of whom were enthusiastic. Indeed, either personally or through Canadian officials, I met with all of the countries that would eventually make up the Leaders' G20. Japan and the United States were the most reluctant. In my meeting with Prime Minister Koizumi, he eventually agreed to try a Leaders' G20 once, but would not commit himself to anything beyond that until he saw how the first meeting played out. By contrast, while I had discussed the concept with President George W. Bush very early on in the process and on numerous occasions thereafter, I was unable to bring him onside. He remained ambivalent, and would say neither yes nor no.

That being said, despite this rather inhibiting hiccup, I continued to push the idea with those governments who were favourably inclined, all the while working with a series of universities and think tanks to build a network supporting the concept. Indeed, I kept at it after stepping down from government in 2006. Canadian think tanks played a pivotal role globally in this effort led by the Centre for International Governance Innovation in Kitchener/Waterloo, Ontario; the Centre for Global Studies at the University of Victoria, British Columbia, and the G8/G20 Research Group at the Munk School for Global Affairs at the University of Toronto.[4] The role of the Brookings Institution in Washington, DC was crucial in the effort as was the Organization for Economic Co-operation and Development (OECD). Institutions and individuals from Brazil, China, France, Germany, India, Korea, Mexico, and the United Kingdom (where Oxford University was an important driver), were major contributors to the development of the network as well.[5]

All of us were convinced that the absence of China, India, and others from the G8 table meant that the creation of the Leaders' G20 was only a question of time. Many felt as I did that its coming into being would inevitably arise out of one of the world's periodic financial crises. As we now know, that is what happened.

Ultimately, President George W. Bush—and I congratulate him for this given his earlier reservations—faced with a global financial crisis many of whose roots were found at home, convened the first G20 summit in Washington on 14–15 November 2008.

Since then, there have been several G20 meetings at the leaders' level. The first three confirmed its position as a crisis responder. The London summit in April 2009 chaired by Prime Minister Gordon Brown prevented a damaging outbreak of protectionism, and it was at the third summit in Pittsburgh in September 2009 that President Obama, speaking for all the leaders present, designated the G20 as 'the premier forum for our international economic cooperation'.[6]

With the success of the G20 as a crisis responder having been established, I believe it has already started its transition to becoming a global steering committee. Following the Toronto summit, the 2010 meeting in Korea was the first time a G20 Leaders' summit was held in an Asian country, and the first chaired by a non-G8 member. This solidified the recognition that the G20 had come of age—a recognition further solidified by both the Korean and French summits, which put development aid on the G20 table whereas in previous meetings it had been largely absent.

At the time of writing, the 2012 Mexican meeting has only recently concluded. This was the first G20 summit chaired by a Latin American country. Given the inclusive approach the Mexican Sherpa took to the tasks at hand such as the need for pre-summit outreach, there is every reason to believe the G20's evolution will continue favourably as Russia inherits the chair for 2013.

This will, of course, depend on how successive summits respond to a number of issues, some of which I have set out here. First, while clearly the G20 must set its priorities, there can be no upfront restrictions placed on its scope. The reason the group came into being was because the G8 without China, India, Mexico, and others at the table was no longer able to function as the world's steering committee. Thus, as the G8's role becomes more and more limited, there can be no issue of global concern that is not within the G20's purview.

In short, now and over the years to come, the issues the G20 will have to confront will be as varied as there are pebbles on the beach. These will certainly include the pressing financial issues of the day. But they will also include issues that range from the threat of pandemic disease to cybercrime, from endemic poverty to climate change. They will also include issues that none of us can predict, such as the possible need to help re-estab-lish devastated economies if the Arab Spring is to bloom.

A second issue for the G20 is the need for it to consult beyond its immediate member-ship. G20 multilateralism must mean more than a camouflaged concern only for a restricted group of countries' narrow national interests. The influence of the G20 may lie in the importance of its members as they speak for themselves and as they lead by example. However those 19 countries must always remember that they are not there to speak only for their own needs but also for the needs of the 174 countries that are not at the G20 table. In short, the G20 members have a responsibility to the rest of the world, a responsibility they must live up to, a responsibility that begins by listening to what others have to say.

Others have raised the question of whether the G20 needs a permanent secretariat. At some point a secretariat may become necessary to ensure continuity from one summit to the next. One proposal is to have a rotating troika, a 'non-secretariat' consisting of representatives of the previous host country, the current host, and its successor.[7] There is some merit to this but whatever the answer is, the G20 must avoid creating a large bureaucracy at all costs. The G20 is an informal forum of international leaders. National bureaucracies do not need a rival at the G20 level, neither does the United Nations nor its Bretton Woods institutions.

Finally, on certain issues the leaders will be required to take a direct role, as was done during the London summit. On other issues, however, its role will be to send strong signals to the actual negotiating tables such as the World Trade Organization (WTO) and the United Nations Convention on Climate Change (UNCCC). In the same vein, the G20's priorities should be to complement or infuse global institutions with the capacity to act. This is what it did with the IMF during the recent financial crisis, and hopefully what it will continue to do with the Financial Stability Board (FSB).

40.4 CRITICISMS AND RESULTS

Following a summit, to the extent that there is critical comment, much of it stems from a variation upon two themes. The first is the charge that the leaders failed to resolve immediately whatever issue happened to be the flavour of the month. The Korean summit comes to mind here. It succeeded in putting the need for global financial safety nets and development aid on the G20 table to stay. These were major accomplishments. Yet it was a new instalment in the ongoing 'currency wars' that blew up a few weeks before only to return to volatile normalcy two weeks later that dominated the headlines.

Let's face it, few of the issues that land on the G20 table at the last minute will lend themselves to instant success.

The second criticism that crops up with regularity following a G20 summit is the lack of 'compatibility' on some issues among G20 members—an apparent 'flaw' in the G20 make-up when compared to the mythical harmony among seven of the eight G8 members about which I will refrain from commenting.

It is true that the G20 is not a club of compatible economies and learning to work together has not been easy. It is an ongoing process.

When you see how difficult it is for the eurozone economies to reconcile their differences, you can imagine how much more difficult it will be for the G20, which is crisscrossed with far greater cultural, historical, political, and economic differences among its members. But this is not a flaw. These differences are what made the G20 necessary, because that is the reality with which the world has to contend.

That being said—the question remains what is the measure by which the new steering committee should be judged? The answer, I believe, lies in the degree to which it improves the way globalization works in the here and now to be sure, but also in the way it prepares for the road ahead. This is not a theoretical yardstick. The original goal was to relieve the gridlock that was paralysing the international system. Thus on issue after issue, not only the resolution of crises, but also their prevention, are the litmus tests by which the success of the G20 should be measured.

To illustrate this last point, let me touch briefly on two very different instances: first, food security and African infrastructure, and second, the financial crisis of 2008–2011 and the Financial Stability Board.

40.4.1 Food Security and African Infrastructure

The issues of poverty and food security in Africa are such that the on-and-off switch of the international community focuses primarily, when it does so, on immediate relief. In times of crisis this is as it should be. It is beyond belief in this day and age that famine can still stalk the land, or that medicines that can prevent or cure are not available to those who need them. Here there is no excuse for inaction.

But as well one must ask about the structural initiatives that will lead to longer-term solutions to Africa's dilemma, such as the construction of regional and pan-African infrastructure. What about it? It doesn't exist and many observers believe that one of the most important determinants to Africa's success in relieving poverty could be the speed with which such infrastructure comes into being. They are right.

Africa is made up of fifty-four states; the average GDP of these counties is only about $4 billion. This fragmentation is one of the most devastating consequences of colonization. As a result, Africa's small, shallow markets offer no economies of scale, and its collective share of world trade is minimal. In truth, however, Africa has an even bigger problem than its inability to export to the world's markets. Due to a lack of road and rail infrastructure, African countries cannot even trade internally with each other.

What does this have to do with African food security? In 2008, the price of the world's food staples tripled, and the budgets of Africa's governments were decimated as they struggled to import food. Again in 2011–2012, commodity and food prices soared, this time coupled with the worst drought in sixty years in the Horn of Africa. True, conflict plays a terrible role in all of this but even without the consequences of war, the inability of Africa to respond to its own needs is tragically evident. One of the key reasons for this is a virtually non-existent transportation infrastructure, and without it the inability to move agricultural produce from areas of surplus to areas of need.

What should be done? At the Korean and French summits the G20 leaders agreed to coordinate the generation and diversification of financing for the infrastructure needs of developing countries. This must not become another unfulfilled promise.[8]

If the G20 took the initiative in conjunction with institutions like the African Development Bank, and if those African countries that have large financial reserves invested abroad were to repatriate them, a large public–private 'mezzanine fund' could be created to invest in the agriculture, energy, and transportation infrastructure that is so desperately required. On its own, this may not be a sufficient condition for the alleviation of poverty on the continent, but it is a necessary condition, and every African leader I have spoken to supports it.

40.4.2 Global Coordination of Financial Regulation— Avoiding Contagion

The second example of an issue where the G20 needs to play a preventative role arises from the current financial crisis—the issue that called the Leaders' G20 into existence in the first place.

Despite all the discussion about globalization over the last twenty-five years, the continuing financial crisis that started in 2008 has shown just how unprepared the world's governments were and still are, when faced with global problems that lie beyond the scope of purely national solutions. Currently, the G20 is engaged in debates on global imbalances, the volatility of capital flows, exchange rates, and excessive reserves in an effort to reform the international financial system. Hopefully these debates will lead to better global coordination, as should the G20 Mutual Assessment Programs and the IMF's spillover studies that flow from the aforementioned issues. Indeed the need for greater coordination becomes even more critical as the sovereign debt squeeze in both Europe and the United States evolves further. Thus the need to include China, India, and the other resurgent economies in the search for answers has become more than essential.

That being said, however, the differences in perceived domestic needs in many of these areas between G20 members are so deep, that the debates they engender regrettably will not be brought to ground quickly.

Nevertheless, there are issues that the G20 can resolve much sooner if the will to do so is there. First among these is the need for the global coordination of national bank regulation, the lack of which bears much of the responsibility for the world's escalating financial crisis.

The great strength of the free market is its ability to innovate. Its great weakness is the tendency every so often to take that innovation a bridge too far. The 2008 recession was not simply another cyclical economic downturn. It mutated into a 'perfect storm' because at its core was a banking crisis of unprecedented global reach. In the never-ending cycle of financial downturns, bubbles, and implosions, banking crises are undoubtedly the worst, for they are essentially crises of confidence and trust, and nothing is more damaging to the economic system.

That is why the moral hazard posed by institutions that violate that trust will eventually eat away at the very foundations of the free market. For instance, as a result of the crisis, the Bank of Canada released a report in 2010 which concluded that 'financial crises are normally followed by financial repression; economic downturns, by increased protectionism. Without credible, coordinated financial reforms, we risk losing the open trading and financial system that has underpinned the economic miracle of recent times.'[9]

I suspect that in this chapter there is no need to make the argument for the unequivocal need to deal with issues such as that of financial institutions that are 'too big to fail', of inadequate bank equity, or of the perils of unregulated market-based financing, commonly known as 'shadow banking'. However each of these issues has one thing in common that must be pointed out. Despite the fact that the banking industry globally is virtually seamless, the legislators of the countries where the problems arose continue to seek solutions that pay little attention to the need for coordination. For instance, the financial press is full of stories detailing the different responses to the aforementioned issues by Europe and the United Kingdom, and who can fail to note that the Dodd–Frank Act was negotiated in the US Congress as if the rest of the world did not exist.

It is true there is some light on the horizon. The announcement midway through writing this chapter that the United States and Europe had formed a 'temporary' task force to deal with their differences was welcomed. However, we should be under no illusion. The differences that exist are not temporary, for they arise from national pressures which will not go away.

It is here that the G20 must rise to the occasion. After all, the G20 came into being because of two banking crises: the Finance Ministers' G20 following the Asian crisis and the Leaders' G20 following the American and European debacle. To be blunt, on the question of bank regulation, the answers the new steering committee must provide go straight to its *raison d'être*. If it cannot deal with the issue that led to its creation, why should the world have confidence it will provide the leadership on the other issues that will come before it?

A single global regulator is simply not workable. Such a body could never have the domestic insight and intuition required to provide adequate national regulation. Furthermore, under normal circumstances financial sector regulation should follow the currency. Here of course lies the paradox of the eurozone and one more reason for a eurozone bank union.

That being said, however, we must recognize that national regulation alone cannot deal with the gaps in the global financial system. For this reason we must ensure that the effectiveness of national regulation is monitored by an international coordinating body, both for scope and competence. Never again must the world stand by as passive observers of the inability or unwillingness of national regulators to follow the trail of the private sector when it invents new ways of financial innovation beyond the reach of needed regulation.

Fortunately, the organization to do all of this is in place, at least in embryonic form. It is the Financial Stability Board (FSB), which the G20 established in April 2009. Since its creation it has more than lived up to its advance billing. However, there are a number of problem areas that inhibit its effectiveness and remain to be solved.

For instance, the G20 leaders appear to be repeating the mistake of the G7 Finance Ministers a decade ago when they limited the membership of the FSB's predecessor, the Financial Stability Forum (FSF), to the G7 countries and a few others. At the present time, the FSB's membership is limited to the G20 members and five others. While this is myopic, the FSB itself has started moving in the right direction with the creation of six regional consultative groups (RCG).[10] This has been endorsed by the G20 as reflecting 'the global nature of our financial system'.[11] The first meeting of the regional consultative bodies met in November 2011.

A second issue arises from the fact that the FSB's authority has yet to be confirmed by treaty, and that it is understaffed. As such, the implementation of its resolutions remains an issue as does its capacity to assess the effectiveness of the measures it itself advocates let alone those adopted by national governments.

Finally the FSB must have the capacity to enforce its rules. At the present time, its means of enforcement are peer review and possibly public shaming. The first works. The second will not. It is virtually impossible to shame a great power. Whether enforcement occurs through a form of WTO-type sanctions, or through host country regulations that apply to banks from recalcitrant countries such that the private sector itself will insist that international standards be observed, is open to debate. What must not be open to debate is that the application of the rules be mandatory.

It is here that the G20 faces its greatest challenge—the reluctance of its members to accept any infringement on what they deem to be their sovereign rights.

40.5 NATIONAL INTEREST AND SOVEREIGNTY

So where does this leave us? So far we have touched on the G20's litmus test as it makes its transition from crisis responder to modern diplomacy's steering committee—that is to say the capacity to confront early in the piece the potential causes of global upheaval—with reference to two examples: food security and African infrastructure on the one hand, and the global financial crisis and the Financial Stability Board on the other.

In each case, the jury remains out, but the grounds for optimism are there. In each case as well, however, the starting point for discussion will inevitably be the need to move the negotiations beyond the constraints of narrow self-interest to the common good as the essential foundation for national well-being in the 21st century.

For instance, why should Africa and its infrastructure be on the G20 agenda? The answer is clearly a question of morality, but it is also very much in the common good. Africa currently has a population of just under 1 billion. In 2030, it is projected to have a population of 1.5 billion, equal to or more than the anticipated populations of China or India. At that time, Africa will also have the largest population of young people anywhere on the planet. Hopefully that massive percentage of young people will be the world's engine of growth, comparable to what China and India are today. However, if that is not the case, if they are unemployed and rootless—millions of desperate young people, with little hope but plenty of anger, they will be the most disruptive source of the world's chaos. The choice is ours, but the cost of failure will be borne by our children, and the G20 cannot allow that to happen.

At the end of section 40.4.2 on the Financial Stability Board I posed the problem somewhat differently—stating that what it will take to make globalization work can no longer be squared with the traditional exercise of sovereignty.

This becomes evident when one examines global issues such as the halting progress on climate change, the greater advance on pandemic disease, and the breakthrough, at least in concept, arising out of the UN resolution on the Responsibility to Protect (R2P).

However, for the purposes of this chapter let me return to the financial crisis. The traditional definition of sovereignty was established in 1648 through the Peace of Westphalia, and it was centred solely on sovereign rights. If we have learned one thing from the 2008 banking fiasco, it is that the threat of contagion, which is the inevitable consequence of the interdependence of nations, means that the recasting of sovereignty today must go beyond rights to include duties.

For instance, when American and European financial players created toxic assets and sold them around the world to everyone's detriment, was that not an infringement on the rest of the world's sovereignty? Was the global recession itself not partially the result of the infringement on the sovereignty of every country that was affected by the failure of the American and European banking systems to exercise minimum standards of prudence? Or again, was the refusal to allow competent financial sector stress tests from the outset not a failure by certain European countries to recognize their duty to others whose stress tests for their banks called it like it was?

Indeed, what has happened in the European Union with the bailouts of its illiquid if not insolvent states is yet another instance of how the unthinkable can become real. Since the current crisis, markets have stripped away sovereignty's last remaining economic veneer from some of the oldest countries in the world. Quite simply the issue is: are market forces going to dictate a country's economic and social policy, or are national governments going to work with their counterparts so that the fear of contagion ceases to be the sword of Damocles hanging over an increasingly integrated system?

Even more to the point, looking ahead the need to recognize sovereign duties becomes increasingly dramatic when we see how quickly the global landscape continues to change. Prior to the financial crisis the United States and the United Kingdom used a weakening of bank regulation as a means of luring major financial institutions to New York and London, as each competed to become the world's financial capital. What do we think will happen if Hong Kong and Shanghai combine their efforts in order to become the world's 'new' financial capital, and they decide to emulate the means used by their Western predecessors? The answer does not require much conjecture. The entire structure of global bank regulation which is now being so painfully constructed will come tumbling down around our ears.

What European and North American legislators must come to grips with, as they engage in incessant argument to no apparent end, is the reality that in the years to come, when the Chinese and Indian economies become as large as the American, and a Chinese bank fails or a mortgage meltdown occurs in India, there will be no stimulus package big enough to rescue any of us. This will especially be the case if we hide behind the traditional interpretation of sovereignty to frustrate the effective resolution of global issues now when memories of the causes of the crisis are fresh, and when we have the opportunity to improve the rules of the game.

It is for this reason I believe the G20 must empower the FSB with the authority called for to ensure the coordination of the principles and minimum regulatory standards required to govern its members' innovative and very ambitious financial industry. History has taught us that the damage a poorly regulated financial sector can cause is simply too great for the world to run further risk. No one expects the G20 leaders at a summit to monitor the ongoing evolution of bank regulation but they do expect them to ensure that somebody does.

Indeed it is because of instances such as this that I hope to show in the concluding section of this chapter that an important priority for the G20 at the present time should be the strengthening of all the institutions created to make globalization work.

Effective global coordination and governance does not mean the slow road to global government, as some seem to fear. Nor do global institutions and standards with teeth infringe on national sovereignty. In fact, they are the reaffirmation of national sovereignty, in that they allow sovereign governments to deal with problems that affect the common good, problems that transcend their borders and which they could otherwise never solve.

40.6 Conclusion: The Multipolar World and the G20

At the close of the Second World War, the economic and military might of the United States meant that it had no peer in the free world and, following the break-up of the Soviet Union in the 1990s, it was confirmed as the world's only superpower.

Building on the earlier progressive internationalism of many pre-war Western governments, as the war drew to an end the great institutions of global governance, beginning with the United Nations system, came into being. While the United States was by no means alone in causing this to happen, no one can deny that without the use of its power and influence the gains arising from progressive internationalism from 1944 to the present would have been much fewer.

Today, however, the 'unipolar era' is drawing to a close and so is the ease with which the United States is able to provide a sense of direction.

There are two reasons given for the return to multipolarity. One, as set out by G.J. Ikenberry, is that

> The Bush Administration...articulated a dramatic reorganization of the world security order...The United States would be the global Leviathan...It would also stand above other states, less constrained by multilateral rules and institutions. The United States would have an open ended license to deploy power...In effect, the United States was offering a new hegemonic bargain to the world. In the end, however, the world did not accept the terms of the new bargain. As a grand conception of a reorganized world order, it was ultimately unwelcome and unsustainable.[12]

The second reason given for the end of the unipolar era is, as we discussed earlier, the home-grown financial crisis of 2008–2011, which caused the United States to cede ground to the emerging economies of Asia—beginning with China.

While both reasons explain why the pace of multipolarity is accelerating, they do not explain why there is no turning the clock back. That, in my opinion, arises not from any failure of the superpower but from the growing presence of the middle class in the populous nations of the world.

Why is it important to emphasise this? It is because if multipolarity is inevitable, then finding the means whereby the great powers can share sovereignty in the global interest becomes essential.

The strength of a nation will be found in the strength of its middle class and in the ability of its poor to achieve that status. For instance, the gigantic leap forward of the United States occurred during the second half of the 19th century when the British Empire was at its peak. It was then that the middle class of the former colony began to grow, because of good governance, because of the hard work of its people, and most importantly because of the sheer growth in the numbers of its underlying population.

Quite simply, given sound governance (which is most certainly not a given), the economic might of a nation will bear an important relationship to the size of its population because a country with a large population is capable of spawning a larger middle class in absolute terms than can a smaller country. Of course there are other factors as well—the age of a country's population, its geography, its innovative capacity, its neighbours, but the basic proposition still stands, and what that means is that we will be hearing more and more from an ever-increasing number of countries in Asia, Latin America, and Africa.

Thus, the need to address a world where for the first time in well over a century there will be not one or two, but five or six giant economies and any number of wealthy economies at the table. This is already a more complex world than anyone living today is used to and it's only going to get more so. The solution does not require genius, but it does require a level of diplomatic 'give and take' that improved in Pittsburgh but failed in Copenhagen and Durban as the world sought to address the issues of climate change.

This is why the G20 is so necessary and it is also why, despite the disappointment at past attempts, its priority must be to strengthen the great institutions created to make globalization work—the United Nations and all of its agencies including those born at Bretton Woods, carrying on through to the WTO and any other pertinent acronyms that are rapidly exhausting the alphabet.

The fundamental issue we face today is the breath-taking speed and spread of contagion—financial contagion, climate change contagion, pandemic disease, transnational crime, you name it. Whatever it is, no nation can deal with it alone.

In the multipolar world, the catalyst responding to the spread of global risk will be the G20. Indeed that is why it was created. It can take decisive action. It can also use the influence of its members to encourage others to follow.

But ultimately, lasting implementation will come from those institutions with truly global membership. Some like the IMF may already exist. Others like the FSB will have to be created. But in either case, whether it is responding to crisis or preventing it, the need for the G20 to strengthen the great global institutions is self-evident.

Thus the need for the G20 to succeed is paramount. The interdependence of nations is now so pervasive that globalization has become freighted with significant contradictory characteristics—one of great hope, anchored in the benefit of states working together, and one of great fear, based on the seeming inevitability of contagion across borders. It is for this reason that it is critical that the G20 complete its passage from economic crisis responder to diplomatic steering committee. For if globalization is to benefit the many as opposed to the few, action must be taken long before crises reach the tipping point.

This does not require prophetic powers of biblical proportions. What it does require is the recognition that as the world's population approaches its anticipated 9 billion this small planet is going to require better management.

This means governments that can lead their people to understand that their national interest will not be achieved in a world in disarray and that for globalization to work, sovereignty cannot be exercised as a territorial imperative. This means leaders who recognize that with a plethora of major economic powers and no single dominant power setting the direction, sovereignty can only be protected if it is shared.

As the G20 seeks to fulfil its role, it is here that the battle lines will be drawn and it is here that for diplomacy to be effective it will have to be at its most creative. For, with the designation of the G20 as the world's new steering committee, the debate is no longer about what will replace the G8. The question is rather, can any steering committee succeed under the old rule of sovereign rights without sovereign duties? This is the issue the G20 must confront if it is to succeed.

Notes

1. Peter I. Hajnal, *The G8 System and the G20: Evolution, Role and Documentation* (Burlington, VT: Ashgate Publishing Limited, 2007), 12.
2. John Kirton, 'The G8: Legacy, Limitations and Lessons', in Colin I. Bradford and Wonhyuk Lim (eds), *Toward Consolidation of the G20: From Crisis Committee to Global Steering Committee* (Washington: Korean Development Institute and Brooking Institution Press, 2010), 22.
3. Argentina, Australia, Brazil, Canada, China, France, Germany, India, Indonesia, Italy, Japan, Mexico, Russia, Saudi Arabia, South Africa, Korea, Turkey, the United Kingdom, and the United States.
4. The G8/G20 Research Group has been for well over a decade the historian of the G8 and has assumed that role now for the G20.
5. The importance of think tanks in the evolution of the G20 has been given added impetus by Mexico's pre-summit decision to create the '*Think 20*', i.e. an ongoing meeting of think tanks from both G20 and non-G20 countries in order to provide a deeper construct for the debates that flow from the G20's activities. For instance, the Mexican Sherpa was an active participant in the first *Think 20* meeting in Mexico City where strong support was given to President Calderon's proposal to put Green Growth on the summit agenda and to make it an essential element of the Millennium Development Goals— both major steps forward in a debate that had become stillborn.
6. The G20, *The G 20 Leaders Statement*, Pittsburg, 24–25 September 2009.
7. Barry Carin, 'A G20 "Non-Secretariat"', in Bradford and Lim (eds), *Toward the Consolidation of the G20*.

8. As expressed in the *Seoul Summit Document*, the G20 has committed 'to work in partnership with other developing countries, and [Least Developed Countries] in particular, to help them build the capacity to achieve and maximize their growth potential, thereby contributing to global rebalancing... to make a tangible and significant difference in people's lives, including in particular through the development of infrastructure in developing countries' (The G20, *G20 Seoul Document*, Seoul, 11–12 November 2010, 3). The French chair at the Cannes summit in 2011 reinforced this commitment by encouraging and endorsing the work being done by the multinational development banks (MDB) to develop and strengthen public–private partnership (PPP) and enhance information-sharing on infrastructure projects to better link sponsors and financiers. Indeed the Mexican chair made it clear that infrastructure would continue to be a priority on the G20 agenda at the 2012 summit in Los Cabos.

9. Mark Carney, 'Bundesbank Lecture 2010: The Economic Consequences of Reform', <http://www.bankofcanada.ca/en/speeches/2010/sp140910.html>.

10. The six regional consultative groups are: Americas, Asia, Commonwealth of Independent States, Europe, Middle East and North Africa, and Sub-Saharan Africa.

11. The Leaders' G20, *The G-20 Toronto Summit Declaration*, Toronto, 26–27 June 2010, 20.

12. G.J. Ikenberry, *Liberal Leviathan: The Origins, Crisis and Transformation of the American World Order* (Princeton, NJ: Princeton University Press, 2011), 269.

CHAPTER 41

....

DIPLOMACY AND THE INTERNATIONAL CRIMINAL COURT

....

BENJAMIN N. SCHIFF

41.1 INTRODUCTION

....

THE International Criminal Court (ICC; alternatively, the Court) combines traditional 'club' diplomacy with 'network' interactions. This young international organization, dedicated to the norm of anti-impunity for perpetrators of genocide, crimes against humanity, war crimes, and aggression, came into being because of a combination of civil society and interstate diplomatic efforts. Its operations receive support, cooperation, and pressure from states, as well as from international governmental and non-governmental organizations (NGOs). Even as it pursues what its founding documents propound as universal values, constraints imposed by the international power hierarchy open it to the charge of discriminating against weak countries. Along similar lines, although the ICC is perhaps the international organization to which NGOs matter most, appearing to imbue it with a degree of global democracy, the non-representative nature and primarily Western base of those organizations limit the Court's claim to egalitarianism.

This chapter first describes how the Court came into being during what appeared to be an unusual historical period of reduced interstate tensions and increased attention to norms long championed by non-state actors. It then describes the ICC network and the range of roles in it played by Court officials and other major participants. The chapter argues that this new organization and its network demonstrate a decline in 'club' diplomacy and a rise in 'network' diplomacy,[1] but concludes that states retain dominant leverage within this nexus of interaction.

41.2 ESTABLISHMENT OF THE COURT

The Statute of the International Criminal Court[2] was negotiated during an interregnum between two metaphorical wars, the cold war and the 'Global War on Terror' (GWOT). Cold war human rights diplomacy was warped by the polarization of East and West. With the cold war's end, human rights initiatives blossomed, enlarging the realm of NGOs' participation in international affairs, and embracing an anti-impunity norm articulated by national truth commissions and, once the wars of Yugoslavia's disintegration heated up, in calls for international justice.[3] Negotiations over international criminal court proposals, largely stalled since the 1950s, were reinitiated and succeeded despite considerable scepticism about their chances and over the objections, in the end, of the United States.

Motivated largely by NGOs, in 1989 the United Nations General Assembly (UNGA) requested that the International Law Commission (ILC) develop a draft statute for an international criminal court. Formal and informal negotiations culminated in the diplomatic conference in Rome during June–July 1998 that produced the Rome Statute of the ICC. At Rome a coalition of countries called the 'like-minded' states pressed for the Statute, including Canada, many European, African, and Latin American states, urged on by NGOs and ultimately including UN Security Council (UNSC) permanent members France and the United Kingdom.[4] Negotiations revolved crucially around how independent the Court, and especially its prosecutor, would be. Negotiators adopted the principle of 'complementarity', under which the Court would act only if domestic investigations and prosecutions were not being pursued,[5] as one concession to state sovereignty. The UNSC was given the capacity to refer conflict situations to the Court[6] and to suspend ICC proceedings,[7] in a compromise between some states' desire for a completely independent ICC and the UN Security Council permanent members' quest to subordinate the Court to the Council. As further protection for states, the ICC prosecutor's actions were subjected to scrutiny by the Court's judiciary.[8] The US opposed the final draft; nonetheless, the Rome Statute was opened for accession on 18 July 1998.

While the Court moved towards realization, the international context changed. The post-cold war trend of multilateralism and active US support for humanitarian and human rights objectives waned due to opposition in the Senate, and halted when George W. Bush took office as US president in January 2001. On the last day of 2000 (still during Bill Clinton's presidency), the US signed the Rome Statute to enable continued US participation in related negotiations; President Bush entered office proclaiming active opposition to the ICC.

The Statute came into effect following ratification by sixty countries, on 11 April 2002, and the Court came into being on 1 July. In the fall, judges were elected by the ICC's Assembly of States Parties to the Rome Statute (ASP) and the first chief prosecutor, elected in spring 2003, began work in July. As with all international organizations, the ICC became a realm of contention and cooperation for a wide range of states and other parties.

41.3 Explaining States' Motives Regarding the ICC

At the simplest level, adherents to the Statute proclaim their intent to fight impunity and uphold international law, seeking to deter mass crimes and to punish perpetrators. Since the Court operates in a world of sovereign states reluctant to cede control over domestic law enforcement, it must cooperate with them. It has no independent enforcement capacity, and it is a Court of 'last resort', to be invoked only when states that should exercise jurisdiction over a crime don't do so.[9]

Theorists propose various explanations for states' joining the ICC. Liberal institutionalists argue that states should support the Court to the extent that it reduces political and financial costs of countering perpetrators' impunity for atrocity crimes.[10] For realists, states join (or at least do not oppose) the ICC because costs of opposition exceed sovereignty benefits, while the benefits of benign or cooperative relations are politically useful and cheap.[11] Joining the Rome Statute may improve a state's international standing, and its interests may be served if its adversaries are targeted by the Court for suspected transgressions. On the other hand, the Court may threaten states whose officials it might target as perpetrators. Rational choice analysts have argued that post-transitional states join the ICC because their leaders seek to signal their intention to abjure atrocity crimes, in order to build regime legitimacy.[12] From a constructivist standpoint, adherence to the Statute shows state leaders' internalization of anti-impunity norms as part of their leadership identities.[13] Finally, from a discursive standpoint, the logic of arguments for fighting impunity are so normatively compelling as to override most states' reluctance to cede even small amounts of sovereignty.[14]

41.4 Power versus Globalism

The record of the ICC demonstrates tensions between traditional state power, on the one hand, and the rise of global norms, multilateralism, and network diplomacy on the other. Although US power and unilateralism appears to have waned under global pressures, international influence in the ICC remains skewed towards the West, both in the form of states' leverage, exemplified by the US, and by NGO activity, dominated by Western-based, global organizations.

Because of their sway in the Security Council, and international power more generally, the actions of the UNSC Permanent Five (the P5: US, UK, France, Russia, and China) are particularly important for the ICC. France and Britain joined the Statute, while the US demurred from ratifying but remained engaged in negotiations during the Clinton administration. Russia signed but did not move conclusively to ratify, while China declined to sign. Because of its overwhelming power during the late 1990s and beginning of the 21st century, participants and observers believed the Court's relationship with the US to be particularly important to the ICC.

The Bush administration and its Congressional allies sought to choke the ICC. On 6 May 2002, long-time ICC opponent and Under-Secretary of State for Arms Control and International Security (later Ambassador to the United Nations) John Bolton conveyed to UN Secretary-General Kofi Annan the US's intention not to become party to the Statute[15] thereby absolving the US of compliance responsibilities under customary treaty law.[16] From Bolton's viewpoint, the ICC was a threat to sovereignty, a challenge to the US Constitution, and an invitation to internationally politicized judicial interference in US overseas engagement. Later in the month, the Congress passed the American Servicemembers Protection Act,[17] outlawing cooperation with the Court and authorizing the president to use all means necessary to release from the custody of the Court US citizens that might be brought before it. The US pressed states to conclude bilateral immunity agreements (BIAs) that would guarantee they would not transfer US citizens to the Court and threatened US aid cut-offs to countries that refused.

While some observers claimed that advent of the 'Global War on Terror' marked a revolution in US foreign affairs, its constraining effect upon international diplomacy proved to be more the transient product of a particular US administration than a structural shift in international relations. The European Union, US NGOs, and other international supporters of the Court excoriated the Bush administration's opposition to the ICC, and the US position proved to have significant diplomatic costs.

Condemning widespread violence in Darfur, Sudan, in 2004 and early 2005, the US advocated creating a new forum in which to prosecute Sudanese suspected of atrocity crimes to avoid legitimating the Court. When the issue came up for a UNSC vote, however, the US abstained. The Council resolution referred the situation to the ICC.[18] Attributed to Secretary of State Condoleezza Rice's increasing and pragmatic influence within the administration, the abstention was followed by a US call for compliance with ICC warrants for arrest of Lord's Resistance Army officials in Uganda.[19] Again showing that diplomatic costs of opposition were too high, in 2006 the Department of Defense called for review of US legislation forbidding military assistance to countries that had failed to sign BIAs because it was poisoning military cooperative arrangements with important potential partners, especially in Latin America.[20]

Entering office in 2009, Barack Obama's administration broke with the previous administration's anti-ICC policy, sending an observer delegation to the November 2009 ICC Assembly of States Parties.[21] The US subsequently engaged in the preparatory process for the June 2010 Kampala Rome Statute Review Conference and sent a large delegation to the conference that became deeply involved in substantive negotiations. US negotiators successfully pursued a cooperative strategy on the controversial question of implementing ICC jurisdiction over the crime of aggression.[22] The Conference agreed on a definition of the crime and developed a mechanism for the Court's exercise of jurisdiction, while delaying enforcement pending further decisions and a minimum seven-year interregnum. The spirit of atrocity crime accountability was upheld, while in practice sovereignty continued to reign supreme.[23]

The dynamics of Rome were repeated at Kampala. NGOs were closely involved and highly active. States negotiated substantively, making at least symbolic concessions to political sensitivities and opening the door to inroads into sovereignty, while postponing the date for implementation. Although the complexity of the issues and the multiplicity of participants continued the Rome negotiations' pattern of network diplomacy, as at Rome, ultimately states' objectives and diplomats' priorities reigned supreme.

By Kampala, even with the return of the US to multilateralism, the hierarchical quality of the international system ensnared the Court in an uncomfortable bind. Of the UNSC P5, only the UK and France had joined the Statute. Most member states were from Europe, Latin America, or Africa, with few large Asian, South Asian, or Middle Eastern members.[24] The Court was carrying out formal investigations and prosecutions only on the African continent. Critics charged that the Court was operating in a discriminatory fashion despite its ostensibly universalist norms, raising the larger question of whether institutionalization and implementation of international criminal law constituted global values convergence or was merely extending the hegemony of the West.

41.5 The ICC Network

The ICC's establishment demonstrated creation of a new node for wide-ranging interactions among a broadening group of state and non-state actors.[25] The legal-judicial core of the new Court means that its central functions are not themselves diplomatic and political; however, the support structure that empowers the ICC entails both old and new forms of diplomacy.

In 1989, the UNGA assigned to the ILC the job of developing a draft statute for such a court. Advocacy at the UNGA and assignment to the ILC were not new ways for international legal issues to be brought into international consideration. What looked new and different was the intense involvement of non-governmental organizations;[26] nonetheless, to be effective, NGOs had to influence and work through states' official delegations. The negotiations that led to the final Rome Statute incorporated traditional diplomatic representation and formal meetings with legal experts, commentators both from and outside of states' employment, and non-diplomatic expert conferences, gatherings,[27] and NGO publications.[28]

This had happened before, as early as the 1919 negotiations over the International Labor Organization which were largely motivated by international trade unions. More recently, at the 1972 United Nations Conference on the Human Environment (UNCHE, the Stockholm Conference that led to establishment of the UN Environment Programme) the official intergovernmental forum was accompanied by a separate NGO forum where, however, state leaders also spoke and consulted. As at Stockholm, at Rome final decisions were made by state representatives; however, participants and observers agree that the NGOs played crucial roles.[29] Similar to the 1990s negotiations over the Mine Ban Treaty,[30] NGOs were influential because they formed common cause with a group of 'like-minded' states and were important sources of information and argument. In the Mine Ban and ICC negotiations, NGO personnel occasionally joined state delegations,[31] but it was the NGOs' mastery of electronic information collection, collation, and dissemination that enabled them to became key suppliers of information to their own memberships, their coalition, and to state delegations, and thus significantly to shape the discussions.[32]

41.6 COURT STRUCTURE, REPRESENTATION, AND TRANSPARENCY

The ICC that came into formal being in July 2002 structurally resembles standard international organizations. Based on an international treaty, its budget is provided by states party to its founding document, and those states annually meet in a legislative body (the Assembly of States Parties, ASP) that oversees the organization. In its operational structure, the ICC resembles the antecedent International Criminal Tribunals for the former Yugoslavia (ICTY) and for Rwanda (ICTR). Like the Tribunals, the Court is made up of four organs—Chambers (judges), the Presidency (president and two vice president judges, elected by the judges), the Office of the Prosecutor (OTP), and the Registry.[33] The Tribunals were established by the UN Security Council under UN Charter Chapter VII ('Action with respect to threats to the peace, breaches of the peace, and acts of aggression') to deal with crimes committed in specified territories and over specified periods.[34] The ICC, however, is a free-standing, permanent organization, a court with jurisdiction beginning in 2002 over citizens of states that accede to its Statute, perpetrate crimes in conflict situations on their territories, or in situations referred to the Court by the UNSC.[35]

Lacking legislative bodies, the Tribunals' funding was determined by the UNSC, while their rules and regulations were developed by their judges even while the Tribunals operated. In contrast, the Rome Statute's ASP approves the Court's rules and regulations, annually considers its budget, operations, and relationships with states, and performs 'any other function consistent with [the] Statute or the Rules of Procedure and Evidence'.[36]

The Court's three top officials—president, prosecutor, and registrar—each have important diplomatic roles linking the Court to its environments; all three also have technical roles internal to the Court that, while they may require the management and negotiating skills of diplomats, are judicial-legal in nature and circumscribed by the Court's extensive regulations. The president is the formal administrative and judicial head of the organization and its external representative. Presidents are elected by their fellow judges to three-year (once renewable) terms. The chief prosecutor has the highest international visibility and is generally considered to be the Court's most important driving force because the prosecutor initiates and pursues investigations and prosecutions. The prosecutor serves a nine-year, non-renewable term (as do judges). Although the registrar is elected (to five-year, once-renewable terms) by the judges and 'exercises his or her functions under the authority of the President',[37] the office's role is functionally coordinate with, rather than subordinate to, the president and prosecutor because of the division of labour between the three units of the Court. The registrar has important representational and diplomatic responsibilities under the Statute as the 'channel of communication of the Court' to states.[38]

These Court officials' duties bring them into frequent contact with representatives of states and non-governmental organizations. The first ICC Prosecutor Luis Moreno-Ocampo negotiated informally with top Ugandan and Democratic Republic of the Congo (DRC) officials before their presidents referred their conflict situations to the Court.[39] The prosecutor's quest for information and cooperation from states also means interaction with state officials at political and operational levels. The prosecutor, moreover, reports to the Security Council when it so requests (as it has on the Darfur, Sudan, and Libya situations).[40] The prosecutor has become an international diplomat as well as an officer of the court.

As its most visible official, the prosecutor's behaviour is key to the image of the Court. In this respect, Moreno-Ocampo, was controversial. He was the subject of debate regarding the impartiality, targets, and speed of his investigations and his own motives in pursuing the strategies that he did. For example, his appearance in 2004 with Ugandan President Yoweri Museveni to announce Uganda's referral of its conflict with the Lord's Resistance Army to the ICC struck some observers as unwise.[41] His warrant for Congolese suspect Thomas Lubanga Dyilo was criticized as overly narrow[42] and possibly opportunistic. Regarding the Darfur situation, Moreno-Ocampo came under fire from prominent international human rights experts for proceeding too slowly,[43] while other detractors argued that his motives for seeking a warrant against President al-Bashir for genocide included self-aggrandizement, and that his management of OTP was capricious and destructive.[44] Following election by the ASP in December 2011, ICC Deputy Chief Prosecutor (2005–2012) Fatou Bensouda of Gambia became Chief Prosecutor on 1 July 2012, succeeding Moreno-Ocampo upon the completion of his nine-year (non-renewable) term.

In an apparent response to concerns about the prosecutor and to improve the ASP's ability to monitor the internal workings of the Court, the eighth ASP (November 2009) decided to establish an 'independent oversight mechanism' (IOM) for the purposes of 'investigation, evaluation and inspection' of the conduct of ICC officials and contractors.[45] A 2010 ASP resolution established initial duties of personnel in the IOM office and recruitment for IOM officers began in March 2011, while state negotiators in The Hague continued to consider the office's specific mandate.[46]

The president of the Court is the formal head of the organization, speaking for the Court and signing agreements on its behalf, and is also the chief judge, assigning the other judges to chambers. The president has signed agreements approved by the ASP formalizing the Court's relationships with the UN and the Netherlands, respectively. The president and prosecutor can report upon appropriate matters to the UN Secretary-General, and the president has been making annual reports to the General Assembly.

The diplomatic functions of Court officials have been contentious within it. As the official 'channel' to states, the registrar has played a diplomatic role, but one that the prosecutor early on attempted to thwart. Under the Statute, the registrar has the duty to convey to states summonses for appearance and warrants for arrest issued by the Pre-Trial Chambers. In a clash between the OTP and the registrar resolved by the Pre-Trial Chamber in favour of the registrar in 2006, the OTP sought authority to determine the timing of publicizing an arrest warrant and to negotiate for the transfer of a suspect to the Court.[47] Recognizing the fissiparous qualities of the Court's tripartite leadership, the Committee on Budget and Finance in 2004 articulated a 'one-court' principle, pressing the ICC leadership as much as possible to coordinate their activities and operate as a single unit.[48] The president, prosecutor, and registrar constituted an Executive Committee, meeting to coordinate their activities to the extent possible (without compromising prosecutorial independence or judicial neutrality).[49]

The ICC touts itself as an 'e-court', making vast numbers of documents available on the Web and seeking to limit its internal paper flow by using electronic communications. The development into the 'e-court' built on several bases—the efforts undertaken by the ICTY and ICTR to move as much of their internal documentation as possible into database form to ease the chaos of early dependence upon paper files, the NGOs' adroit use of information technology during the Rome Conference and thereafter, and upon the general effort in international organizations, particularly the United Nations, to move into the electronic era and be more accessible to outsiders. For the Court, this has meant that many of its early tensions and challenges can be gleaned from sources that in the past would have likely remained obscure to all but the most devoted of document dredgers. For its high officials and the representatives of states and non-state organizations that deal with it, however, much can still take place within the 'club' of casual discussions and unofficial paper. While transparency has increased, much of the day-to-day operation, the legal core, and diplomatic exchanges carried out face-to-face remain out of the public eye.

41.7 State Diplomacy

Traditional diplomats have been at the centre of states' activities in negotiating for, and then interacting with, the Court. Depending upon the diplomatic resources of the individual states, some have established representations in The Hague that specialize in the legal matters at issue in organizations headquartered there (including the ICC, the International Court of Justice, the Permanent Court of Arbitration, the ICTY) along with the standard representative duties of plenipotentiaries to the Dutch capital. ASP annual meetings have taken place both at The Hague and in New York at the UN, with delegations from small states particularly interested in maintaining the New York venue since many are underrepresented at The Hague.

The ASP elects its own president, two vice presidents, and eighteen members for three-year terms to serve as the ASP Bureau on the basis of geographical distribution and representation of the 'principal legal systems of the world'.[50] The Bureau meets between the annual ASP meetings 'to assist the Assembly in the discharge of its duties', setting the ASP agendas, developing reports, and interacting with Court officials on matters of common concern. The ASP also elects a Committee on Budget and Finance, board members of the ICC's Trust Fund for Victims, and can 'establish such subsidiary bodies as may be necessary'.[51] The ASP has a small secretariat housed at the Court's headquarters that is technically not part of the Court, since the Court is subordinate to the ASP. The ASP in action in its annual meetings looks much like any other international organization assembly. Under the Statute, the ASP seeks to reach decisions on the basis of consensus. If that proves impossible, substantive matters are to be settled with a two-thirds majority of states present and voting, procedural matters by simple majority.[52] ASP presidents have so far been diplomats from small, non-EU countries and have been involved with the ICC and diplomacy surrounding it for several years.[53]

A series of ASP working groups have considered plans, operations, and problems, presenting draft proposals to the ASPs. The first ASP established the Special Working Group on the Crime of Aggression (SWGCA) to continue negotiations begun in the Preparatory Committee.[54] Annual meetings sponsored by the Liechtenstein Institute on Self-Determination at Princeton University brought together officials (mostly from New York representations to the UN) to discuss definitions and mechanisms for implementing ICC jurisdiction over aggression. Continuing negotiations in annual SWGCA meetings narrowed differences on the issue, leading to agreement at the 2010 Kampala Review Conference. In addition to the SWGCA, meetings about the developing text on aggression were held in non-state forums, such as at the Cox International Law Institute at Case Western Reserve University in Cleveland, Ohio in fall 2008.[55]

Other working groups were set up to enable informal discussions on particularly pressing matters, for example, the development of a strategic plan for the Court, formulation of recommendations for a transition from rented to permanent headquarters, and formalization of the ICC's relationship with the Dutch government. Each of these working groups' progress hinged on informal discussion of suggestions and ideas in conversation, often with commentary from NGOs, and gradual convergence on substantive matters. Final decision-making for the Court remains in the hands of the ASP and within the administration of the Court.

41.8 NON-GOVERNMENTAL ORGANIZATIONS AND THE ICC

From the commencement of negotiations towards the Rome Statute, non-governmental organizations have played an important role in generating ideas and political and operational support for the ICC. The significance of the NGO coalition to the ICC is figuratively demonstrated by the annual address of the Convener of the NGO Coalition for the ICC (CICC) to ASP plenary sessions that takes place along with speeches from the Court's top officials. Although some local civil society organizations have protested ICC involvement in conflict situations—such as Ugandans who were convinced that the ICC was reducing chances for a negotiated settlement between the Lord's Resistance Army and the Ugandan government[56]—the Court has received strong support from global NGOs. This raises the question of whether these primarily Western-based organizations are representative of a global interest or whether they are further extensions of Western hegemony.[57]

41.9 Trilateral NGO–State–ICC Relations

Once past the Statute Conference, NGOs continued actively to contribute to discussions of the ICC Preparatory Committee, commented upon drafts of the Rules of Procedure and Evidence, pressed for planning to get underway for the establishment of the Court, and urged states—particularly the Netherlands—to prepare for the organization's imminent creation. The head of the CICC, William Pace, became an actor at least on a par with representatives of major states that were boosters of the ICC. Working as the 'convener' of an ever-expanding group of non-governmental organizations, Pace parlayed his knowledge of, involvement in, and advocacy for the creation of the Court into an influential position that commanded the attention of both governmental representatives and, once the Court came into being, ICC officials. What established clout in the precincts of the ICC was his familiarity with the broad range of national delegations, detailed knowledge of the problems confronting the Court, and the CICC's growing membership. By 2011, the CICC counted more than 2,500 NGO coalition members from 150 countries.[58]

NGO influence at the Court also springs from NGOs' roles promoting states' accession to the Statute. Affiliated with the CICC, national-level NGOs operate as advocacy groups for the Court, informing parliamentarians and government officials about the mechanics of joining the Statute. In July 2003, CICC founding member Amnesty International announced its intention to target one country per month to advocate ICC Statute ratification, a campaign adopted by the CICC.[59] Local, national, and international CICC affiliates seek to contact legislators and generate public awareness of the ICC and promote joining the Statute. While Court officials themselves do not campaign for ratification, they are often invited to NGO functions where they can explain the Court and its operations. The ratification campaign accords with an ASP goal[60] of generating more accessions to the Statute, but it is the NGOs that have played the most visible role in promoting Statute adherence.

41.10 Bilateral NGO–ICC Relations

Early recognizing the importance of continued contact with NGOs, ICC Prosecutor Luis Moreno-Ocampo initiated semi-annual briefings with NGOs and continued frequent contact particularly with William Pace and other leading NGO representatives. Because NGO interactions with the Court are generally between supporters of the Court and the organization they are in business to support, their public messages are generally carefully gauged to express even critical views without giving ammunition to the Court's critics. From the Court's side, officials are sometimes exasperated by the close attention of the NGOs, but aware that they are important sources of support and information and thus must be dealt with as inoffensively as possible.

Perhaps the best-known knuckle-rapping undertaken by NGOs early in the Court's existence was Amnesty International's and Human Rights Watch's reaction to the chief prosecutor's appearance with Ugandan President Yoweri Museveni in 2004 to announce the Ugandan referral, implicitly expressing their concern that the prosecutor maintain ICC impartiality.[61] More recently, NGOs close to the Court have been concerned about the operations of the prosecutor's office. In a 2008 publication reviewing the first five years of the Court's operations, Human Rights Watch noted that 'In addition to using more investigators, it is essential that the teams include enough experienced investigators to guide investigations in the field.'[62] Related concerns were expressed privately in rather less euphemistic terms in a letter to the OTP at about the same time. Human Rights Watch noted the high turnover of OTP personnel, claiming that one of the reasons, besides 'burnout', for the departure of experienced investigators was 'the perception that the input of investigators is not sufficiently valued within the OTP, leading to dissatisfaction.'[63] The prosecutor and other Court officials publicly praise the NGOs for their support and close involvement, even while sometimes chafing in private at their presumptions of rectitude. The NGOs, they sometimes argue, were crucial during the Rome process, but in its wake, looking to stay relevant, arrogate to themselves too much authority in judging the Court's behaviour.

41.11 NGOs as Operational Extensions of the ICC

One of the clearest lessons of the Yugoslavia and Rwanda Tribunals was that their abilities to function were constrained by their reputations in the areas where they pursued investigations. While NGOs dealing with the ICC recognized early on that deficiencies in the Court's 'outreach' activities could damage its operations, the ICC's outreach capacities are constrained because of limited funding and local connections. NGOs help in two ways. Their advocacy at the ASP reversed Budget and Finance Committee recommendations on outreach budget reductions, and international and local NGOs work on the ground in conflict areas to provide some of the outreach services that the Court can't. NGOs have become adjuncts to the organization.

A second area of NGO operational involvement is in promoting the Court's consideration of the needs and interests of victims. At Rome, NGOs pressed for victim-oriented innovations in the Statute; subsequently, they have continued to press victims' rights and interests through pressure on the Court to expand its outreach into conflict areas to inform victims and their larger communities about the Court and their potential roles in its proceedings.

The Statute gives victims the right to make representations to Pre-Trial Chambers when the prosecutor seeks authorization to initiate formal investigations.[64] If a case's admissibility to the Court is challenged, victims may 'submit observations to the Court'.[65] The Statute mandates the Registry to set up a Victims and Witnesses unit to protect those who might be jeopardized by testimony in Court and to provide psychological counselling and support to witnesses.[66] Victims are mentioned in many provisions, establishing the prosecutor's, Registry's, and Pre-trial Chambers' responsibilities,[67] regarding reparations,[68] and establishing the Trust Fund for Victims.[69]

In addition to efforts to inform people in situation areas about the Court, in order to pave the way for investigators, NGOs have helped to bring victims to The Hague and to provide them with legal counsel to participate in proceedings. For example, in the Democratic Republic of Congo, after Thomas Lubanga Dyilo was transferred to the ICC, with international foundation support, the International Federation for Human Rights (FIDH) and its affiliates informed people and accumulated affidavits and requests for victim participation even before the Court itself developed a process for victims to apply for participant status.[70]

41.12 Links to International Organizations

41.12.1 United Nations

The ICC is connected to the United Nations system by the Security Council's abilities under the Statute both to refer situations to the Court and to suspend the Court's proceedings under UN Charter Chapter VII (international peace and security).[71] Under a formal agreement, the UN and ICC recognize each other and pledge cooperation, give the ICC observer status at the UN, and grant the UN Secretary-General the right to attend or send a representative to ICC meetings. At the UNSC's request the prosecutor and president of the Court can report to the Security Council.[72] Operationally, ICC personnel have interacted with peacekeeping forces, for example, in the DRC. In administrative matters, the ICC has recognized the jurisdiction of the International Labor Organization Administrative Tribunal and has been represented before it in at least one labour dispute.[73]

41.12.2 European Union

The European Union has been a consistent supporter of the ICC. It has observer status at the ASP and, in addition to the bilateral relationships between the Court and its members, has also played a major role in seeking support for and cooperation with the Court. A particularly sore point in US–EU relations during the Bush administration was the EU's criticism of the US stance against the Court.

41.12.3 African Union

The ICC has also interacted extensively with the African Union (AU). Of the AU's fifty-three members, forty-three are signatories of the Statute and thirty have fully acceded to the Statute. Two AU member states—Uganda and the DRC—were the first to refer conflict situations to the Court, leading to the Court's first arrest warrants. The ICC subsequently issued summonses and warrants in connection with conflicts in AU member states Sudan, Central African Republic, Kenya, Republic of Côte d'Ivoire, and Libya.

The ICC's relationship with the AU became fraught following the Security Council's 2005 Darfur, Sudan, referral and particularly due to the warrants against Sudanese President Omar Al-Bashir in 2009 for war crimes and crimes against humanity and in 2010 for genocide.[74] The AU officially denounced the warrant as an impediment to resolving the Darfur situation, sought Security Council suspension of the proceeding, and officially stated that AU member states' obligations to the Union supersede those to the Court.[75] Some African countries, including ICC members, have entertained President Al Bashir at official functions notwithstanding their Statutory obligation to cooperate with the Court.[76]

In 2011, the AU criticized the UNSC and ICC for the former's referral of the Libyan situation to the Court following uprisings against Muammar Gaddafi's government, and attacked the latter when the Court issued warrants against Gaddafi, one of his sons, and his security chief. The AU statement[77] expressed the members' intention to 'not cooperate in the execution of the arrest warrant', and requested the UNSC to defer ICC proceedings on Libya, along with deferring proceedings regarding the Al Bashir warrants in the Sudan situation and the investigations and prosecutions in Kenya.

41.13 CONCLUSIONS

Interactions between the ICC and its interlocutors combine 'club' and 'network' diplomacy. Traditional diplomacy characterizes interstate relations in the ASP and between the Court's president and high diplomatic officials of states and international organizations. Despite the 'one-court' principle, however, several ICC officials represent the Court to the outside world, and they pursue multiple roles. Each of them participates in public informational and outreach efforts, in addition to their more formal activities. They interact with ASP and non-ASP state representatives, international governmental and non-governmental organizations, and their actions are scrutinized by a wide range of observers.

Since states pursue a variety of objectives with the Court, their diplomats use the usual panoply of club diplomatic strategies as well as the more public forums provided by the Court and surrounding NGOs. The legal-judicial objectives of the Court give its representatives and supporters a basis for making claims on states and their functionaries that transcend traditional interest politics and may make the operation of the Court less amenable to logrolling or issue-linkage than the operations of non-judicial organizations. The AU protestations of ICC actions manifest the dilemmas of competing state interests: the AU pledges its support for anti-impunity norms (especially as embraced it its own Charter) but argues that states' obligations to the ICC are secondary to AU decisions.

NGOs remain of vital and long-standing importance to the Court. NGOs supported and promoted the idea of the Court long before it came into existence, they crucially facilitated the Statute negotiations, they continue to campaign for Statute adherence, support investigations, and assist outreach to witnesses and victims. As a result of this long and close relationship, NGOs' criticisms and suggestions are taken seriously by Court officials, even if direct responses are not always evident.

The prosecutor's calls, in the Security Council and on public platforms, for states to uphold their commitments to the Court by apprehending and turning suspects over to the Court, combine diplomatic, prosecutorial, and public advocacy roles to invoke the pressures of embarrassment and publicity to move states to action. In a similar way, NGOs seek to pressurize states and to steer the prosecutor, the former in the direction of Statute accession and cooperation with the Court, the latter in the direction of investigations, charges, and prosecutions in various conflict situations.

Although for this new organization there is a relative decline in 'club' diplomacy because of the increased density of network interactions, the final reins of control remain in the hands of the Assembly of States Parties, a quintessentially traditional diplomatic structure. The rise of international criminal justice and the embedding of ICC diplomacy in a globalized normative framework may portend the transformation of traditional sovereignty and diplomacy, but as demonstrated by the Kampala outcome on the crime of aggression, states remain innovative and largely successful as they seek to retain control of this new, more complex diplomatic environment.

Notes

1. For more on the 'club' versus 'network' distinction, see Chapter 2, this volume.
2. Rome Statute of the International Criminal Court (opened for accession on 18 July 1998; entered into force following the 60th ratification, on 1 July 2002) A/CONF.183.9, 17 July 1998, as corrected 1999–2002, hereinafter, RS.
3. Benjamin Schiff, *Building the International Criminal Court* (Cambridge: Cambridge University Press, 2008), ch. 1.
4. William Schabas, *An Introduction to the International Criminal Court*, 4th edition (Cambridge: Cambridge University Press, 2011), 16–22.
5. RS Article 17(a), (b).
6. RS Article 13(b).

7. RS Article 16.

8. RS Articles 15, 19, 58, 61.

9. This is the Court's 'complementarity' principle.

10. For the general case, see Kenneth W. Abbott and Duncan Snidal, 'Why States Act through Formal Organizations', *The Journal of Conflict Resolution* 42:1 (1998), 3–32.

11. Schiff, *Building the International Criminal Court*, 192–3.

12. Allison Danner and Beth Simmons, 'Credible Commitments and the International Criminal Court', *International Oganization* 64:2 (Spring 2010), 225–56.

13. Schiff, *Building the International Criminal Court*, 89.

14. Michael Struett, *The Politics of Constructing the International Criminal Court NGOs, Discourse, and Agency* (Basingstoke: Palgrave MacMillan, 2008).

15. US Department of State, Letter to UN Secretary-General Kofi Annan from Under-Secretary of State for Arms Control and International Security John R. Bolton, 6 May 2002, commonly referred to as the US's 'unsigning' of the Statute.

16. Under Vienna Convention on the Law of Treaties, 23 May 1969 (entered into force 27 January 1980), Article 18, a signatory to a treaty that has not fully acceded is nonetheless obligated to uphold its objectives.

17. US Public Law No. 107-206, 116 Stat. 820, 'American Servicemembers Protection Act of 2002'.

18. UNSC Res. 1593 (2005).

19. Reuters, 'US Wants to Rid Uganda of LRA Rebels This Year', 16 May 2006, <http://platform.blogs.com/passionofthepresent/2006/05/us_wants_to_rid.html>.

20. US Department of Defense, 'Quadrennial Defense Review Report', 6 February 2006, 91.

21. John L. Washburn, 'From Anxiety to Complacency: Prospects for the US-ICC relationship', *The Hague Justice Portal*, 24 September 2010, <http://www.haguejusticeportal.net/Docs/Commentaries%20PDF/Washburn_From%20Anxiety%20to%20Complacency_EN.pdf>.

22. American Society of International Law, 'The US and the International Criminal Court: Report from the Kampala Review Conference', transcript, 16 June 2010, <http://www.asil.org/files/Transcript_ICC_Koh_Rapp_Bellinger.pdf>.

23. Beth Van Schaak, 'Negotiating at the Interface of Power & Law: The Crime of Aggression', <http://works.bepress.com/cgi/viewcontent.cgi?article=1001&context=beth_van_schaack>; Claus Kreß and Leonie Claus and von Holtzendorf, 'The Kampala Compromise on the Crime of Aggression', *Journal of International Criminal Justice* 8:5 (November 2010), 1179–218.

24. As of 2012, 121 states had acceded to the Rome Statute, 31 had signed but not ratified. United Nations Treaty Collection Database, <http://treaties.un.org/Pages/ViewDetails.aspx?src=TREATY&mtdsg_no=XVIII-10&chapter=18&lang=en>.

25. For the view of NGOs as democratizing forces, see Cameron Maxwell, 'Democratization of Foreign Policy: The Ottawa Process as a Model', in Robert Lawson Cameron and Brian Tomilin (eds), *To Walk without Fear: The Global Movement to Ban Landmines* (Toronto: Oxford University Press, 1998). For a contrary perspective, see Kenneth Anderson, 'The Ottawa Convention Banning Landmines, the Role of International Non-governmental Organizations and the Idea of International Civil Society', *European Journal of International Law* 11:1 (2000), 91–120.

26. Marlies Glasius, *The International Criminal Court: A Global Civil Society Achievement* (New York: Routledge, 2005); Michael Struett, *The Politics of Constructing the International Criminal Court: NGOs, Discourse, and Agency* (New York: Palgrave MacMillan, 2008).

27. For instance, 17–21 September 1997 Siracusa Conference, 'Reining In Impunity for International Crimes and Serious Violations of Fundamental Human Rights', of the International Institute of higher Studies in Criminal Sciences, proceedings published by the International Association of Penal Law (1998).

28. For example, Amnesty International, 'The International Criminal Court: Making the Right Choices', Parts I–III, IOR 40/001/1997, <http://www.amnesty.org/en/library/info/IOR40/001/1997>, <http://www.amnesty.org/en/library/info/IOR40/011/1997>, <http://www.amnesty.org/en/library/info/IOR40/013/1997>.

29. Adriaan Bos, 'The International Criminal Court: A Perspective', in Roy S. Lee (ed.), *The International Criminal Court: The Making of the Rome Statute—Issues, Negotiations, Results* (The Hague: Kluwer Law International, 1999).

30. Convention on the Prohibition of the Use, Stockpiling, Production and Transfer of Anti-Personnel Mines and on their Destruction (opened for signature 3 December 1997; entered into force 1 March 1999).

31. Nicola Short, 'The Role of NGOs in the Ottawa Process to Ban Landmines', *International Negotiation* 4 (1999), 481–500; Fanny Benedetti and John L. Washburn, 'Drafting the International Criminal Court Treaty: Two years to Rome and an Afterword on the Rome Diplomatic Conference', *Global Governance* 5 (January–March 1999), 1–37.

32. William Pace and Mark Thieroff, 'Participation of Non-Governmental Organizations', in Lee (ed.), *The International Criminal Court.*

33. RS Articles 34–43.

34. Statute of the ICTY, <http://www.icty.org/x/file/Legal%20Library/Statute/statute_sept08_en.pdf>; Statute of the ICTR, <http://www2.ohchr.org/english/law/itr.htm>.

35. RS Article 13.

36. RS Article 112.2.

37. RS Article 43.2.

38. ICC Rules of Procedure and Evidence 13.1.

39. See Schiff, *Building the International Criminal Court*, ch. 7; Angelo Izama, 'Accomplice to Impunity? Rethinking the Political Strategy of the International Criminal Court in Central Africa', *SAIS Review* 29:2 (Summer–Fall 2009), 51–60.

40. ICC web site, <http://www.icc-cpi.int/Menus/ICC/Situations+and+Cases/Situations/Situation+ICC+0205/Reports+to+the+UNSC/>; UN Security Council Resolution 1970 (2011) on Libya <http://daccess-dds-ny.un.org/doc/UNDOC/GEN/N11/245/58/PDF/N1124558.pdf?OpenElement>.

41. Amnesty International, 'Uganda: First Steps to Investigate Crimes Must Be Part of Comprehensive Plan to End Impunity', AFR 59/001/2004 (30 January 2004), <http://www.amnestyusa.org/countries/uganda/document.do?id=80256DD400782B8480256E2B005E9689>; Human Rights Watch, 'Investigate All Sides in Uganda—Chance for Impartial ICC Investigation into Serious Crimes a Welcome Step', (4 February 2004), <http://www.iccnow.org/documents/02.04.2003-HRW-Uganda.pdf>.

42. Frank Petit, 'Minimalist Investigation in Lubanga's Case', *International Justice Tribune* 53, 25 September 2006.

43. Richard Waddington, 'Arbour Urges ICC to Act on Darfur Crimes', *Reuters*, 11 May 2006, <http://news.scotsman.com/latest.cfm?id=707822006>; Antonio Cassese, 'Is the ICC Still Having Teething Problems?', *Journal of International Criminal Justice* 4:3 (July 2006), 434–41.

44. Julie Flint and Alex de Waal, 'Case Closed: A Prosecutor without Borders', *World Affairs Journal* online (Spring 2009), <http://www.worldaffairsjournal.org/articles/2009-Spring/full-DeWaalFlint.html>.

45. ICC ASP, 'Establishment of an independent oversight mechanism', Resolution ICC-ASP/8/Res.1, document ICC-ASP/8/20 and annex paragraph 6, <http://www.icc-cpi.int/iccdocs/asp_docs/Resolutions/ICC-ASP-8-Res.1-ENG.pdf>.

46. ICC ASP, 'Independent Oversight Mechanism', Resolution ICC-ASP/9/Res.5, document ICC-ASP/9/20, (10 December 2010),<http://212.159.242.181/iccdocs/asp_docs/ASP9/OR/ICC-ASP-9-20-Vol.I-Part.III-ENG.pdf>.

47. Schiff, *Building the International Criminal Court*, 122, 219.

48. ICC, Assembly of States parties, Third Session, 'Report of the Committee on Budget and Finance', ICC-ASP/3/CBF.1/L4 (2004).

49. Schiff, *Building the International Criminal Court*, 134.

50. RS 122.3.

51. RS 122.4.

52. RS 122.7 a, b.

53. The first ASP President (2002–2005) was Jordan's ambassador to the UN, HRH Prince Zeid Ra'ad Zeid al Hussein; second (2005–2008) was Costa Rica's UN ambassador, H.E. Mr. Bruno Stagno Ugarte; third was Liechtenstein's ambassador to the UN, H.E. Christian Wenaweser (2008–2011); fourth is Estonia's Ambassador to the UN, H.E. Tiina Intelmann (2011–2014).

54. Resolution ICC-ASP/1/Res.1, 9 December 2002.

55. 'Cleveland Experts Meeting on the International Criminal Court and the Crime of Aggression', 25–26 September 2008. *Case Western Reserve Journal of International Law* 41: 2–3.

56. Acholi Religious Leaders Peace Initiative, 'International Criminal Court's (ICC) Role in Uganda: ALRPI's Position on the International Criminal Court' (9 July 2009), <http://www.arlpi.org/international-criminal-court-s-icc-uganda>.

57. James Petras, 'NGOs: In the service of imperialis', *Journal of Contemporary Asia* 29:4 (1999), 429–40.

58. CICC web site, 'About the Coalition', <http://www.iccnow.org/?mod=coalition>.

59. Amnesty International, Letter to the Rt. Hon. P.J. Patterson, Prime Minister, Jamaica, (17 July 2003), <http://www.amnesty.org/en/library/info/AMR38/014/2003/en>; Coalition for the International Criminal Court, *ICC Update* 35 (August, September 2003) 7, <http://www.iccnow.org/documents/ICCUpdate35.pdf>.

60. ASP, 'Strengthening the International Criminal Court and the Assembly of States Parties' Resolution ICC-ASP/5/Res.3 (1 December 2006), document ICC-ASP/5/32, <http://www2.icc-cpi.int/iccdocs/asp_docs/Resolutions/ICC-ASP-ASP5-Res-03-ENG.pdf>.

61. See footnote 41.

62. Human Rights Watch, *Courting History: The Landmark International Criminal Court's First Years* (New York: HRW, 2008), 48.

63. Human Rights Watch, Letter to the Executive Committee, Office of the Prosecutor of 15 September 2008, <http://www.article42-3.org/Secret%20Human%20Rights%20Watch%20Letter.pdf>.

64. RS Article 15.3.

65. RS Article 19.3.

66. RS Article 43.6.

67. Including Article 63, 'Protection of the victims and witnesses and their participation in the proceedings'.
68. RS Article 75.
69. RS Article 79.
70. MacArthur Foundation press release, 1 November 2006, <http://www.annualreport.mac-found.org/press/press-releases/human-rights-organizations-recieve-more-than-12-million-to-monitor-and-support-first-cases-before-the-international-criminal-court/>.
71. RS Articles 13.b, 16.
72. 'Negotiated Relationship Agreement between the International Criminal Court and the United Nations', <http://www.icc-cpi.int/NR/rdonlyres/916FC6A2-7846-4177-A5EA-5AA9B-6D1E96C/0/ICCASP3Res1_English.pdf>.
73. International Labor Organization Administrative Tribunal 105th session, Palme v. ICC Judgment 2757 (9 July 2008), <http://www.haguejusticeportal.net/Docs/ICC/ILO_Palme_9-7-2008.pdf>.
74. ICC Pre-Trial Chamber 1, 'Warrant of Arrest for Omar Hassan Ahmad Al Bashir' (4 March 2009), <http://www.icc-cpi.int/iccdocs/doc/doc639078.pdf>; 'Second Warrant of Arrest for Omar Hassan Ahmad Al Bashir' (12 July 2010), <http://www.icc-cpi.int/iccdocs/doc/doc907140.pdf>.
75. Report of the Ministerial Meeting on the Rome Statute of the ICC, AU Document Min/ICC/Legal/Rpt. (II) (6 November 2009), African Union, Decision on the Report of the Commission on the Meeting of African States Parties to the Rome Statute of the International Criminal Tribunal (ICC), 10, O.A.U. Doc.Assembly/AU/13(XIII) (1–3 July 2009), <http://www.google.com/url?sa=t&rct=j&q=decision%20on%20the%20report%20of%20the%20commission%20on%20the%20meetings%20of%20african%20states%20par-ties%20to%20the%20rome%20statute%20of%20the%20international%20criminal%20tribunal&source=web&cd=2&ved=0CFAQFjAB&url=http%3A%2F%2Fwww.africa-union.org%2Froot%2Fau%2FConferences%2F2009%2Fjuly%2FPress%2520Release%2520-%2520ICC.doc&ei=HXEhULqWJIae2QXwg4G4CA&usg=AFQjCNHIBHXd7UgHaXl7S Hu6mBn3qjIBuQ>; African Union Communique (February 2010), <http://www.africa-union.org/root/ar/index/Communique%20Feb%204%202010%20eng.pdf>.
76. 'Obama criticizes Kenya over Bashir's visit, local divisions emerge in Nairobi', *Sudan Tribune*, 28 August 2010, <http://www.sudantribune.com/spip.php?article36078>.
77. African Union, 'Decisions Adopted During the 17th African Union Summit', 1 July 2011, <http://www.au.int/en/sites/default/files/17th%20_SUMMIT_-_DECISIONS_DECLARATIONS_and_RESOLUTIONS_-_eng%20FINAL.pdf>, 2–3.

....

CHAPTER 42

THE RESPONSIBILITY TO PROTECT (R2P) AND MODERN DIPLOMACY

....

THOMAS G. WEISS

RAMESH Thakur and this author argue that the responsibility to protect is 'the most dramatic normative development of our time'.[1] Indeed, with the exception of Raphael Lempkin's efforts as a normative entrepreneur and the resulting 1948 Convention on the Prevention and Punishment of the Crime of Genocide, no idea has moved faster or farther in the international normative arena. Commonly called 'R2P', the title of the 2001 report from the International Commission on Intervention and State Sovereignty (ICISS)[2] refers to the conceptual framework to halt mass atrocities through a three-pronged international responsibility—to prevent, to react, to rebuild.

Here, the emphasis is not on the commission's normative efforts but rather its efforts at the time and by others since as an intriguing example of contemporary network diplomacy that contrasts starkly with the clubby, state-centric approaches.[3] The former director of the Policy Planning Staff in the US State Department, Anne-Marie Slaughter, tells us that 'managing international crises...requires mobilizing international networks of public and private actors'.[4] The emergence of the R2P norm results from inputs by a host of actors who would have been kept away from the policy-formulation and policy-making circles of the past—that is, this dynamic process was neither hierarchical nor dominated by the secretive diplomacy of powerful states. The use of R2P by the United Nations (UN) Security Council, the General Assembly, and the Human Rights Council in 2011 illustrated the operational power of the norm under the right political circumstances.[5]

This chapter begins with a short history of independent commissions as a vehicle for moving ideas from the periphery into the mainstream of international public policy discourse. Next is an overview of humanitarian crises resulting from wars in the turbulent 1990s that led, on occasion, to valuing the sovereignty of individuals more than that of states. The following sections deal with the ICISS process itself and the results since of contemporary multilateral diplomacy to halt mass atrocities. In the interests of full disclosure, I was the research director for ICISS and also direct the Ralph Bunche Institute for International Studies that houses the Global Centre for the Responsibility to Protect.

42.1 INDEPENDENT COMMISSIONS, A SHORT HISTORY

Much of international relations scholarship consists of attempting to determine whether continuity or change is the more accurate label to characterize a dramatic event, approach, or era that is path-breaking if not paradigm-shattering. On the one hand, the International Commission on Intervention and State Sovereignty was unusual in that it catalysed exceptional energy among like-minded states, international secretariats, civil society, and individuals. The result was a significant reframing of state sovereignty: rather than being absolute, it was viewed as contingent on a modicum of respect for human rights. On the other hand, the ICISS was a continuation of a three-decade long experiment with independent, blue-ribbon international commissions. Later this chapter explores the unusual character of ICISS, but a brief history of the phenomenon of such commissions is appropriate.

A particular type of expertise—which combines knowledge and political visibility—has been influential in nourishing ideas that emanate from reports of independent commissions composed of eminent persons, usually with a high dose of former politicians.[6] They are intended to help raise the visibility of particular global challenges and possible solutions through a consensus view from prominent individuals who represent a spectrum of opinion and nationalities. But unlike official or semi-official UN reports, the commissioners speak in their individual capacities and may be able to move beyond what passes for politically correct or conventional wisdom in UN circles. A cornucopia of ideas typically requires more space for imagination and experimentation than is found in the confines of UN secretariats and diplomatic missions. Commissions are a tool to move beyond lowest-common-denominator thinking, which can result when seeking to run the fool's errand of trying to please 193 UN member states. Their reports are normally presented to the Secretary-General, who decides on their follow-up within the constraints of daily multilateral diplomacy, but who can point to new-fangled wisdom in an independent commission's prose.

Oftentimes such reports are named after their chairs. This custom began with *Partners in Development*, headed by former Canadian Prime Minister Lester B. Pearson.[7] Commissioned by Robert McNamara as the new president of the World Bank to move beyond the confines of routine development thinking, the so-called Pearson Commission was followed by a host of others, including: the two commissions on development issues chaired by former German Chancellor Willy Brandt;[8] on common security by former

Swedish Prime Minister Olav Palme;[9] on environment and development by serving Norwegian Prime Minister Gro Harlem Brundtland;[10] on humanitarian problems by Iranian and Jordanian princes, Sadruddin Aga Khan and Hassan bin Talal;[11] on South–South cooperation by serving Tanzanian President Julius Nyerere;[12] on global governance by former Swedish Prime Minister Ingvar Carlsson and Guyana's Shridath Ramphal;[13] on intervention and state sovereignty by former Australian Foreign Minister Gareth Evans and former Algerian ambassador Mohamed Sahnoun; on human security by Sadako Ogata and Amartya Sen.[14] There are also commissions that are recalled more by the names of their sponsors than of the chairs—for example, the first report to the Club of Rome[15] and the Carnegie Commission on preventing deadly conflict.[16] Some observers have argued that more official and less autonomous UN-backed panels like the one chaired by Lahkdar Brahimi on peace operations, when properly composed and staffed, can also push out the envelope of ideas.[17] The judgement about the High-Level Panel on Threats, Challenges, and Change (HLP) in preparation for the 2005 World Summit usually gets less high marks.[18]

The ideas in the reports from independent commissions and sometimes more official panels help alter world views and values, and they often lead to new policies and concrete actions—in short, as additional steps in the unfinished journey of global governance.[19] The way that reports from such commissions are received and subsequently put to work by diplomats and decision-makers depends upon factors that are impossible to control, including changes in the world economy (e.g. the financial and economic meltdown of 2008) and domestic politics (e.g. elections in major powers) as well as unforeseen events (e.g. the fall of the Berlin Wall or 11 September 2001).

From interviews with many persons who served on them or observed their impact, the decade-long United Nations Intellectual History Project identified three useful functions of independent, blue-ribbon international commissions: awareness and consciousness-raising; advocacy for particular ideas; and legitimacy to programmes and ideas.[20] Some interviewees qualified their judgements by arguing that such commissions could be successful, provided that these initiatives were backed by major powers, and when the subject matter was narrowly focused. Most agreed that these commissions and their 'blockbuster' reports were of some significance regardless of the backgrounds of the commissioners. *The Responsibility to Protect* provides an illustrative case study of a useful item in the contemporary diplomatic tool-kit.

42.2 THE TURBULENT 1990S, HUMANITARIANISM UNCHAINED

This is not the place to unpack the substantial changes brought about by the end of the cold war, but certainly 'sovereignty was no longer sacrosanct'[21] after humanitarian crises led to the use of military force to come to the rescue of civilians in northern Iraq and Somalia and less robustly in the Balkans. The cumulative effect of what Nicholas Wheeler called 'saving strangers'[22] posed significant conceptual, policy, and operational challenges to the notion of state sovereignty and international society. The ICISS responded to the humanitarian challenges of what became known as 'new wars'[23] and military-civilian interactions;[24] the commission's challenge was to directly confront the divergent reactions—or rather, the non-reactions—by the Security Council.

Rwanda and Kosovo were crucial. In 1994, international intervention was too little and too late to even slow the pace of murder for what may have been as many as 800,000 people in the Great Lakes region of Africa. In 1999, the North Atlantic Treaty Organization (NATO) bypassed the paralysed Security Council and waged war for the first time in Kosovo. But many observers saw the seventy-eight-day bombing effort as being too much too soon, as well as subsequently being too little (after ruling out the use of ground troops) and too counterproductive (perhaps creating as much human suffering among internally displaced persons, internationally displaced persons (IDPs), and refugees as it relieved). In both cases, the Security Council failed to act expeditiously and authorize the use of deadly force to protect vulnerable populations. Many—but not all—human rights advocates and humanitarian agencies supported military protection of civilians whose lives were threatened. The glaring normative gap for collective action was exposed for all to see more clearly than in the past.

I should make my own view clear: the absence of reaction in Rwanda represented a far more serious threat to international order and justice than the Security Council's paralysis in Kosovo where NATO fulfilled the international responsibility to protect. Past or potential victims undoubtedly would agree. For instance, the most thorough survey to date of victims in war zones suggests that there is too little rather than too much military humanitarianism. Fully two-thirds of civilians under siege who were interviewed in twelve war-torn societies by the International Committee of the Red Cross (ICRC) wanted more intervention and only 10 per cent wanted none.[25] In addition, a 2005 mapping exercise of operational contexts for humanitarian agencies found, not unsurprisingly, that recipients 'are more concerned about *what* is provided than about *who* provides it'.[26] Moreover, an examination of 'cultural perspectives from the global South' suggests widespread support for coming to the rescue of war-affected societies in traditional religions, philosophies, and art throughout the third world.[27]

In order not to be irrelevant, the United Nations had to find a way to justify its involvement in the ugly civil wars that produced conscience-shocking suffering. The earlier debate about whether humanitarian disasters qualified as 'threats to international peace and security' (the basis for coercion spelled out in Chapter VII of the UN Charter) had resolved itself because so many crises of the 1990s had been the object of Security Council action precisely on humanitarian grounds. The UN's reactions in Rwanda and Kosovo reflected, to be sure, the paucity of political will; but they also reflected the shield of traditional state sovereignty.

The turbulent period meant that ideas were already fermenting prior to mobilizing the ICISS in 2000. In particular, two prior conceptual efforts had broken new ground between state sovereignty and human rights and paved the way for *The Responsibility to Protect*. First was the normative work by Francis M. Deng and Roberta Cohen on the issue of internally displaced persons. Second was UN Secretary-General Kofi Annan's activism in promoting individual alongside state sovereignty.

Concerned to find a way to protect the ever-increasing number of IDPs, Deng and Cohen sought to reframe sovereignty already at the end of the 1980s. Their 'sovereignty as responsibility' stipulated that when states are unable to provide life-supporting protection and assistance for their citizens, they are expected to request and accept outside offers of aid.[28] Should they refuse or deliberately obstruct access to their displaced populations and put large numbers of them at risk, there is an international responsibility to respond. Sovereignty entails accountability to two separate constituencies: internally to one's own population and internationally to the community of responsible states in the form of compliance with human rights and humanitarian standards. In short, sovereignty is not absolute but contingent. When a government massively abuses the fundamental rights of its citizens, its sovereignty is temporarily suspended.

The second key conceptual contribution came from UN Secretary-General Kofi Annan, who took human rights far more seriously than any of his predecessors and preached about humanitarian justifications for intervention from his bully pulpit. With the help of his scribe, Edward Mortimer, a series of hard-hitting speeches in 1998–1999 placed the issue squarely on the intergovernmental agenda.[29]

Annan's black-and-white challenge reflected changing the balance between states and people as the source of legitimacy and authority. Like Deng and Cohen, he sought to broaden the concept of sovereignty to encompass both the rights *and* responsibilities of states. The Secretary-General's clarion call was hard to muffle especially after *The Economist* published his 'two concepts of sovereignty' on 18 September 1999:

> State sovereignty, in its most basic sense, is being redefined ... States are now widely understood to be instruments at the service of their peoples, and not vice versa ... When we read the Charter today, we are more than ever conscious that its aim is to protect individual human beings, not to protect those who abuse them.

Later that month in opening the General Assembly, the future Nobel laureate's moral plea reached member states in six official UN languages.[30] He put forward his views more delicately a year later at the Millennium Summit.[31]

The reactions in the General Assembly hall were raucous and predictable from China, Russia, and much of the global South. Unilateral intervention—that is, without a Security Council authorization, however many countries are involved in a coalition—for whatever reasons, including genuine humanitarian ones, remains taboo. As the enthusiastic R2P champion Gareth Evans tells us, 'sovereignty thus hard won, and proudly enjoyed, is sovereignty not easily relinquished or compromised'.[32]

Annan's reframing helped shift the balance away from the absolute rights of state leaders and towards respect for international standards, at least in the face of mass atrocities.[33] In brief, the sovereignty of a state does not stand higher than the human rights of its inhabitants. That this argument came from the world's top international civil servant resonated loudly, perhaps too loudly. The stage was thus set for the Canadian government to take the initiative to convene the International Commission on Intervention and State Sovereignty.

42.3 ICISS, LAUNCHING A DIPLOMATIC PROCESS, 2000–2001

Canada championed R2P. Its voice was resonant as a country strongly committed to UN-centred multilateral diplomacy with a history of close engagement with the world organization, political credibility in both North and South, and a tradition of successful global initiatives. Foreign Minister Lloyd Axworthy initiated the commission after the high-decibel-level attacks on Annan in fall 1999. He presided when the ICISS assembled for the first of its five sessions in Ottawa in November 2000 but retired from politics shortly thereafter.[34] The commission's work continued under his successors, Foreign Ministers John Manley and Bill Graham. When Paul Martin succeeded Jean Chrétien as prime minister, again there was no break in leadership on this issue. Several other like-minded countries, including Norway and Switzerland, as well as such major foundations as MacArthur and other actors like the ICRC, worked closely with ICISS in supportive advocacy; but Canada led the way in mobilizing resources and providing logistics.

The commission acted as a norm broker. Its mandate was to find a way to manoeuvre around the barrier between standing on the sidelines to respect non-intervention and state sovereignty, on the one hand, and military intervention to support humanitarian objectives, on the other hand. Humanitarian imperatives and principles of sovereignty were reconciled through the responsibility to protect, with substantial conceptual and political consequences.

A wide range of actors engaged during the commission's deliberations and afterwards, which helps explain R2P's movement from the periphery to the centre of international relations in general and UN diplomacy in particular. The initiative provided an answer to Annan's poignant question: 'If humanitarian intervention is, indeed, an unacceptable assault on sovereignty, how should we respond to a Rwanda, to a Srebrenica—to gross and systematic violations of human rights that offend every precept of our common humanity?'[35]

Given the supposedly wide disparity of views across the North–South divide—industrialized countries more enthusiastic in principle, developing countries more wary about providing a rationale for outside intervention—Ottawa asked a person from each camp (Gareth Evans and Mohamed Sahnoun, respectively) to act as co-chairs and asked a balanced group to fill the other ten spots as commissioners (Gisèle Côté-Harper, Lee Hamilton, Michael Ignatieff, Klaus Naumann, and Cornelio Sommaruga from the North with Cyril Ramaphosa, Fidel Ramos, Eduardo Stein, and Ramesh Thakur from the South and Vladimir Lukin from Russia).

Even though that is how it, like so many other international issues, is usually parsed in UN circles, is responsible sovereignty really an issue that pits the North versus the South?[36] Extensive ICISS outreach and consultations offered evidence that differences across and within developing regions—Africa, Asia, and Latin America—and between governments and civil society within countries had more subtle hues than the stereotypical black-and-white tones attributed to the North and the South.

Ten consultations in both the Northern and Southern hemispheres sought the views of governments, scholars, intergovernmental and non-governmental humanitarian actors, and journalists in order to put them in the R2P hopper.[37] The cacophony cannot be summarized except to say that nowhere did anyone argue that intervention to sustain humanitarian objectives was never justifiable. After the genocide in Rwanda, very few policy-makers, pundits, or practitioners were willing to exclude protective intervention in the face of mass murder.

The ICISS report was finalized in August 2001 and published with especially bad timing in December 2001, shortly after the 9/11 terrorist attacks on the United States when the world's attention was focused on the consequences and responses to that horrific event. The subsequent invasion of Iraq and ousting of Saddam Hussein by a US-led coalition acting without UN authorization was doubly damaging. First, as tensions mounted over 2002 and early 2003, few had the time to focus on R2P. Second, as the 'weapons of mass destruction' (WMDs) justification for the war fell apart and claims of close links between Saddam's regime and al-Qaeda also proved spurious, the coalition of the willing—with Washington and London as the main belligerents—began to apply ex post facto humanitarian language and even R2P as the main justification for their actions in Iraq. Richard Haass, the former director of policy planning unit in the US State Department and president of the Council on Foreign Relations, spoke of sovereignty as responsibility and argued that when states fail to discharge their responsibility to fight terrorism, 'America will act—ideally with partners, but alone if necessary—to hold them accountable.'[38] Military intervention would have been justifiable in self-defence against cross-border terrorism, to be sure, but that was not the case. Human protection was an all-too-transparent rationalization. Indeed, the promising diplomatic process begun by ICISS almost ground to a halt. The war in Iraq became a temporary conversation stopper for R2P.

Some ICISS commissioners argued strenuously that Iraq would not have met the R2P test for intervention.[39] Co-chair Evans, commissioner Thakur, and research director Weiss addressed the multiple audiences who could help move the conversation along: policy (intergovernmental and government officials), scholarly, and civil society.[40] The Canadian government organized consultations with governments, regional organizations, and civil society forums to help promote the report. As the message resonated, many civil society organizations began advocacy and dissemination work on their own. Kofi Annan remained fully engaged with the issue as well.

42.4 R2P, CONTINUING THE DIPLOMATIC PROCESS SINCE 2002

In what Gareth Evans correctly calculates to be 'a blink of the eye in the history of ideas,'[41] the results of multilateral diplomacy since the release of the ICISS report in December 2001 suggest that R2P has moved from the prose and passion of an international commission's report towards being a mainstay of international public policy. And it has substantial potential to evolve further in customary international law and to contribute to ongoing conversations about the responsibilities of states as legitimate, rather than rogue, sovereigns.

The multifaceted diplomatic follow-up process began when the ICISS report was presented to the Secretary-General in December 2001. At that point and still nursing his wounds from the 1999 General Assembly, Annan exclaimed to those gathered, 'I wish I had thought of that.' Prior to the World Summit's agreement to R2P, in 2004 the UN's HLP issued *A More Secure World: Our Shared Responsibility*, which supported 'the emerging norm that there is a collective international responsibility to protect.'[42] Annan endorsed it in his 2005 report, *In Larger Freedom*.[43] In addition to the official blessing by the General Assembly in October 2005, the Security Council made specific references to R2P on two occasions: the April 2006 resolution 1674 on the protection of civilians in armed conflict expressly 'reaffirms the provisions of paragraphs 138 and 139', and the August 2006 resolution 1706 on Darfur, which was the first to link R2P to a particular conflict.

But it would be worthwhile to probe beyond rather than merely list the headlines. The HLP included Evans and reaffirmed the importance of the terminological change from the deeply divisive 'humanitarian intervention' to 'the responsibility to protect'. Their report explicitly endorsed the ICISS argument that 'the issue is not the "right to intervene" of any State, but the "responsibility to protect" of *every* State.'[44] It proposed five criteria of legitimacy: seriousness of threat, proper purpose, last resort, proportional means, and balance of consequences.[45] In a breakthrough of sorts that suggested the widening acceptance of the norm, China's official June 2005 paper on UN reforms noted that 'Each state shoulders the primary responsibility to protect its own population..... When a massive humanitarian crisis occurs, it is the legitimate concern of the international community to ease and defuse the crisis.'[46] In the meantime in the United States, the Gingrich–Mitchell task force also endorsed the responsibility to protect, including calls for the norm to be affirmed by the Security Council and the General Assembly.[47]

In his own report before the World Summit, Annan made an explicit reference to ICISS and R2P as well as to the HLP, endorsed the legitimacy criteria, and urged the Security Council to adopt a resolution 'setting out these principles and expressing its intention to be guided by them' when authorizing the use of force. He continued that this approach would 'add transparency to its deliberations and make its decisions more likely to be respected, by both Governments and world public opinion.'[48]

The responsibility to protect was one of the few substantive items to survive negotiations at the World Summit in New York in September 2005.[49] Some supporters criticized the summit's emphasis on the state and the requirement for coercive measures to be authorized by the Security Council as constituting 'R2P lite', and others thought that the language in paragraphs 138–139 of the *World Summit Outcome Document* was wordier and woollier than the original ICISS version.[50]

Notwithstanding criticisms, the document was a step forward in a long itinerary. The concept was given its own sub-section and title, which makes clear the need for international intervention when countries fail to shield their citizens from, or more likely actively are perpetrators of, mass-atrocity crimes. The language reflects an unambiguous and unanimous acceptance of individual state responsibility specifically to protect populations from genocide, war crimes, ethnic cleansing, and crimes against humanity. Member states further declared that they 'are prepared to take collective action, in timely and decisive manner, through the Security Council . . . and in cooperation with relevant regional organizations as appropriate, should peaceful means be inadequate and national authorities are manifestly failing to protect their populations'. The heads of state and government gathered in New York 'stress[ed] the need for the General Assembly to continue consideration of the responsibility to protect populations from genocide, war crimes, ethnic cleansing, and crimes against humanity'.[51] However, the legitimacy criteria—which would simultaneously make the Security Council more responsive to outbreaks of humanitarian atrocities than hitherto and make it more difficult for individual states or ad hoc coalitions of the willing to appropriate the language of humanitarianism for geopolitical and unilateral interventions—were dropped.[52]

Since that time, the idea has been embedded in the UN. Secretary-General Ban Ki-moon appointed a full-time special adviser for the prevention of genocide (Francis M. Deng) and special adviser tasked with promoting R2P (Edward C. Luck). He has referred to the implementation of R2P as one of his priorities and released *Implementing the Responsibility to Protect* in January 2009,[53] which spells out a three-pillar approach that encompasses the protection responsibilities of individual states, international assistance and capacity-building for weak ones, and timely and decisive international responses to mass atrocities. The emphasis by the Secretary-General and the Secretariat has been on the first two pillars, thereby attempting to finesse the controversy remaining about the topic that launched the debate in the first place, namely the use of military force when necessary to halt mass atrocities.

While the R2P norm has moved quickly, it is still in its infancy, and Luck provides a note of caution: 'like most infants, R2P will need to walk before it can run'.[54] Nonetheless, many victims will suffer and die if R2P's adolescence is postponed. Vigilance is required to keep up the pressure. The process begun by ICISS continues to be a central cause for civil society and supportive governments to push sceptical countries and the UN bureaucracy to take seriously Secretary-General Ban Ki-moon's words: 'R2P speaks to the things that are most noble and most enduring in the human condition. We will not always succeed in this cardinal enterprise, and we are taking but the first steps in a long journey. But our first responsibility is to try.'[55]

In mid-2009, 2010, 2011, and 2012, the General Assembly engaged in 'informal interactive dialogues', additional steps in R2P's normative journey. States members of the 'Group of Friends' of the responsibility to protect in New York, the UN special adviser, and civil society have picked up the mantle from previous 'norm entrepreneurs'.[56] They have drawn upon the example of successful campaigns to forge wider constituencies for such issues as banning landmines and establishing the International Criminal Court and mobilized around the Secretary-General's report.

Initially, many observers feared that the debate would lead to diluting the September 2005 commitment. Fears about normative back-pedalling seemed concrete enough; for instance on the eve of the 2009 debate, *The Economist* described opponents who were 'busily sharpening their knives'.[57] The Nicaraguan president of the General Assembly, Father Miguel d'Escoto Brockmann, unsheathed his Marxist dagger and suggested 'a more accurate name for R2P would be the right to intervene' or 'redecorated colonialism'.[58]

However, R2P-naysayers must have been deeply disappointed by the discernible shift from antipathy to wider public acceptance of the norm.[59] Close reading of the remarks by diplomats from ninety-two countries and two observers who addressed the first interactive dialogue, for example, showed scant support for undermining R2P. Only Venezuela directly questioned the 2005 World Summit agreement, and only four of the usual suspects sought to roll back the earlier consensus (Venezuela, Cuba, Sudan, and Nicaragua). Countries that had suffered terrible atrocities continued to make rousing pleas to strengthen and implement R2P—for example, Rwanda, Bosnia, Guatemala, Sierra Leone, and East Timor. A wide variety of other countries such as Chile, South Korea, and the entire West continued to express their firm support. More surprising was the widening consensus and support from major regional powers that had previously been reticent or even hostile—including Brazil, Nigeria, India, South Africa, and Japan. Concerns of course remained about implementation, thresholds, and inconsistency.

The 2009 General Assembly resolution 63/208 registered tepid but still clearly widespread support for R2P across regions, and in August 2010 the conversation continued around the Secretary-General's report on early warning and resulted in December with the creation of a new joint office. In July 2011, the conversation addressed regional organizations and in 2012 on pillar three. Over the four years of interactive dialogues, the vast majority of member states reaffirmed support for the emerging norm and supported continued discussions. Not surprisingly, the usual detractors continued to question the definition of R2P and earlier agreements.

Operationally, the results of network diplomacy have also advanced. Reference was made, in section 42.4, to 2006 Security Council resolutions 1674 on the protection of civilians in armed conflict and 1706 on Darfur. R2P was also important behind the scenes in helping to move beyond electoral violence in Kenya in 2007–2008.[60] It was misapplied temporarily in Myanmar, Georgia, and Iraq, but even these almost universally contested abuses actually strengthened the norm.[61]

However, the first meaningful operational references came against Libya in 2011: resolution 1970 had unanimous support for a substantial package of Chapter VII efforts (arms embargo, asset freeze, travel bans, and reference of the situation to the International Criminal Court); and resolution 1973 authorized 'all necessary measures' to enforce a no-fly zone and protect civilians. In addition, the Human Rights Council referred to R2P for the first time in resolution S-15/1, which led to the General Assembly's resolution 65/60 that suspended Libyan membership in that council.

The international efforts—not just NATO's rhetorical and military support from the region—to halt Muammar el-Qadafi's threat to crush the 'cockroaches' who opposed him was noteworthy because since the publication of the ICISS report we have witnessed too little, not too much, armed force to protect human beings. The efforts in Libya remain contested and uncertain as of this writing, but the international hesitancy to oust Laurent

Gbagbo and install Alassane Ouattara in Côte d'Ivoire provided a stark contrast. The departure of Gbagbo in April 2011 followed a half-year of dawdling as Côte d'Ivoire's unspeakable disaster unfolded. Three times in the previous month alone, the Security Council emptily threatened the loser of the November 2010 elections and repeated its authorization to 'use all necessary means to carry out its mandate to protect civilians'. Prior to the early April UN action spearheaded by the 1,700-strong French Licorne contingent, the unwillingness to deploy armed force had abetted Gbagbo's intransigence. Was it necessary to endure war crimes, crimes against humanity, a million refugees, and a ravaged economy? Should robust international military action not have occurred earlier?

In addition to hard-core defenders of sovereignty and military critics, a different type of naysayer is found among supporters of humanitarian action who emphasise the potential of the responsibility to protect to backfire. Alan Kuperman, for instance, is one of the contrarians who has argued that the expectation of benefiting from possible outside intervention—including sanctions, embargoes, judicial pursuit, and military force under his rubric—emboldens sub-state groups of rebels either to launch or continue fighting.[62] International mumbling has perhaps affected the calculations of local militias and elites, even causing them to take action that perhaps has had the effect, intended and unintended, of prolonging violence. But does this mean that robust humanitarianism is destined to constitute a moral hazard? There might be a problem were there an insurance policy for humanitarians as there is for banks that can be reckless with other peoples' money. But there is no such global life insurance policy. Indeed, the opposite problem is more likely: combatants know that humanitarian talk is cheap.

If the ICC arrest warrant for Sudanes President Omar al-Bashir is as empty a threat as the use of outside military force to halt the slow-motion genocide in Darfur, then the problem is not moral hazard but empty rhetoric and collective spinelessness. The moral hazard argument, if taken seriously, would lead to the conclusion that pledging to do nothing is appropriate, thereby re-issuing wannabe thugs a license to kill.[63]

42.5 CONCLUSION

The contemporary multilateral diplomacy emanating from the work by the International Commission on Intervention and State Sovereignty has involved many more moving parts than the bilateral variety that is the core curriculum in most diplomatic academies. It is also quite different from the big-power secret diplomacy that is the bread and butter of most economic and political negotiations within the United Nations. This chapter has argued that network diplomacy has helped to transform the normative landscape for halting mass atrocities. Rather than a small number of state representatives in a hierarchical structure employing opaque communications, the ICISS began a process that mobilized individuals, a research directorate, civil society, and worldwide consultations with academics, NGOs, and the media. Since 2001 the R2P idea moved through wide-ranging intergovernmental processes with support and monitoring from a large number of private organizations and individuals. It is now part of the discourse used by states (or rejected by some of them, itself an indication of its importance) as well as by public and private actors.

However, this author feels compelled to ask whether multilateral diplomatic efforts should not rediscover the passionate collective *mea culpa* following the Rwandan genocide. Since the Iraq war and especially with the administration of Secretary-General Ban Ki-moon, the acceptable middle ground has shifted away from the view that there was too little too late in terms of using military force to halt the murder of some 800,000 Rwandans. The fulcrum of attention has shifted towards the most backward-looking critics of the so-called new militarism—a revived third-world criticism of R2P as the Trojan Horse of Western neo-imperialism; the too-much-too-soon of numerous international lawyers in relationship to Kosovo; and the totally disingenuous justification of Iraq in humanitarian terms after the evaporation of other justifications (the links to Al-Qaeda and WMDs).

Many analysts point to Clausewitz's dictum that soldiers take over when diplomacy fails; diplomats step aside then and leave the terrain to the military to pursue politics by other means. Ironically, the responsibility to protect requires diplomats to succeed either in securing agreement on preventive measures or on the use of force. In the latter case, diplomats stand aside after they have succeeded, and soldiers do what diplomats cannot, namely halt atrocities.

Even a cursory glance at Darfur, the Democratic Republic of the Congo, Zimbabwe, or Syria suggests that the central problem in halting mass atrocities today is not too little normative basis for military intervention for human protection purposes. Military force, with or without an R2P justification, is obviously not a panacea; and its use is not a cause for jubilation. Yet if negotiations are to be successful, other preventive measures credible, and ultimately civilians safe, then halting mass atrocities occasionally necessitates applying military force and always the threat to do so.

If the Libyan intervention goes well, it will put additional teeth in the fledgling R2P norm, and the non-violent and democratic revolutions in Tunisia and Egypt may have greater traction elsewhere. If the Libyan intervention goes badly, it will redouble international opposition and make future decisions even more difficult. Nonetheless, international action in 2011 suggests that contemporary network diplomacy has led to a concrete result: the R2P norm has not only emerged and cascaded but also is being internalized by states. Perhaps it's not quixotic within the contemporary confines of minilateral and multilateral diplomacy to say no more Holocausts, Cambodias, and Rwandas—and occasionally to mean it.

NOTES

1. Ramesh Thakur and Thomas G. Weiss, 'R2P: From Idea to Norm—and Action?', *Global Responsibility to Protect* 1:1 (2009), 22–53, at 22.
2. International Commission on Intervention and State Sovereignty, *The Responsibility to Protect* (Ottawa: International Development Research Centre, 2001). See also, Thomas

G. Weiss and Don Hubert, *The Responsibility to Protect: Research, Bibliography, Background* (Ottawa: International Development Research Centre, 2001). For the interpretations of one of the co-chairs, see Gareth Evans, *The Responsibility to Protect: Ending Mass Atrocity Crimes Once and For All* (Washington, DC: Brookings, 2008); and of one of the commissioners, Ramesh Thakur, *The United Nations, Peace and Security: From Collective Security to the Responsibility to Protect* (Cambridge: Cambridge University Press, 2006). See also Alex J. Bellamy, *Responsibility to Protect: The Global Effort to End Mass Atrocities* (Cambridge: Polity Press, 2009); and Cristina Badescu, *Humanitarian Intervention and the Responsibility to Protect: Security and Human Rights* (London: Routledge, 2010). The author's own interpretation is found in *Humanitarian Intervention: Ideas in Action*, 2nd ed. (Cambridge: Polity, 2012).

3. For more on this distinction, see Chapter 2, this volume.

4. Anne-Marie Slaughter, 'America's Edge', *Foreign Affairs* 88:1 (January/February 2009), 94–113, at 94.

5. See Thomas G. Weiss, 'R2P Is Alive and Well after Libya', *Ethics & International Affairs* (2011), 1–6. In the same issue, also see essays by Alex Bellamy, Simon Chesterman, James Pattison, and Jennifer Welsch.

6. See Ramesh Thakur, Andrew F. Cooper, and John English (eds), *International Commissions and the Power of Ideas* (Tokyo: UN University Press, 2005).

7. Commission on International Development, *Partners in Development* (New York: Praeger, 1969).

8. Independent Commission on International Development Issues, *North-South: A Programme for Survival* (London: Pan Books, 1980) and *Common Crisis North-South: Co-operation for World Recovery* (Cambridge: MIT Press, 1983).

9. Independent Commission on Disarmament and Security Issues, *Common Security: A Blueprint for Survival* (New York: Simon & Schuster, 1982).

10. World Commission on Environment and Development, *Our Common Future* (Oxford: Oxford University Press, 1987).

11. Independent Commission on International Humanitarian Issues, *Winning the Human Race?* (London: Zed Books, 1988).

12. South Commission, *The Challenge to the South* (Oxford: Oxford University Press, 1990).

13. Commission on Global Governance, *Our Global Neighbourhood* (Oxford: Oxford University Press, 1995).

14. Commission on Human Security, *Human Security Now* (New York: Commission on Human Security, 2003).

15. D.H. Meadows et al., *The Limits To Growth: A Report to the Club of Rome's Project on the Predicament of Mankind* (New York: Universe Books, 1972). This was reviewed two decades later by D.H. Meadows, D.L. Meadows, and J. Randers, *Beyond the Limits: A Global Collapse or a Sustainable Future* (London: Earthscan, 1992).

16. Carnegie Commission on Preventing Deadly Conflict, *Preventing Deadly Conflict* (New York: Carnegie Corporation of New York, 1997).

17. *Report of the Panel on United Nations Peace Operations*, UN document A/55/305-S/2000/809, dated 21 August 2000.

18. High-level Panel on Threats, Challenges and Change, *A More Secure World: Our Shared Responsibility* (New York: United Nations, 2004).

19. Thomas G. Weiss and Ramesh Thakur, *Global Governance and the UN: An Unfinished Journey* (Bloomington: Indiana University Press, 2010).

20. See Thomas G. Weiss, Tatiana Carayannis, Louis Emmerij, and Richard Jolly, *UN Voices: The Struggle for Development and Social Justice* (Bloomington: Indiana University Press, 2005), 381–7.

21. Jarat Chopra and Thomas G. Weiss, 'Sovereignty Is No Longer Sacrosanct: Codifying Humanitarian Intervention', *Ethics & International Affairs* 6 (1992), 95–117.

22. Nicholas J. Wheeler, *Saving Strangers: Humanitarian Intervention in International Society* (Oxford: Oxford University Press, 2000).

23. The phrase is Mary Kaldor's in her *New and Old Wars: Organized Violence in a Global Era* (Stanford, CA: Stanford University Press, 1999). See also Mark Duffield, *Global Governance and the New Wars: The Merging of Development and Security* (London: Zed, 2001); and Robert Kaplan, 'The Coming Anarchy', *Atlantic Monthly* (February 1994), 44–76 and *The Coming Anarchy: Shattering the Dreams of the Post-Cold War* (New York: Random House, 2000). In relationship to humanitarian action and the use of military force, see Peter J. Hoffman and Thomas G. Weiss, *Sword & Salve: Confronting New Wars and Humanitarian Crises* (Lanham, MD: Rowman & Littlefield, 2006).

24. See Thomas G. Weiss, *Military-Civilian Interactions: Humanitarian Crises and the Responsibility to Protect*, 2nd ed. (Lanham, MD: Rowman & Littlefield, 2004), 191–214.

25. Greenberg Research, *The People on War Report* (Geneva: ICRC, 1999), xvi.

26. Antonio Donini, Larry Minear, Ian Smillie, Ted van Baarda, and Anthony C. Welch, *Mapping the Security Environment: Understanding the Perceptions of Local Communities, Peace Support Operations, and Assistance Agencies* (Medford, MA: Feinstein International Famine Center, June 2005), 53.

27. Rama Mani and Thomas G. Weiss (eds), *The Responsibility to Protect: Cultural Perspectives in the Global South* (London: Routledge, 2011).

28. See, for example, Roberta Cohen and Francis M. Deng, *Masses in Flight: The Global Crisis of Internal Displacement* (Washington, DC: Brookings Institution, 1998); and Roberta Cohen and Francis M. Deng (eds), *The Forsaken People: Case Studies of the Internally Displaced* (Washington, DC: Brookings Institution, 1998). For an historical account of the IDP phenomenon, see Thomas G. Weiss and David A. Korn, *Internal Displacement: Conceptualization and its Consequences* (London: Routledge, 2006).

29. James Traub, *The Best Intentions: Kofi Annan and the UN in the Era of American World Power* (New York: Farrar, Straus and Giroux, 2006).

30. Kofi A. Annan, *The Question of Intervention—Statements by the Secretary-General* (New York: UN, 1999). For an analysis of the implications of his September 1999 speech to the General Assembly, see Thomas G. Weiss, 'The Politics of Humanitarian Ideas', *Security Dialogue* 31:1 (2000), 11–23.

31. Kofi A. Annan, 'We the Peoples': *The United Nations in the 21st Century* (New York: UN, 2000).

32. Gareth Evans, 'Foreword', in Thakur, *The United Nations, Peace and Security*, xiv.

33. Michael Reisman, 'Sovereignty and Human Rights in Contemporary International Law', *American Journal of International Law* 84: 4 (1990), 866–76; and Louis Henkin, 'Kosovo and the Law of "Humanitarian Intervention"', *American Journal of International Law* 93: 4 (1999), 824–8.

34. Commission meetings were held in Ottawa (November 2000), Maputo (March 2001), New Delhi (June 2001), Wakefield, Canada (August 2000), and Brussels (September 2001). See Weiss and Hubert, *The Responsibility to Protect: Research, Bibliography, and Background*, 341–4.

35. *Report of the Secretary-General on the Work of the Organization*, UN document A/54/1 (1999), p. 48.

36. See Thomas G. Weiss, 'Moving Beyond North-South Theatre', *Third World Quarterly* 30:2 (2009), 271–84.

37. Round tables and consultative meetings were held, in chronological order, in Ottawa, Geneva, London, Maputo, Washington DC, Santiago, Cairo, Paris, New Delhi, Beijing, and St. Petersburg. See Weiss and Hubert, *The Responsibility to Protect: Research, Bibliography, and Background*, 349–98.

38. Richard Haass, 'When Nations Forfeit their Sovereign Privileges', *International Herald Tribune*, 7 February 2003.

39. Gareth Evans, 'Humanity Did Not Justify this War', *Financial Times*, 15 May 2003; Ramesh Thakur, 'Chrétien Was Right: It's Time to Redefine a "Just War"', *Globe and Mail*, 22 July 2003 and 'Iraq and the Responsibility to Protect', *Behind the Headlines* 62:1 (Toronto: Canadian Institute of International Affairs, October 2004). However, one of the commissioners, Michael Ignatieff, justified the war before later retracting that support.

40. Evans's thoughts on R2P are summarized in his book, *The Responsibility to Protect*, and on the web site of the International Crisis Group: <http://www.crisisgroup.org>. Thakur's writings encompass a wide range of formats from his book, *The United Nations, Peace and Security*, to scholarly articles brought together in *The Responsibility to Protect: Norms, Laws and the Use of Force in International Politics* (London: Routledge, 2011), and newspaper op-eds assembled in *The People vs. the State: Reflections on UN Authority, US Power and the Responsibility to Protect* (Tokyo: United Nations University Press, 2011).

41. Evans, *The Responsibility to Protect*, 28.

42. HLP, *A More Secure World*, para. 203.

43. Kofi A. Annan, *In Larger Freedom: Towards Development, Security and Human Rights for All* (New York: United Nations, 2005).

44. HLP, *A More Secure World*, para. 201, emphasis in original.

45. HLP, *A More Secure World*, para. 207.

46. *Position Paper of the People's Republic of China on the United Nations Reforms* (Beijing, 7 June 2005), downloaded from <http://news.xinhuanet.com/english/2005-06/08/content_3056817_3.htm>, Part III.1, 'Responsibility to Protect'.

47. *American Interests and UN Reform: Report of the Task Force on the United Nations* (Washington DC: US Institute of Peace, 2005), 15.

48. Annan, *In Larger Freedom*, paras. 122–35.

49. Thomas G. Weiss and Barbara Crossette, 'The United Nations: The Post-Summit Outlook', in *Great Decisions 2006* (New York: Foreign Policy Association, 2006), 9–20.

50. Alex J. Bellamy, 'Whither the Responsibility to Protect?', *Ethics and International Affairs* 20:2 (2006), 143–69.

51. *2005 World Summit Outcome*, adopted by UN General Assembly Resolution A/RES/60/1, 24 October 2005, paras. 138–40.

52. See Alex J. Bellamy, 'R2P and the Problem of Military Intervention', *International Affairs* 84:4 (2008), 625–30.

53. Ban Ki-moon, *Implementing the Responsibility to Protect*, Report from the Secretary-General, UN document A/63/677, 12 January 2009.

54. Edward C. Luck, 'The United Nations and the Responsibility to Protect', *Policy Analysis Brief* (Muscatine, Iowa: Stanley Foundation, 2008), 8.

55. Ban Ki-moon, 'Address of the Secretary-General, Berlin, 15 July 2008', UN document SG/SM/11701.

56. See Martha Finnemore and Kathryn Sikkink, 'International Norm Dynamics and Political Change', *International Organization* 52:4 (1998), 887–917; Thomas Risse, Stephen Ropp, and Kathryn Sikkink, *The Power of Human Rights: International Norms and Domestic Change* (Cambridge: Cambridge University Press, 1999); and Margaret Keck and Kathryn Sikkink, *Activists beyond Borders: Advocacy Networks in International Politics* (Ithaca: Cornell University Press, 1998).

57. 'An Idea whose Time Has Come—And Gone?', *The Economist*, 23 July 2009.

58. 'Statement by the President of the General Assembly, Miguel d'Escoto Brockmann, at the Opening of the 97th Session of the General Assembly', 23 July 2009.

59. For summaries, see reports from the Global Centre for the Responsibility to Protect, available at: <http://globalr2p.org/advocacy/index.php>.

60. Thomas G. Weiss, 'Halting Atrocities in Kenya', in *Great Decisions 2010* (New York: Foreign Policy Association, 2010), 17–30.

61. Cristina Badescu and Thomas G. Weiss, 'Misrepresenting R2P and Advancing Norms: An Alternative Spiral?', *International Studies Perspectives* 11:4 (2010), 354–74.

62. See Alan J. Kuperman, 'Mitigating the Moral Hazard of Humanitarian Intervention: Lessons from Economics', *Global Governance* 14:2 (2008), 219–40; 'The Moral Hazard of Humanitarian Intervention: Lessons from the Balkans', *International Studies Quarterly* 52 (2008), 49–80; and 'Darfur: Strategic Victimhood Strikes Again?', *Genocide Studies and Prevention* 4:3 (2009), 281–303.

63. For more on the previous argument, see Michael Barnett and Thomas G. Weiss, *Humanitarianism Contested: Where Angels Fear to Tread* (London: Routledge, 2011), ch. 10.

CHAPTER 43

....

UN PEACEKEEPING

....

PIERRE SCHORI

43.1 A Dramatic Shift in UN Peacekeeping

A dramatic shift in United Nations (UN) peacekeeping has occurred in the first decade of the 21st century. The shift has taken place in the political environment conditioning UN peacekeeping operations, both in the field and on the global stage, most notably in the Security Council and in concerned regional organizations such as the African Union (AU), the Economic Community of West African States (ECOWAS), the North Atlantic Treaty Organization (NATO), and within the group of troop-contributing countries.

A major game-changer was the hard-power reaction by the Bush administration following the terrorist attacks by non-state actors in the United States on 11 September 2001. Multilateral diplomacy, including important and ambitious global commitments like the Millennium Development Goals, was negatively affected by the so-called Global War on Terror (GWOT), announced by President George W. Bush in an address to Congress nine days after September 11: 'Our war on terror will not end until every terrorist group of global reach has been found, stopped and defeated.'

This seemingly never-ending objective was reversed by President Barack Obama in March 2009. In a memo emailed to Pentagon staff members, the Defense Department's office of security review noted that 'this administration prefers to avoid using the term "Long War" or "Global War on Terror"' [GWOT.] Please use "Overseas Contingency Operation".'[1]

Another, unintended, side effect of the GWOT and the war in Afghanistan has been the emergence of a new North–South divide, in the field of troop-contributing countries. The overwhelming majority of peacekeepers under UN flag come from the global South, and notably from an African–Asian nexus, while Western troops are extremely few in UN-led peacekeeping operations. Western solders can instead be found in great numbers in the NATO-led operation in Afghanistan.

On the other hand, in what must be seen as a more logical stance and in the spirit of articles 52–54 of Chapter 8 of the UN Charter, the regional organizations ECOWAS and AU have, during the evolving power struggle and escalating violence in Côte d'Ivoire, shown unprecedented resolve and determination in the crisis-management of a major regional crisis. On 1 November 2006, after years of calculated obstruction and violent acts mainly by the presidential camp, the Security Council adopted the ambitious Resolution 1721, which renewed and strengthened the mandate of the prime minister and extended the president's term for a 'new and final transition period not exceeding 12 months'. It is noteworthy that Resolution 1721, which in an African context was unique for its imposed conditions on an AU member state, did not originate in New York or, as the presidential camp alleged, in Paris, but after the decision of the AU Peace and Security Council acting upon recommendations of an ECOWAS summit.

An additional strong factor of change was the rise of the global South and emerging powers, engaging in what Andrew F. Cooper, Jorge Heine, and Ramesh Thakur in the introduction to this *Handbook* call 'new forms of post-imperialist diplomacy', and whose roles were accentuated by the 2008 global financial crisis.

These new developments have undoubtedly had significant effects, both negative and positive, on the image and influence of the United Nations itself but also on 'the diplomacy of UN peacekeeping' understood as the diplomacy and mediation efforts initiated by impartial UN representatives in conflict and post-conflict situations.

43.2 UN Peacekeeping—A Prominent Feature of the Contemporary International Diplomatic Landscape

There are currently some 120,000 military, police, and civilian personnel serving in sixteen UN Department of Peacekeeping Operations (DPKO)-led peace operations, with 115 countries—60 per cent of the UN membership!—contributing uniformed personnel. The peacekeeping budget hovers around US$ 7–8 billion a year.

Since 1948, hundreds of thousands of military personnel, and tens of thousands of UN police and civilian personnel, from 120 countries have participated. So approximately two-thirds of the UN's member states have either hosted or contributed to UN peace operations. And of course peace operations are injected into situations of armed conflicts and disputes, the big issues of war and peace diplomacy.

In other words, whether voting in the UN Security Council to establish, renew, or terminate a UN peacekeeping operation; debating and voting in the UN General Assembly to finance a UN peacekeeping mission; or hosting or contributing troops, police, or civilian personnel to a UN peace operation, the reality of UN peacekeeping is a prominent feature of the contemporary international diplomatic landscape.

43.3 UN Diplomacy and Mediation

Among the many UN mediation efforts two stand out: Secretary-General Dag Hammarskjöld's successful negotiations in 1955 with Chinese Prime Minister Zhou En-lai for the release of American prisoners, and the UN-facilitated Geneva Accords that paved the way for the Soviet withdrawal from Afghanistan in 1988.

At the end of the Korean War a number of American pilots were held captive by the Beijing government accused of having violated 'Chinese territorial air'.[2] At the time mainland China was not a member of the UN and US diplomatic relations with the country were non-existent. President Dwight Eisenhower, resisting domestic calls for US unilateral action, argued that it was a UN responsibility to ensure that the pilots were released as they had served under UN command.

The UN General Assembly considered that the Secretary-General was the most appropriate person to conduct any negotiations. On 10 December 1954, Hammarskjöld, accepting the responsibility, sent a letter to Zhou, on behalf of the General Assembly, asking for the release of the UN Command personnel captured by Chinese forces. Zhou's response was positive and Hammarskjöld went to China. After many months and several exchanges of correspondence between Hammarskjöld and Zhou, four prisoners were released. The remainder were released on Hammarskjöld's fiftieth birthday, and Zhou pointed out that it was not a concession to the United States. It was instead Dag Hammarskjöld's 'quiet diplomacy' that received credit for the release.[3]

Another major UN success came thirty-five years later. After the failure of the Security Council to produce a resolution on the Soviet invasion Afghanistan on 27 December 1979, the matter was referred to the General Assembly under a 'Uniting for Peace' procedure. The General Assembly strongly deplored the intervention and called for the immediate, unconditional, and total withdrawal of the foreign troops from Afghanistan.

On 11 February 1981, Secretary-General Kurt Waldheim appointed Under-Secretary-General Javier Pérez de Cuéllar as his Personal Representative on the Situation Relating to Afghanistan. After extensive discussions with the governments of Afghanistan and Pakistan, Pérez de Cuéllar managed to get his four-point agenda accepted as the basis for a negotiating process. After assumption of the post of Secretary-General in January 1982, de Cuéllar designated Diego Cordovez as his successor. Over the next six years Cordovez acted as intermediary in indirect negotiations ('proximity talks'—putting each side into a separate room and 'shuttling' back and forth between them) in Geneva and the region between Kabul and Islamabad. The conclusion of the 'Geneva Accords' led to the announcement by the Soviet government in February 1988 to start withdrawing its forces in May of the same year.[4]

The Accords, worth recalling today, consisted of four instruments: a bilateral agreement between the Republic of Afghanistan and the Islamic Republic of Pakistan, on the principles of non-interference and non-intervention; a declaration on international guarantees, signed by the Soviet Union and the United States; a bilateral agreement between Afghanistan and Pakistan on the voluntary return of refugees; and an agreement on the interrelationships for the settlement of the situation relating to Afghanistan, signed by Afghanistan and Pakistan and witnessed by the Soviet Union and the United States. The last instrument contained provisions for the timetable and modalities for the withdrawal of Soviet troops.

43.4 UN Peacekeeping at a Crossroad

Though the term 'peacekeeping' is not found in the UN Charter, the authorization is generally considered to lie in (or between) Chapters 6 and 7. Chapter 6 describes the Security Council's power to investigate and mediate disputes, while Chapter 7 discusses the power to authorize economic, diplomatic, and military sanctions, as well as the use of military force, to resolve disputes.

The first use of peacekeeping troops on a wider scale occurred during the Suez crisis in 1956. According to Max Harrelson,[5] it was Lester B. Pearson who proposed to the General Assembly that Hammarskjöld should organize an 'international police force that would step in until a political settlement could be reached'. Together with Ralph Bunche and Brian Urquhart, the Secretary-General turned the proposal into reality. Hammarskjöld coined the phrase 'Chapter six and a half' to describe the stretching of the original meaning of Chapter 6.[6]

From 1948 to 1988, the UN deployed thirteen peacekeeping missions, while over the next ten years not a single mission materialized due to the tension between the superpowers. Following the end of the cold war, peacekeeping dramatically increased, with the UN authorizing more missions between 1991 and 1994 than in the previous forty-five years combined.

In the 1950s, peacekeepers mostly came from Europe. During the 1990s, the profile changed as developed countries shrank their militaries and/or became reluctant to commit their soldiers to UN-commanded operations. The largest troop contributors, in 2012, were in Asia (Pakistan, Bangladesh, India, Nepal, and China) and Africa (Ethiopia, Nigeria, Egypt, Rwanda, Ghana, and Senegal).

Initially deploying unarmed or lightly armed military personnel mainly from small or non-aligned countries, peacekeepers were called in order to observe an existing peace process or to separate conflicting forces. But this has dramatically changed as stated by the UN DPKO itself:

> In addition to military functions, today's UN peacekeeping undertakes a wide variety of other complex tasks. Peacekeepers now are administrators and economists, police officers and legal experts, de-miners and electoral observers, human rights monitors and specialists in civil affairs, gender, governance, humanitarian workers and experts in communications and public information.[7]

At the turn of the 21st century, the Secretary-General appointed a panel on United Nations Peace Operations to make recommendations for change. The result, the

'Brahimi Report', called for increased staffing and more robust rules of engagement. The Security Council must provide peacekeeping operations with *clear, credible, and achievable mandates*. Brahimi also insisted that the UN needed to learn to say no rather than agree to impossible mandates without sufficient resources.

As a result, UN member states and the Secretariat made major efforts for reform, including through the High-Level Panel on Threats, Challenges, and Change, the 2005 World Summit, the reform strategy of DPKO entitled 'Peace Operations 2010', and most recently the 'Capstone Doctrine', a DPKO manual for strategic and tactical guidance of UN peacekeepers in the field. To strengthen DPKO's capacity to manage and sustain new peace operations, a separate Department of Field Support was established in 2007.

Other reforms have come about in the field of conduct and discipline. Following investigations of sexual exploitation and abuse by UN peacekeepers, the Secretary-General declared a zero tolerance policy for any violation of UN rules, which includes a ban for UN personnel on sex with children under eighteen and sex with a prostitute.

After a decade of unprecedented growth, United Nations peacekeeping had essentially become 'a victim of its own success', said Alain le Roy, the head of DPKO. 'We are often unable to find the resources we need, and we grapple with increasingly complex, robust mandates in difficult and often hostile environments.' He warned that, while the Brahimi Panel's landmark reforms nearly a decade ago had envisioned the launch of only one new mission a year, DPKO was today 'operating far above that pace'.[8]

Despite concrete successes in providing essential security and support to millions of people, persistent 'political realities' are reflected in the fact that the first two peacekeeping operations are still active today, more than sixty years later. In the Middle East, the UN Truce Supervision Organization (UNTSO), established in 1948, remains to monitor ceasefires and supervise armistice agreements. Likewise, UN Military Observer Group in India and Pakistan (UNMOGIP), launched in January 1949, is still tasked to monitor the ceasefire line between India and Pakistan following the conflict over the State of Jammu and Kashmir.[9]

43.5 BUILDING ON BRAHIMI: THE GAP BETWEEN INTENT AND IMPLEMENTATION

The UN Security Council adopted several provisions relating to peacekeeping following the Brahimi Report, in Resolution 1327 (2000).[10] The Council wanted to be regularly informed by the Secretary-General about military operations and humanitarian factors in countries where peacekeeping operations were ongoing. It underlined that the mandates of peacekeeping missions had to be appropriate for the situation on the ground, including the need to protect civilians and prospects for success, and requested Kofi Annan to prepare a doctrine for the military component of peacekeeping operations. Furthermore, the Council said that the roots of conflict had to be addressed with sustainable development and a democratic society with respect for human rights.

The Brahimi Report was the broadest review and reform proposal for UN peacekeeping since the end of the cold war. Impartiality, consent, and non-use of force except for situations of self-defence, which the Report recognized as the 'bedrock principles' of UN peacekeeping, were put to the test when confronted with intra-state transnational conflicts.

The 2009 FRIDE *Security Council Resolutions under Chapter VII: Design, Implementation and Accountabilities. The Cases of Afghanistan, Côte d'Ivoire, Kosovo and Sierra Leone* noted that 'During the immediate post-Cold War period, the rich countries allied with the West had in the eyes of many experts gone beyond the level of international consensus. The original basic tenets of UN peacekeeping were altered by intervention in situations where there was no peace to keep.'[11]

The study examines four widely different interventions approved by the UN Security Council in the past decade. The aim was to analyse how Security Council resolutions for Chapter 7 missions were implemented at mission, national, and regional level and to what extent they were backed up by adequate financial and human resources and sustained Security Council interest and political pressure on the concerned parties. In reviewing the mandates, the political and material support for their implementation, the contribution of regional actors to the peace process, and the consideration given to the local context, the research largely followed the broad lines set out in the Brahimi Report. It also tested its findings against the DPKO document *A New Partnership Agenda: Charting a New Horizon for UN Peacekeeping* in July 2009.

The FRIDE study provides evidence-based material to the above so-called 'New Horizon' debate. The four cases illustrate the fluctuating priorities of member states in the past decade. The Council's role was characterized by decisive involvement in Sierra Leone; legitimization followed by virtual paralysis in Kosovo; unanimous endorsement turning into increasing enquiries as the security situation deteriorated in Afghanistan; and half-hearted support in Côte d'Ivoire. In sum, it asked for mission mandates that are clear and credible, transparent and achievable, realistic budgets and adequate resources, and increased involvement of the troop-contributing countriesl.

43.6 GENDER—THE MISSING LINK

The distance between prescription and action may be best evidenced by the level of implementation of resolution 1325 (2000) on women, peace, and security. The Resolution, with application in its three dimensions—protection, participation, and promotion of women—constitutes a strong potential for increased security and change in post-conflict societies. Yet, the four case studies showed beyond any doubt that the UN and its member states have failed in implementing Resolution 1325.

In my end-of-assignment report from Côte d'Ivoire of February 2007 to Ban Ki-moon, I recommended that a special task force should be set up, preferably led by a Special Envoy, with the task of mainstreaming gender issues into peacekeeping operations in accordance with resolution 1325.

The violence that followed the disputed presidential election in November 2010 caused the most serious humanitarian and human rights crisis in Côte d'Ivoire since the de facto partition of the country in September 2002.[12] Hundreds of people were unlawfully killed, often only on the grounds of their ethnicity or presumed political affiliation. Women and adolescents became victims of sexual violence, including rape, and hundreds of thousands of people were forced to flee their homes to seek refuge in other regions of Côte d'Ivoire or in neighbouring countries, especially Liberia.

Evidence collected by Amnesty International clearly demonstrated that crimes under international law, including war crimes and crimes against humanity, were committed by all sides during the conflict.

The International Rescue Committee (IRC) came to the same conclusion in a June 2011 report. Strong patriarchal traditions and a history of violence against women and girls indicate that they had faced issues of marginalization and gender-based violence prior to the conflict in 2002, the civil war in 2004–2006, and during the recent post-election crisis. Based on a study conducted by the IRC and its partners in Côte d'Ivoire, 60 per cent of interviewed women had experienced violence in their lifetimes.[13] Gender-based violence was also proven to be a defining feature of the 2011 crisis in Côte d'Ivoire. 66 per cent, or 85 of all respondents, reported an increase in gender-based violence since the crisis.[14]

Experience and research show the need for the UN member states and Secretariat, as well as academia, to be more proactive in bringing the role of women into the discussion of the present and future of UN peacekeeping and diplomacy. The establishment of the entity UN Women and the appointment of a Secretary-General Special Representative on Sexual Violence in Conflict in 2010 are welcome improvements.

> If UN member states, particularly those represented in the Security Council, are serious about their commitments to women's equality and to stopping rape and violence, they would individually and collectively ensure outreach to women and their full participation at all decision-making levels in all arenas where issues of peace and security are being decided. This would enhance the protection, participation, and empowerment of women, which in turn would contribute to sustainable peace.[15]

43.7 THE CASE OF AFGHANISTAN

UN peacekeeping today is faced with two major risks: the outsourcing of Security Council control and creation of a new North–South divide. The 'outsourcing' to NATO in the Balkans in 1999 had a regional logic. So did the initial interventions in the late 1990s by the ECOWAS Monitoring Group (ECOMOG) in Sierra Leone and by ECOWAS in 2003 in Côte d'Ivoire. But the NATO military intervention in Afghanistan, enabled by the 2001 terrorist attacks in the US, defies regional logic.

The FRIDE study examines how the situation in Afghanistan has slipped out of UN control and how there was a strategic uncertainty whether the international intervention was aiming at a political or a military solution. The three missions (NATO/ISAF, UNAMA, and the American OEF) also undermined each other and created confusion among the population and within the donor community.

The relationship between NATO forces and the Security Council is characterized by a paradox: the Council has neither a say in determining their rules of engagement nor effective authority over them, yet these military operations have the power to enable or jeopardize the political and peace-building strategies that underlie UN peacekeeping operations, according to Shahrbanou Tadjbakhsh, editor of the first National Human Development Report (2005) in Afghanistan and FRIDE researcher.

The Security Council resolutions have made the peace-enforcement operation legal, but a combination of problems has made it ineffective and in some respects lacking in legitimacy. The peace-building process in Afghanistan from early 2002 was not based on a genuine peace agreement, but on the assumption that the Taliban had been permanently defeated through military intervention before the UN authorized an International Security Assistance Force (ISAF) and a political mission (the UN Assistance Mission in Afghanistan, UNAMA).

Tadjbakhsh points to the imbalance of resources and attention. The UN mission itself was underfunded, whereas the NATO-run military contingents—and even more so the US's Operation Enduring Freedom (OEF)—were the recipients of inflated resources, personnel, and equipment; the latter increased even more as the operation moved from security assistance to full-fledged combat. Yet, UNAMA was expected to coordinate aid from a large and fragmented international community while at the same time implementing its own projects and advocating peace and reconciliation, all in an environment where insecurity, civilian casualties, and institutional weaknesses were reversing the democratizing gains made in the early post-Taliban period.

The foray of the military into development and humanitarian-aid delivery, as well as the reaction of insurgents to the massive military presence and operations, have ensured that the political and development role of the UN is—at best—ineffective, claims Tadjbakhsh's study. The role of the UN is in the end vital to bringing stability to a volatile region. The UN alone can be perceived as an impartial actor able to act as a legitimate third party, broker negotiations within Afghanistan, and lead a political strategy for the region.

In practice, a role of this kind for the UN should entail the international community finding ways to put Afghanistan and Afghans at the heart of peace-building efforts and the creation of a regional solution. A unified and UN-led political strategy, in coordination with key international and regional stakeholders (Russia, China, Iran, and Pakistan, in addition to the US and Europe), could address the main regional challenges and create a peace-conducive atmosphere.

The UN's role of 'junior partner' in Afghanistan was evident in the long policy discussions that took place from 13 September to the end of November 2009 in the White House leading up to president Obama's major speech at West Point on 1 December, where Obama presented the gist of his Afghan strategy: 'And as Commander-in-Chief, I have determined that it is in our vital national interest to send an additional 30,000 US troops to Afghanistan. After 18 months, our troops will begin to come home.'[16] The UN was not consulted before the final decision and got no mention in the detailed article in the *New York Times* of the extended White House strategy sessions.[17]

Symptomatic of the NATO mission's discreet UN character is the fact that it has no UN symbols, but this situation is most likely advantageous for the image and identity of the world organization. Indicative of the *Beruhrungsangst* (fear of contact) you can sense in UN corridors is the fact that NATO/ISAF does not figure in the DPKO list of UN operations.

43.8 UN PEACEKEEPING WITHOUT THE WEST?

> Concerns had been voiced...that United Nations peacekeeping was dysfunctional, because the troops the United Nations deployed—troops mostly from developing countries—were often ill-equipped, ill-trained and ill-prepared...if developing countries would stop responding to the frantic calls of the United Nations today there would be no peacekeeping tomorrow, barring a few choicest areas in the world of strategic interest to major powers. Blaming the failure on the peacekeepers was the easy way out of meeting the Organisation's collective responsibility.[18]

Since NATO took command of ISAF in August 2003, the Alliance has gradually expanded the reach of its mission, originally limited to Kabul, to cover all of Afghanistan's territory. As of August 2011, the number of ISAF troops grew from the initial 5,000 to more than 130,000 troops from forty-eight countries, including all twenty-eight NATO member nations.[19] Out of these troops 90, 000 are Americans. The top positions were mostly manned by high-ranking US military. The Command in Kabul is led by three Americans.

The 'coalition of the willing' that serve under the NATO flag in Afghanistan is composed overwhelmingly of NATO member states, candidates to the alliance, or countries that have a bilateral defence agreement with the US. To the published NATO so-called placemats[20] should be added that the Netherlands ended its military mission in August 2010, that Canada announced that it would do the same in 2011, that Poland planned to leave in 2012, and the UK in 2014 or 2015. Also, after the elections in 2012, President Hollande announced that all French troops would be withdrawn during 2012. Some countries also seem to have a mere symbolic presence: Jordan accounted for zero soldiers in 2010 and 2011 but was still registered as member of the coalition, while Austria, Iceland, Ireland, and Luxembourg deployed no more than twenty-five soldiers together.

In 2008, when UN forces were unable to contain rebels in the eastern Congo, Secretary-General Ban Ki-moon asked the EU for a European Security and Defence Policy mission to help but was turned down. Britain and Germany, despite having forces available on stand-by as part of the EU's 'battle groups', blocked the proposal. They feared military overstretch in case NATO needed more soldiers in Afghanistan. In early 2009, Poland announced that it would pull out of some UN operations to save money, according to UN expert Richard Gowan.[21]

Sweden, to give an example from my own country, having had a UN Secretary-General, Dag Hammarskjöld, who institutionalized the blue helmets, and whose soldiers used to provide about 10 per cent of UN peacekeepers in the first decades, is an example of this dilemma. During 2009–2012, Sweden had not a single blue helmet under the UN flag; all armed Swedish soldiers on foreign missions were deployed in Afghanistan fighting under the NATO flag.

In other words, Afghanistan absorbed all Western potential for UN-led peacekeeping. Europe and other Western countries are in Afghanistan under the NATO flag and not in Africa where most of the UN peacekeeping is deployed.

The question could be raised why the other 150 member states of the UN have not rallied under NATO in Afghanistan. One reason is that they have answered the repeated calls by the UN Secretary-General to come and strengthen the insufficient ranks of the blue helmets. It is the Africa–Asian nexus that provides nearly 90 per cent of UN peacekeeping. As of December 2010 UN peacekeeping accounted for a total of 99,245 peacekeepers deployed (of whom 82,973 were soldiers) from 118 countries.[22]

43.9   BACK TO THE FUTURE: HAMMARSKJÖLD AND BRAHIMI?

'What sorts of mandates were appropriate for peacekeeping? What were the benchmarks against which success could be measured? Was the Organization equipped with the right systems, rules and regulations to grapple effectively and accountably the challenges of deploying at huge scale and high speed into remote and dangerous areas', Alain Le Roy asked on 23 February 2009.[23]

Similar questions (and answers) were presented in the *UK–France Initiative on Peacekeeping* in January 2009. The Initiative was later endorsed by a presidential statement of the Security Council on 5 August 2009. Among the suggestions were the following:

• Ensuring that mandates for peacekeeping operations are clear, credible, and achievable and matched by appropriate resources;
• The Council stresses the need regularly to assess in consultation with other stakeholders, the strength, mandate, and composition of peacekeeping operations with a view to making the necessary adjustments where appropriate, according to progress achieved or changing circumstances on the ground;
• Earlier and more meaningful engagement with troop- and police-contributing countries before the renewal or modification of the mandate of a peacekeeping operation;
• The Council requests that where a new peacekeeping mission is proposed, or where significant change to a mandate is envisaged, an estimate of the resource implications for the mission be provided to it;

- The Council recognizes the priority of strengthening the capacity of the African Union, and the role of regional and sub-regional organizations, in maintaining international peace and security in accordance with Chapter VIII of the UN Charter.

In fact, these ideas were at the centre of the Brahimi report more than a decade ago and they have been part of all UN reform literature since then. They all focus on more responsibility, accountability, and transparency in the planning and managing of UN peacekeeping, primarily from the Security Council itself, but also from the General Assembly and its budget committee.

43.10 UN Peacekeeping and New Diplomacy: A Look Back at Côte d'Ivoire

Côte d'Ivoire became a test case for Security Council authority and responsibility. The Ivorian crisis has over the years become regionalized (ECOWAS), Africanized (AU), and globalized (UN). For too long it lacked its essential component: to be internalized, nationalized, and taken seriously by the national players.

In their introduction to this *Handbook,* the editors draw attention, among other developments in diplomacy, to the proliferating numbers and types of actors engaged in international diplomacy; to the expanding domain and scope of the subject matter or content of diplomacy; and to the multiple levels at which diplomatic engagement and activity take place. The case of UN peacekeeping in Côte d'Ivoire can illustrate these changes as well.

The Special Representative of the Secretary-General (SRSG), in his or her capacity as the head of a UN peacekeeping mission, functions as the node of a complex web of diplomatic actors and activities that links the international community organically to a variety of actors in a theatre of operation experiencing or recovering from armed conflict.

Elsewhere, Ramesh Thakur has observed that the Secretary-General is required to be a politician, diplomat, and international civil servant all rolled into one, playing administrative, political, and symbolic roles simultaneously. In an organization of, by, and for states, he/she must have the backing of almost all governments but owe no allegiance to any.[24] Acting with the delegated authority of the Secretary-General, the SRSG too must reflect similar impartiality yet not lose the confidence of any of the key local, regional, or international stakeholders.

When Kofi Annan asked me to take over the leadership of the UN Operation in Côte d'Ivoire (ONUCI), he explained that he needed a Francophone person who knew the UN and European Union (EU) from the inside, a diplomat and a politician, with experience from government and parliament, who came from a country with no colonial past and knew South African President and AU mediator Thabo Mbeki and other African leaders. These are not the skill-sets one would have associated with the traditional diplomat in the 19th-century world of club diplomacy.

The competing demands, pressures, and expectations of the international community at UN headquarters in New York can be gleaned from the fact that, since its involvement in the Ivorian peace process in 2003, the Security Council has adopted more than fifty resolutions and presidential statements on Côte d'Ivoire. In 2011 alone the Council adopted seven resolutions on Côte d'Ivoire.

No less than fifteen resolutions and ten presidential statements were adopted during my 22-month tenure, each one of them asking for more but without allocating necessary material, financial and human resources. This was one of the reasons for the gap between intent and implementation. In my *End of Assignment Report* and its thirty-five recommendations, I argued that much more would have been needed to implement the detailed and ambitious operative paragraphs of the Security Council Resolutions and, not least, to meet the high expectations of the conflict-tired peoples of Côte d'Ivoire.

The mandate assigned to UNOCI since its first resolution 1528 (2004) provided for the following tasks:

- Monitoring of the cessation of hostilities and movements of armed groups;
- Disarmament, demobilization, reintegration, repatriation, and resettlement;
- Disarmament and dismantling of militias;
- Operations of identification of the population and registration of voters;
- Reform of the security sector;
- Protection of United Nations personnel, institutions, and the civilian population;
- Monitoring of the arms and diamonds embargo;
- Support for humanitarian assistance;
- Support for the redeployment of State administration;
- Support for the organization of open, free, fair, and transparent elections;
- Assistance in the field of human rights;
- Public information;
- Assistance in maintaining law and order, including restoring a civilian policing presence, and advising the Government on the restructuring of the internal security services; assisting the Government in conjunction with the African Union, ECOWAS, and other international organizations in re-establishing the authority of the judiciary and the rule of law throughout Côte d'Ivoire; and supporting the Government in ensuring the security of the premises of the Radio Television Ivoirienne (RTI).

All these tasks were to be implemented throughout Côte d'Ivoire in cooperation with a 'government of national reconciliation', which was only reconciled in name, and with the support of Africa and a former colonial power.

Taking over an ongoing mission is not always easy for a new SRSG. The mission has often developed its own life and trends, dynamics, and human relationships. You may also inherit a certain mission 'culture' with established and resilient structures. And, consequently, when change is needed, it takes a lot of time to implement it.

The UN policy on 'mission integration' gives the SRSG the main responsibility for coordinating the efforts of the whole UN family in the field in order to promote the peace process. The intention was to achieve a better use of the combined resources of the world organization, a demand not least from donor counties. The SRSG thus chaired the regular meetings of the country team, which represented some ten organizations. However, the coordination exercise was faced with an almost permanent obstacle: the tendency of some UN agencies to protect their turf vis-à-vis the Mission's perceived interference with their areas of responsibility.

The interaction with *national actors* was facilitated by the periodic organization of seminars/workshops on issues relevant to the overall peace process, including identification, preparations for the elections, involvement of civil society in the peace efforts, and gender perspective. To counter the frequent hate media attacks on ONUCI and other forms of international presence, the mission defined and implemented a sensitization campaign which was also used to explain the nature, scope, and limitations of ONUCI's mandate and resources. To that end, the UN Radio 'ONUCI FM' was an invaluable asset in spite of the fact that the government denied ONUCI adequate resources to enable it to ensure a nationwide coverage.

At the *regional level*, the work of the Abidjan-based Mediation Group (where ECOWAS and AU were represented) became complicated by the fact that its members did not always reflect the views of their original organizations. The day-to-day functioning of the Mediation Group also imposed a huge burden on the Mission in terms of providing substantive and logistical support. Because getting access to the regional organizations and their leaders was of course of vital importance for the head of ONUCI, I participated in several ministerial and summit meetings of ECOWAS and the African Union. These meetings provided unique and valuable information to present to the regular SRSG briefings (every third month) of the Security Council.

The multiplicity of *external actors* with sometimes diverging and competing political agendas, including noticeable disagreements among key actors within the Security Council, made it difficult to promote a strong and coordinated international response to the emerging risks and challenges, situations in which the SRSG had to facilitate dialogue among the Ivorian parties and the different international players. One important example of diverging agendas was the failure to agree to the imposition of targeted sanctions against identified spoilers of the peace process, due to apparent disagreement within the Security Council on the timing, the target, and scope of those sanctions. This contributed to our difficulties but more seriously also to emboldening those spoilers and their followers, and diminished thus the credibility of the threat of sanctions provided for in Security Council resolutions.[25]

Regular and close interaction with bilateral and multilateral *donors* has become essential in view of the significant amount of support (technical expertise, financial assistance, etc.) they pledge towards the implementation of key processes of the peace process. In this context, the need to establish a mechanism for coordinating donor support is urgent. In Côte d'Ivoire it would have been useful to get the support of the International Monetary Fund, the World Bank, and the EU to monitor and audit public budgeting and the oil and cocoa sectors, in the context of promoting transparency and accountability.

Finally, without regular and smooth contacts between UN headquarters and the field, a mission is doomed to failure. The Security Council should think strategically—and consult the Secretary-General in advance—when setting up a chapter 7 peacekeeping mission. Furthermore, having opted for a resolution with clear 'interference in internal affairs' as part of the mission mandate, as the case was and is with Côte d'Ivoire, the Council texts must avoid ambiguities and clearly spell out the relationship between chapter 7 obligations and national law. The continued resistance from the presidential camp to Security Council resolutions was built on the unclear wording and ambiguity.

The last quarter of 2006 was marked by mounting tensions between the president and his political allies on one hand and the prime minister and the international actors on the other. The frustration of the Secretary-General at the political stalemate was perceptible in his tenth progress report on ONUCI:

> At every critical turn of the peace process, some of the main political leaders have resorted to calculated obstruction of the peace process, exploiting loopholes in the peace agreements, using legal technicalities and often inciting violent acts by their followers. Consequently the second transition period, like the first, is coming to a close without elections... In this context, it would be necessary for the Council to review the mandate of ONUCI and to augment its resources. It is also important for the Security Council to closely monitor the implementation of the road map during the new transition period, in particular, with a view to imposing targeted sanctions against those obstructing the peace process, or seizing the International Criminal Court.[26]

When elections finally took place in November 2010 (six years later than requested by the Security Council, ECOWAS, and the AU), which was mandated to certify the election process and the results, the president lost but refused to accept defeat and precipitated a fresh national and international crisis. The defeated government, holding tenaciously to power, ordered the UN mission to leave. To do so would have been to give up a just cause and encourage and reward those who want to cling illegitimately to power against the will of the people. It would also have been a victory for violence, a blow to regional crisis-management, and a defeat for the United Nations.

Backed by regional, African, and international actors, the United Nations stayed put—a sequence of events involving a coalition of actors that would have been unimaginable to the diplomats of a mere hundred years ago.

After months of political deadlock, forces loyal to president-elect Alassane Ouattara launched an offensive from their stronghold in the north. As they closed in on Laurent Gbagbo's bunker in the presidential residence in Abidjan on 11 April 2011, ONUCI and French attack helicopters targeted heavy weapons being used by his forces.

UN Secretary General Ban Ki-moon underlined that the UN and the French Licorne forces had acted strictly within the framework of the principle of Responsibility to Protect.[27] The Security Council had indeed on 30 March, in its Resolution 1975 on Côte d'Ivoire, recalled 'its authorization to use all necessary means... to protect civilians under imminent threat of physical violence, including to prevent the use of heavy weapons against the civilian population'. Alain Le Roy, head of DPKO, agreed, stressing that Gbagbo's forces had sharply escalated the shelling of both civilians and the UN in the days leading up to the air strikes.

President Nicolas Sarkozy was also keen to say that he waited for a specific request for help with the air strikes from Ban Ki-moon before he authorized Licorne to join the attacks. It can be argued that Resolution 1975 would not have been adopted without the preceding Resolution 1973 on Libya, which was adopted on 17 March 2011 by a vote of ten in favour with five abstentions (Brazil, China, Germany, India, Russian Federation). Resolution 1973 authorized member states 'to take all necessary measures to protect civilians under threat of attack in the country, including Benghazi, while excluding a foreign occupation force of any form on any part of Libyan territory'.

Shortly before the fall of the Gbagbo regime BBC UN correspondent Barbara Plett echoed the reservations from different quarters to the UN military action.[28] Russian Foreign Minister, Sergei Lavrov, questioned the legality of the air strikes, suggesting the UN peacekeepers may have overstepped their mandate to be neutral. The chairman of the African Union declared that foreign military intervention was unjustified.

And no less a person than the former AU mediator for Côte d'Ivoire, South African ex-President Thabo Mbeki, joined in with a strongly worded essay titled 'Why is the United Nations entrenching former colonial powers on our continent? Africans can and should take the lead in resolving their own disputes.'[29]

Ms Plett ended her article with a remark which will most likely continue to haunt and divide the UN and its member states: 'What is clear is that if the UN continues to sanction military interventions in national conflicts, there will be continuing questions about whether it is acting to protect civilians, or using humanitarian justifications as a smokescreen to force political change.'[30]

43.11 A 'NEW HORIZON' FOR UN PEACEKEEPING DIPLOMACY?

[W]e need mission mandates that are more credible and achievable. We need peacekeeping operations to be planned expertly, deployed quickly, budgeted realistically, equipped seriously, led ably, and ended responsibly.[31]

Susan Rice's declaration represents a positive and dramatic change of the US position, compared to the Bush years. Add to that that President Obama presided over a Security Council meeting on how to rid the world of nuclear weapons on 24 September 2009, and then met with the top ten troop-contributing countries.

There is, however, also a contradiction in the principled and positive stance taken at the UN in favour of reform and strengthening of UN-led peacekeeping, and the fact that the three permanent members of the Security Council advocating change

(France, UK, and US), are themselves heavily engaged in counter-insurgency in Afghanistan. This runs counter to the basic tenets of the still much supported and respected 'Brahimi rules' and the spirit of most reform ideas that followed in the ten years after the report. Therefore, in the eyes of many, not least public opinion globally, the credibility and motives of the nations behind the initiatives could be questioned.

The most urgent issue in terms of international peacekeeping is the growing inequality in the world. Issues such as the rise of food costs, the youth bulge, social injustices, and climate change have the potential to produce pervasive internal conflicts in the developing world. In environments like Somalia, it is very hard to impose order—it takes 'crack troops'. Very few countries produce these troops, yet in a significant number of cases, the world wants order restored.

A decade after foreign troops arrived in Afghanistan, NATO is preparing its exit, leaving the country to an uncertain future. In Côte d'Ivoire, almost ten years after the outbreak of the civil war, SRSG Bert Koenders underlined the post-election fragility, against the backdrop of the killing of seven peacekeepers from Niger in June 2012: 'Despite advances, Côte d'Ivoire needs continued support on the path to stability. The root causes of the conflict—land-related issues, unreformed security forces, impunity and lack of national reconciliation and political dialogue—need to be tackled urgently and in a transparent manner.'[32]

The *2012 SIPRI Yearbook* added new questions regarding the future of peacekeeping:

> 'Despite the levelling out of both mission and peacekeeper numbers, new operations launched in 2011—particularly those in Côte d'Ivoire, Libya and Syria—appeared to signal the beginnings of a commitment on the part of the international community to the concepts of the responsibility to protect (R2P) and the protection of civilians (POC) in armed conflict, but illustrated the lack of consensus on the appropriate form of implementation. The UN's 2012–2013 budget for peacekeeping is expected to be substantially cut. This could have consequences for already deployed operations and the UN's ability to take on new missions, and might even lead to a slow-down in UN activities in the future', stated Senior Researcher Sharon Wiharta, Head of the SIPRI project on Peace Operations, on 4 June 2012.

Will we see more outsourcing to NATO as was the case in Afghanistan and Libya in this century and in the Balkans during the 1990s? Or to 'coalitions of the willing' like the one President George H.W. Bush mobilized in 1991 after Saddam Hussein's invasion and occupation of Kuwait? Will regional organizations play a more proactive role as ECOWAS and AU did in the Côte d'Ivoire crisis? And what role will the United Nations have in this changing political landscape?

A key question remains: Can the 'four bedrock principles'—impartiality, consent, non-use of force except for situations of self-defence, and a peace to keep—still be seen as valid after the outsourcing to NATO in Afghanistan and Libya? An end to the war in Afghanistan seems to be a prerequisite for solving the North–South divide of UN troop-contributing countries and thus preventing a 'clash of civilizations'. Maybe the time has come to restore the diplomacy of Dag Hammarskjöld and to fully implement the peacekeeping recommendations of the Brahimi Report. In any case, a frank, honest, and transparent debate is called for. The very soul of UN peacekeeping is at risk.

NOTES

1. Scott Wilson and Al Kamen, ' "Global War On Terror" Is Given New Name, Bush's Phrase Is Out, Pentagon Says', *Washington Post*, 25 March 2009.

2. Brian Urquhart, *Dag Hammarskjöld, Secretary-General* (New York: United Nations, 1972), 96.

3. <http://www.daghammarskjold.se/biography/#china>.

4. <http://www.un.org/en/peacekeeping/missions/past/ungomap/background.html>.

5. Max Harrelson, *Fires all around the Horizon* (New York: Praeger, 1989), 89.

6. Quoted in Richard Jolly, Louis Emmerij, and Thomas G. Weiss, *UN Ideas that Changed the World* (Bloomington: Indiana University Press, 2009), 172.

7. <http://www.un.org/events/peacekeeping60/60years.shtml>.

8. <http://www.un.org/News/Press/docs/2009/gapk199.doc.htm>.

9. <http://www.un.org/Depts/dpko/missions/untso/background.html>.

10. <http://www.un.org/News/Press/docs/2000/20001113.sc6948.doc.html>.

11. (Madrid: FRIDE, 2009), xx.

12. Amnesty International, *'They look at his identity card and* shot him dead'—Six months of post-electoral violence in Côte d'Ivoire, May 2011.

13. M. Hossain, C. Zimmerman, L. Kiss, and C. Watts, *Violence against women and men in Côte d'Ivoire: Results from a community survey* (London, UK: London School of Hygiene & Tropical Medicine (LSHTM), 2010).

14. International Rescue Committee, Impact of the Post-Election Crisis on Gender-Based Violence among Women and Girls in Côte d'Ivoire, June 2011.

15. Excerpts from an *Open Letter to Member States of the Security Council regarding Resolution 1960 and the need for focus on full implementation of resolution 1325* (Global Network of Women Peace-builders, 7 January 2011).

16. <http://www.whitehouse.gov/the-press-office/remarks-president-address-nation-way-forward-afghanistan-and-pakistan>.

17. Peter Baker, 'How Obama Came to Plan for "Surge" in Afghanistan', *New York Times*, 6 December 2009.

18. Ambassador Anwarul Chowdhury, Permanent Representative of Bangladesh in the United Nations Security Council, on 11 May 2000.

19. <www.NATO.int>.

20. <http://www.isaf.nato.int/troop-numbers-and-contributions/index.php>.

21. *CER Bulletin*, July 2009, <www.cer.org.uk>.

22. <http://www.un.org/en/peacekeeping/contributors/2010/nov10_2.pdf>.

23. <http://www.un.org/News/Press/docs/2009/gapk199.doc.htm>.

24. Ramesh Thakur, *The United Nations, Peace and Security: From Collective Security to the Responsibility to Protect* (Cambridge: Cambridge University Press, 2006), ch. 14.

25. Gilles Yabi, *Côte d'Ivoire* (Madrid: FRIDE, 2009).

26. Tenth Progress Report of the Secretary General, 17 October 2006.

27. 'Ivory Coast: Gbagbo held after assault on residence', <http://www.bbc.co.uk/news/world-africa.April 11, 2011>.

28. Barbara Plett, 'Did UN forces take sides in Ivory Coast?', <http://www.bbc.co.uk/news/world-africa>, 7 April 2011.

29. Mbeki Thabo, 'What the World Got Wrong in Côte D'Ivoire', <http://www.foreignpolicy.com/articles>, 29 April 2011.

30. Plett, 'Did UN forces take sides in Ivory Coast?'.
31. 'A New Course in the World, a New Approach at the UN', remarks by Susan E. Rice, US Ambassador to the United Nations, at NYU's Center for Global Affairs and Center on International Cooperation, 12 August 2009.
32. Bert Koenders, presentation to the Security Council, 19 July 2012.

CHAPTER 44

....

THE OTTAWA CONVENTION ON ANTI-PERSONNEL LANDMINES

....

JOHN ENGLISH

THE Ottawa Treaty or, as it is properly known, the Convention on the Prohibition on the Use, Stockpiling, Production, and Transfer of Anti-Personnel Mines and on their Destruction was signed by 122 governments in Ottawa, Canada, on 3–4 December 1997. On 18 September 1997 a diplomatic conference at Oslo had concluded the convention and article 15 of the convention provided for the opening of the signature of the convention in Ottawa. The convention required that forty states must ratify the convention before it entered into force. On 1 March 1999 Burkino Faso ratified the convention thus triggering the entry into force of the convention a six-month delay, which the terms of the convention had prescribed. After its entry into force, states no longer signed the convention but became bound by their accession; by November 2011 there were 158 states parties to the agreement. Poland and the Marshall Islands signed the treaty but did not ratify. There were thirty-seven other counties that neither ratified nor acceded to the treaty.[1]

44.1 THE INTERNATIONAL CAMPAIGN TO BAN LANDMINES: A MULTI-ACTOR PARTNERSHIP

....

The momentum for the Ottawa treaty arose in the aftermath of the cold war, increased during the early 1990s as non-governmental organizations united around the notion of a ban on anti-personnel mines, and sped to its conclusion when major governments embraced the movement. The Nobel Peace Prize committee awarded the 1997 prize to the International Campaign to Ban Landmines (ICBL) and to Jody Williams, an American activist who had been recruited by the Washington-based Vietnam Veterans against the

War to organize a campaign to ban landmines. The prize recognized the significant contribution Americans made to the campaign but many contemporary observers pointed out that the Americans had not convinced their own government to sign the treaty. The refusal of not only the dominant superpower but also Russia, China, and India to sign the treaty deeply troubles the treaty's proponents. Nevertheless, they correctly argue that the treaty has fulfilled its fundamental purpose; it has greatly reduced the number of victims of landmines. It also has acquired symbolic significance as an innovative partnership between non-governmental organizations (NGO) and governments and to some is a model of how significant change can occur in stagnant international waters.[2]

The International Committee of the Red Cross (ICRC) first drew attention to the growing use of landmines in the 1970s because of 'the magnitude of human suffering' caused by their proliferation in civilian areas in developing countries.[3] The development of 'scatterable' mines had drastically changed the use of anti-personnel mines, which had previously been restricted to protection of perimeters. As Lloyd Axworthy notes in Chapter 4, this volume, the ICRC with its close ties to military officers and legitimacy as a neutral intermediary based upon international conventions was uniquely situated to act as convenor and an animator. It did so throughout the last decade of the cold war, bringing together its medical practitioners who treated the shattered limbs and lifeless bodies, the high human toll of landmines in Cambodia, Afghanistan, Mozambique, Angola, and many other poor countries, with soldiers, diplomats, and concerned NGOs. The human costs, borne mainly by innocent civilians, were detailed, and the military utility of such indiscriminate killing questioned.[4] These discussions penetrated the political world in the late 1980s, most notably in the United States where Vermont Democratic Senator Patrick Leahy developed a strong interest in the subject after he encountered a young disabled boy in a Central American hospital in the late 1980s. The boy told a shaken Leahy that he did not know who had placed the landmine or who had made it but that it meant that he would be on crutches all his life. Leahy returned to Washington determined to effect change and in 1988 used the exceptional powers an American senator possesses to establish a War Victims Fund from the American development assistant budget. The fund provided $5 million annually for landmine victims and also supported organizations contemplating a broader campaign to reduce the human costs of landmine proliferation.[5]

Spurred on by Leahy's support and by the innovative atmosphere after the cold war's end, Human Rights Watch and Physicians for Human Rights published *Landmines in Cambodia: A Coward's War* whose impact was magnified by the celebrated 1984 Roland Joffé film, *The Killing Fields*, which itself did not focus on the landmine question in Cambodia but did draw Western attention to the Cambodian tragedy and did offer its title as an effective metaphor for a campaign against landmine proliferation. Shortly after the publication of *Landmines in Cambodia*, Bobby Muller, the founder and president of the Vietnam Veterans of America Foundation (VVAF), and Thomas Gebauer, the head of Medico International, a German NGO who shared with VVAF recent experience with Cambodian mine victims, discussed the possibility of together leading a campaign to ban anti-personnel landmines. Muller hired Jody Williams, a Vermonter, who quickly contacted her senator, Leahy. On 4 December 1991 Williams and Leahy aide Tim Rieser agreed that Leahy would offer congressional support for the NGO's effort.[6]

The fruits of the collaboration quickly became evident when Leahy pressed forward the issue in Congress and sponsored an amendment requiring a moratorium on the export of landmines. The amendment, which was signed into law by President George H.W. Bush on 23 October 1992, echoed the tone of the NGO meetings and called upon the United States to 'seek verifiable international agreements prohibiting the sale, transfer, or export, and further limiting the use, production, possession, and deployment of antipersonnel landmines'. This statement of purpose quickly became the goal of the ICBL, which was also created in October 1992 in New York by six NGOs: Handicap International (France); Human Rights Watch (US), Medico International (Germany), Mines Advisory Group (UK), Physicians for Human Rights (US), and VVAF (US). Williams became the coordinator, and the campaign drew its first breath as Democrat Bill Clinton became president of the United States and Congress, in the last days of George H.W. Bush's presidency, showed unanimity in supporting Leahy's landmine moratorium.[7]

While Leahy's role remained central in the landmine ban campaign, the United States government under Clinton was to become continuously more reluctant to give leadership. Nevertheless, the ICBL moved beyond its American roots and became remarkably effective in organizing the campaign. It took shrewd advantage of intellectual trends emphasising the role of non-state actors in the early 1990s, not only in the West but also in the developing world. Aware of waning American government support, the ICBL appeared to take pains to distance itself from the United States government as the campaign progressed. It increasingly associated itself with what *New York Times* foreign affairs correspondent Flora Lewis hailed in 1989 as the 'rise of "civil society"' through which people were 'groping for a way of organizing their societies to give more satisfaction both to the community and the individual'. It was for the landmine activists an invigorating concept as they came to define themselves as a 'third force' beyond states and traditional international structures and a movement that attended to the security of individuals.[8] This aspect of the landmine campaign, noted by Axworthy and Kathryn Hochstetler in this *Handbook* (Chapters 4 and 9, respectively), in which traditional diplomacy drew upon 'expanding networks of communication' and new sources of influence, has attracted considerable attention as a possible model.

In its retrospective analysis of its achievement the ICBL credits its achievement to its intense focus on the landmine issue, its successful though loose linking of diverse NGOs throughout the world, and, not least, its effective use of new communication technologies, notably email. The Web and email allowed integration of efforts in developing countries with crucial joint planning and strategies with campaigners in developed countries.[9] And it worked. The memory of the motley groups with various dress, languages, and faces coming to Ottawa in December 1997 endures as the dominant image of the landmine campaign.

Despite the important role of NGOs, the official photographs of Ottawa reveal mainly older men in dark suits representing their governments. In their absence the force of the landmine ban would have lacked substance and force. Civil society and the emergence of the Internet were not enough.

44.2 THE ICRC

As mentioned in section 44.1, the ICRC was critical to the success of the movement because it possessed direct access not only to foreign offices but also to defence ministries which held the existing landmines and from which resistance to the loss of a weapon and suspicion of NGOs advocating such a programme could be expected. The highly capable ICRC President Cornelio Sommaruga took up the landmine issue as a personal cause and devoted significant ICRC resources to its advocacy. With its links to military and mine eradication and mine victim assistance in developing countries, the ICRC brought together members of the growing ICBL coalition with military officers and aid workers who had direct experience of the hideous impact of landmines on civilian populations. A typical ICRC initiative was a symposium it held in Montreux in April 1993 to which it invited the president of Human Rights Watch, and representatives of Medico International, Handicap International, Physicians for Human Rights, Mines Advisory Group, and VVAF (Jody Williams). There they encountered Russian and French diplomats, Kuwaiti, British, Egyptian, American, and Russian military officials, and deminers, including an influential group of British deminers (mainly former soldiers) who came to oppose the landmine campaign. Among the fifty-five participants were, tellingly, journalists from the BBC, *The Observer*, *The Economist*, *The New Yorker*, and the Paris-based foreign affairs correspondent of the *New York Times*.[10]

The ICRC since its mid-19th-century foundation had played a central role in the development of humanitarian law and, at certain times, in the prohibition of weapons. The greatest successes had occurred before the Second World War with the ban on exploding bullets and poison gas; the cold war stalled most progress and had taken weapons restrictions out of the humanitarian law forums and into direct negotiations between the two superpowers. The relevant UN institutions were often sidelined or ignored, limited by their dependence upon consensus. Nevertheless, the United Nations Convention on Certain Conventional Weapons (CCWC) was concluded in 1980, partly in response to ICRC concerns about the impact of landmines upon civilians. Protocol II of the CCWC imposed restrictions upon landmine use, particularly remotely delivered mines, which had such horrendous civilian impact in Southeast Asia. In the aftermath of the American congressional landmine initiative, the Geneva-based Conference on Disarmament (CD) faced pressure to expand the scope of Protocol II, and the ICBL, the ICRC, and other states developed a strong interest in advancing their cause in Geneva.

The campaigners quickly became aware that two particular objections had to be met for their cause to move forward. First, they had to establish that the military utility of landmines was limited. Secondly, they needed to reinvigorate the tradition of international humanitarian law and construct powerful arguments that the concept of 'proportionality' embraced within the Geneva Conventions of 1949, whereby weapons that were 'of a nature to cause superfluous injury or unnecessary suffering', included anti-personnel landmines. The former goal was facilitated by the experience of Operation Desert Storm (the First Gulf War) when prominent American soldiers questioned the military utility of mines. For example, General Alfred Gray, the retired commandant of the United States Marine Corps, reflected on his own military experience including Desert Storm and declared mines largely irrelevant in pursuing military objectives. He bluntly declared: 'We kill more Americans with our own mines than we do anyone else.'[11] Desert Storm commander-in-chief Norman Schwartzkopf reportedly shared his views and expressed them in many private conversations. VVAF in cooperation with Lieutenant-General Robert Gard, the former president of the National Defense University, used their close ties with the military to encourage further open expression of such doubts. Simultaneously, think tanks and academic centres such as the highly reputable Centre for Defence Studies at the University of London published academic studies that set out the case against the military utility of landmines.[12]

The ICRC continued to hold seminars and meetings where military officers mingled with landmine activists and diplomats, and research papers accumulated making the arguments for proportionality. At ICRC gatherings nearly all participants granted that landmines might have a very specific military use but those few cases were far outweighed by the difficulty of removal, the danger to innocent civilians, and, increasingly, the economic costs of landmines to poor nations such as Cambodia and Angola. NGOs associated with the campaign used highly evocative images of victims and stories of individual human suffering to focus public attention on the issue.

More important for the CD debates than emotional pleas were the legal arguments based upon humanitarian law. Here too the ICRC played a central part, particularly its legal adviser Peter Herby who carefully formulated arguments that placed landmines, like exploding bullets and poison gas, within the tradition of international humanitarian law.

44.3 HUMAN SECURITY NETWORK

Although President Clinton initially had indicated his support for a ban on anti-personnel landmines, his increasing confrontations with the military over such issues as homosexuals in the military caused him to become increasingly reluctant. The ICBL was already eager to escape from its own American origins and American political leadership, and it quickly found accomplices in its quest. While attributing the landmine campaign's success primarily to the work of the ICBL, Jody Williams and Human Rights Watch advocate Stephen Goose acknowledge that governments were essential to its success:

> Historically, NGOS and governments have often seen each other as adversaries not colleagues—and in many cases rightly so. And at first many in the NGO mine ban community worried that governments were going to 'hijack' the issue in order to undermine a ban. But a relationship of trust among the relatively small 'core group' of governments (most notably Canada, Norway, Austria, and South Africa) and ICBL leadership quickly developed . . . Eventually this relationship became known as 'citizen diplomacy' and the coalition of small and middle rank states who formed the core of the landmine initiative within international organizations established the 'human security network'.[13]

The ties between the Canadians and the Scandinavians were historically strong; in the 1950s the close relationship between Canadian Foreign Minister Lester Pearson and UN Secretary-General Dag Hammarskjold created the acronym of the 'Scandicanadians', a group of smaller mainly northern countries committed to UN peacekeeping and to resolution of conflicts where the superpowers were on the sidelines or too compromised to interfere. The end of the cold war reinvigorated these relationships, and the landmine cause captured the imagination of the relevant foreign ministries in the mid-1990s.

The coalition formed around the review of the 1980 Convention on Certain Conventional Weapons in Vienna in September–October 1995. ICBL members carrying petitions with 1.7 million signatures and church groups crammed the hotel lobbies, rang bells for landmine victims, and badgered delegates in the bars and Gaststaette of the old imperial capital. But the results were disappointing as governments, including the United States, failed to go beyond the limited restrictions placed on landmines in Protocol II.

After the meetings, the discouraged ICBL leadership met with some government officials who shared the disappointment. Together they determined to press ahead with informal gatherings, as early as early winter in Geneva; and, furthermore, to organize a broader conference involving states and NGOs to press for a fuller ban. Their actions attracted attention.

Veteran politician Lloyd Axworthy, who became Canada's foreign minister on 25 January 1996, was uniquely placed and trained to give leadership to the landmine movement. At Princeton, where he obtained a doctorate in political science, he had studied with Richard Falk, a strong critic of the Vietnam War and proponent of a strengthened international law regime. Within liberal cabinets, he was correctly perceived as a strong voice on the left, a critic of nuclear weapons, and a strong supporter of international development and multilateralism. He had close ties with the Canadian NGOs, who had become prominent in the ICBL. His support for a landmine ban was unequivocal, although ICBL leadership was initially wary of a Canadian initiative to hold a conference to discuss how the ban movement might move forward. Canada was a member of NATO, whose leading members were clearly opposed to the ban, and the close ally of the increasingly reluctant United States.

In spring 1996, the ICBL's suspicions waned and Canadians began to seek out diplomatic support for further action. On the last day of the CCW meetings on 3 May 1996 the Canadians along with representatives of the UN Department of Humanitarian Affairs and UNICEF appeared together to encourage those who were dissatisfied with the CD result to come to Ottawa in October.[14] With that announcement, in Axworthy's words, 'the bailiwick of the land-mine movement' shifted away from Geneva: 'the battle over strategy was rejoined, with Canada at centre court'. Most governments, Axworthy admits, favoured remaining in Geneva and working through traditional institutions, but many dissented such as Belgium and Norway who had recently and unilaterally announced a complete ban on use, production, and export of landmines. Moreover, developing countries had begun to raise their voices in the debate and to provide ever more vivid images and personal testimony of the human devastation caused by landmines. These images and words had a significant impact. In Britain, for example, the Cambodia Trust, organized by Catholic NGO leader Stan Windass, collected tens of thousands of small donations to support victim rehabilitation in a land with tens of thousands of victims and millions of unexploded mines.[15]

44.4 OTTAWA CALLING

The structure of the October 1996 Ottawa conference reflected, on the one hand, the importance of global networks and, on the other, the willingness of some NGOs and some governments to work together for common international purpose. Such cooperation was hardly new: the anti-slavery movement of the 19th century and the peace movement of the early 20th century had built on such collaboration. Nevertheless, the hybrid of the 1990s was different in its global character, secular emphasis, technological spirit, and fluidity of structures. By 1996 funding for the NGO campaign came directly from some governments, including the US government through the Leahy direction of State Department funds. In Canada, NGO activists accompanied Canadian diplomats to official meetings and some were hired to work for the cause in its foreign affairs department. The 'new diplomacy' is an ancient cliché, but the landmine campaign's approach did signal the impact of new media and of social and political networks of broad geographical range and technical sophistication. Critics have attacked the non-representativeness of NGOs and their disregard for the character of relationships between states and the international system more generally, but few dispute that the landmine campaign startled diplomats of the time, captured public attention, created new coalitions, and roiled international meetings, particularly when NGOs penetrated gatherings where they had never been seen or heard before.[16]

Tensions pervaded the meeting at Ottawa on 3–5 October 1996 where, in Axworthy's own words, 'the mixture of NGOs and government proved combustible'. There were fifty participant states, the majority of them favouring a ban, twenty-four observer states who were nearly all opposed, and far more NGO representatives in the former Ottawa train station transformed into a cavernous conference hall. Several of Canada's NATO allies, most notably France and the United States, expressed open dismay when Williams, in clear collaboration with some Canadian officials, vituperatively attacked the French delegate for a statement that stressed traditional approaches and reflected French reluctance to ban landmines. Throughout the conference Canadian officials worked closely with ICBL leadership but avoided their French, American, and Russian colleagues who were increasingly horrified by the style and the substance of the conference. Axworthy accepted his diplomats' defiance of their profession's traditions and on the final day announced that, despite the strong opposition to abandoning the Geneva roadmap, Canada would hold a conference in 1997 whose purpose would be to sign a treaty to ban anti-personnel landmines. The media, Axworthy later wrote, 'couldn't decide if this was a bold stroke or if I had just lost it'.[17] He wasn't sure himself.

Axworthy had gained resolve before his statement not only from other pro-ban countries from Western Europe but also several from Africa and Asia. Moreover, he had
strong public support from Sommaruga of the ICRC and privately from UN Secretary-
General Boutros Boutros-Ghali. With his words, the so-called Ottawa Process—a series
of meetings convened firstly to develop and negotiate a convention to ban landmines
and secondly to build the political will to sign it—began, leading to a dramatic conference in Ottawa in early December 1997. The principle for participation would be self-
selection: those states that wanted to attend could come; those opposed could be absent
or attend as observers. In the meantime, the ICBL would have the principal responsibility of rallying landmine foes around the world to press their governments to come to
Ottawa while the pro-ban states would work closely to develop treaty language and to
push forward the ban in official forums.

The bold stroke brought forth strong critics. Some ridiculed the Western-dominated
leadership of the movement. Victims' voices did not have the American accents that
dominated the NGO leadership, and Norwegians, Canadians, and Belgians were not, in
recent times, victims of landmines and none of the hidden killers lay in their fields.
Others worried about the cavalier disregard of the CD and the blunt attack upon traditional institutions and diplomatic decorum.[18]

But fate fell upon the path of the Ottawa Process. In January 1997 Kofi Annan, an
African and a veteran UN diplomat, became its Secretary-General, and he gave immediate and enthusiastic support for a landmine ban. With the invaluable moral support of
South Africa, the ICBL held its fourth annual conference on landmines in Mozambique
on 25–28 February 1997. It proved to be invaluable in creating a powerful 'story' as victims told tales of lives lost, limbs shattered, and governments helpless in facing the challenge of clearing mines. Most African states participated and endorsed a landmine ban
as South Africa had unilaterally a week before the conference. It was a powerful endorsement for the campaign and a certain indicator that most of the African states would trek
northwards in December to back a landmine ban.

Other conferences followed, notably in March in Japan whose government was
opposed and where it was believed NGOs played an insignificant role in the political
system. The government hosted a conference but NGOs were permitted to attend only
the opening session. In response, the ICBL and some Japanese NGOs sponsored a
counter-conference that led to the creation of an indigenous anti-landmine group that
effectively lobbied the Japanese government to attend the forthcoming Ottawa conference. The ICRC continued to play its critical part sponsoring conferences that brought
in military officials as well as many others with field experience. The Canadian and other
governments often sent delegates and provided indirect support through their embassies. In Australia, where opposition within the defence and foreign ministries was strong,
the Canadian embassy impishly encouraged local landmine campaigners to lobby the
government. Controversially, the Canadian ambassador brought a Canadian NGO representative with him when he met with the Australian foreign minister. After the official
meeting, the Canadian NGO representative promptly told Australian NGOs that their
foreign office was strongly opposed to the landmine ban. In response, they quickly

organized a conference chaired by the eminent academic Ramesh Thakur to which the Canadian government sent representatives to argue for the landmine ban. Australian politicians, journalists, church groups, and NGOs tilted the balance strongly in favour of a ban and slowly the government began to shift its position as fall began.[19]

By the fall Australian leaders were not alone in sensing political danger or, conversely, opportunity in joining the landmine campaign. Backbenchers signed on in the meetings of the International Parliamentary Associations where politicians from ban-supporting countries put forward resolutions that many representatives from states whose governments opposed a ban approved. As they returned to their homes for the summer, politicians heard from constituents, many of who had watched the 'public service' television advertisements produced by the ICRC and the ICBL and financed by private donations and pro-ban governments. Rock stars, spurred on by the success of Live Aid, raised their voices in support, but no celebrity attracted more attention than Princess Diana who, wearing a ballistic helmet and a flak jacket, walked through an Angolan minefield in January 1997. The image persisted in the public mind and then was magnified in the public imagination when she died in an automobile crash on 31 August 1997. The British had previously opposed the landmine ban. After Diana's death, they moved dramatically towards support as Diana's minefield image became ubiquitous and the new Labour government under Tony Blair clung closely to her popular memory.[20]

As Ottawa approached, there remained uncertainty about how many states would commit to the convention. Despite the dominance of Americans among ban leaders, the United States was increasingly wary. President Clinton's relationship with Jody Williams was particularly bad despite her numerous ties to major Democrats. Clinton found military leaders increasingly intractable as they pointed to Korea as the stumbling block to American signature. When the British agreed to support the convention, there were some caveats related to the treaty's entry into force that were accepted by the ICBL, but a similar attempt to find a compromise with the American government failed. Meanwhile the process leading to Ottawa developed in Western Europe in meetings of diplomats concerned with treaty wording and verification. The final negotiating session took place in Oslo in September. Two members of the Security Council, Britain and France (under a newly elected Socialist government) were now on board, but the Americans remained outside. Axworthy met often with Madeline Albright, the new American secretary of state, who told him she personally supported the ban but had to find a way to accommodate American military interests. Clinton continued to hesitate. The pro-ban states tried to find a way to deal with the Korea question, but the NGO leaders became increasingly suspicious of these manoeuvres. No exceptions or exemptions for Americans, they declared, even though some special provisions had been allowed for others. When Axworthy arrived in Oslo, rumours swirled about his attempts to weaken the treaty to win American acceptance. Some campaigners loudly booed him as he entered the conference hall to give his speech. Axworthy and others were strongly seeking some way the Americans could join. Just before Oslo, Albright and other senior American officials told Axworthy that Clinton was ready to sign. But his bar remained too high. The demand that the United States be permitted to use anti-personnel mines not simply attached to the permitted anti-tank mines but, separately, on a perimeter around them was a bridge too high to cross not only for the ICBL but also the Canadians.[21]

A Canadian winter welcomed over 2,400 delegates and 500 journalists to Ottawa on 3 December 1997 where representatives of 122 nations signed the Ottawa Convention. At the final ceremony, Williams, now a Nobel Peace laureate, joined Axworthy, Canadian Prime Minister Jean Chrétien, whose support had been crucial, Sommaruga of the ICRC, whose commitment to the cause had been essential, and UN Secretary-General Kofi Annan, who boldly cast aside objections that the Ottawa process had pushed aside the CD and the UN system to endorse the landmine ban. In the exuberance of the moment, the landmine ban seemed the harbinger of a major transformation; one where NGOs could work with like-minded states to advance a 'human security agenda' whose focus was on the individual. The final speeches celebrated the extraordinary cooperation between nations and NGOs to save lives and to make the world a safer place for all of its people.

44.5 CONCLUSION

The landmine treaty did save lives, opened fields, and inspired change in international institutions. The NGOs created the *Landmine Monitor*, which has reported yearly on the substantial progress made in clearing minefields and preventing export and production of mines. In 2009 only one nation, Myanmar, still used mines, and the number of producing nations had fallen from over forty to an estimated four. The number of deaths and serious wounds has dropped dramatically since 1997. In 2009, the number of landmine-related deaths or woundings was less than 4,000 in comparison with more than 20,000 per year in the early 1990s. As Axworthy had predicted, the shame of defying the treaty made nearly all non-signatories compliant with the Ottawa aims. The United States, while refusing to sign the convention, became the leading funder for mine eradication. Russia and China, which had been among the largest producers, ceased to export anti-personnel landmines. Rwanda and Nicaragua, nations where children walked in fear, could report by 2010 that they were totally cleared.[22] The Ottawa Process brought life where its loss threatened; hope where there was none.

In 2008 the *Landmine Monitor* became the *Landmine and Cluster Munition Monitor* in recognition of the Convention on Cluster Munitions that was adopted by 108 countries in Dublin on 30 May 2008. That change recognized the broader impact of the landmine campaign, which includes not only the cluster munitions convention but also the International Criminal Court. It too developed through the efforts of a coalition of NGOs, international legal networks, and like-minded states. Soon after the Ottawa conference, a 'human security network' took form to advance issues such as the Court, a ban on small arms trade, and cluster munitions. The participating states were those who were most prominent in the Ottawa Process, and they argued in international organizations and elsewhere that the Ottawa experience provided a model for future human security initiatives. In a 2004 preface to a book on *Landmines and Human Security* Axworthy wrote that the Ottawa Process 'spawned a new politics, new partnerships, new ways of thinking about the international environment'. It was, he argued, 'an unconventional, bottom-up approach to diplomacy, instead of the classic top-down, undemocratic approach'. Nevertheless he recognized that it was no longer as powerful a force as it had been before the terrorist assault on the World Trade Centre and the attack on Saddam Hussein.[23]

By the time he wrote, the Canadian Liberal government had abandoned the term 'human security' and the network atrophied significantly in the new century. Under George W. Bush, the landmine treaty remained unsigned and the International Criminal Court was rejected. The broader reform of international institutions spearheaded by Kofi Annan foundered upon traditional state rivalries, bureaucratic lethargy, and the loss of the post-cold war spirit which had animated the marriage between NGOs and governments. The landmine campaign was a product of a particular moment when traditional power formations crumbled and new possibilities emerged. After 9/11 and Iraq, human security had become, in Jody Williams' regret 2008 words 'in many ways,...largely reduced to political rhetoric and academic analysis rather than an agenda for action'.[24]

The superpowers of the past, Russia and the United States, remained outside the treaty; the future pretenders, India and China, gave no indication they would ever sign. Even the Canadians under a new Conservative government did not celebrate the Ottawa Treaty on its tenth anniversary in 2007.

Still, its memory endures. Because of the landmine ban, tens of thousands live who would have died or suffered horrible dismemberment and disability. Moreover, the model of Ottawa with its activists linked together by new technology in global networks remains a powerful force for international change. Indeed, as several chapters in this *Handbook* point out, the technology now permits transnational networks much stronger electronically than those that worked on the landmine campaign. In retrospect, the Ottawa Process gains significance because of its context. It took place just as the Internet was becoming widely available in Western nations and establishing a presence in non-OECD capitals. There were not yet smart phones, and diplomats could not have imagined the nightmare of WikiLeaks. As Axworthy and others have noted, the end of the cold war also brought a new landscape, one where the concept of human security could emerge. Other legacies of the period are the International Criminal Court and the Arctic Council, the latter a body on which indigenous peoples are 'permanent participants'.

In the new century, the war on terror and the conflicts in Iraq and Afghanistan shifted the terrain once more, but the dramatic changes in communication, the role of civil society, and the new understanding of the responsibility to protect remain. And most significantly, every year landmines are fewer and fear is less. The Ottawa Convention may reflect a unique moment but its monuments remain.

NOTES

1. The best source for the ratification process is the web site of the International Campaign to ban Landmines: <http://www.icbl.org/index.php>. The site also provides a short history of the landmine campaign and traces the success of mine eradication efforts. The major history of the landmine ban was compiled shortly after the treaty was signed in Ottawa: Maxwell A. Cameron, Robert J. Lawson, and Brian W. Tomlin (eds), *To Walk Without Fear: The Global Movement to Ban Landmines* (Toronto: Oxford University Press, 1998).

2. Several of the leading activists make these arguments in Jody Williams, Stephen D. Goose, and Mary Wareham, *Banning Landmines: Disarmament, Citizen Diplomacy, and Human Security* (Lanham, Maryland: Rowan & Littlefield Publishers, 2008). They are accepted by Lloyd Axworthy, foreign minister of Canada between 1996 and 2000, in his *Navigating a New World: Canada's Global Future* (Toronto: Knopf Canada, 2004).

3. International Committee of the Red Cross, *Symposium on Anti-Personnel Mines*. Montreux, 21–23 April 1993.

4. This argument was later developed as a major explanation for the successful achievement of the mine ban by Ramesh Thakur and William Maley, 'The Ottawa Convention on Landmines: A Landmark Humanitarian Treaty in Arms Control?', *Global Governance* 5:3 (July–September 1999), 273–302.

5. Leahy describes his personal efforts at a Senate hearing whose testimony was published: 'The Global Landmine Crisis', Subcommittee of the Committee on Appropriations United States Senate, One Hundred Third Congress, Second Session, 13 May 1994 (Washington: US Government Printing Office, 1994), 1–3.

6. *Landmines in Cambodia* is available at: <http://physiciansforhumanrights.org/library/report-cambodialandmines-1991.html>. The best description of Leahy's role and the early organizational efforts is found in Mary Wareham, 'Rhetoric and Policy Realities in the United States', in Cameron et al., *Walk Without Fear*, 212–15.

7. Williams and Stephen Goose of Human Rights Watch have written their own account of the creation of the ICBL: 'The International Campaign to Ban Landmines', in Cameron et al. *Walk Without Fear*.

8. Lewis' important article was published on 25 June 1989. On the third force, see Ann Florini, Nihon Kokusai, and Kōyū Sentā (eds), *The Third Force: The Rise of Transnational Civil Society* (Washington: Carnegie Endowment for International Peace, 2000). Jody Williams and Stephen Goose later wrote about a 'new diplomatic model' that was 'inspiring people of all stripes around the world to explore new possibilities of multilateral responses to global issues', 'Citizen Diplomacy and the Ottawa Process: A Lasting Model?', in Williams et al., *Banning Landmines*, 182.

9. Williams and Goose, 'The International Campaign to Ban Landmines', 24.

10. ICRC, *Report: Symposium on Anti-Personnel Mines*.

11. Quoted in Human Rights Watch, *In Its Own Words: The US Army and Antipersonnel Mines in the Korean and Vietnam Wars* (New York: Human Rights Watch, 1997), 13. This history is described well in Robert G. Gard Jr., 'The Military Utility of Anti-Personnel Mines', in Cameron et al., *Walk Without Fear*.

12. See, for example, Chris Smith, *The Military Utility of Landmines* (London: Centre for Defence Studies, University of London, 1996).

13. Williams and Goose, 'Citizen Diplomacy and the Ottawa Process', 188. See also, Richard A. Matthew, 'Human Security and the Mine Ban Movement: Introduction', in Richard A.

Matthew, Bryan McDonald, and Kenneth R. Rutherford (eds), *Landmines and Human Security: International Politics and War's Hidden Legacy* (Albany, New York: State University of New York Press, 2004), 3–20.

14. Williams and Goose, 'The International Campaign to Ban Landmines', 33.

15. Axworthy, *Navigating a New World*, 135.

16. One exchange which captured the differences is found in Lloyd Axworthy, 'Canada and Human Security: The Need for Leadership', *International Journal* 52 (1997), 183–96; and Fen Hampson and Dean Oliver, 'Pulpit Diplomacy: A Critical Assessment', *International Journal* 53 (1998), 379–406. See also David Lenarcic, *Knight-Errant: Canada and the Crusade to Ban Anti-personnel Landmines* (Toronto: Irwin, 1998). I have argued that the role of the pro-ban states was essential and has been obscured by the focus on the NGO leadership; 'The Ottawa Process: Paths followed, paths ahead' *Australian Journal of International Affairs* 52:2 (1998), 121–32. Jody Williams has considered criticisms and responded in 'New Approaches in a Changing World: The Human Security Agenda', in Williams et al., *Banning Landmines*.

17. Axworthy, *Navigating a New World*, 138. See also Brian Tomlin, 'On a Fast Track to a Ban', in *To Walk Without Fear*, 200ff, for a detailed account of the Ottawa conference based on extensive discussion and interviews with participants.

18. A strong criticism arguing that the landmine campaign represented the same type of unilateralism many NGOs and governments condemned in the George W. Bush administration is found in Adam Chapnick, 'The Ottawa Process Revisited: Unilateralism in the post-Cold War world', *International Journal* 58:3 (2003), 281–93. He writes: 'it is simply ironic that [Canada], which had previously taken great pride when Jody Williams and the ICBL received the 1997 Nobel Peace Prize for actions that blatantly disregarded traditional diplomatic fora, would now have any international credibility in condemning similar American actions six years later [in Iraq]' (p. 292).

19. Interviews and personal knowledge.

20. The Halo Trust took Diana to Angola and the Landmine Survivors Network escorted Diana to Bosnia just weeks before her death.

21. The best account of this negotiation is in Axworthy, *Navigating a New World*, 144ff. In interviews with *Ottawa Citizen* reporter Chris Cobb on the tenth anniversary of the Ottawa Treaty, Williams and Axworthy gave very different accounts of what happened. Williams told Cobb that Stephen Goose was speaking to Canadian government representatives before the Oslo meeting and he told Williams as he covered the receiver that the Canadians were 'caving'. Williams claims that the Canadians intended to compromise the treaty, and Robert Lawson, a Canadian official, appears to indicate that he at least shared Williams' view at the time. Axworthy indicates that the booing deeply offended him and he believes it was a major reason he lost the Nobel Prize to Williams whom Goose (later her husband) nominated. The incident reveals how fragile the NGO–government relationship could be and, in Axworthy's view, how sometimes the pursuit of the ideal made practical advances, notably American acceptance of the treaty, much more difficult. Chris Cobb, 'The Canuck, the landmines, and the bombshell', *Ottawa Citizen*, 2 December 2007; address by Lloyd Axworthy to Canadian Landmine Foundation, 1 November 2011.

22. These statistics are presented in the yearly reports of the *Landmine Monitor*. The most recent edition is available digitally: <http://www.the-monitor.org/>.

23. Lloyd Axworthy, 'Foreword', in Matthew et al., *Landmines and Human Security*, xvi–xvii.

24. Jody Williams, 'New Approaches in a Changing World', in Williams et al., *Banning Landmines*, 282.

CHAPTER 45

....

THE PERMANENT EXTENSION
OF THE NPT, 1995

....

JAYANTHA DHANAPALA

THE assessment of a month-long international conference which took place several years ago can have two main purposes. The first is to evaluate its political impact at the time and ask if that impact continues today, and if so how and why. The second is to examine the conference proceedings from the professional diplomat's point of view, identifying the elements that led to the success or failure of the conference so as to draw general conclusions and lessons for the practice of diplomacy.

Thus, the 1995 Non-Proliferation Treaty Review and Extension Conference (NPTREC) will continue to have a fascination for the disarmament community, as well as for historians of multilateral diplomacy. The NPTREC was intrinsically an important event for the reason that the Nuclear Non-Proliferation Treaty (NPT) was, and continues to be, in conception and implementation, the hub of multilateral nuclear disarmament and non-proliferation. Whatever the outcome of the 1995 Conference, there would have been a global impact. If the decision taken in 1995 was to ensure the NPT's permanent or indefinite extension, it was of critical importance. If, on the other hand, the decision was to extend it for a fixed period or periods, that too would have had immense significance. If there was no decision, the non-proliferation regime would have ended in disarray and international lawyers would have different interpretations on the applicability of the NPT after 1995.

This analysis must perforce begin with the NPT itself, briefly recounting its history before proceeding to the immediate global environment in 1995 and the actual proceedings of the NPTREC. Thereafter, the proceedings of the conference must be discussed to identify the ingredients of success. It will conclude with a reference to the most recent Non-Proliferation Treaty Review Conference (NPTREVCON) and an assessment of the future of the NPT in order to evaluate the historical value of the NPTREC. In other words how permanent is the indefinite extension of the NPT that was achieved in 1995?

45.1 THE NPT IN HISTORICAL CONTEXT

The emergence in the 20th century of chemical, biological, and nuclear weapons as weapons of mass destruction (WMD), as distinct from conventional weapons, marked a watershed. These weapons were shown to be vastly more destructive of human life and of material property with long-lasting ecological and genetic effects. Thus, the elimination or control of WMD became the priority of the United Nations (UN) and the international community. The very first UN General Assembly resolution adopted on 24 January 1946 called for the establishment of a commission 'to deal with the problems raised by the discovery of atomic energy' whose terms of reference included 'the elimination from national armaments of atomic weapons and of all other major weapons adaptable to mass destruction'.[1] The 1972 Biological and Toxin Weapons Convention with 171[2] parties and the 1993 Chemical Weapons Convention with 188 parties[3] banned these two categories of WMD. In 1995 the only WMD not subject to a universal ban was the nuclear weapon.

The invention of the nuclear weapon and its first use in Hiroshima and Nagasaki in 1945 by the United States (US) has been a 'game changer' for the last sixty-five years and more. After the Soviet Union and the United Kingdom acquired the weapon, France and China did so too. The alarming prospect of nuclear weapon proliferation to the 'Nth state' led President John F. Kennedy to speculate over a future of 20–25 nuclear weapon armed states.[4] This led to agreement between the two superpowers to take steps to halt proliferation.

Bilateral treaties between the two largest nuclear-weapon states, the US and the USSR, who had an estimated 95 per cent of these weapons, and multilateral treaties negotiated to ban nuclear tests (first the Partial Test Ban Treaty of 1963 and later the Comprehensive Nuclear Test Ban Treaty—CTBT of 1996) and the proliferation of these weapons (through the NPT) have sought to regulate their vertical and horizontal proliferation. The Natural Resources Defence Council's (NRDC) archive of nuclear data estimates that there were 27,131 nuclear weapons in the possession of US, USSR, UK, France, and China in the year 1995.[5] The Democratic People's Republic of Korea (DPRK), India, and Pakistan were yet to 'cross the nuclear threshold', although their ambitions to be nuclear-weapon states were widely known.

The normative structure with regard to all weapons has two aspects. One is to seek disarmament in terms of universal bans on inhumane weapons or particular categories of weapons for humanitarian and collective security reasons. The other is to seek arms control in terms of levels of arsenals or prevention of new possessors. Disarmament requires verifiable destruction of existing weapons, cessation of production, sale, storage, transfer, or acquisition.

Thus, the total outlawing (as distinct from arms limitation or reduction) of biological weapons, chemical weapons, anti-personnel land mines, cluster munitions, laser weapons, and other categories has been achieved globally even though the multilateral treaties negotiated for these purposes may not be universal and the verification of their observance not always reliable. General and complete disarmament has been the agreed goal of the UN. Whether disarmament results in security or whether security must precede disarmament remains an inconclusive 'which comes first chicken-or-egg' argument.

The one treaty that attempts a combination of the disarmament and arms control aspects is the NPT, which is the world's most widely subscribed to disarmament treaty. It openly accepts two categories of state parties—Nuclear-Weapon States (NWS) and Non-Nuclear-Weapon States (NNWS). In terms of the disarmament approach NWS are only exhorted, as treaty parties, to negotiate the reduction and elimination of their weapons. In contrast, NNWS are totally forbidden to acquire such weapons and the International Atomic Energy Agency (IAEA) is empowered to enter into arrangements with them when peaceful uses of nuclear energy are involved, and to verify that there is no diversion for non-peaceful purposes. In its 1996 Advisory Opinion, the International Court of Justice stated that the NWS had a legal obligation to negotiate nuclear disarmament in good faith, but this has had little impact on the NWS.[6] As far as arms control is concerned, NWS are permitted to retain their weapons with the restraints that apply through other bilateral and multilateral treaties. The only legal commitment by the NWS to nuclear disarmament in a multilateral treaty (apart from the preambular part of the CTBT which has not entered into force as yet) is therefore Article VI of the NPT, explaining why despite all its shortcomings the NPT remains important in the disarmament community.

This discriminatory approach creating an apartheid system between NWS and NNWS has been the cause of tensions within the NPT. By 1995 they had been exacerbated over the twenty-five year history of the treaty. The discovery of Iraq's clandestine nuclear-weapon programme in the early 1990s; the nascent problems over the DPRK within the NPT; and the suspicions over Libya and Iran in 1995 had already weakened the NPT.

Within the ambiguity of the NPT's normative approach, regional conflicts breed insecurity for which nuclear weapons seem an answer to some. For others, nuclear weapons are a badge of great power status.

The NPT regime can be examined in the context of regime theory in international relations.[7] More relevantly, in the context of this *Handbook*, it can be viewed against the conceptual shift from 'club' to 'network' diplomacy. The expansion in the number of states parties was applauded, on the one hand, as a signal that the norm of non-proliferation of nuclear weapons was being universalized. At the same time the motives of the new members of the 'club' could be questioned and their fidelity to the norm would turn out to be doubtful especially with Iraq and DPRK. The expansion of the number of states parties of the NPT led to more networking, especially among the Non-Aligned Movement (NAM) countries who reject the dominance of the NPT regime as a 'club' dominated by the NWS and their allies. Networking with civil society, especially disarmament NGOs, has also been a feature of the NPT regime.

45.2 THE EXERCISE OF DIPLOMACY: THE NPT REVIEW CONFERENCES, 1975–1990

As noted already, the NPT is a unique treaty in many ways. It seeks to combine the outright prohibition aspect of disarmament treaties with regard to NNWS in Articles I–III and the hortatory approach of the arms control treaties as far as the NWS are concerned in Article IV and VI. It thus falls between two stools. This fact was to create tensions within the NPT which the permanent extension has not solved.

The NPT also contains, exceptionally, a provision, in Article X.2, for a conference to be convened twenty-five years after its entry into force to decide whether it should be extended indefinitely or 'for an additional fixed period or periods'.[8]

Moreover, Article VIII.3 of the Treaty provides for Review Conferences at five yearly intervals. If diplomacy is the application of tact, skill, and intelligence in the conduct of international relations among nation states, then both these treaty provisions offer opportunities for the active exercise of diplomacy on the part of the parties to the treaty. Using the definition of diplomacy suggested in the editors' introduction to this *Handbook*, namely as 'the conduct of business, using peaceful means, by and among international actors, at least one of whom is usually governmental', it is obvious that a multilateral conference to review and extend a treaty as vital to international peace and security as the NPT would involve an intensive conduct of that business.

The NPT is, therefore, unlike other treaties, which are usually for an indefinite duration and are frozen in time, except for amendment procedures that are normally difficult to implement. In this situation the internal dynamics of treaty conferences assume special importance while the external context, including instructions from capitals, continues to have its undisputed influence.

Thus, the 1995 NPTREC merits close analysis for the interplay of diplomatic efforts by the NWS and NNWS, and the impact these had on the future course of the treaty.

The content of NPT diplomacy is not merely the interaction of delegations at NPT conferences and in between, but also the management of the conferences by the office bearers elected to the various positions. The success or failure of the conferences often depends on the capability of these office bearers: an often neglected aspect of international diplomacy.

It will be seen that the most intractable issues do not necessarily cause conferences to implode and collapse without agreement if there is sufficient goodwill and creative diplomacy. Likewise a negative personal chemistry among leaders of key delegations and poor conference management are likely to exclude any hope of accommodation or compromise.[9]

The NPT was signed on 1 July 1968 and entered into force in 1970. Its membership has expanded from 91 countries in 1975 to 190 (if we include the DPRK) in 2010. The three depositary states—the US, Russia, and the UK—have strongly encouraged other states to join, contributing to this expansion. However, it is true that assertive US diplomacy has succeeded in convincing many countries to join the NPT as NNWS. At certain stages, opponents of the NPT like India have tried to counteract this diplomacy, especially in South Asia, but without much success.

A dramatic spurt in accessions was visible prior to the 1995 Review and Extension Conference. While of course sovereign countries take such decisions in their national interest, the entry of long-standing holdouts like Argentina, Brazil, and South Africa and the three former Soviet states Belarus, Ukraine, and Kazakhstan, which, at the end of the cold war, had Russian nuclear weapons on their soil, represent a diplomatic success for the depositary states.

Four review conferences were held during this period in Geneva with two of them (1975 and 1985) being able to adopt a final declaration by consensus and two (1980 and 1990) failing to do so. It is, as noted earlier, arguable whether the success or failure of review conferences can be judged by the adoption of a final declaration.

Firstly, although the conference rules of procedure provide for voting, decisions are generally taken by consensus out of an increasing concern not to be divisive in vital issues of global security. This empowers individual delegations or small groups of delegations to obstruct consensus and prevent the adoption of a final declaration. How long this practice will endure is difficult to predict. It has occasionally been broken through exasperation in some forums like in United Nations Conference on Trade and Development (UNCTAD). Therefore, the adoption of a final document by consensus is in itself an undoubted success. That must however depend on the extent to which the treaty parties implement the promises and commitments that are embodied in the final documents.

Secondly, the adoption of a final declaration is regarded by some as less important than a comprehensive discussion of how the treaty has been implemented in all its aspects. That may appear to be an artificial rationalization of a failure in diplomacy. The fact is that the adoption of a final declaration is the expression of a collective political will. Failure to do so could be a symptom of a deeper political malaise or a demonstration of dissatisfaction with specific aspects of the review process such as when the Arab group of countries focuses on a demand for Israel to join the NPT. The adoption of a final declaration is also influenced by the prevailing global atmosphere. Thus a final declaration at a review conference is also undoubtedly a political barometer.

45.2.1 The 1975 Review Conference

The 1975 review conference being the first review conference of the NPT served as a precedent with the non-aligned group of NNWS functioning under the 'Group of 77' title, ready to confront the three NWS in the NPT at the time: the US, USSR, and UK.

Article VI was the key area of dispute and the CTBT was a principal demand in addition to security assurances for the NNWS. The eventual adoption of a final declaration was less a reflection of a political agreement among the parties and more a tribute to the forceful personality of its president, Inga Thorsson of Sweden, who is said to have rammed her own draft through after the drafting committee failed to reach consensus on the nuclear disarmament aspects. Mexico, as spokesman of the 'Group of 77' made an interpretative statement of the final declaration, which was incorporated as a conference document. Thus an uneasy compromise was arrived at.

45.2.2 The 1980 Review Conference

The 1980 review conference followed the remarkable success of the United Nations General Assembly's (UNGA) first Special Session on Disarmament (SSOD I) held in 1978 and expectations were high.

The Carter administration in the US had been weakened considerably by the overthrow of the Shah in Iran and the subsequent student take-over of the US embassy with its staff held in a prolonged hostage crisis. US diplomats were in no mood to be accommodating to non-aligned demands. The relations between the US and the USSR were strained by the Soviet invasion of Afghanistan. The non-aligned themselves were divided with tensions between Iran and Iraq, which erupted into a nasty war after the review conference.

The issues on which sharp divisions arose were on article VI and the CTBT, security assurances, article III, and nuclear sharing as being contrary to articles I and II. After the success of SSOD I the NAM was not going to settle for anything less and so a deadlock resulted with no final declaration emerging.

45.2.3 The 1985 Review Conference

In preparation for the 1985 review conference, this author chaired the third session of the preparatory committee (which decided, following negotiations ably conducted by ambassador Rolf Ekeus of Sweden, on the current structure of three main committees allocating subject areas and apportioning of their chairs to the Western, Eastern, and NAM groups) and went on to chair main committee I of the 1985 review conference, which was held during the first term of US President Reagan.

Israel had attacked and destroyed Iraq's IAEA-safeguarded nuclear reactor. Despite this inclement atmosphere, NPT diplomacy reached one of its heights under the able presidency of ambassador Mohammed Shaker of Egypt (himself an authority on the NPT). His innovative diplomacy included assembling a representative group of advisers who helped to steer the conference to the successful adoption of a final declaration. Before that, however, numerous hurdles had to be cleared as sharp and irreconcilable divisions arose over disarmament issues, especially the CTBT.

It was evident that instructions to the US delegation were very tight and this author conceived of a drafting exercise similar to the Shanghai Communiqué of 28 February 1972 at the end of President Nixon's historic visit to China.[10] Thus a draft with an overwhelming majority of delegations expressing their support for a CTBT and a few delegations holding a contrary view was finally accepted, helping to break the stalemate preventing a consensus.

This formula of 'agreeing to disagree' was unusual but helped to adopt a final declaration, as it was to do twenty-five years later at the 2010 REVCON. The personal diplomacy of the leader of the US delegation, ambassador Lewis Dunn, who painstakingly built relationships with the main office bearers of the review conference throughout all the sessions of the preparatory committee, was another ingredient in the success of the 1985 conference. In the final hours of the conference the hard work on the more substantive issues were almost wrecked over a non-NPT-related dispute between Iran and Iraq. This was also resolved by a drafting exercise, which satisfied both parties, and in the small hours of the morning, with the clock having been stopped, the conference was successfully concluded.

45.2.4 The 1990 Review Conference

The 1990 review conference had to confront a renewed NAM demand for a CTBT, which could not be resolved through drafting tricks or innovative diplomacy. Although the Mexican delegation is accused of having 'wrecked' the conference standing out resolutely against any compromise, it must also be stated that the president of the conference and other key delegations lacked the flexibility to devise diplomatic solutions or procedural fixes.

On the other hand, this is possibly an example of the limits of NPT diplomacy when the political context is so difficult that no diplomacy could overcome the differences among delegations. The lesson to be drawn is that politics and diplomacy must go hand in hand if multilateral conferences are to succeed. There has to be political will to adopt decisions in a conference and creative diplomacy alone will not be enough.

45.3 THE 1995 NPT REVIEW AND EXTENSION CONFERENCE

The preparation for the NPTREC and its month-long conduct presented a huge diplomatic challenge.[11] The NPT depositary states, led by the US, were clear that an indefinite extension was their goal and US diplomats worked in capitals to achieve this end.[12]

No international conference takes place in a vacuum. The prevailing context of international relations must influence its conduct and outcome. This happened with the NPTREC. It was a few years after the end of the cold war. The North Atlantic Treaty Organization (NATO) was nevertheless being enlarged and the 'peaceful ascendancy' of China was well in motion. However, the NAM was also not to be dismissed as an international player.

Ambassador Thomas Graham Jr. of the US visited many capitals.[13] While Russia, UK, and France supported the same objective, there was no evidence of the same organized diplomatic offensive on the part of other delegations. China maintained publicly that it wanted 'a smooth extension' but, with one eye on NAM, declined to be more explicit or active. The political atmosphere around NPTREC was made favourable by the Clinton administration's decision to begin negotiating a CTBT in the Conference on Disarmament, thus removing one of the most contentious issues in NPT conferences. The Carnegie Endowment provided the following assessment:

> The surprising resistance to indefinite extension of the NPT by NAM members prompted the United States to re-evaluate its strategy and make concessions on disarmament and security assurance issues. In a major policy address at the Carnegie Endowment for International Peace on January 30, 1995, then US National Security Advisor Anthony Lake announced that the United States no longer insisted on a provision in a future CTBT that would allow a party to withdraw from the Treaty ten years after it entered into force. He also stated that the United States would extend its existing moratorium on nuclear testing until a CTBT was in place. Lake reiterated the strong US commitment to securing the indefinite and unconditional extension of the NPT.[14]

South Africa was a key target of US diplomacy with the aura that it had acquired following Nelson Mandela's assumption of the leadership of this nation and its emergence as a non-racial democracy replacing the white-minority regime of the past. More significantly, South Africa had joined the NPT as a NNWS after destroying its nuclear devices under IAEA supervision. A special link is said to have been established between US Vice President Al Gore (who addressed the opening of the NPTREC) and South African Vice President Thabo Mbeki on the NPTREC, ensuring South Africa's support for an indefinite extension of the NPT. This was an undoubted diplomatic triumph, especially as South Africa had proposed another twenty-five-year extension during the preparatory committee stage. It proved to be crucial when the key decision was taken.

Similar diplomacy was attempted by the US with the Arab group of countries and Egypt in particular, but was less successful. The then Egyptian Foreign Minister Amr Moussa remained critical of Israel's rejection of the NPT and demanded a solution to this in terms of his president's proposal of the Middle East as a weapons of mass destruction free zone.

Another critic of US NPT policy was the able Mexican diplomat Miguel Marin Bosch, who was marginalized allegedly under US pressure. A series of articles in the *Washington Post* on the eve of the NPTREC outlined US policy and its diplomatic efforts.

In marked contrast to the well-organized US diplomatic offensive, the NAM countries had no similar campaign. No alternative to indefinite extension was conceptualized clearly and pursued vigorously, although many delegations proposed extensions of varying length since an extension of a limited duration would have given their group the leverage it wanted. Even the critics outside the NPT, like India, made no effort to see that its wishes for a deadlocked conference were realized through an organized NAM stance.

The identification of the office bearers of the NPTREC, principally its president, was achieved at an early stage. Two names—Tadeusz Strulak of Poland and Dhanapala of Sri Lanka were proposed at the very first session of the preparatory committee held in New

York on 10–14 May 1993 and the name of this author was confirmed at the second session in New York on 17–21 January 1994. This provided ample time for consultations to be conducted and for diplomatic strategies to be planned. In contrast, the confirmation of the president elect for the 2010 NPT review conference was confirmed at the third session of the preparatory committee in May 2009. Because of the complexity and importance of the NPTREC in comparison to normal five-yearly review conferences, four sessions of the preparatory committee were necessary and yet there was no complete agreement on the rules of procedure.

The diplomatic wrangling on this was on the mode of voting if it came to voting. Was it to be by secret ballot or by open ballot? The NAM countries overwhelmingly preferred the former while the Western group preferred the latter. The importance of this decision revolved around the wording of Article X: 2, which stipulated that the extension decision be taken 'by a majority of the Parties to the Treaty'. This deadlock remained unresolved throughout the NPTREC and it was just as well that the adoption of the final package of three decisions and the resolution on the Middle East was adopted without a vote.

At the opening of the conference it was clear, as a result of the president interviewing delegations who had not openly announced their extension preference in the plenary debate, that a majority did exist for an indefinite extension. It was therefore left to the president to craft a procedure that would legitimize this as well as reflect the overwhelming view that the extension should be conditioned on specific guarantees that nuclear disarmament would be achieved. To respond to that challenge, the conference device of a small group, styled the 'president's consultations', was adopted somewhat along the lines of ambassador Shaker's group in the 1985 review conference.

The group included all the conference office-holders, the five NWS in the NPT, the chairs of the political groups, and key delegations selected by the president. It was conceived as an 'inner cabinet', a focus group, or more accurately, a laboratory to discuss the all-important extension issue which transcended the normal business of the main committees. The device was not entirely undemocratic or lacking in transparency because group leaders (and all delegations belonged to a group except for China) were encouraged to report back to their groups regularly and seek their endorsement on the decisions being taken.

The fact that the results of these consultations were endorsed by the entire conference proved that it was effective multilateral diplomacy. It was certainly better than seeking to arrive at decisions in the plenary through an unwieldy debate. The composition of the group was undoubtedly arbitrary and that was resented by some of the delegations that were excluded, hurting the egos of their ambassadors especially. However, it was flexible too, when Venezuelan ambassador Adolfo Taylhardat quit his delegation over the change of instructions he had received, Peru was invited to replace Venezuela.

In terms of conference diplomacy however, it was the practical and effective thing to do as events turned out. It is doubtful that the same device can be adopted in future with all delegations now asserting their right to participate fully in decision-making. In 1995, it was within this exclusive group that the two decisions 'strengthening the review process for the treaty' and 'principles and objectives for nuclear non-proliferation and disarmament' were drafted over a two-week process.

The president handled the drafting of the key legal decision on the extension and the weaving of the three decisions into a package and announced it to a large representative gathering. The dispute over the rule of procedure on whether the voting should be secret or open was unlikely to have been resolved given the strongly held positions. The president would have had to break the deadlock with a vote and this decision, be it by open or secret vote, would itself have been highly contentious. It was also the president's conviction, voiced repeatedly, that voting on a treaty as important as the NPT would expose the treaty membership as a house divided, eroding the viability of the treaty. The president's main task was to fulfil the terms of Article X.2 that the decision on the extension of the treaty had to be taken by a 'majority of the parties to the treaty'. What better way to do this than by agreeing that there was a consensus that such a majority existed? The formulation thus presented by the president was irrefutable and was met with widespread agreement. In the event the package was not unwrapped but some tinkering of the wording in decision I was agreed upon dropping the word 'a consensus' for simply 'deciding that, as a majority exists...'. This satisfied the befuddled purists among the NAM members who resisted being a part of the consensus. And yet, because they could not deny that a majority did exist for an indefinite extension, they agreed that the entire package would be adopted without a vote, with some registering their disagreement after the adoption.

The contentious issue of the Middle East, which, according to the wishes of the Arab group, had proceeded on a separate track, had not made any progress. The president was approached for a solution at a very late stage of the conference. It was both late and risky to reopen the package of three decisions that had been negotiated. This resulted in special consultations on a resolution on the Middle East with key delegations present and agreement was finally reached. Failure to consult Iran proved almost disastrous when the resolution came up for adoption but was resolved during a tense recess in the plenary on the final day.

While the extension aspect of the conference appeared to have been conducted successfully, the review aspect in the key political areas handled by main committee I was a diplomatic failure[15] (main committees II and III, thanks to the efficiency of their chairmen, concluded their work on technical aspects of the NPT successfully). The president's last minute intervention to rescue the process in main committee I did not succeed. This was not, in the final analysis, a major setback since the main outcome, a decision on the extension, had been achieved.

While the positions of delegations follow instructions from capitals, it is not surprising that some act at their own discretion within the limits of flexibility permitted by their governments. This allows for individuals to show initiative in finding solutions to problems. It is also possible that the stances taken by individual delegations on the conference floor can be changed as a result of diplomatic demarches taken by powerful countries in capitals, compelling delegations to change their positions. Given the confidentiality of diplomatic communications, we do not know what pressures are exerted on NPT parties or what linkages are made as a part of the ongoing diplomatic activity in conferences.

The functioning of various groups within NPT conferences does assist the work of the conferences and is an important element of NPT diplomacy. This was undoubtedly the case in 1995. The groups are the Western group—which includes Japan, Australia, NATO, and the European Union (EU); the Eastern group—which includes Russia and the former USSR states but which has, post cold war, no political role and functions today only to agree on common candidates for NPT positions; and, finally, the NAM, which decides collectively on political issues—but is sub-divided into the Asian, African, and Latin American and Caribbean groups for purposes of agreeing on candidates for NPT conference positions.

In addition, the NAM have within it the Arab group which meets to discuss and decide on Middle East issues and which the NAM generally accepts. The five NWS meet among themselves during conferences and in between. After some of these meetings, joint statements are issued representing common positions.

No group exists uniting all the NNWS and it is left to temporary coalitions like the New Agenda Coalition in the 2000 NPTREVCON to form transcontinental groupings to espouse common positions. Such groupings can be very effective and it has been an omission that more diplomatic energy has not gone into forging alliances, which could serve as 'bridge builders' among the treaty parties and act as a 'fire brigade' to defuse controversies as well as seek negotiated solutions to problems as they arise.[16] Group meetings usually take place prior to the commencement of the day's conference proceedings but can also be held at any moment to coordinate group positions.

The political strength of the NAM derives from its numbers and its solidarity, and the other groups do not always welcome that. It provides protection for the smaller and weaker countries within it. Countries within the Western group also do not always find themselves in agreement, with the NNWS being increasingly critical of the NWS.

45.4 1995 IN RETROSPECT

Writing in the SIPRI Yearbook of 1996 on the NPTREC of 1995, John Simpson said:

> tensions within the regime over non-compliance questions and between treaty parties over progress towards nuclear disarmament became more visible and acute. While the legal foundations of the regime were made permanent, its objectives and the steps that could be taken to reinforce it are likely to cause debate over whether the main task of the regime is to prevent nuclear proliferation by the non-nuclear weapon states within it or to facilitate the disarmament of the five declared nuclear weapon states (China, France, Russia, the UK and the USA) and the removal of the ambiguity that surrounds the nuclear weapon status of India, Israel and Pakistan.[17]

Those tensions have continued. Thus the permanent extension of the NPT did not lay to rest the debates on whether the disarmament, non-proliferation, or peaceful uses of nuclear energy pillars were of equal importance or whether some were more equal than others according to the perception of individual states parties. Simpson presciently added,

The core of the disputes over the NPT is the demand that the division between nuclear and non-nuclear weapon states be eliminated. Disarmament agreements that will reinforce and extend the existing non-proliferation regime by constraining nuclear weapon potentials and inventories are being sought. Measures which can contribute to the disarmament of the existing nuclear weapon states and place constraints on states which remain outside the NPT–e.g. a comprehensive test ban treaty (CTBT) and a fissile material production cut-off–have acquired near-universal support and thus become attainable political goals.[18]

Global trends since 1995 have only strengthened support for the CTBT and the FMCT. Today NGOs are in support of a Nuclear Weapon Convention.

In his article Simpson concluded that the utility of nuclear weapons was questionable other than for deterrence and that the 1995 NPTREC may mark the final stage in making the NPT-based nuclear non-proliferation regime universal, paving the way for a world free of nuclear weapons.[19]

In fact history has probably proved him right. The 2000 NPTREVCON held during the Clinton administration adopted a final declaration by consensus mainly because of the agreement on 13 Steps towards nuclear disarmament and an unequivocal commitment by the NWS to this. Five years later the Bush administration led by ambassador John Bolton scuttled this and the 2005 NPTREVCON ended in disaster. The 2010 REVCON's qualified success is no guarantee that the 1995 achievement will survive into the future. At the end of the 1995 conference the statement by the president from the chair was that 'The permanence of the treaty does not represent a permanence of unbalanced obligations, nor does it represent the permanence of nuclear apartheid between nuclear haves and have-nots.'[20] The regrettable exit of the DPRK from the NPT and its subsequent nuclear testing; the welcome return to compliance of Iraq and Libya; and continuing questions over Iran are some of the experiences we have had to go through since 1995. The non-proliferation norm can be strengthened by encouraging the multilateralization of the fuel cycle and the universalization of the Additional Protocol as voluntary options. Basically though, the failure to implement non-proliferation and disarmament simultaneously is unsustainable. The year 2010 dawned with the promise of being a tipping point for nuclear disarmament after the global surge of public opinion in favour of a nuclear-weapon-free world. Indeed three years after the Prague speech of President Obama, we have seen many events collectively hailed as a 'Prague Spring'. But the prospects of that 'spring' becoming a 'summer' are fading at the time of writing.

The continued modernization of nuclear-weapon arsenals and their delivery systems; the limited reductions achieved by the new Strategic Arms Reduction Treaty (START); the troubling ambiguities over the use of nuclear weapons and negative security assurances in the US Nuclear Posture Review; and the persistence of nuclear deterrence in the doctrines of nuclear-weapon states show that we have progressed very little. Whether it is the pressures of domestic politics and well-entrenched interest groups or a perceived inferiority in conventional weapons, it does not seem as if nuclear-weapon states are ready to eliminate all their weapons, even in a phased programme. Even disarmament commissions and some coalitions for nuclear abolition have set their target dates very far into the distant future building artificial base camps on the way to the total elimination of nuclear weapons. The focus on the DPRK and Iran—and now Syria—and on nuclear terrorism also serves to distract attention from the inherent dangers of nuclear weapons themselves. It has been stated and restated that if there were no nuclear weapons under a verifiable nuclear disarmament regime, there could be no proliferation or nuclear terrorism. How do we exercise our responsibility to protect the goal of a nuclear-weapon-free world?

The only credible alternative appears to be the proposal for a nuclear weapon convention on which negotiations must begin immediately. We already have in the NPT one international compact, which was an agreement between nuclear-weapon states and non-nuclear-weapon states for a transitional period when the former would join the latter in a nuclear-weapon-free world. That has not happened for forty years. The hedging in the statements setting a nuclear-weapon-free world as an objective undermines the determination to reach that goal.

In Chapter 14 of this *Handbook*, A.J.R. Groom points to the growing intervention of global civil society in multilateral conferences. This was also so in the NPT review conferences.[21] While the rules of procedure were tightly controlled by the NWS and their supporters to prevent too much latitude for non-government organizations (NGOs) to participate, some concessions were made to provide them with a session to make their statements and to attend open sessions of plenary meetings. The fact that NGOs are generally against nuclear weapons draws them into an alliance with the NAM which the NWS resent.

45.5 THE FUTURE OF THE NON-PROLIFERATION TREATY

Most observers felt that the 2010 review conference was a success. On the institutional and procedural level, the conference reinforced and strengthened the review process.

States parties agreed on the importance of having an informal and voluntary group of past and incumbent chairs available to pass on the lessons learned to future chairs. In addition, states parties committed to making funding available for one staff officer in the UN Office of Disarmament to monitor and follow non-proliferation matters on a permanent and continuous basis. That said, an objective assessment of the conference involves honest answers to the more political questions related to the future of the regime. In this regard, the divided views attributed in the final declaration to 'a majority of states parties' and to 'numerous parties' cannot be sustained. While the formulation was largely neutral and referred to different groups at procedural level, the conference reinforced and strengthened the review process. These divisions have to be resolved within the NPT.

Two representative opinions that spoke to the success of the conference came from the US delegation's Ellen Tauscher and the Egyptian delegation's Maged Abdel Aziz, respectively. Ellen Tauscher said that the final document adopted advances President Obama's vision and that the forward-looking, balanced action plan establishes benchmarks for future progress and concrete actions.[22] Maged Abdel Aziz, speaking on behalf of the NAM, conceded that while the NAM did not achieve all that it wanted, it had decided to 'take advantage of the emerging goodwill'.[23] Was this a message of thanks by the NNWS in general and the NAM in particular to President Obama for what he had achieved for nuclear disarmament? The final document of the conference was regarded by Egypt as a basis for a future 'deal', and the ambassador promised to pursue NAM priorities in the run up to the 2015 review conference. They include the elimination of all nuclear weapons by 2025 and the beginning of negotiations for a nuclear weapons convention (NWC) and a negative security assurances treaty.

Although the relief of the NWS over the adoption of the final declaration's conclusions and recommendations and the lukewarm reaction by the NAM states and the pro-disarmament NGOs has bought the NPT another five years, the tensions endemic in the central bargain remain. Good-faith implementation of the document's action plan will be crucial, as will progress on the new START, and ratification of the CTBT by the United States. The future course of the Six-Nation Talks on DPRK, the resolution of the questions over Iran's nuclear programme, and the outcomes of the 2012 Middle East conference will also determine the future of the NPT. The NPT has survived another challenge, but without further action by the NWS, the non-proliferation regime may well fray.

The states parties to the NPT clearly cannot rest on the laurels of this qualified success and have equal responsibility not only to fulfil the commitments made at the 2010 review conference but also to reinforce the NPT as the world's most important nuclear non-proliferation and disarmament treaty. The challenge will be to reach that 'balance of interests' that Ramesh Thakur has explained in Chapter 3 of this *Handbook*. Among the many interests that states parties have to balance are the foreign policy advantages of not provoking the suspicions of both neighbours and NWS by signalling a desire to acquire a nuclear weapon capability even through the acquisition of nuclear power capabilities with the security advantage of having a nuclear weapon option while being within the NPT. How also to balance the interests of acquiescing in the nuclear monopoly of the NWS with the need to have a nuclear-weapon-free world? Perhaps the answer lies in Joseph Nye's claim that 'strategies relate means to ends, and those that combine hard and soft power resources successfully in different contexts are the key to smart power'.[24]

NOTES

1. Resolution on the 'Establishment Of A Commission To Deal With The Problem Raised By The Discovery Of Atomic Energy' (United Nations, 24 January 1946), <http://www.un.org/documents/ga/res/1/ares1.htm>.
2. 'Status of the Convention', BTWC, <http://www.opbw.org/>.
3. 'Chemical Weapons Convention Signatories and State Parties', Arms Control Association, <http://www.armscontrol.org/factsheets/cwcsig>.

4. See: 'Face-to-Face, Nixon-Kennedy', Vice President Richard M. Nixon and Senator John F. Kennedy Third Joint Television-Radio Broadcast, John F. Kennedy Presidential Library and Museum, 13 October 1960, <http://www.jfklibrary.org/Research/Ready-Reference/~/link.aspx?_id=F10BA350861349DF93AD8927A452A4F2&_z=z>.

5. Archive of Nuclear Data, Table of Global Nuclear Weapons Stockpiles, 1945–2002, NRDC, last modified 25 November 2002, <http://www.nrdc.org/nuclear/nudb/datab19.asp>.

6. See: ICJ Reports Of Judgments, Advisory Opinions And Orders Legality Of The Threat Or Use Of Nuclear Weapons Advisory Opinion Of July 8, 1996, <http://www.icj-cij.org/docket/files/95/7497.pdf>.

7. Stephen D. Krasner, 'Structural Causes and Regime Consequences: Regimes as Intervening Variables', in S.D. Krasner (ed.), *International Regimes* (Ithaca, NY: Cornell University Press, 1983).

8. 'NPT-The Full Text', IAEA, <http://www.iaea.org/Publications/Magazines/Bulletin/Bull104/10403501117.pdf>.

9. Jayantha Dhanapala, with Randy Rydell, *Multilateral Diplomacy and the NPT—An Insider's Account* (Geneva: United Nations Publications, 2005), 16.

10. That communiqué had stated China's position and the US position on many controversial issues separately with no attempt to bridge the differences.

11. A detailed description is provided by this author in *Multilateral Diplomacy and the NPT*.

12. See Rebecca Johnson, 'Indefinite Extension of the Non-Proliferation Treaty: Risks and Reckonings', *Acronym Reports*, <http://www.acronym.org.uk/acrorep/acro7.htm>. See also Jim Wurst, 'NPT extended indefinitely with greater accountability', *Disarmament Times* 18:4 (18 May 1995), <http://www.jayanthadhanapala.com/content/newsroom/DisaramamentTimes-pg1.jpg>.

13. See Thomas Graham, *Disarmament Sketches, Three Decades of Arms Control and International Law* (Seattle: University of Washington Press, 2002).

14. 'Appendix B, 1995 NPT Review And Extension Conference', Carnegie Endowment.

15. See detailed description in Tariq Rauf and Rebecca Johnson, *After the NPT's Indefinite Extension: The Future of the Global Nonproliferation Regime*, <http://cns.miis.edu/npr/pdfs/raufj031.pdf>.

16. See also Jayantha Dhanapala, 'The NPT Review Process: Identifying New Ideas to Strengthen the Regime', *UNIDIR Newsletter The Enhanced Review Process: Towards 2000*, No 37 (1998), 10.

17. J. Simpson, 'The nuclear non-proliferation regime after the NPT Review and Extension Conference', SIPRI Yearbook 1996 (Stockholm International Peace Research Institute), <http://www.sipri.org/yearbook/1996/13>.

18. Simpson, 'The nuclear non-proliferation regime after the NPT Review and Extension Conference'.

19. Simpson, 'The nuclear non-proliferation regime after the NPT Review and Extension Conference'.

20. '1995 Review and Extension Conference of the Parties to the Treaty on the Non-Proliferation of Nuclear Weapons, VERBATIM RECORD OF THE 19th MEETING', NPT/CONF. 1995/PV.19 (UN, 13 May 1995), <http://www.un.org/Depts/ddar/nptconf/217a.htm>.

21. See Dhanapala, *Multilateral Diplomacy and the NPT*, 136–8.

22. Ellen Tauscher, 'United States Closing Statement at the 2010 NPT Review Conference', US Department of State, New York, 28 May 2010, <http://www.state.gov/t/us/142370.htm>.

23. Maged Abdelaziz, 'Statement of H.E. Ambassador Maged Abdelaziz, Permanent Representative of Egypt to the United Nations, on behalf of the NAM States Parties to the NPT before 16th Plenary Meeting of the Review Conference of the Parties to the Treaty on the Non-Proliferation of Nuclear Weapons' (New York, 28 May 2010), <http://www.eyeo-ntheun.org/assets/attachments/documents/8627NAM.pdf>.

24. See Chapter 30, this volume, p. 559.

CHAPTER 46

··

THE CUBAN MISSILE CRISIS

··

DAVID A. WELCH

As the single most dangerous event in human history, the Cuban missile crisis has attracted (not surprisingly) an unusual degree of scholarly attention. Most commentators would agree that it stands as a particularly good example—and possibly the best example—of successful crisis management.[1] Recent scholarship has qualified this assessment in various ways, not least by making clear that it also stands as a particularly good example of the perils of faulty relationship management. Put another way, while US President John F. Kennedy and Soviet Chairman Nikita S. Khrushchev managed very successfully to step back from the nuclear brink in October 1962, they found themselves on the brink as a result of profound mutual misunderstanding and ineffective channels of communication.[2]

Despite the great deal of attention paid to the Cuban missile crisis, the role of diplomacy as such has received very little of its own. My purpose here is to fill this gap. By describing this as a gap, I do not mean to suggest that scholars have been insensitive either to the role and importance of diplomacy in the missile crisis or to the lessons the crisis might hold for diplomacy. I mean, instead, that the subject has been treated almost entirely in passing and in no particularly systematic way. No one would argue that diplomacy was unimportant in the Cuban missile crisis and few would argue that practitioners of diplomacy have nothing to learn from the event. As yet, however, there has been no attempt at a bird's eye view.

Most readers will be familiar with at least the broad outlines of the crisis and I will refrain from attempting to provide a detailed overview here.[3] For readers unfamiliar with the crisis, it will suffice to say that it arose as a result of rapidly deteriorating US–Cuban relations in the aftermath of the revolution that brought Fidel Castro to power in January 1959. In a series of tit-for-tat moves, Castro sought to reduce American political and economic influence in Cuba and the United States ratcheted up pressure on the Castro regime in an attempt to prevent it from drifting dangerously leftward (suspicions arose either that Castro himself was a communist or that he was under communist influence). Castro became convinced that the United States would not tolerate a genuinely independent Cuba after decades of what was in effect an almost colonial degree of American control. Khrushchev became intrigued by the possibility of cultivating a Soviet client in America's backyard.

As Soviet–Cuban ties broadened and deepened, the United States became increasingly concerned that Castro would turn Cuba into a Soviet outpost in the Western hemisphere. Particularly worrisome was the prospect that he would turn it into a nuclear outpost. American attempts to forestall this served merely to convince Cuba and the Soviet Union of Washington's unwillingness to tolerate the Cuban Revolution. A series of American actions drove this fear home, of which the most worrisome was the disastrous April 1961 Bay of Pigs invasion—an American-sponsored attempt to trigger an anti-Castro uprising by landing a small, ill-equipped, and not particularly well-trained brigade of exiles on Cuba's southern coast, where it was easily defeated by Castro's superior forces.[4] Also ominous were Operation Mongoose—a CIA programme of sabotage, harassment, and attempted assassination—and a series of ostentatious military exercises designed to demonstrate Cuba's vulnerability to American military power. In one such exercise, American marines stormed ashore on the island of Vieques, near Puerto Rico, to liberate a mythical republic from a mythical dictator named Ortsac—'Castro' spelled backwards.

Convinced both that an American attack was inevitable and that the only way to prevent it was by means of a local nuclear deterrent, Khrushchev proposed and Castro accepted precisely the kind of military deployment that President Kennedy wished to forestall.[5] Khrushchev ordered an unprecedented deployment of both conventional and nuclear forces to Cuba. Fatefully, he sought to do so secretly. The gambit nearly worked. American intelligence discovered the deployment just as the first Soviet nuclear missiles in Cuba were about to become operational.[6] After a week of quiet deliberation about how to respond, Kennedy announced on 22 October 1962, that he was imposing a naval 'quarantine' of Cuba and demanded that Khrushchev withdraw his weapons. After six tense days, during which it appeared that the Third World War might break out at any moment, Khrushchev finally agreed to withdraw the weapons that Kennedy considered offensive in return for an American pledge not to invade Cuba. In a private side agreement, Kennedy pledged to withdraw analogous missiles from Turkey 'within a few months'.

46.1 PHASES OF DIPLOMACY

On a narrow understanding of diplomacy—'the conduct of official state-to-state negotiations', or some such formulation—there was very little activity prior to the public week of the crisis, but a great deal during and after. I prefer a broader definition, however, that includes not only official negotiations but communications of any kind intended to signal or convey information. On this understanding, there were five active phases of diplomacy, each with quite distinct characteristics.

The first phase, which we might call the 'pre-discovery' phase, was characterized primarily by ineffective attempts to signal and little in the way of attempts to listen. Diplomacy in this phase, in other words, consisted largely of broadcasting in the form of highly charged rhetoric. The United States warned Cuba against cultivating close ties to the Soviet Union and attempting to export revolution; Cuba railed against the United States for its historical and ongoing attempts to interfere in Cuban domestic affairs; the Soviet Union and the United States traded threats not to meddle.

There was little in the way of real negotiation during this phase, with two notable exceptions: first, US and Cuban officials held talks after the Bay of Pigs fiasco to work out terms for the return of 1,113 captured exiles.[7] Second, the Soviet Union and Cuba negotiated an agreement governing the terms of the Soviet deployment. The former, of course, was narrowly task-specific and afforded no real opportunity for the United States and Cuba to attempt to resolve their differences. The latter, while also task-specific, did have implications for the development of Soviet–Cuban relations. It established early a pattern and a tone that persisted through the crisis: namely, one of Soviet paternalism. The key question that arose as a result of Soviet–Cuban deliberation was whether they ought to keep their agreement secret or announce it publicly. On this issue the Cubans displayed great wisdom and foresight, arguing that since the deployment was perfectly legal under international law, the two countries ought to consider announcing it so as to deprive the Kennedy administration of a potential weapon in the battle for world public opinion. Khrushchev dismissed these concerns out of hand, even flippantly.[8] Events would prove that the secrecy and deception surrounding the deployment was one of the Kennedy administration's greatest assets during the acute phase of the crisis, as it enabled the United States to deflect attention away from the question of the legality of the deployment and towards its apparently sinister aims.

Perhaps the only potentially good-quality channel of communication during this period was a back channel between the White House and the Kremlin: the curious relationship between the president's brother, Attorney General Robert F. Kennedy and Georgi Bolshakov, a Soviet military intelligence officer in Washington. Khrushchev used this channel to assure the president that he would do nothing to rock the boat before the November 1962 midterm congressional elections. In short, Khrushchev squandered on deception the one channel of communication President Kennedy trusted, complicating trust-building during the crisis itself.

The second phase we might call the 'private week'—i.e. the time between the discovery of Soviet strategic nuclear missiles in Cuba on 15 October and Kennedy's announcement of the discovery on 22 October. During this period, American diplomacy, in so far as possible, went to ground. Kennedy wanted as much time as possible to formulate his response and accordingly tried very hard not to tip his hand. He therefore attempted to maintain as much of an air of normalcy as possible. One important and particularly awkward moment during this phase was a previously scheduled meeting at the White House with Soviet Foreign Minister Anatoly Gromyko on 18 October. Kennedy and Gromyko both knew about the Soviet deployment at this point, but neither raised the subject directly. Kennedy did, however, take the trouble to read two of his public statements from September in which he warned of the grave consequences of any attempt on the part of the Soviet Union to deploy 'offensive' weapons in Cuba. Gromyko replied with his government's official line that the Soviet Union was sending only 'defensive' weapons to Cuba. Gromyko, like Khrushchev, may well have believed that the deployment was essentially defensive, intended as it was to protect Soviet interests, but there is no doubt that he was aware of the kinds of weapons Kennedy had in mind and so once again a potentially valuable face-to-face channel of communication was spent primarily on deception. Towards the very end of this phase, once President Kennedy had decided upon a naval quarantine as his initial response to the Soviet deployment, he began the process of notifying allies and laying the groundwork for legal and political support through the Organization of American States (OAS).

The third phase we might call the 'public week' of the crisis. This was characterized by frenetic activity through multiple channels, relatively little of which took the form of broadcasting. A multitude of actors became involved, introducing a degree of confusion into signalling and communication, some of which actually proved to be fortuitous.[9] The overwhelming goal of almost all actors during this period was to find a peaceful resolution to an extremely dangerous nuclear stand-off through mutually acceptable compromise. Most understood this to require clarity and sincerity in communications and a rapid building of trust. Kennedy and Khrushchev continued to be the two key actors, of course, as it was they who bore the responsibility for the outcome by virtue of the fact that it was their countries that possessed the massive nuclear arsenals that threatened to destroy the world. They underwent exactly the same psychological evolution and process of learning, though on somewhat different timetables.[10] Upon learning of the secret, deceptive Soviet deployment a week earlier, Kennedy had reacted with anger and belligerence, but within a few days had calmed down and had begun to focus his attention productively on the question of how he and Khrushchev could have misunderstood each other so profoundly. He became sensitized, in other words, to the dangers of misunderstanding and misperception.

As the public week progressed and as events began to demonstrate to Kennedy the risks of maintaining extremely high levels of military alert over an extended period, he became sensitized also to the danger of hostilities breaking out as a result of accident or inadvertence. He had several lessons towards the end of the public week in the limits of his ability to control the actions of the forces under his nominal command.[11] Khrushchev did as well. Although Khrushchev's moment of anger and belligerence followed Kennedy's by a week, he proved to be a quick learner. Through direct private written correspondence and through good-quality communication between Robert Kennedy and the Soviet ambassador in Washington Anatoly Dobrynin, Kennedy and Khrushchev were able to identify a mutually satisfactory agreement.

There was no significant communication during this period between Washington and Havana. While channels of communication were open between Havana and Moscow, Khrushchev did not seek to elicit Castro's views or engage him in crisis management. Indeed, Khrushchev ultimately did exactly the opposite of what Castro was urging him to do. At the climax of the crisis, on 26 October, believing that an American attack on Cuba was inevitable and most likely imminent, Castro wrote to Khrushchev urging him to stand firm and in the event of a full-scale American invasion to use the nuclear weapons deployed to Cuba for its defence. Khrushchev interpreted this as a call for a nuclear first strike, which he regarded as madness. Castro's efforts to bolster Khrushchev's courage, in other words, inclined Khrushchev to settle.[12]

Khrushchev's agreement on 28 October to withdraw the weapons, as he told Kennedy, 'that you consider offensive', seemed at the time to mark the successful resolution of the crisis and the world breathed a collective sigh of relief. Instead, it signalled the beginning of a fourth, largely behind-the-scenes phase, which we might call 'the November crisis'. During this phase there were three main issues. The first was the question of exactly which weapons Khrushchev had committed to withdraw. It was his understanding that he had committed to withdrawing strategic nuclear missiles alone and this he proceeded to do. But when American and Soviet negotiators met at the United Nations in New York to finalize the terms of the resolution, the Soviets were shocked to discover that the United States considered a long list of things 'offensive', including cruise missiles, obsolete Il-28 jet light bombers, air-to-surface rockets, guided missiles, motor torpedo boats, associated bombs or warheads, and a variety of communications and support equipment. At the end of the day, what Kennedy cared about most were the Il-28s. Kennedy decided to accept Khrushchev's pledge to withdraw these in due course, much as Khrushchev had decided to accept Kennedy's secret pledge to withdraw Jupiter missiles from Turkey.

This was easier said than done, owing to the second issue: namely, the fact that most of the Il-28s had been intended for the Cuban Air Force and Castro was in no mood to agree to their withdrawal, particularly since he was angry at Khrushchev for agreeing to withdraw from Cuba anything whatsoever without first consulting him. To solve this particular issue, Khrushchev dispatched to Havana his most trusted fixer, Anastas Mikoyan, who ultimately succeeded in overcoming Castro's resistance only after great difficulty and almost certainly in part because of Castro's sympathy and personal respect for Mikoyan, who landed in Havana only to be greeted with the news that his wife had died in Moscow. Despite his intense grief, Mikoyan decided to remain in pursuit of his mission.[13]

The third issue was the inspection condition. Kennedy had agreed to pledge not to invade Cuba in return for the Soviet withdrawal of missiles, but only on condition that the United Nations certify their removal. Furious at his mistreatment, Castro refused to accept UN inspection. It is a mark of the trust that Kennedy and Khrushchev had been able to build during the public week of the crisis and the early part of November that they managed a work-around whereby the Soviets permitted American reconnaissance planes to photograph departing weapons on the decks of homebound ships. But while Kennedy declared himself satisfied that the missiles had been withdrawn, the official American view was that Castro's refusal to authorize UN inspections meant that the non-invasion pledge never came into force.

The final phase was clean-up. That the two superpowers could stumble into such an acute nuclear crisis inadvertently and that they could experience such difficulty communicating during the crisis, prompted considerable effort to establish 'rules of the road', or what Jorge Dominguez called a 'security regime', to clarify the kinds of activities that were and were not acceptable within each other's spheres of interest.[14] This was a process that continued right through to the end of the cold war, though not monotonically, by which point the United States and the Soviet Union had developed quite a detailed and robust mutual understanding.

A more immediate concrete measure was the 1963 'Hot Line' agreement, which established secure direct communications between Washington and Moscow, initially in the form of a dedicated teletype machine.[15] Both leaders appreciated the dangers of delay and confusion in communication, in which they had many frustrating lessons during the crisis itself. A particularly important communication towards the climax of the crisis, for example—a long, rambling, very personal and very emotional letter from Khrushchev to Kennedy on 25 October—came in segments that were out of order, the last of which arrived nearly seven hours after Khrushchev had dictated it. To communicate with Moscow, the Soviet embassy in Washington had to encode its cables, summon a bicycle courier from Western Union, and hope for the best.[16]

Arguably, the real unfinished business of the Cuban missile crisis was US–Cuban relations. In many respects, the crisis was a product of their deeper unresolved history. Whether or not there was any prospect of a serious rapprochement after the crisis remains a matter of dispute. Kennedy proffered a number of feelers, not entirely enthusiastically, but he fell to an assassin's bullet in November 1963 before anything could come of them.[17] His successor, Lyndon Johnson, let the matter drop.

46.2 Channels

As my periodization suggests, different diplomatic channels featured more prominently in different phases of the crisis. In the first two phases, most of the relevant attempts at signalling and communication took the form of what I will call 'broadcast' diplomacy. In the third phase, four channels were active: broadcast, private, back-channel, and freelance. The fourth and fifth were marked by a combination of broadcast and private diplomacy.

If we were to evaluate channels of communication strictly in terms of their effectiveness in achieving their intended objectives, we would have to conclude that broadcast diplomacy largely failed. Indeed, it is difficult to identify a single example of a public communication that unequivocally accomplished its objective. Many quite clearly backfired. Public bluff and bluster intended to induce caution often induced risk-taking. In this case, as in others, we see many of the classic difficulties of broadcast diplomacy, of which perhaps the most significant is the question of audience. On 4 September, for example, Press Secretary Pierre Salinger read a statement on Kennedy's behalf in which he said:

There is no evidence of any organized combat force in Cuba from any Soviet bloc country; of military bases provided to Russia; of a violation of the 1934 treaty relating to Guantánamo; of the presence of offensive ground-to-ground missiles; or of other significant offensive capability either in Cuban hands or under Soviet direction and guidance. Were it to be otherwise, the gravest issues would arise.[18]

Khrushchev had no way of knowing whether this statement was intended for a domestic audience or for him. If the former, he may have felt that he stood a good chance of getting away with his gambit as long as the deployment remained secret until after the November midterm elections. If the latter, Kennedy might not be so ready to accept a fait accompli.

Generally speaking, private diplomacy, when undertaken in earnest, was more successful, at least as far as establishing clear communication is concerned. The complete Kennedy–Khrushchev correspondence during and immediately after the public week is particularly instructive in this regard.[19] Kennedy's letters to Khrushchev are written in a simple, clear, direct, businesslike manner, reflecting the fact that he had already had a full week to overcome his shock, anger, and belligerence. Khrushchev's letters evince his full affective evolution. Initially strident and defiant, he moves from intractability to accommodation and from abstract principle to practical problem-solving. Even Khrushchev's famous 25 October letter, which seemed to confuse Kennedy and his advisers because it was so rambling and emotional, managed quite effectively to communicate Khrushchev's state of mind.[20]

But written correspondence, though useful, has its own limitations as well. One may not know, for example, exactly who has penned which words. While the 25 October letter was clearly written in Khrushchev's style, the next letter, which arrived even before Kennedy had had an opportunity to respond, was quite different: firmer, more confident, less emotional. The contrast made Kennedy and his advisers wonder whether hard-liners in Moscow were ascendant.[21]

The single most effective channel of private communication during the crisis was that between Robert Kennedy and Dobrynin. In a crucial meeting in Robert Kennedy's office at the Justice Department on 27 October, the president's brother managed to convey very successfully the urgent need for a resolution. He stressed that if the two sides were unable to find a way out within a few days, military action might be unavoidable. He was careful not to describe this as an ultimatum, but as a simple fact. The president was facing enormous pressure to act, his brother said, and it was unclear how long he could resist. In framing the problem thus, Robert Kennedy was, in effect, eliciting Dobrynin's help as an ally against a common problem: namely, hawks in the US government and military. Finally, Robert Kennedy managed to offer Dobryinin a crucial carrot. When Dobrynin raised the question of US Jupiter missiles in Turkey, Robert Kennedy gave him assurances that they would be withdrawn. From Dobrynin's written report of the meeting to Moscow, we can see that Robert Kennedy's tone and body language were a crucial part of the communication.

Both Kennedy and Khrushchev made use of back-channel diplomacy during the public week of the crisis, though they did so for interestingly different reasons. The president seems to have reached the conclusion earlier than most of his other advisers (almost certainly earlier than everyone but his ambassador to the United Nations, Adlai Stevenson) that he was likely to find a peaceful way out of the crisis only by being willing to trade Jupiter missiles in Turkey for Soviet missiles in Cuba. A strong majority of his own advisory group—the Executive Committee of the National Security Council, or ExComm—rejected the idea of a missile trade. Many felt that it was unnecessary given the US military and diplomatic advantages over the Soviet Union; most thought it unacceptable in view of the fact that Jupiter missiles had been deployed to Turkey openly under the rubric of NATO. There was great concern that agreeing to a public missile trade would be interpreted as a willingness to sell out a NATO ally to solve a local problem, with potentially devastating consequences for the alliance. Indeed, after the crisis the Kennedy administration bent over backwards to insist that there had been no deal with Khrushchev on Jupiter missiles in Turkey

To prepare for the possibility of a missile trade if he felt one was necessary, Kennedy turned to back channels. First, he asked someone—possibly his brother—to ask an American journalist, Frank Holeman, to approach Bolshakov on 24 October with the message that Soviet missiles would have to be withdrawn from Cuba, but that a missile trade might be possible. To make sure that the message got through, the White House asked journalist and close Kennedy family friend Charles Bartlett to speak to Bolshakov as well.[22] Second, on 27 October Kennedy instructed his Secretary of State, Dean Rusk, to contact Andrew Cordier, a colleague from Columbia University who knew Acting UN Secretary-General U Thant well and ask him to be ready upon further signal to ask Thant to propose a public missile trade. Kennedy evidently felt that the idea would be more palatable to the American public and to NATO allies if Kennedy were seen to be responding to a proposal from the United Nations rather than responding to a Soviet offer, or—worse—offering a trade himself.[23]

Khrushchev's use of back channels during the public week was more opportunistic and less strategic. Khrushchev simply seized targets of opportunity as they presented themselves. His most famous impromptu messenger was William Knox, president of Westinghouse International, who just so happened to be in Moscow on 24 October. To Knox he railed against the quarantine as piracy and attempted to signal resolve. Whereas Kennedy's use of back channels during the public week of the crisis was helpful in so far as it enhanced the likelihood of a peaceful resolution by paving the way for a missile trade contingency, Khrushchev's use of back channels appears to have added little, if anything, to other modes of communication.

Finally, there was at least one interesting example of freelance diplomacy during the public week. On 26 October, Aleksandr Feklisov, the KGB *resident* in Washington, who was operating under the pseudonym Aleksandr Fomin, contacted ABC news correspondent John Scali, with whom he was previously acquainted, and insisted that they meet immediately. Over lunch at the Occidental Restaurant, Feklisov asked Scali to find out from his State Department friends whether the United States would be interested in an agreement whereby the Soviet Union would withdraw its missiles from Cuba in return for a non-invasion pledge. Scali immediately took the message to Rusk and returned at 7:30 pm with word that he was authorized 'by the highest authority' to indi-cate interest. Early histories of the crisis credit this channel with facilitating a peaceful resolution. It now appears, however, that Feklisov's report reached Moscow too late to have an impact.[24]

46.3 PLAYERS

To this point I have been concentrating primarily on US and Soviet bilateral diplomacy. By any standard, Kennedy and Khrushchev were the principals in the drama. The United States and the Soviet Union were the two countries who had to reach a resolution if war were to be avoided. However, diplomacy during the missile crisis was multifaceted and many other actors were involved.

America's NATO allies generally stood back and allowed Kennedy to take the lead. This deferential forbearance was quite remarkable, for two reasons. First, if the United States and the Soviet Union had been unable to resolve the crisis peacefully and, if mili-tary conflict could not be confined to Cuba and its immediate vicinity, Europe was the next most likely battleground and stood to face great devastation. Second, many NATO leaders were concerned that Kennedy might not give Khrushchev a face-saving way out. Kennedy did not consult any of his allies prior to deciding upon a quarantine as an ini-tial response, but he did brief most of them prior to his 22 October speech. For the most part, the allies were supportive and understanding. Perhaps most surprising was the reaction of French President Charles de Gaulle—not generally known as pro-American—who was helpfully understanding of Kennedy's decision to inform rather than consult the allies.[25] Kennedy also sent personal emissaries to brief Canadian Prime Minister John Diefenbaker, British Prime Minister Harold Macmillan and West German Chancellor Konrad Adenauer. All responded supportively, though all were wary of pro-voking an adverse Soviet response.[26] Kennedy sent personal messages to Mayor Willy Brandt of West Berlin, Premier Amintore Fanfani of Italy, and Prime Minister Jawaharlal Nehru of India, none of whom sought a major role on the world stage. Kennedy's most significant challenge within NATO was persuading the government of Turkey to agree to the withdrawal of Jupiter missiles. Early feelers elicited flat rejections, but once Italy agreed to the withdrawal of similar Thor missiles and, in return for assurances that Turkish security would be better served by an American Polaris nuclear submarine being stationed permanently in the eastern Mediterranean, Turkey ultimately relented.[27]

Among the most important actors in the crisis was the United Nations, although its role has generally been underplayed.[28] The UN was relevant in two primary respects: first, as the primary field of battle for world public opinion; and second, as a vehicle for facilitating peaceful conflict resolution. With respect to the first, commentators univer-sally agree that the United States won the battle for global sympathy when its ambassa-dor, Adlai Stevenson, badly outperformed his Soviet counterpart, Valerian Zorin in the

Security Council. On 25 October, Stevenson demanded that Zorin admit that his government had attempted to sneak medium- and intermediate-range nuclear missiles into Cuba. Weakened by heart trouble, unaware of the deployment, and operating entirely without instructions from Moscow, Zorin did his best, but he was no match for the articulate and well-prepared Stevenson, who with great dramatic flourish for the very first time unveiled for a transfixed global television audience US reconnaissance photographs of Soviet missile sites in Cuba.[29]

Theatre aside, however, the United Nations played an important substantive role as well. Thant sought to play a constructive, neutral role early and often, beginning with a 24 October 'standstill' proposal by the terms of which, for a period of two to three weeks, the Soviet Union would suspend military shipments to Cuba and the United States would lift the quarantine to give both sides an opportunity to negotiate a settlement. Kennedy rejected the proposal on the ground that it did not include a call for the suspension of ongoing work on Soviet missile sites in Cuba. But Khrushchev embraced it, signalling a willingness to negotiate. Even before Khrushchev responded, however, Kennedy asked Thant to consider representing as his own a second set of proposals enabling Khrushchev without loss of face to order his ships not to challenge the quarantine line. This proposal Khrushchev also accepted.[30] In the fourth phase of the crisis, the UN proved useful as well. It provided good offices for US and Soviet negotiators who were attempting to work out the details of the resolution and it did its best to elicit Castro's cooperation in a peaceful settlement. In pursuit of the latter objective, Thant travelled to Cuba personally. While his mission yielded relatively little in the way of tangible outcomes, it did offer Castro an opportunity to have his voice heard and to represent as a concession to the international community rather than to Kennedy or Khrushchev what limited flexibility he was willing to display.

Another site of intense activity was the OAS. The fact that the Soviet Union wielded a veto in the UN Security Council meant that Washington had no hope of securing that body's blessing for its response to the Soviet deployment. But the UN Charter permitted regional security organizations to take measures in response to threats to peace, so Washington turned to the OAS to bless the quarantine.[31] Dismissed by Cuba as the 'Ministry of Colonies of the United States',[32] the OAS nevertheless did provide necessary legal cover. The delay in securing OAS endorsement also proved helpful: the quarantine came into effect only at noon on 24 October, giving Khrushchev almost two full days to get over his shock and anger at Kennedy's 22 October speech.

The third principal in the drama was Fidel Castro himself. There is little to say of his role in missile crisis diplomacy, quite simply because neither superpower allowed him the stage. From the American perspective, Cuba was merely a parking lot for missiles—the site, as it were, of a superpower confrontation and no more. In any case, no one in Washington considered Castro a free agent and accordingly no one made any effort to engage him directly. Khrushchev, as I have already mentioned, treated Castro paternalistically and at no time seriously solicited his views. At several points Castro offered them freely; but Khrushchev was not inclined to take the young, headstrong Cuban leader's views seriously. The Soviet Union paid dearly for this neglect in the years following the crisis. Castro made clear that the price of his continued loyalty in the face of Khrushchev's gross mistreatment would be billions of dollars' worth of economic and military support year after year.[33]

46.4 Lessons for Diplomacy

One must be careful, when attempting to draw lessons for diplomacy from any single case, not to overestimate their generalizability. The danger of anachronism is particularly acute here. The Cuban missile crisis was unique. Never before and never since has the world stood so close to the precipice of nuclear war. Nor does the 21st century resemble the 1960s in every relevant respect. Considerations such as these prompted Elliot Cohen famously to declare more than twenty-five years ago that the world should simply stop studying the Cuban missile crisis.[34] But bearing these legitimate concerns in mind, I believe that the Cuban missile crisis offers us at least a few timeless truths.[35]

First, neither vague nor duplicitous diplomacy is likely to be useful over the long run. The resolution of grievances or conflicts of interest requires an ability to communicate clearly, a capacity to elicit trust, and an ability to trust in turn. Bluff, bluster, grandstanding, and privileging rhetoric over substance may provide short-term political advantages in highly charged political contexts, but only clear, businesslike communication is capable of focusing one's protagonist's mind both on the issues in need of resolution and on possible ways of resolving them. Broadcast diplomacy accomplished little in the Cuban missile crisis; earnest private diplomacy accomplished a great deal. That the former dominated the period prior to the acute phase of the crisis and the latter dominated the period during and after may go a long way towards explaining the contrast between the inept performance of the principals prior to the American discovery of missiles in Cuba and their generally impressive performance afterwards.

Second, effective diplomacy requires cultivating empathy. It is difficult to solve a tangible conflict of interest without understanding one's protagonist's wants, needs, fears, and general understanding of the world. In the first two phases of the Cuban missile crisis, empathy was in short supply and none of the principals made much effort to acquire it. The shock that both Kennedy and Khrushchev experienced once they realized that they had stumbled inadvertently into a dangerous nuclear crisis as a result of a failure to understand each other motivated them to make up for lost time. That they were able to understand each other so well after just a few days and on the basis of fairly limited exchanges under clearly suboptimal conditions, testifies to the human ability to cultivate empathy once one appreciates the need. It is one of the great tragedies of 20th-century history that neither Kennedy nor Khrushchev remained in office long enough to parlay their newfound empathy into durable structural improvements in US–Soviet relations.

The handmaiden of empathy is trust. Mutual understanding is a precondition for identifying viable settlement of disputes, but without trust settlements are difficult to implement. In the Cuban missile crisis we see several examples of the importance of trust. Perhaps the most noteworthy are Khrushchev's willingness to trust Kennedy's pledge to withdraw Jupiter missiles from Turkey and Kennedy's willingness to trust Khruschev's pledge to withdraw Il-28s from Cuba. But these are not the only examples of trust that we see in this dramatic episode. To be sure, we see many examples of a lack of trust as well; generally speaking, these proved to be costly. Khrushchev's mistreatment of Castro is but one obvious illustration.

Finally, there is the importance of time. And it is on this head that the danger of anachronism is probably most serious. While historical counterfactuals are notoriously difficult to evaluate, it is at least plausible to suggest that if Kennedy had had to decide upon a response to the discovery of Soviet missiles in Cuba quickly, he would have opted for military action. As the audiotapes of deliberations on the first day of the private week make clear, Kennedy's initial inclination was to respond at a minimum with air strikes against Soviet missile sites. Khrushchev's initial response upon hearing Kennedy's speech on 22 October was similarly enraged. The world is fortunate that Kennedy had a full week and Khrushchev nearly two full days in which to calm down and reflect. It is difficult to imagine that the leader of a major superpower in this day and age would have a full week in which to ponder a response to a major international provocation. Nor would today's press defer to a leader's desire for time to ponder. We live now in a world of instant communication and largely unfiltered information.[36]

Put another way, if the Cuban missile crisis were to occur today, leaders would be under a great deal more pressure to act than they were in 1962. As it was, the pressure was nearly unbearable. One can only hope that the speed of communications and abundance of information today would render less likely the very misunderstandings and misperceptions that led to the crisis in the first place.

Notes

1. But cf. Richard Ned Lebow, *Nuclear Crisis Management: A Dangerous Illusion* (Ithaca, NY: Cornell University Press, 1987); Richard M. Pious, 'The Cuban Missile Crisis and the Limits of Crisis Management', *Political Science Quarterly* 116:1 (Spring 2001), 81–105.
2. These insights emerged largely as the result of retrospective dialogue between US and Soviet officials and scholars—later broadened to a trialogue that included Cuban officials and scholars—in a series of 'critical oral history' conferences held between 1987 and 2002. For a history and discussion of the method, see James G. Blight, Bruce J. Allyn, and David A. Welch, *Cuba on the Brink: Castro, the Missile Crisis, and the Soviet Collapse*, rev. and enl. ed. (Lanham, MD: Rowman & Littlefield, 2002), 3–10.
3. For a concise up-to-date account and bibliography, see Don Munton and David A. Welch, *The Cuban Missile Crisis: A Concise History*, 2 ed. (New York: Oxford University Press, 2011).
4. James G. Blight and Peter Kornbluh (eds), *Politics of Illusion: The Bay of Pigs Invasion Reexamined* (Boulder, CO: Lynne Rienner, 1997); Trumbull Higgins, *The Perfect Failure: Kennedy, Eisenhower and the CIA at the Bay of Pigs* (New York: Norton, 1987); Howard Jones, *The Bay of Pigs* (New York: Oxford University Press, 2008).

5. Protecting Cuba was but one of Khrushchev's motives. Also important, in my view, was his desire to redress the US superiority in deliverable strategic nuclear weapons, and, to a somewhat lesser extent, his desire to retaliate for the deployment of US missiles in Turkey, to put Kennedy on the geopolitical defensive, and to demonstrate firmness and decisiveness to both domestic and international audiences, particularly China. Cf. Munton and Welch, *Cuban Missile Crisis*, 21–7; and William Taubman, *Khrushchev: The Man and His Era* (New York: Norton, 2003), 529–32.

6. Raymond L. Garthoff, 'U.S. Intelligence in the Cuban Missile Crisis', in James G. Blight and David A. Welch (eds), *Intelligence and the Cuban Missile Crisis* (London: Frank Cass, 1998).

7. These men were ransomed for $53 million worth of food, medical supplies, and agricultural equipment; Alajandro Quesada, *The Bay of Pigs: Cuba 1961* (Botley, Oxford: Osprey, 2009), 49.

8. According to Emilio Aragonés, who travelled to Moscow with Ernesto 'Che' Guevara to make this case in the summer of 1962, Khrushchev said, 'You don't have to worry; there will be no big reaction from the U.S. And if there is a problem, we will send the Baltic Fleet.' Quoted in James G. Blight and David A. Welch, *On the Brink: Americans and Soviets Reexamine the Cuban Missile Crisis*, 2nd ed. (New York: Noonday, 1990), 334.

9. Kennedy's and Khrushchev's misperceptions during the acute phase of the crisis generally inclined them to overestimate each other's resolve and to seek a peaceful resolution more energetically. See generally Richard Ned Lebow and Janice Gross Stein, *We All Lost the Cold War* (Princeton, NJ: Princeton University Press, 1994).

10. James G. Blight, *The Shattered Crystal Ball: Fear and Learning in the Cuban Missile Crisis* (Savage, MD: Rowman & Littlefield, 1990).

11. Scott D. Sagan, *The Limits of Safety: Organizations, Accidents, and Nuclear Weapons* (Princeton, NJ: Princeton University Press, 1993), 53–116 and 135–40.

12. Blight, Allyn, and Welch, *Cuba on the Brink*, 361–2.

13. Ibid., 219.

14. Jorge I. Domínguez, *To Make a World Safe for Revolution: Cuba's Foreign Policy* (Cambridge, MA: Harvard University Press, 1989).

15. 'The U.S.-Russian "Hot Line" Agreeement', *Current History* 45:265 (September 1963), 178–82.

16. Bruce J. Allyn, James G. Blight, David A. Welch (eds), *Back to the Brink: Proceedings of the Moscow Conference on the Cuban Missile Crisis, January 27–28, 1989* (Lanham, MD: University Press of America, 1992).

17. Stephen G. Rabe, 'After the Missiles of October: John F. Kennedy and Cuba, November 1962 to November 1963', *Presidential Studies Quarterly* 30:4 (December 2000), 714–26.

18. US Department of State, *Bulletin*, Volume XLVII, No. 1213 (24 September 1962), 450.

19. See generally <http://www.state.gov/www/about_state/history/volume_vi/exchanges.html>, 60–84.

20. <http://www.state.gov/www/about_state/history/volume_vi/exchanges.html>, 65. The most famous passages read as follows: 'I see, Mr. President, that you too are not devoid of a sense of anxiety for the fate of the world understanding, and of what war entails. What would a war give you? You are threatening us with war. But you well know that the very least which you would receive in reply would be that you would experience the same consequences as those which you sent us. And that must be clear to us, people invested with authority, trust, and responsibility. We must not succumb to intoxication and petty passions, regardless of whether elections are impending in this or that country, or not impending. These are all

transient things, but if indeed war should break out, then it would not be in our power to stop it, for such is the logic of war. I have participated in two wars and know that war ends when it has rolled through cities and villages, everywhere sowing death and destruction.... [W]e and you ought not now to pull on the ends of the rope in which you have tied the knot of war, because the more the two of us pull, the tighter that knot will be tied. And a moment may come when that knot will be tied so tight that even he who tied it will not have the strength to untie it, and then it will be necessary to cut that knot, and what that would mean is not for me to explain to you, because you yourself understand perfectly of what terrible forces our countries dispose.'

21. Ernest R. May and Philip Zelikow, *The Kennedy Tapes: Inside the White House During the Cuban Missile Crisis* (Cambridge, MA: Harvard University Press, 1997).

22. Aleksandr Fursenko and Timothy Naftali, *'One Hell of a Gamble': Khrushchev, Castro and Kennedy, 1958–1964* (New York: Norton, 1997), 251.

23. Blight and Welch, *On the Brink*, 83–4 and 173–4.

24. Aleksandr Fursenko and Timothy Naftali, 'Using KGB Documents: The Scali-Feklisov Channel in the Cuban Missile Crisis', *Cold War International History Project Bulletin* 5 (Spring 1995), 58 and 60–2.

25. Douglas Brinkley, *Dean Acheson: The Cold War Years, 1953–71* (New Haven: Yale University Press, 1992), 164–8.

26. Perhaps the least cooperative, surprisingly, was Diefenbaker. Peter T. Haydon, *The 1962 Cuban Missile Crisis: Canadian Involvement Reconsidered* (Toronto: Canadian Institute of Strategic Studies, 1993).

27. Philip Nash, *The Other Missiles of October: Eisenhower, Kennedy, and the Jupiters, 1957–1963* (Chapel Hill: University of North Carolina Press, 1997); Süleyman Seydi, 'Turkish-American Relations and the Cuban Missile Crisis, 1957–63', *Middle Eastern Studies* 46:3 (May 2010), 433–55.

28. Walter A. Dorn and Robert Pauk, 'Unsung Mediator: U Thant and the Cuban Missile Crisis', *Diplomatic History* 33:2 (April 2009), 261–92. See also U. Thant, *View from the UN* (Garden City, NY: Doubleday, 1978).

29. The most dramatic moment of Stevenson's speech, which shows Zorin rudderlessly attempting to do his best, is available at <http://www.youtube.com/watch?v=CxDGtu-aMio>.

30. No doubt this episode encouraged Kennedy's confidence in the feasibility of the Cordier Manoeuvre.

31. Abram Chayes, *The Cuban Missile Crisis* (New York: Oxford University Press, 1974).

32. Blight, Allyn, and Welch, *Cuba on the Brink*, 150.

33. Nicola Miller, *Soviet Relations with Latin America 1959–1987* (Cambridge: Cambridge University Press, 1989).

34. Eliot A. Cohen, 'Why We Should Stop Studying the Cuban Missile Crisis', *The National Interest* (Winter 1986), 3–13.

35. My own view that the crisis remains relevant is evident in David A. Welch, 'Lessons of the Cuban Missile Crisis for Nuclear Crisis Management and Their Implications for U.S.-Chinese Relations', in Christopher Twomey (ed.), *Perspectives on Sino-American Strategic Nuclear Issues* (London: Palgrave Macmillan, 2008); and in James G. Blight and David A. Welch, 'Risking "the Destruction of Nations": Lessons of the Cuban Missile Crisis for New and Aspiring Nuclear States', *Security Studies* 4:4 (Summer 1995), 811–50.

36. The American press caught wind of the crisis before Kennedy had decided how to respond, but withheld the story on Kennedy's request.

CHAPTER 47

....

CLIMATE DIPLOMACY

....

LORRAINE ELLIOTT

> Positive moments in international climate diplomacy generally do not
> last very long.[1]

THE 15th Conference of Parties (COP) to the United Nations Framework Convention
on Climate Change (UNFCCC), held in Copenhagen in December 2009, attracted
not only 45,000 delegates and participants but also, as much for its failures as its successes, extensive media and public attention. Much of that attention focused on differences between states parties about national mitigation and global responsibility. In
the shadows of the COP and global efforts to address climate change lurked an equally
important set of questions about institutional architecture, climate diplomacy, and,
for some, the whole United Nations (UN) way of doing things. Climate diplomacy
under the UN followed a fairly conventional path once serious diplomatic efforts
began in the late 1980s—several General Assembly resolutions, an intergovernmental
negotiating committee, a framework convention followed by a protocol, the appointment of subsidiary bodies, a range of other complicated institutional structures, inter-
sessional meetings, annual conferences of parties, the adoption of mandates and
roadmaps, and consensus as the guiding decision-making principle. These were both
the product of climate diplomacy and the venue for it. Following Copenhagen, much
of this seemed to be resting on rocky foundations and commentators and participants
alike openly questioned the value of climate diplomacy based on UN consensus and
inclusive multilateralism.

The purpose of this chapter is not primarily to revisit the history of the climate
change negotiations or the political disputes that have shaped their outcomes
(although that history and politics is not entirely absent either). Those stories have
been told in detail elsewhere.[2] Rather this chapter explores the diplomacy of those
negotiations—their form, structure, and the principles that shaped them. It focuses
on two interacting levels of climate change diplomacy—one empirical and one analytical. The first—the empirical level of analysis—examines the architecture of climate

change negotiations, starting with the UN General Assembly resolution that set the terms of reference for the intergovernmental negotiating committee for a framework convention on climate change (INC) and ending with the 16th conference of parties in Cancún, Mexico in December 2010. The 1992 UNFCCC and the 1997 Kyoto Protocol lie at the heart of this architecture of institutional bargaining on climate change. In formal practice, only states parties can adopt treaties, resolutions, and other agreements under the Convention. But as a quick glance at the UNFCCC web site will reveal, defining diplomacy only as 'channel[s] of communication between sovereigns [and] a means of negotiating agreements between them'[3] is almost certainly too limited to capture the complexity of contemporary climate negotiations. Even under the UNFCCC climate diplomacy has become the bailiwick of a diversity of actors, reflecting what Jorge Heine describes in Chapter 2 of this volume as a move from club diplomacy to network diplomacy[4] and what others refer to as multi-stakeholder diplomacy,[5] 'collective diplomacy',[6] and 'public multilateral diplomacy'.[7]

The second level of analysis locates this move from club to network forms of climate diplomacy on a larger canvas of debate about the nature, relevance, and adequacy of diplomacy in a complex and global world. The story explored here raises questions about legitimacy and effectiveness that are central to debates about global governance. In a globalized world, diplomatic practices are increasingly expected to be open, transparent, participatory, consultative, and accountable if their outcomes are to be broadly accepted, not just by participating governments but also by civil society and global publics. Yet, as some suggested following the 2009 Copenhagen COP, procedural legitimacy runs the risk of overwhelming efficient diplomacy. Peter Haas, for example, argues that 'talks have pursued a norm of fairness...at the expense of efficiency'.[8] Robert Falkner takes a similar view, suggesting that a high degree of participation may produce legitimacy but delivers 'a diminishing rate of return in terms of effective bargaining'.[9]

The focus of this chapter is, however, not *all* of climate diplomacy but what is still the *crux* of climate diplomacy in the UN system. Climate change diplomacy is multilevel. Since 1990 at least, climate diplomacy has been conducted against the backdrop of the regular assessment reports released by the Intergovernmental Panel on Climate Change (IPCC) established jointly by the United Nations Environment Programme (UNEP) and the World Meteorological Organization (WMO) in 1988. The IPCC has confirmed with increasingly greater degrees of confidence the impact of human activity on the climate system. Its Fourth Assessment Report (AR4) reported with 'very high confidence that the net effect of human activities since 1750 has been one of warming'[10] and suggested that 'discernible human influences extend beyond average temperature to other aspects of climate'.[11] Governments have negotiated a range of formal and less formal agreements on bilateral, regional, and plurilateral terms outside the UNFCCC. Private actors in the corporate sector have joined in various structures of dialogue and agreement (diplomacy by any other name) to adopt and implement rules-systems on aspects of climate change. Subnational actors—such as city governments—engage in networks on climate change that bypass national governments altogether. Non-governmental organizations (NGOs) are also active not only as lobbyists or setters of agenda but, in the global governance lexicon, as climate change rule-makers and even enforcers of contracts. Climate change diplomacy has also become more 'public', an 'instrument of soft power wielded by official entities such as states and international organizations and unofficial entities like transnational advocacy groups'.[12] These various activities of non-state, sub-state, and private actors might not be recognized as diplomacy in traditional terms but they inhabit the broad reach of climate change governance arrangements of which formal agreements embedded in international law are only one part. Much of that activity, however, continues to reference or in some way take as its starting point the key UN climate change agreements.

47.1 CLIMATE DIPLOMACY: THIRTY YEARS OF 'URGENCY'

This section examines four phases of climate diplomacy covering a period of more than three decades. It identifies patterns that have persisted over time: last-minute diplomatic breakthroughs, moments of high acclaim usually followed by a tendency to fall back on 'talks about talks about talks',[13] and constant struggles over technical and procedural details.

47.1.1 Setting the Scene

Climate diplomacy—or at least some inchoate form of climate diplomacy—predates the formal negotiations for a legally binding convention mandated by the UN General Assembly in 1990. In these early phases, climate diplomacy was not primarily the function of states or their diplomats. It began as a form of multi-stakeholder or networked diplomacy involving as many scientists and NGOs as government representatives. Demands for formal international negotiations were prefigured in a series of scientific meetings in the 1970s and early 1980s. The rather ponderously titled International Conference on Assessment of the Role of CO_2 and other GHGs [greenhouse gases] in Climate Variation and Associated Impact, held in Villach in Austria in 1985, recommended that UNEP, WMO, and the International Council of Scientific Unions (ICSU) should (if deemed necessary) initiate consideration of a global convention. The then executive director of UNEP, Mostafa Tolba, actively encouraged scientific experts attending the Villach meeting to 'set the ball rolling in the direction of negotiation'.[14] At the Toronto Conference on the Changing Atmosphere three years later, scientists, NGOs, and some government representatives called for a 20 per cent reduction in CO_2 emissions and the negotiation of an international convention. In the same year— 1988—UN General Assembly resolution 42/53 requested the WMO and UNEP, working through the newly established IPCC, to think about a convention on climate change. The 1989 summits of both the G7 industrialized economies and the Non-Aligned Movement called for urgent action to negotiate a framework convention. Member states voting in the UN General Assembly anticipated that such negotiations would involve some form of multi-stakeholder diplomacy. Resolution 44/207 adopted in 1989 urged 'governments, intergovernmental and non-governmental organizations and scientific institutions to collaborate in efforts to prepare, as a matter of urgency, a framework convention on climate and associated protocols containing concrete commitments'.[15]

The *actual* words of resolution 42/53 were that the WMO and UNEP should 'immediately…initiate action leading, as soon as possible, to a comprehensive review and recommendations with respect to…elements for inclusion in a possible future international convention on climate'.[16] In terms of the injunction for diplomatic action, this translates into make haste…but slowly and carefully. Governments certainly understood it this way, becoming more cautious in their approach as the possibility of formal negotiations drew closer. At a ministerial conference in the Netherlands in 1989, delegates could not agree on a Dutch proposal that industrialized countries should stabilize emissions by the year 2000. Japan and the US in particular were strongly opposed. A similar proposal debated at the 2nd World Climate Conference in November 1990—with 1990 as the baseline for stabilization targets—was also rejected.

In September 1990, UNEP and WMO convened an Ad Hoc Working Group of Government Representatives to prepare for negotiations. The final steps in setting the terms and conditions for what was to become the primary site of climate diplomacy came in December 1990 when the UN General Assembly adopted Resolution 45/212. This did two things. First, it took the task of negotiation away from UNEP and the IPCC and established an Intergovernmental Negotiating Committee (INC) under the auspices of the General Assembly (although UNEP and WMO were still expected to provide support). According to Ramakrishna and Young, this was the first time that the General Assembly had taken the decision to 'conduct negotiations on an environmental issue directly under its own auspices'.[17] Haas sees that as a deliberate strategy on the part of governments such as the US to 'avoid exposure to other political forces which may have led to stronger outcomes'.[18] Others are more blunt, seeing Resolution 45/212 as an attempt to marginalize UNEP in a kind of diplomatic 'ozone recoil', an objection to the influential role that the Programme played during the negotiations in the 1980s for the Vienna Convention and Montreal Protocol on ozone depletion.[19] Second, resolution 45/212 stepped away from the broader vision of stakeholder diplomacy that had characterized debates and discussions. While 'relevant non-governmental organizations' were invited to 'make contributions' this was on the specific understanding 'that these organizations shall not have any negotiating role during the process'.[20] The General Assembly locked the negotiations further into a conventional UN diplomatic model of club diplomacy with requirements that each of the five posts in the INC Bureau be filled by a representative of each of the UN regional groupings.

The INC, chaired by French diplomat and UN civil servant Jean Ripert with Raúl Estrada Oyuevala from Argentina as a key vice-chair, met five times in 18 months. Many thought this too tight a schedule to deal adequately with the political, technical, and scientific complexities of climate change.[21] The first two sessions spent most of their time on procedural matters and the final session—sometimes referred to as the 'New York marathon'—actually met twice, in February and April 1992. Negotiations proceeded in two major working groups—one on commitments, financial resources, technology transfer, and the special needs of developing countries, and one on institutional and legal mechanisms for implementation. The head of the INC Secretariat described the whole process as 'two steps forward and one step back'.[22] Governments formed quickly into competing negotiating blocs around key issues such as the inclusion of specific strategies for stabilizing emissions and concentrations, the adoption of formal mitigation targets, the question of whose responsibility it was or should be to act (Resolution 45/212 said that it was the developed countries' responsibility), and how to take account of some degree of scientific uncertainty about the extent of human contributions to climate change.

The UNFCCC was finally adopted at 6:10 pm on Saturday 9 May 1992. It is not a long document—a preamble, 26 articles, and two annexes. Its objective is to stabilize atmospheric GHG concentrations at levels that will prevent human activities from interfering dangerously with the global climate system. Resolution 45/212 had called for 'appropriate commitments' to be included in the Convention. Article 4.2 (a)—which Sands calls possibly 'the most impenetrable treaty language ever drafted'[23]—refers only to the general value of returning emissions to some unspecified 'earlier levels' by 2000, although article 4.2(b) encourages but does not require developed countries to bring emissions to 1990 levels. Much of the Convention is given over to institutional and procedural mechanisms. It establishes what had become by then a fairly standard model for environmental diplomacy—a conference of parties to be the supreme body of the convention, a secretariat, two subsidiary bodies (one on Scientific and Technical Advice and one on Implementation), and a financial mechanism entrusted to the newly established Global Environment Facility (GEF).

47.1.2 The Convention-Protocol Model

The Convention was opened for signature on 4 June 1992 at the UN Conference on Environment and Development in Rio de Janeiro. One hundred and fifty-four countries plus the European Community (as it was then) signed. The required fiftieth ratification was deposited with the United Nations on 21 December 1993 and the Convention entered into force on 21 March 1994. The INC met another six times to prepare for implementation. The first COP met in Berlin in March 1995 and was immediately faced with the contentious issue of commitment and targets. In a replay of earlier disagreements, the Alliance of Small Island States (AOSIS) and the European Union (EU) favoured stringent mitigation targets for industrialized countries. The JUSCANZ group (Japan, the US, Canada, Australia, and New Zealand) was reluctant to accept any commitments beyond the vague ones agreed to in the Convention unless developing countries also accepted legally binding mitigation obligations. China and the G77 continued to argue that developed countries should accept and implement their responsibility for climate change and the oil-exporting countries remained opposed to any action at all. In the absence of any hope of consensus on targets, the COP adopted the Berlin Mandate. Parties recognized that the provisions on reducing emissions (which they had negotiated only three years before) were inadequate and they agreed to 'begin a process to enable [COP] to take appropriate action', including stronger commitments for developed economies, through 'the adoption of a protocol or another legal instrument'.[24] The Mandate specified that there would be no new commitments for developing country parties. The process was to 'begin without delay ... as a matter of urgency, in an open-ended ad hoc group of Parties'[25] with a view to having an agreement on the table for the third COP in 1997. The Ad Hoc Group on the Berlin Mandate met eight times between August 1995 and October 1997. Its ninth and final meeting was held immediately prior to COP-3 in Kyoto on 30 November 1997.

The final draft of the protocol was tabled at COP-3 amid heated and fractious negotiations. When it was finally adopted after a thirty-six-hour non-stop final session on 11 December, the parties listed in Annex B to the Protocol (with only a few exceptions the same as those listed in Annex I to the Convention) had agreed to reduce their overall emissions of six greenhouse gases by an aggregate of at least 5 per cent below 1990 levels by 2008–2012. Targets vary. Three countries—Norway, Australia, and Iceland—were actually allowed to increase their emissions against 1990 levels. The Protocol established incentives for developed countries to reduce their compliance costs—the Clean Development Mechanism, Activities Implemented Jointly, and International Emissions Trading, collectively known as the 'flexible mechanisms'.

47.1.3 Plans, Agreements, and Accords

Just as the UNFCCC had been judged inadequate in terms of its commitments by the very governments that had negotiated it, so was the Kyoto Protocol judged inadequate in terms of its rules about how the various mechanisms would actually operate. As one observer put it, 'the Kyoto structure would require the efficient operation of international institutions that have not yet been established, under rules that have not yet been written'.[26] Few governments were willing to ratify the Protocol without greater clarity on what those institutions and rules would look like. The solution was to begin another round of diplomatic negotiations to work out the details of the 'rulebook'. COP-4 in 1998 adopted the Buenos Aires Plan of Action which established a timetable for negotiating modalities to give practical form to the Protocol's broad strategies. Those rules were supposed to be adopted at COP-6 in The Hague in November 2000. Fundamental disagreements between the EU and a loose coalition of states known as the Umbrella Group (the United States, Japan, Canada, Australia, Norway, and New Zealand, and later Russia and Ukraine) meant that no agreement could be reached despite behind-the-scenes efforts by the Chair, Jan Pronk of the Netherlands, to broker a deal. An informal follow-up meeting was held in Ottawa but a summit between the EU and the Umbrella group, scheduled for Oslo, was cancelled. In March 2001, the US administration announced that it would not ratify the Protocol and the whole diplomatic process seemed to have been entirely derailed.[27] Yet COP-6 resumed in July 2001 to adopt the Bonn Agreements which settled text on some issues (supplementarity, technology transfer, and finance) but deferred decisions on mechanisms, land-use, and compliance.

The rulebook was finally agreed to—in a mood of 'exhaustion and impatience'[28]—at the 7th COP held in Morocco at the end of 2001. The 203 pages of decisions that constitute the Marrakesh Accords expanded activities eligible for funding under the GEF, established two new Convention funds to be managed by the GEF and an Adaptation Fund to operate under the Kyoto Protocol. The Accords also launched an expert group on technology transfer and developed guidelines for the Protocol's Clean Development Mechanism. Climate diplomacy appeared to be getting back on track.

At the 2002 World Summit on Sustainable Development in Johannesburg, Canada and Russia—key to bringing the Kyoto Protocol into effect in the absence of the US—made promises on ratification but sought various concessions to turn their promises into action.[29] COP-8 met in New Delhi in October 2002, overshadowed by uncertainty about when Russia might ratify and by continuing disputes over developing country targets for reducing emissions. Delegates narrowly avoided failing to adopt the final conference declaration. COP-9 was held in Milan in December 2003. Most delegates assumed that this would also serve as the first meeting of parties for the Kyoto Protocol. But the Russian government continued to stall ratification and to send mixed and confusing signals and some commentators were moved to suggest that the Kyoto Protocol was dead.[30] The EU, however, went into diplomatic overdrive, successfully negotiating with Russia on the terms of its admission to the World Trade Organization as a trade-off for ratification of the Protocol.[31] Russia deposited its instrument of ratification on 18 November 2004 and the Kyoto Protocol finally entered into force on 16 February 2005, more than seven years after it had been adopted.

47.1.4 Roadmaps and more Accords

COP-10 in Buenos Aires began with a sense of relief. However, the familiar patterns of climate diplomacy did not stay submerged for long and the conference 'quickly moved back into its...habit of struggling over technical details and worrying about the future of the regime'.[32] Concerns were already being raised about what would happen after the first Kyoto Protocol commitment period expired in 2012. The main impasse at the COP, however, was over what *processes* the parties should adopt to address this challenge. In other words, where should climate diplomacy move next? The apparently practical question of whether discussions should take place under the auspices of the Convention or the Protocol was a highly political one given that the US and a number of other countries were not party to the Protocol. Even a proposal to convene a number of informal seminars to discuss future directions proved controversial.[33]

The first joint COP—MOP (Conference of Parties—Meeting of Parties) for the UNFCCC and the Kyoto Protocol was held in Montreal late in 2005, attracting more than 10,000 participants. Despite some tense moments—the US delegation walked out of one meeting—the idea of a 'dual track' diplomatic process was confirmed as a strategy for discussions on further commitments (the Kyoto track) and long-term cooperation (the Convention track). The former was formalized in the Ad Hoc Working Group on Further Commitments for Annex I Parties. The Convention track was, at this stage, a less formal 'dialogue'. COP-12/MOP-2 was held in Nairobi in November 2006. High expectations were dampened by the 'usual diplomatic ritual' which proceeded at 'an almost surrealistic slow pace'.[34] Some decisions were taken, on the adaptation fund for example, but in the continued absence of consensus, decisions on issues such as technology transfer had to be 'deferred' to later meetings or to working groups that were supposed to have finished their tasks. The 13th COP (and 3rd MOP) in Bali in 2007 was described as 'tense and chaotic'.[35] Despite this, three years of diplomatic efforts dating back to Montréal in 2005 seemed to have paid off when the meeting adopted a series of decisions collectively known as the Bali Roadmap. The Convention dialogue was finally formalized in an Ad Hoc Working Group on Long-term Cooperative Action. Its task was to reach an agreed outcome on a shared vision, on enhanced action on mitigation, adaptation, technology development and transfer, and on the provision of financial resources. The two working groups, although negotiating separately, were expected to converge at the 15th COP in 2009 in Copenhagen. That, of course, is where this chapter started, with an Accord instead of binding commitments, with 'noting' rather than 'adopting', and with claims (not for the first time) that UN climate diplomacy was dead.

The Copenhagen Accord did announce a Technology Mechanism and a Green Climate Fund for transferring increased financial support to developing countries. The sums promised were substantial: something 'approaching' USD 30 billion a year by 2010–2012 rising to USD 100 billion a year by 2020. The Accord also seemed to propel negotiators away from more traditional forms of diplomatic product, relying on voluntary commitments, a kind of pledge-and-review process in contrast to the top-down legally binding model of the Kyoto Protocol.[36] COP-16 met in Cancún, Mexico, in December 2010. The Cancún Agreements adopted there effectively side-stepped but did not remove entirely from the agenda the issue of whether climate diplomacy was heading towards a legally binding agreement on the next phase of mitigation targets. The Agreements gave formal support to mechanisms for Reducing Emissions from Deforestation and Degradation plus measures on conservation and land management (REDD +). They codified the Green Climate Fund, adopted a Cancún Adaptation Framework, and made some progress on monitoring, reporting, and verification. The new UNFCCC Executive Secretary, Christiana Figueres, proclaimed at the closing ceremony that 'the beacon of hope has been ignited and faith in the multilateral climate change process…has been restored'.[37] Even NGOs expressed various degrees of optimism: Greenpeace went so far as to say that governments had chosen 'hope over fear' and saved the multilateral process.[38]

47.2 The End of Climate Diplomacy?

The general view following the Copenhagen COP was that there was something inherently dysfunctional about climate diplomacy under the UNFCCC in particular and under the UN in general. This view was widely shared in the media, among commentators, and a good many participants as well. The apparent 'endgame' failings of Copenhagen should, however, be put into the context of the broader sweep of climate diplomacy. This was not the first time that a climate change COP had been unable to agree on its own declaration. The Geneva Declaration at COP-2 in 1996 was also 'noted' rather than adopted and a similar outcome was only narrowly avoided at COP-8 in 2002. It was also not the first time that a COP was declared to have failed. As noted above, COP-6 in The Hague (November 2000) was 'widely denounced as a failure'[39] after it collapsed because of fundamental disagreements over sinks, compliance, finance, supplementarity, and carbon credits.

Rather than making less of the 'failures' of Copenhagen, however, these observations might equally suggest that climate diplomacy has long been dysfunctional. The puzzle is whether there is something about the structure and management of climate diplomacy that has almost inevitably resulted in sub-optimal diplomatic and environmental outcomes. Diplomatic breakthroughs in climate negotiations, when they occur, are usually very last minute. Procedural issues frequently take precedence over substantive ones. Nevertheless, there is no agreement on what the actual problems of climate diplomacy are. Debates have focused on four sometimes overlapping fields of enquiry. Moving from the allegedly weakest to strongest areas of dysfunction, those fields cover the institutional framework and the way it is managed; the question of leadership; the problem of framing; and the vexed issue of the value of inclusive forms of UN multilateralism.

47.2.1 Institutional Framework

The discussion so far has focused on the public face of climate diplomacy, reported by hundreds of journalists and monitored in various ways by NGOs, civil society organizations, local governments, and corporate institutions. However this public face would not happen without an institutional framework to support it. The day-to-day management of the climate regime's diplomatic stage is the responsibility of a fairly small and modestly funded Convention secretariat based in Bonn. The first COP decided that the secretariat would be 'institutionally linked to the United Nations [but] not... fully integrated in the work programme and management structure of any particular department or programme'.[40] The secretariat has, therefore, a degree of constrained autonomy. It is not controlled by any national government but it remains 'subject to the collective will of the parties'.[41] The Secretariat's own vision is to 'support cooperative action by States to combat climate change and its impacts on humanity and ecosystems'.[42]

The role of the secretariat and its institutional mechanisms has been generally over-looked in analyses of climate diplomacy. Although generally well regarded by the parties, observers cannot agree whether it is weak or strong in comparison with other environmental secretariats.[43] Institutional strength and weakness has some bearing on how well diplomatic negotiations are organized and supported. A more important issue is whether the secretariat affects the outcomes of the negotiations through subtle and perhaps inadvertent influence. Busch suggests this is limited, although both he and Depledge identify instances (COP-6 and COP-8) in which the secretariat was either 'partial[ly] responsib[le]' for failure or should take 'credit for … skillful support' in keeping climate diplomacy alive.[44]

47.2.2 Diplomatic Leadership

The question of leadership functions at multiple levels in the climate diplomacy story-book. Commentators have discussed the imperatives of EU leadership,[45] US leadership,[46] and developing country leadership.[47] They investigate conditions for particular styles of leadership including middle power leadership,[48] entrepreneurial leadership, structural leadership, and intellectual leadership.[49] The most widely held view is that 'successful' diplomatic outcomes—judged variously from getting an actual agreement on paper through to things not falling completely apart—require entrepreneurial leadership or structural leadership.[50] Less attention is paid to more prosaic managerial leadership. Yet, as Swedish environmental diplomat Bo Kjellen has argued, without active management by key diplomatic leaders, 'the whole machinery [of climate diplomacy] gets out of hand and no meaningful results can be achieved'.[51]

The political management of climate diplomacy and the success or failure of any particular diplomatic negotiation drills down to the role of individuals. Leadership in the hotbed of climate diplomacy has required a combination of managerial expertise and entrepreneurial skill. This particular type of leadership, which involves circumventing bargaining problems through 'facilitation, conciliation, [and] mediation' has been most successful when leaders are 'not protagonists in the bargaining process itself'.[52] This has placed particularly high expectations on the 'hierarchy of Chairpersons' who preside over different formal and informal groups to manage climate negotiations.[53] Several individuals have been identified as crucial to making climate diplomacy work through their chairing roles. Jean Ripert, for example, is described by one insider as having maintained 'exquisite control' over the INC negotiations for the framework convention.[54] Raúl Estrada Oyuevala has been called not only a 'grandmaster of diplomacy' but the 'godfather of Kyoto', with a former US assistant secretary of state claiming that the Protocol 'wouldn't have happened without his leadership, excellent judgment and good humor'.[55] Others, who can remain nameless here, have generally been viewed as a key factor in the failure of important meetings.

Tallberg suggests that the role of the chair in diplomatic negotiations is designed to overcome the problems of 'agenda failure, negotiation failure and representation failure'.[56] In climate negotiations, as in other forms of intergovernmental diplomacy, the procedures for appointing chairs can themselves exacerbate these very kinds of failure. The COP president is almost always a senior minister from the country that is hosting the negotiations; vice-chairs are elected on a two-year rotation to ensure adequate representation from all UN regional groupings. Informal groups are chaired by co-chairs, one each from a developed and developing country. While this helps to generate some form of politically acceptable representation in the leadership cohort—even though chairs are supposed to leave 'their passports at the door'[57] and act in the best interests of the Convention and the parties collectively—it has also caused problems in the absence of skill, deftness, and sophisticated understanding of just exactly what is going on. Keukeleire et al. suggest that leadership in climate diplomacy really requires expertise 'beyond that of diplomats'.[58]

47.2.3 Framing Climate Diplomacy

The proposition that the ways in which climate change has been framed as a political issue can either constrain or facilitate successful diplomatic outcomes (more usually the former than the latter) draws attention to two problems. The first is that the social construction by diplomats of climate change as 'a global problem requiring global solutions' has inevitably meant that climate diplomacy is assumed to require not just 'institutions with global membership—the UN' but also 'procedures of global compromise—consensus'.[59] Consensus is assumed to be the cause of lowest common denominator outcomes with weak compliance and enforcement mechanisms. There is, however, nothing specific in the framing of a problem as global that necessarily leads to sub-optimal outcomes of these kinds. The problem is less that climate change has been framed as global and more that national interests have continued to take priority over climate change as a common concern of humankind (as the very first paragraph of the UNFCCC puts it). The problem is located in 'club diplomacy'—that the 'climate talks are dominated by professional negotiators who consider defending historical and national positions more important than progress. The rules of procedure invite delay and obstruction.'[60] Haas suggests that this is not accidental. He says that this 'weak diplomatic context' has been 'one of choice', a way to avoid bringing climate diplomacy into a stronger institutional realm such as might be provided by the OECD (with the addition of China and India).[61]

Cooperation has become an end rather than the means and diplomatic success has come to be measured by agreed words on paper rather than by the actual mitigation of GHG emissions and successful adaptation to the impacts of climate change. This helps in part to explain the outcomes of Copenhagen. Negotiators and observers knew months before the COP in December 2009 that a binding agreement on a second commitment period after 2012 was highly unlikely. Yet the impetus for diplomatic success militated against more cautious and realistic expectations. The final version of the Accord was negotiated behind closed doors by a small number of governments and personal diplomatic interventions by US President Obama with the leaders of key developing countries (China, Brazil, India, and South Africa). Even those close to those negotiations tell different stories about why this happened. Dimitrov suggests that by the time heads of state arrived at the 15th COP in Copenhagen in December 2009, negotiators had nothing to give them by way of deliverables or 'announceables' and leaders crafted a declaration themselves rather than face the international embarrassment of having no agreement at all.[62] Falkner is slightly more sympathetic to the negotiators who, he suggests, spent 'two intensive weeks negotiating over heavily bracketed texts, only to see a smaller group of heads of state take over and draft a compromise agreement that was not based on the official negotiation texts' at all.[63]

The second (and related) framing problem is that the principle of common but differentiated responsibilities (CBDR) has allowed climate diplomacy to be characterized and then played out as a stand-off between developed and developing countries. Both the UNFCCC and the Kyoto Protocol make clear distinctions between developed and developing countries in terms of those who are most vulnerable to the impacts of climate change, those who have contributed more over time to global emissions and concentrations, those who have the technological capacity to take robust action to mitigate greenhouse gas emissions and provide support for those for whom technological capacity remains limited, and those who have the responsibility to take the lead in mitigation. This is in part the reason that the climate change negotiations following Bali proceeded in two separate tracks, one under the Convention and one under the Protocol. The G77 and China were determined that negotiations should focus on amending the Protocol rather than replacing it with a new agreement precisely because it continued to recognize this distinction. At the same time, a number of industrialized countries—the US and Australia among the leaders—were able to fall back on the 'global' framing of climate change and refuse to commit to further binding targets until developing countries—or at least the major gross emitters among them—accepted to do likewise.

47.2.4 Inclusive Multilateralism

The UN model of inclusive multilateralism has been built on the idea of 'one state, one vote' or, at least, equal veto rights to all states although theory has never entirely matched practice. Since the 1992 Rio Conference the diplomacy of environmental multilateralism has also become increasingly participatory and networked, open to a vast variety of NGOs and civil society organizations as well as to the private sector. The logic behind this has been twofold. The efficiency argument is that diplomacy and governance are more likely to be successful if all stakeholders are involved in international rule-making. The ethical argument is that climate diplomacy should reflect a deliberative form of global democracy that accounts for and is accountable to those who are most marginalized from political processes and often most affected by climate change. Following the Copenhagen COP, many commentators and participants suggested that this form of open multilateralism had become increasingly dysfunctional. In the very early days of climate negotiations, Irving Mintzer argued that the various political complexities made it impossible 'to work out a simple and quiet arrangement among a few key interest groups familiar with the problem'.[64] Yet this is precisely what was called for following the Copenhagen conference. Observers spoke approvingly of the 'more fluid yet manageable framework' constituted by a small group of heads of state in the final two days of the Copenhagen COP.[65] Coordinated negotiations among small groups of key countries on specific issues were argued to be preferable to open-ended multilateralism because they offered a better chance of getting real agreement and commitment. From a political perspective they were assumed to avoid situations in which 'smaller states [can] make a greater stand or major states [can] escape their responsibility'.[66]

For some, this was simply a realistic reflection of where climate diplomacy should head if effective action was to be achieved. For others, it challenged the very foundation of the UN's multilateral climate diplomacy. Many developing countries opposed the Copenhagen Accord because they were excluded from the final negotiation of an agreement that could have real consequences for their climate vulnerability. The Accord strategy was also described as 'a backlash against civil society, even reinforcing the disenfranchisement of social movements and stakeholders'[67] despite the very large numbers of NGOs and civil society groups who made their way to Copenhagen.

47.3 CONCLUSION

Once the initial enthusiasm over the quick entry into force of the UNFCCC had passed, few climate meetings were unequivocal successes, despite efforts to generate diplomatic glory. Haas has argued that 'climate change is the limiting case...for the multilateral diplomacy approach,...economically and politically more difficult than other issues...so it is not surprising that the diplomatic efforts to date have been disappointing'.[68] Climate diplomacy has been called 'painstakingly slow and cumbersome'[69] and 'often tortuous',[70] on the one hand, but also trying to 'do too much too fast'[71] on the other. It has been decried as being too open and participatory to be effective, and too closed and dominated by key interests to be legitimate. Demands for finding better ways of negotiating on the complexity of issues on the climate change agenda have certainly been warranted. As this chapter has shown, however, there was little agreement on what the 'new paradigm' for climate diplomacy should be. Various proposals were made to move core climate negotiations from the UN into some other plurilateral forum, either one designed specifically as an alternative form of climate diplomacy involving key emitters and the leading economies (akin to the Major Economies Forum), or to a more generic institutional setting such as the G20. But climate diplomacy is not divorced from the competing political interests that underpin it. This is part of the problem. As Purvis and Stevenson argue, 'moving the climate negotiations to a new forum with the same nations [sic] would change neither their national interests nor the outcome'.[72] Little can be gained, however, from a return to the old, elite style of secret, club diplomacy behind closed doors.

Notes

1. Hermann E. Ott, Bernd Brouns, Wolfgang Sterk, and Bettina Wittneben, 'It takes two to tango—climate policy at COP 10 in Buenos Aires and beyond', *Journal for European Environmental and Planning Law* 2:2 (2005), 84–91 at 84.

2. See, for example, Harriet Bulkeley and Peter Newell, *Governing climate change* (Abingdon: Routledge, 2010); Joanna Depledge, *The organization of global negotiations: constructing the climate change regime* (Sterling, VA: Earthscan, 2005); and Irving M. Mintzer and J. Amber Leonard (eds), *Negotiating climate change: the inside story of the Rio convention* (Cambridge: Cambridge University Press, 1994).

3. Ian Hall, 'The transformation of diplomacy: mysteries, insurgencies and public relations', *International Affairs* 86:1 (2010), 247–56 at 249.

4. See also Jorge Heine, *On the manner of practicing the new diplomacy*, Working Paper no. 11 (Waterloo: The Centre for International Governance Innovation, 2006).

5. See Brian Hocking, 'Multistakholder diplomacy: forms, functions and frustrations', in Jovan Kurbalija and Valentin Katrandjiev (eds), *Multistakeholder diplomacy: challenges and opportunities* (Malta: DiploFoundation 2006).

6. Peter Haas, 'Climate change governance after Bali', *Global Environmental Politics* 8:3 (2008), 1–7 at 7.

7. Karin Bäckstrand, 'Accountability of networked climate governance: the rise of transnational climate partnerships', *Global Environmental Politics* 8:3 (2008), 74–102 at 84.

8. Haas, 'Climate change', 4.

9. Robert Falkner, *The new geopolitics of climate change after Copenhagen*, World Economic Forum Industry Vision, January 2010, 4.

10. Intergovernmental Panel on Climate Change, *Fourth Assessment Report—Climate Change 2007: Synthesis report Summary for Policymakers* (Geneva: Intergovernmental Panel on Climate Change, 2007), 5.

11. IPCC, *Fourth Assessment Report*, 6.

12. Donna Marie Oglesby, *Spectacle in Copenhagen: public diplomacy on parade*, CPD Perspectives on Public Diplomacy Working Paper, no. 4 (2010), 11.

13. Ott et al., 'It takes two to tango', 85.

14. Steinar Andresen and Shardul Agrawala, 'Leaders, pushers and laggards in the making of the climate regime', *Global Environmental Change* 12:1 (2002), 41–51 at 43.

15. United Nations General Assembly, *Protection of global climate for present and future generations of mankind*, A/RES/44/207, 22 December 1989, recommendation 12.

16. UN General Assembly 1988, recommendation 10.

17. Kilaparti Ramakrishna and Oran R. Young, 'International organizations in a warming world: building a global climate regime', in Irving M. Mintzer (ed.), *Confronting climate change: risks, implications and responses* (Cambridge: Cambridge University Press, 1992), 254.

18. Haas, 'Climate change', 5.

19. Andresen and Agrawala, 'Leaders, pushers and laggards', 43.

20. UNGA 1990, recommendation 19.

21. See Ramakrishna and Young, 'International organisations'.

22. UN INC/FCCC 1991, 2.

23. Philippe J. Sands, 'The United Nations Convention on Climate Change', *Review of European Community and International Environmental Law* 1:3 (1992), 270–7 at 273.

24. UN Framework Convention on Climate Change, *Report of the Conference of the Parties on its first session, held at Berlin from March 28 to April 7, 1995*, FCCC/CP/1995/7/Add.1, (6 June 1995), 4.

25. UNFCCC, *Report*, 6.

26. J. W. Anderson, 'Climate change diplomacy: the next step', *Resources* 142 (2001), 11–13 at 11.

27. Entry into force required ratification by at least fifty-five countries including those who together contributed 55 per cent of 1990 carbon dioxide emissions.

28. Emily Boyd and Emma Lisa Schipper, 'The Marrakech Accord—at the crossroad to ratification: seventh conference of parties to the United Nations Framework Convention on Climate Change', *Journal of Environment and Development* 11:2 (2002), 184–90 at 184.

29. Japan, another key party, had deposited its instrument of ratification in June 2002.

30. See Stavrosa Afionis and Ioannis Chatzopoulos, 'Russia's role in UNFCCC negotiations since the exit of the United States in 2001', *International Environmental Agreements* 10 (2010), 45–63 at 53.

31. See John Vogler and Charlotte Bretherton, 'The European Union as a Protagonist to the United States on Climate Change', *International Studies Perspectives* 7:1 (2006), 1–22.

32. Ott et al., 'It takes two to tango', 84.

33. See Ott et al., 'It takes two to tango'.

34. Wolfgang Sterk, Hermann E. Ott, Rie Watanabe, and Bettina Wittneben, 'The Nairobi climate change summit (COP 12—MOP 2): taking a deep breath before negotiating post-2012 targets', *Journal for European Environmental and Planning Law* 4:2 (2007), 139–48 at 139.

35. Pew Center on Global Climate Change, *Summary: Thirteenth Session of the Conference of the Parties to the UN Framework Convention on Climate Change and Third Session of the Meeting of the Parties to the Kyoto Protocol, December 3–15, 2007, Bali, Indonesia 2007* (Arlington, VA: Pew Center, 2007), 1.

36. Proposals of this kind had been regularly raised during negotiations for the Kyoto Protocol.

37. UN Framework Convention on Climate Change Secretariat, 'UN Climate change conference in Cancún delivers balanced package of decisions, restores faith in multilateral process', *Press Release* (11 December 2010), 1.

38. Greenpeace International (2010), Cancun agreement builds towards a global climate deal (11 December 2010), <http://www.greenpeace.org/international/en/news/features/COP16_111210/>.

39. Anderson, 'Climate change diplomacy', 11.

40. Decision 14/CP.1 in UNFCCC, *Report*, 42.

41. Joanna Depledge, 'A special relationship: chairpersons and the secretariat in the climate change negotiations', *Global Environmental Politics* 7:1 (2007), 45–68 at 48.

42. Cited in Per-Olof Busch, 'The climate secretariat: making a living in a straitjacket', in Frank Biermann and Bernd Siebenhüner (eds), *Managers of global change: the influence of international environmental bureaucracies* (Cambridge, MA: The MIT Press, 2009), 245.

43. See, for example, Haas, 'Climate change', 3 and Joanna Depledge, 'A special relationship: chairpersons and the secretariat in the climate change negotiations', *Global Environmental Politics* 7:1 (2007), 45–68 at 62–3.

44. Busch, 'Climate secretariat', 249.
45. Simon Schunz, *Beyond leadership by example: towards a flexible European Union foreign climate policy*, Working Paper FG6 2011/1 (Berlin: German Institute for International and Security Affairs, 2011).
46. Nigel Purvis, *US global leadership to safeguard our climate, security and economy* (Washington DC: Better World Campaign, 2008).
47. Mark Lutes, *Emerging leaders: how the developing world is starting a new era of climate change leadership* (Gland: WWF-World Wide Fund for Nature, 2009).
48. Norichika Kanie, 'Middle power leadership in the climate change negotiations: foreign policy of the Netherlands', in Paul G. Harris (ed.), *Europe and global climate change: politics, foreign policy and regional cooperation* (Cheltenham: Edward Elgar 2007).
49. Oran P. Young, 'Political leadership and regime formation: on the development of institutions in international society', *International Organization* 45:3 (1991), 281–308.
50. See, for example, Andresen and Agrawala, 'Leaders, pushers and laggards'.
51. Cited in Depledge, 'A special relationship', 55.
52. Young, 'Political leadership', 807.
53. Depledge, 'A special relationship', 47.
54. Bo Kjellen, 'A personal assessment', in Irving M. Mintzer and J. Amber Leonard (eds), *Negotiating climate change: the inside story of the Rio convention* (Cambridge: Cambridge University Press, 1994), 164.
55. Ira Boudway, J.J. Helland, Sarah Karnasiewicz, Aaron Kinney, Amanda Griscom Little, Katharine Mieszkowski, and Page Rockwell 'Climate warriors and heroes', *Salon/Rolling Stone*, 4 November 2005, <http://www.salon.com/writer/a_special_salonrolling_stone_report/>.
56. Jonas Tallberg, 'Formal leadership in multilateral negotiations: a rational institutionalist theory', *The Hague Journal of Diplomacy* 1 (2006), 117–41 at 121.
57. Cited in Depledge, 'A special relationship', 48.
58. Stephan Keukeleire, Robin Thiers, and Arnout Justaert, 'Reappraising diplomacy: structural diplomacy at the case of the European Union', *The Hague Journal of Diplomacy* 4 (2009), 143–65 at 144.
59. Haas, 'Climate change', 4–5.
60. Nigel Purvis and Andrew Stevenson, *Rethinking climate diplomacy: new ideas for transatlantic cooperation post-Copenhagen* (Washington DC: The German Marshall Fund of the United States (2010), 19.
61. Haas, 'Climate change', 4.
62. Radoslav S. Dimitrov, 'Inside Copenhagen: the state of climate governance', *Global Environmental Politics* 19:2 (2010), 18–24 at 20.
63. Falkner, *The new geopolitics*, 4.
64. Introduction to Ramakrishna and Young, 'International organisations', 253.
65. Falkner, *The new geopolitics*, 4.
66. Thomas Wright, 'Toward effective multilateralism: why bigger may not be better', *The Washington Quarterly* 32:3 (2009), 163–80 at 168.
67. Karin Bäckstrand, 'Legitimacy of Global Governance after Copenhagen', in John S. Dryzek, Richard B. Norgaard, and David Schlosberg (eds), *The Oxford Handbook of Climate Change and Society* (Oxford: Oxford University Press, 2011), 669–84, at 677.
68. Haas, 'Climate change', 2.
69. Falkner, *The new geopolitics*, 4.

70. Daniel Bodansky, 'Climate commitments: assessing the options', in Joseph E. Aldy et al. (eds), *Beyond Kyoto: advancing the international effort against climate change* (Arlington, VA: Pew Center on Global Climate Change, 2003), 37.
71. Anderson, 'Climate change diplomacy', 11.
72. Purvis and Stevenson, *Rethinking climate diplomacy*, 19.

CHAPTER 48

THE DOHA DEVELOPMENT AGENDA

AMRITA NARLIKAR

AN urban legend of the diplomatic world speaks part in jest of the 'Curse of Geneva': each trade round lasts longer than the previous one! In some ways, this so-called curse is a product of increasing complexity of the negotiations: as average tariffs have fallen, negotiators have inevitably been faced with the remaining and more difficult tasks of removing tariff peaks, reducing non-tariff barriers (NTBs) to trade, and addressing the issue of liberalization in politically sensitive and highly protected areas.[1] However, as this chapter argues, the complexity and political sensitivity of issues under negotiation do not suffice as an explanation for the persistence of deadlock in the Doha negotiations. The fact that Doha diplomacy must occur over particularly complex and controversial areas renders a breakthrough admittedly even more difficult, but the fundamental causes of delay and deadlock in the negotiation are a product of an altered international context that has precipitated changes within the institution, and some parallel changes on a dramatic scale in international trade diplomacy in the Doha negotiations.

My analysis proceeds in four sections. Following this introduction, I present a brief overview of the problems that the Doha development agenda (DDA) has encountered over the past decade (section 48.1). In Section 48.2, I highlight changes in the internal workings of the World Trade Organization (WTO), which in turn are partly a response to systemic changes. While vital in improving transparency and fairness of trade negotiations, their unintended consequence has been a reduction in the efficiency of the system. They do not present a direct cause of the problems of the DDA, but they exercise an important impact upon the nature of diplomacy as practised in this round. Section 48.3 analyses the new features of the Doha diplomacy. I identify four as particularly prominent, and central to understanding the malaise in the multilateral trading system: the rise and growing dominance of collective bargaining from the developing countries via coalitions (48.3.1), the use of normative and highly politicized framing of demands

(48.3.2), the disengagement of the governments of developed countries and lobbies within them (48.3.3), and the difficulties of reaching a trade deal in times of economic crises (48.3.4). Section 48.4 concludes. While this chapter highlights the failings of trade diplomacy in the last decade, the end product of the analysis is not a counsel of despair but of hope. Structural changes and issue complexity may have heightened the challenges, but in good measure, the problems caused by failures of diplomacy can also be fixed through diplomatic skill and compromise.

48.1 PERSISTENT DEADLOCK IN THE DDA

As per the 'Curse of Geneva', it is perhaps to be expected that the DDA would realistically take longer to conclude than its preceding round. The Kennedy Round took three years (1964–1967) to complete, the Tokyo Round lasted for six years (1973–1979), while the Uruguay Round was concluded after eight years (1986–1994) of hard diplomatic graft. This pattern persists: the DDA has been plagued by deadlock and has exceeded the duration of the Uruguay Round. It is now well past its multiple and sliding deadlines, and a decade of negotiations and progressively lowered ambition have failed to produce a deal. It is true that each of these rounds has involved increasing degrees of complexity and difficulty: slowly but surely, the multilateral trade regime has expanded very significantly beyond its attention to tariff reduction in the early rounds and a preliminary attention to some NTBs via the Kennedy Round, to a full-blown development round launched at Doha that can no longer brush away awkward issues (such as agriculture, or indeed certain aspects of Non-Agricultural Market Access, NAMA) under the carpet. But the Curse of Geneva should not lull us into a false sense of complacency that is underpinned by the belief that the deadlocks of Doha represent business-as-usual at the WTO. There are at least three causes for concern.

First, the deadlocks themselves are multiple, recurrent, and span several areas of negotiation via issue linkage. The DDA was launched in 2001 and is now into its eleventh year of negotiation. The Cancun ministerial of 2003 ended in failure. The 'July Package' of 2004 was agreed upon, but this involved a considerable watering down of the DDA, particularly the removal of three of the four Singapore Issues entirely from the negotiations. In July 2006, after further failures to break deadlocks, particularly over agriculture, negotiations had to be indefinitely suspended. Although negotiations were renewed a few months later, the failures became even more public and damaging to the credibility of the organization, especially as they followed in the wake of well-intentioned and high-profile attempts by Director-General Pascal Lamy to rouse members into action.[2] A good gauge of the despair in the organization is the ministerial process. The Agreement establishing the WTO decrees that ministerial conferences will be held every two years. Not only was there a four-year gap between the Hong Kong ministerial of 2005 and the Geneva ministerial of 2009, but the latter was focused almost entirely on systemic issues (and was based on the theme of 'The WTO, the multilateral trading system, and the current global economic environment') rather than geared towards reaching a conclusion to the DDA negotiations. The latest ministerial of 2011—again held in Geneva—also failed to close a deal on the DDA after a weak, lacklustre, and lethargic show of effort by members. The costs of these negotiation deadlocks are not only a delay in reaping the benefits of the round, which are significant, but also take the shape of declining credibility of a trade regime that has served the world well for the last sixty years and is needed more than ever before.[3]

Second, the problems of the DDA are illustrated and reinforced by the proliferation of regional trade agreements (RTAs). As Figure 48.1 indicates, RTAs have grown exponentially in recent years. The turn to regional trade alternatives is at least partly an *effect* of the stalled Doha negotiations as it is a *cause*: as the goal of multilateral trade liberalization becomes increasingly elusive, politicians seeking to deliver results for their pro-liberalization business interests end up resorting to 'easier' and sub-optimal regional alternatives. Importantly, as regional alternatives increase, they provide governments with powerful BATNAs (Best Alternative to Negotiated Agreement), thereby creating a vicious cycle that further decreases the probability of achieving a Doha deal more easily.

Third, the dented credibility of the WTO as a result of the Doha failures risks receiving another battering with the rise of protectionist measures as a response to the financial crisis of 2008. Writing in 2009, Baldwin and Evenett noted:

> Trade is experiencing a sudden, severe and globally synchronised collapse . . . Protectionist forces have already emerged and will strengthen as the recession gets

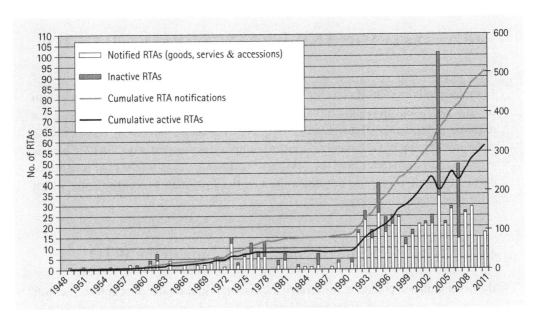

FIGURE 48.1. Evolution of RTAs during 1948–2011. This Figure shows all RTAs notified to the GATT/WTO (1948–2011), including inactive RTAs, by year of entry into force.

Source: <www.wto.org/english/tratop_e/region_e/regfac_e.htm>.

worse. But this is not 1930s-style protection. Governments' crisis-fighting measures have spawned new, murkier forms of protection, which discriminate against foreign firms, workers and investors, often in subtle ways. The use of WTO-legal protection, such as antidumping measures is also up sharply.[4]

In the context of deteriorating macroeconomic conditions in the European Union and China and also poor signs of recovery in the US in 2011, Evenett further reported 'initial reports of the incidence of protectionism in the third quarter of 2011 are as high as in the most troubling quarters of 2009, when protectionist fears were at their peak early in the crisis'.[5] The trade liberalizing aims of the DDA face even greater resistance than before.

What this adds up to is the following. The deadlocks of the DDA are unprecedented in their multiplicity and relentlessness. By reinforcing the turn to regionalism and thereby improving the BATNAs of governments, they are even more difficult to break than the stalemates of the previous rounds. And while these issues would raise serious cause for concern even in prosperous times, they acquire extraordinary urgency in the aftermath of the financial crisis of 2008 and the sovereign debt crises of 2011. International trade offers one of the few ways out of a global economic crisis, and is especially important to sustain when the temptation to raise protectionist barriers is high. The deadlocks, RTAs, and rise in protectionist measures—despite all rational considerations pointing to the urgency of completing the DDA, privileging multilateralism, and avoiding protectionism—are together indicative of the fact that trade diplomacy is somehow failing.

48.2 SYSTEMIC AND INSTITUTIONAL CHANGES

To understand the DDA diplomacy and its limited successes thus far we must take into account two major developments within the WTO. These institutional changes are a response to fundamental exogenous changes at the systemic level. The result of these changes is that the WTO has come to differ in important ways from the GATT. Changes in the institutional workings of the WTO are not directly a cause of the poor progress of the DDA, but they have had a strong impact on the diplomatic process of Doha, which in turn has affected outcomes.

48.2.1 The Rise of Brazil, India, and China in the WTO

The first significant change at the level of the system is in the balance of power. The shift of economic power away from the EU and the US and towards the so-called 'BRICs' (Brazil, Russia, India, China)[6] has been well-documented elsewhere and does not need reiteration here. For our purposes however, the important point to note is that the growing power of the BICs takes at least three very visible shapes in the WTO: (a) their rising trade shares, (b) their increasing activism in the Dispute Settlement Mechanism, (c) their presence and voice in all the crucial small-group consultations and consensus-building meetings of the WTO. I provide a brief outline of these in what follows.

First, the change in the balance of power in the WTO is most easily evident in altered trade shares. China has replaced the US as the world's lead exporter of merchandise trade. If intra-EU trade is excluded, then Brazil occupied the sixteenth position and cornered 1.7 per cent of the world's merchandise export market in 2010; India appeared as the fourteenth largest exporter at 1.9 per cent; China occupied a whopping 13.3 per cent of merchandise exports and thereby stood second only to the European Union. In the area of commercial services, China appeared as the third largest exporter (occupying 6.1 per cent of the market), followed by India as the fifth largest exporter (4.4 per cent), and Brazil as eighteenth (1.1 per cent). These are impressive figures in themselves. But they are rendered even more impressive by the fact that in 1997 neither Brazil nor India featured in the list of top twenty-five exporters of merchandise or services, while China ranked as tenth largest exporter of merchandise (and 3.3 per cent share of the export market) and sixteenth largest exporter of commercial services (1.9 per cent share of the export market).[7] These are clearly powers on the rise, and one of the areas into which their rising power translates most directly is that of international trade. Of course much depends on how these countries will be affected by the latest crisis of the eurozone and the persistent slump in the US economy, but all the evidence thus far points to a clear shift in power away from the former Quad group that had dominated the GATT (the EU, US, Canada, and Japan) and towards the BICs and others.

The second obvious change in the WTO as a result of the evolving balance of power is the increasingly savvy and frequent use of the Dispute Settlement Mechanism (DSM) by the BICs. Brazil and India are amongst the most avid developing country users of the DSM, with Brazil appearing as complainant in twenty-five cases to date and as third party to sixty-five cases and India as complainant in nineteen cases and third party to seventy-two cases. China too, despite being a relatively new entrant into the system, is learning to use the DSM quickly and efficiently, as evidenced in its appearance as third party to eighty-seven cases and complainant in eight (and also having the arguably dubious distinction of appearing as respondent on the largest number of cases, i.e. twenty-three cases, amongst the BICS, in contrast to twenty for India and fourteen for Brazil).

Third, and perhaps of utmost importance in terms of both the proof of the improved influence of the BICs in the WTO as well as the resulting alterations in the Doha diplomacy, the rising powers have acquired seats at all key small group meetings in the WTO. This is partly a product of their improved activism, but it is also a testimony to the governance mechanisms of the WTO that have proven more adaptable and responsive to the changes in the balance of power than all other international organizations (see for instance, the limited changes accommodated by the IMF changing balance to marginally increase the quota shares of the rising members, or indeed the absence of change in the decision-making structures or processes of the UN Security Council).[8] In the Doha negotiations, as a result Brazil and India have been present and vocal at different permutations of consensus-building forums in Geneva, such as the so-called 'New Quad', the Five Interested Parties, the G6, the G7, and so forth. And contrary to expectations that offering them a place at the high table of trade negotiations would secure greater buy-in and regime conformity from them, all three at different points and with differing degrees of vitriol have demonstrated their ability and willingness to exercise their veto power.[9]

48.2.2 The Newfound Centrality of Development to Trade Negotiations

The second major change involves the growing prominence of development concerns within the central mandate of the WTO. This is the product of several factors: a change in the international normative context via initiatives such as the Millennium Development goals that makes it very difficult for international organizations to completely disregard development concerns; a profound dissatisfaction of many developing countries with the 'Grand Bargain' of the Uruguay Round that provided the prelude to the launch of the Doha Round in 2001;[10] and the growing power of the BICs, which have espoused the cause of their own development as well as that of their middle-income and least-developed (LDC) allies.[11] The centrality of development to the current round is indicated both by its name—the Doha *Development* Agenda—and its mandate. Moreover, the focus on development presents a far cry from the GATT, whose commitment to such concerns was minimal: at its most expansive, it took the shape of the inclusion of Part IV to the GATT in 1965 and the Enabling Clause in 1979, whereas the DDA frames the entire liberalization process of Doha in terms of development. The fact that the WTO prioritizes development in this round is borne out not only in the expanse of issues that it covers, and the attention that it accords to development-oriented issues such as agriculture and cotton as part of the mandate, but also its first-time embrace of aid policies via the Aid for Trade agenda.

Together, the rise of the BICs and the centrality attached to development render the WTO significantly different from its predecessor, the GATT. In fact, the WTO in 2011 differs markedly also from its early years as an organization, including the WTO in 1999 when developing countries had complained vehemently about their marginalization from the process and when the proposed 'Millennium Round' agenda had shown scant regard for the concerns of development. One might expect that both sets of changes might result in the emergence of a more cooperative pattern of diplomatic behaviour in the DDA. But this has not been the case.

48.3 Features of the Doha Diplomacy

The change in the balance of power in the WTO along with the prioritization of development concerns in the DDA should have contributed to greater buy-in from the great majority of the organization's membership that had long complained of marginalization. So why has cooperation over a legitimate and important issue i.e. development, via a more inclusive negotiation process, been so difficult to achieve? There are four features that have come to characterize Doha diplomacy, as discussed in the following, which have in different ways exacerbated the difficulty of reaching cooperative outcomes.

48.3.1 Coalition Diplomacy of Developing Countries[12]

A particularly important feature of Doha diplomacy is that at least from the side of the developing world, it is organized and orchestrated via coalitions. This produces interesting consequences of empowerment but also deadlock.

Coalitions are not new to the Doha Round.[13] But collective bargaining in the Uruguay Round had oscillated from bloc-type coalitions on the one hand and issue-based coalitions on the other. The cement binding the bloc-type coalitions was a set of ideas and identity that went beyond immediate instrumentality, which meant that coalitions could address several different issues over time; issue-based coalitions were bound together by a more focused and instrumental aim. A flurry of collective activism notwithstanding, neither type displayed a consistent or reliable record of success.[14]

The reason for the limited successes of the bloc-type coalitions lay in their heterogeneity. Bloc-type coalitions normally brought together countries with some very diverse interests; the coalition thereby would manage to acquire collective market power, but also risked being bought off through side-deals.[15] In effect, such coalitions enjoyed external weight but they ran the risk of fragmentation due to their limited internal coherence. Issue-based coalitions suffered from the opposite problem. Such coalitions benefited from internal coherence, but were difficult to sustain when large and diversified economies (with multiple and competing issue-specific interests) were involved. With loyalties shared across multiple coalitions in competing issue-areas, the coalitions became difficult to sustain.[16] This problem could have been overcome by creating very narrow and focused coalitions involving smaller economies, but then such coalitions lacked external weight. The Uruguay Round demonstrated the dangers and limitations of both bloc-type and issue-specific coalitions.

The Doha coalitions of developing countries, having learnt from the experiences of the previous round and also from the pre-negotiation phase of the DDA, combine the strengths of the different coalitions of the past to produce 'smart coalitions'.[17] The fact that sixteen of the twenty-six coalitions listed by the WTO (see Table 48.1 in the appendix) are constituted entirely by developing countries (defined broadly to include the LDCs, middle-income countries, and economies in transition) offers us a useful insight: the 'stickiness' of Southern activism persists (driven by a mix of ideas, identity, and interests, which varies between coalitions). Contrary to the classic issue-based coalitions of the Uruguay Round, many do not transcend North—South boundaries. Those that restrict themselves to Southern allies benefit from the cement of ideational unity that had united some of the old blocs and also enjoy external weight. But unlike the old blocs, several of these also have an issue-specific focus (such as the G20 and G33 on agriculture, or the NAMA-11 on non-agricultural market access).[18] This helps them address some of the problems of internal coherence that had affected former bloc-type coalitions. Other Southern coalitions—such as the LDC group or the Africa Group—transcend issue areas but concertedly emphasise the specificity and distinctiveness of problems that affect their members. And in sharp contrast to the famous defensiveness of the third world in the past (the G10 providing the classic example of this), the new coalitions of the DDA have emerged as aggressive demandeurs and agenda-setters.[19]

The improved influence of the coalitions of the DDA derives from several factors besides their structure, as outlined in the preceding paragraphs. First, the fact that they are either led by countries like Brazil, India, and China, or are allied with other coalitions led by these large emerging markets, is a source of empowerment. Initiatives led by Brazil and India today as rising powers naturally carry more force than they did in the past. Second, bargaining strategies within coalitions have also improved to facilitate greater cohesion. These include the offer of side payments to smaller members within the coalition that help prevent defection and fragmentation. Third, when cohesiveness and unity of the coalition is assured via effective internal bargaining towards a united front, a large number and diversity of members can assist in the legitimization of one's demands in bargaining with the outside party. The resulting coalitions are ones that have proven to be 'strong coalitions', i.e. coalitions that are able to withstand attempts by the outside party and stand firm in the endgame. In this, the Doha coalitions are unprecedented, and they offer a source of dramatic empowerment for developing countries. The empowerment offered by coalition diplomacy, however, also comes at a significant cost: strong coalitions find it difficult to make the compromises necessary to reach agreement.

The reason why it is difficult for strong coalitions to make concessions, especially when they comprise developing countries, is that the collective agenda of such coalitions is necessarily arrived at through considerable logrolling that allows the coalition external weight. But this expansive and ambitious agenda also makes it difficult for the coalition to negotiate with flexibility. A concession made in any one issue area, or a sub-issue, risks antagonizing at least some members of a coalition, and thereby triggering defection. Bernard Hoekman has also noted this problem: 'The move towards the creation of negotiating coalitions of groups of countries may reduce the number of "principals" but possibly at the cost of greater inflexibility and a higher risk of breakdown, especially in a setting where there is little time to consult.'[20]

The G20 coalition on agriculture gives us an example of the dangers inherent in making concessions for coalition unity and credibility. In the Geneva talks of July 2008, Brazil (the coordinator of the G20) urged its allies to accept the proposed 'July Package'. China and especially India, with their defensive interests in agriculture, along with other allies both within the G20 and the G33, refused to accept the deal until the North improved its offer. At issue were the deep differences within the G20 over the proposed trigger for the Special Safeguard Mechanism, and also over the adequacy/ inadequacy of the US offer to cap its overall trade-distorting support to USD 14.5 billion.[21] China and India took a firm stance against compromise. Brazil was brought round quickly to resume a negotiating position that was sensitive to the concerns of its more defensive allies. The G20 did not collapse in the July 2008 talks, but it certainly came close to it.

And by managing to avoid fragmentation, it also lost out on a promising deal. Effectively, the G20 faced the problem that afflicts most strong coalitions: a willingness to compromise by some players over particular issues may be seen as a sign of potential defection by allies and a sign of weakness of the coalition by the outside party. The alternative, of standing firm, heightens the systemic problem of deadlock.

Doha diplomacy, in good measure, has taken the shape of coalition diplomacy. This is evident not only in the many coalitions that have emerged and continue to thrive through the negotiation process, but also via the unprecedented institutional recognition that they have come to receive. Pascal Lamy's model of consultation towards consensus-seeking via 'concentric circles' accords a prominent position to coalitions.[22] These coalitions present a source of empowerment for developing countries, and also assist in injecting greater legitimacy and transparency into the decision-making process. But as argued in this section, coalition diplomacy has also heightened the tendency of the system to deadlock by making it difficult for members of coalitions to make the compromises necessary to reach agreement.

48.3.2 Normative Framing

The second reason why diplomacy of the DDA has heightened the proclivity of the system to deadlock has to do with the use of normative development-oriented and fairness-based framing tactics. Coalitions of developing countries have resorted to such normative frames (for instance 'food security' as a principle for the G33 group, or Less Than Full Reciprocity as a principle for the LDC group). Developing countries have individually also repeatedly and explicitly appealed to the causes of development and 'policy space' when explaining their reluctance to make concessions.

Normative framing of demands may help coalitions and countries persuade the other party of the legitimacy of their claims. Indeed, such tactics have been used with considerable effectiveness in the past, for example by the TRIPS and public health coalition.[23] But it can also lead the negotiating parties to dig their heels in and refuse agreement until *all* their demands are met. This may be because principles are often regarded as rights not subject to compromise.[24] Max Bazerman and Margaret Neale have argued that 'fairness considerations can lead negotiators to opt for joint outcomes that leave both parties worse off than they would have been had fairness considerations been ignored'.[25] A recent study confirms that ideational considerations and explicitly normative framing tend to exacerbate conflict among parties.[26] While more research is needed in this area, it does seems plausible to argue, for instance, that were coalitions and countries fighting for 'interests' rather than 'causes' (such as development or fairness or global justice), they would find it easier to make compromises. It is also true that while some countries have been more willing to use normative frames than others with higher degrees of frequency and over long periods of time, passions over the DDA discourse have run considerably higher than over the early GATT rounds on tariff reduction or even in the Kennedy, Tokyo, or Uruguay Rounds.

48.3.3 Disengagement of the Developed world

While the developed countries have been quick to place the blame on developing countries, particularly the rising powers,[27] their own Doha diplomacy too has scarcely been cooperative. Jagdish Bhagwati is incisive in his indictment of the role of the US administration in the recent years of the Doha negotiations:

> In place of what the economist Charles Kindleberger once called an "altruistic hegemon", the America that the world now faces is what I call a "selfish hegemon". Thus, the US has virtually pulled out of the Doha Round of multilateral trade negotiations, with Obama acquiescing to greedy business lobbies that will not settle unless more of their demands are met.[28]

There are several reasons for the disengagement of the developed countries, especially when compared against the proactive agenda-setting of business lobbies in the US and EU and the activism of Northern governments in the Uruguay Round. I offer four below.

First, at least in the early phases of the Doha negotiations, it is likely that the deadlocks were a result of the unknown and untested power and determination of the South. Coalitions at Cancún in 2003, for instance the G20 and the G33 on agriculture, reiterated their determination to stand firm on their collective demands and resist side-deals. But given that these claims came in the wake of a history of failed coalitions, whose members had succumbed all too easily to bilateral arm-twisting in the past, there was little reason for the North to believe that the claims of Southern coalitions were little more than cheap talk, bluffing, or wishful thinking. In effect, poor signalling mechanisms and high levels of uncertainty (which were exacerbated because of the importance of coalition diplomacy in the DDA) contributed to at least the first phases of deadlock.[29]

Second, the emphasis on the development content of this round detracts attention away from the mutual gains that trade liberalization offers to both developed and developing country members of the organization, and gives rise to the impression that the Doha *Development* Agenda is less about reciprocity and more about charity. Such a round has little intuitive value for business interests in the North. Add to this the narrowing agenda of the DDA: the launch of this round had offered at least some attractions to governments and businesses in the US, the EU, and other OECD via the basket of Singapore Issues. By 2004, as a result of the July Package negotiations, three of the four Singapore Issues were taken off the negotiating table as a result of the resistance to them by developing countries. The NAMA-agriculture linkage, teamed up with the principle of Less Than Full Reciprocity, have made it difficult for Northern interests to secure an easy deal on market access in the large emerging economies. In other words, the perceived gains of the DDA have diminished in value for the developed world, while regional and bilateral arrangements offer quicker fixes.

Third, there is little doubt that the balance of power has changed in the WTO. The shift from the Old Quad to the New Quad/G7 has improved the representativeness and transparency of the decision-making process in the organization. But for the developed countries, especially those that had either constituted the Old Quad or otherwise played a central role in the decision-making process, the costs are twofold. First, and more directly, their own influence is considerably reduced relative to that of the others. Second, multipolarity might result in the creation of a more equitable governance structure, but by introducing a diversity of multiple voices, it reduces the efficiency of decision-making. Consensus-based decision-making worked effectively in the 'Rich Man's Club' of the GATT, but decisions using the same consensus rule are much harder to arrive at when multiple players are involved, especially players at diverse stages of development and working in cooperation with a large group of other developing countries via coalitions. This author recalls a discussion with a WTO official in 1997, who was quick to emphasise the distinctiveness of the WTO's consensus-based decision-making as an efficient and valuable procedure, and contrasted it with the inefficiencies of majoritarian institutions and especially the group-based diplomacy of the UNCTAD. The same official would today be unimpressed with the importation of similar inefficiencies in the WTO. In some ways, the disillusionment of the developed countries with the multilateral negotiation process bears potentially alarming resemblance to their disillusionment with the UN General Assembly, the ECOSOC, and the UNCTAD.

Finally, the extended length of the negotiation of the DDA thus far means that the negotiation cycle has already outlasted the political cycles of most major players, and that too by a margin. The most immediate consequence of this 'misalignment' is the increased pressure on governments to seek solutions outside the multilateral system.[30] It introduces further uncertainties into the negotiation process, and a risk that previous steps towards compromise might be disregarded amidst altered economic circumstances. It also exposes the multilateral diplomacy to radical ideological switches. A classic example of these costs can be found in the US role in the DDA. The US has been, as a hegemon in relative decline, much less willing in the DDA than in previous rounds to carry a large share of the burden of providing the public good of free trade. But this reserve has taken a turn for the worse under the Obama administration, as highlighted eloquently in the quotation by Jagdish Bhagwati cited at the start of this sub-section. Under the Obama regime in times of financial crisis, the prospects for Doha look especially bleak; a compromise deal under a shortened negotiation cycle, arrived at in July 2008 for instance when agreement was a realistic possibility, could have avoided this problem.

48.3.4 Diplomacy in Hard Times

In addition to all of the features discussed so far, we must take into account the impact that the financial crisis has exercised on the DDA in recent years. It is worth recalling that writing in 2007, scholars had pointed out that one of the reasons for the apathy of negotiators towards the DDA was the minimal gains that it offered: for example, Evenett argued that were the DDA not concluded, China would effectively incur losses no more than losing just three days of growth. Evenett thus argued that 'Blocking or a nonchalant attitude to negotiating progress is surely easier when a country is experiencing accelerating economic growth.'[31] In other words, for several years into the Doha negotiations, the booming global economy provided attractive BATNAs to politicians and diplomats, making them reluctant to make concessions at the multilateral level.

The financial crisis altered this calculation dramatically. The risk that countries might now actually make use of the 'water in the tariffs', and hike up trade barriers from their low applied to rates to their much higher bound rates, became much more real. The threat of increased protectionism effectively presented a potentially serious worsening of BATNA for all parties, and thus one might have expected negotiators to renew their commitment to multilateralism. In practice, however, historically and today, this has been far from the case.

While all governments recognize the importance of keeping markets open in tough economic times, every government also has a short-term political incentive to meet domestic hardship and austerity with populist measures of protectionism. If boom times presented difficulties for diplomats in the early Doha years due to the availability of superior BATNAs outside and thereby made it harder for them to galvanize the support of pro-liberalization interests, times of economic crises present even greater difficulties for diplomats fighting protectionist interests at home.

48.4 Conclusion

The DDA is—even in its watered-down form—the most ambitious trade negotiation since the failed attempt to create the International Trade Organization. This naturally makes the DDA even more susceptible to the so-called Curse of Geneva than previous rounds: issue complexity and expansion into development-related trade concerns have inevitably extended the duration of the negotiation.

To some extent, the difficulties of the DDA are a product of altered systemic and derivative institutional factors. The first systemic change with institutional consequences that this chapter identified was the change in the balance of power, while the second was the growing and unavoidable prominence of development concerns. Regarding the first, the growing power of the BICs in the international system, and the

WTO's responsiveness to these changes in the balance of power, have together introduced a multiplicity and diversity of voices into key decision-making forums. The most obvious way to retain the benefits of improved representativeness, inclusiveness, and transparency but address the problem of inefficiency is to introduce new decisionmaking procedures in the WTO. Old GATT-style consensus-based decision-making has perhaps outlived its utility in a world of multipolarity and diversity. The second systemic change—the growing prominence and legitimacy of development concerns across international organizations—has improved the legitimacy concerns associated with the WTO but has also taken the organization considerably beyond its area of expertise and mandate. This mission creep necessitates a careful rethinking of the mandate and capability of the WTO in relation to those of other international organizations and in the context of the broader issue of the coherence of global economic governance. Admittedly, both sets of reform measures to address these systemically-derived institutional issues will not happen overnight. More immediately, though, diplomatic solutions to the diplomatic problems identified in this chapter would also generate positive steps towards reaching agreement.

First, as has been argued in this chapter, a characteristic feature of the Doha diplomacy is that especially from the side of developing countries, it is conducted via coalitions. These coalitions are a source of great empowerment for the large emerging economies and also their weaker allies. But in an attempt to demonstrate the unity of their collective bargaining positions, developing countries using coalition diplomacy also find it harder to make concessions to reach agreement. Improved signalling mechanisms to convey one's bottom-lines with credibility would be an effective step towards facilitating a more conciliatory dynamic.[32] Second, normative framing was perhaps useful in the agenda-setting phase, but now concerns of development and fairness are deeply ingrained in the negotiation process. Rather than spend further time and effort grandstanding on ideas, it would now be more useful if all parties— developed and developing—were to bargain over specific interests. Third, we know that developed countries have been significantly less engaged on the DDA than developing countries. The reduction in normative framing will contribute to re-emphasising the gains that governments and lobbies stand to make from the DDA, over and above what RTAs have to offer them. Clear signals from all the major players—rather than the cheap talk that has been prevalent in G20 summitry—that they are committed to completing the DDA are also vital. Finally, the global economic downturn could be used to considerable advantage by politicians and negotiators. Amidst austerity measures worldwide, binding one's hands multilaterally offers governments the only safeguard against the temptation to resort to beggar-thy-neighbour policies. Visionary diplomats may still be able to use the financial crisis as a frame to emphasise the urgency of completing the DDA.

Table 48.1. Coalitions listed on the WTO website[1]

Groups	Description/issues	Countries
ACP	African, Caribbean, and Pacific countries with preferences in the EU	*WTO members (58):* Angola, Antigua and Barbuda, Barbados, Belize, Benin, Botswana, Burkina Faso, Burundi, Côte d'Ivoire, Cameroon, Cape Verde, Central African Republic, Chad, Congo, Cuba, Democratic Republic of the Congo, Djibouti, Dominica, Dominican Republic, Fiji, Gabon, Gambia, Ghana, Grenada, Guinea, Guinea Bissau, Guyana, Haiti, Jamaica, Kenya, Lesotho, Madagascar, Malawi, Mali, Mauritania, Mauritius, Mozambique, Namibia, Niger, Nigeria, Papua New Guinea, Rwanda, Saint Kitts and Nevis, Saint Lucia, Saint Vincent and the Grenadines, Senegal, Sierra Leone, Solomon Islands, South Africa, Suriname, Swaziland, Tanzania, Togo, Tonga, Trinidad and Tobago, Uganda, Zambia, Zimbabwe
	Issues: Agricultural preferences	*WTO observers (10):* Bahamas, Comoros, Equatorial Guinea, Ethiopia, Liberia, Samoa, Sao Tomé and Principe, Seychelles, Sudan, Vanuatu
	Nature: Geographical	
	Website: <www.acpsec.org>	*Not WTO members or observers (11):* Cook Islands, Eritrea, Kiribati, Marshall Islands, Micronesia (Federated States of), Nauru, Niue, Palau, Somalia, Timor-Leste, Tuvalu
African group	African members of the WTO	*WTO members (41):* Angola, Benin, Botswana, Burkina Faso, Burundi, Côte d'Ivoire, Cameroon, Cape Verde, Central African Republic, Chad, Congo, Djibouti, Egypt, Gabon, Gambia, Ghana, Guinea, Guinea Bissau, Kenya, Lesotho, Madagascar, Malawi, Mali, Mauritania, Mauritius, Morocco, Mozambique, Namibia, Niger, Nigeria, Rwanda, Senegal, Sierra Leone, South Africa, Swaziland, Tanzania, Togo, Tunisia, Uganda, Zambia, Zimbabwe
	Issues: General	
	Nature: Regional	
APEC	Asia-Pacific Economic Cooperation forum	*WTO members (20):* Australia, Brunei Darussalam, Canada, Chile, China, Chinese Taipei, Hong Kong, China, Indonesia, Japan, Korea (Republic of), Malaysia, Mexico, New Zealand, Papua New Guinea, Peru, Philippines, Singapore, Thailand, United States of America, Viet Nam
	Issues: General	*WTO observers (1):* Russian Federation
	Nature: Regional	
	Website: <www.apec.org>	

1. The WTO website lists the majority of the coalitions involved in the current negotiations on its web site, and further states the following: 'A number of countries have formed coalitions in the WTO. These groups often speak with one voice using a single coordinator or negotiating team. These are some of the most active groups in the WTO.' Accessed at <www.wto.org/english/tratop_e/dda_e/negotiating_groups_e.htm.>

EU	European Union	*WTO members (28):* Austria, Belgium, Bulgaria, Cyprus, Czech Republic, Denmark, Estonia, European Union (formerly EC), Finland, France, Germany, Greece, Hungary, Ireland, Italy, Latvia, Lithuania, Luxembourg, Malta, Netherlands, Poland, Portugal, Romania, Slovak Republic, Slovenia, Spain, Sweden, United Kingdom
	Issues: General	
	Nature: Customs union	
	Website: <http://ec.europa.eu>	
Mercosur	Common Market of the Southern Cone, a customs union (Mercosul in Portuguese)	*WTO members (4):* Argentina, Brazil, Paraguay, Uruguay
	Issues: General	
	Nature: Customs union	
	Website: <www.mercosur.int>	
G-90	African Group + ACP + least-developed countries	*WTO members (65):* Angola, Antigua and Barbuda, Bangladesh, Barbados, Belize, Benin, Botswana, Burkina Faso, Burundi, Côte d'Ivoire, Cambodia, Cameroon, Cape Verde, Central African Republic, Chad, Congo, Cuba, Democratic Republic of the Congo, Djibouti, Dominica, Dominican Republic, Egypt, Fiji, Gabon, Gambia, Ghana, Grenada, Guinea, Guinea Bissau, Guyana, Haiti, Jamaica, Kenya, Lesotho, Madagascar, Malawi, Maldives, Mali, Mauritania, Mauritius, Morocco, Mozambique, Myanmar, Namibia, Nepal, Niger, Nigeria, Papua New Guinea, Rwanda, Saint Kitts and Nevis, Saint Lucia, Saint Vincent and the Grenadines, Senegal, Sierra Leone, Solomon Islands, South Africa, Suriname, Swaziland, Tanzania, Togo, Trinidad and Tobago, Tunisia, Uganda, Zambia, Zimbabwe
	Issues: General	*WTO observers (14):* Afghanistan, Bahamas, Bhutan, Comoros, Equatorial Guinea, Ethiopia, Lao People's Democratic Republic, Liberia, Samoa, Sao Tomé and Principe, Seychelles, Sudan, Vanuatu, Yemen
		Not WTO members or observers (11): Cook Islands, Eritrea, Kiribati, Marshall Islands, Micronesia (Federated States of), Nauru, Niue, Palau, Somalia, Timor-Leste, Tuvalu

(Continued)

Table 48.1. (Continued)

Groups	Description/issues	Countries
Least-developed countries (LDCs)	Least-developed countries: the world's poorest countries. The WTO uses the UN list.	*WTO members (32):* Angola, Bangladesh, Benin, Burkina Faso, Burundi, Cambodia, Central African Republic, Chad, Democratic Republic of the Congo, Djibouti, Gambia, Guinea, Guinea Bissau, Haiti, Lesotho, Madagascar, Malawi, Maldives, Mali, Mauritania, Mozambique, Myanmar, Nepal, Niger, Rwanda, Senegal, Sierra Leone, Solomon Islands, Tanzania, Togo, Uganda, Zambia
	Issues: General	*WTO observers (12):* Afghanistan, Bhutan, Comoros Equatorial Guinea, Ethiopia, Lao People's Democratic,
	Website: <http://www.ldcgroups.org>	*Not WTO members or observers (5):* Eritrea, Kiribati, Somalia, Timor-Leste, Tuvalu
Small, vulnerable economies (SVEs)— agriculture	This list is based on sponsors of proposals. See also: list in Annex I of the 10 July 2008 revised draft agriculture modalities, and footnote 9 (paragraph 65) and paragraph 151.	*WTO members (14):* Barbados, Bolivia, Cuba, Dominican Republic, El Salvador, Fiji, Guatemala, Honduras, Mauritius, Mongolia, Nicaragua, Papua New Guinea, Paraguay, Trinidad and Tobago
	Issues: Agriculture	
Small, vulnerable economies (SVEs)—NAMA	This list is based on sponsors of proposals. See also: definition in paragraph 13 of the 10 July 2008 revised draft NAMA modalities.	*WTO members (19):* Antigua and Barbuda, Barbados, Bolivia, Dominica, Dominican Republic, El Salvador, Fiji, Grenada, Guatemala, Honduras, Jamaica,
	Issues: NAMA	Mongolia, Nicaragua, Papua New Guinea, Paraguay, Saint Kitts and Nevis, Saint Lucia, Saint Vincent and the Grenadines, Trinidad and Tobago
Small, vulnerable economies (SVEs)—rules	Sponsors of TN/RL/W/226/Rev.5	*WTO members (14):* Barbados, Cuba, Dominica, Dominican Republic, El Salvador, Fiji, Honduras, Jamaica, Mauritius, Nicaragua, Papua New Guinea, Saint Lucia, Saint Vincent and the Grenadines, Tonga
	Issues: Rules (fisheries subsidies)	
	Documents: TN/RL/W/226/Rev.5	

Recent new members (RAMs)	Recently acceded members (RAMs), i.e. countries that negotiated and joined the WTO after 1995, seeking lesser commitments in the negotiations because of the liberalization they have undertaken as part of their membership agreements. Excludes least-developed countries because they will make no new commitments, and EU members. *Issues*: General	*WTO members (19)*: Albania, Armenia, Cape Verde, China, Chinese Taipei, Croatia, Ecuador, Former Yugoslav Republic of Macedonia, Georgia, Jordan, Kyrgyz Republic, Moldova, Mongolia, Oman, Panama, Saudi Arabia (Kingdom of), Tonga, Ukraine, Viet Nam
Low income transition	Seeking to secure the same treatment as least-developed countries. (Georgia formally withdrew, but in the agriculture draft the full list is: Albania, Armenia, Georgia, Kyrgyz Rep, Moldova). *Issues*: Agriculture/NAMA	*WTO members (3)*: Armenia, Kyrgyz Republic, Moldova
Cairns group	Coalition of agricultural exporting nations lobbying for agricultural trade liberalization. *Issues*: Agriculture *Website*: http://www.cairnsgroup.org	*WTO members (19)*: Argentina, Australia, Bolivia, Brazil, Canada, Chile, Colombia, Costa Rica, Guatemala, Indonesia, Malaysia, New Zealand, Pakistan, Paraguay, Peru, Philippines, South Africa, Thailand, Uruguay

(Continued)

Table 48.1. (Continued)

Groups	Description/Issues	Countries
Tropical products	Coalition of developing countries seeking greater market access for tropical products. *Issues:* Agriculture	*WTO members (8):* Bolivia, Colombia, Costa Rica, Ecuador, Guatemala, Nicaragua, Panama, Peru
G-10	Coalition of countries lobbying for agriculture to be treated as diverse and special because of non-trade concerns (not to be confused with the Group of Ten Central Bankers). *Issues:* Agriculture	*WTO members (9):* Chinese Taipei, Iceland, Israel, Japan, Korea (Republic of), Liechtenstein, Mauritius, Norway, Switzerland
G-20	Coalition of developing countries pressing for ambitious reforms of agriculture in developed countries with some flexibility for developing countries (not to be confused with the G-20 group of finance ministers and central bank governors, and its recent summit meetings). *Issues:* Agriculture *Website:* <http://www.g-20.mre.gov.br>	*WTO members (23):* Argentina, Bolivia, Brazil, Chile, China, Cuba, Ecuador, Egypt, Guatemala, India, Indonesia, Mexico, Nigeria, Pakistan, Paraguay, Peru, Philippines, South Africa, Tanzania, Thailand, Uruguay, Venezuela (Bolivarian Republic of), Zimbabwe
G-33	Also called 'Friends of Special Products' in agriculture. Coalition of developing countries pressing for flexibility for developing countries to undertake limited market opening in agriculture. *Issues:* Agriculture	*WTO members (46):* Antigua and Barbuda, Barbados, Belize, Benin, Bolivia, Botswana, Côte d'Ivoire, China, Congo, Cuba, Dominica, Dominican Republic, El Salvador, Grenada, Guatemala, Guyana, Haiti, Honduras, India, Indonesia, Jamaica, Kenya, Korea (Republic of), Madagascar, Mauritius, Mongolia, Mozambique, Nicaragua, Nigeria, Pakistan, Panama, Peru, Philippines, Saint Kitts and Nevis, Saint Lucia, Saint Vincent and the Grenadines, Senegal, Sri Lanka, Suriname, Tanzania, Trinidad and Tobago, Turkey, Uganda, Venezuela (Bolivarian Republic of), Zambia, Zimbabwe

Cotton-4	West African coalition seeking cuts in cotton subsidies and tariffs. *Issues:* Agriculture (Cotton)	*WTO members (4):* Benin, Burkina Faso, Chad, Mali
NAMA-11	Coalition of developing countries seeking flexibilities to limit market opening in industrial goods trade. *Issues:* NAMA	*WTO members (10):* Argentina, Brazil, Egypt, India, Indonesia, Namibia, Philippines, South Africa, Tunisia, Venezuela (Bolivarian Republic of)
Paragraph 6 (NAMA)	In NAMA (refers to paragraph 6 of the first version of the NAMA text), for reducing the number of new bindings they would have to contribute and to increase the average target from 27.5%. (Except Macao, China.) *Issues:* NAMA	*WTO members (12):* Côte d'Ivoire, Cameroon, Congo, Cuba, Ghana, Kenya, Macao, China, Mauritius, Nigeria, Sri Lanka, Suriname, Zimbabwe
Friends of Ambition (NAMA)	Seeking to maximize tariff reductions and achieve real market access in NAMA. (Some nuanced differences in positions.) *Issues:* NAMA	*WTO members (36):* Australia, Austria, Belgium, Bulgaria, Canada, Cyprus, Czech Republic, Denmark, Estonia, European Union (formerly EC), Finland, France, Germany, Greece, Hungary, Ireland, Italy, Japan, Korea (Republic of), Latvia, Lithuania, Luxembourg, Malta, Netherlands, New Zealand, Norway, Poland, Portugal, Romania, Slovak Republic, Slovenia, Spain, Sweden, Switzerland, United Kingdom, United States of America
Middle Ground Group (NAMA)	Moderate ambition, seeking to improve market access into both developed and developing countries. *Issues:* NAMA	*WTO members (12):* Chile, Colombia, Costa Rica, Hong Kong, China, Israel, Malaysia, Mexico, Morocco, Pakistan, Peru, Singapore, Thailand

(Continued)

Table 48.1. (Continued)

Groups	Description/issues	Countries
Friends of A-D Negotiations (FANs)	Coalition seeking more disciplines on the use of anti-dumping measures. *Issues:* Rules (anti-dumping)	*WTO members (15):* Brazil, Chile, Chinese Taipei, Colombia, Costa Rica, Hong Kong, China, Israel, Japan, Korea (Republic of), Mexico, Norway, Singapore, Switzerland, Thailand, Turkey
Friends of Fish (FoFs)	Coalition seeking to significantly reduce fisheries subsidies. Previously included Ecuador, Philippines. *Issues:* Rules (fisheries subsidies)	*WTO members (10):* Argentina, Australia, Chile, Colombia, Iceland, New Zealand, Norway, Pakistan, Peru, United States of America
'W52' sponsors	Sponsors of TN/C/W/52, a proposal for 'modalities' in negotiations on geographical indications (the multilateral register for wines and spirits, and extending the higher level of protection beyond wines and spirits) and 'disclosure' (patent applicants to disclose the origin of genetic resources and traditional knowledge used in the inventions). The list includes as groups: the EU, ACP, and African Group.* Dominican Rep. is in the ACP and South Africa is in the African Group, but they are sponsors of TN/IP/W/10/Rev.2 on geographical indications. *Issues:* Intellectual property (TRIPS) *Documents:* TN/C/W/52	*WTO members (109):* Albania, Angola, Antigua and Barbuda, Austria, Barbados, Belgium, Belize, Benin, Botswana, Brazil, Bulgaria, Burkina Faso, Burundi, Côte d'Ivoire, Cameroon, Cape Verde, Central African Republic, Chad, China, Colombia, Congo, Croatia, Cuba, Cyprus, Czech Republic, Democratic Republic of the Congo, Denmark, Djibouti, Dominica, Dominican Republic, Ecuador, Egypt, Estonia, European Union (formerly EC), Fiji, Finland, Former Yugoslav Republic of Macedonia, France, Gabon, Gambia, Georgia, Germany, Ghana, Greece, Grenada, Guinea, Guinea Bissau, Guyana, Haiti, Hungary, Iceland, India, Indonesia, Ireland, Italy, Jamaica, Kenya, Kyrgyz Republic, Latvia, Lesotho, Liechtenstein, Lithuania, Luxembourg, Madagascar, Malawi, Mali, Malta, Mauritania, Mauritius, Moldova, Morocco, Mozambique, Namibia, Netherlands, Niger, Nigeria, Pakistan, Papua New Guinea, Peru, Poland, Portugal, Romania, Rwanda, Saint Kitts and Nevis, Saint Lucia, Saint Vincent and the Grenadines, Senegal, Sierra Leone, Slovak Republic, Slovenia, Solomon Islands, South Africa, Spain, Sri Lanka, Suriname, Swaziland, Sweden, Switzerland, Tanzania, Thailand, Togo, Tonga, Trinidad and Tobago, Tunisia, Turkey, Uganda, United Kingdom, Zambia, Zimbabwe

| Joint proposal | Sponsors of TN/IP/W/10/Rev.2 proposing a database that is entirely voluntary.

Issues: TRIPS GI register

Website: <www.wto.org/english/tratop_e/trips_e/gi_background_e.htm>

Documents: TN/IP/W/10/Rev.2 | *WTO members (19):* Argentina, Australia, Canada, Chile, Chinese Taipei, Costa Rica, Dominican Republic, Ecuador, El Salvador, Guatemala, Honduras, Japan, Korea (Republic of), Mexico, New Zealand, Nicaragua, Paraguay, South Africa, United States of America |

Source: www.wto.org

Notes

1. Robert E. Baldwin, *Non Tariff Distortions to International Trade* (Washington DC: Brookings, 1970); Bernard Hoekman, 'Focal Points in Multilateral Negotiations on the Contestability of Markets', in Keith Maskus, Peter Hooper, Edward Learner, and David Richardson (eds), *Quiet Pioneering: Robert M. Stern and his International Economic Legacy* (Ann Arbor: University of Michigan Press, 1998).

2. Games of brinkmanship can be dangerous to play. In March 2006, Pascal Lamy announced: 'We approach the moment of truth', as he referred to the deadline of the negotiations that were intended to be completed at the end of 2006 (as renegotiated at the Hong Kong ministerial 2005). On 28 June 2006, he reiterated at a press conference: 'It is the moment of truth. I don't think we can postpone the decision anymore.' In March 2007, after negotiations were resumed, at a speech in Mexico City, he declared that the negotiations were in their 'final stretch', albeit admitting that 'as in so many human endeavours, the last part is the most difficult'. In his report to the General Council on 5 February 2008, he said 'we are on the last lap and we have now started the final sprint towards establishing modalities'. In the run-up to the July Package negotiations of 2008, at a speech on 5 June, he again declared, 'we are getting to the moment of truth'. And then, reproducing for his audience a sense of more déjà vu, in an attempt to resolve differences in April 2009 to facilitate an agreement, he stated, 'In politics, as in life, there is always a moment when intentions and reality face the test of truth. We are nearly there today.' At the time of writing this paper, i.e. December 2011, the round had still not been concluded. For a selection of the DG's speeches, see <www.wto.org/english/news_e/sppl_e/sppl_e.htm>.

3. On the benefits of the DDA, see for instance Bernard Hoekman, Will Martin, and Aaditya Mattoo, 'Conclude Doha: It Matters!', *World Trade Review* 9:3 (2010), 505–30.

4. Richard E. Baldwin and Simon Evenett, 'Introduction and Recommendations for the G20', in Richard Baldwin and Simon Evenett (eds), *The Collapse of Global Trade, Murky Protectionism, and the Crisis: Recommendations for the G20* (London: CEPR and Voxeu. org, 2009).

5. Simon Evenett, *Trade Tensions Mount: 10th GTA Report*, Executive Summary, p. 1, accessed at <www.globaltradealert.org/gta-analysis/trade-tensions-mount-10th-gta-report>.

6. The popular acronym of the BRICs was coined by Jim O'Neill of Goldman Sachs. South Africa has recently been included in the grouping. The analysis in this chapter does not include Russia as it completed its accession process to the WTO only as recently as November 2011. For more on the BRICs, see Jim O'Neill, Roopa Purushothaman, and Dominic, Wilson, *Dreaming with the BRICS: The Path to 2050* (Goldman Sachs, Global Economics Paper 99, 2003), <www.gs.com/insight/research/reports/99.pdf>.

7. International Trade Statistics, <www.wto.org>.

8. Amrita Narlikar, 'New Powers in the Club: The Challenges of Global Trade Governance', *International Affairs* 86:3 (May 2010), 717–28.

9. Amrita Narlikar, *New Powers: How to become one and how to manage them* (New York: Columbia University Press, 2010).

10. Sylvia Ostry, *The Uruguay Round North-South Grand Bargain: Implications for Future Negotiations*, Political Economy of International Trade Law, University of Minnesota (September 2000); available at <http://www.utoronto.ca/cis/ostry.html>.

11. Amrita Narlikar and John Odell, 'The Strict Distributive Strategy for a Bargaining Coalition: The Like Minded Group in the World Trade Organization', in John Odell (ed.),

Negotiating Trade: Developing Countries in the WTO and NAFTA (Cambridge: Cambridge University Press, 2006); Narlikar, 'New Powers in the Club'.

12. This section draws on the analysis presented in detail in Amrita Narlikar, 'Collective Agency, Systemic Consequences: Bargaining Coalitions in the WTO', in Amrita Narlikar, Martin Daunton, and Robert M. Stern (eds), *The Oxford Handbook on the World Trade Organization* (Oxford: Oxford University Press, 2012).

13. For works on coalitions in the GATT, see Amrita Narlikar, *International Trade and Developing Countries: Bargaining Coalitions in the GATT and WTO* (London: Routledge, 2003); Richard Higgot Andrew Cooper, 'Middle Power Leadership and Coalition Building: Australia, the Cairns Group, and the Uruguay Round of Trade Negotiations', *International Organization* 44:4 (1990), 589–632; Colleen Hamilton and John Whalley, 'Coalitions in the Uruguay Round', *Weltwirtschaftliches Archiv* 125:3 (1989), 547–56.

14. For the theoretical and empirical analysis of coalitions in the GATT and the WTO, see Narlikar, *International Trade and Developing Countries*.

15. Narlikar and Odell, 'Strict Distributive Strategy'; Narlikar, *International Trade and Developing Countries*.

16. This point was first made in Hamilton and Whalley, 'Coalitions in the Uruguay Round'.

17. For one of the first analyses of the Doha coalitions, see Amrita Narlikar and Diana Tussie, 'The G20 at the Cancun Ministerial: Developing countries and their evolving coalitions in the WTO', *The World Economy* 27:7 (July 2004), 947–66.

18. For the membership composition of these coalitions, see Table 48.1 in the appendix.

19. Faizel Ismail, 'Reflections on the July 2008 Collapse', in Amrita Narlikar and Brendan Vickers (eds), *Leadership and Change in the Multilateral Trading System* (Leiden: Martinus Nijhoff; Dordrecht: Republic of Letters Publishing, 2009); Narlikar and Tussie, 'The G20 at the Cancun Ministerial'.

20. Bernard Hoekman, *Cancún: Crisis or Catharsis?* (September 20), <http:// siteresources. worldbank.org/ . . . /Hoekman-CancunCatharsis-092003.pdf>. Also for a legal analysis of coalitions see Sonia Rolland, 'Developing Country Coalitions at the WTO: In Search of Legal Support', *Harvard International Law Journal* 48:2 (2007), 483–551.

21. Ismail, 'Reflections on the July 2008 Collapse'; Amrita Narlikar, 'A Theory of Bargaining Coalitions', in Amrita Narlikar and Brendan Vickers (eds), *Leadership and Change in the Multilateral Trading System* (Leiden: Martinus Nijhoff, 2009).

22. See <www.wto.org> for details of these processes, and also Mateo Diego-Fernandez, 'Trade Negotiations make Strange Bedfellows', *World Trade Review* 7:2 (2008), 423–53 and Ismail, 'Reflections on the July 2008 Collapse', for useful accounts by practitioners.

23. John Odell and Susan Sell, 'Reframing the Issue: The WTO Coalition on TRIPs and Public Health, 2001', in John Odell (ed.), *Negotiating Trade: Developing Countries in the WTO and NAFTA* (Cambridge: Cambridge University Press, 2006).

24. Andrew Gamble, 'The Politics of Deadlock', in Amrita Narlikar (ed.), *Deadlocks in Multilateral Negotiations: Causes and Solutions* (Cambridge: Cambridge University Press, 2010).

25. Max Bazerman and Margaret Neale, 'The Role of Fairness Considerations and Relationships in a Judgemental Perspective of Negotiations', in Kenneth Arrow, Robert Mnokin, and Amos Tversky (eds), *Barriers to Conflict Resolution* (New York: W.W. Norton, 1995).

26. Narlikar, 'New Powers in the Club'.

27. The finger-pointing began in 2003 with the failure of the Cancun ministerial, and has continued largely unabated, with Susan Schwab writing the following in 2011: 'At Doha, these

emerging economies have minimized their own difficult market-opening decisions by seeking maximum flexibility for developing countries. And they have found it easier to avoid confronting their own needs for greater access to one another's markets by focusing on what they can all agree on—namely, the market-opening obligations of developed countries. The result is what one African ambassador to the WTO once described as "the elephants hiding behind the mice".' See SusanSchwab, 'After Doha: why the negotiations are doomed, and what we should do about it', *Foreign Affairs* 90:3 (2011), 96–103.

28. Jagdish Bhagwati, 'Deadlock in Durban: Will COP-17 Produce Substance?', *Economic Times*, 2 December 2011, <http://articles.economictimes.indiatimes.com/2011-12-02/news/30467869_1_climate-change-climate-change-kyoto-protocol>.

29. Amrita Narlikar and Pieter van Houten, 'Know the Enemy: Uncertainty and Deadlock in the WTO', in Amrita Narlikar (ed.), *Deadlocks in Multilateral Negotiations: Causes and Solutions* (Cambridge: Cambridge University Press, 2010).

30. Warwick Commission, *The Multilateral Trade Regime: Which Way Forward? The Report of the First Warwick Commission* (Coventry: University of Warwick, 2007).

31. Simon Evenett, 'Receiprocity and the Doha Round Impasse: Lessons for the Near Term and After' (2007), <www.crei.cat/activities/sc_conferences/33/Papers/**Evenett**.pdf>.

32. Narlikar and Van Houten, 'Know the Enemy'. Amrita Narlikar, 'Collective Agency, Systemic Consequences: Bargaining Coalitions in the WTO', in Amrita Narlikar, Martin Daunton, and Robert Stern (eds), *The Oxford Handbook on the WTO* (Oxford: Oxford University Press, 2012). A more ambitious solution would be an institutionalization of coalitions; see Rolland, 'Developing Country Coalitions at the WTO'; Narlikar, 'A Theory of Bargaining Coalitions'.

CHAPTER 49

THE ECONOMIC DIPLOMACY OF THE RISING POWERS

GREGORY CHIN[*]

THIS chapter examines the economic diplomacy of the BRIC rising powers. Whereas the tendency in the literature is to treat the 'BRICs' countries (i.e. Brazil, Russia, India, and China) as a bloc or a collective 'threat',[1] the approach taken here is to instead analyse how the differing diplomatic styles of the BRIC states have produced a range of international outcomes, some trending towards interstate rivalry, and others more cooperative. Such analysis combines the agency of economic diplomacy with the structural determinants of political economy. In this chapter, we give special attention to how the differing diplomatic cultures of the rising powers have been brought together in complementary ways to achieve shared foreign policy goals.

In section 49.1 we discuss how the intellectual problem of the rising powers has been studied heretofore in the predominant literature, and argue instead for a political economy interpretation of how the global financial crisis (2007–2009) has induced mutual socialization and learning between the BRIC states, as rising powers. We turn in section 49.2 to the differences in the diplomatic cultures of Brazil and China in particular, and assess their respective national diplomatic styles. In section 49.3 we analyse how the differing diplomatic approaches of Brazil and China have coalesced, in combination with support from India and Russia, for common foreign policy goals, particularly Bretton Woods reform.

The analyses highlights that diplomacy is both an *instrument* of foreign policy for states, and a *learning* or *socializing* process that fosters change in the international behaviour of states.[2] The diplomatic interventions of the BRIC states further provide a *midrange* indication of their future roles in the politics of the world economy.

49.1 THE RISING POWERS AS CONCEPT

What do we mean by 'rising powers'—how useful is the concept? To what degree, or in what ways, is this abstraction generalizable from particular national instances? In the burgeoning literature on the 'rising powers', 'emerging powers', and 'would-be great powers', there is a tendency to treat the BRICs as a generic group, or a bloc, that exhibits similarities, or enough shared characteristics to classify them as a collective phenomenon. This practice started in 2001 when Jim O'Neil of Goldman Sachs first coined the term 'BRICs' to classify the most dynamic economies for the foreseeable future into a grouping, as a sound bet for financial investors. Eventually, the BRIC countries themselves gave legitimacy to the narrative when Brazil agreed to join Russia, India, and China at the Russian city of Yekaterinburg in June 2009 for the inaugural BRICs summit, and when South Africa joined the club in April 2011 for the first 'BRICS' summit in Hainan Island, China.[3] As a consultative forum, the BRICS summits and their related ministerial meetings have grown into a regularized process of international policy coordination that parallels the gatherings of the Group of Eight ('G8') traditional powers. Russia is the only country that is a member of the G8, and also of the BRIC.

Although there is still no widely accepted definition of 'rising powers', some criteria are commonly featured. The most frequent is their growing weight in the world economy. In the academic literature, some studies stand out for their persuasiveness in depicting a collection of rising powers. In a 2006 article, Hurrell[4] suggests that a group of 'would-be-great powers' have four attributes in common, in addition to economic heft: first, a relatively high degree of hard power capacity or potential, with sufficient national political cohesion to affect global change; second, ambition to exert more regional or global influence; third, growing ties with other rising powers; and fourth, a lack of full integration or 'buy-in' to the Western liberal order. While Hurrell does acknowledge the particularities of the individual countries, he argues convincingly that there is enough commonality across the national cases to draw broader generalizations. Narlikar[5] similarly sees the 'new powers', specifically Brazil and India, as different from China for their potential willingness to integrate into the existing order, but focuses ultimately on advising more generically on 'how to be one [a new power], and how to manage them'. Ikenberry[6] writes of 'new power centers' in the liberal international order, and the Unites States needing to reconstruct the global institutions of the 'Liberal Leviathan', to better incorporate the rising 'non-western powers'. In the related literature, the lexicon of terms such as 'BRICSAM', 'BASIC', and 'CIBS' also suggest that a grouping of nations are *collectively* reshaping the global map of the 21st century.[7]

We see frequent usage of the term 'rising powers' in the think-tank literature. In an early *Reader* from the Center for International and Strategic Studies, Lennon and Kozlowski[8] discuss a group of 'major powers' who were seeking to strengthen their presence on the global stage. The sceptics of engaging the rising powers refer to these states in a general sense. For example, in an article in *Foreign Affairs* magazine (2010), former

Mexican Foreign Minister Jorge Castenada argues that the 'emerging powers' share the quality of being 'the prime candidates' for inclusion in a retooled international order; but they are 'not ready for prime time'.[9] Patrick at the Council on Foreign Relations in Washington, DC, similarly observes a group of rising powers in a piece entitled 'Irresponsible Stakeholders',[10] and emphasises the difficulties of 'bringing-in' these nations into existing arrangements. Shorr from The Stanley Foundation rebuts the sceptics, arguing the US has little choice but to keep close-by this group of 'potential defectors' from the system.[11] Jones at the Brookings Institution analyses the collective threat from the 'rise of the rest' and adds the nuance that 'the United States confronts not a rigid bloc of emerging powers, but complex and shifting coalitions of interest'.[12] He concludes, nonetheless, that the redistribution of influence attached to the simultaneous rise of Brazil, China, and India 'carries risks for the U.S., even if Ikenberry is correct in stating that they are rising within the existing international order'.

In contrast to the aforementioned academic studies, which tend to emphasise the shared characteristics of the BRICs states, and the think-tank literature that frames the debate in terms of 'collective threat' to American supremacy, the approach taken in this chapter is to examine how the shared global economic concerns and differences of diplomatic style between the BRIC countries have coalesced in complimentary ways to achieve shared foreign policy goals among the rising states. The analyses of international financial reform expands upon previous studies of international coordination between India, Brazil, and China in world trade negotiations, and research on how the diplomatic idiosyncrasies of the respective rising states have been leveraged for shared objectives.[13]

49.1.1 Shared Global Concerns

The global financial crisis that started in 2007 exposed flaws in the existing system of global economic governance. It drew a spotlight on the fact that the global architecture—the Bretton Woods institutions—that was first created six decades ago to manage the world economy had proved ineffective during the most severe financial crisis since the Great Depression of the 1930s. In the BRICs countries and across the South, analysts drew the source of the failure to the inability of the Group of Seven (G7) countries to lead.

The severity of the crisis in the advanced economies brought into question the assumptions and rules of the global financial order, as well as norms and procedures of global integration that were held as sacrosanct in recent decades.[14] The freefall of Anglo-American finance from 2007–2009, and the ongoing troubles of European finance, have brought about a return to the big themes of world order, hegemony, capitalism, democracy, and culture/identity,[15] and the emergence of newer challenges such as climate change and corruption. The answers, and the international leadership needed to address the issues, are no longer obvious.

The global economic crisis put the rising powers face to face with unprecedented foreign policy challenges. It has been a long time since Brazil, India, and China have taken a *proactive* stance in global affairs, and looked to reshape the dominant norms and ideas of international society. For most of the 1970s, China and India pursued self-sufficient development paths. Brazil was an active participant in the 'North—South' negotiations of the period, and in the Southern demands for a 'new international economic order'. However, for two generations, China, India, and Brazil had largely *reacted* to the ideas of global governance which were advanced by other states.

The global posture of the rising powers has changed during the past decade. Especially since the global financial crisis, the BRICs states have found that it will not do anymore to simply react to ideas produced in Washington, New York, or London. As they have become more integrated into the global economy, the rising states—out of necessity—have been compelled to be more proactive, more involved in finding solutions to the worsening financial turmoil, and the downturn in the world economy. As their economic weight has increased, so have the expectations from other states that the new powers will take on more global responsibilities.[16] As the rising powers have joined the global 'high table', BRICs diplomacy is being pushed beyond pre-existing modes of thought and behaviour.

49.2 CONTRASTING DIPLOMATIC CULTURES

The shared historical experiences of Brazil, China, and India in overcoming economic backwardness, poverty reduction, and anti-colonial struggle have resulted in commonalities in their diplomacy. 'Anti-hegemony' is a shared overarching sentiment, as well as a continuing desire to self-identify with 'the South'. Governments in each of these countries have been attuned to protecting their sovereignty and autonomy while pursuing national development. They are sceptical of universalist models such as the so-called 'Washington Consensus'. Leaders in all three countries equate going to the International Monetary Fund (IMF) for emergency liquidity with humiliation.

The diplomatic cultures of Brazil, China, and India have placed a premium on 'respect for sovereignty', 'equal treatment', and 'peaceful means' for resolving interstate conflicts. However, these nations also exhibit marked differences in their diplomatic styles, and the particularities *also* define their economic diplomacy in profound ways.

49.2.1 Brazil's Can-Do Style

One of the characteristics of Brazilian diplomacy is activism and robust style, which contrasts sharply with China's measured 'cool-headed' diplomacy. Analysts have written of a new era of Brazilian diplomacy, emerging from 'the Lula era', and Brazil's more prominent stance in the international arena. *The Economist* magazine has gone so far as to call Brazil a 'diplomatic giant'.

It is not hubris to suggest that Brazilian diplomacy has learned how to ride the wave of Brazil's rise over the past two decades, where the country has achieved *quality* growth, pulled millions out of poverty and into the middle class, increased access for more of the population to higher education or technical training, become a large and diversified economy, brought order to the domestic fiscal situation, kept inflation under control, opened new export markets (with China a key export market for Brazil's natural resources and commodities), reduced and domesticated sovereign debt, improved overall income distribution—while strengthening a vibrant democracy.[17] Brazilian authorities, with support from key national developmental institutions such as *Banco nacional do desenvolvimento* (BNDES, Brazil's national development bank) and *Embrapa* (The Brazilian Agricultural Research Center), have created space for Brazil's leading firms such as Petrobras, Vale, and billionaire Eike Batista's LLX Logistica, to grow into global contenders.

What are the origins of Brazil's diplomatic rise? The rise of Brazilian diplomacy is the result of a conjuncture of external interventions and internal strengths. Some factors are objective, structural, such as Brazil's dramatic and sustained growth of the past two decades.[18] Credit must also go to the organizational capacities of the Brazilian foreign ministry—'Itamarty'—for selecting and cultivating a cadre of high-calibre diplomats to represent the country. Other factors are more subjective. Brazil's recent former Foreign Minister, Celso Amorim[19] has noted (2011) that Brazil suffered historically from a lack of self-esteem, and a diplomatic culture that was hamstrung by excessive caution and self-reinforced inhibitions.[20] This tradition constrained 'bolder-than-usual' and innovative diplomacy, even during the 'independent foreign policy' period of Janio Quadros and Joao Goulart, and into the Geisel-Silveira period. According to Amorim, this disposition re-emerged periodically during the Lula period: 'We had a preconceived notion of our place in the world and our ability to influence international events.'[21] In contrast, the 'imaginative' diplomacy of the presidency of Luiz Inacio Lula da Silva elevated Brazil's regional and global profile. At the same time, the critics of Lula have not relented in their criticism of Brazil's diplomatic ambitions under Lula.

From the start of the Lula presidency, Brazilian authorities and its diplomats began to demonstrate that they would no longer be self-constrained by overly cautious foreign policy or timid diplomacy. An early indication was the Lula administration's opposition to the Iraq invasion. Leading government officials, including President Lula da Silva, Amorim, and the critical legal scholar Roberto Mangabeira Unger (who served as Minister of Strategic Affairs), explain that the shift in the country's diplomacy did not happen overnight; that it was preconditioned by important subterranean changes in Brazilian society, that resulted from a lengthy process of democratic maturation and rising self-confidence within the Brazilian people. In other words, the 'can-do' attitude of Brazilian foreign policy and diplomacy is the result of a political movement that started with the successful impeachment of President Collor in 1992, and taming inflation in 1994. People slowly started to believe that the political system could be a vehicle for positive change, and the demonstration effect of the reforms introduced by the Cardoso governments (1995–2003), and then the Lula presidencies (2003–2010) reinforced the mindset.

Brazil's can-do diplomacy mirrors the *transformational* and *imaginative* state of mind of the populace at large. Brazilian diplomats transferred this mood into concrete actions to influence regional arrangements and the global scene. Societal transformation thus lays behind the transition to a more proactive diplomatic agenda. Examples include the derailment of the most powerful actor in the hemisphere, the United States, when it tried to establish a Free Trade Area of the Americas (FTAA), in which Brazil did not overtly obstruct, but rather sought to *redefine* the terms of the agreement to give Brazil and the other signatories more autonomy to define their own development path. This goal was consistent with Brazil's aforementioned foreign policy principles of non-intervention and maintaining national developmental control.[22]

In 2003, the Lula administration asserted Brazil's role in the global arena at the WTO ministerial negotiations in Cancún, Mexico. Brazilian diplomats worked proactively with other developing nations in a joint diplomatic, coalitional effort to avert a protectionist treaty, which, if passed, would have legally sanctioned large subsidies for European and US farmers.[23] Diplomatic success led to the formation of the 'G-20 Trade' group, with a mandate to negotiate on agricultural matters in the Doha Round of trade negotiations.

Brazilian diplomats also translated the atmosphere of domestic transformation into promoting 'regional solidarity' and new global caucusing mechanisms between the rising powers, namely the 'IBSA' Dialogue Forum and the BRICS (discussed later). Another initiative was transforming South America into a 'Peace Zone'. Brazil attempted to re-inject confidence in Mercusor. The Lula administration built on earlier plans from the Cardoso period (2000), to initiate the twelve-nation process that became the Union of South American Nations (UNASUR), which runs the length of the continent from Columbia to Argentina. UNASUR's core foundations are trade and economic agreements, but it has also developed a political component in facilitating region-wide responses to the global financial crisis, and regional coordination in meeting human health needs such as HIV-AIDs vaccines. At the Sauipe summit in Bahia, Brazil in March 2009, the UNASUR 'spirit' of regional cooperation was extended to encompass all of Latin America *and* the Caribbean nations. US diplomats noted, at the time, how this two-day multi-summit illustrated that the Brazilian government is 'able and willing to exercise increasingly visible regional leadership, with an eye toward gaining legitimacy as the principal regional representative on the global stage'.[24]

Also at the global level, starting in the first years of the Lula administration, Brazil established and strengthened new strategic partnership arrangements with China, India, South Africa, and Russia. Brazilian diplomats were active in creating platforms and channels for international cooperation between the rising powers, such as the aforementioned IBSA—a mechanism for encouraging cooperation and diplomatic consultation between India, Brazil, and South Africa. Brazil also established a summit process between Arab countries and South America, and one for African countries and South America. Involvement in BRICS summitry has associated Brazil with the world's rising economies. Its other strategic initiatives with other emerging countries, such as Turkey, and their joint intervention in Middle East conflict management led the European Union and the US to take notice of Brazil's role in international security. Much of the diplomatic effort on the security side was tied to Brasilia's desire to gain permanent membership in the UN Security Council.

In brief, as a result of their imaginative foreign policy, and proactive diplomacy, Brazilian diplomats have strengthened the image of Brazil as a nation with influence and interests, within its region and beyond.

49.2.2 China's 'Principled, Cool-Headed' Diplomacy

The long sweep of China's diplomatic quest over the modern period has been defined by the goal of 'returning China to its rightful place', and in this regard, China has achieved considerable diplomatic success during the last six decades. Not unlike Brazil, China's recent strong economic performance and its particular organizational advantages have been leveraged diplomatically for foreign policy gains. Beijing has created space for China's rise; not an easy task considering the added burden of dealing with 'China threat' perceptions on the part of its regional neighbours, and the US, and Europe.

Chinese diplomatic theorists suggest that the systems, practices, and forms of diplomacy that China follows today are generally those which are accepted by the international community, with roots in European tradition. However, Chinese diplomatic scholars also emphasise that modern China has made 'special contributions' to world diplomacy, since the founding of the People's Republic (1949), under the 'direct leadership' of Mao Zedong, Zhou En-lai, Deng Xiaoping, and Jiang Zemin. Huang[25] highlights 'distinct characteristics' of Chinese diplomacy such as the 'two combinations': the 'perfect and adroit combination' of consistency in principle and flexibility in tactics; and the 'perfect and correct combination' of internationalism and patriotism.

One of the characteristics of Chinese diplomacy, in contrast to Brazil for instance, is a high degree of continuity. The Chinese diplomatic norm of 'consistency in principle, and flexibility in tactics', has placed strong emphasis on highlighting continuity in foreign policy principles and diplomatic practice since the establishment of 'new China' in 1949. The model of professional diplomatic conduct remains that of the legendary Premier Zhou En-lai. Chinese diplomats continue to hearken back to Zhou's 'new China' diplomatic model—that China follows a 'general foreign policy of peace', and takes a 'principled approach' to foreign affairs. Zhou En-lai[26] emphasised: 'Comrade Mao Zedong announced that we would establish diplomatic relations with foreign countries on the basis of equality, mutual benefit and mutual respect for territorial integrity and sovereignty.'[27] Chinese diplomats continue to reiterate that China's foreign relations are guided by the 'Five Principles for Peaceful Coexistence', first worked out in the early 1950s to engage a newly independent India, and credited to Premier Zhou: (1) mutual respect for sovereignty and territorial integrity; (2) mutual non-aggression; (3) non-interference in each other's internal affairs; (4) equality and mutual benefit; and (5) peaceful coexistence. Chinese diplomats remain steadfast that 'all unresolved problems can be discussed, providing the negotiators abide by these principles.'[28]

The latest iteration of the Chinese Communist Party's foreign policy line and the basic diplomatic posture was outlined by Party General Secretary and State President Hu Jintao in his 'Report at the Seventeenth Party Congress' in October 2007:

> The Chinese nation is a peace-loving people, and China is always a staunch force *safe-guarding world peace*. We are committed to combining the interests of the Chinese people with the common interests of the people of other countries, and always stand for *fairness and justice*. We maintain that all countries, big and small, strong and weak, rich and poor, are *equal*. We *respect* the right of the people of all countries to independently choose their own development path. We will *never interfere* in the internal affairs of other countries *or impose our own will* on them. China works for peaceful settlement of international disputes and hotspot issues, promotes international and regional security cooperation, and opposes terrorism in any form. China follows a *national defence policy* that is *defensive* in nature, and it does not engage in arms race or pose a military threat to any other country. China *opposes* all forms of *hegemonism* and power politics and *will never seek hegemony* or engage in expansion.[29]

In other words, together with continuity in policy, China's leaders have consistently emphasised diplomatic traits such as non-aggression, non-aggressiveness, being respectful and modest when engaging other countries, big and small.

In addition to continuity, Chinese diplomatic culture places a premium on being 'cool-headed' when facing a world of swirling developments. For example, when former Foreign Minister Li Zhaoxing was asked, 'What are China's major diplomatic achievements this year in the complex and changing international environment?', he answered: 'This year, led by the Chinese Government and with the support of the Chinese people, we have, with the firm belief that the conduct of diplomacy should serve the people and China's national interest, responded to changes in international developments in a *cool-headed way* and properly handled difficult issues.'[30] For Chinese diplomats, having a 'cool-headed' approach means having the patience, confidence, and the strategic intelligence to 'play the long game' in world affairs, as well as at the personal level, engaging in a non-ostentatious style, with diligent effort, and focusing on far-sighted goals for self-motivation.

The strong emphasis placed on a 'principled approach', combined with so-called cool-headedness has resulted in a *highly formalistic style* as the norm in Chinese diplomatic practice. China's diplomats have often given the impression at international meetings that they are sticking close to Beijing's rule-book. As the venerable Premier Zhou instructed: 'Since diplomats represent the state, they should always bear in mind the collective interest. It would be very dangerous if they proceeded from their personal interests...We should never allow personal considerations to intervene in diplomatic work.'[31] He added:

> We emphasize the conscientious observance of *discipline* in the interest of the Party. We cannot permit any liberalism. *Irresponsible remarks* and acts will cause *trouble*. Diplomacy deals with relations between states, so in this work we *should ask for instructions before making statements* and submitting reports afterwards...it's *better not to say too much*...We can be flexible to some degree, providing we keep to certain principles...there's nothing wrong with postponing dealing with certain new problems: when we don't have sufficient experience, it's better not to act too hastily.[32]

This behavioural code, in general, mirrors established diplomatic norms elsewhere. Diplomats of all countries are not supposed to 'go rogue'. However, for the People's

Republic, these norms have been elevated to disciplinary guidelines and control procedures such as 'cadres in the foreign ministry are People's Liberation Army men out of uniform', 'there are no trifles in diplomacy', 'diplomatic work is highly political as well as technical', and 'diplomatic authority is limited'.[33] Although there are countervailing guidelines such as 'We should be flexible in our diplomatic work',[34] the prevailing instruction is to stick to the 'correct line'. In brief, the cautious formalism in the Chinese diplomatic approach has its origins in cool-headedness, but also in the dictates of centralized political control.

Despite the predilection to formalism, China's principled, measured, and cool-headed diplomacy has actually produced a *duality* of outcomes. In many instances, Chinese diplomatic style—when backed up by concrete national power capabilities, and marshalled by sophisticated diplomats—has proven beneficial in achieving desired foreign policy results. This entails playing the strategic 'long game', starting at the level of principles, but combining it with tactical flexibility. The cool-headed, long-game approach was used effectively, for example, by the Chinese leadership to break the diplomatic isolation that China was placed under after the tragic events at Tiananmen Square on 4 June 1989. When Deng Xiaoping was told by President George H. W. Bush's envoy, Brent Scowcroft, that the G7 would soon impose sanctions on China, Deng retorted:

> Not even seventy countries can daunt us, let alone seven! . . . we are not afraid of the Americans. Fear will not help us. The Chinese people should have a backbone and aspirations. Have we ever feared anybody? After liberation, we fought a war with the United States, which had an overwhelming advantage over us, with air supremacy. But we were not afraid of them.

Deng insisted to all Chinese diplomats to keep these points in mind, and that 'China, as a nation, does not fear evil spirits nor any blusters.'[35]

Going into secret discussions with the US on 2 July 1989, Deng instructed the other Chinese representatives that: 'We will talk only about *principles* today. We shall not talk about specifics. We don't care about sanctions. We are not scared by them.'[36] Right after stabilizing the tense situation with the Americans (and despite the ongoing public denunciations), Chinese authorities shifted their focus, *tactically*, onto Japan as the 'weak link' in the G7 sanctions, and then onto the European Community representatives, to 'divide and demoralize' the 'anti-China forces'. In the early 1990s, Beijing also put concerted attention into restoring diplomatic ties with nations in the Asian region and the South as the medium- to long-term strategy to prevent any future attempts by the Western alliance to impose diplomatic isolation on China.[37]

More recently, the methodical and principled, but flexible and proactive approach to diplomacy was used effectively again by Chinese officials when negotiating the China—ASEAN Free Trade Area (CAFTA) agreement with Southeast Asian states.[38] In the late 1990s, during the lead up to China's WTO accession, governments and companies in Southeast Asia grew increasingly anxious about the impact of China's WTO entry on their own economies, there were fears that their exports would lose out to Chinese rivals, and that foreign multinationals would relocate away from Southeast Asia to China to take advantage of increased access to the Chinese market. The sense of 'China threat' had *shifted* from geopolitics to economic security threat. Chinese strategists responded by devising a Chinese 'peaceful rise' theory, and the so-called 'win-win' trade strategy for China—ASEAN economic cooperation. At the ASEAN—China Leaders meeting in 2001, Chinese Premier Zhu Rongji surprised ASEAN counterparts by suggesting a new preferential trade agreement, in which China would include 'principled' South—South cooperation clauses, such as 'Early Harvest' arrangements so that ASEAN trading partners would gain early benefits, as well as a longer phase-in period for trade liberalization reforms for the least developed member countries of the ASEAN grouping (Cambodia, Laos, Vietnam). These measures, combining principled and flexible diplomacy, proved useful for calming anxiety among China's neighbours.

The behavioural code for China's diplomats has led, however, to another tendency where initiative and innovation have been stifled on the world stage. In the hands of inexperienced, overly cautious, or hesitant personalities, the code has the effect of constraining individuals from taking a more robust stance in diplomatic situations, when action—or the *perception* of action—is needed.

One example is China's role in the G20 Leaders process, where the operational norm is informal, personalized diplomacy between the national leaders. Despite its growing activism in the global summitry process, and although the responsible officials have mastered their files, China has been accused of being less active than needed within the G20 process. Beijing's cautious diplomacy in the G20—its unwillingness to bandwagon on the *status quo* agenda of the G7—has led foreign observers to suggest that China is deliberately 'punching below its weight', or consciously trying to avoid carrying its 'fair' share of global stewardship. Chinese officials, in contrast, highlight that China is working with other developing countries to advance a more fundamental reorientation of the system, and to correct institutionalized 'biases' that privilege the developed nations.[39] Whether the image of China as laggard is accurate or not, the perception exists, and needs to be addressed by China's diplomats. Another example of Chinese diplomacy underperforming is in managing foreign perceptions of China's presence in Africa. Brazilian diplomats, in contrast, have excelled in portraying Brazil's growing presence in the continent as noble and constructive. China's diplomats have been hamstrung by a reactive diplomacy that has relied on 'explaining better, China's good intentions', *after* the criticism has gone public.

Even updates of Chinese thinking on behavioural guidelines, such as the following from Huang Jinqi in 2004,[40] that encourage a more active diplomatic stance, nonetheless end with disciplined centralism:

> China's diplomacy now requires our diplomats to show greater initiative in their work and practice, so to speak, an 'active diplomacy'. This does not mean, however, that our diplomats may act as they think fit. The active diplomacy we advocate only means that our diplomats should display initiative in implementing foreign policy decided upon by the top leadership, and they should actively and promptly ascertain new developments and report to the senior leadership so that decision can be made. Diplomacy at all times and in all countries demands invariably and exactingly, centralism and discipline.[41]

The result of the behavioural code is that Chinese officials of all ranks are often reduced to reading prepared statements that must be cleared by central authorities—including when senior officials are supposed to be engaging in frank discussions with foreign counterparts. Unfortunately for Beijing, perception carries a lot of weight in diplomacy.

The differences in diplomatic styles between the BRICs countries have been marshalled for interstate rivalry, for example, in their outreach to Africa. At the same time, however, as we shall see in section 49.3, these differences can coalesce in complementary ways for cooperation between the rising powers—especially in reaction to the obstinacy of the traditional powers.

49.3 Cooperative Outcomes

Prior to the onset of the global financial crisis in 2007, China and Brazil directed their diplomatic outreach at strengthening ties to nations within their own regions, and across the global South. The rising powers turned their attention to building intra-BRIC connectivity, as well as ties of goods exchange, capital, people, and ideas across the developing world—so-called 'routing-around' options.[42] However, the global crisis revealed the limits of Southern networking to Brazil, India, and China, when they faced a crisis of *global* proportions. The crisis further showed that the rising powers were not yet willing or able to play the role of alternative global lender-of-last-resort. Rather, Brazil, India, and China joined the global-level G20 Leaders' process to contain the freefall of Anglo-American finance, and re-strengthen the IMF.

The turn back to 'the global' was signified in the Joint Statement of the G20 finance ministers in Sao Paulo, Brazil (November 2008), which declares that 'the global crisis requires global solutions'. Brazil's global turn was seen in the statements from President Lula da Silva, that nations struggling with the crisis must 'avoid temptations to take unilateral measures', and he stressed that 'new universal mechanisms are needed'.[43] Finance Minister Guido Mantega called for 'joint and coordinated action', 'greater regulation of financial markets', and 'total agreement' on policies to restore financial stability.[44]

Brazilian authorities escalated their diplomatic power when President Lula called for an overhaul of the existing global financial system, saying that it 'collapsed like a house of cards' in the credit crisis, and that the emerging countries must have more say in key decisions. He emphasised: 'We need new, more inclusive governance and Brazil is ready to face up to its responsibilities. It is time for a pact between governments to build a new financial architecture for the world.'[45] Brazilian representatives pressed for the G20 to replace the 'rich-country G7' as the global crisis committee. Mantega added, 'We refuse to take part in the G7 merely to drink coffee and we have to have a more important role in discussions.'[46]

India added its voice to Brazil's demands for reform when Minister Manmohan Singh highlighted that reform of the financial system was needed, and that countries should acknowledge the 'economically damaging role of excessive speculative activity'.[47] Indian diplomats highlighted that poorer countries faced big risks as the crisis grew and mutated, notably in commodity export prices, lack of liquidity, and foreign exchange volatility. Singh emphasised that, 'when the capital development of a country becomes a by-product of the activities of a casino, the job is likely to be ill-done'.[48]

Similar calls for reform from China and Brazil at the major Bretton Woods meetings (IMFC) prior to 2007–2008, had been largely ignored by the G7 finance grouping. Even during the height of the global crisis, G7 finance ministers continued to deflect the calls for fundamental systemic reform. Canadian Finance Minister Jim Flaherty, for example, argued against the need 'for a major shake-up' of the way global finance is managed, stating: 'Now is the time to be putting out the fire, not to be planning for grand new schemes. We're in the midst of a crisis and certain things need to be done now.'[49] The former head of the IMF, Dominique Strauss-Kahn, stated in a media interview that 'expectations should not be oversold' of a successor to the 1944 Bretton Woods system being agreed to; that 'things are not going to change overnight… The words sound nice but we are not going to create a new international treaty'.[50]

Despite the diplomatic stonewalling, the BRIC governments agreed in their first *Joint Statement*, that the IMF and other institutions created from the 1944 Bretton Woods accord 'must be comprehensively reformed so that they can more adequately reflect changing economic weights in the world economy'.[51] Particularly noteworthy, however, was how—coinciding with these joint diplomatic statements from Brazil and India in the forefront—China flexed its new financial muscle at the G20 finance meeting in Sao Paulo, when it announced before the end of the meeting that it would immediately introduce a US$586 billion domestic stimulus package to respond to the worsening global credit crisis.[52] Beijing sent stock markets spinning upwards. What this situation showed was that unlike previous Southern campaigns to reform the world economic order, such as Bandung in the late 1950s, or the call for a New International Economic Order in the 1970s, this time, the emerging countries were not coming with cap in hand. They have resources—and are learning how to influence world financial and trade markets, as sellers, buyers, and investors; and, in turn, they are figuring out how to leverage this systemic influence for diplomatic gains.[53]

At the first G20 Leaders summit in Washington DC in November 2008, the BRIC representatives restated that the Bretton Woods institutions were outdated, and should be reformed to more adequately reflect changing economic weights in the world economy, and be more responsive when facing future challenges. Although the American hosts at the Washington summit put off the debate on bigger questions of the system, the rising powers did secure the following in the official Communiqué:

> The G20 Leaders are committed to advancing the reform of the Bretton Woods Institutions so that they can more adequately reflect changing economic weights in the world economy in order to increase their legitimacy and effectiveness. In this respect, emerging and developing economies, including the poorest countries, should have greater voice and representation. The Financial Stability Forum (FSF) must expand urgently to a broader membership of emerging economies, and other major standard setting bodies should promptly review their membership.

Moreover, as a result of lobbying from India and Indonesia,[54] G20 Leaders also agreed in the Washington Summit Communiqué to 'help emerging and developing economies gain access to finance in current difficult financial conditions, including through liquidity facilities and program support. We stress the IMF's important role in crisis response, welcome its new short-term liquidity facility, and urge the ongoing review of its instruments and facilities to ensure flexibility.'[55]

In the lead up to the London G20 (2 April 2009), the finance ministers of the BRIC group issued their *first pre-summit* joint statement, which called on the G20 'leading economies of the world' to rebuild confidence, and maintain and support credit flow to help restore growth.[56] The London G20 (2 April 2009) followed up on commitments made in Washington first when China, Brazil, India, and Russia were admitted into the Financial Security Board (FSB) as members, immediately after the London summit, and when 'the 20' agreed that IMF representational changes would be settled by 2011; and second, when the G20 committed to establish a $1.1 trillion pool of emergency financing, and pledged to help developing countries to respond to the spreading liquidity crisis. In his post-summit interviews in London, President Lula stated that the G20 London was an important 'first step' in recognizing that there can be no long-term solution to the global financial crisis without bringing developing countries on board.

The complimentary diplomacy of the BRICs countries can be seen in the fact that although Brazil, India, and China had emphasised, together, that developing countries needed to be 'part of the solution', David Miliband, theBritish Foreign Secretary, singled out the moment when Chinese President Hu Jintao spoke in London as pivotal:

> China's president arrived as the head of the only major power still enjoying strong growth (expected to be 8% this year), backed by substantial financial reserves...If you looked around the 20 people sitting at the table...what was striking was that when China spoke everybody listened.[57]

In other words, China's financial capabilities underpin its 'indispensable' clout, and bolster the collective diplomatic efforts of the BRICs. Miliband also highlighted that 'Hu [Jintao] helped support Gordon Brown's position against protectionism, and China's economic stimulus package (equivalent to 16 percent of its GDP over two years) is widely seen as among the world's best hopes for a recovery.'[58] Beijing's economic weight serves to strengthen its diplomatic positioning.

The other BRICs drew lessons from the Chinese announcements at the Sao Paulo and London meetings at the London Summit to declare that it could be willing to purchase a significant amount of IMF bonds (one estimate was $US40 billion); but also to stipulate that it wanted to see the promised Bretton Woods representational reforms. In early June 2009, Russia and Brazil followed the Chinese example, by announcing that they would join China as the first countries to buy the new IMF bonds, denominated in SDRs, each offered to purchase $10 billion worth of the IMF bonds. President Lula suggested that the $10 billion pledge 'gives us moral authority to keep pushing for the changes that are needed at the IMF'.[59] In June 2012, India followed suit, after prolonged internal debate, Prime Minister Singh announced at the Cancun G20 summit in Mexico that India would contribute $10 billion to the IMF to help tackle the fallout from the crisis in the Eurozone.

As another example of their complimentary diplomacy, one Brazilian participant-observer described the following situation to the author, about China providing key backing at the IMF Board meetings for Brazil's vocal demands for IMF representational reforms:

> The Chinese sat quietly at the table throughout the quota negotiations. In contrast, Brazil's representative took a very active role, making extremely verbose demands for representational changes—with some of the demands going far beyond what most members were considering. These changes, if they were actually made, would mean major changes in the criteria for determining voting shares in the IMF. China sat quietly throughout these tense and extended discussions. However, when it came time to vote, China acted. When it was time for the Chinese representative to speak, everyone listened. The Chinese representative said a few words. And then he voted in support of the Brazilian position. The debate was over.[60]

In these instances, Beijing can be seen as taking the diplomatic tactic of 'leading from behind', of assuming a non-aggressive posture that appears less threatening to the traditional powers. One long-time British military historian described it aptly as Beijing leaving the 'charge of the cavalry' to its BRICS partners, while China takes on the role of the 'infantry' in providing sustained force.[61]

Mutual learning between the BRICS countries can also be observed in their forays into great power monetary statecraft and diplomacy, in the wake of the global financial crisis. The leaders of the BRICs reinforced their calls for systemic reform by raising the premise of de-dollarization. In the lead up to the inaugural 'BRIC' Leaders summit in June 2009, President Lula da Silva highlighted the instability in the US dollar, and dollar's role as the de facto global reserve currency. The BRIC summit host, Russian President Dmitry Medvedev also noted to the foreign media before the start of the summit that the existing reserve currencies, including the dollar, have not performed their proper function, and that 'we are likely to witness the creation of a supranational currency...which will be used for international settlements'.[62] The dollar fell 0.9 per cent against a basket of currencies on world markets.

The interventions of the individual BRICs leaders in monetary diplomacy have been a learning experience, i.e. how to use this *form* of diplomatic leverage with the necessary caution and nimbleness. Beijing's socialization started earlier, from 2004 onwards, when its foreign currency reserves started accumulating massively, and caught the attention of American politicians. Chinese representatives came to learn that they must choose their words very carefully when discussing currency with the foreign media after they saw the consequence of their words, and were reprimanded for speaking 'carelessly'; that, as creditors and holders of a massive amount of international currency, they could 'move money markets' in unanticipated ways.[63] More recently, Russia's leaders have apparently come to better appreciate how their words can also affect foreign currency markets in unintended ways. Their statements on currency have become more measured.

Brazil, Russia, and China reasserted their diplomatic pressure at the July 2009 G8 summit in L'Aquila, Italy, when the 'Group of Five' emerging countries ('G5', including Brazil, India, China, South Africa, and Mexico) were invited again for side meetings at the G8 summit. On the eve of the G8+G5 meeting, at the behest of President Lula, the G5 discussed the use of their own currencies to settle a portion of their trade accounts. As a sign of mutual socialization, 'the 5' issued a 'G5 Political Declaration' at the end of their preparatory meeting in L'Aquila. The Declaration called for the 'full, immediate implementation of the G20 Summit Declaration of London, with no delay', and declared their shared intention to 'continue promoting the reform of the international financial system', and to 'establish a new international financial order' that will be 'just, fair, inclusive, and well-administered'. The G5 pledged to 'dedicate the necessary efforts to resolve the issue of the inadequate representation of developing countries in international financial institutions', which they added, 'must be carried out immediately'.[64]

The next day, at the G8 + G5 meeting, Chinese State Councillor Dai Bingguo, delivered the message on behalf of his President Hu Jintao—that was discussed beforehand with the G5 members—calling unequivocally for the world to diversify the reserve currency system, and to restore exchange rate stability. Looking across to President Obama and the other G7 leaders, Dai told the summit: 'We should have a better system for reserve currency issuance and regulation, so that we can maintain relative stability of major reserve currencies' exchange rates and promote a diversified and rational international reserve currency system.'[65]

In the lead-up to the next gathering of the G20 Leaders, the Pittsburgh summit (September 2009), Brazil and the other developing countries again pushed for a 7 per cent shift in voting power in the IMF.[66] However, according to Marco Aurelio Garcia (foreign policy adviser to President Lula), the proposal to reform voting power at the IMF faced increasing opposition from rich countries, especially European nations. By the end of the second day in Pittsburgh, the leaders had only agreed to shift 5 per cent of the voting rights in the IMF from the rich members to the rising powers.[67] It would actually take another full year of BRIC's collective advocacy to move the voting shares another percentage further. The year included a missed opportunity at the Toronto G20 Summit in June 2010, where IMF reforms were given less priority on the summit agenda than banking reforms, and President Lula took a pass on attending. The shift in IMF voting shares was given more attention by the South Korean hosts for the first G20 summit to be held outside of the G7, and agreement was finally announced at the 23 October 2010 meeting of G20 finance ministers and central banks governors in Gyeongju, South Korea, at the preparatory meeting before the Leaders Summit in Seoul in November 2010. The outcome (6 per cent) was still not the 7 per cent shift that the BRICs had requested. This result, after all of the diplomatic bargaining around three global Leaders summits, sent a sobering message to the rising powers about just how difficult it was going to be, to get the traditional powers to relinquish some of their outdated privilege.

49.4 CONCLUDING REMARKS

This chapter highlights three main points. First, the rising powers can be understood as a grouping of nations that share the characteristic of being the fastest growing, most dynamic large economies in the world economy, as well as a common bond of needing to respond to the current global economic crisis, to sustain their own respective rises. The global crisis has induced mutual socialization among the BRIC rising states, in terms of their common need to re-engage in global crisis management. But they are doing so not to re-establish or reinforce status quo arrangements. Rather they are advocates for change in the representational arrangements of the formal institutions that govern the world economy.

Second, the diplomatic interventions of the BRIC states are a mid-range indicator of their future roles in the politics of the world economy. In some instances, differences in diplomatic cultures among these rising states have been marshalled for interstate contestation—for example in their outreach to Africa. However, in other cases, differences of diplomatic style have coalesced to produce cooperative outcomes, as seen within the G20 process, in their push for IMF reforms.

As discussed earlier, China has provided important backing to Brazil, when the latter has led the call for institutional reform at the Fund. In their collective diplomacy, Brazilian, Russian, and Indian representatives have often been at the forefront, diplomatically, in pushing for Bretton Woods reforms, whereas the Chinese have provided material power for a sustained push —a form of 'leadership from behind'.[68] China's material capabilities have proven crucial to bolstering the diplomacy of the group as a whole. Chinese monetary statecraft has, in turn, had a socializing effect on Brazil and Russia, starting with their 2009 contributions to the IMF, and seen most recently, when India announced in June 2012 that it would make a sizable contribution to the Fund.

It should be noted that just as Brazilian diplomacy has changed over the past two decades, there are signs that China's diplomatic culture is evolving, though gradually. Whereas China specialists have detailed how Chinese diplomacy faces challenges in managing the rising tide of nationalism inside China,[69] or how changing international security concerns are reshaping Chinese diplomacy,[70] this chapter has described how modern Chinese economic diplomacy may be converging towards a more proactive diplomatic style. Although Chinese foreign ministry officials continue to faithfully deliver their prescribed talking points, it is also dawning on the authorities that the inherent conservatism in China's diplomatic approach has, at times, left the country open to international criticism. This realization, and the space afforded by the country's ongoing reforms, likely explain the urgings from the esteemed former Chinese ambassador to the UN, and France, Wu Jianmin for China's diplomats to 'improve their communications'. In the realm of public diplomacy, and especially on Africa, China is catching up fast.

Third, there is no denying the limits that remain in the collective will and cooperative action of the BRICS. Although their advocacy did produce a 6 per cent quota shift in

IMF voting shares, it was still not the 7 per cent they had pushed for, starting back in 2009.[71] Although the BRICS did exercise some collective voice in challenging European efforts to anoint another European as the IMF executive director in June 2011, they did not advance their own BRICS' sanctioned candidate. The collective diplomacy of the BRICS is still emerging at this stage. While this may bring comfort to the traditional powers, it *should* be noted that what is at stake is the future viability of the existing institutional arrangements, in terms of securing the buy-in of the rising powers, and their eventual willingness to take a sense of ownership in the existing global arrangements—rather than pursuing default options. Time will not stand still for the traditional powers.

NOTES

* I thank Maxwell Brem, Katherine Hochstetler, and Robert Latham for their comments. Special thanks to Marcel Fortuna Biato, Audo Araujo Faleiro, Wang Yong, and Wu Jianmin for sharing their insight, to Andrew Cooper, Jorge Heine, and Ramesh Thakur for their editorial suggestions, and Andrew Schrumm for the research support. My thanks to the Social Sciences and Humanities Research Council of Canada for supporting the research. Any errors of interpretation are the author's responsibility alone.

1. Andrew Hart and Bruce Jones, 'How Do Rising Powers Rise?', *Survival* 53:6 (2011), 63–88.

2. For a similar argument for Chinese diplomacy specifically see Pauline Kerr, Stuart Harris, and Qin Yaqing (eds), *China's 'New' Diplomacy: Tactical or Fundamental Challenge?* (New York: Macmillan, 2008).

3. Chris Buckley, 'Much-Trumpeted BRIC Summit Ends Quietly', *Reuters*, 17 June 2009.

4. Andrew Hurrell, 'Hegemony, Liberalism and Global Order: What Space for Would-Be Great Powers?', *International Affairs* 82:1 (2006), 1–19.

5. Amrita Narlikar, *Rising Powers: How to be One, How to Manage Them* (London: Hirst & Columbia University Press, 2010).

6. G. John Ikenberry, *Liberal Leviathan* (Princeton: Princeton University Press, 2011).

7. Leslie Elliot Armijo, 'The BRICs Countries as Analytical Category: Mirage or Insight?', *Asian Perspectives* 31:4 (2007), 7–42; Andrew F. Cooper and Agata Antkiewicz (eds), *Emerging Powers and Global Governance* (Waterloo: Wilfred Laurier University Press, 2008).

8. Alexander Lennon and Amanda Kozlowski (eds), *Global Powers in the 21st Century: Strategy and Relations* (Cambridge, MA: MIT Press, 2008).

9. Jorge Castenada, 'Not Ready for Prime Time; Why Including the Emerging Powers Will Hurt Global Governance', *Foreign Affairs*, September–October 2010, <http://www.foreignaffairs.com/articles/66577/jorge-g-castaneda/not-ready-for-prime-time>.

10. Stewart Patrick, 'Irresponsible Stakeholders: The Difficulty of Integrating Rising Powers', *Foreign Affairs*, November–December 2010, <http://www.foreignaffairs.com/articles/66793/stewart-patrick/irresponsible-stakeholders>.

11. David Shorr, 'Make Room for the Rising Powers', *The Globalist*, 22 September 2010.

12. See Bruce Jones, 'Managing a Changing World', *Foreign Policy*, 14 March 2011.

13. Amrita Narlikar and Brendan Vickers (eds), *Leadership and Change in the Multilateral Trading System* (Leiden: Martinus Nijhoff, 2009); Gregory Chin, 'The Emerging Countries and China in the G20: Reforming Global Economic Governance', *Studia*

Diplomatica (Brussels Journal of International Relations), LXIII, Number 2–3 (2010), 105–24.

14. Gregory Chin and Ramesh Thakur, 'Will China Change the Rules of Global Order?', *The Washington Quarterly* 33:4 (2010), 119–38.

15. Steven Weber and Bruce Jentleson, *The End of Arrogance: America in the Global Competition of Ideas* (Cambridge, MA: Harvard University Press, 2010).

16. Andrew F. Cooper and Thomas Fues, 'Do Asian Drivers Pull Their Diplomatic Weight?: China, India and the United Nations', *World Development* 36:2 (2008), 293–307.

17. Lael Brainard and Leonardo Martinez-Diaz (eds), *Brazil as an Economic Superpower?: Understanding Brazil's Changing Role in the Global Economy* (Washington, DC: Brookings Institution Press, 2009).

18. Luiz Pedone, '*Quo vadis*, Brazil?', in A. Cooper and J. Heine (eds), *Which Way Latin America?: Hemispheric Politics Meets Globalization* (Tokyo: United Nations University Press, 2009), 262–80.

19. Celso Amorim, 'Reflections on Brazil's Global Rise', *Americas Quarterly* (2011), 50–5.

20. Amorim, 'Reflections on Brazil's Global Rise', 52.

21. Amorim, 'Reflections on Brazil's Global Rise', 52.

22. I thank Kathryn Hochstetler for highlighting this point.

23. Amrita Narlikar and Diana Tussie, 'The G20 and the Cancun Ministerial: Developing Countries and Their Evolving Coalitions in the WTO', *The World Economy* 27:7 (2004), 947–66.

24. <http://www.cablegatesearch.net/cable.php?id=08BRASILIA1636>.

25. Huang Jinqi, *What is Diplomacy?: A Bilingual Course* (Beijing: World Affairs Press, 2004).

26. Zhou En-lai, 'Our Foreign Policies and Our Tasks', *Selected Works of Zhou Enlai, Volume II* (Beijing: Foreign Languages Press, 1952; reprinted 1989).

27. Zhou, 'Our Foreign Policies', 94–5.

28. Zhou En-lai, 'Five Principles for Peaceful Coexistence', *Selected Works of Zhou Enlai, Volume II* (Beijing: Foreign Languages Press, 1953; reprinted 1989), 128.

29. Full Text of Hu Jintao's 'Report to the Seventeenth Party Congress', 15 October 2007, *Documents of the Seventeenth National Congress of the Communist Party of China* (Beijing: Foreign Languages Press, 2007), 60, 61 (emphasis added).

30. 'Foreign Minister Li Zhaoxing Gives Year-End Interview to People's Daily', *Ministry of Foreign Affairs*, 20 December 2005.

31. Zhou, 'Our Foreign Policies', 100.

32. Zhou, 'Our Foreign Policies', 101 (emphases added).

33. See Huang, *What is Diplomacy?*, 208–14.

34. Zhou, 'Our Foreign Policies', 99.

35. Qian Qichen, *Ten Episodes in China's Diplomacy* (New York: Harper Collins, 2005), 134.

36. Qian, *Ten Episodes in China's Diplomacy*, 134 (emphasis added).

37. Zhao Suisheng, 'Beijing's Perception of the International System and Foreign Policy Adjustment after the Tiananmen Incident', S. Zhao (ed.), *Chinese Foreign Policy: Pragmatism and Strategic Behaviour* (Armonk: M.E. Sharpe, 2004).

38. Gregory Chin and Richard Stubbs, 'China, Regional Institution-Building and the China-ASEAN Free Trade Area', *Review of International Political Economy* 18:3 (2011), 277–98.

39. For the details see Gregory Chin, 'What Next for China in the G20?: Reorienting the Core Agenda', *CIGI Commentary*, 9 November 2011, <http://www.cigionline.org/publications/2011/11/what-next-china-g20-%E2%80%94-reorienting-core-agenda>.

40. Huang Jinqi, *What is Diplomacy?*.

41. Huang, *What is Diplomacy?*, 214 (emphasis added).
42. Naazneen Barma, Ely Ratner, and Steven Weber, 'A World without the West', *The National Interest* 90 (2007), 23–30.
43. Quoted in 'G20 Proposes Joint Action on Global Financial Crisis', <http://news.xinhuanet.com/english/2008-11/10/content_10334142.htm>.
44. The statements by Guido Mantega are quoted in "G20 Proposes Joint Action on Global Financial Crisis", *Xinhua News Agency*, 10 November 2008, <http://news.xinhuanet.com/english/2008-11/10/content_10334142.htm>.
45. Louise Egan and Renato Andrade, 'Brazil's Lula Calls for Shake-Up of Global Finance', *Reuters*, 9 November 2008, <http://www.reuters.com/article/2008/11/09/us-financial-g-idUSTRE4A67NF20081109>.
46. <http://www.reuters.com/article/2008/11/09/us-financial-g-idUSTRE4A67NF20081109>.
47. Manmohan Singh's statements are quoted in 'Emerging Countries Looking for Equal Say at G20 Summit', *The Economic Times*, 13 November 2008, <http://articles.economictimes.indiatimes.com/2008-11-13/news/28483159_1_bric-countries-bretton-woods-world-economic-growth>.
48. <http://articles.economictimes.indiatimes.com/2008-11-13/news/28483159_1_bric-countries-bretton-woods-world-economic-growth>.
49. Louise Egan and Renato Andrade, 'Brazil's Lula Calls for Shake-Up of Global Finance', *Reuters*, 9 November 2008.
50. 'G20 Looks to Expand Emerging Nations Role in the Global Economy', *AFP*, 8 November 2008.
51. 'Emerging Economies Press for Greater Role in Financial Overhaul', *AFP*, 8 November 2008.
52. 'Emerging Economies Press for Greater Role in Financial Overhaul'.
53. David M. Lampton, *The Three Faces of Chinese Power: Might, Money, and Minds* (Berkeley: University of California Press, 2008).
54. Gregory Chin, 'The Emerging Countries and China in the G20: Reforming Global Economic Governance', *Studia Diplomatica* (Brussels Journal of International Relations), LXIII, Number 2–3 (2010), 105–24.
55. 'Statement from the G20 Summit', published in *The New York Times*, 15 November 2008, <http://www.nytimes.com/2008/11/16/washington/summit-text.html?pagewanted=all>.
56. 'Full Text of BRIC Countries Joint Communiqué', published in Reuters, 14 March 2009, <http://www.reuters.com/article/2009/03/14/g20-brics-text-idUSLE47000820090314>.
57. <http://www.guardian.co.uk/politics/2009/may/17/david-miliband-china-world-power>.
58. <http://www.guardian.co.uk/politics/2009/may/17/david-miliband-china-world-power>.
59. Todd Benson, 'Brazil Lends IMF Money Ahead of BRIC Summit', *Reuters*, 11 June 2009.
60. The author's discussion with Brazilian finance official; Cambridge, UK, 2010.
61. The author's notes from a discussion on the rising powers at the University of Cambridge in May 2010.
62. Guy Faulconbridge, 'Emerging Powers Try to Wean Themselves Off U.S. Dollars', *Reuters*, 17 June 2009; Naomi Tajitsu, 'FOREX-Dollar Falls on Russia Comments, BRICs Awaited', *Reuters*, 16 June 2009; Wanfeng Zhou, 'Dollar Slides after Russia Comments, BRIC Summit', *Reuters*, 16 June 2009.
63. Gregory Chin and Eric Helleiner, 'China as a Creditor: Rising Financial Power?', *Journal of International Affairs* (2008), 87–102.

64. 'G5 Declaration' (online), G8 L'Aquila Summit website, <http://portal3.sre.gob.mx/group-five/images/stories/laquila/G5_Pol_Dec_ENG.pdf>.

65. Simon Rabinovitch and Matt Falloon, 'China Demands Currency Reform at G8 Summit, Britain Skeptical', *Reuters*, 9 July 2009.

66. <http://www.reuters.com/article/2009/09/24/g20-imf-brazil-idUSN2446868620090924>.

67. <http://www.reuters.com/article/2009/09/25/us-g20-communique-institutions-text-sb-idUSTRE58O6PD20090925>.

68. Siddharth Varadarajan, 'BRIC Should Create Conditions for Fairer World Order', *The Hindu* (online), 17 June 2009.

69. Peter Hays Gries, *China's New Nationalism: Pride, Politics and Diplomacy* (Berkeley: University of California Press, 2003).

70. Bates Gill, *Rising Star: China's New Security Diplomacy* (Washington, DC: Brookings Institution Press, 2007).

71. Walter Brandimarte, 'Must Reform IMF to Fix Global Economy', *Reuters*, 24 September 2009.

INDEX

Note: Bold entries refer to figures, tables or boxes.